Evolutionary Psychology

Series Editors
Todd K. Shackelford
Rochester, Michigan, USA

Viviana A. Weekes-Shackelford
Rochester, Michigan, USA

The Springer Series in Evolutionary Psychology is the first series of volumes dedicated to this increasingly important discipline within psychology. The series will reflect the multidisciplinary nature of this field encompassing evolutionary theory, biology, cognitive psychology, anthropology, economics, computer science, and paleoarchaeology. It will explore the underlying psychological mechanisms, and information processing systems housed in the brain as well as the various triggers for their activation. Its scientific assumptions rest on The concept that evolution is the only known causal process capable of creating complex organic mechanisms as are exhibited in human and animal life. Further, it seeks to show how information processing is adaptively influenced by input from the environment. Overall, the series will address the range of functionally specialized evolved mechanisms, mediated by contextual circumstances, that become combined and integrated to produce manifest behavior. The Series will address key areas of research within the field, including sexual behavior; conflict between the sexes; parenting; kinship; cooperation and altruism; aggression; warfare; and status and prestige. A premier resource in evolutionary psychology for researchers, academics and students, this series will provide. the field continuing and comprehensive coverage of this high profile area.

More information about this series at http://www.springer.com/series/10583

Virgil Zeigler-Hill • Lisa L. M. Welling
Todd K. Shackelford
Editors

Evolutionary Perspectives on Social Psychology

Editors
Virgil Zeigler-Hill
Department of Psychology
Oakland University
Rochester
Michigan
USA

Todd K. Shackelford
Department of Psychology
Oakland University
Rochester
Michigan
USA

Lisa L. M. Welling
Department of Psychology
Oakland University
Rochester
Michigan
USA

ISSN 2197-9898 ISSN 2197-9901 (electronic)
Evolutionary Psychology
ISBN 978-3-319-12696-8 ISBN 978-3-319-12697-5 (eBook)
DOI 10.1007/978-3-319-12697-5

Library of Congress Control Number: 2015938452

Springer Cham Heidelberg New York Dordrecht London

Printed on acid-free paper

Springer is part of Springer Science+Business Media (www.springer.com)

Contents

Part IX Individual Differences

Part X Conclusion

Contributors

Scott Atran Centre National de la Recherche Scientifique, Institut Jean Nicod-Ecole Normale Supérieure, Paris, France

H. Clark Barrett Department of Anthropology, University of California Los Angeles, Los Angeles, CA, USA

Pieter van den Berg Theoretical Biology Group, Groningen Institute for Evolutionary Life Sciences, University of Groningen, Groningen, The Netherlands

David F. Bjorklund Department of Psychology, Florida Atlantic University, Boca Raton, FL, USA

Candace J. Black Department of Psychology, University of Arizona, Ethology and Evolutionary Psychology, Tucson, AZ, USA

Jessica J. Cameron Department of Psychology, University of Manitoba, Winnipeg, MB, Canada

Carlos Ernesto Gómez Ceballos Department of Psychology, University of Arizona, Tucson, AZ, USA

Victoria Della Cioppa Department of Psychology, Queen's University, Kingston, ON, Canada

Julie C. Coultas Department of Psychology, University of Sussex, Falmer, UK

Centre for the study of Cultural Evolution, Stockholm University, Stockholm, Sweden

Catharine P Cross School of Psychology & Neuroscience, University of St Andrews, Fife, UK

M. Brent Donnellan Department of Psychology, Texas A&M University, College Station, TX, USA

Megan Earle Department of Psychology, Brock University, St. Catharines, ON, Canada

Ann H. Farrell Department of Psychology, Brock University, St. Catharines, ON, Canada

Laurence Fiddick School of Psychology, James Cook University, Townsville, Australia

Aurelio Jos é Figueredo Department of Psychology, University of Arizona, Tucson, AZ, USA

Corey L. Fincher Department of Psychology, University of Warwick, Coventry, UK

John M. Friend Department of Political Science, University of Hawai'I at Mānoa, Honolulu, HI, USA

Bjørn Grinde Division of Mental Health, Norwegian Institute of Public Health, Nydalen, Oslo, NORWAY

Joseph Hackman School of Human Evolution and Social Change, Arizona State University, Tempe, AZ, USA

Sarah E. Hill Department of Psychology, Texas Christian University, Fort Worth, TX, USA

Christopher J. Holland Department of Psychology, Texas Christian University, Fort Worth, TX, USA

Nicholas S. Holtzman Department of Psychology, Georgia Southern University, Statesboro, GA, USA

Daniel Hruschka School of Human Evolution and Social Change, Arizona State University, Tempe, AZ, USA

Eric T. Huang Department of Psychology, University of Victoria, Victoria, BC, Canada

Jacqui Hutchison School of Psychology, University of Aberdeen, Old Aberdeen, UK

Gordon P. D. Ingram School of Society, Enterprise, and Environment, Bath Spa University, Bath, UK

Zoe Johnson-Ulrich Department of Psychology, Oakland University, Rochester, MI, USA

Tatsuya Kameda Department of Social Psychology, The University of Tokyo, Bunkyo-ku, Tokyo, Japan

Phillip S. Kavanagh School of Psychology, Social Work, and Social Policy, University of South Australia, Adelaide, SA, Australia

Timothy Ketelaar Department of Psychology, New Mexico State University, Las Cruces, NM, USA

Lee A. Kirkpatrick Department of Psychology, College of William and Mary, Williamsburg, VA, USA

Dennis L. Krebs Department of Psychology, Simon Fraser University, Burnaby, British Columbia, Canada

Edwin J. C. van Leeuwen Department of Developmental Psychology, University of Jena, Jena, Germany

Florian van Leeuwen Dynamique du Langage, University of Lyon, Lyon, France

Anthony C. Little School of Natural Sciences, Psychology, Stirling University, Stirling, Scotland, UK

Charles G. Lord Department of Psychology, Texas Christian University, Fort Worth, TX, USA

Tong Lu Department of Psychology, Texas Christian University, Fort Worth, TX, USA

Shane Macfarlan Department of Anthropology, University of Utah, Salt Lake City, UT, USA

Karin Machluf Department of Psychology, Florida Atlantic University, Boca Raton, FL, USA

Douglas Martin School of Psychology, University of Aberdeen, Old Aberdeen, UK

Allan Mazur Maxwell School, Syracuse University, Syracuse, NY, USA

Molly McGuire Department of Psychology, Oakland University, Rochester, MI, USA

Thomas J. H Morgan Department of Psychology, University of California, Berkeley, CA, USA

Raymond L. Neubauer Molecular Cell & Developmental Biology, University of Texas at Austin, AustinTX, USA

Sylis C. A. Nicolas Department of Psychology, Oakland University, Rochester, MI, USA

Justin H. Park School of Experimental Psychology, University of Bristol, Bristol, UK

Emily Anne Patch Department of Psychology, University of Arizona, Phoenix, AZ, USA

Jared R. Piazza Department of Psychology, University of Pennsylvania, Philadelphia, PA, USA

Mike Prentice Department of Psychology, University of Missouri, Columbia, MO, USA

Luke E Rendell Biomedical Sciences Research Complex, School of Biology, University of St. Andrews, Fife, UK

Catherine Salmon Department of Psychology, University of Redlands, Redlands, CA, USA

Thomas C. Scott-Phillips School of Psychology, Philosophy, & Language Sciences, Durham University, Edinburgh, Scotland, UK

Hayley E. Scrutton School of Psychology, Social Work, and Social Policy, University of South Australia, Adelaide, SA, Australia

Jon A. Sefcek Department of Psychology, Kent State University, Kent, OH, USA

Todd K. Shackelford Department of Psychology, Oakland University, Rochester, MI, USA

Hammad Sheikh John Jay College of Criminal Justice, City University of New York, New York, NY, USA

Kennon M. Sheldon Department of Psychology, University of Missouri, Columbia, MO, USA

Danu Anthony Stinson Department of Psychology, University of Victoria, Victoria, BC, Canada

Bradley Thayer Department of Political Science, Utah State University, Logan, UT, USA

Randy Thornhill Department of Biology, University of New Mexico, Albuquerque, NM, USA

R. Scott Tindale Department of Psychology, Loyola University Chicago, Chicago, IL, USA

Doug P. VanderLaan Gender Identity Service, Child, Youth and Family Services, Centre for Addiction and Mental Health, Beamish Family Wing, Intergenerational Wellness Centre, Toronto, ON, Canada

Paul L. Vasey Department of Psychology, University of Lethbridge, Lethbridge, AB, Canada

Anthony A. Volk Department of Child and Youth Studies, Brock University, St. Catharines, ON, Canada

Jennifer Vonk Department of Psychology, Oakland University, Rochester, MI, USA

Mark Van Vugt Department of Psychology, VU University Amsterdam, Amsterdam, The Netherlands

Franz J. Weissing Theoretical Biology Group, Groningen Institute for Evolutionary Life Sciences, University of Groningen, Groningen, The Netherlands

Lisa L. M. Welling Department of Psychology, Oakland University, Rochester, MI, USA

Hippel William von School of Psychology, University of Queensland, Brisbane, QLD, AUSTRALIA

Pedro S. Wolf Department of Psychology, University of Cape Town, Humanities Graduate School Building, Rondebosch, South Africa

Kristin Yoke Department of Psychology, Texas Christian University, Fort Worth, TX, USA

Virgil Zeigler-Hill Department of Psychology, Oakland University, Rochester, MI, USA

Part I
Introduction

How Can an Understanding of Evolutionary Psychology Contribute to Social Psychology?

1

Virgil Zeigler-Hill, Lisa L. M. Welling and Todd K. Shackelford

There has been conflict and tension between social psychology and evolutionary psychology over the past few decades. This is understandable given that it is difficult to avoid conflict between different scientific approaches, with the emergence of string theory in physics being one recent example (e.g., Kuhn 1962). It is easy for scholars to become so focused on their own approaches and the sorts of questions that they care about that they fail to appreciate the value of other perspectives. As an illustration of the tension between social psychology and evolutionary psychology, we recently heard an evolutionary psychologist publicly discount the entire field of social psychology during a presentation at a conference as a "cabinet of curiosities" that has limited value because there is no overarching theory that connects the disparate pieces. He suggested that an evolutionary framework would be the best way to correct what he perceived as deep flaws in the approach that social psychologists have taken to understanding human behavior during the past century. Social psychologists, in turn, have charged evolutionary psychologists with telling "just so stories" that can never be tested empirically.

This tension between social psychology and evolutionary psychology is similar in many respects to the turmoil that surrounded the emergence of social cognition within social psychology in the 1980s. The focus on social cognition transformed some areas of research in social psychology over a remarkably brief period of time (e.g., attitudes, stereotyping). In fact, advocates of the "social cognitive approach" believed that social cognition should be applied far more broadly with some especially enthusiastic supporters—such as Ostrom (1984)—arguing that social cognition should have sovereignty over the entire field of social psychology. These sorts of claims concerning the sovereign status of social cognition—and the not-so-subtle implication that other approaches were inadequate—sparked controversy and led to a great deal of resistance from social psychologists who were less enthusiastic about the idea that all social psychologists should be forced to adopt a social cognitive perspective. The social cognition enthusiasts were adamant that their perspective would revolutionize the field, which led to them being perceived by other social psychologists as having an almost evangelical zeal (e.g., Carlston 2010). There were a wide variety of conflicts that emerged over the years concerning various issues, such as the topics of conferences, editorial positions at journals, and funding priorities for federal agencies. The tension between the social cognition enthusiasts and the rest of the field eventually dissipated,

V. Zeigler-Hill (✉) · L. L. M. Welling ·
T. K. Shackelford
Department of Psychology, Oakland University,
212A Pryale Hall, Rochester MI 48309, USA
e-mail: zeiglerh@oakland.edu

L. L. M. Welling
e-mail: welling@oakland.edu

T. K. Shackelford
e-mail: shackelf@oakland.edu

V. Zeigler-Hill et al. (eds.), *Evolutionary Perspectives on Social Psychology,* Evolutionary Psychology,
DOI 10.1007/978-3-319-12697-5_1,

however, and social cognition has been integrated into the broader field of social psychology. In fact, social cognition has become such a fundamental part of modern social psychology that younger scholars are likely unaware of the fact that this conflict existed. It is likely that something similar will occur with regard to evolutionary reasoning becoming a fundamental aspect of social psychology such that young scholars 20 years from now will be unaware that there was any tension about the integration of an evolutionary perspective.

It has been clear since the time of Charles Darwin that evolutionary processes have shaped the physical characteristics of humans, including our opposable thumbs, relatively large brain, and upright body posture. However, it was not until the 1970s that researchers began to seriously consider the possibility that the same evolutionary processes that led to the physical characteristics possessed by humans may have also engineered our mental processes (e.g., Wilson 1975). The application of an evolutionary framework to psychological phenomena was initially controversial because most explanations for behavior and mental processes at that time focused on a form of unconstrained learning. That is, it was often assumed that individuals were born as relatively "blank slates" that were molded by their social environments. The possibility that our thoughts, feelings, and behaviors were enabled by biological processes over the course of human evolution was a radical departure from this tabula rasa view of the human mind. During the intervening decades, the application of an evolutionary perspective to our understanding of psychological phenomena has become common and has offered insights that have deepened our understanding of human psychology and behavior. Despite this integration, there is still an uneasy tension that exists between evolutionary psychology and social psychology.

Evolutionary psychology is a metatheoretical perspective that influences how researchers approach questions about psychological phenomena (Buss 1999). The most basic assumptions of evolutionary psychology (e.g., biological processes play a role in the thoughts, feelings, and behaviors of individuals and these biological processes have acted over evolution) are widely accepted and supported by research from various fields. Evolutionary psychology is most often concerned with mid-level theories or models derived from an evolutionary framework, such as life history theory (e.g., Ellis et al. 2009) or parasite-stress theory (Fincher and Thornhill 2012). These mid-level theories and models have already been used to enhance our understanding of social psychological phenomena and an evolutionary perspective has the potential to make additional contributions to social psychology.

The purpose of this volume is to continue the dialogue between social psychologists and evolutionary psychologists initiated in other forums (e.g., Cosmides et al. 1992; Forgas et al. 2007; Kenrick et al. 2005; Schaller et al. 2006; Simpson and Kenrick 1997). This is an important exchange of ideas because social psychologists may be able to learn valuable lessons and gain important insights from those who have adopted an evolutionary perspective that may further strengthen the field of social psychology. We are not advocating that an evolutionary perspective must have sovereignty over the field of social psychology. Rather, we are suggesting that social psychology would benefit from more often incorporating an evolutionary perspective when considering social psychological phenomena. Both social psychology and evolutionary psychology have made important contributions to our understanding of human psychology and behavior, and we expect that both areas will continue to do so in the future. However, neither of these approaches is perfect or able to offer complete explanations for all psychological phenomena at the present time.

At the most basic level, the adoption of an evolutionary framework acknowledges that many thoughts, feelings, and behaviors are due, at least in part, to psychological adaptations built by natural selection acting over the course of human evolution. An evolutionary perspective may be able to offer insights and facilitate understanding of an array of topics included within social psychology, such as romantic relationships, stereotyping and prejudice, aggression, prosocial behavior, and social influence. Kenrick et al.

(2005) suggested that social psychologists may be able to benefit from learning the following lessons from evolutionary psychologists: (1) focus less on proximate triggers of behavior and devote more effort to understanding ultimate causes of behavior, (2) pay more attention to domain-specific processes rather than focusing exclusively on domain-general processes, and (3) reconsider the current conceptualization of culture by explicitly recognizing that it has coevolved with humanity. The points suggested by Kenrick et al. could be helpful for broadening and improving the field of social psychology. For example, culture clearly plays a role in shaping behavior, but culture does not develop arbitrarily. Rather, culture has coevolved with biological processes (i.e., gene–culture coevolution) and both exert influence over how humans think, feel, and behave (see Kenrick et al. 2003 or Mesoudi 2009, for extended discussions).

There are already many psychologists pursuing research at the intersection of social psychology and evolutionary psychology or who are applying some of the ideas and approaches from evolutionary psychology to their work in social psychology. For example, studies have found that pathogen exposure is associated with political orientations (Fincher et al. 2008), ovulating women prefer the scent of symmetrical men (Thornhill and Gangestad 1999), and humans are more easily conditioned to fear snakes or spiders than guns (see Öhman and Mineka 2001, for a review). However, there is still the potential for greater integration of an evolutionary perspective into the field of social psychology. The goal of the present volume is to facilitate this integration by (1) offering current evolutionary perspectives on some of the most widely researched topics in social psychology, (2) collecting discussions of prominent programs of research that bridge social psychology and evolutionary psychology, and (3) identifying areas for which evolutionary psychology may offer novel insights into phenomena at the core of social psychology. We also hope that the present volume will serve as a reference for researchers interested in perusing research at the intersection of social psychology and evolutionary psychology. Toward these ends, this volume brings together chapters written by influential scholars who consider the application of an evolutionary perspective to social psychological phenomena. It is our hope that readers will come away from this volume with an appreciation for other perspectives that can be adopted when considering familiar topics. We hope that this volume will demonstrate to readers the importance of continuing to integrate an evolutionary perspective into social psychology.

Overview of the Volume

This volume consists of parts that address specific areas of research within the field of social psychology. Part 1 (Chaps. 2–7) considers social cognition, with chapters addressing issues such as modularity, religiosity, and comparative views of social cognition across species. Part 2 (Chaps. 8–13) examines processes related to the self, with chapters concerning topics such as self-esteem, self-deception, and self-presentation in social media. Part 3 (Chaps. 14–17) examines attitudes and attitude change, with chapters covering issues such as conformity, feminism, and the role of culture in shaping behavior. Part 4 (Chaps. 18–24) considers interpersonal processes, with chapters dealing with issues such as prosocial behavior, cooperation, coalitions, and the use of stereotypes. Part 5 (Chaps. 25–28) examines mating and relationships, with chapters on topics such as romantic attraction, familial relationships, and androphilia. Part 6 (Chaps. 29–31) addresses violence and aggression, with chapters concerning bullying, war, and terrorism. Part 7 (Chaps. 32 and 33) considers health and psychological adjustment, with chapters that address the behavioral immune system and subjective well-being. Finally, Part 8 (Chaps. 34–36) examines individual differences, with chapters concerning personality features and evolutionary game theory.

Part 1: Social Cognition

Part 1 (Chaps. 2–7) examines social cognition, which refers to cognitive processes that enable individuals to understand and interact with others in their social environment (Adolphs 1999; Frith 2007; Olson and Dweck 2008). The term "social cognition" is used in a few different ways in the literature (e.g., a set of cognitive abilities, a subarea within social psychology, a general approach to understanding social psychological phenomena), which has sometimes led to confusion (see Macrae and Miles 2012, for an extended discussion). Regardless of how the term is used, the common thread that binds those who are interested in social cognition is an interest in the social consequences of cognitive processes (e.g., attributions, stereotyping). The authors in this part of the volume present their views concerning how an evolutionary perspective can deepen our understanding of social cognition.

Fiddick (Chap. 2) argues that social psychology has adopted an intentional stance as its primary mode for explaining behavior. He suggests that social psychology should adopt a design stance because this would lead to more integration with other cognitive disciplines. The author argues that this transition would not necessitate an abandonment of social behavior because social psychologists could focus on mental faculties that have evolved to solve social problems.

Machluf and Bjorklund (Chap. 3) focus on the role that social cognitive development has played in the evolution of the human mind. Humans are an extremely social species, and social cognition may have served as a driving force in the evolution of human intelligence. Machluf and Bjorklund review work showing that humans have a strong preference for social stimuli from the earliest days of life. They also review work showcasing the developmental changes that occur in the social cognitive capacities of individuals as they mature. The development of human social cognition during the earliest years of life is compared and contrasted with the social cognitive abilities of chimpanzees (*Pan troglodytes*) because these are the closest living relatives of humans.

Barrett (Chap. 4) reviews the contentious idea that the human mind consists of modules. He adopts a biological view of modularity and argues that this perspective is indispensable for considering the structure and function of the human brain. The author explains how a hierarchical view of brain modularity may lead to a reconsideration of the traditional view of modules as being autonomous and independently shaped.

Ketelaar (Chap. 5) considers the evolutionary functions of emotion. He provides an historical review of evolutionary approaches to understanding human emotions that includes early theories proposed by Charles Darwin and William James as well as contemporary ideas by scholars such as Robert Trivers and Randy Nesse. The author argues that emotions serve as strategic commitment devices that are capable of influencing decisions and behaviors in various areas of life (e.g., economic decisions, social behaviors).

Kirkpatrick (Chap. 6) reviews the application of an evolutionary perspective to religiosity. He argues that an evolutionary approach is essential for considering questions that deal with whether religiosity is driven by basic needs or motives. This chapter considers explanations for religiosity that stem both from the individual and from broader social influences.

Vonk, McGuire, and Johnson-Ulrich (Chap. 7) discuss the role that comparative psychology may play in improving our understanding of social cognitive abilities. They review hypotheses and research concerning the evolution of a set of foundational social cognitive skills. The authors suggest that researchers make more of an effort to appreciate the social cognitive skills of other species rather than searching for evidence of humanlike traits in nonhuman research subjects.

Part 2: Self

Part 2 (Chaps. 8–13) examines processes related to the self. The self is an essential part of the interface between our physical bodies and the social environment (Baumeister 2010). According to Baumeister (1998), there are three sets of phenomena that serve as the basis of the self. The first set of phenomena concerns *self-knowledge,* which captures issues such as self-awareness (i.e., the extent to which individuals reflect on who they are), self-concept (i.e., the information that individuals actually hold regarding who they are), and self-esteem (i.e., the value that individuals place on their mental representations of themselves). The second set of phenomena concerns the *interpersonal self,* which captures self-presentation (i.e., how individuals portray themselves to others) and self-concept change (i.e., the consequences that interpersonal contexts have for how individuals think about themselves). The third set of phenomena deal with the *executive function of the self,* which refers to the ability of individuals to alter their own behavior (i.e., self-regulation) and behave in accordance with their own desires (i.e., self-determination). The authors in this part of the volume present their views concerning how to apply an evolutionary perspective to the scientific study of the self.

Neubauer (Chap. 8) considers the link between large relative brain size and the ability to deal with the challenges of a changing environment through learning and behavioral flexibility. He considers the cognitive abilities and behaviors of a small number of species that have relatively large brains and long life spans (e.g., chimpanzees, African elephants). These species are similar to humans with regard to their delayed maturation and extended period of brain development.

Park and van Leeuwen (Chap. 9) consider the evolution of psychological mechanisms concerning social identification processes. Their chapter predominantly focuses on coalitional social identity (e.g., nationality, ethnicity, religious affiliation). The authors suggest that this form of social identity may constitute a set of loyalty-signaling characteristics that indicate membership in the coalition and the intention to behave in a cooperative fashion.

Kavanagh and Scrutton (Chap. 10) consider the evolutionary function of self-esteem. They focus primarily on the sociometer model, which argues that self-esteem reflects the extent to which an individual believes that he or she is valued as a relational partner. Empirical support for the sociometer model is reviewed and areas that require further investigation are identified (e.g., the number of sociometers that exist, domain-specific versus domain-general nature of these sociometers).

Stinson, Cameron, and Huang (Chap. 11) argue that self-esteem has evolved to assist individuals with the formation and maintenance of interpersonal relationships. In addition to reflecting the extent to which individuals are valued by their social environments, these authors suggest that self-esteem may also influence how individuals are perceived by others. Stinson et al. suggest that the self-esteem system helps humans to successfully navigate their social worlds.

Von Hippel (Chap. 12) reviews the evolution of self-deception. He argues that self-deception evolved to allow individuals to facilitate the deception of others and avoid the cognitive costs associated with deceit. This chapter also provides a review of recent studies concerning self-deception and the role that self-deception plays in deceiving others.

Piazza and Ingram (Chap. 13) consider the application of an evolutionary perspective to cyberpsychology. The chapter focuses on six areas that have been a traditional focus of evolutionary psychology: mating, intrasexual competition, parenting and kinship, friendship, personal information management, and trust and social exchange. The authors are particularly attentive to research concerning Internet-based social networking.

Part 3: Attitudes and Attitudinal Change

Part 3 (Chap. 14–17) examines attitudes, which refer to the relatively general and enduring evaluation of an object (i.e., the extent to which we judge something as being "good" or "bad"). There are few topics that have been as influential to the field of social psychology as the study of attitudes and attitude change. The reason that attitudes have generated so much interest is the potential they have for predicting the future behavior of individuals. However, the connections between attitudes and behaviors are complex and impacted by issues such as the accessibility, strength, and stability of the attitude (reviewed in Fabrigar and Wegener 2010; Petty and Briñol 2010). The chapters in this part of the volume concern the advantages of applying an evolutionary framework to attitudes and attitudinal change.

Lord, Hill, Holland, Yoke, and Lu (Chap. 14) consider construal models of attitudes, which suggest that individuals construct their evaluative responses online. When considered from this perspective, attitudes are able to serve evolutionary functions because they can be influenced by the temporary salience of evolutionary motives. This chapter reviews past research in which the experimental manipulation of motives such as disease avoidance, self-protection, and mate acquisition have led to changes in the attitudes adopted by individuals.

Coultas and van Leeuwen (Chap. 15) present an evolutionary perspective on conformity. The authors outline gene–culture coevolutionary models and review research on nonhuman animals that may shed light on conformity processes in humans. They suggest that accounting for the prior behavior of individuals in gene–culture models may improve their ability to predict and explain conformity.

Nicolas and Welling (Chap. 16) attempt to integrate evolutionary psychology and feminism. They argue that the reservations that many feminists have concerning evolutionary psychology may be based on misconceptions concerning the science behind evolutionary theory (e.g., the mistaken belief that evolutionary psychologists are arguing that human behavior is driven exclusively by genes). This chapter outlines the contributions that evolutionary psychology and feminism have made to women's issues and offers suggestions for reconciling these disciplines.

Morgan, Cross, and Rendell (Chap. 17) describe the field of cultural evolution, which treats culture as a shared body of knowledge that evolves in a manner that can be independent of genes. This process allows for gene–culture coevolution. The authors argue that there is potential for ideas concerning cultural evolution to influence social psychology (e.g., biases to copy the behavior of others when uncertain about how to behave).

Part 4: Interpersonal Processes

Part 4 (Chaps. 18–24) examines interpersonal processes. Social behavior can often be conceptualized as group behavior. Individuals go about their lives trying to satisfy their personal goals (e.g., finding a mate, raising their children, earning more money) while also being bound to members of social collectives (e.g., sharing a racial/ethnic background, working for the same corporation, living in the same community). The authors in this part of the volume consider how an evolutionary framework can provide a richer understanding of interpersonal processes.

Krebs (Chap. 18) suggests that the views of prosocial behavior adopted by social psychologists can be improved by considering an evolutionary framework. An evolutionary perspective suggests that prosocial behaviors are produced by cognitive mechanisms that allowed early humans to solve adaptive problems. The chapter considers the possibility that prosocial behavior may have emerged due to sexual selection, kin selection, group selection, or as a by-product of other adaptations.

Kameda, Van Vugt, and Tindale (Chap. 19) present an evolutionary perspective on group behavior. They argue that group behavior is a fundamental aspect of human evolution and that humans have evolved adaptations to deal with the challenges associated with living in complex groups. The authors apply an evolutionary framework to a range of group tasks, including coordination, social exchange, status, and group cohesion.

Hruschka, Hackman, and Macfarlan (Chap. 20) consider how an evolutionary perspective may be applied to our understanding of friendship. The authors pay special attention to evolutionary explanations for the helping and sharing behaviors often found among close friends. Evolutionary hypotheses concerning friendship are evaluated using existing evidence from psychology, anthropology, and biology.

Prentice and Sheldon (Chap. 21) review the application of an evolutionary framework to our understanding of human cooperation. They blend evolutionary ideas with observations from social psychology to gain a better understanding of the ubiquitous nature of cooperation. This is accomplished by focusing on the conflict between the interests of the individual and those of the broader social environment.

Scott-Philips (Chap. 22) applies an evolutionary framework to social cognition and other proximate mechanisms in human language and communication. He is particularly attentive to the idea that human communication is a form of mutually assisted mind reading and mental manipulation. The author also considers proximate mechanisms associated with language structure and explanations for the stability of human communication.

Hutchison and Martin (Chap. 23) examine stereotypes from an evolutionary perspective. The authors suggest that stereotypes are produced by cognitive adaptations that allow humans to deal more effectively with their social environments. They also consider the possibility that cultural evolution may provide unique insights into the origins and nature of stereotypes.

Mazur (Chap. 24) applies an evolutionary framework to human status hierarchies. An important aspect of this chapter is the consideration of the similarities and differences between human status hierarchies and those found among the other African apes. The author considers how individuals of various species signal their status to other members of the group and the ways in which groups resolve disagreements concerning the status of particular members.

Part 5: Mating and Relationships

Part 5 (Chaps. 25–28) examines mating and relationships. Intimate relationships—whether they are romantic relationships, platonic friendships, or familial relationships—involve a sense of interdependence. As a result, a considerable amount of human life revolves around forming and maintaining our relationships with others (e.g., finding a romantic partner, reconnecting with old friends, fulfilling familial obligations). The authors in this part outline how an evolutionary perspective may contribute to our understanding of these relationships.

Little (Chap. 25) outlines an evolutionary perspective for the consideration of attractiveness in humans. He argues that attractiveness is vital to the human social world for a variety of reasons, including our interest in mating with partners who will impart benefits to us and our shared hypothetical offspring. The author reviews research that has demonstrated the importance of attractiveness, considers several characteristics that have been found to impact attractiveness, and discusses variability in personal preferences concerning attractive features.

Vasey and VanderLaan (Chap. 26) consider evolutionary explanations for male androphilia (i.e., men who have a predominant sexual attraction to other men). Male androphilia presents an interesting evolutionary conundrum because it appears to have a genetic component even though it compromises reproduction. The authors consider the cross-cultural expression of male androphilia and review evidence concerning the kin selection hypothesis as a possible explanation for its persistence.

Salmon (Chap. 27) applies an evolutionary framework to familial relationships. The author argues that the understanding of family dynamics can be improved by considering humans as nepotistic strategists. This approach provides insights into a range of behaviors, including the extent to which parents invest in offspring, parent–offspring conflict over the allocation of investments, and sibling conflict and cooperation.

Figueredo, Patch, and Ceballos (Chap. 28) propose a model of multilevel selection to explain the ways in which life history influences social evolution and development. This model describes a cascade of consequences in which selective pressures at one level (e.g., natural selection) generate selective pressures at other levels (e.g., social selection). The authors argue that this sort of multilevel model can improve our understanding of the pressures that drive both life history evolution and development.

Part 6: Violence and Aggression

Part 6 (Chaps. 29–31) examines violence and aggression. Given the seemingly ubiquitous violence taking place in the world around us (e.g., armed conflict in the Middle East, the threat of terrorist attacks), it is easy to lose sight of the fact that the world is a far less violent place today than it has been at any point in human history (e.g., Gurr 1981; Pinker 2012). For example, the murder rate in England dropped from 24 per 100,000 in the fourteenth century to less than 1 per 100,000 in the twentieth century. However, these general trends offer little comfort to the victims of violence or their families. Research concerning aggression and violence is generally concerned with understanding the potential causes, correlates, and consequences of these behaviors. The authors in this part of the volume argue that an evolutionary framework can shed light on the nature of violence and aggression.

Friend and Thayer (Chap. 29) argue that war and aggression are produced by cognitive adaptations. As a result, the authors contend that an evolutionary framework has the potential to provide key insights into intergroup conflict and competition. They consider a range of issues, including the fact that aggression is often sensitive to context, the neurobiology of aggression, and the role that xenophobia plays in intergroup conflict.

Volk, Cioppa, Earle, and Farrell (Chap. 30) apply evolutionary explanations to bullying. They argue that it is important to consider how individual differences and social influences interact to contribute to bullying behavior. An important aspect of the chapter is the consideration of an expanding ring of social influences that may impact bullying behavior, which range from the immediate environment (e.g., joining friends in the bullying of a classmate) to the broader culture (e.g., the depiction of bullying in popular media).

Atran and Sheikh (Chap. 31) review recent studies related to violent extremism. The authors suggest that many violent extremists are devoted actors who are motivated by "sacred values" that render them highly resistant to material tradeoffs, normative social influence, or exit strategies. Evolutionary explanations are considered for the willingness of individuals to make costly sacrifices (e.g., die as a suicide bomber) to provide benefits for the larger social group.

Part 7: Health and Psychological Adjustment

Part 7 (Chaps. 32 and 33) examines health and psychological adjustment. Health can be defined as the "state of complete physical, mental, and social well-being and not merely the absence of disease or infirmity" (World Health Organization 1948, p. 100). There have been tremendous changes in the nature of health in the USA and other prosperous nations during the past century such that the major causes of morbidity and mortality have shifted from acute disorders and infectious diseases (e.g., tuberculosis, pneumonia) to chronic illnesses (e.g., heart disease, diabetes). That is, individuals who live in developed countries have experienced a rapid shift from a situation in which infectious agents were the biggest threat to their health to one in which behavioral regulation is increasingly important (e.g., eating a balanced diet, getting adequate exercise, managing stress). The authors in this part highlight how an evolutionary framework can deepen our understanding of behavior surrounding health and psychological adjustment.

Thornhill and Fincher (Chap. 32) outline the parasite-stress theory of sociality. A central aspect of this theory is the behavioral immune system, which includes psychological features and behaviors for avoiding contact with infectious disease and managing the negative effects of infectious diseases. The authors argue that this framework has implications for understanding a broad array of behaviors, including mate selection, interactions with pets, culinary behaviors, and political beliefs.

Grinde (Chap. 33) applies an evolutionary framework to our understanding of happiness. The author presents a model of happiness based on the idea that affective states have evolved as part of a system of rewards and punishments used for evaluating behavioral options. He reviews recent studies which suggest that affective states are associated with shared neural circuits involved in generating mood.

Part 8: Individual Differences

Part 8 (Chaps. 34–36) examines individual differences, with considerable attention devoted to personality features. An understanding of personality is important to social psychology because these internal qualities often have implications for how individuals interact with others in their social environment. That is, it does not appear that there are any important human behaviors that are due exclusively to situational causes, because behavior appears to always be influenced by psychological processes such as personality features (e.g., Buss 1991). The authors in this part of the volume apply an evolutionary perspective to our understanding of personality.

Van den Berg and Weissing (Chap. 34) discuss the connections between evolutionary game theory and personality research. Recent studies concerning evolutionary game theory have suggested that differences in personality features may have adaptive explanations. The authors consider the evolutionary causes and consequences of personality differences using evolutionary game theory.

Sefcek, Black, and Wolf (Chap. 35) apply evolutionary principles to the understanding of personality features. The authors review contemporary evolutionary models of personality traits. An important feature of the chapter is the consideration of the function of personality differences within populations as well as the evolutionary mechanisms that produce this variability.

Holtzman and Donnellan (Chap. 36) provide an overview of the possible evolutionary origins of narcissism. The authors focus on the idea that narcissism is related to numerous genes that have been subjected to selection pressures over the course of human evolutionary history. They suggest that narcissism is the result of selection for attributes that promote short-term mating and social dominance.

Conclusion

Despite the sometimes uneasy relationship that exists between social psychology and evolutionary psychology, these two areas have a tremendous amount to offer each other. For example, evolutionary psychologists are able to draw upon a diverse set of theories that have been generated using an evolutionary perspective. It is not our intention to suggest that social psychologists are unable to draw upon their own set of theories. Rather, we suggest that social psychologists may benefit from drawing on an evolutionary perspective more frequently when considering their own work. To illustrate this point, studies have revealed various patterns of behavior that are difficult—or even impossible—to adequately explain using conventional theories from social psychology, even though these findings are readily explained using an evolutionary framework (e.g., women in long-term relationships being more likely to cheat on their partner when they are ovulating, people being more easily conditioned to fear snakes than guns; Maner and Kenrick 2010). We hope that this volume will serve as another step toward more fully integrating an evolutionary perspective into the field of social psychology.

References

Adolphs, R. (1999). Social cognition and the human brain. *Trends in Cognitive Sciences, 3,* 469–479.

Baumeister, R. F. (1998). The self. In D. T. Gilbert, S. T. Fiske, & G. Lindzey (Eds.), *Handbook of social psychology* (4th ed., pp. 680–740). New York: McGraw-Hill.

Baumeister, R. F. (2010). The self. In R. F. Baumeister & E. J. Finkel (Eds.), *Advanced social psychology: The state of the science* (pp. 139–175). New York: Oxford University Press.

Buss, D. M. (1991). Evolutionary personality psychology. *Annual Review of Psychology, 42,* 459–491.

Buss, D. M. (1999). Evolutionary psychology: A new paradigm for psychological science. In D. H. Rosen & M. C. Luebbert (Eds.), *Evolution of the psyche: Human evolution, behavior, and intelligence* (pp. 1–33). Westport: Praeger.

Carlston, D. (2010). Social cognition. In R. F. Baumeister & E. J. Finkel (Eds.), *Advanced social psychology: The state of the science* (pp. 63–99). New York: Oxford University Press.

Cosmides, L., Tooby, J., & Barkow, J. (1992). Evolutionary psychology and conceptual integration. In J. Barkow, L. Cosmides, & J. Tooby (Eds.), *The adapted mind: Evolutionary psychology and the generation of culture*. New York: Oxford University Press.

Ellis, B. J., Figueredo, A. J., Brumbach, B. H., & Schlomer, G. L. (2009). Fundamental dimensions of environmental risk: The impact of harsh versus unpredictable environments on the evolution and development of life history strategies. *Human Nature, 20,* 204–268.

Fabrigar, L. R., & Wegener, D. T. (2010). Attitude structure. In R. F. Baumeister & E. J. Finkel (Eds.), *Advanced social psychology: The state of the science* (pp. 177–216). New York: Oxford University Press.

Fincher, C. L., & Thornhill, R. (2012). The parasite-stress theory may be a general theory of culture and sociality. *Behavioral and Brain Sciences, 35,* 99–119.

Fincher, C. L., Thornhill, R., Murray, D. R., & Schaller, M. (2008). Pathogen prevalence predicts human cross-cultural variability in individualism/collectivism. *Proceedings of the Royal Society of London Biological Sciences, 275,* 1279–1285.

Forgas, J. P., Haselton, M. G., & von Hippel, W. (2007). *Evolution and the social mind: Evolutionary psychology and social cognition.* New York: Psychology Press.

Frith, C. D. (2007). *The social brain? Philosophical Transactions of the Royal Society B: Biological Sciences, 362,* 671–678.

Gurr, T. R. (1981). Historical trends in violent crime: A critical review of the evidence. *Crime and Justice, 3,* 295–353.

Kenrick, D. T., Becker, D. V., Butner, J., Li, N. P., & Maner, J. K. (2003). Evolutionary cognitive science: Adding what and why to how the mind works. In J. Fitness & K. Sterelny (Eds.), *From mating to mentality: Evaluating evolutionary psychology* (pp. 13–38). New York: Psychology Press.

Kenrick, D. T., Maner, J. K., & Li, N. P. (2005). Evolutionary social psychology. In D. Buss (Ed.), *The handbook of evolutionary psychology.* Hoboken: Wiley.

Kuhn, T. S. (1962). *The structure of scientific revolutions.* Chicago: University of Chicago Press.

Macrae, N., & Miles, L. (2012). Revisiting the sovereignty of social cognition: Finally some action. In S. Fiske & N. Macrae (Eds.), *The SAGE handbook of social cognition* (pp. 1–11). Thousand Oaks: Sage.

Maner, J. K., & Kenrick, D. T. (2010). Evolutionary social psychology. In R. F. Baumeister & E. J. Finkel (Eds.), *Advanced social psychology: The state of the science* (pp. 613–653). New York: Oxford University Press.

Mesoudi, A. (2009). How cultural evolutionary theory can inform social psychology and vice versa. *Psychological Review, 116,* 929–952.

Öhman, A., & Mineka, S. (2001). Fears, phobias, and preparedness: Toward an evolved module of fear and fear learning. *Psychological Review, 108,* 483–522.

Olson, K. R., & Dweck, C. S. (2008). A blueprint for social cognitive development. *Perspectives on Psychological Science, 3,* 193–202.

Ostrom, T. M. (1984). The sovereignty of social cognition. In R. S. Wyer & T. K. Srull (Eds.), *Handbook of social cognition* (Vol. 1, pp. 1–38). Hillsdale: Erlbaum.

Petty, R. E., & Briñol, P. (2010). Attitude change. In R. F. Baumeister & E. J. Finkel (Eds.), *Advanced social psychology: The state of the science* (pp. 217–259). New York: Oxford University Press.

Pinker, S. (2012). *The better angels of our nature: Why violence has declined.* New York: Penguin Press.

Schaller, M., Simpson, J. A., & Kenrick, D. T. (2006). *Evolution and social psychology.* New York: Psychology Press.

Simpson, J. A., & Kenrick, D. T. (1997). *Evolutionary social psychology.* Mahwah: Erlbaum.

Thornhill, R., & Gangestad, S. W. (1999). The scent of symmetry: A human sex pheromone that signals fitness? *Evolution and Human Behavior, 20,* 175–201.

Wilson, E. O. (1975). *Sociobiology: The new synthesis.* Cambridge: Harvard University Press.

World Health Organization. (1948). *Constitution of the World Health Organization.* Geneva: World Health Organization Basic Documents.

Part II

Social Cognition

Social by Design: How Social Psychology Can Be More Cognitive Without Being Less Social

2

Laurence Fiddick

Despite popular misconceptions that evolutionary psychology is simply the study of mating, murder, and perhaps morality, the field is not defined by its topics of investigation, but by its approach to psychological research. In their landmark book, *The Adapted Mind,* Cosmides et al. (1992, p. 3) define evolutionary psychology as "simply psychology that is informed by the additional knowledge that evolutionary biology has to offer, in the expectation that understanding the process that designed the human mind will advance the discovery of its architecture." What this definition omits, but Tooby and Cosmides (1992) would subsequently argue, is an emphasis on natural design. What I aim to clarify in this chapter is how this emphasis on design strongly allies evolutionary psychology with cognitive psychology and how, following evolutionary psychology's lead, social psychology might become more deeply integrated with the cognitive sciences.

The Physical, Intentional, and Design Stances

The philosopher Daniel Dennett (1978) has proposed that there are three basic strategies that one might adopt to try to explain and predict the behavior of complex systems, such as those found in humans. The simplest in principle, though the most unwieldy in practice, is the physical stance. "From this stance our predictions are based on the actual physical state of the particular object, and are worked out by applying whatever knowledge we have of the laws of nature" (Dennett 1978, p. 4). Arguably this was the approach taken previously by the behaviorists. I, however, intend to focus instead on Dennett's two other explanatory strategies: the intentional stance and the design stance.

In applying the intentional stance to humans, one assumes that a person will rationally act to satisfy their desires given what they believe and the constraints under which they must act. In the wider philosophical and psychological literatures, this explanatory strategy is widely referred to as "folk psychology" or "theory of mind." Empirical investigations of folk psychology have been particularly prominent in the comparative, developmental, and neuroscientific literatures, especially after the discovery that persons with autism appear to be specifically impaired in their ability to make folk psychological predictions (Baron-Cohen et al. 1985). What these psychological investigations of folk psychology suggest is that it is an innate explanatory framework possessed and intuitively used by all neurologically normal human adults—hence the term, *folk* psychology. I will argue that folk psychology, or the intentional stance, remains the default theory of the mind for much of social psychology, and

L. Fiddick (✉)
School of Psychology, James Cook University, Townsville 4811, Australia
e-mail: larry.fiddick@my.jcu.edu.au

V. Zeigler-Hill et al. (eds.), *Evolutionary Perspectives on Social Psychology,* Evolutionary Psychology,
DOI 10.1007/978-3-319-12697-5_2, © Springer International Publishing Switzerland 2015

in this it contrasts with much of cognitive psychology and a prominent strand of evolutionary psychology. Hence, to appreciate how these evolutionary psychologists approach cognition, it is important to consider not only the influence of evolutionary biology but also the fundamental differences in the ways in which social psychologists, on the one hand, and cognitive and evolutionary psychologists, on the other, approach psychological explanation.

The explanatory stance explicitly adopted by evolutionary psychologists and at least implicitly adopted by cognitive psychologists is the design stance. "Different varieties of design-stance predictions can be discerned, but all of them are alike in relying on the notion of *function*, which is purpose-relative or teleological. That is, a design of a system breaks it up into larger or smaller functional parts, and design-stance predictions are generated by assuming that each functional part will function properly" (Dennett 1978, p. 4, emphasis in original). Some cognitive psychologists might object that they do not assume that the human mind is designed, that this would constitute unwarranted teleological speculation that runs contrary to blind evolutionary processes. Yet, this is precisely the assumption made by evolutionary psychologists, that the mind bears evidence of evolved natural design. In treating the mind as designed, evolutionary psychologists are not adopting some heterodox approach to evolutionary theorizing. On the contrary, the search for special design is a widely accepted methodological approach to the study of adaptation (Dawkins 1986; Williams 1966). The hesitation to impute design to nature is simply an anachronistic concern that one thereby subscribes to the view that the designer is an intelligent agent (e.g., God). Evolutionary biologists see no contradiction in proposing that the blind, materialistic forces driving natural selection can result in natural design. If one is troubled by the conceptual baggage riding with the term *teleology,* one can substitute, as many evolutionary biologists have, the term *teleonomy* instead (Mayr 1974; Pittendrigh 1958). Both terms refer to end-directedness, but the latter explicitly carries no assumption that the cause of such end-directedness is an intelligent agent.

Put another way, Cummins (1975) has argued that the design stance (which he calls functional analysis) has traditionally involved two assumptions: (A) The point of the design stance is to explain the origins of a functionally characterized item, and (B) "For something to perform its function is for it to have certain effects on a containing system, which effects contribute to the performance of some activity of, or the maintenance of some condition in, that containing system" (p. 741). Cummins' purpose in making this distinction was to argue that, though B might be a valid explanatory framework, it does not justify A, and so Cummins argued for keeping B and jettisoning A. Most cognitive psychologists adopt B as an explanatory framework. For example, in their influential account of human memory, (Atkinson and Shiffrin 1968; Shiffrin & Atkinson, 1969) divided human memory into a collection of functional parts: sensory register, short-term store, long-term store, control processes, and response generator, and a glance at any recent cognitive psychology textbook will reveal the same approach to the human mind, more generally. The mind is divided into a collection of functional parts: perception, attention, memory, imagery, language, problem solving, reasoning, etc.—functionally, if not neurologically, differentiated components that work as part of a system. Where cognitive psychology differs from evolutionary psychology is in its reservations about assumption A. Cognitive psychology is largely uncommitted to any specific theory about the origins of mental faculties and talk of design seems to presuppose a theory about their origins. Evolutionary psychology, on the other hand, has no such qualms about accepting assumption A—functional explanations play an important role in accounting for the origins of the traits in question. Despite their differences, it is cognitive psychology's and evolutionary psychology's commitment to assumption B, regardless of whether they also subscribe to A, that justifies labeling their approach to psychological explanation the design stance.

While it might seem that folk psychology treats beliefs and desires as distinct mental faculties, viewing these as such would be mistaken.

Beliefs and desires are not powers of the mind; they are mental representations—the contents of the folk psychological mind—just as concepts, propositions, spatial representations, and so on are the purported contents of the various mental faculties. The closest equivalent to a mental faculty in folk psychology is rationality. It is by virtue of the rational organization of the mind that beliefs and desires can be invoked in the derivation of a behavioral prediction. What I will argue is that social psychologists have, to a large extent, treated the mind as a black box—not because they are behaviorists, but because they have largely adopted the intentional stance as their primary mode of psychological explanation. While this has not impeded the development of social psychology, it has forestalled a meaningful engagement with the cognitive sciences on social psychology's own terms. In arguing this, my aim is not to pass judgment, but to provide advice gleaned from the transition of human evolutionary research from sociobiology, which similarly employed the intentional stance, to evolutionary psychology, which has embraced the design stance.

How Is Social Psychology Folk Psychological?

In arguing that social psychology is folk psychological, I do not mean that it is thoroughly so, or that cognitive psychology, by contrast, is completely free of folk psychological speculation. Dennett (1987), for example, has suggested that cognitive psychologists continue to use the intentional stance as a competence theory (i.e., a benchmark by which the cognitive faculties they postulate are judged). Hence, when speaking more broadly, beyond the usual narrow focus on a particular mental faculty, or when engaging non-psychologists like philosophers or the lay public, cognitive psychologists often adopt the intentional stance. Steven Pinker, who is both a cognitive psychologist and an advocate for evolutionary psychology, rarely, if ever, invokes folk psychological concepts in his technical works. Yet, in his best-selling popular work, *How the Mind Works,* he explicitly defends folk psychology as "the most useful and complete science of behavior there is" (Pinker 1997, p. 63). Conversely, within social psychology, social cognition in particular is influenced by cognitive psychology and, thereby, less folk psychological. Therefore, when I claim that social psychology is folk psychological, whereas cognitive and evolutionary psychology are not, this should be read more as a difference in relative focus.

Caveats aside, the differences between social psychology and cognitive psychology are striking at times. For example, Gordon Allport (1935) once claimed that attitudes are the "most distinctive and most indispensable concept in contemporary social psychology"—a quote that is still cited approvingly in social psychology textbooks and a sentiment that is echoed in the technical writings of contemporary social psychologists. Fazio and Olson (2003) write:

> It is difficult to imagine a psychological world without attitudes. One would go about daily life without the ability to think in terms of "good" and "bad," "desirable" and "undesirable," or "approach" and "avoid." There would be no activation of positivity or approach tendencies upon approaching objects that would engender positive outcomes, but, perhaps more seriously, there would be no mental faculty for avoiding negative objects in one's environment. Our environment would make little sense to us; the world would be a cacophony of meaningless blessings and curses.

Apparently, though, it is not all that difficult to imagine a psychological world without attitudes, because cognitive psychology progresses perfectly well without ever invoking the construct. Turn to any cognitive psychology textbook and one would be hard-pressed to find any mention of attitudes. The reason cannot be that attitudes are inherently social (and, therefore, left to social psychologists to study) because it is not clear what is social about an attitude like "I like chocolate." True, people could hold attitudes for value-expressive or social-adjustive reasons, but Fazio and Olson's object-appraisal approach to attitudes would appear to touch on themes dear to cognitive psychologists, like how people understand their world. Yet, cognitive psychologists have found little use for the attitude construct.

Conversely, all of those cognitive psychology textbooks that do not even mention the word "attitude" will typically include a whole chapter on language. As our species' primary means of communication, language is inherently social. Yet, one finds little discussion of language in the typical social psychology textbook. Why is that? Why is it that social psychologists are fascinated with attitudes—even attitudes of no obvious social import like one's attitude towards chocolate—and yet they seem uninterested in language, one of our species' most remarkable social faculties? The answer, I would argue, is precisely that language is a mental faculty and not readily explained in terms of the intentional stance. If one wants to explain why, for example, "no mere mortal has ever flown out to center field"—why instead we say that they "flied out" (Kim et al. 1991), it will be more useful to consider the functional organization of the language faculty rather than explanations couched in terms of a person's beliefs and desires, if for no other reason than the fact that much of linguistic processing appears to be fast, automatic, and unconscious—i.e., not the sort of thing that we likely have beliefs about. Indeed, Pinker (1994), who would later vigorously defend folk psychology, devoted a whole book to the design of the language faculty without saying much about the role that beliefs play in its functioning.

Attitudes, despite Fazio and Olson's assertion, are not a mental faculty. Attitudes, defined as one's evaluation of a target along a good–bad dimension, play roughly the same role in social psychology that desires do in folk psychology. People desire that for which they have a positive attitude and do not desire that for which they have a negative attitude. Like desires, attitudes are not mental faculties—powers of the mind—but the contents of the mind. Attitudes might appear to have the power to prompt action, but they are behaviorally inert without the rational apparatus of folk psychology. Even if one knows that someone likes chocolate, one would be at a loss to make any behavioral predictions about the person unless one also assumed that the person is rational and will rationally pursue their desires, because without the presumption of rationality, one could just as easily predict that someone desiring chocolate would go swimming as one would predict that the person would buy chocolate.

Although seldom discussed in the psychological literature, the role that the assumption of rationality plays in the ascription of belief and desire is a common theme in the philosophical literature (e.g., Dennett 1987; Stich 1983). Moreover, it is a particular form of rationality that a person is assumed to exhibit. It is the internal consistency of one's beliefs and desires that is most important and not, say, their correspondence with reality. Consider, for example, the intensively studied Sally–Anne false-belief task (Baron-Cohen et al. 1985). Sally places a marble in a basket and then leaves. While she is gone, Anne moves the marble from the basket to a box. The question posed to participants is: Where will Sally look for the marble when she returns? The answer is straightforward, Sally will act in a way that is consistent with her belief that the marble is in the basket, and not in a way that is consistent with reality, that the marble is in the box. It is precisely because persons with autism fail to predict that Sally will act in a way that is consistent with her beliefs that they are suggested to have problems with folk psychology (Baron-Cohen et al. 1985).

The same principle of internal consistency is invoked when we try to determine our own beliefs. Asked, for example, whether one believes there are more pink flamingos on the Earth or on the moon, most people will assert that there are more pink flamingos on Earth. As Sperber (1996, p. 86) notes, it is highly unlikely that this is explained by the fact that one had previously represented this belief in one's head such that one could just consult one's memory to find the belief: *There are more pink flamingos on Earth than on the moon.* Instead, in this case, we determine what we believe inferentially, based on what would be rationally consistent with other mental representations that are explicitly represented in memory.

The point of this digression into the assumption of internal consistency is that, compared with cognitive psychologists, social psychologists have a strong interest in internal consistency. Festinger's (1957) cognitive dissonance theory and Heider's (1958) balance theory, for example, both stress the consistency of belief, desire (attitudes), and behavior. By contrast, cognitive consistency is not a topic that is frequently discussed by cognitive psychologists, with the notable exception of the reasoning and decision-making literatures. Of course, it is not surprising that the topic of cognitive consistency should arise in the reasoning and decision-making literatures given that performance in these domains should conform to norms stressing internal consistency, such as the rules of logic. However, these norms were originally advocated by philosophers and economists and not psychologists. The more common position held by cognitive psychologists is that people do not, in fact, exhibit cognitive consistency (Kahneman et al. 1982).

Finally, outside of the laboratory, the primary use of folk psychology is to predict and explain *individual* behavior, not the behavior of people in general. In other words, the function of folk psychology is to predict how, or to explain why, a particular person, situated as they are, acts as they do and not how it is possible for people, in general, to act. Design stance explanations generally do just the opposite. They are more focused on how a complex mechanism functions, in general, as opposed to how the system will act in any specific situation. Here, too, the differences between social psychology and cognitive psychology are striking. A major focus of social psychology is individual differences that are typically assessed by a myriad of scales measuring the individual's beliefs or attitudes. In cognitive psychology, there is far less interest in individual differences outside of the intelligence and expertise literatures. However, these are possibly exceptions that prove the rule, as in neither literature is there a strong tendency to postulate corresponding mental faculties as opposed to invoking mental faculties, such as working memory, that have been proposed on other grounds. Even individual difference constructs, like need for cognition (Cacioppo and Petty 1982), that would presumably be of some relevance to cognitive psychology are rarely considered in cognitive research. Compared with social psychologists, cognitive psychologists are much less interested in individual differences.

To summarize, social psychology is folk psychological in that it routinely employs the concepts of belief and desire/attitude; it routinely stresses the internal consistency of a person's beliefs, desires/attitudes, and actions; and individual differences play an important role in social psychological research. In all three respects, cognitive psychology is quite different. The reason it is different is that cognitive psychology is focused instead on elucidating the functions of mental faculties that are presumed to be universal. In practice, this seldom draws upon the explanatory constructs of beliefs, desires, or attitudes, and the basic design of mental faculties is not presumed, a priori, to be internally consistent, though perhaps the ultimate goal of cognitive psychology is to describe a system that in its global functioning approximates folk psychology (i.e., adopting folk psychology as a competence theory; Dennett 1978).

Why Might Social Psychologists Want to Adopt the Design Stance?

Even if one accepts the argument that social psychologists tend to adopt the intentional stance, while cognitive psychologists tend to adopt the design stance, this, in itself, provides no reason for social psychologists to likewise adopt the design stance.

Moreover, by adopting the design stance, the possibility arises that that which most interests social psychologists—the social—will be lost. Would not the adoption of the design stance ultimately reduce social psychology to asocial, cognitive psychology? If this is what social psychologists have to look forward to in adopting the design stance, perhaps they might choose, instead, to continue the same basic program of research that they are engaged in now, investigating "how the thoughts, feelings, and behaviors of individuals are influenced by the actual, imagined, or implied presence of other human beings"

(Allport 1954, p. 5). In other words, studying the social might require social psychologists to treat the mind somewhat as a black box, the details of which are left to cognitive psychologists to study, for to study mental faculties properly would mean setting aside the social, to investigate mental processes independent of the information they process. The error in this line of reasoning is that it privileges a particular conception of faculty psychology, which, though the most common conception, is not the only one possible.

There are, in fact, two different schools of thought with respect to mental faculties. Fodor (1983) has labeled these horizontal faculty psychology and vertical faculty psychology, or, as these are more commonly known, mainstream cognitive psychology and mental modularity, respectively. According to Fodor, horizontal faculties are distinguished on the basis of their typical effects, whereas vertical faculties are distinguished on the basis of their domain of application. For example, the horizontal faculties of short-term and long-term memory are distinguished by the duration over which they hold information, their storage capacity, etc. They are not distinguished by the content domain of the information that they store—any information that can be stored in short-term memory can also be stored in long-term memory, what distinguishes these memory stores is how long information is held within each, etc.

Vertical faculties, on the other hand, are distinguished less by the effects they have on information, such as whether the information is stored (e.g., memory) versus highlighted (e.g., attention), but by the content of the information that they process. For example, Kanwisher et al. (1997) have shown that a region of the fusiform gyrus, the fusiform face area (FFA), is preferentially activated by visual displays of faces as opposed to other comparable visual displays, such as displays of houses or other common objects. Based on these findings, Kanwisher et al. proposed that the FFA is a face *perception* module. Subsequent research has implicated the same brain region in explicit working memory for faces (Druzgal and D'Esposito 2003), implicit memory for faces (Henson et al. 2000), and the mental imagery of faces (O'Craven and Kanwisher 2000). In other words, what predicts activation of the FFA is not the type of processing effect—e.g., perception versus memory versus imagery—but the content of the information processed, faces versus other objects. The FFA is, therefore, a content-specialized vertical faculty, not a content-independent horizontal faculty.

I do not intend to provide a general argument in favor of vertical faculty psychology over horizontal faculty psychology. Instead, I will argue for the particular advantages of adopting the former as opposed to the latter in further integrating social psychology and cognitive psychology, without social psychology thereby surrendering the social.

Suppose, for example, that social psychologists choose horizontal faculty psychology as their guiding model of mental structure. There would then be little that social psychologists qua social psychologists could contribute to the study of mental faculties. Social information is no different from any other information from the perspective of horizontal faculty psychology, as mental processes are, by hypothesis, domain general in their application. Social psychology would remain in the position it finds itself in now, investigating the influence of social information on mental faculties, with nothing to say about the design and function of those mental faculties. The discovery of the mind's structure would remain the privileged task of cognitive psychologists.

Suppose, on the other hand, that social psychologists adopted vertical faculty psychology as their guiding model of the mind. The most straightforward implication would be that social psychologists would go about the business of proposing and studying *social* faculties. In other words, social psychologists could, indeed, adopt the design stance and investigate mental faculties without giving up the social. Is this a viable prospect? Not only is it viable, but it has been done and it has been enormously successful. However, it has not been done by "social psychologists."

In proposing that language is a domain-specific mental faculty, a linguist, Chomsky (1965), had an enormous influence on cognitive psychology. According to Jackendoff (2002), "This hypothesis [specifically the proposal that there is a language module] is what connects linguistic theory most closely to biology, cognitive development, ethology, and evolutionary psychology. It also has been the main driving force in research on language typology, language acquisition, and linguistic change, not to mention day-to-day research on the structure of language" (p. 68). Yet, despite the inherently social nature of language, social psychologists have played a relatively minor role in the scientific study of language. One cannot dismiss the above observations by arguing that it is trivially obvious that a linguist would have more of an influence on the psychology of language than a social psychologist would. Chomsky (1957) had already revolutionized linguistics with the publication of his *Syntactic Structures* before he truly engaged psychologists by proposing a language-specific mental module in *Aspects of the Theory of Syntax* (Chomsky 1965). This suggests that it was not simply his influence within linguistics that made his proposals influential on cognitive psychology. Moreover, it was cognitive psychologists who subsequently investigated Chomsky's proposal, not social psychologists. Arguably, the reason why social psychologists have contributed little to subsequent research is that Chomsky's proposal was cast in terms of a mental faculty and social psychologists tend not to be faculty psychologists.

By the same reasoning, social psychology is not likely to have much influence on cognitive psychology until its proposals are framed in terms of (social) mental faculties. Consider, for example, the fate of attribution theory. The theories of attribution developed by Heider (1958), Kelley (1973), and Weiner (1985) have been enormously influential within social psychology, but their influence outside of social psychology has been much more limited. There is now a burgeoning literature on folk psychology within the cognitive developmental, cognitive neuroscience, primatology, and autism literatures, yet these three social psychologists are rarely mentioned within these literatures, despite the fact that attribution theory is typically viewed as the attempt to account for naive psychology (i.e., folk psychology). In part, this lack of influence may be due to misguided emphases on distinguishing the person from the situation and covariation data, but equally important is the failure to distinguish behavior from other events (i.e., to distinguish naive psychology as a distinct domain of human understanding; Malle 2011).

Where Kelley has had an influence in cognitive psychology is in the causal cognition literature (e.g., Ahn et al. 1995; Cheng 1997). This is hardly surprising given that Kelley (1973) explicitly equated social attribution with nonsocial causal cognition. In so doing, Kelley effectively argued that social psychology has nothing unique to contribute to the understanding of causal cognition, and as a result cognitive psychologists were free to, and did, ignore social influences on causal cognition. In other words, Kelley engaged cognitive psychologists on their own terms and what got lost in the process was the social.

What animates much current research on naive psychology beyond social psychology is the proposal the folk psychology is a distinct *social* faculty (e.g., Baron-Cohen 1997; Frith and Frith 1999). By contrast with Kelley's legacy in the causal cognition literature, the social has not been sidelined in the folk psychology literature, even though it is primarily nonsocial psychologists, such as clinical and developmental psychologists, who are engaged in this literature (e.g., Caputi et al. 2012; Dodell-Feder et al. 2013; Slaughter et al. 2013). Moreover, the folk psychology literature is being belatedly invoked to reinterpret well-established work in social psychology (e.g., Bazinger and Kühberger 2012; Malle 2011).

To summarize, there is more than one way to adopt the design stance. Mainstream cognitive psychology has adopted horizontal faculty psychology, which sidelines the social due to its emphasis on domain-general mechanisms. An equally viable option, though, is vertical faculty psychology or modularity, which focuses on domain-specific mechanisms. Among the social modules that have been proposed and have generated a vibrant literature are language, face processing, and folk psychology. Yet, none of these literatures intersect much with standard social psychology. Hence, I argue that by similarly adopting the design stance, particularly a modular perspective, standard social psychologists might likewise engage a much broader audience.

The Illustrative Example of Evolutionary Psychology

How might social psychologists go about adopting the design stance? In practice, would it mean social psychologists doing anything different from what they do now? Would they, say, need to be more cognitive and, if so, why and what would this look like? Answers to these questions can be found in the history of evolutionary psychology's development.

Prior to the emergence of evolutionary psychology in the late 1980s, the evolutionarily inspired investigation of human behavior was dominated by sociobiology. More specifically, a large measure of sociobiology fell within a program of research initiated by Richard Alexander, dubbed Alexander's program by Kitcher (1985), but also known as Darwinian anthropology (Symons 1989). In contrast to Wilson's (1978) somewhat pessimistic view of human behavior kept on a short tether by our genes, Alexander (1979) proposed that humans flexibly respond to their local environment with the unconscious desire to increase their fitness. In effect, Darwinian anthropology unwittingly melded evolutionary theorizing with folk psychology (Kitcher 1985; Tooby and Cosmides 1990). Rather than people acting to rationally satisfy their desires given their beliefs and various constraints on their actions, people act to rationally maximize their fitness given the various constraints on their actions. Furthermore, these proposals were tested by correlating individual differences in behavior with individual differences in reproductive success.

On the surface, Darwinian anthropology might seem to have little in common with social psychology, but the larger explanatory frameworks of both are similar. Both fields generally assume that people act to satisfy some desire and that they highlight individual differences. Where they contrast is in the content of the desires that they attribute to people. The overarching desire that Darwinian anthropology attributes to people, albeit an unconscious one, is the desire to increase one's reproductive success, whereas the desires attributed to people by social psychology are much more varied. Regardless, both fields typically assume that these desires are rationally and individually pursued, subject to the constraints under which a person must act.

In the late 1980s, Leda Cosmides, John Tooby, and Donald Symons published a series of papers that were critical of Darwinian anthropology and argued for a different approach to studying the influence that evolution has had on the human mind and behavior (Cosmides and Tooby 1987; Symons 1987, 1989, 1990; Tooby and Cosmides 1989, 1990). Evolutionary psychology is the realization of this alternate program of research that Cosmides, Symons, and Tooby advocated.

In essence, Cosmides, Symons, and Tooby advocated adopting the design stance, but in so doing, they followed the lead, not of Dennett, but of Williams (1966). Williams argued that evolutionary theorists must distinguish between adaptations and fortuitous effects. Adaptations are the end products of a history of natural selection. Hence, they are anatomical, physiological, or behavioral solutions to ancestral problems, which one demonstrates by showing how the trait shows evidence of special design for solving the problem.

In evolutionary terms, solving a problem ultimately means promoting fitness—i.e., differential reproductive success. However, differential reproductive success in the present is not the mark of adaptation. An adaptation undergoes many generations of selection in which it contributes to the differential reproductive success of its bearers, yet the contemporary environment may have changed such that the adaptation no longer conveys a fitness advantage or, perhaps more importantly, precisely because the adaptation conferred a fitness advantage it displaced all rival designs such that now every member of the species possesses the trait. In the latter case, the adaptation no longer contributes to differential reproductive success precisely because there are no differences between individuals with respect to the trait. Regardless of the reason, current reproductive success provides no evidence that the trait in question is an adaptation. Current reproductive success may simply be the fortuitous effect of some trait. Hence, evidence for adaptation must be sought elsewhere. Special design (i.e., complex functional organization) does not change when an adaptation saturates a population. It also disappears slowly—as slowly as it appeared, all else being equal—when the environment changes such that the trait no longer fits its environment. But even if one has determined to seek evidence of special design, there is still the question of where one is most likely to find it.

Cosmides and Tooby (1987) and Symons (1989; see also Daly and Wilson 1984) argued that overt behavior is too variable in most cases to be the locus of design. Consider, for example, food acquisition. Few would deny that finding nourishment is a long-standing problem with clear fitness consequences. Where, then, would one look for evidence of special design for procuring nourishment? At the level of overt behavior, there is too much variability for behavior to have been the target of selection and the locus of design. People can grow their own food, they can hunt and gather, and they can buy food at a supermarket. For one meal a person might eat a salad, for another they might eat pasta, and so on. Couched at the behavioral level, there are too many different ways of acquiring nourishment and their expression is too variable for each behavior to have been the target of selection and for each to be considered an aspect of our species' evolved design.

Instead, stable invariance is more likely to be found at the physiological or psychological level of description. For example, hunger might be regulated by the same motivation system across all humans, despite the fact that how they eventually act to satisfy their hunger varies enormously. Therefore, if one wants to explain behavior from an evolutionary perspective, one will need to look to the physiological and psychological mechanisms that motivate behavior to demonstrate evidence of special design. Moreover, due to the functional nature of cognitive descriptions—cognitive descriptions specify the role that psychological states and processes play in solving a problem—the cognitive level of description is particularly suited for analyzing the design of a system (Cosmides and Tooby 1987).

The above argument generalizes to any attempt to apply the design stance. In other words, even if a social psychologist is not committed to an evolutionary account of the origins of mental faculties, if instead one adopts Cummins' (1975) more agnostic stance towards the origin of functional components, it would still make practical sense to couch one's proposals at the cognitive level because cognitive-level descriptions best capture functional relationships. Where social psychologists might part ways with evolutionary psychologists is in the latter's emphasis on special design. The emphasis on special design is driven more by evolutionary concerns (Dawkins 1986; Williams 1966). However, social psychologists might, likewise, choose to focus on special design for other reasons.

In psychology, special design for solving problems is naturally aligned with vertical faculty psychology and so it was that Cosmides and Tooby (1987) and Symons (1987) argued that special design was to be found in the modularity of the mind. The interested reader can refer to the chapter in this volume on modularity for scientific arguments in favor of modularity (see Chap. 4). Instead, I consider whether social psychologists might likewise wish to focus on special design and mental modularity. The answer I give here is that which I have already raised above. It is primarily by adopting mental modularity that social psychologists can adopt the design stance without letting go of the social. In other words, if social psychologists were to postulate specifically social faculties, like language, face processing, and folk psychology, they would, in effect, be invoking special design—they would, de facto, be postulating mental faculties are specially designed for social ends.

But does one need an evolutionary account of the origin of such faculties? Much vision research, for example, is modular without being (explicitly) committed to an evolutionary account of the origins of the visual system. As

Symons (1987) acknowledges, a little common sense goes a long way towards understanding the design of our perceptual systems. However, Symons also argues that this is less likely to be the case for social faculties. To begin with, unlike the physical world that our perceptual systems were designed to report on, the social world is rife with conflicts of interest. Consider, for example, mating psychology. From an evolutionary perspective, males and females should have quite different views about mating (Symons 1979). Hence, a male social psychologist consulting only his own intuitions about mating psychology is likely to have only a partial and biased understanding of human mating. Of course, a male evolutionary theorist is just as likely to have partial and biased intuitions about mating, but an evolutionary perspective acts as a corrective because it starts with the presumption that there will be conflicts of interest; it, therefore, encourages one to consider the perspective of both sexes; and it encourages one to consider other species with different life histories in which the selective forces acting on males and females can be different from those acting on humans.

Second, an evolutionary perspective suggests that our minds were designed for past environments, not present environments (Symons 1987; Tooby and Cosmides 1990). As Symons notes, the past was probably not all that different from the present with respect to those features of the environment that our perceptual mechanisms are attuned to. The social environment, however, has changed enormously. Therefore, intuitions based on contemporary social environments may be poor guides as to the design of our social faculties.

There is no denying that social psychology has been enormously successful; nor is it generally in the throes of some crisis that might prompt a major rethink of current practice. Nevertheless, in adopting the intentional stance as its primary mode of psychological explanation, social psychology has forestalled a deeper integration with the cognitive sciences. Research topics that should naturally concern social psychology such as language, face processing, and folk psychology have been largely ignored by social psychologists. The corrective to this situation is for social psychologists to adopt the design stance. This would naturally lead social psychologists to adopt a more cognitive orientation, but it need not be at the expense of the social, provided that social faculties are investigated from a modular perspective. In so doing, social psychology would be following the lead of evolutionary psychology, which itself made the transition from folk psychological sociobiology. While it is not necessary for social psychologists to explicitly adopt an evolutionary perspective in making this transition, were they to do so, they would avail themselves of a wealth of evolutionary theorizing on social matters.

Acknowledgment Many thanks to Mark Young and the editors, Lisa Welling, Virgil Zeigler-Hill, and Todd Shackelford, for many helpful comments and suggestions.

References

Ahn, W., Kalish, C. W., Medin, D. L., & Gelman, S. A. (1995). The role of covariation versus mechanism information in causal attribution. *Cognition, 54,* 299–352.

Alexander, R. (1979). *Darwinism and human affairs.* Seattle: University of Washington Press.

Allport, G. (1935). Attitudes. In C. Murchison (Ed.), *The handbook of social psychology* (pp. 798–844). Worchester: Cark University Press.

Allport, G. (1954). The historical background of modern social psychology. In G. Lindzey (Ed.), *Handbook of social psychology* (pp. 3–56). Reading: Addison-Wesley.

Atkinson, R. C., & Shiffrin, R. M. (1968). Human memory: A proposed system and its control processes. In K. W. Spence (Ed.), *The psychology of learning and motivation* (pp. 89-195). New York, NY: Academic Press.

Baron-Cohen, S. (1997). *Mindblindness: An essay on autism and theory of mind.* Cambridge: MIT Press.

Baron-Cohen, S., Leslie, A., & Frith, U. (1985). Does the autistic child have a "theory of mind"? *Cognition, 21,* 37–46.

Bazinger, C., & Kühberger, A. (2012). Is social projection based on simulation or theory? Why new methods are needed for differentiating. *New Ideas in Psychology, 30,* 328–335.

Cacioppo, J. T., & Petty, R. E. (1982). The need for cognition. *Journal of Personality and Social Psychology, 42,* 116–131.

Caputi, M., Lecce, S., Pagnin, A., & Banerjee, R. (2012). Longitudinal effects of theory of mind on later peer relations: The role of prosocial behavior. *Developmental Psychology, 48,* 257–270.

Cheng, P. (1997). From covariation to causation: A causal power theory. *Psychological Review, 104,* 367–405.

Chomsky, N. (1957). *Syntactic structures*. The Hague: Mouton.

Chomsky, N. (1965). *Aspects of the theory of syntax*. Cambridge: MIT Press.

Cosmides, L., & Tooby, J. (1987). From evolution to behaviour: Evolutionary psychology as the missing link. In J. Dupre (Ed.), *The latest on the best: Essays on evolution and optimality* (pp. 277–306). Cambridge: Bradford Book

Cosmides, L., Tooby, J., & Barkow, J. (1992). Introduction: Evolutionary psychology and conceptual integration. In J. Barkow, L. Cosmides, & J. Tooby (Eds.), *The adapted mind: Evolutionary psychology and the generation of culture* (pp. 3–15). New York: Oxford University Press.

Cummins, R. (1975). Functional analysis. *Journal of Philosophy, 72,* 741–765.

Daly, M., & Wilson, M. (1984). A sociobiological analysis of human infanticide. In G. Hausfater & S. B. Hrdy (Eds.), *Infanticide* (pp. 487–502). New York: Aldine.

Dawkins, R. (1986). *The blind watchmaker*. New York: Norton.

Dennett, D. (1978). *Brainstorms*. Cambridge: Bradford Books.

Dodell-Feder, D., Tully, L. M., Lincoln, S. H., & Hooker, C. I. (2013). The neural basis of theory of mind and its relationship to social functioning and social anhedonia in individuals with schizophrenia. *NeuroImage: Clinical*. Available online 27 November 2013.

Druzgal, T. J., & D'Esposito, M. (2003). Dissecting contributions of prefrontal cortex and fusiform face area to face working memory. *Journal of Cognitive Neuroscience, 15,* 771–784.

Fazio, R. H., & Olson, M. A. (2003). Attitudes: Foundations, functions, and consequences. In M. A. Hogg & J. Cooper (Eds.), *The Sage handbook of social psychology* (pp. 139–160). London: Sage.

Festinger, L. (1957). *A theory of cognitive dissonance*. Stanford: Stanford University Press.

Fodor, J. (1983). *The modularity of mind*. Cambridge: Bradford Book.

Frith, C. D., & Frith, U. (1999). Interacting minds—A biological basis. *Science, 286,* 1692–1695.

Heider, F. (1958). *The psychology of interpersonal relations*. New York: Wiley.

Henson, R., Shallice, T., & Dolan, R. (2000). Neuroimaging evidence for dissociable forms of repetition priming. *Science, 287,* 1269–1272.

Jackendoff, R. (2002). *Foundations of language: Brain, meaning, grammar, evolution*. New York: Oxford University Press.

Kahneman, D., Slovic, P., & Tversky, A. (1982). *Judgment under uncertainty: Heuristics and biases*. New York: Cambridge University Press.

Kanwisher, N., McDermott, J., & Chun, M. M. (1997). The fusiform face area: A module in human extrastriate cortex specialized for face perception. *Journal of Neuroscience, 17,* 4302–4311.

Kelley, H. H. (1973). The process of attribution. *American Psychologist, 28,* 107–128.

Kim, J., Pinker, S., Prince, A., & Prasada, S. (1991). Why no mere mortal has ever flown out to center field. *Cognitive Science, 15,* 173–218.

Kitcher, P. (1985). *Vaulting ambition: Sociobiology and the quest for human nature*. Cambridge: MIT Press.

Malle, B. (2011). Time to give up the dogmas of attribution: An alternative theory of behavior explanation. *Advances in Experimental Social Psychology, 44,* 297–352.

Mayr, E. (1974). Teleological and teleonomic: A new analysis. *Boston Studies in the Philosophy of Science, 15,* 91–117.

O'Craven, K. M., & Kanwisher, N. (2000). Mental imagery of faces and places activates corresponding stimulus-specific brain regions. *Journal of Cognitive Neuroscience, 12,* 1013–1023.

Pinker, S. (1994). *The language instinct*. New York: William Morrow and Co.

Pinker, S. (1997). *How the mind works*. New York: Norton.

Pittendrigh, C. S. (1958). Adaptation, natural selection, and behaviour. In A. Roe & G. G. Simpson (Eds.), *Behavior and evolution* (pp. 390–416). New Haven: Yale University Press.

Shiffrin, R. M., & Atkinson, R. C. (1969). Storage and retrieval processes in long-term memory. *Psychological Review, 76,* 179–1793.

Slaughter, V., Peterson, C. C., & Moore, C. (2013). I can talk you into it: Theory of mind and persuasion behavior in young children. *Developmental Psychology, 49,* 227–231.

Sperber, D. (1996). *Explaining culture: A naturalistic approach*. Cambridge: Blackwell.

Stich, S. (1983). *From folk psychology to cognitive science: The case against belief*. Cambridge: Bradford Book.

Symons, D. (1979). *The evolution of human sexuality*. New York: Oxford University Press.

Symons, D. (1987). If we're all Darwinians, what's the fuss about? In C. B. Crawford, M. F. Smith, & D. L. Krebs (Eds.), *Sociobiology and psychology* (pp. 121–146). Hillsdale: Erlbaum.

Symons, D. (1989). A critique of Darwinian anthropology. *Ethology and Sociobiology, 10,* 131–144.

Symons, D. (1990). Adaptiveness and adaptation. *Ethology and Sociobiology, 11,* 427–444.

Tooby, J., & Cosmides, L. (1989). Evolutionary psychology and the generation of culture, part I. Theoretical considerations. *Ethology and Sociobiology, 10,* 29–49.

Tooby, J., & Cosmides, L. (1990). The past explains the present: Emotional adaptations and the structure of ancestral environments. *Ethology and Sociobiology, 11,* 375–424.

Tooby, J., & Cosmides, L. (1992). The psychological foundations of culture. In J. Barkow, L. Cosmides, & J. Tooby (Eds.), *The adapted mind: Evolutionary psychology and the generation of culture* (pp. 19–136). New York: Oxford University Press.

Weiner, B. (1985). An attributional theory of achievement motivation and emotion. *Psychological Review, 92,* 548–573.

Williams, G. (1966). *Adaptation and natural selection.* Princeton: Princeton University Press.

Wilson, E. O. (1978). *On human nature*. Cambridge: Harvard University Press.

Social Cognitive Development from an Evolutionary Perspective

3

Karin Machluf and David F. Bjorklund

Humans are among the most social of mammals; they cooperate, compete, imitate, and teach to a degree that is unmatched by any other known species. They transmit information to group members and across generations with great fidelity. *Homo sapiens* have developed technologies to make such transmission fast and efficient, including alphabets, numbers, books, and computers, but it is our species' social nature, less so than our technological acumen, that is responsible for our global hegemony. We contend, as others have (e.g., Alexander 1989; Dunbar 2003; Hare 2011), that it was changes in social cognition over hominin evolution that was the driving force in human intelligence. Moreover, the origins of humans' social nature and cognition are found in infancy and childhood, placing social cognitive development at center stage in understanding the evolution of the human mind.

Darwin (1871) recognized the significance of sociality to human intellectual evolution, writing, "It serves notice that as soon as the progenitors of man became social…the advancement of the intellectual facilities will have been aided and modified in an important manner, of which we see only traces in the lower animals" (p. 161). Extending the *social brain hypothesis* (Dunbar 2003), Bjorklund and his colleagues argued that it was the confluence of a large brain, an extended juvenile period, and social complexity that was responsible for the development of human social intelligence (e.g., Bjorklund and Bering 2003; Bjorklund et al. 2005), and that these three factors interacted synergistically over hominin evolution, with large brains and an extended juvenile period being necessary for mastering the ways of one's group, and social complexity in turn exerting selection pressures for increased brain size and an extension of the preadult life span.

The core of human social cognition is the ability to view others as *intentional agents,* individuals whose actions are purposeful and goal directed (see Bandura 2006; Tomasello 2009; Tomasello and Carpenter 2007). Although viewing others as intentional agents may not seem to be such a momentous cognitive accomplishment, it is the foundation for *theory of mind,* the ability to model the psychological states of others—understanding that others' behavior is based on what they know, or believe, and what they want, or desire, termed *belief–desire reasoning* (Wellman 1990). Human children develop theory-of-mind abilities over the preschool years, culminating in solving explicit false-belief tasks around 4 years of age, and display a very different ontogenetic pattern of social cognition from the extant great apes (Bjorklund et al. 2010; Hare 2011). Human infants are oriented toward social stimuli, leading ineluctably—given a species-typical environ-

K. Machluf (✉)
Department of Psychology, Florida Atlantic University, 777 Glades Road, Boca Raton, FL 33431, USA
e-mail: kmachluf@fau.edu

D. F. Bjorklund
Department of Psychology, Florida Atlantic University, 112 Behavioral Science, 777 Glades Road, Boca Raton, 33431-0991FL, USA
e-mail: dbjorklu@fau.edu

V. Zeigler-Hill et al. (eds.), *Evolutionary Perspectives on Social Psychology,* Evolutionary Psychology, DOI 10.1007/978-3-319-12697-5_3, © Springer International Publishing Switzerland 2015

ment—to an ability to anticipate and understand the thoughts, perspectives, and actions of others, resulting in the development of distinctly human social intelligence. In this chapter, we review the development of human social cognition during the early years of life, contrast it with the social cognitive abilities of humans' closest genetic relatives, chimpanzees (*Pan troglodytes*), and speculate why such a unique cognitive system may have evolved.

Newborns' Attention to Social Stimuli

Infancy is a highly vulnerable time for survival for all mammals, including humans. Infants are highly dependent on their primary caregiver, typically the mother, for nutrition, shelter, and care. Given this dependency, human infants have evolved ways of attaining such care and forming strong bonds with their caretaker in some ways that are seemingly unique in the animal kingdom.

One important set of adaptations possessed by human neonates and other vertebrate newborns is the tendency to orient toward and process information related to animate creatures, presumably their own species (reviewed in Johnson 2007). For example, 2-day-old human infants will preferentially look at light displays that depict biological motion (Bardi et al. 2011; Simion et al. 2008). In these studies, infants were shown point-light displays of a walking hen with 13 light patches at the main joints. This was contrasted with a display of rigid motion, in which a single point-light frame of a hen was moved around the screen. Using both visual preference (Bardi et al. 2011; Simion et al. 2008) and habituation procedures (Bardi et al. 2011), newborns were able to distinguish between the two displays and were more attentive to the one depicting biological motion. Human infants do not differentiate between displays of human and nonhuman biological motion until about 9 months (Bertenthal et al. 1987), and by 12 months, infants will follow the "gaze" of a point-light human figure, indicating that such displays convey sufficient information for babies to treat them as intentional agents (Yoon and Johnson 2009).

Human newborns also show biases to attend to faces. Numerous studies have shown that neonates will selectively attend to face-like stimuli relative to other equally complex stimuli (e.g., Goren et al. 1975; Mondloch et al. 1999). Other research indicates that newborns can discriminate among human faces and look longer at faces of their mothers than of other women (Bushnell et al. 1989) and will modify their rate of sucking to see a picture of their mother's face than that of another woman (Walton et al. 1992). This seeming early learning of an ecologically important social stimulus is not unique to humans and has also been reported in a 4-week-old gibbon (Myowa-Yamakoshi and Tomonaga 2001).

The eyes seem to be especially important for newborns. For example, neonates look longer at faces with eyes opened rather than closed (Batki et al. 2000) and are more attentive to direct gaze than averted gaze (Farroni et al. 2002). This latter finding caused Farroni and colleagues to conclude that infants' bias for direct gaze "is probably a result of a fast and approximate analysis of the visual input, dedicated to find socially relevant stimuli for further processing" (p. 9604). The eyes also seem to be important in infants' bias to attend to upright versus upside-down faces. In one study, newborns were shown upright and upside-down photos of partially occluded faces, some showing the eyes and others not. The infants looked significantly longer at the upright than the upside-down faces, as do older infants and adults, but only when they could see the eyes. They showed no differential attention for either the upright or upside-down faces when the eyes were occluded (Gava et al. 2008). In other research, newborns were more attentive to attractive than less attractive faces (Slater et al. 1998), but only when faces were presented in an upright orientation (Slater et al. 2000).

Newborns have also been shown to match facial expressions made by adults, termed *neonatal imitation*. However, rather than being an indication that human infants are born with the rudiments of sophisticated social learning abilities as originally proposed by Meltzoff and Moore (1977), such "imitation" more likely reflects an ontogenetic adaptation, a behavior that serves an adaptive function at a specific time in development and then disappears when it is no longer functional (Bjorklund 1997; Oppenheim 1981). For example, the imitation of tongue protrusion, the most studied facial gesture when examining neonatal imitation, disappears around 2 months of age (e.g., Abravanel and Sigafoos 1984; Jacobson 1979). Similar patterns of imitation of facial expressions at birth followed by decline later have been shown for chimpanzees (Bard 2007; Myowa-Yamakoshi et al. 2004) and rhesus monkeys (Ferrari et al. 2006).

Rather than reflecting a subtle version of true selective imitation, others have interpreted neonatal imitation as a transient adaptation to solve specific problems of early infancy. For example, Jacobson (1979) suggested that neonatal imitation may be functional in nursing, while others have proposed that such behavior serves to facilitate social interaction between newborns and their mothers (e.g., Bjorklund 1987; Byrne 2005; Nagy 2006). Infants may reflexively match some facial expressions, fostering social interaction with a caretaker at a time when they are not able to control their own social behavior intentionally. Byrne (2005) referred to such matching behavior as *social mirroring,* in which the infant copies the action of his or her caretaker to stay "in tune" with one another, consolidating the social interaction. As infants gain greater neurological control over their behavior, the reflexive matching of facial expressions disappears. Consistent with this interpretation, Heimann (1989) showed that neonates who showed higher levels of facial imitation had higher-quality social interactions with their mothers 3 months later.

It seems clear that human babies enter the world with biases to attend to socially relevant stimuli. The research also demonstrates that infants' learning about faces begins early and "with a vengeance" (Karmiloff-Smith 1996, p. 10). Given the importance of faces (or more properly, the people possessing the faces) to a highly dependent infant, it should not be too surprising that natural selection has made this so.

Viewing Others as Intentional Agents

Beyond the neonatal period, infants are able to exert greater intentional control of their actions, as control is shifted from subcortical to cortical brain areas (Nagy 2006). Among the "social" behaviors infants control are sustained eye contact and social smiling, reflective of positive mood, which is not frequently and unambiguously seen until about 3 months (Reilly et al. 1995). Smiling before this time, which is sometimes observed during rapid eye moment (REM) sleep, is best thought of as reflections of some positive bodily state, such as being fed or being gently touched. These positive social cues are seen universally and promote repeated social interaction with their caretakers, fostering infant–mother attachment and, thus, survival. These cues also serve as reinforcements to caregivers, promoting a mother's feelings of competence, which may serve to increase the quantity and quality of the maternal care infants receive (see Goodman et al. 2005; Murray and Trevarken 1986).

Despite infants' improved abilities to control their own behaviors and facilitate social interaction with their caregivers, human social interaction requires, at its most basic, the ability to view other people as *intentional agents*—individuals who *cause* things to happen and whose behavior is designed to achieve some goal (see Bandura 2006; Tomasello 2009). Related to viewing others as intentional agents is *perspective taking,* the ability to take the point of view of others. Despite young infants' social orientation and considerable social skill in manipulating their parents, they seem to not treat others as intentional agents until the latter part of the first year (see Tomasello 2009; Tomasello and Carpenter 2007). The first sign of this is in the form of *shared attention* (e.g., Carpenter et al. 1998), which involves a three-way interaction between the infant, another person, and an object. This is apparent during parent–infant interaction, with parents pointing out objects to infants (referential communication). Although many parents start engaging in such behavior in the first months of life, infants only begin to engage in shared interaction beginning around 9 months of age, when they will participate in repetitive give-and-take with an adult and an object, look in the direction adults are looking or pointing, and point or hold up objects to another person (e.g., Carpenter et al. 1998). This ability improves over infancy into toddlerhood so that by 12 months of age, infants will point to objects to inform others about events they do not know (Liszkowski et al. 2007). Between 12 and 18 months, children will point to objects to direct an adult's attention to something he or she is searching for (Liszkowski et al. 2006) and will use another person's gaze to direct their own attention (Brooks and Meltzoff 2002). Being able to share a perceptual experience may hardly seem like a task of great cognitive complexity or consequence, but it is one that is seemingly not possessed by other great apes (Herrmann et al. 2007; Tomasello and Carpenter 2005).

Viewing others as intentional agents is a foundational ability for effective social learning. As we will see, the nature of children's social learning changes as they enter childhood, but well before their second birthdays, infants and toddlers are attentive to the behavior of others and will reproduce others' actions, often based on their assumed intentions.

Social Learning in Infants and Children

Childhood is about learning and accruing those skills and behaviors necessary for successful adult functioning and, ultimately, for successful reproduction. The work for such adaptations is done in childhood, but does not necessarily pay off immediately. Rather, their benefits can be apparent in childhood as *ontogenetic adaptations* or as *deferred adaptations* in adulthood (for a discussion of ontogenetic vs. deferred adaptation, see Hernández Blasi and Bjorklund 2003). Prolonged childhoods, like those found in higher primates, would be a monumental waste of time and resources if they did not provide any added evolutionary value to mature life. The social complexity of hominin life is likely one such major driving force behind human cognitive evolution and development (Joffe 1997; Konner 2010) as the variety and intricacy of social behaviors required for functioning is quite substantial, with an extended juvenile period providing the opportunity for acquiring such knowledge, often through social learning.

At its most general, social learning can be defined as occurring in a situation "in which one individual comes to behave similarly to another" (Boesch and Tomasello 1998, p. 598). This is typically achieved through observation, although there are a variety of different types of mechanisms underlying observational learning. For the most part, there is little evidence of social learning in the first half of the first year of life. As mentioned earlier, neonates will engage in neonatal imitation, imitating facial expressions of adults. Older infants will later engage in what Piaget (1962) described as *mutual imitation,* with an infant matching the behavior of an adult who is imitating the infant, but nothing new is acquired by the infant in these situations, and so although the context is clearly social, it does not involve learning new behaviors via observation (Nagy and Molnar 2004). Once infants become aware that others behave intentionally, they seem to use this information to determine which modeled behaviors to copy (e.g., Carpenter et al. 1998; Meltzoff 1995). For example, in one study, 14–18-month-old infants watched adults perform a series of actions on objects, some of which appeared intentional and others accidental, based on what the model said (Carpenter et al. 1998). Carpenter and her colleagues reported that infants subsequently imitated twice as many "intentional" as "accidental" behaviors.

In other research, 14-month-old infants imitated a model who turned on a light by touching her head against a box rather than using her hands, a seemingly more straightforward method (Meltzoff 1988). However, subsequent research suggested that infants were not copying behaviors blindly, but assumed the model used her head for a reason. When 14-month-old infants saw a model whose hands were wrapped in a blanket and later given the chance to interact with the apparatus, most used their hands, not their heads, to turn on the light (Gergely et al. 2002). Gergely and colleagues referred to this as *rational imitation,* suggesting that infants copy the actions of a model in relation to his or her goal. The model used his head because his hands were occupied, so, in this context, infants used the more conventional means of reproducing the model's goal and not necessarily his precise behavior.

Many 2-year-olds show selectivity in their social learning, displaying *emulation* learning in which they presumably recognize the goal of a model, but do not necessarily copy the exact behaviors to achieve that goal (e.g., McGuigan and Whiten 2009; Nielsen 2006). This is contrasted with "true" imitation in which the learner identifies the model's goal and uses the same behaviors as the model to achieve this goal (Tomasello et al. 1993a). Emulation, used by most pre-2-year-old children, is also the typical style of social learning displayed by chimpanzees (e.g., Horner and Whiten 2005; Nagell et al. 1993). For example, when shown how to use a tool to retrieve out-of-reach food, chimpanzees will fail to copy irrelevant actions of a model if there is a more efficient means of achieving the goal.

Children's social learning begins to change sometime during the third year of life. Children are now apt to imitate all the behaviors of a model, including those that are irrelevant to attaining the goal (e.g., Horner and Whiten 2005; Lyons et al. 2007; Nielsen 2006). For instance, in a study by Lyons et al. (2007), preschool children watched an adult perform a series of actions on objects in order to retrieve a toy locked inside. Children copied all the actions, both relevant and irrelevant ones, even after being warned to avoid "silly," unnecessary actions. Such *overimitation* has been observed in a number of studies, including those with 2–6-year-old Kalahari Bushman children (Nielsen and Tomaselli 2010).

Young children are not necessarily imitating blindly, however, and will imitate selectively when they know the goal of a task beforehand (Williamson and Markman 2006) or when they have some awareness of the intentions of the model (Gardiner 2014; Gardiner et al. 2011), for example. Despite the contextual nature of overimitation, its prevalence during the preschool years and its persistence into adulthood in some contexts (e.g., McGuigan et al. 2011) are compelling and counterintuitive, and a number of researchers believe that it reflects an evolved adaptation.

A somewhat analogous phenomenon to overimitation can be found in young children's ready compliance to follow adults' suggestions when trying to recall events from the past. People of all ages are susceptible to forming "false memories" when an interviewer asks misleading questions in a memory interview (e.g., "The boy was wearing a black jacket, wasn't he?"), but preschool children are especially likely to fall prey to such questions (Ceci and Bruck 1995). This is similar to overimitation in that both types of "errors" reflect young children's ready compliance to adult requests, which, in more cases than not, will likely result in the acquisition of useful information, even though it will occasionally result in some false memories and taking extra steps in solving problems (Bjorklund and Sellers 2013). As interpreted by Bjorklund and Sellers (2013), "In general, children seem biased to believe the credibility of kindly adults, something that was likely adaptive for our ancestors, and their cognitive systems are also biased to retain many of these false memories (and of course many of the 'true memories') that adults suggest to them" (p. 140).

Although most research on preschool children's social learning has focused on children imitating adults, children learn socially from other children as well. In a series of studies, target children were shown one of two ways ("lift" and "poke" methods) to operate a set of panpipes to receive a treat, shown in Fig. 3.1 (e.g., Flynn and Whiten 2012; Hopper et al. 2010; Whiten and Flynn 2010). In one study, the apparatus was then moved into the preschool classroom and target children operated the panpipes, serving as potential models for other children (Whiten and Flynn 2010). Many children played with the panpipes, usually after watching the target child operate it, and 83 % of these children were successful. Most children initially used the same method used by the target child, showing the high degree of imitative fidelity that preschool children typically dis-

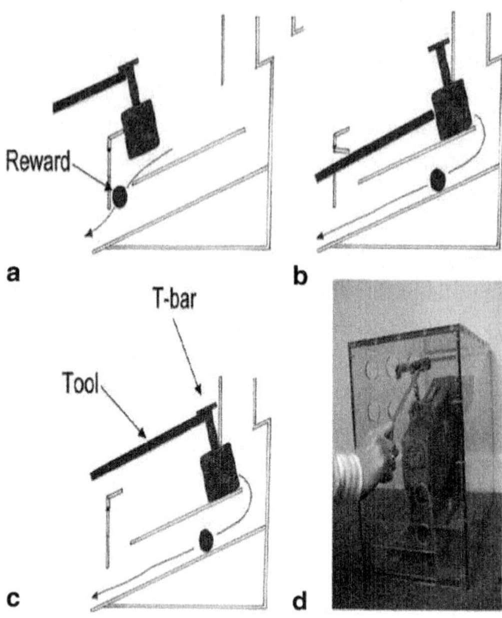

Fig. 3.1 Panpipes apparatus. **a** The stick tool inserted under the T-bar for the lift method, **b** the stick tool inserted into the top hole for the poke method, and **c** the push-slide method by using the stick tool pushing the T-bar back. In **d**, the panpipes viewed from the child's perspective, inside the clear plastic box with the access holes, with lift being demonstrated. (From Hopper et al. 2010)

play. However, some children discovered alternative methods (e.g., the "poke" if they watched the "lift," or even the "push-slide" method, modeled by no child), showing flexibility, realizing the same goal as the model, but achieving it via different means (i.e., emulation as opposed to imitation). The panpipes were a topic of conversation among the children, which was one source of innovation in operating the apparatus. Thus, this research indicates both young children's tendency to copy faithfully the actions of a model, in this case a peer, and also to show some innovation after initial exposure to the task.

One particularly important type of cultural artifact that children learn about through observation is tools. Although infants and children can learn to use tools by manipulating objects and discovering an object's properties and affordances as a tool, they are more apt to learn to use a tool by watching more experienced others interacting and sometimes specifically demonstrating them. For example, in one study, 2- and 3-year-old children either watched as an adult demonstrated how to extract a toy from an apparatus with a tool, had specific haptic (i.e., "hands-on") experience with the tools, or some combination of the two (Gardiner et al. 2012). Children learned about the tools better through observation than by manual exploration. The authors argued that "Evolutionarily, learning tool use through observation would have been selected over modes of independent learning for the efficient and accurate transmission of crucial, adaptive tool-use knowledge" (p. 252).

Social Learning in Chimpanzees

Chimpanzees and bonobos also display substantial levels of social learning, yet such learning is clearly different in both quantity and quality from that shown by human preschool children. For example, as we mentioned previously, chimpanzees tend to emulate the actions of a model—working to achieve the same goal, but often by using different means—as opposed to engaging in "true" imitation. Moreover, although there is some debate about whether nonhuman apes ever engage in true imitation, there is no evidence that they engage in overimitation (Nielsen 2012).

An exception to this general pattern is for enculturated apes, raised much as human children are. Such animals have been unequivocally shown to engage in true imitation, both immediately after viewing a human model's behavior (e.g., Buttelmann et al. 2007; Tomasello, Savage-Rumbaugh, and Kruger 1993) and following a significant delay (e.g., Bjorklund et al. 2002; Tomasello et al. 1993a). These findings are consistent with the *enculturation hypothesis*—that chimpanzees raised with adult humans engaging them in shared attention, teaching, and using language will develop some social cognitive abilities more similar to those of humans (Bjorklund and Rosenberg 2005; Call and Tomasello 1996). These findings suggest that our common ancestor with chimpanzees likely possessed the rudiments for cognitively advanced social learning, but it would be revealed only when the animals were raised in a socially atypical environment (atypical for another ape, not for a human).

In the opening paragraphs of this chapter, we introduced the social brain hypothesis. Humans evolved the impressive brain that they did in large part to deal with other members of their species. In having to cooperate and compete with conspecifics, *H. sapiens* also expanded on the more general primate abilities of learning from one another. This impressive learning ability, possibly the cognitive basis for humans' ecological dominance, has its origins in infancy and childhood. In fact, Nielsen (2012) has proposed that humans essentially invented the stage of childhood, coming between infancy and the juvenile period (see also Bogin 2001), and with two important social cognitive adaptations, permitting human intelligence and accomplishments. One adaptation was pretense and counterfactual thinking as reflected in pretend play. The second was enhanced social learning abilities, particularly imitation. Using anthropological evidence, Nielsen identified correlations between cultural innovation (mainly tool manufacture) and evidence for a stage of childhood (using mainly evidence from dental ontogeny). From this, Nielsen proposed that it was only because of humans' prolonged childhood that imitative abilities, and thus the high-fidelity transmission of nongenetic information between individuals and across generations, could be achieved.

Plasticity of Social Cognition

To this point, we have been addressing mainly species-typical patterns of development and how human social cognition in children differs from that of the other great apes. Yet, although social cognition follows a species-typical developmental trajectory across all cultures, there are individual differences. At the extreme, children with autism show significant deficits in social cognition, providing support for the argument that human social intelligence is not simply derivative of our species' general cognitive abilities, but rather represents dedicated, evolved abilities. Individual differences in the rate of development or in the effectiveness of a variety of social cognitive abilities, including shared attention, empathy, social learning, and theory of mind, have been associated with parents' use of language, quantity and quality of parents' social responsivity, the extent to which parents imitate their infants, and the presence of older siblings, among others (reviewed in Bjorklund et al. 2010). Moreover, despite the universality of theory of mind, individual differences associated with culture and sex are frequently found (see Wellman et al. 2001), attesting to the plasticity of human social cognition. For example, Sabbagh et al. (2006) found that Chinese preschoolers outperform American preschoolers on executive function tasks that predicted their theory-of-mind performance. This effect seems to linger into adulthood, with Chinese adults consistently outperforming American adults in perspective-taking tasks (Wu and Keysar 2007).

Aspects of social cognition also seem to be subject to the environment in other great apes as well, at least under extreme conditions. As we mentioned earlier, enculturated apes are uniquely able to acquire humanlike social cognitive abilities, such as true imitation. An exciting implication of such robust and sophisticated social learning abilities found in both humans and primates is the possibility that socially learned behaviors can serve as the fodder for epigenetic evolutionary change. Under particular circumstances, the reciprocal interaction between action and observer can create a novel behavioral phenotype upon which selection pressures can act (Bjorklund 2006; Gottlieb 1991). This could promote the spread of a novel behavior throughout a group, selecting for the abilities required to engage in that behavior. If this behavior provides a survival benefit, it could create a new paradigm within the group where the cognitive or social cognitive abilities necessary for its transmission or enaction are selected for. For example, a group of Japanese macaques have been observed engaging in the novel behavior of potato washing. This behavior had never been observed before, but reliably spread throughout the young members of the group through observational learning (Kawamura 1959; see also De Waal 1999). Another notable example, some groups of chimpanzees have been observed to use rocks as anvils or hammers for cracking nuts. A chimpanzee will set a flatter stone on the ground and place the nut on top, then grab another tool, typically a stick or rock, and use it to hammer the nut until it cracks. Interestingly, these tools are not random. Chimpanzees seem to understand that different tools serve different functions. For example, a small twig will not serve the purpose of cracking a nut, but might be useful in prying the nut open once it is fractured. Although never explicitly instructed, young chimpanzees will observe older members of the group, practicing with small rocks and sticks until they themselves master this skill (Boesch-Achermann and Boesch 1993).

Conclusion

Here, we examined only a few of the important social cognitive abilities exhibited by humans, as well as other primates, as a full discussion of every aspect of the evolution and development of social cognition is beyond the scope of this chapter. Some of the topics absent from this chapter are the emergence of theory of mind (see Wellman et al. 2001), the importance of tool use on social cognition (see Nagel et al. 1993; Rosati et al. 2010), and the evolutionary developmental roots of prosociality (see Warneken and Tomasello 2013), among many others. We hope to relay the importance of the social world over hominin evolution as the driving force in shaping the human mind with evidence of the origins of this social nature and cognition unfolding over infancy and childhood. Newborns' attentional bias for biological motion and the later preference for attending to human faces—and eyes, specifically—are just two examples of the evolutionary origins of humans' social mind. As they enter early childhood, children are able to view others as intentional agents, and eventually guide their own behaviors by mimicking, imitating, and emulating others. Even though these abilities do not seem very profound, they are not observed in other species, at least not to the extent they are in humans. However, as our discussion of social cognition in other primates submits, these animals possess some substantial social cognitive competencies. Moreover, enculturated primates seem to exhibit behaviors and cognitions closer to those of *H. sapiens,* suggesting that our closest common ancestors also possess the plasticity to adapt their cognitions and behavioral responses depending on their environmental conditions.

References

Abravanel, E., & Sigafoos, A. D. (1984). Exploring the presence of imitation during early infancy. *Child Development, 55,* 381–392.

Alexander, R. D. (1989). Evolution of the human psyche. In P. Mellers & C. Stringer (Eds.), *The human revolution: Behavioural and biological perspectives on the origins of modern humans* (pp. 455–513). Princeton: Princeton University Press

Bandura, A. (2006). Toward a psychology of human agency. *Perspectives on Psychological Science, 1,* 164–180.

Bard, K. A. (2007). Neonatal imitation in chimpanzees (*Pan troglodytes*) tested with two paradigms. *Animal Cognition, 10,* 233–242.

Batki, A., Baron-Cohen, S., Wheelwright, S., Connellan, J., & Ahluwalia, J. (2000). Is there an innate gaze module? Evidence from human neonates. *Infant Behavior and Development, 23,* 223–229.

Bardi, L., Regolin, L., & Simion, F. (2011). Biological motion preference in humans at birth: Role of dynamic and configural properties. *Developmental Science, 14,* 353–359.

Bertenthal, B. I., Proffitt, D. R., & Kramer, S. J. (1987). Perception of biomechanical motions by infants: Implementation of various processing constraints. *Journal of Experimental Psychology: Human Perception and Performance, 13,* 577.

Bjorklund, D. F. (1987). How age changes in knowledge base contribute to the development of children's memory: An interpretive review. *Developmental Review, 7,* 93–130.

Bjorklund, D. F. (1997). The role of immaturity in human development. *Psychological Bulletin, 122,* 153–169.

Bjorklund, D. F. (2003). Evolutionary developmental psychology: A new tool for better understanding human ontogeny. *Human Development, 46,* 259–281.

Bjorklund, D. F. (2006). Mother knows best: Epigenetic inheritance, maternal effects, and the evolution of human intelligence. *Developmental Review, 26,* 213–242.

Bjorklund, D. F., & Bering, J. M. (2003). Big brains, slow development, and social complexity: The developmental and evolutionary origins of social cognition. In M. Brane, H. Ribbert, & W. Schiefernhvel (Eds.), *The social brain: Evolution and Pathology* (pp. 111–151). New York: Wiley.

Bjorklund, D. F., & Rosenberg, J. S. (2005). The role of developmental plasticity in the evolution of human cognition. In B. J. Ellis & D. F. Bjorklund (Eds.), *Origins of the social mind: Evolutionary psychology and child development* (pp. 45–75). New York: Guilford Press.

Bjorklund, D. F., & Sellers, P. D., II. (2013). Memory development in evolutionary perspective. In P. J. Bauer & R. Fivush (Eds.), *The Wiley handbook on the development of children's memory* (pp. 126–150). Hoboken: Wiley.

Bjorklund, D. F., Yunger, J. L., Bering, J. M., & Ragan, P. (2002). The generalization of deferred imitation in enculturated chimpanzees (Pan troglodytes). *Animal Cognition, 5,* 49–58.

Bjorklund, D. F., Cormier, C., & Rosenberg, J. S. (2005). The evolution of theory of mind: Big brains, social complexity, and inhibition. In W. Schneider, R. Schumann-Hengsteler, & B. Sodian (Eds.), *Young children's cognitive development: Interrelationships among executive functioning, working memory, verbal ability and theory of mind* (pp. 147–174). Mahwah: Erlbaum.

Bjorklund, D. F., Causey, K., & Periss, V. (2010). The evolution and development of human social cognition. In P. Kappeler & J. Silk (Eds.), *Mind the gap: Tracing the origins of human universals* (pp. 351–371). Berlin: Springer Verlag.

Boesch-Achermann, H., & Boesch, C. (1993). Tool use in wild chimpanzees: New light from dark forests. *Current Directions in Psychological Science, 2,* 18–21.

Boesch, C., & Tomasello, M. (1998). Chimpanzee and human cultures. *Current Anthropology, 39,* 591–614.

Bogin, B. (2001). *The growth of humanity.* New York: Wiley.

Brooks, R., & Meltzoff, A. N. (2002). The importance of eyes: How infants interpret adult looking behavior. *Developmental Psychology, 38,* 958–966.

Bushnell, I. W. R., Sai, F., & Mullin, J. T. (1989). Neonatal recognition of the mother's face. *British Journal of Developmental Psychology, 7,* 3–15.

Buttelmann, D., Carpenter, M., Call, J., & Tomasello, M. (2007). Enculturated chimpanzees imitate rationally. *Developmental Science, 10,* F31–F38.

Byrne, R. W. (2005). Social cognition: Imitation, imitation, imitation. *Current Biology, 15,* R489–R500.

Call, J., & Tomasello, M. (1996). The effect of humans on the cognitive development of apes. In A. E. Russon, K. A. Bard, & S. T. Parker (Eds.), *Reaching into thought: The minds of the great apes* (pp. 371–403). New York: Cambridge University Press.

Carpenter, M., Akhtar, N., & Tomasello, M. (1998). Fourteen-through 18-month-old infants differentially imitate intentional and accidental actions. *Infant Behavior and Development, 21,* 315–330.

Ceci, S. J., & Bruck, M. (1995). *Jeopardy in the courtroom: A scientific analysis of children's testimony.* Washington: American Psychological Association.

Darwin, C. (1871). *The descent of man.* D. Appleton and Company.

De Waal, F. B. (1999). Cultural primatology comes of age. *Nature, 399,* 635–636.

Dunbar, R. I. (2003). The social brain: Mind, language, and society in evolutionary perspective. *Annual Review of Anthropology, 32,* 163–181.

Farroni, T., Csibra, G., Simion, F., & Johnson, M. H. (2002). Eye contact detection in humans from birth. *Proceedings of the National Academy of Sciences, 99,* 9602–9605.

Ferrari, P. F., Visalberghi, E., Paukner, A., Fogassi, L., Ruggiero, A., & Suomi, S. J. (2006). Neonatal imitation in rhesus macaques. *PLoS Biology, 4,* e302.

Flynn, E., & Whiten, A. (2012). Experimental "microcultures" in young children: Identifying biographic, cognitive, and social predictors of information transmission. *Child Development, 83,* 911–925.

Gardiner, A. K. (2014). Beyond irrelevant actions: Understanding the role of intentionality in children's imitation of relevant actions. *Journal of experimental child psychology, 119,* 54–72.

Gardiner, A. K., Greif, M. L., & Bjorklund, D. F. (2011). Guided by intention: preschoolers' imitation reflects inferences of causation. *Journal of Cognition and Development, 12,* 355–373.

Gava, L., Valenza, E., Turati, C., & Schonen, S. D. (2008). Effect of partial occlusion on newborns' face preference and recognition. *Developmental Science, 11,* 563–574.

Gergely, G., Bekkering, H., & Király, I. (2002). Developmental psychology: Rational imitation in preverbal infants. *Nature, 415,* 755–755.

Goodman, E., McEwen, B. S., Dolan, L. M., Schafer-Kalkhoff, T., & Adler, N. E. (2005). Social disadvantage and adolescent stress. *Journal of Adolescent Health, 37,* 484–492.

Goren, C. C., Sarty, M., & Wu, P. Y. (1975). Visual following and pattern discrimination of face-like stimuli by newborn infants. *Pediatrics, 56,* 544–549.

Gottlieb, G. (1991). Experiential canalization of behavioral development: Theory. *Developmental Psychology, 27,* 4.

Hare, R. D. (2011). From hominoid to hominid mind: What changes and why? *Annual Review of Anthropology,* 40, 293–309.

Heimann, M. (1989). Neonatal imitation, gaze aversion, and mother-infant interaction. *Infant Behavior and Development, 12,* 495–505.

Hernández Blasi, C., & Bjorklund, D. F. (2003). Evolutionary developmental psychology: A new tool for better understanding human ontogeny. *Human Development, 46,* 259–281.

Herrmann, E., Call, J., Hernández-Lloreda, M. V., Hare, B., & Tomasello, M. (2007). Humans have evolved specialized skills of social cognition: The cultural intelligence hypothesis. *Science, 317,* 1360–1366.

Hopper, L. M., Flynn, E. G., Wood, L. A., & Whiten, A. (2010). Observational learning of tool use in children: Investigating cultural spread through diffusion chains and learning mechanisms through ghost displays. *Journal of Experimental Child Psychology, 106,* 82–97.

Horner, V., & Whiten, A. (2005). Causal knowledge and imitation/emulation switching in chimpanzees (*Pan troglodytes*) and children (*Homo sapiens*). *Animal Cognition, 8,* 164–181.

Jacobson, S. W. (1979). Matching behavior in the young infant. *Child Development, 50,* 425–430.

Joffe, T. H. (1997). Social pressures have selected for an extended juvenile period in primates. *Journal of Human Evolution, 32,* 593–605.

Johnson, M. H. (2007). The social brain in infancy: A developmental cognitive neuroscience approach. In D. Coch, K. W. Fischer, & G. Dawson (Eds.), *Human behavior, learning, and the developing brain: Typical development* (pp. 115–137). New York: Guilford.

Karmiloff-Smith, A. (1996). The connectionist infant: Would Piaget turn in his grave? *Society for Research in Child Development, (Newsletter, Fall), 10,* 1–3.

Kawamura, S. (1959). The process of sub-culture propagation among Japanese macaques. *Primates, 2,* 43–60.

Konner, M. (2010). *Evolution of childhood: Relationships, emotion, mind.* New York: Harvard University Press.

Liszkowski, U., Carpenter, M., Striano, T., & Tomasello, M. (2006). 12- and 18-month-olds point to provide information for others. *Journal of Cognition and Development, 7,* 173–187.

Liszkowski, U., Carpenter, M., & Tomasello, M. (2007). Pointing out new news, old news, and absent referents at 12 months of age. *Developmental Science, 10,* F1–F7.

Lyons, D. E., Young, A. G., & Keil, F. C. (2007). The hidden structure of overimitation. *Proceedings of the National Academy of Sciences, 104,* 19751–19756.

McGuigan, N., & Whiten, A. (2009). Emulation and "overemulation" in the social learning of causally opaque versus causally transparent tool use by 23-and 30-month-olds. *Journal of Experimental Child Psychology, 104,* 367–381.

McGuigan, N., Makinson, J., & Whiten, A. (2011). From over-imitation to super-copying: Adults imitate causally irrelevant aspects of tool use with higher fidelity than young children. *British Journal of Psychology, 102,* 1–18.

Meltzoff, A. N. (1988). Imitation of televised models by infants. *Child Development, 59,* 1221–1229.

Meltzoff, A. N. (1995). Understanding the intentions of others: Re-enactment of intended acts by 18-month-old children. *Developmental Psychology, 31,* 838–850.

Meltzoff, A. N., & Moore, M. K. (1977). Imitation of facial and manual gestures by human neonates. *Science, 198,* 75–78.

Mondloch, C. J., Lewis, T. L., Budreau, D. R., Maurer, D., Dannemiller, J. L., Stephens, B. R., & Kleiner-Gathercoal, K. A. (1999). Face perception during early infancy. *Psychological Science, 10,* 419–422.

Murray, L., & Trevarthen, C. (1986). The infant's role in mother-infant communication. *Journal of Child Language, 13,* 15–29.

Myowa-Yamakoshi, M., Tomonaga, M., Tanaka, M., & Matsuzawa, T. (2004). Imitation in neonatal chimpanzees (*Pan troglodytes*). *Developmental Science, 7,* 437–442.

Myowa-Yamakoshi, M., & Tomonaga, M. (2001). Development of face recognition in an infant gibbon (Hylobates agilis). *Infant Behavior and Development, 24,* 215–227.

Nagell, K., Olguin, R. S., & Tomasello, M. (1993). Processes of social learning in the tool use of chimpanzees (*Pan troglodytes*) and human children (Homo sapiens). *Journal of Comparative Psychology, 107,* 174–186.

Nagy, E. (2006). From imitation to conversation: The first dialogues with human neonates. *Infant and Child Development, 15,* 223–232.

Nagy, E., & Molnar, P. (2004). Homo imitans or homo provocans? Human imprinting model of neonatal imitation. *Infant Behavior and Development, 27,* 54–63.

Nielsen, M. (2006). Copying actions and copying outcomes: Social learning through the second year. *Developmental Psychology, 42,* 555–565.

Nielsen, M. (2012). Imitation, pretend play, and childhood: Essential elements in the evolution of human culture? *Journal of Comparative Psychology, 126,* 170–181.

Nielsen, M., & Tomaselli, K. (2010). Overimitation in Kalahari Bushman children and the origins of human cultural cognition. *Psychological Science, 21,* 729–736.

Oppenheim, R. W. (1981). Ontogenetic adaptations and retrogressive processes in the development of the nervous system and behavior. In K. J. Connolly & H. F. R. Prechtl (Eds.), *Maturation and development: Biological and psychological perspectives* (pp. 73–108). Philadelphia: International Medical Publications

Piaget, J. (1962). *Play, dreams and imitation* (Vol. 24). New York: Norton.

Reilly, J., Harrison, D., & Klima, E. S. (1995). Emotional talk and talk about emotions. *Genetic Counseling, 6,* 158–159.

Rosati, A., Hare, B. A., & Santos, L. R. (2010). Primate social cognition: Thirty years after Premack and Woodruff. *Primate Neuroethology, 1,* 117–144.

Sabbagh, M. A., Xu, F., Carlson, S. M., Moses, L. J., & Lee, K. (2006). The development of executive functioning and theory of mind a comparison of Chinese and US preschoolers. *Psychological Science, 17,* 74–81.

Simion, F., Regolin, L., & Bulf, H. (2008). A predisposition for biological motion in the newborn baby. *Proceedings of the National Academy of Sciences, 105,* 809–813.

Slater, A., Von der Schulenburg, C., Brown, E., Badenoch, M., Butterworth, G., Parsons, S., & Samuels, C. (1998). Newborn infants prefer attractive faces. *Infant Behavior and Development, 21,* 345–354.

Slater, A., Quinn, P. C., Hayes, R., & Brown, E. (2000). The role of facial orientation in newborn infants' preference for attractive faces. *Developmental Science, 3,* 181–185.

Tomasello, M. (2009). *Why we cooperate*. Cambridge: MIT Press.

Tomasello, M., & Carpenter, M. (2005). The emergence of social cognition in three young chimpanzees: III. Understanding intentional action. *Monographs of the Society for Research in Child Development.*

Tomasello, M., & Carpenter, M. (2007). Shared intentionality. *Developmental Science, 10,* 121–125.

Tomasello, M., Savage Rumbaugh, S., & Kruger, A. C. (1993). Imitative learning of actions on objects by children, chimpanzees, and enculturated chimpanzees. *Child development, 64*(6), 1688–1705.

Tomasello, M., Kruger, A. C., & Ratner, H. H. (1993a). Cultural learning. *Behavioral and Brain Sciences, 16,* 495–495.

Tomasello, M., Savage-Rumbaugh, S., & Kruger, A. C. (1993b). Imitative learning of actions on objects by children, chimpanzees, and enculturated chimpanzees. *Child Development, 64,* 1688–1705.

Walton, G. E., Bower, N. J. A., & Bower, T. G. R. (1992). Recognition of familiar faces by newborns. *Infant Behavior and Development, 15,* 265–269.

Warneken, F., & Tomasello, M. (2013). The emergence of contingent reciprocity in young children. *Journal of Experimental child Psychology, 116,* 338–350.

Wellman, H. M. (1990). *The child's theory of mind*. Cambridge: MIT Press.

Wellman, H. M., Cross, D., & Watson, J. (2001). Meta-analysis of theory-of-mind development: The truth about false belief. *Child Development, 72,* 655–684.

Whiten, A., & Flynn, E. (2010). The transmission and evolution of experimental microcultures in groups of young children. *Developmental Psychology, 46,* 1694–1709.

Williamson, R. A., & Markman, E. M. (2006). Precision of imitation as a function of preschoolers' understanding of the goal of the demonstration. *Developmental Psychology, 42,* 723–731.

Wu, S., & Keysar, B. (2007). The effect of culture on perspective taking. *Psychological Science, 18,* 600–606.

Yoon, J., & Johnson, S. C. (2009). Biological motion displays elicit social behavior in 12-month-olds. *Child Development, 80,* 1069–1075.

Modularity

4

H. Clark Barrett

The history of psychology is, to a first approximation, the history of debates about the mind's parts. What are the processes, mechanisms, and abilities of which the mind is composed? How is the apparently seamless flow of our day-to-day thoughts, decisions, and behavior constructed by the underlying mechanisms of our brains?

The way that many evolutionary psychologists would frame these questions is in terms of modularity: What are the modules of which the mind is composed, and how do they interact to produce human thought and behavior? On this view, modules are defined simply as the mind's functional parts or processes, whatever these might be. Our job as evolutionary psychologists is to discover and describe them, using the full range of tools available to the biological and brain sciences. This is decidedly not how modules are viewed by many psychologists, however. This is evidenced by the fact that what should be a relatively uncontroversial statement—that a key task of psychology is the functional deconstruction of the mind—is treated as one of the most controversial statements one could make, when the term "module" is used. Clearly, there is some kind of disconnect: the way that evolutionary psychologists think about modules is not the same as everyone else. Something has to give.

H. C. Barrett (✉)
Department of Anthropology, University of California Los Angeles, 341 Haines Hall, Box 951553, Los Angeles, CA 90095-1553, USA
e-mail: barrett@anthro.ucla.edu

One solution would be to simply stop using the term "module." That might be a reasonable solution, but it is worth pausing before we do so for several reasons. First, we would need to replace it with some other word to refer to the brain's evolved functional mechanisms. Second, we would have to retain all that the idea of functionally organized division of labor can explain about brain function—potentially, nearly all of it. Third, we would still need some way to interface usefully with the area of biology that has the potential to connect the dots between the evolution of gene regulatory systems and the functional organization of phenotypes: evolutionary developmental biology, or "evo-devo." As it turns out, there is a term that is used in that literature to describe the decomposition of phenotypes into underlying components and processes: modularity.

Rather than discard the concept of modularity, then, it might make more sense to stop using it in ways that make little or no biological, psychological, or neurological sense, and start using it in ways that do. In this chapter, I outline a sketch of how this can be done (for more details see Barrett 2005, 2006, 2012, 2015; Barrett and Kurzban 2006). First, I describe what might be thought of as the "classical" view of modularity—the view that has led to the terminological bickering that has plagued evolutionary psychology. Then, I describe what I call the "biological" view of modularity, rooted in the idea that biological traits evolve through descent with modification as a function of the role they play in a system of interacting parts, with plasticity and self-organi-

V. Zeigler-Hill et al. (eds.), *Evolutionary Perspectives on Social Psychology,* Evolutionary Psychology,
DOI 10.1007/978-3-319-12697-5_4, © Springer International Publishing Switzerland 2015

zation as key components of how phenotypes are constructed. This shifts the focus from properties such as innateness and rigidity to the properties that matter most in biology: properties related to function. Next, I focus in detail on several elements of this view of modularity that are largely or entirely missing from the classical view: hierarchical specialization, functional diversity, and interaction. Finally, I summarize some of the implications of this view for theoretical and empirical work in social psychology, and conclude with thoughts about future directions within the study of modularity.

The Classical View of Modularity

The classical view of modularity in psychology is due largely to philosopher Jerry Fodor's influential 1983 volume, *The Modularity of Mind,* and related technical literature (Fodor 1983). Fodor's view of modularity is based in part on functional decomposition of cognitive processes into underlying components—hence, its affinity to the evolutionary psychological view of modularity. However, it also brings with it substantial conceptual baggage due to its dependence on several unfortunate dichotomies, especially the conscious/unconscious dichotomy and the innate/learned dichotomy.

Fodor viewed modules as, in essence, cognitive reflexes: little bits of neural machinery operating automatically and rapidly, outside of conscious awareness, with narrowly prespecified input–output relationships and little or no room for learning or contextually modifiable interaction with other modules. A paradigmatic case for him would be speech parsing, in which almost entirely unconscious and automatic processes intervenes between the early stage of auditory processing and the phenomenological experience of the meaning of spoken words. In his view, following from Chomsky, little or no learning was involved in the construction of these mechanisms. Moreover, the signature features of processes such as these—automaticity, speed, and inaccessibility to consciousness of the underlying computations—became synonymous with modularity, and could therefore be turned into a kind of litmus test to diagnose it.

This logic has made its way into social psychology. A variety of empirical tools have been developed in order to diagnose whether a process is classically modular or not—and, via an alarming leap of logic, to ostensibly diagnose whether a biological adaptation is involved. One, for example, is the "cognitive load" method, in which mechanisms of working memory are kept occupied by one task, such as keeping a string of digits in mind, while participants are asked to perform another task ostensibly involving a modular process (DeSteno et al. 2002). According to Fodor's logic, modules operate independently of conscious processes, including processes such as consciously rehearsing a string of digits. Therefore, if the second task is interfered with by cognitive load, it is not (entirely) modular. Here, how we theorize modularity has direct and important consequences for the conclusions we draw. If "module" is synonymous with "evolved adaptation," then any process that can be interfered with by repeating a string of numbers to oneself cannot be a biological adaptation. Indeed, if we interpret Fodor's criterion of processing independence strictly, then any process that can be modified by the operation of another process is not modular—and therefore, not an adaptation.

Several points are worth noting here, that bear directly on contemporary theorizing in social psychology. First and foremost, the latter conclusion—that any processes in the mind that contextually modify each others' operations cannot be biological adaptations—is almost certainly one that no psychologist who reflected carefully on it would want to draw (Barrett et al. 2006). This should be especially clear to social psychologists: Whatever adaptations may exist for social judgment and decision making, they are likely to include adaptations that are interactive and context-sensitive. Indeed, one of the primary adaptive problems of a social life is contextual adjustment: What is good in one situation is not necessarily good in another. Moreover, conscious deliberation probably plays a role in much if not most social decision making, and there is no reason to think that natural selection has not shaped such processes of deliberation. Finally, the idea that learning is not involved is a non-starter.

A second and related point is that it is a mistake, albeit an apparently beguiling one, to equate the unconscious with evolution and consciousness with something else. While this idea has a distinguished history in psychology, one would have thought that a thoroughly contemporary treatment of brain evolution would have laid it to rest. Unfortunately, it is seeing something of a resurgence in at least some varieties of "dual systems" views of the mind, which treat unconscious, automatic modules as akin to evolved instincts, and consciousness as akin to reason, or whatever else instincts are not (Stanovich 2004). This is not characteristic of all dual systems views, of course, but the flavor of the idea—our unconscious minds are automatic robots programmed by natural selection via our genes, to be overridden, when possible, by the flexible, human, general-purpose faculty of reason—can be seen lingering throughout psychology. As described below, while consciousness is certainly a real phenomenon, there is no reason why a functionalist view of mind need equate the unconscious with the products of natural selection, and consciousness with something else.

In summary, while the classical Fodorian view of modularity might describe some of the mind's processes, there is no question that there are many (and probably most) that it does not describe. This does not mean that processes that are interactive, flexible, and shaped by learning are not also the products of natural selection. In fact, no biologist would argue that there cannot be biological adaptations that are all those things: interactive, flexible, and shaped by learning. Therefore, we are going to need a concept of biological adaptations in the mind that can account for this broader category of evolved mechanisms, whether you want to call them "modules" or not.

The Biological View of Modularity

A psychologist might be surprised to discover that while the idea of modularity is alive and well in biology, it bears only a faint resemblance to Fodor's view. Among other things, Fodor's conception of modularity, as he himself recognized, virtually mandates that only a small part of the mind is modular (Fodor 2000). That other psychologists agree with this can be seen in the scorn heaped on the idea of "massive modularity," the idea that much (or all) of the mind is or might be composed of modules (Buller and Hardcastle 2000; Carruthers 2006; Frankenhuis and Ploeger 2007; Machery 2008; Panksepp and Panksepp 2000; Samuels 1998; Sperber 1994, 2001). Fodor himself has called this "modularity theory gone mad" (Fodor 1987, p. 27).

Compare this with the following statement by evolutionary developmental biologist Craig Nelson: "Modularity pervades every level of biological organization. From proteins to populations, larger biological units are built of smaller, quasi-autonomous parts" (Nelson 2004, p. 17). Clearly, Nelson has something else in mind than Fodor and critics of massive modularity. His view is not atypical in the literature in evolutionary developmental biology. Indeed, the mainstream view in evo-devo is precisely that organisms are composed of modular components at many levels of organization and that modularity may even be a prerequisite for the evolution of complexity (Wagner and Altenberg 1996).

What is the source of this disjuncture? Fundamentally, it stems from the fact that Fodor and most psychologists adopt an a priori definition of modularity—as automatic, innate, etc.—and then ask what, if anything, in the mind fits that definition. In contrast, the biologist's approach to modularity is empirical. Nelson's statement above, for example, is fundamentally a statement about what biologists have *observed.* Theory and modeling work in this area have been driven by the observed ubiquity of modularity in biological systems, asking *why* modularity is so biologically pervasive, how and when modularity evolves, and what new insights can be gained by understanding the modular nature of complex, interactive systems (Callebaut and Rasskin-Gutman 2005; Raff 1996; Schlosser and Wagner 2004; Wagner and Altenberg 1996).

As might be expected from this disciplinary difference, in biology (unlike psychology) there is no simple, unitary definition of modularity. Generally speaking, biological concepts of modularity tend to turn on the idea of decomposability, or separability. However, unlike in psychology, decomposability tends to be defined functionally. As such, it can occur at many levels of organization simultaneously (as Nelson's quote implies) and is quite different from the intuitive notion of a module as a physical "part" that can be snapped into or out of a system (a notion that underlies much naïve thinking about localization in brain mapping; Shallice 1988; Uttal 2001). Wagner et al. (2005), for example, distinguish between *developmental, evolutionary,* and *functional* modularity. Developmental modularity refers to the separability of developmental processes and is motivated by the observation that specialized subprocesses in embryogenesis can often be dissociated, as in the experimental induction of organ formation via alterations in gene regulation. Evolutionary modularity refers to the degree to which aspects of the phenotype can be independently varied during evolution. Functional modularity, on the other hand refers to the degree to which parts of an interacting whole carry out separable functions.

As Wagner et al. (2005) note, "the precise definition of all these concepts is somewhat difficult and still controversial" (p. 34), and they are careful to point out that they are not necessarily mutually exclusive. For example, it is still not clear, theoretically or empirically, whether evolutionary and developmental modularity are different things. As we will see in more detail below, different kinds of modules can be nested within each other, so that aspects of organisms can be part of the same module on one level, and different modules on another (Ravasz et al. 2002; Thomas 2005). For example, because the genes that control development of the left and right arms in humans are nearly entirely overlapping, the left and right arms are different developmental modules, but part of the same evolutionary module (Wagner et al. 2005). To some degree, especially because of handedness in humans, they are also partly distinct functional modules (for some functions, e.g., writing, yes; for other functions, e.g., push-ups, no). This *hierarchical* nature of modularity is likely to be crucial for understanding brain modules, which likely evolved through processes of descent with modification as brains expanded and differentiated relative to simpler ancestral brains (Allman 2000; Barrett 2012, 2015; Kaas 1984; Krubitzer and Huffman 2000).

The technical literature on modularity in biology—concerning when, why, and how modularity evolves, and how it is instantiated in phenotypes via underlying developmental processes—is difficult and complex. Moreover, much of what is known about the biological modularity of brains, and human brains in particular, is still in the early stages. For many social psychologists, much of this literature is probably too distant from the phenomena they study to be of much use or interest. However, there are major, basic differences between what a biological modularity view might lead a psychologist to expect about brain organization, and what a classical modularity view might imply. As hinted at in the discussion of cognitive load techniques above, these can have a direct impact on the conclusions about modularity that psychologists might draw from their data. Here I highlight the most important features of what a biological modularity view offers for our understanding of cognitive architecture and how this differs from the classical view. Then I turn to the implications of the biological modularity view for current and future research in social psychology.

Hierarchical Specialization, Functional Diversity, and Interaction

It is a basic fact of biology that adaptations evolve through descent with modification. This is true both for phenotypes and for the gene regulatory systems that give rise to them during development. Nothing appears de novo; all evolutionarily new things are modified versions of older things. Roughly speaking, this novelty can appear in one of two ways. A single thing—a trait, a gene, a developmental process—can be modified over evolutionary time, so that the derived version is different in some ways from the ancestral version. This results in the basic phenomenon of *homology*, the evolutionary relatedness of traits via descent. Additionally—and not necessarily independently—what was once a single thing can become multiple things, which can then (sometimes) diverge evolutionarily. Processes of this kind give rise to *serial homologies*, or *paralogies*, distinct traits within an organism that can be traced back to common ancestral traits (Hall 2003). Evolutionary biology has revealed that parts of organisms that might not appear to be evolutionarily related, such as distinct limbs, organs, and tissue types, have in fact evolved through such an evolutionary process of diversification from common ancestral features. For example, there is evidence that the nervous system, with all of its functional complexity, ultimately evolved from skin (Holland 2003). Indeed, given that all multicellular life evolved from single-celled organisms, most of the functional complexity of organisms such as ourselves, including our brains, has probably evolved through processes of descent and diversification from simpler ancestral traits.

These facts have important implications for the modularity and functional organization of the brain that are often not recognized in discussions of modularity. First, unlike the way they are often treated in psychology, brain modules are not likely to be sui generis phenomena, each one evolving from scratch, and requiring its own large and unique complement of genes. Instead, like most products of descent with modification, brain modules are likely to be hierarchically related, with some features shared across broad categories of modules, and smaller families within them that are characterized by (some) uniquely derived features. Second, brain modules are not likely to be characterized by a rigid, uniform checklist of features, such as automaticity, encapsulation, shallow inputs, etc., as the strictly classical view would have it (Fodor himself stressed this in his original monograph, but the point has largely been forgotten; Fodor 1983). Instead, just as limbs, livers, and lungs are all related by relationships of homology yet exhibit substantial differences in their functional features, so we would expect mechanisms in the brain to differ because of the different functions they have been selected to carry out—some fast, some slow, some broad, some narrow, some highly learning-dependent, others less so. Third, because brain modules evolve as do-all biological traits, within a network of interacting parts, brain modules are likely to be largely interactive *by design*, both developmentally and phenotypically (where "by design" I mean because selection has shaped them because of the interactive role they play within a larger system). This is, again, in stark contrast to the classical view of modularity, which rules out properties like plasticity and contextual interactivity as a matter of definition. On a biological view, in contrast, such features are often expected, especially for modules within a complex behavior-regulation organ such as the brain. Briefly, I elaborate on each of these three features of the biological modularity perspective and then turn to their implications for the practice of social psychology.

Among the most remarkable lessons of evolutionary developmental biology and comparative genomics has been that evolutionary conservatism and evolutionary innovation are not nearly as zero-sum as once thought. The most undeniable finding of genomics research is that the relationship between genes and phenotypes is far from obvious. To us, at least, fruit flies appear radically unlike humans, and yet genetically, they are more similar than different. When it comes to humans and chimpanzees, of course, the genetic differences are less than two percent. How can this be? And how can we reconcile it with a massively modular view of the mind?

If you had not looked carefully at evolutionary developmental biology, you might be forgiven for thinking that it is hopeless to expect brain architecture to be closely related to genes. But what evo-devo has increasingly made clear is that underlying the astounding diversity of life lies a remarkable amount of conservatism in genes themselves. While gene sequences do (and indeed must) change over evolutionary time, the relationship between genetic and phenotypic change is far from one-to-one, and the reason lies—perhaps ironically, depending on one's point of view—in the modularity of the genome and processes of gene regulation that give rise to phenotypic structures. In essence, genes and the biochemical networks within which they are embedded are a kind of combinatorial system that can give rise to incredible novelty and diversity of phenotypes by turning the existing knobs of development (Carroll 2008). Over the long run, natural selection shapes the biochemical machinery of life to be so well-designed—as well as causally interdependent in its function—that the basic building blocks are remarkably conserved over evolutionary time. Yet, these building blocks, because of what they can do, become the source of evolutionary innovation.

The reason this can give rise to hierarchically organized modularity is as follows. Consider, as an analogy, the processes of descent with modification that give rise to patterns of similarity and difference across species. Taxonomic diversity originates in speciation events in which one taxon splits into two, which then diversify through a combination of selection, mutation, and drift. Because of the evolutionary conservatism described above, even as these species diverge they will share many, many similarities—more similarities than differences, in fact, except over enormous stretches of evolutionary time. The similarities and differences will be patterned, phylogenetically, such that species that share a recent common ancestor are more similar to each other than to species that share a more distant common ancestor, creating a nested hierarchy of similarity and difference. Similar patterns of similarity and difference are likely to be observed in modules that have evolved through processes of descent with modification from common ancestral traits, some recently and some long ago (Barrett 2012).

To be clear, the descent with modification of brain modules, or any traits within an organism for that matter, is not entirely analogous to this. For one, populations of organisms following a speciation event no longer share gene flow, whereas the modular parts of a single organism arise from a single genome. However, at least some of the hierarchical properties that arise from descent with diversification are likely to hold true for brain modules. For example, because all brain modules are subcomponents of the nervous system, they share many, many features in common due to this deep homology. However, the longer ago different parts of the brain and nervous system diverged, the more differences they are likely to have. For relatively recently differentiated parts of the brain, such as separate modules within the mammalian neocortex, one would expect very high degrees of overlap in functional design features. One would also expect varying degrees of functional differentiation as a function of time since divergence, strength of selection for functional distinctness, and the evolutionary separability of these components. Think about, for example, how natural selection has differentially modified the forelimbs and hind limbs of primates (part of the same evolutionary and developmental modules at some level, different at one level down)—and then how these have been further modified, in turn, in humans. One can recognize nested patterns of similarity and difference both within and across species, due to relationships of homology; the same is what one might expect in the brain. This is what I mean by *hierarchical specialization:* mammalian limbs are, at one level, a single module, with many shared features of development, motor control, etc.; but there are separate fore- and hind- limb modules within this module, and these lead to differences in specialization between, e.g., human hands and feet. And within these modules are yet more, such as the specialized modules of thumb, index finger, and other digits, along with the neural structures that control them. In the brain, examples might include nested hierarchical specialization within systems of object recognition (e.g., faces, places, bodies, words), motor control (facial expressions gestures, object manipulation, locomotion), and more (Barrett 2012, 2015).

Contrasting with this principle of hierarchical specialization—but not in contradiction to it—is *functional diversity.* Here what I have in mind is a contrast with the high degree of design uniformity implied by the classical, Fodorian view of modules as a battery of rigid, narrow, innate cognitive reflexes. In fact, we already know that many brain structures that comparative embryologists and neuroanatomists would take to be modular in the sense described above—e.g., the hippocampus, the amygdala, the cerebellum—have substantially different organization and functional design features (to the extent that these are understood). And in neuroscience, it is becomingly increasingly well-understood that different brain regions and networks carry out substantially different functions, and exhibit different functional features as a consequence. On the question of conscious and unconscious processes, for example, we are increasingly coming to understand some of the neural bases of these processes, which, by definition, violate the Fodorian definition of modularity (e.g., they can be relatively slow, nonautomatic, influenced by volition, etc.). Certainly, such processes satisfy at least some aspects of the biological modularity criterion of *separability* from other processes—otherwise, we would not be able to study the differences between conscious and unconscious properties as such. Moreover, it seems likely that mechanisms involved in processes of conscious deliberation and choice—even, perhaps, uniquely human ones—are products of the evolutionary process. It is currently a question of considerable interest, for example, whether some regions of the neocortex, such as the frontal lobes, have been differentially modified in humans—as well as other features, such as white matter pathways and putative "language areas" (Friederici 2009; Rilling et al. 2008; Schoenemann et al. 2005). On the view presented here, if some regions have been differentially modified then some degree of modularity is implied, and an important and interesting question for psychology and neuroscience is: What exactly are the biological modules that have been (at least partly) differentially selected for? The idea of functional diversity allows us to think about these possible derived changes in the human lineage under the same rubric that we use to think about the evolution of other aspects of brain and body, without banishing conscious processes from evolutionary explanation.

A third and vitally important feature of the biological modularity view is *interactivity*. Again, interactivity between brain parts is not only a well-documented empirical fact but also an expectation of the view that brain modules evolve and have always operated within an interacting system of parts, both developmentally and phenotypically. By "developmentally," I mean that there is every reason to expect that brain modules emerge in development, at least in part through interaction with their neighbors, and as a function of information passing through them (in the form of biochemical activity, of course). Note that, in contrast to some views in developmental psychology, this does not imply that the environment alone, in combination with general-purpose plasticity, shapes the brain. Another clear lesson from evolutionary developmental biology is that development is orchestrated by patterns of gene regulation, and that these are in turn regulated by interactions within a developmental network—but this is a far cry from saying that these processes are necessarily "general purpose," nor that the shaping of development is being done exclusively by the environment. Developmental contingency and interactivity are hallmarks of all developmental systems and are what we should expect in the development of brain modules as well. Developmental contingency and interactivity are shaped by natural selection, not the opposites of it.

At the phenotypic level, too, interactivity between brain modules is likely to be the norm. At a minimum, of course, this means that information is passed from one place to another, as expected in a behavior-regulation organ such as the brain. However, it also means that in many cases, we expect information processing to be heavily distributed across parallel systems and for these systems to make use of the virtues of parallel distributed processing, such as robustness and context-sensitivity. Brain mapping is increasingly revealing that the operation of brain networks is, in real time, modular; but this modularity is not necessarily the same as implied by a classical view (Bullmore and Sporns 2009). Modules are not (mostly) individual, isolated, reflex-like chunks of neural tissue; they are spread out over the brain, alter themselves dynamically on short timescales, and the "same" tissue can do different things in different contexts. Again, the hallmark of biological organization is function, and so it is this functional modularity that should be of interest to us, not cartoon versions of modules as stereo components that are self-contained, independent, and can be snapped into and out of the system, leaving everything else intact.

Implications for Social Psychology

A shift from a classical to a biological view of modularity entails changes in how the mind's parts and processes are theorized and studied in social psychology. We have already seen, in the case of cognitive load, how a non-biology-based definition of modularity can lead to unwarranted conclusions if strict Fodorian modularity is equated with biological adaptation. More positively, an expanded and biologically realistic view of modularity also has the potential for leading to new advances in social psychology by widening the scope of phenomena that can be studied under the evolutionary lens, and properly situating human brains and behavior in the continuum of the natural world.

As mentioned above, "dual systems" or "dual process" models of cognition are currently popular in social psychology (Evans 2008). On one hand, the basic idea underlying such models—that cognitive processes can involve the interaction of distinct parts, with the parts carrying out different functions—is easily accommodated within a biological modularity framework. However, what is not particularly biologically plausible is the "me versus the modules" view of dual systems, in which the rational, conscious self battles the ruthless biological instincts encoded in automatic, unconscious modules (a view illustrated by Fodor's statement that, "If, in short, there is a community of computers living in my head, there had also better be somebody who is in charge; and, by God, it had better be me"; Fodor 1998, p. 11).

There are at least two things wrong with "me versus the modules." One is that the existence of a distinction between conscious and unconscious processes, whatever that might turn out to be at a neural level, does not necessarily imply anything like a unified "self" who oversees the modules (Kurzban 2010). Another arises from the fact that whatever conscious processes are, they evolved via natural selection within a system of interacting parts and processes that all share a common fate, in fitness terms. Colloquially put, the interests of "me" are not evolutionarily different from the interests of my "modules," because we live, die, and reproduce together. This does not mean, of course, that organisms cannot act in ways that are fitness-reducing, even deliberately, in the case of humans. Even in cases where they do, it is incorrect to think of certain parts of the cognitive system as having different interests, or—except in special evolutionary cases—to have design features that are mutually antagonistic by design (special cases include those in which different parts of an organism do not have entirely shared fates, e.g., in maternal–fetal conflict).

A second mistaken notion that requires revision in light of a properly biological view of modularity is the idea that there are one or a few "bits" which, when added on to an ancestral brain, make us human. It might be tempting, for example, to think that if you add something like a capacity for self-reflection, or language, or impulse control to a chimp brain, you get us. There are several things that are probably incorrect about this view. First is the idea that there are radical discontinuities between humans, chimps, and other primates, in the sense of something being "snapped on," entirely *de novo*, to a chimp brain; instead, whatever design features differ between human and chimp brains reflect evolutionary modifications to traits that existed in the chimp–human common ancestor. Second is the idea that whatever differences exist between human and nonhuman primate brains need to be in just one or a few biological modules. An evo-devo perspective suggests that human and non-human primate brains are likely to be overwhelmingly similar in many respects, but the number of tweaks to developmental knobs need not be small or limited to just one or a few systems and mechanisms. Indeed, comparative work on gene expression in human and chimpanzee brains suggest many differences in gene expression, varying across brain regions and portions of the genome (Khaitovich et al. 2004). Chimp–human brain differences are still poorly understood, but there is every reason to expect that the differences involve modified homologies of many kinds, and not a small number of novel, evolutionarily discontinuous modules that explain the difference.

Work in brain mapping and social cognitive neuroscience is also beginning to paint a picture of the architecture of social cognition that is quite consistent with a biologically appropriate view of "massive modularity": namely, that social cognition is carried out by the distributed interaction of many specialized networks, which collaborate to produce the apparently seamless whole of social judgment and decision making. Frith and Frith (2007), for example, review work on eight different brain areas (anterior cingulate cortex, medial prefrontal cortex, inferior frontal gyrus, interparietal sulcus, temporo-parietal junction, posterior superior temporal sulcus, anterior insula, and amygdala) that interact in various combinations to produce things like social valuations, social emotions, mentalizing, perspective-taking, observing others' actions and expressions, and other forms of intersubjectivity (and this is only at the relatively non-fine-grained level observable by Functional magnetic resonance imaging (fMRI) and electroencephalography (EEG); there is likely to be finer-grained specialization as well). This work suggests that, contrary to some popular views in neuroscience, the cortex is indeed functionally specialized, and many if not most of the regions are likely to be modified homologs of regions present in other primates that carry out similar functions. Thus, there is likely to be no "magic bullet" that explains human social cognition, or human–chimp cognitive differences. Instead, a biologically informed multi-modular view of the mind—where modules are conceptualized as evolving via descent with modification in the developmental systems that give rise to them, due to their functional properties within a complex system of interacting parts—seems the most promising candidate for bridging social psychology with evolutionary developmental biology, neuroscience, and genetics.

Finally, it is important to emphasize that a biological modularity view, when properly construed, renders moot one of the most heated points of conflict between evolutionary psychology and other social sciences: namely, the supposed conflict between plasticity and specialization. Just as it is an empirical fact that the human brain contains a high degree of functional specialization, it is an equally undeniable fact that it contains a high degree of plasticity. Indeed, brain research over the past decades has revealed increasingly mounting evidence for both things. Thus, contrary to what is for many a deep-seated intuition, specialization and plasticity are not necessarily at odds. Not only does this empirically appear to be the case, there is nothing in biological theory that suggests otherwise: plasticity and adaptation are not antonyms.

That said, however, much work remains to be done in order to understand the specifics of how human plasticity emerges from our modularly organized brains. In principle, it is not hard to see how it could be the case that high degrees of plasticity could emerge from a system of flexibly interacting parts, each of which is developmentally and phenotypically plastic in its own right. Indeed, the history of computing technology shows that the accelerating flexibility of computing devices such as computers and cellular phones generally results from the addition, not removal, of more and more specialized functionality—including increasingly flexible interfaces between specialized systems (Baldwin and Clark 2000, Kurzban 2010). Recent evidence of modifications in brain wiring between specialized brain systems in humans—in particular, in white matter pathways—is particularly interesting in this regard (Rilling et al. 2008; Schoenemann et al. 2005). It is consistent with the possibility that evolutionary advances in human cognition, including increases in our flexibility and the diversity of our behavioral and cognitive repertoires, have come about through descent with modification within hierarchically specialized brains. And at least some of this might be due to a kind of runaway evolutionary feedback process between human brains, culture, and the increasingly complex ways that we have structured our environments (Barrett 2012, 2015; Laland et al. 2000; Richerson and Boyd 2005).

Conclusion

At the beginning of this chapter, I suggested that we may be at a kind of crossroads when it comes to modularity. On the one hand, classical Fodorian modularity appears to be largely dead or dying, because it simply cannot account for most of human cognition. In biology, however, modularity is not only alive and well, it is considered to be a ubiquitous feature of organisms, and perhaps even a prerequisite for the evolution of complexity. An important reason for the difference is that in psychology, the classical view of modularity begins with an a priori definition that makes it inapplicable for many cognitive phenomena. Biologists, on the other hand, view modularity as an empirical phenomenon, and adopt a broad working definition that allows them to explore modularity as a natural phenomenon to be studied and understood using the tools of evolutionary biology. If modules are broadly defined as semi-separable or decomposable functional components of a system that can exist simultaneously at multiple levels of brain organization and can take different forms depending on their functions, then the study of modularity in the brain and cognition can easily be merged with the study of modularity in biology, rendering the seemingly intractable "modularity debate" in psychology obsolete (Barrett and Kurzban 2006). More than that, a biologically realistic view of modularity is increasingly consistent with current knowledge of the brain gleaned through genetics, neuroscience, and psychology. If modularity seen in this light is embraced rather than ignored by psychologists, it is likely to lead to progress beyond what the venerable but biologically suspicious dichotomies of psychology have so far allowed.

References

Allman, J. M. (2000). *Evolving brains*. New York: Scientific American Library.

Baldwin, C. Y., & Clark, K. B. (2000). *Design rules: Vol. 1. The power of modularity*. Cambridge: MIT Press.

Barrett, H. C. (2005). Enzymatic computation and cognitive modularity. *Mind & Language, 20,* 259–287.

Barrett, H. C. (2006). Modularity and design reincarnation. In P. Carruthers, S. Laurence, & S. Stich (Eds.), *The innate mind: Vol. 2. Culture and cognition* (pp. 199–217). New York: Oxford University Press.

Barrett, H. C. (2012). A hierarchical model of the evolution of human brain specializations. *Proceedings of the National Academy of Sciences, 109*(Suppl. 1), 10733–10740.

Barrett, H. C. (2015). The shape of thought: How mental adaptations evolve. New York: Oxford University Press.

Barrett, H. C., & Kurzban, R. (2006). Modularity in cognition: Framing the debate. *Psychological Review, 113,* 628–647.

Barrett, H. C., Frederick, D. A., Haselton, M. G., & Kurzban, R. (2006). Can manipulations of cognitive load be used to test evolutionary hypotheses? *Journal of Personality and Social Psychology, 91,* 513–518.

Buller, D. J., & Hardcastle, V. G. (2000). Evolutionary psychology, meet developmental neurobiology: Against promiscuous modularity. *Brain and Mind, 1,* 307–325.

Bullmore, E., & Sporns, O. (2009). Complex brain networks: Graph theoretical analysis of structural and functional systems. *Nature Reviews Neuroscience, 10,* 186–198.

Callebaut, W., & Rasskin-Gutman, D. (Eds.). (2005). *Modularity: Understanding the development and evolution of natural complex systems*. Cambridge: MIT Press.

Carroll, S. B. (2008). Evo-devo and an expanding evolutionary synthesis: A genetic theory of morphological evolution. *Cell, 134,* 25–36.

Carruthers, P. (2006). *The architecture of the mind*. New York: Oxford University Press.

DeSteno, D., Bartlett, M. Y., Braverman, J., & Salovey, P. (2002). Sex differences in jealousy: Evolutionary mechanism or artifact of measurement? *Journal of Personality and Social Psychology, 83,* 1103–1116.

Evans, J. S. B. (2008). Dual-processing accounts of reasoning, judgment, and social cognition. *Annual Review of Psychology, 59,* 255–278.

Fodor, J. A. (1983). *The modularity of mind*. Cambridge: MIT Press.

Fodor, J. A. (1987). Modules, frames, fridgeons, sleeping dogs, and the music of the spheres. In J. L. Garfield (Ed.), *Modularity in knowledge representation and natural-language understanding* (pp. 26–36). Cambridge: MIT Press.

Fodor, J. (1998). The trouble with psychological Darwinism. *London Review of Books, 20,* 11–13.

Fodor, J. (2000). *The mind doesn't work that way: The scope and limits of computational psychology*. Cambridge: MIT Press.

Frankenhuis, W. E., & Ploeger, A. (2007). Evolutionary psychology versus Fodor: Arguments for and against the massive modularity hypothesis. *Philosophical Psychology, 20,* 687–710.

Friederici, A. D. (2009). Pathways to language: Fiber tracts in the human brain. *Trends in Cognitive Sciences, 13,* 175–181.

Frith, C. D., & Frith, U. (2007). Social cognition in humans. *Current Biology, 17*(16), R724–R732.

Hall, B. K. (2003). Descent with modification: The unity underlying homology and homoplasy as seen through an analysis of development and evolution. *Biological Reviews, 78,* 409–433.

Holland, N. D. (2003). Early central nervous system evolution: An era of skin brains? *Nature Reviews Neuroscience, 4,* 617–627.

Kaas, J. H. (1984). Duplication of brain parts in evolution. *Behavioral and Brain Sciences, 7,* 342–343.

Khaitovich, P., Muetzel, B., She, X., Lachmann, M., Hellmann, I., Dietzsch, J., Steigele, S., Do, H. H., Weiss, G., Enard, W., Heissig, F., Arendt, T., Nieselt-Struwe, K., Eichler, E. E., & Pääbo, S. (2004). Regional patterns of gene expression in human and chimpanzee brains. *Genome Research, 14,* 1462–1473.

Krubitzer, L., & Huffman, K. J. (2000). Arealization of the neocortex in mammals: Genetic and epigenetic contributions to the phenotype. *Brain, Behavior and Evolution, 55,* 322–335.

Kurzban, R. (2010). *Why everyone (else) is a hypocrite: Evolution and the modular mind.* Princeton: Princeton University Press.

Laland, K. N., Odling-Smee, J., & Feldman, M. W. (2000). Niche construction, biological evolution, and cultural change. *Behavioral and Brain Sciences, 23,* 131–146.

Machery, E. (2008). Massive modularity and the flexibility of human cognition. *Mind & Language, 23,* 263–272.

Nelson, C. (2004). Selector genes and the genetic control of developmental modules. In G. Schlosser & G. P. Wagner (Eds.), *Modularity in development and evolution* (pp. 17–33). Chicago: University of Chicago Press.

Panksepp, J., & Panksepp, J. B. (2000). The seven sins of evolutionary psychology. *Evolution and Cognition, 6,* 108–131.

Raff, R. A. (1996). *The shape of life: Genes, development, and the evolution of animal form.* Chicago: University of Chicago Press.

Ravasz, E., Somera, A. L., Mongru, D. A., Oltvai, Z. N., & Barabási, A. L. (2002). Hierarchical organization of modularity in metabolic networks. *Science, 297*(5586), 1551–1555.

Richerson, P. J., & Boyd, R. (2005). *Not by genes alone: How culture transformed human evolution.* Chicago: University of Chicago Press.

Rilling, J. K., Glasser, M. F., Preuss, T. M., Ma, X., Zhao, T., Hu, X., & Behrens, T. E. J. (2008). The evolution of the arcuate fasciculus revealed with comparative DTI. *Nature Neuroscience, 11,* 426–428.

Samuels, R. (1998). Evolutionary psychology and the massive modularity hypothesis. *British Journal for the Philosophy of Science, 49,* 575–602.

Schlosser, G., & Wagner, G. P. (Eds.). (2004). *Modularity in development and evolution.* Chicago: University of Chicago Press.

Schoenemann, P. T., Sheehan, M. J., & Glotzer, L. D. (2005). Prefrontal white matter volume is disproportionately larger in humans than in other primates. *Nature Neuroscience, 8,* 242–252.

Shallice, T. (1988). *From neuropsychology to mental structure.* New York: Cambridge University Press.

Sperber, D. (1994). The modularity of thought and the epidemiology of representations. In L. A. Hirschfeld & S. A. Gelman (Eds.), *Mapping the mind: Domain specificity in cognition and culture* (pp. 39–67). New York: Cambridge University Press.

Sperber, D. (2001). In defense of massive modularity. In E. Dupoux (Ed.), *Language, brain, and cognitive development: Essays in honor of Jacques Mehler* (pp. 47–57). Cambridge: MIT Press.

Stanovich, K. E. (2004). *The robot's rebellion: Finding meaning in the age of Darwin.* Chicago: University of Chicago Press.

Thomas, R. D. K. (2005). Hierarchical integration of modular structures in the evolution of animal skeletons. In W. Callebaut & D. Rasskin-Gutman (Eds.), *Modularity: Understanding the development and evolution of natural complex systems* (pp. 239–258). Cambridge: MIT Press.

Uttal, W. R. (2001). *The new phrenology: The limits of localizing cognitive processes in the brain.* Cambridge: MIT Press.

Wagner, G. P., & Altenberg, L. (1996). Complex adaptations and the evolution of evolvability. *Evolution, 50,* 967–976.

Wagner, G. P., Mezey, J., & Calabretta, R. (2005). Natural selection and the origin of modules. In W. Callebaut & D. Rasskin-Gutman (Eds.), *Modularity: Understanding the development and evolution of natural complex systems* (pp. 33–50). Cambridge: MIT Press.

Evolutionary Psychology and Emotion: A Brief History

5

Timothy Ketelaar

The first rumblings of a modern evolutionary psychology of the emotions began in the late 1880s in the form of William James' writings on instinct and emotion. James' most notable attempt to combine Darwin's insights on human nature with a scientific discussion of emotion appeared in his 1890 textbook, *The Principles of Psychology*. Although James' writings on emotion published in the *Principles* (and in his 1984 paper, "What is an Emotion?") were arguably the first modern scientific accounts of human emotion, his writings did not constitute an "adaptationist" approach to emotion in the sense that evolutionary psychologists use that term today.

Although he was familiar with Darwin's views on evolution and human nature, James was not Darwin's bulldog when it came to theorizing about human emotions. In many instances, James' use of Darwin's insights revealed more sympathy than willingness to carry Darwin's evolutionary insights to their full conclusion. James' reticence in his evolutionary theorizing about emotion was not due to a lack of sophistication in his psychological thinking; indeed, the *Principles of Psychology* was hailed at the time as "the most important contribution that has been made to the subject for many years" (Perry 1935, p. 104) and James' theory of emotion "is still the starting point for much contemporary theory and research into emotions" (Dixon 2003, p. 231). Nor is it plausible to claim that James' restraint in applying Darwinian thinking to the study of emotion was due to a lack of familiarity with Darwin's writings. As a medical student at Harvard in the 1860s, James published two reviews of Darwin's (1868) book *The Variation of Animals and Plants under Domestication* in the same year it was published. James' reticence in exploring the ultimate causes of human emotion appears to be due less to a lack of familiarity with Darwin's views on evolution and more to James' peculiar views on teleology (discussed below).

James' failure to apply an adaptationist analysis to human emotion can perhaps be forgiven by modern evolutionary psychologists because it turns out that Darwin was, despite numerous erroneous modern claims to the contrary, among the least "Darwinian" of emotion scholars in the past 150 years (Dixon 2003; Fridlund 1994; Griffith 1997). If by employing the term "Darwinian" one refers to an evolutionary account of a psychological trait that invokes evidence of special design in biology, then Darwin's views on emotional expression did not constitute an "adaptationist" treatment of emotion (Dixon 2003; Fridlund 1994). In his 1872 book, *The Expression of Emotions in Man and Animal,* Darwin focused instead on rejecting the theological account of emotional expressions that had been popularized by Sir Charles Bell. Bell, a Scottish surgeon and theological philosopher, was well known for his anatomical expertise, and published a number of works on facial expression, including his (1806)

T. Ketelaar (✉)
Department of Psychology, New Mexico State University, MSC 3452, Las Cruces, NM, 88001-8001, USA
e-mail: ketelaar@nmsu.edu

V. Zeigler-Hill et al. (eds.), *Evolutionary Perspectives on Social Psychology,* Evolutionary Psychology, DOI 10.1007/978-3-319-12697-5_5, © Springer International Publishing Switzerland 2015

Essays on the Anatomy of Expression in Painting and his even more popular (1824) *The Anatomy and Philosophy of Expression.* In the latter, Bell argued that God had endowed humans alone with the capacity to express their inner states through facial displays, a claim which famously prompted Darwin to scribble in the margins of his copy of Bell's text: "I suspect he never dissected [a] monkey."[1]. For Bell, God was the only force in the universe capable of rendering such biological designs.

Bell (1824) had argued that it was a mistake to assume that nonhuman animals possessed the capacity to express their inner states with outer displays of emotion. The mistake, according to Bell, was to confuse various instinctive reflex-like movements (e.g., the opening of the mouth and protruding of the tongue while expelling a disgusting food) with signaling systems "designed" to convey to conspecifics inner feeling states (such as disgust; Dixon 2003). In a review of Darwin's writings on emotional expression, Dixon (2003) wrote:

> Darwin was determined to deny Bell's claim that expressions were boons to the human race and evidence of divine design.... Thus, Darwin's anti-theological agenda required him to deny the utility of expression and so to miss the (to us) obvious fact that most expressions are very useful (because socially communicative). (p. 172)

As a result, Dixon (2003) noted that:

> Darwin, in order to undercut the idea that the muscles and nerves were specially designed and endowed on humans by the Deity, argued that they were not for communicating our feelings. (p. 171)

Despite his rejection of Bell's design-theology, Darwin did not dismiss all that Bell offered regarding emotional expression. Bell's (1824) *Anatomy and Philosophy of Expression* contained detailed descriptions of the nerves and muscles involved in the expression of emotion. Darwin and his contemporaries (e.g., Alexander Bain) incorporated numerous examples from Bell's research into their own work (see Dixon 2003, for a review). As Dixon (2003) notes, Darwin was not striving to articulate a theory of the emotions per se, so much as he wished to provide a natural science account of the behaviors referred to as "emotional expressions." To achieve this goal, Darwin (1872) proposed three different explanatory principles, including the *principle of serviceable associated habits,* the *principle of antithesis,* and the *principle of the direct action of the nervous system*. None of these "Darwinian" principles of facial signals invoked an explicitly adaptationist portrayal of facial displays as evolved signaling systems; rather, these principles were Darwin's attempt at grounding our understanding of facial behaviors associated with emotion into known facts about the physiology of our nervous system, an approach that would soon be echoed by James (1884, 1890).

Darwin's "non-Darwinian" treatment of emotions is almost as striking as the list of modern emotion scholars who have incorrectly portrayed Darwin as having offered an adaptationist account of facial expressions (reviewed in Dixon 2003; Fridlund 1994). The list of influential emotion scholars who have presented Darwin's view of emotional expression in an adaptationist light range from Richard Lazarus (1993) and Klaus Scherer (1994, 2000) to Carroll Izard (Izard and Ackerman 2000), Paul Ekman[2] (1973; Keltner et al. 2000), and Tooby and Cosmides (1990), all of whom either suggest that Darwin's writings on emotion were the origins of the

[1] From the third edition of Darwin's (1872/1998) *The Expression of the Emotions in Man and Animals,* an annotated anniversary edition containing an introduction, afterword, and commentaries by Paul Ekman.

[2] The claim here is not that Ekman's writings on facial expression provide an inaccurate account of Darwin's writings on emotions. Indeed, Ekman has been one of the most perceptive Darwin scholars [see Ekman's annotated edition of Darwin's (1879/1998) *Expressions*]. Rather, the claim is that Ekman's early writings, like many contemporary emotion scholars, provides an incomplete portrayal of Darwin's view. For example, in the introduction to his edited volume *Darwin and Facial Expression: A century of review*, Ekman (1973) lists five reasons why Darwin's book on facial expression "had so little influence" (p. 2). These reasons include Darwin's anthropomorphism and his reliance on anecdotal data. Interestingly, the fact that Darwin argued against an adaptationist account of facial expression is not listed among the reasons for the lack of influence of Darwin's theory of emotion.

modern view that "facial expressions evolved to elicit distinct behaviors in conspecifics" (Keltner et al. 2000, p. 424) or explicitly portray Darwin's view of expressions as adaptationist (e.g., Lazarus, Scherer). Some of these mistaken references to Darwin's "adaptationist" view of emotional expression may simply be attributed to ambiguous statements contained in reviews of Darwin's writings on emotion; However, several modern textbooks and edited volumes on emotion provide explicit citations to Darwin's putatively adaptationist stance regarding emotional expressions in (for examples, see Kalat and Shiota 2007; Petri and Govern 2004; Reeve 2005). By contrast with these all-too-common mistaken claims, emotion scholar and historian Dixon (2003) opined that:

> As this brief summary of Darwin's principles shows, the *Expression of the Emotions in Man and Animals* might have been more appropriately entitled *The Inheritance of Useless Habits in Man and Animals*. (p. 168)

Although Darwin failed to offer an adaptationist account of emotional expressions, his insights into natural and sexual selection did not stop him from seeing the utility of adaptationist thinking for psychology more broadly. In the final chapter of his 1859 *Origin of the Species,* Darwin famously remarked:

> In the distant future I see open fields for far more important researches. Psychology will be based on a new foundation, that of the necessary acquirement of each mental power and capacity by gradation. (p. 449)

Darwin's observations proved prescient, as James soon took up Darwin's call to eschew design-theology accounts of emotion in favor of explanations drawn from the natural sciences of physiology and medicine. Yet James, like Darwin, stopped short of offering a fully adaptationist account of human emotion.

After Darwin: Emotions as Perceptions of Instinctual Bodily Movements

James' discussion of emotional states in the *Principles of Psychology* focused on the proximate physiological mechanisms underlying emotional experiences rather than their ultimate evolutionary functions. In fact, James used the phrase "evolutionary psychology" just once in his 1700-page, two-volume *Principles of Psychology*. By contrast, James' discussion of the functions of emotion was more extensive, encompassing two chapters in the *Principles of Psychology,* including a review of "The Emotions" (Chap. 25) and "Instinct" (Chap. 24), in which he provided an extensive discussion of emotions such as fear. Yet James' focus on the functions of emotion was limited to a description of proximate (not ultimate) mechanisms.

With the exception of his anecdotal account of the adaptive problem of "running from a bear" (see Ellsworth 1994), James (1884/1994) provided little discussion of how emotions might be considered psychological mechanisms that were biologically "designed" to solve a particular recurrent problems of survival or reproduction (Dixon 2003; Prinz 2004). Instead, James (1884) argued that emotions were best described as *perceptions* of instinctual bodily reflexes, proposing that "bodily changes follow directly the PERCEPTION of the exciting fact" and that "our feeling of the same changes as they occur IS the emotion." (p. 189, emphasis in original). James argued that it is only after we become fully aware of our instinctual bodily preparations for flight or fight—which occur when we encounter an exciting stimulus—that we can claim to be experiencing the psychological state that we call an emotion. Just as Darwin had offered a vehement critique of Bell's design-theology account of emotional displays, James took theologians to task for their portrayal of biological instincts as God-given traits. James (1890) illustrated his point with his example of the broody hen for whom "the notion would probably seem monstrous that there should be a creature in the world to whom a nestful of eggs was not the utterly fascinating and precious and never-to-be-too-much-sat-upon object which it is to her" (p. 268). In discussing the biological basis of these instincts, James (1890, emphasis added) criticized theological accounts of such phenomena, writing:

> The older writings on instinct are ineffectual wastes of words, because their authors never came down to this definite and simple point of view but smoth-

> ered everything in vague wonder at the clairvoyant and prophetic power of the animals—so superior to anything in man—and at the beneficence of God in endowing them with such a gift. *But God's beneficence endows them first of all with a nervous system;* and, turning our attention to this, makes instinct immediately appear neither more nor less wonderful than all the other facts of life. (p. 267)

James' brand of teleology did not allow him to take Darwin's insights about these biologically based instincts to their full conclusions. Instead, James mistakenly argued that explanations of ultimate causes for instinctual tendencies such as "care for eggs" required that the broody hen was consciously aware of the evolutionary goals that its behavior was "designed" to achieve. On that basis, James' teleological stance led him to dismiss ultimate causal accounts of instincts outright, arguing that explanations focusing on the proximate physiological mechanisms of these instinctual behaviors were to be preferred. In his 1887 paper "What is an instinct?" James wrote:

> A very common way of talking about these admirable definite tendencies to act is by naming abstractly the purpose they subserve, such as self-preservation, or defense, or care for eggs…. But this represents the animal as obeying abstractions which, not once in a million cases is it possible it can have framed. (p. 2)

After James's early scientific writings on emotion, it would take almost another two decades before the terms "emotion" and "evolution" would appear together in the same volume of psychological work. This occurred when social psychologist William McDougall (1908/1921) published his textbook *An Introduction to Social Psychology*. Following James' writings on the subject, McDougall argued that emotions were biologically grounded instincts. McDougall (1908/1921) maintained that each instinct produces a "kind of emotional excitement whose quality is specific or peculiar to it" (p. 47) and, moreover, that "each primary emotion accompanies the excitement of an instinctive disposition of specific tendency" (p. 80). McDougall was following James' lead in viewing emotions as instincts. Compare McDougall's (1908/1921) writings to James' (1890) claim that: "every object that excites an instinct incites an emotion!" (p. 304). Another way in which McDougall followed in the footsteps of James was in his failure to offer a sophisticated adaptationist account of emotion. To be fair, McDougall offered a more explicitly Darwinian view of emotions than did James; However, McDougall's account of emotion was naïve (by modern standards), invoking the argument that emotions evolved "for the good of the species." These sorts of "for the good of the group" or "for the good of the species" arguments have largely fallen out of favor since the late 1960s, in large part due to the influential writings of evolutionary biologist George Williams (see Williams 1966; but see Wilson and Wilson 2008 for an alternative view). As evolutionary biologist Richard Dawkins (1976/1989) notes:

> …the best way to look at evolution is in terms of selection occurring at the lowest level of all…the fundamental unit of selection, and therefore of self-interest, is not the species, nor the group, nor even, strictly, the individual. It is the gene, the unit of heredity. (pp. 11–12)

Today most evolutionary psychologists can appreciate how McDougall's (1908) "survival of the species" arguments and James' (1890) flawed teleology may have impeded their development of sophisticated adaptationist accounts of emotion. Almost exactly a century after James reiterated his views of emotion in his revised (1892) textbook, *Psychology: A Briefer Course,* evolutionary psychologists published their flagship treatise, *The Adapted Mind* (Barkow et al. 1992), in which they described how a sophisticated evolutionary psychological explanation necessarily entails providing an argument for how a putative evolved psychological mechanism displays evidence of special biological design (e.g., Barkow et al. 1992; Buss et al. 1998; Thornhill 1990, 1997; Williams 1966). By contrast with the less sophisticated approaches to emotion scholarship witnessed in the late nineteenth century, it is now more widely appreciated that determining whether there is sufficient evidence to invoke a claim of special biological design involves determining:

> whether a *presumed function* is served with sufficient *precision, economy, efficiency,* etc., to rule out pure chance (i.e., any possibility other than

> adaptation for a particular effect) as an adequate explanation. (Williams 1966, p. 10, emphasis in original)

More specifically, sophisticated evolutionary psychologists now argue that there are three products of the evolutionary process that can be invoked when attempting to characterize a complex trait such as human emotion: (1) adaptations, (2) byproducts of adaptations, and (3) random effects or noise (see Buss et al. 1998; Tooby and Cosmides 1990). Even Williams (1966) cautioned:

> This biological principle [adaptation] should be used only as a last resort. It should not be invoked when less onerous principles such as those of physics and chemistry or that of unspecific cause and effect, are sufficient for a complete explanation. (p. 11)

By this standard, James was appropriately cautious in choosing not to apply the label "adaptation" to emotions, showing a preference instead for descriptions of the proximate physiological mechanisms underlying human emotional experiences.

James' reticence to carry Darwinian insights to their full conclusions might be more properly understood, however, by considering the historical context of his contributions to the psychological science of human emotion. Like many of the early psychological scientists (including Wilhem Wundt, Alexander Bain, Herbert Spencer, Walter Cannon, and William McDougall), James was familiar and impressed with Darwin's thinking about human nature, yet as already noted, Darwin's writings on emotion hardly constituted a "Darwinian" approach to emotion—in the sense of an explicitly adaptationist account—upon which a James (or a McDougall) could build a sophisticated evolutionary psychology of the emotions (Dixon 2003; Fridlund 1994). Given the lack of evolutionary models in psychology upon which to construct an adaptationist account of emotion, James' failure to provide a sophisticated evolutionary account of emotion is perhaps not surprising. Two centuries earlier, Isaac Newton (1676) famously described how the process of scientific advancement often proceeds by virtue of one scientist building upon the work of their predecessors, writing: "If I have seen further, it is by standing on the shoulders of giants" (Letter to Robert Hooke, February 15, 1676; c.f. Gould 2003, p. 70). Although Darwin was arguably an intellectual giant upon whose shoulders many modern adaptationists have stood, it turns out that the theory of emotion proposed by James (1884, 1890), and then subsequently echoed by McDougall (1908), and more recently embraced by neuroscientist Antonio Damasio (1994, 1999, 2003; see also Prinz 2004), owes more to James' standing on the shoulders of Medieval and Renaissance scholars of emotion such as St. Augustine, Thomas Aquinas, René Descartes, and Baruch Spinoza than it owes to the writings of Darwin (see Dixon 2003). It was the writings of these medieval emotion scholars that set the stage for Enlightenment philosophers such as David Hume and Adam Smith, scholars who might rightfully be considered the "giants" of emotion scholarship upon whose shoulders have stood modern scholars such as Robert Trivers, Randy Nesse, and Robert Frank.

From Hume to Trivers: The Ancient Origins of Our Modern Evolutionary View of Emotion

As widely read as James was, he apparently failed to note that his view of emotion was essentially a repetition of the insights of ancient Stoic philosophers (see Oatley 2004). Writing in the first century AD, Seneca, for example, argued—in works such as *On Anger*—that all emotions comprise at least two movements (see Oatley 2004; Sorabji 2010). The *first* movement, according to Seneca, was a reflex-like, automatic, and involuntary (often bodily) response, while the *second* movement, was a conscious evaluation, consisting of a consideration of how to act upon the actions resulting from the first movement. It is not hard to see how Seneca's ancient description of *first and second movements* bears a striking resemblance to James' (1884) nineteenth-century proposal that "the bodily changes [first movements] follow directly the PERCEPTION of the exciting fact, and that our feeling of the same changes as they occur [second movements] IS the emotion" (pp. 189–190, emphasis in original). Almost 500 years after Seneca introduced this "two movements" account of emotion, St. Augustine of Hippo, a Christian theologian, referred to emotions as movements in several theological works such as *City of God* and *Confessions* (both written in the fifth century AD, see Dixon 2003). St. Augustine wrote:

> Our affections are motions of souls. Joy is the extending of the soul; sadness the contraction of the soul; desire the soul's going forward; fear the soul's flight. (St. Augustine, c.f. O'Daly 1987, p. 48)

St. Augustine's writings, however, did not generate an immediate burst of scholarly activity developing the idea that emotions were movements, perhaps due in large part to the ensuing fall of the Roman Empire (fifth century AD) and the subsequent decline in many forms of scholarship during the Dark Ages, which extended from the fifth to early thirteenth centuries.

The Dark Ages were not devoid of scholarly thinking and writing (e.g., witness the development of algebra and astronomy in the Arab world during this period), yet scholarship in much of the Western world was restricted to theologically driven writings (scholasticism) rather than secular philosophizing about human nature (Dixon 2003; Pagden 2013). The Dark Ages were nearing their end in the thirteenth century when Thomas Aquinas, a philosopher and theologian, attempted to synthesize classic Aristotelian philosophy with principles of Christianity. In his *Summa Theologiae,* Aquinas (1273/2013) echoed the view of Seneca that emotions corresponded to movements, writing that:

> Virtues are not emotions. Emotions are movements of appetite, virtues dispositions of appetite towards movement. Moreover emotions can be good or bad, reasonable or unreasonable; whereas virtues dispose us only to good.[3] (pt. 1, 2nd pt., qu. 59, art. 1)

Aquinas, like other medieval scholars, used the Latin phrase "motus animae" (rather than the modern word "emotion") to refer to these movements of the soul in relation to one's deity (e.g., moving toward or away from God). In this light, it is not difficult to see how the writings of scholars such as Augustine and Aquinas gave rise to the modern scientific term "emotion" as a derivation of the Latin word "motus" which refers to "movement". In this regard, the writings of Aquinas are seen by some emotion historians as the bridge linking theological writings on passions and sentiments to the more secular scientific view of human emotion that developed in the centuries that followed (see Cates 2009; Dixon 2003; Oatley 2004). Aquinas essentially opened the door to a gradual shift away from a predominantly theological worldview in which scholars looked to God for the origins of natural laws and toward a more secular view in which philosophers (e.g., recall Seneca) returned to the idea that fallible human reasoning was a better guide to understanding the rules that might be governing our mental processes (Dixon 2003).

Perhaps the most influential of these renaissance scholars was René Descartes, who argued that human reasoning, rather than God's laws, was a more reliable guarantor of truth. Descartes's writings influenced not only fellow renaissance emotion scholars such as Baruch Spinoza but also set the stage for the most influential Enlightenment writings on emotion, including the works of David Hume and Adam Smith, which followed in the eighteenth century (see Dixon 2003 for a review). After Descartes, the idea that passions and affects were "movements" was quickly replaced with a more "cognitive" view in which emotions were best characterized as "perceptions" (see Dixon 2003). Baruch Spinoza, a Dutch philosopher who was influenced by Descartes, proposed that mental life comprised three forces which he labeled *conatus* (akin to what we today refer to as will or motivation), *affectus* (emotion), and *intellectus* (cognition). Over the next two centuries, the shift in thinking to a more secular view of the mind was reflected in a profound change in the terminology employed by scholars studying emotion. Renaissance writing on affects, sentiments, and passions would continue through the Enlightenment (see below), but just as the con-

[3] Excerpt from Aquinas, T. (1273), *Summa Theologica,* pt. 1, 2nd pt., qu. 59, art. 1.

cepts of God and soul were being replaced with the concepts of cognition and emotion, theologically inspired terms such as passions and sentiments were increasingly being replaced in the 1800s with more scientific terms such as affect and emotion (see Dixon 2003).

At the dawn of this period of Enlightenment, otherwise known as the Scientific Revolution, Newton's writing on natural philosophy (i.e., science) captured the zeitgeist of scholarly thinking as it shifted away from theologically driven accounts of natural law (and toward natural science accounts of the same). In the final paragraph of his book *Opticks,* Newton (1704/1979) wrote:

> if natural Philosophy and all its Parts, by pursuing this Method, shall at length be perfected, the Bounds of Moral Philosophy will also be enlarged. (p. 405)

Newton's insights were soon echoed by Enlightenment philosophers David Hume and Adam Smith, who took up the challenge of developing a mental science of moral reasoning and moral sentiments, an effort that laid the groundwork for the twentieth century writings of evolution-minded emotion scholars such as Robert Trivers, Randy Nesse, and Robert Frank.

Among the most influential participants in the Enlightenment debate concerning the proper role of emotion in mental science was David Hume. In his *Treatise on Human Nature,* Hume (1740) espoused the radical view that reason was the "slave of the passions," but later modified his position in his *Enquiries Concerning Human Understanding and Concerning the Principles of Morals* (1777), portraying moral sentiment and moral reasoning on more equal footing (see Haidt 2001). Among the Enlightenment emotion scholars influenced by Hume's arguments was eighteenth century economist–philosopher Adam Smith, who argued that moral sentiments such as resentment and guilt can exert a powerful influence on judgment that often competes with more rational deliberations in determining our behavior. In his (1759/2000) *Theory of Moral Sentiments,* Smith wrote:

> The man who acts according to the rules of perfect prudence, of strict justice, and of proper benevolence, may be said to be perfectly virtuous. But the most perfect knowledge of those rules will not alone enable him to act in this manner, his own passions are very apt to mislead him—sometimes to drive him, and sometimes to seduce him, to violate all the rules which he himself, in all his sober and cool hours, approves of. (p. 349)

By arguing that moral passions and emotions (e.g., gratitude, guilt) can motivate an individual to make choices that sometimes conflict with their immediate self-interest, Smith's theory of moral sentiments foreshadowed much of the twentieth century social psychology literature on emotion and judgment. In particular, research in the social cognitive tradition has demonstrated that the influence of emotion on judgment depends on cognitive factors specific to each emotion (reviewed in Clore et al. 1994; Ketelaar and Clore 1997). For example, in a study of the effects of emotion on risk perception, Lerner and Keltner (2001) showed that angry individuals tend to appraise future events as more probable (compared to fearful individuals), in part because anger brings with it cognitive appraisals of "certainty," whereas the emotion of fear covaries with cognitions regarding uncertainty (Ortony et al. 1988; Smith and Ellsworth 1985).

Although Enlightenment philosophers such as Hume and Smith were among the first emotion scholars to portray moral sentiments as strategic influences on moral decision-making, emotion scholarship in the centuries that followed (e.g., Darwin, James, and McDougall) placed more emphasis on articulating the proximate physiological mechanisms underlying emotional sentiments, at the expense of identifying ultimate evolutionary purposes that such psychological machinery might serve. It would be more than two centuries after Hume's and Smith's portrayals of the strategic role of emotions in reasoning—and almost a century after Darwin's and James's writings on the physiology of emotional expression—that the first modern evolutionary psychology of emotions would arrive. This was in the form of evolutionary biologist Robert Trivers's (1971) pathbreaking paper on *reciprocal altruism* in which he presented prescient speculations regarding the evolutionary functions of moral sentiments such as guilt and gratitude.

Trivers's (1971) View of Social Emotions

It is often not appreciated that over one third of Robert Trivers's (1971) paper on *reciprocal altruism* was devoted to a discussion of the role of emotions in cooperative exchanges. Trivers (1971) wrote:

> It seems plausible, furthermore, that the emotion of guilt has been selected for in humans partly in order to motivate the cheater to compensate his misdeed and to behave reciprocally in the future, and thus to prevent the rupture of reciprocal relationships. (p. 50)

Trivers's (1971) paper had a profound impact on the scientific study of cooperation in both evolutionary psychology and behavioral economics. One might even speculate that Trivers's reciprocal altruism paper played a significant role in the early discipline-defining empirical research on "cheater detection" that dominated the early development of evolutionary psychology.[4] Trivers's modern take on moral sentiments opened the door to a number of game-theoretic insights into how cooperation could be achieved in indefinitely repeated social interactions. Trivers proposed that reciprocal altruism, a strategy that would later become known as *tit for tat,*[5] was the equivalent of a social contract in which one individual bestowed a benefit upon a second individual with the expectation of being repaid (by the recipient) in the future. Prior to Trivers's introduction of the strategy of reciprocal altruism, cooperation between genetically unrelated individuals was difficult to explain in terms of the calculus of selfish genes. Trivers's paper demonstrated that as long as the eventual benefit to the individual who provided the aid (by cooperating) was greater than the cost of this initial act of cooperation, neither individual had an incentive to defect from this ongoing, reciprocal tit-for-tat exchange.

Trivers (1971) employed the now familiar prisoner's dilemma game to speculate about the role of moral emotions in sustaining reciprocal exchange agreements. Game theorists (mainly evolutionary biologists, political scientists, and behavioral economists) soon began exploring Trivers's insights regarding cooperation by considering the implications of his ideas for understanding cooperative behavior in economic bargaining games that resembled real-world social dilemmas. Among the insights suggested by Trivers was the recognition of the *folk theorem,* which argues that there exists an infinite number of equilibrium (best) strategies in any indefinitely repeated noncooperative game (such as an indefinitely repeated prisoner's dilemma). This is the case, so argues the folk theorem, because there is always an incentive for both players to coordinate on *any* alternative strategy that generates a larger payoff than what can be obtained by continuous mutual defection (see Binmore 1998; Ketelaar 2004). Spurred on by Trivers's writings on reciprocal altruism, recognition of the *folk theorem* soon allowed game theorists to identify a central problem underlying how two players might coordinate on these more profitable alternative strategies, namely, the problem of credibility: How do you determine that your partner's display of their intention to cooperate (rather than defect) is credible (see Hirschleifer 1987, 2001; Schelling 2001)? Trivers argued that your partner's expression of hard-to-fake moral emotions—such as guilt or gratitude—could guarantee the credibility of their commitment to play one of these alternative strategies, as when feelings of guilt compel "the cheater to compen-

[4] Trivers's writings on cooperation and cheater detection helped set the stage for the development of "evolutionary psychology" in the mid 1980s, a period in which evolutionary approaches to human behavior began shifting away from the study of behavioral mechanisms per se (an approach emphasized in sociobiological accounts of human nature, see Wilson 1975) and toward the study of the evolved psychological mechanisms that generated "adaptively patterned" behavior (see Barkow et al. 1992; Buss 1995). Trivers (1971, p. 50) devoted several pages to the problem of cheater detection, arguing that "Selection should favor the ability to detect and discriminate against subtle cheaters." This idea would later be tested empirically by Cosmides and colleagues (Cosmides 1985; Gigerenzer and Hug 1987) and provided a substantial portion of the early empirical support for claims regarding the utility of an adaptationist approach for understanding human psychology (see Barkow et al. 1992).

[5] The strategy of tit for tat entails that the organism begins cooperatively in the first interaction and on all subsequent interactions copies the action taken by their interaction partner in the previous round (see Axelrod 1984).

sate his misdeed and to behave reciprocally in the future" (p. 50). Trivers argued:

> If an organism has cheated on a reciprocal relationship and this fact has been found out, or has a good chance of being found out, by the partner and if the partner responds by cutting off all future acts of aid, then the cheater will have paid dearly for his misdeed. It will be to the cheater's advantage to avoid this.... The cheater should be selected to make up for his misdeed and to show convincing evidence that he does not plan to continue his cheating sometime in the future. In short, he should be selected to make a reparative gesture. (p. 46)

Trivers proposed that moral emotions such as guilt and gratitude constitute these reparative gestures. Guilt, Trivers argued, can serve the function of signaling a credible commitment to future reparations. Trivers argued that *if* these emotional displays could be considered credible signals, *then* moral sentiments such as guilt and gratitude could unravel the perpetual series of retaliations and tit-for-tat counterretaliations that characterize Hatfield and McCoy-like feuds which erupt whenever one party appears to have violated the terms of social contract resembling a social dilemma.

Trivers's (1971) solution to the problem of achieving cooperation in social dilemmas followed from the realization that both parties have a strong incentive to defect on any promise of future cooperation. The core logic of Trivers's solution to the problem of establishing the credibility[6] of *an emotional signal of commitment to future cooperation* was subsequently worked out by evolution-minded scholars such as Jack Hirschliefer (1987, 2001) and Robert Frank (1988, 2001). Following the lead of Trivers (1971) and Adam Smith (1759), Hirschliefer (1987) sketched out how moral emotions—such as anger (in the case of threats) or gratitude (in the case of promises)—could function as commitment devices that served as the guarantors of promises (to cooperate) and threats (to retaliate). Moreover, Hirshleifer demonstrated how commitment devices were not restricted to pro-social emotions (such as guilt and gratitude) that guarantee promises, but can also include more contrarian moral sentiments, such as anger, an emotion that serves to guarantee threats. In short, the crux of the problem described by the *folk theorem* centers on how to communicate a credible promise (or threat) so that both parties will be rationally motivated to coordinate on a more profitable course of action (specified in the social contract), rather than simply adopting the default strategy of ruthlessly pursuing one's immediate short-term self-interest through defection. Hirshleifer (1987, 2001) showed how moral emotions could guarantee promises (and threats) such that both parties in a social contract would benefit from sticking to a proposed alternative (to defection) strategy that could lead to a more profitable pay-off than that obtained by the short-sighted strategy of self-interested defection.

From Trivers to Nesse to Frank: Emotions as Commitment Devices

The decades following Trivers's (1971) reciprocal altruism paper saw a resurgence of evolutionary accounts of reciprocity and cooperation. In the final two decades of the twentieth century, a number of Trivers's insights were further developed by psychiatrist Randy Nesse. Nesse's early research focused on a variety of evolutionary topics, including senescence and anxiety. In the final decades of the twentieth century, Nesse produced two broad-reaching works that summarized the state of sophisticated evolutionary thinking regarding emotions.

Nesse (1990) summarized three important adaptationist approaches to human emotion. These approaches included: (1) evidence that

[6] The problem of guaranteeing the credibility of one's commitment to play an alternative strategy (one that is more profitable than continuous defection), is the rather simple realization that most promises to play an alternative strategy correspond to what biologists and economists refer to as *cheap talk*. In other words, what is to prevent the sender of this promise from defecting on their promise? The problem of credibility centers on the notion that the recipient of a promise must determine whether the sender has an incentive to defect on their promise (see Ketelaar 2004). Hirschleifer (1987, 2001), following Adam Smith, proposed that the presence of certain emotional states could guarantee various promises and threats that would otherwise be viewed as *cheap talk*.

specific fears (i.e., phobias) operated as domain-specific psychological mechanisms for coping with specific kinds of threat (see Marks 1987; also Seligman 1971) and (2) the idea that moods may be functional psychological processes for coping with propitious and unpropitious environments (a view that has proved to generate a number of promising evolutionary models of depression; see Hagen 2002, 2003; McGuire et al. 1997; Nesse 1991, 2009). Finally, Nesse (1990) touched on (3) the claim that social emotions provide the psychological machinery underlying cooperation in reciprocal relations/cooperative exchanges. Following Trivers's (1971, 1981) insights into emotions and cooperation, Nesse used the prisoner's dilemma game to identify specific social emotions that were expected to covary with particular combinations of strategies, such as "anger," which is predicted to occur when the principal agent cooperates while their partner defects, or "guilt," which is predicted to occur when the principal agent defects while their partner cooperates (see Nesse 1990, Table 4).

Nesse and Williams (1994) provided another contribution to evolutionary approaches to emotion scholarship by discussing evolutionary perspectives on a variety of topics in medicine and physiology ranging from fever and infection to cancer and obesity. Among the most influential contributions to our understanding of the adaptive basis of human emotion was their discussion of the distinction between defects and defenses. Nesse and Williams (1994) discussed the possible biological design features and adaptive benefits associated with the symptoms of affective disorders such as phobia, panic attacks, and depressed mood (see also Nesse 1997). This distinction between *defects* (design flaws) and *defenses* (mechanisms or processes specifically designed to cope with a particular challenge) allowed Nesse and Williams to pose the question of whether a variety of unpleasant symptoms associated with affective disorders (e.g., loss of pleasure, rumination) might constitute evidence of special design, in the form of evolved psychological defenses for combatting specific threats. Nesse and Williams pondered whether physicians and social scientists are often too quick to categorize unpleasant psychological states (e.g., depression, anxiety) as mental defects and disorders. By contrast, Nesse and Williams echoed Tooby and Cosmides' (1990) proposal that emotions—including many of their affiliated symptoms—might actually constitute "Darwinian algorithms of the mind" designed to provide the psychological machinery for coping with specific threats and challenges in one's social environment. One of the most promising avenues of research into the "Darwinian algorithm" view of emotions concerns the role of moral sentiments, such as guilt, in compelling cooperative behavior in economic bargaining games such as the prisoner's dilemma and ultimatum game.

Although the prisoner's dilemma had traditionally been used to model the conflict between individual and collective self-interest, economist Robert Frank (1988) used this two-person bargaining game to illustrate the role of moral sentiments in an entirely different, but equally important, set of conflicts known as commitment problems. Frank showed how the moral sentiments discussed by Adam Smith and Jack Hirshleifer could, in principle, solve the conflict between immediate and long-term self-interest. Consistent with Hirshleifer (1987) and Schelling's (1960) earlier analysis of these issues, Frank referred to these sorts of conflicts as *commitment problems*. Commitment problems (see Hirshleifer 2001; Schelling 2001; reviewed in Nesse 2001) arise whenever immediate incentives run contrary to one's long-term interests. The dieter, for example, faces the immediate attraction of a piece of cake, weighed against the long-term costs of gaining weight. The diner in a restaurant faces the immediate benefit of not leaving a tip, weighed against the potential long-term damage to their reputation (or future service) for being less than generous. The key "problem" of a commitment problem centers on the fact that the psychological reward mechanism displays the short-term benefits (rewards) right now (see Frank 1988). The activation of this reward mechanism can be a tempting lure for behavior that is not in one's long-term self-interest.

Frank (1988; see also Hirshleifer 1987) proposed that moral sentiments such as guilt function as commitment devices, mechanisms that provoke individuals to make binding commitments to strategies that maximize their long-term payoffs, often at the expense of sometimes forgoing short-term rewards. Citing the familiar prisoner's dilemma scenario, Frank (1988) argued that moral sentiments could explain why we live in a world where some individuals shirk the immediate payoff associated with defection in favor of more cooperative strategies. According to Frank, if an individual experiences feelings of guilt while contemplating defection, then his feelings can serve as a potent counterweight to the immediate payoffs reaped by not cooperating. Frank (1988) observed that moral sentiments:

> can and do compete with feelings that spring from rational calculations about material payoffs.... Consider, for example, a person capable of strong guilt feelings. This person will not cheat even when it is in her material interests to do so. The reason is not that she fears getting caught but that she simply does not *want* to cheat. Her aversion to feelings of guilt effectively alters the payoffs she faces. (p. 53)

Because these feelings coincide with the activation of the reward mechanism, the individual has two concurrent sources of information that can be taken into account when deciding how to behave. One source of information (from the immediate reward mechanism) informs the individual about the immediate consequences of a given strategy and the second source of information (from the consciously accessible moral sentiments such as feelings of guilt) informs the individual about the future (in this case negative) consequences of the same strategy choice.

Subjecting Frank's translation of Adam Smith and Jack Hirshleifer to empirical test turned out to be relatively straightforward. A central prediction of Frank's model, that guilt feelings can provoke a commitment to more cooperative strategies, has been tested by examining whether individuals who experience guilt feelings while considering "defection" in a repeated prisoner's dilemma are more likely to forgo this initially attractive strategy in favor of alternative (more cooperative) strategies. In one study, Ketelaar and Au (2003) subjected participants to a standard laboratory mood manipulation (in the form of a guilt induction) and observed the effects of these manipulated "guilt" feelings on subsequent strategy choice in a repeated prisoner's dilemma game. In a study inspired by Isen et al.'s (1976; Isen and Simmonds 1978) influential research on mood and cooperation and Schwarz and Clore's (1983, 2003) "Affect as information" model, Ketelaar and Au (2003) found that when previously noncooperative individuals were experimentally manipulated into a guilty mood they subsequently displayed higher levels of cooperation (53 % cooperative responses) in a repeated prisoner's dilemma compared to individuals who were experimentally placed into a more neutral mood (39 % cooperation).

In a second study, Ketelaar and Au (2003) replicated these findings by exploring the impact of "naturalistic" feelings of guilt that occurred during a repeated ultimatum game.[7] Participants in this study played two ultimatum games over a 2-week period and were instructed to divide US$19 into whole dollar increments. Of primary interest was whether selfish proposers (those who kept most of the money for themselves in week one) would subsequently propose more generous offers when the ultimate game was repeated 1 week later, but *only* if they had reported feelings of guilt over their selfish offer the previous week. Consistent with Trivers's (1971) views on emotion in reciprocal exchanges, Nesse's predictions about emotions in social dilemmas, and Frank's (1988) predictions about guilt and commitment problems, the results revealed that the largest effects of guilty feelings were seen among individuals who tended to play uncooperatively in the earlier rounds of the ultimatum game. Not surprising, none of the individuals who proposed a generous division of the money reported feelings of guilt, whereas over half (57 %) of individuals who made a selfish offer reported such feelings.

[7] The ultimatum game is a two-person economic-bargaining game in which one individual (the proposer) is asked to offer a proposal to a second individual regarding how to split a sum of money (Guth et al. 1982). The second individual (the receiver) has the task of either accepting the offer as is (in which case the money is divided as proposed) or rejecting the offer (in which case neither party receives any money).

More important, the vast majority (91 %) of these guilty-feeling individuals subsequently gave a more generous offer to their partner in the final round of the ultimatum game (see Ketelaar and Au 2003). By contrast, only 22 % of the selfish proposers who reported no feelings of guilt behaved in such a generous fashion in the second round. In other words, individuals who had previously behaved in a noncooperative fashion now appeared to be motivated by their feelings of guilt to compensate for their earlier uncooperative behavior. Such findings lend empirical support to evolutionary accounts of emotions as commitment devices. Whereas the first examples of modern evolutionary accounts of emotion and cooperation (Frank 1988; Hirschliefer 1987; Nesse 1990; Trivers 1971) offered considerably more logic and theory than actual data or empirical tests, more recent research on emotion and economic decision-making has provided increasing empirical evidence for the adaptationist claim that social emotions such as guilt, anger and regret may have been biologically "designed" to regulate—rather than simply disrupt—strategic behavior in social interactions (see Ketelaar 2006, for a review).

The journey from Charles Darwin and William James to Robert Trivers and his contemporaries (Nesse, Hirshliefer, Frank, etc.) traverses an interesting path in the intellectual history of emotion scholarship. The current retelling of this history suggests that adaptationist accounts of human emotion—especially those with empirical support for their theoretical propositions—are not much older than the discipline of evolutionary psychology itself (see Barkow et al. 1992; Wang 2011). Despite their relatively recent emergence, evolutionary accounts of emotion have evolved from nineteenth-century adaptation—agnostic descriptions of the proximate physiological mechanisms of emotional expressions to twenty-first-century empirically validated accounts of emotions as strategic commitment devices capable of influencing economic and social decisions that were once viewed as the sole province of cold-hearted reasoning processes (see Ketelaar 2004, 2006; Ketelaar and Koenig 2007; also Haidt 2001, 2003 for reviews). To the degree that many of our everyday judgment and decision-making processes are based on moral intuitions and emotional perceptions rather than an emotionless capacity for logic and rational deliberation, one might suspect that the impact of emotion in everyday psychological experience has been greatly underestimated. In this regard, I conclude this chapter with a brief review of two areas of emotion scholarship that appear to be fruitful avenues for future adaptationist exploration.

Promising Future Directions for the Evolutionary Psychology of Emotion

Individual differences in strategic emotional commitments. Some of the most compelling empirical support for adaptationist accounts of emotion (i.e., the claim that emotions are defenses rather than defects) involves demonstrations of the strategic influence of emotions on social and economic decision-making (Ketelaar 2006). As previously noted, this evidence includes empirical demonstrations that particular emotions can compel individuals to maximize long-term payoffs by sometimes forgoing immediate rewards (Fehr and Gaetcher 2002; Ketelaar and Au 2003). Although it is now clear that certain social–moral emotions can compel increases in direct reciprocity (e.g., guilt increases cooperation among noncooperators in the prisoners' dilemma and ultimatum games), as well as increases in indirect reciprocity (e.g., anger is associated with increased punishment of under-contributors in public goods games), these systematic influences of emotion on strategic behavior are not universal patterns of human behavior. Instead, individual differences are observed in these studies (see Ketelaar 2006; Ketelaar and Koenig 2007). For example, in an influential study of anger and punishment (Fehr and Gächter 2002), only one third of the sample consistently (across several rounds of play) punished group members who made deviant contributions, and these costly acts of punishment were shown to be strongly linked to individual differences in the experience of anger. Similarly, Ketelaar and Au (2003) observed that only 57% of individuals reported feelings of guilt after proposing an unfair split of the money in the first round of a repeated ultimatum game. Before one would want to conclude that moral emotions such as guilt function as species-typical adaptations for repairing the harm done by failure to cooperate in a reciprocal exchange, one must first account for the robust findings that certain moral sentiments—such as guilt—are reliably absent in a stable segment of the human population known as psychopaths or sociopaths (3–4% of males and 1–2% of females; see Mealey 1995). As originally formulated, the commitment device view of moral emotions does not explain why certain individuals (e.g., guilt-free individualists and emotionless sociopaths; see Ketelaar 2004, 2006; Ketelaar and Au 2003) lack these emotional commitment devices. Evolutionary psychologist Linda Mealey (1995) conjectured that individual differences in the deployment of such commitment devices might reflect a polymorphic population structure, rather than noise around a single adaptive norm, noting that:

> as long as evolutionary pressures for emotions as reliable communication and commitment devices leading to long-term cooperative strategies coexist with counter pressures for cheating, deception and 'rational' short-term selfishness, *a mixture of phenotypes* will result, such that some sort of statistical equilibrium will be approached. (p. 524, emphasis added)

In sum, an intriguing possibility for future research into the adaptationist logic of emotional commitment devices involves the claim that individual differences in moral sentiments constitute evidence for a stable polymorphic distribution of distinct emotion-based strategy types (Ketelaar 2004, 2006; Ketelaar and Koenig 2007).

Emotional mechanisms underlying the behavioral immune system. Another area where evolutionary theorizing about emotion has provided novel insights involves research into the origins of xenophobia, defined as a dislike or fear of strangers or foreign people (Kirkpatrick and Navarrete 2006; Navarrete et al. 2007; Schaller and Park 2011; Schaller and Neuberg 2012). To explain some of the robust, systematic features of xenophobia—such as disgust reactions to foreigners—evolutionary psychologists have posited a behavioral immune system that evolved to serve as a first line of defense (ahead of the internal physiological immune system) in response to pathogens (Schaller and Neuberg 2012; Schaller and Park 2011). Central to the behavioral immune system view of xenophobia is the well-established finding that contact with out-group members has historically been associated with increased exposure to novel pathogens, which tend to be especially virulent when introduced to the local population (reviewed in Fincher and Thornhill 2012; Schaller and Neuberg 2012; Schaller and Park 2011). Moreover, members of out-groups are less likely to be familiar with local norms pertaining to hygiene and food preparation, behavioral norms that "serve as barriers to pathogen transmission" (Schaller and Neuberg 2012, p. 36). In this light, evolutionary psychologists have hypothesized that humans evolved a behavioral immune system to facilitate avoidance of pathogens through a number of mechanisms including emotion systems that respond specifically to contagion threats (e.g., disgust) and perceptual systems designed to identify and avoid "people who appear especially likely to pose some risk of pathogen transmission" (Schaller and Park 2011, p. 100).

Positing a behavioral immune system has been instrumental in explaining why xenophobic reactions are often better conceptualized by the emotion of disgust rather than fear, as might be implied by the term *xenophobia* (Cottrell and Neuberg 2005; Park et al. 2007). In this regard, a number of studies have begun exploring the links between geographic and historical variation in pathogen prevalence and cultural differences in xenophobia (see Schaller and Park 2011). Other lines of research have begun investigating contextual (e.g., life history and developmental) variation in susceptibility to disease and suppression of the immune system as it covaries with behavioral indicators of ethnocentrism and racism (Navarrete et al. 2007, 2010). Such research promises to shed light on emotional processes that might exacerbate and ameliorate several forms of social prejudice, including xenophobia and ethnic hatred.

Final Comments

The first attempts at an evolutionary psychology of the emotions—at the end of the nineteenth century—began as a series of adaptation-agnostic accounts of the proximate machinery of emotional expression. By contrast, the first modern evolutionary accounts of emotion have been much more recent phenomena, appearing near the close of the twentieth century (e.g., Frank 1988; Hirshliefer 1987; Nesse 1990; Trivers 1971). In this regard, sophisticated adaptationist accounts of human emotion are not much older than the discipline of evolutionary psychology itself. The current review of the history of evolutionary approaches to emotion scholarship suggests a promising future for the evolutionary psychology of human emotion as the ratio of interesting data to interesting theoretical propositions appears to be steadily increasing.

Acknowledgments Portions of this chapter have been adapted from the following sources:
Ketelaar, T. (2004). Ancestral emotions, current decisions: Using evolutionary game theory to explore the role of emotions in decision-making. In C. Crawford & C. Salmon (Eds.), *Evolutionary psychology, public policy and personal decisions* (pp. 145–168). Mahwah, NJ: Lawrence Erlbaum Associates.
Ketelaar, T. (2006). The role of moral sentiments in economic decision making. In D. de Cremer, M. Zeelenberg, & K. Murnighan (Eds.), *Social psychology and economics* (pp. 97–116). Mahwah, NJ.: Lawrence Erlbaum Associates.
Ketelaar, T. (in press). Evolutionary theories. In B. Gawronski & G. Bodenhausen (Eds.), *Theory and explanation in social psychology*. New York, NY: Guilford Press

References

Aquinas, T. (1273/2013). *Summa theologica*. New York: Cosimo Classics.
Axelrod, R. (1984). *The evolution of cooperation*. New York: Basic Books.
Barkow, J., Cosmides, L., & Tooby, J. (1992). *The adapted mind*. Oxford: Oxford University Press.
Bell, C. (1806) *Essays on the anatomy of expression in painting*. London: Longman, Hurst, Rees, and Orme, Paternoster-Row.
Bell, C. (1824/1844) *The anatomy and philosophy of expression as connected with the fine arts* (3rd ed.). London: Murray.
Binmore, K. (1998). *Game theory and the social contract; Volume 2. Just playing*. Cambridge: MIT Press.
Buss, D. M. (1995). Evolutionary psychology: A new paradigm for psychological science. *Psychological Inquiry, 6*, 1–30.
Buss, D. M., Haselton, M. G., Shackelford, T. K., Bleske, A. L., & Wakefield, J. C. (1998). Adaptations, exaptations, and spandrels. *American Psychologist, 53*, 533–548.
Cates, D. F. (2009). *Aquinas on emotion: A religious-ethical inquiry*. Washington, DC: Georgetown University Press.
Clore, G. L., Schwarz, N., & Conway, M. (1994). Affective causes and consequences of social information processing. In R. S. Wyer & T. Srull (Eds.), *The handbook of social cognition* (2nd ed., pp. 323–417). Hillsdale: Erlbaum.
Cosmides, L. (1985). *Deduction or Darwinian algorithms? An explanation of the "elusive" content effect on the Wason Selection task*. Doctoral dissertation, Department of Psychology, Harvard University. University Microfilms, #86-02206.
Cosmides, L., & Tooby, J. (2000). Evolutionary psychology and the emotions. In M. Lewis & J. M. Haviland-Jones (Eds.), *Handbook of emotions* (2nd ed., pp. 91–115). New York: Guilford.
Cottrell, C. A., & Neuberg, S. L. (2005). Different emotional reactions to different groups: A sociofunctional threat-based approach to 'prejudice'. *Journal of Personality and Social Psychology, 88*, 770–789.
Damasio, A. R. (1994). *Descartes error: Emotion, reason, and the human brain*. New York: Grosset/Putnam.
Damasio, A. R. (1999). *The feeling of what happens: Body and emotion in the making of consciousness*. New York: Harcourt.
Damasio, A. R. (2003). *Looking for Spinoza: Joy, sorrow, and the feeling brain*. New York: Harcourt.
Darwin, C. (1859). *On the origins of the species*. London: Murray.
Darwin, C. (1868). *The variation of animals and plants under domestication*. London: John Murray.
Darwin, C. (1872/1998). *The expression of emotions in man and animals*. Oxford: Oxford University Press.
Darwin, C. (1879). *The descent of man and selection in relation to sex*. London: Murray.
Dawkins, R. (1976/1989). *The selfish gene*. Oxford: Oxford University Press.
Dennett, D. C. (1991). *Consciousness explained*. Boston: Little, Brown, and Company.
Dixon, T. (2003). *From passions to emotions: The creation of a secular psychological category*. Cambridge: Cambridge University Press.
Ekman, P. C. (1973). *Darwin and facial expression: A century of research in review*. Cambridge: Malor Books.
Ellsworth, P. C. (1994). William James and emotion: Is a century of fame worth a century of misunderstanding? *Psychological Review, 101*, 222–229.
Fehr, E., & Gäetcher, S. (2002). Altruistic punishment in humans. *Nature, 10*, 137–140.

Fincher, C. L., & Thornhill, R. (2012). Parasite-stress promotes in-group assortative sociality: The cases of strong family ties and heightened religiosity. *Behavioral and Brain Sciences, 35,* 61–79.

Frank, R. H. (1988). *Passions with reason: The strategic role of the emotions*. New York: W. W. Norton.

Frank, R. H. (2001). Cooperation through emotional commitment. In R. M. Nesse (Ed.), *Evolution and the capacity for commitment* (pp. 57–76). New York: Russell Sage Foundation.

Fridlund, A. (1994). *Human facial expression: An evolutionary view*. New York: Academic.

Gigerenzer, G., & Hug, K. (1987). Domain specific reasoning: Social contracts, cheating, and perspective change. *Cognition, 43,* 127–171.

Gould, S. J. (2003). *The hedgehog, the fox, and the Magister's Pox*. New York: Harmony Books.

Griffith, P. E. (1997). *What emotions really are*. Chicago: The University of Chicago Press.

Guth, W., Schmittberger, R., & Schwarz, B. (1982). An experimental analysis of ultimatum bargaining. *Journal of Economic Behavior and Organization, 3,* 367–388.

Hagen, E. H. (2002). Depression as bargaining: The case postpartum. *Evolution and Human Behavior, 23,* 323–336.

Hagen, E. H. (2003). The bargaining model of depression. In P. Hammerstein (Ed.), *Genetic and cultural evolution of cooperation* (pp. 95–123). Cambridge: MIT Press.

Haidt, J. (2001). The emotional dog and its rational tail: A social intuitionist approach to moral judgment. *Psychological Review, 108,* 814–834.

Haidt, J. (2003). The moral emotions. In R. J. Davidson, K. R. Scherer, & H. H. Goldsmith (Eds.), *Handbook of affective sciences* (pp. 852–870). Oxford: Oxford University Press.

Hirschleifer, J. (1987). On the emotions as guaranteers of threats and promises. In J. Dupre (Ed.), *The latest on the best: Essays in evolution and optimality* (pp. 307–326). Cambridge: MIT Press.

Hirschleifer, J. (2001). Game-theoretic interpretations of commitment. In R. M. Nesse (Ed.), *Evolution and the capacity for commitment* (pp. 77–93). New York: Russell Sage Foundation.

Hume, D. (1740/1978). *A treatise of human nature*. Oxford: Clarendon Press.

Hume, D. (1777/1996). *Enquiries concerning human understanding and concerning the principles of morals*. Oxford: Oxford University Press.

Isen, A. M., & Simmonds, S. F. (1978). The effect of feeling good on a helping task that is incompatible with good mood. *Social Psychology, 41,* 346–349.

Isen, A. M., Clark, M. S., & Schwartz, M. F. (1976). Duration of the effect of good mood on helping: "Footprints on the sand of time". *Journal of Personality and Social Psychology, 34,* 385–393.

Izard, C. E., & Ackerman, B. P. (2000). Motivational, organizational, and regulatory functions of discrete emotions. In M. Lewis & J. Haviland-Jones (Eds.), *Handbook of emotion* (pp. 253–264). New York: Guilford Press.

James, W. (1884). What is an emotion? *Mind, 9,* 188–205.

James, W. (1887). What is an instinct? *Scribner's Magazine, 1,* 355–366.

James, W. (1890). *Principles of psychology*. New York: Henry Holt.

James, W. (1892/1948). *Psychology: A briefer course*. Cleveland: Fine Editions Press.

Kalat, J. W., & Shiota, M. N. (2007). *Emotion*. Belmont: Thomson Wadsworth.

Keltner, D., Ekman, P., Gonzaga, G. C., & Beer, J. (2000). Facial expression of emotion. In M. Lewis & J. Haviland-Jones (Eds.), *Handbook of emotion* (pp. 236–249). New York: Guilford Press.

Ketelaar, T. (2004). Ancestral emotions, current decisions: Using evolutionary game theory to explore the role of emotions in decision-making. In C. Crawford & C. Salmon (Eds.), *Evolutionary psychology, public policy and personal decisions* (pp. 145–168). Mahwah: Lawrence Erlbaum Associates.

Ketelaar, T. (2006). The role of moral sentiments in economic decision making. In D. de Cremer, M. Zeelenberg, & K. Murnighan (Eds.), *Social psychology and economics* (pp. 97–116). Mahwah: Lawrence Erlbaum Associates.

Ketelaar, T., & Au, W. T. (2003). The effects of guilty feelings on the behavior of uncooperative individuals in repeated social bargaining games: An Affect-as-information interpretation of the role of emotion in social interaction. *Cognition & Emotion, 17,* 429–453.

Ketelaar, T., & Clore, G. L. (1997). Emotions and reason: The proximate effects and ultimate functions of emotions. In G. Matthews (Ed.), *Personality, emotion, and cognitive science* (pp. 355–396). Amsterdam: Elsevier.

Ketelaar, T., & Koenig, B. (2007). Justice, fairness, and strategic emotional commitments. In D. de Cremer (Ed.), *Justice and emotions: Current developments* (pp. 133–154). Mahwah: Lawrence Erlbaum Associates.

Kirkpatrick, L. A., & Navarrete, C. D. (2006). Reports of my death anxiety have been greatly exaggerated: A critique of terror management theory from an evolutionary perspective. *Psychological Inquiry, 17,* 288–298.

Lazarus, R. S. (1993). *Emotion and adaptation*. New York: Oxford University Press.

Lerner, J., & Keltner, D. (2001). Fear, anger, and risk. *Journal of Personality and Social Psychology, 81,* 146–159.

Mealey, L. (1995). The sociobiology of sociopathy: An integrated evolutionary model. *Behavioral and Brain Sciences, 18,* 523–599.

McDougall, W. (1908/1921). *An introduction to social psychology*. London: Methuen & Co., Ltd.

McGuire, M. T., Troisi, A., & Raleigh. M. (1997). Depression in evolutionary context. In S. B. Cohen (Ed.), *The maladapted mind: Classic readings in evolutionary psychopathology* (pp. 255–282) Psychology Press.

Marks, I. M. (1987). *Fears, phobias and rituals*. New York: Oxford University Press.

Navarrete, C. D., Fessler, D. M. T., & Eng, S. J. (2007). Elevated ethnocentrism in the first trimester of pregnancy. *Evolution and Human Behavior, 28,* 60–65.

Navarrete, C. D., McDonald, M. M., Mott, M. L., Cesario, J., & Sapolsky, R. (2010). Fertility and race perception predict voter preference for Barack Obama. *Evolution and Human Behavior, 31,* 394–399.

Nesse, R. M. (1990). Evolutionary explanations of emotions. *Human Nature, 1,* 261–289.

Nesse, R. M. (1991). What good is feeling bad? The evolutionary utility of psychic pain. *The Sciences, November./December,* 30–37.

Nesse, R. M. (1997). An evolutionary perspective on panic disorder and agoraphobia. In S. B. Cohen (Ed.), *The maladapted mind: Classic readings in evolutionary psychopathology* (pp. 73–84). Hove: Psychology Press.

Nesse, R. M. (2001). Natural selection and the capacity for subjective commitment. In R. M. Nesse (Ed.), *Evolution and the capacity for commitment* (pp. 1–44), New York: Russell Sage Foundation.

Nesse, R. M. (2009). Explaining depression: Neuroscience is not enough, evolution is essential. In C. M. Pariente, R. M. Nesse, & L. Wolpert (Eds.), *Understanding depression: A translational approach* (pp. 17–36). Oxford: Oxford University Press.

Nesse, R. M., & Ellsworth P. C. (2009). Evolution, emotions, and emotional disorders. *American Psychologist, 64,* 129–139.

Nesse, R. M. & Williams, G. C. (1994). *Why we get sick: The new science of Darwinian medicine.* New York: Random House.

Newton, I. (1704/1979). *Opticks.* London: G. Bell and Sons, Ltd.

Oatley, K. (2004). *A brief history of emotion.* Oxford: Blackwell Publishing.

O'Daly, G. (1987). *Augustine's philosophy of mind.* Berkeley: University of California Press.

Ortony, A., Clore, G. L., & Collins, A. (1988). *The cognitive structure of emotion.* Cambridge: Cambridge University Press.

Pagden, A. (2013). *The enlightenment and why it still matters.* New York: Random House.

Park, J. H., Schaller, M., & Crandall, C. S. (2007). Pathogen-avoidance mechanisms and the stigmatization of obese people. *Evolution and Human Behavior, 28,* 410–414.

Perry. (1935). *The thought and character of William James: As revealed in unpublished correspondence and notes, together with published writings* (Vol. 2). Boston: Little Brown and Company.

Petri, H. L., & Govern, J. M. (2004). *Motivation: Theory, research, and application* (5th ed.). Belmont: Thomson Wadsworth.

Prinz, J. (2004). *Gut reactions: A perceptual theory of emotion.* Oxford: Oxford University Press.

Reeve, J. M. (2005). *Understanding motivation and emotion* (4th ed.). Hoboken: Wiley.

Schaller, M., & Neuberg, S. L. (2012). Danger, disease, and the nature of prejudice(s). *Advances in Experimental Social Psychology, 46,* 1–54.

Schaller, M., & Park, J. H. (2011). The behavioral immune system (and why it matters). *Current Directions in Psychological Science, 20,* 99–103.

Schelling, T. C. (1960). *The strategy of conflict.* Cambridge: Harvard University Press.

Schelling, T. C. (2001). Commitment: Deliberate versus involuntary. In R. M. Nesse (Ed.), *Evolution and the capacity for commitment* (pp. 48–56). New York: Russell Sage Foundation.

Schwarz, N., & Clore, G. L. (1983). Mood, misattribution, and judgments of well-being: Informative and directive functions of affective states. *Journal of Personality and Social Psychology, 45,* 513–523.

Schwarz, N., & Clore, G. L. (2003). Mood as information: 20 years later. *Psychological Inquiry, 14,* 296–303.

Scherer, K. R. (1994). Emotion serves to decouple stimulus and response. In P. Ekman & R. J. Davidson (Eds.), *The nature of emotion: Fundamental questions* (pp. 127–130). Oxford: Oxford University Press.

Scherer K. R. (2000). Psychological models of emotion. In J. C. Borod (Ed.), *The Neuropsychology of Emotion* (pp. 137–162) Oxford: Oxford University Press.

Seligman, M. E. P. (1971). Phobias and preparedness. *Behavior Therapy, 2,* 307–320.

Smith, A. (1759/2000). *The theory of moral sentiments.* New York: Prometheus.

Smith, C. A., & Ellsworth, P. C. (1985). Patterns of cognitive appraisal in emotion. *Journal of Personality and Social Psychology, 48,* 813–838.

Sorabji, R. (2010). *Emotion and peace of mind: From stoic agitation to Christian temptation.* Oxford: Oxford University Press.

Thornhill, R. (1990). The study of adaptation. In Bekoff & D. Jamieson (Eds.), *Interpretation and explanation in the study of behavior* (Vol. II, pp. 31–62) Boulder: Westview Press.

Thornhill, R. (1997). The concept of an evolved adaptation. In G. Bock & G. Cardew (Eds.), *Characterizing human psychological adaptations* (pp. 4–13). London: CIBA Foundation.

Tooby, J., & Cosmides, L. (1990). The past explains the present: Emotional adaptations and the structure of ancestral environments. *Ethology and Sociobiology, 11,* 375–424.

Tooby, J., & Cosmides, L. (2008). The evolutionary psychology of the emotions and their relationship to internal regulatory variables. In M. Lewis, J. M. Haviland-Jones, & L. F. Barrett (Eds.), *Handbook of emotions* (3rd ed., pp. 114–137). New York: Guilford.

Trivers, R. (1971). The evolution of reciprocal altruism. *Quarterly Review of Biology, 46,* 35–57.

Trivers, R. (1981). Sociobiology and politics. In E. White (Ed.), *Sociobiology and politics* (pp. 1–43). Lexington: Lexington Books.

Wang, X. T., & Yan-Jie, S. (2011). *Thus spake evolutionary psychologists: Evolutionary psychology for Chinese students*. Peking: Peking University Press.

Williams, G. C. (1966). *Adaptation and natural selection*. Princeton: Princeton University Press.

Wilson, D. S., & Wilson, E. O. (2008). Evolution "For the Good of the Group". *American Scientist, 96,* 380–389.

Wilson, E. O. (1975). *Sociobiology*. Boston: Belknap Press of the Harvard University Press.

Religiosity

6

Lee A. Kirkpatrick

Religion, as far as we know, is universal across human cultures and time. People's religious beliefs profoundly affect their perceptions of the world, morals and values, goals and aspirations, social interactions, group affiliations, and daily behavior. Nevertheless, religion has received scant attention in mainstream psychology. Browse any textbook in introductory psychology—or any textbook or journal in any subdiscipline of psychology—and you will find few (if any) references to religion. In fact, you might not even find the word "religion" in the index.

The reasons for this unfortunate state of affairs are probably legion, but for present purposes I suggest two. First, given its multifaceted nature, the topic of religion does not neatly fit within any of the traditional subdisciplines of psychological science. The study of religion requires an approach that integrates perspectives from social psychology, developmental psychology, cognitive psychology, and so on, rather than a piecemeal approach. Relatedly, the topic transcends traditional boundaries between psychology, sociology, and anthropology, but until recently no higher-order paradigm has been available within which to integrate perspectives at these equally valid but distinct levels of analysis. I suspect that many psychologists think of religion as a "cultural" phenomenon—something that people learn via socialization from their parents and local culture—and that religion therefore falls outside their intellectual jurisdiction.

Despite (or because of) its exclusion from mainstream psychology, a substantial field of study referred to as the "psychology of religion" has emerged over the last several decades with its own textbooks, conferences, and journals. Unfortunately, progress in this field has been hamstrung by the same problems noted above. Much work has been done examining religiosity or religious affiliation, as both a dependent and an independent variable, in relation to a variety of other psychological variables, but little attention has been paid to such "big questions" as why people are (nearly) universally religious, and why religious beliefs, though variable across cultures and time, take certain typical forms rather than others. The most common kind of answer to these questions in this literature (to the extent they are addressed) is that religious beliefs are embraced because they address certain postulated "fundamental" needs or motives. For example, researchers have proposed that religious beliefs satisfy needs for self-esteem, control, meaning, anxiety reduction (in general, or with respect to fear of death, in particular), and so on. Hypotheses about such motives or needs tend to be post hoc and lack a strong theoretical foundation, and many appear dubious when examined carefully from a Darwinian perspective. For example, an evolutionary perspective suggests that self-esteem is not a goal or motive, but rather an internal gauge of one's current status with respect to adaptively

L. A. Kirkpatrick (✉)
Department of Psychology, College of William and Mary, P.O. Box 8795, Williamsburg, VA, 23187-8795, USA
e-mail: lakirk@wm.edu

V. Zeigler-Hill et al. (eds.), *Evolutionary Perspectives on Social Psychology,* Evolutionary Psychology,
DOI 10.1007/978-3-319-12697-5_6, © Springer International Publishing Switzerland 2015

important social relationships: People are motivated to strive for dominance, attractiveness as a mate, inclusion in social groups, and so forth—success in which is reflected in feelings of high self-esteem—but not to strive for self-esteem, per se (Kirkpatrick and Ellis 2001; Leary and Downs 1995).

An evolutionary psychological approach represents a potential solution to these problems. An evolutionary perspective transcends arbitrary subdisciplinary boundaries and serves to integrate issues and approaches across such boundaries; similarly, it provides a theoretical basis for drawing connections between the psychological level of analysis and the cultural level of analysis pursued by (evolutionary-minded) anthropologists and sociologists. Moreover, any discussion of "fundamental" human needs or motives is inherently (if implicitly) an evolutionary one, begging the question as to why humans should be designed in this way rather than some other way.

Fortunately, a new paradigm has emerged over the last 20 years—the *cognitive science of religion* (CSR; Barrett 2007)—that has proved enormously successful at motivating and organizing social scientific research on religion in a manner compatible with—and often (though not always) grounded explicitly in—an evolutionary perspective. This success, relative to previous approaches, owes largely to two sets of organizing principles and assumptions. First, the cognitive science perspective is predicated on the assumption that there exists a species-universal psychological architecture or "human nature," comprising numerous functionally domain-specific mechanisms or systems; these mechanisms and systems are conceptualized as analogous to computer programs within the context of a computational model of the mind. The central problem for the psychology of religion, in this view, is to determine how and why religious belief and behavior emerge from this species-specific psychology.

Second, the CSR approach bridges the historical gap between psychology and anthropology by recognizing that a complete understanding of religious belief must comprise processes at both the individual (psychological) and cultural levels of analysis. A popular approach for integrating these perspectives is Sperber's (1996) *epidemiological* model of culture, which emphasizes the role of individual psychology in the process of cultural transmission of ideas, values, and practices. The transmission of an idea from one person to another is not analogous to copying a file from one computer to another. Rather, countless psychological processes are involved in determining whether and how a person communicates an idea to another, how the receiver interprets the communication to create his or her own mental representation, and how this representation is evaluated. This integrative perspective has enabled CSR to become an interdisciplinary field in which religion can be understood simultaneously at the psychological and cultural levels of analysis.

Religion as a Psychological Adaptation

The first obvious question arising from an evolutionary psychological approach to religion is that of whether religious belief or behavior reflects an adaptation designed for this purpose (i.e., whether we possess a religious "instinct") or whether these emerge instead as by-products of adaptations designed for other (nonreligion-specific) purposes. Although the notion that humans possess some kind of religious instinct has a long history in (traditional) psychology (e.g., Hood et al. 2009), adaptationist explanations for religion have largely fallen into disfavor among contemporary evolutionary psychologists and CSR researchers for a variety of reasons. For example, the idea that humans possess one or more religion-specific adaptations has been proposed as a (post hoc) explanation for the facts that religion (1) appears to be a human universal, (2) is associated (in part) with activity in particular brain areas, and/or (3) is moderately heritable (e.g., Harris and McNamara 2008). None of these observations requires an adaptationist explanation, however. For instance, people (or cultures) can independently converge on "good ideas," such as wearing more clothing in cold weather or building canoes to traverse bodies of water, in the absence of a cognitive adaptation designed specifically to motivate such behavior, and genetic variability in religiosity is, if anything, contrary to what one would expect if religion is a species-universal adaptation (see Kirkpatrick 2006, 2008, for a detailed discussion).

One of the most common claims is that religious beliefs provide psychological benefits, such as relief from anxiety and fear—particularly fear of death—which in turn lead to physical health benefits and thus, presumably, greater reproductive success. Proponents of this view often point to evidence that religiosity is correlated, in contemporary societies, with measures of mental and physical health (including longevity), and that religious people tend to have more children (e.g., Sanderson 2008). However, Symons (1989, 1992) long ago marshalled numerous arguments to show that apparent "adaptiveness" in contemporary populations is irrelevant to the question of adaptation, per se. For example, mental and physical health are undoubtedly correlated in the modern West with gym memberships and access to medical care, neither of which is reasonably attributed to cognitive adaptations designed to produce them.

Another commonly postulated adaptive function of religion is that of promoting within-group cooperation. Explaining cooperation among unrelated humans is a difficult problem for evolutionary-minded researchers in light of inclusive fitness theory, and researchers have generated many hypotheses about the ways in which religion may provide a solution. Wilson (2002) draws upon group selection—contrary to the objections of most contemporary evolutionists—as an explanation for the evolution of religion as an adaptation designed for this purpose. Other researchers, unpersuaded by Wilson to adopt a group selectionist model, have attempted to find other ways around the problem. According to one theory, beliefs in omniscient, moralizing gods reflect an adaptation whose function is to discourage people from engaging in behaviors that would lead to moral condemnation if discovered by others, the potential costs of which were increased by the evolution of language (Bering 2006; Bering and Shackelford 2004; Johnson and Bering 2006). If one believes that he or she is constantly being watched by an omniscient, moralizing god who punishes infractions, then one should be less likely to engage in selfish, antisocial behaviors—and thus less likely to suffer the costs of reputational damage within the community.

A second adaptationist argument draws upon *costly signaling theory*. According to this view, religious beliefs and practices represent costly, and thus "honest," signals of commitment to one's social group which rests on the assumption that one would not be willing to incur the considerable costs of religious belief and participation in the absence of such a commitment (e.g., Alcorta and Sosis 2005, 2006; Irons 2001; Sosis 2006). By demonstrating one's willingness to incur these costs, the individual gains access to the benefits of social inclusion. At the same time, one also benefits from the ability to exclude potential *free riders* from the group, thereby ensuring that one's investments in the group are not undermined by "cheaters."

Kurzban and Christner (2011) have pointed to serious problems with both of these latter theories from an evolutionary perspective. Specifically, they note that the Sosis–Alcorta model is not strictly analogous to the costly signaling model of evolutionary biology because a beautiful, symmetrical peacock's tail functions as an "honest" signal of genetic quality, not merely because the peacock has incurred considerable expense to produce it, but because peacocks of lower genetic quality are *incapable* of producing it. The Bering–Johnson model, while emphasizing the adaptive benefits of avoiding reputational damage, overlooks the adaptive benefits of engaging opportunistically in "bad behavior" when one is not being watched. Kurzban and Christner offer a variation on the Sosis–Alcorta model designed to circumvent these problems: Their suggestion is that because the religious beliefs of one community typically seem "crazy" to members of other religious communities, public commitment to one group's beliefs render one unacceptable for membership in other groups, in the same way that other signs of disease, mental instability, or "abnormality" might. Religious beliefs are akin to a tattoo signaling membership in a particular gang; it serves as an "honest" signal of commitment to that gang that precludes the possibility of being accepted by a competing gang. This is an intriguing idea that warrants more attention than it has received in the literature.

Although the Sosis–Alcorta and Bering–Johnson hypotheses are problematic as theories of psychological adaptations that have evolved via natural selection, their major weaknesses may be solved by being reconceptualized in terms of a *cultural evolutionary* model—an idea to which I return later in this chapter.

Religion as an Evolutionary By-product

Both adaptationist theories and traditional psychology-of-religion theories seem to be based on the (largely implicit) assumption that in the absence of certain postulated cognitive mechanisms or motives, people would "by default" be nonreligious. In mainstream psychology, for example, people are often portrayed as "naive scientists" who use their empirical observations about the world to evaluate the relative merit of alternative truth claims. In contrast, much contemporary CSR research is predicated on the assumption that religious thinking emerges spontaneously and effortlessly from our (evolved) psychology.

The underlying assumption of most such approaches is that our species' evolved psychology includes a number of functionally domain-specific systems for reasoning about the natural and social world (e.g., Pinker 1997; Wellman and Inagaki 1997). According to our evolved *folk* (or *naive*) *physics,* for example, inanimate objects tend to fall down if unsupported, and otherwise move only when acted upon by other forces. According to our evolved *folk biology,* (many) living things are capable of self-locomotion, behave in functional ways (e.g., avoiding predators or seeking prey), and exist in the world as "natural kinds" (e.g., lions, as a group, are different from giraffes). Our *folk psychology,* designed for processing information about other humans, leads us to interpret behavior in terms of beliefs, desires, and goals. Theories about religion as an evolutionary by-product generally involve various kinds of errors in the application of these systems to stimuli outside their respective natural domains.

For example, Guthrie (1993) reviewed many examples of ways in which people commonly misapply these psychological models beyond their natural domains. *Psychological animism* results from the application of folk-biology thinking to inanimate objects, as when we get angry and curse at our computer for crashing or our car for failing to start. *Psychological anthropomorphism* results from the application of folk psychology to nonhuman agents, such as when we imbue our pets with human-like thoughts and emotions. Such errors are readily generated when, for example, inanimate objects appear to violate expectations of folk physics, such as apparent self-propulsion (Premack 1990). It is therefore no surprise that gods are widely associated across cultures with such phenomena as the moon, sun, and stars. Moreover, these cognitive systems appear to be calibrated to err on the side of caution, like a fire alarm, in light of the asymmetrical costs of false-negative and false-positive errors (cf. Haselton and Buss 2000). As Guthrie (1993) put it, it is generally a safer bet to mistake a stick for a snake than vice versa.

A second (but not incompatible) approach suggests that religious beliefs involve various other kinds of violations of "intuitive" inferences vis-á-vis these evolved psychological systems. According to Pinker (1997), for example, supernatural beliefs typically involve the perception of objects or deities as essentially human-like in most ways (i.e., in ways consistent with our folk psychology) but that violate our intuitions in other ways, such as being invisible or able to fly (Pinker 1997). Boyer (1994, 2001), along with numerous other researchers (e.g., Atran 2002; Atran and Norenzayan 2004; Barrett 2004), argued that human minds find such ideas particularly intriguing, memorable, and worthy of transmitting to others. The ideas that are most memorable and transmittable are those that comprise an optimal balance of intuitive and counterintuitive components.

A third (and, again, compatible) approach has been to focus on specific psychological mechanisms and processes associated with folk biology and psychology. For example, a central component of our evolved folk biology appears to be *psychological essentialism*. As summarized by Gelman et al. (1994), people seem to believe implicitly that…

> categories are discovered rather than arbitrary or invented; they carve up nature at its joints. The underlying nature, or category *essence*, is thought to be the causal mechanism that results in those properties that we can see. For example, the essence of tigers causes them to grow as they do—to have stripes, large size, capacity to roar, and so forth. (p. 344)

Based on this kind of reasoning, even second graders understand that bleaching the stripes of a tiger and adding a mane would not turn it into a lion because its essential "tigerness" has not been altered (Keil 1989). Such essentialist thinking might be responsible for animistic beliefs about spirits residing in trees and animals, totems, and the perception of certain objects as "sacred" (Kirkpatrick 1999, 2005).

Similarly, a central component of our evolved folk psychology is what has come to be known as *theory of mind*. Once a supernatural agent is recognized as human-like, a host of inferential processes whir into action to discern the agent's beliefs, motives, emotions, and goals. Bering (2011) has recently explored a variety of ways in which theory-of-mind processes give rise to religious beliefs. For example, we perceive events in the world as being purposeful, reflecting the gods' desires and goals, and our ability to think about another person's mind as distinct from their body leads readily to the notion that mental capacities may survive (bodily) death, giving rise to beliefs about an afterlife.

My own contribution to this literature (Kirkpatrick 1999, 2005) has been to suggest that the specific kinds of beliefs and desires people project onto supernatural agents are further shaped by a variety of functionally domain-specific, *social*-psychological cognitive adaptations. Many of the most-challenging adaptive problems faced by humans over their evolutionary history involve negotiating and manipulating relationships with other people. As a consequence, we possess evolved systems corresponding to many functionally distinct kinds of interpersonal relationships. For example, the *attachment system* (Bowlby 1969) appears to be of particular importance in modern Christianity for supporting perceptions of (and individual differences in) God as a parent-like figure who loves and cares for his children (see Granqvist and Kirkpatrick 2013, for a review of this burgeoning attachment-to-God literature).

Numerous other social cognitive systems are at least as important as attachment for understanding the kinds of religious beliefs that likely have characterized most humans across time and place (see Kirkpatrick 1999, 2005, for detailed discussions). In polytheistic belief systems, relationships with gods frequently take the form of *social-exchange* relationships in which gods offer specific benefits to people in exchange for people performing particular rituals, offering sacrifices, or observing certain codes of behavior (Burkert 1996). Such social-exchange reasoning may also undergird and guide beliefs about rewards forthcoming in an afterlife if one behaves in certain ways in the here and now. Our evolved *coalitional psychology*—which is designed to maintain and monitor alliances and coalitions both within and between groups—plays an important role in promoting cooperation within religious communities or cultures as well as conflict between them. Psychological mechanisms dedicated to identifying *kinship* relations and treating kin preferentially may underlie the ubiquitous phenomenon of ancestor worship, and promote intragroup cooperation by encouraging the perception of in-group members as fictive kin (Batson 1983; Crippen and Machalak 1989). Other cognitive systems dedicated to *intrasexual competition*—for dominance, prestige, and mates—may underlie some of the seamier aspects of religion, such as the ways in which religious authority is translated into political power, control over mates, and so forth (Buss 2002), as well as perceptions of God or gods as awesome, dominant figures to be worshipped and offered subservience.

The Mickey Mouse Problem

The preceding discussion illustrates ways in which beliefs about anthropomorphized supernatural agents emerge spontaneously from, and are deemed plausible by, our species-specific psychology. However, these same kinds of processes also explain how we think about—and are entertained by—stories about Santa Claus, superheroes, and other fictional characters. The comic book hero Superman, for example, is human-like in nearly every way—a point further underscored by his alter ego, Clark Kent—except that he has immense physical strength, the ability to leap over tall buildings in a single bound, and X-ray vision. This raises a problem for by-product theories of religion, however, known as the *Mickey Mouse problem*: Few people believe that Superman or Mickey Mouse actually exists—much less that one could have some kind of social relationship with them or that they could exert important influences on one's life. For that matter, even the most ardent believers within any particular religion reject the countless other gods that characterize religions other than their own. It is one thing to explain why people find the existence of supernatural agents plausible and interesting, but another to explain why they believe in the ontological existence of some but not (most) others.

One obvious response to the Mickey Mouse problem is that the gods we believe in are those that are endorsed by our parents and other trusted members of our local culture: We acquire our particular beliefs via acculturation or social learning. Although natural selection has equipped us with many abilities to negotiate the physical and social world, it has also equipped us with an extraordinary ability to learn from others. Our evolved food preferences tend to steer us from foods that taste bitter or sour (and thus are likely to contain toxins or illness-inducing bacteria), and toward sweet and fatty foods (that provide essential nutrients), but these individual-level adaptations provide only a rough guide to the offerings and dangers of any particular local ecology. For details, we rely heavily on culturally accumulated knowledge. Analogously, we find some ideas about the world (including supernatural agents) more or less intuitively plausible than others, but rely on our local culture to determine which to believe and which to reject. The effects of *conformity bias* plays a central role in all theories of cultural evolution and gene–culture coevolution (e.g., Boyd and Richerson 1985; Richerson and Boyd 2005). In one sense, the answer to the Mickey Mouse problem is that you probably have never met anybody who believes that Mickey Mouse really exists. You probably believed in Santa Claus for the first few years of your life—for as long as the adults around you played along, anyway—but then you probably stopped believing in Santa Claus when those adults abandoned the charade.

The Santa Claus example is useful for making another important point: Contrary to my simplistic depiction immediately above, I'll bet that you did not just suddenly abandon a strongly held belief about Santa the moment a parent told you otherwise. What probably happened instead is that at some point in your early cognitive development, you began to spontaneously develop your own doubts about the story. How does he manage to service the entire world in one night or be in multiple shopping malls at the same time? Flying reindeer? Elves? You probably began peppering your parents with questions about these "counterintuitive" elements of the story that seemed problematic, and for a while they probably succeeded in assuaging some of those doubts. Eventually, though, you wore them down, and they finally admitted that the whole story was a (well-meaning) hoax.

So what is the difference between beliefs about Santa Claus and those about God or gods? Why is it that counterintuitive elements in the Santa story inevitably sow the seeds of their own demise, but not in the "story" about God or gods? I suggest that the answer is the same as it is to this question: Why is it that after you have cursed in anger at your computer for freezing, or your car for not starting, you quickly (I hope) realize that the offending object is not really a sentient agent who can be persuaded by physical threat to treat you better in the future? The reason is that you have, readily available at your disposal, a more intuitively plausible mental model of the computer or car as an inanimate object that is occasionally subject to electronic or mechanical failure. (It is also worth noting that despite this realization, you might still find yourself angry at the computer or car: In a modular mind, it is entirely possible for multiple, mutually inconsistent beliefs to coexist. See Kurzban 2010, for a thorough discussion). In the case of Santa Claus, a more intuitively plausible explanation for the facts is that your parents drank the milk and left the presents, and that shopping malls hire people to dress up and pretend to be Santa.

Religious beliefs, in contrast, are notoriously immune to empirical disconfirmation, and alternative explanations for the same phenomena often are either not readily available or not any more intuitively plausible. For most of human history, there simply did not exist a better explanation for the sun's and moon's apparent self-propulsion and immunity to gravity than that they are, or are inhabited or driven by, supernatural agents. Although scientific explanations for many such phenomena are available in the modern world, such explanations are often more counterintuitive than religious explanations. Consequently, intuitively appealing religious explanations are not easily trumped by alternative, naturalistic explanations in the same way as is the immediate but short-lived perception of your computer or car as a sentient being that is deliberately frustrating your goals.

Cui Bono?

Although there is little doubt that people tend to adopt the specific religious beliefs of their family and/or local culture, this explanation begs the question as to why particular sets of beliefs become widespread within and across cultures while others do not. Dennett (2006) suggests that, from an evolutionary perspective (broadly defined), the question should be framed in terms of "cui bono?"—that is, who or what benefits? In this section, I briefly sketch some of the many kinds of answers that have been offered to this question.

Memes

Dawkins (1976) introduced the term "meme" to represent an analog to the "gene" as a unit of selection and suggested that the evolution of memes—ideas behaviors, beliefs, etc.—might be explained by processes analogous to natural selection. From this perspective, one can think about the differential success of alternative memes in terms of properties of the memes themselves that favor or disfavor their transmission (i.e., their "reproductive success"), relative to alternative memes, in a given cultural milieu. Some memes are popular because they have features that make them attractive to human minds, such as catchy jingles or trendy musical acts, irrespective of the costs or benefits to the individuals or social groups adopting them. Dawkins (1993) has argued that religion memes have certain properties that enhance the likelihood of their own transmission not only irrespective of any benefits that such memes might have but despite being harmful to the individuals and social groups that adopt them: They are, in his words, "viruses of the mind."

Although it is not typically presented in these terms, much of the research in contemporary CSR discussed earlier—for example, the notion that religious ideas reflect an optimal balance of intuitive and counterintuitive beliefs—exemplifies this memetic perspective in a crucial sense: Religious ideas succeed merely because they are good at getting themselves reproduced, irrespective of any benefits (and perhaps despite costs) conferred on the individuals who contribute to their reproduction. To answer the "cui bono?" question, perhaps we need to look no further than the memes themselves: Perhaps religion memes have other characteristics that cause them to be more "believable" than Mickey Mouse. Dawkins (1993) suggests, for example, that religion memes often contain ancillary instructions, such as "I am true" or "do not doubt me" that contribute to their success.

On the other hand, there are several reasons to think that this is only part of the answer. For one, whereas cartoon characters and hair styles come and go in popularity, religious ideas evince a considerably greater level of staying power that requires explanation. Second, even seemingly arbitrary cartoon-character memes and hairstyles may owe at least part of their success to functions for which they were initially created or that they subsequently come to acquire. The catchy commercial jingle that gets stuck in your head was created by clever marketers to do exactly that (and increase the likelihood that you will purchase a product). Viral cat videos are beneficial to the individuals who find them amusing, if only by helping them to enjoy themselves. These videos are memorable and readily transmitted in part because of the psychological benefits they offer. Hair, clothing, and musical styles may start out as completely arbitrary, but often come to take on important social functions related to status and coalitional boundaries. In sum, it seems likely that religion memes owe their success not only to their intrinsic memorability or transmitability but also to other functions or benefits that they come to provide for individuals or groups.

Individuals

I argued earlier in this chapter against the idea that humans possess religion-specific cognitive adaptations—that the answer to the "cui bono" question is "genes"—by virtue of postulated benefits to individuals. However, this is not to say that religion does not provide such benefits. There is no doubt that beliefs about an afterlife are comforting to those approaching death or coping with the death of loved ones, for example, or that beliefs about a creator god satisfy the curiosity of people wondering about the mysteries of the universe. The traditional psychology-of-religion literature is replete with examples of psychological benefits purported to be associated with religion, many of which are probably true. People who have experienced such psychological benefits are likely to not only retain them but also pass them along to their children and other relatives and loved ones. A worthy goal for future research would be to reevaluate and reconceptualize this previous work from an evolutionary psychological perspective.

At the same time, however, religious ideas can be employed in the service of other functions that benefit selfish individuals in more nefarious ways: They can serve as powerful tools for manipulating the behavior of others. Many religious ideas, such as moral and sexual proscriptions, would be highly beneficial to an individual (and/or his or her reproductive success) if *everyone else* accepted them: It benefits you, for example, to persuade everyone around you that God wants them to behave altruistically toward their neighbors. Kings and other rulers throughout history have promulgated the belief that their power and status is sanctioned by the gods—or even that they are deities themselves. Buss (2002) calls attention to the fact that religious leaders sometimes promulgate beliefs that provide them with mating opportunities or regulate other people's sexual behavior in other ways that benefit themselves. In their haste to document the purported benefits of religion, psychology-of-religion researchers have given scant attention to this seamier side of religion.

Another intriguing hypothesis has been offered by Weeden et al. (2008). Contrary to the usual assumption that people's participation in religion leads them to hold particular beliefs about sexuality (e.g., to support committed, monogamous marriage, and other "family values"), Weeden et al. argue that the causal direction might be reversed such that religious institutions have evolved (in a cultural evolutionary sense) to provide a "family-friendly" home that attracts individuals pursuing long-term, monogamous mating strategies. In two empirical studies, they show that moral views about sexual behavior are more strongly linked to religious attendance than are other moral issues and that individual differences in mating strategies are more powerful than standard personality variables in predicting religious attendance. Although this theory might be limited with respect to explanatory breadth—beliefs about sex and morality represent a part of "religion"—it offers a unique way of thinking about how cultural evolution, in general, and the cultural evolution of religion, in particular, can be shaped by individual differences in adaptive strategies.

Groups

The idea that religious serves the function of enhancing cooperation and cohesion of cultural groups has a long history in anthropology and sociology (e.g., Durkheim 1995; Turner 1995) and continues to be a central focus of much contemporary research in CSR and related fields. Many of these modern approaches draw heavily upon evolutionary ideas, although they do so in a dizzying variety of ways. Given that a review of these literatures is well beyond the scope of the present chapter, I offer only a few brief comments.

First, I suggest that some of the adaptationist hypotheses reviewed earlier in this chapter are better conceptualized as the result of cultural evolutionary processes that benefit groups, rather than as (genetically) evolved adaptations that benefit individuals. Wilson's (2002) demonstrations of religion enhancing cooperation, enabling cultures to accomplish remarkable feats that would be impossible otherwise, would be decidedly less controversial if conceptualized this way. Although evolutionary biologists have raised serious doubts about Wilson's model with respect to natural selection (e.g., West et al. 2011), the idea that cultural practices can evolve via group selection by virtue of intergroup competition is less controversial (though it also has its share of detractors; e.g., Pinker 2012). Similarly, the Alcorta–Sosis model seems uncontroversial when viewed as a cultural evolutionary model rather than a biological evolutionary one: That is, costly rituals are a "good idea" that many cultures have invented (or discovered) that are effective in promoting group solidarity and cooperation, in much the same way as modern state societies have invented such things as police forces, security cameras, and taxation systems to "encourage" cooperation.

Similarly, the shortcomings of the Bering–Johnson hypothesis about moralizing gods as an adaptation are readily resolved by reconceptualizing the model as a cultural evolutionary rather than biological-evolutionary one. Indeed, Norenzayan (2013) has recently done exactly this. Like Bering and Johnson, Norenzayan proposes that beliefs about omniscient, moralizing gods function to encourage prosocial behavior and discourage selfish ("cheating") behavior. However, Norenzayan argues that beliefs about "big gods" have, over time, outcompeted alternative kinds of beliefs in a process of cultural or memetic evolution, because cultures that have adopted such belief systems have historically outcompeted cultures that did not. Moreover, he offers an important empirical observation that favors his cultural evolutionary hypothesis over Bering and Johnson's cognitive adaptation hypothesis: "Big gods" are a recent invention. In a sweeping review, he shows that for most of human history, gods were perceived as either indifferent to human behavior, incapable of punishing wrongdoing, or both.

Conclusions

The emergence of CSR as an interdisciplinary approach to religion has already produced far more creative and promising ideas about religion than did a previous century of psychologists and anthropologists working in isolation. Religion cannot be understood at either level of analysis alone. As I have argued throughout this chapter, the explanation for the breadth and diversity of religious phenomena cannot be found exclusively in terms of cognitive adaptations designed by natural selection to produce them. Rather, other levels of analysis—including cultural evolutionary models of various sorts—are needed. On the other hand, such cultural models must be based on a solid psychological foundation which, in turn, must be grounded in evolutionary theory. Much progress has been made in the short history of CSR: Psychologists are gradually incorporating more cultural-level thinking into their work, while anthropologists are gradually incorporating more psychological-level thinking into theirs. Moreover, researchers from other disciplines have joined the cause and brought unique perspectives from their own disciplines. There is still a long way to go, but the future is bright.

References

Alcorta, C. S., & Sosis, R. (2005). Ritual, emotion, and sacred symbols: The evolution of religion as an adaptive complex. *Human Nature, 16,* 323–359.

Alcorta, C. S., & Sosis, R. (2006). Why ritual works: A rejection of the by-product hypothesis. *Behavioral and Brain Sciences, 29,* 613–614.

Atran, S. (2002). *In gods we trust.* Oxford: Oxford University Press.

Atran, S., & Norenzayan, A. (2004). Religion's evolutionary landscape: Counterintuition, commitment, compassion, communion. *Behavioral and Brain Sciences, 27,* 713–770.

Barrett, J. L. (2004). *Why would anyone believe in God?* Walnut Creek: AltaMira Press.

Barrett, J. L. (2007). Cognitive science of religion: What is it and why is it? *Religion Compass, 1,* 768–786.

Batson, C. D. (1983). Sociobiology and the role of religion in promoting prosocial behavior: An alternative view. *Journal of Personality and Social Psychology, 45,* 1380–1385.

Bering, J. M. (2006). The folk psychology of souls. *Behavioral and Brain Sciences, 29,* 453–462.

Bering, J. M. (2011). *The belief instinct: The psychology of souls, destiny, and the meaning of life.* New York: Norton.

Bering, J. M., & Shackelford, T. (2004). The causal role of consciousness: A conceptual addendum to human evolutionary psychology. *Review of General Psychology, 8,* 227–248.

Bowlby, J. (1969). *Attachment and loss. Vol. 1. Attachment.* New York: Basic.

Boyd, R., & Richerson, P. J. (1985). *Culture and the evolutionary process.* Chicago: University of Chicago Press.

Boyer, P. (1994). *The naturalness of religious ideas: A cognitive theory of religion.* Berkeley: University of California Press.

Boyer, P. (2001). *Religion explained: The evolutionary origins of religious thought.* New York: Basic Books.

Burkert, W. (1996). *Creation of the sacred: Tracks of biology in early religions.* Cambridge: Harvard University Press.

Buss, D. M. (2002). Sex, marriage, and religion: What adaptive problems do religious phenomena solve? *Psychological Inquiry, 13,* 201–203.

Crippen, T., & Machalek, R. (1989). The evolutionary foundations of the religious life. *International Review of Sociology, 3,* 61–84.

Dawkins, R. (1976). *The selfish gene.* New York: Oxford University Press.

Dawkins, R. (1993). Viruses of the mind. In B. Dahlbohm (Ed.), *Dennett and his critics: Demystifying mind* (pp. 13–27). Oxford: Blackwell.

Dennett D. C. (2006). *Breaking the spell: Religion as a natural phenomenon.* New York: Viking.

Durkheim, E. (1995). *The elementary forms of religious life.* New York: Free Press. (Original work published 1912).

Gelman, S. A., Coley, J. D., & Gottfried, G. M. (1994). Essentialist beliefs in children: The acquisition of concepts and theories. In L. Hirschfeld & S. Gelman (Eds.), *Mapping the mind: Domain specificity in cognition and culture* (pp. 341–365). Cambridge: Cambridge University Press.

Granqvist, P., & Kirkpatrick, L. A. (2013). Religion, spirituality, and attachment. In K. I. Pargament, et al. (Eds.), *APA handbook for the psychology of religion and spirituality* (Vol. 1, pp. 129–155). Washington, DC: American Psychological Association.

Guthrie, S. (1993). *Faces in the clouds: A new theory of religion.* New York: Oxford University Press.

Harris, E., & McNamara, P. (2008). Is religiousness a biocultural adaptation? In J. Bulbulia, R. Sosis, E. Harris, R. Genet, C. Genet, & K. Wyman (Eds.), *The evolution of religion: Studies, theories, and critiques* (pp. 79–85). Santa Margarita: Collins Foundation Press.

Haselton, M. G., & Buss, D. M. (2000). Error management theory: A new perspective on biases in cross-sex mind reading. *Journal of Personality and Social Psychology, 78,* 81–91.

Hood, R. W, Jr., Hill, P. C., & Spilka, B. (2009). *The psychology of religion: An empirical approach* (4th ed.). New York: Guilford.

Irons, W. (2001). Religion as a hard-to-fake sign of commitment. In R. Nesse (Ed.), *Evolution and the capacity for commitment* (pp. 292–309). New York: Russell Sage Foundation.

Johnson, D. D. P., & Bering, J. M. (2006). Hand of God, mind of man: Punishment and cognition in the evolution of cooperation. In J. Schloss & A. Platinga (Eds.), *The nature of belief: Scientific and philosophical perspectives on the evolution of religion* (pp. 26–43). New York: Oxford University Press.

Keil, F. C. (1989). *Concepts, kinds, and cognitive development.* Cambridge: MIT Press.

Kirkpatrick, L. A. (1999). Toward an evolutionary psychology of religion. *Journal of Personality, 67,* 921–952.

Kirkpatrick, L. A. (2005). *Attachment, evolution, and the psychology of religion.* New York: The Guilford Press.

Kirkpatrick, L. A. (2006). Religion is not an adaptation. In P. McNamara (Ed.), *Where God and Science meet: How brain and evolutionary studies alter our understanding of religion* (Vol. 1, pp. 159–179). Westport: Praeger Perspectives.

Kirkpatrick, L. A. (2008). Religion is not an adaptation: Some fundamental issues and arguments. In R. Sosis, et al. (Eds.), *The evolution of religion: Studies, theories, and critiques* (pp. 47–52). Santa Margarita: Collins Foundation Press.

Kirkpatrick, L. A., & Ellis, B. J. (2001). An evolutionary-psychological approach to self-esteem: Multiple domains and multiple functions. In G. Fletcher & M. Clark (Eds.), *The Blackwell handbook of social psychology: Vol. 2: Interpersonal processes* (pp. 411–436). Oxford: Blackwell.

Kurzban, R. (2010). *Why everyone (else) is a hypocrite: Evolution and the modular mind*. Princeton: Princeton University Press.

Kurzban, R., & Christner, J. (2011). Are supernatural beliefs commitment devices for intergroup conflict? In J. P. Forgas, A. W. Kruglanski, & K. D. Williams (Eds.), *The psychology of social conflict and aggression* (pp. 285–300). New York: Psychology Press.

Leary, M. R., & Downs, D. L. (1995). Interpersonal functions of the self-esteem motive: The self-esteem system as a sociometer. In M. H. Kernis (Ed.), *Efficacy, agency, and self-esteem* (pp. 123–144). New York: Plenum.

Norenzayan, A. (2013). *Big gods: How religion transformed cooperation and conflict*. Princeton: Princeton University.

Pinker, S. (1997). *How the mind works*. New York: Norton.

Pinker, S. (2012) The false allure of group selection. *Edge*, June 18. http://edge.org/conversation/the-false-allure-of-group-selection. Accessed 14 Aug 2014.

Premack, D. (1990). Do infants have a theory of self-propelled objects? *Cognition, 36,* 1–16.

Richerson, P. J., & Boyd, R. (2005). *Not by genes alone: How culture transformed human evolution*. Chicago: University of Chicago Press.

Sanderson, S. K. (2008). Adaptation, evolution, and religion. *Religion, 38,* 141–156.

Sosis, R. (2006). Religious behaviors, badges, and bans: Signaling theory and the evolution of religion. In P. McNamara (Ed.), *Where God and science meet: How brain and evolutionary studies alter our understanding of religion* (pp. 61–86). Westport: Praeger Perspectives.

Sperber D. (1996). *Explaining culture: A naturalistic approach*. Oxford: Blackwell.

Symons, D. (1989). A critique of Darwinian anthropology. *Ethology and Sociobiology, 10,* 131–144.

Symons, D. (1992). On the use and misuse of Darwinism in the study of behavior. In J. H. Barkow, L. Cosmides, & J. Tooby (Eds.), *The adapted mind* (pp. 137–159). New York: Oxford University Press.

Turner V. (1995). *The ritual process*. Chicago: Aldine. (Original work published 1969).

Weeden, J., Cohen, A. B., & Kenrick, D. T. (2008). Religious attendance as reproductive support. *Evolution and Human Behavior, 29,* 327–334.

Wellman, H. M., & Inagaki, K. (1997). *The emergence of core domains of thought: Children's reasoning about physical, psychological, and biological phenomena*. San Francisco: Jossey-Bass.

West, S. A., El Mouden, C., & Gardner, A. (2011). Sixteen common misconceptions about the evolution of cooperation in humans. *Evolution and Human Behavior, 32,* 231–262

Wilson, D. S. (2002). *Darwin's cathedral: Evolution, religion and the nature of society*. Chicago: University of Chicago Press.

The Evolution of Social Cognition

7

Jennifer Vonk, Molly McGuire and Zoe Johnson-Ulrich

A recent focus in comparative research has been the identification of social cognitive skills in nonhumans. Researchers have sought evidence for traits traditionally deemed unique to humans, such as the capacity for theory of mind (i.e., the ability to represent and reason about mental states in other organisms; Premack and Woodruff 1978). Some capacity for theory of mind might facilitate other social cognitive skills and behaviors, such as cooperation, prosocial behavior, and reputation formation. Research on each of these topics has been accumulating at a frenetic pace, including tests of various previously understudied species. However, there remain significant gaps in the literature. Namely, researchers have focused on the social intelligence hypothesis (Humphrey 1976; Jolly 1966) as the best predictor of advanced social cognitive skills to the neglect of studies with other species that do not live in large, social groups. Such studies are necessary to determine whether group-living is a necessary, or merely sufficient, condition of social cognitive skills. We briefly review various hypotheses regarding the emergence of social cognitive capacities, followed by a synopsis of the most recent and controversial comparative research in several key areas. We conclude that the field has been hindered by an anthropocentric focus on human-like capacities and that other interesting species-specific cognitive mechanisms may remain just out of sight when viewed only through our human-centric lens.

Machiavellian Hypothesis

The Machiavellian intelligence hypothesis (Whiten and Byrne 1988) has been presented as an explanation for the advanced social skills of group-living species, in particular, humans. It purports that humans evolved a keen intellect to outcompete conspecifics through their superior social skills (Whiten and Byrne 1997). For group-living to persist, it must be beneficial to individuals. Natural selection will not directly select behaviors that are best for the group, which can lead to an environment that favors individuals capable of social manipulation at the expense of group-mates. A key element of the Machiavellian hypothesis is the use of deception, which protects manipulative individuals from the possible threat of ejection from the group for promoting their own interests. It would also be beneficial for manipulations to result in compensatory gains for group members through cooperation (Bryne and Whiten 1997), which would result in benefits to all those involved, minimizing any costs associated with being deceived. The Machiavellian hypothesis predicts the greater use of deception and

J. Vonk (✉)
Department of Psychology, Oakland University, 211 Pryale Hall, Rochester, MI 48309, USA
e-mail: vonk@oakland.edu

M. McGuire · Z. Johnson-Ulrich
Department of Psychology, Oakland University, 130 Pryale Hall, Rochester, MI 48309, USA
e-mail: mcmcguir@oakland.edu

Z. Johnson-Ulrich
e-mail: zjohnson@oakland.edu

V. Zeigler-Hill et al. (eds.), *Evolutionary Perspectives on Social Psychology*, Evolutionary Psychology, DOI 10.1007/978-3-319-12697-5_7, © Springer International Publishing Switzerland 2015

social manipulation in species that have evolved for group-living, regardless of whether deception is used to alter mental states as well as behavior.

Social Intelligence Hypothesis

The social intelligence hypothesis proposes that the ability to reason about group-mates and predict their behavior affords greater benefits in social settings (Humphrey 1976; Jolly 1966). Social intelligence can be defined as intelligence applied to the social world and to other living organisms (Whiten and Van Schaik 2007). It is key to organizing and maintaining complex social environments through the representation of reciprocal, altruistic, and kin relationships. As with the Machiavellian hypothesis, the social intelligence hypothesis assumes that greater complexity in groups predicts greater cognitive complexity as well, at least in the social domain. Whereas Machiavellianism refers to outcompeting group members through social manipulation, social intelligence more broadly refers to the ability to track and utilize knowledge about various group members to facilitate cohesive group-living in navigating both affiliative and agonistic relationships.

Although early field and lab studies focused on social cognition in nonhuman primates, social intelligence can also be found in many nonprimate group-living species, such as cetaceans, corvids, chiroptera, and canines. Bottlenose dolphins live in fission–fusion societies, much like chimpanzees, which require the ability to recognize many individuals and their relationships with others (Connor 2007). Male bottlenose dolphins form alliances with other males, often to defend females from other alliances. Therefore, male bottlenose dolphins that are able to form and maintain these complex social relationships have increased fitness via increased mating opportunities compared with males who fail to form such relationships. This same strategy has also been found in bats (Carter and Wilkinson 2013a), particularly in polygynous species. Dominant male bats will tolerate the presence of subordinate males as they help them ward off foreign males. With the help of subordinates, who are often relatives, the dominant male can defend larger groups of females. Although the cognitive abilities of bats have seldom been tested, dolphins have, for example, been shown to excel at tests of social learning (Jaakola 2012).

The study of social skills in such a diverse range of social species is a welcome contribution to the literature. However, one can neither confirm nor dispute the social intelligence hypothesis unless, in addition to showing evidence for sophisticated social cognition in social animals, we also show a lack of such abilities in less social animals. Even in nonhuman primates, less research has been conducted on *relatively* less social species, such as pair-bonded species like gibbons, titi monkeys, owl monkeys, and some callitrichids (marmosets and tamarins). Orangutans are the most studied of the relatively solitary primates, and their social cognitive skills thus far do not appear appreciably different from those of the other great apes based on research from the Tomasello–Call research group at the Wolfgang Kohler Institute at Maxx Planck in Leipzig (Herrmann et al. 2007).

Outcompeting More Physically Dominant Species

The preceding hypotheses focus on the emergence of social cognitive skills as an adaptation for outcompeting group-mates. An alternative hypothesis is that advanced social cognitive skills, particularly mind reading, may have emerged in order to allow humans to predict the behaviors of both nonhuman competitors and prey (see also Vonk and Aradhye in press). *Homo sapiens* outcompeted all of the hominid species that have been discovered in the fossil record. This seems counterintuitive given that most other hominid species that lived alongside early *H. sapiens* were larger and more robust, suggesting that they would have been physically dominant (Haviland et al. 2005).

One explanation could be that *H. sapiens* had the evolutionary advantage of intelligence. As early humans evolved larger brains capable of more complex reasoning, they started making and using tools. From the fossilized remains of the brain cavity, certain features of the brains of early *Homo* species such as *Homo habilis* suggest that they may have had rudimentary language skills. This hypothesis is supported by evidence of the tools they made, most of which appear to have been made by right-handed individuals. Handedness is associated with lateralization of the brain, which is associated with language skills (Haviland et al. 2005). Their combined intelligence, language skills, and tool use would have enabled them to compete with the larger and more physically dominant hominid species during that time period. It is also possible that these advances in cognitive abilities allowed *H. sapiens* to occupy a different ecological niche and to exploit different resources such that they may not have been in direct competition with other *Homo* species with whom they coexisted.

Reinterpretation Hypothesis

The preceding hypotheses allow for the possibility that other group-living species may have evolved similar cognitive abilities, dependent on the complexity of their social groups. Alternatively, the reinterpretation hypothesis posits a stricter cognitive divide between humans and even their closest living relatives (Povinelli and Giambrone 1999). This hypothesis suggests that the foundation for advanced mind-reading skills was present in the most recent common ancestor of humans and other primates and is present in our closest relatives today. This basic foundation for theory of mind is the ability to interpret the behaviors of others and make predictions about future behaviors based on these observable behaviors. For instance, a chimpanzee may have learned that the direction of another's eye gaze predicts the presence of something interesting. The chimpanzee can thus form an abstraction of a likely subsequent behavior or event based on behaviors that he directly observes. The foundation for predicting future behaviors based on observed behaviors may be shared widely in the animal kingdom, but, alongside this ability, the capacity to infer internal mental states as causes for behaviors may have emerged only in the human lineage (Povinelli and Giambrone 1999; Povinelli et al. 2000).

A human might infer that the chimpanzee's gaze is directed at something that he sees and is interested in. Thus, the human interprets the gaze to reflect an internal state of seeing, on which internal states of knowing may also be based. This reinterpretation hypothesis allows that chimpanzees and other primates have sophisticated social reasoning skills that they share with humans: the ability to reason about others' behaviors. The ability to reason about and reinterpret the behaviors as arising from mental states—such as emotions, desires, beliefs, goals, and knowledge—evolved later in humans and is merely an additional aid to behavioral interpretation. It is presumed that this additional capacity allows humans to make more flexible predictions in a variety of contexts because mental states may form the basis for a range of behaviors widely applied. Reasoning about behaviors alone may allow one to form inferences only in closely related contexts. There is no existing hypothesis by which a system for mind reading bypasses the presumed earlier system for interpreting and making predictions from observable behaviors (see also Povinelli and Vonk 2003, 2004). The mind-reading system depends upon the behavior-reading system in that mental states, being unobservable, can only be inferred from observable behavioral states. Thus, an organism must first reason about and understand the implications of observable states and only then can make an additional inference about the underlying cause of the behavioral state—namely, a mental state.

The Unobservability Hypothesis

A related idea is the hypothesis that humans alone can reason about unobservable entities, such as causal forces, which include mental states such as feelings, beliefs, desires, and intentions (Vonk and Povinelli 2006). Evidence that nonhumans reason about underlying motives for behavior, including knowledge states, would argue against the unobservability hypothesis, but, to date, experimental "evidence" has been subject to multiple interpretations (Penn and Povinelli 2007; Povinelli and Vonk 2003, 2004).

Enculturation Hypothesis

Initially, researchers found that human-like rearing may engender chimpanzees with human-like abilities, such as mind reading. These researchers focused on the unique rearing histories of captive individuals under the notion that human rearing might allow for the expression of cognitive capacities not witnessed in wild counterparts, or in captive individuals raised under less cognitively enriched circumstances. The enculturation hypothesis assumes that other apes might share the basic neural architecture for cognitive capacities, such as theory of mind, but require a particular environment rich in dyadic interactions in order for these capacities to be fully realized. This hypothesis initially received strong support from studies indicating that apes reared by humans displayed stronger evidence for social learning, theory of mind, and other cognitive skills (Call and Tomasello 2008). However, when revisited years later, the growing "evidence" for equivalent capacities in nonenculturated apes called the emphasis on rearing environment into question. Langer (2000) proposed that enculturation may instill quantitative, but not qualitative, changes in great ape cognitive development. Similarly, Bering (2004) proposed that the early-seen advantage for enculturated apes on cognitive tests may have to do more with exposure to, and subsequent proficiency with, human cultural artifacts than to the nature of early social interactions.

Vygotskian Cultural Intelligence

A related hypothesis shares the emphasis on early interactions between parents and their offspring in facilitating the emergence of sophisticated social reasoning skills. The Vygotskian cultural intelligence model suggests that, whereas the development of cognitive abilities among primates in general was probably driven by social competition (Humphrey 1976), the development of humans' unique cognitive abilities was driven by social cooperation (Moll and Tomasello 2007). Humans are equally capable of reasoning about both competitive and cooperative social interactions. In addition, during development, humans acquire cooperative social reasoning skills from a very early age (for a review, see Moll and Tomasello 2007). This hypothesis builds upon the influential Vygotskian framework that stressed the importance of sociocultural interactions in shaping human cognitive development. In particular, Vygotsky stressed learning traditions and culture from others with more expertise within a given culture. This hypothesis suggests that chimpanzees and other nonhuman primates will do best on studies that require them to reason about social cues in competitive, rather than cooperative, paradigms because this is the situation that is most typical in their native social groups (see also Hare 2001; Hare and Tomasello 2004). For humans, however, cooperative interactions, necessary for trade and commerce, for example, are critical. The Vygotskian cultural intelligence hypothesis focuses on the tendency of human caregivers to engage in joint attention, gaze sharing, and other dyadic interactions that emphasize communicative intent and foster the development of abilities, such as theory of mind (Moll and Tomasello 2007).

This hypothesis is supported by findings that chimpanzees more easily utilize social cues such as gaze following in competitive paradigms rather than in more traditional cooperative paradigms (Hare and Tomasello 2004). For example, they excel in studies testing their ability to choose which piece of food to approach first, when only one piece can be seen by a dominant conspecific who will have access to the same enclosure (Hare et al. 2000, 2001). In tests requiring them to ask a human for food (Povinelli and Eddy 1996), they have been less skilled (Hare and Tomasello 2004). In addition, they are less likely than human children to actively engage others in cooperative ventures, although there is some evidence that they are willing to help both human experimenters and other chimpanzees (Warneken and Melis

2012). Recently, researchers found that chimpanzees provided help to both humans and conspecifics, but, compared to children, helped less in collaborative compared to noncollaborative tasks (Greenberg et al. 2010). This finding supports the supposition that chimpanzees, unlike young humans, are more prepared to cooperate when focused on their own unique goals, rather than when focused on dyadic interactions. Important differences in the cooperative skills of chimpanzees and children suggest that either biological or environmental differences engender discontinuity in social cognitive skills (Warneken and Melis 2012). The Vygotskian cultural intelligence hypothesis focuses more heavily on environmental factors.

Domestication Hypothesis

In contrast, the domestication hypothesis focuses on the shaping of particular behaviors and cognitive traits over the course of a long process by which characteristics that aid in human/domestic animal interactions are selectively bred (Hare et al. 2002; Hare and Tomasello 2004). Notably, the process of domestication selects for strong social skills with regard to interactions with humans rather than interactions with conspecifics (Agnetta et al. 2000; Hare et al. 2010). In addition, strong social skills found in animals that humans interact with regularly are due to innate abilities selected for during domestication, rather than ontogenetic effects, such as "enculturation" or having extensive experience with humans. This hypothesis suggests that the nonhuman animals with the most sophisticated social reasoning skills will be the ones with the longest evolutionary history with humans that involves working in situations where following human cues and directions would be advantageous. It predicts that even young domestic dogs will be better at reading human social cues than wolves and other wild canids, and chimpanzees (Agnetta et al. 2000; Bräuer et al. 2006; Hare et al. 2002, 2010).

Support for the domestication hypothesis has largely come from the object choice task. The subject must use a human pointing cue to locate a piece of food hidden in one of (usually) two locations. Dogs are excellent at these tasks and can use even subtle cues, such as head turning, nodding, or even gaze, and they seem to understand something of the intentional, communicative nature of pointing (Kaminski and Nitzschner 2013). Adult wolves perform similarly to dogs; however, they require intensive socialization and are slower to develop the ability as pups (Gácsi et al. 2009; Udell et al. 2008, 2012; Virányi et al. 2008). Coyotes (Udell et al. 2012), dingoes (Smith and Litchfield 2010), and Pampas foxes (Barrera et al. 2011) have shown some ability to follow points, although the dingoes (the only canid in which other cues were tested) struggled with gaze cues. Overall, domestic dogs are better than their closest relatives—and our closest relatives, chimpanzees—at following human social cues (Bräuer et al. 2006; Kirchhofer et al. 2012).

Other domesticated animals show some ability to follow human gestures, including cats, horses, and goats (Kaminski et al. 2005; Maros et al. 2008; Miklósi et al. 2005). Cats follow points comparably to dogs, but have not been tested on other cues. Horses and goats appear to rely on stimulus enhancement when following points. Some nondomesticated animals can follow human pointing cues as well, including dolphins (Pack and Herman 2007) and fur seals (Scheumann and Call 2004). Although many animals are capable of using human cues to some extent, dogs stand out as being superior at reading human communicative gestures. Dogs and humans share a long, rich evolutionary history, even compared to other domesticated animals. That they are excellent at reading human social gestures speaks to this history and supports the hypothesis that domestication is responsible for strong social skills. However, given the debate about comparisons between domestic dogs and enculturated wolves, as well as between stray dogs and house pets (Hare et al. 2010; Udell et al. 2008; Wynne et al. 2008), the contribution of the longer evolutionary history of canid social organization should not be ignored. It seems probable that only those species that have already evolved the capacity for particular social skills will have those skills enhanced through the process of domestication such that they can be applied to human interactions.

Experimental Evidence

Emotion State Understanding

Living in large social groups demands the ability to predict behavior from outward signs of internal emotional states. This ability helps regulate social interactions between individuals and is pronounced in primates. Parr (2001) found that chimpanzees were able to categorize emotional videos by selecting the appropriate corresponding photograph of expression in a conspecific. For example, chimpanzees watched videos of chimpanzees being darted by veterinarians and selected the fear grimace rather than the play-face expression. However, matching videos of chimpanzees reacting either negatively or positively to a corresponding photograph of a chimpanzee's positive or negative facial expression may be nothing more than an artifact of having formed associations between negative (or positive) experiences and negative (or positive) emotions on the faces of conspecifics. Thus, they may not have needed to reason about the underlying mental state giving rise to the expression. As with studies of theory of mind, it is difficult to tease apart when animals are learning associations based on observed physical features and when they are reasoning about underlying internal states, such as emotions, in a way that reflects an abstract conceptual representation of the causes and consequences of different emotional states (see also Vonk and Povinelli 2006).

Gácsi et al. (2004) found that dogs were able to recognize the role of their owner's facial orientation in social contexts, outperforming chimpanzees tested in previous studies. When humans reacted emotionally (happy, neutral, or disgusted) to objects in containers hidden from dogs' view, dogs were able to appropriately distinguish between the containers, choosing the one that the human had reacted to positively (Buttelmann and Tomasello 2013). Again, these studies suggest that dogs are able to make accurate predictions based on the outward expression of emotions, but do not require that the dogs infer the causal role of different emotional states in producing those cues. The difficulty in discriminating between these different possible mechanisms underlying performance in these tasks recurs throughout the literature on the broader ability to read mental states (Sect. 2.2 below).

Theory of Mind

The term "theory of mind" was introduced by Premack and Woodruff (1978) as the ability to ascribe mental states (i.e., beliefs, thoughts, goals, emotions, and other internal mental processes) to others and to predict their behavior based on knowledge of these internal states. It allows intentional communication, including attempts to repair failed communication, teaching others, intentional persuasion, deception, pretense, shared goals, and attention (Baron-Cohen 1999). In typically developing children, theory of mind develops between the ages of 3–4 years as assessed by false-belief tasks (Wimmer and Perner 1983), which assess a child's ability to understand that someone might have a belief that does not correspond to reality. In addition, it is beliefs (regardless of their truth) that cause behavior, rather than objective reality. For example, a story character, Maxi, puts chocolate into a cupboard. In his absence, his mother displaces the chocolate from the cupboard into a drawer. Subjects have to indicate the place where Maxi will look for the chocolate when he returns (Wimmer and Perner 1983). Children with theory of mind will correctly predict that Maxi will look in the cupboard. Younger children with an undeveloped theory of mind will incorrectly predict that Maxi will look in the drawer, not understanding that Maxi could hold a belief that does not match reality and that is different from their own.

Whether nonhuman animals have a theory of mind is still under contention, largely due to the difficulty of creating tests for nonverbal subjects that are not confounded by behavior-reading explanations (Penn and Povinelli 2007). This is because reasoning about mental states is not independent of reasoning about behaviors, even in humans. When one infers an underlying, internal mental state, this inference is necessarily predicated on observable cues that correlate with the underlying state. It is this actuality that makes it difficult to tease these two explanatory mechanisms apart in studies with nonverbal organisms. To test their understanding of mental states, one must present the observable cues on which such inferences would be based (see Povinelli and Vonk 2004; Penn and Povinelli 2007). Consequently, tests of theory of mind need to distinguish between performance based on reasoning about behavior alone and performance that could arise only as a result of additionally reasoning about mental states, which has yet to be accomplished with existing methods.

Visual perspective-taking is a common focal point for testing "low-level" theory of mind. Indeed, many animals succeed at gaze-following tasks with varying degrees of sophistication (reviewed in Shepherd 2010), as well as visual perspective-taking tasks (Krachun and Call 2009), including both dogs and wolves (Call et al. 2009; Kaminski et al. 2013; Udell et al. 2011). Chimpanzees can follow the gaze of humans and conspecifics, even around barriers (Bräuer et al. 2005), to locate food (Call et al. 1998), recognize that barriers impede gaze (Povinelli and Eddy 1996), and prefer to approach food that is occluded from a dominant subject's or experimenter's gaze (Bräuer et al. 2007; Hare et al. 2000, 2001; but see Karin-D'Arcy and Povinelli 2002). It is clear that chimpanzees have highly sophisticated visual perspective-taking skills. However, there are currently no experimental designs that can discriminate whether chimpanzees attribute seeing to others (mind reading) on top of associating visual cues of attention with interesting outcomes (behavior reading; Povinelli and Vonk 2004). In all of these studies, the subjects had access to behaviors of either conspecifics or humans that could have led them to make accurate responses, making it impossible to discriminate whether they were reasoning about mental states or the behaviors. Indeed, Reaux et al. (1999) found that chimpanzees appear to attend to a hierarchy of observable cues (such as body direction, presence of a face, and presence of eyes) when choosing which experimenter to beg from. In control conditions, they prioritized observable cues, even when they were not predictive of an experimenter's attentional state (e.g., begging to someone facing forward with eyes closed rather than someone looking over their shoulder with eyes open).

Penn and Povinelli (2007) suggest two methods that can discriminate between behavior reading and mind reading with regard to visual perspective taking. One of these methods (experience-projection task) was implemented by Vonk and Povinelli (2011). Enculturated chimpanzees were given the opportunity to wear two visually identical (except for color) buckets, one that could be seen out of and another that could not. After the experience of wearing the buckets, the subjects were presented with experimenters, each wearing one of the buckets. Because the subjects had no experience observing the behaviors of other individuals wearing the buckets, the only way to correctly predict the behavior of the experimenters was for the subjects to project their own experience to infer the visual state of the experimenters. Two enculturated chimpanzees displayed no preference to beg from the experimenter who could see, in line with the previous evidence suggesting that chimpanzees attend to behavioral cues, rather than attributing mental states, when interacting with both conspecifics and human experimenters.

Although chimpanzees have made accurate inferences involving a conspecific's visual perspective when required to compete with that conspecific for food in some tasks (Bräuer et al. 2007; Hare et al. 2000, 2001), these competitive paradigms suffer from the same interpretive difficulties outlined above. In addition, there is no reason that chimpanzees should be able to reason about mental states in one context and be completely unable to use this ability in another context. Situations of high ecological validity are the ones where it is most likely that an organism will have evolved specific, fixed responses; it is new and unusual situations that call for the most flexible and least "hard-wired" explanations and reactions, such as mental state attribution. Ecologically valid tests may thus be the least valid for assessing whether subjects have theory of mind (Povinelli and Giambrone 1999; Vonk and Subiaul 2009).

In addition to the focus on visual perspective-taking, early studies with chimpanzees revealed a capacity for deception. As with other theory of mind tasks, there has been extensive debate in the literature about whether the ability to engage in deceptive behavior requires the ability to reason about underlying mental states in other agents (Whiten and Byrne 1988). A subordinate baboon might learn that when hiding out of sight he is less likely to receive retaliation from a dominant male for mating with a female (Whiten and Byrne 1988). His reasoning could be based entirely on his own viewpoint (behind an opaque barrier) rather than on making inferences about what the dominant male sees. Thus, he may be successful at manipulating the dominant's behavior without attempting to alter his thinking. Teasing apart these two types of explanations for animal behavior is arguably the biggest challenge in the field of comparative psychology. Woodruff and Premack (1979) found that chimpanzees learned to withhold information and misled human "competitors" in a food-searching paradigm. They suggested that chimpanzees' success on this task implies intentional communication (or miscommunication). However, behavior reading seems likely such that the chimpanzees learned that their own behaviors, pointing, looking, etc., toward the baited containers caused a behavior in the human competitor, taking the food. This task was clearly difficult for chimpanzees; it took tens to hundreds of trials for the chimpanzees to become successful at inhibiting nondeceitful information and then to develop misleading communicative cues. In contrast, human children deceive on similar tasks by the age of 5 years (Sodian 1991). Whiten and Byrne (1988) discussed the concept of tactical deception, in which normal behaviors are used in new contexts, such that others are likely to misinterpret the behaviors to the agent's advantage. They cite numerous examples of tactical deception by chimpanzees in both wild and captive environments, but, although they discuss the necessary mental state attribution that would be involved in certain scenarios of deceit, they acknowledge that the evidence is not clear either way. There continue to be examples of strong deceptive abilities of nonhuman animals, such as a chimpanzee hiding rocks for future throwing (Osvath and Karvonen 2012), chimpanzees and dogs hiding approaches to food (Bräuer et al. 2013; Hare et al. 2006), and dogs stealing food in darkened, but not illuminated, areas of rooms (Kaminski et al. 2013). All of these behaviors can be explained through the mechanism of behavioral abstractions. Thus, there is still no strong evidence that any nonhuman animals have a theory of mind—at least not the same level of theory of mind that allows humans to behave flexibly in a wide variety of novel situations (Penn and Povinelli 2007).

Reputation Formation

Somewhat less abstract than inferring the mental states of others is the ability to form and reason about reputations attributed to others (i.e., reputation formation). An individual's reputation can be derived from direct interactions with the individual or from the indirect experience of observing that individual interact with others (Nitzschner et al. 2012). Knowledge of another individual's reputation allows individuals to make decisions about engaging with a known cooperative individual or avoiding interaction with a known defector, without having to learn directly via potentially deleterious consequences of having made the wrong choice. Herrmann et al. (2013) found that some apes predicted the future behaviors of others based on their direct experience with them as well as the past interactions of another with a third party, preferring to approach an experimenter they had observed behaving generously to another individual over an experimenter that had behaved selfishly (see also Russell et al. 2008; Subiaul et al. 2008). This phenomenon can be found even in animals more evolutionarily distant from humans, such as fish and dogs. Reef fish, which maintain a mutualistic relationship with cleaner fish, have been found to seek out cleaner fish with which they had previously had a positive interaction. If the cleaner fish, which the reef fish visit to have parasites and dead tissue removed, had previously ignored or cheated the reef fish (by ingesting healthy tissue instead of the dead tissue), the reef fish was less likely to revisit that cleaning station (Bshary and Schäffer 2002). Dogs are also able to make reputation-like inferences of strangers after observing third party exchanges even when researchers altered certain components of the interaction, such as available visual social cues and the nature (using both living and inanimate agents) and behaviors (begging or neutral) of the recipient (Kundey et al. 2011). Although, in a more recent study (Freidin et al. 2013), dogs' behaviors seemed driven by observable cues rather than recognition of individuals.

In addition to chimpanzees' preferences for "generous" over "selfish" partners in simple choice tasks, chimpanzees have also been shown to recruit the most effective collaborators over other individuals in cooperative tasks (Melis et al. 2006, 2009). However, this preference might again be mediated by a simpler associative preference for individuals who are more strongly associated with a successful outcome, rather than involving an underlying reputation judgment. The finding that "reputation judgments" may be widely distributed in the animal kingdom may suggest that there are simpler mechanisms by which animals attend to the past behaviors of others, without inferring that they maintain representations for continuous characteristics in social partners. Indeed, Subiaul et al. (2008) found that chimpanzees did not easily generalize selfish and generous behaviors to novel contexts.

Cooperation

If animals are able to attribute reputations, this would enable them to more flexibly plan social behavior by taking into account likely future behaviors of conspecifics. As Melis et al. (2006) found, individuals could selectively recruit partners to cooperate with. Cooperation should emerge only in complex societies and should be absent in solitary species. Yet even in those species that live in complex social groups, cooperation is liable to be rare because it requires that individuals relinquish some of their potential fitness to achieve a joint goal, providing resources that also benefit others. For cooperation to persist, it must overcome the inherent competition that drives natural selection. Mechanisms that work to support cooperation include kin selection, where helping ones relatives increases an individual's inclusive fitness, reciprocation, whereby helping an individual increases the chance of receiving help in the future, and group selection, where a group of cooperators is more successful than a group of defectors (Nowak 2006). An acceptance of short-term inequalities could be explained by the fact that most cooperative relationships are long term and so most individuals can expect that their supportive behavior will be reciprocated later on. Chimpanzees, for instance, will punish another individual that steals food from them, yet fail to react when another group mate receives a disproportionate amount of the shared food (Cheney and Seyfarth 2012; although chimpanzees' tolerance of inequities likely depends on their social relationships, Brosnan et al. 2005). Lionesses will take on different roles in risk assessment, with some allowing others to take on greater risks, but there is no punishing of the freeloaders. Tolerance of such freeloading may reflect the fact that freeloaders participate in other cooperative activities, such as hunting, or that the risk-averse lionesses increase their sisters' inclusive fitness by avoiding dangerous situations (Heinsohn and Packer 1995). Alternatively, lions may not possess the cognitive capacity to keep track of and punish defectors.

There are many other examples of apparent cooperative behaviors in the wild, such as group hunting efforts of social carnivores like the spotted hyena. Chimpanzees also frequently hunt and share meat, using the shared meat as a social tool, strengthening social bonds and alliances between males (Mitani and Watts 2001). Additionally, researchers have recently started collecting experimental evidence of cooperation in the laboratory. Captive hyena pairs coordinate their behaviors to solve problems (Drea and Carter 2009). Hyenas with more cooperative experience were found to modify their behavior when paired with a less experienced individual to promote the pair's coordination. Learned cooperation has also been demonstrated in chimpanzees, elephants, and parrots. When given a cooperation task that requires two individuals to work together by simultaneously pulling ropes to obtain a reward, chimpanzees (Chalmeau and Gallo 1996; Hirata and Fuvva 2007) and elephants (Plotnik et al. 2011) acted together, and elephants would even delay attempting the rope task until their partner arrived. This inhibition of the pulling response until their partner was available shows an understanding that the task could not be completed without help. Chimpanzees showed mixed levels of understanding in that they did not always solicit help when required (Hirata and Fuvva 2007). African grey parrots were also able to coordinate their actions to solve tasks, but did not inhibit their response when their partner was delayed (Péron et al. 2011). These studies suggest that most individuals learn contingencies associated with success, but may not fully appreciate the collaborative nature of the tasks (Chalmeau and Gallo 1996). More recent work, however, indicates that chimpanzees may be cognizant of strategies used by their partners in collaborative tasks and can work to achieve mutually beneficial outcomes (Melis et al. 2009). Work in this exciting area continues to accumulate.

Prosociality

Cooperation might emerge because individuals recognize that their own payoffs will be greater if they work with others, or because individuals are concerned with the welfare of group-mates. Prosocial preferences encompass behaviors that are intended to benefit others at some cost to the self, and are distinct from kin selection (selectively helping family members to indirectly increase inclusive fitness) and mutualism (where two individuals benefit directly from a relationship). Researchers have frequently investigated the prosocial preferences of primates through the use of the prosocial choice test (Silk et al. 2005), where an actor is given the choice between an option that rewards both the actor and a potential recipient or an option that rewards only the actor. To control for bias towards the shared option (which would contain a larger amount of food), experimenters include a nonsocial condition in which the adjacent cage is empty, yet the actor still has the option to reward the empty cage (Silk et al. 2005). Using this paradigm, de Waal et al. (2008) found that brown capuchin monkeys systematically preferred the prosocial option if their partner was familiar, visible, and receiving equal rewards. This preference increased even more if the pair was related and decreased if the recipient was a stranger.

Interestingly, some monkey species, such as capuchins, demonstrate a clear pattern of prosocial behavior directed down the hierarchy, whereas rank does not appear to influence prosocial behavior in chimpanzees (Cronin 2012). In cotton-top tamarins, a species of cooperatively breeding monkeys, researchers found no preference to reward mates (even when doing so was at no cost to themselves) and tamarins were even less likely to reward their mate if the mate showed interest in the reward (Cronin et al. 2009). This finding has cast doubt on the likelihood that other primates share prosocial sentiments.

A more recent study has been championed as providing evidence for prosocial tendencies in chimpanzees using a token-based task (Horner et al. 2011). Chimpanzees were given the choice between a token that resulted in a "selfish" choice (rewarding only the actor) and another that represented the "prosocial" choice (rewarding both the actor and the recipient). All of the chimpanzees showed a bias for the prosocial token. Yet when the recipient directly solicited and pressured the actor, this actually reduced the tendency of the actor to behave prosocially, similar to previous studies that failed to find evidence for prosocial preferences (Silk et al. 2005; Vonk et al. 2008) and suggests that another mechanism explains the chimpanzees' preferences. Perhaps they learned to associate the "prosocial" token with the appearance of a greater amount of food. Even when testing mother–offspring pairs, chimpanzees showed no prosocial tendencies (Yamamoto and Tanaka 2010), further calling into question the conclusion that chimpanzees behave prosocially.

Researchers have more recently begun to explore the possibility of prosocial sentiments in nonprimate mammals. In a highly publicized finding, Bartal et al. (2011) found that rats, when placed in a container with a restrained cage-mate, would free their cage-mate from the restraint container while ignoring empty restraint containers. Furthermore, when a free rat encountered both a restrainer with a cage-mate and a restrainer containing a chocolate treat, the free rat then opened both containers and would share the chocolate treat with their companion. Silberberg et al. (2013) have suggested that the "rescue" behaviors described in rats may result from a desire for social contact. They showed that the rats may have been conditioned to release rats in a social contact condition, but did not release rats into an adjacent enclosure where contact was not possible if this condition was presented first. Furthermore, rats may be attempting to reduce their own stress caused by the distress signals given off by their restrained cage-mate. The same argument has been made regarding prosocial behaviors in chimpanzees, where the actor may give to the recipient to stop them from begging. Yet this argument is not supported by some studies that showed that chimpanzees did not show a significant response to begging behaviors (Silk et al. 2005; Vonk et al. 2008). More distantly related species, such as bats, may produce stronger evidence for prosocial sentiments. For instance, Wilkinson (1984) found that vampire bats, which require frequent blood meals to avoid starvation, routinely share blood meals with other bats, even unrelated individuals. Bats that fail to obtain a meal are fed by their roost mates upon return. Interestingly, blood sharing is more often initiated by the donor, making harassment an unlikely cause (Carter and Wilkinson 2013b). Given that the best predictor of food-sharing behavior was previous meal-sharing interaction and not relatedness, it is possible that such behaviors are determined by reciprocity, in which bats keep track of their own future benefits, and do not truly reflect prosocial sentiments. Therefore, whether other species really possess sentiments such as prosociality is still a controversial topic.

Conclusions

We have provided a brief synopsis of the issues surrounding the comparative study of social cognition. We hope to have shed light on the possible mechanisms underlying the emergence of various social cognitive skills in a wide range of species, while cautioning the reader to avoid the temptation of assigning human-like qualities to other species. It is quite possible that different mechanisms produce similar manifest behaviors without requiring similar levels of conceptual understanding of constructs, such as mental states. Thus, it appears that there is some degree of continuity across the animal kingdom with regard to behaviors that play an important role in the evolution of human social cognition. At the same time, there are important discontinuities where even our closest relatives do not appear to apply the same level of social understanding to problem solving in the social realm. This is a rapidly evolving area of research and we hope that collaborations between researchers working from a variety of perspectives will facilitate further understanding of both the similarities and differences between various animal minds.

References

Agnetta, B., Hare, B., & Tomasello, M. (2000). Cues to food location that domestic dogs (*Canis familiaris*) of different ages do and do not use. *Animal Cognition, 3,* 107–112.

Baron-Cohen, S. (1999). The evolution of a theory of mind. In M. C. Corballis & S. E. G. Lea (Eds.), *The descent of the mind* (pp. 261–275). New York: Oxford University Press.

Barrera, G., Jakovcevic, A., Mustaca, A., & Bentosela, M. (2011). Learning interspecific communicative responses in Pampas foxes (*Lycalopex gymnocercus*). *Behavioural Processes, 89,* 44–51.

Bartal, I. B. A., Decety, J., & Mason, P. (2011). Empathy and pro-social behavior in rats. *Science, 334,* 1427–1430.

Bering, J. M. (2004). A critical review of the "enculturation hypothesis": The effects of human rearing on great ape social cognition. *Animal Cognition, 7,* 201–212.

Bräuer, J., Call, J., & Tomasello, M. (2005). All great ape species follow gaze to distant locations and around barriers. *Journal of Comparative Psychology, 119,* 145–154.

Bräuer, J., Kaminski, J., Riedel, J., Call, J., & Tomasello, M. (2006). Making inferences about the location of hidden food: Social dog, causal ape. *Journal of Comparative Psychology, 120,* 38–47.

Bräuer, J., Call, J., & Tomasello, M. (2007). Chimpanzees really know what others can see in a competitive situation. *Animal Cognition, 10,* 439–448.

Bräuer, J., Keckeisen, M., Pitsch, A., Kaminski, J., Call, J., & Tomasello, M. (2013). Domestic dogs conceal auditory but not visual information from others. *Animal Cognition, 16,* 351–359.

Brosnan, S. F., Schiff, H. C., & de Waal, F. B. M. (2005). Chimpanzees' (*Pan troglodytes*) reactions to inequity during experimental exchange. *Proceedings of the Royal Society of London, Series B, 1560,* 253–258.

Bshary, R., & Schäffer, D. (2002). Choosy reef fish select cleaner fish that provide high-quality service. *Animal Behaviour, 63,* 557–564.

Buttelmann, D. & Tomasello, M. (2013). Can domestic dogs (*Canis familiaris*) use referential emotional expressions to locate hidden food? *Animal Cognition, 16,* 137–145.

Byrne, R. W., & Whiten, A. (1997). Machiavellian intelligence II: Extensions and evaluations. In A. Whiten & R. W. Byrne (Eds.), *Machiavellian intelligence II* (pp. 1–23).

Call, J., & Tomasello, M. (2008). Does the chimpanzee have a theory of mind? 30 years later. *Trends in Cognitive Sciences, 12,* 187–192.

Cambridge: Cambridge University Press.

Call, J., Hare, B. A., & Tomasello, M. (1998). Chimpanzee gaze following in an object-choice task. *Animal Cognition, 1,* 89–99.

Call, J., Kaminski, J., Bräuer, J., & Tomasello, M. (2009). Domestic dogs are sensitive to a human's perspective. *Behaviour, 146,* 979–998.

Carter, G. G., & Wilkinson, G. S. (2013a). Cooperation and conflict in the social lives of bats. In R. A. Adams & S. C. Pedersen (Eds.), *Bat evolution, ecology, and conservation* (pp. 225–242). New York: Springer Science Press.

Carter, G. G., & Wilkinson, G. S. (2013b). Food sharing in vampire bats: Reciprocal help predicts donations more than relatedness or harassment. *Proceedings of the Royal Society B: Biological Sciences, 280.*

Chalmeau, R., & Gallo, A. (1996). What chimpanzees (*Pan troglodytes*) learn in a cooperative task. *Primates, 37,* 39–47.

Cheney, D. L., & Seyfarth, R. M. (2012). The evolution of a cooperative social mind. In J. Vonk & T. K. Shackelford (Eds.), *The Oxford handbook of comparative evolutionary psychology* (pp. 507–528). New York: Oxford University Press.

Connor, R. C. (2007). Dolphin social intelligence: Complex alliance relationships in bottlenose dolphins and a consideration of selective environments for extreme brain size evolution in mammals. *Philosophical Transactions of the Royal Society B: Biological Sciences, 362,* 587–602.

Cronin, K. A. (2012). Prosocial behaviour in animals: The influence of social relationships, communication and rewards. *Animal Behaviour, 84,* 1085–1093.

Cronin, K. A., Schroeder, K. K. E., Rothwell, E. S., Silk, J. B., & Snowdon, C. T. (2009). Cooperatively breeding cottontop tamarins (*Saguinus oedipus*) do not donate rewards to their long-term mates. *Journal of Comparative Psychology, 123,* 231–241.

de Waal, F. B., Leimgruber, K., & Greenberg, A. R. (2008). Giving is self-rewarding for monkeys. *Proceedings of the National Academy of Sciences, 105,* 13685–13689.

Drea, C. M., & Carter, A. N. (2009). Cooperative problem solving in a social carnivore. *Animal Behaviour, 78,* 967–977.

Freidin, E., Putrino, N., D'Orazio, M. & Bentosela, M. (2013). Dogs' eavesdropping from people's reactions in their party interactions. *PLoS one.* doi:10.1371/journal.pone.0079198.

Gácsi, M., Miklósi, Á., Varga, O., Topál, J., & Csányi, V. (2004). Are readers of our face readers of our minds? Dogs (*Canis familiaris*) show situation-dependent recognition of human's attention. *Animal Cognition, 7,* 144–153.

Gácsi, M., Györi, B., Virányi, Z., Kubinyi, E., Range, F., Belényi, B., & Miklósi, A. (2009). Explaining dog wolf differences in utilizing human pointing gestures: Selection for synergistic shifts in the development of some social skills. *PloS One, 4*(8), e6584.

Greenberg, J. R., Hamann, K., Warneken, F., & Tomasello, M. (2010). Chimpanzee helping in collaborative and noncollaborative contexts. *Animal Behaviour, 80,* 873–880.

Hare, B. (2001). Can competitive paradigms increase the validity of social cognitive experiments on primates? *Animal Cognition, 4,* 269–280.

Hare, B., & Tomasello, M. (2004). Chimpanzees are more skillful in competitive than cooperative cognitive tasks. *Animal Behaviour, 68,* 571–581.

Hare, B., Call, J., Agnetta, B., & Tomasello, M. (2000). Chimpanzees know what conspecifics do and do not see. *Animal Behaviour, 59,* 771–785.

Hare, B., Call, J., & Tomasello, M. (2001). Do chimpanzees know what conspecifics know? *Animal Behaviour, 61,* 139–151.

Hare, B., Brown, M., Williamson, C., & Tomasello, M. (2002). The domestication of social cognition in dogs. *Science, 298,* 1634–1636.

Hare, B., Call, J., & Tomasello, M. (2006). Chimpanzees deceive a human competitor by hiding. *Cognition, 101,* 495–514.

Hare, B., Rosati, A., Kaminski, J., Bräuer, J., Call, J., & Tomasello, M. (2010). The domestication hypothesis for dogs' skills with human communication: A response to Udell et al. (2008) and Wynne et al. (2008). *Animal Behaviour, 79,* e1–e6.

Haviland, W. A., Prins, H. E., Walrath, D., & McBride, B. (2005). *Anthropology: The human challenge.* Belmont: Wadsworth/Thomson Learning.

Heinsohn, R., & Packer, C. (1995). Complex cooperative strategies in group-territorial African lions. *Science, 269,* 1260–1262.

Herrmann, E., Call, J., Hernández-Lloreda, M. V., Hare, B., & Tomasello, M. (2007). Humans have evolved specialized skills of social cognition: The cultural intelligence hypothesis. *Science, 317,* 1360–1366.

Herrmann, E., Keupp, S., Hare, B., Vaish, A., & Tomasello, M. (2013). Direct and indirect reputation formation in nonhuman great apes (*Pan paniscus, Pan troglodytes, Gorilla gorilla, Pongo pygmaeus*) and human children (*Homo sapiens*). *Journal of Comparative Psychology, 127,* 63–75.

Hirata, S., & Fuvva, K. (2007). Chimpanzees (*Pan troglodytes*) learn to act with other individuals in a cooperative task. *Primates, 48,* 13–21.

Horner, V., Carter, J. D., Suchak, M., & de Waal, F. B. M. (2011). Spontaneous prosocial choice by chimpanzees. *PNAS Proceedings of the National Academy of Sciences of the United States of America, 108,* 13847–13851.

Humphrey, N. (1976). The social function of intellect. In P. P. G. Bateson & R. A. Hinde (Eds.), *Growing points in ethology* (pp. 303–317). Cambridge: Cambridge University Press.

Jaakola, K. (2012). Cetacean cognitive specializations. In J. Vonk & T. K. Shackelford (Eds.), *The Oxford handbook of comparative evolutionary psychology* (pp. 144–165). New York: Oxford University Press.

Jolly, A. (1966). Lemur social behavior and primate intelligence. *Science, 153,* 501–506.

Kaminski, J., & Nitzschner, M. (2013). Do dogs gct thc point? A review of dog-human communication ability. *Learning and Motivation, 44,* 294–302.

Kaminski, J., Riedel, J., Call, J., & Tomasello, M. (2005). Domestic goats, *Capra hircus*, follow gaze direction and use social cues in an object choice task. *Animal Behaviour, 69,* 11–18.

Kaminski, J., Pitsch, A., & Tomasello, M. (2013). Dogs steal in the dark. *Animal Cognition, 16,* 385–394.

Karin-D'Arcy, R. M., & Povinelli, D. J. (2002). Do chimpanzees know what each other see? A closer look. *International Journal of Comparative Psychology, 15,* 21–54.

Kirchhofer, K. C., Zimmermann, F., Kaminski, J., & Tomasello, M. (2012). Dogs (*Canis familiaris*), but not chimpanzees (*Pan troglodytes*), understand imperative pointing. *PloS One, 7,* e30913.

Krachun, C., & Call, J. (2009). Chimpanzees (*Pan troglodytes*) know what can be seen from where. *Animal Cognition, 12,* 317–331.

Kundey, S. M. A., De, L. R., Royer, E., Molina, S., Monnier, B., German, R., & Coshun, A. (2011). Reputation-like inference in domestic dogs (canis familiaris). *Animal Cognition, 14(2),* 291–302.

Langer, J. (2000). The descent of cognitive development. *Developmental Science, 3,* 361–378.

Maros, K., Gácsi, M., & Miklósi, A. (2008). Comprehension of human pointing gestures in horses (*Equus caballus*). *Animal Cognition, 11,* 457–466.

Melis, A. P., Hare, B., & Tomasello, M. (2006). Chimpanzees recruit the best collaborators. Science, *311,* 1297–1300.

Melis, A. P., Hare, B., & Tomasello, M. (2009). Chimpanzees coordinate in a negotiation game. *Evolution and Human Behavior, 30,* 381–392.

Miklósi, A., Pongrácz, P., Lakatos, G., Topál, J., & Csányi, V. (2005). A comparative study of the use of visual communicative signals in interactions between dogs (*Canis familiaris*) and humans and cats (*Felis catus*) and humans. *Journal of Comparative Psychology, 119,* 179–186.

Mitani, J. C., & Watts, D. P. (2001). Why do chimpanzees hunt and share meat? *Animal Behaviour, 61,* 915–924.

Moll, H., & Tomasello, M. (2007). Cooperation and human cognition: The Vygotskian intelligence hypothesis. *Philosophical Transactions of the Royal Society of London. Series B, Biological sciences, 362,* 639–648.

Nitzschner, M., Melis, A. P., Kaminski, J., & Tomasello, M. (2012). Dogs (Canis familiaris) evaluate humans on the basis of direct experiences only. *PloS One, 7,* e46880.

Nowak, M. A. (2006). Five rules for the evolution of cooperation. *Science, 314,* 1560–1563.

Osvath, M., & Karvonen, E. (2012). Spontaneous innovation for future deception in a male chimpanzee. *PloS One,* 7(5), e36782.

Pack, A. A., & Herman, L. M. (2007). The dolphin's (*Tursiops truncatus*) understanding of human gazing and pointing: Knowing what and where. *Journal of Comparative Psychology, 121,* 34–45.

Parr, L. A. (2001). Cognitive and physiological markers of emotional awareness in chimpanzees (*Pan troglodytes*). *Animal Cognition, 4,* 223–229.

Penn, D. C., & Povinelli, D. J. (2007). On the lack of evidence that non-human animals possess anything remotely resembling a "theory of mind". *Philosophical transactions of the Royal Society of London. Series B, Biological sciences, 362,* 731–744.

Péron, F., Rat-Fischer, L., Lalot, M., Nagle, L., & Bovet, D. (2011). Cooperative problem solving in African grey parrots (*Psittacus erithacus*). *Animal Cognition, 14,* 545–553.

Plotnik, J. M., Lair, R., Suphachoksahakun, W., & de Waal, F. B. (2011). Elephants know when they need a helping trunk in a cooperative task. *Proceedings of the National Academy of Sciences, 108,* 5116–5121.

Povinelli, D. J., & Eddy, T. J. (1996). Chimpanzees: Joint visual attention. *Psychological Science, 7,* 129–135.

Povinelli, D. J., & Giambrone, S. (1999). Inferring others minds: Failure of the argument by analogy. *Philosophical Topics, 27,* 167–201.

Povinelli, D. J., & Vonk, J. (2003). Chimpanzee minds: Suspiciously human? *Trends in Cognitive Science, 7,* 157–160.

Povinelli, D. J., & Vonk, J. (2004). We don't need a microscope to explore the chimpanzee's mind. *Mind and Language, 19,* 1–28.

Povinelli, D. J., Bering, J. M., & Giambrone, S. (2000). Toward a science of other minds: Escaping the argument by analogy. *Cognitive Science, 24,* 509–541.

Premack, D., & Woodruff, G. (1978). Does the chimpanzee have a theory of mind? *Behavioral and Brain Sciences, 4,* 515–526.

Reaux, J. E., Theall, L. a., & Povinelli, D. J. (1999). A longitudinal investigation of chimpanzees' understanding of visual perception. *Child Development, 70,* 275–290.

Russell, Y. I., Call, J., & Dunbar, R. I. (2008). Image scoring in great apes. *Behavioural Processes, 78,* 108–111.

Scheumann, M., & Call, J. (2004). The use of experimenter-given cues by South African fur seals (*Arctocephalus pusillus*). *Animal Cognition, 7,* 224–230.

Shepherd, S. V. (2010). Following gaze: Gaze-following behavior as a window into social cognition. *Frontiers in Integrative Neuroscience, 4,* 1–13.

Silberberg, A., Allouch, C., Sandfort, S., Kearns, D., Karpel, H., & Slotnick, B. (2014). Desire for social contact, not empathy, may explain "rescue" behavior in rats. *Animal Cognition, 17,* 609–618.

Silk, J. B., Brosnan, S. F., Vonk, J., Henrich, J., Povinelli, D. J., Richardson, A. S., Lambeth, S. P., Mascaro, J., & Schapiro, S. J. (2005). Chimpanzees are indifferent to the welfare of unrelated group members. *Nature, 437,* 1357–1359.

Smith, B. P., & Litchfield, C. A. (2010). Dingoes (*Canis dingo*) can use human social cues to locate hidden food. *Animal Cognition, 13,* 367–376.

Sodian, B. (1991). The development of deception in young children. *British Journal of Developmental Psychology, 9,* 173–188.

Subiaul, F., Vonk, J., Okamoto-Barth, S., & Barth, J. (2008). Do chimpanzees learn reputation by observation? Evidence from direct and indirect experience with generous and selfish strangers. *Animal Cognition, 11,* 611–623.

Udell, M. A. R., Dorey, N. R., & Wynne, C. D. (2008). Wolves outperform dogs in following human social cues. *Animal Behaviour, 76,* 1767–1773.

Udell, M. A. R., Dorey, N. R., & Wynne, C. D. L. (2011). Can your dog read your mind? Understanding the causes of canine perspective taking. *Learning & Behavior, 39,* 289–302.

Udell, M. A. R., Spencer, J. M., Dorey, N. R., & Wynne, C. D. L. (2012). Human-socialized wolves follow diverse human gestures … and they may not be alone. *International Journal of Comparative Psychology, 25,* 97–117.

Virányi, Z., Gácsi, M., Kubinyi, E., Topál, J., Belényi, B., Ujfalussy, D., & Miklósi, A. (2008). Comprehension of human pointing gestures in young human-reared wolves (*Canis lupus*) and dogs (*Canis familiaris*). *Animal Cognition, 11,* 373–387.

Vonk, J., & Aradhye, C. (in press). Evolution of cognition. In M. Simon & J. Abelson (Eds.), *Encyclopedia of human biology* (3rd ed.). Amsterdam: Elsevier.

Vonk, J., & Povinelli, D. J. (2006). Similarity and difference in the conceptual systems of primates: The unobservability hypothesis. In E. Wasserman & T. Zentall (Eds.), *Comparative cognition: Experimental explorations of animal intelligence* (pp. 363–387). New York: Oxford University Press.

Vonk, J., & Povinelli, D. J. (2011). Social and physical reasoning in human-reared chimpanzees. In J. Roessler, H. Lerman, & N. Eilan (Eds.), *Perception, causation, and objectivity* (pp. 342–367). New York: Oxford University Press.

Vonk, J. & Subiaul, F. (2009). Do chimpanzees know what others can and cannot do? Reasoning about 'capability'. *Animal Cognition, 12,* 267–286.

Vonk, J., Brosnan, S. F., Silk, J. B., Henrich, J., Richardson, A. S., Lambeth, S. P., Schapiro, S. J., & Povinelli, D. J. (2008). Chimpanzees do not take advantage of very low cost opportunities to deliver food to unrelated group members. *Animal Behaviour, 75,* 1757–1770.

Warneken, F., & Melis, A. P. (2012). The ontogeny and phylogeny of cooperation. In J. Vonk & T. K. Shackelford (Eds.), *The Oxford handbook of comparative evolutionary psychology* (pp. 399–418). New York: Oxford University Press.

Whiten, A., & Byrne, R. W. (1988). Tactical deception in primates. *Behavioral and Brain Sciences, 11,* 233–273.

Whiten, A., & Byrne, R. W. (1997). *Machiavellian intelligence II: Extensions and evaluations* (Vol. 2). Cambridge: Cambridge University Press.

Whiten, A., & Van Schaik, C. P. (2007). The evolution of animal 'cultures' and social intelligence. *Philosophical Transactions of the Royal Society B: Biological Sciences, 362,* 603–620.

Wilkinson, G. S. (1984). Reciprocal food sharing in the vampire bat. *Nature, 308,* 181–184.

Wimmer, H., & Perner, J. (1983). Beliefs about beliefs: Representation and constraining function of wrong beliefs in young children's understanding of deception. *Cognition, 13,* 103–128.

Woodruff, G., & Premack, D. (1979). Intentional communication in the chimpanzee: The development of deception. *Cognition, 7,* 333–362.

Wynne, C. D. L., Udell, M. A. R., & Lord, K. A. (2008). Ontogeny's impacts on human-dog communication. *Animal Behaviour, 76,* e1–e4.

Yamamoto, S., & Tanaka, M. (2010). The influence of kin relationship and reciprocal context on chimpanzees' other-regarding preferences. *Animal Behaviour, 79,* 595–602.

Part III
Self

The Emergent Self

8

Raymond L. Neubauer

Life deals with change chiefly with two information systems: genes and nervous systems. Genes came first; nervous systems did not get underway until the Cambrian explosion, about 535 million years ago (mya). Both systems respond to their environment and allow an organism to change its behavior to optimize survival and reproductive success. Neurons have the potential to respond faster than genes and to integrate more data. A gene is controlled by the accumulation of transcription factors, which may number from a few to several dozen, while a neuron may receive input at 100,000 synapses with other neurons (Neubauer 2011).

There has been an increase in brain size relative to body size in vertebrates over geologic time. On average, mammals and birds have increased tenfold in brain-to-body ratio compared to fish, reptiles, and amphibians (see Fig. 8.1). The increased encephalization of mammals took place mainly during the Cenozoic, but was not a linear change. The variance between large- and small-brained species increased, as did the average brain-to-body ratio over time (Boddy et al. 2012; Finarelli 2011).

Various evolutionary advantages have been linked to increased encephalization, including greater behavioral flexibility and adaptability to novel environments (Finarelli and Flynn 2009). In mammals and birds, species with higher relative brain size have higher survival rates when introduced into novel environments (Sol et al. 2005, 2008). Rates of anatomical change correlate with relative brain size, suggesting that behavioral flexibility may lead species into new niches where they undergo new selective pressures (Cherry et al. 1982; Wyles et al. 1983).

Large brains are expensive metabolically. In humans, they make up only 2 % of body mass, but consume 20 % of resting metabolism (Dunbar 1998). Life-history changes compensate for this expensive tissue. Large brains take a long time to develop, which leads to delayed reproduction, but an extension of the lifespan compensates for this loss in fertility (Gonzalez-Lagos et al. 2010). Slowly developing brains require high parental care via nurturing and protection, since immature young are vulnerable to predators (Snell-Rood 2012, 2013). Litter size will be small with long intervals between reproduction. However, these characteristics favor a strategy of behavioral flexibility. A slowly maturing brain allows for extended periods of learning and fosters the transfer of skills across generations.

This contrasts with an alternative relationship in mammals between small body size, high fecundity, short lifespan, and rapid turnover of generations (Bromham 2011). This is part of the "fast-slow continuum" (Bielby et al. 2007; Ricklefs and Wikelski 2002). There even is a difference in the rate of molecular evolution, with small, short-lived mammals having higher rates than large-bodied mammals (Bromham 2011). There is evidence for lower rates of DNA repair in small mammals, so they present greater amounts of genetic variability per generation. We may think of this as large-brained animals developing behavioral flexibility to deal with change,

R. L. Neubauer (✉)
Molecular Cell & Developmental Biology, University of Texas at Austin, 1 University Station, A6700, Austin TX 78712-0183, USA
e-mail: rneubauer@utexas.edu

V. Zeigler-Hill et al. (eds.), *Evolutionary Perspectives on Social Psychology*, Evolutionary Psychology,
DOI 10.1007/978-3-319-12697-5_8, © Springer International Publishing Switzerland 2015

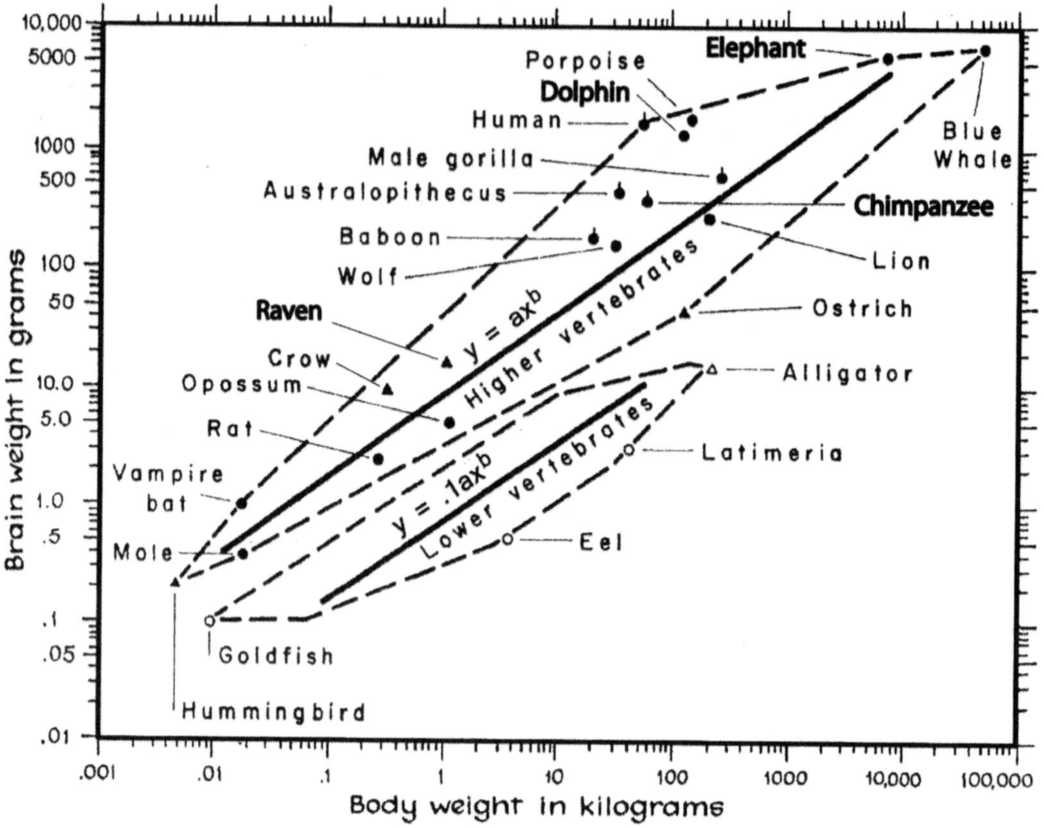

Fig. 8.1 Minimum convex polygons drawn around brain and body data for 198 vertebrate species. Regression lines in each polygon represent average brain size for animals at a particular body size. Animals above this line have an encephalization quotient (EQ) greater than 1, and animals below it have an EQ less than 1. Species in **boldface** are discussed in this chapter. (Adapted with permission from Jerison 1969. © 1969 by the University of Chicago Press, with data from Striedter 2005)

while small-bodied, small-brained animals rely on faster turnover of generations with greater genetic variability.

Many of these differences have been summarized in the concepts of *r*- and *K*-selection (Pianka 2000). While the ecological conditions that foster one kind of selection or the other have been challenged, the behavioral characteristics associated with each kind of selection have found support (Boyce 1984; Mauseth 1995; Snell-Rood 2012). In both plants and animals, one can distinguish *r*-selected opportunistic species that can quickly take over an environment via rapid development, small size, and many small offspring, from *K*-selected species that combine slow development, delayed reproduction, and few progeny with high competitive ability due to behavioral flexibility. In animals, this flexibility is provided mainly by a large, slowly maturing brain.

The four animal groups reviewed here share qualities of large brains and a *K*-selected suite of characteristics. Chimpanzees (*Pan troglodytes*) live about 50 years in the wild and females do not begin to reproduce until about age 14 years, with 5-year intervals between young. They lactate until infants are about 4–5 years old, but the young do not become independent of the mother until about age 14 years (Boesch 2009).

Bottlenose dolphins (*Tursiops truncatus*) live into their 50s and females become sexually mature around the age of 8 years. They have one calf at a time, several years apart, which remain with their mothers for 3–5 years (Connor 2007; Jaakkola 2012). Elephants live about 60 years; the African species first gives birth at about 14 years and continues at intervals of 4–5 years. The young are nutritionally dependent until about 4 years, but remain socially dependent on their mothers until 10–16 years (Lee and Moss 1999; Payne 2003). I discuss the behavior of the African species (*Loxodonta africana*) and the Asian species (*Elephas maximus*). The common raven (*Corvus corax*) lives up to 21 years in the wild and does not breed until at least 3 years. It is part of the family Corvidae, which has the longest mean maximum lifespan in the order Passeriformes (Wasser and Sherman 2010). Ravens associate with their parents for 2–3 months after fledging, while many passerines are independent immediately or within days after fledging (Heinrich 2011; van Horik et al. 2012). I also review behavioral studies of two other corvids, the New Caledonian crow (*Corvus moneduloides*) and the magpie (*Pica pica*).

Relative Brain Size

Figure 8.1 shows an average regression line through the data for mammals and birds. This line is described by the formula $y=ax^b$, where x is the body weight of the animal and y is the brain weight. When logs are taken of both sides (as in the graph), b becomes the slope of the line and a is the y-intercept. Encephalization quotient (EQ) is a measure of how far a species' brain weight deviates from an average animal of its body weight. An EQ = 1 means it has an average brain weight for its body weight, and an EQ = 2 means it has twice the brain weight of an average animal of that body weight.

EQ has been proposed as a measure of the computational power of a brain (Jerison 1973, 2001). If an average animal can survive with an EQ of 1, higher EQ values may represent "extra neurons" that could be devoted to functions beyond physiological control (Jerison 1969, 1973; Striedter 2005). Advanced cognitive abilities, such as innovation, tool use, and social learning, have been correlated with greater EQ (Lefebvre and Sol 2008). There are, however, problems in drawing a single regression line as the average for many taxa because different groups have different slopes (e.g., primates: 0.756; cetaceans: 0.376; all mammals without primates and cetaceans: 0.718; Manger 2006). Jerison (1973) calculated 0.67 for a sample set of 198 mammals and birds, while Eisenberg (1981) found 0.74 for 547 mammalian species. A recent calculation using 630 extant mammalian species in 21 orders found a slope of 0.75 (Boddy et al. 2012).

Different types of measurements have been proposed to compare changes in brain size, including the size of the forebrain or neocortex, forebrain/brainstem ratio, and absolute brain size (Gonzalez-Lagos et al. 2010; Herculano-Houzel 2012; Reader et al. 2011). Many different metrics yield similar results. Several brain component volumes, especially those involved in higher-order cognition, correlate with whole brain size (Gonzalez-Lagos et al. 2010; Lefebvre and Sol 2008, but see Deaner et al. 2007). A study of primate general and cultural intelligence found a correlation with three measures of brain size: neocortex size, neocortex ratio (neocortex/rest of brain), and executive brain ratio (neocortex + striatum/brainstem; Reader et al. 2011).

The four animal groups reviewed here may not have the highest EQ values for their body weight, but they are species for which a large number of ethological studies have been published so that detailed behavioral comparisons can be made. Boddy et al. (2012) use a regression line specific to mammals and give EQ values for bottlenose dolphins (3.51), chimpanzees (2.18), the Asian elephant (1.46), and African elephant (1.09). By comparison, humans have an EQ of 5.72. Using a regression line specific for birds (van Dongen 1998) gives an EQ for ravens of 1.98 (Armstrong and Bergeron 1985) and for the New Caledonian crow of 2.26 (Mehlhorn et al. 2010). Corvids have the highest EQ values of all the songbirds, and the basic architecture of the avian brain is similar to that of mammals, though without the six-layered cortex (Emery 2006; Striedter 2013). Elephants do not have an EQ much above the regression line shown in Fig. 8.1, but it is the largest at that body size and variance at these large body sizes is much less than among smaller animals. Elephants have the largest brains of any terrestrial animal, and there is evidence that as brains become larger, a smaller proportional area is devoted to physiological functions, so that large brains may have many "extra neurons" for advanced cognitive functions (Striedter 2005). Elephants are also among the few species (including humans, dolphins, and chimpanzees) that have been found with Von Economo neurons, especially large spindle-shaped neurons in the forebrain that receive input from many other neurons and are involved in social behavior (Hakeem et al. 2009; Spocter et al. 2012).

These four animal groups differ in phylogeny and ecology, yet they display a remarkable convergence of behavior. They all possess high relative brain size and a *K*-selected life history that provides a slowly maturing brain that relies on learning and behavioral flexibility to survive. They are also capable of what Matsuzawa (1996) calls third-order relationships; they not only use tools but may also use a tool to modify another tool. They engage in complex social interactions and appear to recognize abstractions (i.e., patterns that are higher derivatives of the raw data). This objectivity is reflected in mirror self-recognition. Higher-order cognition is evident in both their social relationships and in manipulation of their environment.

Tool Use

Tool use is found in only 0.01 % of nonprimate mammals (Mann et al. 2008). Primates have the highest frequency of tool use among mammals, and it is present in all great apes (Iwaniuk et al. 2009). A review of tool use among 104 species of birds found the most cases among the large-brained corvids (Lefebvre et al. 2002). Rates of tool use in primates and birds correlate with relative brain size (Seed and Byrne 2010). Researchers distinguish between proto-tool use, such as smashing shellfish against a hard surface, and true tool use that involves modifying an object to use as a tool. True tool users have larger brain size than proto-tool users, and proto-tool use involves more stereotyped and repetitive actions than complex manipulations with true tools (Iwaniuk et al. 2009).

Chimpanzees

The most complex and diverse tool use outside humans has been found in chimpanzees (Dora Biro et al. 2010). In the Taï forest of West Africa, 26 different kinds of tools have been catalogued for activities as diverse as honey dipping, termite fishing, sponging liquids, and pounding nuts (Boesch and Boesch-Achermann 2000). The combination of tools used varies across Africa, leading to local cultures (McGrew 2010). Bossou et al. (1996) found "metatool" use; that is, one tool used to modify another. Besides a stone anvil and hammer used to crack nuts, a third stone was used to prop up the anvil to a level angle. Researchers have also found a case in which two stones on opposite sides were used to prop up the anvil to a level angle (Biro et al. 2010).

Sequential tool use may also be thought of as a kind of metatool use that suggests a conceptual understanding of materials. Tools must be the proper hardness and length to obtain the desired result, and they must be used in the proper sequence (Brewer and Mcgrew 1990). In the Congo, wild chimpanzees use different tools in sequence to break into termite nests and then extract the insects (Sanz et al. 2004). Not all chimpanzee communities go termite fishing, and groups in East and West Africa use different tool kits, so this is likely a learned behavior that is culturally passed on in each chimpanzee community (Biro et al. 2010a).

Corvids

A wide variety of birds use tools in the wild, but the most numerous examples cited are among corvids (Emery and Clayton 2004; Lefebvre et al. 2002). The most intricate modifications of tools have been found in the New Caledonian crow (Hunt and Gray 2004). Two different kinds of tools are produced to extract food from crevices in trees. In the first, a hooked tool is made by multiple cuts on a twig, leaf stripping, and sharpening the end with the bill. This is the most modifications in tool manufacturing by any known bird (Hunt and Gray 2004). A second tool is produced from leaves of the *Pandanus* tree. A set of crosscuts and rip cuts are made to produce a spear-like tool to probe into tree holes for food. Finished tools may be stored on perches for later use, and there are differences in tool production in different parts of the islands in the Pacific where these birds are found (Hunt 2000). Common ravens also show insight in tool use. Hand-reared naive birds were able to lift meat dangled from strings by holding multiple loops in place with the foot to get at the meal (Heinrich 2011).

Elephants

Both Asian and African elephants use tools for at least six different functions, though they are mostly related to bodily care (Bates et al. 2009). A common practice is to break branches from trees to use as fly swatters. Wild elephants in India use the branches of at least five different plants in this way and have been observed to hold down a branch with a foot while twisting off the side branches with the trunk to make it a suitable size (Hart et al. 2001), thereby demonstrating an advanced form of tool use (i.e., tool modification). They are also able to throw objects accurately with the trunk to ward off animals, including bothersome humans. In captivity, elephants have been observed using sticks to pull food closer, open faucets, and make piles of tires to stand on to reach high branches (Poole and Moss 2008). A study of Asian elephants found that they learned to pull cooperatively on a rope to retrieve a food reward (Plotnik et al. 2011).

Dolphins

In Shark Bay, Western Australia, some bottlenose dolphins have been observed wearing marine sponges on the rostra (beak)—presumably to protect the rostrum from the sharp surface of the sea bottom (Mann et al. 2008; Patterson and Mann 2011)—while they hunt. When the prey swim out from hiding, the dolphin drops the sponge, catches the fish, and then returns to the sponge to continue foraging. A minority of females use this technique and it is passed on to young by social learning. Not all calves take up the habit, but those who do may continue the technique for a decade or more. Thirteen different foraging techniques are known among bottlenose dolphins, and at least three of them are passed on by social learning (Sargeant and Mann 2009).

Social Relations

A study of 206 species of mammals in three orders, including primates (Dunbar 1998) and cetaceans (van Horik et al. 2012), found a positive relationship between relative brain size and sociality (Perez-Barberia et al. 2007). Long-term relationships with single individuals make high demands on cognitive powers. Among carnivores, ungulates, bats, and birds, species that are pair bonded have relatively larger brains than species with other mating systems (Dunbar and Shultz 2007). In birds, long-term monogamous species and cooperative breeders have the largest relative brain sizes (van Horik et al. 2012).

Complex social life involves not only affiliation but also deception. A study of 18 species of primates living in the wild found that forebrain size predicted the frequency of deceptive tactics used for social manipulation (Byrne abd Corp 2004). The four species described here are characterized by unusually large social groups that include individual recognition. In some cases, they involve third-party relationships in complex "politics" of group life.

Elephants

Elephants have been described as having the largest network of vocal recognition of any mammal (McComb et al. 2000). An adult female may be familiar with the calls of up to 100 adults, with one report indicating that as many as 650 individuals know each other (Moss 1988). African and Asian elephants live in multitiered societies whose core is the family: a mother and her subadult offspring. Families are often joined into larger "family units," comprising up to 20 mothers and their young, and these form larger aggregations called clans, which may number up to several hundred individuals. At the clan level, elephants may not be closely related, apparently forming for social reasons and to attract mates (Archie et al. 2006). The age of the matriarch in a family unit predicts the number of calves per female in her group, indicating that an experienced leader provides direct fitness advantages to group members (Douglas-Hamilton et al. 2006). Elephant society, therefore, especially for females, exists in a nested hierarchy from the family up to the clan level in which hundreds of individuals may know each other.

Dolphins

Bottlenose dolphins have been found in social networks of more than 400 individuals. Each dolphin has 60–70 associates (Connor 2007; Connor et al. 2001). Adult males form strong associations with two to three others that may cooperate in hunting, defense, and herding of females. Two of these groups may join against a third group and there can be "super-alliances" of up to 14 males. Dolphin hunting often involves divisions of labor, and they also cooperate in driving fish onto the shore, then beaching themselves in order to feed (Smolker 2000). In southern Brazil, cooperative hunting may include humans. At certain times of the year, bottlenose dolphins herd fish into nets which humans throw at just the right cues, and the dolphins feed on those that try to escape (Pryor et al. 1990). The fishermen maintain they have not trained the cetaceans, and episodes are initiated and cued by the dolphins.

Chimpanzees

Chimpanzees in the wild live in fission–fusion societies of 30–120 individuals where small groups may go off for several days before rejoining their troop (Boesch 2012; Goodall 1986). Troops have dominance hierarchies with an alpha male, but his position depends on alliances within the troop. Retaining power depends not only on the alliances of the dominant male but also on the coalitions of males and females within the troop in complex patterns of "chimpanzee politics." According to de Waal, an enduring leader is often more interested in keeping peace in the troop than favoring particular allies or relatives. In disputes, he must place himself "*above* the conflicting parties" (de Waal 1996, p. 129) and decide what is best for the troop.

The complexity of chimpanzee relationships can be seen during a hunt. In some parts of Africa, meat is an important part of the diet, and the colobus monkey (*Colobus badius tephrosceles*) is favored prey. Males form coordinated hunts where some flush monkeys out of the trees, others block escape routes, and finally an ambusher, who must anticipate where the quarry will flee, comes from hiding to grab prey. It takes a chimpanzee about 20 years to become a good ambusher. The skills involved have been described as an understanding of "tertiary relationships," for it requires the ambusher to keep track of the movements of conspecifics and anticipate the reaction of the quarry (Boesch and Boesch-Achermann 2000). Similarly, leadership ability also involves understanding tertiary relationships because the alpha male must keep track of his own coalitions and those arrayed against him.

Ravens

Ravens mate for life and may live up to 30 years. Monogamy in birds is one of the factors correlated with large relative brain size. Before they become sexually mature, ravens live in loose flocks of both sexes that often have strong individual bonds. A study of ravens in the wild found an individual interacting on average with 3 +/– 2 partners over a 2-year period, usually with a member of the opposite sex. Seventy-one percent of marked ravens switched partners during this 2-year period (Braun and Bugnyar 2012). Bonded birds support each other in conflicts with other birds and console each other (e.g., via preening and contact sitting with the partner) after conflicts (Fraser and Bugnyar 2010).

Epimeletic Behavior

Consolation of an individual who has lost a fight is rare in animal societies but characteristic of species with large relative brain size (van Horik et al. 2012). Even rarer is tending to wounded animals or individuals that have died. Along with intense, long-lasting bonds, there appears to be a special recognition of the value of the individual that is expressed in care for conspecifics who may not even be kin and in what looks like mourning behavior for deceased group members.

Chimpanzees

Alliance partners in chimpanzee society may help each other in aggressive encounters with others or offer consolation after a conflict (e.g., via grooming or sitting near the victim; Romero and de Waal 2010). Consolers may be kin or allied nonkin. The quality of the relationship, as measured by previous affiliative behavior, affects the frequency of consolation. Wounds may be inflicted by either another chimpanzee or a predator. In the Taï forest, leopards are a major predator which waits in ambush for chimpanzees. Wounded individuals who have escaped attack may be cared for by anyone in the troop, regardless of kinship. Aid may include licking wounds with saliva (which has antibiotic properties), removing dirt, and chasing away flies (Boesch 2012).

Care is also extended to orphans, who may not be kin, suggesting that the individual is valued regardless of genetic relatedness. Of 18 adoptions reported in the Taï forest, half were by males, of which only one was the sire (Boesch et al. 2010). This is especially unusual since males in this polygynous society normally show little paternal behavior. Caring behavior includes carrying the infant and sharing food and the nest at night, and it may extend over several years. The value of the individual may also be evident in attitudes toward death. When a 10-year-old female died of wounds, males guarded her body for 6 h. None licked her wounds, indicating they understood this state as different from being wounded. Troop members have been observed cutting leafy branches to place over dead bodies; one high-ranking female was found almost entirely covered by especially large branches (Boesch 2012). Similarly, females will continue to carry dead infants for days, even when the body has become swollen and begun to smell (Boesch and Boesch-Achermann 2000). At Gombe, a mother was recorded carrying a 2.6-year-old for 19 days after death, and another mother held a 1.2-year-old for 68 days after death (Biro et al. 2010b).

Dolphins

Caregiving in dolphins is extended to nonrelatives and even to other species (Connor and Norris 1982). Supporting behavior often involves lifting a sick or wounded dolphin to the surface to breathe (Connor and Norris 1982). In an experiment with bottlenose dolphins, a young male received an overdose of Nembutal and developed breathing difficulties. Two females supported him at the surface for more than 20 min until he was able to swim on his own; only one of the females was believed to be related to him (Caldwell and Caldwell 1966). A report from the wild relates an incident when dynamite exploded near a school of dolphins, stunning one of them. Two adult males supported him at the surface, and when they needed to catch a breath, other adult pairs took their places until the male could swim on his own (Caldwell and Caldwell 1966).

Female bottlenose dolphins have been reported to carry dead calves on their rostra, both in the wild and in captivity. A female who lost her calf a day after birth circled him for an hour and a half, repeatedly lifting his body to the surface and making whistling sounds (Wells 1991). A report from South Africa cited two dolphins who repeatedly lifted a dead calf to the surface (Cockcroft and Sauer 1990). While these reports of caregiving in dolphins are anecdotal, Connor and Norris (1982) claim the evidence "…is so common as to be overwhelming in its broad detail" (p. 372).

Elephants

Elephants go to great lengths to help stricken members of their group. In an incident in which an African elephant had been shot, two family members got on either side of her to help her stand up. When she fell over nevertheless, they tried to lift her to a sitting position by working their tusks under her back and head (Moss 1988). Similar helping behavior has been observed between unrelated matriarchs (Hart et al. 2008), and in removing foreign objects from wounded companions (Bates et al. 2008a).

Elephants appear to have a unique sense of death. Elephants are famously attracted to bones of their own species (Moss 1988). McComb et al. (2006) presented 17 different family groups of wild African elephants with a choice of the skulls of an elephant, buffalo, and rhino. Subjects showed nearly twice as much interest in the elephant skull compared to the other species, but did not differ in their choice to examine either the buffalo or rhino skulls. When an African elephant was shot and killed, family members stood around her and kept vigil through the night, only moving on the next day. Some sprinkled loose dirt on her body and others broke branches from bushes and nearly covered her entire body with them (Douglas-Hamilton et al. 2006). Payne (2003) describes the reactions of 129 visitors to the body of a recently deceased African elephant calf in the wild. One hundred and twenty eight changed their behavior in some way (e.g., lifting the body with a trunk or foot, trumpeting, showing guarding behavior) and relatedness did not predict whether males or females visited the body.

Ravens

Ravens show consolation behavior to others who have been in a fight. Within 2 min after an aggressive encounter, a bystander was likely to provide consoling behavior to a victim through preening and sitting closely, during which low soft comfort sounds are often heard (Fraser and Bugnyar 2010; Heinrich 2011). The bystander is likely to be an affiliate from the flock of young ravens that form before they separate into breeding pairs. Ravens also have unusual reactions to other dead ravens. They are fond of the meat of all kinds of birds, but appear reluctant to eat a dead raven. When Heinrich (1999) provided ravens with a dead raven shot by a hunter, they would not touch it. When he gave them a dead, headless crow, they would not go near it either. But when he removed the feathers, head, wings, and legs from a crow, they accepted the meat readily. Apparently, something about the physical resemblance to a dead raven deters them.

Communication

Complexity of communication can be seen as a correlate of complex social relationships. These species have much to communicate to each other, and they do it both vocally and nonvocally. A higher conceptual order appears to be present in some species as shown by the ability to understand syntax within sound communication. Self-expression also comes through the use of appendages: for referential gestures and modification of the environment. The appendage used may be different, depending on the evolutionary histories of these species: a hand, trunk, beak, or rostrum. What seems to be constant is that species with large relative brain size have much to express, both to conspecifics and in manipulation of their surroundings.

Dolphins

Each dolphin develops a distinct signature whistle in the first few months of life that is learned.

Wild dolphins use whistle matching in a kind of imitation, as a way of addressing different individuals up to 580 m away (Janik 2000). In some cases, bottlenose dolphins appear to understand complex sentences and syntax in communicated signals. Herman et al. have trained dolphins with both verbal instructions and sign language. They respond correctly to sentences that include both modifiers and verbs with up to five terms and understand the difference in how they orient their activities when direct and indirect objects are exchanged with each other (Herman 1986; Marino et al. 2008). Dolphins also respond correctly to reversed sentences and to novel word combinations that they have not heard before, and they can generalize classes of objects. The term "hoop," for example, was understood whether the hoop was square, round, larger, smaller, lighter, or darker than the exemplar (Herman 1986; but see Manger 2006). Moreover, dolphins understand the referential meaning of gestures. They can use the rostrum or body alignment to point out an object to a human attendant, and they monitor whether the person is paying attention (Jaakkola 2012; Marino et al. 2007).

Chimpanzees

Goodall (1986) distinguished 32 different chimpanzee calls used to express 13 different emotional states. These calls can be graded in intensity by changes in loudness, pitch, and duration. There are dialect differences across different communities in Africa, reflecting the learned nature of vocalizations (Reynolds 2005). Individuals that join a new troop will gradually take on the accent of their adopted group.

Most remarkable are the language abilities shown by some primates raised in captivity. Typically, they are taught with either American Sign Language or keyboards with symbols for words since the chimpanzee throat is not bent at the right angle that allows humans to produce a wide variety of sounds. Lana, a captive-born chimpanzee, learned to use a keyboard with symbols for nouns and verbs, and was able to generalize familiar terms to new objects. For example, she spontaneously described her first cucumber as the "banana which- is green" and her first orange was termed the "apple which-is orange" (Rumbaugh and Washburn 2003). Similar achievements were noted in a captive-born bonobo named Kanzi who learned hundreds of lexigram symbols and understood complex sentences with syntax so that "pour the juice in the egg" could be distinguished from "pour the egg in the juice" (Rumbaugh and Washburn 2003).

Neither primate nor dolphin vocalizations in nature are known to include syntax. The ability of both species to master instructions of this kind may indicate a general ability to comprehend patterns in nature. There may be innate cognitive abilities that do not appear until they have a cultural context to evoke them. For example, rooks (*Corvus frugilegus*) are not known to use tools in the wild, but readily do so in experiments in captivity (Reader et al. 2011).

The ability of dolphins and chimpanzees to use novel combinations of words and understand syntax indicates the animals have learned in more than a simple associative manner. Their comprehension has some of the key factors that we associate with comprehending language. An arbitrary sound or symbol represents an object in nature. An order of words in a sentence represents an order of actions in the real world. This is symbolic behavior and a form of abstraction by which sounds or symbols and their relationships stand for real objects in the external world.

Ravens

One study of ravens reported 81 different call types, many specific to individual raven pairs (Conner 1985; Heinrich 1999), as well as local dialects in different parts of the USA. A study of food calls of 18 marked wild ravens showed individually distinctive characteristics of pitch and harmonic structure. Playback experiments indicate that ravens can identify particular individuals on the basis of their calls (Boeckle et al. 2012). Besides the familiar harsh caw, ravens will sing for hours in a kind of musical warble (Heinrich 1989). Ravens are one of the few birds that have been recorded to use referential gestures. They may pick up a nonfood item with the beak (e.g., a stone) and show it to a conspecific, who then usually engages in an affiliative interaction (Pika and Bugnyar 2011).

Elephants

Elephants have a complex vocal repertoire that includes rumbles, snorts, growls, roars, barks, and trumpets (Sukumar 2003). At least 30 different calls are reported depending on the social context, including contact calls, distress, alarm, and sexual signaling (Bates et al. 2008b). Elephants also make infrasounds that travel long distances (Shoshani 1997). At least 27 different low-frequency rumbles have been identified (Payne 2003). Playback experiments show that wild African elephants can distinguish acoustic cues in human voices and identify threatening humans by gender, age, and the language spoken by different local tribes (McComb et al. 2014). Besides sound, elephants have complex chemical communication from temporal glands on either side of the head (Sukumar 2003). Eighty different visual and tactile displays have been recorded in elephants. Together with chemical and vocal signals, these offer a rich repertoire of communication between individuals (Bates et al. 2008b).

Dexterity

A high-EQ brain appears to express itself not only in complex communication and highly personalized, multifaceted relationships but also with intricate manipulation of its environment. All four of the species described here have unusual dexterity in dealing with their surroundings, but it comes via very different appendages.

Chimpanzees

There are overall similarities in the neural, skeletal, and muscular anatomy of the hand between chimpanzees and humans (Crast et al. 2009). They have an opposable thumb and independent movement of the other digits, but the chimpanzee thumb is short compared to the other fingers, hindering its maneuverability (Pouydebat et al. 2011). In nut-cracking technology alone, chimpanzees use six different grips in holding hammers and five different hand postures in manipulating the kernels (Lazenby et al. 2011).

Elephants

The trunk is a unique appendage that has been compared to the human hand in dexterity (Shoshani 1997). The end of an African elephant's trunk has two extensions that can hold objects by a pinching method similar to what humans do with an opposable thumb. The trunk can hold objects as thin as a straw or carry up to 600 pounds between the trunk and tusks. There are no bones in the trunk and it is operated by a rich network of muscles and nerves. The trunk of the Asian elephant has about 150,000 muscle subunits along its length (Shoshani 1997). It can be used to break and modify tree branches and throw objects quite accurately (Hart et al. 2001).

Ravens

Like most birds, ravens build intricate nests, but they also use their bills in a variety of ways to manipulate their surroundings. They dig in snow or dirt to cache food, grip and tear meat from carcasses, pry and break wood, and comb and caress the feathers of a conspecific (Heinrich 1999).

Dolphins

Dolphin appendages have evolved to fin-like form, yet they are used with a dexterity beyond that of any known fish. Grooming is an important part of bonding in dolphin social affiliations, as it is in chimpanzee society. Dolphins touch and stroke each other with their pectoral fins in grooming. Dexterity is expressed during sex: foreplay may include stroking with the pectoral fins or flukes, back and forth rubbing of the pectoral fins, and rubbing of the genitalia (Wells et al. 1999).

Imitation

Vocal mimicry is under neuronal control and may have various degrees of plasticity. For some bird species, a song is heard while it is a nestling and then imitated as an adult. Thus, a "template" is stored in memory that the bird tries to match as it matures (Ballentine et al. 2013; Brenowitz 2002). For some species, this song crystallizes at maturity and does not change thereafter. Other species, such as the mockingbird, can go on imitating other birds their entire adult life.

The idea of a template suggests a mental pattern that the bird is trying to match. Plasticity suggests that this is not entirely under genetic control, but involves flexible learning. All four of the species discussed here have flexible mimicry, which accords with a conceptual understanding suggested by other abilities, such as flexible tool manufacturing. That is, the animal appears to have a model in mind and then takes actions to match that mental model. The ability to imitate other species, and even sounds of inanimate objects, indicates an unusual cognitive plasticity in these species.

Dolphins

Dolphins are one of the few mammal species that have both vocal and motor imitation capabilities (Herman 2012; Marino et al. 2008; Xitco et al. 2004). In the wild, each dolphin has a distinct signature whistle and can imitate the whistle of conspecifics, apparently as a way of addressing specific individuals (Janik 2000). In captivity, dolphins can imitate computer-generated sounds, sometimes copying new sounds accurately on the first try. In a study where the computer sound was outside the dolphin's range, she was able to transpose the sound an octave higher or lower while still maintaining the sound contours of the original (Herman 2006).

Captive dolphins are able to imitate complex physical movements demonstrated by either another dolphin or a human model, including analogous movements that suggest a conceptual understanding of the instruction to "mimic" (Herman 2012). For example, when a human demonstrator waved his hand, the dolphin waved the analogous pectoral fin, and when the human walked forward by the side of the pool, the dolphin stood erect on its tail and moved forward by small hopping motions, including reversing direction when the human turned around. Herman (2012) proposes that this shows a conceptual understanding in which the dolphin has an image of its own body and how it can best match the human model.

Ravens

Ravens have a remarkable ability to mimic other birds and sounds from their environment. When missing a mate, they may call out with the partner's own individually specific call (Heinrich 1989). In the wild, they are known to imitate songs of other birds, human speech, and even the sounds of inanimate sources (Pika and Bugnyar 2011), such as sounds similar to radio static and a motorcycle engine. In Olympic National Park, they were observed sitting atop outdoor urinals that had automatic flushing. Elsewhere in the woods, they could be heard making the gurgling sound of water rushing down a drain (Heinrich 1999).

Elephants

Elephants are capable of vocal imitation, an ability that is rare in mammals. One study reports a female living in a camp in Kenya that appeared to imitate the sound of nearby trucks, with frequency characteristics more similar to the truck motor than to elephant calls (Poole et al. 2005). An African elephant living with two Asian elephants in a zoo made chirping sounds characteristic of the Asian species that are not heard in its own species. Statistical analysis showed sound qualities similar to those of its Asian "mentors" (Poole et al. 2005).

Chimpanzees

Young chimpanzees watch older members of the troop, especially their mothers, during nut cracking and learn how to use the tools of the trade (Matsuzawa 2010). It may be debated whether imitation, emulation, or mere social facilitation is taking place during the learning process (Biro et al. 2010). Cultural differences between different chimpanzee troops in the wild, both in how they use tools and the particular food items they process (Boesch 2012), argue for a model-based system where some members imitate others in their group (Whiten et al. 2005).

Mirror Self-Recognition

Mirror self-recognition (MSR), as originated by Gordon Gallup (1970), involves putting a colorless, odorless mark on an animal in a place it cannot normally view directly and testing whether it recognizes that mark on its body in a mirror. All four groups discussed here provide evidence of MSR (corvids in this case are represented by magpies, *P. pica*). Most other species treat the image in the mirror as a conspecific and may react aggressively to it. The different reactions of these four groups suggest something different in their cognition, and it accords with higher level representations that we saw in other areas, such as in tool making and imitation. That is, the animal appears to have a mental image of itself, and when this is compared with what it sees in the mirror, it can tell that something is amiss.

Chimpanzees

In tests with wild-born chimpanzees, marks were put on (during sedation) over the eyebrow and on top of the ear in places not normally visible to the subject without a mirror. After waking up and looking in a full-length mirror in front of their cage, they could be seen touching the marked parts of their bodies and smelling their fingers much more than other parts of their bodies. Other great apes have passed this mark test, but no small apes or monkeys have reliably passed it (Suddendorf and Butler 2013).

Corvids

Ravens have not yet been tested for MSR, but another corvid, the magpie, has passed the test. Five hand-reared adult birds had their eyes shielded while brightly colored adhesive markers were placed on black throat feathers under the bill where they could not normally be seen. For controls, black markers were put on black feathers in the same place. When supplied with a mirror in the cage, birds with bright marks showed repeated self-directed actions, reaching with the beak or foot as though trying to remove the marks. Birds without a mirror, or with black marks on the throat with a mirror, showed little or no self-directed behavior (Prior et al. 2008).

Dolphins

In a test of MSR, two dolphins were marked with nontoxic black ink on a part of the body not normally visible without a mirror. At other times, they were sham-marked in the same way with a marker that left no visible mark. The dolphins spent more time looking at themselves in mirrors in areas where they had been marked than when they had sham marks (Reiss and Marino 2001).

Elephants

Three Asian elephants were tested with a full-length mirror at the Bronx zoo. All showed self-directed movements in front of the mirror. Only one elephant showed clear evidence of MSR after all three had a large white mark placed under one eye and a sham mark under the other eye. She repeatedly touched the white mark, both in front of the mirror and within 90 s after viewing herself in the mirror. This was significantly different from the number of times she touched the sham mark and the number of times she touched that area of her head when no mirror was present (Plotnik et al. 2006).

Summary and Conclusions

All animals must have some sense of self because they are not constantly bumping into their environment, or each other, as they move about. But a response at this level can be built into a simple servomechanism, such as a robot that turns aside when it approaches a wall. It only takes a signal source, receptor, and transducer to interpret the returning signal. Why then should so few species pass the mirror test?

Suddendorf and Butler (2013) propose that it is part of a general capacity to form mental images and compare them. They note that before about the age of 15 months, human children do not pass the MSR test, and the ability to do so appears about the same time that children express embarrassment and shame (Lewis 2011). This suggests the emergence of an image of themselves as it may appear to others as well as a sense of what others are thinking. By comparing the expected image of themselves with what they see in the mirror, they can tell what is amiss. Herman (2002, 2012) suggests a similar mechanism when discussing mimicry in dolphins. When a dolphin gets the instruction to "mimic" a human waving his arms, he waves his pectoral fins, and when told to mimic a human slapping his legs against the water, he slaps his tail in a similar motion. The dolphin appears to have an image of his own body as well as that of the human, and he can compare them to form analogies. He also seems to have a conceptual understanding of the instruction "mimic" because he is not applying it in a literal way, as operant conditioning would suggest, but with the closest conceptual approximation to the instruction. We cannot know what goes on in another animal's mind, but this appears to be the most parsimonious explanation (Herman 2012).

A concept can be thought of as an abstraction from raw data. From viewing a variety of round objects—a peach, an apple, a cherry—one might abstract the concept of a circle. This is a form of feature extraction and neurons are ideally suited to such a task because they can take a large variety of inputs and make yes/no decisions on whether a set of criteria have been met. These behavioral results suggest a hierarchy of circuits. What species with high relative brain size may have in common are extra neurons that can be devoted to higher levels of processing (Jerison 1973, 2001) that can take higher derivatives of the raw data. They are able to see a pattern of patterns, as the abstract idea of a circle might be lifted from the study of many round objects. As the brain enlarges in primate evolution, a larger percentage of cortex is devoted to association areas compared to primary sensory and motor areas (Buckner and Krienen 2013), providing extra neurons for higher-order processing.

Conceptual thinking also seems to be at work in some of the examples of tool use reviewed here. When chimpanzees make tools of just the right hardness to puncture a termite nest, or use one tool to modify another, it suggests a conceptual understanding of the tools and the materials they will be used on (Brewer and Mcgrew 1990; Sanz et al. 2004). It can also be seen in flexible mimicry that is applied to other species and even inanimate objects. There seems to be a conceptual sense of a sound pattern they are trying to match.

While there is a remarkable convergence of behavior in the four animal groups considered here, we should not expect all large-brained species to share the same qualities. Depending on ecology and phylogeny, one set of qualities may be emphasized over another. If indeed a hierarchy of circuits is involved, we may find some species of low relative brain size that have one or a few of these qualities. What we should expect of high EQ species is many of these qualities occurring together. They may also occur in species of lower total brain mass, such as corvids or honeybees (Avargues-Weber et al. 2012), that have high relative brain size for their body size, and use extra neurons to build hierarchical circuits that allow higher levels of abstraction.

The other main conclusion from this survey is that species with high relative brain size have much to express both to conspecifics and in manipulating their environment. We see this in the elaborate communication systems of all four groups and in the unusual dexterity with which they alter their surroundings. The appendage may vary greatly—a hand, trunk, flipper, or beak—but what is constant is a large brain expressing itself. These species also appear to value each other to an unusual degree compared to other species. We see this in care of wounded conspecifics, consolation after fights, and what looks like mourning behavior for deceased members of the group. These species have much to express to conspecifics, form long-lasting, individualized bonds with each other, and appear to value each other highly as individuals.

This interpretation may seem like an exercise in anthropomorphism, but it might equally be called corvidism or dolphinism. We are all *K*-selected, high-information species that use learning and behavioral flexibility as a way to deal with the challenges of a fluctuating environment. We do this chiefly with high relative brain size and an extended period of maturation. This involves high parental investment in individual young, lowered fertility, and an extended lifespan. Humans currently represent the most extreme form of this strategy, but it is emerging in a variety of other species, and is one of the fundamental ways evolution deals with a world in flux. This outlook accords with the view of Darwin who expected cognitive abilities would differ in degree but not in kind between humans and other species (Darwin 1871). An evolutionary view implies that there may be an emergent self in other species that is comparable to qualities of personality we find in humans.

I began by viewing genes and brains as information systems that build up responses to their environment. Culture is a third system that gathers information that can be passed on to the next generation. We saw the rudiments of culture in these high EQ species that, for example, have tool-making techniques that are passed on by social learning. Humans, with the highest EQ of any species, have capitalized on this third method of gathering cultural information, and the amount of data now stored in books, computers, and the Internet vastly exceeds the capacity of any individual genome or nervous system (Sagan 1977). Our dominance on the planet, for good and for ill, is testimony to the power of information to master the vagaries of nature. In this sense, we are not just some peculiar language-specialized primate, but an extension of one of the fundamental strategies of life in dealing with the challenges of a changing environment.

References

Archie, E. A., Moss, C. J., & Alberts, S. C. (2006). The ties that bind: Genetic relatedness predicts the fission and fusion of social groups in wild African elephants. *Proceedings of the Royal Society B-Biological Sciences, 273,* 513–522.

Armstrong, E., & Bergeron, R. (1985). Relative brain size and metabolism in birds. *Brain Behavior and Evolution, 26,* 141–153.

Avargues-Weber, A., Dyer, A. G., Combe, M., & Giurfa, M. (2012). Simultaneous mastering of two abstract concepts by the miniature brain of bees. *Proceedings of the National Academy of Sciences of the United States of America, 109,* 7481–7486.

Ballentine, B., Gkoo, K. W. & Greenberg, R. (2013). *Mechanisms of song divergence between swamp sparrow subspecies. Behaviour, 150,* 1165–1181.

Bates, L. A., Lee, P. C., Njiraini, N., Poole, J. H., Sayialel, K., Sayialel, S., et al. (2008a). Do Elephants show empathy? *Journal of Consciousness Studies, 15,* 204–225.

Bates, L. A., Poole, J. H., & Byrne, R. W. (2008b). Elephant cognition. *Current Biology, 18,* R544–R546.

Bates, L. A., Poole, J. H., & Byrne, R. W. (2009). Elephant cognition in primate perspective. *Comparative Cognition & Behavior Reviews, 4,* 65–79.

Bielby, J., Mace, G. M., Bininda-Emonds, O. R. P., Cardillo, M., Gittleman, J. L., Jones, K. E., et al. (2007). The fast-slow continuum in mammalian life history: An empirical reevaluation. *American Naturalist, 169,* 748–757.

Biro, D., Carvalho, S., & Matsuzawa, T. (2010a). Tools, traditions, and technologies: Interdisciplinary approaches to chimpanzee nut cracking. In E. Lonsdorf, S. R. Ross, T. Matsuzawa, & J. Goodall (Eds.), *The mind of the chimpanzee: Ecological and experimental perspectives* (pp. 141–155). Chicago: University of Chicago Press.

Biro, D., Humle, T., Koops, K., Souse, C., Hayashi, M., & Matsuzawa, T. (2010b). Chimpanzee mothers at Bossou, Guinea carry the mummified remains of their dead infants. *Current Biology, 20,* R351–R352.

Boddy, A. M., McGowen, M. R., Sherwood, C. C., Grossman, L. I., Goodman, M., & Wildman, D. E. (2012). Comparative analysis of encephalization in mammals reveals relaxed constraints on anthropoid primate and cetacean brain scaling. *Journal of Evolutionary Biology, 25,* 981–994.

Boeckle, M., Szipl, G., & Bugnyar, T. (2012). Who wants food? Individual characteristics in raven yells. *Animal Behaviour, 84,* 1123–1130.

Boesch, C. (2009). *The real chimpanzee: Sex strategies in the forest*. Cambridge: Cambridge University Press.

Boesch, C. (2012). *Wild cultures: A comparison between chimpanzee and human cultures*. Cambridge: Cambridge University Press.

Boesch, C., & Boesch-Achermann, H. (2000). *The chimpanzees of the Taï Forest: Behavioural ecology and evolution*. New York: Oxford University Press.

Boesch, C., Bole, C., Eckhardt, N., & Boesch, H. (2010). Altruism in forest chimpanzees: The case of adoption. *PLoS One, 5*(1), e8901.

Boyce, M. S. (1984). Restitution of R-selection and K-selection as a model of density-dependent natural-selection. *Annual Review of Ecology and Systematics, 15,* 427–447.

Braun, A., & Bugnyar, T. (2012). Social bonds and rank acquisition in raven nonbreeder aggregations. *Animal Behaviour, 84,* 1507–1515.

Brenowitz, E. A. (2002). Birdsong: Integrating physics, physiology, and behavior. *Journal of Comparative Physiology a-Neuroethology Sensory Neural and Behavioral Physiology, 188,* 827–828.

Brewer, S. M., & Mcgrew, W. C. (1990). Chimpanzee use of a tool-set to get honey. *Folia Primatologica, 54,* 100–104.

Bromham, L. (2011). The genome as a life-history character: Why rate of molecular evolution varies between mammal species. *Philosophical Transactions of the Royal Society B-Biological Sciences, 366,* 2503–2513.

Buckner, R. L., & Krienen, F. M. (2013). The evolution of distributed association networks in the human brain. *Trends in Cognitive Sciences, 17,* 648–665.

Byrne, R. W., & Corp, N. (2004). Neocortex size predicts deception rate in primates. *Proceedings of the Royal Society B-Biological Sciences, 271,* 1693–1699.

Caldwell, M. C., & Caldwell, D. K. (1966). Epimeletic (caregiving) behavior in Cetacea. In K. S. Norris & American Institute of Biological Sciences (Eds.), *Whales, dolphins, and porpoises* (pp. 755–789). Berkeley: University of California Press.

Cherry, L. M., Case, S. M., Kunkel, J. G., Wyles, J. S., & Wilson, A. C. (1982). Body shape metrics and organismal evolution. *Evolution, 36,* 914–933.

Cockcroft, V. G., & Sauer, W. (1990). Observed and inferred epimeletic (nurturant) behaviour in bottlenose dolphins. *Aqatic mammals, 16*(1), 31–32.

Conner, R. N. (1985). Vocalizations of common ravens in Virginia. *Condor, 87,* 379–388.

Connor, R. C. (2007). Dolphin social intelligence: Complex alliance relationships in bottlenose dolphins and a consideration of selective environments for extreme brain size evolution in mammals. *Philosophical Transactions of the Royal Society B-Biological Sciences, 362,* 587–602.

Connor, R. C., & Norris, K. S. (1982). Are dolphins reciprocal altruists. *American Naturalist, 119,* 358–374.

Connor, R. C., Heithaus, M. R., & Barre, L. M. (2001). Complex social structure, alliance stability and mating access in a bottlenose dolphin 'super-alliance'. *Proceedings of the Royal Society B-Biological Sciences, 268,* 263–267.

Crast, J., Fragaszy, D., Hayashi, M., & Matsuzawa, T. (2009). Dynamic in-hand movements in adult and young juvenile chimpanzees (Pan troglodytes). *American Journal of Physical Anthropology, 138,* 274–285.

Darwin, C. (1871). *The descent of man, and selection in relation to sex*. London: J. Murray.

Deaner, R. O., Isler, K., Burkart, J., & van Schaik, C. (2007). Overall brain size, and not encephalization quotient, best predicts cognitive ability across non-human primates. *Brain Behavior and Evolution, 70,* 115–124.

de Waal, F. B. M. (1996). *Good natured: The origins of right and wrong in humans and other animals*. Cambridge: Harvard University Press.

Douglas-Hamilton, I., Bhalla, S., Wittemyer, G., & Vollrath, F. (2006). Behavioural reactions of elephants towards a dying and deceased matriarch. *Applied Animal Behaviour Science, 100,* 87–102.

Dunbar, R. I. M. (1998). The social brain hypothesis. *Evolutionary Anthropology, 6,* 178–190.

Dunbar, R. I., & Shultz, S. (2007). Evolution in the social brain. *Science, 317,* 1344–1347.

Eisenberg, J. F. (1981). *The mammalian radiations: An analysis of trends in evolution, adaptation, and behavior*. Chicago: University of Chicago Press.

Emery, N. J. (2006). Cognitive ornithology: The evolution of avian intelligence. *Philosophical Transactions of the Royal Society B-Biological Sciences, 361,* 23–43.

Emery, N. J., & Clayton, N. S. (2004). The mentality of crows: Convergent evolution of intelligence in corvids and apes. *Science, 306,* 1903–1907.

Finarelli, J. A. (2011). Estimating endocranial volume from the outside of the skull in Artiodactyla. *Journal of Mammalogy, 92,* 200–212.

Finarelli, J. A., & Flynn, J. J. (2009). Brain-size evolution and sociality in Carnivora. *Proceedings of the National Academy of Sciences of the United States of America, 106,* 9345–9349.

Fraser, O. N., & Bugnyar, T. (2010). Do ravens show consolation? Responses to distressed others. *PLoS One, 5, e10605*.

Gallup, G. G. (1970). Chimpanzees: Self-recognition. *Science, 167,* 86–87.

Gonzalez-Lagos, C., Sol, D., & Reader, S. M. (2010). Large-brained mammals live longer. *Journal of Evolutionary Biology, 23,* 1064–1074.

Goodall, J. (1986). *The chimpanzees of Gombe: Patterns of behavior*. Cambridge: Belknap Press of Harvard University Press.

Hakeem, A. Y., Sherwood, C. C., Bonar, C. J., Butti, C., Hof, P. R., & Allman, J. M. (2009). Von economo neurons in the elephant brain. *Anatomical Record-Advances in Integrative Anatomy and Evolutionary Biology, 292,* 242–248.

Hart, B. L., Hart, L. A., McCoy, M., & Sarath, C. R. (2001). Cognitive behaviour in Asian elephants: Use and modification of branches for fly switching. *Animal Behaviour, 62,* 839–847.

Hart, B. L., Hart, L. A., & Pinter-Wollman, N. (2008). Large brains and cognition: Where do elephants fit in? *Neuroscience and Biobehavioral Reviews, 32,* 86–98.
Heinrich, B. (1989). *Ravens in winter*. New York: Summit Books.
Heinrich, B. (1999). *Mind of the raven: Investigations and adventures with wolf-birds* (1st ed.). New York: Cliff Street Books.
Heinrich, B. (2011). Conflict, cooperation, and cognition in the Common Raven. *Advances in the Study of Behavior, 43,* 189–237.
Herculano-Houzel, S. (2012). The remarkable, yet not extraordinary, human brain as a scaled-up primate brain and its associated cost. *Proceedings of the National Academy of Sciences of the United States of America, 109,* 10661–10668.
Herman, L. M. (1986). Cognition and language competencies in bottlenosed dolphins. In R. J. Schusterman, J. A. Thomas, F. G. Wood, & Hubbs Marine Research Institute (Eds.), *Dolphin cognition and behavior: A comparative approach* (pp. 221–252). Hillsdale: L. Erlbaum Associates.
Herman, L. M. (2002). Vocal, social, and self-imitation by bottlenosed dolphins. In C. L. Nehaniv & K. Dautenhahn (Eds.), *Imitation in animals and artifacts* (pp. 63–108). Cambridge: MIT Press.
Herman, L. M. (2006). Intelligence and rational behavior in bottlenosed dolphins. In S. L. Hurley & M. Nudds (Eds.), *Rational animals?* (pp. 239–267). New York: Oxford University Press.
Herman, L. M. (2012). Body and self in dolphins. *Consciousness and Cognition, 21,* 526–545.
Hunt, G. R. (2000). Human-like, population-level specialization in the manufacture of pandanus tools by New Caledonian crows Corvus moneduloides. *Proceedings of the Royal Society B-Biological Sciences, 267,* 403–413.
Hunt, G. R., & Gray, R. D. (2004). The crafting of hook tools by wild New Caledonian crows. *Proceedings of the Royal Society B-Biological Sciences, 271,* S88–S90.
Iwaniuk, A. N., Lefebvre, L., & Wylie, D. R. (2009). The comparative approach and brain-behaviour relationships: A tool for understanding tool use. *Canadian Journal of Experimental Psychology-Revue Canadienne De Psychologie Experimentale, 63,* 150–159.
Jaakkola, K. (2012). Cetacean cognitive specializations. In J. Vonk & T. K. Shackelford (Eds.), *The Oxford handbook of comparative evolutionary psychology* (pp. 144–165). New York: Oxford University Press.
Janik, V. M. (2000). Whistle matching in wild bottlenose dolphins (Tursiops truncatus). *Science, 289,* 1355–1357.
Jerison, H. J. (1969). Brain evolution and dinosaur brains. *American Naturalist, 103,* 575–588.
Jerison, H. J. (1973). *Evolution of the brain and intelligence*. New York: Academic.
Jerison, H. J. (2001). The evolution of neural and behavioral complexity. In G. Roth & M. F. Wullimann (Eds.), *Brain evolution and cognition* (pp. 523–553). New York: Wiley.
Lazenby, R. A., Skinner, M. M., Hublin, J. J., & Boesch, C. (2011). Metacarpal trabecular architecturevVariation in the Chimpanzee (Pan troglodytes): Evidence for locomotion and tool-use? *American Journal of Physical Anthropology, 144,* 215–225.
Lee, P. C., & Moss, C. J. (1999). The social context of learning and behavioural development among wild African elephants. In H. O. Box & K. R. Gibson (Eds.), *Mammalian social learning: Comparative and ecological perspectives* (pp. 102–125). Cambridge: Cambridge University Press.
Lefebvre, L., & Sol, D. (2008). Brains, lifestyles and cognition: Are there general trends? *Brain Behavior and Evolution, 72,* 135–144.
Lefebvre, L., Nicolakakis, N., & Boire, D. (2002). Tools and brains in birds. *Behaviour, 139,* 939–973.
Lewis, M. (2011). The origins and uses of self-awarenesss or the mental representation of me. *Consciousness and Cognition, 20,* 120–129.
Manger, P. R. (2006). An examination of cetacean brain structure with a novel hypothesis correlating thermogenesis to the evolution of a big brain. *Biological Reviews, 81,* 293–338.
Mann, J., Sargeant, B. L., Watson-Capps, J. J., Gibson, Q. A., Heithaus, M. R., Connor, R. C., et al. (2008). Why do dolphins carry sponges? *PLoS One, 3*(12), e3868.
Marino, L., Connor, R. C., Fordyce, R. E., Herman, L. M., Hof, P. R., Lefebvre, L., et al. (2007). Cetaceans have complex brains for complex cognition. *Plos Biology, 5,* 966–972.
Marino, L., Butti, C., Connor, R. C., Fordyce, R. E., Herman, L. M., Hof, P. R., et al. (2008). A claim in search of evidence: Reply to Manger's thermogenesis hypothesis of cetacean brain structure. *Biological Reviews of the Cambridge Philosophical Society, 83,* 417–440.
Matsuzawa, T. (1996). Chimpanzee intelligence in nature and in captivity. In W. C. McGrew, L. F. Marchant, & T. Nishida (Eds.), *Great ape societies* (pp. 196–209). Cambridge: Cambridge University Press.
Matsuzawa, T. (2010). The chimpanzee mind: Bridging fieldwork and laboratory work. In E. Lonsdorf, S. R. Ross, T. Matsuzawa, & J. Goodall (Eds.), *The mind of the chimpanzee: Ecological and experimental perspectives* (pp. 1–19). Chicago: University of Chicago Press.
Mauseth, J. D. (1995). *Botany: An introduction to plant biology* (2nd ed.). Philadelphia: Saunders College Publishers.
McComb, K., Baker, L., & Moss, C. (2006). African elephants show high levels of interest in the skulls and ivory of their own species. *Biology Letters, 2,* 26–28.
McComb, K., Moss, C., Sayialel, S., & Baker, L. (2000). Unusually extensive networks of vocal recognition in African elephants. *Animal Behaviour, 59,* 1103–1109.
McComb, K., Shannon, G., Sayialel, K. N., & Moss, C. (2014). Elephants can determine ethnicity, gender, and age from acoustic cues in human voices. *Proceedings*

of the National Academy of Sciences of the United States of America. doi:10.1073/pnas.1321543111.

McGrew, W. C. (2010). Chimpanzee technology. *Science, 328*, 579–580.

Mehlhorn, J., Hunt, G. R., Gray, R. D., Rehkamper, G., & Gunturkun, O. (2010). Tool-making new caledonian crows have large associative brain areas. *Brain, Behavior and Evolution, 75*, 63–70.

Moss, C. (1988). *Elephant memories: Thirteen years in the life of an elephant family* (1st ed.). New York: W. Morrow.

Neubauer, R. L. (2011). *Evolution and the emergent self: The rise of complexity and behavioral versatility in nature*. New York: Columbia University Press.

Patterson, E. M., & Mann, J. (2011). The ecological conditions that favor tool use and innovation in wild bottlenose dolphins (Tursiops sp.). *PLoS One, 6*(7), e22243.

Payne, K. (2003). Sources of social complexity in the three elephant species. In F. B. M. de Waal & P. L. Tyack (Eds.), *Animal social complexity: Intelligence, culture, and individualized societies* (pp. 57–85). Cambridge: Harvard University Press.

Perez-Barberia, F. J., Shultz, S., & Dunbar, R. I. M. (2007). Evidence for coevolution of sociality and relative brain size in three orders of mammals. *Evolution, 61*, 2811–2821.

Pianka, E. R. (2000). *Evolutionary ecology* (6th ed.). San Francisco: Benjamin Cummings.

Pika, S., & Bugnyar, T. (2011). The use of referential gestures in ravens (Corvus corax) in the wild. *Nature Communications, 2*, 560–564.

Plotnik, J. M., de Waal, F. B. M., & Reiss, D. (2006). Self-recognition in an Asian elephant. *Proceedings of the National Academy of Sciences of the United States of America, 103*, 17053–17057.

Plotnik, J. M., Lair, R., Suphachoksahakun, W., & de Waal, F. B. M. (2011). Elephants know when they need a helping trunk in a cooperative task. *Proceedings of the National Academy of Sciences of the United States of America, 108*, 5116–5121.

Poole, J. H., & Moss, C. J. (2008). Elephant sociality and complexity: The scientific evidence. In C. M. Wemmer & C. A. Christen (Eds.), *Elephants and ethics: Toward a morality of coexistence* (pp. 69–98). Baltimore: Johns Hopkins University Press.

Poole, J. H., Tyack, P. L., Stoeger-Horwath, A. S., & Watwood, S. (2005). Elephants are capable of vocal learning. *Nature, 434*, 455–456.

Pouydebat, E., Reghem, E., Borel, A., & Gorce, P. (2011). Diversity of grip in adults and young humans and chimpanzees (Pan troglodytes). *Behavioural Brain Research, 218*, 21–28.

Prior, H., Schwarz, A., & Gunturkun, O. (2008). Mirror-induced behavior in the magpie (Pica pica): Evidence of self-recognition. *Plos Biology, 6*, 1642–1650.

Pryor, K., Lindbergh, J., Lindbergh, S., & Milano, R. (1990). A dolphin-human fishing cooperative in Brazil. *Marine Mammal Science, 6*, 77–82.

Reader, S. M., Hager, Y., & Laland, K. N. (2011). The evolution of primate general and cultural intelligence. *Philosophical Transactions of the Royal Society of London. Series B: Biological Sciences, 366*, 1017–1027.

Reiss, D., & Marino, L. (2001). Mirror self-recognition in the bottlenose dolphin: A case of cognitive convergence. *Proceedings of the National Academy of Sciences of the United States of America, 98*, 5937–5942.

Reynolds, V. (2005). *The chimpanzees of the Budongo Forest: Ecology, behaviour, and conservation* (Oxford biology). New York: Oxford University Press.

Ricklefs, R. E., & Wikelski, M. (2002). The physiology/life-history nexus. *Trends in Ecology & Evolution, 17*, 462–468.

Romero, T., & de Waal, F. B. M. (2010). Chimpanzee (Pan troglodytes) consolation: Third-party identity as a window on possible function. *Journal of Comparative Psychology, 124*, 278–286.

Rumbaugh, D. M., & Washburn, D. A. (2003). *Intelligence of apes and other rational beings*. New Heaven: Yale University Press.

Sagan, C. (1977). *The dragons of Eden: Speculations on the evolution of human intelligence* (1st ed.). New York: Random House.

Sanz, C., Morgan, D., & Gulick, S. (2004). New insights into chimpanzees, tools, and termites from the Congo basin. *American Naturalist, 164*, 567–581.

Sargeant, B. L., & Mann, J. (2009). Developmental evidence for foraging traditions in wild bottlenose dolphins. *Animal Behaviour, 78*, 715–721.

Seed, A., & Byrne, R. (2010). Animal tool-use. *Current Biology, 20*, R1032–R1039.

Shoshani, J. H. (1997). It's a nose! It's a hand! It's an elephant's trunk! *Natural History, 106*, 36–45.

Smolker, R. (2000). Keeping in touch at sea: Group movement in dolphins and whales. In S. Boinski & P. A. Garber (Eds.), *On the move: How and why animals travel in groups* (pp. 559–586). Chicago: University of Chicago Press.

Snell-Rood, E. C. (2012). Selective processes in development: Implications for the sosts and benefits of phenotypic plasticity. *Integrative and Comparative Biology, 52*, 31–42.

Snell-Rood, E. C. (2013). An overview of the evolutionary causes and consequences of behavioural plasticity. *Animal Behaviour, 85*, 1004–1011.

Sol, D., Duncan, R. P., Blackburn, T. M., Cassey, P., & Lefebvre, L. (2005). Big brains, enhanced cognition, and response of birds to novel environments. *Proceedings of the National Academy of Sciences of the United States of America, 102*, 5460–5465.

Sol, D., Bacher, S., Reader, S. M., & Lefebvre, L. (2008). Brain size predicts the success of mammal species introduced into novel environments. *American Naturalist, 172*, S63–S71.

Spocter, M. A., Hopkins, W. D., Barks, S. K., Bianchi, S., Hehmeyer, A. E., & Anderson, S. M., et al. (2012). Neuropil distribution in the cerebral cortex differs between humans and chimpanzees. *Journal of Comparative Neurology, 520*, 2917–2929.

Striedter, G. F. (2005). *Principles of brain evolution*. Sunderland: Sinauer Associates.

Striedter, G. F. (2013). Bird brains and tool use: Beyond instrumental conditioning. *Brain Behavior and Evolution, 82,* 55–67.

Suddendorf, T., & Butler, D. L. (2013). The nature of visual self-recognition. *Trends in Cognitive Sciences, 17,* 121–127.

Sukumar, R. (2003). *The living elephants: Evolutionary ecology, behavior, and conservation*. New York: Oxford University Press.

van Dongen, P. A. M. (1998). Brain size in vertebrates. In R. Nieuwenhuys, H. J. t. Donkelaar, & C. Nicholson (Eds.), *The central nervous system of vertebrates* (Vol. 3, pp. 2099–2134). New York: Springer.

van Horik, J. O., Clayton, N. S., & Emery, N. J. (2012). Convergent evolution of cognition in corvids, apes and other animals. In J. Vonk & T. K. Shackelford (Eds.), *The Oxford handbook of comparative evolutionary psychology* (pp. 80–101). New York: Oxford University Press.

Wasser, D. E., & Sherman, P. W. (2010). Avian longevities and their interpretation under evolutionary theories of senescence. *Journal of Zoology, 280,* 103–155.

Wells, R. S. (1991). Bringing up baby. *Natural History, 8,* 56–62.

Wells, R. S., Boness, D. J., & Rathbun, G. B. (1999). Behavior. In J. E. Reynolds & S. A. Rommel (Eds.), *Biology of marine mammals* (pp. 324–422). Washington, DC: Smithsonian Institution Press.

Whiten, A., Horner, V., & de Waal, F. B. M. (2005). Conformity to cultural norms of tool use in chimpanzees. *Nature, 437,* 737–740.

Wyles, J. S., Kunkel, J. G., & Wilson, A. C. (1983). Birds, behavior, and anatomical evolution. *Proceedings of the National Academy of Sciences of the United States of America-Biological Sciences, 80,* 4394–4397.

Xitco, M. J., Gory, J. D., & Kuczaj, S. A. (2004). *Spontaneous pointing by bottlenose dolphins (Tursiops truncatus). Animal Cognition, 4,* 115–123.

Evolutionary Perspectives on Social Identity

9

Justin H. Park and Florian van Leeuwen

Here is a hypothetical conversation between two psychology students:

"What is identity?"

"I think an individual's identity is made up of their self-concept, which is like a list of attributes they associate with themselves."

"OK. Does the self-concept have any form or structure? Can the list of attributes be organized in any way?"

"There seems to be some organization. Some attributes are related to individual characteristics, such as favorite foods and personality traits; other attributes are related to the groups an individual belongs to, such as nationality and occupation. I think the latter are what psychologists call *social* identity."

"Alright, so what does an individual's social identity do? I mean, assuming that it results from the operation of psychological mechanisms, what do those mechanisms do? What would be their function? We know that we have eyes for seeing and a motor cortex for moving—what are the psychological mechanisms underlying social identity *for*?"

"I think you're asking two separate questions. Regarding what social identity *does,* we can try to answer this by investigating its effects on other psychological processes and behaviors. This is about *how* social identity works. I think we can learn about this by reading the social psychological literature. Your question about what social identity mechanisms are *for* is interesting. You're asking *why* we have social identity at all. I don't know. Let's ask our social psychology professor."

The scientific study of behavior and the mind took an important step forward with the recognition that complete explanations require not only investigations of how mental and behavioral processes work but also analyses of why they may have evolved. In the realm of human behavior, this approach—most vigorously advocated by evolutionary psychologists—has been highly fruitful, not only offering ultimate explanations for many behavioral tendencies but also stimulating the generation of entirely new hypotheses (Barkow et al. 1992; Buss 2005; Dunbar and Barrett 2007). In this chapter, we apply this perspective to the phenomenon of *social identity,* attempting to shed some light on how it works and, more crucially, *why it exists.* To give away the ending, we do not have definitive answers to the why question, but we aim to highlight the sorts of questions that must be asked and issues that must be considered in order for psychologists to move toward a complete account of the phenomenon. Let us begin with a quick overview of phenomena that seem related to social identity and that any good theory of social identity should be able to explain.

Most conspicuously, social identity plays a role in human conflict: Numerous wars and genocides throughout human history have focused on conquering or destroying some "other" people. Such conflicts may take place on the

J. H. Park (✉)
School of Experimental Psychology,
University of Bristol, Bristol BS8 1TU, UK
e-mail: j.h.park@bristol.ac.uk

F. van Leeuwen
Dynamique du Langage, University of Lyon, 14 avenue Berthelot, 69007 Lyon, France
e-mail: f.van.leeuwen.84@gmail.com

V. Zeigler-Hill et al. (eds.), *Evolutionary Perspectives on Social Psychology,* Evolutionary Psychology,
DOI 10.1007/978-3-319-12697-5_9,

scale of nations, tribes, gangs, or families (e.g., Pinker 2011). Analyses of deadly ethnic riots suggest that enraged individuals who are ready to commit atrocities may attend to identity and refrain from harming members of untargeted ethnic groups (Horowitz 2001). Even between nations who are on friendly terms, simply being foreign usually entails restrictions on individuals, such as not being allowed to enter the country, not being allowed to work, not being entitled to the full set of social benefits, and not being allowed to vote in elections, to name only a few. As both authors of this chapter have experienced firsthand, foreignness imposes difficulties when interacting with formal institutions. For instance, not being able to provide standard documentation (e.g., tax return, utility bill) makes it difficult to secure accommodation, open a bank account, obtain health insurance, and sign contracts with utility providers. One can easily imagine the proverbial Martian observing the people of Earth and wondering why people treat those born on one side of an imaginary line so differently from those born on the other side of the imaginary line.

Of course, social identity is not limited to geographical origin, ethnicity, and nationality because it can also be associated with religion, ideology, social status, and occupation. Furthermore, many social identities are associated with rituals—for example, Thanksgiving for North Americans, *Oktoberfest* for Bavarians, *Koningsdag* for nonrepublican Dutch, or pierced-and-barefooted mountain climbing for some Mauritian Hindus (Xygalatas et al. 2013). Social identity can engender feelings of pride (e.g., when your team wins) and anger (e.g., when a foreigner insults your nation) as well as efforts to retaliate against perceived wrongdoings or insults. In addition, people are very curious about other people's social identity. Most people who have migrated or traveled have been asked where they are from. While this may seem trivial, there are many other (probably more informative) idiosyncratic data (e.g., medical or psychiatric conditions, political preference) that seem to have lower priority or are not part of common inquiry at all. This intense interest in social identity can sometimes be problematic; at least anecdotally, many children of immigrants resent constantly being asked where they are from.

Finally, rudiments of social identity are evident across animal species. Many animals appear capable of distinguishing between kin and nonkin (e.g., Buchan et al. 2003; Sherman 1977; Todrank et al. 1998). And nonhuman primates display behaviors suggesting more advanced forms of social identity, distinguishing members of their own group from those of other groups. Observations of an island colony of rhesus macaques revealed that most of the copulations involved members of the same group, whereas between-group interactions were often agonistic (Boelkins and Wilson 1972). Japanese macaques also seem capable of a sense of group membership. Although these monkeys tend to live in groups with overlapping nomadic ranges (i.e., the range of one group overlaps with the range of another group), intergroup contact observed at feeding places frequently involved monkeys driving away members of other troops and responding to attacks on their troop members from other troops (Kawanaka 1973). Similarly, male chimpanzees form coalitions, and they raid other coalitions and attack intruders (e.g., Boehm 1999). As humans seem to possess a more elaborate psychology of social identity than do other primates, any good theory of social identity should be able to account for why human psychology is more—rather than less—entangled with social identity.

Psychological Approaches to Social Identity

As noted above, there are many different kinds of social identity. This implies that people are capable of (and have a penchant for) carving up the social world in multiple ways. To account for the diverse instances of social identification, one approach is to prioritize parsimony and attempt to specify a common mechanism underlying all the varieties of social identity. This approach is epitomized by *social identity theory* (Tajfel and Turner 1979, 1986), which invokes a stripped-down, all-purpose mechanism to explain the antecedents and consequences of social identification. This approach has conferred certain benefits, and it has propelled social psychological research on this important phenomenon. However, just as domain-general approaches to emotions can mask important nuances (e.g., not all "negative" emotions are alike), invoking a general social-identity mechanism may mask important nuances as well. This is because the groups and categories that separate people in the real world are of many qualitatively different types which are often grounded in distinct evolutionary foundations (Park 2012).

Consider the case of gender identity. In all known human cultures, people divide themselves up into sex-based categories and have sex-based division of labor (Brown 1991). While some aspects of gender identification are undoubtedly due to culture, it is likely that heterosexual mating underlies much of the basic perceptions of the two sexes, and it is likely that sex differences in dispositions (e.g., aggressiveness, upper-body strength) give rise to different perceptions of men and women. For most humans, their gender identity may be the earliest developing, most robust, and longest-lasting social identity (Martin and Ruble 2004). At the same time, sex-based identity lacks some of the key characteristics of social identity described above, such as intergroup conflict and segregation (even the most sex-segregated societies are not interested in keeping men and women apart permanently—no society attempts to keep men and women on different sides of a guarded border). It is thus unlikely that psychological processes underlying gender identity overlap fully with those underlying identities based on nationality, ethnicity, religion, etc.

A similar argument might be made for age-based identity, which seems to be distinct from gender identity. Identification with an age group varies across life stages and cohorts (e.g., young vs. old, adult, born in the 1960s). Like gender identity, age identity is not associated with intergroup conflict or total segregation. In contrast to gender identity, age identity necessarily changes over time. For the remainder of the chapter, we set aside gender and age identities (which have qualitatively distinct characteristics) and focus on the type of social identity associated with nationality, ethnicity, religion, and class—which has received the most attention in social psychology and which appears to be a manifestation of *coalitional* (or "tribal") psychology (Cosmides et al. 2003).

Much social psychological research has attempted to understand *groups* (e.g., Reicher et al. 2012). Social psychologists have used this term somewhat loosely, and it is important to distinguish groups (a collective of individuals with a capacity for cooperating toward a common goal) from social categories (the categories or stereotypes individuals employ during person perception and impression formation, e.g., male vs. female, young vs. old, White vs. Black; Brubaker 2002; Fiske and Neuberg 1990; Kinzler et al. 2010) and social identities (those parts of individuals' self-concepts derived from groups and social categories). Whereas most groups may be based on or give rise to social categories, most social categories are not groups (Brubaker 2002). Furthermore, whereas all groups and social categories may give rise to social identities, not all social identities are based on actual groups or commonly employed social categories. Below, we focus on the psychological mechanisms underlying an individual's social identity.

A useful tool afforded by an evolutionary psychological perspective is the "function-to-form" approach, which consists of "reverse engineering" a trait (e.g., Buss 1995; Pinker 1997; Tooby and Cosmides 1992). Consider how the proverbial Martian would attempt to understand a human-engineered system, such as an automobile. One strategy would involve taking it apart and listing the properties of all of its parts (e.g., material, shape, location inside the automobile, and connections with other parts). Another strategy would be starting with a conjecture about the *function* of the automobile. For example, the Martian might conjecture that the function of an automobile is locomotion[1]. The Martian may

[1] For some, it might seem obvious that the function of an automobile is locomotion. However, for a naïve observer, the function may not be obvious at all. The observer may note that an automobile burns fuel, disrupts airflow, makes noise, and sometimes causes accidents, and take

then combine this conjecture with other knowledge and assumptions to formulate hypotheses regarding the characteristics of the automobile and the mechanisms that make it move—its *form*. (For example, knowledge about aerodynamics might be used to formulate hypotheses about the external shape of the automobile, and knowledge of mechanics might be used to formulate hypotheses about the characteristics of those parts of the car touching the terrain.) Of course, during the process of investigating how the automobile moves, the function-to-form approach will benefit from a catalog of all the parts and their properties. However, in the absence of knowledge about function, even the most thorough cataloging is unlikely to lead to a proper understanding of the automobile.

Conjecture About Function: Tribal Social Identity May Be For Forging Group Loyalty

To the extent that social identification involves forming a representation of oneself as a member of a collective, what functions might be served by this process? This question touches on a broader question regarding what functions are served by possessing self-representations at all. Various views have been expressed on this issue, and one influential theory is that humans evolved to experience *symbolic self-awareness,* which allows humans to regulate their own behavior in accordance with expectations regarding the consequences of their actions (Sedikides and Skowronski 1997). A key component of this argument is that symbolic self-awareness allows humans to anticipate how their behavior will impact their social standing—that is, how they are evaluated by others. Given the importance of social acceptance (Baumeister and Leary 1995), it is indeed plausible that a sense of public self (the self as seen by others) became highly developed in humans, along with affective mechanisms—such as the sociometer (Leary 2012)—designed to motivate context-specific adaptive behavior.

Of course, social identity, in its fully fledged form, involves more than a motivation to be socially accepted—it involves a readiness to incur costs for the collective (Van Vugt and Hart 2004). This phenomenon is readily observed in competitive intergroup contexts in which competition drives up both group identification and (potentially personally costly) intragroup cooperation (Van Vugt et al. 2007). The links between social identity, intergroup competition, and intragroup cooperation imply that a key driver of human social identity may be contexts involving competitive (and often hostile) intergroup encounters that have featured throughout human evolution (Bowles 2009). We can thus begin to get a handle on why identification with "tribal" groups (or their contemporary analogues, such as national and ethnic groups) is associated with psychological processes that are largely absent in identification with nontribal social categories (such as genders and ages). In short, tribal social identity may serve the function of solidifying coalitional alliances, allowing members to reap the benefits of intragroup cooperation (and intergroup competition).

The finding *that* group identification is associated with a readiness to incur costs for the collective does not in itself explain *why* reaping the benefits of intragroup cooperation would be contingent on such identification. In other words, it is not obvious why reaping the benefits of intragroup cooperation is facilitated by solidifying alliances and, crucially, what role social identity plays in solidifying alliances. Could not a few individuals simply agree to cooperate on an ad hoc basis? No, because there is a key evolutionary problem: For each of those individuals, there is always a risk of cooperating with cheaters (i.e., nonreciprocators), such that unconditional cooperation is not an evolutionarily stable strategy (e.g., Cosmides and Tooby 2013). A capacity to *signal* coalitional membership and cooperative intent would be beneficial, and social identity may serve this function.

Imagine three individuals, two of whom have already formed an alliance (say, the "Reds"). The

any one of these to be its function. Obviously, different conjectures regarding function (e.g., locomotion vs. fuel burning) yield different hypotheses regarding form.

third individual (X) might want to join the alliance and reap the benefits of cooperation. From the perspective of the Reds, cooperating with X may end up being costly (if X is a cheater). Therefore, X must do something to convince the Reds that she can be trusted to cooperate so that the Reds will allow her to join the alliance. As a start, X can signal to the Reds something like: "I am like you, and I will cooperate exclusively with you." Is there any reason why the Reds would believe in the veracity of this signal? If X publicly signals that she is like the Reds and will cooperate with them, then an alliance that is in competition with the Reds—say, the "Blues"—will have all the more reason to distrust X and will likely exclude X from their alliance of Blues. Thus, by publicly signaling identification with the Reds, X forfeits any potential benefits of cooperating with the Blues. In other words, in an environment of competing alliances, signaling membership (or loyalty) to one alliance carries inherent opportunity costs. That X incurs costs by proclaiming social identification with the Reds thus provides a reason for the Reds to start trusting X. The opportunity costs create an incentive for X to cooperate, as becoming excluded from the Reds may result in X not being part of any alliance. Therefore, social identification may both signal and motivate cooperation.

Importantly, the signaling of tribal social identity need not involve a verbal statement as in the example above. The signals may involve publicly observable characteristics that the individual can modify to some extent, such as dress, language, accent, rituals, and nonstandard beliefs and attitudes, to the extent that the signals entail (opportunity) costs that motivate the individual to remain in the alliance. Given the need to signal potentially shifting alliances, humans are unlikely to have evolved to perceive unchangeable characteristics—such as skin color—as reliable social-identity signals, although they may serve as proxies under certain circumstances (Kurzban et al. 2001). Tribal social identity, then, may be a *self-represented summary of the loyalty-signaling characteristics that one has acquired.* The fact that signals work best when they are "honest" and genuinely internalized (e.g., Von Hippel and Trivers 2011; Zahavi and Zahavi 1997) helps explain why individuals possess social identity that simultaneously imposes costs and motivates behavior.

Predictions About Form: The Psychology of Social Identification

To the extent that tribal social identity serves the function of signaling and motivating cooperation, a number of hypotheses can be formulated regarding its psychological characteristics (i.e., its form). First, as signaling one's loyalties is superfluous in a social environment in which intergroup competition is absent, and as signaling one's loyalties may be especially likely to yield benefits in a social environment with intergroup competition, tribal social identification may increase under conditions of intergroup competition. Second, tribal social identification is likely to lead to discriminatory behavior with regard to alternative groups—not only in-group favoritism but also antipathy toward out-groups. As already mentioned, there is evidence that (perceived) intergroup competition/conflict increases social identification with familiar "tribal" groups (Van Vugt and Hart 2004; Van Vugt and Park 2010). There is also ample evidence that social identification results in discrimination—indeed, this is the focal phenomenon studied by researchers inspired by social identity theory (Brewer 1999). An evolutionary perspective introduces additional nuances to these processes. Most notably, antipathies toward tribal out-groups are specific, characterized by psychological mechanisms that facilitate avoidance and exclusion (Kurzban and Leary 2001; Schaller et al. 2003). More generally, perceived threats from out-groups lead to greater in-group favoritism and xenophobia (Faulkner et al. 2004). Also, consistent with the *male warrior hypothesis* (i.e., males have historically been more highly involved in intergroup conflict, and thus men's psychology is relatively more specialized for intergroup conflict), the effect of intergroup competition on social identification is stronger in men than women (Van

Vugt et al. 2007). We would also expect men to be more frequent targets of social identity–based discrimination, which has been empirically demonstrated (Navarrete et al. 2010).

More speculatively, because the risk of cooperating with cheaters is ever present, there may have evolved psychological features that allow individuals to maximize their fitness gains in cooperative contexts: (a) sensitivity to other group members' levels of loyalty, which can be used to calibrate one's own level, (b) slightly exaggerated perceptions of one's own level of loyalty and commitment, which is readily displayed to others, and (c) tactics intended to increase other group members' levels of sacrifice. In other words, social identification may be strategic, with individuals aiming for beneficial rather than disadvantageous memberships, and being highly sensitive to context.

The idea that individuals may strategically perceive and display exaggerated levels of group loyalty is consistent with recent theoretical perspectives suggesting that the self may be organized in a modular, functionally specialized manner, comprising a part of the mind whose key function is to represent the self in the best possible light, allowing individuals to more effectively persuade others (Kurzban and Aktipis 2007). This perspective proposes that while there may be parts of the mind that represent true beliefs (and serve to influence one's own behavior), there may be parts that hold plausibly distorted beliefs (and serve to influence others' behavior). For example, recent research on social-welfare attitudes suggests that individuals may harbor seemingly contradictory motivations for the purposes of optimizing their own goal-directed behavior while attempting to strategically influence others' behavior to their own advantage. Aarøe and Petersen (2013) manipulated participants' blood glucose levels (with lower blood glucose levels serving as a physiological proxy for hunger) and assessed their attitudes toward social welfare (which are essentially attitudes about sharing) and their actual sharing behavior in an economic game. Hunger increased support for social welfare, but had no effect on sharing behavior (in fact, controlling for social-welfare attitudes, hunger decreased sharing behavior). As such, the manipulation seems to have triggered two distinct psychological responses, one private (reduced intentions to share, consistent with the goal of obtaining resources for oneself) and one public (increased advocacy of sharing, presumably aimed at influencing others' behavior for one's own gain).

Likewise, in the realm of moral psychology, a distinction has been made between moral *conscience* (which regulates one's own behavior) and moral *condemnation* (which specializes in judging others in order to influence their behavior; DeScioli and Kurzban 2013). We suggest that an analogous distinction might be usefully made between "private" social identity (which regulates one's own behavior with respect to incurring costs for the group) and "public" social identity (which specializes in signaling one's commitments to others in order to persuade them to incur greater costs for the group).

A private social identity that motivates cooperation at the risk of incurring costs would be associated with at least three measurable aspects of how individuals *think* and *feel* about social identities. First, individuals should feel that some memberships are more important for them than other memberships, with group memberships that are more beneficial being perceived as more important. Second, individuals should feel greater loyalty toward the more beneficial groups, characterized by greater willingness to incur costs. Third, individuals should feel an increase in the importance of a particular social identity (and increase in willingness to incur costs) if the loss of that membership becomes more costly.

A public social identity specializing in signaling one's loyalties in order to persuade others to incur greater costs for the group would be associated with at least three observable aspects of how individuals *express* their social identity. First, signals of the importance of memberships (i.e., displays of loyalty) need not be highly correlated with the benefits associated with membership. Rather, the expression of loyalties should be a function of both identification with a group *and* whether the situation allows for signals of loyalty to persuade others to incur costs for the group.

Second, similarly, contributions or sacrifice to the group should be contingent on both willingness to incur costs *and* the extent to which the situation allows that the sacrifice persuades others to sacrifice for the group as well. Third, increases in the expression of loyalties and publicly incurring costs for the group should be influenced by the costs of losing the membership for the individual as well as the costs that would be incurred by the individual if others left the coalition.

Furthermore, an important part of social identity may be inflated beliefs regarding the superiority of one's own group. Not only would such beliefs help to solidify private commitment but they would also be enthusiastically expressed to signal one's commitment to both in-group members and competitors. As such, proclamations may be used to influence other group members' behavior; publicly expressed social identity may be associated with especially exaggerated views concerning the superiority of the in-group.

These conjectures point to some intriguing theoretical and empirical implications. Because self-reports of social identification are necessarily "public," previous findings relying on self-reports may have been focused specifically on aspects of social identification related mostly to exaggerated beliefs and persuasion of others. From this perspective, it is not surprising that social psychological investigations of social identity (focusing mostly on the public aspect) have recurrently highlighted positive in-group distinctiveness as a central intergroup motive. It follows that investigations of "private" social identity may require measurements that circumvent self-presentation, such as assessment of anonymous costly behavior (e.g., Aarøe and Petersen 2013).

As noted above, a good model of social identity should be able to explain social-identity phenomena. Indeed, the perspective outlined above permits elaborations that explain several social-identity phenomena. The conjecture that social identity is a (self-represented) summary of individuals' group loyalties seems compatible with the association between identity and intergroup conflict, institutional distrust toward members of out-groups, and individuals' curiosity about others' identity. In addition, the association of identity with traditions and rituals can be explained. Individuals in an alliance might use traditions and rituals as a way to place (opportunity) costs on group membership, and thus increase or maintain loyalty and cooperation (Xygalatas et al. 2013). Because social identity plays a crucial role in cooperation, the observation that humans are more influenced by social identity than are less interdependent primates also makes sense (cf., Brewer 1999).

Alternative Perspectives on Social-Identity Phenomena

Are there alternative perspectives that better account for the phenomena associated with social identity? This is, ultimately, an empirical question. However, we would argue that the function-to-form approach delineated above has an important conceptual advantage over explanations that rely on "intrapsychic needs" (e.g., self-esteem that needs to be protected, maintained, or increased; cf. Tajfel and Turner 1979). Invoking intrapsychic needs raises the more basic question of why humans possess such needs, thus pushing back the explanatory burden. We briefly discuss what we believe is currently the most important alternative theory of tribal social identity.[2]

Optimal distinctiveness theory (Brewer 1999, 2003; Brewer and Caporael 2006) starts from the premise that in-group–out-group distinctions do not always involve competition or conflict, and thus aims to provide an explanation for group identification that does not invoke intergroup competition. As humans rely on cooperation for

[2] There are several influential perspectives that are relevant to social identity and intergroup psychology. One notable perspective is terror management theory (TMT), which explains many human psychological phenomena—including intergroup bias—as resulting from motivations to uphold cultural worldviews (which, in turn, exist to assuage anxieties about death). Interestingly, evolutionary psychologists have attempted to explain many of the TMT-related phenomena as manifestations of coalitional psychology (e.g., Navarrete and Fessler 2005). Thus, this is another example of an explanation relying on intrapsychic needs being updated by a more contemporary evolutionary psychological perspective.

survival, individuals must rely on others for information, help, and resources, and individuals must be willing to share information, help, and resources with others. Such cooperation requires that individuals trust others to cooperate in return. However, trusting others indiscriminately is a suboptimal strategy, as this leaves one vulnerable to exploitation by cheaters. A more optimal strategy would be to trust others contingently on the probability that they will cooperate in return. Social differentiation and group boundaries might be a way for individuals to achieve cooperation, by limiting the costs of trusting indiscriminately. Optimal distinctiveness theory holds that for the purpose of creating cooperative groups through social differentiation, humans have evolved opposing needs for inclusion (assimilation in groups) and differentiation from other individuals:

> When a person feels isolated or detached from any larger social collective, the drive for inclusion is aroused; on the other hand, immersion in an excessively large or undefined social collective activates the search for differentiation and distinctiveness. Equilibrium is achieved through identification with distinctive social groups that meet both needs simultaneously. (Brewer 1999, p. 434)

Optimal distinctiveness theory shares certain assumptions with our arguments outlined above (e.g., that it would be maladaptive to trust indiscriminately, that a more optimal strategy would be to trust others contingently on the probability that they will cooperate in return). However, our perspective differs in the specification of how individuals may determine the probabilities that others will reciprocate. Optimal distinctiveness theory proposes that individuals may use a somewhat crude heuristic to lower the probability of providing benefits to someone who will not reciprocate—that by limiting cooperation to a subset of all available others, individuals may reduce the costs of cooperation and still enjoy the benefits of cooperation (Brewer 1999, 2003). By contrast, our argument outlined above entails more specific proposals regarding how individuals might signal cooperative intent and specify the reasons other individuals might have for responding favorably to such signals. The key difference between optimal distinctiveness and our perspective is that we see intergroup competition/conflict as providing a necessary footing for the evolution of motivations to cooperate with a particular group of individuals (see also Boyd and Richerson 2009; Van Vugt and Park 2010). Also, our perspective attempts to explain why individuals who consider themselves part of a group would be motivated to trust each other. Specifically, it attempts to explain why individuals seeking alliances might be motivated to trust individuals who claim to be or are considered to be in-group members. (In optimal distinctiveness theory, trust is a defining characteristic of in-groups, but it is not explained why this would be so.) Furthermore, the hypotheses regarding the distinction between private and public social identity (with each having a specific function in balancing group contributions and benefits) are novel and not predicted by optimal distinctiveness theory.

To support their perspective, Brewer and Caporael (2006) referred to the findings that in-group positivity does not necessarily predict out-group negativity and that in-group favoritism is often observed in the absence of out-group prejudice. We believe there are a couple of crucial points to note. First, social context matters. It is not the case that all possible “intergroup” situations will give rise to antipathy toward out-groups. Humans likely possess mechanisms allowing them to learn (via socialization in their in-groups) which out-groups are the most insidious and demand vigilance. Thus, even within ecological contexts with multiple coalitional social identities, some out-groups may be distrusted more than others. Second, to say that a key evolutionary cause of in-group cooperation was intergroup competition is not to imply that, at the level of proximate psychological mechanisms, one necessarily should observe a correlation between in-group favoritism and out-group prejudice. While intergroup conflict may sometimes lead to both outcomes, antipathy toward out-groups is expected to be functionally strategic, and thus separable from in-group favoritism.

Additional Issues Highlighted by an Evolutionary Perspective

A key assumption in evolutionary psychology is that the mind is functionally specialized (Barrett and Kurzban 2006). From such a perspective, one would predict that the mechanisms underlying coalitional social identity would be programmed to develop and become calibrated around the time when they are most functional (as it would be suboptimal to invest in the development of these mechanisms when they are not yet useful and when resources can be channeled toward processes more important for survival). Thus, the development of social identity and possible sensitive periods in identity development are topics that fall within the scope of evolutionary analyses of social identity. If the mechanisms underlying coalitional social identity serve to forge group loyalty, then one might predict that the mechanisms underlying coalitional social identity will involve sensitive periods that coincide with when children have their first interactions with peers in the absence of parents (which plausibly is a situation in which they would need to forge alliances themselves, rather than relying on their parents for resources or cooperative benefits). For example, sports fandom—identifying as a supporter of a sports team—seems to be an expression of coalitional social identity (Winegard and Deaner 2010). At least anecdotally, it would appear that fandom develops and solidifies during adolescence (the period of heightened independence from parents). The sports teams that one becomes a supporter of during adolescence (e.g., the Red Sox for a teenager growing up in Boston) seem to be those that one supports later in life, even after moving to a different city. (Note that one could make a similar argument for gender identities developing during adolescence, as from that age individuals might engage in potentially reproductive romantic relationships. However, gender identities actually develop at a much younger age. As this chapter focuses on tribal identities, we only mention this puzzle.) The development of social identity and the presence of sensitive periods may be a fruitful topic for further research.

Conclusion

Psychological investigations of social identity might usefully make a distinction between social identities associated with coalitional ("tribal") groups, such as ethnicity and social class, and identities associated with noncoalitional categories, such as sex and age, as the mechanisms underlying these different identities are unlikely to overlap completely. We have described an evolutionary psychological perspective on coalitional social identity that started with a conjecture about an ultimate function of social identity. In a social ecology with intergroup competition, social identification may involve opportunity costs and, thus, both signal and motivate cooperation. Based on this conjecture about function, we derived predictions about form—the proximal psychology of social identification. Many questions remain. In particular, further research may examine whether social identity involves private social identities (for balancing costs and benefits of group membership) and public social identities (for strategically influencing the behaviors of others).

Acknowledgments We would like to thank Pascal Boyer for his helpful comments.

References

Aarøe, L., & Petersen, M. B. (2013). Hunger games: Fluctuations in blood glucose levels influence support for social welfare. *Psychological Science, 24,* 2550–2556.

Barkow, J. H., Cosmides, L., & Tooby, J. (Eds.). (1992). *The adapted mind: Evolutionary psychology and the generation of culture*. New York: Oxford University Press.

Barrett, H. C., & Kurzban, R. (2006). Modularity in cognition: Framing the debate. *Psychological Review, 113,* 628–647.

Baumeister, R. F., & Leary, M. R. (1995). The need to belong: Desire for interpersonal attachments as a fundamental human motivation. *Psychological Bulletin, 117,* 497–529.

Boehm, C. (1999). *Hierarchy in the forest*. London: Harvard University Press.

Boelkins, R. C., & Wilson, A. P. (1972). Intergroup social dynamics of the Cayo Santiago rhesus (*Macaca mulatta*) with special reference to changes in group membership by males. *Primates, 13,* 125–140.

Bowles, S. (2009). Did warfare among ancestral hunter-gatherers affect the evolution of human social behaviors? *Science, 324,* 1293–1298.

Boyd, R., & Richerson, P. J. (2009). Culture and the evolution of human cooperation. *Philosophical Transactions of the Royal Society B, 364,* 3281–3288.

Brewer, M. B. (1999). The psychology of prejudice: Ingroup love or outgroup hate? *Journal of Social Issues, 55,* 429–444.

Brewer, M. B. (2003). Optimal distinctiveness, social identity, and the self. In M. R. Leary & J. P. Tangney (Eds.), *Handbook of self and identity* (pp. 480–491). New York: Guilford Press.

Brewer, M. B., & Caporael, L. R. (2006). An evolutionary perspective on social identity: Revisiting groups. In M. Schaller, J. A. Simpson, & D. T. Kenrick (Eds.), *Evolution and social psychology* (pp. 143–162). New York: Psychology Press.

Brown, D. E. (1991). *Human universals.* Philadelphia: Temple University Press.

Brubaker, R. (2002). Ethnicity without groups. *Archives Européenes de Sociologie, 43,* 163–189.

Buchan, J. C., Alberts, S. C., Silk, J. B., & Altmann, J. (2003). True paternal care in a multi-male primate society. *Nature, 425,* 179–181.

Buss, D. M. (1995). Evolutionary psychology: A new paradigm for psychological science. *Psychological Inquiry, 6,* 1–30.

Buss, D. M. (Ed.). (2005). *The handbook of evolutionary psychology.* Hoboken: Wiley.

Cosmides, L., & Tooby, J. (2013). Evolutionary psychology: New perspectives on cognition and motivation. *Annual Review of Psychology, 64,* 201–229.

Cosmides, L., Tooby, J., & Kurzban, R. (2003). Perceptions of race. *Trends in Cognitive Sciences, 7,* 173–179.

DeScioli, P., & Kurzban, R. (2013). A solution to the mysteries of morality. *Psychological Bulletin, 139,* 477–496.

Dunbar, R. I. M., & Barrett, L. (Eds.). (2007). *The Oxford handbook of evolutionary psychology.* Oxford: Oxford University Press.

Faulkner, J., Schaller, M., Park, J. H., & Duncan, L. A. (2004). Evolved disease-avoidance mechanisms and contemporary xenophobic attitudes. *Group Processes and Intergroup Relations, 7,* 333–353.

Fiske, S. T., & Neuberg, S. L. (1990). A continuum of impression formation, from category-based to individuating processes: Influences of information and motivation on attention and interpretation. *Advances in Experimental Social Psychology, 23,* 1–74.

Horowitz, D. L. (2001). *The deadly ethnic riot.* Berkeley: University of California Press.

Kawanaka, K. (1973). Intertroop relationships among Japanese monkeys. *Primates, 14,* 113–159.

Kinzler, K. D., Shutts, K., & Correll, J. (2010). Priorities in social categories. *European Journal of Social Psychology, 40,* 581–592.

Kurzban, R., & Aktipis, C. A. (2007). Modularity and the social mind: Are psychologists too self-ish? *Personality and Social Psychology Review, 11,* 131–149.

Kurzban, R., & Leary, M. R. (2001). Evolutionary origins of stigmatization: The functions of social exclusion. *Psychological Bulletin, 127,* 187–208.

Kurzban, R., Tooby, J., & Cosmides, L. (2001). Can race be erased? Coalitional computation and social categorization. *Proceedings of the National Academy of Sciences, 98,* 15387–15392.

Leary, M. R. (2012). Sociometer theory. In L. Van Lange, A. W. Kruglanski, & E. T. Higgins (Eds.), *Handbook of theories of social psychology* (Vol. 2, pp. 141–159). Los Angeles: Sage.

Martin, C. L., & Ruble, D. (2004). Children's search for gender cues: Cognitive perspectives on gender development. *Current Directions in Psychological Science, 13,* 67–70.

Navarrete, C. D., & Fessler, D. M. T. (2005). Normative bias and adaptive challenges: A relational approach to coalitional psychology and a critique of terror management theory. *Evolutionary Psychology, 3,* 297–325.

Navarrete, C. D., McDonald, M. M., Molina, L. E., & Sidanius, J. (2010). Prejudice at the nexus of race and gender: An outgroup male target hypothesis. *Journal of Personality and Social Psychology, 98,* 933–945.

Park, J. H. (2012). Evolutionary perspectives on intergroup prejudice: Implications for promoting tolerance. In S. C. Roberts (Ed.), *Applied evolutionary psychology* (pp. 186–200). Oxford: Oxford University Press.

Pinker, S. (1997). *How the mind works.* New York: Norton.

Pinker, S. (2011). *The better angels of our nature: The decline of violence in history and its causes.* London: Penguin Books.

Reicher, S. D., Haslam, S. A., Spears, R., & Reynolds, K. J. (2012). A social mind: The context of John Turner's work and its influence. *European Review of Social Psychology, 23,* 344–385.

Schaller, M., Park, J. H., & Faulkner, J. (2003). Prehistoric dangers and contemporary prejudices. *European Review of Social Psychology, 14,* 105–137.

Sedikides, C., & Skowronski, J. J. (1997). The symbolic self in evolutionary context. *Personality and Social Psychology Review, 1,* 80–102.

Sherman, P. W. (1977). Nepotism and the evolution of alarm calls. *Science, 197,* 1246–1253.

Tajfel, H., & Turner, J. C. (1979). An integrative theory of intergroup conflict. In W. G. Austin & S. Worchel (Eds.), *The social psychology of intergroup relations* (pp. 33–47). Monterey: Brooks/Cole.

Tajfel, H., & Turner, J. C. (1986). The social identity theory of intergroup behavior. In S. Worchel & W. G. Austin (Eds.), *Psychology of intergroup relations* (pp. 7–24). Chicago: Nelson-Hall.

Tooby, J., & Cosmides, L. (1992). The psychological foundations of culture. In J. Barkow, L. Cosmides, & J. Tooby (Eds.), *The adapted mind* (pp. 19–136). New York: Oxford University Press.

Todrank, J., Heth, G., & Johnston, R. E. (1998). Kin recognition in golden hamsters: Evidence for kinship odours. *Animal Behaviour, 55,* 377–386.

Van Vugt, M., & Hart, C. M. (2004). Social identity as social glue: The origins of group loyalty. *Journal of Personality and Social Psychology, 86,* 585–598.

Van Vugt, M., & Park, J. H. (2010). The tribal instinct hypothesis: Evolution and the social psychology of intergroup relations. In S. Sturmer & M. Snyder (Eds.), *The psychology of prosocial behavior: Group processes, intergroup relations, and helping* (pp. 13–32). Chichester: Wiley-Blackwell.

Van Vugt, M., De Cremer, D., & Janssen, D. P. (2007). Gender differences in cooperation and competition: The male-warrior hypothesis. *Psychological Science, 18,* 19–23.

Von Hippel, W., & Trivers, R. (2011). The evolution and psychology of self-deception. *Behavioral and Brain Sciences, 34,* 1–56.

Winegard, B., & Deaner, R. O. (2010). The evolutionary significance of Red Sox nation: Sports fandom as a by-product of coalitional psychology. *Evolutionary Psychology, 8,* 432–446.

Xygalatas, D., Mitkidis, P., Fischer, R., Reddish, P., Skewes, J., Geertz, A. W., Roepstorff, A., & Bulbulia, J. (2013). Extreme rituals promote prosociality. *Psychological Science, 24,* 1602–1605.

Zahavi, A., & Zahavi, A. (1997). *The handicap principle: A missing piece of Darwin's puzzle*. Oxford: Oxford University Press.

Self-Esteem

10

Phillip S. Kavanagh and Hayley E. Scrutton

Perhaps more ink has been devoted to the issue of self-esteem...than to any other single topic in psychology.
Kirkpatrick and Ellis (2001, p. 411)

The above quote captures the essence of research and writing on the psychology of self-esteem, and, ironically, we are going to devote even more ink to the topic. Self-esteem is not a new concept or area of research by any stretch of the imagination and can be found in some of the earliest psychological writings (e.g., James 1890). Indeed, a simple search on Google Scholar will produce approximately 1.3 million results, with close to 32,000 for the year 2014 alone. Despite this large body of literature, few researchers address self-esteem within an explanatory theoretical framework. While most agree that self-esteem refers to how positively or negatively we evaluate ourselves (our self-concept), after that, the agreement typically stops. The topic of self-esteem is so pervasive that it is not restricted to just psychology—many parents, teachers, retail assistants, talk show hosts, bloggers, and most other people in the population have their own concept of self-esteem. It is not unusual to hear phrases such as "they need more self-esteem" or "I need to protect my children's self-esteem by not letting them fail" spoken on radio talk shows, in classrooms, and in coffee shops, as if self-esteem is a tangible resource that requires saving and protecting. So why is self-esteem so important? What is the role and function of self-esteem? Can we "get" more self-esteem? Can we "protect" it? Evolutionary psychology provides a framework for conceptualizing and understanding the role and function of self-esteem (Hill and Buss 2006; Kirkpatrick and Ellis 2001; Leary and Downs 1995).

An evolved human psyche is not a new concept, having been mentioned in the broader scientific literature for well over a century (e.g., Darwin 1880) and in some of the earliest psychological writings (i.e., James 1890). More recently, contemporary researchers (e.g., Buss 1995, 2004; Cosmides and Tooby 1997) explicitly describe a framework of conceptualizing and explaining human cognitive processes and behavior within an evolutionary psychological framework, with this paradigm slowly gaining acceptance in the psychological arena. The last two decades have been described as "the period of the evolution revolution in psychology" (Geher et al. 2008, p. 8). Indeed, an evolutionary approach to psychology has found its way into most branches of contemporary psychology, from the psychology of intimate relationships (Fletcher 2002) to mental health Nesse 2005). It is not surprising, then, that evolutionary psychology has something to offer in conceptualizing and understanding self-esteem.

P. S. Kavanagh (✉) · H. E. Scrutton
School of Psychology, Social Work, and Social Policy, University of South Australia, Magill Campus, GPO Box 2471, Adelaide, SA 5001, Australia
e-mail: Phil.Kavanagh@unisa.edu.au

V. Zeigler-Hill et al. (eds.), *Evolutionary Perspectives on Social Psychology,* Evolutionary Psychology,
DOI 10.1007/978-3-319-12697-5_10, © Springer International Publishing Switzerland 2015

Fundamentals of Evolutionary Psychology

Before discussing an evolutionary perspective on self-esteem, it is important to keep in mind the fundamentals of an evolutionary psychology approach. At the conceptual level of evolutionary psychology, it is proposed there exists an interplay between adaptive problems, cognitive problems, and neuropsychological processes (Cosmides and Tooby 1997). Alongside this proposition, there are three key premises within evolutionary psychology: domain specificity, numerousness, and functionality (Buss 1995). Domain specificity is the concept that all evolved mechanisms are designed through selective pressures to solve specific adaptive problems. That is, there exist different decision rules for different contexts or environmental problems, as different problems require different solutions. Having one or two global strategies for solving multiple distinct adaptive problems would be maladaptive. Numerousness is the concept that there is more than one psychological mechanism for the various adaptive problems faced by humans; for example, psychological mechanisms for mate selection, assessment of danger, or parenting. Each of these psychological mechanisms is distinct and domain specific. That is, the psychological mechanism for the selection of mates should not be relevant for the assessment of danger; first, because the adaptive problems are different, and second, this would make one or the other of the mechanisms redundant. The premise of functionality is that each psychological mechanism is designed to fulfill a precise adaptive process (Buss 1995). It is these premises that are important to be mindful of when thinking about an evolutionary psychology account of self-esteem.

Sociometer Theory

One of the most influential theories of self-esteem from an evolutionary psychology perspective is sociometer theory (Leary and Downs 1995). While the original intent of this chapter was not to review sociometer theory per se, it is the theory most grounded in an evolutionary psychology framework. By reviewing the research findings associated with premises of sociometer theory, one can have a better understanding of the contributions of evolutionary psychology to conceptualizing self-esteem. Although it has to be acknowledged that there are other evolutionary accounts of self-esteem, such as terror management theory (Greenberg et al. 1986), as MacDonald (2007) clearly articulated, terror management theory does not offer a thorough evolutionary account of self-esteem and lacks parsimony—a key component of a successful theory (see MacDonald 2007, for a full discussion).

The original sociometer research demonstrated converging evidence for sociometer theory by revealing links between perceived social exclusion and state self-esteem (Leary et al. 1995b). This research and the subsequent theoretical chapter (Leary and Downs 1995) were the platforms for the launch of sociometer theory. Sociometer theory (Leary and Downs 1995) was born out of an attempt to answer two fundamental questions that at the time had rarely been considered: (1) what is self-esteem?, and (2) what is its function? Based on his earlier work, Leary had observed that self-esteem was highly correlated with social anxiety, jealousy, loneliness, and depression (Leary 1990, 2003). Along with these observations—and consistent with earlier theorists such as Cooley (1902) and Rosenberg (1979)—Leary proposed that self-esteem is a reflection of an individual's perceptions of how others view oneself. Specifically, Leary proposed that state self-esteem is an interpersonal monitor that had evolved to gauge an individual's level of social acceptance, based on the premise that a key adaptive problem faced by our ancestors was group inclusion. Exclusion from a group could result in reduced survival due to loss of resources and benefits associated with group living. Using the analogy of a fuel gauge in a car, which is designed to alert the driver when to refill, Leary proposed that state self-esteem monitors the environment to alert an individual when social acceptance is low, thus motivating the person to take corrective action—a sociometer (Leary and Downs 1995; Leary et al. 1995b).

In an important extension to the original work of Leary and his colleagues, Kirkpatrick and Ellis (2001) proposed a domain-specific model of sociometer theory. Although acknowledging the merits of the original model, Kirkpatrick and Ellis noted several theoretical weaknesses. They proposed that if self-esteem is a barometer of social acceptance evolved through natural selection, then key premises of evolutionary psychology need to apply to this theoretical mechanism (i.e., domain specificity, numerousness, and functionality). While Leary and Downs (1995) covered the functionality premise within an evolutionary psychological framework, they had not completely addressed the domain specificity and numerousness premises.

Kirkpatrick and Ellis (2001) expanded where Leary and colleagues had left off theoretically by proposing multiple domain-specific sociometers, each designed to monitor acceptance in distinctly different group settings that have their own set of adaptive problems (e.g., instrumental coalitions, mating relationships, family relationships). Kirkpatrick and Ellis did not address the question of exactly how many distinct sociometers there might be, but they did suggest that any group affiliation that is important for human survival may have its own sociometer. Kirkpatrick and Ellis argue that, similar to a dashboard with several gauges, there exist an array of sociometers with each designed to measure inclusion in a particular group and motivate specific corrective action (sometimes automatically) that is relevant to that particular group.

In a further extension of sociometer theory, Hill and Buss (2006) suggested caution when invoking a domain-specific model of sociometers. They argued that in some instances the argument for domain specificity overlooks the fact that some attributes contribute to successfully solving problems across domains. Hill and Buss use the example of social status, which is important in both the mating domain and the coalitional domain. They argue that using a separate mechanism for each self-esteem domain may not be parsimonious.

Hill and Buss's (2006) cautionary note regarding domain specificity offers an explanation for the positive correlations found across self-esteem domains. That is, the extent to which an attribute raises self-esteem in one domain (a reflection of greater social value, hence social inclusion) should be associated with increases in another domain in which that attribute is also valued. However, when valued attributes differ markedly across domains, there should be weak correlations, thus establishing relative domain specificity. One example is physical attractiveness. Physical attractiveness is an important attribute in the mating domain, although it is not nearly as important as other attributes, such as cooperativeness, in the coalitional domain (Cottrell et al. 2007). Hill and Buss's model expanded Kirkpatrick's and Ellis's (2001) approach and provides a framework for predicting specificity versus generality across conditions.

Sociometer Research

A mounting body of research has supported a sociometer theory account of self-esteem. Detailed in the following paragraphs are research findings that directly or indirectly support a sociometer account of self-esteem, organized according to the key premises of evolutionary psychology and sociometer theory.

According to sociometer theory, trait self-esteem is calibrated by experiencing relatively consistent levels of state self-esteem based on feedback from the social environment (Hill and Buss 2006). There is typically a moderate to strong correlation between state and trait self-esteem (Haupt and Leary 1997; Leary 1999a, b; Leary et al. 2001). Levels of trait self-esteem are representative of an idling sociometer (a sociometer at rest). Therefore, it is important to consider both trait and state self-esteem when reviewing the evidence regarding sociometer theory. The research is presented according to the three premises of evolutionary psychology (i.e., functionality, numerousness, and domain specificity).

Evolutionary Psychology Premise: Functionality

Each psychological mechanism has evolved to solve a specific adaptive problem recurrently confronted by our ancestors. For example, to understand how the experiences of rejection and acceptance affect the self-concept, we first need to understand the function of self-esteem. That is, identifying the adaptive problem that a psychological mechanism such as self-esteem has evolved to solve should help us to understand the proximal processes involved in how experiences like acceptance or rejection impact self-concept.

Sociometer Premise: The Need to Belong

A core premise of sociometer theory contends that there is an innate need for humans to belong (Leary and Downs 1995). Belongingness is positively and uniquely associated with self-esteem (Gailliot and Baumeister 2007). Individuals who have a high need to belong (i.e., a high need to experience social connectedness) are more sensitive to and accurate in detecting and interpreting social cues (Pickett et al. 2004). Consistent acceptance leads to increases in self-esteem compared to increasing acceptance, and consistent rejection leads to lower levels of self-esteem compared to increasing rejection (Buckley et al. 2004). Furthermore, rejection versus acceptance from someone who is less familiar with you results in lower self-esteem compared to someone who is more familiar (Snapp and Leary 2001). Ostracism—a form of exclusion—has an impact on both self-esteem and belongingness, with lower self-esteem associated with ostracism (Sommer et al. 2001; Williams et al. 2000) and higher ostracism associated with lower perceived belongingness and self-esteem (Williams et al. 2000). Finally, dominance and acceptance within a group—independent of each other—are also associated with higher levels of self-esteem (Leary et al. 2001). Although dominance within a group (which presupposes acceptance) is important, perceived acceptance within a group accounts for substantially more variance in trait self-esteem than perceived dominance (Leary et al. 2001).

Universal Need to Belong

Any robust evolutionary account of self-esteem also needs to pass the cultural test (Henrich et al. 2010). Although there are differences in the source of self-esteem between Western and Eastern cultures (i.e., individual vs. collective, respectively), the self-esteem motive appears universal (Leary et al. 1995a). Perceived emotional support has a strong effect on self-esteem, regardless of culture (Uchida et al. 2008). For those who identify strongly with their cultural group, people with low collective self-esteem are particularly reactive to evaluations of their cultural group (Downie et al. 2006), suggesting that the sociometer is sensitive to threats associated with collectivist sources of self-esteem. Westerners are more attuned to feedback reflecting social commodities (i.e., traits such as physical attractiveness, popularity, and social skills), as opposed to communal qualities (i.e., personality traits such as kindness, warmth, responsiveness, and honesty; Anthony et al. 2007a), suggesting the sociometer within Westerners is more sensitive to threats associated with individualistic sources of self-esteem. Finally, self-esteem appears most sensitive to rejection when it is accompanied by having one's worldview validated (Gailliot and Baumeister 2007).

Biological Sex

Sex differences are often investigated in the evolutionary psychology literature given the different selective pressures on men and women (Schmitt 2005). The self-esteem literature is no exception and sex differences appear to exist in relation to attributes most relevant to mate value, or relative desirability as a mate. For example, males report lower state self-esteem after competence and status rejections, whereas physical attractiveness is reportedly more important for women (Pass et al. 2010). Further, self-esteem is more attuned to self-perceived mate value in men who pursue short-term mating approaches, as compared to men who were already in relationships or have fathered a child (Penke and Denissen 2008).

Sociometer Premise: A Signal Detection System

According to sociometer theory, state self-esteem acts as an early warning system, alerting the individual to changes in the social environment before exclusion takes place. Research has demonstrated (e.g., Sommer and Baumeister 2002) that people with lower trait self-esteem are more sensitive to changes in the social environment. Further, people with lower trait self-esteem are less likely to join a new social group unless acceptance is guaranteed, whereas people with high self-esteem will join regardless of whether acceptance is guaranteed (Anthony et al. 2007b). Other studies have found that positive regard and acceptance by others is associated with higher levels of self-esteem (Buckley et al. 2004; Leary et al. 2001, 2003; Lemay and Ashmore 2006; Srivastava and Beer 2005), even for people who claim that acceptance by others is not important to them (Leary et al. 2003; Lemay and Ashmore 2006). Finally, self-esteem is sensitive to social cues, such as eye contact (Wirth et al. 2010), with perceived inclusion associated with direct eye contact and perceived exclusion associated with averted eye gaze, leading to reduced self-esteem and lowered perceived relational value (Wirth et al. 2010).

State self-esteem is most sensitive to rejection when others' evaluations are ambivalent (Leary et al. 1998). A history of rejection by others can increase an individual's sensitivity to future rejection, and has been associated with lower trait self-esteem (Carnelley et al. 2007; Srivastava and Beer 2005). While rejection sensitivity may appear a useful tool for low trait self-esteem individuals, it has been associated with negative consequences (e.g., Cikara and Girgus 2010), with people high in social hypersensitivity experiencing greater levels of negative affect. It appears that people with low self-esteem experience an attentional bias towards negative social cues and people with fewer friends display a heightened ability to decode social cues (Gardner et al. 2005). Finally, people with low self-esteem experience more social pain after experiencing ostracism and display more activity in the dorsal anterior cingulate and prefrontal cortices (Onoda et al. 2010), indicating a higher reactivity and sensitivity to rejection based on previous experiences.

Sociometer Premise: A Corrective Action System

The final proposed function of a sociometer, after detecting social exclusion or rejection, is to motivate behavior to avoid or address the threatened exclusion. Along those lines, research findings indicate that after being ostracized, people attempted to counteract the threat to belongingness by conforming to a new group to reestablish a sense of belonging (Williams et al. 2000). The threat of exclusion also leads people to express a greater desire to affiliate with others, form increased positive impressions of other possible social targets, and perceive greater rewards from interacting with new people (Maner et al. 2007). Self-protection is used by people with low self-esteem in the romantic context (Cameron et al. 2010). People with low self-esteem, in their desire to avoid rejection, tend to underestimate acceptance from potential romantic partners as a means of self-protection, whereas people with high self-esteem tend to overestimate their acceptance (Cameron et al. 2010). Finally, the expression of pride may be an indicator to others that a person is deserving of greater social inclusion (Tracy et al. 2010).

The research investigating the associations between self-esteem and various aspects of social inclusion and belongingness, as outlined, supports the sociometer model of self-esteem. People are sensitive to their social environments and the degree of inclusion or belonging experienced, and this sensitivity is reflected in levels of state (and trait) self-esteem. Self-esteem is therefore linked to the degree to which we are socially included or excluded, especially by those with whom we are strongly connected or with whom we identify. Moreover, after inclusionary status is threatened, people take behavioral action to counteract the threat, including withdrawal and seeking inclusion in another group.

Evolutionary Psychology Premise: Numerousness

There is more than one psychological mechanism for the various adaptive problems faced by humans (e.g., mate selection, assessment of danger, parenting) and each of these mechanisms is distinct and relatively domain specific. That is, a mechanism motivating selection of mates should not be relevant for the assessment of danger, for example.

Mating

The mate value sociometer is a mechanism whereby one can track one's relative mate value through experiences of accepted and rejected mating attempts. That is, people face the adaptive problem of securing partners with a mate value that is comparable to their own mate value (Penke et al. 2008). Within the mating domain, there is a strong link between those traits that males and females consider valuable for mating and, therefore, impact their self-esteem. As a result, both men and women experience a decrease in self-esteem after rejection and an increase in self-esteem after acceptance for a potential dating situation, and this in turn influences their mating aspirations (Kavanagh et al. 2010). Men and women experience decreases in self-esteem when they are devalued on mating ideals that are valued in their sex (i.e., status/resources for males and attractiveness/vitality for females; Campbell and Wilbur 2009). Self-esteem is positively associated with mate value for women (Hill and Durante 2009), especially self-perceived attractiveness (Bale and Archer 2013).

Attachment

As sociometer theory presupposes an innate need to belong and form relationships with others, it is plausible that attachment working models or styles (i.e., a family relationships sociometer; Kirkpatrick and Ellis 2001) play a role in the function of the sociometer system, especially since early attachment styles are correlated with adult relationship attachment (Murray et al. 2000). As such, higher levels of insecure attachment predict lower self-esteem, and people with higher levels of anxious attachment are more reactive to both acceptance and rejection (Foster et al. 2007; Srivastava and Beer 2005)—that is, they have more reactive sociometers. Lower self-esteem is associated with negative feedback from an intimate partner for those higher in attachment anxiety (Carnelley et al. 2007), and higher self-esteem is associated with secure attachment (Foster et al. 2007).

Current Intimate Relationships

There is a large literature examining the associations between trait self-esteem and features and processes of current intimate relationships. As such, trait self-esteem is positively associated with relationship satisfaction (Aune and Wong 2002; Cramer 2003a, b; Lemay et al. 2007; Murray et al. 2000, 2001; Shackelford 2001; Voss et al. 1999), playfulness in a relationship (Aune and Wong 2002), sexual satisfaction in a relationship (Barnett and Nietzel 1979), perceived acceptance in a relationship (Cramer 2003a), perceived regard in a relationship (Murray et al. 2000), and marital adjustment (Voss et al. 1999). Trait self-esteem has also been found to be negatively associated with need for approval in a romantic relationship (Cramer 2003a), misperceptions of partner's mood and intentions (Bellavia and Murray 2003), anxiety about partner acceptance, sensitivity to threats (Murray et al. 2002), insecurities about partner's positive regard (Murray et al. 2005), need for affiliation (Rudich and Vallacher 1999), and lower quality relationships (Denissen et al. 2008). These findings are all broadly consistent with sociometer theory. That is, higher trait self-esteem is associated with being included and valued in relationships and with relationship security.

Coalitions

One domain proposed by Kirkpatrick and Ellis (2001) that may have a distinct sociometer is coalitional relationships. Examples of coalitions in a modern context would be friendships, sports teams, or work relationships. Lower levels of inclusion (self-esteem) are associated with lower friendship quality (Denissen et al. 2008). Procedural fairness within an organization is associated with information about relational value (e.g., De Cremer 2003; De Cremer et al. 2004). People with lower self-esteem report self-attributions that are more negative and show less commitment to their organization when there is inconsistent leadership. Leadership inconsistency appears to elicit concerns about one's social worth (De Cremer 2003; De Cremer et al. 2004). Findings from the belongingness literature (Lavigne et al. 2011) suggest there exist two belongingness need orientations—one directed towards seeking relationships for enrichment and personal development, and one seeking others to fill a social void. Individuals in collegial relationships who are seeking belongingness to fill a social void were perceived by colleagues to be less socially accepted and to have lower self-esteem (Lavigne et al. 2011).

Evolutionary Psychology Premise: Domain Specificity

All evolved mechanisms are a product of selective pressures to solve specific adaptive problems. That is, there exist different decision rules for different contexts or environmental problems, as different problems require different solutions. To our knowledge, there are only two studies (i.e., Kavanagh et al. 2010, 2014) that have explicitly tested the domain specificity of the sociometer advanced by Kirkpatrick and Ellis (2001). For sociometer theory to fit in a modern evolutionary psychological framework, calibrations of mate value as represented by mating aspirations should be independent of friendship aspirations, for example. In a critical test of the domain specificity proposition of the sociometer, individuals who were single had their mating self-esteem manipulated by being accepted or rejected for a potential date and had both their mating and friendship aspirations measured (Kavanagh et al. 2010). Rejected individuals reported a decrease in mating aspirations, whereas those who were accepted reported an increase, with this association mediated by state self-esteem. Importantly, however, there were no differences between the rejected and accepted group for friendship aspirations (Kavanagh et al. 2010). Similar findings were reported with participants currently in an intimate relationship (Kavanagh et al. 2014). After experiencing either mating acceptance or rejection from a potential date, those who were rejected reported greater satisfaction and commitment to their current relationship, whereas those who were accepted reported less satisfaction and commitment. Again supporting the domain specificity premise, there was no difference between groups for dedication to their current friendships (Kavanagh et al. 2014).

Conclusions

Sociometer theory provides a comprehensive and parsimonious account of self-esteem from an evolutionary psychological perspective. There is a plethora of research supporting the basic premise that self-esteem is linked to social acceptance and a sense of belongingness. This research provides support for the functionality aspect of sociometer theory. However, what is lacking is research examining other premises (e.g., numerousness) and the extent to which sociometers are domain specific or domain general. We conclude that researchers must continue examining the domain specificity aspects of self-esteem if we are to continue down the path of an evolutionary psychological model for understanding self-esteem. There is already a large literature examining mating relationships and intimate relationships. However, as suggested by Kirkpatrick and Ellis (2001), there are other domains for which gauging one's level of social acceptance is equally important. At the same time, researchers also need to be mindful of the potential overlap across domains (e.g., Hill and Buss 2006).

In sum, sociometer theory provides an excellent framework for conceptualizing and understanding variability and stability in self-esteem, while adhering to the core premises of evolutionary psychology. Nevertheless, like most theories, it requires further testing.

References

Anthony, D. B., Holmes, J. G., & Wood, J. V. (2007a). Social acceptance and self-esteem: Tuning the sociometer to interpersonal value. *Journal of Personality and Social Psychology, 92,* 1024–1039.

Anthony, D. B., Wood, J. V., & Holmes, J. G. (2007b). Testing sociometer theory: Self-esteem and the importance of acceptance for social decision-making. *Journal of Experimental Social Psychology, 43,* 425–432.

Aune, K. S., & Wong, N. C. H. (2002). Antecedents and consequences of adult play in romantic relationships. *Personal Relationships, 9,* 279–286.

Bale, C., & Archer, J. (2013). Self-perceived attractiveness, romantic desirability and self-esteem: A mating sociometer perspective. *Evolutionary Psychology, 11,* 68–84.

Barnett, L. R., & Nietzel, M. T. (1979). Relationship of instrumental and affectional behaviors and self-esteem to marital satisfaction in distressed and nondistressed couples. *Journal of Consulting and Clinical Psychology, 47,* 946–957.

Bellavia, G., & Murray, S. L. (2003). Did I do that? Self esteem-related differences in reactions to romantic partner's mood. *Personal Relationships, 10,* 77–95.

Buckley, K. E., Winkel, R. E., & Leary, M. R. (2004). Reactions to acceptance and rejection: Effects of level and sequence of relational evaluation. *Journal of Experimental Social Psychology, 40,* 14–28.

Buss, D. M. (1995). Evolutionary psychology: A new paradigm for psychological science. *Psychological Inquiry, 6,* 1–30.

Buss, D. M. (2004). *Evolutionary psychology: The new science of the mind* (2nd ed.). Boston: Allyn & Bacon.

Cameron, J. J., Stinson, D. A., Gaetz, R., & Balchen, S. (2010). Acceptance is in the eye of the beholder: Self-esteem and motivated perceptions of acceptance from the opposite sex. *Journal of Personality and Social Psychology, 99,* 513–529. doi:10.1037/a0018558.

Campbell, L., & Wilbur, C. J. (2009). Are the traits we prefer in potential mates the traits they value in themselves? An analysis of sex differences in the self-concept. *Self and Identity, 8,* 418–446.

Carnelley, K. B., Israel, S., & Brennan, K. A. (2007). The role of attachment in influencing reactions to manipulated feedback from romantic partners. *European Journal of Social Psychology, 37,* 968–986.

Cikara, M., & Girgus, J. S. (2010). Unpacking social hypersensitivity: Vulnerability to the absence of positive feedback. *Personality and Social Psychology Bulletin, 36,* 1409–1423. doi:10.1177/0146167210383288.

Cooley, C. H. (1902). *Human nature and the social order.* New York: Scribner.

Cosmides, L., & Tooby, J. (1997, Jan 13). Evolutionary psychology: A primer. http://www.psych.ucsb.edu/research/cep/primer.html. Accessed April 1999.

Cottrell, C. A., Neuberg, S. L., & Li, N. P. (2007). What do people desire in others? A sociofunctional perspective on the importance of different valued characteristics. *Journal of Personality and Social Psychology, 92,* 208–231.

Cramer, D. (2003a). Acceptance and need for approval as moderators of self-esteem and satisfaction with a romantic relationship or closest friendship. *Journal of Psychology: Interdisciplinary and Applied, 137,* 495–505.

Cramer, D. (2003b). Facilitativeness, conflict, demand for approval, self-esteem, and satisfaction with romantic relationships. *Journal of Psychology, 137,* 85–98.

Darwin, C. (1880). *Descent of man, and selection in relation to sex: New edition, revised and augmented.* New York: D Appleton & Company.

De Cremer, D. (2003). Why inconsistent leadership is regarded as procedurally unfair: The importance of social self-esteem concerns. *European Journal of Social Psychology, 33,* 535–550.

De Cremer, D., van Knippenberg, D., van Dijke, M., & Bos, A. E. R. (2004). How self-relevant is fair treatment? Social self-esteem moderates interactional justice effects. *Social Justice Research, 17,* 407–419.

Denissen, J. J. A., Penke, L., Schmitt, D. P., & van Aken, M. A. G. (2008). Self-esteem reactions to social interactions: Evidence for sociometer mechanisms across days, people, and nations. *Journal of Personality and Social Psychology, 95,* 181–196. doi:10.1037/0022-3514.95.1.181.

Downie, M., Mageau, G. A., Koestner, R., & Liodden, T. (2006). On the risk of being a cultural chameleon: Variations in collective self-esteem across social interactions. *Cultural Diversity and Ethnic Minority Psychology, 12,* 527–540.

Fletcher, G. J. O. (2002). *The new science of intimate relationships.* Malden: Blackwell Publishers.

Foster, J. D., Kernis, M. H., & Goldman, B. M. (2007). Linking adult attachment to self-esteem stability. *Self and Identity, 6,* 64–73. doi:10.1080/15298860600832139.

Gailliot, M. T., & Baumeister, R. F. (2007). Self-esteem, belongingness, and worldview validation: Does belongingness exert a unique influence upon self-esteem? *Journal of Research in Personality, 41,* 327–345.

Gardner, W. L., Pickett, C. L., Jefferis, V., & Knowles, M. (2005). On the outside looking in: Loneliness and social monitoring. *Personality and Social Psychology Bulletin, 31,* 1549–1560. doi:10.1177/0146167205277208.

Geher, G., Miller, G. F., & Murphy, J. (2008). Mating intelligence: Toward an evolutionarily informed construct In G. Geher & G. F. Miller (Eds.), *Mating intelligence: Sex, relationships, and the mind's reproductive system* (pp. 3–34). New York: Lawrence Erlbaum Associates.

Greenberg, J., Pyszczynski, T., & Solomon, S. (1986). The causes and consequences of a need for self-esteem: A terror management theory. In R. F. Baumeister (Ed.), *Public self and private self* (pp. 189–212). New York: Springer-Verlag.

Haupt, A. L., & Leary, M. R. (1997). The appeal of worthless groups: Moderating effects of trait self-esteem. *Group Dynamics: Theory, Research, and Practice, 1,* 124–132.

Henrich, J., Heine, S. J., & Norenzayan, A. (2010). The weirdest people in the world? *Behavioral and Brain Sciences, 33,* 61–83.

Hill, S. E., & Buss, D. M. (2006). The evolution of self-esteem. In M. H. Kernis (Ed.), *Self-esteem issues and answers: A sourcebook of current perspectives* (pp. 328–333). New York: Psychology Press.

Hill, S. E., & Durante, K. M. (2009). Do women feel worse to look their best? Testing the relationship between self-esteem and fertility status across the menstrual cycle. *Personality and Social Psychology Bulletin, 35,* 1592–1601. doi:10.1177/0146167209346303.

James, W. (1890). *The principles of psychology* (Vol. 1). New York: Dover.

Kavanagh, P. S., Robins, S. C., & Ellis, B. J. (2010). The mating sociometer: A regulatory mechanism for mating aspirations. *Journal of Personality and Social Psychology, 99,* 120–132. doi:10.1037/a0018188.

Kavanagh, P. S., Fletcher, G. J. O., & Ellis, B. J. (2014). The mating sociometer and attractive others: A double-edged sword in romantic relationships. *The Journal of Social Psychology, 99,* 120–132. doi:10.1080/00224545.2013.872594.

Kirkpatrick, L. A., & Ellis, B. J. (2001). An evolutionary-psychological approach to self-esteem: Multiple domains and multiple functions. In G. J. O. Fletcher & M. S. Clark (Eds.), *Blackwell handbook of social psychology: Interpersonal processes* (pp. 411–436). Oxford: Blackwell Publishers.

Lavigne, G. L., Vallerand, R. J., & Crevier-Braud, L. (2011). The fundamental need to belong. *Personality and Social Psychology Bulletin, 37,* 1185–1201. doi:10.1177/0146167211405995.

Leary, M. R. (1990). Responses to social exclusion: Social anxiety, jealousy, loneliness, depression, and low self-esteem. *Journal of Social and Clinical Psychology, 9,* 221–229.

Leary, M. R. (1999a). Making sense of self-esteem. *Current Directions in Psychological Science, 8,* 32–35.

Leary, M. R. (1999b). The social and psychological importance of self-esteem. In R. M. Kowalski & M. R. Leary (Eds.), *The social psychology of emotional and behavioral problems: Interfaces of social and clinical psychology* (pp. 197–221). Washington, DC: American Psychological Association.

Leary, M. R. (2003). Commentary on self-esteem as an interpersonal monitor: The sociometer hypothesis (1995). *Psychological Inquiry, 14,* 270–274.

Leary, M. R., & Downs, D. L. (1995). Interpersonal functions of the self-esteem motive: The self-esteem system as a sociometer. In M. H. Kernis (Ed.), *Efficacy, agency, and self-esteem* (pp. 123–144). New York: Plenum Press.

Leary, M. R., Schreindorfer, L. S., & Haupt, A. L. (1995a). The role of low self-esteem in emotional and behavioral problems: Why is low self-esteem dysfunctional? *Journal of Social and Clinical Psychology, 14,* 297–314.

Leary, M. R., Tambor, E. S., Terdal, S. K., & Downs, D. L. (1995b). Self-esteem as an interpersonal monitor: The sociometer hypothesis. *Journal of Personality and Social Psychology, 68,* 518–530.

Leary, M. R., Haupt, A. L., Strausser, K. S., & Chokel, J. T. (1998). Calibrating the sociometer: The relationship between interpersonal appraisals and the state self-esteem. *Journal of Personality and Social Psychology, 74,* 1290–1299.

Leary, M. R., Cottrell, C. A., & Phillips, M. (2001). Deconfounding the effects of dominance and social acceptance on self-esteem. *Journal of Personality and Social Psychology, 81,* 898–909.

Leary, M. R., Gallagher, B., Fors, E., Buttermore, N., Baldwin, E., Kennedy, K., & Mills, A. (2003). The invalidity of disclaimers about the effects of social feedback on self-esteem. *Personality and Social Psychology Bulletin, 29,* 623–636.

Lemay, E. P., & Ashmore, R. D. (2006). The relationship of social approval contingency to trait self-esteem: Cause, consequence, or moderator? *Journal of Research in Personality, 40,* 121–139.

Lemay, E. P., Clark, M. S., & Feeney, B. C. (2007). Projection of responsiveness to needs and the construction of satisfying communal relationships. *Journal of Personality and Social Psychology, 92,* 834–853.

MacDonald, G. (2007). Self-esteem: A human elaboration of prehuman belongingness motivation. In C. Sedikides & S. J. Spencer (Eds.), *The self* (pp. 235–257). New York: Psychology Press.

Maner, J. K., DeWall, C. N., Baumeister, R. F., & Schaller, M. (2007). Does social exclusion motivate interpersonal reconnection? Resolving the "porcupine problem". *Journal of Personality and Social Psychology, 92,* 42–55.

Murray, S. L., Holmes, J. G., & Griffin, D. W. (2000). Self-esteem and the quest for felt security: How perceived regard regulates attachment processes. *Journal of Personality and Social Psychology, 78,* 478–498.

Murray, S. L., Holmes, J. G., Griffin, D. W., Bellavia, G., & Rose, P. (2001). The mismeasure of love: How self-doubt contaminates relationship beliefs. *Personality and Social Psychology Bulletin, 27,* 423–436.

Murray, S. L., Rose, P., Bellavia, G. M., Holmes, J. G., & Kusche, A. G. (2002). When rejection stings: How self-esteem constrains relationship-enhancement processes. *Journal of Personality and Social Psychology, 83,* 556–573.

Murray, S. L., Rose, P., Holmes, J. G., Derrick, J., Podchaski, E. J., Bellavia, G., & Griffin, D. W. (2005). Putting the partner within reach: A dyadic perspective on felt security in close relationships. *Journal of Personality and Social Psychology, 88,* 327–347.

Nesse, R. M. (2005). Evolutionary psychology and mental health. In D. M. Buss (Ed.), *The handbook of evolutionary psychology* (pp. 903–927). Hoboken: Wiley.

Onoda, K., Okamoto, Y., Nakashima, K., Nittono, H., Yoshimura, S., Yamawaki, S., Yamaguchi, S., & Ura, M. (2010). Does low self-esteem enhance social pain? The relationship between trait self-esteem and anterior cingulate cortex activation induced by ostracism. *Social Cognitive and Affective Neuroscience, 5,* 385–391. doi:10.1093/scan/nsq002.

Pass, J. A., Lindenberg, S. M., & Park, J. H. (2010). All you need is love: Is the sociometer especially sensitive to one's mating capacity? *European Journal of Social Psychology, 40,* 221–234.

Penke, L., & Denissen, J. J. A. (2008). Sex differences and lifestyle-dependent shifts in the attunement of self-esteem to self-perceived mate value: Hints to an adaptive mechanism? *Journal of Research in Personality, 42,* 1123–1129.

Penke, L., Todd, P. M., Lenton, A. P., & Fasolo, B. (2008). How self-assessments can guide human mating decisions. In G. Geher & G. F. Miller (Eds.), *Mating intelligence: Sex, relationships, and the mind's reproductive system* (pp. 37–75). New York: Lawrence Erlbaum Associates.

Pickett, C. L., Gardner, W. L., & Knowles, M. (2004). Getting a cue: The need to belong and enhanced sensitivity to social cues. *Personality and Social Psychology Bulletin, 30,* 1095–1107.

Rosenberg, M. (1979). *Conceiving the self.* New York: Basic.

Rudich, E. A., & Vallacher, R. R. (1999). To belong or to self-enhance? Motivational bases for choosing interaction partners. *Personality and Social Psychology Bulletin, 25,* 1387–1404.

Schmitt, D. P. (2005). Fundamentals of human mating strategies. In D. M. Buss (Ed.), *The handbook of evolutionary psychology* (pp. 258–289). Hoboken: Wiley.

Shackelford, T. K. (2001). Self-esteem in marriage. *Personality and Individual Differences, 30,* 371–390.

Snapp, C. M., & Leary, M. R. (2001). Hurt feelings among new acquaintances: Moderating effects of interpersonal familiarity. *Journal of Social and Personal Relationships, 18,* 315–326.

Sommer, K. L., & Baumeister, R. F. (2002). Self-evaluation, persistence, and performance following implicit rejection: The role of trait self-esteem. *Personality and Social Psychology Bulletin, 28,* 926–938.

Sommer, K. L., Williams, K. D., Ciarocco, N. J., & Baumeister, R. F. (2001). When silence speaks louder than words: Explorations into the intrapsychic and interpersonal consequences of social ostracism. *Basic and Applied Social Psychology, 23,* 225–243.

Srivastava, S., & Beer, J. S. (2005). How self-evaluations relate to being liked by others: Integrating sociometer and attachment perspectives. *Journal of Personality and Social Psychology, 89,* 966–977.

Tracy, J. L., Shariff, A. F., & Cheng, J. T. (2010). A naturalist's view of pride. *Emotion Review, 2,* 163–177. doi:10.1177/1754073909354627.

Uchida, Y., Kitayama, S., Mesquita, B., Reyes, J. A. S., & Morling, B. (2008). Is perceived emotional support beneficial? Well-being and health in independent and interdependent cultures. *Personality and Social Psychology Bulletin, 34,* 741–754. doi:10.1177/0146167208315157.

Voss, K., Markiewicz, D., & Doyle, A. B. (1999). Friendship, marriage and self-esteem. *Journal of Social and Personal Relationships, 16,* 103–122.

Williams, K. D., Cheung, C. K. T., & Choi, W. (2000). Cyberostracism: Effects of being ignored over the Internet. *Journal of Personality and Social Psychology, 79,* 748–762.

Wirth, J. H., Sacco, D. F., Hugenberg, K., & Williams, K. D. (2010). Eye gaze as relational evaluation: Averted eye gaze leads to feelings of ostracism and relational devaluation. *Personality and Social Psychology Bulletin, 36,* 869–882.

Your Sociometer Is Telling You Something: How the Self-Esteem System Functions to Resolve Important Interpersonal Dilemmas

11

Danu Anthony Stinson, Jessica J. Cameron and Eric T. Huang

Human beings are the quintessential social animals. Through generations of evolution, this aspect of human nature has left an indelible impression on almost every aspect of human psychology, including *the self*: the collection of traits, qualities, schema, roles, beliefs, and attitudes that form the core of one's identity (e.g., Markus 1977). The link between the self and one's social world is fundamental. Cooley (1956) posited that people observe others' treatment of—and reactions to—oneself. The self is then formed through this social "looking glass." Once formed, the self becomes an organizing structure that helps people to make sense of their past experiences, guide present behavior, and predict future experiences (Swann 1987, 2012). These functions are essential for social animals. Success in a social world relies upon one's ability to understand and anticipate others' behavior and reactions to oneself. Although people certainly look to their social worlds to form such vital perceptions, we argue that people also look to the internal world of the self for this social guidance. Specifically, we suggest that humans have evolved a quick and readily available system for understanding and anticipating their social world: the self-esteem system.

Sociometer theory contends that the self-esteem system is an evolved regulatory system aimed at helping people form and maintain high-quality social bonds (e.g., Leary and Baumeister 2000); bonds that were and are essential for survival (Tooby and Cosmides 1996). As such, the motivational heart of the self-esteem system is the fundamental need to form lasting and satisfying interpersonal attachments. This *need to belong* is one of the most basic of human needs, and its satisfaction is essential for normal development (Bowlby 1973), continued well-being (Baumeister and Leary 1995), and maintaining physical health (e.g., Stinson et al. 2008b). Thus, the self-esteem system evolved to help people gain acceptance from others and avoid social exclusion (e.g., Leary and Guadagno 2011). We suggest that the self-esteem system accomplishes these tasks, in part, by providing answers to four pressing interpersonal dilemmas concerning *relational value,* which is one's value as an interpersonal partner: (a) What is my relational value? (b) Should I believe social feedback about my relational value? (c) If my relational value is threatened, should I pursue connection or self-protection? (d) How can I judge the relational value of others before committing to a long-term bond? As we detail below, the self-esteem system helps to resolve these interpersonal dilemmas by monitoring the social world for cues that are relevant

D. A. Stinson (✉) · E. T. Huang
Department of Psychology, University of Victoria,
PO Box 1700 STN CSC, Victoria, BC V8W 2Y2, Canada
e-mail: dstinson@uvic.ca

E. T. Huang
e-mail: huange@uvic.ca

J. J. Cameron
Department of Psychology, University of Manitoba,
Winnipeg, MB R3T 2N2, Canada
e-mail: Jessica.Cameron@umanitoba.ca

V. Zeigler-Hill et al. (eds.), *Evolutionary Perspectives on Social Psychology,* Evolutionary Psychology,
DOI 10.1007/978-3-319-12697-5_11, © Springer International Publishing Switzerland 2015

to each question and then signaling a response. In turn, the signals produced by the self-esteem system in response to each dilemma provoke motivations and behaviors that service the need to belong. Thus, we suggest that the self-esteem system is a multifaceted drive system shaped by evolution to provide humans with the tools they need to successfully navigate their social worlds.

"What Is My Relational Value?"

The self-esteem system services the need to belong, in part, by maintaining an internal barometer of the quality of one's social bonds. This *sociometer* indexes one's *perceived relational value,* which is the degree to which one perceives that one is valued by others as a social partner (Leary and Baumeister 2000). Thus, the sociometer monitors the environment for cues regarding one's relational value. Such cues may come from the external environment in the form of current social feedback from interpersonal experiences. For example, the aloof and rejecting behavior of a coworker during a conversation is real-time feedback suggesting that one has low relational value (e.g., Stinson et al. 2009). The self-esteem system responds to such relational-value cues and provides real-time feedback concerning the quality of one's social bonds (e.g., Leary et al. 1998). The signal produced by the self-esteem system in response to higher or lower perceived relational value is referred to as *state self-esteem* (SSE), which is one's in-the-moment feelings of self-worth or self-directed affect (i.e., feeling good or bad about oneself). If feedback suggests that one's relational value is high, the sociometer signals this desirable state of affairs with positive affect and increases in SSE. In contrast, if feedback suggests that one's relational value is low, the sociometer signals this threat to the need to belong with negative affect and decreases in SSE. There is ample empirical evidence to suggest that social feedback concerning one's relational value prompts changes in SSE (e.g., Leary et al. 1998; Stinson et al. 2008b; Stinson et al. 2010). For example, when participants interacted socially with a cold and rejecting confederate during an experimental session, they reported lower levels of SSE than did participants who had interacted with a warm and friendly confederate (Stinson et al. 2010). This example is consistent with a recent meta-analytic review; across 192 studies of social exclusion, accepted participants reported more positive affect, less negative affect,[1] and higher SSE than rejected participants (Blackhart et al. 2009).

The sociometer view of SSE is unique, in that it not only proposes the specific experiences that will provoke fluctuations in state feelings of self-worth—specifically, experiences that yield social cues concerning one's relational value—but also suggests an adaptive reason why SSE exists in the first place. In the sociometer view, decreases in SSE alert the individual that his or her social bonds are in jeopardy (e.g., Leary and Baumeister 2000; Stinson et al. 2010), a state of affairs that would have threatened ancestral human's very survival. Reflecting the importance of maintaining social bonds, the response of the sociometer to relational-value feedback is biased: Once relational-value feedback becomes neutral or mildly negative, people's SSE has already reached its lowest point and does not become more negative, even as feedback becomes increasingly unfavorable (Leary et al. 1998). Thus, it appears that the self-esteem system does not distinguish between a moderate threat to one's belonging, such as a rebuke from a romantic partner for bad behavior, and outright rejection. For any social animal, both threats to belonging are equally perilous and worthy of attention.

The SSE signal produced in response to relational value prompts motivational and behavioral responses aimed at meeting the need to belong. In two experiments, Murray et al. (2008, Studies 1

[1] Variation in affect as a function of acceptance–rejection may also reflect changes in SSE as a function of acceptance–rejection, at least in part, because many affect measures include items tapping self-directed feelings (e.g., "proud," "ashamed," "nervous," and "guilty," are included in the widely used short-form PANAS (positive and negative affect schedule); Watson et al. 1988).

and 2) demonstrated this process experimentally.[2] Participants in the experimental threat condition recalled a time when their romantic partner had hurt their feelings or had let them down, a task that we suggest constitutes low-relational-value feedback (see also Leary et al. 1998, and Stinson et al. 2010, for similar experimental threats to belonging). Consistent with this interpretation, compared to the control condition, participants in the experimental threat condition reported more hurt feelings (i.e., an affective response consistent with the proposed sociometer response to low-relational-value feedback; MacDonald and Leary 2005). In turn, and again compared to participants in the control condition, participants whose belongingness was threatened were faster to name connection words on a lexical decision task and reported stronger connection goals, results that we believe are consistent with the activation of the need to belong. Hence, the sociometer model of self-esteem not only describes the nature of SSE but also proposes an evolutionarily adaptive function for feelings (i.e., signals) of high or low self-worth: To alert the individual to threats to the need to belong and prompt behaviors aimed at correcting that undesirable state of affairs (see Williams 2007). But what behaviors are prompted by a threatened need to belong? We will return to this question shortly. First, we discuss another pressing interpersonal dilemma: How do people determine whether or not they can trust the relational-value feedback they receive?

"Should I Believe Social Feedback About My Relational Value?"

Relational-value feedback prompts the affective SSE signal without the use of regulatory effort or conscious deliberation (Swann and Schroeder 1995). However, when people receive relational-value feedback, a second, independent, deliberative level of processing also occurs in parallel to the effortless, affective processing of the feedback (Stinson et al. 2010). This deliberation aims to determine whether the relational feedback is trustworthy and believable, and therefore worthy of action. This function of the self-esteem system relies not on the state component of self-esteem but on the trait component. Over time, specific experiences of acceptance and rejection are internalized to form a relatively stable, and global, view of one's relational value, which sociometer theorists call *global self-esteem* (Stinson and Holmes 2010). Individuals with higher global self-esteem (HSEs) feel that they were, are, and will be valued by others, whereas individuals with lower global self-esteem (LSEs) doubt their value as relational partners and project these doubts onto future relationships (e.g., Murray et al. 2000). As with other central aspects of the self-concept (Swann 1987), people rely on their global self-esteem to make sense of their worlds, to explain past social experiences, and to predict the outcome of future social experiences (e.g., Stinson et al. 2010). Thus, not only does sociometer theory describe the nature of global self-esteem but it also implies an important function of global perceived relational value (i.e., to lend coherence and predictability to one's world). One way that the self-esteem system accomplishes this goal is by helping people to evaluate the validity of incoming relational-value feedback.

When feedback concerning one's relational value is detected, the self-esteem system compares the feedback to one's global self-esteem to determine if the feedback is consistent or inconsistent with existing self-views (Stinson et al. 2010). If the social feedback in question is consistent with one's global self-esteem, then, for better or worse, this causes people to conclude that the feedback is accurate and valid. In contrast, if feedback is inconsistent with self-esteem, then this causes people to conclude that the feedback is inaccurate and possibly invalid. For example, in one study, Stinson et al. (2010) provided participants with false feedback from their romantic partner, indicating that their romantic partner either agreed with the participants' own self-views of a particular socially valued trait or viewed the participant much more positively than the participants' rated themselves (i.e., the partner held

[2] The authors offered a different, but related, risk-regulation interpretation of their results, but we think that a belongingness account also fits their data.

positive illusions about the participant; Murray et al. 2001). This feedback constituted relational-value feedback, and thus was either self-esteem consistent or self-esteem inconsistent. Conceptually replicating past research (e.g., Swann 1997), participants rated the self-esteem-consistent feedback as more accurate than the self-esteem-inconsistent feedback. Thus, the self-esteem system helped people to evaluate whether or not they should believe the relational-value feedback by providing a benchmark against which the relational-value feedback was compared (i.e., feedback that deviated from participants' global self-esteem benchmark was deemed inaccurate).

Rejecting self-esteem-inconsistent relational-value feedback is a safe response. Existing self-views reflect years of experience, so one should not change them to reflect new relational-value feedback precipitously. Therefore, although SSE is influenced by any social experience that connotes acceptance or rejection, global self-esteem is more selective. Once solidified around age 12 (Harter 2003), global self-esteem is quite stable during adulthood (Trzesniewski et al. 2003).

However, maintaining one's self-esteem in the face of self-esteem-inconsistent relational-value feedback could have a maladaptive downside. Recall that people rely on their global self-esteem to make sense of their worlds, explain past social experiences, predict the outcome of future social experiences, and even judge the validity of incoming relational-value feedback. Therefore, miscalibrated self-esteem that is grossly out of touch with one's true relational value can have negative social repercussions (Leary and Guadagno 2011; Murray et al. 2003; see Sedikides 1993, for related arguments). For example, incorrectly overestimating one's social value could cause one to attempt to initiate relationships with people who are not interested or trust people who do not have one's best interests at heart. Either one of these possibilities could lead to humiliation, embarrassment, and social pain. In contrast, incorrectly underestimating one's social value is painful by its very nature and could cause one to overlook social opportunities with interested others, initiate or maintain poor-quality relationships, or feel unwarranted insecurities within one's close relationships. Any of these possibilities could lead to depression, anxiety, loneliness, and social isolation. Thus, both overestimating and underestimating one's relational value could lead to negative interpersonal consequences.

Therefore, it is essential that one's chronic global self-esteem is in touch with social reality. So at the same time that the self-esteem system was leading participants in Stinson et al. (2010) study to conclude that self-esteem-inconsistent feedback was inaccurate, another deliberative process was evident in the participants' spontaneous thoughts about the feedback. After receiving the self-esteem-consistent or -inconsistent feedback, participants freely listed their thoughts about the feedback and coders rated the thought lists for epistemic (i.e., knowledge) uncertainty (e.g., "Doesn't make sense?!," "Maybe there is something I never saw?;" Stinson et al. 2010, p. 1006) or epistemic certainty (e.g., "Typical," "I expected it;" p. 1006). Compared to the self-esteem-consistent condition, the self-esteem-inconsistent relational-value feedback caused participants to experience feelings of epistemic confusion and uncertainty. Although participants explicitly declared that the self-esteem-inconsistent feedback was inaccurate, on another, perhaps implicit level, the feedback shook participants' confidence in their self-views. Stinson and colleagues replicated this effect in a number of experiments. Across studies, if the relational-value feedback was consistent with participants' global self-esteem, it provoked comfortable and safe feelings of epistemic certainty and confidence. In contrast, if feedback was inconsistent with participants' self-esteem, then it provoked aversive and uncomfortable feelings of epistemic confusion and uncertainty.

Stinson et al. (2010) suggested that such feelings of epistemic confusion may reflect the first step on the road towards self-esteem change aimed at keeping global self-esteem in touch with social reality. Epistemic confusion feels uncomfortable, and people are motivated to alleviate such discomfort. In a sense, self-verification is the "easy way out" of epistemic confusion, providing a safe and quick way to reestablish epistemic confidence (e.g., Sedikides 1993).

However, what happens when feedback that is inconsistent with one's self-esteem becomes more frequent, especially over a long period of time? For example, if a woman with low self-esteem forms a romantic bond with a partner who has positive illusions about her relational value, then over time, frequent self-esteem-inconsistent feedback from her partner would cause the woman to experience chronic epistemic confusion concerning her relational value. In such a state, the benchmark against which novel relational-value feedback is compared becomes unstable and unreliable. Moreover, one's ability to determine the validity of incoming relational-value feedback becomes compromised, as does one's ability to benefit from the social-predictive function of global self-esteem. The "easy way out" of such epistemic uncertainty is also untenable: What type of relational-value feedback will verify unstable and uncertain global self-esteem?

In such a state of chronic epistemic confusion, individuals may experience self-evaluative motivations that prompt them to seek any and all feedback about the self, regardless of whether it verifies or contradicts existing self-views (Sedikides 1993). In turn, they may relieve the chronic psychological discomfort caused by epistemic confusion by changing their self-views to be more consistent with the feedback they obtain from the social environment. Thus, a woman's low self-esteem might begin to change (i.e., increase) to bring it into alignment with the positive feedback she constantly receives from her adoring romantic partner. By changing her global self-esteem, her epistemic certainty will increase because now the positive relational-value feedback she receives from her romantic partner is self-concept consistent, rather than inconsistent. In line with these predictions, Stinson et al. (2010) observed that participants who received self-esteem-inconsistent relational-value feedback from their romantic partner shifted their self-views to become more positive. Furthermore, Murray et al. (1996) demonstrated that lower self-esteem individuals who are loved by a partner who sees more virtue in them than they see in themselves experienced increases in self-esteem over the course of a year. Thus, the self-esteem system not only includes a mechanism to maintain much needed stability by urging people to reject self-esteem-inconsistent feedback but also includes a mechanism to facilitate change by generating feelings of epistemic confusion. In this way, the self-esteem system maintains its ability to perform important social-regulatory functions, such as determining one's behavioral response to self-threats.

"When My Relational Value Is Threatened, Should I Pursue Connection or Self-Protection?"

Responses to relational threats are not straightforward. As implied by previous sociometer theorists (Leary and Baumeister 2000; Leary and Guadagno 2011; MacDonald and Leary 2005), belongingness is a two-sided coin comprising both the desires to attain acceptance and avoid rejection. These relational *connection* and *self-protection* goals (Murray et al. 2006) exert opposing pressures. Connection goals push people to pursue social rewards, like commitment (e.g., Rusbult 1980), relatedness (Reis et al. 2000), and sex (Muise et al. 2013), that will satisfy their need to belong, whereas self-protection goals pull people to distance themselves from negative emotions (Lemay et al. 2012), real or anticipated rejection (Stinson et al. 2009), and social pain (e.g., MacDonald and Leary 2005). Although connection and self-protection goals are conceptually independent (Murray et al. 2008), they are often linked in everyday life. That is, securing social connections that satisfy the need to belong and yield rewards—such as acceptance, love, and positive regard—usually means exposing oneself to the possibility of rejection and social costs, including humiliation, exclusion, and negative evaluation (e.g., Kelley and Thibault 1978; Murray et al. 2006). For example, self-disclosure increases intimacy between social partners, but it simultaneously leaves one vulnerable to rejection by exposing one's inner thoughts, feelings, or dreams, which can be exploited by an untrustworthy partner (Gaucher et al. 2012). Thus, when both motivations are activated, as they are when one's relational value is threatened (Murray et al.

2008), people experience a motivational conflict between wanting to approach connectedness and wanting to avoid rejection. How people typically resolve this conflict is largely determined by the self-esteem system.

A large body of research suggests that global self-esteem is a key determinant of people's chronic patterns of responding to real, imagined, past, or future threats to their relational value (e.g., Baumeister et al. 1989; Cavallo et al. 2009; Lemay and Clark 2009; Murray et al. 2006; Murray et al. 2008; Wood and Forest 2011). In general, LSEs adopt a self-protective style, whereas HSEs adopt a connection-promoting style of responding to social threats. Therefore, when they experience a motivational approach–avoid conflict, LSEs suppress the goal of pursuing connection in favor of the goal of protecting the self from rejection (Murray et al. 2008). In contrast, the same motivational conflict prompts HSEs to suppress the goal of protecting the self from rejection in favor of the goal of pursuing connection with others. For example, Cavallo et al. (2012; Study 1) threatened participants' confidence in their perceived regard from their romantic partner, and then measured participants' connection motivations. When threatened, HSEs reported greater connection motivations than LSEs. Similarly, Cameron et al. (2010) made salient the possibility of rejection (a threat to relational value), and then measured participants' recall of words related to self-protection. Compared to a no-threat control condition, LSEs recalled more protection words when threatened. In contrast, HSEs appeared to suppress self-protection goals when threatened (see also Murray et al. 2008, Study 7). Thus, global self-esteem plays a social-regulatory role by determining whether people respond to belonging threats with connection or self-protection.

Just as global self-esteem determines signature social motivations, it also determines signature social behavior. Across a wide range of social contexts and for a wide range of behaviors, when relational value is threatened (in either a real or imagined way), HSEs behave in ways that increase closeness to their interaction partner, whereas LSEs behave in ways that protect the self from the rejection that they seem to anticipate. Such self-esteem differences in social behavior are evident in romantic relationships (Murray et al. 2006), platonic friendships (Gaucher et al. 2012), and during relationship initiation (Cameron et al. 2010). Self-esteem differences are also evident for a wide range of behaviors, including communicating with friends (Gaucher et al. 2012), romantic-partner reports of people's critical behavior (e.g., Marigold et al. 2010), group-joining decisions (Anthony et al. 2007a), likeable behavior (Cameron et al. 2010), warm or agentic behavior (Stinson et al. 2012), and directness of initiation behavior (Cameron et al. 2013a). For example, on the day following a conflict in their romantic relationships (a threat to one's relational value), HSEs attempt to repair their relationship by seeking closeness with their romantic partner, whereas LSEs attempt to limit their risk of rejection by emotionally distancing themselves from their partner (Murray et al. 2002). In addition, when the possibility of rejection by one's partner is present during romantic relationship initiation, HSEs use very direct and obvious methods of relationship initiation, whereas LSEs remain cautious and circumspect in their initiation behaviors (Cameron et al. 2013a).

The preceding discussion may lead readers to question the evolutionary adaptiveness of global self-esteem: If global self-esteem is adaptive, how can one explain LSEs' seemingly chronic use of maladaptive, self-protective social strategies (i.e., strategies that likely hurt their social bonds and well-being; Stinson et al. 2008b)? First, we concede that LSEs' self-protective responses to social threats are probably maladaptive if one's goal is to repair a damaged social bond and maximize one's relational value. These are goals that HSEs are likely to espouse. However, if one's goal is to avoid additional damage to one's social bonds and protect oneself from further hurt and social pain—goals that are typically at the forefront of LSEs' minds (e.g., Baumeister et al. 1989)—then LSEs' self-protective response to social threats is indeed adaptive. In fact, given LSEs' diminished resources for coping (Baumeister et al. 2003) and their typically pessimistic expectations concerning the likelihood of acceptance in a given situation (Stinson et al. 2009), self-protection seems especially adaptive. Second, LSEs' signature self-protective behavior is not immutable. Across a variety of social contexts and for a variety of behaviors, when the threat of rejection is absent, and instead the security of acceptance is guaranteed, LSEs will behave in connection-promoting ways (e.g., Anthony et al. 2007a; Cameron et al. 2010; Cameron et al. 2013). For example, when people are induced to think about compliments from a friend in an abstract manner, a technique that bypasses LSEs' typical defenses and allows them to accurately perceive the high relational value conveyed by the compliment (Marigold et al. 2007), LSEs are just as open and self-disclosing as HSEs (a connection-promoting behavior; Gaucher et al. 2012). When the specter of possible rejection is eliminated, LSEs seem to seize the opportunity to safely satisfy their connection motives by engaging in connecting behaviors like self-disclosure (Gaucher et al. 2012), direct relationship initiation behaviors (Cameron et al. 2013), or the pursuit of novel social opportunities (Anthony et al. 2007a). Thus, for LSEs, connection behaviors are most likely to occur in response to strongly positive relational-value feedback and assured belonging, whereas for HSEs, connection behaviors are most likely to occur in response to negative relational-value feedback and threats to belonging.

"How Can I Judge the Relational Value of Others Before Committing to A Long-Term Bond?"

Thus far, we have described how the self-esteem system monitors cues and provides intrapersonal signals concerning one's relational value, how the system determines whether relational-value feedback is valid and thus actionable, and how the system determines motivational and behavioral responses to threats to relational value. Each of these functions relies on *one's own* self-esteem (either state or trait) to resolve important interpersonal dilemmas. However, we suggest that people also rely on *their interaction partners'* self-esteem to resolve yet another important interpersonal dilemma: "How can I judge the relational value of others?"

Determining the relational value of potential interpersonal partners is a crucial social task. Forming a social bond with another person, be it a romantic, platonic, or workplace bond, requires that one invest in that bond. If one chooses well, then one's investment will be returned in benefits afforded by that bond. However, if one chooses poorly, then one's investments into the bond may not be returned, and one's relational outcomes will suffer (e.g., Thibaut and Kelley 1959). Thus, the ability to form an impression of potential partners' relational value early in a relationship would be highly adaptive. Indeed, the earlier such an evaluation can occur, the better. The economics of human relationships dictate that as time passes, investments increase, and increasing investments result in increasing commitment (Rusbult et al. 1994). Hence, the longer one spends in a relationship with a poorly chosen partner, the harder it is to end that relationship, and the greater costs one will incur as a result of the original poor choice.

Sadly, assessing a potential interaction partners' relational value is easier said than done. With the exception of easily observable traits, like physical attractiveness and social skills, evaluating the many traits, skills, and abilities that comprise relational value takes time and a depth of person knowledge that is simply not possible during relationship formation (e.g., Anthony et al. 2007a). For example, the traits most desired in a romantic partner include loyalty and kindness (e.g., Fletcher et al. 2000), yet those same traits take about 9 months to assess accurately (Stinson et al. 2008a). This unfortunate reality creates a "catch-22" situation: People should not commit to a relationship until they can assess a potential partners' relational value, but people cannot assess relational value until they are in a long-term (and presumably committed) relationship.

Humans have developed a few solutions to this dilemma. One solution is that people tend to rely on easily observable traits like physical attractiveness to judge others' relational value

(Anthony et al. 2007b). However, we suggest that humans have evolved yet another solution to the "catch-22" situation of judging others' relational value. To determine the relational value of a potential interaction partner, an observer will rely on the opinion of the person who knows that potential partner better than anyone else: The potential partner him or herself. Thus, an observer will use a *sociometer proxy* to judge the relational value of the potential partner, relying on the partner's own chronic perceived relational value (i.e., global self-esteem) to judge the potential interaction partner's relational value (Cameron et al. 2013). Knowing a potential interaction partner's self-esteem would convey meaningful information about their relational value. People with lower self-esteem are more depressed, neurotic, less satisfied with life (see Baumeister et al. 2003), less healthy (e.g., Stinson et al. 2008b), and more likely to engage in delinquent, antisocial (Donnellan et al. 2005) activities. All of those traits and behaviors are undesirable, suggesting that a sociometer proxy would be adaptive, allowing individuals to avoid undesirable relational partners.

Growing evidence suggests that observers do rely on others' self-esteem to judge others' relational value. For example, observers led to believe that an preferred-sex target has lower self-esteem will conclude that the target is lower in mate value (i.e., sex-specific, consensually desired traits) than an ostensibly higher-self-esteem, preferred-sex target (Zeigler-Hill and Myers 2011). More generally, when explicitly labeled as possessing lower self-esteem, targets are evaluated more negatively on socially valued traits like warmth and competence, compared to their ostensibly higher self-esteem counterparts (Cameron et al. 2013). For example, Cameron et al. (2013) asked observers to rate male and female targets' warmth based on short 1-min videos of very warm and friendly, or cold and aloof, behavior. Importantly, participants were told that the targets had either lower or higher self-esteem. Results revealed a main effect of target behavior, such that targets exhibiting warmer behavior were perceived to be warmer than targets exhibiting colder behavior. But participants also applied the sociometer proxy, rating the lower self-esteem targets as lower in warmth than the higher self-esteem targets, even though the actual behavior of the lower and higher self-esteem targets was identical (indeed, it was the same target in both self-esteem conditions). Thus, observers apply the sociometer proxy even when diagnostic information about particular traits is readily available. People also use the sociometer proxy to make important social decisions. For example, people are more likely to vote for political candidates said to possess higher self-esteem than candidates said to possess lower self-esteem (Zeigler-Hill and Myers 2009), and people anticipate that they will like higher self-esteem-interaction partners more than lower self-esteem-interaction partners (Cameron et al. 2013).

The adaptiveness of the sociometer proxy rests on two assumptions. First, people must possess lay theories of self-esteem that generally map onto the sociometer model; that is, people must be aware that self-esteem reflects one's worth as a person. This appears to be the case. Wikipedia defines self-esteem as an individual's "evaluation of his or her own worth" ("Self-Esteem," 2013), and individuals raised within North American culture can readily relay a similar definition when asked (Cameron and Allary 2013). Second, people must be able to observe and judge others' self-esteem. This also appears to be true. People use a variety of social cues to infer others' self-esteem, including appearance (Naumann et al. 2009), and the possession of socially valued traits (Zeigler-Hill et al. 2013). However, the accuracy of these observations may be questionable. The cues that people utilize to judge self-esteem are not ideal indicators (Naumann et al. 2009). Thus, in both brief interactions (e.g., a three-minute video; Zeigler-Hill et al. 2013) and in long-term relationships (e.g., Lemay and Dudley 2011), observer impressions of self-esteem are only modestly correlated with the actual self-esteem of targets (i.e., correlations around 0.30). However, the sociometer proxy may be calibrated to err on the side of false alarms when detecting low self-esteem, because incorrectly rejecting a higher-self-esteem partner may be less costly than incorrectly accepting a lower-self-esteem partner.

Simple correlations between observer ratings and actual self-esteem cannot detect such a complex model. So, although it is clear that people's absolute judgments of others' self-esteem contain only a kernel of truth, it is still possible that people's judgments of others' self-esteem are adaptive and perform an important social-regulatory function.

Summary

We suggest that the self-esteem system helps people optimize their interactions with others in part by providing answers to four pressing interpersonal dilemmas concerning relational value. First, the self-esteem system assesses one's own relational value by monitoring the environment for cues concerning one's relational value, and signaling high relational value with increases in SSE and low relational value with decreases in SSE. Second, the self-esteem system provides a stable benchmark—in the form of global self-esteem—against which incoming relational-value feedback can be compared, deeming inconsistent feedback to be unbelievable. Yet, self-esteem-inconsistent feedback also causes feelings of uncertainty that may prompt changes in self-esteem if such inconsistent feedback is encountered repeatedly over time, thus keeping global self-esteem in touch with social reality. Third, global self-esteem provides guidance for action, with higher self-esteem pushing individuals to pursue connection and lower self-esteem pulling individuals to pursue self-protection; or the reverse pattern of action when social risk is very low. Fourth, people use a sociometer proxy to judge the relational value of potential interaction partners, relying on a potential partner's own global self-esteem to judge his or her value. These functions of the self-esteem system reveal that self-esteem is not merely an epiphenomenon. Instead, the self-esteem system can be conceptualized as a multifaceted drive system shaped by evolution to provide humans with the tools they need to successfully navigate their social worlds.

References

Anthony, D. B., Holmes, J. G., & Wood, J. V. (2007a). Social acceptance and self-esteem: Tuning the sociometer to interpersonal value. *Journal of Personality and Social Psychology, 92,* 1024–1039.

Anthony, D. B., Wood, J. V., & Holmes, J. G. (2007b). Testing sociometer theory: Self-esteem and the importance of acceptance for social decision-making. *Journal of Experimental Social Psychology, 43,* 425–432.

Baumeister, R. F., & Leary, M. R. (1995). The need to belong: Desire for interpersonal attachments as a fundamental human motivation. *Psychological Bulletin, 117,* 497–529.

Baumeister, R. F., Tice, D. M., & Hutton, D. G. (1989). Self-presentational motivations and personality differences in self-esteem. *Journal of Personality, 57,* 547–579.

Baumeister, R. F., Campbell, J. D., Krueger, J. I., & Vohs, K. D. (2003). Does high self-esteem cause better performance, interpersonal success, happiness, or healthier lifestyles? *Psychological Science in the Public Interest, 4,* 1–44.

Blackhart, G. C., Nelson, B. C., Knowles, M. L., & Baumeister, R. F. (2009). Rejection elicits emotional reactions but neither causes immediate distress nor lowers self-esteem: A meta-analytic review of 192 studies on social exclusion. *Personality and Social Psychology Review, 13,* 269–309.

Bowlby, J. (1973). *Attachment and loss, Vol. 2: Separation.* New York: Basic Books.

Cameron, J. J., & Allary, A. (2013). *Lay theories of self-esteem: Defining Characteristics, Source, and Controllability.* Unpublished manuscript, University of Manitoba, Winnipeg, Canada.

Cameron, J. J., Stinson, D. A., Gaetz, R., & Balchen, S. (2010). Acceptance is in the eye of the beholder: Self-esteem and motivated perceptions of acceptance from the opposite sex. *Journal of Personality and Social Psychology, 99,* 513–529.

Cameron, J. J., Stinson, D. A., & Wood, J. V. (2013a). The bold and the bashful: Self-esteem, gender, and relationship initiation. *Social Psychological and Personality Science, 4,* 685–691.

Cameron, J. J., MacGregor, J. C. D., Hole, C., & Holmes, J. G. (2013b). *Is low self-esteem a stigma? The extremity of the self-esteem signal.* Unpublished manuscript, University of Manitoba, Winnipeg, Canada.

Cameron, J. J., Stinson, D. A., Hole, C., Reddoch, L., Allary, A., & Holmes, J. G. (2013c). *The sociometer proxy: Self-esteem as an interpersonal signal of worth.* Unpublished manuscript, University of Manitoba, Winnipeg, Canada.

Cavallo, J. V., Fitzsimons, G. M., & Holmes, J. G. (2009). Taking chances in the face of threat: Romantic risk regulation and approach motivation. *Personality and Social Psychology Bulletin, 35,* 737–751.

Cavallo, J. V., Holmes, J. G., Fitzsimons, G. M., Murray, S. L., & Wood, J. V. (2012). Managing motivational conflict: How self-esteem and executive resources influence self-regulatory responses to risk. *Journal of Personality and Social Psychology, 103,* 430–451.

Cooley, C. H. (1956). *Human nature and the social order.* New York: Schocken Books.

Donnellan, M. B., Trzesniewski, K. H., Robins, R. W., Moffitt, T. E., & Caspi, A. (2005). Low self-esteem is related to aggression, antisocial behavior, and delinquency. *Psychological Science, 16,* 328–335.

Fletcher, G. J. O., Simpson, J. A., & Thomas, G. (2000). Ideals, perceptions, and evaluations in early relationship development. *Journal of Personality and Social Psychology, 79,* 933–940.

Gaucher, D., Wood, J. V., Stinson, D. A., Forest, A. L., Holmes, J. G., & Logel, C. (2012). Perceived regard explains self-esteem differences in expressivity. *Personality and Social Psychology Bulletin, 38,* 1144–1156.

Harter, S. (2003). The development of self-representations during childhood and adolescence. In M. R. Leary & J. P. Tangney (Eds.), *Handbook of self and identity* (pp. 610–642). New York: Guilford Press.

Kelley, H. H., & Thibaut, J. W. (1978). *Interpersonal relations: A theory of interdependence.* New York: Wiley-Interscience.

Leary, M. R., & Baumeister, R. F. (2000). The nature and function of self-esteem: Sociometer theory. *Advances in Experimental Social Psychology, 32,* 1–62.

Leary, M. R., & Guadagno, J. (2011). The sociometer, self-esteem, and the regulation of interpersonal behavior. In R. F. Baumeister & K. Vohs (Eds.), *Handbook of self-regulation* (2nd ed., pp. 339–354). New York: Guilford.

Leary, M. R., Haupt, A. L., Strausser, K. S., & Chokel, J. T. (1998). Calibrating the sociometer: The relationship between interpersonal appraisals and state self-esteem. *Journal of Personality and Social Psychology, 74,* 1290–1299.

Lemay, E. P., Jr., & Clark, M. S. (2009). Self-esteem and communal responsiveness toward a flawed partner: The fair-weather care of low-self-esteem individuals. *Personality and Social Psychology Bulletin, 35,* 698–712.

Lemay, E. P., Jr., & Dudley, K. L. (2011). Caution: Fragile! Regulating the interpersonal security of chronically insecure partners. *Journal of Personality and Social Psychology, 100,* 681–702.

Lemay, E. P., Jr., Overall, N. C., & Clark, M. S. (2012). Experiences and interpersonal consequences of hurt feelings and anger. *Journal of Personality and Social Psychology, 103,* 982–1006.

MacDonald, G., & Leary, M. R. (2005). Why does social exclusion hurt? The relationship between social and physical pain. *Psychological Bulletin, 13,* 202–223.

Marigold, D. C., Holmes, J. G., & Ross, M. (2007). More than words: Reframing compliments from romantic partners fosters security in low self-esteem individuals. *Journal of Personality and Social Psychology, 92,* 232–248.

Marigold, D. C., Holmes, J. G., & Ross, M. (2010). Fostering relationship resilience: An intervention for low self-esteem individuals. *Journal of Experimental Social Psychology, 46,* 624–630.

Markus, H. (1977). Self-schemas and processing information about the self. *Journal of Personality and Social Psychology, 35,* 63–78.

Muise, A., Impett, E. A., & Desmarais, S. (2013). Getting it on versus getting it over with: Sexual motivation, desire, and satisfaction in intimate bonds. *Personality and Social Psychology Bulletin, 39,* 1320–1332.

Murray, S. L., Holmes, J. G., & Griffin, D. W. (1996). The self-fulfilling nature of positive illusions in romantic relationships: Love is not blind, but prescient. *Journal of Personality and Social Psychology, 71,* 1155–1180.

Murray, S. L., Holmes, J. G., & Griffin, D. W. (2000). Self-esteem and the quest for felt security: How perceived regard regulates attachment processes. *Journal of Personality and Social Psychology, 78,* 478–498.

Murray, S. L., Holmes, J. G., Griffin, D. W., Bellavia, G., & Rose, P. (2001). The mismeasure of love: How self-doubt contaminates relationship beliefs. *Personality and Social Psychology Bulletin, 27,* 423–436.

Murray, S. L., Rose, P., Bellavia, G. M., Holmes, J. G., & Kusche, A. G. (2002). When rejection stings: How self-esteem constrains relationship-enhancement processes. *Journal of Personality and Social Psychology, 83,* 556–573.

Murray, S. L., Griffin, D. W., Rose, P., & Bellavia, G. M. (2003). Calibrating the sociometer: The relational contingencies of self-esteem. *Journal of Personality and Social Psychology, 85,* 63–84.

Murray, S. L., Holmes, J. G., & Collins, N. L. (2006). Optimizing assurance: The risk regulation system in relationships. *Psychological Bulletin, 132,* 641–666.

Murray, S. L., Derrick, J. L., Leder, S., & Holmes, J. G. (2008). Balancing connectedness and self-protection goals in close relationships: A levels-of-processing perspective on risk regulation. *Journal of Personality and Social Psychology, 94,* 429–459.

Naumann, L. P., Vazire, S., Rentfrow, P. J., & Gosling, S. D. (2009). Personality judgments based on physical appearance. *Personality and Social Psychology Bulletin, 35,* 1661–1671.

Reis, H. T., Sheldon, K. M., Gable, S. L., Roscoe, J., & Ryan, R. M. (2000). Daily well-being: The role of autonomy, competence, and relatedness. *Personality and Social Psychology Bulletin, 26,* 419–435.

Rusbult, C. E. (1980). Commitment and satisfaction in romantic associations: A test of the investment model. *Journal of Experimental Social Psychology, 16,* 172–186.

Rusbult, C. E., Drigotas, S. M., & Verette, J. (1994). The investment model: An interdependence analysis of commitment processes and relationship maintenance phenomena. In D. J. Canary & L. Stafford (Eds.), *Communication and relational maintenance* (pp. 115–139). San Diego: Academic Press.

Sedikides, C. (1993). Assessment, enhancement, and verification determinants of the self-evaluation process. *Journal of Personality and Social Psychology, 65,* 317–338.

Self-Esteem. (2013). In Wikipedia. http://en.wikipedia.org/wiki/Self-esteem. Accessed 10 Aug 2013.

Stinson, D. A., & Holmes, J. G. (2010). Sociometer Model. In J. M. Levine & M. A. Hogg (Eds.), *Encyclopedia of group processes and intergroup relations* (pp. 830–832). Thousand Oaks: Sage.

Stinson, D. A., Wood, J. V., & Doxey, J. R. (2008a). In search of clarity: Self-esteem and domains of confidence and confusion. *Personality and Social Psychology Bulletin, 34,* 1541–1555.

Stinson, D. A., Logel, C., Zanna, M. P., Holmes, J. G., Cameron, J. J., Wood, J. V., & Spencer, S. J. (2008b). The cost of lower self-esteem: Testing a self- and social-bonds model of health. *Journal of Personality and Social Psychology, 94,* 412–428.

Stinson, D. A., Cameron, J. J., Wood, J. V., Gaucher, D., & Holmes, J. G. (2009). Deconstructing the "reign of error": Interpersonal warmth explains the self-fulfilling prophecy of anticipated acceptance. *Personality and Social Psychology Bulletin, 35,* 1165–1178.

Stinson, D. A., Logel, C., Holmes, J. G., Wood, J. V., Forest, A. L., Gaucher, D., Fitzsimons, G. M., & Kath, J. (2010). The regulatory function of self-esteem: Testing the epistemic and acceptance signaling systems. *Journal of Personality and Social Psychology, 99,* 993–1013.

Stinson, D. A., Gaucher, D., Wood, J. V., Reddoch, L. B., Holmes, J. G., & Little, D. C. G. (2012). Sex, 'lies,' and videotape: Self-esteem and successful presentation of gender roles. *Social Psychological and Personality Science, 3,* 503–509.

Swann, W. B., Jr. (1987). Identity negotiation: Where two roads meet. *Journal of Personality and Social Psychology, 53,* 1038–1051.

Swann, W. B., Jr. (1997). The trouble with change: Self-verification and allegiance to the self. *Psychological Science, 8,* 177–180.

Swann, W. B., Jr. (2012). Self-verification theory. In P. Van Lange, A. W. Kruglanski, & E. T. Higgins (Eds.), *Handbook of theories of social psychology* (pp. 23–42). London: Sage.

Swann, W. B., Jr., & Schroeder, D. G. (1995). The search for beauty and truth: A framework forunderstanding reactions to evaluations. *Personality and Social Psychology Bulletin, 21,* 1307–1318.

Thibaut, J. W., & Kelley, H. H. (1959). *The social psychology of groups*. New York: Wiley.

Tooby, J., & Cosmides, L. (1996). Friendship and the banker's paradox: Other pathways to the evolution of adaptations for altruism. In W. G. Runciman, J. M. Smith, & R. I. M. Dunbar (Eds.), *Evolution of social behaviour patterns in primates and man* (pp. 119–143). New York: Oxford University Press.

Trzesniewski, K. H., Donnellan, M. B., & Robins, R. W. (2003). Stability of self-esteem across the life span. *Journal of Personality and Social Psychology, 84,* 205–220.

Watson, D., Clark L. A., & Tellegen, A. (1988). Development and validation of brief measures of positive and negative affect: The PANAS scales. *Journal of Personality and Social Psychology, 54,* 1063–1070.

Williams, K. D. (2007). Ostracism. *Annual Review of Psychology, 58,* 425–452.

Wood, J. V., & Forest, A. L. (2011). Seeking pleasure and avoiding pain in interpersonal relationships. In M. D. Alicke & C. Sedikides (Eds.), *Handbook of self-enhancement and self-protection* (pp. 258–278). New York: Guilford Press.

Zeigler-Hill, V., & Myers, E. M. (2009). Is high self-esteem a path to the White House? The implicit theory of self-esteem and the willingness to vote for presidential candidates. *Personality and Individual Differences, 46,* 14–19.

Zeigler-Hill, V., & Myers, E. M. (2011). An implicit theory of self-esteem: The consequences of perceived self-esteem for romantic desirability. *Evolutionary Psychology, 9,* 147–180.

Zeigler-Hill, V., Besser, A., Myers, E. M., Southard, A. C., & Malkin, M. L. (2013). The status-signaling property of self-esteem: The role of self-reported self-esteem and perceived self-esteem in personality judgments. *Journal of Personality, 81,* 209–220.

Self-Deception

12

William von Hippel

Self-deception has traditionally been viewed as a strategy that people adopt to protect themselves from a psychologically threatening reality. In this sense, self-deception is classically considered an *intra*personal process that defends the individual. In contrast to this view, this chapter adopts the perspective that self-deception evolved for the ROM. purpose of facilitating the deception of others (Trivers 1976/2006). Thus, in this sense, self-deception might be considered to have evolved for offensive rather than defensive purposes. Following from this perspective, this chapter also considers secondary gains provided by self-deception. Specifically, self-deception also benefits deceivers by enabling them to lie without the costly cognitive load induced by holding truth and lie simultaneously in mind and by minimizing retribution if their lies are discovered.

Deception and Self-Deception

In the struggle to accrue resources, a strategy that has emerged over evolutionary time is deception. For example, people frequently lie to those on whom they depend to receive resources that might not otherwise be provided (Steinel and De Dreu 2004). Indeed, approximately half of people's daily deceptions are intended to gain a resource for the self (DePaulo and Kashy 1998). Such deceptive practices instigate a coevolutionary struggle, because selection favors the deceived evolving new means of detection and the deceiver evolving new means of deception. Self-deception may be an important tool in this coevolutionary struggle, by allowing deceivers to circumvent detection efforts.

In the case of deception among humans, there are several categories of cues (beyond fact-finding itself) that people can use to detect deception in others, including signs of nervousness, suppression, and cognitive load. Despite the availability of these cues, research suggests that people perform poorly in detecting deception (Bond and DePaulo 2006). Nevertheless, the literature on deception may have underestimated people's ability to detect deception through reliance on studies where (a) the deception is of little or no consequence, (b) the deceived has no opportunity to cross-examine the deceiver, (c) deceiver and deceived are strangers to each other, and (d) there are no repeated interactions between deceiver and deceived. Furthermore, recent research suggests that detection of deception may also be much higher when people rely on unconscious, rather than conscious, processes to detect deceivers (Reinhard et al. 2013). Thus, rates of deception detection may be higher outside the laboratory than in it.

Because successful deception can lead to substantial benefits for deceivers and costs for the deceived, and vice versa for unsuccessful deception (Boles et al. 2000; Schweitzer et al. 2006),

W. von Hippel (✉)
School of Psychology, University of Queensland, MC-323, St. Lucia, Brisbane, QLD 4072, AUSTRALIA
e-mail: billvh@psy.uq.edu.au

V. Zeigler-Hill et al. (eds.), *Evolutionary Perspectives on Social Psychology*, Evolutionary Psychology, DOI 10.1007/978-3-319-12697-5_12, © Springer International Publishing Switzerland 2015

those who would deceive are in a perennial struggle against those who would not be deceived. Self-deception offers an important tool in this coevolutionary struggle by allowing the deceiver the opportunity to deceive without cognitive load, conscious suppression, and increased nervousness. That is, to the degree that people can convince themselves that a deception is true or that their motives are beyond reproach, they are no longer in a position in which they must knowingly deceive others. Thus, by deceiving themselves people can better deceive others, because they no longer emit the cues of consciously mediated deception that could reveal their deceptive intent (Trivers 2011; von Hippel and Trivers 2011).

Beyond this primary role that self-deception plays in facilitating the deception of others, self-deception should lead to two additional interpersonal benefits as well. First, cognitive load not only reveals deception but it has other costs as well: Demands on working memory reduce performance in challenging domains (Schmader and Johns 2003) and disrupt social functioning (von Hippel and Gonsalkorale 2005). When people are forced to maintain both truth and lie in working memory, they are likely to show reduced ability to engage in other tasks and access other opportunities. This cognitive load required to maintain conscious deception is difficult to avoid, because many deceptions require the deceiver to keep fact and fiction in mind simultaneously in an effort to ensure that the former is hidden and the latter is disseminated. Self-deception provides a way to avoid this cognitive load. To the degree that deceivers can convince themselves that their deception is indeed true, they are no longer required to maintain the real facts of the case in mind while they focus on promulgating the fiction. Rather, by believing the fiction that they are expressing to others, they can free their mind to concentrate on other matters.

Second, the best-laid plans often go awry and lies are no exception to this rule; even careful and well-rehearsed deceptions can be uncovered. This ever-present possibility of detection poses a problem for would-be deceivers, as retribution and exclusion are common responses to detected deceptions. One solution to the threat of punishment when an apparent deception is uncovered is to co-opt legitimate reasons for having led people astray by pleading ignorance or ineptitude rather than deception. When people feel deceived, they typically become angry and seek retribution, but when they feel that they were unintentionally misled they are much more willing to forgive (Schweitzer et al. 2006; Stouten et al. 2006). For this reason, people who accompany their deception of others with deception of the self are better placed to avoid retribution if discovered. By arguing that they had not intentionally deceived, self-deceivers are more likely than conscious deceivers to avoid retribution. Of course, conscious deceivers can also deceive about their original knowledge and intent, but the cues that reveal deception can also reveal deception about their earlier lies. Thus, by deceiving themselves, people can reduce retribution if their deception of others is discovered.

Self-Deception in Service of Social Advancement

Self-deception can also facilitate the deception of others in a more general sense, in that it can help us convince others that we are better (e.g., more moral, stronger, smarter) than we really are. Thus, the benefits of self-deception go beyond convincing others of specific lies, as self-deception can also help us accrue the more general social advantages of self-inflation or self-enhancement. To the degree that people can bolster their image of themselves to themselves and enhance their self-confidence, they increase the chances that they will be able to influence others and will be chosen for socially important roles. For this reason, self-enhancement should be commonplace, and people should believe their own self-enhancing stories. Evidence supports both of these possibilities.

With regard to ubiquity, self-enhancing biases are evident in a wide variety of domains and strategies among a wide variety of peoples (Alicke and Sedikides 2009). Even East Asians, who value humility and harmony over individualistic self-aggrandizement, show self-enhancement in their claims of the superiority of their collectivist qualities (Sedikides et al. 2003; Sedikides et al. 2005). Furthermore, like Westerners, East Asians who are low in depression and stress show this self-enhancement to a greater degree than those who have these problems (Gaertner et al. 2008).

People not only self-enhance the world over, but the average person appears to be convinced that he or she is better than average (Alicke and Sedikides 2009). Most of the research on self-enhancement does not allow one to assess whether these aggrandizing claims are self-deceptive or only intended to deceive others, but some of the measures used in this research support the idea that people believe their own self-enhancing stories. For example, Epley and Whitchurch (2008) photographed participants and then morphed these photographs to varying degrees with attractive or unattractive photos of same-sex individuals. Epley and Whitchurch then presented participants with these morphed or unaltered photos of themselves under different circumstances. In one experiment, participants were asked to identify their true photo in an array of actual and morphed photographs of themselves. Participants were more likely to choose their photo morphed 10–20% with the more attractive image than either their actual photo or their photo morphed with the unattractive image. This effect emerged to a similar degree with a photo of a close friend, but it did not emerge with a photo of someone they had just met. Because people often perceive their close friends in an overly positive light (Kenny and Kashy 1994), these findings suggest that people do not have a general bias to perceive people as more attractive than they really are, but rather a specific bias with regard to themselves and close others.

In a second experiment, participants were presented with an array of photos of other individuals, among which was a single photo of themselves (either their actual photo or a photo morphed 20% with the attractive or unattractive image). Epley and Whitchurch found that people were able to locate photographs of themselves most rapidly if they were morphed with an attractive photo, at an intermediate speed if they were not morphed, and most slowly if they were morphed with an unattractive photo. These findings suggest that the enhanced photo most closely matches how people see themselves in their mind's eye, suggesting that they are deceiving themselves about their own attractiveness. Were they aware of this inaccuracy, they would be unlikely to claim the attractive photo to an experimenter who has the truth at her disposal and unlikely to locate their enhanced self more rapidly than their actual self. Thus, self-enhancement appears to be self-deceptive and not a conscious effort to deceive others.

Varieties of Self-Deception

If deceiving others can be facilitated by self-deception, the question then arises: how are people able to deceive themselves? At first, it seems paradoxical that the same individual could be both the teller and the believer of a lie, but the answer to this question can be found in a variety of information-processing biases that favor welcome over unwelcome information.

Amount of Searching

There are many situations in which people avoid searching for further information because they may encounter news that is incompatible with their goals or preferences. For example, on the trivial end of the continuum, some people avoid checking alternative products after they have made a purchase that cannot be undone (Olson and Zanna 1979). On the more important end of the continuum, some people avoid AIDS testing out of concern that they might get a result that they do not want to hear, particularly if they believe the disease is untreatable (Dawson et al. 2006; Lerman et al. 2002). This sort of self-deceptive information avoidance can be seen in the aphorism, "What I don't know can't hurt me." Although a moment's reflection reveals the fallacy of this statement, it is nonetheless psychologically compelling.

Similar sorts of biased information search can be seen in laboratory studies. Perhaps the clearest examples can be found in the research by Ditto and Lopez (1992), in which people are confronted with the possibility that they may have a proclivity for a pancreatic disorder. In their experiments, people expose a test strip to their saliva and are led to believe that a color change is indicative of either a positive or negative health prognosis (actually the test strip is inert and the color never changes). When people are led to believe that a color change is a good thing, they wait 60 % longer for the test strip to change color than when they believe color change is a bad thing. Thus, people sometimes do not tell themselves the whole truth, if a partial truth seems preferable.

Selective Searching

The type of information gathered can also be biased. Although one never knows for sure what lies around the next corner, some corners are more likely to yield welcome information than others. Thus, politically liberal people might choose the *New York Times* as their information source, whereas politically conservative individuals might choose *Fox News* (Frey 1986). In such a manner, people can be relatively confident that the brunt of the information they gather will be consistent with their worldview, even if they do not know what tomorrow's headlines will bring.

Laboratory studies have examined this sort of biased information search, in part by assessing the conditions under which people are interested in learning negative information about themselves. One conclusion from this research is that the better people feel about themselves, the more willing they are to face criticism. For example, Trope and Neter (1994) told participants that they were going to take a social sensitivity test and asked whether they would like feedback on their assets or liabilities. When participants had ostensibly failed an unrelated spatial abilities test, or had not taken the test, they showed a slight preference for feedback on their assets. In contrast, when bolstered by the experience of ostensibly performing well on the spatial abilities test, participants were more interested in learning about their liabilities, presumably in service of self-improvement. Such data suggest that people search for welcome information, but are capable of searching for unwelcome information when their self-enhancement goals have been met. Thus, people are often able to avoid telling themselves the whole truth by searching out those bits of truth that they want to hear, but they are also willing to face uncomfortable truths when feeling confident in their other assets.

Selective Attention

When information is perceptually available and need not be actively discovered, people can still bias their encoding by selectively attending to aspects of the information that they would prefer to be true. For example, if a person is at a dinner party where one conversation concerns the dangers of smoking and the other concerns the dangers of alcohol, she can choose to attend to one conversation or the other and may do so selectively if she is a smoker or a drinker. In such a case, she would likely be aware of the general tone of the information she is choosing not to gather, but by not attending to one of the conversations she could avoid learning details that she may not want to know.

This sort of effect has been documented in a variety of different types of experiments. For example, in a study of proactive coping, Wilson et al. (2004) convinced participants that they might be chosen or were highly unlikely to be chosen for a date. When participants believed they might be chosen, they spent slightly more time looking at positive than negative information about their potential partner. In contrast, when they believed that they were highly unlikely to be chosen, they spent more time looking at negative information about their potential partner. Thus, when people faced almost certain disappointment, they directed their attention to information that would make their upcoming rejection more palatable.

Eye-tracking studies provide some of the clearest evidence that people are often strategic in their attentional decisions (Isaacowitz 2006). For example, older adults look toward positive stimuli and away from negative stimuli when in a bad mood (Isaacowitz et al. 2008). This effect did not emerge among younger adults, suggesting that older adults are more likely than younger adults to rely on selective attention for mood repair. Thus, it seems that older adults sacrifice informational content in service of emotional goals. This strategy may be sensible for older adults, who face greater immune challenges than their younger counterparts, because happiness is associated with better immune functioning (Marsland et al. 2007). Consistent with this possibility, older adults who showed positivity biases in recall also showed cluster of differentiation antigen 4 (CD4) counts and activation levels indicative of better immune functioning at 1–2-year follow-ups (Kalokerinos et al. 2014).

Biased Interpretation

Despite the strategies just described for avoiding unwelcome information, there remain a variety of circumstances in which such information is nevertheless faithfully encoded. Under such circumstances, unwelcome information can still be dismissed through biased interpretation of information. In the classic study of this phenomenon (Lord et al. 1979), people who were preselected for their strong attitudes on both sides of the capital punishment debate were exposed to a mixed bag of information about the efficacy of capital punishment. Some of the data with which they were presented suggested that capital punishment was an effective crime deterrent, whereas other data suggested that it was not. Given that the data were new to participants, logic would suggest that the two groups would coalesce at least to some degree in their attitudes. In contrast, people ended the experiment more polarized than they began it.

Lord et al. (1979) discovered that this attitude polarization was a product of biased interpretation of the data. People who were in favor of capital punishment accepted the data that supported capital punishment as sound, but rejected the data that opposed capital punishment as flawed. Those who were against capital punishment showed the opposite pattern of skepticism. This selective skepticism appears self-deceptive, as it is attenuated or eliminated by self-affirmation (Reed and Aspinwall 1998) and cognitive load (Ditto et al. 1998). These findings suggest that people rely on their motivational and mental resources to be differentially skeptical of welcome and unwelcome information. Thus, selective skepticism appears to be a form of self-deception rather than simply an objective devaluation of new information to the degree that it is inconsistent with a large body of prior experience.

As a consequence of this selective skepticism, people are able to encounter a mixed bag of evidence, but nevertheless walk away with their original beliefs intact and potentially even strengthened. Because they are unaware that a person with a contrary position would show the opposite pattern of acceptance and rejection, they are able to convince themselves that the data support their viewpoint. By relying on their considerable powers of skepticism only when information is uncongenial, people are able to prevent themselves from learning the whole truth.

Misremembering

Even if people attend to unwanted information, and even if they accept it at the time of encoding, this does not guarantee that they will be able to retrieve it later. Rather, information that is inconsistent with their preferences may simply be forgotten or misremembered later as preference-consistent or neutral. Thus, a person might have great memory for the details of his victory in the championship tennis match but very poor memory for the time he lost badly. Indeed, this latter memory might also be distorted to implicate his doubles partner or the unusual talents or luck of his opponent. Various lines of research support such a possibility.

For example, when people put effort into self-improvement, but the improvement does not materialize, they can manufacture the gains they wish they had made by misremembering how they used to be. In a classic demonstration of this effect, Conway and Ross (1984) found that after taking a study skills class, people misremembered their prior study skills as lower than they rated them originally, thereby supporting their belief that their skills have improved. They then later misremembered their subsequent course performance as better than it was to maintain the fiction of improvement. Through processes such as these, people are able to purge their memories of inconvenient truths, thereby preventing themselves from knowing the whole truth, even if they accurately encoded it in the first instance.

This sort of memory bias can also be seen in recollection of daily experiences, whereby people have better recall of their own good than bad behavior, but do not show this bias in their recall of the behaviors of others (D'Argembeau and Van der Linden 2008). This self-enhancing recall is also eliminated by information that bolsters people's self-image (Green et al. 2008). Thus, people's memories are self-enhancing, sometimes containing information that is biased to be consistent with preferences and sometimes just failing to contain the whole truth.

Rationalization

Even if one's prior misdeeds are accurately recalled by self and others, it is still possible to avoid telling oneself the whole truth by reconstructing or rationalizing the motives behind the original behavior to make it more socially acceptable. For example, after eating a second helping of cake that leaves none for those who have not yet had dessert, a person could explain that he had not noticed that there was no other cake, or that he thought more cakes were available elsewhere. Here it is not memory of the misdeed that is critical, but interpretation of the motive that underlies the deed.

Again, laboratory evidence supports this sort of rationalization process. For example, von Hippel et al. (2005) demonstrated that when cheating could be cast as unintentional, people who showed a self-serving bias in another domain were more likely to cheat, but when cheating was clearly intentional, self-serving individuals were no more likely to cheat than others. These data suggest that some types of self-serving biases involve rationalization processes that are also common to some types of cheating. Indeed, people also cheat more when they are told that free will is just an illusion (Vohs and Schooler 2007), suggesting that they rationalize their cheating in these circumstances as caused by life situations rather than their own internal qualities.

More direct evidence for this sort of rationalization can be found in the hypocrisy research of Valdesolo and DeSteno (2008). In their study, participants were given the opportunity to (a) choose whether to give themselves or another individual an onerous task or (b) randomly assign the onerous task to self versus other. When given this opportunity, nearly all participants chose to give the onerous task to the other participant rather than rely on random assignment. Observers were not asked to make the choice themselves, but rather watched a confederate make this same self-serving choice. When asked how fair the choice was, observers rated the act of choosing rather than relying on random assignment as less fair than it was rated by those who had actually made this choice. This hypocrisy shown by those who chose to assign the onerous task to another was eliminated by cognitive load, suggesting that participants rely on their cognitive resources to reconstrue the fairness underlying their judgments.

Convincing the Self that an Untruth Is True

The classic form of self-deception is convincing oneself that an untruth is true. An example of this sort of self-deception can be found in research on perceptions of control. When people are deprived of control, they often endeavor to regain a sense of control. In a self-deceptive example of this effect, Whitson and Galinsky (2008) found that when people are led to feel low levels of personal control, they perceive illusory patterns in random configurations and are more likely to endorse conspiracy theories to explain world events. Importantly, these effects did not emerge when people had self-affirmed, suggesting that people have the potential to be aware of the absence of patterns and conspiracies. Similar findings have been documented by Kay et al. (2008), who argue that beliefs in a controlling God and a strong government serve people's need for control. Consistent with their reasoning, differences in the percentage of people who believe in God between countries can be predicted by the insecurities of existence within countries (e.g., availability of health care, food, and housing), with increased insecurity associated with increased religiosity (Norris and Inglehart 2004). Such a finding suggests the possibility of important forms of self-deception on a worldwide scale.

Experiments in cognitive dissonance also suggest that people are facile at lying to others and then coming to believe their own lies. For example, when they believe that they have freely chosen to tell another person that a tedious task is interesting, people soon believe that the task really is interesting (Festinger and Carlsmith 1959), and again this effect is eliminated by self-affirmation (Steele and Liu 1983).

Preliminary Evidence for Self-Deception to Deceive Others

If these information-processing biases that favor welcome over unwelcome information have evolved to facilitate deception of others, then it should be the case that people show these biases when they endeavor to deceive someone else. Additionally, if people have evolved to self-enhance due to the positive effects their inflated self-image has on others, then self-enhancement biases should be associated with more positive impressions on the part of others. The final section of this chapter describes some of the preliminary evidence that supports of these possibilities.

If self-deception serves the deception of others, then three predictions can be made regarding self-deceptive biases. First, people should be more likely to show such biases when they endeavor to deceive others, particularly when those deceptions are important. Second, these self-deceptive biases should create in the self a convincing picture of reality that is consistent with the upcoming deception. And third, these self-deceptive biases should facilitate interpersonal deception. To date, we have conducted two experiments to test the first of these predictions (Smith et al. 2014).

To test whether people self-deceive in service of deceiving another, participants in our experiments were told that their task was to convince an expert lie detector that a drink contained either sugar or artificial sweetener. To ensure that participants were motivated to convince the expert, they were told that being convincing in tasks such as these has been shown to predict future personal and career success. Prior to trying to convince the expert, participants tested the drink themselves by exposing it to an ostensibly sugar-sensitive test strip under the belief that the test strip would change color if the drink contained sugar. As in Ditto and Lopez (1992), the test strip was inert and thus, from their perspective, the absence of color change indicated that the drink did not contain sugar. Consistent with the possibility that people self-deceive in an effort to deceive others, participants tested the drink for longer and rechecked the results more frequently when their task was to convince someone that the drink contained sugar than when their task was to convince someone that the drink did not contain sugar. In other words, participants attempted to bias the test result so that it was consistent with their upcoming claim.

Although the results of this experiment were consistent with predictions, it is possible that this biased information processing may have been motivated by a desire to avoid lying and the self-image threat associated with lying rather than a desire to convince the expert. To provide clearer evidence that this bias was borne of the motive to convince another, we replicated the first experiment with an additional manipulation. Rather than telling people that it was personally important to be convincing, their motivation to convince the expert was varied by telling them that they would receive either US$ 20 or US$ 1 if they convinced the expert that the drink contained sugar or artificial sweetener.

If the results of our first experiment are the product of people's desire to avoid lying and the consequences for their self-concept, self-deceptive information processing should be more pronounced when US$ 1 versus US$ 20 is at stake because a lack of external justification for lying should enhance the threat to the self (Festinger and Carlsmith 1959). However, if people's self-deceptive information gathering was motivated by a desire to convince the expert, then the extent of self-deceptive information gathering should be greater when they could earn US$ 20 than when they could only earn US$ 1 for convincing the expert. That is, with US$ 20 at stake, people should be much more motivated to convince the expert, and that motivation in turn should translate into a larger bias in the manner in which they gather information (which on average would translate into a greater chance of finding their preferred conclusion). Consistent with this latter possibility, biased information searching only emerged when US$ 20 was at stake, as only then did people test longer and recheck more frequently when the results with the test strip were inconsistent rather than consistent with their upcoming claim. These findings suggest that when people know that they need to potentially deceive someone else about a particular issue, they are likely to take the opportunity to deceive themselves first. In so doing, these findings suggest that people intuitively believe that they are more convincing to others if they believe the claim they are making.

Beyond its role in specific deceptions, self-deception should also lead others to believe that we are generally better than we really are. Consistent with this possibility, across a series of studies, Anderson et al. (2012) found that people who were overconfident in their knowledge were more persuasive in convincing others of their beliefs. Indeed, overconfident individuals displayed more behavioral cues of competence than did knowledgeable individuals, and the benefits of overconfidence were not limited to short-term interactions (Anderson et al. 2012). Thus, overconfidence appears to be an interpersonally effective self-deceptive strategy.

If overconfidence evolved for these interpersonal effects, then it should be particularly evident (and particularly effective) in the mating marketplace, where any interpersonal advantage that people can gain will have a substantial impact on their fitness. To test this possibility, Murphy et al. (2014) ran a series of studies in which overconfidence was measured via Paulhus et al. (2003) overclaiming scale (which assesses the degree to which people claim to know information that does not actually exist).

After completing the overclaiming scale, people were asked to create a dating profile. Results revealed that the profiles written by overclaimers demonstrated greater confidence in their dating profiles, which in turn was associated with greater desirability as a romantic partner. Nevertheless, despite the positive effects of confidence on desirability, overclaimers were not perceived as more romantically desirable overall. This null effect was apparently caused by the fact that overclaimers were also perceived as more arrogant, which in turn was associated with less desirability as a romantic partner. A final study revealed that although arrogance has costs in terms of desirability, it also has benefits in terms of intrasexual competition, as men and women both reported that they would be less likely to compete with the overclaimers for the attentions of a romantic interest, and this effect was driven in part by the increased arrogance displayed by the overclaimers. Although further research is necessary to demonstrate the role of self-deception in overconfidence, intersexual attraction, and intrasexual competition, these preliminary results are consistent with the possibility that overconfidence evolved due to its interpersonal benefits.

Conclusions

There is a long history of treating self-deception in psychology as if it is an intrapersonal defense mechanism, designed to protect the individual from an imperfect world. In contrast to this tradition, we have argued that self-deception is an interpersonal strategy, intended to facilitate the deception of others. This deception can be about something specific, such as whether a soft drink contains sugar, or about something very general, such as whether one is knowledgeable and romantically desirable. In both cases, self-deception might be better conceived as a strategy intended to influence the information available to others than as a strategy intended to protect the self.

References

Alicke, M. D., & Sedikides, C. (2009). Self-enhancement and self-protection: What they are and what they do. *European Review of Social Psychology, 20,* 1–48.

Anderson, C., Brion, S., Moore, D., & Kennedy, J. (2012). A status-enhancement account of overconfidence. *Journal of Personality and Social Psychology, 103,* 718–735.

Boles, T., Croson, R., & Murnighan, J. K. (2000). Deception and retribution in repeated ultimatum bargaining. *Organizational Behavior and Human Decision Processes, 83,* 235–259.

Bond, C. F., Jr., & DePaulo, B. M. (2006). Accuracy of deception judgments. *Personality and Social Psychology Review, 10,* 214–234.

Conway, M. & Ross, M. (1984). Getting what you want by revising what you had. *Journal of Personality and Social Psychology, 47,* 738–748.

D'Argembeau, A., & Van der Linden, M. (2008). Remembering pride and shame: Self-enhancement and the phenomenology of autobiographical memory. *Memory, 16,* 538–547.

Dawson, E., Savitsky, K., & Dunning, D. (2006). "Don't tell me, I don't want to know": Understanding people's reluctance to obtain medical diagnostic information. *Journal of Applied Social Psychology, 36,* 751–768.

DePaulo, B. M., & Kashy, D. A. (1998). Everyday lies in close and casual relationships. *Journal of Personality and Social Psychology, 74,* 63–79.

Ditto, P. H., & Lopez, D. F. (1992). Motivated skepticism: Use of differential decision criteria for preferred and nonpreferred conclusions. *Journal of Personality and Social Psychology, 63,* 568–584.

Ditto, P. H., Scepansky, J. A., Munro, G. D., Apanovitch, A. M., & Lockhart, L. K. (1998). Motivated sensitivity to preference-inconsistent information. *Journal of Personality and Social Psychology, 75,* 53–69.

Epley, N., & Whitchurch, E. (2008). Mirror, mirror on the wall: Enhancement in self recognition. *Personality and Social Psychology Bulletin, 34,* 1159–1170.

Festinger, L., & Carlsmith, J. M. (1959). Cognitive consequences of forced compliance. *Journal of Abnormal and Social Psychology, 58,* 203–211.

Frey, D. (1986). Recent research on selective exposure to information. In L. Berkowitz (Eds.), *Advances in experimental social psychology* (Vol. 19, pp. 41–80). Maryland Heights: Academic Press.

Gaertner, L., Sedikides, C., & Chang, K. (2008). On pan-cultural self-enhancement: Well-adjusted Taiwanese self-enhance on personally valued traits. *Journal of Cross-Cultural Psychology, 39,* 463–477.

Green, J. D., Sedikides, C., & Gregg, A. P. (2008). Forgotten but not gone: The recall and recognition of self-threatening memories. *Journal of Experimental Social Psychology, 44,* 547–561.

Isaacowitz, D. M. (2006). Motivated gaze: The view from the gazer. *Current Directions in Psychological Science, 15,* 68–72.

Isaacowitz, D. M., Toner, K., Goren, D. & Wilson, H. R. (2008). Looking while unhappy: Mood-congruent gaze in young adults, positive gaze in older adults. *Psychological Science, 19,* 848–853.

Kalokerinos, E. K., von Hippel, W., Henry, J. D., & Trivers, R. (2014). The aging positivity effect and immune functioning: Positivity in recall predicts higher CD4 counts and lower CD4 activation. *Psychology and Aging, 29,* 636–641.

Kay, A. C., Gaucher, D., Napier, J. L., Callan, M. J. & Laurin, K. (2008). God and government: Testing a compensatory control explanation for the support of external systems. *Journal of Personality and Social Psychology, 95,* 18–35.

Kenny, D. A. & Kashy, D. A. (1994). Enhanced co-orientation in the perception of friends: A social relations analysis. *Journal of Personality and Social Psychology, 67,* 1024–1033.

Lerman, C., Croyle, R. T., Tercyak, K. P., & Hamann, H. (2002). Genetic testing: Psychological aspects and implications. *Journal of Consulting and Clinical Psychology, 70,* 784–797.

Lord, C. G., Ross, L., & Lepper, M. R. (1979). Biased assimilation and attitude polarization: The effects of prior theories on subsequently considered evidence. *Journal of Personality and Social Psychology, 37,* 2098–2109.

Marsland, A. L., Pressman, S. D., & Cohen, S. (2007). Positive affect and immune function. In R. Ader (Ed.), *Psychoneuroimmunology* (pp. 261–279). Philadelphia: Elsevier.

Murphy, S. C., Barlow, F. K., Dubbs, S. L., & von Hippel, W. (2014). *The role of overconfidence in sexual attraction and competition.* Unpublished manuscript, University of Queensland.

Norris, P., & Inglehart. R. (2004). *Sacred and secular: Religion and politics worldwide.* New York: Cambridge University Press.

Olson, J. M., & Zanna, M. P. (1979). A new look at selective exposure. *Journal of Experimental Social Psychology, 15,* 1–15.

Paulhus, D. L., Harms, P. D., Bruce, M. N., & Lysy, D. C. (2003). The over-claiming technique: Measuring self-enhancement independent of ability. *Journal of Personality and Social Psychology, 84,* 890–904.

Reed, M. B., & Aspinwall, L. G. (1998). Self-affirmation reduces biased processing of health-risk information. *Motivation and Emotion, 22,* 99–132.

Reinhard, M-A., Greifeneder, R., & Scharmach, M. (2013). Unconscious processes improve lie detection. *Journal of Personality and Social Psychology, 105,* 721–739.

Schmader, T., & Johns, M. (2003). Converging evidence that stereotype threat reduces working memory capacity. *Journal of Personality and Social Psychology, 85,* 440–452.

Schweitzer, M. E., Hershey, J., & Bradlow, E. (2006). Promises and lies: Restoring violated trust. *Organizational Behavior and Human Decision Processes, 101,* 1–19.

Sedikides, C., Gaertner, L., & Toguchi, Y. (2003). Pancultural self-enhancement. *Journal of Personality and Social Psychology, 84,* 60–70.

Sedikides, C., Gaertner, L., & Vevea, J. L. (2005). Pancultural self-enhancement reloaded: A meta-analytic reply to Heine (2005). *Journal of Personality and Social Psychology, 89,* 539–551.

Smith, M. K., von Hippel, W., & Trivers, R. (2014). *Self-deception as an interpersonal strategy.* Unpublished manuscript, University of Queensland.

Steele, C. M., & Liu, T. J. (1983). Dissonance processes as self-affirmation. *Journal of Personality and Social Psychology, 45,* 5–19.

Steinel, W., & De Dreu, C. K. W. (2004). Social motives and strategic misrepresentation in social decision making. *Journal of Personality & Social Psychology, 86,* 419–434.

Stouten, J., De Cremer, D., & van Dijk, E. (2006) Violating equality in social dilemmas: Emotional and retributive reactions as a function of trust, attribution, and honesty. *Personality and Social Psychology Bulletin, 32,* 894–906.

Trivers, R. (1976/2006). Foreword. In R. Dawkins (Ed.) *The selfish gene* (pp. 19–20). New York: Oxford University Press.

Trivers, R. (2011). *The folly of fools: The logic of deceit and deception in human life.* New York: Basic Books.

Trope, Y., & Neter, E. (1994). Reconciling competing motives in self-evaluation: The role of self-control in feedback seeking. *Journal of Personality and Social Psychology, 66,* 646–657.

Valdesolo, P., & DeSteno, D. (2008). The duality of virtue: Deconstructing the moral hypocrite. *Journal of Experimental Social Psychology, 44,* 1334–1338.

Vohs, K. D., & Schooler, J. W. (2007). The value of believing in free will: Encouraging a belief in determinism increases cheating. *Psychological Science, 19,* 49–54.

von Hippel, W., & Gonsalkorale, K. (2005). "That is bloody revolting!" Inhibitory control of thoughts better left unsaid. *Psychological Science, 16,* 497–500.

von Hippel, W., Lakin, J. L., & Shakarchi, R. J. (2005). Individual differences in motivated social cognition: The case of self-serving information processing. *Personality and Social Psychology Bulletin, 31,* 1347–1357.

von Hippel, W., & Trivers, R. (2011). The evolution and psychology of self-deception. *Behavioral and Brain Sciences, 34,* 1–16.

Whitson, J. A., & Galinsky, A. D. (2008). Lacking control increases illusory pattern perception. *Science, 322,* 115.

Wilson, T. D., Wheatley, T. P., Kurtz, J. L., Dunn, E. W., & Gilbert, D. T. (2004). When to fire: Anticipatory versus post-event reconstrual of uncontrollable events. *Personality and Social Psychology Bulletin, 30,* 340–351.

Evolutionary Cyberpsychology 2.0: Revisiting Some Old Predictions and Posting Some New Ones in the Age of Facebook

13

Jared R. Piazza and Gordon P. D. Ingram

The past two decades have witnessed the success of evolutionary psychology (EP) as a powerful framework for understanding and generating hypotheses about human cognition and behavior. Yet, in 2008, one of the authors was dismayed to find a lack of EP-based applications to one of the fastest growing areas of psychology: *cyberpsychology,* the study of computer-mediated behavior. Responding to this situation, a brief primer was developed that outlined several directions for applying evolutionary perspectives to the study of cyber-behavior (see Piazza and Bering 2009). At that time, there were only a handful of papers published in the more popular cyberpsychology journals (e.g., *Computer in Human Behavior*) that utilized an EP perspective, and 5 years later the situation has not much changed. Meanwhile, cyberpsychology as a discipline has rapidly grown, partly because of the widespread success of social networking software. In 2008, scientific interest in social networking behavior was just taking off (e.g., Boyd and Ellison 2007), and Facebook had just over 90 million active monthly users; by September 30, 2013, Facebook had 1.19 billion active monthly users (Facebook Newsroom 2013). The growth of social networking has generated a wealth of social scientific research (Wilson et al. 2012). Indeed, reflecting the mass impact of social networking on public life, and mounting interest among researchers, *Cyberpsychology and Behavior,* one of the field's flagship journals, at the start of 2010 re-branded itself, *Cyberpsychology, Behavior, and Social Networking.*

The goal of the present chapter is to revisit some of the predictions of Piazza and Bering (2009), take stock of relevant research conducted in the interim, and offer some ways forward, with a particular eye on the topic of social networking. Our aim is to provide the field with a road map of what has been done in the application of EP to cyberpsychology and to highlight areas that deserve further attention. We have adopted the basic structure used by Piazza and Bering, which covers five broad themes from EP that have direct application for cyberpsychology, including mating, intrasexual competition, parenting and kinship, personal information management, trust and social exchange. We have also added a sixth theme: friendship. We hope our review will illustrate how an evolutionary approach can help illuminate how people conduct themselves in cyberspace.

J. R. Piazza (✉)
Department of Psychology, Lancaster University, Fylde College, Lancaster LA1 4YF, UK
e-mail: j.piazza@lancaster.ac.uk

G. P. D. Ingram
School of Society, Enterprise, and Environment, Bath Spa University, Bath BA2 9BN, UK
e-mail: gordoning@gmail.com

Mating and Dating

According to a recent Pew Internet report, one in ten Americans has used an online dating site or mobile dating app, and 5% of Americans who are

V. Zeigler-Hill et al. (eds.), *Evolutionary Perspectives on Social Psychology,* Evolutionary Psychology,
DOI 10.1007/978-3-319-12697-5_13,

currently married or in a long-term partnership met their partner online (Pew Internet and American Life Project 2013). Online dating appeals to people for several reasons. First, it provides people with access to a larger pool of potential mates than is accessible through direct channels, increasing the likelihood of finding someone who will reciprocate interest (Valkenburg and Peter 2007). Second, online dating profiles provide users with substantial control over the initial impressions they make to prospective partners (Whitty 2007). However, online dating is not without challenges, and many online daters report negative experiences (Pew 2013). In addition to online dating and the pursuit of long-term partnerships, the Internet provides virtual spaces for individuals to engage in other sexual pursuits, including flirting (Whitty 2003), initiating sexual interest through "sexting" (sending sexually suggestive electronic messages; Drouin et al. 2013), achieving sexual gratification via hot chat, cybersex, or pornography (Spink et al. 2004), and arranging to have sex offline (Daneback et al. 2007). With the advent of social networking sites (SNSs), individuals often use the Internet as a form of surveillance technology to monitor their romantic partner's activity (e.g., a partner's Facebook contacts, posted photos, or comments they made on a contact's "wall") for signs of relational dissatisfaction or indiscretion (Clayton et al. 2013; Elphinston and Noller 2011; Muise et al. 2009). Thus, there are many ways people today use the Internet to pursue short-term and long-term sexual interests, making it a rich domain for testing evolutionary theories of courtship and intersexual competition.

Drawing on Buss and Schmitt's (1993) sexual strategies theory, Piazza and Bering (2009) hypothesized that men would be more likely than women to use Web-based technologies, such as chat rooms and text messaging, to initiate short-term sexual encounters. This would be a consequence of women having a much greater obligatory parental investment (Trivers 1972) and thus having less to gain than men by pursuing a short-term mating strategy. Consistent with this hypothesis, several studies found that men are the primary initiators of "sexting" behaviors, such as sending a sexually suggestive text or a partially nude self-photo (Delevi and Weisskirch 2013; Gordon-Messer et al. 2012). Sexting occurs frequently within committed relationships, but it also occurs with some frequency within casual and extra-pair relationships (Drouin et al. 2013). Thus, the use of sexting to signal sexual interest or initiate offline sexual interactions may reflect men's greater orientation to short-term mating.

Another important sex difference stemming from differences in parental investment (and paternity certainty) is the way that men and women react to different forms of infidelity (Buss 1994). Converging evidence suggests that men are more distressed than women by envisioning their current romantic partner having sex with someone else, whereas women are more distressed than men by envisioning their partner forming a close emotional attachment to someone of the opposite sex (Buss et al. 1992; Shackelford et al. 2002). Assuming that computer-mediated activities may approximate "real" forms of infidelity (Whitty 2005), Piazza and Bering (2009) suggested that evolutionary predictions about sex differences in jealousy could be tested in relation to online sexual or romantic behaviors, such as men and women engaging in cybersex versus forming an emotional attachment with someone whom they met online. However, a study by Whitty and Quigley (2008) suggested that computer-mediated forms of sexual conduct may only weakly approximate offline infidelity. Northern Irish college students selected from among four scenarios which would be most distressing: their partner's offline sexual infidelity, online sexual infidelity (cybersex), offline emotional infidelity, or online emotional infidelity (falling in love with a person they have only known online). The study replicated the well-established pattern that men are more distressed by their partner's offline sexual infidelity while women are more distressed by their partner's offline emotional infidelity. No participants selected either cybersex or online emotional attachment as the most distressing scenario. Nevertheless, since this study did not exclusively contrast cybersex and online emotional infidelity, it remains to be seen whether the typical sex difference might emerge when directly contrasting these two cases.

More recently, Muscanell et al. (2013) had American undergraduates imagine that they discovered on their romantic partner's Facebook page a photograph of their partner with someone of the opposite sex. Consistent with the notion that women are more distressed by the thought of a budding emotional relationship between their partner and a rival, they found that women, compared to men, experienced more feelings of jealousy, hurt, and anger over the discovered photo, though this sex difference vanished when the partner had set the photo to be "private" (implying he or she was attempting to conceal the relationship). Lastly, McAndrew and Shah (2013) found that female college students were more likely than men to report jealousy in response to their romantic partner's Facebook activities. The Facebook activities involved behaviors that could signal the blossoming of a new relationship or the rekindling of an old one (e.g., partner posting pictures with a previous partner); thus, the researchers interpreted the results as being consistent with the evolutionary prediction that Facebook-mediated triggers of emotional jealousy are more distressing for women than for men.

Another form of intersexual behavior that EP may be useful in addressing is cyberstalking and cyber-harassment. Victims of cyberstalking tend to be female, whereas perpetrators tend to be men who are acquaintances or ex-partners of the victims (Dreßing et al. 2014; Sheridan and Grant 2007), as is the case with offline stalking patterns. The perpetration of cyberstalking by acquainted men is consistent with one prominent evolutionary perspective, which argues that stalking and other forms of sexual harassment arise from an evolved male psychology that motivates feelings of proprietary sexual jealousy, as men attempt to control a romantic partner or ex-partner's sexual behavior (Wilson and Daly 1993). This perspective also makes the prediction that the main victims of cyberstalking should be young, reproductive-age females (Daly and Wilson 1988; Peters et al. 2002). We are not aware of research specifically testing the possibility that rates of cyberstalking diminish with age for women.

A robust finding in EP is that men consistently overperceive the degree to which a woman is sexually interested in them (Haselton and Buss 2000), whereas women tend to underperceive sexual interest (Perilloux et al. 2012). The Internet presents a rich context in which sexual misperception biases might be studied. Signals communicated via electronic text are ambiguous insofar as a presenter's true intentions are hidden and unobservable (Donath 2008). This is also true, to some extent, of face-to-face (FTF) communication (Silk et al. 2000); nevertheless, text-based computer-mediated communication (CMC) is more ambiguous than FTF in that several modes of CMC (e.g., instant messaging and e-mail) typically involve only one sensory modality, whereas FTF involves a multiplicity of sensory cues perceivers may use to help disambiguate the presenter's intent, including speech prosody and facial expressions (Dunbar 2012). The deprivation of sensory cues within various CMC media may create an environment in which perceptual biases of sexual intent are inflated—with men overperceiving sexual interest, and women underperceiving sexual interest, to an even greater extent—due to the ambiguity of the signals exchanged. Another possibility is that users of CMC understand the limitations of CMC, and engage in deliberate efforts to disambiguate their true intent within these channels by using more explicit signals. Males in particular may signal sexual interest using more explicit means of communication with a prospective partner, to avoid missing a potential opportunity.

Lastly, sexual aspects of the Internet (e.g., pornography; Spink et al. 2004) may pose a particular challenge to men in committed relationships, given the attentional biases men display towards attractive mating alternatives (Becker et al. 2005; Duncan et al. 2007). One strategy committed individuals employ to maintain their current investment in a partner is to depreciate the attractiveness of a mating alternative (Miller and Maner 2010). Another strategy is to be selectively inattentive to, and/or deliberately avoid, contexts in which attractive alternatives are present. At least one study of men's and women's Facebook activity found evidence for a mate-maintenance strategy among men. McAndrew and Jeong (2012) showed that men in committed relationships spent less time than single men perusing and/or posting on the Facebook pages of women. Relationship status, by contrast, had no association with women's Facebook activities. Committed and single women were just as likely to view men's Facebook pages, though women were predominantly interested in viewing the pages of other women as a means of making social comparisons or gathering information about same-sex friends and rivals—activities theorized to be particularly important for female intrasexual competition (McAndrew and Milenkovic 2002).

Intrasexual Competition

Computer-mediated self-presentations, particularly those found on SNSs such as Facebook, provide an excellent testing ground for psychological theories pertaining to intrasexual competition. Facebook, for example, offers a number of uses, including the opportunity to keep in touch with preexisting friends and family, interact (e.g., via Facebook chat or wall posts), initiate new social connections, and self-enhance via user pages (Raacke and Bonds-Raacke 2008; Tosun 2012). In this section, we are particularly interested in the self-enhancement function of Facebook. Piazza and Bering (2009) hypothesized that young men more than young women would stress their skills, creativity, and resources in their personal online profiles and homepages, whereas young women more than young men would stress their physical appearance and prosocial reputations, reflecting general sex differences in intrasexual competition (e.g., Geary 1998; Hill et al. 2012). This hypothesis should apply no less to SNS profiles. We assume that one goal people have for creating and updating an SNS profile is to signal their desirable qualities to others. This goal need not be explicit, but an evolutionary perspective suggests that the motivations men and women bring to their online social networking may differ due to distinct adaptive problems faced by ancestral males and females (Buss 1994; Geary 1998).

Some recent research findings may be brought to bear on these predictions. Haferkamp et al. (2012) analyzed the publicly accessible profiles of 106 StudiVZ (the German equivalent of Facebook) users. Consistent with the idea that men are more motivated to "show off" their unique skills, while women are more motivated to highlight their physical appearance, men spent more time editing their profile picture in creative ways, perhaps as a means to display their technical skills, while women preferred using portrait photography, presumably to present their physical appearance in the most attractive light. Mehdizadeh (2010) observed a similar pattern among a sample of Facebook users. Men were more likely to share self-promotional content in the "About Me" and "Notes" sections of their profile, while women were more inclined to self-promote via their physical appearance (e.g., by using a professional photograph).

Other research suggests that women are better than men at refraining from risky online behavior, such as posting compromising images of themselves on Facebook, consistent with the idea that sex differences in executive functioning have a basis in parental investment differences, whereby men have more to gain than women from risk-taking (Bjorklund and Shackelford 1999; Campbell 1999). For example, Peluchette and Karl (2008) found that male college students were more likely than their female counterparts to post to their Facebook accounts pictures of their sexual exploits, partying, and drinking behavior. One prediction that has not yet been tested but deserves further investigation is whether men (but not women) are more likely to engage in risky Internet behavior (e.g., posting compromising photos of themselves) when placed in a mating mindset or when their social status is challenged.

"Cyberbullying" refers to computer-mediated forms of relational aggression, such as forwarding private e-mails or posting embarrassing photos without permission. Offline relational aggression is a common form of aggression used by adolescents (as well as adults) to manipulate the status and reputation of a peer competitor through indirect, social channels (e.g., spreading rumors), as opposed to direct physical conflict (Archer 2004). Piazza and Bering (2009) predicted that as with offline bullying, cyberbullying would be perpetrated primarily by adolescents and teens who tend to be high-status (or "popular") within a peer group, while their victims would tend to be relatively low-status individuals on the "fringe" of various peer groups. They also predicted, however, that the relative invisibility and social distance of cyber-aggression would be empowering for low-status teens, leading to greater status challenges being made by low-status teens than would traditionally occur offline. Somewhat inconsistent with the first hypothesis, Calvete et al. (2010) found that levels of perceived peer support decreased as the frequency of self-reported cyberbullying increased, suggesting that the status of many of the cyberbullies in their sample may have been quite low. But in line with Piazza and Bering's (2009) hypotheses, other studies have shown that victims of cyberbullying have low status. In a sample of 12–19-year-old high school students, Festl and Quandt (2013) found that position in the social network was a strong predictor of cyber-victimization. "Pure" victims reported having more friends than either perpetrators or perpetrators/victims, yet were less often named as friends themselves, suggesting that they may have been vulnerable because they did not belong to well-defined cliques that could support them. Finally, a study of German secondary school pupils elucidated context as an important moderator: Falling victim to major school bullying was negatively predicted by popularity in the classroom, while falling victim to major cyberbullying was negatively predicted by popularity in online chat rooms (Katzer et al. 2009).

While more research is needed, there are some tentative signs that the status differentials implicated in FTF bullying—which seems to be practiced more by dominant individuals with secure friendship networks—are less of a predictor for online bullying. This is borne out by evidence that cyberbullying, on account of its indirect and relational nature, may be more often utilized by females than is traditional bullying (Dooley et al. 2009). There thus appears to be a similar pattern with sex to that which exists for dominance: Individuals who are physically dominant or who are supported by a network of friends may be better able to bear the risks of FTF bullying, but these risks are reduced for cyberbullying. Similarly, although girls engage in FTF bullying less than boys because of the physical risks (Campbell 1999), communicating through virtual means reduces these physical risks and so permits girls to engage in more online than FTF bullying.

Parenting and Kinship

Alongside finding a mate and competing with conspecifics, successfully socializing children into a community is a challenge facing humans everywhere. There are strong selective pressures on parents to monitor their children's social interactions, particularly with regards to their choice of sexual partners. The Internet presents new challenges for parental monitoring, partly because it vastly widens the pool of individuals with whom their children can interact, and partly because virtual interactions may be less easily scrutinized by parents than physical interactions (Lenhart and Madden 2007). Evolutionary theory predicts that mothers will be more concerned with their children's social interactions than fathers, due to their certainty about their maternity and their greater levels of parental care (Bjorklund and Shackelford 1999; Geary 1998). Accordingly, Piazza and Bering (2009) hypothesized that "women would take a more active role than men, overall, in monitoring their children's online behavior" (p. 264). In a study of Dutch parents' mediation of their 2–12-year-old children's Internet use, Nikken and Jansz (2012) found that mothers were much more likely than fathers to supervise, actively intervene, and implement restrictions on children's Internet-based activities; somewhat more likely to co-use the Internet with them; slightly more likely to provide specific restrictions about which websites they could or could not visit; but not more likely to provide technical guidance to their children. Also supporting Piazza and Bering's hypothesis, Vasalou et al. (2012) documented a trend for mothers to be more likely than fathers to use a location-tracking tool to monitor their children's whereabouts, though this trend was not statistically significant. On the other hand, Wang et al. (2005) found that fathers were more likely than mothers to check which websites their children had been visiting, and there were no effects of parental sex in the use of monitoring software or the promotion of rules about online activity. These findings highlight that any sex effects in this area are likely to be contextual and dependent on the type of monitoring that is taking place: for example, men's particular interest in certain more technical forms of monitoring might offset a stronger evolved tendency of women to monitor offspring.

Men who doubt their paternity feel less connected to the child in their care and as a consequence reduce their investment in the child (Apicella and Marlowe 2004; Burch and Gallup 2000). Likewise, stepparents, who are certain of their nonpaternity or nonmaternity, invest less in their partners' offspring (Daly and Wilson 1988; Marlowe 1999). This suggests that, controlling for Internet access in the home and technical acumen with computers, men who doubt their paternity may spend less time and energy on mediating their children's online activity—that is, less time checking the web pages their children have visited, participating in online activities with children, and establishing and enforcing rules about children's Internet use. It also suggests that stepparents will expend less effort, compared to genetic parents, mediating stepchildren's online activity. Neither of these predictions has been tested.

Individuals promote their own genetic fitness not only by caring for children but also by investing in the welfare of nondependent kin (Hamilton 1964). People tend to provide high-cost support to individuals they identify as close biological kin (e.g., full siblings; Pollet 2007; Stewart-Williams 2007). Piazza and Bering (2009) hypothesized that due to kin investment mechanisms, people would tend to use high-cost communication technologies (such as video chat) to contact related individuals more than non-kin, a difference that would not be as apparent when considering low-cost communication technologies (e.g., text-based chat or e-mail). Part of the logic of this argument was based on the high financial costs, at the time, of securing the bandwidth necessary for video or audio communication. Since that article was written, bandwidth costs have fallen dramatically, to the extent that financial costs are unlikely to be much of a consideration when deciding whom to contact over an internet-based service. However, video or audio communication may still be more costly in the sense of being more time-consuming or cognitively demanding (Dunbar 2012), and they may still be more financially costly when taking place over a mobile phone, due to the loss of inclusive minutes or data allowances.

Support for Piazza and Bering's kin investment hypothesis comes from Hampton et al. (2010), who surveyed wireless Internet users in public spaces (e.g., parks, plazas, and markets) in four major North American cities. They found that Internet-based phone calls were mostly made with family (especially spouses), whereas communication by e-mail and instant messaging more often took place with friends, or with coworkers (in the case of e-mail). Similarly, Mok et al. (2010) showed that their participants phoned relatives more than friends, even intimate ones.

One unresolved question is whether spending time using virtual technology detracts from time spent on FTF contact, and whether this might have a detrimental effect for some relationships more than others. In a long-term longitudinal study of various forms of contact in a Toronto neighborhood, Mok et al. (2010) found that frequency of FTF contact was unchanged between the 1970s and the 2000s, even as e-mail was introduced and the frequency of telephone use increased. Affirming the importance of frequent contact for maintaining friends, a study by Roberts and Dunbar (2011) tracked kin relationships and friendships over an 18-month period and found that friendships were more susceptible than kin relationships to decreases in emotional closeness due to failure to contact either FTF, by phone or e-mail, or through participation in joint social or physical activities. Thus, new technologies may be more important in maintaining long-distance friendships, but less important for kin relationships, though people voluntarily use these technologies to affiliate with kin. At the same time, digital technologies may interfere with the development of new friendships by redirecting efforts into maintaining long-distance friendships that would have otherwise naturally decayed (Dunbar 2012).

Friendship

Friendships differ from kin relationships in that they are not based on the emotional bonds that form between a parent and child, the sharing of a mutual caregiver early in life, phenotype matching, or other kin-identification mechanisms. Rather, friendships usual form around shared interests (homophily) or shared experiences (Schneider 2000). Intimacy (emotional closeness), loyalty, exclusivity, and tolerance are the core features of friendship that distinguish it from the casual, cordial, low-tolerance relationships we have with other non-kin individuals in our social spheres (Amichai-Hamburger et al. 2013; DeScioli and Kurzban 2009; Silk 2003). Recent work suggests that friendships are distinct from kin relationships in that the intimacy and loyalty that define friendships require a great deal of social interaction to maintain (Roberts and Dunbar 2011). Furthermore, friends may be distinguished from acquaintances in that people are much more tolerant of short-term asymmetries (imbalances) in the giving and receiving of services with friends, due to the longer horizon of interaction that friendships entail (Xue and Silk 2012). Finally, friendships are defined by a high degree of loyalty and exclusivity (DeScioli and Kurzban 2009), whereby the perception of a stronger tie between a close friend and another person, relative to the strength of the tie between that friend and the self, may evoke feelings of betrayal, jealousy, and disappointment (Piazza and DeScioli 2012).

Traditionally, friendships are maintained through direct forms of "social grooming," such as FTF communication or joint activities (Roberts and Dunbar 2011). Social media and communication technology may offer the potential for friendships to persist that would have otherwise faded in the absence of direct contact (Armichai-Hamburger et al. 2013; Dunbar 2012). This may be particularly the case for women who, according to one study, rely more heavily on communication, as opposed to joint activity (e.g., playing sports), for friendship maintenance (Roberts and Dunbar 2011). Nevertheless, multiplayer online games, such as World of Warcraft, offer at least one channel by which activity-based "grooming" might occur in the virtual world (Barnett and Coulson 2010). CMC technologies, such as video chat via Skype, offer sensory-rich mediums for creating a sense of co-presence and real-time social feedback, and as a result are comparably effective as FTF communication for sustaining levels of intimacy among geographically distant friends (Vlahovic et al. 2012). The benefits of other, less-rich CMC media, such as SNSs or IM (instant message), for sustaining friendships are less clear. Some research suggests that friendships benefit from these technologies, for example, by allowing friends to monitor and track each other's weekly activities, update one another about important events, and share photos, gossip, and express opinions (e.g., Tosun 2012). Other research suggests that social networking in particular can have a negative effect on preexisting relationships by promoting relational jealousy, betrayal, and disappointment (Muise et al. 2009). Indeed, Tokunaga (2011) uncovered ten different kinds of "negative events" that users of SNSs report, including being denied friend requests, being "unfriended," disparities in perceived friend rankings on "Top Friends" applications, deletion of messages, ignored questions or remarks, and disparaging remarks posted on message boards.

Steijn and Schouten (2013) found that personal information sharing on SNSs (Facebook or Hyves) had both positive and negative interpersonal outcomes. Many participants reported greater benefits than costs of engaging in public posts on a weak-tie friend's SNS profile. However, more participants reported negative outcomes than positive ones resulting from making public posts on the profile of "close friends." These authors did not examine the content of what was shared within the public posts, thus it is not entirely clear what the cause of the conflict was between close friends. One possibility is that SNS use might erode a close friendship as a direct result of disclosure-based violations of perceived friendship rank (Piazza and DeScioli 2012). For example, if a person posts positive news or personal information to their public wall prior to sharing the news with a close friend, this might cause hurt feelings if it is interpreted by the friend as a violation of their perceived friendship rank, which serves as an indicator of the kinds of privileges and services a person is entitled to within a friendship (DeScioli and Kurzban 2009). Any activity that might be construed as a violation of these "rules of privilege" should be distressing, as it may signal a potential reorganization (e.g., demotion) of the friendship hierarchy.

One form of rank reversal that is likely to occur often on SNSs is *disclosure-based rank reversal* (Piazza and DeScioli 2012). This happens when a piece of privileged social information is communicated to a person of lower friendship rank prior to reception by a person of higher friendship rank. Rank reversals of this sort are probably common among SNS users insofar as communications within SNSs are often one-to-many (Chiou et al. 2013), and therefore obscure the sequential flow of one-to-one communication; for example, when a person posts a message on their Facebook wall, this is a one-to-many communication, as any "friend" logged into Facebook and monitoring that person's wall is a potential recipient. Depending on the newsworthiness of the post, a close friend who first learns of the news via the person's wall, as opposed to some one-to-one channel, may feel betrayed or hurt by the oversight.

Studies by Piazza and DeScioli (2012) found some evidence for the disruptive effects of disclosure-based rank reversals within friendships. In one study, participants imagined a situation in which they received a privileged piece of information from a friend (information about a friend's secret affair). They learned that a third person also received the same information either before or after them. Among participants who received the secret *after* another person, those who experienced a downward rank reversal (i.e., who were higher rank than the other person) felt less close to the friend and significantly more negative emotion than participants who were of lower friendship rank. Among those who received the secret *before* another person, those who experienced an upward rank reversal (i.e., who were lower rank than the other person) felt closer to the friend than participants who were of higher friendship rank.

The implications of this study for CMC are clear: Technologies such as Facebook that enable disclosure-based rank reversals may be causing undue strain on existing friendships. At the same time, public posting on SNSs may help enhance weak-tie relationships, as weak ties may benefit more from one-to-many communications (Steijn and Schouten 2013). Thus, a related (and much debated) question is whether social media and other Internet technologies are helping people forge new, meaningful friendships (Boase et al. 2006). Research by Pollet et al. (2011) suggests that this may not be the case. These authors highlight the inherent cognitive constraints that present a ceiling on how many intimates a person can maintain at high or "strong-tie" levels. Pollet et al. (2011) surveyed 117 Europeans about their offline and online relationships, their use of SNS and IM technology, how often they contacted them, and their emotional closeness to each contact. They found absolutely no relationship between time spent using IM or SNS and either the size of participants' offline networks or the emotional closeness of their offline relationships. In other words, CMC did not provide any social gain that could not be achieved simply via traditional communication channels. Similar null findings are reported by Dunbar (2012).

Although Internet use may not translate into larger networks or stronger ties, other research has shown that relationships formed on the Internet can be as deep and lasting as offline relationships (McKenna et al. 2002). Despite these findings, people continue to voice skepticism about the benefits of their online interactions, doubting the quality of these computer-mediated experiences (Schiffrin et al. 2010). Thus, only time will tell whether emerging technologies will enable friendships forged online to have the same depth and staying power as those managed through traditional means. While social technologies do keep friends connected over geographical distances, it remains unclear whether these technologies can match the social-bonding power of actual physical contact.

Personal Information Management

The decision to disclose negative personal information poses a dilemma: While negative self-disclosure can bring with it helpful insights (Kelly et al. 2001) and increase relational intimacy (Altman and Taylor 1973), it can also lead to relational conflict, negative gossip, reputational damages, and stigmatization (Kelly and McKillop 1996; Piazza and Bering 2010). An evolutionary approach to personal information management highlights the target-specific consequences of decisions to self-disclose personal information that could impact negatively on a long-term relationship, especially a romantic partner or close friend, who unlike kin have no investment in one's inclusive fitness (Bering and Shackelford 2004; Piazza and Bering 2010). From this perspective, people should be sensitive to the content of their personal information, take care to track which individuals in their network are in possession of this information, and engage in countermeasures (e.g., deliberate secrecy, selective disclosure) to interrupt or forestall the transmission of such information to those targets that would be most impacted or distressed by the news. This might involve the recruitment of allies or kin who are not directly affected by the information as "conspirators" (co-secret-keepers), or as intermediaries to help manage any conflict that ensues when the secret is revealed. A complementary perspective on human friendship (DeScioli and Kurzban 2009) suggests that close friends are those one perceives as having a stronger allegiance with oneself than with others. Thus, selective disclosure of negative secrets to close friends may be a crucial strategy in garnering support in the event that the secret reaches its target.

On the basis of this evolutionary approach, Piazza and Bering (2009) hypothesized that most people would not disclose "personal secrets" (i.e., negative personal information) online even under fairly anonymous conditions. This hypothesis was guided by the assumption that people would be skeptical of the allegedly private or "anonymous" nature of CMC, and mindful of the archival and retrievable nature of Internet-based communications (Solove 2007), despite the reduced sensory nature of CMC technology, which might provide users with a temporary sense of invisibility. How then do we reconcile this prediction with recurrent findings that CMC technology often *enhances* levels of self-disclosure between individuals, compared to FTF communication, as a result of the reduced social-presence cues and controllable features of text-based communication (Joinson 2001; Tidwell and Walther 2002; Valkenburg and Peter 2009)?

First, we should point out that a recent meta-analysis of research looking into the online disinhibition effect found that the actual size of the effect may be overstated (Nguyen et al. 2012). That is, people may not self-disclose on the Internet as much as some theorists have suggested. Second, it is unclear whether any gain in self-disclosure that may occur via CMC technology involves the disclosure of negative self-content. Our suspicion is that most of the personal content Internet users are presenting to the cyberworld is positive, self-promotional content, while much less is negative content that a person has a stake in concealing. Indeed, SNSs in particular encourage *positive* self-disclosures (Ljepava et al. 2013; Toma and Hancock 2013). By contrast, Internet users do not use CMC for discussing personal information such as "personal habits, fears, and relationships" (Schiffrin et al. 2010, p. 302), but prefer to discuss such sensitive topics FTF. Consistent with Piazza and Bering's prediction, Frye and Dornisch (2010) reported a negative correlation between amount of online self-disclosure and the level of "intimacy" of the information (most of the non-shared "intimate" content in their study largely had to do with private sexual matters). Thus, while some researchers find that the apparent invisibility of CMC helps foster self-disclosure, which in turn can foster relational intimacy, it seems likely that the majority of this online self-disclosure is positive or neutral in content.

Another possibility is that disclosure of potentially stigmatizing personal secrets does occur over the Internet but only within select cyber-environments where individuals perceive they are communicating with trusted allies only, where privacy concerns are highly satisfied (i.e., the disclosing party trusts the website to maintain the anonymity of its users and the content exchanged between its users), and there is control over the target audience (Joinson et al. 2010). Researchers have long noticed the level of self-disclosure that occurs on personal blogs (Hollenbaugh 2010; Viegas 2005). Despite the publicly accessible nature of blogs, research suggests that most bloggers are concerned about privacy (Viegas 2005) and write with a particular audience in mind—often, friends and family (Stefanone and Jang 2007). SNSs provide public, one-to-many modes of communication through wall posts, where users have little control over the flow of information once it is posted. Although Facebook offers users some modes of private communication (e.g., private chat) and various privacy settings, anyone with a Facebook account and who has viewer privileges has access to one's online profile and public comments (Christofides et al. 2009). By contrast, private online chat rooms and online groups or "communities" provide greater privacy and audience controls, which may foster the disclosure of personal secrets over the long term, once a deep, trusting relationship is formed. Many online groups are devoted to a specific topic or issue, which enable Internet users to easily locate individuals who may possess similar stigmatizing secrets, thus creating an environment of nonjudgment and trust (McKenna and Bargh 1998). Thus, the extent to which a given CMC technology is thought to provide sufficient levels of privacy and audience control is probably an important moderator on the hypothesis originally proposed by Piazza and Bering.

Some extant research may be brought to bear on this qualified hypothesis. According to a study by Christofides et al. (2009) of Canadian college students, Facebook users reported being concerned about privacy and were likely to use a variety of privacy settings to manage the consumption of their personal information. They also reported being very unlikely to post pictures of themselves or their friends doing something illegal, or photos of themselves naked or partially nude. We might infer from the general lack of negative personal information being posted to Facebook that the communication of personal secrets to SNSs is either uncommon, or that the *possession* of negative personal secrets is uncommon. Given the high rates of offline secret-keeping reported in past research (Kelly et al. 2001; Piazza and Bering 2010), we think the former is more likely.

Importantly, an evolutionary perspective on personal information management also makes the prediction that complete secrecy (i.e., total concealment of personal information from everyone) is often not the best policy, as secrets often involve at least one other person, who may not be trusted to maintain the secret, particularly when their interests oppose one's own. For this reason, we might expect natural selection to have favored psychological mechanisms for promoting secrets disclosure (i.e., "confessions") to trusted kin and allies as a means of preempting inevitable conflict that would ensue from the secret's public revelation (Bering and Shackelford 2004). Extant research suggests that negative personal secrets are often shared to at least one other person (Piazza and Bering 2010), and that "secondary disclosures" (secrets passed on to unintended third parties) occur with some frequency despite the best intentions of the receiver (Christophe and Rimé 1997). Secrets are often provocative and newsworthy—they stir emotions, such as surprise or outrage, within the recipient, which makes them salient, accessible, and difficult to forget, and as a consequence, the vast majority of personal secrets are passed along. Because secrets are newsworthy, secrets also represent a tradable good. This presents the confidant with a dilemma whereby they might receive some benefit by sharing the secret, while at the cost of damaging a relationship.

The ecology of secret sharing suggests that the human mind has not evolved for total secrecy, but to selectively reveal negative personal secrets to loyal kin and allies who may be counted on to defend the self against retaliations from offended parties. Thus, while natural selection likely favored mechanisms for controlling the transmission of negative personal information (e.g., conscious concealment from select targets), total secrecy may not be an adaptive strategy insofar as: (1) most secrets are likely to be inadvertently revealed through various channels outside the secret-keeper's control and (2) revealing secrets to close allies and kin may serve to hasten support in anticipation of the negative reverberations of the secret's eventual revelation. This perspective thus suggests that selective disclosure of secrets is likely to occur in online contexts where a secret-keeper encounters sufficient cues indicating that the receiving party may be trusted to remain loyal to the discloser over and above any conflicting loyalties that person may have to the secret's target. This implies that contacts made online, for example, within private online groups, who have nonoverlapping social networks with the secret-keeper, may make ideal confidants for distressing secrets, more so than individuals with overlapping social networks.

Trust and Social Exchange

Despite initial and persistent concerns about electronic shopping, e-commerce continues to grow (Horrigan 2008). In 2008, Amazon had around 88 million active registered customers worldwide; by 2012 that number was 200 million (Statista 2013). eBay, one of the largest online marketplaces/auction sites, has a global customer base of 233 million (eBay Worldwide 2013). Anxieties about online shopping revolve mainly around issues of trust (e.g., that a seller can be trusted to accurately represent the nature or quality of a product and honor their end of an online transaction), privacy (e.g., concerns about online companies sharing users' personal information to third parties), and consumer satisfaction (e.g., that the purchased item will not be defective; Chen et al. 2010; Yang and Lester 2004). The risks associated with purchasing goods and sharing personal information over the Internet include loss of money and resources (e.g., paying for something that never gets sent, identity theft), loss of time (e.g., time spent bidding on an item in an auction or browsing for an item in an online market), and loss of control (e.g., having personal information circulated against one's wishes), among others. Online transactions often occur between anonymous or pseudo-anonymous strangers where buyers and sellers know little about each other and the likelihood of future interaction is uncertain (Resnick and Zeckhauser 2002), thus prompting the questions: Why has e-commerce been so successful? What mechanisms have enabled online shoppers to trust e-vendors whom they encounter online?

A number of evolutionary perspectives suggest that cooperation among strangers is an unnatural or unusual occurrence, since for most of human history humans have cooperated with members of their own tribe or community who they interacted with on a recurrent basis FTF, and thus had a larger stake in reciprocating contributions over time (as opposed to defecting on a stranger one is unlikely to see again; Piazza and Bering 2009). Still, trade between groups probably occurred often enough that high-risk cooperation under conditions of low-frequency interaction (and thus minimal reputational information) was not unheard of in the ancestral past among neighboring groups (Fehr and Henrich 2003). Expectations about future interaction, even if these interactions are spread out over time and sporadic, may be helpful to induce cooperation between strangers. Indeed, behavioral economists have shown that humans are more inclined to cooperate with individuals they know little or nothing about if they expect frequent future interactions than if future interactions are unlikely (e.g., Gächter and Falk 2002). Thus, one mechanism that may be driving the success of e-commerce is for online sellers to capitalize on a well-established offline reputation. Consistent with this idea, research by Chen et al. (2010) has shown that online shoppers are more inclined to trust e-vendors that have cultivated a brand name image, and which buyers have had past experiences with, and so they can be expected to stick around, to invest in the quality of their products and the reputation of the company.

Another mechanism that evolutionary game theorists have highlighted as essential to human cooperation among nonrelatives and non-friends is reputation-based partner choice, also referred to as "competitive altruism" (Barclay 2004; Roberts 1998; Sylwester and Roberts 2013). Competitive altruism occurs when individuals compete with one another for the most lucrative partnerships via the reputations they acquire through their previous interactions. Online marketplaces, such as Amazon, and auction sites, such as eBay, exploit the principles of reputation-based partner choice through the institution of electronic "feedback" mechanisms, or reputation systems, such as eBay's Feedback Forum (Resnick et al. 2006). Online feedback mechanisms collect, aggregate, and distribute feedback about buyers and sellers' past experiences within the marketplace. Buyers and sellers rate each other and leave comments upon completion of an online transaction. A feedback profile is automatically generated for registered sellers, which displays the net ratings they receive across their various transactions for a given period of time (e.g., eBay currently has a 12-month cap on their feedback system). Buyers may also leave comments and sometimes sellers are allowed to leave comments in turn.

Leaving feedback about a seller imposes a minimal cost on buyers (e.g., the time required to rate and comment about a completed transaction); thus, it remains a puzzle why buyers would ever leave feedback, given the costs entailed. (Although we could not find any official statistics on buyer feedback percentages, discussions about the low levels of buyer feedback are quite common on Amazon Seller Forums.) One possibility is that individuals who experience strong emotions, such as gratitude or outrage, on account of unanticipated transaction outcomes (i.e., unusually positive or negative experiences), may be more inclined to leave feedback than buyers whose expectations are simply met by the seller. If this is the case, then we might expect buyer feedback to be skewed towards larger end tails with overall fewer middle ratings. We find this outcome unlikely. Another possibility is that buyers who leave feedback are invested in the reputation they imagine they receive for leaving feedback. Buyer feedback is a public good in that feedback about prospective sellers is available to all buyers and maintained through voluntary contributions. As such, the feedback system is vulnerable to exploitation by free riders who freely benefit from the feedback of other buyers without themselves contributing to the system. Online feedback systems help solve this public goods dilemma by allowing buyers leaving feedback to identify themselves (e.g., by name) and thus cultivate a reputation for providing useful feedback within the system. Amazon's feedback system also allows buyers to rate the usefulness of other buyers' feedback when making purchasing decisions within the marketplace—which provides buyers reputational incentives to provide high-quality feedback to other buyers, despite the costs of time and effort required to contribute quality feedback.

As far as we are aware, no systematic investigation of buyers' motivations to leave feedback has been undertaken; thus, the question of what exactly motivates buyers to leave feedback remains an interesting direction for future research. One testable prediction which stems from the above discussion is that online feedback systems which capitalize on the ability for users to develop a reputation for making positive contributions to the system, and that offers benefits to users for leaving helpful feedback (e.g., in the form of user ratings, discounts, or monetary rewards), will thrive in relation to systems that do not provide these reputational incentives (e.g., systems that overly conceal the identities of buyers who leave feedback).

One additional aspect of online trust and exchange has to do with the reliability of information people encounter, whether from sellers making claims about a given product, buyers leaving feedback about their transactions with sellers, or Facebook users posting assertions to a public wall. Perspectives from EP can help illuminate the decisions people make regarding whether to trust the veracity of information they receive online. Hess and Hagen (2006) have argued that humans evolved psychological adaptations for assessing the veracity of gossip they encountered in order to counteract deceptive communication. One strategy in particular that people consistently use to counteract deceptive communications is to doubt statements made by single and interdependent sources (Hess and Hagen 2006). Over the Internet, this might play out in e-shoppers seeking out feedback information from multiple, independent sources before making a final purchasing decision or auction bid, or discounting feedback submitted by a single buyer, as hypothesized by Piazza and Bering (2009). Although we are unaware of any research to date that has directly tested these predictions, Walther et al. (2009) recently showed that Internet users tend to be skeptical of self-disclosures posted on Facebook that are not confirmed by independent parties, which is consistent with Piazza and Bering's hypothesis. Apparently, there is a great deal more work that needs to be done on this topic.

Conclusion

Improvements to digital media occur year-round as developers seek to provide users with satisfying experiences. An evolutionary perspective suggests that for emerging technologies to be most effective they must consider the fundamental motives humans have as a vestige of their evolutionary history, and not just their idiosyncratic tastes and interests. Humans have evolved to behave in adaptive ways as a function of the species-typical conditions they find themselves living in. This implies a degree of regularity to human motivation, and the cyberworld is no exception to this rule. Real improvements to computer technology may only occur when developers hone in on these fundamental motives and engineer new ways for users to satisfy them.

References

Altman, I., & Taylor, D. A. (1973). *Social penetration: The development of interpersonal relationships*. New York: Irvington.

Amichai-Hamburger, Y., Kingsbury, M., & Schneider, B. H. (2013). Friendship: An old concept with a new meaning? *Computers in Human Behavior, 29,* 33–39.

Apicella, C. L, & Marlowe, F. W. (2004). Perceived mate fidelity and paternal resemblance predict men's investment in children. *Evolution and Human Behavior, 25,* 371–378.

Archer, J. (2004). Sex differences in aggression in real-world settings: A meta-analytic review. *Review of General Psychology, 8,* 291–322.

Barclay, P. (2004). Trustworthiness and competitive altruism can also solve the "tragedy of the commons". *Evolution and Human Behavior, 25,* 209–220.

Barnett, J., & Coulson, M. (2010). Virtually real: A psychological perspective on massively multiplayer online games. *Review of General Psychology, 14,* 167–179.

Becker, D. V., Kenrick, D. T., Guerin, S., & Maner, J. M. (2005). Concentrating on beauty: Sexual selection and sociospatial memory. *Personality and Social Psychology Bulletin, 12,* 1643–1652.

Bering, J. M., & Shackelford, T. K. (2004). The causal role of consciousness: A conceptual addendum to human evolutionary psychology. *Journal of General Psychology, 8,* 227–248.

Bjorklund, D. F., & Shackelford, T. K. (1999). Differences in parental investment contribute to important differences between men and women. *Current Directions in Psychological Science, 8,* 86–89.

Boase, J., Horrigan, J. B., Wellman, B., & Rainie, L. (2006). The strength of internet ties: The internet and email aid users in maintaining their social networks and provide pathways to help when people face big decisions. http://www.pewinternet.org/. Accessed 7 April 2008.

Boyd, D. M., & Ellison, N. B. (2007). Social network sites: Definition, history, and scholarship. *Journal of Computer-Mediated Communication, 13,* 210–230.

Burch, R. L., & Gallup, G. G., Jr. (2000). Perceptions of paternal resemblance predict family violence. *Evolution and Human Behavior, 21,* 429–435.

Buss, D. M. (1994). *The evolution of desire*. New York: Basic Books.

Buss, D. M., & Schmitt, D. P. (1993). Sexual strategies theory: A contextual evolutionary analysis of human mating. *Psychological Review, 100,* 573–587.

Buss, D. M., Larsen, R., Westen, D., & Semmelroth, J. (1992). Sex differences in jealousy: Evolution, physiology, and psychology. *Psychological Science, 3,* 251–255.

Calvete, E., Orue, I., Estévez, A., Villardón, L., & Padilla, P. (2010). Cyberbullying in adolescents: Modalities and aggressors' profile. *Computers in Human Behavior, 26,* 1128–1135.

Campbell, A. (1999). Staying alive: Evolution, culture and women's intrasexual aggression. *Behavioral and Brain Sciences, 22,* 203–252.

Chen, Y.-H., Chien, S.-H., Wu, J.-J., & Tsai, P.-Y. (2010). Impact of signals and experience on trust and trusting behavior. *Cyberpsychology, Behavior, and Social Networking, 13,* 539–546.

Chiou, W.-B., Chen, S. W., & Liao, D.-C. (2013). Does Facebook promote self-interest? Enactment of indiscriminate one-to-many communication on online social networking sites decreases prosocial behavior. *Cyberpsychology, Behavior, and Social Networking*. doi:10.1089/cyber.2013.0035.

Christofides, E., Muise, A., & Desmarais, S. (2009). Information disclosure and control on Facebook: Are they two sides of the same coin or two different processes? *Cyberpsychology and Behavior, 12,* 341–345.

Christophe, V., & Rimé, B. (1997). Exposure to the social sharing of emotion: Emotional impact, listener responses and secondary social sharing. *European Journal of Social Psychology, 27,* 37–54.

Clayton, R. B., Nagurney, A., & Smith, J. A. (2013). Cheating, breakup, and divorce: Is Facebook use to blame? *Cyberpsychology, Behavior, and Social Networking*. doi:10.1089/cybr.2012.0424.

Daly, M., & Wilson, M. (1988). Evolutionary psychology and family homicide. *Science, 242,* 519–524.

Daneback, K., Minsson, S.-A., & Ross, M. W. (2007). Using the Internet to find offline sex partners. *Cyberpsychology and Behavior, 10,* 100–107.

Delevi, R., & Weisskirch, R. S. (2013). Personality factors as predictors of sexting. *Computers in Human Behavior, 29,* 2589–2594.

DeScioli, P., & Kurzban, R. (2009). The alliance hypothesis for human friendship. *PLoS ONE, 4,* e5802.

Donath, J. (2008). Signals in social supernets. *Journal of Computer-Mediated Communication, 13,* 231–251.

Dooley, J. J., Pyzalski, J., & Cross, D. (2009). Cyberbullying versus face-to-face bullying: A theoretical and conceptual review. *Zeitschrift für Psychologie, 217,* 182–188.

Dreßing, H., Bailer, J., Anders, A., Wagner, H., & Gallas, C. (2014). Cyberstalking in a large sample of social network users: prevalence, characteristics, and impact upon victims. *Cyberpsychology, Behavior & Social Networking, 17,* 61–67.

Drouin, M., Vogel, K. N., Surbey, A., & Stills, J. R. (2013). Let's talk about sexting baby: Computer-mediated sexual behaviors among young adults. *Computers in Human Behavior, 29,* A25–A30.

Dunbar, R. I. M. (2012). Social cognition on the Internet: Testing constraints on social network size. *Proceedings from the Royal Society, B, Biological Sciences, 367,* 2192–2201.

Duncan, L.A., Park, J.H., Faulkner, J., Schaller, M., Neuberg, S. L., & Kenrick, D. T. (2007). Adaptive allocation of attention: Effects of sex and sociosexuality on visual attention to attractive opposite-sex faces. *Evolution and Human Behavior, 28,* 359–364.

eBay Worldwide. (2013). eBay—the world's online marketplace. Retrieved November 2013 from http://pages.ebay.co.uk/aboutebay/thecompany/company-overview.html.

Elphinston, R. A., & Noller, P. (2011). Time to face it! Facebook intrusion and the implication for romantic jealousy and relationship satisfaction. *Cyberpsychology, Behavior, and Social Networking, 14,* 631–635.

Facebook Newsroom. (2013). Key facts. Retrieved November 2013 from http://newsroom.fb.com/Key-Facts.

Fehr, E., & Henrich, J. (2003). Is strong reciprocity a maladaptation? On the evolutionary foundations of human altruism. CESifo Working Paper, No. 859. Retrieved February 2015 from http://hdl.handle.net/10419/76253.

Festl, R., & Quandt, T. (2013). Social relations and cyberbullying: The influence of individual and structural attributes on victimization and perpetration via the Internet. *Human Communication Research, 39,* 101–126.

Frye, N. E., & Dornisch, M. M. (2010). When is trust not enough? The role of perceived privacy of communication tools in comfort with self-disclosure. *Computers in Human Behavior, 26,* 1120–1127.

Gächter, S., & Falk, A. (2002). Reputation and reciprocity: Consequences for the labor relation. *Scandinavian Journal of Economics, 104,* 1–25.

Geary, D. C. (1998). *Male, female: The evolution of human sex differences*. Washington, DC: American Psychological Association.

Gordon-Messer, D., Bauermeister, J., Grodzinski, A., & Zimmerman, M. (2012). Sexting among young adults. *Journal of Adolescent Health, 52*(3), 301–306. http://dx.doi.org/10.1016/j.jadohealth.2012.05.013.

Haferkamp, N., Eimler, S. C., Papadakis, A.-M., & Kruck, J. V. (2012). Men are from Mars, women are from Venus? Examining gender differences in self-presentation on social networking sites. *Cyberpsychology, Behavior, and Social Networking, 15,* 91–98.

Hamilton, W. D. (1964). The genetical evolution of social behavior: I & II. *Journal of Theoretical Biology, 7,* 1–52.

Hampton, K. N., Livio, O., & Goulet, L. S. (2010). The social life of wireless urban spaces: Internet use, social networks, and the public realm. *Journal of Communication, 60,* 701–722.

Haselton, M. G., & Buss, D. M. (2000). Error management theory: A new perspective on biases in cross-sex mind reading. *Journal of Personality and Social Psychology, 78,* 81–91.

Hess, N. H., & Hagen, E. H. (2006). Psychological adaptations for assessing gossip veracity. *Human Nature, 17,* 337–354.

Hill, S. E., Rodeheffer, C. D., Griskevicius, V., Durante, K., & White, A. E. (2012). Boosting beauty in an economic decline: Mating, spending, and the lipstick effect. *Journal of Personality and Social Psychology, 103,* 275–291.

Hollenbaugh, E. E. (2010). Personal journal bloggers: Profiles of disclosiveness. *Computers in Human Behavior, 26,* 1657–1666.

Horrigan, J. B. (2008). Online shopping: Internet users like the convenience but worry about the security of their financial information. http://www.pewinternet.org/. Accessed 7 April 2008.

Joinson, A. N. (2001). Self-disclosure in computer-mediated communication: The role of self- awareness and visual anonymity. *European Journal of Social Psychology, 31,* 177–192.

Joinson, A. N., Paine, C. B., Buchanan, T., & Reips, U.-R. (2010). Privacy, trust and self- disclosure online. *Human-Computer Interaction, 25,* 1–24.

Katzer, C., Fetchenhauer, D., & Belschak, F. (2009). Cyberbullying: Who are the victims? *Journal of Media Psychology: Theories, Methods, and Applications, 21,* 25–36.

Kelly, A. E., & McKillop, K. J. (1996). Consequences of revealing personal secrets. *Psychological Bulletin, 120,* 450–465.

Kelly, A. E., Klusas, J. A., von Weiss, R. T., & Kenny, C. (2001). What is it about revealing secrets that is beneficial? *Personality and Social Psychology Bulletin, 27,* 651–665.

Lenhart, A., & Madden, M. (2007). Teens, privacy and online social networks. Retrieved from , April 18 2007 Pew Internet & American Life Project. http://www.pewinternet.org/.

Ljepava, N., Orr, R. R., Locke, S., & Ross, C. (2013). Personality and social characteristics of Facebook non-users and frequent users. *Computers in Human Behavior, 29,* 1602–1607.

Marlowe, F. (1999). Male care and mating effort among Hazda foragers. *Behavioral Ecology and Sociobiology, 46,* 57–64.

McAndrew, F. T., & Jeong, H. S. (2012). Who does what on Facebook? Age, sex and relationship status as predictors of Facebook use. *Computers in Human Behavior, 28,* 2359–2365.

McAndrew, F. T., & Milenkovic, M. A. (2002). Of tabloids and family secrets: The evolutionary psychology of gossip. *Journal of Applied Social Psychology, 32*(5), 1064–1082.

McAndrew, F. T., & Shah, S. S. (2013). Sex differences in jealousy over Facebook activity. *Computers in Human Behavior, 29,* 2603–2606.

McKenna, K. Y. A., & Bargh, J. A. (1998). Coming out in the age of the Internet: Identity "demarginalization" through virtual group participation. *Journal of Personality and Social Psychology, 75,* 681–694.

McKenna, K. Y. A., Green, A. S., & Gleason, M. E. J. (2002). Relationship formation on the Internet: What's the big attraction? *Journal of Social Issues, 58,* 9–31.

Mehdizadeh, S. (2010). Self-presentation 2.0: Narcissism and self-esteem on Facebook. *Cyberpsychology, Behavior, and Social Networking, 13,* 357–364.

Miller, S. L., & Maner, J. K. (2010). Evolution and relationship maintenance: Fertility cues lead committed men to devalue relationship alternatives. *Journal of Experimental Social Psychology, 46,* 1081–1084.

Mok, D., Wellman, B., & Carrasco, J. (2010). Does distance matter in the age of the Internet? *Urban Studies, 47,* 2747–2783.

Muise, A., Christofides, E., & Desmarais, S. (2009). More information than you ever wanted: Does Facebook bring out the green-eyed monster of jealousy? *Cyberpsychology & Behavior, 12,* 441–444.

Muscanell, N. L., Guadagno, R. E., Rice, L., & Murphy, S. (2013). Don't it make my brown eyes green? An analysis of Facebook use and romantic jealousy. *Cyberpsychology, Behavior, and Social Networking, 16,* 237–242.

Nguyen, M., Bin, Y. S., & Campbell, A. (2012). Comparing online and offline self disclosure: A systematic review. *Cyberpsychology, Behavior, and Social Networking, 15,* 103–111.

Nikken, P., & Jansz, J. (2012). Parental mediation of young children's Internet use. http://111.lse.ac.uk/media%40lse/research/EUKidsOnline/Conference%202011/Nikken.pdf. Accessed 8 Oct 2013.

Peluchette, J., & Karl, K. (2008). Social networking profiles: An examination of student attitudes regarding use and appropriateness of content. *Cyberpsychology & Behavior, 11,* 95–97.

Perilloux, C., Easton, J. A., & Buss, D. M. (2012). The misperception of sexual interest. *Psychological Science, 23,* 146–151.

Peters, J., Shackelford, T. K., & Buss, D. M. (2002). Understanding domestic violence against women: Using evolutionary psychology to extend the feminist functional analysis. *Violence and Victims, 17,* 255–264.

Pew Internet & American Life Project. (2013). Online dating and relationships. http://www.pewinternet.org/Reports/2013/Online-Dating/Summary-of-Findings.aspx.

Piazza, J., & Bering, J. M. (2009). Evolutionary cyberpsychology: Applying an evolutionary framework to Internet behavior. *Computers in Human Behavior, 25,* 1258–1269.

Piazza, J., & Bering, J. M. (2010). The coevolution of secrecy and stigmatization: Evidence from the content of distressing secrets. *Human Nature, 21,* 290–308.

Piazza, J., & DeScioli, P. (2012). *Who else knows? The strategic significance of secrets.* Poster presented at the Meeting for the Society of Personality and Social Psychology, San Antonio, TX.

Pollet, T. V. (2007). Genetic relatedness and sibling relationship characteristics in a modern society. *Evolution and Human Behavior, 28,* 176–185.

Pollet, T. V., Roberts, S. G. B., & Dunbar, R. I. M. (2011). Use of social network sites and instant messaging does not lead to increased offline social network size, or to emotionally closer relationships with offline network members. *Cyberpsychology, Behavior, and Social Networking, 14,* 253–258.

Raacke, J., & Bonds-Raacke, J. (2008). MySpace and Facebook: Applying the uses and gratifications theory to exploring friend-networking sites. *Cyberpsychology and Behavior, 11,* 169–174.

Resnick, P., & Zeckhauser, R. (2002). Trust among strangers in internet transactions: Empirical analysis of eBay's reputation system. In M. R. Baye (Ed.), *The economics of the Internet and e-commerce* (pp. 127–157). Amsterdam: Elsevier Science.

Resnick, P., Zeckhauser, R., Swanson, J., & Lockwood, K. (2006). The value of reputation on eBay: A controlled experiment. *Experimental Economics, 9,* 79–101.

Roberts, G. (1998). Competitive altruism: From reciprocity to the handicap principle. *Proceedings of Royal Society London B, 265,* 427–431.

Roberts, S. G. B., & Dunbar, R. I. M. (2011). The costs of family and friends: An 18-month longitudinal study of relationship maintenance and decay. *Evolution and Human Behavior, 32,* 186–197.

Schiffrin, H., Edelman, A., Falkenstern, M., & Stewart, C. (2010). The associations among computer-mediated communication, relationships, and wellbeing. *Cyberpsychology, Behavior, and Social Networking, 13,* 299–306.

Schneider, B. H. (2000). *Friends and enemies: Peer relations in childhood*. London: Arnold.

Shackelford, T. K., Buss, D. M., & Bennett, K. (2002). Forgiveness or breakup: Sex differences in responses to a partner's infidelity. *Cognition and Emotion, 16,* 299–307.

Sheridan, L. P., & Grant, T. (2007). Is cyberstalking different? *Crime & Law, 13,* 627–640.

Silk, J. B. (2003). Cooperation without counting: The puzzle of friendship. In P. Hammerstein (Ed.), *Genetic and cultural evolution of cooperation* (pp. 37–54). Cambridge: MIT Press.

Silk, J. B., Kaldor, E., & Boyd, R. (2000). Cheap talk when interests conflict. *Animal Behavior, 59,* 423–432.

Solove, D. J. (2007). *The future of reputation: Gossip, rumor, and privacy on the Internet*. London: Yale University Press.

Spink, A., Koricich, A., Jansen, B. J., & Cole, C. (2004). Sexual information seeking on web search engines. *Cyberpsychology and Behavior, 7,* 65–72.

Statista. (2013). Number of worldwide active Amazon customer accounts from 2007 to 2012 (in millions). Retrieved November 2013 from http://www.statista.com/statistics/237810/number-of-active-amazon-customer-accounts-worldwide/.

Stefanone, M. A., & Jang, C.-Y. (2007). Writing for friends and family: The interpersonal nature of blogs. *Journal of Computer-Mediated Communication, 13*(1), 123–140 (article 7).

Steijn, W. M. P., & Schouten, A. P. (2013). Information sharing and relationships on social networking sites. *Cyberpsychology, Behavior, & Social Networking, 16,* 582–587.

Stewart-Williams, S. (2007). Altruism among kin vs. nonkin: Effects of cost of help and reciprocal exchange. *Evolution and Human Behavior, 28,* 193–198.

Sylwester, K., & Roberts, G. (2013). Reputation-based partner choice is an effective alternative to indirect reciprocity in solving social dilemmas. *Evolution and Human Behavior, 34,* 201–206.

Tidwell, L. C., & Walther, J. B. (2002). Computer-mediated communication effects on disclosure, impressions, and interpersonal evaluations. *Human Communication Research, 28,* 317–348.

Tokunaga, R. S. (2011). Friend me or you'll strain us: Understanding negative events that occur over social networking sites. *Cyberpsychology, Behavior, & Social Networking, 14,* 425–432.

Toma, C. L., & Hancock, J. T. (2013). Self-affirmation underlies Facebook use. *Personality and Social Psychology Bulletin, 39,* 321–331.

Tosun, L. P. (2012). Motives for Facebook use and expressing "true self" on the Internet. *Computers in Human Behavior, 28,* 1510–1517.

Trivers, R. (1972). Parental investment and sexual selection. In B. Campbell (Ed.), *Sexual selection and the descent of man* (pp. 136–179). New York: Aldine de Gruyter.

Valkenburg, P. M., & Peter, J. (2007). Who visits online dating sites? Exploring some characteristics of online daters. *Cyberpsychology and Behavior, 10,* 849–852.

Valkenburg, P. M., & Peter, J. (2009). Social consequences of the Internet for adolescents. *Current Directions in Psychological Science, 18,* 1–5.

Vasalou, A., Oostveen, A.-M., & Joinson, A. N. (2012). A case study of non-adoption: The values of location tracking in the family. *Proceeding of the ACM 2012 Conference on Computer Supported Cooperative Work*, 779–788.

Viegas, F. B. (2005). Bloggers' expectations of privacy and accountability: An initial survey. *Journal of Computer-Mediated Communication, 10*(3), (article 12). DOI: 10.1111/j.1083-6101.2005.tb00260.x

Vlahovic, T. A., Roberts, S., & Dunbar, R. (2012). Effects of duration and laughter on subjective happiness within different modes of communication. *Journal of Computer-Mediated Communication, 17,* 436–450.

Walther, J. B., Van Der Heide, B., Hamel, L., & Shulman, H. (2009). Self-generated versus other-generated statements and impressions in computer-mediated communication: A test of warranting theory using Facebook. *Communication Research, 36,* 229–253.

Wang, R., Bianchi, S. M., & Raley, S. B. (2005). Teenagers' internet use and family rules: A research note. *Journal of Marriage and Family, 67*, 1249–1258.

Whitty, M. T. (2003). Cyber-flirting: Playing at love on the internet. *Theory & Psychology, 13,* 339–357.

Whitty, M. T. (2005). The realness of cybercheating: Men's and women's representations of unfaithful internet relationships. *Social Science Computer Review, 23,* 57–67.

Whitty, M. T. (2007). Revealing the 'real' me, searching for the 'actual' you: Presentations of self on an internet dating site. *Computers in Human Behavior, 24,* 1707–1723.

Whitty, M. T., & Quigley, L. (2008). Emotional and sexual infidelity offline and in cyberspace. *Journal of Marital and Family Therapy, 34,* 461–468.

Wilson, M., & Daly, M. (1993). An evolutionary psychological perspective on male sexual proprietariness and violence against wives. *Violence and Victims, 8,* 271–294.

Wilson, R. E., Gosling, S. D., & Graham, L. T. (2012). A review of Facebook research in the social sciences. *Perspectives on Psychological Science, 7,* 203–220.

Xue, M., & Silk, J. B. (2012). The role of tracking and tolerance in relationship among friends. *Evolution and Human Behavior, 33,* 17–25.

Yang, B., & Lester, D. (2004). Attitude toward buying online. *Cyberpsychology and Behavior, 7,* 85–91.

Part IV
Attitudes and Attitudinal Change

Attitudes: An Evolutionary Perspective

14

Charles G. Lord, Sarah E. Hill, Christopher J. Holland, Kristin Yoke and Tong Lu

In the 1800s, a 29-year-old man sat down to consider his attitude toward getting married versus staying single. He took a scrap of paper and drew two columns labeled "Marry" and "Not Marry." Then he listed his thoughts in favor of marriage in one column and his thoughts against marriage in the other (see Table 14.1). After listing these thoughts, the young man wrote at the bottom of the left-hand column "Marry—Marry—Marry Q.E.D." Soon after, he courted and wed his first cousin Emma Wedgwood.

The young man's name was Charles Darwin. By age 29, he had already completed his famous voyage of discovery on the *Beagle* and had formulated many of his ideas that would provide the groundwork for the theory of evolution by natural selection. What we can never know for sure is how Darwin reached such an extremely positive overall evaluation from the thoughts that he wrote. He did not use numbered lists, but there seem to be approximately as many cons as pros. Some of the pros (e.g., "better than a dog") seem like very faint praise. Some of the cons (e.g., a possible lifetime of "banishment and degradation") seem extremely negative. It is hard to see how these ideas about getting married, in total, could lead to anything better than a lukewarm endorsement, and certainly not to "Marry—Marry—Marry Q.E.D." unless he attached overwhelming importance to some of the items on that list, including what was probably the first thing he wrote —"Children (if it Please God)."

Given the overlap in dates, it is possible that before making his list, Charles Darwin had just been writing about his theory of evolution by natural selection, in which reproduction plays a central role. He may have put down his pen after writing about his theory and within minutes begun his list of pros and cons in the top left corner by listing "Children" simply because he had been writing about reproduction merely moments before. His list—and therefore his attitudes about marriage—may have been quite different if something else had come to mind when he began his list. That one positive association to getting married—having children—may have been primed by his recent thoughts about reproduction and made him adopt a more positive attitude toward marriage than he would have had he considered it in a different time and place. As it turns out, he and Emma had ten children, three of whom went on to become accomplished Fellows of the Royal Society.

C. G. Lord (✉) · S. E. Hill · C. J. Holland · K. Yoke · T. Lu
Department of Psychology, Texas Christian University, Fort Worth, TX 76129, USA
e-mail: c.lord@tcu.edu

S. E. Hill
e-mail: s.e.hill@tcu.edu

C. J. Holland
e-mail: c.holland@tcu.edu

K. Yoke
e-mail: kristin.yoke@tcu.edu

T. Lu
e-mail: t.lu@tcu.edu

V. Zeigler-Hill et al. (eds.), *Evolutionary Perspectives on Social Psychology,* Evolutionary Psychology,
DOI 10.1007/978-3-319-12697-5_14,

Table 14.1 A young man's list of reasons to either "Marry" or "Not Marry"

Marry	Not Marry
Children—(if it Please God)—Constant companion, (& friend in old age) who will feel interested in one—object to be beloved & played with—better than a dog anyhow.—Home & someone to take care of house—Charms of music & female chitchat.—These things good for one's health—but terrible loss of time—My God, it is intolerable to think of spending one's whole life, like a neuter bee, working, working, & nothing after all.—No, no won't do.—Imagine living all one's day solitarily in smoky dirty London House—Only picture to yourself a nice soft wife on a sofa with good fire, & books & music perhaps—Compare this vision with the dingy reality of Grt. Marlbro' St	Freedom to go where one liked—choice of Society & little of it—Conversation of clever men at clubs—Not forced to visit relatives, & to bend in every trifle.—to have the expense & anxiety of children—perhaps quarrelling—Loss of time.—cannot read in the Evenings—fatness & idleness—Anxiety & responsibility—less money for books, etc.—if many children forced to gain one's bread—(But then it is very bad for one's health to work too much). Perhaps my wife won't like London; then the sentence is banishment & degradation with indolent, idle fool—

Attitude Models

That idea—that Darwin's attitude toward a topic as important as getting married might have been influenced without his awareness by events in the recent environment —flies in the face of traditional attitude theories that depict attitudes as traits or dispositions. Allport (1935), for instance, famously defined attitude as "a mental and neural state of readiness, organized through experience, exerting a directive and dynamic influence upon the individual's response to all objects and situations with which it is related" (p. 810). Such definitions emphasize the stable, enduring nature of attitudes, which are seen as summary evaluations stored in and later retrieved from memory to "direct" an individual's responses to an attitude object. According to these storage and retrieval models, Darwin would have earlier in life developed an overall summary evaluation of "getting married" and would have simply retrieved that attitude to inform his decision, without having to consider the pros and cons of marriage each time a relevant situation arose.

Tempting as it may be to accept this traditional storage and retrieval model of attitudes, it entails serious logical problems, including how cognitively costly it would be to remember summary evaluations for the huge array of attitude objects that people encounter in their lifetimes, plus doing the mental work necessary to update each summary evaluation with each new piece of relevant information one might glean. In addition, the traditional model of attitudes explains instances of stability, when people evaluate the same attitude object the same way—either favorably or unfavorably—across times and situations, but it has difficulty explaining instances of instability, when the same person evaluates the same attitude object differently at different times and in different contexts (Schwarz 2007). Traditional models would have difficulty, for example, explaining a hypothetical scenario in which Charles Darwin might have evaluated marriage unfavorably in the morning, did not think about marriage for the next few hours, and yet evaluated marriage very favorably after writing a few paragraphs in the afternoon about the role of reproduction in human evolution.

In contrast to the traditional model of attitudes are construal models. A construal model of attitudes, explains both stability and instability within the same explanatory framework (Schwarz 2006). According to construal models, people do not need to store, update, and retrieve summary evaluations for a vast array of attitude objects. Instead, each time they evaluate an attitude object, it brings to mind a few associations—e.g., "marriage means children and nice soft wife on the sofa"—and those activated associations inform the evaluation of the moment (Lord and Lepper 1999; Schwarz and Bohner 2001; Smith and DeCoster 1998). Evaluations tend to be stable across times and situations when the attitude object activates similar associations and different when it activates dissimilar associations (Sia et al. 1997). Thus, Darwin might evaluate "getting married" more favorably at a time when having children

Table 14.2 Studies that have manipulated three fundamental evolutionary motives and measured effects on attitudes

Article	Study	Motive	Manipulation	Persons affected	Attitude displayed	Toward
Lee et al. 2010	Study 1	Disease avoidance	Encountering a sneezing person	Men and women	Negative	The health-care system
	Study 2	Disease avoidance	Encountering a sneezing person	Men and women	Positive	Federal funding for flu vaccines
Tybur et al. 2011		Disease avoidance	Smelling foul odor	Men and women	Positive	Condoms
Faulkner et al. 2004	Study 5	Disease avoidance	Slide show on contagious diseases	Men and women	Negative	Immigrants from Nigeria
Park et al. 2007	Study 2	Disease avoidance	Viewing slide show on pathogens	Men and women	Negative	Obese people
Griskevicius et al. 2011	Study 2	Self-protection	News story about violent crime	Men and women	Positive if low SES childhood; negative if high	Having children soon
	Study 4	Self-protection	News story about violent crime	Men and women	Positive if low SES childhood; negative if high	Starting family vs. career
Roney 2003		Mate acquisition	Rated ads with attractive models	Men	Positive	Having large income and being financially successful
Hill and Durante 2011	Study 1	Mate acquisition	Rating photos of attractive men	Women	Positive	Tanning and diet pills
	Study 2	Mate acquisition	Recall competing for partner	Women	Positive	Tanning and diet pills
Griskevicius et al. 2007	Study 1	Mate acquisition	Rating desirability of attractive opposite-sex others	Men (not women)	Positive	Conspicuous expensive products
	Study 2	Mate acquisition	Rating desirability of attractive opposite-sex others	Women (not men)	Positive	Volunteering for good causes
Sundie et al. 2011	Study 2	Mate acquisition	Reading short romantic story	Men (not women)	Positive	Buying fake "expensive" wallet
Hill et al. 2012	Study 2	Mate acquisition	Reading about job scarcity	Women	Positive	Beauty-enhancing products

Table 14.2 (continued)

Article	Study	Motive	Manipulation	Persons affected	Attitude displayed	Toward
	Study 3	Mate acquisition	Reading about job scarcity	Women	Positive	Beauty-enhancing products and wealthy men
Durante et al. 2012	Study 2	Mate acquisition	Viewing local dating web-site with few men	Women	Positive	Pursuing a career
	Study 3	Mate acquisition	News story about scar-city of men	Women	Positive	Pursuing a career
	Study 4	Mate acquisition	News story about scar-city of men	Women who thought they were not attractive to men	Positive	Pursuing a lucrative career

SES socioeconomic status

comes to mind than at a different time when loss of time and money for books come to mind. The construal model of attitudes avoids the fundamental attribution error (Ross 1977; see also Mesquita et al. 2010; Richardson et al. 2010) of thinking the cause of evaluative responses must be a relatively permanent fixture of the actor, and offers greater parsimony by explaining both stability and instability of attitudes with the same cognitive process mechanism (Schwarz 2006).

The construal model of attitudes predicts that temporary changes in the immediate context can sway current attitudes. People might respond favorably to an attitude object in one context that primes positive associations, and respond unfavorably in another context that primes negative associations (Förster and Lieberman 2007; Higgins 1996; Lord and Lepper 1999; Schwarz 2007; Tesser and Martin 1996; Wilson and Hodges 1992; Wyer and Srull 1986). Darwin, for instance, might adopt a different attitude toward getting married if he were seated in a nursery than in a library, because one context reminds him of the association between marriage and children, whereas the other reminds him of all those books that he could no longer afford to buy.

Because different contexts can make different associations to an attitude object salient, and thus promote different attitudes toward that object (Schwarz 1999; Schwarz and Sudman 1992), people are free to behave in ways that are flexible and adaptive (Brooks 2008; Smith and Collins 2010). They can exercise situated cognition (Barsalou 1999) and cope with changing contexts in ways that overly stable, enduring attitudes would not allow. The construal model of attitudes, in contrast to the traditional model, depicts people as adept at coping with changing times and circumstances by adopting different attitudes (Lord in press). They might not realize that their associations and evaluations have been affected by something in their immediate environment, but they can shift their evaluative response of the moment to one that is different from what it might otherwise have been. In this sense, the construal model of attitudes seems more compatible than traditional storage and retrieval models with evolutionary theory.

There is another sense, however, in which construal models of attitudes fit well with evolutionary theory, and that is in the relevance to context effects of fundamental evolutionary motives. Throughout evolutionary history, humans have faced a number of fundamental challenges to their survival and reproduction (Buss and Schmitt 1993; Kenrick et al. 2010b; Neuberg et al. 2005). To survive, for instance, humans have had to be adept at avoiding a range of physical dangers, such as violence and disease. To reproduce, they have had to master the art of acquiring and retaining a desirable mate. The human cognitive system has thus been hypothesized to be attuned to environmental cues that direct our attention to the threats and opportunities afforded by an attitude object within the context encountered (Kenrick et al. 2010a). If, as described by construal theories of attitudes, people construct their current evaluations on the spot (Schwarz 2006, 2007) and base their evaluations of the moment on temporarily salient associations to an attitude object (Lord and Lepper 1999; Tourangeau and Rasinski 1988), then the environmental context might be unchanged, and yet people might evaluate differently depending on whether one or more of these evolutionarily significant motives happens to be salient for them at that particular time (Griskevicius and Kenrick 2013; Maner et al. 2005).

Table 14.2 lists several recent studies that are consistent with this view of the human cognitive system. In each case described, a fundamental evolutionary motive was made temporarily salient by a brief experimental manipulation, after which participants evaluated an attitude object that posed either an opportunity or a threat relevant to that motive. In each of these studies, experimental manipulations of evolutionarily significant motives altered how participants evaluated the attitude object in ways that would facilitate an adaptive response to the stimulus in question. Participants evaluated attitude objects that presented an opportunity to satisfy the motive more positively than they would have otherwise, and evaluated attitude objects that threatened the motive more negatively than they would have otherwise.

Indeed, it is easy to see why the process of evolution by selection would shape attitudes to be flexibly constructed depending on the adaptive problems one is currently confronting. Take, for example, one's attitudes toward having children. In a harsh, unpredictable environment, it is adaptive to adopt a positive attitude toward having children early in life ("do it now or possibly never"), but in a safe, predictable environment adopting a negative attitude toward having children early in life would work better because it takes time to accumulate resources that will ensure the children's health and survival (Chisholm 1993). A stubbornly consistent attitude—either positive or negative—would not work as well as one that alters with the situation. Table 14.2 is divided into studies that manipulated disease-avoidance, self-protection, and mate-acquisition motives, because disease avoidance is often considered separately from self-protection (Griskevicius and Kenrick 2013).

Disease Avoidance

The construal model of attitudes can be applied to situations in which cues to infectious disease are present. In one such study (Lee et al. 2010), participants who had passed a sneezing, coughing confederate in a public place were then approached by an experimenter who asked them to evaluate the country's health-care system. They reported more negative attitudes than did participants in a control group, and rated their likelihood of contracting a serious disease as higher. In a second study, participants who met a sneezing, coughing experimenter reported more positive attitudes toward the federal government spending money on flu vaccines instead of on creating green jobs. Participants in both studies were unaware that another person's sneezing and coughing had influenced their attitudes. In these two studies, priming fundamental evolutionary motives had selective effects: Attitudes toward a government health system that might threaten disease avoidance became more negative and attitudes toward government spending that might help disease avoidance became more positive.

Contaminants that carry disease often emit a foul odor, so foul odors might prime disease-avoidance motives. In a relevant study (Tybur et al. 2011), randomly selected students participated in a room that had been sprayed with "Liquid ASS," a fluid that smells like feces. Compared to participants in a control group, those in the foul-odor condition subsequently reported greater intentions to use condoms. Participants in the experimental versus control groups did not differ in their reported positive or negative affect, so the "Liquid ASS" manipulation did not alter attitudes of the moment by eliciting different levels of general affect. The more positive attitudes appear to have been directed only at the disease-avoidance attributes of condoms.

Momentary salience of disease-avoidance motives can also affect attitudes toward possibly unhealthy out-groups. Faulkner et al. (2004, study 5), had students view one of two slide shows—either on the ways that diseases can be transmitted in everyday life or on accidents that can happen in every life. Those who viewed the disease slide show subsequently reported less favorable attitudes (compared to those who viewed the accidents slide show) toward the government allowing immigrants from Nigeria to live in their city. Participants displayed no such bias toward immigrants from Scotland, whom other students described as more sanitary. Similarly, students in another study (Park et al. 2007, study 2) who viewed a diseases slide show were faster than those who viewed an accidents slide show to display negative attitudes by associating disease-related words with photos of obese versus normal-weight people.

The take-home message from these studies seems clear. Temporary salience of disease-avoidance motives accentuates the connection between contamination and out-groups that are suspected of being unsanitary, which in turn causes people to adopt functionally adaptive unfavorable attitudes toward those particular out-groups. Evolutionarily significant motives, when triggered by cues from the immediate environment, can magnify attitudinal tendencies to avoid out-groups that might pose a danger.

Self-Protection and Having Children

The superiority of the construal model of attitudes is also apparent when one considers the effects of self-protective motives on the question confronted by Charles Darwin in the opening vignette—whether to marry and have children. Humans have always faced the twin challenges of personal survival and reproduction, but self-enhancing activities that promote personal survival can be seen as a stepping stone—as ensuring that the person accumulates enough personal fitness and resources to produce children who will be born healthy and thrive. During their reproductive years, both men and women face a trade-off between expending energy on their own personal survival and fitness versus on finding a mate and having children—essentially the dilemma faced by Charles Darwin at age 29. Suppose that something in the immediate environment were to make self-protective motives more salient than usual. What effect might that momentary salience of self-protective motives have on attitudes toward getting married and having children?

Griskevicius et al. (2011) examined this question in studies where, to prime self-protection motives, some participants (not others) read a news story claiming that random shootings and deaths were becoming an everyday occurrence. All participants then reported their attitudes toward having children "in the next few years." Interestingly, the effects of priming self-protective motives depended on participants' childhood socioeconomic status (SES). It led those who grew up poor to report more positive attitudes toward having children soon (study 2), and toward starting a family at the expense of furthering their education and career (study 4), but it had exactly the opposite effects on those who grew up in relatively wealthy homes. These results are consistent with a functional analysis of the relationship between salient evolutionary motives and current attitudes. People who grew up in a wealthy environment might interpret rampant violence in their cities as something they can control by waiting before they begin any new ventures like having children; people who grew up in a poor environment might interpret the same level of violence as uncontrollable—a sign that they had better have children quickly, before it is too late.

Mate Acquisition

It is unlikely that self-protective motives had been momentarily cued at the time when Darwin was compiling his list of pros and cons. It is much more likely that writing about reproduction within his theory of evolution primed mate-acquisition motives.

Table 14.2 shows several studies in which mating-related motives were made temporarily salient by a brief manipulation for randomly selected participants, who then evaluated an attitude object differently than they might have otherwise. Some of these studies primed mate-acquisition motives by drawing participants' attention to desirable members of the opposite sex. Roney (2003), for instance, had men rate the effectiveness of ads containing photos of either very attractive or less attractive women, after which the men reported their attitudes toward having a large income and being financially successful. Men who viewed photos of sexy, desirable women expressed more positive attitudes toward making a lot of money—an activity that both men and women agree would help them to satisfy mate-acquisition motives.

Like men, women who have mate-acquisition motives made temporarily salient also adopt more positive attitudes toward activities that will increase their chances of acquiring a high-quality mate. Hill and Durante (2011, study 1), for instance, had women rate the attractiveness of highly desirable "local" men and then had them report their interest in tanning and taking diet pills—two activities that carry health risks but make women more attractive to prospective mates. Compared with women who had not yet seen the photos, those who had just rated photos of sexy men reported more positive attitudes toward tanning and taking diet pills. In a follow-up study (study 2), women who were asked to recall or imagine a time when they had to compete with other women for a desirable romantic partner estimated the health risks of tanning and taking diet pills as less likely and adopted more favorable attitudes toward those specific activities, but not toward other risky behaviors irrelevant to mate acquisition. Hill and Durante's results highlight the selective functionality of mate-acquisition primes and also suggest that when people have an evolutionary motive made momentarily salient they tend to display positive attitudes toward anything that satisfies that specific motive, even when they incur costs by doing so.

In a study of adopting seemingly costly attitudes, Griskevicius et al. (2007, study 1) had men and women rate photos showing three attractive members of the opposite sex and then describe a perfect first date with their favorite. They were then asked how much money they would spend on several "flashy" items that signaled how well-off they were (a costly signal men send to attract women) and how much volunteering they would do for good causes (a costly signal women send to attract men). Relative to a control group, making mate-acquisition motives salient caused men (not women) to adopt more positive attitudes toward buying items that would show off how much money they had, and caused women (not men) to adopt more positive attitudes toward benevolent volunteering. Follow-up studies showed that these more positive attitudes are adopted only when they can be displayed in public (study 2), and that even men will adopt more positive attitudes toward benevolent acts when those acts can be made to appear heroic (study 3) or as evidence of their dominance (study 4)—in other words, when it will help them get women. Finally, other studies have shown that men (not women) who have just read a short story about passionately kissing a new acquaintance on a moonlit beach express greater willingness to buy a fake "knock-off" wallet that looks like a very expensive one (Sundie et al. 2011, study 2), indicating that it is the "show off" property of the object that matters and not just how much it costs.

Women are not immune to the effects of mate-acquisition motives on attitudes toward costly signals. Hill et al. (2012, study 2) had men and women read an article saying that the current economy was in recession and good jobs were scarce—implying that high-income mates were hard to find. Women (not men) who read the recession article subsequently reported greater desire to purchase products that would enhance their physical attractiveness. They were also more likely to say they wanted to look attractive to men, valued a potential marriage partner's financial stability, and would purchase products like cosmetics, perfume, and fitted jeans while cutting back on other purchases (study 3). Furthermore, these positive attitudes applied only to costly luxury brand products likely to attract a quality mate (study 4). These studies illustrate how making mate-acquisition motives momentarily salient affects current attitudes toward specific objects that help satisfy those motives.

Mate Acquisition and Having Children

In a study of threats to mate acquisition, Durante et al. (2012, study 2) showed college women photos "from a local dating website" that had either 70 % men or 70 % women. The researchers reasoned that people often confront a tradeoff between expending energy on looking after themselves versus on having children (Griskevicius et al. 2011), so thinking there were few eligible men might make women put off plans to get married and have children, concentrating instead on pursuing a lucrative career.

That is exactly what the researchers found. Compared to the "many-men" condition, women in the "few-men" condition reported more positive attitudes toward pursuing a career relative to starting a family. These attitude effects were mediated by changes in the women's perceptions of how difficult it would be to find a suitable mate (Durante et al. 2012, study 3), and driven primarily by women who viewed themselves as less attractive (study 4)—the very women who would find it most difficult to acquire a mate in an environment composed of 70 % women and only 30 % men.

Discussion

Many of the described studies found the predicted effects only for certain people and only for specific attitude objects. Looking back at the "participants affected" column of Table 14.2, men and women reacted the same way to manipulations that made disease-avoidance and self-protective motives salient, whereas the two sexes often reacted differently to manipulates that made mate-acquisition motives salient. These differences in how men and women responded to the activation of mate-acquisition motives were predictable based on empirically verified differences in men's and women's mating strategies and preferences.

Because of the sex-differentiated mating benefits available to men and women from displaying cues to wealth and fertility, for example, men and women differed in the degree to which mating goals influenced their attitudes toward buying conspicuously costly items and their desire to buy beauty products. In addition, participants reacted differently to these mating manipulations depending on their interest in short-term versus long-term relationships and whether they had grown up relatively poor or relatively rich. Finally, the effects of priming evolutionary motives on attitudes were highly dependent on the nature of the attitude objects themselves. When evolutionary motives were made temporarily salient, participants reported no changes in positive or negative affect or in moods. Instead, their attitudes changed only toward attitude objects that might play a role in successfully or unsuccessfully solving the adaptive challenge implied by the specific motive primed. These findings demonstrate the specificity of the participants affected and the attitude objects affected are also consistent with recent advances in understanding how priming works.

The situated inference model of priming (Loersch and Payne 2011) holds that priming manipulations increase the cognitive accessibility of specific mental content. An individual might spontaneously associate condoms, for example, more with "prevent pregnancy" than with "prevent spread of sexually transmitted diseases (STDs)." Being in a room that smells like feces, however, reverses that hierarchy of associations and makes STDs more accessible than pregnancy. Similarly, a woman might spontaneously associate diet pills more with "health risks" than with "attracts men," but having recently viewed photos of sexy local men reverses the relative accessibility of these mental contents. Once a priming manipulation has made prime-relevant content unusually accessible, people will use that temporarily activated mental content to inform their judgments and behaviors, but only if they think the specific associations were self-generated, without any external influence. That is why all the reviewed studies went out of their way to disguise the intended connection between the manipulation of evolutionary motives and the attitudinal measures.

Finally, people apply the preferentially accessed mental content only to objects that are relevant to solving problems afforded by the current situation. If the task in the current situation is to evaluate taking diet pills and painting in a closed room (both risky activities), for instance, "attracts men" seems relevant to evaluating one of these activities but not the other. Similarly, viewing photos of attractive others might render thoughts like "attracts women" to be preferentially associated with "flashy" consumer products, but thoughts about attracting women would affect the attitudes of men more than women, because such thoughts would seem more task relevant for men than for women. Different contexts afford different concerns for different participants, so the meaning and impact on attitudes of the specific mental content that was primed can vary greatly.

The general principle, however, is that when people believe the primed mental content was accessed spontaneously, they apply that mental content to whichever current evaluative judgment or behavior affords relevance (Loersh and Payne 2011)—a principle that is consistent with both evolutionary theory (Chisholm 1993; Haselton and Buss 2000) and the construal model of attitudes. Although we have no way to know, by applying the situated inference model of priming to the studies in Table 14.2, we might suspect that Charles Darwin had been writing about reproduction, took a break to compose his list, remained unaware that his recent writing had temporarily increased the accessibility of thoughts like "Children—if it please God," perceived that marriage afforded the opportunity of having children, and thus adopted an extremely positive attitude.

References

Allport, G. W. (1935). *Attitudes*. Worcester: Clark University Press.

Barsalou, L. W. (1999). Perceptual symbol systems. *Behavioral and Brain Sciences, 22,* 577–660. doi:10.1017/S0140525X99002149.

Brooks, R. A. (2008). Intelligence without representation. In W. G. Lycan & J. J. Prinz (Eds.), *Mind and cognition: An anthology* (pp. 298–311). Malden: Blackwell Publishing.

Buss, D. M., & Schmitt, D. P. (1993). Sexual strategies theory: An evolutionary perspective on human mating. *Psychological Review, 100,* 204–232. doi:10.1037/0033-295X.100.2.204.

Chisholm, J. S. (1993). Death, hope, and sex: Life-history theory and the development of reproductive strategies. *Current Anthropology, 34,* 1–24. doi:10.1086/204131.

Durante, K. M., Griskevicius, V., Simpson, J. A., Cantú, S. M., & Tybur, J. M. (2012). Sex ratio and women's career choice: Does a scarcity of men lead women to choose briefcase over baby? *Journal of Personality and Social Psychology, 103,* 121–134. doi:10.1037/a0027949.

Faulkner, J., Schaller, M., Park, J. H., & Duncan, L. A. (2004). Evolved disease-avoidance mechanisms and contemporary xenophobic attitudes. *Group Processes and Intergroup Relations, 7,* 333–353. doi:10.1177/1368430204046142.

Förster, J., & Liberman, N. (2007). Knowledge activation. In A. W. Kruglanski & E. T. Higgins (Eds.), *Social psychology: Handbook of basic principles* (2nd ed., pp. 201–231). New York: Guilford Press.

Griskevicius, V., & Kenrick, D. T. (2013). Fundamental motives: How evolutionary needs influence consumer behavior. *Journal of Consumer Psychology, 23,* 372–386. doi:10.1016/j.jcps.2013.03.003.

Griskevicius, V., Tybur, J. M., Sundie, J. M., Cialdini, R. B., Miller, G. F., & Kenrick, D. T. (2007). Blatant benevolence and conspicuous consumption: When romantic motives elicit strategic costly signals. *Journal of Personality and Social Psychology, 93,* 85–102. doi:10.1037/0022-3514.93.1.85.

Griskevicius, V., Tybur, J. M., Delton, A. W., & Robertson, T. E. (2011). The influence of mortality and socioeconomic status on risk and delayed rewards: A life history theory approach. *Journal of Personality and Social Psychology, 100,* 1015–1026. doi:10.1037/a0022403.

Haselton, M. G., & Buss, D. M. (2000). Error management theory: A new perspective on biases in cross-sex mind reading. *Journal of Personality and Social Psychology, 78,* 81–91. doi:10.1037/0022-3514.78.1.81.

Higgins, E. T. (1996). Knowledge activation: Accessibility, applicability, and salience. In E. T. Higgins & A. W. Kruglanski (Eds.), *Social psychology: Handbook of basic principles* (pp. 133–168). New York: Guilford Press.

Hill, S. E., & Durante, K. M. (2011). Courtship, competition, and the pursuit of attractiveness: Mating goals facilitate health-related risk taking and strategic risk suppression in women. *Personality and Social Psychology Bulletin, 37,* 383–394. doi:10.1177/0146167210395603.

Hill, S. E., Rodeheffer, C. D., Griskevicius, V., Durante, K., & White, A. E. (2012). Boosting beauty in an economic decline: Mating, spending, and the lipstick effect. *Journal of Personality and Social Psychology, 103,* 275–291. doi:10.1037/a0028657.

Kenrick, D. T., Griskevicius, V., Sundie, J. M., Li, N. P., Li, Y. J., & Neuberg, S. L. (2009). Deep rationality: The evolutionary economics of decision making. *Social Cognition, 27,* 764–785. doi:10.1521/soco.2009.27.5.764.

Kenrick, D. T., Griskevicius, V., Neuberg, S. L., & Schaller, M. (2010a). Renovating the pyramid of needs: Contemporary extensions built upon ancient foundations. *Perspectives on Psychological Science, 5,* 292–314. doi:10.1177/1745691610369469.

Kenrick, D. T., Neuberg, S. L., Griskevicius, V., Becker, D. V., & Schaller, M. (2010b). Goal-driven cognition and functional behavior: The fundamental-motives framework. *Current Directions in Psychological Science, 19,* 63–67. doi:10.1177/0963721409359281.

Lee, S. W. S., Schwarz, N., Taubman, D., & Hou, M. (2010). Sneezing in times of a flu pandemic: Public sneezing increases perception of unrelated risks and shifts preferences for federal spending. *Psychological Science, 21,* 375–377. doi:10.1177/0956797609359876.

Loersch, C., & Payne, B. K. (2011). The situated inference model: An integrative account of the effects of primes on perception, behavior, and motivation. *Perspectives on Psychological Science, 6,* 234–252. doi:10.1177/1745691611406921.

Lord, C. G. (in press). Attitudes: Constructions versus disposition. In R. A. Scott & S. M. Kosslyn (Eds.), *Emerging trends in the social and behavioral sciences.* New York: Wiley.

Lord, C. G., & Lepper, M. R. (1999). Attitude representation theory. In M. P. Zanna (Ed.), *Advances in experimental social psychology* (Vol. 31, pp. 265–343). San Diego: Academic. doi:10.1016/S0065-2601(08)60275-0.

Maner, J. K., Kenrick, D. T., Becker, D. V., Robertson, T. E., Hofer, B., Neuberg, S. L., Delton, A. W., Butner, J., & Schaller, M. (2005). Functional projection: How fundamental social motives can bias interpersonal perception. *Journal of Personality and Social Psychology, 88,* 63–78. doi:10.1037/0022-3514.88.1.63.

Mesquita, B., Barrett, L. F., & Smith, E. R. (2010). The context principle. In B. Mesquita, L. F. Barrett, & E. R. Smith (Eds.), *The mind in context* (pp. 1–24). New York: Guilford Press.

Neuberg, S. L., Kenrick, D. T., Maner, J. K., & Schaller, M. (2005). From evolved motives to everyday mentation: Evolution, goals, and cognition. In J. P. Forgas, K. D. Williams, & S. M. Laham (Eds.), *Social motivation: Conscious and unconscious processes* (pp. 133–152). New York: Cambridge University Press.

Park, J. H., Schaller, M., & Crandall, C. S. (2007). Pathogen-avoidance mechanisms and the stigmatization of obese people. *Evolution and Human Behavior, 28,* 410–414. doi:10.1016/j.evolhumbehav.2007.05.008.

Richardson, M. J., Marsh, K. L., & Schmidt, R. C. (2010). Challenging the egocentric view of coordinated perceiving, acting, and knowing. In B. Mesquita, L. F. Barrett, & E. R. Smith (Eds.), *The mind in context* (pp. 307–333). New York: Guilford Press.

Roney, J. R. (2003). Effects of visual exposure to the opposite sex: Cognitive aspects of mate attraction in human males. *Personality and Social Psychology Bulletin, 29,* 393–404. doi:10.1177/0146167202250221.

Ross, L. (1977). The intuitive psychologist and his shortcomings: Distortions in the attribution process. *Advances in Experimental Social Psychology, 10,* 173–220.

Schwarz, N. (1999). Self reports: How the questions shape the answers. *American Psychologist, 54,* 93–105.

Schwarz, N. (2006). Attitude research: Between Ockham's razor and the fundamental attribution error. *Journal of Consumer Research, 33,* 19–21.

Schwarz, N. (2007). Attitude construction: Evaluation in context. *Social Cognition, 25,* 638–656. doi:10.1521/soco.2007.25.5.638.

Schwarz, N., & Bohner, G. (2001). The construction of attitudes. In A. Tesser & N. Schwarz (Eds.), *Blackwell handbook of social psychology: Intraindividual processes* (pp. 436–457). Malden, MA: Blackwell Publishers.

Schwarz, N., & Sudman, S. (Eds.). (1992). *Context effects in social and psychological research.* New York: Springer Verlag. http://hdl.handle.net/2027.42/64020, 04–03-2009.

Sia, T. L., Lord, C. G., Blessum, K. A., Ratcliff, C. D., & Lepper, M. R. (1997). Is a rose always a rose? The role of social category exemplar change in attitude stability and attitude-behavior consistency. *Journal of Personality and Social Psychology, 72,* 501–514. doi:10.1037/0022-3514.72.3.501.

Smith, E. R., & Collins, E. C. (2010). Situated cognition. In B. Mesquita, L. F. Barrett, & E. R. Smith (Eds.), *The mind in context* (pp. 126–145). New York: Guilford Press.

Smith, E. R., & DeCoster, J. (1998). Knowledge acquisition, accessibility, and use in person perception and stereotyping: Simulation with a recurrent connectionist network. *Journal of Personality and Social Psychology, 74,* 21–35. doi:10.1037/0022-3514.74.1.21.

Sundie, J. M., Kenrick, D. T., Griskevicius, V., Tybur, J. M., Vohs, K. D., & Beal, D. J. (2011). Peacocks, Porsches, and Thorstein Veblen: Conspicuous consumption as a sexual signaling system. *Journal of Personality and Social Psychology, 100,* 664–680. doi:10.1037/a0021669.

Tesser, A., & Martin, L. (1996). The psychology of evaluation. In E. T. Higgins & A. W. Kruglanski (Eds.),

Social psychology: Handbook of basic principles (pp. 400–432). New York: Guilford Press.

Tourangeau, R., & Rasinski, K. A. (1988). Cognitive processes underlying context effects in attitude measurement. *Psychological Bulletin, 103,* 299–314. doi:10.1037/0033-2909.103.3.299.

Tybur, J. M., Bryan, A. D., Magnan, R. E., & Hooper, A. E. C. (2011). Smells like safe sex: Olfactory pathogen primes increase intentions to use condoms. *Psychological Science, 22*(4), 478–480. doi:10.1177/0956797611400096.

Wilson, T. D., & Hodges, S. D. (1992). Attitudes as temporary constructions. In L. L. Martin & A. Tesser (Eds.), *The construction of social judgments* (pp. 37–65). Hillsdale: Lawrence Erlbaum Associates, Inc.

Wyer, R. S., & Srull, T. K. (1986). Human cognition in its social context. *Psychological Review, 93,* 322–359. doi:10.1037/0033-295X.93.3.322.

15 Conformity: Definitions, Types, and Evolutionary Grounding

Julie C. Coultas and Edwin J. C. van Leeuwen

Conformity is the act of fitting in with the group. As a group-living species, much of our behavior is focused on preserving group cohesion. The tendency to change one's behavior to match the responses of others is often adaptive (Cialdini and Goldstein 2004). If we want to join a group, then we monitor and copy the responses and actions of those we observe. This copying behavior is not always conscious (Chartrand and Bargh 1999), but it is often functional. If we copy those around us when we are unsure of ourselves, we will often adopt successful behavior, especially when individually acquired information is costly (Boyd and Richerson 1985; Henrich and Boyd 1998). In the past 25 years, there has been a burgeoning interest in conformist behavior from diverse disciplines including psychology, anthropology, evolutionary biology, behavioral ecology, mathematics, and economics.

The grounding of conformist behavior in evolutionary theory proved justified when nonhuman species were similarly observed to be drawn to majorities (e.g., Claidière and Whiten 2012). For instance, chimpanzees behave as if they desire to be like others (Hopper et al. 2011; Whiten et al. 2005), capuchin monkeys develop group-specific foraging traditions (Perry 2009), and vervet monkeys acquiesce to local foraging techniques upon entering a new group (van de Waal et al. 2013). That these closely related species show behavioral patterns that resemble crowd-following in humans marked a starting point for exploring the evolutionary roots of human conformity. When even more distantly related species like rats (Galef and Whiskin 2008; Jolles et al. 2011) and fish (Day et al. 2001; Pike and Laland 2010) were found to show conformity, it led to an interest in the evolutionary roots of human conformity as well as the robustness of conformity as a social learning heuristic (Laland 2004).

Recent investigations into conformity, however, have exposed several issues that may distort our understanding of conformist behavior, even in humans. Notably, "conformity" has not been defined unequivocally across disciplines (e.g., Haun et al. 2013). Whereas conformity in humans has been defined in terms of forgoing personal convictions in the face of a majority of peers expressing a different stance (e.g., Asch 1956; Sherif 1936), "conformity" has been used to describe the process by which individual nonhumans acquire the foraging strategy that becomes the most common variant (e.g., Hopper et al. 2011; Perry 2009). Moreover, whereas some conformity studies have produced conclusions by investigating the effects of one large group (i.e., the majority) on the focal individuals in the absence of minori-

J. C. Coultas (✉)
Centre for the study of Cultural Evolution, Stockholm University, 106 91 Stockholm, Sweden
e-mail: julie.coultas@gmail.com

Department of Psychology, University of Sussex, Falmer BN1 9QH, UK

E. J. C. van Leeuwen
Department of Developmental Psychology, University of Jena, Am Steiger 3/1, 07743 Jena, Germany
e-mail: edwin.vanLeeuwen@mpi.nl

V. Zeigler-Hill et al. (eds.), *Evolutionary Perspectives on Social Psychology,* Evolutionary Psychology, DOI 10.1007/978-3-319-12697-5_15,

ties (e.g., van de Waal et al. 2013), others have investigated the effects of one conspecific on the behavioral perseverance of the focal individuals (e.g., Galef and Whiskin 2008). The plethora of definitions used across these "conformity" studies has hampered assessment of the evolutionary roots of conformist behavior and thwarted between-species comparisons (van Leeuwen and Haun 2014). To clarify the study of conformity, a proposal has been made for a streamlined set of definitions (see Haun et al. 2013; van Leeuwen and Haun 2014). In the following paragraphs, we present this set of definitions and put the disparate body of terms in line with this classification. Another issue distorting understanding of conformist behavior is that many "conformity" findings can similarly be explained by (unbiased) social influences (van Leeuwen and Haun 2014). Social influence can be a potent force in shaping individuals' behavior, even in the absence of majorities. In this chapter, however, we focus on streamlining the study of conformity by delineating its definitions and arguing for a detailed consideration of the *type* of influence that generates the conformity effect.

First, it is important to consider that individuals can acquire the behavior of the majority through mechanisms that *do* or *do not* concern the meta-fact that it is "the majority" that is being observed (as opposed to "a minority" or any separate individual). The majority strategy could be adopted for the reason that it is the majority strategy, or for any other reason. Examples of nonmajority targeted reasons are *random copying,* where individuals randomly copy a member of their group, or the heuristic that guides individuals to *copy successful group members* (e.g., Laland 2004). Both these mechanisms do not concern targeted majority copying, yet likely cause the social learner to end up with the majority strategy (see Haun et al. 2013). Since both targeted and nontargeted majority copying can produce similar behavioral signatures (i.e., within-group homogeneity; Boyd and Richerson 1985), it is important to distinguish their mechanisms accordingly.

Another aspect to consider in labeling conformist behavior is whether the social learner had preestablished convictions or behavior regarding the observed phenomenon. Humans and many other animals form routines or habits. These habits may hinder the adoption of observed behavior (van Leeuwen and Haun 2014). Compare this to the situation in which individuals are ignorant to the affordances (e.g., when people visit a new city and want to find a good restaurant)—the impact of observing the choice of the local majority (i.e., the restaurant with the most customers on a given square) would be larger than when the visitors had acquired local preferences. A powerful situational incentive to adopt the behavior of conspecifics seems to be naivety or uncertainty (Kendal et al. 2009). Given the potential impact of these different starting points (i.e., experienced or naïve) on the tendency to use social information, it might improve accuracy to organize conformity labels accordingly.

The term *majority influence* refers to any effect that the majority has on its observers (Haun et al. 2013). This term includes targeted and nontargeted majority copying, just like effects on experienced and naïve observers. Under the majority influence umbrella, we first identify *majority-biased transmission* as a general, nontargeted way in which majorities can affect its naïve observers. In this case, the mere presence of a majority increases the likelihood that the observers acquire the strategy of the majority compared to the expectancy of acquiring this same strategy in the absence of the majority (Haun et al. 2012; also see Haun et al. 2013). Different strategies could lead to majority-biased transmission, including random copying or copying successful individuals. Scholars across disciplines have used different terms to capture processes that fall under the term "majority-biased transmission." For instance, *unbiased transmission* refers to random copying (Boyd and Richerson 1985), just like *linear transmission* (e.g., Boyd 1988), *linear imitation* (McElreath et al. 2005), and *linear conformity* (Claidière and Whiten 2012). Majority-biased transmission was proposed to refer to the process where naïve individuals face a majority.

This scrutiny of naïve individuals' behavior has been the trademark of scholars studying cultural evolution (e.g., Boyd and Richerson 1985;

Cavalli-Sforza and Feldman 1981; Henrich and Boyd 1998; see Aoki avd Feldman 2013). Moreover, the study of cultural evolution has produced a more stringent version of majority-biased transmission. In search of processes that could change rather than perpetuate the distribution of cultural variants over generations, notably towards (asymptotic) within-group homogeneity, the hallmark of culture, it was found that within the scope of majority influences only targeted majority copying yielded the respective change, not any form of majority-biased transmission (e.g., Boyd and Richerson, 1985; Laland 2004). This targeted majority copying was coined *conformist bias* (Boyd and Richerson 1985; Eriksson and Coultas 2009; Eriksson et al. 2007), *copy-the-majority* (Laland 2004), or *hyper-conformity* (Claidière and Whiten 2012). The related change in the distribution of cultural variants within populations was referred to as *conformist transmission,* or *conformity* (Boyd and Richerson 1985). Thus, the discovered impetus towards cultural differentiation was described by a disproportionate increase in the tendency to copy the majority with increasing majority sizes (e.g., Henrich and Boyd 1998). This version of conformity has been central to studies of cultural evolution (Morgan and Laland 2012; van Leeuwen and Haun 2014).

The term *conformity* has also been used in the study of human psychology, defined as the modification of an individual's statements or behavior towards matching the majority (Kiesler and Kiesler 1969). Psychologists have long been interested in the extent to which humans are susceptible to group pressure, especially in scenarios where people have good reasons to believe that their group expresses an erroneous statement (e.g., Asch 1956; Jenness 1932; Sherif 1936). This version of conformity has become common within popular culture. The human psychology version of conformity differs from the cultural evolution version in that individuals with pre-established preferences, knowledge, or behavior are being scrutinized, as opposed to naïve ones (for more details, see van Leeuwen and Haun 2014). This aspect of forgoing personal strategies in favor of the majority has led researchers to use the equivalent term *strong conformity* (Haun and Tomasello 2011). Most human psychology studies have not been accurate or explicit in their analyses regarding targeted and nontargeted majority copying (Mesoudi 2009; van Leeuwen and Haun 2014). Instead, different forms of majority influences have been subsumed under the general phenomenon of conformity, with the exception of the distinction between two different motivations to conform: acquiring valuable information (*informational conformity*) and inducing social approval (*normative conformity*; Deutsch and Gerard 1955; also see Claidière and Whiten 2012). The lack of scrutiny on the level of targeted and nontargeted majority copying has resulted in a common usage of the term "conformity" for instances in which humans (and nonhuman animals) adopt another strategy without it being clear whether the majority was responsible for the strategy shift or any nonmajority influence (see van Leeuwen and Haun 2014).

Another majority influence aspect that remained incompletely assessed is its evolutionary framework. When the diversity of majority influence definitions hampers cross-species comparisons, it remains unclear if there are any nonhuman animal equivalents to human conformity patterns. There is a fast-growing body of studies reporting cultural group differences in nonhuman animals, which is indicative of majority influences accordingly (reviewed in Galef 2012; Hoppitt and Laland 2013). The study of cultural evolution has shown that potent majority influences (specifically, conformist transmission) can result in relative within-group homogeneity and between-group heterogeneity, which in common language amounts to "cultural differences" (reviewed in Aoki and Feldman 2013). Hence, it could be inferred that nonhuman animal culture arises through similar majority influence principles. Although this hypothesis is currently under investigation (e.g., van Leeuwen et al. 2013; Luncz and Boesch 2013; van de Waal et al. 2013), the impetus to view majority influences from an evolutionary perspective seems plausibly justified (see also Richerson and Boyd 2005). It was the seminal work on modeling the evolution of culture by anthropologists Boyd and Richerson (1985) that highlighted the importance of placing conformity in an evolutionary framework. Their work not only showed that the targeted form of majority influence (i.e., conformist transmission) could lead to cultural group differences, but was able to explain phenomena that had been evolutionary puzzles until then, most prominently large-scale human cooperation (Boyd and Richerson 1991). To streamline the proximate forms of conformity, however, and provide the data-driven tools to advance the current models of gene-culture coevolution, we focus on clarifying the plethora of conformity definitions and progress in the next section by delineating different *types* of conformity and reviewing the existing evidence accordingly.

Types of Conformity

Early conformity experiments within social psychology (e.g., Asch 1951, 1956; Gerard et al. 1968; Milgram et al. 1969; Sherif 1935) and theory (e.g., Deutsch and Gerard 1955; Latané 1981; Tanford and Penrod 1984) are still important in our thinking about conformity, but more recent accounts informed by evolutionary theory challenge us to take another look at the phenomenon (e.g., Boyd and Richerson 1985; Cladière and Whiten 2012; Henrich and Boyd 1998; Richerson and Boyd 2005) and empirical work (e.g., Coultas 2004; Efferson et al. 2008; Eriksson and Coultas 2009; Griskevicius et al. 2006; McElreath et al. 2005).

Because most studies of human psychology have focused on the "conformity" operationalization as outlined in the previous section, we focus on research shedding light on this phenomenon, with an occasional excursion to the "conformist transmission" operationalization when studies are of particular relevance. There has been a recent proposal to separate conformity research into two categories: studies where informational social influence comes into play and studies where the influence is normative (Campbell and Fairey 1989; Cladière and Whiten 2012; Deutsch and Gerard 1955). There is utility in thinking about different types of social influence, but informational and normative influences can often be theoretically and empirically intertwined (Cialdini and Goldstein 2004; David and Turner 2001). To tease apart the social influences on conformist behavior, we first consider Deutsch and Gerard's (1955) informational and normative social influence, then review relevant conformity experiments focusing on three types: conformity in perceptual judgment, behavioral conformity, and conformity in opinions and attitudes. The foundational contribution of conformity research to both early theoretical models in social psychology (Social Impact Theory, Latané 1981; Social Influence Model, Tanford and Penrod 1984) and a later gene-culture coevolutionary model (Conformist Transmission Model; Boyd and Richerson 1985) is acknowledged. However, the context of the experiment (e.g., field or laboratory) and the prior "habits" and self-perceptions of the participants (self-categorization theory; Turner 1991) need to be taken into account.

In a recent review of conformity, Cialdini and Goldstein (2004) focus on Deutsch and Gerard's (1955) concept of informational and normative social influence. This approach to conformity has been influential, as it draws attention to the fact that different processes of influence could be present in different situations. Deutsch and Gerard describe *normative* social influence as an influence to conform to the positive expectations of another person or group, which can lead to solidarity and *informational* social influence (i.e., to accept information obtained from another person or group as evidence about reality). They recognize that these two types of influence often emerge together, but that it is possible to conform behaviorally by agreeing publically with the beliefs of others even though they are counter to one's own beliefs (normative influence; see also Kelman 1961; Mann 1969). In addition, it is possible to accept an opponent's belief as evidence about a particular aspect of reality (informational influence) even though there may be no intention of accepting all the opponent's beliefs (Deutsch and Gerard 1955).

Festinger's (1950, 1954) social comparison theory encourages us to be cautious in accepting the distinction between normative and informational influence without acknowledging some additional factors. People tend not to evaluate their opinions or abilities by comparing themselves to others who are divergent from themselves (Festinger 1950). We are more strongly influenced by people who are similar to us. Turner (1991) also argues that the processes of normalization, conformity, and innovation are interconnected with the formation, maintenance, and change of in-group norms. Conversely, Campbell and Fairey (1989) argue for the relative importance of normative and informational influences in conformity experiments where they manipulate public and private agreement using an Asch-type paradigm. Cladière and Whiten (2012) base their argument for dissecting conformity research into these two categories on Campbell and Fairey's (1989) work. However, although normative and informational influences are important notions, we argue for an explicit appraisal of the *type* of conformity experiment in which the respective behavior is elicited.

Conformity experiments are not homogeneous; some studies take place in laboratories (e.g., Allport 1924; Asch 1951 1956; Sherif 1935), others in natural environments where participants are unaware that they are in an experiment (e.g., Allport 1934; Coultas and Eriksson 2014; Mann 1977; Milgram et al. 1969), others use naturalistic methods in a formal setting (e.g., Coultas 2004), whereas other studies influence people's opinion in the laboratory or in the natural environment (Crutchfield 1955; Eriksson and Coultas 2009; Latané and Davis 1974). This methodological variation creates problems for making comparisons across conformity studies. For instance, group size needs to be greater than three for naturalistic experiments when people are unaware that they are taking part in a study; both Mann (1977) and Coultas (2004) found that there needed to be at least five or six models of the target behavior before any conformist behavior was observed.[1] Similarly, most behavioral conformity experiments take place in the field, whereas perceptual judgment experiments focusing on conformity take place in the laboratory. The flexible nature of conformity studies on attitudes and opinions means that they can take place in the laboratory or in naturalistic environments. Next, we address the evidence for conformity classified by the type of experiment, both regarding task features and the context in which the study takes place.

Conformity in Perceptual Judgment

Earlier conformity studies (e.g., Asch 1951, 1956; Crutchfield 1955; Sherif 1935) were explorations of situational uncertainty where people sometimes denied the evidence of their own senses and accepted others' perceptual judgments. The effect of different group sizes on people's conformist tendencies was measured in these experiments, but not always systematically (Bond 2005). Additionally, the proportion of people producing the target behavior (majority) compared to those who were producing the minority behavior was not always clearly reported (e.g., Moscovici et al. 1969; Nemeth et al. 1977). One earlier perceptual judgment study did systematically manipulate unanimous and nonunanimous majorities to measure the level of conformist behavior (Jacobs and Campbell 1961), but it is only in the past decade, inspired by gene-culture coevolutionary models, that conformity experiments have begun to systematically manipulate both group size and proportion.

Perceptual judgment experiments have a special place in social psychology, where Asch's work on perceptual judgment is most frequently reported. However, in an earlier experiment, Allport (1924) had participants judge—both alone and in groups—the pleasantness or unpleasantness of odors, ranging from putrid to perfumes. Participants judged the putrid odors as less unpleasant when they were in a group than when they were on their own and the pleasant smells as less pleasant when they made their judgment in the group rather than on their own. People modified their opinion about the odors when working in a group and avoided extreme judgments. The reported olfactory experiences changed depending on whether they were in a group or

[1] Asch proposed that conformity leveled off at a group size of three in perceptual judgment experiments.

on their own which indicates that a group norm was formed. Sherif's (1935) perceptual judgment experiments using the "autokinetic" effect also demonstrated that artificially created norms or judgments in groups could alter the judgment of an individual. He presented a stationary point of light at a distance of about 5 m from participants in a darkened room and asked them (both in groups and alone) to make oral estimations about the movement of the light. The participants in groups were influenced by the overestimation of confederates.

Utilizing the situational ambiguity of Sherif's (1935) autokinetic effect, Jacobs and Campbell (1961) asked groups of two, three, or four participants to make judgments on how far the light had moved. In the first set of 30 trials, all but one of the participants were confederates and gave widely discrepant judgments compared to that of the one naïve participant. In subsequent blocks of 30 trials (generations), a confederate was removed and another naïve participant was included in the group. By the second, third, or fourth generation, there were no confederates left in the group. Jacobs and Campbell (1961) continued their experiment by replacing the most experienced naïve participant with another naïve participant up to the 11th generation. They found that control groups estimated the light movement around the 4-inch mark, but naïve participants in the presence of confederates who were radically overestimating the light movement (e.g., 16 inches) would provide much greater estimates than those in the control condition (e.g., 14 inches). Even when all the confederates had been replaced, the influence of the confederates remained, with naïve participants estimating the light movement at around the 10-inch mark. Jacobs and Campbell's results indicate that the majority can have a significant effect on how others make perceptual judgments even after those who made up the majority are no longer present. The experimental procedures used by Jacobs and Campbell (1961) suggest the existence of conformist transmission (Boyd and Richerson 1985; Henrich and Boyd 1998).

Asch (1951) wanted to test conformity in a situation where, unlike Sherif's autokinetic effect, there was a right or wrong answer. He asked participants to match the length of a line on one card with one line out of three lines of unequal length on another card. In a control group, Asch found that the error rate was very small. In the main study, confederates made unanimously incorrect line judgments two thirds of the time (on 12 out of 18 trials). Naïve participants were then asked to give their answer. Three quarters of participants were influenced by the incorrect majority some of the time. In total, just over two thirds of the choices made by the real participants were correct despite the pressure of the majority. Asch used unanimous groups of various sizes (1, 2, 3, 4, 8, 16) and found that when there was one confederate and one naïve participant the majority effect all but disappeared. Asch was convinced that the effect was present in full force when there was a majority of three (though it is important to note that Asch's assertion was based on a sample of ten participants). The larger majorities of four, eight, and sixteen did not produce effects that were substantially greater than a majority of three. He therefore predicted a nonlinear effect of conformity. It would be judicious to accept these results with a note of caution due to the small sample size and concerns about consistency across Asch's studies (Bond 2005). Another reason for caution is that an early Asch replication (Gerard et al. 1968) found that conformity increased linearly with group size, although the first few models of the behavior had the most impact.

One of the defining characteristics of perceptual judgment tasks is that there is often scope for situational ambiguity. In Sherif's autokinetic technique, even the control participants believed that the stationary light had moved a short distance. Recently, there have been critical assessments of Asch's studies in a meta-analysis of Asch-type perceptual judgment task studies (Bond and Smith 1996). Bond and Smith also note that conformist behavior as defined by performance on the Asch perceptual judgment task has declined in the USA since the 1950s. Bond (2005) comments that "given the pre-eminent status of Asch's (1951,1955, 1956) conformity experiments, it is surprising to find inconsistencies in the reports of what size of majority was employed" (p. 338). A large number of perceptual judgment experiments have used nonunanimous majorities, but have not systematically tested proportion (e.g., Asch 1951, 1956; Moscovici et al. 1969; Nemeth et al. 1977). The predictions made by theoretical models (Boyd and Richerson 1985; Latané 1981; Tanford and Penrod 1984) encourage researchers to carefully plan studies where both group size and proportion are varied systematically.

Behavioral Conformity

A key aspect of many behavioral conformity experiments is that participants are unaware that they are taking part in a study. Bargh and Chartrand's (1999) work on automatic imitation, in which people adopt the behavior of those around them without being aware, has made a contribution to our thinking about conformity experiments in naturalistic environments. Our predisposition for affiliative (Cialdini and Goldstein 2004) or docile (Simon 1990) behavior means we often copy those around us without any conscious intent. This form of behavioral conformity would fall under the heading of the ethological approach to human behavior—observing humans in their natural habitat (Hinde 1982). Many years before Asch's studies, Allport (1934) had developed his J-curve conformity hypothesis by observing people stopping their cars at street crossings, people parking their cars, the degree of kneeling in two Catholic churches, and participation in congregational singing. He argued that in order for conformity to occur there had to be a purpose for the behavior, there had to be some rule in society related to it, and over half the population needed to be behaving in that particular way. Allport's main conformity hypothesis was that if over half the population were producing a particular behavior then that behavior was likely to be adopted. This is similar to the predictions made by Boyd and Richerson's (1985) conformist transmission model.

Following the tradition of naturalistic observation, Milgram et al. (1969) sent out groups of stooges (group sizes 1, 2, 3, 5, 10, and 15) to stare up at a building in New York and counted how many people looked up as they walked past or stopped and stared alongside the group. They found that the size of the stimulus group significantly affected the proportion of passersby who looked up or stopped alongside the group. The larger the stimulus crowd staring up at the building, the greater the effect.[2] More recently, this field study has been replicated in the UK and Sweden (Coultas and Eriksson 2014; Gallup et al. 2012) producing a similar linear pattern of influence with increase in group size. However, far fewer people were influenced to stare up at a building in the UK and Sweden compared to the earlier New York study, leading to the question of whether these differences in conformity are situational. Potential influences on behavioral conformity include location (e.g., city size; Milgram 1970; Newman and McCauley 1977; Mullen et al. 1990), change in conformist behavior across time (Bond and Smith 1996), and different types of groups or entities. Knowles and Bassett (1976) manipulated the type of stimulus groups in a similar field experiment to Milgram et al. and found that those standing silently while staring up had greater influence on passersby compared to groups who interacted with one another. Coultas and Eriksson's (2014) replication of Milgram et al.'s (1969) study, which ran in three different locations in the UK and one in Sweden, also established that the type of stimulus group is an important factor.

The fundamental difference between conformity field studies and laboratory experiments is that participants in the laboratory *know* that they are taking part in an experiment. The ethological method focuses on humans in their natural habitat—walking along the street, sometimes making decisions consciously, while at other times automatically following the crowd. Mann (1977) looked at the influence of stimulus groups on people's queue-joining behavior in Jerusalem where this was not the social norm. Mann observed the effect of stimulus queues of two, four, six, and eight confederates on 569 commuters waiting at a bus stop. Congruent

[2] Lumsden and Wilson (1981) used these findings when constructing their trend-watcher curve.

with findings by Milgram et al., Mann found that a larger stimulus queue had a greater influence on commuters. However, unlike in Milgram et al.'s study, Mann found that a six-person queue was required to induce a reliable level of queue-joining behavior. These findings reinforce the need to take the situation into account when designing experiments and manipulating group size.

Field studies are used extensively to demonstrate how humans behave in everyday life. In their naturalistic study of environmental conservation, Aronson and O'Leary (1983) found that a sign instructing students to save water by turning off the shower while they soaped up had little effect, whereas two thirds turned off the shower with two models of the behavior. Similarly, two field experiments by Goldstein et al. (2008) found that hotel guests were not influenced by a sign in their room encouraging environmental conservation (e.g., reuse their towels), but were influenced by the information that the majority of hotel guests reuse their towels. Situational influence was also present, as hotel guests who were informed that the majority of guests who had stayed in their current room had reused their towels were more likely to produce the same behavior than those guests who only saw the sign encouraging environmental conservation.

Goldstein et al. (2008) report a study of conformity to the unseen and anonymous majority. Inevitably, there will be studies of conformist behavior that do not fall easily into the categories of behavioral conformity, perceptual judgment, or attitudes. An unpublished study by Latané and Davis (1974 cited in Latané and Wolf 1981) is an example of conformity to the anonymous majority's opinion. In this field experiment, college students were approached and asked to sign a questionnaire concerning the adequacy of local newspapers. Each page of the questionnaire had one question at the top and two columns labeled "yes" and "no" below. This dichotomous choice was a constrained behavior with little commitment required other than to sign one's name in a column. The questionnaires already contained a varying number of signatures before being presented to the respondent. These signatures were either all in the "yes" column or all in the "no" column and were counterbalanced so that they appeared in both columns an equal number of times. Even though a proper baseline measure was absent in their study (i.e., how people would behave if there were no signatures), they found that conformity increased systematically with the number of signatures up to a majority of 12.

Importantly, individuals' habitual behavior will influence how they respond to a novel behavior. In a study of behavior in a computer laboratory, participants—unaware that they were taking part in an experiment—were influenced to place their keyboard covers in an unusual position (on top of their computers) by the presence of models of that behavior (Coultas 2004). However, contrary to Asch's findings, group size needed to be greater than three before anyone copied the novel behavior and conformed to the majority which demonstrated that the strongest predictor of conformity, once group size was greater than five, was the proportion of individuals who were already producing the behavior. In a subsequent experiment, participants who had signed up for clinical psychology experiments also (unknowingly) took part in a conformist transmission study in which they were influenced to change the way they wrote the date by those who had filled in the sheets and signed the date before them (a common method, e.g., "14/5/96,"[3] and a rare method, e.g., "14th May 1996"; Coultas 2004). The relative size of the majority (i.e., proportion) was shown to be a significant predictor of conformity and participants were more likely to be influenced by the majority if their behavior was rare (e.g., 14th May 1996) and the majority behavior was the common behavior (e.g., 14/5/96). In this case, the data fitted the conformist transmission curve. However, when an individual who wrote the date in the most common form (14/5/96) was presented with a sheet where the majority of people (forged) had written the date analogically (14th May 1996), conformity occurred only when approximately three quarters of the forged dates were written analogically. People were less likely to adopt a rare behavior even if that behavior was common in the context of the experiment.

[3] Note that this is the UK numerical version of the date. US version would be 5/14/96. The difference in US/UK date-signing was used as a variable in an unpublished study by Moore and Coultas (2010).

The two studies by Coultas (2004) were a direct test of the conformist transmission model (Boyd and Richerson 1985), as both the influence of group size and proportion was measured for each individual. Recapitulating, conformist transmission is the disproportionately increasing tendency to adopt the majority strategy with increasing relative majority size and can thus only be measured when group size and majority proportion are varied. Its importance follows from the fact that only this disproportionate tendency to copy the majority will yield behavioral patterns typical of what we consider to be "culture" (i.e., relative within-group homogeneity and between-group heterogeneity; see also Richerson and Boyd 2005). The computer laboratory and date-signing studies also illustrate that the conformist transmission model needs to be modified on the basis of the "habits" that people bring with them to naturalistic experiments. Our predispositions to behave in certain ways can override the influence of the majority if we are strongly attached to our personal strategy (van Leeuwen and Haun 2014) or the specific behavior that is being studied is not a social norm. In their review, Cialdini and Goldstein (2004) also acknowledge that pre-existing attitudes, prior behaviors, and commitments will influence our behavior towards novel stimuli. These habits or predispositions that people bring to a situation are related to the concept of social identity (Tajfel and Turner 1979; Turner et al. 1987); the phenomenon that describes how people's perception of who they are is based on their identifying with certain groups (see also the concept of *self-categorization* (Turner 1991) and the drive to maintain a favorable self-concept (Cialdini and Goldstein 2004). However, the adoption of a group norm may not always be a conscious action (Bargh and Chartrand 1999; Chartrand and Bargh 1999; Nisbett and Wilson 1977).

Conformity in Opinion and Attitude

The terms *opinions* and *attitudes* are sometimes incorrectly used interchangeably (e.g., Nowak et al. 1990; Haddock and Maio 2008). Attitudes have affective, cognitive, and behavioral components and involve favoring or disfavoring some particular entity (e.g., Eagly and Chaiken 1993). Moreover, attitudes are relatively deep-rooted and change only gradually over time. Opinions are more flexible and prone to change and therefore are the most relevant in a review of conformity research. However, there is empirical evidence that both people's opinions and attitudes are influenced by those around them (Crutchfield 1955; Eriksson and Coultas 2009; Newcomb et al. 1967; Wolf and Latané 1983).

Most of the studies in this section focus on participants changing their opinion about a particular aspect within an experiment. However, in a longitudinal study begun in 1935, Newcomb (1943) studied attitude change across time at a college with predominantly conservative students and liberal professors. Over time, students increasingly adopted the liberal attitudes of their new reference group, the professors. When Newcomb et al. (1967) interviewed the students 25 years later, they found that the adopted attitudes persisted. Indeed, opinion change has been a topic within social psychology for many years (e.g., Allport 1924; reviewed in Cialdini and Goldstein 2004). Opinions can be manipulated both in the laboratory (e.g., Crutchfield 1955) and in the field (e.g., Eriksson and Coultas 2009; Latané and Davis 1974; Stang 1976; White 1975). For instance, in Crutchfield's (1955) study, where participants agreed or disagreed with particular statements, there was a shift to change opinion and agree with the unanimous majority, but when participants provided a subjective judgment (preference) about two simple line drawings they were not influenced by the majority.

The study of the effects of different motivations on tendencies to conform has been extended beyond the distinction between informational and normative influences. In a coherent set of experiments, two motives pivotal to evolutionary success were studied in the context of conformity: self-protection (survival) and mate attraction (reproduction; Griskevicius et al. 2006). By theorizing about the possible ramifications of conformity in light of these two motives, these scholars were able to predict the existence of (sex-specific) behavioral patterns likely shaped by evolutionary processes. In line with these predictions, being primed with a self-protective mindset caused both males and females to increase their conformist responses. This finding was interpreted to be evolutionarily advantageous in the sense that avoiding standing out from the crowd lowers predation risk (Griskevicius et al. 2006). Additionally, the activation of mate attraction motives resulted in sex-specific conformity responses, congruent with predictions based on sex-specific mating strategies where men chose to stand out of the crowd to highlight the qualities generally preferred by women (assertiveness, independence, leadership; see Buss 2003) and women preferred to emphasize the qualities generally liked by men (agreeableness, facilitating group cohesion; see Campbell 2002) by conforming to the majority (Griskevicius et al. 2006).This study nicely illustrates how evolutionary theory could be used to set up specific empirical studies revolving around conformist tendencies.

A useful approach to understanding different types of influence is to examine the situations in which conformist behavior occurs. Why would conformist behavior have been useful in our evolutionary past? In situations where there is uncertainty about the correct behavior, the best strategy is often to adopt the most common behavior (Boyd and Richerson 1985). From this perspective, both group size and proportion are important factors in conformity research. Two theoretical models in social psychology sought to formalize predictions of conformist behavior, using both group size and proportion; whereas Latané (1981) used the findings from Asch (1951) and Milgram et al. (1969) as the foundations of social impact theory (SIT), Tanford and Penrod (1984) used jury decision making in the development of their social influence model (SIM).[4] This means that SIT used both laboratory (e.g., Asch) and field studies (e.g., Milgram et al.) synonymously, whereas social influence theory used jury decision making to represent social influence in general. In an alternative approach, Boyd and Richerson (1985) used the gene-culture coevolutionary theory, inspired by population genetics and past research within social psychology, to develop their conformist transmission model. This evolutionary model of conformity made predictions about behavior which had echoes of an earlier model of conformity within social psychology (Allport 1934). Boyd and Richerson's conformist transmission model emphasized the importance of proportion (frequency) in conformity research and enabled researchers to formalize their empirical work in order to test the model both in simulations (Henrich and Boyd 1998) and in the field (Coultas 2004; Eriksson and Coultas 2009). However, for reasons of direct relevance to the evolution of culture, their theoretical focus has not been on the aspect of *changing* perceptions, behavior, or opinions, but rather on the more pronounced form of conformist behavior (i.e., "conformist transmission") in which typically naïve individuals are under investigation. At the intersection of social psychology's focus on "conformity" and the conformist variant central to analyses of cultural evolution ("conformist transmission"), we would envision fruitful cross-fostering leading to the incorporation of individuals' habits or predispositions, and the evidenced circumstances under which they would be abandoned, into models of cultural evolution (cf. Strimling et al. 2009; see also van Leeuwen and Haun 2014).

This section has aimed to emphasize the importance of taking into account the type (perception, behavior, or opinion) and context (laboratory, field) of conformity, while at the same time advancing the idea that individuals' current habits or mind-sets need to be factored in when interpreting any kind of conformist or nonconformist behavior.

Concluding Remarks

In this chapter, we hope to have conveyed how evolutionary theory can elucidate the study of conformity. By taking seriously the predictions and ramifications of the early gene-culture coevolution models (Boyd and Richerson 1985; Henrich and Boyd 1998) and by appreciating the conformity evidence from nonhuman animal studies, our understanding of conformist behavior

[4] The SIM equation in Tanford and Penrod (1984) is incorrect (see Coultas, 2004; MacCoun, 2012).

can transcend the unfounded sphere of plausible evolutionary scenarios to become a substantiated research endeavor including testable hypotheses stemming from evolutionary theory. However, we have identified several proximate issues that cloud our current appreciation of the scope of conformity. In order to achieve a coherent field of conformity research in the future, we have three simple pieces of advice for researchers. Firstly, define conformity in the context of your experimental manipulation. Social psychology typically focuses on another form of conformity than scholars investigating cultural evolution, and even within social psychology, there are several different definitions; only by specifying the operationalization of conformity will we be able to interpret and compare the phenomena validly. Secondly, make sure that different types of conformity are not subsumed under the same heading. Different patterns are expected based on whether the conformity scenario entails perceptual, behavioral, or opinion features. Moreover, field studies and laboratory studies yield very different results. In general, group size needs to be larger in field studies than in the laboratory before conformist behavior is elicited. Furthermore, it would be fruitful to formally acknowledge that participants' preestablished views and habits will inevitably influence the outcome of any conformity study. By operationalizing this idiosyncratic aspect and incorporating this measure into conformity models, in both social psychology and the study of cultural evolution, we will gain a more fine-grained understanding of the effects of majorities. Finally, taking an evolutionary perspective on conformity is an exciting proposition, but take care not to overestimate the presence of conformity based on models and simulations. It makes good sense to conform to the group in some situations, but nonconformity and independence are also adaptive under certain circumstances.

References

Allport, F. H. (1924). *Social psychology*. Boston: Houghton Mifflin.

Allport, F. H. (1934). The j-curve hypothesis of conforming behavior. *Journal of Social Psychology, 5,* 141–185.

Aoki, K., & Feldman, M. W. (2013). Evolution of learning strategies in temporally and spatially variable environments: A review of theory. *Theoretical Population Biology, 90,* 64–81.

Aronson, E., & O'Leary, M. (1983). The relative effectiveness of models and prompts on energy conservation. *Journal of Environmental Systems, 12,* 219–224.

Asch, S. E. (1951). Effects of group pressure upon the modification and distortion of judgment. In H. Guetzkow (Ed.), *Groups, leadership and men* (pp. 117–190). Pittsburgh: Carnegie Press.

Asch, S. E. (1955). Opinions and social pressure. *Scientific American, 193,* 31–35.

Asch, S. E. (1956). Studies of independence and conformity: A minority of one against a unanimous majority. *Psychological Monographs, 70,* 1–70.

Bargh, J. A., & Chartrand, T. L. (1999). The unbearable automaticity of being. *American Psychologist, 54,* 462–479.

Bond, R. (2005). Group size and conformity. *Group Processes & Intergroup Relations, 8,* 331–354.

Bond, R., & Smith, P. B. (1996). Culture and conformity: A meta-analysis of studies using Asch's (1952b, 1956) line judgment task. *Psychological Bulletin, 119,* 111–137.

Bonnie, K. E., Horner, V., Whiten, A., & de Waal, F. B. M. (2007). Spread of arbitrary conventions among chimpanzees: A controlled experiment. *Proceedings of the Royal Society B-Biological Sciences, 274,* 367–372.

Boyd, R. (1988). Is the repeated prisoner's dilemma game a good model of reciprocal altruism? *Ethology and Sociobiology, 9,* 211–221.

Boyd, R., & Richerson, P. J. (1985). *Culture and the evolutionary process*. Chicago: University of Chicago Press.

Boyd, R., & Richerson, P. J. (1991). Culture and cooperation. In R. A. Hinde & J. Groebel (Eds.), *Cooperation and prosocial behavior* (pp. 27–48). Cambridge: Cambridge University Press.

Buss, D. M. (2003). *The evolution of desire: Strategies of human mating* (2nd ed.). New York: Basic Books.

Campbell, A. (2002). *A mind of her own: The evolutionary psychology of women*. Oxford: Oxford University Press.

Campbell, J. D., & Fairey, P. J. (1989). Informational and normative routes to conformity: The effect of faction size as a function of norm extremity and attention to the stimulus. *Journal of Personality and Social Psychology, 57,* 457–468.

Cavalli-Sforza, L. L., & Feldman, M. W. (1981). *Cultural transmission and evolution: A quantitative approach*. Princeton: Princeton University Press.

Chartrand, T. L., & Bargh, J. A. (1999). The chameleon effect: The perception—b ehavior link and social interaction. *Journal of Personality and Social Psychology, 76,* 893–910.

Cialdini, R. B., & Goldstein, N. J. (2004). Social influence: Conformity and compliance. *Annual Review of Psychology, 55,* 591–621.

Claidière, N., & Whiten, A. (2012). Integrating the study of conformity and culture in humans and nonhuman animals. *Psychological Bulletin, 138,* 126–145.

Claidière, N., Bowler, M., & Whiten, A. (2012). Evidence for weak or linear conformity but not for hyper-conformity in an everyday social learning context. *PLoS One, 7,* e30970.

Coultas, J. C. (2004). When in Rome… An evolutionary perspective on conformity. *Group Processes & Intergroup Relations, 7,* 317–331.

Coultas, J. C., & Eriksson, K. (May, 2014). Milgram revisited: Imitative behaviour is influenced by both the size and entitativity of the stimulus group. Paper presented at the *Annual British Psychological Society*, Birmingham.

Crutchfield, R. S. (1955). Conformity and character. *American Psychologist, 10,* 191–198.

Darley, J. M. (1966). Fear and social comparison as determinants of conformity behavior. *Journal of Personality and Social Psychology, 4,* 73–78.

David, B., & Turner, J. C. (2001). Majority and minority influence: a single process self-categorisation analysis. In C. K. W. De Dreu & N. K. de Vries (Eds.), *Group consensus and minority influence: Implications for innovation* (pp. 91–121). Malden: Blackwell.

Day, R. L., MacDonald, T., Brown, C., Laland, K. N., & Reader, S. M. (2001). Interactions between shoal size and conformity in guppy social foraging. *Animal Behaviour, 62,* 917–925.

Deutsch, M., & Gerard, H. B. (1955). A study of normative and informational social influences upon individual judgment. *Journal of Abnormal and Social Psychology, 51,* 629–636.

Dindo, M., Whiten, A., & de Waal, F. B. M. (2009). In-group conformity sustains different foraging traditions in capuchin monkeys (*Cebus apella*). *PloS One, 4,* e7858.

Eagly A. H., & Chaiken S. (1993). *The psychology of attitudes*. Fort Worth: Harcourt Brace.

Efferson, C., Lalive, R., Richerson, P. J., McElreath, R., & Lubell, M. (2008). Conformists and mavericks: The empirics of frequency-dependent cultural transmission. *Evolution and Human Behavior, 29,* 56–64.

Eriksson, K., & Coultas, J. C. (2009). Are people really conformist-biased? An empirical test and a new mathematical model. *Journal of Evolutionary Psychology, 7,* 5–21.

Eriksson, K., Enquist, M., & Ghirlanda, S. (2007). Critical points in current theory of conformist social learning. *Journal of Evolutionary Psychology, 5,* 67–87.

Festinger, L. (1950). Informal social communication. *Psychological Review, 57,* 271–282.

Festinger, L. (1954). A theory of social comparison processes. *Human Relations, 7,* 117–140.

Galef, B. G. (2012). Social learning and traditions in animals: Evidence, definitions, and relationship to human culture. *Wiley Interdisciplinary Reviews-Cognitive Science, 3,* 581–592.

Galef, B. G., & Whiskin, E. E. (2008). 'Conformity' in Norway rats? *Animal Behaviour, 75,* 2035–2039.

Gallup, A. C., Hale, J. J., Sumpter, D. J. T., Garnier, S., Kacelnik, A., Krebs, J. R., & Couzin, I. D. (2012). Visual attention and the acquisition of information in human crowds. *PNAS, 109,* 7245–7250.

Gerard, H. B., Wilhelmy, R. A., & Connolley, E. S. (1968). Conformity and group size. *Journal of Personality and Social Psychology, 8,* 79–82.

Goldstein, N. J., Cialdini, R. B., & Griskevicius, V. (2008). A room with a viewpoint: Using social norms to motivate environmental conservation in hotels. *Journal of Consumer Research, 35,* 472–482.

Griskevicius, V., Goldstein, N. J., Mortensen, C. R., Cialdini, R. B., & Kenrick, D. T. (2006). Going along versus going alone: When fundamental motives facilitate strategic (non)conformity. *Journal of Personality and Social Psychology, 91,* 281–294.

Haddock, G., & Maio, G. R. (2008). Attitudes: Content, structure and function. In M. Hewstone, W. Stroebe, & K. Jonas (Eds.), *Introduction to social psychology: A European perspective* (4th ed.). Oxford: Blackwell.

Haun, D. B. M., & Tomasello, M. (2011). Conformity to peer pressure in preschool children. *Child Development, 82,* 1759–1767.

Haun, D. B. M., Rekers, Y., & Tomasello, M. (2012). Majority-biased transmission in chimpanzees and human children, but not orangutans. *Current Biology, 22,* 727–731.

Haun, D. B. M., van Leeuwen, E. J. C., & Edelson, M. G. (2013). Majority influence in children and other animals. *Developmental Cognitive Neuroscience, 3,* 61–71.

Henrich, J., & Boyd, R. (1998). The evolution of conformist transmission and the emergence of between-group differences. *Evolution and Human Behavior, 19,* 215–241.

Hinde, R. (1982). *Ethology: Its nature and relations with other sciences*. Glasgow: Fontana Press.

Hopper, L. M., Schapiro, S. J., Lambeth, S. P., & Brosnan, S. F. (2011). Chimpanzees' socially maintained food preferences indicate both conservatism and conformity. *Animal Behaviour, 81,* 1195–1202.

Hoppitt, W., & Laland, K. N. (2013). *Social learning: An introduction to mechanisms, methods, and models*. Oxfordshire: Princeton University Press.

Jacobs, R. C., & Campbell, D. T. (1961). The perpetuation of an arbitrary tradition through several generations of a laboratory culture. *Journal of Abnormal and Social Psychology, 12,* 649–658.

Jenness, A. (1932). The role of discussion in changing opinion regarding a matter of fact. *Journal of Abnormal Social Psychology, 27,* 279–296.

Jolles, J. W., de Visser, L., & van den Bos, R. (2011). Male Wistar rats show individual differences in an animal model of conformity. *Animal Cognition, 14,* 769–773.

Kameda, T., & Nakanishi, D. (2002). Cost-benefit analysis of social/cultural learning in a nonstationary uncertain environment—An evolutionary simulation and an experiment with human subjects. *Evolution and Human Behavior, 23,* 373–393.

Kelman, H. C. (1961). Processes of opinion change. *Public Opinion Quarterly, 25,* 57–78.

Kendal, R. L., Coolen, I., & Laland, K. N. (2004). The role of conformity in foraging when personal and social information conflict. *Behavioral Ecology, 15,* 269–277.

Kendal, R. L., Coolen, I., & Laland, K. N. (2009). Adaptive trade-offs in the use of social and personal information. In R. Dukas & J. Ratcliffe (Eds.), *Cognitive ecology II* (pp. 249–271). Chicago: University of Chicago Press.

Kiesler, C., & Kiesler, S. B. (1969). *Conformity.* Reading: Addison Wesley.

King, A. J., & Cowlishaw, G. (2007). When to use social information: the advantage of large group size in individual decision making. *Biology Letters, 3,* 137–139.

Knowles, E., & Bassett, R. (1976). Groups and crowds as social entities: Effects of activity, size and member similarity on nonmembers. *Journal of Personality and Social Psychology, 34,* 837–845.

Krützen, M., Willems, E. P., & van Schaik, C. P. (2011). Culture and geographic variation in orangutan behavior. *Current Biology, 21,* 1808–1812.

Laland, K. N. (2004). Social learning strategies. *Learning & Behavior, 32,* 4–14.

Latané, B. (1981). The psychology of social impact. *American Psychologist, 36,* 343–356.

Latané, B., & Wolf, S. (1981). The social impact of majorities and minorities. *Psychological Review, 88,* 438–453.

Lumsden, C. J., & Wilson, E. O. (1981). *Genes, mind and culture: The coevolutionary process.* London: Harvard University Press.

Luncz, L., & Boesch, C. (2013). Tradition over trend: Neighboring chimpanzee communities maintain differences in cultural behavior despite frequent immigration of adult females. *American Journal of Primatology, 76,* 649–657.

MacCoun, R. J. (2012). The burden of social proof: Shared thresholds and social influence. *Psychological Review, 119,* 345–372.

Mann, L. (1969). *Social psychology.* London: Wiley.

Mann, L. (1977). The effect of stimulus queues on queue-joining behavior. *Journal of Personality and Social Psychology, 6,* 437–442.

McElreath, R., Lubell, M., Richerson, P. J., Waring, T. M., Baum, W., Edsten, E., et al. (2005). Applying evolutionary models to the laboratory study of social learning. *Evolution and Human Behavior, 26,* 483–508.

Mesoudi, A. (2009). How cultural evolutionary theory can inform social psychology and vice versa. *Psychological Review, 116,* 929–952.

Milgram, S. (1970). The experience of living in cities. *Science, 167,* 1461–1468.

Milgram, S., Bickman, L., & Berkowitz, L. (1969). Note on the drawing power of crowds of different sizes. *Journal of Personality and Social Psychology, 13,* 79–82.

Moore, C., & Coultas, J. C. (March, 2010). Strangers in a strange land: Social norms, situational variables and the conformist bias. Paper presented at the 5th *European Human Behaviour and Evolution Association Conference*, University of Wroclaw, Poland.

Morgan, T. J. H., & Laland, K. (2012). The biological bases of conformity. *Frontiers in Neuroscience, 6,* 87.

Morgan, T. J. H., Rendell, L., Ehn, W., Hoppitt, W., & Laland, K. (2011). The evolutionary basis of human social learning. *Proceedings of the Royal Society B-Biological Sciences, 279,* 653–662.

Moscovici, S., Lage, E., & Naffrechoux, M. (1969). Influence of consistent minority on the responses of a majority in a color perception task. *Sociometry, 32,* 365–379.

Mullen, B., Copper, C., & Driskell, J. E. (1990). Jaywalking as a function of model behavior. *Personality and Social Psychology Bulletin, 16,* 320–330.

Nemeth, C., Wachtler, C., & Endicott, J. (1977). Increasing the size of the minority: Some losses and some gains. *European Journal of Social Psychology, 7,* 15–27.

Newcomb, T. M. (1943). *Personality and social change.* New York: Dryden Press.

Newcomb, T. M., Koenig, K. E., Flacks, R., & Warwick, D. P. (1967). *Persistence and change: Bennington College and its students after twenty five years.* New York: Wiley.

Newman, J. & McCauley, C. (1977). Eye contact with strangers in city, suburb and small town. *Environment and Behavior, 9,* 547–558.

Nisbett, R. E., & Wilson, T. D., (1977). Telling more than we can know: Verbal reports on mental processes. *Psychological Review, 84,* 231–259.

Nowak, A., Szamrej, J., & Latané, B. (1990). From private attitude to public opinion. *Psychological Review, 97,* 362–376.

Perry, S. (2009). Conformism in the food processing techniques of white-faced capuchin monkeys (Cebus capucinus). *Animal Cognition, 12,* 705–716.

Pike, T. W., & Laland, K. N. (2010). Conformist learning in nine-spined sticklebacks' foraging decisions. *Biology Letters, 6,* 466–468.

Richerson, P. J., & Boyd, R. (2005). *Not by genes alone: How culture transformed human evolution.* Chicago: University of Chicago Press.

Sherif, M. (1935). A study of some social factors in perception. *Archives of Psychology, 27,* 187.

Sherif, M. (1936). *The psychology of social norms.* Oxford: Harper.

Simon, H. (1990). A mechanism for social selection and successful altruism. *Science, 250,* 1665–1668.

Stang, D. J. (1976). Group size effects on conformity. *Journal of Social Psychology, 98,* 175–181.

Strimling, P., Enquist, M., & Eriksson, K. (2009). Repeated learning makes cultural evolution unique. *Proceedings of the National Academy of Sciences, 106,* 13870–13874.

Tajfel, H., & Turner, J. C. (1979). An integrative theory of intergroup conflict. In W. G. Austin & S. Worchel (Eds.), *The social psychology of intergroup relations* (pp. 33–47). Monterey: Brooks/Cole.

Tanford, S., & Penrod, S. (1984). Social influence model: A formal integration of research on majority and minority influence processes. *Psychological Bulletin, 95,* 189–225.

Turner, J. C. (1991). *Social influence*. Belmont: Wadsworth.

Turner, J. C., Hogg, M. A., Oakes, P. J., Reicher, S. D., & Wetherell, M. S. (1987). *Rediscovering the social group: A self-categorization theory*. Oxford: Blackwell.

van de Waal, E., Borgeaud, C., & Whiten, A. (2013). Potent social learning and conformity shape a wild primate's foraging decisions. *Science, 340,* 483–485.

van Leeuwen, E. J. C., & Haun, D. B. M. (2013). Conformity in primates: Fad or fact? *Evolution and Human Behavior, 34,* 1–7.

van Leeuwen, E. J. C., & Haun, D. B. M. (2014). Conformity without majority? The case for demarcating social from majority influences. Animal Behaviour, *96,* 187–194.

van Leeuwen, E. J. C., Cronin, K. A., Schütte, S., Call, J. & Haun, D. B. M. (2013). Chimpanzees flexibly adjust their behaviour in order to maximize payoffs, not to conform to majorities. *PloS One, 8*(11), e80945. doi:10.1371/journal.pone.0080945.

White, G. M. (1975). Contextual determinants of opinion judgments: Field experimental probes of judgmental relativity boundary conditions. *Journal of Personality and Social Psychology, 32,* 1047–1054.

Whiten, A., Horner, V., & de Waal, F. B. M. (2005). Conformity to cultural norms of tool use in chimpanzees. *Nature, 437*(7059), 737–740.

Wolf, S., & Latané, B. (1983). Majority and minority influences on restaurant preferences. *Journal of Personality and Social Psychology, 45,* 282–292.

16 The Darwinian Mystique? Synthesizing Evolutionary Psychology and Feminism

Sylis C. A. Nicolas and Lisa L. M. Welling

Feminism is a social and political philosophy maintaining that women should enjoy the same rights and opportunities as men (Campbell 2006; Schuster and Van Dyne 1984; Sommers 1994). Feminist movements have traditionally sought to bolster women's status to the same standing that men hold in education, employment, politics, and social roles, and have also pursued justice concerning issues that women experience disproportionately as compared to men, such as rape and intimate partner violence (IPV; e.g., Estrich 1987; MacKinnon 1987). Certainly, feminist movements still have considerable obstacles to overcome. For instance, men still generally outearn women across the globe (e.g., Antonczyka et al. 2010; Lips 2013); the face of poverty is disproportionally female (especially minority group females, e.g., Ezeala-Harrison 2010); and men are judged as more competent and hirable, are offered a higher hypothetical starting salary, and are offered more career mentoring than women with identical qualifications, regardless of the sex of the rater (Moss-Racusin et al. 2012). Clearly, feminist goals and policies still need support and are of the utmost relevance to current society.

Importantly, feminism is not a homogeneous entity because many branches of feminism exist (Pollis 1988). Rosser (1997) identified at least nine different types of feminism, although DeKeseredy (2011) more recently suggested a figure closer to 20 variations. Despite these distinctive branches of feminism, feminist perspectives are united in advancing the idea that gender (i.e., the characteristics that a given culture delineates as related to biological sex) is an indispensable characteristic to be examined in its relation to other factors, such as biology, sexual orientation, social class, or race (Rosser 1997). Most notably, feminists are allied in their sociopolitical desire for equality between the sexes. This view alone, the desire for improving women's position in society, is sometimes referred to as "liberal" or "equity feminism" (Sommers 1994; Vandermassen 2005), though other branches of feminism extend this view. For example, socialist feminists emphasize the importance of social class, whereas African-American feminists center on heightening awareness about race (Rosser 1997). Although a full overview of all feminist subgroups is beyond the scope of this chapter, other examples of well-known branches of feminism include postmodern feminism (an experience-oriented approach incorporating postmodern and post-structuralism theory), essentialist feminism (which stresses intrinsic biological differences between the sexes), and radical feminism (which contends that male supremacy oppresses women; see Campbell 2013; Rosser 1997).

L. L. M. Welling (✉)
Department of Psychology, Oakland University,
212 Pryale Hall, Rochester, MI 48309, USA
e-mail: welling@oakland.edu

S. C. A. Nicolas
Department of Psychology, Oakland University,
130 Pryale Hall, Rochester, MI 48309, USA
e-mail: canicolas@oakland.edu

V. Zeigler-Hill et al. (eds.), *Evolutionary Perspectives on Social Psychology*, Evolutionary Psychology,
DOI 10.1007/978-3-319-12697-5_16, © Springer International Publishing Switzerland 2015

Historically, scientific claims have at times been misconstrued to subjugate women and cast them as inferior to men (e.g., Hodson 1929; Moore 1930). Indeed, Darwin's (1871) theory of evolution has previously been misused—particularly by scientists who investigated sex differences (discussed in Butler 1997)—to argue that women are innately subordinate to men (e.g., Geddes and Thomson 1889; Romanes 1887; Spencer 1862). Such supposed "scientific" claims fuelled skepticism and increased distrust for evolution-derived theories of human behavior. This distrust resurfaced in the twentieth century in response to sociobiological work by Trivers (1972), Dawkins (1976), and, notably, Wilson (1975; see Gowaty 2003; Rosser 1997). Wilson's (1975) proposal that sex differences have evolutionary origins was misinterpreted by some as an attempt to justify the societal practice of confining women to oppressive gender roles, and was ardently rejected by several feminist scholars (e.g., Fausto-Sterling 1985; Hubbard 1979; Rosser 1982). The fundamental criticism surrounds disagreement with the *essentialist* view, which posits that biological underpinnings are partially responsible for psychological and behavioral sex differences (Campbell 2013). Those who argue against essentialism predominantly adopt either extreme environmentalist or social constructionist ideologies (Campbell 2013; Vandermassen 2005). While both perspectives share either a partial or complete refutation of biological sex differences (e.g., Eagly and Wood 2011; Epstein 1997; Muldoon and Reilly 1998), the extreme environmentalist position holds that human behavior and psychology are exclusively the products of sociocultural reinforcement, whereas social constructionism postulates that objective knowledge about human nature cannot be obtained because humans generate sociocultural dialogues (referred to as "discourse") through which such concepts as gender or human nature are created (Epstein 1997; Hollway 1984). During the second wave of feminism, social constructionism emerged as the dominant perspective among feminists, arguably because it directly contradicted biological determinism (Kruger et al. 2013).

Although many liberal feminists embrace a scientific approach to obtaining knowledge about women's issues, a mistrust of evolution-derived theories of human sex differences is still present among many (Daly and Wilson 1988; Vandermassen 2005), and many principles within evolutionary psychology (EP) have been met with resistance (see Liesen 2008). Critics of EP often hold misconceptions of the science or argue that EP is politically motivated (i.e., used to justify and continue unequal, oppressive practices; Cassidy 2007; Contratto 2002; Crane-Seeber and Crane 2010; Hyde and Durik 2000; Segal 2000; Tang-Martinez 1997). Yet, EP theorists frequently identify as feminists or have argued that feminism is compatible with EP (e.g., Buss and Schmitt 2011; Gowaty 1997; Hannagan 2008; Kuhle 2012; Lancaster 1991; Smuts 1995; Vandermassen 2008). *Feminist Darwinians* refers to evolutionary theorists who are sensitive to the roles of gender and biological sex in the sciences and allow feminist concerns to inspire their empirical research (Vandermassen 2008). However, Vandermassen (2008) explains that there is a distinction to be made between feminist Darwinism and *Darwinian feminism*. Darwinian feminism is, by contrast, a political philosophy that seeks to apply evolutionarily based research to guide social action (see also Gowaty 1997; Hrdy 1999a). Essentially, feminist Darwinians take caution to be scientists first and feminists second (i.e., to not allow feminist ideology to cloud their scientific objectivity), but believe feminist concerns can be examined through an evolutionary lens to arrive at a more comprehensive understanding of the sources of gender/sex inequality and how to correct these injustices (e.g., Johnson 2012; Smuts 1995; Vandermassen 2005). Hereafter, we use the term *evolutionary feminists* to refer to both Darwinian feminists and feminist Darwinians.

In this chapter, we argue that feminism and EP are compatible and together have the potential to offer valuable insights for rectifying sex-based inequality. First, we discuss how the feminist movement has made contributions to science and society by increasing social equality, potentially reflecting (along with other human rights movements) how our species is evolving on a social level. Next, we outline misconceptions about EP and examine proposed strategies to reconcile EP and feminist perspectives. Finally, we describe how an evolutionary perspective can shed light on how to approach important feminist issues, using patriarchy and IPV as examples.

Feminism's Contributions to Science and Society

The contributions of feminist movements on society and within the sciences are not lost on evolutionary psychologists. Traditionally, women have been excluded from having roles within science, as both researchers and participants (Eagly and Wood 2011; Hager 1997). Feminist social programs that endeavored to inspire greater inclusion of women in the workforce can be credited for the increase of women entering scientific disciplines, including the field of evolutionary biology (Rosser 1997). The feminist emphasis on women's roles in science also led to an increase in the previously scarce research on female human and nonhuman animals (e.g., Angier 1999; Hrdy 1997; Zuk 2002). As a result, some formerly accepted theories were overturned, and this may not have occurred were it not for this shift in focus (Hrdy and Williams 1983). Additionally, because feminism is not solely focused on the greater inclusion of women in society, but other marginalized groups as well (e.g., minorities, homosexuals, transgendered individuals; e.g., Heywood 2006; Ingraham 1994), feminist movements have been credited with increasing inclusion in science from diverse populations (Sokol-Chang and Fisher 2013).

Feminist movements may have also inspired greater attention to researcher biases in science. Some maintain that male bias has exerted partiality in scientific methods via an exclusion of female participants and scientists, androcentrism, and a minimization of women's issues (reviewed in Sokol-Chang and Fisher 2013; Vandermassen 2004). Gowaty (2003) argues that feminism facilitates a heightened recognition of political biases, which can then be used to implement controls for the improvement of rigorous experimental designs. Where evolutionary science is concerned, feminists have highlighted how women's roles in evolution have often been underrated or discounted (e.g., Tanner and Zhilman 1976), compelling researchers to pursue topics often left unexamined by male scientists (Campbell 2013; Fisher et al. 2013), such as the evolution of patriarchy (e.g., Hrdy 1997; Smuts 1995), female coalitions (e.g., Hrdy 2009), femicide (e.g., Daly and Wilson 1988), female intrasexual competition (e.g., Fisher 2013), mothering and children (e.g., Lancaster 1991), and women's physiology (e.g., Vitzthum 2008). Accordingly, feminism has elucidated sources of scientific bias, enabling both women and minorities to enter formerly inaccessible scientific professions and allowing for a more comprehensive and inclusive examination of scientific topics.

Society has also benefited from feminist movements. In an examination of the global decline in violence over the past 10,000 years, Pinker (2011) argues that the increasing value placed on women's interests, what he terms *feminization,* is one of the five key historical forces responsible for the significant drop in rates of worldwide violence. He lists the varieties of feminization that have contributed to this decline, including "direct political empowerment, the deflation of manly honor, the promotion of marriage on women's terms, the rights of girls to be born, and women's control over their own reproduction" (p. 688). Furthermore, Pinker observes that the rates of violence are lower in both contemporary and traditional societies where women are treated more equitably, and he credits feminist movements with the plummeting instances of rape and the general drop in crime during the 1990s. Of course, men also benefit from feminism. Kruger et al. (2014) recently found that women's social and economic empowerment across nations is negatively related to the disparity between male and female mortality, even when accounting for general economic inequality and the prevalence of polygyny.

Other social movements—also known as *Rights Revolutions* (Pinker 2011)—such as the civil rights, children's rights, and animal rights movements, have likewise had a significant role in the global decline of violence. Pinker (2011) asserts that there is a dearth of evidence that biological evolution of the human species is responsible for such a trend away from violence, specifically because natural selection at the level of the gene takes an exceptionally long time. Instead, given the rapidity of the decline in violence that coincides with humanistic movements that aim to minimize aggression towards others, it is far more likely that social revolutions have curbed our violent inclinations and are a reflection of human cultural evolution (for a full discussion, see Morgan, Cross, & Rendell, this volume). Thus, feminist theorists who argue that cultural and social input influence human behavior are at least partially correct. Campbell (2006) succinctly explains that social learning evolved "because its superiority over individual trial-and-error learning brought fitness benefits" (p. 73). Pinker contends that overcoming our biological predispositions was necessary for each social movement to be effective. Indeed, social movements alter people's attitudes and behavior, yet the capacity to change and act ethically lies in our evolved biology (Alexander 1987; Cosmides and Tooby 2006).

Although it is in our nature to act selfishly (Korsgaard and de Waal 2006), humans are also capable of prosocial and cooperative behavior (Dovidio et al. 2006; see also Krebs, this volume). The related cognitive faculties of learning and rationality may be at the root of this trend toward peace given that moral judgment is elicited in part by brain regions associated with abstract thought (Greene et al. 2001) and that individuals with greater reasoning abilities tend to be more tolerant, cooperative, and less violent (Burks et al. 2009; Deary et al. 2008). Contemporary Rights Revolutions are likely to have contributed to the decline in worldwide violence by means of appealing to human rationality through mass media messages. While pamphlets and best-selling books arguing for the humane treatment of animals, children, and women have historically led to sociopolitical change and legislative reforms (Hunt 2007), contemporary Rights Revolutions are aided by modern technological tools that allow for the quick dispersal of ideas (see Joyce 2011). Perhaps the success of activists in drawing attention to issues during recent revolutions, such as the Occupy Movement or the numerous political uprisings known as Arab Spring, can be attributed in part to the increase in recent mobile and Internet technologies and the rapid dissemination of ideas. Widespread stigmatizing of discriminating behavior may be an effective way of changing attitudes because individuals noticing a majority shift toward a less discriminating attitude may then adopt it themselves to avoid social exclusion (Kurzban and Leary 2001).

The various Rights Revolutions demonstrate that cultural evolution, whereby cultural norms and ideas evolve in a way akin to the selection of physical traits within a population, is ongoing. Social movements have already transformed cultural mores, reducing violence and discrimination. Nonetheless, social contexts interact with our evolved predispositions to elicit behavioral responses (Lenroot and Giedd 2011; Rose 1995). Understanding social problems, like those tackled by feminism, from an evolutionary perspective may help define strategies that are effective in public policy.

Misconceptions Surrounding EP

Perhaps the leading conflict between evolutionary psychologists and those feminists opposed to evolution-derived theories of human behavior concerns the existence of behavioral and psychological differences between men and women. Opposition to EP does not mean opposition to the theory of evolution by natural selection, per se. Rather, those who dispute EP tend to take issue with the application of evolutionary theory to behavior, specifically (Campbell 2012, 2013). Although behavioral sex differences are not wholly innate (Schmitt 2005; Smuts 1995) and many traits do overlap considerably between the sexes (see Nelson 2011; but see Del Giudice et al. 2012), EP has fallen under criticism via the incorrect assumption that their theories support *genetic determinism* (e.g., Condit 2008; Crane-Seeber and Crane 2010; Rogers 1999; Rosser 1992).

Genetic determinism is the untenable idea that one's genes are solely responsible for behavior, rendering behavior unchangeable (Rogers 1999). Evolutionary scientists repeatedly reject the notion of genetic determinism (e.g., Buss 1996; Campbell 2013; Gowaty 1997; Pinker 2002), arguing instead that the knowledge of how environmental inputs influence our evolved psychological mechanisms will lead to better understanding of how to address social problems and change human behavior (Confer et al. 2010; Ridley 1993). Moreover, several studies grounded in EP have found that cultural and social input are substantially important to human behavior and, thus, that behavior is environmentally responsive (e.g., Buss and Schmitt 2011; Pinker 2002; Tooby and Cosmides 1992). Therefore, the EP framework maintains that humans are not fated by genes to behave in a certain way; an individual's survival hinges on making context-dependent decisions that take environmental cues into consideration (Pinker 2002). Correspondingly, many feminist scholars endorse a social constructionist perspective (see Kruger et al. 2013), which garners empirical support within a number of constructs (e.g., sex differences in competitive behavior; Gneezy et al. 2009). Nonetheless, the existence of social and cultural impacts on traits does not eliminate potential contributions of biology on facets of behavior.

Another key misinterpretation of EP is the logical fallacy known as the "appeal to nature" (Fisher et al. 2013, p. 8), also referred to as "the naturalistic fallacy" (Buss 1996; Gowaty 1997; Ridley 1993). This fallacy can be summarized by "what is natural must therefore be good or right." For instance, people who commit the logical fallacy of the appeal to nature erroneously interpret the finding that men's higher tendency toward violence, hypothesized by evolutionary theory to be a form of intrasexual competition (e.g., Archer 2009), is a "free pass" or justification for men's physical aggression (Eagly 1987). Instead, the intrasexual competition explanation for sex differences in violence is an empirically supported explanation, not a prescription for how to behave (Pinker 2002; Ridley 1993). In other words, EP aims to provide *explanations* of—and not *limitations* on—human behavior. Next, we explore how EP and feminist theory can be integrated in practical terms.

Reconciling Feminism with EP

The key misunderstandings outlined above hinder the intersection of some social disciplines, such as women's studies, with EP (Campbell 2013; Geary 2010; Mealey 2000; Pinker 2002). Evolutionary feminists agree with the assertion that female psychology and behavior have frequently been secondary in empirical and evolutionary research (Campbell 2013; Fisher et al. 2013, Hrdy 1999b; Jennions and Petrie 2000; Stockley and Bro-Jorgensen 2011). Unfortunately, it is difficult for any research, including EP, to be entirely impartial because of human error and bias (Gowaty 1997). Some researchers are undoubtedly influenced by the culture in which they were raised and results in scientific disciplines can be subject to corresponding experimenter bias. However, the scientific method continues to be the best method by which ideas can be systematically tested and falsified. Since findings can be supported or refuted through additional testing and replication using various methods (Smith and Davis 2007), science, by its very nature, is self-correcting and fashioned by evidence (discussed in Hannagan 2008). Because feminism is not itself a science, but, rather, an ethical philosophy concerned with social and political agendas, it is not subject to these principles. This categorical distinction is critical in integrating feminism and EP because although feminist evolutionary psychologists may encourage feminist perspectives to inspire scientific work, EP does not seek to promote social goals within society as feminism does. Scientific work generally refrains from prescribing moral action to best uphold the traditional standard of neutrality (discussed in Buss and Schmitt 2011; Vandermassen 2005).

Natural and sexual selection are fundamental tools for comprehending the oppression of women and better comprehension can in turn be applied to political action. In general, evolutionary psychologists share with feminists a concern for patriarchy, male bias in science, inequality, and injustices committed toward women (Campbell 2013). As a result, attempts have been made by evolutionary theorists to reconcile EP and feminism (e.g., Buss and Malamuth 1996; Morbeck et al. 1997; Smuts 1995; Tate 2013; Vandermassen 2005, 2011). For instance, evolutionary feminists have illustrated the benefits of applying an evolutionary perspective to feminist concerns by proposing strategies for tackling specific issues based on evolution-informed predictors (e.g., IPV, patriarchy, rape; Johnson 2012; Smuts 1995; Vandermassen 2011) and have made suggestions for how the two perspectives can operate together to reach their respective goals (e.g., Nier and Campbell 2013). To test hypotheses relating to feminist issues, such as disparity in equality, power relations, and social structures, empirical approaches based in the scientific method should be used (Campbell 2006; Gowaty 1997, 2003; Low 2005; Vandermassen 2005, 2008). EP can provide a unified, comprehensive theoretical framework to help explain why sex differences exist and this knowledge can guide political activism. To arrive at an informed public policy that has an empirical basis for what strategies will be effective in promoting equality, an accurate understanding of human nature is required and EP can serve as an evidence-based framework for political agendas.

However, thought must be given to ultimate and proximate causes (Nettle 2011; Vandermassen 2011) and although EP can elucidate the ultimate causes for human behavior, it does not address the proximate causes; rather, EP uses evidence of proximate cause to inform theories of ultimate causation. Vandermassen (2004) suggests that most variations of feminism can provide partial, proximate accounts of sex differences. She explains, "the various strands of feminism may help us to discover how exactly cultural and socialization practices (i.e., explanations on the proximate level) magnify or attenuate the psychosexual predispositions of women and men" (Vandermassen 2004, p. 22). A multidisciplinary approach that utilizes outside perspectives for a more complete understanding of behavioral phenomena and appropriate practical applications is ideal within science and in social activism (see Buunk and van Vugt 2007; Klatzky 2009). Thus, the disciplines of feminism and EP should merge on shared issues (Hannagan 2008; Vandermassen 2005). Below, using patriarchy and IPV as examples, we briefly describe how evolutionary perspectives can be beneficial to the goals of feminism by revealing the contexts in which they most frequently occur.

What EP Can Offer Feminism

Patriarchy

Common among evolutionary theorists (e.g., Buss 1996; Hrdy 1997; Smuts 1995) and feminist scholars (e.g., Dworkin 1997; Lerner 1986; MacKinnon 1987; Richards 2013) is the observation that sexual control and coercion are central to patriarchy (i.e., male control over women). Evolutionary theory surrounding human sexual strategies may explain why men seek to control women's sexuality (Smuts 1992). Based on data in nonhuman primates, Hrdy (1997) reasons that prehominid females likely solicited several male partners, which may have led to male counterstrategies aimed at controlling female sexuality to ensure paternal certainty. Men who were better able to attract and retain a mate and prevent cuckoldry were more likely to reproduce successfully than other men (Buss 1994). Thus, men who were better able to control women may have been more successful in the mating market. Similarly, men's intrasexual competition is also hypothesized to be central to patriarchy. Buss (1994) reasons that the roots of patriarchy can be explained by the coevolution of women's preferences for men with access to resources and men's competition with one other for sexual access to women. That is, because women preferentially selected male partners with resources, men may have competed more fiercely to acquire status and resources to attract female partners, leading to men having primary control over available resources. However, Buss (1996) notes that causality in this relationship may be reversed and that it is more likely that men's competitive strategies and women's preferences coevolved concurrently.

Because feminism neither offers a theory for the origins of patriarchy nor identifies the contexts in which the subjugation of women is most customary (Campbell 2006; Vandermassen 2004, 2005), Smuts (1995) proposes that evolution-derived theories be employed to test hypotheses that examine why men began to seek control over women. She outlines six factors that have impacted the evolution of inequality between women and men: weak female–female coalitions, strong male alliances, male control over resources, hierarchical relationships among men, female complicity with patriarchy, and use of language and ideology to perpetuate patriarchy. In these contexts, women have less power over their lives and sexuality. Smuts (1995) offers counterstrategies to minimize patriarchy, such as giving women access to media outlets and positions of power to feminize social and cultural dialogue, ensuring that women have economic opportunities, and assuring access to legal protection of property rights to minimize men's control over resources. Smuts suggests that by altering the contexts (e.g., laws) in societies where patriarchy is observed to be more prevalent, oppressive conditions for women can be alleviated. For instance, Smuts proposes that because patriarchy thrives in conditions in which men have strong coalitions with one another but women do not, establishing female political solidarity—in collaboration with male supporters—to institutionalize policies that protect women (e.g., against rape and sexual harassment) may decrease men's control over women's lives, bodies, and resources (see also, Estrich 1987; MacKinnon 1987). Smut's proposal is in contradiction to the legitimacy of genetic determinism that some (e.g., Condit 2008; Crane-Seber and Crane 2010; Segal 2000) have accused EP of advancing. She stresses that an evolutionary perspective does not support the notion that men's control over women is inevitable, but, rather, is critical for identifying crucial environmental factors. Accordingly, both proximate and ultimate causes of sex-based inequality may be instrumental to a more complete understanding of patriarchy (Hrdy 1997; Smuts 1995; Vandermassen 2004, 2011).

Intimate Partner Violence

A related area of concern that benefits from an evolutionary perspective is IPV. Evolutionary theorists concur with feminists (e.g., Adams 1988; Walker 1994) that controlling women is at the core of domestic abuse, but have provided strong empirical evidence that this concern is not generalized, but instead focused explicitly on women's sexuality (e.g., Buss and Malamuth 1996; Daly and Wilson 1988). Throughout our evolutionary past, men have faced the problem of paternity uncertainty, whereby they were unable to know for certain whether their putative children were indeed genetic relatives. Males who were cuckolded by their female partners and unknowingly invested in offspring who were not their genetic kin were less reproductively successful and may have even incurred reputational damage that diminished their future mating opportunities (for review, see Buss 2000). Therefore, IPV is likely motivated by a proprietary desire to control women's reproductive capacity and sexuality to avoid incurring the costs associated with female cuckoldry (Goetz et al. 2008; Wilson and Daly 1992).

In other words, the threat of physical violence may be a mating tactic to coerce women into remaining faithful to their partner (Buss and Duntley 2011). Support for this hypothesis comes from research documenting that instances of IPV are positively correlated with younger age in women, when they have the greatest fertility and reproductive ability (Buss 2002; Buss and Shackelford 1997; Rennison and Welchans 2000), and findings that possessiveness and male sexual jealousy—theorized strategies that increase men's probability of paternity—are strong predictors of IPV (Daly et al. 1982; Wilson and Daly 1992). A woman's actual or perceived infidelity is also a strong predictor of IPV (Daly et al. 1982); however, it is crucial to note that this finding in no way implies that victims of IPV are to blame for the inexcusable violence they experience (see also Buss and Duntley 2011). More exactly, an evolutionary perspective has successfully identified the contexts in which IPV is likely, including how other aspects of the perpetrator, such as neurological predispositions (Wilson and Daly 1993), life history strategy (discussed in Figueredo et al. 2012), and socioeconomic status (Flynn and Graham 2010), are linked to IPV.

Following arguments by Wilson and Daly (1998), Johnson (2012) asserts that the evolutionary perspective "identifies what it is about the actions of female partners that men try to control, why women may be motivated to pursue these actions despite the potential for violence, and the personal characteristics of the victim and perpetrator (as well as the social and environmental factors) affecting the risk that men will respond violently toward their partners" (p. 336). Just as Smuts (1995) argues of patriarchy, Johnson (2012) maintains that an evolutionary framework has and will continue to accurately predict the factors associated with IPV and supposes that instances of IPV will decrease when the associated contexts are changed. For example, Wilson and Daly (1998) found that men are much less likely to be violent toward their partners in societies where violence is socially stigmatized and generally not tolerated. This pattern highlights a need for greater institutionalization of policies that protect women, as Smuts and many others contend (e.g., Estrich 1987; MacKinnon 1987). In addition to informing policy, using an evolutionary framework to make predictions about the precursors of IPV and employing proximate solutions derived from feminist theorizing (e.g., implementing policies, derived from an integrative feminist model, that reduce male privilege; see McPhail et al. 2007) could inform rehabilitation and prevention models. Consistent with feminist aims, educating women about the precursors to IPV may help prevent its occurrence, in particular if women are better able to discern IPV-associated qualities in potential and current romantic partners. Hypothesis testing using an evolutionary perspective provides the empirical basis for this education. For instance, evidence suggests that men who are chronically jealous and engage in possessive behaviors are more likely to commit domestic abuse (Daly et al. 1982; Wilson and Daly 1992). Furthermore, education may enable women in abusive relationships to adopt strategies to protect themselves while transitioning to a safer environment, such as ensuring the presence of kin or other "bodyguards" (e.g., Figueredo et al. 1998; McKibbin et al. 2011).

Concluding Remarks: Evolutionary Science, Social Movements, and Public Policy

The feminist and other human rights movements have played a role in the global decline of violence (Pinker 2011), attesting to the importance of social and cultural learning in affecting human behavior. The examination of women's issues from a combined evolutionary-feminist perspective will likely have important implications for society, whereby evolutionary analyses of women's issues may provide practical and defensible solutions that could potentially translate into public policies. Evolutionary feminists use empirical techniques to explore feminist concerns and highlight the active role women have had in the evolutionary process (Sokol-Chang and Fisher 2013). Moreover, the objective of aiding women to obtain sociopolitical equality with men is an inspiring research opportunity that may have practical and theoretical value. EP has already generated important feminist-related research by identifying predictors of IPV and environments in which patriarchal systems are most prevalent. Both male and female scientists use empirical methods to test hypotheses that are relevant to women's sociopolitical equality and opportunities to test these hypotheses are growing (Campbell 2013; Gowaty 2003). Evolutionary theorizing shows promise for revealing further useful findings on human nature that are relevant to feminist goals.

In this chapter, we have argued that—far from being incompatible perspectives—evolutionary theory and feminism can be reconciled in an effort to improve women's lives. While feminists are correct to decry the historical relationship between science and women's rights, these missteps should not define the future of science. We hope we have demonstrated that it is not the intentions of EP to perpetuate gender roles and neither does EP exclude feminist scholars from engagement with the social sciences. EP and feminist philosophy are deeply compatible, and combining these perspectives will positively encourage the continued social progression of our species.

References

Adams, D. (1988). Feminist-based interventions for battering men. In L. Caesar & K. Hamberger (Eds.), *Therapeutic interventions with batterers* (pp. 3–23). New York: Springer.

Alexander, R. S. (1987). *The biology of moral systems*. Hawthorne: Aldine de Gruyter.

Angier, N. (1999). *Woman: An intimate geography*. London: Virago.

Antonczyka, D., Fitzenberger, B., & Sommerfeld, K. (2010). Rising wage inequality, the decline of collective bargaining, and the gender wage gap. *Labour Economics, 17,* 835–847.

Archer, J. (2009). Does sexual selection explain human sex differences in aggression? *The Behavioral and Brain Sciences, 32,* 249–311.

Burks, S. V., Carpenter, J. P., Goette, L., & Rustichini, A. (2009). Cognitive skills affect economic preferences, strategic behavior, and job attachment. *Proceedings of the National Academy of Sciences, 106,* 7745–7750.

Buss, D. M. (1994). *The evolution of desire: Strategies of human mating*. New York: Basic Books.

Buss, D. M. (1996). Sexual conflict: Evolutionary insights into feminism and the "battle of the sexes". In D. M. Buss & N. M. Malamuth (Eds.), *Sex, power, conflict: Evolutionary and feminist perspectives* (pp. 296–318). New York: Oxford University Press.

Buss, D. M. (2000). *The dangerous passion*. New York: The Free Press.

Buss, D. M. (2002). Understanding domestic violence against women: using evolutionary psychology to extend the feminist functional analysis. *Violence Victims, 17,* 255–264.

Buss, D. M., & Duntley, J. D. (2011). The evolution of intimate partner violence. *Aggression and Violent Behavior, 16,* 411–419.

Buss, D., & Malamuth, M. (1996). *Sex, power, conflict: Evolutionary and feminist perspectives*. Oxford: Oxford University Press.

Buss, D. M., & Schmitt, D. P. (2011). Evolutionary psychology and feminism. *Sex Roles, 64,* 769–787.

Buss, D. M., & Shackelford, T. K. (1997). From vigilance to violence: Mate retention tactics in married couples. *Journal of Personality and Social Psychology, 72,* 346–361.

Butler, J. (1997). *The psychic life of power: Theories in subjection*. Redwood City: Stanford University Press.

Buunk, A. P., & van Vugt, M. (2007). *Applying social psychology: From problems to solutions*. London: Sage.

Campbell, A. (2006). Feminism and evolutionary psychology. In J. H. Barkow (Ed.), *Missing the revolution: Darwinism for social scientists* (pp. 63–99). New York: Oxford University Press.

Campbell, A. (2012). The study of sex differences: Feminism and biology. *Zeitschrift für Psychologie, 220,* 137–143.

Campbell, A. (2013). *A mind of her own: The evolutionary psychology of women* (2 ed.). Oxford: Oxford University Press.

Cassidy, A. (2007). The (sexual) politics of evolution: Popular controversy in the late 20th-century United Kingdom. *History of Psychology, 10,* 199–226.

Condit, C. M. (2008). Feminist biologies: Revising feminist strategies and biological science. *Sex Roles, 59,* 492–503.

Confer, J. C., Easton, J. E., Fleischman, D. S., Goetz, C., Lewis, D. M., Perilloux, C., & Buss, D. M. (2010). Evolutionary psychology: Controversies, questions, prospects, and limitations. *American Psychologist, 65,* 110–126.

Contratto, S. (2002). A feminist critique of attachment theory and evolutionary psychology. In M. Ballou & L. Brown (Eds.), *Rethinking mental health and disorder: Feminist perspectives* (pp. 29–47). New York: Guilford.

Cosmides, L., & Tooby, J. (2006). Evolutionary psychology, moral heuristics, and the law. In G. Gigerenzer & C. Engel (Eds.), *Heuristics and the law* (pp. 175–205). Cambridge: MIT Press.

Crane-Seeber, J., & Crane, B. (2010). Contesting essentialist theories of patriarchal relations: Evolutionary psychology and the denial of history. *Journal of Men's Studies, 18,* 218–237.

Daly, M., & Wilson, M. (1988). *Homicide*. New York: Aldine de Gruyter.

Daly, M., Wilson, M. I., & Weghorst, S. J. (1982). Male sexual jealousy. *Ethology and Sociobiology, 3,* 11–27.

Darwin, C. (1871). *The descent of man and selection in relation to sex*. London: John Murray.

Dawkins, R. (1976). *The selfish gene*. New York: Oxford University Press.

Deary, I. J., Batty, G. D., & Gale, C. R. (2008). Bright children become enlightened adults. *Psychological Science, 19,* 1–6.

DeKeseredy, W. S. (2011). Feminist contributions to understanding woman abuse; Myths, controversies, and realities. *Aggression and Violent Behavior, 16,* 297–302.

Del Giudice, M., Booth, T., & Irwing, P. (2012). The distance between mars and venus: Measuring global sex differences in personality. *PLoS One, 7,* 1–8.

Dovidio, J. F., Piliavin, J. A., Schroeder, D. A., & Penner, L. (2006). *The social psychology of prosocial behavior*. Mahwah: Lawrence Erlbaum.

Dworkin, A. (1997). *Life and death: Unapologetic writings on the continuing war against women*. New York: Free Press.

Eagly, A. H. (1987). *Sex differences in social behavior: A social-role interpretation*. Hillsdale: Lawrence Erlbaum.

Eagly, A. H., & Wood, W. (2011). Feminism and the evolution of sex. *Sex Roles, 64,* 758–767.

Epstein, C. F. (1997). The multiple realities of sameness and difference: Ideology and practice. *Journal of Social Sciences, 53,* 259–278.

Estrich, S. (1987). *Real rape*. Cambridge: Harvard University Press.

Ezeala-Harrison, F. (2010). Black feminization of poverty: evidence from the U.S. cross-regional data. *The Journal of Developing Areas, 44,* 149–166.

Fausto-Sterling, A. (1985). The new research on women: How does it affect the natural sciences? *Women's Studies Quarterly, 13,* 30–32.

Figueredo, A. J., Corral-Verdugo, V., Frías-Armenta, M., Bachar, K., Goldman-Pach, J., & McNeill, P. L. (1998). La influencia de la familia consanguínea de la mujer en la ocurrencia de violencia intramarital: Una comparación de muestras piloto de Madrid y Hermosillo. *Enseñanza e Investigación en Psicología, 3,* 103–117.

Figueredo, A. J., Gladden, P. R., & Beck, C. J. (2012). Intimate partner violence and life history strategy. In T. K. Shackelford & A. T. Goetz (Eds.), *The Oxford handbook of sexual conflict in humans* (pp. 72–99). New York: Oxford University Press.

Fisher, M. L. (2013). Women's intrasexual competition for mates. In M. L. Fisher, J. R. Garcia, & R. Sokol-Chang (Eds.), *Evolution's empress: Darwinian perspectives on the nature of women* (pp. 19–42). New York: Oxford University Press.

Fisher, M., Sokol-Chang, R., & Garcia, J. (2013). Introduction to Evolution's Empress. In M. Fisher, J. Garcia, & R. Sokol-Chang (Eds.), *Evolution's empress: Darwinian perspectives on the nature of women* (pp. 1–16). New York: Oxford University.

Flynn, A., & Graham, K. (2010). "Why did it happen?" A review and conceptual framework for research on perpetrators' and victims' explanations for intimate partner violence. *Aggression and Violent Behavior, 15,* 239–251.

Geary, D. C. (2010). *Male, female: The evolution of human sex differences (2nd edition)*. Washington, DC: American Psychological Association.

Geddes, P., & Thomson, J. A. (1889). *The evolution of sex*. London: Walter Scott.

Gneezy, U., Leonard, K. L., & List, J. A. (2009). Gender differences in competition: Evidence from a matrilineal and a patriarchal society. *Econometrica, 77,* 1637–1664.

Goetz, A. T., Shackelford, T. K., Starratt, V. G., & McKibbin, W. F. (2008). Intimate partner violence. In J. D. Duntley, & T. K. Shackelford (Eds.), *Evolutionary forensic psychiatry* (pp. 65–78). New York: Oxford University Press.

Gowaty, P. A. (1997). Introduction: Darwinian feminists and feminist evolutionists. In P. A. Gowaty (Ed.), *Feminism and evolutionary biology* (pp. 1–17). New York: Chapman & Hall.

Gowaty, P. A. (2003). Sexual natures: How feminism changed evolutionary biology. *Signs, 28,* 901–921.

Greene, J. D., Sommerville, R. B., Nystrom, L. E., Darley, J. M., & Cohen, J. D. (2001). An fMRI investigation of emotional engagement in moral judgment. *Science, 293,* 2105–21-8.

Hager, L. D. (Ed.). (1997). *Women in human evolution*. London: Routledge.

Hannagan, R. (2008). Gendered political behavior: A Darwinian feminist approach. *Sex Roles, 59,* 465–475.

Heywood, L. L. (2006). *The women's movement today: An encyclopedia of third-wave feminism* (Vol. 1, A-Z). Westport: Greenwood.

Hodson, C. B. (1929). Feminism and the race. *Eugenics, 2,* 3–5.

Hollway, W. (1984). Gender difference and the production of subjectivity. In J. Henriques, W. Hollway, C. Urwin, C. Venn, & V. Walkerdine (Eds.), *Changing the subject: Psychology, social regulation and subjectivity* (pp. 227–263). London: Methuen.

Hrdy, S. (1997). Raising Darwin's consciousness: Female sexuality and the prehominid origins of patriarchy. *Human Nature, 8,* 1–49.

Hrdy, S. B. (1999a). *The woman that never evolved* (2nd ed.). Cambridge: Harvard University Press.

Hrdy, S. B. (1999b). *Mother nature: Natural selection and the female of the species*. London: Chatto & Windus.

Hrdy, S. B. (2009). *Mothers and others: The evolutionary origins of mutual understanding*. Cambridge: Harvard University Press.

Hrdy, S., & Williams, G. C. (1983). Behavioral biology and the double standard. In S. K. Wasser (Ed.), *Social behavior of female vertebrates* (pp. 3–17). New York: Academic Press.

Hubbard, R. (1979). Introduction. In R. Hubbard & M. Lowe (Eds.), *Genes and gender II: Pitfalls in research on sex and gender* (pp. 9–34). New York: Gordian Press.

Hunt, L. (2007). *Inventing human rights: A history*. New York: W.W. Norton & Company.

Hyde, J. S., & Durik, A. M. (2000). Gender differences in erotic plasticity—evolutionary or sociocutural forces? Comment on Baumeister. *Psychological Bulletin, 126,* 375–379.

Ingraham, C. (1994). The heterosexual imaginary: Feminist sociology and theories of gender. *Sociological Theory, 12,* 203–219.

Jennions, M. D., & Petrie, M. (2000). Why do females mate multiply? *Biological Reviews, 75,* 21–64.

Johnson, H. (2012). When feminism meets evolutionary psychology: The enduring legacy of Margo Wilson. *Homicide Studies, 16,* 332–245.

Joyce, D. (2011). New media witnessing and human rights. *Human Rights Defender, 20,* 23–26.

Klatzky, R. L. (2009). Giving psychological science away. *Perspectives on Psychological Science, 4,* 522–530.

Korsgaard, C. M., & de Waal, F. (2006). Morality and the distinctiveness of human action. In S. Macedo & J. Ober (Eds.), *Primates and philosophers: How morality evolved* (pp. 98–119). Princeton: Princeton University Press.

Kruger, D. J., Fisher, M. L., & Wright, P. (2013). A framework for integrating evolutionary and feminist perspectives in psychological research. *Journal of Social, Evolutionary, and Cultural Psychology, 7,* 299–303.

Kruger, D. J., Fisher, M. L., & Wright, P. (2014). Patriarchy, male competition, and excess male mortality. *Evolutionary Behavioral Sciences, 8,* 3–11.

Kuhle, B. X. (2012). Evolutionary psychology is compatible with equity feminism, but not with gender feminism: A reply to eagly and wood. *Evolutionary Psychology, 10,* 39–43.

Kurzban, R., & Leary, M. R. (2001). Evolutionary origins of stigmatization: The functions of social exclusion. *Psychological Bulletin, 127,* 187–208.

Lancaster, J. B. (1991). A feminist and evolutionary biologist looks at women. *Yearbook of Physical Anthropology, 34,* 1–11.

Lenroot, R. K., & Giedd, J. N. (2011). Annual research review: Developmental considerations of gene by environment interactions. *Journal of Child Psychology and Psychiatry, 52,* 429–441.

Lerner, G. (1986). *The creation of patriarchy*. Oxford: Oxford University Press.

Liesen, L. (2008). The evolution of gendered political behavior: Contributions from feminist evolutionists. *Sex Roles, 59,* 476–481.

Lips, H. M. (2013). The gender pay gap: challenging the rationalizations. Perceived equity, discrimination, and the limits of human capital models. *Sex Roles, 68,* 169–185.

Low, B. S. (2005). Women's lives there, here, then, now: A review of women's ecological and demographic constraints cross-culturally. *Evolution and Human Behavior, 26,* 64–87.

MacKinnon, C. (1987). *Feminism unmodified*. Cambridge: Harvard University Press.

McKibbin, W. F., Shackelford, T. K., Miner, E. J., Bates, V. M., & Liddle, J. R. (2011). Individual differences in women's rape avoidance behaviors. *Archives of Sexual Behavior, 40,* 343–349.

McPhail, B. A., Busch, N. B., Kulkarni, S., & Rice, G. (2007). An integrative feminist model: The evolving feminist perspective on intimate partner violence. *Violence Against Women, 13,* 817–841.

Mealey, L. (2000). *Sex differences: Developmental and evolutionary strategies*. San Diego: Academic Press.

Moore, H. T. (1930). Women's colleges and race extinction. *Schribner's, 87,* 280–284.

Morbeck, M. E., Galloway, A., & Zihlman, A. (1997). *The evolving female: A life-history perspective*. Princeton: Princeton University Press.

Moss-Racusin, C. A., Dovidio, J. F., Brescoll, V. L., Graham, M. J., & Handelsman, J. (2012). Science faculty's subtle gender biases favor male students. *Proceedings of the National Academy of Sciences of the United States of America, 109,* 16474–16479.

Muldoon, O., & Reilly, J. (1998). Biology. In K. Trew & J. Kremer, *Gender and psychology* (pp. 55–65). London: Arnold.

Nelson, R. J. (2011). Sex differences in behavior: Sex determination and differentiation. In R. J. Nelson (Ed.), *An Introduction to Behavioral Endocrinology* (4th ed., pp. 89–142). Sunderland: Sinauer Associates.

Nettle, D. (2011). Flexibility in reproductive timing in human females: Integrating ultimate and proximate explanations. *Philosophical Transactions of the Royal Society B, 366,* 357–365.

Nier, J. A., & Campbell, S. D. (2013). Two outsiders' view on feminism and evolutionary psychology: An opportune time for adversarial collaboration. *Sex Roles, 69,* 503–506.

Pinker, S. (2002). *The blank slate: The modern denial of human nature*. New York: Penguin.

Pinker, S. (2011). *The better angels of our nature: Why violence has declined*. New York: Penguin.

Pollis, C. A. (1988). An assessment of the impacts of feminism on social science. *Journal of Sex Research, 25,* 86–105.

Rennison, C. M., & Welchans, S. (2000). Intimate partner violence. Washington, DC: U.S. Department of Justice, Office of Justice Programs, Bureau of Justic Statistics.

Richards, D. A. (2013). Liberal democracy and the problem of patriarchy. *Israel Law Review, 46,* 169–191.

Ridley, M. (1993). *The red queen: Sex and the evolution of human nature*. New York: Harper Perennial.

Rogers, L. (1999). *Sexing the brain*. London: Weidenfeld & Nicholson.

Romanes, G. J. (1887). Mental differences between men and women. *The Nineteenth Century, 21,* 654–672.

Rose, R. J. (1995). Genes and human behavior. *Annual Review of Psychology, 46,* 625–654.

Rosser, S. V. (1982). Androgyny and sociobiology. *International Journal of Women's Studies, 5,* 435–444.

Rosser, S. (1992). *Biology and feminism: A dynamic interaction*. New York: Twayne Publishers.

Rosser, S. (1997). Possible implications of feminist theories for the study of evolution. In P. Gowaty (Ed.), *Feminism and evolutionary biology: Boundaries, intersections, and frontiers* (pp. 21–41). New York: Chapman & Hall.

Schmitt, D. P. (2005). Sociosexuality from Argentina to Zimbabwe: A 48-nation study of sex, culture, and strategies of human mating. *Behavioral and Brain Sciences, 28,* 247–275.

Schuster, M., & Van Dyne, S. (1984). Placing women in the liberal arts: Stages of cirriculum transformation. *Harvard Educational Review, 54,* 413–428.

Segal, L. (2000). Gender, genes and genetics: from Darwin to the human genome. In C. Squire (Ed.), *Culture in psychology* (pp. 31–43). London: Routledge.

Smith, R. A., & Davis, S. F. (2007). *The psychologist as detective*. Upper Saddle River, New Jersey: Pearson Education, Inc.

Smuts, B. (1992). Male aggression against women: An evolutionary perspective. *Human Nature, 3,* 1–44.

Smuts, B. (1995). The evolutionary origins of patriarchy. *Human Nature, 6,* 1–32.

Sokol-Chang, R., & Fisher, M. L. (2013). Letter of purpose of the feminist evolutionary psychology society. *Journal of Social, Evolutionary, and Cultural Psychology, 7,* 286–294.

Sommers, C. H. (1994). *Who stole feminism?* New York: Simon and Schuster.

Spencer, H. (1862). *First principles*. London: Williams and Norgate.

Stockley, P., & Bro-Jorgensen, J. (2011). Female competition and its evolutionary consequences in mammals. *Biological Reviews, 86,* 341–366.

Tang-Martinez, Z. (1997). The curious courtship of sociobiology and feminism: A case of irreconcilable differences. In P. A. Gowaty (Ed.), *Feminism and evolutionary biology* (pp. 116–150). New York: Chapman & Hall.

Tanner, N., & Zihlman, A. (1976). Women in evolution. Part I. Innovation and selection in human origins. *Signs, 1,* 585–608.

Tate, C. C. (2013). Addressing conceptual confusions about evolutionary theorizing: How and why evolutionary psychology and feminism do not oppose each other. *Sex Roles, 69,* 491–502.

Tooby, J., & Cosmindes, L. (1992). The psychological foundations of culture. In J. Barkow, L. Cosmides, & J. Tooby (Eds.), *The adapted mind: Evolutionary psychology and the generation of culture* (pp. 19–136). New York: Oxford University Press.

Trivers, R. L. (1972). Parental investment and sexual selection. In B. Campbell (Ed.), *Sexual selection and the descent of man: The Darwinian pivot* (pp. 136–179). Chicago: Aldine-Atherton.

Vandermassen, G. (2004). Sexual selection: A tale of male bias and feminist denial. *European Journal of Women's Studies, 11,* 1–26.

Vandermassen, G. (2005). *Who's afraid of Charles Darwin? Debating feminism and evolutionary theory.* Lanham: Rowman & Littlefield.

Vandermassen, G. (2008). Can Darwinian feminism save female autonomy and leadership in egalitarian society? *Sex Roles, 59,* 482–491.

Vandermassen, G. (2011). Evolution and rape: A feminist darwinian perspective. *Sex Roles, 64,* 732–747.

Vitzthum, V. J. (2008). Evolutionary models of women's reproductive functioning. *Annual Review of Anthropology, 37,* 53–73.

Walker, L. (1994). *Abused women and survivor therapy*. Washington, DC: American Psychological Association.

Wilson, E. O. (1975). *Sociobiology: The new synthesis*. Cambridge: Harvard Universiy Press.

Wilson, M., & Daly, M. (1985). Competitiveness, risk-taking and violence: The young male syndrome. *Ethology & Sociobiology, 6,* 59–73.

Wilson, M. I., & Daly, M. (1992). The man who mistook his wife for a chattel. In J. Barkow, L. Cosmides, & J. Tooby (Eds.), *The adapted mind* (pp. 289–326). New York: Oxford University Press.

Wilson, M. I., & Daly, M. (1993). An evolutionary perspective on male sexual proprietariness and violence against wives. *Violence and Victims, 8,* 271–294.

Wilson, M., & Daly, M. (1996). Male sexual proprietariness and violence against wives. *Current Directions in Psychological Science, 5,* 2–7.

Wilson, M., & Daly, M. (1998). Lethal and non-lethal violence against wives and the evolutionary psychology of male proprietariness. In R. E. Dobash & R. P. Dobash (Eds.), *Rethinking violence against women* (pp. 199–230). Thousand Oaks: Sage.

Zuk, M. (2002). *Sexual selections: What we can and can't learn about sex from animals*. Berkeley/Los Angeles: University of California Press.

Nothing in Human Behavior Makes Sense Except in the Light of Culture: Shared Interests of Social Psychology and Cultural Evolution

17

Thomas J. H. Morgan, Catharine P. Cross and Luke E. Rendell

We would hope that at least some readers would already agree with the first part of our chapter's title, paraphrased from the words of evolutionary biologist Theodosius Dobzhansky, who first stated that "nothing in biology makes sense except in the light of evolution" (Dobzhansky 1964, p. 449). In the animal kingdom, human culture is extraordinary. Over the past 100,000 years, we have cumulatively acquired the abilities necessary to colonize every terrestrial ecosystem on Earth, profoundly affect those systems (for better or worse), escape the embrace of Earth's gravity, and alter our own evolutionary trajectory. Culture permeates our lives profoundly. It affects, for example, some of our most basic psychological processes—many thought to be human universals—such as how our eyes take in information (Chua et al. 2005; Kitayama et al. 2003), how we reason about objects in space (Henrich et al. 2010), and how we recall our memories (Ross and Wang 2010). In our view, as evolutionary biologists and psychologists, any account of human evolution that did not include culture as a major factor would be necessarily depauperate.

Our field, though fundamentally interdisciplinary, has become generally known as *cultural evolution,* or *gene–culture coevolution,* and is one of the modern fields of scientific research that aims to understand human behavior in the light of evolution. While sharing common descent from human sociobiology with its sibling fields, evolutionary psychology and human behavioral ecology, cultural evolution differs considerably in its approach, methods, and underlying assumptions. In this chapter, our aim is to convince the reader that the second part of our title is true. We outline the cultural evolutionary approach for a social psychology audience, highlighting where it differs from those of evolutionary psychology and human behavioral ecology, and the developing areas where we believe there is fertile soil for interaction, collaboration, and exchange between social psychology and cultural evolution. For readers interested in learning more about the potential for crossovers between cultural evolution and social psychology, we suggest the article "How cultural evolutionary theory can inform social psychology and vice versa" (Mesoudi 2009) as an excellent next step.

T. J. H. Morgan (✉)
Department of Psychology, University of California, Tolman Hall, Berkeley, CA 94720, USA
e-mail: thomas.morgan@berkeley.edu

C. P. Cross
School of Psychology & Neuroscience, University of St Andrews, St Mary's Quad, St Andrews, Fife, KY16 9JP, UK
e-mail: cpc2@st-andrews.ac.uk

L. E. Rendell
Centre for Social Learning and Cognitive Evolution, School of Biology, University of St. Andrews, St Andrews, Fife, KY16 9TH, UK
e-mail: ler4@st-andrews.ac.uk

V. Zeigler-Hill et al. (eds.), *Evolutionary Perspectives on Social Psychology,* Evolutionary Psychology,
DOI 10.1007/978-3-319-12697-5_17, © Springer International Publishing Switzerland 2015

The Cultural Evolution Approach

The social sciences have occasionally had a tense relationship with the word "evolution," largely because of the way Darwinian ideas have sometimes been applied to human societies (Laland and Brown 2011). It is therefore worth beginning our outline of cultural evolution by drawing some clear lines between what cultural evolution is and what it is not. Firstly, the modern field of cultural evolution has nothing at all to do with the nineteenth-century "progressive" conception of cultural evolution sometimes known as *Spencerian,* after its principal articulator Victorian anthropologist Herbert Spencer. Under this empirically untenable view, cultural evolution progressed up a fixed series of steps on a ladder from barbarism to the height of Victorian civilization, handily justifying the ongoing colonial exploitation of "less evolved" societies. Progressivism, the idea that all life is evolving toward some single, perfect, form, and the notion of the Spencerian "ladder of life," have been utterly rejected by modern evolutionary biology and have nothing to do with the field of cultural evolution as we understand it.

More subtly, cultural evolution can and should be distinguished from memetics. The word "meme" was coined by Dawkins (1976) to describe a neatly packaged particle of culture, directly analogous to a gene. Despite "memes" having a lasting legacy as part of internet culture, the science of memetics is not thriving (Laland and Brown 2011; Mesoudi et al. 2004), perhaps because it was overly committed to an inflexible, gene-inspired model of transmission of discrete units and a meme's eye view of cultural change to match the gene's eye view of genetic evolution espoused by Dawkins. In contrast, cultural evolution has adopted a broader approach with fewer a priori assumptions about how culture is transmitted—indeed, this question is one area where cultural evolution can potentially learn a lot from social psychology.

Perhaps the defining feature of cultural evolution, with respect to other contemporary, evolutionary approaches to human behavior, is its treatment of culture as being influenced by pressures that operate at least partially independently from those acting on genes (Boyd and Richerson 1985; Mesoudi 2011). To make this clear, we need to introduce some terminology to distinguish the various evolutionary processes that cultural evolution researchers recognize as occurring in human societies (see also Fig. 17.1). The first process is regular genetic evolution—changes in gene frequencies within a given population over time; this can result from a number of processes, including natural selection, neutral drift, and others (Endler 1986). Through development, a genotype interacts with the environment to manifest as a phenotype, but developing humans also acquire cultural content—their language, their values, knowledge of their environment, various technologies, and their material inheritance. As culture thus constitutes another heritable system, parallel to the genetic system, then, alongside genetic evolution, there is cultural evolution. Cultural evolution is the change in the cultural content of a given population over time as certain practices or ideas become more or less common, new knowledge is generated, retained, and elaborated, and so forth. Understanding the range of processes by which this happens is a major concern of cultural evolution as a scientific field. Finally, we can distinguish a process by which genes and culture interact with each other, with each (sometimes profoundly) influencing the evolution of the other. This process is called *gene–culture coevolution,* and it is a cornerstone of the modern study of cultural evolution (Boyd and Richerson 1985; Cavalli-Sforza and Feldman 1981; Lumsden and Wilson 1981).

Cultural evolution's emphasis on gene–culture coevolution can be seen as a point of departure from sociobiology. Founding sociobiologist E. O. Wilson famously described culture as being held on a genetic leash (Wilson 1978), with the obvious intention to evoke the image of a person walking a dog and to leave no doubt which is in control. While cultural evolutionists would not dispute that the link between the two—the leash—exists, they would dispute that the implied control is unidirectional. Consider, as an analogy, host–parasite coevolution where two species are engaged in an evolutionary arms

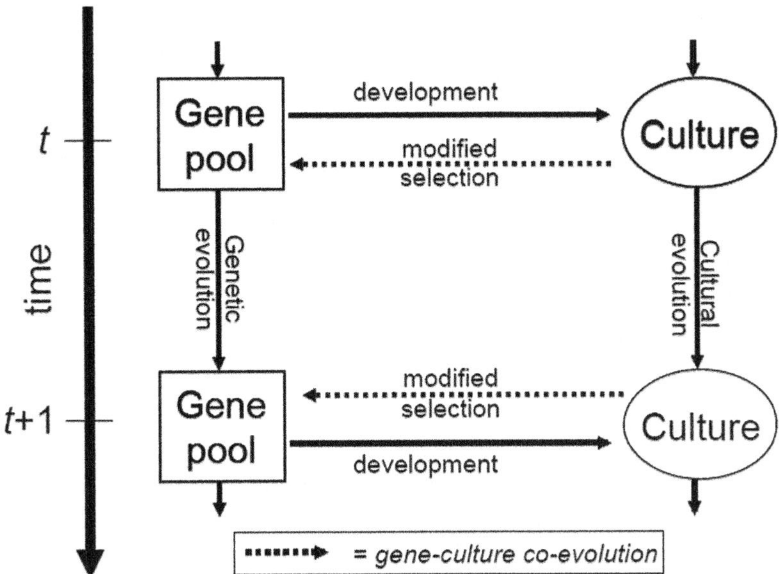

Fig. 17.1 Genetic evolution, cultural evolution, and gene–culture coevolution. Both genes and culture constitute forms of inheritance that are passed down across generations over time. Changes to genes and culture are genetic evolution and cultural evolution, respectively. The influence of genes on culture through development is a classic part of evolutionary theory; however, gene–culture coevolutionary theory extends this model by allowing culture to have an effect upon the gene pool. This occurs by culture modifying the selection acting on genes leading to different future compositions of the gene pool. Several examples of gene–culture coevolution are given in this chapter

race: the parasite evolving to take advantage of the host, the host to repel the parasite. Just as it would be inappropriate to argue that the parasite is controlling the evolution of the host, while ignoring the impact the host is having on the evolution of the parasite, cultural evolution argues that it is inappropriate to focus solely on the influence that genes have on culture, to the extent that the influence of culture on genes is ignored. So it is a central tenet of cultural evolution theory that the relationship between genetic and cultural evolution is mutual in that both forms of inheritance can alter the other's evolution. In support, there is good evidence that culture can alter the rate, dynamics, direction, and steady states of genetic evolution (Boyd and Richerson 1985; Feldman and Cavalli-Sforza 1989; Feldman and Laland 1996; Laland et al. 1995; Laland et al. 2010; Laland 1994; Richerson et al. 2010). A familiar example is the selection of alleles for lactose tolerance following the spread of cultural traits for dairy farming (Tishkoff et al. 2007)—a clear case where cultural evolution subsequently drove genetic evolution. Other examples include the spread of genes for malaria resistance (and in turn sickle cell anemia) following the spread of the cultural practice of yam farming (Durham 1991), and the prevalence of the 230C *thrifty* allele, which impedes the elimination of cholesterol, in Central American populations whose ancestors first domesticated maize. The reliance on maize for dietary proteins was fine when growing conditions were good, but if crops failed, this generated a strong selection for any genetic variants that increased survivability in times of famine, such as the *thrifty* allele. Since then, further cultural evolution has generated a modern nutritional environment rich in fats, with adverse survival consequences for individuals inhibited in their ability to eliminate cholesterol (Hünemeier et al. 2012). Recently, exploration of the human genome has revealed scores of genes that have undergone strong and very recent (i.e., within the past 50,000 years) selection. A good number of these genes have functions likely to have been affected by cultural developments over this period, such as the creation of information-rich environments affecting genes involved in brain development (Laland et al. 2010; Richerson et al. 2010).

Despite viewing culture as partially independent of genes, cultural evolutionists do not deny that there is any genetic influence on culture. Indeed, such a denial would be clearly untenable. Culture could not exist in a species that had not already evolved brains and cognitive systems capable of acquiring culture and effectively passing it on, such as what Csibra and Gergely (2011) call *natural pedagogy*. Csibra and Gergely argue that natural pedagogy is a human adaptation by which infants acquire, and their adult carers pass on, locally relevant cultural information. For a more specific example of a genetic influence on culture, consider cross-cultural work examining variation in color naming systems. Whilst such systems do show tremendous variation across cultures, cultures that have the same number of terms for different colors tend to show consistency across cultures in which colors relate to which terms (Kay et al. 2009; Regier and Kay 2009). Further work found that the corresponding colors can be understood as providing optimal partitioning of color space given a certain number of partitions (i.e., color names) and human visual processing neuro-circuitry (Regier et al. 2007).

In addition to the instances of genetic influences on the content of a culture, however, cultural evolutionists seek to understand the cultural influences on the evolution of behavior. To illustrate this, consider the evolution of language (Mesoudi 2011). One could explain the evolution of language in terms of the genetic loci involved and relevant selection pressures. However, one could also explain it in terms of why a particular individual speaks Urdu instead of French, the cultural evolutionary histories of the languages involved, how Mandarin has changed over time, or why English more closely resembles German than it does Navajo. These different approaches to the question are complementary, not conflicting, and a central theme of cultural evolution is that a full understanding of the evolution of human behavior will involve both types of answers. From this perspective, culture and genes are both simultaneously proximate and ultimate causes of evolution in humans and possibly other animals (Laland et al. 2011; Whitehead 1998) and, at least in the case of humans, have been for at least the past 100,000 years. This perspective contrasts with others from evolutionary psychology and human behavioral ecology that cast culture as a proximate means to a genetically specified end (Barkow et al. 1992; Mace 2000; Tooby and Cosmides 1989).

How Culture Evolves: An Overview of Social Learning Strategies

Cultural evolution aims to understand the mechanisms by which culture evolves. Part of this process involves considering the extent to which cultural evolution operates like genetic evolution and where the major points of departure can be found (e.g., Strimling et al. 2009). For the purposes of this chapter, however, we focus on the role of cultural evolution in the persistence and spread of the culture of *social learning*—the suite of processes by which an individual's learning is influenced by the behavior or products of another individual (Heyes 1994; Hoppitt and Laland 2013). In particular, we focus on the study of social learning strategies (Laland 2004; Rendell et al. 2011) or transmission biases (Boyd and Richerson 1985; Henrich and Mcelreath 2003); evolved learning rules that guide individual reliance on either social or individual/asocial information and so are central to understanding how culture evolves. Taking an evolutionary perspective, it is also important to understand and show the adaptive value of social learning mechanisms and biases—through, for example, showing their positive effects on the effectiveness and accuracy of decision making—that would favor their evolution and, in turn, the evolution of a human psychology capable of supporting culture as we know it today. The result has been the development of a strong theoretical tradition, using mathematical models of evolution to generate predictions that can then be tested empirically.

In addition to the corpus of theoretical work, we also briefly touch on the burgeoning experimental literature within cultural evolution on social learning strategies. This work bears a great deal in common with studies of conformity from social psychology (e.g., Asch 1956; Jenness 1932; Raafat et al. 2009). The differences typically lie in the specific variables considered by the two fields, but also in the general view of social information use. The view of copying others as an adaptive behavior (if used strategically) contrasts with traditional social psychology, which has often viewed conformity in a negative light—an abandonment of individual beliefs (Asch 1952; but see Krueger and Funder 2004, for a more positive overview). Next, we outline some of the wide variety of social learning strategies that have been considered by cultural evolutionists, both theoretically and empirically.

Copy When Uncertain

The existence of a bias to copy when uncertain has been a key assumption of many theoretical models of cultural evolution. Boyd and Richerson (1988) constructed a simple mathematical model to demonstrate the utility of this bias, which we describe in conceptual terms here to provide an example of the kind of theoretical work that typically underpins this kind of cultural evolution research. The model simulated an environment inhabited by individuals who could earn payoffs depending on the match between their behavior and the state of the environment, and these payoffs determined their likelihood of reproducing. Individuals died periodically and were replaced with a new generation of offspring such that selection—and hence evolution—could take place. The environment changed between two possible states (which Boyd & Richerson called *habitat 1* and *habitat 2*). Individuals in the model had to determine which habitat they were in at any given time in order to perform the appropriate behavior, and those that got it right received higher payoffs. Individuals were given both imperfect personal information (information that they acquired independently of other individuals) about the habitat and the opportunity to learn from a member of the previous generation. Boyd and Richerson then explored what mix of individual and social learning would be favored by natural selection under varying degrees of imperfection in personal information and rates of switching between the habitat states. They found that when an individual's personal information was unsatisfactory (i.e., it left them uncertain), individuals should adopt the decisions of others. Although uncertainty may be generated through an unsuccessful attempt at collecting personal information (i.e., one that results in insufficient evidence to make a decision), uncertainty in real life could also result from poor performance on the same task on previous occasions or on related tasks. Thus, an individual who makes a poor mating decision may come to doubt their ability to identify high-quality mates and so be more inclined to copy the decisions of others when required to make another decision (i.e., a reduction in confidence). There is strong empirical evidence to support such a role for uncertainty in adult humans. When tested using both a simulated foraging task and a mental rotation task, individuals who expressed higher levels of uncertainty in their individual decision making were more likely to adopt the decisions of others (Morgan et al. 2011). Furthermore, the same study documented that individual certainty correlated with whether or not individuals were correct. Accordingly, this social learning strategy can be seen to improve the accuracy of individual decision making, as it guided individuals who were actually likely to be incorrect to copy the correct decisions of other individuals (Morgan et al. 2011).

Payoff- and Prestige-Biased Social Learning

Payoff-biased social learning refers to any form of selective social learning where an individual's social learning is guided by the payoffs to themselves or to other individuals (Kendal et al. 2009; Schlag 1998). Here, "payoff" is shorthand for what an individual gets as a result of their choice of behavior in a given context (e.g., food, safety).

Theoretical analyses have indicated that strategies where an individual's use of social information is guided by their own payoff ("proportional reservation"), the payoff to demonstrators ("proportional observation"), or the difference between the two ("proportional imitation") can all be highly effective in particular contexts (Schlag 1998, 1999). There is also good empirical evidence that humans are sensitive to such information and do use it to direct social learning (Apesteguia et al. 2007; Caldwell and Millen 2008; Mesoudi and O'Brien 2008; Mesoudi 2008; Pike et al. 2010). For example, in a computer-based tool-design task, in which participants could alter four different parameters before receiving feedback on the efficacy of their design, participants were found to selectively copy the design of the individual who was performing the best in the group (Mesoudi and O'Brien 2008). Similarly, in a pitch-discrimination task, individuals were observed to copy a potential demonstrator in relation to the latter's performance ranking, but were particularly influenced when they themselves were performing poorly (Morgan et al. 2011).

"Prestige" has been defined as noncoerced within-group human status asymmetry, and the idea that prestige might influence social learning biases has been studied by cultural evolutionists (Henrich and Gil-White 2001). The "prestige-bias" hypothesis holds that because specific payoffs are often hard to obtain, individuals have a general tendency to copy the decisions of those who have been successful—though not necessarily in the relevant domain—and who are afforded associated prestige. Prestige is distinguished from dominance on the basis that prestige is noncoercive, whereas dominance is coercive (Henrich and Gil-White 2001), and this mirrors the distinction between hedonic and agonistic social hierarchies observed in nonhuman primates (Barkow et al. 2012). The copying of generally successful individuals may be easier to implement than relying on knowledge of the specific payoffs associated with particular decisions and so could be a widespread phenomenon. For example, a handful of Fijian *yalewa vuku,* or wise women, had a disproportionate impact on the cultural evolution of the population, largely through the high general prestige in which they were held (Henrich and Henrich 2010).

Conformist Transmission

Although this learning rule is sometimes referred to as *conformity,* we shall use the term *conformist transmission* here, because what cultural evolutionists refer to as conformist transmission differs from the term "conformity" as used in a social psychology context. In social psychology, conformity typically means "yielding to group pressure" (Crutchfield 1955), and there is a long history in social psychology of studying how people will change their expressed views in apparent attempts to "fit in" to a group context. In cultural evolution, conformist transmission is a learning rule by which individuals are *disproportionately* likely to adopt the decisions of majorities at the expense of minorities (Boyd and Richerson 1985; Morgan and Laland 2012). Consider the case of a naïve individual choosing between options A and B who is presented with seven informants advocating option A and three informants advocating option B. In this case, the majority amongst the informants makes up 70 % of the group. If the naïve individual were to use conformist transmission (we shall henceforth refer to such individuals as "conformists," and when we do so, we mean in the cultural evolution sense) they would have a *greater* than 70 % chance of choosing option A. An individual with a 70 % chance of adopting the behavior of the majority would be using unbiased transmission (behaviorally indistinguishable from picking an individual at random from the environment and copying them) and would *not* be said to be conformist even though they might have altered their behavior to match the majority.

Conformist transmission is of particular interest to cultural evolutionists as it results in popular views coming to dominate the population and so can have considerable population-level consequences (Boyd and Richerson 1985). This interest stems originally from a theoretical model in which groups of individuals occupied a spatially variable environment. The model found that if an individual moved from its existing group to a new group in an unfamiliar part of the environment, conformist transmission was a very effective means by which the migrant individual could accurately hone in on locally adaptive behavior (Boyd and Richerson 1985), so effective in fact that the model predicted that anytime social learning itself would be favored, so would conformist transmission. More recent theory (Nakahashi et al. 2012) has added to this, finding that spatial variation, errors in learning, and the number of options between which individuals choose, all favor the evolution of conformist transmission. This is because conformist transmission uses the decisions of a large group of individuals to identify potentially weak signals across multiple decisions. Both errors in learning and a larger number of options to choose between make each individual's decision less reliable, but when offered to a group of individuals the correct option will still most likely be the most prevalent decision in the population and so conformist transmission will be a successful strategy.

Interest in conformist transmission has persisted because of theoretical studies that suggest it offers a framework to help understand the comparatively extraordinary levels of cooperation seen in human societies (e.g., Boyd et al. 2011). To sketch the argument, conformist transmission sharpens and maintains distinctions between groups. This in theory can produce the conditions for what Boyd and Richerson have called *cultural group selection* to operate. Whereas genetic group selection breaks down when individuals move between groups and bring their behavioral genes with them, thus allowing uncooperative behavior to take advantage of a cooperative group, in a cultural context, with conformist transmission, immigrants to the group change their behavioral culture to match the group they are moving into.

On the other hand, a potential pitfall of conformist transmission is that favoring the already dominant view can be an obstacle to the spread of new information or innovations (Eriksson et al. 2007). As even very good ideas must initially start at very low frequencies, the prevalence of conformist transmission can act to block their spread. This is particularly problematic in temporally variable environments where the discovery and spread of new behaviors is essential to success (Eriksson et al. 2007; Kandler and Laland 2013; Nakahashi et al. 2012). Because weak conformist transmission hinders the spread of innovations less than strong conformist transmission, Kandler and Laland (2013) argue that conformist transmission is likely to be weak. Thus, the extent to which conformist transmission is expected to be adaptive is contested, but the theoretical models lead us to expect a broad range of conditions under which conformity will be utilized.

Given the predictions made by evolutionary models concerning the success of conformist transmission, several experiments on adult human participants have been carried out to distinguish a disproportionate tendency to adopt the majority decision from other rules that lack the same population level consequences. Efferson et al. (2008) carried out an experiment in which, over many rounds, participants repeatedly chose between two "technologies." The participants knew the alternative technologies had different expected payoffs, but did not know which was better. Although conformist transmission was found to be an effective strategy in this context, Efferson et al. (2008) found that only some participants used it. They characterize this difference in terms of a mixed population of conformists and "mavericks," the latter being individuals who typically prefer to rely on their own information. However, the data imply that individuals vary continuously in the extent to which they utilize social information and/or are conformist, such that a dichotomy would not be an appropriate way to interpret the data (Efferson et al. 2008). In a similar experiment, Mcelreath et al. (2005) also used a simple two-choice task, where participants were required to choose between planting two types of virtual crop. Although participants did again show some evidence of a conformist tendency, they were better characterized by unbiased transmission when the environment was stable across time, a result at odds with theory that suggests environmental stability over time favors conformist transmission (Nakahashi et al. 2012). More recent empirical work found that although the response of adult participants to consensus alone was consistent with conformist transmission, the additional effects of other variables, such as individual confidence and group size, acted to mask this effect at the behavioral level (Morgan et al. 2011). The data and the theory concerning conformist transmission are therefore complex, but there is good evidence to think that it is a feature of at least some human social learning.

Age- and Kin-Biased Social Learning

Another bias that could guide social learning is age. Such a bias is likely to be adaptive to the extent that older individuals have had more time to acquire valuable information, but also have demonstrated, through their survival, that they have not been overly reliant on poor information. Thus, one might surmise that any remaining old individuals are more likely than young individuals to be in the possession of high-quality information. There is also evidence for such a bias in humans. For example, in the case of the Fijian population, although *yalewa vuku* (i.e., wise women) were particularly influential, to a lesser extent, so were *qase*—nonspecific elders (Henrich and Henrich 2010). In the traditional societies of the Solomon Islands, elders are valuable sources of information on the edibility of various plants, which can prove crucial when the gardens that are the usual source of food fail (Diamond 1997).

Individuals may also show a bias to copy the decisions of kin. There are at least three reasons as to why this is likely adaptive and hence favored by selection. First, in a structured population, which most are, related individuals typically live nearer to each other than the average unrelated individual does and so the information they possess may be of greater relevance than that offered by unrelated individuals. Second, kin are readily available, accessible, and tolerant to close proximity. Third, due to the accrual of indirect fitness, individuals may be more likely to donate information to their kin, either by making such information more readily available, or by directly teaching them (Fogarty et al. 2011). In the Fijian population, in addition to the influence of *yalewa vuku* and *qase* (wise women and elders), food taboos were identified as primarily learned from mothers, grandmothers, or mothers-in-law (Henrich and Henrich 2010). Similarly, craftsmen of the New Guinean Langda people report passing on the prized skill of stone-adze construction "only to close relatives" (Stout 2002, p. 702). In the case of vertical transmission from parents to offspring, however, it is possible that such a copying bias may not be the result of a psychological mechanism, but instead the result of behavioral practices concerning childrearing. In species with parental care of offspring, including humans, it is typically the parents with whom offspring interact most frequently. Thus, even unbiased social learning might be expected to lead to a greater cultural transmission between parent–offspring pairs than between other members of the population.

Random Copying

Of course, cultural transmission does not necessarily have to be biased. A number of studies have highlighted areas of human culture where the copying decisions of individuals produce no net effect on the population distribution, consistent with a model in which individuals copy at random. Such models fit observed data for the popularity of baby names, music, and dog breeds very well (Bentley et al. 2007). In spite of all of the thought and care that individual parents put into choosing their child's name, parents, as a group, behave in a manner that is identical to a population of parents who choose names at random—in both cases, new parents are more likely to adopt baby names they have been exposed to more often. Such an approach has also illustrated the interactions between independent decisions and social transmission in the spread of interest in disease pandemics, such as H5N1 and bird flu virus (Bentley et al. 2007). These studies also reveal how the results of apparently random copying can be perturbed by the influence of key events, such as a spike in popularity of the Dalmatian dog breed observed after the rerelease of the film *101 Dalmatians* (Bentley et al. 2007). However, a recently developed model investigating the social transmission of neolithic German pottery designs, which previously had been considered an example of random copying (Bentley et al. 2004), was able to detect collective forces guiding decision making (Kandler and Shennan 2013). This raises the possibility that more sensitive models may yet find trends guiding other decisions currently considered random at the population level.

Maladaptive Culture

Culture has typically been viewed as an evolved adaptation, and thus to be highly beneficial to individuals. However, the only requirement is that culture be adaptive as a whole; many specific cultural traits may in fact be maladaptive to the individuals who possess them. Accordingly, the study of the appearance, spread, and persistence of maladaptive cultural practices has been another focus of cultural evolution. For example, Tanaka et al. (2009) modeled the evolution of maladaptive practices for treating disease. They found that the inefficacy of poor treatments, paradoxically, allowed them to spread. Individuals who use effective treatments are likely to seek treatment less frequently than individuals who use ineffective or maladaptive treatments (because effective treatments will cure problems whilst ineffective treatments allow them to persist, causing the individual to seek further bouts of treatment). Provided the ineffective treatments do not immediately lead to the death of their users, undecided individuals will observe the use of ineffective treatments more often than they observe the use of effective treatments. If the relative efficacy of treatments is not obvious then the maladaptive medical treatments may spread throughout the population at the expense of superior ones. As described above, the prevalence of conformist transmission can also lead to maladaptive consequences because it inhibits the spread of beneficial innovations (Eriksson et al. 2007; Morgan and Laland 2012). The view of culture as a blend of adaptive and maladaptive traits evolving both independently and in interaction with genetic evolution can be contrasted with the other subfields studying human evolution and behavior. For example, in evolutionary psychology, the role of what is termed *epidemiological culture*—the transmitted culture studied most often by cultural evolutionists—is de-emphasized. Instead, evolutionary psychology conceptualizes human minds as possessing *evoked culture,* analogous to a jukebox, where "evoked" behavior is selected from a library of genetically determined alternatives according to inputs from the environment in which the individual finds themselves. In this case, culture is generally expected to be adaptive as long as the environment is not too different from that in which the library evolved (Brown et al. 2011). In human behavioral ecology, culture is viewed as a proximate mechanism; a highly flexible strategy allowing individuals to tailor behavioral responses in order to ultimately maximize fitness in any environment, but with little creativity beyond the complex matching of behavior to environment (Brown et al. 2011). Accordingly, it suggests that the vast majority of culture should be adaptive. Both approaches struggle to accommodate empirical phenomena such as the demographic transition (the switch from having many children with low life expectancy, to fewer children with greater life expectancy) seen in populations across the world, that does not increase long-term fitness and seems to result from the prioritization of socioeconomic competitiveness over fitness (Goodman et al. 2012). Cultural evolution, in contrast, expects culture to contain a mix of adaptive and maladaptive behavior, and as a result the demographic transition can more easily be modeled within its assumptions (Kolk et al. 2014).

Comparative Work

A feature of many of the social learning strategies considered by cultural evolutionists is that their adaptive value is likely to be very general. For example, copying other individuals when you are uncertain is likely to be an effective strategy across many different contexts and even for multiple species. Accordingly, there has been much work investigating social learning strategies in nonhuman animals (e.g., Kendal et al. 2005). Such work can help our understanding of the evolution of social learning and culture in two ways. First, it can help piece together the evolutionary history of certain human traits. Studies of nonhuman primates may be particularly informative in this regard. Second, comparative work can give insights into the conditions that favor reliance on social information or the evolution of particular social learning strategies. In this case, a much wider range of species can be fruitfully studied. For example, a bias to copy when uncertain has received empirical support across a variety of nonhuman taxa, including rats (Galef et al. 2008), gerbils (Forkman 1991), capuchin monkeys (Visalberghi and Fragaszy 1995), ants (Grüter et al. 2011), and nine-spined sticklebacks (Kendal et al. 2005). There is also evidence for a bias to copy older individuals in guppies (Amlacher and Dugatkin 2005) where female mating preferences were influenced to a greater degree by the equivalent decisions of older conspecific females than they were by the decisions of younger conspecific females. Other studies have found that young birds (Biondi et al. 2010) and chimpanzees (Biro et al. 2003; Biro et al. 2006) are more reliant on social information than older conspecifics. More recently, vervet monkeys have been observed to adopt group norms when choosing food, going with the group even when the choice contradicts previously acquired preferences (van de Waal et al. 2013). Understanding the functional consequences of social learning across species helps us understand the generality of conditions under which various strategies may or may not be adaptive and feeds into an understanding of the evolution of human culture, even while debates continue about the relationship between cultural processes in humans and nonhumans (Laland and Galef 2009).

Integrating Social Psychology and Cultural Evolution

Cultural evolution has a strong theoretical tradition of mathematical modeling, but has only relatively recently, compared to social psychology, begun experimentally exploring how culture is passed from individual to individual. It is here that we see the clearest opportunities for the two fields to inform each other in developing the science of cultural evolution. Mathematical models of cultural transmission have to incorporate complex cognitive processes and the array of environmental and social factors that potentially affect them. If a model is to be tractable, that is, suitable for analyzing to understand the processes it is designed to represent, then these intricacies must be dramatically simplified. This simplification can often be in tension with the complexities of psychological findings on how people actually acquire cultural information (Barkow et al. 2012). Current models do not, for example, reflect the possibility that different informational domains will favor different learning biases, and that these biases are likely to change over the life-course. Empirical evidence for this possibility exists, however. For example, among the many social learning biases observed in young children (referred to as "trust" by developmental psychologists) are a bias to trust familiar caregivers over strangers and a bias to trust individuals who have shown themselves to be reliable informants over those exposed as unreliable. Whilst 3-year-olds prioritize familiarity over reliability, this changes in 4-year-olds who favor reliability (Corriveau and Harris 2009; Harris 2012).

A second complexity not covered by extant models is membership of individuals to different groups within the same population. The likelihood that an adult will adopt the behavior of a group depends on how strongly they identify with that group (Louis et al. 2007), and individuals might actively reject the influence of a majority if it conflicts with information already learned from a more salient social group (Smith and Louis 2008). Similar behavior has been observed in young children where they preferentially trust an adult informant with the local accent over an informant with a foreign accent (Kinzler et al. 2011). Given that the processes underlying group identification already have a rich literature devoted to them (e.g., Tajfel 1982), this could be a fertile area for integration between cultural evolution and social psychology.

One recent study (Cross et al. 2013; under review) attempted to integrate cultural evolution and social psychology approaches to the question of sex differences in conformity. The finding that women are more susceptible than men to conform to a majority is well demonstrated within social psychology (Bond and Smith 1996), yet was not explicitly addressed within the cultural evolution approach. As noted above, social learning rules are typically assumed to be used similarly by all members of a population, and both men and women did indeed adopt a copy-when-uncertain rule in two different experimental tasks. However, gender stereotypes—well studied in social psychology—about performance on these tasks affected women's confidence independently of any effect of accuracy. That is, women consistently underestimated their ability to perform the task when it was stereotypically "masculine." Using the copy-when-uncertain strategy, they therefore copied the majority more often than men. Conversely, where gender stereotypes about a task were absent, uncertainty related to accuracy similarly for both sexes, such that the copy-when-uncertain rule produced similar levels of copying for men and women.

Incorporating experimental findings from social psychology into general models of cultural transmission is a major challenge for cultural evolution researchers. The modelers are mindful of the likelihood of informational and cognitive intricacy, and work on these kinds of complexities has increased in recent years (Rendell et al. 2011). Nonetheless, we still do not know how general current mathematical models of cultural transmission are. Each model might only be valid for specific domains of information in specific circumstances. A model that works for language transmission and change, for example, may have quite different assumptions, structure, and evolutionary outcomes than a model of religious learning, or cultural transmission of diet, or changes in fashion mediated by mass media. The implication is that we need increased collaboration between social psychologists who study social learning and cultural transmission, and the theoreticians of cultural evolution (Mesoudi 2009), so that model builders are challenged to incorporate the complexities found by cognitive scientists. Culture, after all, can only be the cumulative result of cognitive processes occurring in the brains of a population of individuals, so for a complete understanding of how it evolves and coevolves, a concurrent understanding of human psychology is essential.

Another area where cultural evolution could benefit from collaboration with social psychology is in the details of what cultural transmission involves. Cultural evolutionary models, for simplicity's sake, typically model cultural transmission the same way population geneticists model genetic transmission—the clean and instantaneous transmission of a trait from one individual to another (give or take some chance mutation or learning error). Yet, culture clearly does not "transmit" like DNA or electrons (Strimling et al. 2009); there is no material continuity between the brains in the way that there is when DNA enters gametes and then zygotes. Instead, culture is a melange of information, various types of which may or may not be processed and acquired in different ways. What looks like cultural transmission at the macro level is built at the individual level upon cultural editing and reconstruction processes in the brain that we still understand little about. This should not be taken as a reason to dismiss cultural evolution theory out of hand. Just as the modern evolutionary synthesis was developed using models based on a conceptual understanding of genes before their chemical basis was identified, the success of cultural evolutionary models in predicting behavior is proof that they have been fruitful tools. By implication, there is tremendous opportunity for collaboration between cultural evolution and social psychology as the impact of a proper understanding of cultural transmission on our understanding of culture could be as profound as the impact of the discovery of DNA on evolutionary biology.

Conclusion

Social psychologists continue to generate significant insights into how human behavior is affected by the behavior of others, describing how conformity works, understanding how human cultural acquisition is biased, how it can be fooled, what contexts these biases are sensitive to, and so on. What cultural evolution has to offer is a conceptual and theoretical framework within which to understand these features of human psychology as the product of a complex and ongoing coevolutionary dynamic between genes and culture. We believe that increased interactions between these fields will result in further progress in generating hypotheses that encompass evolutionary timescales and ultimately help to explain those features of modern human behavior that social psychologists are in the process of revealing.

References

Amlacher, J., & Dugatkin, L. (2005). Preference for older over younger models during mate-choice copying in young guppies. *Ethology Ecology & Evolution, 17,* , 161–169.

Apesteguia, J., Huck, S., & Oechssler, J. (2007). Imitation—theory and experimental evidence. *Journal of Economic Theory, 136,* 217–235.

Asch, S. (1952). *Social psychology*. Englewood cliffs: Prentice Hall.

Asch, S. (1956). Studies of independence and conformity. A minority of one against a unanimous majority. *Psychological Monographs, 70,* 1–70.

Barkow, J., Cosmides, L., & Tooby, J. (1992). *The adapted mind: Evolutionary psychology and the generation of culture*. New York: Oxford University Press.

Barkow, J., O'Gorman, R., & Rendell, L. (2012). Are the new mass media subverting cultural transmission? *Review of General Psychology, 16,* 121–133.

Bentley, R. A., Hahn, M. W., & Shennan, S. J. (2004). Random drift and culture change. *Proceedings Biological Sciences/The Royal Society, 271*(1547), 1443–1450.

Bentley, R. A., Lipo, C. P., Herzog, H. A., & Hahn, M. W. (2007). Regular rates of popular culture change reflect random copying. *Evolution and Human Behavior, 28,* 151–158.

Biondi, L. M., García, G. O., Bó, M. S., & Vassallo, A. I. (2010). Social learning in the Caracara Chimango, Milvago chimango (Aves: Falconiformes): An age comparison. *Ethology, 116,* 722–735.

Biro, D., Inoue-Nakamura, N., Tonooka, R., Yamakoshi, G., Sousa, C., & Matsuzawa, T. (2003). Cultural innovation and transmission of tool use in wild chimpanzees: evidence from field experiments. *Animal Cognition, 6,* 213–223.

Biro, D., Sousa, C., & Matsuzawa, T. (2006). Ontogeny and cultural propagation of tool use by wild chimpanzees at Bossou, Guinea: Case studies in nut cracking and leaf folding. In T. Matsuzawa, M. Tomonaga, & M. Tanaka (Eds.), *Cognitive development in chimpanzees* (pp. 476–508). Tokyo: Springer.

Bond, R., & Smith, P. B. (1996). Culture and conformity: A meta-analysis of studies using Asch's (1952b, 1956) Line judgment task. *Psychological Bulletin, 119,* 111–137.

Boyd, R., & Richerson, P. J. (1985). *Culture and the Evolutionary Process. American Anthropologist* (Vol. 89, p. 331). Chicago: University of Chicago Press.

Boyd, R., & Richerson, P. J. (1988). An evolutionary model of social learning: the effects of spatial and temporal variation. In T. R. Zentall & B. G. Galef (Eds.), *Social Learning: Psychological and Biological Perspectives* (pp. 29–48). Mahwah: Lawrence Erlbaum.

Boyd, R., Richerson, P. J., & Henrich, J. (2011). Rapid cultural adaptation can facilitate the evolution of large-scale cooperation. *Behavioral Ecology and Sociobiology, 65,* 431–444.

Brown, G. R., Dickins, T. E., Sear, R., & Laland, K. N. (2011). Evolutionary accounts of human behavioural diversity. *Philosophical Transactions of the Royal Society of London. Series B, Biological Sciences, 366*(1563), 313–324.

Caldwell, C. a., & Millen, A. E. (2008). Experimental models for testing hypotheses about cumulative cultural evolution. *Evolution and Human Behavior, 29,* 165–171.

Cavalli-Sforza, L. L., & Feldman, M. W. (1981). *Cultural transmission and evolution: A quantitative approach.* Princeton: Princeton University Press.

Chua, H. F., Boland, J. E., & Nisbett, R. E. (2005). Cultural variation in eye movements during scene perception. *Proceedings of the National Academy of Sciences of the United States of America, 102,* 12629–12633.

Corriveau, K. H., & Harris, P. L. (2009). Choosing your informant: Weighing familiarity and recent accuracy. *Developmental Science, 12,* 426–437.

Cross, C. P., Brown, G. R., Morgan, T. J. H., & Laland, K. N. (2013). *Sex differences in conformity: The role of confidence*. Paper presented at the Annual Meeting of the Human Behavior and Evolution Society, Miami Beach, FL.

Cross, C. P., Brown, G. R., Morgan, T. J. H., & Laland, K. N. (under review). *Sex differences in conformity: The role of confidence.*

Crutchfield, R. (1955). Conformity and character. *American Psychologist, 10,* 191–198.

Csibra, G., & Gergely, G. (2011). Natural pedagogy as evolutionary adaptation. *Philosophical Transactions of the Royal Society of London. Series B, Biological Sciences, 366*(1567), 1149–1157.

Dawkins, R. (1976). *The selfish gene*. Oxford: Oxford University Press.

Diamond, J. (1997). *Why is sex fun? The evolution of human sexuality*. New York: Basic Books.

Dobzhansky, T. (1964). Biology, molecular and organismic. *American Zoologist, 4,* 443–452.

Durham W. (1991). *Coevolution: Genes, culture and human diversity*. Redwood City: Stanford University Press.

Efferson, C., Lalive, R., Richerson, P. J., Mcelreath, R., & Lubell, M. (2008). Conformists and mavericks: The empirics of frequency-dependent cultural transmission. *Evolution and Human Behavior, 29,* 56–64.

Endler, J. A. (1986). *Natural selection in the wild.* Princeton: Princeton University Press.

Eriksson, K., Enquist, M., & Ghirlanda, S. (2007). Critical points in current theory of conformist social learning. *Journal of Evolutionary Psychology, 5,* 67–87.

Feldman, M. W., & Cavalli-Sforza, L. L. (1989). On the theory of evolution under genetic and cultural transmission with application to the lactose absorption problem. In M. W. Feldman (Ed.), *Mathematical Evolutionary Theory* (pp. 145–173). Princeton: Princeton University Press.

Feldman, M. W., & Laland, K. N. (1996). Gene-culture coevolutionary theory. *Trends in Ecology & Evolution, 5347*(96), 453–457.

Fogarty, L., Strimling, P., & Laland, K. N. (2011). The Evolution of teaching. *Evolution, 65,* 2760–2770.

Forkman, B. (1991). Social facilitation is shown by gerbils when presented with novel but not with familiar food. *Animal Behaviour, 42,* 860–861.

Galef, B. G., Dudley, K. E., & Whiskin, E. E. (2008). Social learning of food preferences in "dissatisfied" and "uncertain" Norway rats. *Animal Behaviour, 75,* 631–637.

Goodman, A., Koupil, I., & Lawson, D. W. (2012). Low fertility increases descendant socioeconomic position but reduces long-term fitness in a modern post-industrial society. *Proceedings of the Royal Society B—Biological Sciences, 279*(1746), 4342–4351.

Grüter, C., Czaczkes, T. J., & Ratnieks, F. L. W. (2011). Decision making in ant foragers (Lasius niger) facing conflicting private and social information. *Behavioral Ecology and Sociobiology, 65,* 141–148.

Harris, P. L. (2012). *Trusting what you're told: How children learn from others.* Boston: Harvard University Press.

Henrich, J., & Gil-White, F. (2001). The evolution of prestige—Freely conferred deference as a mechanism for enhancing the benefits of cultural transmission. *Evolution and Human Behavior, 22,* 165–196.

Henrich, J., & Mcelreath, R. (2003). The evolution of cultural evolution. *Evolutionary Anthropology, 12,* 123–135.

Henrich, J., & Henrich, N. (2010). The evolution of cultural adaptations: Fijian food taboos protect against dangerous marine toxins. *Proceedings of the Royal Society B-Biological Sciences, 277*(1701), 3715–3724.

Henrich, J., Heine, S. J., & Norenzayan, A. (2010). The weirdest people in the world? *The Behavioral and Brain Sciences, 33,* 61–83.

Heyes, C. M. (1994). Social learning in animals: categories and mechanisms. *Biological Reviews, 69,* 207–231.

Hoppitt, W. J. E., & Laland, K. N. (2013). *Social Learning: An introduction to mechanisms, methods, and models.* Princeton: Princeton University Press.

Hünemeier, T., Amorim, C. E. G., Azevedo, S., Contini, V., Acuña-Alonzo, V., Rothhammer, F., Bortolini, M. C. (2012). Evolutionary responses to a constructed niche: Ancient Mesoamericans as a model of gene-culture coevolution. *PloS One, 7*(6), e38862.

Jenness, A. (1932). The role of discussion in changing opinion regarding a matter of fact. *Journal of Abnormal and Social Psychology, 27,* 279–296.

Kandler, A., & Laland, K. N. (2013). Tradeoffs between the strength of conformity and number of conformists in variable environments. *Journal of Theoretical Biology, 332C,* 191–202.

Kandler, A., & Shennan, S. J. (2013). A non-equilibrium neutral model for analysing cultural change. *Journal of Theoretical Biology, 330,* 18–25.

Kay, P., Berlin, B., Maffi, L., Merrifield, W. R., & Cook, R. (2009). *The World Color Survey.* Stanford: CSLI Publications.

Kendal, R. L., Coolen, I., van Bergen, Y., & Laland, K. N. (2005). Trade-offs in the adaptive use of social and asocial learning. *Advances in the Study of Behavior, 35,* 333–379.

Kendal, J. R., Giraldeau, L.-A., & Laland, K. N. (2009). The evolution of social learning rules: Payoff-biased and frequency-dependent biased transmission. *Journal of Theoretical Biology, 260,* 210–219.

Kinzler, K. D., Corriveau, K. H., & Harris, P. L. (2011). Children's selective trust in native-accented speakers. *Developmental Science, 14,* 106–11.

Kitayama, S., Duffy, S., Kawamura, T., & Larsen, J. T. (2003). Perceiving an object and its context in different cultures: A cultural look at New Look. *Psychological Science, 14,* 201–206.

Kolk, M., Cownden, D., & Enquist, M. (2014). Correlations in fertility across generations: can low fertility persist? *Proceedings of the Royal Society B: Biological Sciences, 281,* 1–8.

Krueger, J. I., & Funder, D. C. (2004). Towards a balanced social psychology: Causes, consequences, and cures for the problem-seeking approach to social behavior and cognition. *Behavioral and Brain Sciences, 27,* 313–327.

Laland, K. N. (1994). Sexual selection with a culturally transmitted mating preference. *Theoretical Population Biology, 45,* 1–15.

Laland, K. N. (2004). Social learning strategies. *Learning and Behavior, 32,* 4–14.

Laland, K. N., & Galef Jr., B. G. (2009). *The question of animal culture.* Cambridge: Harvard University Press.

Laland, K. N., & Brown, G. (2011). *Sense and nonsense: Evolutionary perspectives on human behaviour.* Oxford: Oxford University Press.

Laland, K. N., Kumm, J., & Feldman, M. W. (1995). Gene-culture coevolutionary theory: A test case. *Current Anthropology, 36,* 131–156.

Laland, K. N., Odling-Smee, J., & Myles, S. (2010). How culture shaped the human genome: bringing genetics and the human sciences together. *Nature Reviews Genetics, 11,* 137–148.

Laland, K. N., Sterelny, K., Odling-Smee, J., Hoppitt, W., & Uller, T. (2011). Cause and effect in biology revisited: Is Mayr's proximate-ultimate dichotomy still useful? *Science, 334*(6062), 1512–1516.

Louis, W., Davies, S., Smith, J., & Terry, D. (2007). Pizza and pop and the student identity: The role of referent group norms in healthy and unhealthy eating. *Journal of Social Psychology, 147*, 57–74.

Lumsden, C. J., & Wilson, E. O. (1981). *Genes, mind, and culture: The coevolutionary process*. Cambridge: Harvard University Press.

Mace, R. (2000). Evolutionary ecology of human life history. *Animal Behaviour, 59*, 1–10.

Mcelreath, R., Lubell, M., Richerson, P. J., Waring, T. M., Baum, W., Edsten, E., Efferson, C., & Paciotti, B. (2005). Applying evolutionary models to the laboratory study of social learning. *Evolution and Human Behavior, 26*, 483–508.

Mesoudi, A. (2008). An experimental simulation of the "copy-successful-individuals" cultural learning strategy: Adaptive landscapes, producer-scrounger dynamics, and informational access costs. *Evolution and Human Behavior, 29*, 350–363.

Mesoudi, A. (2009). How cultural evolutionary theory can inform social psychology and vice versa. *Psychological Review, 116*, 929–952.

Mesoudi, A. (2011). *Cultural evolution: How Darwinian theory can explain human culture and synthesize the social sciences*. Chicago: University of Chicago Press.

Mesoudi, A., & O'Brien, M. J. (2008). The cultural transmission of Great Basin projectile-point technology I: An experimental simulation. *American Antiquity, 73*, 3–28.

Mesoudi, A., Whiten, A., & Laland, K. N. (2004). Perspective: Is human cultural evolution Darwinian? Evidence reviewed from the perspective of the Origin of Species. *Evolution, 58*, 1–11.

Morgan, T. J. H., & Laland, K. N. (2012). The biological bases of conformity. *Frontiers in Neuroscience, 6*, 1–7.

Morgan, T. J. H., Rendell, L., Ehn, M., Hoppitt, W. J. E., & Laland, K. N. (2011). The evolutionary basis of human social learning. *Proceedings of the Royal Society B: Biological Sciences, 279*, 653–662.

Nakahashi, W., Wakano, J. Y., & Henrich, J. (2012). Adaptive social learning strategies in temporally and spatially varying environments†¯: How temporal vs. spatial variation, number of cultural traits, and costs of learning influence the evolution of conformist-biased transmission, payoff-biased transmission. *Human Nature, 23*, 386–418.

Pike, T. W., Kendal, J. R., Rendell, L., & Laland, K. N. (2010). Learning by proportional observation in a species of fish. *Behavioral Ecology, 21*, 1–18.

Raafat, R. M., Chater, N., & Frith, C. (2009). Herding in humans. *Trends in Cognitive Sciences, 13*, 420–428.

Regier, T., & Kay, P. (2009). Language, thought, and color: Whorf was half right. *Trends in Cognitive Sciences, 13*, 439–446.

Regier, T., Kay, P., & Khetarpal, N. (2007). Color naming reflects optimal partitions of color space. *Proceedings of the National Academy of Sciences of the United States of America, 104*, 1436–1441.

Rendell, L., Fogarty, L., Hoppitt, W. J. E., Morgan, T. J. H., Webster, M. M., & Laland, K. N. (2011). Cognitive culture: theoretical and empirical insights into social learning strategies. *Trends in Cognitive Sciences, 15*, 68–76.

Richerson, P. J., Boyd, R., & Henrich, J. (2010). Gene-culture coevolution in the age of genomics. *Proceedings of the National Academy of Sciences of the United States of America, 107*, 8985–8992.

Ross, M., & Wang, Q. (2010). Why we remember and what we remember: Culture and autobiographical memory. *Perspectives on Psychological Science, 5*, 401–409.

Schlag, K. H. (1998). Why imitate, and if so, how? A boundedly rational approach to multi-armed bandits. *Journal of Economic Theory, 78*, 130–156.

Schlag, K. H. (1999). Which one should I imitate? *Journal of Mathematical Economics, 31*, 493–522.

Smith, J. R., & Louis, W. R. (2008). Do as we say and as we do: The interplay of descriptive and injunctive group norms in the attitude-behaviour relationship. *The British Journal of Social Psychology, 47*, 647–66.

Stout, D. (2002). Skill and cognition in stone tool production: An ethnographic case study from Irian Jaya. *Current Anthropology, 43*, 693–723.

Strimling, P., Enquist, M., & Eriksson, K. (2009). Repeated learning makes cultural evolution unique. *Proceedings of the National Academy of Sciences of the United States of America, 106*(33), 13870–13874.

Tajfel, H. (1982). Social psychology of intergroup relations. *Annual Review of Psychology, 33*, 1–39.

Tanaka, M. M., Kendal, J. R., & Laland, K. N. (2009). From traditional medicine to witchcraft: Why medical treatments are not always efficacious. *Plos One, 4*(4), e5192.

Tishkoff, S., Reed, F., Ranciaro, A., Voight, B. F., Babbitt, C. C., Silverman, J. S., Powell, K., Mortensen, H. M., Hirbo, J. B., Osman, M., Ibrahim, M., Omar, S. A., Lema, G., Nyambo, T. B., Ghori, J., Bumpstead, S., Pritchard, J. K., Wray, G. A., & Deloukas, P. (2007). Convergent adaptation of human lactase persistence in Africa and Europe. *Nature Genetics, 39*, 31–40.

Tooby, J., & Cosmides, L. (1989). Evolutionary psychology and the generation of culture, part I. *Ethology and Sociobiology, 10*, 29–49.

Van de Waal, E., Borgeaud, C., & Whiten, A. (2013). Potent social learning and conformity shape a wild primate's foraging decisions. *Science, 340*(6131), 483–485.

Visalberghi, E., & Fragaszy, D. (1995). The behaviour of capuchin monkeys, Cebus apella, with novel food: The role of social context. *Animal Behaviour, 49*, 1089–1095.

Whitehead, H. (1998). Cultural selection and genetic diversity in matrilineal whales. *Science, 282*(5394), 1708–1711.

Wilson, E. O. (1978). *On human nature*. Cambridge: Harvard University Press.

Part V

Interpersonal Processes

Prosocial Behavior

18

Dennis L. Krebs

Antisocial behaviors tend to grab the headlines, but to a great extent this is because they are exceptional. As people go about the routine business of their everyday lives, they display a wide array of prosocial behaviors, defined as behaviors that benefit others. People tip at restaurants, give up their seats on busses, donate blood, help friends in need, donate to charity, and so on. In addition, people sometimes seem to behave in altruistic ways, intervening in emergencies at great risk to themselves, donating their organs to others, and sacrificing their lives for their countries at war. Three questions arise from these observations: (a) what variables affect the probability of people behaving in prosocial ways, (b) why do people help others, and (c) how altruistic are the prosocial acts that people emit—are they aimed at helping others as ends in themselves, or are they means to egoistic ends? In this chapter, I will review the main answers that social psychologists have given to these questions, identify several limitations of traditional accounts, and demonstrate how an evolutionary approach is equipped to redress these limitations.

D. L. Krebs (✉)
Department of Psychology, Simon Fraser University, Burnaby, British Columbia V5A1S6, Canada
e-mail: krebs@sfu.ca

Traditional Social Psychological Accounts of Prosocial Behavior

Accounts of prosocial behavior contained in social psychology textbooks can be grouped into five main categories: (a) social learning, (b) social norms, (c) situational variables, (d) cognitive construal processes, and (e) emotional states.

Social Learning

The basic idea underlying social learning accounts of prosocial behavior is that people teach others to behave in prosocial ways by rewarding and punishing them, preaching to them, and modeling prosocial forms of conduct. For example, Rushton (1975) found that children who observed models who preached generous or selfish behaviors and behaved in generous or selfish ways were more likely than children who did not undergo these experiences to behave in more generous or selfish ways 2 months later in a different situation from the one in which they originally were tested. Rushton (1975) also found that children who were exposed to models who preached prosocial behavior but behaved selfishly were more inclined than children who were exposed to consistent models to behave in a hypocritical manner. Liebert and Sprafkin (1988) found that children who were exposed to prosocial models on television subsequently emitted more incidents of prosocial behavior while they were playing than children in a control group did.

V. Zeigler-Hill et al. (eds.), *Evolutionary Perspectives on Social Psychology*, Evolutionary Psychology,
DOI 10.1007/978-3-319-12697-5_18, © Springer International Publishing Switzerland 2015

Other studies have produced evidence for prosocial modeling in adults (e.g., Rushton and Campbell 1977).

Social Norms

Social norm accounts of prosocial behavior are based on the assumption that societies contain norms such as the norm of social responsibility, the norm of reciprocity, and the norm of equity that prescribe prosocial behaviors, and that making these norms salient to people and embedding them in personal values increase the probability that people will behave in accordance with them (Schwartz 1977). Studies have concluded that some norms are universal (e.g., norm of reciprocity), whereas other norms vary across cultures (e.g., norm of responsibility; Gouldner 1960). For example, Ma (1985) found that people from collectivist cultures were more likely than people from individualistic cultures to feel that they have an obligation to help in-group members.

Situational Variables

Most traditional social psychological research is based on experiments that manipulate aspects of situations and assesses their effect on social behaviors (Zimbardo 2005). Consider research on bystander intervention, for example. In early studies, social psychologists varied the number of bystanders present in emergencies and observed what came to be called "the bystander effect"—individuals were more likely to intervene in emergencies when they were alone than when others were present (Latané and Nida 1981). In subsequent studies, investigators found that an array of situational variables affected the probability that bystanders would help in emergencies—variables such as whether a victim was bloody, whether a victim had a physical stigma, the amount of pain or danger involved in helping, how real the emergency seemed, how close participants were standing to a victim, whether the victim screamed or asked for help, whether the victim was similar to bystanders, and so on (reviewed in Piliavin et al. 1981). Some social psychologists attempted to organize such variables under overriding constructs, such as diffusion of responsibility, cost of helping, and tension reduction. For example, Piliavin et al. (1981) concluded that "the bystander will choose that response to an emergency that will most rapidly reduce his or her arousal, incurring in the process as few net costs…as possible" (p. 83).

Cognitive Construal Processes

In interpreting findings from research on prosocial behaviors, social psychologists have created decision-making models that connect situational variables to actors' cognitive and emotional reactions. Consider two examples. First, Darley and Latané (1968) suggested that the probability of people intervening in emergencies is affected by factors that influence (a) whether they notice that someone needs help, (b) whether they interpret the situation as an emergency, (c) whether they feel that they are responsible for helping, and (d) whether they know how to help. Second, Piliavin et al. (1981) suggested that people's decisions about whether or not to help in emergencies are affected by their awareness of others' need, the amount of physiological arousal they experience, how they label the arousal, and a cost–benefit analysis of the options available to them.

Emotional States

Social psychologists have found that emotions such as love, gratitude, forgiveness, sympathy, empathy, and guilt induce people to behave in prosocial ways (Batson 1991; McCullough 2008; McCullough et al. 2001; Regan 1971). Among the emotions studied by social psychologists, empathy has received the most attention. A spate of studies has found that inducing people to empathize with victims increases the probability that they will take measures to relieve the victims' distress, sometimes at considerable cost to themselves (reviewed in Batson 1991). Social psychologists have found that "the empathic response is amplified by similarity, familiarity, social closeness, and positive experience with the other.... Subjects empathize with a confederate's pleasure or distress if they perceive the relationship as cooperative" (de Waal 2008, p. 16).

Social Psychological Research on the Relation Between Empathy and Altruism

Most prosocial behaviors investigated in traditional social psychological studies do not qualify as altruistic, because they are aimed at improving the welfare of the individuals performing the prosocial acts. People help others for a large number of nonaltruistic reasons, such as conforming to social norms, avoiding being ostracized by their groups, ingratiating, building credit, brightening their mood, and relieving vicariously experienced distress. The greater the costs associated with helping, the lower the probability of helping. A notable exception to this trend has been found in research concerning empathy and altruism.

Batson (2000) has found that when people focus on the plight of others in need, they may experience either "personal distress," which they can reduce not only by helping the person in need but also by looking away, leaving the scene, and so on, or "an other-oriented emotional response...[such as] empathy, sympathy, compassion, etc. [that engenders] a motivational state with the ultimate goal of increasing another's welfare" (pp. 207–208). According to Batson, people seek to help those with whom they empathize as an end in itself, as opposed to wanting to help them instrumentally in order to relieve their own vicariously experienced personal distress or to achieve other egoistic goals such as obtaining approval or avoiding disapproval from self or others. Batson and his colleagues have conducted more than two dozen experiments that they claim support the link between empathy and altruism (reviewed in Batson 1991).

Although it is always possible that an investigator will find that empathic people who help victims are motivated to obtain some hidden gain (Schaller and Cialdini 1988), Batson and his colleagues have been remarkably successful at demonstrating that the relation between empathy and altruism cannot be accounted for by any of the most obvious egoistic alternatives. Batson (1998) concurred with Piliavin and Charng's (1990) conclusion that a "paradigm shift" is occurring in psychology, "away from the earlier position that behavior that appears to be altruistic must, under closer scrutiny, be revealed as reflecting egoistic motives. Rather, theory and data now being advanced are more compatible with the view that true altruism—acting with the goal of benefiting another—does exist and is a part of human nature" (p. 27).

An Evaluation of Traditional Social Psychological Accounts of Prosocial Behavior

Traditional social psychological research has contributed a great deal to our understanding of the proximate causes of prosocial behavior. It has identified variables that increase the frequency with which people help others and it has improved our ability to predict when people will behave in prosocial ways. This work has also identified mental states and processes that mediate prosocial decisions and offered some insight into the altruism question. However, traditional social psychological research on prosocial behavior is limited in several ways.

First, social psychologists have tended to report findings pertaining to prosocial behavior in a piecemeal, descriptive manner. If someone asked how a traditional social psychologist would answer the question of why people behave in prosocial ways, you could give a large array of independent answers, such as, "because they observe prosocial models; because they are behaving in accordance with a prosocial norm; because the costs of helping are low and the rewards high; because they are feeling empathic or guilty," and so on. The question is what, if anything, do the variables that affect prosocial behavior have in common? It would be helpful to have an overriding theoretical framework to tie them together.

Second, social psychological researchers rarely consider the origins of the processes they study. For example, although social psychologists have established that social learning plays an important role in inducing people to behave in prosocial ways and in the transmission of prosocial norms, social psychologists have not explained how social learning abilities and prosocial norms originated. In a similar vein, traditional social psychologists have not attended to how people acquired the capacity to experience prosocial emotions.

Finally, although traditional social psychological research may increase our ability to predict prosocial behavior, it is not particularly good at explaining it. Why do people (sometimes) model the prosocial behavior of others? Why do people (sometimes) conform to prosocial norms? Why do people experience prosocial emotions, and why do these emotions dispose people to behave in prosocial ways?

An Evolutionary Approach to Prosocial Behavior

Viewing prosocial behavior from an evolutionary perspective helps redress the limitations of traditional social psychological approaches and increase their explanatory power. Evolutionary theory offers an overriding theoretical umbrella under which the findings from social psychological research can be organized. It offers an account of how mental mechanisms originated, and in the process it supplies a basis for deriving hypotheses about how they should be designed. Evolutionary theory is equipped to answer ultimate "why" questions and to supply a basis for understanding how mental mechanisms that motivate people to behave in altruistic ways could have evolved, thus offering insights into human nature.

The theory of evolution is the most powerful and pervasive theory in the biological and human sciences. In its essence, it accounts for human social behavior in terms of mental mechanisms that evolved because they helped archaic humans survive, reproduce, and propagate their genes. As explained by Buss (2008), when evolutionary psychologists attempt to map the mental mechanisms that mediate social behaviors, they attend to the fact that they were designed through natural selection to solve recurring adaptive problems. Evolutionary psychologists expect the inputs that activate evolved mental mechanisms to offer information about the types of adaptive problems that the mechanisms evolved to solve. They expect people to process these inputs in terms of "if–then" decision rules and, therefore, they expect people's decision-making strategies to be conditional, flexible, and attentive to the adaptive implications of alternative courses of action. Note that the "if" in these if–then sequences usually pertains to situational variables, or environmental triggers.

Evolutionary psychology offers answers to "why" questions by attending to the ultimate functions that evolved mental mechanisms were designed to fulfill. In answer to the question "why do people intervene in emergencies?" a social psychologist might say "in order to meet their social responsibilities" or "in order to avoid the costs of disapproval." However, such proximate explanations leave more ultimate questions unanswered. Why are people motivated to meet their social responsibilities? Why are people motivated to avoid disapproval? If you keep asking why questions about human behavior, you will end up either with some nonscientific explanation, such as God, or the theory of evolution. Evolutionary theory implies that the best answer to the final why question is, "because the form of conduct under consideration helped early humans adapt to their environments, solve the problems they faced, and propagate their genes."

An Evolutionary Reconceptualization of Traditional Social Psychological Accounts of Prosocial Behavior

Interpreting prosocial behaviors in terms of evolutionary theory does not entail rejecting traditional social psychological theory and research. The empirical findings and proximate explanations that social psychologists have offered are of great value. Viewing prosocial behavior from an evolutionary perspective implies reframing traditional theory and research in ways that embed them in evolutionary theory (see Krebs 2011, for an extended discussion of this issue). Consider the five areas of research discussed above, for example.

Reframing Social Learning Accounts of Prosocial Behavior

The social learning theorist, Bandura (1989) was attentive to the adaptive value of social learning: "Because people can learn approximately what to do through modeling before they perform any behavior, they are spared the costs and pain of faulty effort. The capacity to learn by observation enables people to expand their knowledge and skills on the basis of information exhibited and authored by others" (p. 47). As explained by Simon (1990), social learning is highly adaptive because it is impossible for people to learn on their own all the beneficial knowledge accumulated by members of their cultures and passed down through the generations. The main difference between traditional social learning accounts of prosocial behavior and evolutionary accounts is that evolutionary theorists embed proximate costs and benefits in considerations of ultimate fitness. Richerson and Boyd (2005) have advanced an account of the role that social learning plays in gene-culture coevolution that discusses the adaptive value of social learning and presents a mathematical model outlining the conditions under which social learning pays off better biologically than individual learning does.

Evolutionary theory generates the expectation that social learning should be selective—individuals should have evolved to learn from and copy types of people and types of behavior that fostered the fitness of early humans. As expressed by Flinn and Alexander (1982), the mental mechanisms that regulate people's responses to inputs from others should be designed in terms of such decision rules as "accept advice and instruction from those with an interest in one's success" and "view skeptically advice and instruction from those with conflicting interests with regard to the topic being instructed." Viewed from an evolutionary perspective, the reason that people are disposed to model the prosocial behaviors of people whom they like and respect, who are similar to them, whom they view as nurturing, who have control over their fates, and who have high status (Burton and Kunce 1995) is because copying the forms of conduct displayed by these people paid off biologically in early environments. In a similar vein, the reason that people are disposed to conform to prosocial norms is because it is usually adaptive to go along with the crowd.

Research revealing differences between people's reactions to prosocial forms of conduct that are preached and practiced by others also makes sense from the perspective of evolutionary theory. We would expect members of groups to preach prosocial values in order to manipulate others into behaving in ways that foster their interests, but we would not expect people to be inclined to conform to these injunctions when they ran contrary to their interests. We also would expect people to be more influenced by what others do than by what others say. Words are cheap and easily employed to produce false representations.

A great deal of social learning occurs in families. Evolutionary theory encourages us to view family relations as microcosms of social relations in larger groups. Members of families experience confluences and conflicts of interest. It is in members' interest to cooperate with other members in order to advance their common good, but it also is their interest to favor themselves and those who are best qualified to help them propagate replicas of their genes. Conflicts of interest precipitate strategic social interactions in which family members attempt to induce one another to behave in ways that maximize their biological and genetic benefits, though they usually are not conscious of their motives. The ways in which members of families resolve their conflicts of interest affect the ways in which their prosocial dispositions are structured and calibrated. In attending to strategic social interactions within families, evolutionary theory sensitizes us to the fact that social learning is often a two-way process—an insight embraced by contemporary social learning theorists (Grusec 2006). Children are both agents and objects, sending as well as receiving persuasive communications.

Reframing Normative Accounts of Prosocial Behavior

Evolutionary theorists view prosocial norms, such as the norm of reciprocity, as instantiations of genetically coded social strategies that members of groups preach to others and invoke to foster their fitness. Effective strategies generate replicas of themselves in both verbal and behavioral forms, increasing in frequency until they constitute social norms. A notable implication of this process is that as populations become flooded with effective strategies, these strategies interact increasingly frequently with one another. It follows that an important characteristic of evolved social strategies is that they pay off well when interacting with replicas of themselves.

Research using the Prisoner's Dilemma game has modeled the evolution of the norm of reciprocity (Axelrod and Hamilton 1981). Evolutionary game theory research has found that reciprocity-based strategies such as *tit for tat* are equipped to defeat more selfish and more altruistic strategies in iterated evolutionary games, thereby evolving into social norms. Tit for tat is effective because it induces individuals to initiate mutually beneficial cooperative exchanges while protecting them from exploitation. Tit-for-tat strategies pay off well when interacting with one another. Game theory research also has found that although unconditional altruism is a losing strategy, variations of *tit-for-tat* strategies that render them more generous, more forgiving, and more contrite may end up paying off better than rigid *tit-for-tat* strategies, because one selfish mistake in cooperative *tit-for-tat* exchanges locks players into an endless iteration of vindictiveness (Ridley 1996).

People are disposed to conform to prosocial norms such as the norm of reciprocity because conforming to them produced greater biological benefits than failing to conform to them in the environments in which they evolved. People are most likely to conform to such norms in conditions that maximize their fitness—conditions such as those that affect the cost to the benefactor, the benefit to the recipient, the ability of recipients to repay, the likelihood of meeting a recipient in the future, the likelihood of making a good impression on observers, and so on.

Reframing Situational Accounts of Prosocial Behavior

The situational variables studied by traditional social psychologists are viewed by evolutionary psychologists as "if" conditions that trigger the evolved mental mechanisms that induce people to behave in prosocial ways. For example, findings indicating that the probability of bystanders intervening in emergencies is affected by variables that signal the costs and benefits of intervening are interpreted by evolutionary theorists as identifying the conditions under which helping others in emergencies paid off biologically in the environments in which the mental mechanisms that mediate this form of conduct evolved. Sensitivity to such conditions is built into the mechanisms. Note that prosocial behaviors that were adaptive in archaic social environments (because, for example, they helped early humans save the lives of members of their groups on whom they were dependent for survival) may be maladaptive in modern environments.

Reframing Cognitive Construal Accounts of Prosocial Behavior

Evolutionary theory directs us to view the cognitive construal processes that traditional social psychologists have found to mediate prosocial behavior as features of mental mechanisms that evolved to increase individuals' fitness. Evolutionary theorists expect people to process information in ways that enable them to solve adaptive problems. Viewed in this way, the reason that people attend to others in emergencies, react differently to victims they view as similar to them from those they view as dissimilar to them, and perform cost–benefit analyses of the options available to them (Piliavin et al. 1981) is because early humans who inherited mental mechanisms that gave rise to these cognitive and affective reactions fared better biologically than early humans who did not.

Reframing Emotional Accounts of Prosocial Behavior

Evolutionary theorists assume that emotions evolved because they induced individuals to behave in fitness-increasing ways. Prosocial emotions tend to help people foster their fitness by inducing them to resist the temptation to promote their short-term personal interests at the expense of their long-term biological welfare (Frank 2001). Consider the suite of emotions that uphold the norm of reciprocity, for example.

Emotions such as sympathy, empathy, and feelings of solidarity dispose people to initiate prosocial exchanges by helping those with whom they associate. Emotions such as appreciation, gratitude, and a sense of indebtedness induce recipients to return the favors. Emotions such as guilt induce individuals to correct their mistakes and make amends when they fail to pay others back. Emotions such as forgiveness enable individuals to reestablish mutually beneficial social exchanges.

McCullough (2008) reviews evidence showing that forgiveness mediates reconciliation in chimpanzees and other primates, and that it constitutes a cultural universal in the human species. He suggests that there is no reason to expect humans to derive decisions about forgiving others in more rational ways than other primates do. As we would expect from an evolutionary standpoint, social psychologists have found that judgments about whether victimizers intended to inflict harm, whether victimizers could have avoided inflicting harm, whether they regret inflicting harm, and whether they are likely to repeat the offence affect people's tendency to forgive (McCullough 2008).

With respect to empathy, de Waal (2008) has suggested that "emotional connectedness in humans is so common, starts so early in life... and shows neural and physiological correlates... as well as a genetic substrate...that it would be strange indeed if no continuity with other species existed. Evolutionary continuity between humans and apes is reflected in the similarity of emotional communication...as well as similar changes in brain and peripheral skin temperatures in response to emotionally charged images" (p. 5). De Waal reviews evidence indicating that personal distress stems from a primitive core of empathy, whereas sympathetic and empathic concern stem from later-evolved layers of the brain. De Waal (2008) concludes that, "the empathy mechanism is biased the way evolutionary theory would predict. Empathy is (a) activated in relation to those with whom one has a close or positive relationship, and (b) suppressed, or even turned into Schadenfreude, in relation to strangers and defectors" (p. 16).

Social Investment Theory

Brown and Brown (2006) have advanced an integrative evolutionary theory—social investment theory—that accounts for a great deal of social psychological research on prosocial behavior under one overriding principle, namely that individuals are naturally disposed to help those with whom they share fitness interdependence. They adduce evidence that mental mechanisms have evolved in many species that give rise to emotionally mediated social bonds between mates, offspring, friends, and members of groups, and that these bonds dispose them to treat one another in prosocial ways. With respect to the cognitive construal processes in the mental mechanisms that dispose people to behave in prosocial ways, Brown and Brown suggest that the emotions engendered by social bonds induce people to overestimate the benefits of helping those on whom their fitness is dependent, and to underestimate the costs. With respect to altruism, Brown and Brown (2006) argue that social scientists have erred in viewing costly long-term social investments as selfish, and accounting for them in terms of the proximate benefits they purvey.

Brown and Brown assert that people who help those with whom they have bonded are driven by genuinely altruistic motives.

Psychological and Biological Altruism

Although such social scientists as Batson (1991), Brown and Brown (2006), Piliavin and Charng (1990), and McCullough (2008) have concluded that humans are capable of behaving in genuinely altruistic ways, it is important to recognize that these social scientists define altruism in a quite different way from how biologists define altruism. Whereas psychological altruism is defined by the goals, intentions, and motivational states of actors—the proximate effects actors are trying to achieve—biological altruism is defined by the ultimate biological consequences of behavioral decisions. Psychologically altruistic behaviors are biologically selfish when they increase actors' fitness. Seeking to improve the welfare of others, as an end in itself, often reaps biological rewards for helpers. For example, it may increase the probability that helpers will receive help from others, and it may increase helpers' attractiveness as mates. Good intentions may produce beneficial consequences, even though those with good intentions were not trying to obtain the beneficial consequences.

Even if most of the prosocial behaviors investigated by social psychologists—including those that are psychologically altruistic in nature—are biologically selfish (that is to say, they improve the biological welfare of the individuals emitting them), this does not mean that all forms of prosocial conduct are biologically selfish, or that biologically altruistic dispositions could not have evolved. Evolutionary theorists have mapped four routes to biological altruism—(a) misfiring of evolved mechanisms, (b) sexual selection, (c) kin selection, and (d) group selection (Krebs 2011). Let us consider each in turn.

The Evolution of Biological Altruism

The Evolution of Altruism Through the Misfiring of Evolved Mechanisms

Two features of evolved mental mechanisms open the door for biologically altruistic behaviors. First, all evolved mechanisms contain imperfections. The refinement of mental mechanisms as they evolve is an ongoing process that is dependent on the random occurrence of favorable mutations, as well as other factors. Although it is reasonable to assume that the evolved mechanisms that we inherit were the best of those that were available during the process of natural selection, they may induce individuals to emit biologically maladaptive forms of altruistic behavior under certain conditions. For example, Simon (1990) has argued that simple social learning heuristics such as "believe what others say," and "go along with the crowd" were so adaptive to early humans that these heuristics evolved even though they sometimes induced early humans to behave in biologically altruistic ways.

Second, the mechanisms inherited by contemporary humans were selected and evolved in environments ("if" conditions) that differed in important ways from most contemporary environments and may, as a result, "misfire" in modern environments. For instance, social learning heuristics such as "obey the injunctions of powerful leaders" that may have been adaptive in the relatively small hunter-gatherer bands in which humans evolved may be maladaptive in modern environments.

An important implication of this point is that we would expect members of groups to be disposed to prey on the imperfections in others' evolved mental mechanisms in order to advance their own interests. Like cuckoo birds that trick neighboring birds into sitting on their eggs, humans may manipulate others into behaving in biologically altruistic ways by inducing them to believe that they are worthy recipients, by preaching altruistic norms, by praising altruistic martyrs, and so on.

The Evolution of Altruism Through Sexual Selection

The second way in which dispositions to behave in biologically altruistic ways could have evolved is through sexual selection. The basic idea here is that altruistic traits that are a burden to survival can evolve if they increase an animal's reproductive success. Altruistic traits may be attractive to potential mates for two reasons—(a) as signals that the mate will make sacrifices for them, their offspring and other kin, and (b) as signals that the mate possesses "good genes." Costly signaling theorists such as Zahavi (1995) have suggested that animals put on costly displays of altruism for much the same reason that peacocks grow costly plumages. In effect, such animals are saying, "I will make a good mate because I am powerful enough to survive even though I am able to handicap myself by behaving altruistically."

Note that in species that seek altruistic mates, it is in the biological interest of suitors to put on displays that exaggerate their capacity for altruism (Alcock 1998). However, by the same token, it is in the interest of the choosers to see through such ruses. We would expect these interacting processes to lead to arms races in which actors become increasingly good at creating false impressions and observers become increasingly good at detecting them.

We would expect sexual selection to have exerted a significant effect on the evolution of altruism in the human species. Humans produce a relatively small number of offspring that require a great deal of care over a long period of time. Therefore, it is in the biological interest of members of both sexes to select partners with good genes who are willing and able to make the sacrifices necessary to ensure that their offspring survive and thrive (Miller 2007). Note that even though prosocial dispositions that evolved through sexual selection may qualify as altruistic in terms of the biological welfare of the individuals emitting the behaviors, they are selfish when defined in terms of reproductive success and genetic propagation.

The Evolution of Altruism Through Kin Selection

In the same way that individuals who survive but fail to reproduce will not propagate their genes (at least via sexual reproduction), individuals who reproduce but do not have fecund offspring will fail to propagate their genes. Evolutionary theory draws our attention to a significant fact masked in social psychological research employing college students as participants, namely that by far the greatest incidence of prosocial behavior in the world—not only among humans, but in other species as well—occurs when parents invest in their offspring. If parents from species that produce dependent offspring were not evolved to care for, nurture, and make sacrifices for their offspring, they would go extinct.

In 1964, Hamilton published a groundbreaking paper based on the insight that helping one's offspring survive and reproduce is not the only way in which individuals can propagate replicas of their genes; individuals can also accomplish this by helping more distant relatives. Hamilton (1964) argued that what counts in evolution is "inclusive fitness," defined in terms of the total number of genes an individual propagates, both directly (through reproducing) and indirectly (by helping relatives reproduce). Hamilton asserted that altruism should evolve when the fitness costs to animals of behaving altruistically are lower than the fitness benefits they bestow on blood relatives, weighted by their degree of relatedness. Degree of relatedness reflects the probability that the donor and recipient inherited the genes that code for altruism from an immediate common ancestor, such as a parent or grandparent.

What has come to be called kin selection is a complex process that is widely misunderstood. Hamilton's rule does not imply that individuals will distribute their helping to others in accordance with how closely related they are; rather, it implies that individuals will favor themselves and relatives who are most likely to share the genes that code for altruism and to transmit them to future generations. Hamilton's rule implies that individuals will be most likely to help their relatives when the genetic costs of helping them are low and the genetic benefits of helping them are high.

There is a great deal of evidence that humans and other animals are disposed to behave in accordance with Hamilton's rule by, for example, sacrificing their interests for the sake of their kin and favoring those who are most closely related to them and those with the highest reproductive potential (reviewed in Burnstein 2005). Studies (reviewed in Kurland and Gaulin 2005) have found that humans (and many other animals) rely on three cues to identify their kin—how much they look (and smell) like them, how familiar they are, and how close to them they reside. Note that traditional social psychologists have found that these cues increase the probability of prosocial behavior. It is also important to note that because non-kin may display and fake these cues, the mechanisms that mediate kin selection may misfire, and people may end up helping others who look and act like their kin, thus contributing little or nothing to the propagation of their genes and rendering the prosocial behaviors altruistic at a genetic level.

Evolutionary theorists disagree about the extent to which kin selection supplies a plausible account of the tendency for modern humans to help people other than their kin. Theorists such as Johnson et al. (2003) argue that kin recognition mechanisms that reliably signaled kinship in ancestral environments misfire in modern environments, inducing people to help those who are familiar to them, similar to them, members of their in-groups, and so on. In contrast, theorists such as Fehr and Gächter (2003) argue that contemporary humans are quite good at distinguishing between kin and non-kin, and that it is implausible that the mechanisms that dispose people to help non-kin—especially strangers whom they never expect to see again—evolved through kin selection.

The Evolution of Altruism Through Group Selection

The final route to biological altruism mapped out by evolutionary theorists involves group selection. The basic idea underlying the group selection of altruism was advanced by Darwin (1874) in *Descent of Man*: Groups replete with individuals who inherit dispositions to sacrifice their survival and reproductive interests for the sake of their groups will out-compete groups replete with selfish individuals, and through this process the altruistic dispositions possessed by members of altruistic groups who benefit from the altruism of their fellows will be preserved and passed on to future generations. However, Darwin immediately saw a problem with this idea, namely that if the selfish individuals within altruistic groups were more likely to survive and to reproduce than their altruistic compatriots were, then the proportion of selfish members of groups would increase until they eventually replaced all the altruists.

Although virtually all evolutionary theorists agree that group selection could occur under ideal conditions, skeptical evolutionary theorists have raised two main arguments against invoking it as an explanation for the evolution of altruism. First, they have argued that when you boil group selection down to its mathematical essence, it reduces to kin selection (Grafen 1984). The idea underlying this argument is that the action in group selection stems from the genetic benefits that individuals who possess genes that code for altruism bestow on recipients who possess copies of these genes. West et al. (2006) offer an insightful analysis of the similarities and differences between kin selection and group selection models of social evolution, and come down solidly in favor of kin selection models.

Second, skeptical evolutionary theorists have argued that the conditions necessary for group selection to occur are very demanding and unlikely to be met in nature. To outpace within-group selection for selfishness, the probability of stably selfish individuals infiltrating altruistic groups would have to be low. The between-group variance in altruism would have to be relatively large, compared to the within-group variance, because the rate of natural selection is dependent on the amount of variation in populations. Altruistic groups would have to produce groups like themselves at a relatively rapid rate, and the benefits of selfishness within altruistic groups would have to be prevented from escalating in an exponential manner. One way in which this could occur is for groups to break up and re-form at some optimal point in time.

Although many, if not most, evolutionary theorists consider it unlikely that these conditions were met in groups of early humans, especially in view of the consistent trend among other primates to change groups in a "fission and fusion" manner (de Waal 2006), some theorists have argued that, with the aid of cultural evolution, group selection has exerted a significant effect on the evolution of altruism in the human species (Boehm 2010; Richerson and Boyd 2005; Sober and Wilson 1998; Wilson and Wilson 2007).

Conclusion

In conclusion, evolutionary theory offers a framework for interpreting the findings from traditional social psychological accounts of prosocial behavior by embedding the proximate explanations offered by social psychologists in ultimate principles of evolution. Attending to the fact that humans have evolved in ways that enable them to solve adaptive problems and foster their inclusive fitness supplies a basis for hypotheses about when people will, and will not, behave in prosocial ways and directs social psychologists to attend to the biological costs and benefits of helping others. Evolutionary theory also offers a basis for distinguishing among different forms of prosocial conduct by attending to the types of adaptive functions they serve, and it offers a basis for explaining how different forms of altruism could have evolved. Humans are social for a reason. Contemporary humans develop mental mechanisms that dispose them to help others in certain "if" conditions because behaving in prosocial ways in these conditions helped their ancestors survive, reproduce, and propagate their genes.

References

Alcock, J. (1998). *Animal behavior: An evolutionary approach* (6th ed.). Sunderland: Sinauer Associates.

Axelrod, R., & Hamilton, W. D. (1981). The evolution of cooperation. *Science, 211,* 1390–1396.

Bandura, A. (1989). Social cognitive theory. *Annals of Child Development, 6,* 1–60.

Batson, C. D. (1991). *The altruism question: Toward a social-psychological answer*. Hillsdale: Erlbaum.

Batson, C. D. (1998). Altruism and prosocial behavior. In D. T. Gilbert, S. T. Fiske, & G. Lindzey (Eds). *The handbook of social psychology* (4th ed., pp. 282–315). Boston: McGraw-Hill.

Batson, C. D. (2000). Unto others: A service...and a disservice. *Journal of Consciousness Studies, 7,* 207–210.

Boehm, C. (2010). *Moral origins*. New York: Basic Books.

Brown, S. L., & Brown, M. (2006). Selective investment theory: Recasting the functional significance of close relationships. *Psychological Inquiry, 17,* 30–59.

Burnstein, E. (2005). Altruism and genetic relatedness. In D. Buss (Ed.), *The handbook of evolutionary psychology* (pp. 528–551). Hoboken: John Wiley & Sons

Burton, R. V., & Kunce, L. (1995). Behavioral models of moral development: A brief history and integration. In W. M. Kurtines & J. L. Gewirtz (Eds.), *Moral development: An introduction* (pp. 141–172). Boston: Allyn and Bacon.

Buss, D. (2005). *The handbook of evolutionary psychology*. New York: Wiley & Sons.

Buss, D. (2008) *Evolutionary psychology: The new science of the mind* (3rd ed.). Boston: Pearson Education.

Cialdini, R. B., Schaller, M., Houlihan, D., Arps, J., Fultz, J., & Beaman, A. L. (1987). Empathy-based helping: Is it selflessly or selfishly motivated? *Journal of Personality and Social Psychology, 52,* 749–758.

Darley, J. M., & Latane, B. (1968). Bystander intervention in emergencies: Diffusion of responsibility. *Journal of Personality and Social Psychology, 8,* 377–383.

Darwin, C. (1874). *The descent of man and selection in relation to sex*. New York: Rand, McNally & Company.

de Waal, F. B. M. (2006). *Primates and philosophers: How morality evolved.* Princeton: Princeton University Press.

de Waal, F. B. M. (2008). Putting the altruism back in altruism. *Annual Review of Psychology, 59,* 279–300.

Essock-Vitale, S., & McGuire, M. (1985). Women's lives viewed from an evolutionary perspective II: Patterns of helping. *Ethology and Sociobiology, 6,* 155–173.

Fehr, E., & Gächter, S. (2003). Reply. *Nature, 421,* 912.

Flinn, M. V., & Alexander, R. D. (1982). Culture theory: The developing synthesis from biology. *Human Ecology, 10,* 383–400.

Frank, R. H. (2001). Cooperation through emotional commitment. In R. Nesse (Ed.), *Evolution and the capacity for commitment* (pp. 57–76). New York: Russell Sage Foundation.

Gouldner, A. W. (1960). The norm of reciprocity: A preliminary statement. *American Sociological Review, 25,* 161–78.

Grafen, A. (1984). Natural selection, kin selection and group selection. In J. R. Krebs & N. B. Davies (Eds.), *Behavioural ecology: An evolutionary approach* (pp. 62–84). Oxford: Blackwell Scientific Publications.

Grusec, J. (2006). The development of moral behavior and conscience from a socialization perspective. In M. Killen & J. Smetana (Eds.), *Handbook of moral development* (pp. 243–266). Mahwah: Lawrence Erlbaum Associates.

Hamilton, W. D. (1964). The evolution of social behavior. *Journal of Theoretical Biology, 7,* 1–52.

Johnson, D. D. P., Stopka, P., & Knights, S. (2003). The puzzle of human cooperation. *Nature, 421,* 911–912.

Krebs, D. L. (2011). *The origins of morality.* New York: Oxford University Press.

Kurland, J. A., & Gaulin, S. J. C. (2005). Cooperation and conflict among kin. In D. Buss (Ed.), *The handbook of evolutionary psychology* (pp. 447–482). New York: John Wiley & Sons.

Latané, B., & Nida, S. (1981). Ten years of research on group size and helping. *Psychological Bulletin, 89,* 308–324.

Liebert, R. M., & Sprafkin, J. (1988). *The early window.* New York: Random House.

Ma, V. (1985). Cross-cultural study of altruism. *Psychological Reports, 57,* 337–338.

McCullough, M. E. (2008). *Beyond revenge: The evolution of the forgiveness instinct.* San Francisco: Jossey-Bass.

McCullough, M. E., Kilpatrick, S. D., Emmons, R. A., & Larson, D. B. (2001). Is gratitude a moral affect? *Psychological Bulletin, 127,* 249–266.

Miller, G. F. (2007). The sexual selection of moral virtues. *Quarterly Review of Biology, 82,* 97–125.

Piliavin, J. A., Dovidio, J. F., Gaertner, S. L., & Clark, R. D. (1981). *Emergency intervention.* New York: Academic Press.

Piliavin, J., & Charng, H. (1990). Altruism—A review of recent theory and research. *Annual Review of Sociology, 16,* 27–65.

Regan, J. (1971). Guilt, perceived injustice and altruistic behavior. *Journal of Personality and Social Psychology, 18,* 124–132.

Richerson, P. J. & Boyd, R. (2005). *Not by genes alone: How culture transformed human evolution.* Chicago: University of Chicago Press.

Ridley, M. (1996). *The origins or virtue: Human instincts and the evolution of cooperation.* New York: Viking

Rushton, J. P. (1975). Generosity in children: immediate and long-term effects of modeling, preaching, and moral judgment. *Journal of Personality and Social Psychology, 31,* 459–466.

Rushton, J. P., & Campbell, A. C. (1977). Modeling, vicarious reinforcement and extraversion on blood donating in adults: Immediate and long term effects. *European Journal of Social Psychology, 7,* 297–306.

Schaller, M., & Cialdini, R. B. (1988). The economics of empathic helping: Support for a mood management motive. *Journal of Experimental Social Psychology, 24,* 163–181.

Schwartz, S. H. (1977). Normative influences on altruism. In L. Berkowitz (Ed.), *Advances in experimental social psychology* (Vol. 10, pp. 221–279). New York: Academic Press.

Simon, H. (1990). A mechanism for social selection of successful altruism. *Science, 250,* 1665–1668.

Sober, E., & Wilson, D. S. (1998). *Unto others: The evolution and psychology of unselfish behavior.* Cambridge: Harvard University Press.

West, S. A., Griffin, A. S., & Gardner, A. (2007). Social semantics: altruism, cooperation, mutualism, strong reciprocity and group selection. *Journal of Evolutionary Biology, 20,* 415–432.

Wilson D. S., & Wilson E. O. (2007). Rethinking the theoretical foundation of sociobiology, *Quarterly Review of Biology, 82,* 327–348.

Zahavi, A. (1995). Altruism as a handicap—the limitations of kin selection and reciprocity. *Journal of Avian Biology, 26,* 1–3.

Zimbardo, P. (2005). A situationalist perspective on the psychology of good and evil: Understanding how good people are transformed into perpetrators. In A. G. Miller (Ed.), *The social psychology of good and evil* (pp. 21–50). New York: Guilford Press.

19 Groups

Tatsuya Kameda, Mark Vugt and R. Scott Tindale

Imagine that you live in an unaltered natural environment. Your survival hinges on securing food and fuel resources, finding shelter, understanding your local geography, acquiring knowledge about animals and plants, guarding against predators and enemies, possibly making allies with out-groups, and so on. It is unlikely that any single individual can perform these tasks adequately. There is no doubt that groups have been one of the most frequently used adaptive devices to manage these challenges throughout hominid evolution, as well as in modern human history. Given this fact, social psychologists would be well served by revisiting various group behaviors and group phenomena from an evolutionary, adaptationist perspective, which in turn may provide for a common conceptual ground with biologists and neuroscientists interested in human social behaviors.

A growing body of research in this area has applied evolutionary principles in understanding group behaviors (Kameda and Tindale 2006; Van Vugt and Kameda 2013, 2014). One impetus behind this shift is the "social brain hypothesis." Comparative studies of primates and other mammals have found a positive relationship between the size of the prefrontal cortex and the average group size of a species. Humans are ranked at the top of this scale, with a large prefrontal cortex and associated large group size, extrapolated to be around 150 individuals based on the observed trend. Given the high metabolic costs of maintaining a large brain (for human adults, the brain makes up only 2 % of body mass, but consumes more than 20 % of daily energy intake), the social brain hypothesis posits that humans have evolved large brains in order to manage complicated social interactions—competitive as well as cooperative, in large groups including non-kin members (Dunbar 1993). In other words, many of our core cognitive and emotional faculties are likely to have been tuned to solve recurrent adaptive problems that ancestral humans encountered in group life. Thus, the primary aim of an evolutionary approach to group behaviors is to identify and analyze specific adaptive group interactions, and the psychological architectures that have evolved to solve these problems.

T. Kameda (✉)
Department of Social Psychology, The University of Tokyo, Bungakubu, 7-3-1, Hongo, Bunkyo-ku , Tokyo 113-0033, Japan
e-mail: tatsuyakameda@gmail.com

M. VanVugt
Department of Psychology, VU University Amsterdam, De Boelelaan 1105, Amsterdam 1081 HV, The Netherlands
e-mail: m.van.vugt@vu.nl

R. S. Tindale
Department of Psychology, Loyola University Chicago, 1032 W Sheridan Rd, Chicago, IL 60660, USA
e-mail: rtindal@luc.edu

V. Zeigler-Hill et al. (eds.), *Evolutionary Perspectives on Social Psychology,* Evolutionary Psychology,
DOI 10.1007/978-3-319-12697-5_19, © Springer International Publishing Switzerland 2015

Key Adaptive Problems in Group Life

Van Vugt and Kameda (2013, 2014) have proposed six key adaptive problems that ancestral humans were likely to have encountered recurrently in group life: (1) coordinating members' activities (group coordination), (2) exchanging resources (social exchange), (3) negotiating group hierarchies (status), (4) keeping groups together (group cohesion), (5) making collective decisions (group decision making), and (6) interacting with members of out-groups (intergroup relations).

Of course, this list is neither exhaustive nor mutually exclusive, but it serves as a reasonable starting point for building an evolutionary framework for analyzing group processes. The list also corresponds closely to the core themes of group dynamics identified in textbooks such as Forsyth's (2010) *Group Dynamics*. Although none of these adaptive group challenges has been fully analyzed using an evolutionary framework, various research programs have contributed to developing such analyses by providing evidence for evolved psychological mechanisms that address a particular group challenge. The promise of an evolutionary group dynamics lies in the generativity and productivity of this approach in formulating novel hypotheses and providing empirical evidence. This chapter provides an illustrative set of findings from evolution-inspired research programs for each of these core adaptive challenges.

Group Coordination

Coordinating members' cognitive and physical resources is a key to effective group performance (Steiner 1972). As a nomadic, group-living species, early humans would have had to solve problems associated with coordinating activities between individuals in groups. For instance, when migrating, they would have had to decide where to move to, and when, and how long to stay there. To solve such problems would have required mechanisms for identifying situations requiring coordination, developing rules for how to achieve coordination (e.g., turn-taking, leadership), and then carrying them out.

Leadership

There are multiple indications that leadership might be an adaptive solution to coordinate members' actions (Van Vugt 2006). Whenever organisms must collaborate to achieve their adaptive goals, they face a critical coordination problem: how do they decide what to do and when? A simple thought experiment illustrates that leadership—where one individual takes the initiative and others follow—is a powerful solution to such coordination problems. Suppose that two individuals who are thirsty must find a water hole to drink from. They must stay together as a form of protection, but how do they decide which water hole to go to? In such cases, it is most efficient for one individual to take the initiative to go to a particular hole, which leaves the other no option but to follow. Coordinating on the same water hole is the equilibrium solution to this game. An implication would be that leadership–followership interaction emerges spontaneously without much cognitive computation. Indeed, the emergence of leadership of this sort has been documented across many different animal species that face functionally important coordination problems, including house hunting by social insects (e.g., ants, honeybees), movement in stickleback guppies, and peacekeeping in nonhuman primates (King et al. 2009; Sumpter 2010).

Among humans, similar kinds of coordination problems also result, predictably, in the emergence of leader–follower relations. This occurs quickly and spontaneously, and does so across many different situations and cultures, suggesting evidence for adaptation (Brown 1991). Of course, the exact system of leadership varies across different situations. There is evidence for both highly democratic leadership structures and highly despotic leadership structures in humans, which may represent different adaptive solutions to various local group conditions. For instance, dictatorial leadership might have emerged in response to immediate crises where quick and decisive actions were required (Van Vugt 2009).

Transactive Memory

Another coordination device that may have evolved to support group coordination is the transactive memory system. Wegner (1987) argued that groups can store and process more information than individuals because they can share the responsibility of knowledge storage. However, in order to retrieve the information efficiently, a shared knowledge system must exist that identifies who in the group knows what—a transactive memory system. Once such a system exists, each individual member only needs to store information for which they are responsible, easing the memory load on each member, but increasing the total amount of information available to the group. Division of cognitive labor is common in social insects; one famous example is the honeybee waggle dance displayed by scout bees, a group decision-making device for house hunting (Seeley 2010). Research on humans also suggests that members working in the same group often specialize in different areas, and group members are very quick at recognizing and using each other's expertise (Littlepage et al. 2008). Experts not only have more information on their respective topics, but they are also the ones who are responsible for storing new information in their areas of expertise. A set of experiments by Moreland et al. (1996) showed that teams performed better on a group task to the extent that the team members divided their cognitive tasks better. Furthermore, members of teams with better transactive memory systems also trusted each other's expertise more. There is also evidence that such systems begin to form quite quickly through normal group interaction (Moreland et al. 1996).

Structural and Social Focal Points

The game-theoretic concept of focal points discussed by Schelling (1960) plays an important role in group coordination. Early work had shown that certain game solutions (e.g., equal outcomes—see "Social Exchange" section below) tend to receive greater support than would be expected by rational game-playing assumptions (Komorita and Chertkoff 1973). Schelling argued that such outcome distributions "stood out" and were salient because of their normative or focal nature. It appears that humans may have learned to use some specific structural characteristics of their environments to help coordinate action (e.g., meeting in the center of the village or at the water's edge). More recent research has shown that "social focal points" are also useful in coordinated action (Abele and Stasser 2008). Thus, normative preferences among the group members or exhibited by high-status members (leaders) can be used to guide action in ambiguous situations. Abele and Stasser (2008) showed that people were quite good at coordinating actions around social focal points and successful coordination led to greater liking among group members. More recent research (Abele and Chartier 2012) has also shown that groups are substantially better than individuals at locating and using social focal points. The superiority of groups in this regard seems to stem from both majority processes as well as the group's ability to recognize appropriate focal points even when proposed by a single group member (see related discussions under "Group Decision Making").

Following Group Norms

Group norms can also be helpful for coordinating behavior. Recent research has supported the idea of evolved hormonal mechanisms to insure greater conformity to in-group norms (Stallen et al. 2012). Participants in their study were administered either oxytocin or a placebo and were asked to rate stimuli in terms of attractiveness. They were also shown ratings of each symbol by both in-group and out-group members. When ratings differed for the in-group and out-group, participants' ratings were more similar to the in-group ratings but only when administered oxytocin. Thus, a hormone that has been linked to in-group trust and cooperation (Kemp and Guestella 2011) also seems to help coordination by enhancing norm-abiding behavior.

Social Exchange

Social exchange—cooperation for mutual benefit—is a pervasive and culturally universal feature of human group life. Exchanging vital resources with others is fundamental for any gregarious species, yet humans are unique in being able to establish large-scale cooperation with genetically unrelated individuals. Social norms related to cooperation are robust across various cultures, ranging from hunter–gatherer, horticultural, tribal, and agricultural, to highly industrialized societies (Henrich et al. 2004). Such norms specify how individuals should behave in group situations where incentives for free riding exist, including when to cooperate, how to distribute group outcomes, and how to punish uncooperative group members.

Cooperation Norms

Human collective action is often governed by a norm of "conditional cooperation" (Fehr and Fischbacher 2004). This norm dictates that an individual should cooperate if other group members cooperate, but is not required to cooperate if others defect. Fischbacher et al. (2001) examined participants' willingness to contribute in a one-shot public-goods experiment as a function of the average contribution of the other group members. Despite the economic incentives to free ride (i.e., contribute nothing), 50 % of the participants matched their contributions with the average contribution of other members. Furthermore, when participants simply observed the interaction of two players in a Prisoner's Dilemma game, they spent their own endowments to punish players who defected unilaterally, but *not* players who defected bilaterally (Fehr and Fischbacher 2004). This pattern indicates that the norm of conditional cooperation ("unilateral defection is not acceptable") is enforced by neutral observers. Such selective sanctioning includes not only physical punishment but also social exclusion, collectively denying the violator's access to interpersonal relations in a group (Sasaki and Uchida 2013).

The evolutionary perspective suggests a novel hypothesis about the psychological mechanisms underlying enforcement of cooperation norms. Given that exchanges of valuable resources occur mainly within groups, violations of cooperation norms committed by another in-group member should be considered more serious than those committed by an out-group member. If this is the case, then noncooperative behavior by in-group members should be punished more severely than noncooperative behavior by out-group members. Using the third-party punishment paradigm, Shinada et al. (2004) confirmed this prediction.

Distribution Norms

Distribution norms refer to a set of shared beliefs that prescribes how resources should be distributed among group members. Evidence suggests that motives for egalitarian sharing often operate strongly in resource distribution (Fehr and Schmidt 1999; Kameda et al. 2010). For example, results from numerous one-shot Ultimatum Game experiments indicate that modal offers by a proposer for a responder's share are around 40–50 % and that offers in this range are rarely rejected (Camerer 2003). Although there are some cultural differences (Henrich et al. 2004), extremely small offers (1–10 %) are rarely seen in ultimatum bargaining experiments conducted in a wide range of contexts, including primordial as well as industrialized societies. Violators of the egalitarian distribution norm are also punished. Henrich et al. (2006) conducted a third-party punishment experiment, where participants could spend their own endowments to punish an unfair proposer in the Ultimatum Game. The experimental results from 15 diverse populations showed that costly punishment as a third party was common, although the magnitude of punishment varied substantially across cultures.

Ethnographic studies show that egalitarian sharing of hunted meat constitutes a core feature of hunter–gatherer life. Compared to collected resources (e.g., cassava), hunted meat is often subject to communal sharing. Kaplan and Hill (1985) argued that the sharing system, once established, functions as a collective risk-reduction device. While acquisition of collected resources is relatively stable and dependable, acquisition of meat is a highly variable, uncertain event. By including many individuals in the sharing group, the variance in meat supply decreases exponentially (Gurven 2004). This may imply that our minds are built to be highly sensitive to cues of uncertainty in resource acquisition. Kameda et al. (2002) showed that such uncertainty cues promoted people's willingness to share with others beyond their personal distributive ideologies. Using an evolutionary game model, Kameda et al. (2003b, 2005) analyzed how such psychological mechanisms contribute to solving the free-rider problem inherent in egalitarian sharing (see also Kameda et al. 2013 for the neural basis of the egalitarian-sharing norm).

Status

Competition for status, especially among males, is a robust phenomenon across cultures (e.g., Geary et al. 2004). Even in modern ad hoc groups such as juries, status competition is often observed, where some jurors "show off" their toughness for the purpose of establishing their prestige in the group, while sacrificing factual discussions about the case (Hastie et al. 1983). Evolutionarily, with increases in the size and complexity of social groups, competition for scarce resources including food, water, and mates would have intensified, paving the way for the emergence of status hierarchies (Boehm 1999; Dunbar 2004). To climb the group hierarchy or maintain one's current status in the group (and thus secure privileged access to scarce resources), one would need to closely monitor one's relative standing in the hierarchy and behave strategically in group interactions.

Signaling and Status Emotions

Along with other group-living animals, humans display various cues to signal their relative status to others. For example, nonverbal cues such as a firm handshake, a poised posture, gaze maintenance, and taking initiatives in conversations are among the characteristics of high-status individuals when they interact with others. Some of these cues are culture specific, but other cues (e.g., poised posture, gaze maintenance) are easily recognizable even by outsiders who do not belong to the culture (Ridgeway et al. 1985), which may suggest that they have evolutionary origins.

Besides sensitivities to subtle status signals displayed during interaction, our own emotional experiences are also closely linked to changes in relative status in a group. For example, when people experience a status gain (e.g., winning an award), they tend to feel pride. Recent research has shown that, like the "basic" emotions, pride is associated with a distinct, universally recognized, nonverbal expression, which is spontaneously displayed during pride experiences (Tracy and Robins 2004). It has also been argued that self-esteem may be an evolved internal gauge ("sociometer") that monitors people's standing in a group and motivates actions when people feel their status is threatened (Leary 1999).

Competitive Altruism

When individuals can select social exchange partners freely in a group, status competition can arise for establishing a reputation as a generous person. This phenomenon is called competitive altruism (Barclay and Willer 2007; Roberts 1998), as people compete to be chosen as exchange or coalition partners through their generosity. The anthropological literature documents many examples of ostentatious public displays of altruism and generosity. Experimental evidence also shows that generous individuals receive more status than nongenerous individuals and are preferred as group leaders (Hardy and Van Vugt 2006).

Competitive altruism requires psychological mechanisms to monitor and enhance one's relative standing in a group in terms of generosity. People are highly sensitive to social cues that suggest their reputation is under scrutiny. For example, experimental evidence shows that people behave more generously when they think they are being watched by others (Bateson et al. 2006; Haley and Fessler 2005). Men also behave more generously to a stranger when they are watched by a potential female partner (Iredale et al. 2008).

Group Cohesion

Group cohesion has been defined as "the resultant of all forces acting on the members to remain in the group" (Festinger 1950, p. 274). In light of the importance of staying together as a unit in a hostile environment, our ancestors had to evolve mechanisms to preserve social cohesion. Furthermore, as human social networks increased in size and complexity over the course of human evolution, we would expect these bonding mechanisms to have become increasingly sophisticated. To maintain group cohesion would require specialized mechanisms to recognize oneself and others as belonging to the same group as well as mechanisms to feel emotionally connected with others in increasingly large groups (Kameda et al. in press).

Social Identity

Thinking of people who are not necessarily around each other all the time as belonging to the same group requires the capacity for symbolic thought, through which language or rituals become markers of shared group membership. A symbolic social identity allowed our ancestors to connect with a larger, spatially distributed network of individuals, and this may have been quite helpful in sharing resources as well as in competing with other groups. Human social identity is highly group based, and people spontaneously make "us versus them" categorizations (Tajfel and Turner 1979). Preserving group cohesion also requires a deeply ingrained sense of group loyalty, whereby individuals are prepared to forego attractive alternatives in favor of staying with their group.

Religion, Music, and Dance

Humans seem to have many specialized behavioral mechanisms for fostering group cohesion, which may have deep evolutionary roots. Religion, for instance, is an effective method to promote cohesion between strangers and mobilize them for joint action on behalf of a group (Atran 2002). Similarly, dance and music have ancient historical origins; according to evolutionary anthropologists, these activities may have evolved as adaptations for connecting large networks of genetic strangers (Dunbar 2004).

Group Decision Making

Along with our highly sophisticated faculty for language, the complexity, variety, and ubiquity of group decision making across many societies may seem to indicate that "real" group decisions are uniquely human. However, recent research on animal behavior suggests that this is not the case. Group decision making seems to be common in the animal kingdom as well, including social insects (e.g., ants, termites, honeybees), fish, and some mammals (Conradt and List 2009; Seeley 2010). Although "animal group decision making" may look more like an automated self-organization than a deliberate coordination, the social aggregation processes (e.g., honeybees' waggle dances to recruit more fellow searchers) are in fact highly coordinated, and often lead to efficient group-level outcomes. Evidently, some well-structured social-coordination mechanisms that yield collective wisdom are an outcome of natural selection (Kameda et al. 2012).

Despotism versus Democracy

What is the primary evolved decisional structure that enables collective wisdom in honeybees and in some other animals? Conradt and Roper (2003) compared two contrasting structures, "despotism" and "democracy," in the animal kingdom. Using a stochastic model, they showed that democratic decisions usually yield better fitness outcomes to group members than despotism—even when the despot is the most experienced group member, it pays other members to accept the despot's decision only when group size is small and the difference between their own and the despot's information is large. These findings may be extendable to human group decision making as well. Most naturally occurring environments for humans as well as other animals are characterized by large statistical uncertainties. Given that no single individual (despot) can handle these uncertainties alone, even if highly experienced, the more viable and reliable decisional structure in the long run is to use groups as an aggregation device. By aggregating members' opinions, random errors in individual perceptions and judgments under uncertainty are cancelled collectively, as implied by the law of large numbers in statistics (Surowiecki 2004).

A recent study compared several decision rules differing in computational load in terms of their net efficiencies under uncertainty (Hastie and Kameda 2005). These included the Best Member ("despotism") rule and the Majority ("democracy") rule. Results from both computer simulations and laboratory experiments showed that the majority rule fared quite well, performing at levels comparable to much more computationally taxing rules. Furthermore, the majority rule outperformed the despotic best-member rule, even when members were not forced to cooperate for the group endeavor and free riding was possible (Kameda et al. 2011).

The Robust Beauty of Majority Rules

These results indicate that, despite its computational simplicity, the majority rule can achieve surprisingly high levels of performance (see also Wolf et al. 2013; Kameda and Nakanishi 2003 for *individual* computational algorithms required for the "wisdom of crowds" phenomenon at the collective level). Such observations may explain the popularity of the majority rule across the full spectrum of human groups, from hunter–gatherer and tribal societies (Boehm 1999) to modern industrial democracies (Kerr and Tindale 2004), as well as the animal cases in which democratic decisions are often more beneficial than despotism (Conradt and Roper 2003). Of course, phylogenetically, humans are quite distant from honeybees and other "lower" species. Yet, the striking similarities in decision styles between the two most social species on the earth suggest that humans and honeybees have evolved structurally similar group aggregation mechanisms (i.e., utilizing the law of large numbers) to solve similar adaptive problems such as foraging. Dealing with uncertainty is the key challenge underlying the evolution and use of these mechanisms (Kameda et al. 2012; Wolf et al. 2013).

Social Sharedness

The majority processes discussed above can be seen as prime examples of "social sharedness" (Kameda et al. 2003a; Tindale and Kameda 2000). Social sharedness is a term for the phenomena associated with shared cognitions and preferences playing an inordinate role in group decision making and problem solving. Majority rules are an instantiation of sharedness at the preference level. However, there is now a large amount of evidence that shared knowledge and motives can play important roles in how groups reach consensus. It is often through shared cognition and information that groups can perform even better than simple majority processes (e.g., a minority faction being able to use such information to "demonstrate" the correctness of their position to a majority that had previously coalesced around a less-than-optimal alternative; see Laughlin 2011; Tindale et al. 2012).

Intergroup Relations

A final problem that both modern humans and our ancestors have faced is how to deal with members of other groups. As population densities increased in human evolution, so did the likelihood of contact and competition for scarce resources with members of rival groups. Interactions with out-groups provided opportunities for beneficial exchange of resources such as food, mates, and information, but could also be a source of tension and conflict over the same resources. As a consequence, humans likely possess highly specialized mechanisms that enable them to reap the benefits of intergroup relations while avoiding the costs.

Fear of Strangers

As part of this evolved intergroup psychology, humans are often relatively suspicious and even fearful of strangers. Fear of strangers is an innate response observed among young children. Fear is strongest toward out-group males, presumably because they constituted a considerable physical threat in ancestral times (McDonald et al. 2012). Beyond the physical threat out-groups posed in ancestral environments, there was also the threat of unfamiliar diseases. A recent study showed that ethnocentrism is strongest among women who are in the early stage of pregnancy, presumably because they (and their fetus) are most at risk of catching a disease (Navarrete et al. 2007).

Intergroup Aggression and Warfare

An adaptive solution to intergroup competition is engaging in organized violence against members of out-groups. Humans and chimpanzees use coalitional aggression to gain access to reproductively relevant resources, such as territories and mates (Brosnan et al. 2009). In both species, such coalitions usually consist of males, arguably because males have more to gain from participating in intergroup conflict—what has been dubbed the "male warrior hypothesis" (Van Vugt 2009). Research on the male warrior hypothesis indicates that men are more "tribal" than women: They are more aggressive in intergroup encounters and have a stronger inclination to dehumanize out-group members. Men are also more likely to make sacrifices on behalf of their group during intergroup conflict (Johnson et al. 2006; Lehmann and Feldman 2008; Van Vugt et al. 2007). Consistent with the male warrior hypothesis, a recent study suggests that physically formidable men have a stronger preference for intergroup aggression and warfare than do less formidable men (Sell et al. 2009).

Recent game theoretic simulations are consistent with the ideas of in-group sacrifice and out-group aggression (Choi and Bowles 2007). Their simulations showed that neither societies made up of mainly pure aggressors nor pure altruists survived well over time. However, societies with mainly "parochial altruists" (members who sacrifice for in-group members, but shun or aggress against out-group members) proved to be evolutionarily stable (Bernhard et al. 2006; for contrasting perspectives, arguing that out-group hostility may not be essential for evolution of in-group cooperation, see Fu et al. 2012; Mifune et al. 2010; Simunovic et al. 2013). More recent work has begun to isolate the physiological and neurological correlates of these phenomena, and has shown that oxytocin helps to regulate cooperation toward in-group members (De Dreu et al. 2010). Thus, behaving in ways that favor in-group welfare appears to be adaptive for both the group and the individuals that depend on it.

The Promise of an Evolutionary Science of Group Dynamics

An evolutionary approach to group behavior can be fruitful in at least four different ways. First, an evolutionary perspective can provide a more complete understanding of particular group processes by asking fundamental questions about the functions, origins, and evolution of these phenomena. A more complete account inevitably follows from rigorous attempts to establish conceptual linkages between evolutionary processes operating on ancestral populations and psychological processes operating within contemporary groups.

Second, an evolutionary perspective can help overcome biases and blind spots in the study of groups. For example, it strikes us as odd that the social psychology literature on group decision making often focuses on what is wrong with groups, disregarding the fact that the group is the natural environment for humans. Examples include research on groupthink, brainstorming, group polarization, and information sharing. A cursory reading of these literatures all too easily suggests that people are poor collective decision makers. Any such conclusion, however, is inaccurate (or, at the very least, overly simplistic), and we believe that an evolutionary perspective can produce more sophisticated and accurate conclusions about group decision making.

Third, an evolutionary approach is useful in yielding novel hypotheses about group behaviors. As seen in this chapter, evolutionary reasoning has led to a number of new hypotheses about traditional group topics such as status, conformity, and social influence, which are unlikely to have been stimulated by other theoretical frameworks (Kenrick et al. 2003).

Finally, an evolutionary approach can expand the boundaries of scientific inquiry on group dynamics by suggesting important group phenomena that have previously received little, if any, attention from group researchers. Laughter, language, gossip, dance, music, sports, culture, and religion are increasingly being understood as group-level adaptations, that is, as manifestations of psychological processes that connect individuals to each other in large and diverse groups, and these insights have benefited from evolutionarily informed inquiry.

In short, an evolutionary perspective reinforces our awareness that group dynamics are fundamental to the study of human nature. Furthermore, it provides a set of conceptual and empirical tools that can be used to understand and describe group processes more completely and accurately.

References

Abele, S., & Chartier, C. (2012). *Groups outperform individuals in tacit coordination by using consensual and disjunctive salience*. Paper presented at the 7th Annual Conference of the International Network of Groups Researchers, Chicago, IL.

Abele, S., & Stasser, G. L. (2008). Coordination success and interpersonal perceptions: Matching versus mismatching. *Journal of Personality and Social Psychology, 95,* 576–592.

Atran, S. (2002). In gods we trust: The evolutionary landscape of religion. Oxford: Oxford University Press.

Barclay, P., & Willer, R. (2007). Partner choice creates competitive altruism in humans. *Proceedings of the Royal Society-B, 274,* 749–753.

Bateson, M., Nettle, D., & Roberts, G. (2006). Cues of being watched enhance cooperation in a real-world setting. *Biology Letters, 2,* 412–414.

Bernhard, H., Fischbacher, U., & Fehr, E. (2006). Parochial altruism in humans. *Nature, 442,* 912–915.

Boehm, C. (1999). *Hierarchy in the forest: The evolution of egalitarian behavior*. Cambridge: Harvard University Press.

Brosnan, S. F., Newton-Fisher, N. E., & Van Vugt, M. (2009). A melding of minds: When primatology meets personality and social psychology. *Personality and Social Psychology Review, 13,* 129–147.

Brown, D. (1991). *Human universals*. Boston: McGraw-Hill.

Camerer, C. (2003). *Behavioral game theory: Experiments in strategic interaction*. Princeton: Princeton University Press.

Choi, J., & Bowles, S. (2007). The coevolution of parochial altruism and war. *Science, 318,* 636–640.

Conradt, L., & List, C. (Eds.). (2009). Theme issue: Group decision making in humans and animals. *Philosophical Transactions of the Royal Society B, 364,* 719–852.

Conradt, L., & Roper, T. J. (2003). Group decision-making in animals. *Nature, 421,* 155–158.

De Dreu, C. K. W., Greer, L. L., Handgraaf, M. J. J., Shalvi, S., Van Kleef, G. A., Baas, M., Ten Velden, F. S., Van Dijk, E., & Feith, S. W. W. (2010). The neuropeptide Oxytocin regulates parochial altruism in intergroup conflict among humans. *Science, 328,* 1408–1411.

Dunbar, R. I. M. (1993). Coevolution of neocortical size, group size, and language in humans. *Behavioral and Brain Sciences, 16,* 681–735.

Dunbar, R. I. M. (2004). *Grooming, gossip, and the evolution of language*. London: Faber & Faber.

Fehr, E., & Fischbacher, U. (2004). Third party sanctions and social norms. *Evolution and Human Behavior, 25,* 63–87.

Fehr, E., & Schmidt, K. M. (1999). A theory of fairness, competition, and cooperation. *Quarterly Journal of Economics, 114,* 817–868.

Festinger, L. (1950). Informal social communication. *Psychological Review, 57,* 271–282.

Fischbacher, U., Gächter, S., & Fehr, E. (2001). Are people conditionally cooperative? Evidence from a public goods experiment. *Economics Letters, 71,* 397–404.

Forsyth, D. (2010). *Group dynamics*. Belmont: Wadsworth.

Fu, F., Tarnita, C. E., Christakis, N. A., Wang, L., Rand, D. G., & Nowak, M. A. (2012). Evolution of in-group favoritism. *Scientific Reports, 2*, 460. doi:10.1038/srep00460

Geary, D. C., Vigil, J., & Byrd-Craven, J. (2004). Evolution of human mate choice. *Journal of Sex Research, 41,* 27–42.

Gurven, M. (2004). To give or not to give: An evolutionary ecology of human food transfers. *Behavioral and Brain Sciences, 27,* 543–559.

Haley, K., & Fessler, D. (2005). Nobody's watching. *Evolution and Human Behavior, 26,* 245–256.

Hardy, C. L., & Van Vugt, M. (2006). Nice guys finish first: The competitive altruism hypothesis. *Personality and Social Psychology Bulletin, 32,* 1402–1413.

Hastie, R., & Kameda, T. (2005). The robust beauty of majority rules in group decisions, *Psychological Review, 112,* 494–508.

Hastie, R., Penrod, S. D., & Pennington, N. (1983). *Inside the jury.* Cambridge: Harvard University Press.

Henrich, J., Boyd, R., Bowles, S., Gintis, H., & Fehr, E. (2004). *Foundations of human sociality: Economic experiments and ethnographic evidence from fifteen small scale societies.* Oxford: Oxford University Press.

Henrich, J., McElreath, R., Barr, A., Ensminger, J., Barrett, C., Bolyanatz, A., Cardenas, J. C., Gurven, M., Gwako, E., Henrich, N., Lesorogol, C., Marlowe, F., Tracer, D., & Ziker, J. (2006). Costly punishment across human societies. *Science, 312,* 1767–1770.

Iredale, W., Van Vugt, M., & Dunbar, R. (2008). Showing off in humans: Male generosity as mate signal. *Evolutionary Psychology, 6,* 386–392.

Johnson, D. D. P., McDermott, R., Barrett, E. S., Cowden, J., Wrangham, R., McIntyre, M. H., & Rosen S. P. (2006). Overconfidence in wargames: Experimental evidence on expectations, aggression, gender and testosterone. *Proceedings of the Royal Society B—Biological Sciences, 273,* 2513–2520.

Kameda, T., & Nakanishi, D. (2003). Does social/cultural learning increase human adaptability? Rogers's question revisited. *Evolution and Human Behavior, 24,* 242–260.

Kameda, T., & Tindale, R. S. (2006). Groups as adaptive devices: Human docility and group aggregation mechanisms in evolutionary context. In M. Schaller, J. A. Simpson, & D. T. Kenrick (Eds.), *Evolution and social psychology* (pp. 317–341). New York: Psychology Press.

Kameda, T., Takezawa, M., Tindale, R. S., & Smith, C. (2002). Social sharing and risk reduction: Exploring a computational algorithm for the psychology of windfall gains. *Evolution and Human Behavior, 23,* 11–33.

Kameda, T., Tindale, R. S., & Davis, J. H. (2003a). Cognitions, preferences, and social sharedness: Past, present and future directions in group decision making. In S. L. Schneider & J. Shanteau (Eds.), *Emerging perspectives on judgment and decision research* (pp. 458–485). New York: Cambridge University Press.

Kameda, T., Takezawa, M., & Hastie, R. (2003b). The logic of social sharing: An evolutionary game analysis of adaptive norm development. *Personality and Social Psychology Review, 7,* 2–19.

Kameda, T., Takezawa, M., & Hastie, R. (2005). Where do norms come from? The example of communal-sharing. *Current Directions in Psychological Science, 14,* 331–334.

Kameda, T., Takezawa, M., Ohtsubo, Y., & Hastie, R. (2010). Are our minds fundamentally egalitarian? Adaptive bases of different sociocultural models about distributive justice. In M. Schaller, A. Norenzyan, S. J. Heine, T. Yamagishi, & T. Kameda (Eds.), *Evolution, culture, and the human mind* (pp. 151–163). New York: Psychology Press.

Kameda, T., Tsukasaki, T., Hastie, R., & Berg, N. (2011). Democracy under uncertainty: The wisdom of crowds and the free-rider problem in group decision making. *Psychological Review, 118,* 76–96.

Kameda, T., Wisdom, T., Toyokawa, W., & Inukai, K. (2012). Is consensus-seeking unique to humans? A selective review of animal group decision-making and its implications for (human) social psychology. *Group Processes and Intergroup Relations, 15,* 673–689.

Kameda, T., Inukai, K., Higuchi, S., Ogawa, A., Kim, H., Matsuda, T., & Sakagami, M. (2013). The maximin rule as a key cognitive anchor in distributive justice and risky decisions: Rawls in our minds. Submitted.

Kameda, T., Inukai, K., Wisdom, T., & Toyokawa, W. (in press). Herd behavior: Its psychological and neural underpinnings, In S. Grundmann, et al. (Eds.), *Contract governance.* Oxford: Oxford University Press.

Kaplan, H., & Hill, K. (1985). Food sharing among Ache foragers: Tests of explanatory hypotheses. *Current Anthropology, 26,* 223–246.

Kemp, A. H., & Guastella, A. J. (2011). The role of oxytocin in human affect: A novel hypothesis. *Current Directions in Psychological Science, 20,* 222–231.

Kenrick, D. T., Li, N. P., & Butner, J. (2003). Dynamical evolutionary psychology: Individual decision-rules and emergent social norms. *Psychological Review, 110,* 3–28.

Kerr, N. L., & Tindale, R. S. (2004). Group performance and decision making. *Annual Review of Psychology, 55,* 623–655.

King, A., Johnson, D. D. P., & Van Vugt, M. (2009). The origins and evolution of leadership. *Current Biology, 19,* 1591–1682.

Komorita, S. S., & Chertkoff, J. M. (1973). A bargaining theory of coalition formation. Psychological Review, 80, 149–162.

Laughlin, P. R. (2011). *Group problem solving.* Princeton: Princeton University Press.

Leary, M. R. (1999). Making sense of self-esteem. *Current Directions in Psychological Science, 8,* 32–35.

Lehmann, L., & Feldman, M. W. (2008). War and the evolution of belligerence and bravery. *Proceedings of the Royal Society B: Biological Sciences, 275,* 2877–2885.

Littlepage, G., Hollingshead, A. B., Drake, L. R., & Littlepage, A. M. (2008). Transactive memory and performance in work groups. *Group Dynamics, 12,* 223–241.

McDonald, M. M., Navarrete, C. D., & Van Vugt, M. (2012). Evolution and the psychology of intergroup conflict: The Male Warrior Hypothesis. *Philosophical Transactions of the Royal Society-Biological Sciences, 367,* 670–679.

Mifune, N., Hashimoto, H., & Yamagishi, T. (2010). Altruism toward in-group members as a reputation mechanism. *Evolution and Human Behavior, 31,* 109–117.

Moreland, R., Argote, L., & Krishnan, R. (1996). Socially shared cognition at work. In J. Nye & A. Brower (Eds.), *What's social about social cognition* (pp. 57–84). Thousand Oaks: Sage.

Navarrete, C. D., Fessler, D. M. T., & Eng, S. J. (2007). Elevated ethnocentrism in the first trimester of pregnancy. *Evolution and Human Behavior, 28,* 60–65.

Ridgeway, C. L., Berger, J., & Smith, L. (1985). Nonverbal cues and status: an expectation states approach. *American Journal of Sociology, 90,* 955–978.

Roberts, G. (1998). Competitive Altruism: From reciprocity to the handicap principle. *Proceedings of the Royal Society of London: Series B, 265,* 427–431.

Sasaki, T., & Uchida, S. (2013). The evolution of cooperation by social exclusion. *Proceedings of the Royal Society-B, 280,* 20122498. http://dx.doi.org/10.1098/rspb.2012.2498.

Schelling, T. (1960). *The strategy of conflict.* Cambridge: Harvard University Press.

Seeley, T.D. (2010). *Honeybee democracy.* Princeton: Princeton University Press.

Sell, A., Cosmides, L., & Tooby, J. (2009). Human adaptations for the visual assessment of strength and fighting ability from body and face. *Proceedings of the Royal Society-B, 276,* 575–584.

Shinada, M., Yamagishi, T., & Ohmura, Y. (2004). False friends are worse than bitter enemies: "Altruistic" punishment of in-group members. *Evolution and Human Behavior, 25,* 379–393.

Simunovic, D., Mifune, N., & Yamagishi, T. (2013). Preemptive strike: An experimental study of fear-based aggression. *Journal of Experimental Social Psychology, 49,* 1120–1123.

Stallen, M., De Dreu, C. K. W., Shalvi, S., Smidts, A., & Sanfey, A. G. (2012). The herding hormone: Oxytocin stimulates in-group conformity. *Psychological Science, 23,* 1288–1292.

Steiner, I. D. (1972). *Group processes and productivity.* New York: Academic.

Sumpter, D. J. T. (2010). *Collective animal behavior.* Princeton: Princeton University Press.

Surowiecki, J. (2004). *The wisdom of crowds: Why the many are smarter than the few and how collective wisdom shapes business, economies, societies and nations.* New York: Doubleday.

Tajfel, H., & Turner, J. (1979). An integrative theory of intergroup conflict. In W. Austin & S. Worchel (Eds.), *The psychology of intergroup relations* (pp. 33–47). Monterey: Brooks/Cole.

Tindale, R. S., & Kameda, T. (2000). "Social sharedness" as a unifying theme for information processing in groups. *Group Processes and Intergroup Relations, 3,* 123–140.

Tindale, R. S., Talbot, M., & Martinez, R. (2012). Group decision making. In J. M. Levine (Ed.), *Group processes* (pp. 165–194). New York: Psychology Press.

Tracy, J. L., & Robins, R. W. (2004). Show your pride: Evidence for a discrete emotion expression. *Psychological Science, 15,* 194–197.

Van Vugt, M. (2006). Evolutionary origins of leadership and followership. *Personality and Social Psychology Review, 10,* 354–371.

Van Vugt, M. (2009). Despotism, democracy and the evolutionary dynamics of leadership and followership. *American Psychologist, 64,* 54–56.

Van Vugt, M., & Kameda, T. (2013). Evolution and groups. In J. M. Levine (Ed.), *Group processes* (pp. 297–332). New York: Psychology Press.

Van Vugt, M., & Kameda, T. (2014). Evolution of the social brain: Psychological adaptations for group living. In M. Mikulincer & P. Shaver (Eds.), *Mechanism of social connection: From brain to group* (pp. 335–355). Washington, DC: American Psychological Association.

Van Vugt, M., De Cremer, D., & Janssen, D. (2007). Gender differences in cooperation and competition: The male warrior hypothesis. *Psychological Science, 18,* 19–23.

Wegner, D. M. (1987). Transactive memory: A contemporary analysis of the group mind. In B. Mullen & G. R. Goethals (Eds.), *Theories of group behavior* (pp. 185–208). New York: Springer-Verlag.

Wolf, M., Kurvers, R. H. J. M., Ward, A. J. W., Krause, S., & Krause, J. (2013). Accurate decisions in an uncertain world: Collective cognition increases true positives while decreasing false positives. *Proceedings of the Royal Society-B, 280,* 20122777. http://dx.doi.org/10.1098/rspb.2012.2777.

20 Why Do Humans Help Their Friends? Proximal and Ultimate Hypotheses from Evolutionary Theory

Daniel Hruschka, Joseph Hackman and Shane Macfarlan

In mythology, novels, and the trenches of everyday life, humans frequently make exceptional sacrifices to help their close friends. Pythias of Greek legend escaped pirates and swam through miles of treacherous seas to save his best friend Damon from execution (Raschen 1919). In the Chinese historical novel *Snow Flower and the Secret Fan,* Snow Flower shelters her best friend for months after she loses her family during the Taiping Rebellion (See 2009). Such exceptional aid is not limited to fiction. Among nineteenth-century maritime traders off the coast of Papua New Guinea, specially designated friends provided safe harbor and lodging in otherwise hostile territory (Malinowski 2003). In East Africa, Maasai herders cultivate selective, enduring relationships, called *osotua,* in which partners share valuable animals with each other when needed (Cronk 2007). Indeed, across documented human groups, people regularly cultivate enduring social ties like close friendships which are grounded in selective and exceptional help (Hruschka 2010).

There is remarkable diversity in the ways that people build and maintain these friendships (Adams et al. 2004; Bell and Coleman 1999; Hruschka 2010). In some societies, parents and elders arrange friendships in the same way they arrange marriages. Friendships can be cemented with official rituals and they can also require formalized procedures—something like divorce—to terminate. The kinds of help that are found to be acceptable also varies. Is it acceptable to lend large sums of money to friends? Is it acceptable to lie for friends in a court of law? Is it acceptable not to? Answers to these questions can change from place to place and person to person (Hruschka 2010). Given the diversity in how people define friendship, how they build friendships, and how friends help each other, one might ask whether it is possible or useful to put all of these relationships under a single umbrella called "friendship." However, in the face of this diversity, there is a common set of features which reliably co-occur in relationships across human societies. Specifically, people regularly build selective and enduring relationships with individuals (who may or may not be genetic kin). Partners in these relationships express selectively positive feelings and goodwill toward each other and they aid these partners in exceptional ways (Hruschka 2010). Here, we refer to such relationships as friendships.

The fact that this suite of relationship features arises reliably across most (if not all) human populations raises numerous evolutionary questions.

D. Hruschka (✉) · J. Hackman
School of Human Evolution and Social Change, Arizona State University, Tempe, AZ 85287, USA
e-mail: Daniel.Hruschka@asu.edu

J. Hackman
e-mail: Joseph.Hackman@asu.edu

S. Macfarlan
Department of Anthropology, University of Utah, Salt Lake City, UT 84112, USA
e-mail: shane.macfarlan@anthro.utah.edu

V. Zeigler-Hill et al. (eds.), *Evolutionary Perspectives on Social Psychology,* Evolutionary Psychology,
DOI 10.1007/978-3-319-12697-5_20, © Springer International Publishing Switzerland 2015

In the short run, what psychological machinery helps people identify who is and who is not a friend and how do people choose to bestow exceptional aid to those they classify as friends? At longer timescales, how do people cultivate relationships that prepare them to provide such special help in times of need? At the deepest time scales, what general or specific evolutionary challenges might have selected for the capacities and propensities needed to make these tough decisions?

In the past two decades, evolutionary scholars have proposed a number of answers to these questions. To sort through these explanations for increased helping among friends, we first outline current theories and parse how these theories differ and converge in their answers to the above questions. We then review how well these different answers fit existing evidence from anthropology, psychology, and behavioral economics. Finally, we examine how these different theories account or fail to account for other aspects of human friendships—including the dark side of friendship—which may not be directly related to mutual aid.

Algorithms, Cues, and Signals in the Decision to Help Friends

Ethnographic and experimental data collected from around the world show that people are often willing to bear substantial costs to help their friends (Hruschka 2010). Without some long-term reproductive return to such sacrifice, it is not immediately clear how such behaviors could have withstood the multiple trials of natural selection. To solve this puzzle, evolutionary accounts identify how such decisions, and the underlying decision-making mechanisms, might have regularly provided a positive net return on investment. From a computational perspective, we might ask what kind of algorithm could prevent exploitation and ensure that one on average reaps a net reward from sacrifices made for friends (Tooby and Cosmides 1996)? Since algorithms depend on inputs and ways of handling those inputs, each theoretical algorithm makes specific predictions about the kinds of cues and signals to which individuals should attend when making these decisions.

Backward-Looking Algorithms

A natural workhorse worth trotting out at this point is the classic algorithm based on *tit-for-tat helping* (Axelrod and Hamilton 1981). According to this algorithm, one pays attention to past help provided by a partner when making the choice to help in the future. Specifically, if a friend helps us, that makes us more likely to help that friend next time around. Conversely, if the friend fails to help, then we will reciprocate with neglect in the future. Numerous modeling exercises and behavioral experiments have shown that following some form of tit-for-tat algorithm is a cheap and efficient way of enforcing cooperation between relative strangers. Using this cue, an agent quickly breaks off draining interactions with an exploitative partner. A related algorithm which also focuses directly on past acts of helping uses as input the long run balance of favors between oneself and one's partner. A person engaging in such *balance-dependent helping* would estimate the balance of past favors and would then choose to help based on how lopsided the balance had recently been in the friend's favor. Each of these algorithms—tit-for-tat and balance-dependent reciprocity—relies on tracking help provided and received by a friend as a guide to current or future behaviors.

Reputational or Forward-Looking Algorithms

More proactive algorithms do not simply depend on past behaviors, but assess how generosity toward a person could shape future events. If the link between current actions and the future effects of those actions is sufficiently tight, then the decision to help should be based on the relative consequences of helping versus not helping. For example, we might choose to help a friend to increase the likelihood of receiving help from that friend in the future. This is perhaps the most straightforward example of forward-looking algorithms, but would-be-helpers can also consider other indirect future benefits. For example, if people are attracted to generous partners, then one may be generous to a friend in order to attract more potential partners and selectively cultivate relationships with the most generous of the crowd. This is precisely a prediction from biological markets theory which envisions that individuals are continually engaged in an open market for good quality partners (Barclay 2013; Noë and Hammerstein 1995). According to this theory, helping a friend is a signal to *other* people that they should be friends with you. Whether trying to shape the future behavior of a friend or the future behavior of others, a key prediction of these *reputational theories* is that people should pay attention to the visibility of a good deed to relevant parties so that they can acknowledge and act on it.

Kin Detection Algorithms

A third kind of algorithm that potentially underwrites helping among friends may have been originally designed to send benefits to closely related kin. According to the *kin detection* argument, in early human societies where people were putatively surrounded by close kin, one could use proximity and frequent interaction as a cue to shared genes (Ackerman et al. 2007). Indeed, individuals appear to use cues of co-residence and closeness, as well as phenotypic similarity, to infer kinship (DeBruine 2005; Lieberman et al. 2007; Park and Schaller 2005) and are consequently less attracted to individuals raised in close proximity to themselves, a phenomenon known as the *Westermarck effect* (Park and Ackerman 2011). In the modern world where people interact on a regular basis with non-kin, this algorithm frequently misfires, sending costly benefits to unrelated individuals who we mistake as kin (e.g., our friends). Thus, according to this hypothesis, we provide exceptional aid to close friends because we mistake them for close genetic kin.

Theory of Mind Algorithms

The final kind of algorithm focuses on signals of a partner's intentions and feelings about the relationship. If you know that your partner sees your relationship as valuable and difficult to replace, then you also know that that person will sacrifice substantial time and effort to protect you and to help you to survive through hard times. Your partner's unique devotion to your relationship in turn makes the relationship irreplaceable to you. Thus, you will make sacrifices to protect your partner so that when you need help in the future, your partner will be around and able to help you. The importance of such mutual signals arises from the notion of *mutual irreplaceability* (Tooby and Cosmides 1996). This algorithm leads to a mutually reinforcing feedback loop that Tooby and Cosmides refer to as runaway friendship, whereby the fact that a partner sees you as irreplaceable makes that partner in turn irreplaceable to you (Tooby and Cosmides 1996). If people follow this algorithm, they should focus on how the other partner values the relationship relative to other relationships and how the partner signals relative devotion to this specific relationship (e.g., through costly gifts and time). Partners in such runaway friendships may also use hard-to-fake external focal points, such as the duration of the friendship, which both partners can use as an objective measure of the irreplaceability of the relationship. Given that there are very few people with whom we can claim a very long relationship, this is a natural focal point for establishing mutual irreplaceability.

For What Purpose Were These Algorithms Designed?

At a deeper level, researchers have also asked why such algorithms might have arisen and for what specific evolutionary challenges they were potentially designed. Here, we review dominant hypotheses about the evolutionary challenges giving rise to exceptional aid among friends.

Mutual Aid Hypotheses

Mutual aid hypotheses propose that the capacity and propensity to cultivate friendships and selectively help friends solved problems of organizing mutual aid in a number of arenas. These include helping partners when sick (Sugiyama 2004), helping buffer food shortages, helping partners gain access to scarce and novel resources (e.g., water, safe haven in foreign groups, rare goods), and supporting partners during interpersonal conflicts (Descioli and Kurzban 2012; Hruschka 2010; Tooby and Cosmides 1996). Within this large umbrella of mutual aid, several of the hypothesized algorithms described above could underwrite the specific acts of mutual aid.

Alliance Hypothesis

The alliance hypothesis is similar to mutual aid hypotheses. However, it focuses specifically on one kind of challenge: finding support during interpersonal and intergroup conflicts (DeScioli and Kurzban 2009, 2012). It rests on the premise that, "The apparent primary purpose of human coalitions is to outcompete other human coalitions" (Flinn et al. 2012, p. 70). Thus, the capacity and propensity for friendship arose out of one specific kind of adaptive challenge, cultivating alliance partners who could provide protection in a world of competing alliances.

Competitive Altruism Hypothesis

The competitive altruism hypothesis (Roberts 1998) arises from biological markets theory (Barclay 2013; Noë and Hammerstein 1995), which views friendship and other kinds of cooperative relationships as arising in a market where people compete for high-quality (e.g., generous) partners (Barclay and Willer 2007; Macfarlan et al. 2012; Sylwester and Roberts 2010). This perspective makes two assumptions: (1) individuals differ in their level of quality, and (2) people prefer high-quality partners to low-quality ones (Nesse 2007). In discussions about friendship, the relevant personal quality is usually generosity or trustworthiness. When generous partners are in short supply, people will engage in bidding wars to be friends with hyper-generous individuals. Thus, hyper-generous individuals can be choosey about their friends. This in turn gives people an incentive to show off their generosity. According to biological markets theory and the competitive altruism hypothesis, exceptional generosity towards a friend is intended for two audiences; on the one hand, it is an act of commitment to the current friend, on the other hand, it is a signal to *others* about one's quality as a partner to attract more friends in the future.

Kin Confusion Hypothesis

A fourth possibility is that we help friends because we have been tricked into thinking that they share our genes. This is directly related to the proximate algorithm described earlier that attends to qualities of relationships, such as frequency of interaction, proximity, and duration of the relationship, that would have been reliable cues to genetic kinship in the ancestral environment (Ackerman et al. 2007).

Empirical Findings on Friendship

Each of the theories outlined above give us expectations about how friendships are formed and how friends treat each other. Here, we examine these different theories in light of current data from anthropology, psychology, and economics, as well as the current understanding of how nonhuman primates and other social animals cultivate selective, enduring relationships.

Psychological and Neurobiological Classification of Close Friends

Researchers in anthropology, psychology, and economics have independently identified "social closeness" as a key concept used by people to evaluate and describe their social partners and, specifically, their friends (Aron et al. 1992; Jones and Rachlin 2006; Leider et al. 2009). Although most existing literature in the social sciences has framed such ranking in terms of spatial metaphors (e.g., "closeness," "inclusion," "merging," "distance"), many languages also provide metaphors based on value (e.g., "dear," "chere") or ordinal ranking (e.g., "best," "prio") for comparing and classifying social partners (Hruschka 2010). Across a range of studies in different cultural settings and using different methodologies, perceived social closeness to a partner consistently predicts how willing one is to sacrifice time or money for a partner (Goeree et al. 2010; Jones and Rachlin 2006; Leider et al. 2009; Strombach et al. in press). Feelings of closeness are also associated with our physiological responses to social interactions with others (Güroğlu et al. 2008). When thinking about a close partner (as opposed to a stranger) engaging in a disgusting act, people report less disgust, their heart rate changes less, and they engage in less avoidant behaviors (Peng et al. 2013). Observing a close friend's (as opposed to a stranger's) social exclusion activates brain regions involved in firsthand experience of the pain of exclusion (Meyer et al. 2013). Males do not experience elevated testosterone levels when they defeat close friends in competition in the same way they do when they beat nonfriends (Flinn et al. 2012). Moreover, sharing with a close friend more strongly activates brain regions associated with reward than does sharing with a stranger or a computer (Fareri et al. 2012).

Perceptions of social closeness are used to organize a range of relationships, including those with genetic kin and mates (Ackerman et al. 2007). Indeed, one possibility is that social closeness is the key psychological cue accounting for heightened generosity across all of these relationships (Korchmaros and Kenny 2001). This is an implicit or explicit assumption of many theories of close relationships (Brown and Brown 2006; Clark et al. 1986; Neyer et al. 2011). Social closeness does appear to fully mediate the increased giving among self-described close and best friends (Hackman and Hruschka 2013; Hackman et al. 2015). However, numerous studies have demonstrated a "kinship premium," whereby people are more generous to genetic kin than non-kin at the same level of social closeness (Curry et al. 2012; Korchmaros and Kenny 2001; Rachlin and Jones 2008). This suggests that people use cues other than social closeness when interacting with genetic kin (e.g., phenotypic similarity; Platek and Kemp 2009). Only one study to date has examined whether there is a comparable "mate premium," whereby people are more generous to mates than other non-kin at the same level of social closeness (Hackman et al. 2015). Figure 20.1 illustrates the current state of knowledge on how social closeness mediates the increased generosity observed in specific kinds of relationships. The sum of current—though limited—evidence suggests that social closeness is the key mediator of increased helping among friends, but that other mechanisms are involved in detecting genetic kin. Thus, if increased helping among friends is a misfiring of kin detection systems, it only recruits one part of those systems, and specifically those systems involved in evaluations of social closeness.

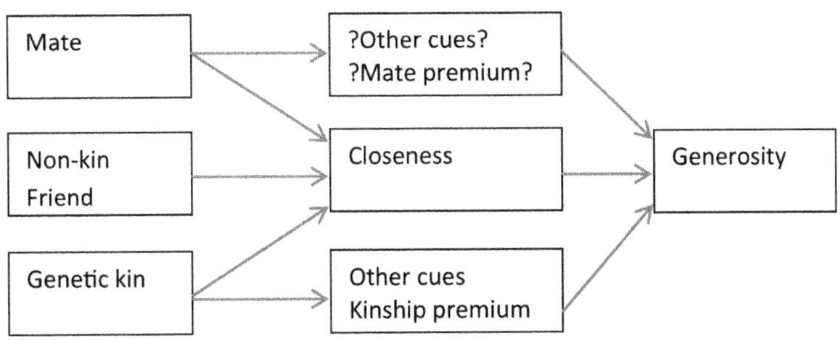

Fig. 20.1 Mediators of increased generosity among specific kinds of relationships

Closeness completely mediates increased helping among non-kin friends, but other cues appear to be important among genetic kin (thus, the kinship premium) and may also be important among mates.

Given the link between feelings of closeness and willingness to help in both real and hypothetical scenarios, and understanding how the brain reckons closeness is a key piece in understanding the evolutionary origins of the proximate machinery of friendship. Current research suggests that the assessment of closeness seems to recruit similar brain networks as assessments of physical distance from self (Yamakawa et al. 2009) and perhaps physical warmth (Ijzerman et al. 2013). Interesting parallels between temporal discounting (giving less to temporally far than temporally close selves) and social discounting (giving less to socially far than socially close selves) also suggest one possible origin for the social discounting system (Jones and Rachlin 2006; Pronin et al. 2008). Given that temporal discounting is phylogenetically ancient (Chung and Herrnstein 1967), this could be the basis for social discounting in humans and perhaps other social animals. However, more research is needed to determine if this connection relies on common neural substrates or is simply an interesting analogy.

How such cues of social closeness are neurally represented and processed are still not clearly understood. However, a number of recent neuroimaging studies that have examined the neural correlates of viewing social partners suggest that images of non-kin friends activate only a subset of the brain systems recruited when viewing either long-term pair bonds or close genetic kin. Specifically, the one functionally relevant system commonly activated by all three kinds of social partners is the periaqueductal gray, a region with a high density of vasopressin receptors and one also recruited when thinking about unconditional love (Acevedo et al. 2012; Cacioppo et al. 2012). As with the kinship premium, it appears that friendship recruits a few neurobiological systems used for genetic kin and pair bonds, but as of yet there do not appear to be any unique systems dedicated to friendships per se (Platek and Kemp 2009).

Decisions to Help Friends and Responses to Help Seeking

Humans weigh many factors when choosing to help others, whether they are close friends, family, or strangers. For example, they can consider how it will affect their reputation, whether they will be punished for not helping, and how much the other person needs it. Our goal here is *not* to understand why humans help any Joe off the street, but rather why people provide exceptional aid to their friends, and especially their close friends. Specifically, why are people *more likely* to help close friends than acquaintances, strangers, or distant family? When discussing decisions to help, it is important to distinguish between reciprocity—a statistical observation of balance in transfers—and the decision mechanisms underlying such balance. For example, if we observe statistical balance, or "reciprocity," in maintenance behaviors among friends (Oswald et al. 2004), this could conceivably be due to many of the decision algorithms proposed below.

Attention to Past Behaviors An important prediction of hypothesized algorithms based on strict reciprocity and balance is that people should pay close attention to their friends' past behaviors and how much they contribute to joint tasks. Interestingly, a number of experiments in the USA and other countries have shown that friends are *less* sensitive to recent favors than are strangers when making decisions to help or to share. (Boster et al. 1995; Cronk 2007; Hruschka 2010, pp. 21–24). One reason people may be less sensitive to past behaviors of friends is that they monitor their friends less. Indeed, when engaged in common activities where a partner can shirk, people are *less* likely to monitor the inputs of close friends than the inputs of strangers (Clark et al. 1986; Xue and Silk 2012). In short, the existing body of data provides no evidence that friends are more likely to pay attention to past behaviors or to reciprocate favors or sharing than are strangers or acquaintances. Thus, although strict reciprocity is an important mechanism underlying helping in humans, it is unlikely the mechanism underlying increased helping among friends (Clark et al. 1986; Silk 2003). The limited data on long-term balance in relationships tells a similar story. Close friends attend less to long-run balances of favors than do acquaintances in evaluating their relationship (cf. Hruschka 2010, pp. 24–25). Thus, current evidence suggests that algorithms based on simply keeping track of past favors are unlikely to be supporting the heightened generosity and helping among friends.

Attention to Future Consequences and Reputation An important prediction of reputational algorithms is that the increased helping and giving to friends should attenuate when no one will find out what one did. When studies have taken away the possibility for reputation by making decisions anonymous, they do indeed find that people help less and give less when no one can see their actions. However, this effect applies equally to strangers and close friends and, even when one removes an audience, people are much more likely to help close friends than strangers or acquaintances. In one recent experiment, researchers asked Harvard College students to identify up to ten mutual best friends on Facebook (Leider et al. 2009). Some students were designated "decision makers," and over the course of several days the researchers asked them to make decisions to help particular partners (with real money provided by the experimenters). Sometimes they were asked about a close friend and sometimes about a distant friend-of-a-friend-of-a-friend-of-a-friend. Sometimes the close friend would be informed about the donor's identity, and sometimes they would remain anonymous. Moreover, since people could receive help from anyone in the experiment, it was never certain in the anonymous condition from whom one could have received help. The researchers found that making the donor's identity known did increase helping and sharing by about 0–35 % over and above an anonymous situation. However, the effect of close friendship was much stronger, with people helping and sharing by 52–95 % more with close friends than with acquaintances. This was independent of any audience effects. We find similar effects of close friendship independent of reputation in a range of tasks, including trust (Vollan 2011) and giving games (Binzel and Fehr 2013a, b; Brañas-Garza et al. 2010), and across several cultural contexts, including Egypt, Namibia, Spain, and the USA. Moreover, these effects are similar whether the close friend or a third party is the audience (Vollan 2011). This suggests that people do indeed pay attention to whether someone is watching when choosing to help people, but that this is relatively unrelated to the increased help and support given to close friends.

Attention to Cues of Kinship Several lines of evidence also suggest that people's decisions to help genetically related kin are fundamentally different from non-kin. For example, the likelihood of helping genetic kin goes up as the cost of help increases, while the likelihood of helping friends (even close friends) goes down (Stewart-Williams 2007; Xue 2013). Thus, the cost of help has the opposite effect on helping among genetic kin and non-kin. Another recurring finding in studies of helping is the "kinship premium." People are on average more likely to help close genetic kin (e.g., siblings, parents) than non-kin partners even when they feel the same level of emotional closeness (Curry et al. 2012; Korchmaros and Kenny 2001; Rachlin and Jones 2008). Interestingly, there is no comparable "friendship premium," as all of the increased giving among self-described friends, close friends, and best friends can be explained by how emotionally close people feel (Hackman and Hruschka 2013; Hackman et al. 2015). Finally, the relative need of a partner appears to influence helping among genetic kin more than among non-kin (Hackman and Hruschka 2013). These findings suggest that mechanisms in place for helping genetic kin operate over and above the mechanisms involved in helping close friends, and sometimes in different ways (such as the role of cost and need in decision making).

Attention to a Partner's View of the Relationship Theory of mind hypotheses suggest that people should pay close attention to cues that a partner finds the relationship irreplaceable, valuing the relationship over and above other relationships. Cues of replaceability would include the duration of the relationship as well as how much one's partner values and needs the relationship. In line with this hypothesis, individuals often have relative rankings of partners in terms of social or emotional closeness, which may be an internal cue to assess the relationship (DeScioli and Kurzban 2009; Schino and Aureli 2009). This assessment of closeness is associated with the duration of the relationship, and it is related to how much one sees a partner valuing the relationship (DeScioli and Kurzban 2009). For example, in a series of studies in the USA and Japan, Niiya et al. (2006; Niiya and Ellsworth 2012) found that people were more upset and felt less close to friends if they found out their friend needed help, but instead asked someone else for help. These findings suggest that people's assessment of closeness depends in an important way on cues to how irreplaceable a partner sees the relationship.

Cultivation and Maintenance of Relationships

The different hypotheses described above also make predictions about how people choose partners and cultivate relationships.

Homophily on Generosity One unique prediction from the competitive altruism model is that friends will be more similar to each other on their baseline generosity—how generous they are to people in general. This prediction is based on the assumption that baseline generosity is perceived as a good indicator of friend quality. Bereczkei et al. (2010) used costly signaling theory to show that baseline generosity, measured as charitable donations to an unfamiliar person, were associated with an increased likelihood of being selected as a good friend candidate (Bereczkei et al. 2010). Thus, increases in baseline generosity tend to improve others' perceptions of the friend quality of the individual. In an experimental study among undergraduates, Schaefer (2012) found that manipulating partner quality in a competitive partner marketplace resulted in homophily on partner quality. Importantly, this homophily emerged through the selective reciprocation exercised by the high-quality individuals. This works shows clearly that in a competitive marketplace, homophily on generosity can arise when high-quality individuals exercise selective cultivation of relationships. However, studies using social network data in naturalistic settings have produced mixed results. Leider et al. (2009) found positive assortment among friends in terms of giving to a stranger in a Dictator Game. However, based on people's inability to predict their partner's baseline generosity, Leider et al. (2009) argued that this resulted from influence of one's social partners, rather than selection of generous partners. Using a Trust Experiment, Winter and Kataria (2013) confirmed this hypothesis, finding that friends are more similar in their trustworthiness to a stranger only when they can observe their friends' behavior. This suggests people do not select friends who display similar levels of baseline trustworthiness, but are rather influenced by the people they interact with. In another field experiment using the Dictator Game in Cairo slums, Binzel and Fehr found that altruistic preferences were not significantly correlated among friends (Binzel and Fehr 2013a). Thus, current evidence from naturalistic settings does not provide much support for selection of friends based on baseline generosity.

Relational Aggression An understudied, but important, element of friendship is its "dark side," including betrayal, ultimatums, jealousy, and relational aggression. Relational aggression is perhaps the most discussed example of friendship's dark side. Research on friendship dissolution suggests that one of the primary reasons friendships dissolve is due to a third friend who enters into an existing dyad (e.g., Casper and Card 2010). Thus, people can become jealous of third parties who threaten to replace them as friends. They can even go so far as to sabotage third party relationships in attempts to increase the value of their own relationship with a partner (DeScioli and Kurzban 2009; Hruschka 2010). Such relational aggression is a prediction of three of the four evolutionary hypotheses described above. The alliance hypothesis predicts that people should be concerned that their partners are not fettered by potentially competing loyalties when disputes arise (Descioli and Kurzban 2012). Mutual aid hypotheses based on mutual irreplaceability would predict that people should try to make themselves as irreplaceable to their partner as possible, and thus remove third party competitors (Hruschka 2010; Tooby and Cosmides 1996). Competitive altruism theories predict that low-quality individuals will experience greater jealousy concerning their existing friends' relationship status and may be more likely to derogate third-party interlopers compared to high-quality individuals, as low-quality individuals are less capable of engaging in bidding wars with third-party members to maintain existing friendships and have fewer opportunities for attracting new friends (Barclay 2013). Given its consistency with so many theories, it is difficult to use relational aggression as a tool for discriminating between them.

Comparative Data

Finally, comparative data from diverse human groups as well as nonhuman primates hold promise in discriminating between different hypotheses and proposed algorithms. For example, recent work on the social organization of small-scale societies challenges a key premise of kin detection explanations. Specifically, in extant human foraging societies, people live in bands where many of their interactions are with genetically unrelated individuals (Hill et al. 2011). Thus, it is not clear that coresidence, common group membership, and frequency interaction would have been very good cues of genetic relatedness even in ancestral human groups.

Recent comparative work on sharing among nonhuman primates also suggests that coalitionary alliances (as proposed by the alliance hypothesis) may have been a key stepping stone to the other kinds of sharing and mutual aid observed among friends in contemporary human groups. Coalitionary support has traditionally been a key kind of aid studied by primatologists (Jaeggi and Van Schaik 2011; Micheletta et al. 2012; Schino 2007). Whether this reflects measurement bias is to be determined. However, one comparative study which examined the phylogenetic ordering of different kinds of support and sharing suggests coalitionary support comes first. Specifically, male–male coalitions appear to be a necessary condition for male–male sharing among non-kin and female–female coalitions appear to be a necessary condition for female–female sharing among non-kin. However, the converse does not appear to be true (Jaeggi and Van Schaik 2011). Future comparative studies will hopefully provide further refinements and greater checks on current assumptions of the different hypotheses.

Conclusion

A number of tentative conclusions can be drawn from the current empirical literature about proximate and ultimate accounts for increased helping and sharing among friends.

1. *Kin detection hypotheses? Unlikely.* If helping among close friends is a misfiring of kin detection mechanisms, then it only recruits one part of that system—the one involving feelings of social closeness. The different effects of the cost of helping also indicate that different algorithms may underlie the increased help among genetic kin and non-kin friends. Finally, a key premise of the kin confusion argument—that people primarily interacted with close genetic kin in early ancestral environments—is not supported by current data on contemporary foraging groups. It is still possible that helping among friends recruits key neural substrates used to detect and interact with kin and mates. However, this substrate would need to have been modified sufficiently to prevent exploitation by non-kin in ancestral environments and to lead to the contemporary differences observed in behavior among genetic kin and non-kin friends.
2. *Reputational hypotheses? Unlikely, but there is room for further exploration.* People do indeed pay attention to their audience when choosing to help others. However, available evidence suggests that increased helping among friends is independent of such

audience effects. Thus, reputational theories may account for generosity in general, but are unlikely to account for the increased helping observed among close friends. An interesting prediction of one reputational theory—competitive altruism's prediction of increased homophily among friends on baseline generosity to strangers—deserves further exploration.

3. *Theory of mind hypotheses? Promising.* A number of lines of evidence suggest that people pay attention to cues of a partner's view of a relationship in assessing one's social closeness to a partner (DeScioli et al. 2011; Niiya and Ellsworth 2012). In turn, social closeness is related to willingness to help a partner. More research is needed to trace this potential chain of causation.
4. *Mutual aid versus alliance hypothesis? Comparative and experimental data may hold the key.* Mutual aid and alliance hypotheses are difficult to tease apart. They are both consistent with current evidence about increased generosity in the absence of audience effects, about attention to a partner's view of the relationship and about relational aggression. A recent comparative study of sharing and coalitionary support among nonhuman primates suggests that coalitionary support is a precursor of sharing among non-kin. Future comparative and experimental work will hopefully provide new informative comparisons of these two hypotheses.

Acknowledgments We thank members of the Laboratory of Culture Change and Behavior for helpful comments on earlier drafts. DJH acknowledges support from the National Science Foundation grant BCS-1150813, jointly funded by the Programs in Cultural Anthropology, Social Psychology Program and Decision, Risk, and Management Sciences.

References

Acevedo, B. P., Aron, A., Fisher, H. E., & Brown, L. L. (2012). Neural correlates of long-term intense romantic love. *Social Cognitive and Affective Neuroscience, 7,* 145–159.

Ackerman, J. M., Kenrick, D. T., & Schaller, M. (2007). Is friendship akin to kinship? *Evolution and Human Behavior, 28,* 365–374.

Adams, G., Anderson, S. L., & Adonu, J. K. (2004). The cultural grounding of closeness and intimacy. In D. J. Mashek & A. Aron (Eds.), *Handbook of Closeness and Intimacy* (pp. 321–339). Mahwah: Lawrence Erlbaum Associates.

Aron, A., Aron, E. N., & Smollan, D. (1992). Inclusion of other in the self scale and the structure of interpersonal closeness. *Journal of Personality and Social Psychology, 63,* 596–612.

Axelrod, R., & Hamilton, W. D. (1981). The evolution of cooperation. *Science, 211,* 1390–1396.

Barclay, P. (2013). Strategies for cooperation in biological markets, especially for humans. *Evolution and Human Behavior, 34,* 164–175.

Barclay, P., & Willer, R. (2007). Partner choice creates competitive altruism in humans. *Proceedings of the Royal Society B: Biological Sciences, 274,* 749–753.

Bell, S., & Coleman, S. (1999). *The anthropology of friendship*. Oxford: Berg.

Bereczkei, T., Birkas, B., & Kerekes, Z. (2010). Altruism towards strangers in need: Costly signaling in an industrial society. *Evolution and Human Behavior, 31,* 95–103.

Binzel, C., & Fehr, D. (2013a). Giving and sorting among friends: Evidence from a lab-in-the-field experiment. *Economics Letters, 121,* 214–217.

Binzel, C., & Fehr, D. (2013b). Social distance and trust: Experimental evidence from a slum in Cairo. *Journal of Development Economics, 103,* 99–106.

Boster, F. J., Rodriguez, J. I., Cruz, M. G., & Marshall, L. (1995). The relative effectiveness of a direct request message and a pregiving message on friends and strangers. *Communication Research, 22,* 475–484.

Brañas-Garza, P., Cobo-Reyes, R., Espinosa, M. P., Jiménez, N., Kovářík, J., & Ponti, G. (2010). Altruism and social integration. *Games and Economic Behavior, 69,* 249–257.

Brown, S. L., & Brown, R. M. (2006). Selective investment theory: Recasting the functional significance of close relationships. *Psychological Inquiry, 17,* 1–29.

Cacioppo, S., Bianchi-Demicheli, F., Hatfield, E., & Rapson, R. L. (2012). Social neuroscience of love. *Clinical Neuropsychiatry, 9*(1), 3–13.

Casper, D. M., & Card, N. A. (2010). "We Were Best Friends, But…": Two studies of antipathetic relationships emerging from broken friendships. *Journal of Adolescent Research, 25,* 499–526.

Chung, S.-H., & Herrnstein, R. J. (1967). Choice and delay of reinforcement. *Journal of the Experimental Analysis of Behavior, 10,* 67–74.

Clark, M. S., Mills, J., & Powell, M. C. (1986). Keeping track of needs in communal and exchange relationships. *Journal of personality and social psychology, 51,* 333–338.

Cronk, L. (2007). The influence of cultural framing on play in the trust game: A Maasai example. *Evolution and Human Behavior, 28,* 352–358.

Curry, O., Roberts, S. G., & Dunbar, R. I. (2012). Altruism in social networks: Evidence for a 'kinship premium'. *British Journal of Psychology, 104,* 283–295.

DeBruine, L. M. (2005). Trustworthy but not lust-worthy: Context-specific effects of facial resemblance. *Proceedings of the Royal Society B: Biological Sciences, 272,* 919–922.

DeScioli, P., & Kurzban, R. (2009). The alliance hypothesis for human friendship. *PLoS One, 4,* e5802.

DeScioli, P., & Kurzban, R. (2012). The company you keep: Friendship decisions from a functional perspective. In J. Krueger (Ed.), *Social judgment and decision-making* (pp. 209–226). New York: Taylor and Francis Group.

DeScioli, P., Kurzban, R., Koch, E. N., & Liben-Nowell, D. (2011). Best frends: Alliances, friend ranking, and the MySpace social network. *Perspectives on Psychological Science, 6*(1), 6–8.

Fareri, D. S., Niznikiewicz, M. A., Lee, V. K., & Delgado, M. R. (2012). Social network modulation of reward-related signals. *The Journal of Neuroscience, 32,* 9045–9052.

Flinn, M. V., Ponzi, D., & Muehlenbein, M. P. (2012). Hormonal mechanisms for regulation of aggression in human coalitions. *Human Nature, 23,* 68–88.

Goeree, J. K., McConnell, M. A., Mitchell, T., Tromp, T., & Yariv, L. (2010). The 1/d law of giving. *American Economic Journal: Microeconomics, 2,* 183–203.

Güroğlu, B., Haselager, G. J., van Lieshout, C. F., Takashima, A., Rijpkema, M., & Fernández, G. (2008). Why are friends special? Implementing a social interaction simulation task to probe the neural correlates of friendship. *Neuroimage, 39,* 903–910.

Hackman, J., & Hruschka, D. J. (2013). *Emotional closeness, need and sacrifice across kin and non-kin relationships*. Chicago: Paper presented at the American Anthropological Association.

Hackman, J., Danvers, A., & Hruschka, D. J. (2015). Closeness is enough for friends, but not mates or kin: Mate and kinship premiums in India and US. *Evolution and Human Behavior, 36,* 137–145.

Hill, K. R., Walker, R. S., Božičević, M., Eder, J., Headland, T., Hewlett, B., Hurtado, A. M., Marlowe, F., Wiessner, P., & Wood, B. (2011). Co-residence patterns in hunter-gatherer societies show unique human social structure. *Science, 331,* 1286–1289.

Hruschka, D. J. (2010). *Friendship: Development, ecology, and evolution of a relationship* (Vol. 5). Berkeley: University of California Press.

Ijzerman, H., Karremans, J. C., Thomsen, L., & Schubert, T. W. (2013). Caring for sharing. *Social Psychology, 44,* 160–166.

Jaeggi, A. V., & Van Schaik, C. P. (2011). The evolution of food sharing in primates. *Behavioral Ecology and Sociobiology, 65,* 2125–2140.

Jones, B., & Rachlin, H. (2006). Social discounting. *Psychological Science, 17,* 283–286.

Korchmaros, J. D., & Kenny, D. A. (2001). Emotional closeness as a mediator of the effect of genetic relatedness on altruism. *Psychological Science, 12,* 262–265.

Leider, S., Möbius, M. M., Rosenblat, T., & Do, Q.-A. (2009). Directed altruism and enforced reciprocity in social networks. *Quarterly Journal of Economics, 124,* 1815–1851.

Lieberman, D., Tooby, J., & Cosmides, L. (2007). The architecture of human kin detection. *Nature, 445,* 727–731.

Macfarlan, S. J., Remiker, M., & Quinlan, R. (2012). Competitive altruism explains labor exchange variation in a dominican community. *Current Anthropology, 53,* 118–124.

Malinowski, B. (2003). *Argonauts of the Western Pacific: An account of native enterprise and adventure in the archipelagoes of Melanesian New Guinea*. New York: Routledge.

Meyer, M. L., Masten, C. L., Ma, Y., Wang, C., Shi, Z., Eisenberger, N. I., & Han, S. (2013). Empathy for the social suffering of friends and strangers recruits distinct patterns of brain activation. *Social Cognitive and Affective Neuroscience, 8*(4), 446–454.

Micheletta, J., Waller, B. M., Panggur, M. R., Neumann, C., Duboscq, J., Agil, M., & Engelhardt, A. (2012). Social bonds affect anti-predator behaviour in a tolerant species of macaque, Macaca nigra. *Proceedings of the Royal Society B: Biological Sciences, 279,* 4042–4050.

Nesse, R. M. (2007). Runaway social selection for displays of partner value and altruism. *Biological Theory, 2,* 143–155.

Neyer, F. J., Wrzus, C., Wagner, J., & Lang, F. R. (2011). Principles of relationship differentiation. *European Psychologist, 16,* 267–277.

Niiya, Y., & Ellsworth, P. C. (2012). Acceptability of favor requests in the United States and Japan. *Journal of Cross-Cultural Psychology, 43,* 273–285.

Niiya, Y., Ellsworth, P. C., & Yamaguchi, S. (2006). Amae in Japan and the United States: An exploration of a "culturally unique" emotion. *Emotion, 6,* 279–295.

Noë, R., & Hammerstein, P. (1995). Biological markets. *Trends in Ecology & Evolution, 10,* 336–339.

Oswald, D. L., Clark, E. M., & Kelly, C. M. (2004). Friendship maintenance: An analysis of individual and dyad behaviors. *Journal of Social and Clinical Psychology, 23,* 413–441.

Park, J. H., & Ackerman, J. M. (2011). Passion and compassion: Psychology of kin relations within and beyond the family. In C. Salmon & T. Shackelford (Eds.), *The Oxford handbook of evolutionary family psychology* (pp. 329–344). Oxford: Oxford University Press.

Park, J. H., & Schaller, M. (2005). Does attitude similarity serve as a heuristic cue for kinship? Evidence of an implicit cognitive association. *Evolution and Human Behavior, 26,* 158–170.

Peng, M., Chang, L., & Zhou, R. (2013). Physiological and behavioral responses to strangers compared to friends as a source of disgust. *Evolution and Human Behavior, 34,* 94–98.

Platek, S. M., & Kemp, S. M. (2009). Is family special to the brain? An event-related fMRI study of familiar, familial, and self-face recognition. *Neuropsychologia, 47,* 849–858.

Pronin, E., Olivola, C. Y., & Kennedy, K. A. (2008). Doing unto future selves as you would do unto others:

Psychological distance and decision making. *Personality and Social Psychology Bulletin, 34,* 224–236.
Rachlin, H., & Jones, B. A. (2008). Altruism among relatives and non-relatives. *Behavioural Processes, 79,* 120–123.
Raschen, J. (1919). Earlier and later versions of the friendship-theme. I "Damon and Pythias". *Modern Philology, 17,* 105–109.
Roberts, G. (1998). Competitive altruism: From reciprocity to the handicap principle. *Proceedings of the Royal Society of London. Series B: Biological Sciences, 265,* 427–431.
Schaefer, D. R. (2012). Homophily through nonreciprocity: Results of an experiment. *Social Forces, 90,* 1271–1295.
Schino, G. (2007). Grooming and agonistic support: A meta-analysis of primate reciprocal altruism. *Behavioral Ecology, 18,* 115–120.
Schino, G., & Aureli, F. (2009). Reciprocal altruism in primates: Partner choice, cognition, and emotions. *Advances in the Study of Behavior, 39,* 45–69.
See, L. (2009). *Snow flower and the secret fan: A novel.* New York: Random House Digital, Inc.
Silk, J. B. (2003). Cooperation without counting. In P. Hammerstein (Ed.), *Genetic and cultural evolution of cooperation* (pp. 37–54). Cambridge: MIT Press.
Stewart-Williams, S. (2007). Altruism among kin vs. nonkin: Effects of cost of help and reciprocal exchange. *Evolution and Human Behavior, 28,* 193–198.
Strombach, T., Jin, J., Weber, B., Kenning, P., Shen, Q., Ma, Q., & Kalenscher, T. (in press). Charity begins at home: Cultural differences in social discounting and generosity. *Journal of Behavioral Decision Making.*
Sugiyama, L. S. (2004). Illness, injury, and disability among Shiwiar forager-horticulturalists: Implications of health-risk buffering for the evolution of human life history. *American Journal of Physical Anthropology, 123,* 371–389.
Sylwester, K., & Roberts, G. (2010). Cooperators benefit through reputation-based partner choice in economic games. *Biology Letters, 6,* 659–662.
Tooby, J., & Cosmides, L. (1996). Friendship and the banker's paradox: Other pathways to the evolution of adaptations for altruism. *Proceedings of the British Academy, 88,* 119–143.
Vollan, B. (2011). The difference between kinship and friendship: (Field-) experimental evidence on trust and punishment. *Journal of Socio-Economics, 40,* 14–25.
Winter, F., & Kataria, M. (2013). You are who your friends are: An experiment on trust and homophily in friendship networks. Available at SSRN 2347536.
Xue, M. (2013). Altruism and reciprocity among friends and kin in a Tibetan village. *Evolution and Human Behavior, 34,* 323–329.
Xue, M., & Silk, J. B. (2012). The role of tracking and tolerance in relationship among friends. *Evolution and Human Behavior, 33,* 17–25.
Yamakawa, Y., Kanai, R., Matsumura, M., & Naito, E. (2009). Social distance evaluation in human parietal cortex. *PLoS One, 4*(2), e4360.

Evolutionary and Social Psychological Perspectives on Human Cooperation

21

Mike Prentice and Kennon M. Sheldon

The interface of evolutionary and social psychological perspectives on human cooperation has provided the basis of a generative conundrum in science for decades. On the one hand, it is clear from both lay and scientific observation and experimentation that people (and many other species) are often very cooperative. For example, recent research suggests that the "canonical model" of the purely self-interested human fails uniformly across cultures (Henrich et al. 2005; see also Caporael et al. 1989). On the other hand, this behavior is hard to square with the fact that cooperative choices almost always produce lesser outcomes for individuals, at least within a single encounter, and it is hard to imagine the adaptive advantages to such behaviors. The past 50 or so years have seen some resolution of the problem through conceptual and empirical progress, particularly thanks to notions of inclusive fitness and reciprocal altruism, which allow for concern beyond the self that can be advantageous over time. Further, the integration of evolutionary and psychological perspectives has provided useful explanations from different directions. The evolutionary explanations are often ultimate and examine how cooperative behavior could reflect advantageous strategy. The psychological perspective often seeks more proximate explanations for cooperative behavior, examining, for example, individual differences in cooperative tendencies and situational factors that influence cooperative behavior. Because these explanations are more proximate, they provide more specific answers to the question of why people cooperate. Combining the two perspectives, then, can provide a more complete answer to why and under what circumstances people cooperate.

And this is an important question as humanity approaches some of the most complex collective dilemmas it has ever faced in the forms of ever greater global interdependence, resource depletion, continued population growth, and climate change. Recently, an entire volume has been dedicated to the subject of human cooperation, and within it entire chapters were dedicated to evolutionary and psychological perspectives in turn (Van Lange et al. 2014). The more circumscribed goal of this chapter is to note some major themes across these perspectives and point to potential areas of integration in the pursuit of understanding human cooperation.

Human Life as an N-person Iterated Dilemma

The Social Dilemma Framework

The view from the evolutionary perspective is typically that individuals compete with one an-

M. Prentice (✉) · K. M. Sheldon
Department of Psychology, University of Missouri, 210 McAlester Hall, Columbia, MO 65211, USA
e-mail: mptg2@mail.missouri.edu

K. M. Sheldon
e-mail: sheldonk@missouri.edu

V. Zeigler-Hill et al. (eds.), *Evolutionary Perspectives on Social Psychology*, Evolutionary Psychology,
DOI 10.1007/978-3-319-12697-5_21, © Springer International Publishing Switzerland 2015

other for limited resources—both material (territory, food) and social (status, reputation). Those behavioral strategies that best serve to navigate these competitive situations toward successful reproductive outcomes should be selected for, such that the genes attending those strategies increase in frequency in the population over the generations. If it was the case that peoples' fates were never interrelated, then there would be no reason to expect that people would deviate from pure competitive strategies because there could be no advantage to this. However, our outcomes are often correlated. In the short term, it is often advantageous to cooperate to solve a specific problem that could potentially be impossible going it alone. In the long term, human groups share resource bases that are subject to exhaustion. Social dilemmas reflect the tension that occurs when self-interest meets correlated outcomes, as these dilemmas are situations in which individuals' outcomes are interdependent with, and thus dependent upon other individuals' actions and choices, as well as their own actions and choices. In social dilemmas, it is often tempting to act primarily according to one's self-interest—particularly due to the allure of short-term gains—but if everyone acted this way then everyone would be worse off over time (Van Dijk et al. 2013).

Thus, a social dilemma perspective—grounded in evolutionary notions of adaptive strategies—can provide a relatively comprehensive framework for considering individual behavior in its social context, broadly speaking. Such a perspective focuses on how decision making in interpersonal contexts leads to different outcomes for the participants in interactions. The paradigmatic dilemma that has historically grounded much research is the prisoner's dilemma (Poundstone 1993). Two men, coconspirators in a crime, are being questioned separately by the district attorney. If both keep quiet, they know that the minimal evidence against them will lead to minimal sentences for each of them. But what if one of the men cuts a deal, confessing to the district attorney in exchange for immunity? In this case, the confessor will go free, and the other man, who tries to cooperate by refusing to confess, will bear the punitive brunt. Given this, can either man afford to take the risk of cooperating, especially in the face of the temptation to "defect" and perhaps get away clean? Maybe so, given that if both men confess (i.e., defect), then things will turn out worse for both of them than if neither had confessed. This is the dilemma.

There is no a priori way to know which choice (cooperation or defection) one should make, because it depends so heavily on what the other person does. Evolutionary game theory attempts to mathematically model the various possible strategies and decision rules in order to understand which strategies and approaches lead to the best outcomes. In principle, the most effective strategies are also the ones that should have evolved, and thus should manifest in human psychology.

Of course, the optimal strategy will vary depending on a wide variety of factors. For example, in addition to two-person prisoner's dilemmas, there are also multiple-person prisoner's dilemmas in which individual payoffs depend on the decisions of several people instead of just one other person. An additional factor is that in any type of dilemma there are a large number of possible payoff matrices, which determine how much each participant receives in a particular dilemma. For example, does mutual defection lead to the worst outcome, or to the second-worst outcome? How large is the numerical value representing the "temptation to defect," or the value representing the "sucker's payoff" that results when a person is exploited? Yet another factor is the wide variety of social-contextual conditions that can surround the game. For example, is there a sanctioning system in place? Have prosocial norms been made salient? Can protagonists communicate with each other? Still another factor is that games can vary widely in their length. For example, is it a one-shot dilemma, or an iterated dilemma that goes on for many trials, such that participants have the opportunity to respond to and adapt to each other? Finally, there are also multiple types of dilemmas besides prisoner's dilemmas.

Another important type of social dilemma is the resource dilemma, in which individuals have the opportunity to draw from a common community pool. Resource dilemmas are multi-person dilemmas, in which the temptation is to take more than one's fair share of the commons. This can happen because of greed (the desire to get something for nothing), fear (that others will exploit the resource, so one should "get while the getting's good"), or both. Unfortunately, the more individuals pursue this over-acquisitive strategy, the more quickly the resource collapses, leading to what Hardin (1968) referred to as "the tragedy of the commons." Indeed, it may be that the twenty-first century will see the playing out of a *global* tragedy of the commons driven by increasing population pressure on available resources and the broadly embraced belief that material success is essential for "the good life" (Myers 2000).

Related to the resource dilemma is the public goods dilemma, in which the problem is to get people to contribute to a public good, rather than keeping people from abusing it. For example, when we suffer an accident, we all hope that there is blood available in the community blood bank. But do we donate blood? Often not—instead, we yield to the temptation not to contribute (i.e., we defect). Similarly, public radio requires the support of public pledges. However, as pledge-drive managers can attest, motivating people to call up the station to give away their money "for nothing" can be a difficult! Thus, public goods dilemmas may be particularly difficult to solve, because they require people to take intentional actions that are somewhat costly.

As these examples illustrate, cooperation is a potentially risky personal strategy within many social dilemmas, even those that are iterated and shared among many individuals. Because of the assumption of individual selfishness made by traditional evolutionary theory, it was long thought that genes coding for cooperative behavior would have a disadvantage in the evolutionary arms race (Axelrod 1984). However, contemporary developments in evolutionary theory have begun to make a clearer place for cooperative behavior and suggest that cooperative tendencies may reflect something of a human default. Below, we outline some general theories that predict when cooperation will emerge in populations and examine some potential instantiations of these in humans.

Inclusive Fitness One important advance for understanding apparent non-self-interest in evolutionary theory was provided by Hamilton's theory of inclusive fitness (Hamilton 1964). Focusing on the gene as the unit of selection (Dawkins 1976), Hamilton recognized that cooperative behavior might evolve because it benefits individuals who are related to the self, even if the behavior incurs some cost to oneself. For example, although a young male may die defending his family against attack, this self-sacrificial behavior could still be selected for because overall it benefits copies of the genes of those who emit them that exist in others, for example, in the young man's brothers and sisters. More specifically, Hamilton proposed that the likelihood of self-sacrificial behavior should follow the degree of relatedness between any two individuals. Thus, the brother should be more willing to exhibit self-sacrificial behavior for a full sibling than for a half sibling. Importantly, nepotistic behavior is only to be expected when the species tends to live among kin; otherwise, there would generally not be opportunities to help individuals with whom one is closely related (Hamilton 1987).

Reciprocal Altruism Inclusive fitness follows straightforwardly from selfish genes, but could cooperative behavior evolve even for unrelated actors? Reciprocal altruism theory (Trivers 1971) suggests that it could. A gene or complex of genes that prompted individuals to help others in need could be adaptive *if* that other would do the same for you, were the situations reversed. In other words, cooperating with others might be advantageous to a person if the cooperation was reciprocated at a future time when one could in turn derive a considerable benefit from the help. Whether that future reciprocation occurs, however, could be very uncertain if those individuals you previously helped are "free riders," capitalizing on your generosity without paying the cost. Despite this threat to reciprocity, it is clear that humans have somehow managed to keep the risk of free riding low enough to maintain public goods. We have social welfare agencies, international relief organizations, charitable foundations, and many less formal supports for the disadvantaged, who are typically unrelated to their benefactors.

How is this reciprocity established and maintained? Reciprocal altruism and the vulnerability it introduces add the requirement of a compensatory sensitivity to the possibility of being exploited by others who might take undue advantage of one's help and charity, otherwise generosity is a sucker's proposition. That is, reciprocity requires the ability to detect cheaters (Cosmides and Tooby 1992). The idea that reciprocal altruism and cheater detection are linked evolved social strategies is well illustrated in Axelrod's computer simulation tournaments. Axelrod's (1984) competition compared the functional efficacy of a wide variety of strategies for playing iterated two-person prisoner's dilemmas, and they demonstrated that the winning strategies tended to have two qualities: They were "nice," meaning that they cooperated on the first move, and they were "punitive," meaning that they did not tolerate the other's defection. If the opponent defects, a tit-for-tat strategy "remembers" and always defects immediately, in retaliation, as it were. In terms of the concepts developed above, "niceness" is analogous to the willingness to seek reciprocal altruism (i.e., mutually beneficial relations). "Punitiveness" is analogous to cheater detection and punishment, a characteristic without which cooperation cannot be maintained.

To better reflect the environments in which organisms can make cooperative decisions, more recent models of reciprocity have incorporated other important variables that help maintain cooperation as a stable strategy: variability, choice, and time. Specifically, when there are both cooperative and competitive prospective exchange partners, some individuals will primarily exchange with cooperative others (i.e., they are choosey), and choosey cooperators will tend to assort over time and thus "lock in" to mutually beneficial relationships (McNamara et al. 2008) and out-compete less cooperative, less choosey interactors. Most of the above can be considered reflections of direct reciprocity in which possibilities of future reciprocation are plausible. However, sometimes people cooperate with no clear chance for reciprocation from the recipient of their initial generosity, simply responding to cooperative reputational information of another. This is a reflection of indirect reciprocity, whereby cooperative acts are initiated to maintain a reputation such that others who may receive your reputational information are inclined to help you out later (Roberts 2008).

Costly Signaling How could one invite cooperative advances from others over time? One way may be to somehow communicate the ability to cooperate in a way that is obvious to all (McAndrew 2002). For example, one could make a donation in one's own name to a local charity, and then it would be clear to all who saw the donor list that you participated to better the public good and they would likely infer that you are generally cooperative. That donation is obviously an expenditure of your own resources, so it is a costly signal that one has the resources to spare and the capacities to acquire them in the first place, as well as the willingness to share. Thus, costly signals tend to be honest signals because there is a fitness cost associated with having the signaled quality (Gintis et al. 2001). As another example, if an individual makes the choice to actively and unilaterally punish a cheater, there is a cost involved through the altercation, but that individual also gains reputation for taking the initiative and having the necessary capacities to punish for the sake of the group.

Advantageous Cooperation in Groups In what other ways might the risks be mitigated, such that cooperation becomes a more viable strategy? Some have posited the possibility of group or multilevel selection (see McAndrew 2002). That is, some cooperation that is costly to oneself may benefit the group and provide group-level advantages. This concept has been controversial in evolutionary biology because of the implication that imperatives beyond the selfish gene could provide a locus for selection pressure. Further, other criticism points out that group selection and inclusive fitness are equivalent (Sober 1999), so it is just a redescription for an already articulated theory. Still, the group process lens may be useful for considering human cooperation, despite whether it is ultimately best captured by the theories outlined above, so we provide an illustrative example. In order for group processes to confer advantages due to cooperation, it must be the case that cooperative groups outperform competitive ones and that cooperators can find each other, as in the computer models by McNamara et al. (2008).

Sheldon and McGregor (2000) demonstrated that cooperative groups can be more advantageous than competitive ones in a laboratory study of the tragedy of the commons. Participants were first placed into groups of four, based on their scores on a measure of prosocial values (i.e., a measure of intrinsic versus extrinsic valuing; Kasser and Ryan 1996). Some groups consisted of four participants with predominantly prosocial values (i.e., community, intimacy, growth); some groups consisted of four participants with predominantly self-serving values (i.e., money, fame, beauty); and some groups consisted of two of each type. Participants made repeated bids concerning a group resource (i.e., a forest). The forest replenished at a 10% rate after each harvest, and each group continued bidding until their forest was gone. Sheldon and McGregor examined whether it was the case that "nice groups finish first," by showing that predominantly prosocial groups received the largest score in the resource dilemma.

Hierarchical modeling revealed support for this idea, but also suggested a more complex picture. Specifically, an individual's value scores had contradictory influence upon individual harvest totals, at within-group and between-group levels of analysis. Group members who were more prosocial than their group mates harvested less, because of their self-restraint, and thus did worse, within-groups. However, members of groups that were more prosocial than the other groups harvested more, because of their group's aggregate ability to preserve the resource. Overall, intrinsic individuals did no better or worse than extrinsic individuals, because the two types of effect essentially cancelled out.

Thus, it appears that the outcomes for dispositional cooperators are crucially dependent on a particular factor: The extent to which cooperators are concentrated within groups, such that would-be exploiters have been excluded from their midst. Without this, they are at a disadvantage. Could prosocial types achieve such an assortative arrangement on their own? If it were not the case that cooperators were also "choosey," then it would be difficult for cooperators to maintain their advantage (McNamara et al. 2008).

Sheldon et al. (2000) addressed the group-assortation question by inviting college students to play an N-person prisoner's dilemma game for movie ticket prizes (which went to the top 15% of game-scorers). Participants completed questionnaires in which they listed three friends, to whom the researchers also sent questionnaires. All participants' values were assessed, including both primary and secondary (participant-selected) participants. Participants and their friends constituted self-selected groups, whose outcomes were pooled over five rounds of bidding in a social dilemma, in order to determine each individual's total outcome.

First, Sheldon et al. (2000) demonstrated that significant value-based assortation had occurred among the groups; specifically, participants with intrinsic values tended to select other intrinsic participants for their groups, and vice versa for participants with more extrinsic values. Such heterogeneity at the group level is an important precondition for group selection to occur (Sober 1999)—if groups do not differ, then there can be no advantage in belonging to one group, rather than another. In particular, this heterogeneity between groups (and homogeneity within groups) indicates that those with prosocial values can indeed successfully assort with each other.

Second, Sheldon et al. (2000) showed that intrinsic values had a significant positive effect on participant game-scores at the between-group level of analysis, and a significant negative effect on game-score at the within-group level of analysis, replicating the finding of Sheldon and McGregor (2000). Because of these largely canceling effects, intrinsic individuals fared no worse than extrinsic individuals, on average. Although this may not sound impressive, it was actually quite striking given the intrinsic types' much greater vulnerability to exploitation. By aggregating themselves into groups, they managed to completely mitigate this disadvantage.

Despite the possible reducibility of group selection to inclusive fitness cited above, appeals to theoretical pluralism are generally for highlighting the heuristic values of the different ways of thinking, rather than maintaining them as separable. One advantage of the group-selection perspective is that in addition to clearly modeling the group-level benefit, it can also model the vulnerabilities of individuals within cooperative groups. For example, what happens to animals that readily perform the sentry duty, compared to animals that shirk this duty (i.e., "free riders" who do not contribute to the public good)? How bad does the within-group free rider problem have to get, before the between-group advantage disappears? In addition, the multilevel perspective allows for more intuitive framing of possible interactions between within- and between-group variables. For example, the within-group effectiveness of a particular individual strategy (e.g., Machiavellianism) may depend upon the particular group-type or context in which the person is nested (i.e., gullible versus savvy groups). Thus, regardless of the debate about theoretical reducibility, the group-selection way of thinking may be particularly useful for psychologists considering group composition and individual strategies within short-term settings.

Another interesting—albeit controversial—idea in the area of evolution of cooperation in humans concerns purposive selection. Specifically, human purposes may have had an effect on natural selection processes in that the maintenance of cooperation in small groups would have required punishing cheaters and rewarding cooperators (Boehm 2008). To the extent that these group processes of punishment and status conferral could influence reproductive success across generations (i.e., become a consistent environmental pressure), then one would expect them to provide a source of selection pressure that follows from the purpose of cooperation maintenance. Indeed, they do seem capable of this, as Boehm notes that political bullies are frequently the subjects of executions, and often the traits that stimulate social approval are willingness to share and cooperate (Boehm 2008). It is important to note that this perspective, like the irreducible perspective on group selection, allows for unorthodox sources of evolutionary causality, which may be grounds for healthy skepticism. But those sources may also hold promise for better explaining the extent of cooperative tendencies and sanctioning processes evident in humans today, in particular.

Summary The preceding sections have outlined the evolutionary game theoretical perspective on cooperation and some theories that address questions of whether we should expect cooperation to arise in certain contexts as well as why we should have those expectations. At the most basic level, evolutionary processes should select for those tendencies that function to maintain many genetic replicates in the population (and their opportunities for replication), for example, through inclusive fitness processes, and to accrue individuals' opportunities to replicate further, for example, through participating reciprocally in mutually beneficial relationships over time and communicating one's value along cooperative dimensions. In the next section, we will examine more proximate explanations of human cooperation by examining the psychology of human cooperation.

Psychological Considerations

Humans are not privy to the calculus of their genetic information or the environments that shaped it, nor do they have foresight of all adaptive challenges their environments will produce over their life spans. Rather, they come equipped with a set of mechanisms that have proven to be adaptive on average given past environments that can be triggered given the appropriate eliciting stimuli. Cooperative behaviors and the thoughts and feelings people experience when they make them are thus far removed from the ultimate questions that guide them. If you ask your friend why she donated to a charity, she is unlikely to say that she calculated her coefficient of relatedness to the recipients. Instead, she is more likely to say that it "felt like the right thing to do" or that she is "just someone who likes to donate to causes like that." These psychological explanations are just as valid as evolutionary ones and not ultimately incompatible, but psychological explanations change the focus from distal fitness imperatives to the individuals with dispositions to think, feel, and behave in particular ways given particular situations and adaptive challenges in their environments.

In the sections that follow, we outline a few major themes of psychological research on cooperation. Specifically, we focus on various situational characteristics that impact cooperative behavior, as well as individual differences in cooperative tendencies. Throughout, we note where we can make sense of the psychological explanations in terms of evolutionary theories.

Like the evolutionary perspective, research in psychology has also wrestled with the abstract question of whether humans are primarily interested in maximizing short-term personal gain. The short answer across numerous studies, like the cross-cultural studies by Henrich et al. (2005), is generally no. People often seek better long-term outcomes that, in the context of group living, require cooperative efforts with others. As alluded to above, there are a few key factors that inform whether individuals cooperate or the extent to which they cooperate: personal dispositions, situational features, and time. Below, we sketch some key considerations along each of these factors.

Individual Differences

Social value orientation is perhaps the most heavily studied individual difference in the social dilemma context in psychology (reviewed in Balliet et al. 2009). Social value orientation measurement is based on decomposed prisoner's dilemma games (Messick and McClintock 1968) in which participants allocate points to self and an imagined other they do not know and will not meet. Unlike the dilemmas outlined above, the payoffs for self and other are wholly dependent on the choices of the participant and the payoff matrix. From this decision making, researchers can categorize participants into prosocials, individualists, and competitors (though others are possible, these are the most common types). Prosocials tend toward decisions that emphasize joint gain. Individualists tend to maximize personal gain without regard to the outcomes of others. Competitors tend to maximize the distance between self and other, negatively weighting others' gains in their decisions.

Thus, it appears that each orientation is informed by a few basic motives. Prosocials appear to pursue not only joint gain but also equality (Van Lange 1999), and competitors and individualists pursue neither (Van Lange and Van Doesum 2012). If anything, the motives of competitors are aimed at inequality. Supporting this motivational view, research has shown that prosocials are angered by exchange violations regardless of the impact those violations have on their own personal outcomes, whereas individualists and competitors do not exhibit this equality violation response if their outcomes are not impacted (Stouten et al. 2005). Further, in everyday life, it appears prosocials donate more to charities in general, and aim their donations especially toward those that help the disadvantaged (Van Lange et al. 2007) and identify with more egalitarian political groups (Van Lange et al. 2012).

Another construct that appears to index the egalitarian motive is found in the values people report to hold dear. If people say that they find helping their communities or being benevolent toward others to be more centrally important than personal financial gain and social power, then this likely reflects the same underlying dimension along which prosocials, individualists, and competitors fall when measured by decomposed games. A potential criticism to this mode of measurement, as suggested by the evolutionary theories above, is that people may pose as more prosocial than they really are to reap the benefits of a good reputation. However, it appears this technique identifies real-world cooperators as well. For example, people who endorse affiliation and community feeling engage in more ecologically responsible behavior in their everyday lives (Brown and Kasser 2005) and identify with egalitarian political groups (Sheldon and Nichols 2009), whereas people who centrally value extrinsic pursuits of money and fame are more antiegalitarian and ethnically prejudiced (Duriez et al. 2007) and experience more interpersonal conflict (Kasser and Ryan 2001). Further, recent research suggests that cooperative primes are more likely to generate cooperative behavior for people identified as more prosocial on this measure than those identified as less prosocial (Prentice and Sheldon 2015). Thus, it may be possible to activate cooperative motives through situational primes, but this will be most effective for those who strongly represent the reward of cooperation in their value systems.

Recent reviews suggest that the majority of people are prosocial and competitors are in the minority (Au and Kwong 2004). Even toddlers exhibit interdependent morality, working together, recognizing joint outcomes, and dividing resources equally (Thomasello and Vaish 2013). What, then, are the roots of an overly competitive or exploitative interpersonal orientation? One explanation may be that it reflects a heritable trait that fills a niche in the midst of high cooperation. But exploitation invites punishment, and risk-conferring heritable genotypes often require releasing stimuli for phenotypic expression. One candidate for the release of competitive phenotypes is psychological insecurity—when environments and relationships are fundamentally unstable and inconsistent. Consistent with this idea, Kasser et al. (1995) showed that children raised in insecure neighborhoods or by cold, controlling parents are more likely to develop competitive values. Similarly, Van Lange et al. (1997) showed that competitive orientations are associated with insecure attachment, and Sheldon and Kasser (2008) provided experimental evidence that insecurity causes a more acquisitive orientation.

Again, competitive or extrinsic orientations may be appropriate strategies given competitive circumstance. The potential problem with dispositional competitiveness comes later on, when circumstances change for the better—in this case the competitor may not be able to reform, feeling that life has handed him a "bum deal," that it is a dog-eat-dog world, and that he is deserving of compensation and special rewards. Still, there is also some reason for optimism regarding peoples' ability to shift towards more cooperative strategies as a result of life experience. For example, Sheldon (1999) conducted repeated prisoner's dilemma tournaments, one month apart, in which all participants faced a tit-for-tat strategy during the first session, and participants were randomly paired against other participants in the second session. Sheldon showed that even those with competitive dispositions switched to more cooperation during the second session, as a result of having faced the "punitive" tit-for-tat in the first session; that is, they had accommodated their strategy to the fact that exploiting the opponent was not feasible.

Situational Factors

We have alluded to the importance of the potential for punishment above, and this is just one example of a situational factor that can impact whether individuals and groups cooperate, and an extremely important one. Other key situational factors include rewards for cooperation, opportunities for sanctions, and the potential payoff matrix that interactors face. Each of these has effects on cooperative behavior, and we detail some examples below.

Payoff matrices determine how much of a dilemma the dilemma really is, or how tempting defection for short-term gain may be. For example, in the context of a group academic project, one may be guaranteed the passing grade that the cooperative members will ensure without putting in much effort oneself. In this situation, conflict is high because a member could stand to gain a great deal for nothing and the other group members could suffer considerably because they are missing the contribution of one member. Thus, the payoff matrix alone exhibits a strong pull on behavior. But people still cooperate in high conflict situations, so how does this come about? One prominent variable is trust, which is the acceptance of vulnerability in the pursuit of dependent outcomes and the maintenance of positive expectations for others' behaviors. Indeed, trust has been shown to attenuate the breakdown of cooperation as dilemma conflict increases (reviewed in Balliet and Van Lange 2013).

But trust is not always present and may be hard to instill in the face of high conflict or interaction histories that were competitive. One way to overcome the problem of low trust is to introduce the opportunity for sanctions or punishments (Yamagishi 1986). In the same way that sanctions can be an effective means of bringing parties to the table to cooperate in international affairs, they can also be used in other dilemmas. However, sanctions do pose some risk to sustaining cooperative outcomes. In some circumstances, sanctions lead people to perceive the dilemma as a business exchange, rather than an ethical exchange in which egalitarian motives may be salient (Tenbrunsel and Messick 1999).

Less formal types of sanctioning could take the form of ostracism and social exclusion or loss of reputation, which suggests that loss of reputation in itself could provide a basis for cooperation maintenance. Thus, the signaling value of cooperative behavior, rather than the immediate cooperative situation, may provide a source of motivation for acting cooperatively. Indeed, it appears that self-sacrificial behavior can win a person reputational gains (McAndrew and Perilloux 2012), and that signaling constitutes something of a market within cooperative dilemmas. Underscoring this, Parks and Stone (2010) demonstrated that people who were *too* cooperative were subject to sanctioning, as it seemed that they were violating norms for how much reputation one could take away from the dilemma. Therefore, a free rider may be the subject of disdain, but perhaps so too the smug saint.

Temporal Considerations

That the situational factors surrounding dilemmas often become important because of long-term reputational concerns points to another important factor impacting social dilemmas: time. As the results of McNamara et al.'s (2008) simulation of choosey cooperators and Sheldon et al.'s (2000) in vivo assortation effects demonstrate, people need time to figure out who has a good reputation or actually is a cooperator through direct experience. Not only does time facilitate assortation but it also weighs on people's decision making within social dilemmas. For example, people who tend to weigh the long-term consequences of their behavior (see Strathman et al. 1994) were more likely to limit consumption in a resource dilemma (Kortenkamp and Moore 2006). Extrapolating from this, shifting participant's time perspective may also impact dilemma behavior, and indeed it appears to do so. In one set of studies, participants with individualist and competitive values who were primed with a long-term perspective exhibited less behavioral greed in take-some dilemmas (Cozzolino et al. 2009). Finally, the temporal dimension also allows for interaction learning to occur such that participants can learn that a cooperative strategy would be more fruitful than a competitive one and make appropriate adjustments (Sheldon 1999) as well as for groups to establish cooperative norms by witnessing the behavior of consistent contributors (Weber and Murnighan 2008).

Conclusion

For the early decades of social psychology, it was difficult to see how the ready cooperation humans could exhibit (e.g., given a shared obstacle; Sherif 1966) could be integrated with the austere survival imperatives implied by Darwinian evolutionary theory. More recent developments now indicate that human nature is deeply cooperative, and that this is not incompatible with evolutionary processes. Pinker (2011), in *The Better Angels of our Nature,* noted not only this cooperative capacity but also something yet more optimistic: Human cooperation has demonstrably improved for centuries, as underlined by declines in violence across the globe. Human culture and modern commerce depend on an incredibly complex network of dependencies and codependencies, as do relationships between individual actors. The questions now are, "how do we manage to pull this off?" and "how can we use this information to pull it off even better?" Hopefully, we can harness our cooperative potentials even further, so that humanity can navigate some of the perilous cooperative bottlenecks looming in the twenty-first century.

References

Au, W. T., & Kwong, J. Y. Y. (2004). Measurements and effects of social-value orientation in social dilemmas. In R. Suleiman (Ed.), *Contemporary psychological research on social dilemmas* (pp. 71–98). New York: Cambridge University Press.

Axelrod, R. (1984). *The evolution of cooperation*. New York: Basic Books.

Balliet, D., & Van Lange, P. A. M. (2013). Trust, conflict, and cooperation: A meta-analysis. *Psychological Bulletin, 139,* 1090–1112. doi:10.1037/a0030939.

Balliet, D., Parks, C., & Joireman, J. (2009). Social value orientation and cooperation in social dilemmas: A meta-analysis. *Group Processes and Intergroup Relations, 12,* 533–547. doi:10.1177/1368430209105040.

Boehm, C. (2008). Purposive social selection and the evolution of human altruism. *Cross-Cultural Research, 42,* 319–352. doi:10.1177/1069397108320422.

Brown, K. W., & Kasser, T. (2005). Are psychological and ecological well-being compatible? The role of values, mindfulness, and lifestyle. *Social Indicators Research, 74,* 349–368. doi:10.1007/s11205-004-8207-8.

Caporael, L. R., Dawes, R. M., Orbell, J. M., & Van de Kragt, A. J. (1989). Selfishness examined: Cooperation in the absence of egoistic incentives. *Behavioral and Brain Sciences, 12,* 683–739. doi:10.1017/S0140525X00025292.

Cosmides, L., & Tooby, J. (1992). Cognitive adaptations for social exchange. In J. H. Barkow, L. Cosmides, & J. Tooby (Eds.), *The adapted mind: Evolutionary psychology and the generation of culture* (pp. 163–228). New York: Oxford University Press.

Cozzolino, P. J., Sheldon, K. M., Schachtman, T. R., & Meyers, L. S. (2009). Limited time perspective, values, and greed: Imagining a limited future reduces avarice in extrinsic people. *Journal of Research in Personality, 43,* 399–408. doi:10.1016/j.jrp.2009.01.008.

Dawkins, R. (1976). *The selfish gene*. New York: Oxford University Press.

Duriez, B., Vansteenkiste, M., Soenens, B., & De Witte, H. (2007). The social costs of extrinsic relative to intrinsic goal pursuits: Their relation with social dominance and racial and ethnic prejudice. *Journal of Personality, 75,* 757–782. doi:10.1111/j.1467-6494.2007.00456.x.

Gintis, H., Smith, E. A., & Bowles, S. (2001). Costly signaling and cooperation. *Journal of Theoretical Biology, 213,* 103–119. doi:10.1006/jtbi.2001.2406.

Hamilton, W. D. (1964). The genetical evolution of social behaviour. I. *Journal of Theoretical Biology, 7,* 1–16.

Hamilton, W. D. (1987). Discriminating nepotism: expectable, common, overlooked. In D. J. C. Fletcher & C. D. Michener (Eds.), *Kin recognition in animals* (pp. 417–437). New York: Wiley.

Henrich, J., Boyd, R., Bowles, S., Camerer, C., Fehr, E., Gintis, H., McElreath, R., Alvard, M., Barr, A., Ensminger, J., Henrich, N. S., Hill, K., Gil-White, F., Gurven, M., Marlowe F. W., Patton J. Q., & Tracer, D. (2005). Models of decision-making and the coevolution of social preferences. *Behavioral and Brain Sciences, 28,* 838–855. doi:10.1017/S0140525X05460148.

Kasser, T., & Ryan, R. M. (1996). Further examining the American dream: Differential correlates of intrinsic and extrinsic goals. *Personality and Social Psychology Bulletin, 22,* 80–87.

Kasser, T., & Ryan, R. M. (2001). Be careful what you wish for: Optimal functioning and the relative attainment of intrinsic and extrinsic goals. In P. Schmuck & K. M. Sheldon (Eds.), *Life goals and well-being: Towards a positive psychology of human striving* (pp. 116–131). Goettingen: Hogrefe & Huber Publishers.

Kasser, T., Ryan, R. M., Zax, M., & Sameroff, A. J. (1995). The relations of maternal and social environments to late adolescents' materialistic and prosocial values. *Developmental Psychology, 31,* 907–914. doi:10.1037/0012-1649.31.6.907.

Kortenkamp, K. V., & Moore, C. F. (2006). Time, uncertainty, and individual differences in decisions to cooperate in resource dilemmas. *Personality and Social Psychology Bulletin, 32,* 603–615. doi:10.1177/0146167205284006.

McAndrew, F. T. (2002). New evolutionary perspectives on altruism: Multilevel-selection and costly-signaling theories. *Current Directions in Psychological Science, 11,* 79–82. doi:10.1111/1467-8721.00173.

McAndrew, F. T., & Perilloux, C. (2012). Is self-sacrificial competitive altruism primarily a male activity? *Evolutionary Psychology, 10,* 50–65.

McNamara, J. M., Barta, Z., Fromhage, L., & Houston, A. I. (2008). The coevolution of choosiness and cooperation. *Nature, 451,* 189–192. doi:10.1038/nature06455.

Messick, D. M., & McClintock, C. G. (1968). Motivational bases of choice in experimental games. *Journal of Experimental Social Psychology, 4,* 1–25. doi:10.1016/0022-1031(68)90046-2.

Myers, D. G. (2000). The funds, friends, and faith of happy people. *American Psychologist, 55,* 56–67. doi:10.1037/0003-066X.55.1.56.

Parks, C. D., & Stone, A. B. (2010). The desire to expel unselfish members from the group. *Journal of Personality and Social Psychology, 99,* 303–310. doi:10.1037/a0018403.

Pinker, S. (2011). *The better angels of our nature: Why violence has declined*. New York: Penguin.

Poundstone, W. (1993). *Prisoner's dilemma*. New York: Anchor Books.

Prentice, M., & Sheldon, K. M. (2015). Priming effects on cooperative behaviors in social dilemmas: Considering the prime and the person. *The Journal of Social Psychology, 155,* 163–181.

Roberts, G. (2008). Evolution of direct and indirect reciprocity. *Proceedings of the Royal Society B: Biological Sciences, 275,* 173–179. doi:10.1098/rspb.2007.1134.

Sheldon, K. M. (1999). Learning the lessons of tit-for-tat: Even competitors can get the message. *Journal of Personality and Social Psychology, 77,* 1245–1253. doi:10.1037/0022-3514.77.6.1245.

Sheldon, K. M., & Kasser, T. (2008). Psychological threat and extrinsic goal striving. *Motivation and Emotion, 32,* 37–45. doi:10.1007/s11031-008-9081-5.

Sheldon, K. M. & McGregor, H. (2000). Extrinsic value orientation and the 'tragedy of the commons.' *Journal of Personality, 68,* 383–411.

Sheldon, K. M., & Nichols, C. P. (2009). Comparing democrats and republicans on intrinsic and extrinsic values. *Journal of Applied Social Psychology, 39,* 589–623. doi:10.1111/j.1559-1816.2009.00452.x.

Sheldon, K.M., Sheldon, M.S., & Osbaldiston, R. (2000). Prosocial values and group-assortation within an N-person prisoner's dilemma. *Human Nature, 11,* 387–404.

Sherif, M. (1966). *In common predicament: Social psychology of intergroup conflict and cooperation*. Boston: Houghton Mifflin.

Sober, E. (1999). *Unto others: The evolution and psychology of unselfish behavior*. Cambridge: Harvard University Press.

Stouten, J., de Cremer, D., & van Dijk, E. (2005). All is well that ends well, at least for proselfs: emotional reactions to equality violation as a function of social value orientation. *European Journal of Social Psychology, 35,* 767–783. doi:10.1002/ejsp.276.

Strathman, A., Gleicher, F., Boninger, D. S., & Scott, C. (1994). The consideration of future consequences: Weighing immediate and distant outcomes of behavior. *Journal of Personality and Social Psychology, 66,* 742–752. doi:10.1037/0022-3514.66.4.742.

Tenbrunsel, A. E., & Messick, D. M. (1999). Sanctioning systems, decision frames, and cooperation. *Administrative Science Quarterly, 44,* 684–707. doi:10.2307/2667052.

Tomasello, M., & Vaish, A. (2013). Origins of human cooperation and morality. *Annual Review of Psychology, 64,* 231–255.

Trivers, R. (1971). The evoluition of reciprocal altruism. *Quarterly Review of Biology, 46,* 35–57.

Van Dijk, E., Parks, C. D., & van Lange, P. A. M. (2013). Social dilemmas: The challenge of human cooperation. *Organizational Behavior and Human Decision Processes, 120,* 123–124. doi:10.1016/j.obhdp.2012.12.005.

Van Lange, P. V. (1999). The pursuit of joint outcomes and equality in outcomes: An integrative model of social value orientation. *Journal of Personality and Social Psychology, 77,* 337–349. doi:10.1037/0022-3514.77.2.337.

Van Lange, P. A. M., & Van Doesum, N. J. (2012). The psychology of interaction goals comes as a package. *Psychological Inquiry, 23,* 75–79. doi:10.1080/1047840X.2012.657566.

Van Lange, P. A. M., Otten, W., & Joireman, J. A. (1997). Development of prosocial, individualistic, and competitive orientations: Theory and preliminary evidence. *Journal of Personality and Social Psychology, 73,* 733–746. doi:10.1037/0022-3514.73.4.733.

Van Lange, P. A. M., Bekkers, R., Schuyt, T. N. M., & Vugt, M. V. (2007). From games to giving: Social value orientation predicts donations to noble causes. *Basic and Applied Social Psychology, 29,* 375–384. doi:10.1080/01973530701665223.

Van Lange, P. A. M., Bekkers, R., Chirumbolo, A., & Leone, L. (2012). Are conservatives less likely to be prosocial than liberals? From games to ideology, political preferences and voting. *European Journal of Personality, 26,* 461–473. doi:10.1002/per.845.

Van Lange, P. A. M., Balliet, D. P., Parks, C. D., & van Vugt, M. (2014). *Social dilemmas: Understanding human cooperation*. New York: Oxford University Press.

Weber, J. M., & Murnighan, J. K. (2008). Suckers or saviors? Consistent contributors in social dilemmas. *Journal of Personality and Social Psychology, 95,* 1340–1353. doi:10.1037/a0012454.

Yamagishi, T. (1986). The provision of a sanctioning system as a public good. *Journal of Personality and Social Psychology, 51,* 110–116. doi:10.1037/0022-3514.51.1.110.

Language and Communication

22

Thomas C. Scott-Phillips

Even by primate standards, humans are a hugely social species. We live in large, highly interactive groups, in which various forms of both competition and collaboration are daily, routine activities. Indeed, this is why social psychology is such a major branch of psychology. Among the most important ways in which we navigate this social environment (if not the most important ways) are communication and language. We use them to lead, persuade, coax, guide, misguide, deceive, argue, promise, organize, liaise, coordinate, and manage almost all our social interactions.

There is a healthy and growing community of researchers studying the origins of language (see, e.g., Christiansen and Kirby 2003; Fitch 2010; Hurford 2007, 2011; Scott-Phillips 2014; Tomasello 2008). The central questions here are how and why language evolved in our species, and why only we have it. Less research asks, as its main focus, how an evolutionary perspective, and in particular an adaptationist perspective, can inform traditional questions about the social cognition and other proximate mechanisms involved in language and communication. This state of affairs is in contrast to, say, evolutionary psychology, whose principle concern is not to study the evolutionary history of the human mind, per se, but rather to use an evolutionary, adaptationist approach as a tool to understand how the human mind works (Cosmides and Tooby 2013).

In this chapter, I outline what an evolutionary perspective can tell us about human communication and language. The coverage is necessarily brief, but sufficient to highlight the main questions and possible answers, and bring attention to some important unanswered questions. In Sect. 2, I distinguish between two different types of communication, and explain why understanding this distinction is critical to understanding the nature of human communication, and, in Sect. 3, I discuss how the distinction relates to language in particular. In Sect. 4, I discuss possible evolutionary explanations of why languages are structured in the ways that they are. In Sect. 5, I explain what human communication should look like if it is adaptive, and survey evidence to show that it is. Finally, in Sects. 6 and 7, I focus on the possibility of misinformation and the associated problem of evolutionary stability: Section 6 is concerned with proximate mechanisms; Sect. 7 with ultimate explanations.

Section 2: Two Models of Communication

Communication is often conceptualized as information that is encoded into a message, which is then transmitted through some communication channel to be decoded at the other end. This approach is called the *code model*

T. C. Scott-Phillips (✉)
School of Psychology, Philosophy, & Language Sciences, Durham University, 3 Charles Street, EH8 9AD Edinburgh, Scotland, UK
e-mail: t.c.scott-phillips@durham.ac.uk

V. Zeigler-Hill et al. (eds.), *Evolutionary Perspectives on Social Psychology*, Evolutionary Psychology, DOI 10.1007/978-3-319-12697-5_22, © Springer International Publishing Switzerland 2015

of communication. The idea at the core of the code model is that communication is made possible by mechanisms of association: between the state of the world and a signal (for signalers); and between a signal and a response (for receivers). The code model has a deep intuitive appeal, and a great deal of research on the evolution of communication, in both humans and animals, uses it as a default background assumption about how communication works (e.g., Skyrms 2010). Indeed, the terminology of codes and information transmission is common in the vast majority of work on the evolution of communication, human or otherwise. Here, for instance, is a description of human linguistic communication, taken from a highly influential paper: "the vocal-auditory *channel* has some desirable features as a medium of communication: it has a *high bandwidth*… however it is essentially a *serial interface*…the basic tools of a *coding scheme* employing it are *an inventory of distinguishable symbols and their concatenation*" (Pinker and Bloom 1990, p. 713, italics added).

However, there is another way of thinking about the very possibility of communication, called the *ostensive-inferential model*. Here, communication is not about encoding and decoding messages, but about expressing and recognizing intentions (Scott-Phillips 2014; Sperber and Wilson 1995, 2002). Specifically, the signaler must express both communicative and informative intentions. An informative intention is an intention to change the mental state of the receiver: When I use my leg to point to the door, I express an informative intention that you believe that I would like you to open the door. A communicative intention is an intention that you recognize that I have an informative intention. When I use my leg to point to the door, I express not only the informative intention described above but also a communicative intention that I have an informative intention; in other words, that you believe that I am trying to communicate with you in the first place. After all, legs point in particular directions all the time. I need to show in some way that the direction my leg is pointing is not just incidental but is in fact a signal that has meaning for you. The technical term is *ostension:* I point my leg in an ostensive way, and in so doing I express my communicative and informative intentions. Similarly, when I tilt my mug to nonverbally ask my waiter for more coffee, I do so in an ostensive way. (I do not simply tilt it and do nothing more.) The flip side of this is *inference:* the recognition, by the receiver, that the signaler has these communicative and informative intentions.

Because it is ultimately about the expression and recognition of intentions, communication of this sort is only possible if the individuals involved possess mechanisms of metapsychology: Signalers must entertain beliefs about the intentions and mental states of listeners, and listeners must do the same for signalers. Pointing is a particularly productive instance of ostensive communication, but any behavior (e.g., shrugs, nods, gestures, facial contortions, burps) can, in principle, be used ostensively so long as it expresses a communicative intention, and hence an informative intention too.

The fundamental difference between the code model and the ostensive-inferential model is, then, a difference about the mechanisms that make each type of communication possible. On the one hand, code model communication is made possible by mechanisms of association. On the other, ostensive-inferential communication is made possible by mechanisms of metapsychology.

As such, ostensive-inferential communication is ultimately a tool for social navigation (Scott-Phillips 2014). For signalers, ostensive-inferential communication is a tool to (more or less) directly influence others' minds; for receivers, it is a tool to more or less directly read others' minds. Both of these objectives obviously require the assistance and acquiescence of the other party, and indeed that is, from both an evolutionary and a social psychology perspective, what linguistic and other forms of ostensive-inferential communication ultimately are: mutually assisted mind reading and mental manipulation. One seminal paper in the history of animal communication theory used mind reading and manipulation as a metaphor to describe the adaptive payoffs available in communication to, respectively, the receivers and the signalers (Krebs and Dawkins 1984). In the case of human ostensive communication, that insight is not metaphorical, but literal: Ostensive communication is a form of extended social navigation. Signalers mentally manipulate their audience, and audiences mind read signalers. These direct functions give rise to numerous derived functions of communication and language, such as gossip, courtship, hunting, and all the other ends we use them for (for the difference between direct and derived functions, see Millikan 1984; Origgi and Sperber 2000).

Ostensive-inferential communication is likely uniquely human (Scott-Phillips 2014; Tomasello 2008). We can divide ostensive-inferential communication into four distinct behaviors: (1) the expression of communicative intentions, (2) the expression of informative intentions, (3) the recognition of communicative intentions, and (4) the recognition of informative intentions. There is clear experimental evidence that children have command of the first three behaviors, and it would be very surprising if they did not have command of the fourth too: The only reasons why such studies have not yet been conducted are methodological (Scott-Phillips 2014). In contrast, there is as yet no evidence that any nonhuman primate has command of any of these four behaviors. Nonhuman primates communicate intentionally, but intentionality is not sufficient for ostension and inference (for detailed discussion, see Scott-Phillips 2014).

Section 3: Language

Where does linguistic communication fit into this distinction between coded and ostensive-inferential communication? The immediate intuition is that it operates according to the code model. After all, there are clearly reliable associations between signals and their meanings: The word "dog" is reliably associated with canine animals, for example. Yet this is equally clearly not the whole story. Metaphors, allusions, and other figurative expressions express far more than the literal, "decoded" meanings of what is said, and these are not atypical uses. On the contrary, they are entirely quotidian. Moreover, listeners use more than just language to determine a speaker's intended meaning. Other aspects of production, such as intonation and body language, are important too. Even an utterance as simple as "How are you?" can express a range of speaker meanings, depending on how it is expressed. To determine between these readings, and to express them appropriately in the first place, speakers and listeners must reason about each other's mental states. Linguistic communication clearly involves some use of ostension and inference.

What, then, is the relationship between ostension, inference, and the linguistic code? One common answer to this question—indeed, the dominant one in mainstream linguistics—is that the linguistic code makes language possible, and ostension and inference make it especially flexible and expressively powerful. There is, however, a long tradition in the philosophy of language which shows that the code model is insufficient as a description of how linguistic communication actually works (see Sperber 1995 for an accessible version of the argument). The basic point can be illustrated rather simply. Consider the following exchange:

Mary: What are you doing later?
Peter: Sally has invited me to dinner.

If it is understood purely in terms of the linguistic code, Peter's utterance does not, *on its own,* answer Mary's question. It is only when context, shared knowledge, and other pragmatic considerations are taken into account that Peter's intended meaning becomes clear. In the jargon of linguistics, literal meaning underdetermines speaker meaning (Carston 2002). The fact of underdeterminacy means that the linguistic code is not, on its own, enough for communication to succeed.

Instead, the linguistic code augments our capacity for ostensive-inferential communication (Sperber and Wilson 2002). I can point to the door with my leg, but with the linguistic code I can be more explicit, and actually ask you to open it. In this way, linguistic communication is an instance of ostensive-inferential communication, one that makes use of a rich set of culturally shared conventions that we call languages. Put another way, ostension and inference make human communication possible, and what the linguistic code does is make it expressively powerful.

Section 4: Mechanisms of Language Structure

These linguistic codes—languages—are structured in interesting, nonrandom ways. Why? Just as the *raison d'être* of, say, biology is to enquire about why nature is the way it is, and not some other way, the *raison d'être* of linguistics is to investigate why languages take the form that they do, and not some other form.

One prominent hypothesis is that we have an innate mechanism—typically called a universal grammar (UG)—that effectively and adaptively prespecifies the form that languages take, and in doing so allows us to acquire language. Central to this claim is the argument that the natural language that children are exposed to does not contain sufficient data for them to actually acquire the whole of (what is to be) their native language. Hence, there must be some cognitive mechanism that primes them to do so (Berwick et al. 2011; Chomsky 1980). Any such mechanism should be recognized as an evolutionary adaptation (Pinker and Bloom 1990).

However, the existence of UG is disputed. In particular, many researchers have argued, against the nativist view, that language acquisition is possible in a purely data-driven way (i.e., that in order to learn their native tongues, children need no more linguistic input than that to which they are naturally exposed; e.g., Goldberg 2006; Tomasello 2003). This is a vexed, contentious, and unresolved debate (Pullum and Scholz 2002)—and if the anti-nativists are correct, then the question of why languages take the forms that they do reasserts itself.

Cultural evolution provides a potential answer to this question, and hence an alternative to nativist explanations of language structure. The basic suggestion is that, as they propagate through a community, languages gravitate towards forms that match the dispositions of the human mind, and the behavior of language users (Christiansen and Chater 2008; Evans and Levinson 2009). If so, this would be an instance of cultural attraction, in which cultural traits (languages, fashions, religious beliefs, etc.) spread through a population to the extent that they fit the natural dispositions of human behavior and the human mind (Claidière et al. 2014; Sperber 1996). The idea is best illustrated with an example.

In one influential experiment, participants were asked to learn an "alien" language of 27 meaning-word mappings. Each "meaning" comprised one of three different shapes (square, triangle, circle), which could each be in one of three different colors (red, blue, black), and which were associated with one of three different types of movement (straight, rotation, bounce). The words associated with these meanings were randomly created, and without meaning in English (e.g., "nohu," "gatuha"). Such languages are effectively sets of 27 distinct associations, between meanings and previously unknown words. Having been shown the language, the first participant was then tested on it: shown all the shapes again, and asked to type the corresponding word. The language the participant produced was then used as the language that the next participant had to learn, and this process was repeated for ten generations, in two different experimental conditions. What happened was that, as they were passed from one participant to another in this way, the languages became more structured. In one condition in particular, each word acquired distinct parts for each part of the meaning: One part described the color (say, black is "ne"), another part described the shape (say, a square is "ho"), and a third part the movement (say, bounce is "pilu"). These different component parts (the technical term is "morphemes") can then be combined in various ways to describe all the different shapes uniquely. The black bouncing square, for instance, was now labeled "nehopilu" (i.e., the combination of "ne," "ho," and "pilu"; Kirby et al. 2008). In short, the meaning of the terms is now given by the meaning of the component parts and the way they are combined. This property is called *compositionality,* and it is a distinctive and basic feature of linguistic structure.

There are many similar findings of this sort. That is, numerous models and experiments illustrate how various features of language, such as compositionality, can emerge as languages propagate through a community (Scott-Phillips 2014). These findings provide good arguments to be skeptical about the existence of an innate mechanism for language, because they explain how it is possible for languages to take the form without any such innate mechanism (Evans and Levinson 2009). In other words, the proximate mechanism involved in the generation of linguistic structure may not be a UG, but rather the process of cultural propagation, which tends to morph languages into structural forms. Of course, these two explanations are not mutually exclusive. It is possible that both play a role.

Section 5: Adaptive Behavior in Ostensive-Inferential Communication

In ostensive-inferential communication, the individual goals of the two distinct parties are not always aligned. In particular, there may be things that I, as a speaker, want you to believe, but which you, the listener, have no interest in, or which you simply do not wish to know or believe. Similarly, there may be aspects of my mind that you want to infer, but which I have no interest in revealing. Interactive, social behaviors of this sort present the adaptationist with a host of interesting questions that involve how the interests of the different parties play off against one another in evolution (Davies et al. 2012).

First, we must understand how the interests of speakers and receivers play off against one another in ostensive communication. For listeners, the main issue is to avoid attending to irrelevant stimuli, since to do otherwise is a waste of time and energy. In short, listeners must filter the stimuli they are exposed to for relevance. If I say to you, "this is a pipe," one thing that follows is that the object I am holding is conventionally referred to as a pipe. But other things logically follow too, for example, that it is not a knife. Or a fork. Or a house, a field, an idea, a lobster, a picture of a pipe…and so on. What this random list illustrates is that the potential new beliefs that follow from even the most simple of stimuli are infinite (this is a serious philosophical problem in computer science, where it goes by the name of the frame problem). Even for the most simple of utterances, listeners must have some way to limit exactly what conclusions they draw. More specifically, they should seek to extract as much worthwhile information from the stimulus as they can, while not wasting undue energy (Sperber and Wilson 1995).

Speakers must also limit their efforts. We do not inform our audiences of everything we have ever known or thought. After all, if listeners filter for relevance, as discussed above, then unnecessary verbosity is just a waste of energy. Moreover, if we are consistently irrelevant, we will lose friends and influence. These are serious consequences in a highly social species like humans. Instead, a speaker should tend to produce stimuli that are as relevant for the listener as possible, given the speaker's own goals and preferences.

In sum, the design features for adaptive ostensive communication are that (1) listeners' cognitive systems should tend to maximize the relevance of incoming stimuli, and (2) speakers should tend to produce ostensive stimuli that are optimally relevant for the intended audience (where optimally relevant means as relevant as possible, given the speaker's own goals and preferences) (Scott-Phillips 2010). That human communication actually exhibits both of these qualities is the central claims of *Relevance Theory*, a prominent approach to pragmatics, the branch of linguistics concerned with how languages are used and the cognitive mechanisms behind linguistic communication. The two qualities are called, respectively, the cognitive and the communicative principles of relevance, and they are, in effect, claims that we use ostensive-inferential communication adaptively (Sperber and Wilson 1995).

Both principles of relevance have been subject to empirical testing (reviewed in van der Henst and Sperber 2004). Probably the most well-known and cleanest test of the communicative principle (that speakers will tend to produce optimally relevant stimuli) concerns telling the time. When approached on the street and asked for the time by somebody who says they have an appointment soon, people will round their answer (e.g., to say "5 to 3" instead of "2:56", or "4 min to 3") if the appointment is between 15 and 30 min from now, but they will give a precise, nonrounded answer if the appointment is within the next 15 min (Gibbs and Bryant 2008; van der Henst et al. 2002). This is because the precise, nonrounded answer is only relevant if the appointment is immediate. This is just one of several experiments whose results are consistent with the predictions of the communicative principle of relevance.

The cognitive principle of relevance (that human cognition will maximize the relevance of incoming stimuli) has also been tested in a variety of ways. One way is with relational reasoning tasks (van der Henst and Sperber 2004). Relational reasoning tasks come in determinate and indeterminate forms. In the determinate form, participants are given premises such as "A is taller than B" and "B is taller than C," and asked about the relation between A and C. Indeterminate forms are the same, except that the premises are indeterminate about the relation between the terms. The most straightforward example is "A is taller than B" and "A is taller than C." Here, nothing follows about the one unstated relationship between these three terms (i.e., the one between B and C). To test the communicative principle of relevance, instead of asking "What is the relationship between B and C?" we can ask a question more like "What conclusions, if any, follow from these premises?" The point here is that many things (in fact, an infinite number) logically follow from these premises, many of them trivial and obvious. For example, and most immediately, the conjunction "A is taller than both B and C" follows. A series of experiments show, however, that participants tend to say that no conclusions follow. In other words, the question they seem to answer is not the one they were literally asked, but this one: "What relevant conclusions, if any, follow from these premises?" (van der Henst and Sperber 2004). In short, the participants interpret the question in a way that it is relevant in the context (of a relational reasoning task, where many of the conclusions are trivial and obvious, and hence irrelevant), just as predicted by the cognitive principle of relevance.

In sum, experimental data suggest that human communicative behavior is indeed adaptive, given the different interests of signaler and receiver. Signalers tend to produce optimally relevant stimuli, given their communicative goals, and receivers maximize the relevance of the stimuli they receive.

Section 6: Vigilance and Argumentation

From an evolutionary perspective, there is one type of irrelevance that is of particular importance: dishonesty. A dishonest signal is one that is presented as having useful (relevant) information, but which in fact does not, because that information is false. Why is deception not widespread? After all, deceiving others can be very beneficial. If it pays a signaler to signal dishonestly, at least on average, then we should expect dishonest signals to evolve. If this occurs, the receiver's best reaction is, again on average, simply to ignore signals from these signalers, and so we should expect this indifference to evolve too. The end result is that the system has collapsed, and no further communication takes place. Under what circumstances does this outcome not come to pass? This question is the defining problem of signaling theory (Maynard Smith and Harper 2003). In this and the next section, I shall address it from both an ultimate and, first, a proximate perspective.

From the receiver's perspective, communication, linguistic or otherwise, is a potentially rich source of useful information. However, there is always the risk of deception and other forms of misinformation. This information must therefore be filtered; false and otherwise useless information should be rejected. Listeners able to do this effectively will make the best use of communication as a source of information.

This filtering of information is called *epistemic vigilance* (Sperber et al. 2010). A critical component of epistemic vigilance is the distinction between comprehension and acceptance: We can comprehend what others say without accepting it (i.e., without changing our mental states in the way that the signaler intends). There are two reasons why we might reject information in this way: because we think the signaler is either (1) malevolent (i.e., liable to deceive) or (2) incompetent (i.e., liable to be misinformed themselves). To the extent that it is possible to detect malevolence and incompetence in advance, we are cautious about accepting information from such sources.

Epistemic vigilance is specific to ostensive communication. Exercising epistemic vigilance involves the listener satisfying the speaker's communicative intention, while at the same time holding open the possibility of not satisfying the corresponding informative intention. In other words, the listener can accept that the speaker intends that the listener understands that the speaker has a particular informative intention, while at the same time the listener can choose not to accept the content of that informative intention. Since there are, by definition, no such similar intentions in code model communication, no such epistemic vigilance is possible there.

Whether the mechanisms involved in epistemic vigilance are adaptive or not is presently unclear. Whether and how we are able to detect misinformation is a much-studied topic in social psychology. There are also sizable literatures on the dissemination and persistence of misinformation, and on how accent and other paralinguistic features of dialects are sometimes used as heuristic markers of group identity, and hence of who one should or should not trust and cooperate with (reviewed in Cohen 2012). In contrast, whether we filter information acquired via ostensive communication as usefully as possible, given the inherent uncertainties involved, is far less studied (Sperber et al. 2010). Given the central role that ostensive communication plays in human life, it is quite plausible that the mechanisms involved in epistemic vigilance are adaptive—but, to the best of my knowledge, we do not have good data on this question at present. In short, nobody has yet done quantitative empirical work on the effectiveness of epistemic vigilance. This is an important topic for future research.

Let us now look at things from the perspective of the signaler. Doing so sheds surprising new light on an aspect of our cognition that does not immediately seem to be of direct relevance to communication. Signalers signal in order to influence others' mental states (Sect. 2). However, epistemic vigilance poses a barrier to this goal: Vigilant listeners, alert to the possibility of deception, will not simply adjust their mental states willy-nilly, just as they are told. This means that signalers must find ways to overcome this barrier. They cannot literally force listeners to adjust their mental representations, so they must instead persuade, argue, and otherwise provide good reasons why listeners really should adopt their point of view. As such, crucial to this signaler's goals is the ability to generate good arguments and other forms of persuasion in the first place; in other words, to reason well. This insight motivates the argumentative theory of reasoning, which states that the proper function of human reasoning skills is not, as is commonly assumed, to improve knowledge and make better decisions, but rather to devise and evaluate arguments intended to persuade (Mercier and Sperber 2011). This does not mean, of course, that reasoning is not used to improve one's own knowledge and make better decisions, or that it does not sometimes serve this purpose; the claim is simply that using reasoning in this way is like using a chair to hold open a door: It works, and often very well, but that is not what it is designed for. The function of reasoning is instead to persuade others in ostensive communication.

The argumentative theory makes a number of specific and otherwise counterintuitive predictions that are supported by the empirical data, and which are hard to account for under the more traditional view (that the proper function of reasoning is to improve knowledge). The most salient example of this is confirmation bias. It is well known that people tend not to systematically evaluate both of the arguments in favor and those against existing beliefs or new ideas. Instead, they interpret new data in a partial way, considering only or predominantly those data that support already existing beliefs (for a review, see Nickerson 1998). If human reasoning is about improving one's own knowledge and making better decisions, confirmation bias is simply a flaw: It hinders rather than aids the purported goal. However, from the perspective of the argumentative theory, it is exactly what should be expected. If the goal of reasoning is to provide listeners with reasons to accept your claims, then our reasoning skills should be designed to seek arguments in favor of our existing view, because it is these arguments that are most useful for the persuasion of others (Mercier and Sperber 2011).

This section has looked at the proximate mechanisms associated with deception and other forms of misinformation in human ostensive-inferential communication. Doing so has highlighted how mechanisms for epistemic vigilance and mechanisms for reasoning are two sides of the same communicative coin. I turn now to ultimate questions.

Section 7: Honesty and Reputation

The theoretical literature contains several possible ultimate-level explanations of evolutionary stability in communication. In this section, I briefly review these and discuss which apply to human communication.

One possibility is indices. With indices, there is a causal relationship between signal form and signal meaning. Dark clouds, for example, are indexical of rain. A biological example is red deer roars, whose acoustic properties are indexical of the deer's size. This is due to the physical constraints of deer vocalization (Fitch and Reby 2001). Specifically, when red deer roar, their larynx descends as far as possible, and this maximizes their apparent size. The deer cannot evolve to descend the larynx any further because this would require a change in the fundamental anatomy of the deer. Another possibility is deterrents, where the payoffs associated with honesty outweigh the payoffs associated with dishonesty.

One special type of index is a handicap: Costs paid to produce a signal, which have no function except as a way to advertise the fact that the signaler can actually produce the signal in the first place. It is critical to the mathematics of handicaps that these costs are *differential:* The costs of signal production must be greater for dishonest rather than honest signalers (Grose 2011; Számadó 2011). This quality is hard to measure, and hence real-world examples are hard to find: "there is not a single biological example that could be claimed as handicap beyond doubt" (Számadó 2012, p. 281). Nevertheless, the peacock tail is often put forward as a possible example (discussed in Maynard Smith and Harper 2003).

Students of human behavior have been far too keen to argue that human communication uses handicaps (Grose 2011). One example is blood donation (Lyle et al. 2009). Another is costly apologies (e.g., gifts), which signal a sincere desire to repair a relationship (Ohtsubo and Watanabe 2009). A third example is self-harm among prisoners, which some researchers argue is used to signal psychological volatility ("if I am crazy enough to do this to myself, what might I do to you?!"; Gambetta 2009). All these examples are costly to some degree or another, but in no case is there good reason to think that they are *differentially costly*. As such, these proposals all ignore a key requirement for a signal to qualify as a handicap. There are further examples still (Grose 2011; Scott-Phillips 2014).

While it is possible that some instances of human communication are kept stable by other means, most are kept stable by deterrents, and in particular by reputation (Lachmann et al. 2001; Scott-Phillips 2008a). Individuals who lie are likely to be ignored or ostracized in the future, and this possibility stops people from lying. The loss of reputation that can result from dishonesty is a major cost in a highly social species like humans, who continually monitor and gossip about each other's behavior. Indeed, Aesop's fable of the boy that cried wolf is designed to illustrate the importance of a reputation for honesty. The importance of reputation for the evolution of human cooperation was recognized some time ago (e.g., Milinski et al. 2002). Its importance for the evolution of human communication is less widely recognized, but should be.

Section 8: Summary

When we study human communication from an evolutionary or zoological perspective, the most important point to keep in mind is that human communication is ostensive-inferential (Sect. 2). What this means is that human communication involves the expression and recognition of intentions. Specifically, these intentions are communicative intentions, the content of which are informative intentions.

As such, human communication is ultimately a form of mutually assisted social navigation. Its direct functions are mind reading (for receivers) and mental manipulation (for signalers). Several researchers have suggested other functions for human communication, such as grooming, courtship, and so on, but these are all derived functions, and should not be confused with its direct functions (Origgi and Sperber 2000; Scott-Phillips 2014). Linguistic communication is a type of ostensive-inferential communication (Sect. 3).

In asking what an adaptationist perspective might tell us about human communication and language, it is important to recognize that communication systems are not psychological traits, nor biological traits of any other sort. Communication is instead the product of two interactive traits, namely mechanisms for signal production and mechanisms for signal reception (Scott-Phillips 2008b; Scott-Phillips et al. 2012). When we consider how the interests of signaler and receiver play off against one another, we derive the following predictions: (1) listeners' cognitive systems should tend to maximize the relevance of incoming stimuli, and (2) speakers should tend to produce ostensive stimuli that are optimally relevant for the intended audience. These are the central claims of relevance theory, and they have stood up to empirical scrutiny (Sect. 5).

It is possible that humans have adaptations for language acquisition, which constrain the possible forms that languages can take. If so, this can help explain why languages take the forms that they do. However, an alternative proximate explanation of this is cultural attraction: It is possible that languages take the forms that they do because as they propagate through a community they change in nonrandom ways, and in doing so they gravitate towards certain forms and away from others (Sect. 4). Which of these explanations is correct (or whether a combination of them is) is a central question for contemporary linguistics, and will remain so for some time.

Communication is of course a social phenomenon, and as such a classic problem is evolutionary stability. What prevents widespread dishonesty? In most human communication, the answer is social reputation: The potential benefits of dishonesty are outweighed by the potential costs of being discovered or known as a liar (Sect. 7). At a proximate level, we have a suite of mechanisms that help to defend themselves against the possibility of misinformation (Sect. 6). This is called epistemic vigilance. An adaptationist approach suggests that our ability to reason may be the flip side of this: A mechanism adapted to persuade others to accept the information we present to them.

This brief survey of what an evolutionary perspective can tell us about human communication and language has highlighted several important questions that require further investigation. Among the most prominent are: How good are we at epistemic vigilance? (This is not the same question as "How good are we at detecting liars?"; Sperber et al. 2010). How widespread are handicaps in human communication? To what extent, exactly, does human communicative behavior satisfy the principles of relevance? Within evolutionary linguistics, adaptationist questions of this sort have received relatively little attention in comparison to questions about the evolutionary origins of language. Research on language origins is certainly to be welcomed, but we should not neglect to study how an evolutionary, adaptationist perspective can inform questions about the nature of language and communication themselves.

References

Berwick, R. C., Pietroski, P., Yankama, B., & Chomsky, N. (2011). Poverty of the stimulus revisited. *Cognitive Science, 35,* 1207–1242.

Carston, R. (2002). *Thoughts and utterances: The pragmatics of explicit communication.* Oxford: Blackwell.

Chomksy, N. (1980). *Rules and representations.* Oxford: Blackwell.

Christiansen, M. H., & Chater, N. (2008). Language as shaped by the brain. *Behavioral and Brain Sciences, 31,* 489–558.

Christiansen, M. H., & Kirby, S. (2003). *Language evolution.* Oxford: Oxford University Press.

Claidière, N., Scott-Phillips, T. C., & Sperber, D. (2014). How Darwinian is cultural evolution? *Philosophical Transactions of the Royal Society of London, 369,* 20130368.

Cohen, E. (2012). The evolution of tag-based cooperation in humans: The case for accent. *Current Anthropology, 53,* 588–616.

Cosmides, L., & Tooby, J. (2013). Evolutionary psychology: New perspectives on cognition and motivation. *Annual Review of Psychology, 64,* 201–229.

Davies, N. B., Krebs, J. R., & West, S. A. (2012). An introduction to behavioural ecology. Oxford: Wiley-Blackwell.

Evans, N., & Levinson, S. C. (2009). The myth of language universals: Language diversity and its importance for cognitive science. *Behavioral and Brain Sciences, 32,* 429–448.

Fitch, W. T. (2010). *The evolution of language.* Cambridge: Cambridge University Press.

Fitch, W. T., & Reby, D. (2001). The descended larynx is not uniquely human. *Proceedings of the Royal Society of London, B, 268,* 1669–1675.

Gambetta, D. (2009). *Codes of the underworld: How criminals communicate.* Princeton: Princeton University Press.

Gibbs, R. W., & Bryant, G. A. (2008). Striving for optimal relevance when answering questions. *Cognition, 106,* 345–369.

Goldberg, A. E. (2006) *Constructions at work: The nature of generalization in language.* Oxford: Oxford University Press.

Grose, J. (2011). Modelling and the fall and rise of the handicap principle. Biology & Philosophy, 26(5), 677–696.

Hurford, J. R. (2007). *Origins of meaning.* Oxford: Oxford University Press.

Hurford, J. R. (2011). *Origins of grammar.* Oxford: Oxford University Press.

Kirby, S., Cornish, H., & Smith, K. (2008). Cumulative cultural evolution in the laboratory: An experimental approach to the origins of structure in human language. *Proceedings of the National Academy of Sciences, 105,* 10681–10686.

Krebs, J. R., & Dawkins, R. (1984). Animal signals: Mind-reading and manipulation. In J. R. Krebs & N. B. Davies (Eds.), *Behavioural ecology: An evolutionary approach* (2nd ed., pp. 380–402). Oxford: Blackwell.

Lachmann, M., Szamado, S., & Bergstrom, C. T. (2001). Cost and conflict in animal signals and human language. *Proceedings of the National Academy of Sciences, 98,* 13189–13194.

Lyle, H. F., Smith, E. A., & Sullivan, R. J. (2009). Blood donations as costly signals of donor quality. *Journal of Evolutionary Psychology, 7,* 263–286.

Maynard Smith, J., & Harper, D. G. C. (2003). *Animal signals.* Oxford: Oxford University Press.

Mercier, H., & Sperber, D. (2011). Why do humans reason? Arguments for an argumentative theory. *Behavioral and Brain Sciences, 34,* 57–111.

Milinski, M., Semmann, D., & Krambeck, H. J. (2002). Reputation helps solve the 'tragedy of the commons'. *Nature, 415,* 424–426.

Millikan, R. (1984). *Language, thought and other biological categories.* Cambridge: MIT Press.

Nickerson, R. S. (1998) Confirmation bias: A ubiquitous phenomena in many guises. *Review of General Psychology, 2,* 175–220.

Ohtsubo, Y., & Watanabe, E. (2009). Do sincere apologies need to be costly? Test of a costly signaling model of apology. *Evolution and Human Behavior, 30,* 114–123.

Origgi, G., & Sperber, D. (2000). Evolution, communication and the proper function of language. In P. Carruthers & A. Chamberlain (Eds.), *Evolution and the human mind: Language, modularity and social cognition* (pp. 140–169). Cambridge: Cambridge University Press.

Pinker, S., & Bloom, P. (1990). Natural language and natural selection. *Behavioral and Brain Sciences, 13,* 707–727.

Pullum, G. K., & Scholz, B. C. (2002). Empirical assessment of stimulus poverty arguments. *Linguistic Review, 18,* 9–50.

Scott-Phillips, T. C. (2008a). On the correct application of animal signalling theory to human communication. In A. D. M. Smith, K. Smith & R. Ferrer i Cancho (Eds.), *The evolution of language: Proceedings of the 7th International Conference* (pp. 275–282). Singapore: World Scientific.

Scott-Phillips, T. C. (2008b). Defining biological communication. *Journal of Evolutionary Biology, 21,* 387–395.

Scott-Phillips, T. C. (2010). The evolution of relevance. *Cognitive Science, 34,* 583–601.

Scott-Phillips, T. C. (2014). *Speaking our minds: Human communication and the evolutionary origins of language.* London: Palgrave MacMillan.

Scott-Phillips, T. C., Blythe, R. A., Gardner, A., & West, S. A. (2012). How do communication systems emerge? *Proceedings of the Royal Society of London, B, 279,* 1943–1949.

Skyrms, B. (2010). *Signals: Evolution, learning, and information.* Oxford: Oxford University Press.

Sperber, D. (1995). How do we communicate? In J. Brockman & K. Matson (Eds.), How things are: A science toolkit for the mind (pp. 191–199). New York: Morrow.

Sperber, D. (1996). *Explaining culture: A naturalistic approach*. Oxford: Blackwell.
Sperber, D., & Wilson, D. (1995). *Relevance: Communication and cognition* (2nd ed.). Oxford: Blackwell.
Sperber, D., & Wilson, D. (2002). Pragmatics, modularity, and mind-reading. *Mind and Language, 17,* 3–23.
Sperber, D., Clément, F., Heintz, C., Mascaro, O., Mercier, H., Origgi, G., & Wilson, D. (2010). Epistemic vigilance. *Mind and Language, 25,* 359–393.
Számadó, S. (2011). The cost of honesty and the fallacy of the handicap principle. *Animal Behaviour, 81,* 3–10.
Számadó, S. (2012). The rise and fall of handicap principle: A commentary on the 'Modelling and the fall and rise of the handicap principle'. *Biology and Philosophy, 27,* 279–286.
Tomasello, M. (2003). *Constructing a language: A usage-based theory of language acquisition*. Cambridge: Harvard University Press.
Tomasello, M. (2008). *Origins of human communication*. Cambridge: MIT Press.
van der Henst, J.-B., & Sperber, D. (2004). Testing the cognitive and the communicative principles of relevance. In I. Noveck & D. Sperber (Eds.), *Experimental pragmatics* (pp. 141–171). London: Palgrave.
van der Henst, J.-B., Carles, L., & Sperber, D. (2002). Truthfulness and relevance in telling the time. *Mind and Language, 17,* 457–466.

The Evolution of Stereotypes

23

Jacqui Hutchison and Douglas Martin

We share our planet with more than 7 billion members of our species, each of whom has their own unique biographical history, personal characteristics, and preferences. Of these seven billion or so other people, how many do we each have individuated knowledge? While it is almost impossible to provide an accurate answer to this question, it is relatively straightforward to demonstrate that this number is far short of the entire population. Estimates of social network size—people we know personally—range from around 100 (Hill and Dunbar 2003) to 5000 people (Killworth et al. 1990; Pool and Kochen 1978). Even when you add in people with whom we are familiar (e.g., famous celebrities, public figures, people we do not know but see regularly in day-to-day life, people we have learned about from others), it seems likely that the number of people we each have individuated knowledge of would be quantified in thousands or tens of thousands, rather than hundreds of thousands or millions—certainly not billions. Yet despite our impoverished person-specific knowledge of our conspecifics, we are remarkably adept at navigating our social environment, successfully interacting with people irrespective of whether we have ever encountered them before or not. Much of this social dexterity can be attributed to our use of stereotypes.

We perceive ourselves and other people not only as unique individuals who possess their own personal characteristics (e.g., *Jill goes running and enjoys fine wine*) but also as members of social groups that are themselves associated with many attributes (e.g., *as a nurse, Jill must be caring and friendly*). The information associated with social groups is commonly referred to as *stereotypes* (Allport 1954; Lippman 1922). Stereotypes are often viewed in terms of their negative influence (i.e., prejudice), most notably when their endorsement leads to discrimination toward people belonging to minority groups (Tajfel 1969). However, in the face of an infinitely complex social world, stereotypes also play a vital positive role by efficiently organizing social information in a way that allows us to rapidly make inferences about other people (Macrae and Bodenhausen 2000; McGarty et al. 2002).

By examining stereotypes from an evolutionary perspective, in this chapter, we present evidence that our reliance on stereotypes is a functional, social, and cognitive adaptation, without which we would be considerably less able to thrive in our social environment. We also explore the extent to which the process of cultural evolution—the way that information changes as it passes from person to person—is influenced by stereotypes, influences the evolution of stereotypes, and might even provide clues to the origins of stereotypes.

J. Hutchison (✉) · D. Martin
School of Psychology, University of Aberdeen, William Guild Building, Room F17, Kings College, Old Aberdeen AB24 3FX, UK
e-mail: jacqui.hutchison@abdn.ac.uk

D. Martin
e-mail: doug.martin@abdn.ac.uk

V. Zeigler-Hill et al. (eds.), *Evolutionary Perspectives on Social Psychology,* Evolutionary Psychology,
DOI 10.1007/978-3-319-12697-5_23, © Springer International Publishing Switzerland 2015

Stereotypes are Adaptive

One of the most compelling arguments in favor of stereotypes as functional, social cognitive adaptations is simply that they exist. Evolutionary biology and cultural evolution provide many examples of attributes that are either vestigial and have no apparent current function or are maladaptive and actually hinder function (e.g., Wisdom teeth and the QWERTY keyboard are two commonly cited examples of biological and cultural maladaptation, respectively; Mesoudi 2011). However, the vast majority of the traits we inherit have some adaptive value. It seems likely that if stereotypes had no adaptive function, then they would never have come into existence in the first place. Similarly, if stereotypes were not a useful tool for us today, then selection pressure would have marginalized them or eliminated them completely. That stereotypes not only endure, but are continually forming and evolving, is testament to their functional value as aids to understanding, as a means of conserving cognitive energy, as culturally shared beliefs, and as a means of protecting self-esteem.

Stereotypes are often described as aids to understanding because, in the absence of readily available person-specific information, they allow us to perceive other people and their behavior in terms of the social groups to which they belong. Just as we have cognitive categories for nonsocial objects, such as vehicles and furniture (Rosch et al. 1976), stereotypes are cognitive categories for social groups, such as sex, age, and ethnicity (Fiske and Neuberg 1990). Once a category is cued, we have access to a wealth of existing knowledge about attributes associated with the category, which influences our subsequent cognitive and behavioral tendencies (Allport 1954; Brewer and Feinstein 1999; Fiske and Neuberg 1990; Rosch et al. 1976). The ability to interpret new information in terms of our previous experience enables us to go beyond that which is available and make inferences based on our existing knowledge (Bartlett 1932; Griffiths et al. 2008; Kalish et al. 2007). As social animals living in large groups, it is vital that we are able to respond rapidly when encountering new people in our environment, paving the way for smooth social interactions (McGarty et al. 2002). Without the aid of stereotypes, this task would be virtually impossible, and so we have evolved to use them as a way of making sense of the complex social world in which we live (Tajfel et al. 1971).

Not only do stereotypes help us to navigate our complex social environment but they also do so in a highly efficient manner; in effect, stereotypes are energy-saving devices (Allport 1954; Brewer 1988; Macrae et al. 1994a). Considering the excessive amount of information we are exposed to in our social environment, we have neither the cognitive capacity nor the time to perceive each person individually. Stereotypes allow us to ignore the individuating information about a person (Fiske and Neuberg 1990), thereby saving effort (Bodenhausen and Lichtenstein 1987; Macrae et al. 1994a) and time (Fiske et al. 1987). As Allport (1954) suggests, "The human mind must think with the aid of categories…. Orderly living depends on it" (p. 20). We use stereotypes to reduce the differences between people to cognitively and behaviorally functional proportions (Rosch et al. 1976). To the extent that a strategy is required which allows us to adapt to frequently changing social situations, our cognitive processes have evolved to use stereotypes as a way of reducing the complexity of the task at hand. In a social environment, where we are often required to perform multiple tasks simultaneously, stereotypes provide us with shortcuts that preserve our precious cognitive resources for other duties (Macrae et al. 1994a).

Stereotypes not only benefit us because of the way they help us structure information within our own minds but they are also adaptive because they are culturally shared knowledge structures, with similar representations in the minds of other people (Devine 1989; Devine and Elliot 1995; Karlins et al. 1969; Katz and Braly 1933; Madon et al. 2001; Schaller and Conway 1999). According to Devine (1989), "… stereotypes are part of the social heritage of a society and no one can escape learning the prevailing attitudes and stereotypes…" (p. 5). Stereotypes have the capacity to influence how we perceive reality because they are shared across the population and guide our expectations of the roles and behaviors that both we and others will undertake. An important function of our shared stereotype knowledge is that it allows us to simplify communication, while at the same time convey information that is rich in implied meaning (i.e., *because I know what you know, and you know what I know, neither of us has to say it*; Stangor and Schaller 1996). Thus, because stereotypes exist not only in the mind of the individual but also in the minds of others, they help regulate social perception and interactions by reducing uncertainty (Hogg and Reid 2006). Because of their value in helping us to intuitively understand one another and act collectively, it has been argued that shared group beliefs, such as stereotypes, provide one of the foundations on which a structured and cohesive society can be built (Bar-Tal 2000).

Even one of the less savory aspects of stereotypes—their relationships with prejudice and discrimination—can have adaptive value through their influence on the social comparisons we make between ourselves and other people. While we all share similar levels of knowledge about cultural stereotypes, people differ in their endorsement of the accuracy of stereotypes, depending on their personal beliefs (Devine 1989). Specifically, people who exhibit lower levels of prejudice tend to refute the accuracy of stereotypes, whereas people with higher levels of prejudice are more likely to believe stereotypes are accurate descriptions of group members. As stereotype content tends to be predominantly negative, people who endorse stereotypes are more likely to evaluate members of other social groups in a negative light. Because we gain an indication of our self-worth by continually comparing our perception of ourselves to our perceptions of other people (Festinger 1954; Tajfel and Turner 1979), negative evaluations of out-group members increase our relative sense of self-worth and can boost our self-esteem (Fein and Spencer 1997). Indeed, when a person's self-esteem is threatened, they are more likely to perceive out-group members in a negative stereotypical manner and experience an associated increase in self-esteem as a consequence (Fein and Spencer 1997).

There can be little doubt that our reliance on stereotypes is due to the adaptive solutions they provide to the challenges we face as members of a cognitively and socially advanced species. Without stereotypes, our interactions with other people would be vastly more cumbersome, time-consuming, and cognitively demanding. Certainly, without the affordances of stereotypes, we might never have had the spare cognitive capacity and social cohesion that have led us to evolve into the culturally advanced society we live in today. While one can only speculate about the relative influence of stereotypes on our evolutionary heritage, there is undoubtedly evidence that stereotypes influence the way that culture evolves today.

Stereotypes Influence the Way Culture Evolves

The past decade has seen an upsurge in interdisciplinary research examining how human knowledge develops through cultural evolution (e.g., Baum et al. 2004; Caldwell and Millen 2008a, b; Flynn 2008; Kirby et al. 2008; recently reviewed in Mesoudi 2009, 2011). One of the central tenets of cultural-evolution theory is that because human culture encompasses *variation* (there is innumerable variance in the forms of human information), *competition* (it is not possible to recall and transmit all information; therefore, some information is passed on, while other information is not), and *inheritance* (we learn from others and they learn from us), it is likely to be subject to the pressures of Darwinian evolution (Campbell 1975; Dennet 1995; Mesoudi 2009). Indeed, evidence suggests that when information is repeatedly passed from person to person, it develops adaptively in a manner broadly analogous to biological evolution (Mesoudi 2009, 2011; Richerson and Boyd 2005). Because stereotypes impact both information competition and its transmission, it seems likely that they influence the way that culture evolves.

While there has been a recent spike in interest in cultural evolution, the idea that information changes as it is socially transmitted is not a new one. In 1932, Sir Frederic Bartlett conducted studies examining the reconstructive nature of memory and the effects of this on the transmission of knowledge. The format of Bartlett's experiments resembled the children's game—"telephone" (also often called "Chinese whispers"); the first person in the experiment was asked to try and learn a story and then after a short delay recall it, whatever the first person recalled was passed on as the to-be-learned story for the second person, whatever the second person recalled was then passed to a third person, the third to a fourth, and so on. This process was repeated to form multiple storytelling chains, each comprising multiple "generations" of participants. Because the information passed along each chain was dependent on the unique memories of the people in them, the stories were very different from one another by the end of the process even though each chain began from the same starting point. In other words, knowledge of the stories had culturally evolved across a series of generations.

Interestingly, while the content of the stories at the end of Bartlett's chains was different from both the original seed story and from one another, there was also evidence that properties of the stories were evolving in similar, predictable ways. Specifically, as the stories were continually retold, they began to get shorter, simpler, and more structured until eventually they could be transmitted successfully word for word. By the end of the chains, the original gist of the stories was often all that remained of the original, with many specific details either lost or replaced across the course of the chain. Bartlett (1932) suggested that what we remember is a continual interaction between past events and the current environment. Bartlett (1932) referred to this process as *conventionalization,* meaning that we use stored knowledge and expectations to assimilate and make sense of new information. As individuals, we show a bias toward internal consistency (Schaller and Conway 1999; Spiro 1980), with inconsistent information often lost from memories and consistent information often more likely to persist or be erroneously added (Bartlett 1932; Sherman and Bessenoff 1999). It seems that as information is repeatedly passed from person to person this individual bias is incrementally amplified and the result is gradual cultural evolution.

Because stereotypes are a rapidly accessible source of stored knowledge (Allport 1954; Fiske and Neuberg 1990; Macrae et al. 1994b), and have the ability to guide our expectations (Bodenhausen and Lichtenstein 1987; Bodenhausen and Wyer 1985), it should come as no surprise that they have the ability to influence the cultural evolution of information. For example, Allport and Postman (1947) demonstrated that stereotypes can have a powerful top-down influence on rumor transmission. Using a serial transmission paradigm akin to Bartlett's (1932), the first participant in a chain was shown pictures of complex scenes and asked to remember these and then verbally describe them to the next participant in the chain; each subsequent generation was asked to remember the verbal description of the previous participant and relay this to the next generation. Consistent with Bartlett's (1932) findings, over successive generations, the volume of information being transmitted reduced, and the content of the information changed. What was particularly striking was how existing stereotype knowledge influenced the way that content changed. For example, in one experiment, participants were shown a scene that depicted a scruffily dressed White man holding a razor and gesticulating aggressively at a smartly dressed Black man. In three of the eight chains, Allport and Postman reported, the final generation believed it was the Black man that was holding the razor. It would seem that the information changed to become consistent with the prevailing negative stereotype of African Americans in the USA at that time (Kashima 2000). These findings suggest that, irrespective of the reality we are presented with, our knowledge of stereotypes can have a profound influence on what we recall and consequently what we are likely to transmit to others.

Our cognitive limitations and the quantity of social information we encounter create the conditions for memory-based competition; some information will survive in memory long enough to be successfully transmitted to others, while other information will be forgotten before it can be reproduced. In this competition for space within our memories, not all information is treated equally, and there exists a substantial body of research demonstrating a bias for recall of stereotype information (Bodenhausen and Lichtenstein 1987; Bodenhausen and Wyer 1985; Dodson et al. 2008). Moreover, as information is transmitted from person to person, stereotype-consistent information is more likely to be remembered than stereotype-inconsistent information (Allport and Postman 1947; Bangerter 2000; Kashima 2000; Kashima et al. 2013; Lyons and Kashima 2001, 2003). As a result, over time and repeated transmissions, information tends to become more consistent with the prevailing attitudes and stereotypes in society (Kashima et al. 2013). Cumulatively, our cognitive limitations and individual biases toward stereotype-consistent information influence what kind of information survives as it is passed from person to person, thus providing a mechanism by which stereotypes can be maintained and reproduced in our culture.

Not only does stereotype knowledge influence the narrative of what we remember and transmit to others but it also manifests itself in subtle and systematic ways in the language we use (Wigboldus et al. 2000). When we describe expectancy-consistent information (e.g., stereotype-consistent information) we do so at a greater level of linguistic abstraction than when describing expectancy-inconsistent information (Maass et al. 1989; Semin and de Poot 1997; Wigboldus et al. 2000). While these linguistic differences are seemingly unintended, they have the power to influence our collocutor's perception of events (Franco and Maass 1996; von Hippel et al. 1997). Wigboldus et al. (2000) were interested in the communicative consequences of our linguistic biases. In one experiment, participants were asked to communicate stereotype-relevant messages using their own words. They found that participants did indeed use a greater level of abstraction when communicating expected information compared to that which was unexpected. Moreover, results indicated that the greater the level of linguistic abstraction, the more likely recipients were to make dispositional inferences about the event, going beyond the specific content of the message. This suggests that stereotypes have the capacity to shape the language we use when we communicate with others, which, in turn, influences how information is perceived by others.

By influencing cognitive competition and the social transmission of information, stereotypes have the power to shape the way that knowledge evolves. Even when people are striving to recall and transmit an accurate account of events, knowledge of existing cultural stereotypes has the ability to distort reality. The extent of these distortions may be very slight within a single individual, but because all individuals have knowledge of the same cultural stereotypes (Devine 1989; Karlins et al. 1969; Katz and Braly 1933; Madon et al. 2001), these distortions grow cumulatively as knowledge is repeatedly relayed across many people. Thus, the selection and transmission bias toward stereotype-consistent information we exhibit as individuals acts to maintain and strengthen existing cultural stereotypes at a societal level. Although stereotypes exert selection pressure on the evolution of information, as a form of socially transmitted knowledge, stereotypes themselves are also subject to the pressures of cultural evolution.

Cultural Evolution Influences Stereotype Content

Many of the adaptive cognitive and social benefits we gain from using stereotypes are derived from the underlying principle that, in an ever-changing world, stereotypes provide a stable knowledge base that can assist us. However, any suggestion that stereotypes are fixed would be quite wrong. Stereotypes are continually evolving; it is only because they tend to change very slowly that gives the impression that they are stable. Cultural stereotypes evolve gradually but continuously in a manner that is similar to the continual but imperceptible change of organisms over many generations in biological evolution. Take the example of the gender stereotype associated with the colors pink and blue. In contemporary Western society, the colors pink and blue are unambiguously associated with girls and boys, respectively. These stereotypes are reflected in the color of clothes that people are able and willing to buy for babies and young children (Cunningham and Macrae 2011), to the extent that it would generally be deemed socially unacceptable to buy pink clothes for a boy. However, it seems this pervasive cultural stereotype linking gender and color only developed in the past 70 years or so. Up until around 1900, there was no apparent color-based sex stereotype for children's clothes, with boys and girls likely to be dressed in white until around the age of 6 (Paoletti 2012). In the first third of the twentieth century, retailers increasingly distinguished boys' and girls' clothes using color, but not consistently—indeed, in 1927, *Time* magazine printed an article on children's fashions telling readers that the majority of retailers recommended dressing boys in pink and girls in blue *(Fashions: Baby's clothes, Time,* 14 November, 1927; cited in Paoletti 2012). It is not until around the 1940s that we see the nascent beginnings of the "pink for a girl/blue for a boy" cultural stereotype of today. Clearly, the stereotype associations of pink and blue changed radically and on multiple occasions throughout the twentieth century.

Social psychological research spanning the past eight decades provides a more detailed analysis of the evolution of cultural stereotypes that are seemingly ubiquitous at a single point in time. The best known of these are the "The Princeton Trilogy" (Devine 1989; Madon et al. 2001), which examined the content and consensus of cultural stereotype knowledge shown by Princeton University students at three different points over a 36-year period. The initial study was conducted by Katz and Braly (1933) who asked a sample of students to select 5 traits from a list of 84 that best described ten ethnic and national groups. Their results indicated that the students held distinct beliefs about the groups in question, as well as showing a high degree of consensus across participants about those beliefs. A replication of this study by Gilbert (1951) found that the content of the stereotypes had remained stable over time, but that the degree of consensus had reduced. However, in the final study, Karlins et al. (1969) found that the content of stereotypes had changed considerably over time, with the degree of consensus across participants remaining stable.

The Princeton Trilogy studies demonstrate considerable change in stereotype content between 1933 and 1969. Subsequent replications of these studies suggest that changes found in stereotype content are reliable (Dovidio and Gaertner 1986; Lepore and Brown 1997). Madon et al. (2001) also replicated the findings of the Princeton Trilogy; their results demonstrated that both the content and consensus of the ten national and ethnic stereotypes reported had changed considerably over the intervening 60 years. In addition to replicating the original results, Madon et al. (2001) extended the findings by using an updated attribute list that included 300 new attributes to ensure that real changes in stereotypes were not being masked by the use of an outdated attribute list. Out of the ten groups, they found that stereotypes had changed significantly for nine of the groups. For example, while Katz and Braly (1933) found that 84% of their participants reported "superstitious" as an attribute of the African American stereotype, none of the European American participants in Madon et al. (2001) reported this attribute. Similarly, 75% of participants in Katz and Braly (1933) reported the African American stereotype to include "lazy," whereas "lazy" was not considered relevant to the current stereotype in Madon et al. (2001). Overall, Madon et al. (2001) reported that the majority of stereotypes had undergone considerable revision over time, with consensus for the current stereotypes remaining high or even increasing.

While it is relatively easy to demonstrate that cultural stereotypes evolve over time, determining exactly what factors influence their evolution is somewhat trickier because stereotypes change gradually over many years. One obvious contributory factor to changes seen in ethnic and national stereotypes is many years of increasing intergroup contact (Allport 1954; Madon et al. 2001). Since Katz and Braly's (1933) original investigation, societal changes in the USA mean there has been a progressive increase in the number of opportunities for people from different social groups to interact with one another. This increase in intergroup contact provides many more opportunities for people to refute the accuracy of stereotypes through their own personal experiences (Allport 1954; Madon et al. 2001). It is also possible that socioeconomic changes in the roles that members of different social groups play in society has altered the structural relationships between groups in such a way that has placed stereotype content under pressure to change. Evidence shows that stereotypes sometimes reflect the actual characteristics of social groups (Judd and Park 1993), thus any changes in the social group status are consequently reflected in a change in the stereotype content over time (Madon et al. 2001).

Examining the content of cultural stereotypes measured at different points in time provides very compelling evidence of the capacity for stereotypes to evolve (Karlins et al. 1969; Katz and Braly 1933; Madon et al. 2001). This by no means implies that stereotype change is either quick or easy to achieve (Devine and Elliot 1995; Lepore and Brown 1997). Stereotype change is a slow process but, over time, it seems stereotypes gradually adapt to reflect changes in cultural attitudes and beliefs (Madon et al. 2001). However, while we have some insight into *why* stereotypes might change over time, the mechanisms underpinning *how* stereotypes evolve are less apparent. How does one change stereotypes that exist in the collective consciousness of all members of society? How does one change stereotype associations that remain pervasive even though there is no obvious basis for their origin in the first place? How does one change stereotype associations that persist even in the minds of those who strenuously refute their accuracy? Indeed, how do stereotypes even form in the first place? It is possible that insights from cultural evolution research might help provide answers to all of these questions.

How Do Stereotypes Form and Evolve?

Theories of cultural evolution suggest that if one wishes to understand the content of human culture at a societal level, one must first understand how information is processed and transmitted at the individual level (Richerson and Boyd 2005; Mesoudi 2011). This acknowledgment that the macroevolution of culture is dependent on microevolution processes could be central to developing an understanding of how cultural stereotypes form and evolve. We see two appealing benefits from adopting this approach. First, explaining macroevolutionary culture by scaling up from microevolutionary processes provides plausible theoretical explanations for both how and why stereotypes form and change. Second, because the individual-level cognitive and social determinants of microevolution can be measured and manipulated within the controlled confines of a laboratory setting, it is possible to empirically test theories of stereotype formation and evolution that have thus far proved too unwieldy to examine in the wild.

A comparable cultural evolution approach has recently been adopted by researchers interested in the origins and evolution of human language. In order to examine the effects of cultural transmission on language, Kirby et al. (2008) developed a novel "alien" language for use in a diffusion-chain paradigm, similar to the methodology used by Bartlett (1932). The first participant in a chain underwent a learning phase where they received training in the alien language; this involved studying artificially created names used to describe pictures of "alien objects" (e.g., an image of a red circle was a "tuge"). Following the learning phase, knowledge of the language was tested by presenting participants with objects to name; some of these objects were ones they had encountered before (seen items) and some were previously unseen (unseen items). Crucially, while unseen items were entirely novel, they did share features with some of the seen items (e.g., shape or color). Whatever words participant 1 used to describe each stimulus during the test phase, whether correct or incorrect, were then carried over for use with participant 2 and were randomly designated as either seen items (i.e., viewed during learning and test) or unseen items (i.e., viewed only at test). This procedure was repeated until the language was transmitted across ten individuals/generations in turn.

The results of these experiments demonstrated that as the output of the language was transmitted from one participant to another, it became increasingly learnable (both for seen and unseen items). There was also evidence that the language became more structured over time. What started out as a set of random pairings of words and pictures (e.g., "tuge" used to describe a red circle), evolved into a structured language with specific words being used to describe certain shared categorical features (e.g., "tuge" incorporated in the description of all red items). Faced with the dual problems of an overwhelming amount of information to process and previously unseen objects, participants made many errors. However, it seems that their memory successes and failures were not random; instead, there was some level of categorical structure to their responses, with people more likely to make within-category confusions than between-category confusions. What began as tiny templates of structure in the episodic recall of one participant were detected and inadvertently and unconsciously amplified in the recollections of the next participant. Over time, these cumulative and systematic biases in recall resulted in a coherent categorical structure that could be used efficiently to infer information about targets even when they had never before been encountered.

There are some obvious conceptual parallels between the way that language and stereotypes function. First, both language and stereotypes rely on cultural consensus. A language cannot function successfully unless there is general agreement about its rules and meanings (Lehrer 1984). Similarly, the very nature of stereotypes requires that their content is widely known, if not necessarily endorsed (Devine 1989; Katz and Braly 1933; Lepore and Brown 1997). Second, both language and stereotypes allow users to make rule-based inferences that can be utilized in new situations. For example, grammatical sentences can be constructed even though the content of the sentence may be entirely novel (Kirby 2001); equally, we can use category-based stereotypes to make inferences about people we have never before encountered (Allport 1954; Brewer 1988; Fiske and Neuberg 1990). Third, both languages and stereotypes have the ability and propensity to change over time (Kirby et al. 2008; Madon et al. 2001). Finally, both languages and stereotypes are culturally learned through iterated learning—that is, rather than being explicitly learned, they can be acquired tacitly through our repeated interactions with other people (Kirby et al. 2008; Stangor and Schaller 1996; Stangor et al. 2001).

Given these parallels, it is possible that stereotypes might culturally evolve in a similar way to language. Any hint of existing linguistic structure and category association is detected and repeatedly amplified as a consequence of the shared cognitive biases and limitations of those who transmit the information (Kirby et al. 2008). Clearly, there are many examples of stereotypes that contain a "kernel of truth," as they are based on a genuine relationship that exists between attributes and categories (e.g., the Scottish stereotype includes attributes that are overrepresented among Scots, such as wearing kilts and having red hair). Where such category-based overrepresentations exist for social information, it seems likely they would be detected and amplified until a stereotype has formed. In addition, cumulative cultural evolution might also provide a mechanism to explain those aspects of stereotypes that are seemingly arbitrary or of no obvious origin (e.g., the stereotype of Scottish people as miserly or the gender stereotypes of the colors of pink and blue). Kirby and colleagues found that even when there was no discernible categorical organization of a language, this structure was imposed unintentionally as people (mis)remembered what they had learned. Where there is no existing association between social categories and information, our shared cognitive biases and limitations might result in the spontaneous creation of relationships as information passes from one mind to the next.

Conclusion

By examining stereotypes from an evolutionary perspective, one begins to get a sense of their broad significance for our species. The adaptive social and cognitive benefits stereotypes provide us as individuals today are well documented (Bodenhausen and Lichtenstein 1987; Brewer 1988; Fiske and Neuberg 1990; Macrae et al. 1994a). What is less clear is the influence that stereotypes have exerted in shaping the substance of our inherited knowledge by subtly changing the content of information as it is passed from person to person. Equally intangible are the mechanisms that facilitated the creation and development of the cultural stereotypes that exist today. However, by utilizing the theoretical and methodological approaches of cultural evolution, we could examine the origins and development of stereotypes in the lab, and further our understanding of how stereotypes might naturally occur or evolve in nature.

References

Allport, G. (1954). *The nature of prejudice*. Reading: Addison-Wesley.

Allport, G. W., & Postman, L. (1947). *The psychology of rumor*. New York: Russell & Russell.

Bangerter, A. (2000). Transformation between scientific and social representations of conception: The method of serial reproduction. *British Journal of Social Psychology, 39,* 521–535.

Bar-Tal, D. (2000). *Shared beliefs in a society: Social psychological analysis*. Thousand Oaks: Sage.

Bartlett, F. C. (1932). *Remembering: A study in experimental and social psychology*. Cambridge: Cambridge University Press.

Baum, W. M., Richerson, P. J., Efferson, C. M., & Paciotti, B. M. (2004). Cultural evolution in laboratory microsocieties including traditions of rule giving and rule following. *Evolution and Human Behavior, 25,* 305–326.

Bodenhausen, G. V., & Lichtenstein, M. (1987). Social stereotypes and information-processing strategies: The impact of task complexity. *Journal of Personality and Social Psychology, 52,* 871–880.

Bodenhausen, G. V., & Wyer, R. S. (1985). Effects of stereotypes in decision making and information-processing strategies. *Journal of Personality and Social Psychology, 48,* 267–282.

Brewer, M. B. (1988). A dual process model of impression formation. In T. K. Scrull & R. S. Wyer, Jr. (Eds.), *Advances in social cognition* (Vol. 1, pp. 1–36). Hillsdale: Erlbaum.

Brewer, M. B., & Feinstein, A. H. (1999). Dual processes in the cognitive representation of persons and social categories. In S. Chaiken & Y. Trope (Eds.), *Dual-process theories in social psychology* (pp. 255–270). New York: Guilford.

Caldwell, C. A., & Millen, A. E. (2008a). Studying cumulative cultural evolution in the laboratory. *Philosophical Transactions of the Royal Society B: Biological Sciences, 363,* 3529–3539.

Caldwell, C. A., & Millen, A. E. (2008b). Experimental models for testing hypotheses about cumulative cultural evolution. *Evolution and Human Behavior, 29,* 165–171.

Campbell, D. T. (1975). On the conflicts between biological and social evolution and between psychology and moral tradition. *American Psychologist, 30,* 1103–1126.

Cunningham, S. J., & Macrae, C. N. (2011). The colour of gender stereotyping. *British Journal of Psychology, 102,* 598–614.

Dennet, D. C. (1995). *Darwin's dangerous idea. Evolution and the meanings of life*. London: Allen Lane.

Devine, P. G. (1989). Stereotypes and prejudice: Their automatic and controlled components. *Journal of Personality and Social Psychology, 56,* 5–18.

Devine, P. G., & Elliot, A. J. (1995). Are racial stereotypes really fading? The Princeton trilogy revisited. *Personality and Social Psychology Bulletin, 21,* 1139–1150.

Dodson, C. S., Darragh, J., & Williams, A. (2008). Stereotypes and retrieval-provoked illusory source recollections. *Journal of Experimental Psychology: Learning, Memory, and Cognition, 34,* 460–467.

Dovidio, J. F., & Gaertner, S. L. (1986). *Prejudice, discrimination, and racism*. New York: Academic.

Fein, S., & Spencer, S. J. (1997). Prejudice as self-image maintenance: Affirming the self through derogating others. *Journal of Personality and Social Psychology, 73,* 31–44.

Festinger, L. (1954). A theory of social comparison processes. *Human Relations, 7,* 117–140.

Fiske, S. T., & Neuberg, S. L. (1990). A continuum of impression formation, from category-based to individuating processes: Influences of information and motivation on attention and interpretation. In M. P. Zanna (Ed.), *Advances in experimental social psychology* (Vol. 23, pp. 1–74). San Diego: Academic.

Fiske, S. T., Neuberg, S. L., Beattie, A. E., & Milberg, S. J. (1987). Category-based and attribute-based reactions to others: Some informational conditions of stereotyping and individuating processes. *Journal of Experimental Social Psychology, 23,* 399–427.

Flynn, E. (2008). Investigating children as cultural magnets: do young children transmit redundant information along diffusion chains? *Philosophical Transactions of the Royal Society B: Biological Sciences, 363,* 3541–3551.

Franco, F. M., & Maass, A. (1996). Implicit versus explicit strategies of out-group discrimination: The role of intentional control in biased language use and reward allocation. *Journal of Language and Social Psychology, 15,* 335–359.

Gilbert, G. M. (1951). Stereotype persistence and change among college students. *Journal of Abnormal and Social Psychology, 46,* 245–254.

Griffiths, T. L., Kalish, M. L., & Lewandowsky, S. (2008). Theoretical and empirical evidence for the impact of inductive biases on cultural evolution. *Philosophical Transactions of the Royal Society B: Biological Sciences, 363,* 3503–3514.

Hill, R. A., & Dunbar, R. I. (2003). Social network size in humans. *Human nature, 14,* 53–72.

Hogg, M. A., & Reid, S. A. (2006). Social identity, self–categorization, and the communication of group norms. *Communication Theory, 16,* 7–30.

Judd, C. M., & Park, B. (1993). Definition and assessment of accuracy in social stereotypes. *Psychological review, 100,* 109–128.

Kalish, M. L., Griffiths, T. L., & Lewandowsky, S. (2007). Iterated learning: Intergenerational knowledge transmission reveals inductive biases. *Psychonomic Bulletin and Review, 14,* 288–294.

Karlins, M., Coffman, T. L., & Walters, G. (1969). On the fading of social stereotypes: studies in three generations of college students. *Journal of Personality and Social Psychology, 13,* 1–16.

Kashima, Y. (2000). Maintaining cultural stereotypes in the serial reproduction of narratives. *Personality and Social Psychology Bulletin, 26,* 594–604.

Kashima, Y., Klein, O., & Clark, A. E. (2007). Grounding: Sharing information in social interaction. In K. Fiedler (Ed.), *Social communication* (pp. 27–77). New York: Psychology Press.

Kashima, Y., Lyons, A., & Clark, A. (2013). The maintenance of cultural stereotypes in the conversational retelling of narratives. *Asian Journal of Social Psychology, 16,* 60–70.

Katz, D., & Braly, K. W. (1933). Racial stereotypes of one hundred college students. *Journal of Abnormal and Social Psychology, 28,* 280–290.

Killworth, P. D., Johnsen, E. C., Bernard, H. R., Ann Shelley, G., & McCarty, C. (1990). Estimating the size of personal networks. *Social Networks, 12,* 289–312.

Kirby, S. (2001). Spontaneous evolution of linguistic structure-an iterated learning model of the emergence of regularity and irregularity. *IEEE Transactions on Evolutionary Computation, 5,* 102–110.

Kirby, S., Cornish, H., & Smith, K. (2008). Cumulative cultural evolution in the laboratory: An experimental approach to the origins of structure in human language. *Proceedings of the National Academy of Sciences, 105,* 10681–10686.

Lehrer, K. (1984). Coherence, consensus and language. *Linguistics and Philosophy, 7,* 43–55.

Lepore, L., & Brown, R. (1997). Category and stereotype activation: Is prejudice inevitable? *Journal of Personality and Social Psychology, 72,* 275–287.

Lippman, W. (1922). *Public opinion.* New York: Harcourt & Brace.

Lyons, A., & Kashima, Y. (2001). The reproduction of culture: Communication processes tend to maintain cultural stereotypes. *Social Cognition, 19,* 372–394.

Lyons, A., & Kashima, Y. (2003). How are stereotypes maintained through communication? The influence of stereotype sharedness. *Journal of Personality and Social Psychology, 85,* 989–1005.

Maass, A., Salvi, D., Arcuri, L., & Semin, G. R. (1989). Language use in intergroup contexts: The linguistic intergroup bias. *Journal of personality and social psychology, 57,* 981–993.

Macrae, C. N., & Bodenhausen, G. V. (2000). Social cognition: Thinking categorically about others. *Annual Review of Psychology, 51,* 93–120.

Macrae, C. N., Milne, A. B., & Bodenhausen, G. V. (1994a). Stereotypes as energy-saving devices: A peek inside the cognitive toolbox. *Journal of Personality and Social Psychology, 66,* 37–47.

Macrae, C. N., Stangor, C., & Milne, A. B. (1994b). Activating social stereotypes: A functional analysis. *Journal of Experimental Social Psychology, 30,* 370–389.

Madon, S., Guyll, M., Aboufadel, K., Montiel, E., Smith, A., Palumbo, P., & Jussim, L. (2001). Ethnic and national stereotypes: The Princeton trilogy revisited and revised. *Personality and Social Psychology Bulletin, 27,* 996–1010.

McGarty, C., Yzerbyt, V. Y., & Spears, S. (2002). *Stereotypes as explanations.* Cambridge: Cambridge University Press.

Mesoudi, A. (2009). How cultural evolutionary theory can inform social psychology and vice versa. *Psychological Review, 116,* 929–952.

Mesoudi, A. (2011). *Cultural evolution: How Darwinian theory can explain human culture and synthesize the social sciences.* Chicago: University of Chicago Press.

Paoletti, J. B. (2012). *Pink and blue: Telling the boys from the girls in America.* Bloomington: Indiana University Press.

Pool, I. S., & Kochen, M. (1978). Contact and influence. *Social Networks, 1,* 5–51.

Richerson, P. J., & Boyd, R. (2005). *Not by genes alone: How culture transformed human evolution.* Chicago: University of Chicago Press.

Rosch, E., Mervis, C. B., Gray, W. D., Johnson, D. M., & Boyes-Braem, P. (1976). Basic objects in natural categories. *Cognitive psychology, 8,* 382–439.

Schaller, M., & Conway, L. G. (1999). Influence of impression management goals on the emerging contents of group stereotypes: Support for a social-evolutionary process. *Personality and Social Psychology Bulletin, 25,* 819–833.

Semin, G. R., & De Poot, C. J. (1997). The question-answer paradigm: You might regret not noticing how a question is worded. *Journal of Personality and Social Psychology, 73,* 472–480.

Sherman, J. W., & Bessenoff, G. R. (1999). Stereotypes as source-monitoring cues: On the interaction between episodic and semantic memory. *Psychological Science, 10,* 106–110.

Spiro, R. J. (1980). Accommodative reconstruction in prose recall. *Journal of Verbal Learning and Verbal Behavior, 19,* 84–95.

Stangor, C., & Schaller, M. (1996). Stereotypes as individual and collective representations. In C. N. Macrae, C. Stangor, & M. Hewstone (Eds.), *Stereotypes and stereotyping* (pp. 3–37). New York: Guilford Press.

Stangor, C., Sechrist, G. B., & Jost, J. T. (2001). Changing racial beliefs by providing consensus information. *Personality and Social Psychology Bulletin, 27,* 486–496.

Tajfel, H. (1969). Cognitive aspect of prejudice. *Journal of Social Issues, 25,* 79–97.

Tajfel, H., & Turner, J. C. (1979). An integrative theory of intergroup conflict. In W. G. Austin & S. Worchel (Eds.), *The social psychology of intergroup relations* (pp. 33–47). Monterey: Brooks-Cole.

Tajfel, H., Billig, M. G., Bundy, R. P., & Flament, C. (1971). Social categorization and intergroup behaviour. *European Journal of Social Psychology, 1,* 149–178.

Von Hippel, W., Sekaquaptewa, D., & Vargas, P. (1997). The linguistic intergroup bias as an implicit indicator of prejudice. *Journal of Experimental Social Psychology, 33,* 490–509.

Wigboldus, D. H., Semin, G. R., & Spears, R. (2000). How do we communicate stereotypes? Linguistic bases and inferential consequences. *Journal of Personality and Social Psychology, 78,* 5–18.

A Biosocial Model of Status in Face-To-Face Groups

24

Allan Mazur

How exactly should we apply an evolutionary perspective to social psychology? A well-known example is the selectionist theory of sex differences in human mating strategy. Men produce offspring via ejaculation; women must invest a prolonged period of pregnancy and nursing (Trivers 1972). The implication is that men and women engage in different mating strategies, with women's comparatively limited reproductive capabilities, relative to men, increasing their choosiness and causing them to be more discerning when selecting a mate. The theory's logic can be extended to gorillas and orangutans, where males seek to mate with multiple females, while females are usually limited to a single male. However, it fails for other apes: Gibbons and siamangs are monogamous, although at least one observer thinks male gibbons compete more than females for mates based on sex differences in song bouts (Cowlishaw 1996). Among chimpanzees, both sexes mate with multiple partners. Among bonobos, females freely seek sexual relations with both sexes and appear as eager as males for coitus.

An alternate approach to the evolution of behavior recognizes that humans are primates, and we share certain behaviors seen in nearly all our primate cousins, especially in those evolutionarily closest to us, the African apes. This strongly suggests that such common behaviors evolved along with the physical changes that produced *Homo sapiens*. But this is only a first step. To be convincing, we may also identify proximate mechanisms in the neurophysiology of humans (and other primates) that underlie these putatively evolved behaviors.

A. Mazur (✉)
Maxwell School, Syracuse University,
419 Crouse-Hinds Hall, 900 S. Crouse Avenue, Syracuse, NY, 13244-1020, USA
e-mail: amazur@maxwell.syr.edu

Dominance/Status Hierarchies in Face-to-Face Groups

Dominance (or status) hierarchies are a reliable feature of primate societies. (To be clear, I am referring to status in face-to-face groups, not to macro-level stratification in large societies, which has no homologue in nonhuman primates.) To avoid an overly simplistic picture of these structures, several qualifications are needed. Status rank may be persistently relevant in species with fairly permanent groups, or only occasionally relevant for animals that forage alone. Rankings are usually, but not necessarily, transitive. The relative status of two individuals may depend, in part, on the proximity of allies. Sometimes the highest-ranking position is shared by a coalition of two or three animals. It is often easier to identify a male ranking than a female ranking. Rankings are usually less clear in the wild than in captive colonies where animals are forced into close contact. Also, some species simply show less overt status behavior than others, and status ranking may become prominent

V. Zeigler-Hill et al. (eds.), *Evolutionary Perspectives on Social Psychology*, Evolutionary Psychology,
DOI 10.1007/978-3-319-12697-5_24, © Springer International Publishing Switzerland 2015

only during the breeding season or in periods of food scarcity. Given these qualifications, it is still clear that there is a general primate pattern of fairly consistent rank ordering with respect to influence, power, and valued prerogatives.

Among humans, face-to-face status (dominance) hierarchies have corollary features long recognized in classical social psychology. Here, I briefly enumerate five corollaries that we now know are also found among nonhuman primates, at least those evolutionarily closest to us, and therefore plausibly having an evolved basis (see Mazur 2005, for an extended treatment).

1. **An individual's rank depends partly on extrinsic attributes that are not obviously prerequisites for status in the group**

Thus, a person may have high status in a small group simply by virtue of being older, or male, or coming from a wealthy family—features Berger and his colleagues have labeled "diffuse status characteristics" (Berger et al. 1972). Sex and age are also reliable status determinants in nonhuman primates but it seems inappropriate to consider them extrinsic attributes (as we do in humans) since they are clearly correlated with strength, size, experience, and perhaps relevant hormonal differences. More relevant is the tendency, known in several primate species, for an animal's status to be influenced, if not fully determined, by the rank of its mother. Broader family connections have similar influence. Troops of Old World monkeys—such as baboons, macaques, and vervets—are composed of different matrilineal families, each arranged in a stable, linear dominance hierarchy. All females of one matriline outrank all females of another. Female baboons recognize that a reversal in the status of two matrilines affects their own status (Bergman et al. 2003).

2. **Over the long run, group members interact more with others of similar rank ("near-peers") than with members of dissimilar rank**

Among nonhuman primates, interaction usually occurs within age–sex categories (excepting sexual and mother–offspring relations). Since males usually dominate females, and adults generally dominate juveniles, the effect is to concentrate interaction among near-peers. Within age–sex categories, monkeys and chimpanzees often form coalitions, their decisions to give or withdraw support seemingly calculated to earn enhanced status (de Waal 1989). Tabulations of pair-wise interactions among monkeys and apes show more interaction with near-peers than would be expected by chance (Mazur 1973).

3. **High-ranked members—particularly the leaders—perform service and control functions for other members and for the group as a whole**

Leaders of baboon and macaque troops are in the forefront during intertroop combat or in defense against a predator. When a dispute breaks out between troop members, the leader may stop it with a threat, and will protect a mother with an infant who is threatened by another animal. High-ranking chimpanzees sometimes adopt a control role, breaking up fights or systematically protecting the weak against the strong (de Waal 2000).

4. **Low-ranked members appear more nervous than higher-ranked members; high-ranked members can manipulate the stress experienced by—and thereby the performance of—low-ranked members**

Early accounts of macaque behavior often describe low-ranking members as "nervous, insecure" or "cowering" (e.g., Southwick 1963). In human groups or gangs, the cool confidence of leaders versus the timidity of lowest-ranked members has become a cliché.

5. **Humans and apes usually establish and maintain status rank without physical fights, aggressive threats, or overt gestures of submission**

Displays of dominance must be viewed within the broader context of communication. Lower primates are limited, repetitive, and stereotypic in their displays; higher primates are more flexible and capable of using diverse and novel forms of expression. Apes are capable of violent dominance displays, but these are relatively infrequent. During her pioneering years of studying chimps in the wild, Jane Goodall found her subjects apparently so uncompetitive that she could not at first discern their dominance relationships. "However, when regular observations became possible on the interactions between the various individuals it gradually became evident that the social status of each chimpanzee was fairly well defined in relation to each other individual" (van Lawick-Goodall 1968, p. 315). Similarly, most human adults are rarely, if ever, violent in face-to-face competition for status.

Overall, we see that these status corollaries—thought by early social psychologists and sociologists to be uniquely human—are in fact common among primates, especially in those most like us physically. We have a prima facie case that these status behaviors evolved along with our physical form and that they might be explained proximately by neurophysiological mechanisms. We turn now to these proximate mechanisms, especially the stress differences that often distinguish high from low rank.

Status Signs

Every individual primate has certain observable *signs* or *signals* that suggest his or her social status is (or ought to be) high or low (Mazur 2005). Those displaying high-status signs are not guaranteed to hold correspondingly high rank in their group's status hierarchy, but if we know an individual's signs we can make a better than random guess about their actual status.

Some status signs are limited to a particular species, such as the silver hair on the back of a dominant male gorilla. Others are similar across primate species. For example, large size, physical strength, vigor, good health, age (i.e., adult vs. juvenile), being male, and (among the higher primates) having a high-ranked mother are all signs associated with high status, whereas their opposites suggest low status. The range and flexibility of status signs are least among the lower primates (prosimians), increase among monkeys, more so in apes with their protocultures, and are most flexible among humans with full cultures. Wearing expensive and fashionable clothing is a signal of high status among humans. A beautiful wife, desirable to other men, or one with a rich dowry, gives prestige to her husband; a rich or powerful husband or protector elevates a woman's rank.

Among humans, the prestige one holds in the larger society—perhaps as a representative of "legitimate" or "official" authority, or by virtue of occupation, wealth, education, or family lineage—carries over into face-to-face interaction, although it may have no relevance in that context. A surgeon and a plumber, meeting casually outside their professional roles, are likely to rank themselves so that the plumber defers to the surgeon, even though medical skills are irrelevant to the situation. (If the toilet is flooding, the plumber will enjoy a temporarily elevated status.) A famous person, like a visibly wealthy one, can usually dominate an intimate social gathering.

It is useful to divide status signs into two categories: *constant* signals that individuals display persistently, whether they want to or not (e.g., size, sex, age), and *controllable* signals that individuals can quickly change by their own (conscious or unconscious) efforts. Among controllable status signals are body postures, facial expressions, direct staring or eye aversion, advancing toward or retreating from another individual, and relaxed and confident demeanor versus nervous fidgeting, growling, grinning, or crying. Among humans, language carries many of these controllable signals, in either tone (command vs. request), semantic content, or nonverbal gestures that accompany speech. Items of dress, cosmetics, and accessories also serve humans as controllable status signs.

Faces

Facial appearance and facial gestures are among the most impressive status signs in higher primates, especially among the apes (including humans) in whom facial musculature is most flexible, subtle, and expressive. Figure 24.1 shows artist John Hyatt's rendition of two facial displays, one dominant, the other deferent (Guthrie 1973). No one has trouble deciding which is which, though neither display is a pure sign. The dominant face additionally signals menace and anger. The deferent face seems vacantly happy in its submissiveness—an Alfred E. Neuman without buckteeth.

My distinction between constant and controllable signs is pertinent here. Comparing

Fig. 24.1 John Hyatt's renderings of dominant and submissive faces. (Guthrie 1973)

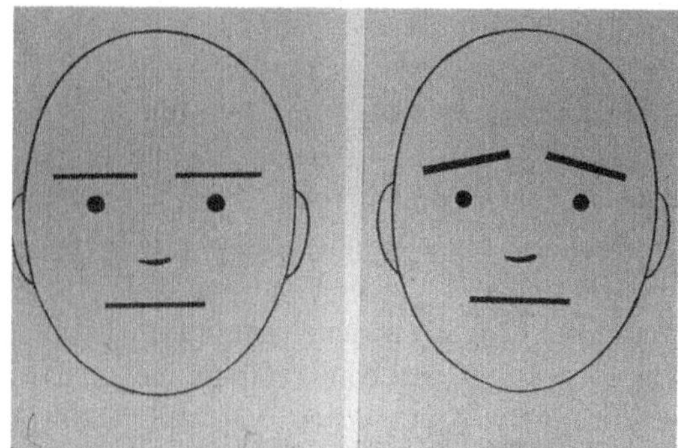

Fig. 24.2 Cartoon expressions of dominance and deference

the controllable expressions on these faces, we see dominance signaled with directly glaring and narrowed eyes beneath lowered eyebrows, taut facial muscles, flared nostrils, and visibly clinched teeth. In contrast, the deferent expression has relaxed musculature, eyes wide open and averted, eyebrows raised, and lips smiling. If these were live faces, their expressions could be reversed in a moment, but doing so would not fully transpose the displays because their faces also differ in constant features that signal dominance or deference. The left face is bearded, suggesting—though we cannot see it—a square jaw; the face is vertically elongated with rugged, muscular features, including a strong browridge emphasized by heavy eyebrows; the skin seems coarse. The right face is round, soft, smooth, with pudgy cheeks, perhaps fittingly termed "baby faced" (Zebrowitz et al. 1993). Even with neutral expressions, the constant features of one face convey a more dominant aspect than those of the other.

Our flexibly expressive eyes, brow, and mouth are the critical features for quickly altering visible demeanor, and their manipulation can blatantly or subtly change the meaning read into a facial signal. Participants shown portraits posed with differing eyebrow positions (raised or lowered) or with differing mouth positions (smiling or neutral), and asked to judge which is more dominant (i.e., which is more respected, more likely to tell others what to do, more leader-like), tend to choose portraits with lowered brows and unsmiling mouths (Keating et al. 1977). The reader may easily see this perceptual difference due to eyebrow position in cartoon faces (Fig. 24.2).

Ulrich Mueller and I wondered if the perception of dominance conveyed by yearbook portraits of the West Point Class of 1950 had any effect on their subsequent careers in the US military. Judges blind to the purpose of our study were asked to rank cadet portraits on a seven-point scale of dominance–submissiveness (1 = *very submissive*, 7 = *very dominant*). Figure 24.3 shows four cadets of varying facial dominance, and formal portraits of the same men after all had achieved the rank of general.

All cadets entered West Point as undifferentiated plebes. The first time they were given ranks was in junior year when nearly half were elevated to corporal, the rest remaining privates. As seniors they were ranked again, with one quarter of the class named cadet officers and the rest sergeants. At graduation, everyone received the rank of second lieutenant. By 1963, nearly everyone remaining on active duty had been promoted to major. During the early 1960s, roughly three quarters of these men were invited to spend an academic year at the army's Command and General Staff College for additional training. This was a critical branching point because men who did not attend this college were almost certain to advance no higher than lieutenant colonel. Graduation from Staff College is an essential but not sufficient requirement for an invitation to a war college, the second crucial branching point. Less than half of the graduates from Staff College

bhec-08-05-06-f01

Fig. 24.3 Men of varying facial dominance who became high-ranked generals, shown as cadets and in late career. From *left*: Wallace Nutting (facial dominance score as cadet = 6), Charles Gabriel (5), John Wickham, Jr. (4), and Lincoln Faurer (3). Cadet portraits are from the West Point yearbook *The Howitzer 1950*; officer portraits are from Pentagon archives

were admitted to a war college to receive training at the level of division command.

Did looks ever affect promotion? Certainly, this appears to have been the case at West Point. In junior year, cadets with the most dominant-looking faces were twice as likely to make corporal as those with the least dominant-looking faces. In senior year, the promotion rate of the most dominant-looking men was five times that of their least dominant-looking classmates.

After West Point, the dynamics of rank attainment changed. Facial dominance did not predict promotion to major or lieutenant colonel, selection to staff or war colleges, nor did it predict the rapidity of these advancements. What did count was the rate of advance; some men were on a fast track, racing through successive promotions ahead of their classmates, but these men did not have especially dominant faces. Promotions in mid-career are decided impersonally by boards of officers who do not know the candidates, but look at their dossiers.

Colonels who entered a war college made up the pool from which generals were drawn. Nearly everyone who reaches this stage has an excellent record, so personnel files do not differentiate very well. The pool is relatively small, about 108 men for the class of 1950. At this level in the hierarchy, someone on the promotion board almost certainly knows each candidate personally and would have heard of others by reputation or through advice from mentors and colleagues. Promotions at this stage are similar to the selection of cadet officers back at West Point in the sense that those making the selection know the men as individuals rather than from impersonal records. Therefore, it is not surprising that the criteria for selection to the highest ranks are again highly personal, including whether the man *looks* like a leader. For war

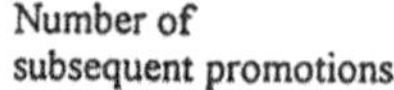

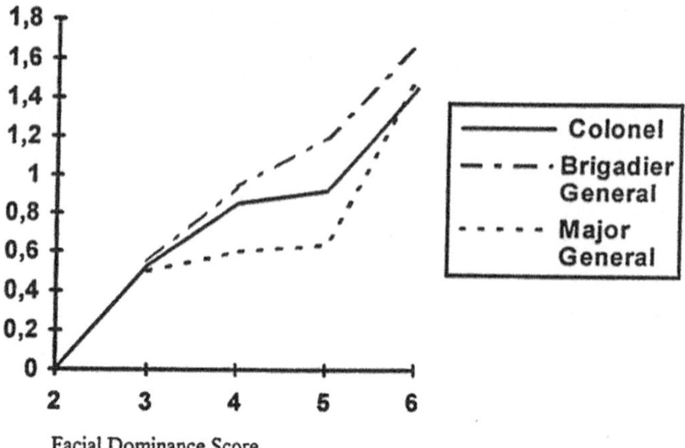

Fig. 24.4 Number of subsequent promotions from each officer rank, by facial dominance score (war college graduates only). (Mueller and Mazur 1996))

college graduates, the number of promotions beyond colonel increased with facial dominance (Fig. 24.4). Men with dominant faces had an advantage in promotion to general.

Considering that cadet faces were rated for dominance by strangers looking quickly at yearbook portraits, it is remarkable that these scores predict promotions made 20 or more years after the portraits were taken. Surely, a fuller and more contemporaneous evaluation of dominant appearance, including not only one's face but also one's body, one's postures and gestures, and one's voice, would more strongly predict the decisions of promotion boards.

A question that inevitably arises is, what do dominant faces look like? Everyone knows because anyone can sort portraits on that basis, but facial dominance is a gestalt concept, difficult to describe in simple terms. Dominant faces often seem muscular, with prominent as opposed to weak chins, and with heavy browridges and deep-set eyes. Submissive faces are often round or narrow, with ears "sticking out," whereas dominant faces are oval or rectangular with close-set ears. Faces identified as dominant are more likely to be handsome than not, though with striking exceptions. Many rate Arnold Schwarzenegger's face (in his prime) as dominant, but not handsome, and actor Hugh Grant's face as handsome, but not dominant.

Allocating Ranks

Dominance hierarchies, once set, are fairly stable. However, when a new group forms, there must be an initial allocation of ranks, and in established groups some individuals occasionally alter their positions. How are these initial rankings, and later changes in rank, determined? The short answer is that ranks are allocated either *cooperatively,* by consensus of those involved, or *competitively,* when there is disagreement over who should be superior.

Primate species vary in the degree to which they allocate ranks competitively. Among the prosimians, as well as baboons and macaques, rank allocation within newly formed groups as well as changes of rank within established groups are usually accompanied by overt conflict that produces a victor and vanquished. Among apes and humans, rank allocation is often cooperative, and when there is competition, it usually stops short of physical attack.

We may explore the decision to compete or cooperate by visualizing two individuals (Ego and Alter) meeting for the first time. If their interaction is very brief or casual, the notion of ranking may never arise. In more extended or serious meetings, each appraises the status signs of the other, forming some idea of their relative standings. If Ego perceives that Alter's status signs exceed his own, he may defer to Alter without any dispute. In a classic study of the American court system, when jury members elected a foreman, they favored men with prestigious occupations, even though sex and occupation were irrelevant to the foreman's task (Strodtbeck et al. 1957). Ego, in explaining such concessions, may offer that Alter *belongs* in the higher rank, or that Alter *deserves* it, or that Alter *could easily take it* if Ego resisted, or that Alter may be more *competent* in the duties of high rank. Indeed, it is a long-established finding that even when no obvious status signs distinguish participants from each other in a newly formed group, they still tend to stratify cooperatively, often within the first minutes of interaction (e.g., Fisek and Ofshe 1970). This was a surprising finding when first reported because social psychologists did not recognize that barely perceptible status signs like those emanating from a face or from postural cues, convey ranking information as effectively as blatant markers like sex, race, and occupation.

The signaling capability of an eye glance was demonstrated decades ago with an experiment devised by Strongman and Champness (1968). Starting with three unacquainted participants and taken two at a time, there are three possible pairs. Seat each pair of participants at a table so they are face to face, but with a screen blocking their view of each other. Remove the screen, telling participants to get to know one another. Typically, as the screen is removed, the pair makes eye contact. One person holds the glance longer than the other and we describe this person as "out-glancing" the other. Repeat the procedure for the other two pairs. A transitive ordering occurs if one person out-glances the other two, one person out-glances one but is out-glanced by another, and one person is out-glanced by two others. Strongman and Champness (1968) found a nearly transitive eye-glance hierarchy among ten subjects, matched pair-wise in a round robin tournament. Eugene Rosa and I found perfect transitivity in a round robin tournament of six subjects (Rosa and Mazur 1979).

Rosa went further by asking if rank in this momentary eye-glance hierarchy predicts rank in the status hierarchy that emerges when the same participants are brought together in prolonged discussion. He ran 20 groups, each composed of three unacquainted college students undifferentiated by age, race, sex, or social class; half the groups were male, half female. First, Rosa put each threesome through a pair-wise round robin to establish the eye-glance hierarchy. Later, he brought the three participants together in a half-hour discussion, measuring each person's status by the amount he or she spoke during the discussion. He corroborated this ranking by afterward asking participants to rate who contributed the most ideas and the best guidance to the group. Sixteen of the 20 groups formed a transitive eye-glance hierarchy. In these transitive groups, Rosa found that eye-glance rank significantly predicted status ranking in the following discussion (Rosa and Mazur 1979). Eye glance is only one of many facial gestures that can signal dominance or deference, and these are usually accompanied by parallel signals in speech and body posture, producing an integrated presentation of high or low status.

People do not always accept their status ranking so easily. Ego's decision to comply or compete depends on his motivation to dominate or the stakes that may be on the table. An individual who has experienced a recent rise in stature, perhaps from a victory or by passing through puberty, may be unusually pugnacious and challenge someone with impressive status. When Ego is on home territory, or protecting group members or valued possessions, and Alter is an intruder, then Ego is particularly likely to rise to a challenge. Among humans, a substantive disagreement—perhaps over a point of information or ideology—may escalate into a dominance competition so that winning becomes an end in itself, with the original substantive disagreement relegated to secondary importance. If both Ego and Alter decide to compete, their relative ranks are then determined by the outcome of one or more short *dominance contests*.

Dominance Contests

Nonhuman primates often establish and maintain their dominance hierarchies through a series of short face-to-face competitions between members of the group. Usually, these are pair-wise contests, but occasionally they involve more than two individuals at once. Some competitions involve fierce combat to determine victor and vanquished. Others are mild, as when one animal is obviously the more powerful or assertive, or the other appears fearful. In such cases, a simple stare by the powerful animal, followed by the fearful animal averting its eyes or yielding something of value (perhaps food or a sitting place), may suffice to determine the winner. Sometimes a single contest is all that is needed to allocate ranks or to verify a preexisting status relationship, but often the outcome is settled only after a series of contests.

A mechanism postulated to operate across this range of competition is the manipulation of discomfort levels during these contests. In this model, a threat or attack is an attempt by one animal to "out-stress" or intimidate the opponent by inducing fear, anxiety, or other discomfort. The animal that out-stresses its adversary is the winner. At first glance, this model seems inappropriate to humans, who usually form status hierarchies politely. Chimpanzees, bonobos, and gorillas—the primates most like us—are more subtle in their status competition than monkeys or prosimians, and humans continue that trend. The emotional distribution of status occurs less stressfully among us than among nonhuman primates, but stresses are not wholly absent.

The model becomes clearer if we consider a concrete example. The eyes of two strangers, Ego and Alter, meet by chance across a room. Let us say that Ego decides to hold the glance. The chance eye contact now becomes a dominance encounter. Ego's stare makes Alter uncomfortable. Alter may avert his eyes, thus relieving his discomfort while in effect surrendering, or he may stare back, making Ego uncomfortable in return. In the latter case, the stare-down continues with each individual trying to out-stress the other until finally one person succumbs to the discomfort (and to the challenger) by averting his eyes. The matter thus settled, the yielder usually avoids further eye contact, though the winner may occasionally look at the loser as if to verify his victory. In this example, Ego's stare is assumed to cause stress in Alter. Alter's eye aversion is assumed to relieve his stress. Typically, in stare-downs of this kind, the levels of discomfort are low and the adversaries may be barely aware of their contest.

In this context, staring is an assertive sign of high status. Eye aversion is a deferent sign associated with low status. In other words, a dominant act (staring) elicits stress in the recipient; a deferent act (eye aversion) relieves stress in the actor. A central assumption of the model is that most dominant and deferent acts work this way, inducing or relieving stress, respectively. These actions are the means through which adversaries wage their dominance contest, aiming "darts" at one another. When the stress becomes too great for one, he switches from dominant to deferent actions, thereby relieving his stress and simultaneously signaling his acceptance of the lower rank. Normally, a dominance-seeking person stresses adversaries through means that are polite or at least socially acceptable, and within the norms of business or sports competition.

Stress

Stress is an organism's subjective plus physiological responses to threatening or demanding stimuli. Subjectively, this response is experienced as discomfort, whether as anxiety, fear, anger, annoyance, or depression. Physiologically, it involves a complex response of the neurohormonal system: release of adrenocorticotropin from the anterior pituitary, glucocorticoids from the adrenal cortex (including cortisol, in humans), epinephrine (adrenaline) from the adrenal medulla, and norepinephrine from the sympathetic nerves of the autonomic nervous system, all of which produce effects on other parts of the body. This total reaction is often called the "fight-or-flight response" because it admirably prepares the organism to flee or face the threat. The central nervous system is aroused, the body provides glucose for quick energy, skeletal muscle increases contractility and loses fatigue, heart output increases, blood is shunted from viscera and the periphery of the body to the heart, lungs, and large muscles, and there is increased ventilation. This is not a wholly stereotyped pattern, its different components coming more or less into play depending on the character of the threat and the previous experience of the organism.

The model assumes that during status contests, Ego's dominant actions are perceived as threatening by Alter and therefore produce a stress response in Alter. That this occurs during violent contests involving overt threats and attacks can hardly be doubted. The occurrence of milder stress responses during more subtle contests, such as stare-downs, is less obvious although well supported by experimental evidence. A decrease in thumb blood volume is a convenient indicator of stress, showing the shift of blood from the periphery of the body to the skeletal muscles, an important feature of the fight-or-flight response. Human subjects engaged in a stare-down report feelings of discomfort, and they experience a significantly greater decrease in thumb blood volume than do subjects in control conditions of no stare or of unreciprocated stare (Mazur et al. 1980).

With stress a central variable in the biosocial model, we can explain some of the corollary features of status hierarchies, described at the beginning of this chapter. In most species, the low-ranked members of a group show more stress symptoms than higher-ranked members during common interactions. Often the low-ranked are described as "nervous, insecure" while those of high rank appear "relaxed, confident." We now see that the processes of rank allocation, especially dominance contests, encourage the upward movement of those group members most able to withstand stress and best equipped to impose stress on others, whereas those with the most difficulty handling stress or with the least interest in stressing others, move downward. Thus, there is a natural sorting that places individuals who are comfortable with stress near the top of the hierarchy and those who are "nervous" at the bottom.

Top-ranked individuals are well equipped with high-status signs and can easily impose stress on those down the hierarchy, enforcing compliance if it is not freely given. The imposition of stress is not only a powerful sanction on those below, but it directly inhibits their performance as well. Although the stress response admirably equips the body for the gross actions of fight or flight, it also produces muscle tension and tremor that interfere with finer actions, such as those required for controlled accuracy in sports or weapons competition. By intimidating our opponent in a duel or tennis match, we degrade his body's usual level of skill, diminishing his chances of scoring against us. Extreme stress can enervate an organism and, if chronic, cause physical morbidity. It is difficult for one of low rank to act dominantly toward a higher-ranked individual, for such an action is "presumptuous" (in human terms) and therefore may produce more stress on the low-status actor than on his higher-status target.

The stress variable also explains why the leaders rather than the low-ranked members of the group are most likely to face external threats such as predators, strange intruders, or hostile conspecifics. Those who handle stress most comfortably have been sorted into the high ranks, so they, rather than the low-ranked nervous individuals, are least intimidated by external threat and therefore most likely to advance against it. In human groups, the individuals who best handle stress are not only prone to become leaders but also, depending on circumstances, may be the thrill seekers and those most willing and able to violate laws or other norms.

Modes of Competition

Nearly all modes of communicating status that commonly appear among nonhuman primates occur among humans too. Excepting warfare, modern societies discourage violent threat and attack, though this remains a useful mode for adolescent males and outlaws. Many primates allocate status in a play mode, which in humans takes form in a variety of competitive games and sports. Humans seem limited only by their ingenuity in devising novel modes of competition, even including the conspicuous consumption of luxury goods.

The concept of modes is important for fitting humans into a general primate model because our most important style of communication is conversation, which is qualitatively different from the behavior of any other primate. Theorists have the choice of treating language-using humans as unique, to be explained on our own terms, or of treating language as simply one of several alternate modes of action, whereby primates communicate with conspecifics. I have chosen the latter course. The commonalities across the status hierarchies of humans and nonhuman primates seem to me a compelling reason for this choice, so I now turn to conversation as a mode of allocating status.

Rules of Conversation

The biosocial model of status works independently of the mode of communication used between Ego and Alter, as long as they can distinguish dominant (high-status) acts from deferent (low-status) ones. To include language as a mode of communicating dominance and deference, we need only specify how the speaker and listener (or signer and recipient) recognize dominance and deferent actions during conversation. One obvious way is through the words that each person speaks, since these may carry lexical meaning indicating that the speaker (or listener) is a high- or low-status person (e.g., "I came, I saw, I conquered," vs. "I am the dust beneath your feet").

Since conversations also carry meaning in their form and action—apart from the particular string of words—we often recognize the relative status of conversing foreigners even though we do not understand their speech. It is these features of form and action, independent of grammar or lexicon, that are sometimes described as a set of rules usually followed in natural conversation (Mazur 2005). Some of these rules are asymmetrical, specifying different actions for a high-status actor than a low-status one. If an individual in conversation takes the high-status role, then he is displaying a dominant sign, whereas if he acts the low-status part, then he displays a deferent sign. Other rules are symmetrical, applying without regard for the status of the actor. It is the *violation* of symmetrical rules that signals a dominant act, whereas strict conformity to them—while others are violating—signals deference (or politeness). The obvious underlying assumption here is that the dominant actor is most likely to assume the prerogative of violating the norms, whereas the deferent person would not dare. (To act dominantly toward one's superior is presumptuous and therefore stressful.) As in all modes, a dominant act is assumed to stress the recipient of the act and a deferent act relieves the stress of the actor. Thus, for Ego to violate any of the following rules would place stress on Alter. Alter would relieve this stress through strict conformity to the rules. These stresses are assumed to be subtle and the actors may barely be aware of their motivating qualities.

Most conversation between familiars is not concerned with achieving or exhibiting status differences, so there is usually adherence to these rules which produces relaxed, polite, and noncompetitive conversations. Violations occur primarily during dominance contests, or when high-status individuals choose to emphasize their superior positions. Conversation between Ego and Alter is, by definition, a series of turns in which each talks to the other in a language that both understand. Here are some common rules:

1. *If one individual is speaking, the other should remain quiet.* If Ego interrupts Alter's speech, Ego has acted dominantly. Sometimes the interruption is inadvertent, as when speaker Alter pauses and Ego, mistaking the pause for an ending, begins to talk, only to have Alter continue speaking. If Ego realizes Alter is not done and aborts a premature speech, Ego has deferred to Alter. If both continue speaking, they are vying for dominance.
2. *A listener who is offered the floor should speak.* A speaker can conclude talking without passing the floor, or may explicitly offer it, as by asking a question of the listener, or by directing his eyes to the listener after concluding a speech. If Ego remains silent after Alter offers the floor, Ego has acted dominantly,

stressing Alter. If silent, Ego then offers the floor back to Alter (by looking at Alter and waiting for Alter to speak), and Alter speaks (relieving his own stress), then Alter has deferentially complied with the same rule that Ego has just violated.

3. *Do not look into another individual's eyes when no one is speaking* (unless in a romantic context or at a distance well beyond conversational range). The violation of this rule, silent staring, is a common dominant act among primates, whereas rule-following eye aversion indicates deference. Conversation complicates these common signals since all listeners, whatever their status, look directly at a speaker's face to maximize comprehension; thus, the rule applies only during silent periods and is the converse of the next rule.
4. *Look at the speaker's face, particularly if the speaker is looking at you.* To look away, suggesting inattention (unless to look at an object of concern), is very hard to do if you respect the person speaking to you. If the person is of minor consequence, it is easy to violate the rule, thus showing your dominance. This rule is inoperative when the listener's averted eyes are a clear signal of submission, as when a child's eyes are downcast while being reprimanded by an adult, or to comply with ritual eye aversion.
5. *Do not speak loudly, sternly, or angrily.* Shouting matches and arguments are obviously dominance contests.
6. *The speaker should direct the listener's actions by request rather than command and should avoid a stern or stubborn tone.* To speak in a commanding or inflexible way implies that the listener is of lower status.
7. *The listener should respond to the speaker's directions for action.* Frequently, the listener responds to the speaker's requests while the speaker continues to hold the floor, as by head nods, laughs, or brief vocalizations. Refusing a request is an assertion of status; refusing a command is an outright challenge.

The next two rules are asymmetrical, treating the high-status participant differently than the low-status person. To take the high-status role is a dominant act; to relinquish it is deferential. If both participants assume the high-status role, there is an obvious dominance contest.

8. *The high-status person sets the pace and mood of the conversation and the low-status person follows.* The dominant person sets these with smiles, jokes, frowns, exclamations, volume, and rapidity of speech. High-status Ego may sustain a lagging conversation by asking questions or otherwise eliciting responses from Alter. If Ego tells a joke, Alter can deferentially laugh or challenge by being unresponsive.
9. *The high-status person introduces and terminates major topics of conversation.* This rule, like the previous one, indicates that the high-status person can take control of the conversation, which is the essence of having high status. If the relative status of the participants is not already set, then either one who assumes control is acting dominantly. If both attempt to control the conversation, there is a dominance contest.

These rules operate within a context of linguistic interaction, and the words actually spoken are an important part of the whole display. When we deferentially compliment someone, our own words are said in strict accordance with the rules, whereas our verbal insults gain emphasis when spoken in violation of the rules of conversation. Also, we accompany our speech with appropriate gestures, perhaps glaring for dominance or smiling for deference. This full array of actions—words, gestures, and rules—constitutes the status display.

Testosterone

There are active research programs on the proximate neurophysiological mechanisms underlying dominance and deference in humans (and other primates). Obviously from the foregoing discussion, the physiology of stress is important; it is the subject of my own current research. Here, I touch briefly on the hormone testosterone, which for decades has been implicated in the dominance/status processes of primates (Mazur 1976) as well as other mammals and even birds (e.g., Wingfield et al. 1990).

Testosterone is the key hormone involved in dominance and deference interactions among mature males, though evidence is equivocal for females (Carré et al. 2013; Mazur and Booth 1998). The precise mechanisms of action and strength of effects in humans remain uncertain (Batrinos 2012). Ethical and practical constraints have limited experiments on humans that compare behavior under testosterone versus placebo treatments; however, there is by now considerable correlational research from surveys and observational studies, and some ingenious experiments that depend on variations in endogamous testosterone.

It is clear that the link between testosterone and dominance is reciprocal. Not only does testosterone affect dominance behavior, but changes in dominance behavior or social status cause changes in testosterone level. We have stronger evidence on this *reverse* effect in humans because studies of it require no drug administration and can therefore be done by researchers other than physicians; also, testosterone levels can be obtained from participants' saliva, which is easily collected. By now there have been several reports of testosterone changes in young men during athletic events, which are convenient research settings because they are stylized dominance contests involving face-to-face competition with a clear winner and loser (e.g., Booth et al. 1989).

Male testosterone varies in predictable ways both before and after competitive matches. First, athletes' testosterone rises shortly before their matches, as if in anticipation of the competition. This pre-competition boost may promote dominant behavior, increasing the chance of victory. Second, for 1 or 2 h after the match, testosterone of winners is usually high relative to that of losers. These effects appear not only in physically taxing sports but also in chess competition, in symbolic changes in social status (graduation from medical school), vicariously in sports fans when their favored team wins or loses a game, and in election partisans when "their" candidate wins or loses an election (reviewed in Mazur 2005; Stanton et al. 2009). The rise in testosterone following a win is associated with the participant's elated mood. If the mood elevation is lessened because the participants have won by luck rather than through their own efforts, or because they do not regard the win as important, then the rise in testosterone is lessened or does not occur at all.

In a dominance contest, Ego's decision to compete with Alter, or to defer, depends on his motivation to dominate, which hypothetically depends on his testosterone level (among other factors). A man who has experienced a recent rise in testosterone, perhaps from a prior victory or a symbolic elevation in status, should be unusually assertive and may challenge someone of relatively high status. If both Ego and Alter decide to compete, their subsequent ranks are determined according to who successfully out-stresses whom.

If the winner (say, Ego) experiences rising testosterone as a result of his victory, this should sustain or increase his assertiveness and his display of dominant signs such as erect posture, sauntering or striding gait, and direct eye contact with others. Thus bolstered, Ego may seek out new dominance encounters and is primed to win them. The feedback between high testosterone and dominant demeanor may explain the momentum often associated with strings of triumphs. Success begets a high testosterone response, which begets more dominant behavior, which begets more success. (Part of this sequence has been demonstrated by Mehta and Josephs 2006; Carré et al. 2009.)

On the other side, Alter (the loser) experiences a drop in testosterone, reducing his assertiveness and increasing his display of deferential signs, such as stooped posture, smiling, or eye aversion. Faced with a new dominance encounter, he is now at a psychological and physiological disadvantage. One defeat begets another. Alter is more likely than before to retreat or submit. This may be an adaptive response, saving Alter from further losses and perhaps from additional damage.

Conclusion

We are past the naiveté of postwar social science when human behavior was regarded as biologically immaculate, the product entirely of cultural socialization and operant conditioning. There is no scientific doubt today that humans are an evolved species, not only in physical form but also to a considerable extent in the underpinnings of our behavioral repertoires. Thus, the present challenge for social psychology is to explicate how evolution is best incorporated into research and theoretical explanations of behavior.

The approach of this chapter is to examine humans in the context of our cousins, the living primates. Focusing on the dominance/status hierarchies of face-to-face groups, we see that many behaviors once considered by social scientists as strictly human phenomena are in fact part of the general primate pattern or appear in those primates most closely related to us, the African apes, giving prima facie grounds that these are evolved tendencies. A stronger (testable) case for homology is made by identifying proximate neurohormonal mechanisms—for status processes, the physiology of stress and testosterone—that underlie these behaviors and function similarly among other primates.

References

Batrinos, M. (2012). Testosterone and aggressive behavior in man. *International Journal of Endocrinology and Metabolism, 10,* 563–568.

Berger, J., Cohen, B., & Zeditch, M. (1972). Status characteristics and social interaction. *American Sociological Review, 37,* 209–219.

Bergman, T., Beehner, J., Cheney, D., & Seyfarth, R. (2003). Hierarchical classification by rank and kinship in baboons. *Science, 302,* 1234–1236.

Booth, A., Shelley, G., Mazur, A., Tharp, G., & Kittok, R. (1989). Testosterone, and winning and losing in human competition. *Hormones and Behavior, 23,* 556–571.

Carré, J., Putnam, S., & McCormick, C. (2009). Testosterone responses to competition predict future aggressive behavior at a cost to reward in men. *Psychoneuroendocrinology, 34,* 561–570.

Carré, J., Campbell, J., Lozoya, E., Goetz, S., & Welker, K. (2013). Changes in testosterone mediate the effect of winning on subsequent aggressive behavior. *Psychoneuroendocrinology, 10,* 2034–2041.

Cowlishaw, G. (1996). Sexual selection and information content in gibbon song bouts. *Ethology, 102,* 272–284.

de Waal, F. (1989). *Chimpanzee politics.* Baltimore: Johns Hopkins University Press.

de Waal, F. (2000). Primates: A natural heritage of conflict resolution. *Science, 289,* 586–590.

Fisek, M, & Ofshe, R. (1970). The process of status evolution. *Sociometry, 33,* 327–346.

Guthrie, J. (1973, April 28). The evolution of menace. *Saturday Review of the Sciences, 1,* 22–28.

Keating, C., Mazur, A., & Segall, M. (1977). Facial gestures which influence the perception of status. *Sociometry, 40,* 374–378.

Mazur, A. (1973). A cross-species comparison of status in small established groups. *American Sociological Review, 38,* 513–550.

Mazur, A. (1976). Effects of testosterone on status in primate groups. *Folia Primatologica, 26,* 214–226.

Mazur, A. (2005). *Biosociology of dominance and deference.* New York: Rowman & Littlefield.

Mazur, A., & Booth, A. (1998). Testosterone and dominance in men. *Behavioral and Brain Sciences, 21,* 353–363.

Mazur, A., Rosa, E., Faupel, M., Heller, J., Leen, R., & Thurman, B. (1980). Physiological aspects of communication via mutual gaze. *American Journal of Sociology, 90,* 125–150.

Mehta, P., & Josephs, R. (2006). Testosterone change after losing predicts the decision to compete again. *Hormones and Behavior, 50,* 684–692.

Mueller, U., & Mazur, A. (1996). Facial dominance of West Point cadets as a predictor of later military rank. *Social Forces, 74,* 823–850.

Rosa, E., & Mazur, A. (1979). Incipient status in small groups. *Social Forces, 58,* 18–37.

Southwick, C. (1963). *Primate social behavior.* Toronto: Van Nostrand.

Stanton, S., Beehner, J., Saini, E., Kuhn, C., & Labar, J. (2009). Dominance, politics, and physiology: Voters' testosterone changes on the night of the 2008 United States presidential election. *PLoS ONE, 4,* e7543.

Strodtbeck, F., James, R., & Hawkins, C. (1957). Social status in jury deliberations. *American Sociological Review, 22,* 713–719.

Strongman, K., & Champness, B. (1968). Dominance hierarchies and conflict in eye contact. *Acta Psychologica, 28,* 376–386.

Trivers, R.L. (1972). Parental investment and sexual selection. In B. Campbell (Ed.), *Sexual selection and the descent of man,* 1871–1971 (pp. 136–179). Chicago: Aldine.

van Lawick-Goodall, J. (1968). A preliminary report on expressive movements and communications in the Gombe Stream chimpanzees. In P. Jay (Ed.), *Primates: Studies in adaptation and variability* (pp. 313–374). New York: Holt, Rinehart and Winston.

Wingfield, J., Hegner, R., Dufty, A. Jr., & Ball, G. (1990). The 'challenge hypothesis': Theoretical implications for patterns of testosterone secretion, mating systems, and breeding strategies. *American Naturalist, 136,* 829–846.

Zebrowitz, L., Olson, K., & Hoffman, K. (1993). Stability of babyfaceness and attractiveness across the life span. *Journal of Personality and Social Psychology, 64,* 453–466.

Part VI

Mating and Relationships

Attraction and Human Mating 25

Anthony C. Little

Our magazines, movies, and television screens are filled with attractive individuals. Despite the fact that an interest in attractiveness may appear shallow, both women and men are concerned with good looks in a potential partner, and spend time, effort, and money in the pursuit of looking more appealing via diet, exercise, fashion, and cosmetics. This begs the question of why humans are so interested in being attractive and wanting to be with attractive others. In the chapter, I discuss the power of attractiveness and the evolutionary logic for why beauty and attractiveness are fundamental aspects of social life in humans. We start with a basic question: Why do we care about attractiveness?

Is Attractiveness Important?

Before discussing *why* attractiveness is important, we should first examine if research suggests attractiveness *is* important. In fact, many studies show that beauty impacts our lives in many ways, not only because we are attempting to attract the attention of beautiful people to be our partners but also because our attractiveness affects the way people behave toward us. For example, beauty is associated with upward economic mobility, especially for women (Elder 1969; Holmes and Hatch 1938), and attractive people also have more dates than less attractive people (Berscheid et al. 1971; Riggio and Woll 1984; Walster et al. 1966). Experimental studies have also demonstrated advantages of attractiveness. It has long been noted that there exists a "What is beautiful is good" stereotype (Dion et al. 1972), whereby attractive individuals are perceived to possess a variety of positive personality attributions. For example, in Dion et al.'s (1972) study, attractive individuals were thought to be able to achieve more prestigious occupations, be more competent spouses with happier marriages, and have better prospects for personal fulfillment. There have been a large number of studies examining this attractiveness stereotype, mainly demonstrating that attractive people are seen in a positive light for a wide range of attributes compared to unattractive people. Feingold (1992) reports that, for both men and women, attractive individuals report more satisfying and more pleasurable interactions with others than do less attractive individuals. Attractive people also appear to lead more favorable lives than do unattractive people. In mock interviews (Cash and Kilcullen 1985), and outside the laboratory (Chiu and Babcock 2002; Marlowe et al. 1996), attractive people are more likely to be hired for jobs than are less attractive individuals. Attractive individuals also pay lower bail than less attractive individuals (Downs and Lyons 1991), and attractiveness can influence judgments about the seriousness of crimes (Sigall and Ostrove 1975). So, not only are there consistent associa-

A. C. Little (✉)
School of Natural Sciences, Psychology,
Stirling University, FK9 4LA, Stirling, Scotland, UK
e-mail: anthony.little@stir.ac.uk

V. Zeigler-Hill et al. (eds.), *Evolutionary Perspectives on Social Psychology,* Evolutionary Psychology,
DOI 10.1007/978-3-319-12697-5_25,

tions between positive traits and attractiveness (see Eagly et al. 1991; Feingold 1992; Langlois et al. 2000 for meta-analytic reviews of research on physical attractiveness stereotypes), attractive people also have many social advantages in their lives. Indeed, the social impact of attractiveness is not restricted to adulthood—attractiveness appears to elicit more positive reactions from infancy. Langlois et al. (1995) found that mothers are more nurturing toward attractive babies than unattractive babies.

In a classic study, Snyder et al. (1977) found evidence that beauty may impact the behavior of the perceived. In a telephone conversation, men who believed the woman they were conversing with was attractive were judged to be more positive and socially interested in the person on the phone by independent judges than those who thought they were conversing with an unattractive person. The behavior of the women interacting with the men also changed according to whether the person talking to them thought they were attractive or unattractive. Those women who had a partner who thought that they were attractive behaved in a more confident way and also believed that the partnered man liked them more than those in the group where the partnered man was told the woman was less attractive. Thus, not only does our attractiveness change the way others interact with us but it also changes the way we interact with them.

Is Attractiveness Arbitrary?

Beauty has major social consequences, but exactly what is attractiveness? Indeed, there is a widespread belief that standards of attractiveness are learned gradually through exposure to culturally presented ideals (e.g., through the media in Western society). If this were true, it would mean that attractiveness was arbitrary and what is beautiful now could, in a different time or place, be considered unattractive. The well-known phrase "beauty is in the eye of the beholder" is a testament to the belief that attractiveness is not something that can be defined.

Darwin (1871) himself was also struck by cultural differences, such as preferences for skin color, body hair, body fat, and practices such as lip ornamentation and teeth filing: "It is certainly not true that there is in the mind of man any universal standard of beauty with respect to the human body" (pp. 353). Such convictions were supported by early cross-cultural work by Ford and Beach (1951), who catalogued differences between cultures in preferences for body weight, breast size, and other aspects of female physique.

While individual and cross-cultural differences exist (discussed later), there are certain features that are attractive to all (or at least the majority of) judges. In fact, agreement between individuals is one of the best-documented and most robust findings in attractiveness research since the 1970s. Across many studies, there is a high degree of agreement from individuals within a particular culture and also high agreement between individuals from different cultures (e.g., Cunningham et al. 1995; see Langlois et al. 2000 for a meta-analytic review). There is even evidence that when infants (3–6 months of age) are shown faces that have been judged by adults for attractiveness, they prefer to look at faces rated more highly for attractiveness than at those faces rated lower (Langlois et al. 1987; Samuels et al. 1994). Before any substantial exposure to cultural standards of attractiveness, infants demonstrate a preference for attractive faces that are in agreement with adult judgments. So, we have seen that attractiveness appears to be an important social trait and that individuals agree on who is and who is not attractive (Fig. 25.1). The next question to examine is why do we care about who is and who is not attractive?

Why Is Attractiveness Important?

Evolutionary theory has been proposed to be able to cast light on what features are attractive and what makes people seek out and desire to mate with attractive individuals. While most people may think first of natural selection, to understand the link between attractiveness and evolution

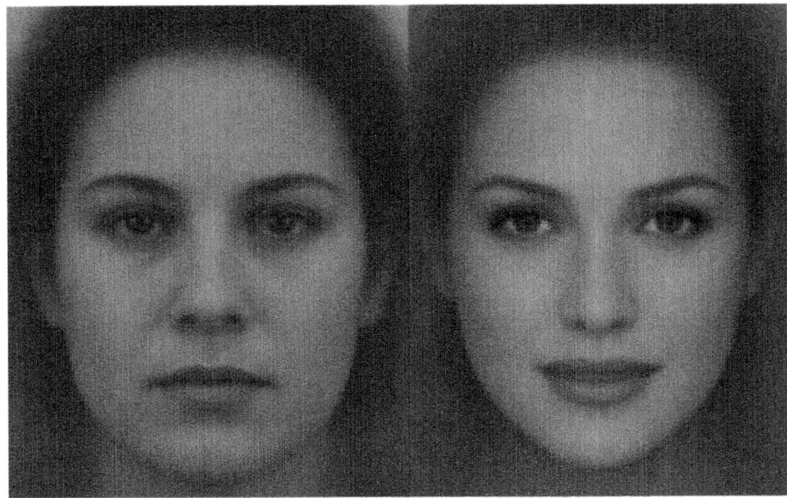

Fig. 25.1 Universal attractiveness? These images represent two composite images made by combining with a number of pictures of students or celebrities. One image is generally seen as more attractive than the other

we turn to sexual selection, the second powerful force postulated in evolutionary theory. The two major problems faced by an organism are survival and reproduction, and it is *differential reproductive success* that is the key to evolution. Reproduction is more important than survival because without offspring an organism's genes die with it—in evolutionary terms, it is better to lead a short life producing lots of offspring than a long life and producing none. From this, it can be seen that evolutionary success can be measured by how well an organism succeeds in passing on its genes into the next generation and beyond. It is unsurprising then that organisms invest so much in efforts to reproduce.

An evolutionary view suggests that choosiness may reflect preferences that drive us to acquire high-quality mates—the traits we find attractive in individuals may be linked to their value as mates (Symons 1987). High-quality, or high value, mates are individuals who will best enhance the reproductive success of their partners. Women and men should both be sensitive to cues that indicate higher mate value because ancestral individuals who were attentive to cues of high mate value, and based mate-choice decisions on them, left behind more offspring, which would be healthier and more fecund, than those who failed to attend to these cues.

Sexual Selection

Darwin (1871) was the first to point to a force he called sexual selection to account for the seemingly inexplicable differences between the sexes of some species and suggested that sexual selection arises from differences in reproductive success caused by competition over mates. Indeed, the selective forces that operate on males and females, as a result of the phenomena of sexual reproduction, have profound effects on the morphology and behavior of animals (for a comprehensive overview, see Andersson 1994).

Mate choice by one sex can exert a selective pressure on both the morphological and behavioral features of the other sex. This is the basis for intersexual selection. It is this form of sexual selection that has been most prominently applied to research on human attractiveness. We can then expect sexual selection to be tied to preferences for morphology and behavior themselves. While preferences may reflect somewhat arbitrary processes, such as the runaway selection proposed by Fisher (1915, 1930), much research has focused on indicator mechanisms. Indicator mechanisms of sexual selection refer to traits that are preferred because they are associated with phenotypic or genotypic quality of individuals possessing them. In other words, individuals find mates attractive because of the advertisement of the quality of their genes or the resources they possess. There is a distinction among the benefits acquired from mating with individuals:

1. Indirect benefits—acquiring "good genes" from partners, which benefit offspring.
2. Direct benefits—acquiring factors other than good genes from partners, which benefit the choosing individual.

For example, choosing a healthy mate may lead to offspring inheriting genes that enable good health in adulthood—an indirect benefit (Møller 1990). Choosing a healthy mate and avoiding a parasitized mate also has obvious direct advantages (Gibson 1990), such as avoiding the parasites. Thus, while indirect and direct benefits may be distinct in some cases, they are not necessarily mutually exclusive.

Traits Associated with Attractiveness

In the previous section, I discussed why physical appearance is important to humans: There are potentially important reproductive consequences based on our preferences. While arbitrary preferences are possible in humans, most evolutionary research has focused on indicator mechanisms in humans, positing that certain traits are attractive because they are linked to benefits for the choosing individual. In this section, I briefly describe some of the traits that are proposed to relate to attractiveness.

Youth

Individuals generally value youth in a potential partner (Kenrick and Keefe 1992). For example, when rating faces, relatively younger adult faces are seen as more attractive than older faces (Korthase and Trenholme 1982). In evolutionary terms, preferences for youthful partners can provide direct benefits. For example, youth is associated with vigor and a longer period of potential parental investment. Further, particularly in women, youth is strongly tied to the ability to produce offspring. Preferences for young partners in both men and women would then appear to have obvious direct benefits to the chooser.

Weight and Body Shape

Much research has examined the role of body weight and shape on judgments of attractiveness (Singh 1993, 1995; Tovee et al. 1998). In many Western societies, thinness is a valued trait. Women with low body mass indices (a standard measure of weight, calculated by dividing weight by height squared) receive higher attractiveness ratings (Tovee et al. 1998). This preference for thinness is likely a recent trend, however. For instance, the average weight of centerfold models has decreased in the last 50 years, with the most striking changes taking place in the past decade (Seifert 2005). Research suggests our preferences for body weight may reflect adaptations to prefer individuals who are best suited to certain environmental conditions. It has been suggested that in societies where individuals experience food shortages, fluctuations in food availability and/or intense workloads, preferences for increased fatness in a mate may be adaptive (Anderson et al. 1992). In line with these ideas, hungry individuals report stronger preferences for higher body weights (Swami and Tovee 2006). Studies of body shape have shown preferences based on waist-to-hip ratio (WHR). WHR is sexually dimorphic and can be seen in women's body shape as an hourglass figure, with men having more similar waist and hip measurements and therefore a straighter appearance (Fig. 25.2). Men generally prefer a low (feminine) WHR in women (Singh 1993) and women prefer a high (masculine) WHR in men (Dixson et al. 2003; Singh 1995). Because differences in body shape may reflect hormonal profiles linked to fertility (Singh 1993), such preferences could be tied to both direct and indirect benefits.

Height

Height and body build are sexually dimorphic, with men typically being taller than women. Many studies suggest a positive relationship

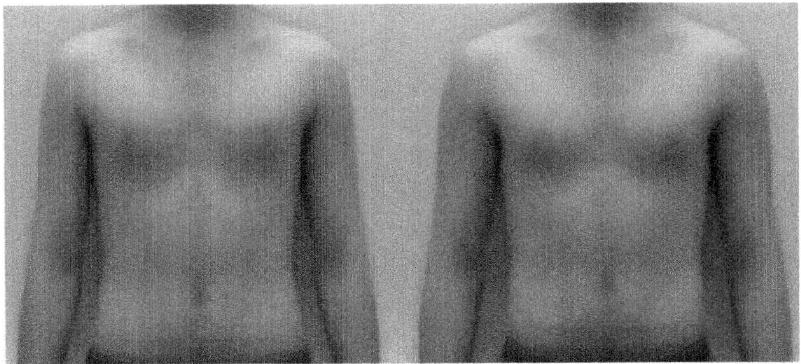

Fig. 25.2 Feminine (*left*) and masculine (*right*) body shapes made using transformations. The images are composites made up of multiple male bodies transformed using the difference between an average male and average female body shape. The feminized version is more hourglass shaped than the masculinized version. (Body images are adapted from a similar figure appearing in Little et al. 2007b)

between height and a variety of positive traits, at least in men. Height is associated with attractiveness, with taller men having an advantage in being selected for dates (Hensley 1994; Shepperd and Strathman 1989) and attracting more attractive partners (Feingold 1982). Meta-analyses suggest that women desire male mates who are as tall or taller than themselves more so than men desire female partners who are of equal or shorter height than themselves (Pierce 1996). Being relatively short in adult life is also associated with lower self-reported health-related quality of life (Christensen et al. 2007). Height is also linked to career success, being positively related to income (Judge and Cable 2004). As height is positively associated with health and economic success (albeit modestly), this is suggestive that height, at least in men, is an advertisement of biological quality and so indirect benefits. There are additional, direct benefits of mating with taller men for women in terms of both avoidance of disease by mating with healthy men and the potentially increased investment of taller, richer men.

Facial Averageness

The averageness of a face is related to how closely it resembles the majority of other faces within a population and may be attractive because the possession of features that are close to a population average in shape, size, or configuration is potentially linked to genetic heterozygosity and genetic diversity (Mitton and Grant 1984; Thornhill and Gangestad 1993). Genetic diversity is linked to pathogen resistance because diversity may result in the owner producing less common proteins to which common pathogens are poorly adapted (Thornhill and Gangestad 1993). Genetic diversity also means that an individual's genotype is more likely to be heterozygous (possess two different alleles of a gene) and so be less likely to be homozygous (possess two of the same alleles of a gene) for deleterious alleles (Thornhill and Gangestad 1993). Both of these theories propose direct and indirect benefits to mating with those possessing average faces. It has been shown that heterozygosity in the major histocompatibility complex (MHC), a suite of genes linked to immune function, is positively related to male facial attractiveness (Roberts et al. 2005) and that facial averageness is positively related to physical health (Rhodes et al. 2001b). Averageness is also associated with attractiveness. Classic early work by Langlois et al. (1994; 1990) has shown that composite faces are judged to be more attractive than the individual faces from which they are constructed. Averageness has also been found to be attractive across different cultures. For example, averageness is attractive in Japanese participants (Rhodes et al. 2001a) and in African hunter-gatherers (Apicella et al. 2007). Overall, then, there is evidence that averageness is a determinant of facial attractiveness.

Facial Symmetry

Symmetry refers to the extent to which one half of a trait (organism, etc.) is the same as the other half. Individuals differ in their ability to maintain the stable development of their morphology under the prevailing environmental conditions (Møller and Swaddle 1997). The ability of an individual to develop successfully in the face of environmental pressures is therefore one proposed indicator of genetic quality. Indeed, facial asymmetry is positively related to self-reported number of occurrences of respiratory disease in men and women (Thornhill and Gangestad 2006), suggesting direct and indirect benefits to individuals that select symmetric partners. Several studies using manipulated faces have also demonstrated that symmetry has a positive influence on attractiveness (Perrett et al. 1999; Rhodes et al. 1998), paralleling the findings of investigations into naturally occurring facial asymmetries (Grammer and Thornhill 1994; Mealey et al. 1999; Scheib et al. 1999). Preferences for symmetry using manipulated faces have also been found in samples of African hunter-gatherers (Little et al. 2007a).

Secondary Sexual Characteristics in Faces

Mature features in adult human faces reflect the masculinization or feminization of secondary sexual characteristics that occurs at puberty. These face shape differences in part arise because of the action of hormones, such as testosterone. Larger jawbones, more prominent cheekbones, and thinner cheeks are all features of male faces that differentiate them from female faces (e.g., Enlow 1982). From an evolutionary perspective, feminine women and masculine men are proposed to be attractive because these traits are associated with hormonal profiles tied to general and reproductive health (Law-Smith et al. 2006; Penton-Voak and Chen 2004). A study by Rhodes et al. (2003) has shown that perceived masculinity correlated positively (if weakly) with actual measures of health in male adolescents, but no relationship was found between femininity and health in female faces (Rhodes et al. 2003). Another study has demonstrated that men's facial masculinity and women's facial femininity are negatively related to self-reports of respiratory disease (Thornhill and Gangestad 2006).

There is considerable evidence that feminine female faces are attractive. Studies measuring facial features from photographs of women (Cunningham 1986; Grammer and Thornhill 1994; Jones and Hill 1993) and studies manipulating facial composites (e.g., Perrett et al. 1998) indicate that feminine features increase the attractiveness of female faces across different cultures. The link between sexual dimorphism and attractiveness in male faces is less clear. Some studies have shown that women preferred large, masculine jaws in males (Cunningham et al. 1990; Grammer and Thornhill 1994), whereas other studies have shown that feminine characteristics are attractive in male faces (Berry and McArthur 1985; Cunningham et al. 1990; Perrett et al. 1998; Rhodes et al. 2000; Swaddle and Reierson 2003). Using techniques to manipulate masculinity and femininity in male faces, several studies have documented preferences for femininity (Little et al. 2001, 2002; Little and Hancock 2002; Rhodes et al. 2000), and some computer graphic studies have reported preferences for masculinity (DeBruine et al. 2006; Little and Mannion 2006). Preferences for male facial masculinity therefore appear variable. The explanation may lie in the personality traits that masculine- and feminine-faced males are assumed to possess. Increasing the masculinity of face shape increased perceptions of dominance, masculinity, and age, but decreased perceptions of warmth, emotionality, honesty, cooperativeness, and quality as a parent (Perrett et al. 1998). It appears that "socially valued" traits (e.g., honesty) that are important for direct benefits are associated with feminized versions of male faces, whereas traits such as dominance are associated with masculinized face shapes. A trade-off between "good dads" and "good genes" may help reconcile varying preferences for masculine-faced men.

Health

Unsurprisingly, people prefer healthy-appearing partners. Perceived health is difficult to relate to any one metric, but people rating faces for perceived health show very high agreement on such ratings (see, e.g., Jones et al. 2001, 2005b). In evolutionary terms, there is a large and obvious selective advantage in preferring healthy partners. Again, as for previous traits, there may be both direct and indirect benefits to partnering with individuals who are perceived to be healthy. There have been several studies that have addressed how facial appearance relates to health in humans. One study examined how well ratings of health from small patches of skin of faces are related to overall rated attractiveness when the whole face image is available. Jones et al. (2004) found that apparent health of facial skin is positively correlated with ratings of male facial attractiveness. In other research, homogeneity of skin color was positively related to attractiveness (Fink et al. 2006). Findings have also suggested that men who are more heterozygous (possess two different alleles of a gene) in their MHC genes also have healthier-appearing skin compared to men with more homozygous alleles (Roberts et al. 2005), suggesting genetic diversity at the MHC is linked to healthy appearance.

"Good" Behavior and Personality

Personality traits are reported cross-culturally to be among the most important factors in partner choice by both sexes (Buss 1989; Buss and Barnes 1986). One study demonstrated that a desire for some personality traits influences judgments of facial attractiveness (Little et al. 2006b). Individuals valuing particular personality traits find faces appearing to display these traits attractive. Thus, desired personality traits influences perceptions of facial attractiveness in opposite-sex faces, such that "what is good is beautiful" (Little et al. 2006b). In terms of benefits to perceivers, it is easy to see why traits, such as appearing trustworthy, would make an individual appear more attractive. For individual-specific traits, such preferences could be related to behavioral compatibility within couples, as people do tend to desire partners with personalities similar to their own (Botwin et al. 1997).

Status

Status is somewhat unusual, in that it is often inferred from the possessions of an individual. For example, dressing in high-status clothing increases male attractiveness (Townsend 1990). In general, wealth and status are positive traits in a potential partner (Buss 1989). The specific trappings of wealth and status are perhaps most likely to be culturally determined. For example, high-end sports cars are not status symbols in cultures that do not rely on automobiles for transportation. High-status individuals are likely to be resource rich and able to provide direct investment to both their partners and their offspring. This does not preclude provisioning of indirect benefits—the genes that lead to acquiring high status may be heritable and so choosing a high-status partner may secure genes for achieving high status for one's offspring.

Variation in Attraction

In the previous section, I reviewed research on a wide variety of traits that have been linked to attraction. Each of the individual traits is plausibly related to some benefit to the choosing individual, although how individuals weight up these different traits has yet to be determined, and it is unlikely that each is equally weighted. Determining someone's attractiveness from this variety of traits is likely complex, and this complexity is further compounded because there are also evolutionary reasons to expect that preferences for these traits may be variable. Despite broad agreement on attractiveness, many factors may influence an individual in determining who they find attractive. In this section, I review some examples of where variation has been found and examined from an evolutionary perspective.

Sex Differences

Women and men may differ in the relative importance of traits (Geary et al. 2004). Of course, both men and women value physical attractiveness, and other positive traits, in a partner. However, the relative balance of certain preferences may not be equal, with members of one sex placing more importance on some traits compared to the other. For example, women value earning potential and ambition/drive more than men do (Buss 1989). Conversely, men value youth and attractiveness more than women do (Buss 1989). Indeed, research on sex differences in age preferences demonstrate that women desire a slightly older man, while men desire younger women (Buunk et al. 2002; Kenrick and Keefe 1992). In general, these sex differences are in line with a difference in priorities related to what is important to each sex. Women value wealth/status more than men as these traits have more bearing on their ability to produce offspring than the attractiveness of the man. Men, on the other hand, value youth and beauty more than women because there is a stronger relationship between age and the ability to produce children in women than in men.

Within-Person Differences

Multiple studies have demonstrated that women's preferences for various traits in several domains, including smell, sound, and vision, shift across the menstrual cycle (Feinberg et al. 2006; Little et al. 2011a; Puts 2005; Rikowski and Grammer 1999). One of the most well-documented phenomena in studies examining cyclical preference shifts is a greater attraction to masculine male faces at peak fertility in the menstrual cycle (Johnston et al. 2001; Jones et al. 2008; Little and Jones 2012; Little et al. 2007c; Penton-Voak et al. 1999), a within-individual shift driven by variation in hormone levels across the cycle. This shift has been proposed to be adaptive in changing the preferences of women when they are most likely to become pregnant towards high-quality men, or in leading to attraction to more cooperative men when they are not likely to become pregnant (Johnston et al. 2001; Jones et al. 2008; Little and Jones 2012; Little et al. 2007c; Penton-Voak et al. 1999). As a different, but potentially complementary, explanation for shifting preferences, rather than acquiring direct benefits for offspring from masculine men, women may maximize investment from feminine men when raised progesterone prepares the body for pregnancy (Jones et al. 2005a).

Relationship context refers to the temporal context of a relationship. For short-term relationships, women are more likely to choose an attractive man who is less cooperative and has worse parenting qualities over a less attractive man who is more cooperative and with better parenting qualities (Scheib 2001). In contrast, in long-term contexts, women choose the less attractive but more cooperative man more often (Scheib 2001). In face and voice preferences, women judging men for short-term relationships prefer more masculinity in faces than those judging for long-term relationships (Little et al. 2002) and prefer lower-pitched, masculine voices for a short-term relationship than for a long-term relationship (Puts 2005). These findings are consistent with the hypothesis that masculinity in men is associated with indirect genetic benefits to offspring: When investment is not an issue, as in short-term relationships, traits associated with indirect benefits would be expected to be valued more highly. In the context of a long-term relationship, however, where investment is an issue, women may be more constrained in their preferences and look for cues to long-term investment that are not necessarily consistent with traits that indicate high genetic quality.

Between-Person Differences

Preferences may be influenced by one's own attractiveness. Condition-dependent mate choice is seen in female fish of several species, whereby higher-quality females are more attentive to cues to male quality (Bakker et al. 1999). In humans, condition-dependent mate choice is potentially adaptive for women of low mate value in order to avoid the costs of decreased parental investment/potential desertion from high-quality partners (Little et al. 2001). Such reasoning arises from notions that high-quality males are least likely to invest in or most likely to desert their partners (Gangestad and Simpson 2000). Little et al. (2001) found that women who thought they were physically attractive preferred more masculine faces and had greater preferences for symmetry than those women who thought they were less physically attractive, and subsequent studies have shown similar effects using more objective measures of attractiveness, such as other-rated facial attractiveness and measured WHR (Penton-Voak et al. 2003; Smith et al. 2009). As in faces, self-rated attractiveness is also positively related to women's preferences for masculinized men's voices (i.e., voices with lower pitch; Vukovic et al. 2010).

Similarity may also change preferences and is dependent on one's own traits. Newcomb (1961) addressed attitudes in a sample of students who were offered free housing. Proximity was found to impact liking of other students; but as time passed, students liked those with similar attitudes to themselves. At the proximate level, people with similar attitudes may find it easier to get along, whereas dissimilar individuals come into conflict over factors such as religion or politics or even over where to eat dinner or what to see at the movies. In the realm of attraction, similarity between partners is referred to as assortative mating and is seen for a variety of measures, both behavioral and physical. Positive assortative mating (pairing with similar partners), at least for long-term relationships, may have benefits in terms of keeping adaptive suites of genes together (Thiessen and Gregg 1980) or increasing behavioral compatibility (Hill et al. 1976). While there are costs to inbreeding, a certain amount of genetic similarity can be beneficial—so-called optimal outbreeding (Bateson 1983). Certainly, there is evidence that members of long-term couples resemble each other facially (Hinsz 1989; Little et al. 2006a).

Cultural Differences

As noted earlier, preferences for high body fat would be adaptive in environments where food shortage was possible and, likewise, higher body weight may be less of an attractive trait where food was plentiful. In line with these ideas, body fat, at least in women, is preferred in cultures that are at greater risk of food shortage (Anderson et al. 1992). Another environmental factor is pathogen risk. In an environment with high pathogen risk, the probability of offspring survival and eventual reproduction decreases. Consequently, there may be few benefits to attracting an attentive/investing partner, because individuals may maximize their reproductive output by focusing on acquiring good genes for their offspring (Belsky et al. 1991). Penton-Voak et al. (2004) found stronger preferences for male masculinity in Jamaicans than in the UK and Japan and suggested that a higher pathogen prevalence may result in increased preferences for masculinity in male faces. The Hadza, a tribe of African hunter-gatherers, have also been found to exhibit stronger preferences for facial symmetry (Fig. 25.3) than do participants in the UK (Little et al. 2007a). Another study examined a larger cross-cultural sample of 30 countries, calculating both the average female preference for male facial masculinity (Fig. 25.3) and a composite health index derived from World Health Organization statistics (DeBruine et al. 2010). This study found that poorer health (i.e., higher mortality and incidence of disease) was related to stronger female preferences for male masculinity (DeBruine et al. 2010). All of these studies are suggestive that under conditions of health risk, female preferences for healthy, masculine partners are stronger, reflecting motivations to secure direct or indirect benefits.

Another source of variation between cultures comes from social learning. Individuals often learn from others and selection for social-learning mechanisms may occur when there are costs to acquiring accurate information via individual learning (Richerson and Boyd 2005). Inspired by work on nonhuman species, recent research also suggests that social learning may influence

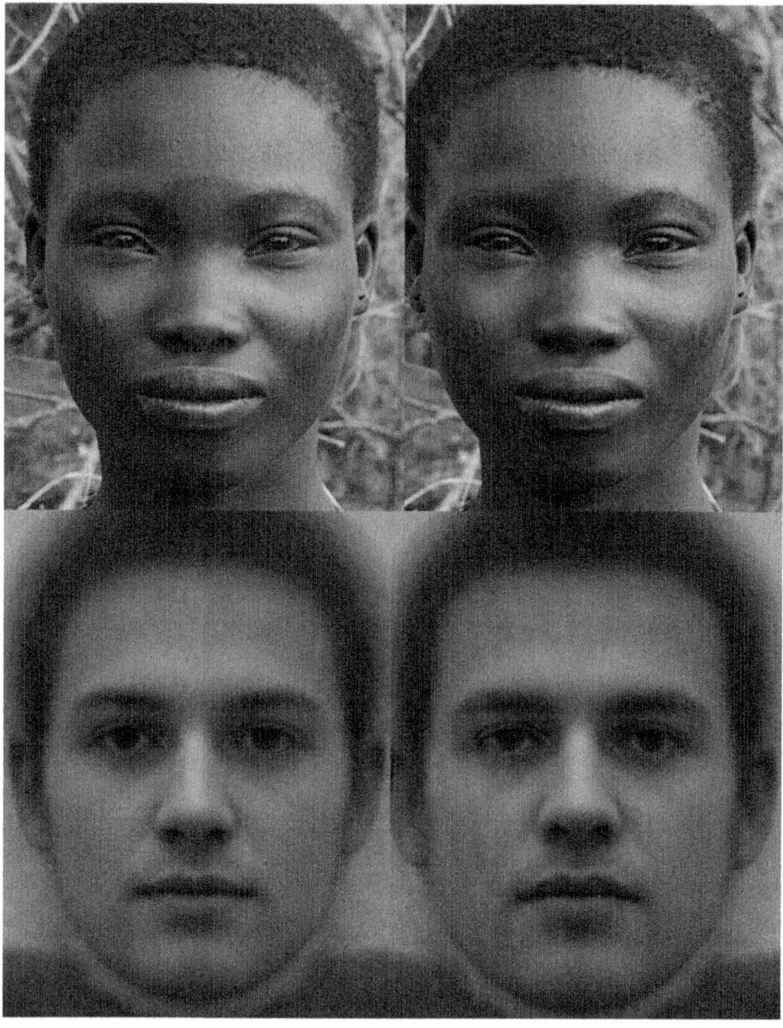

Fig. 25.3 Examples of symmetric (*top left*), asymmetric (*top right*), feminized (*bottom left*) and masculinized (*bottom right*) facial images similar to those used in various studies examining face preferences. (Symmetric and asymmetric Hadza faces are adapted from a similar figure appearing in Little et al. 2007a)

human mate preferences (Little et al. 2011b). Modeling work has shown that social transmission of preferences in humans can result in a directional pressure on both traits and preferences within populations, and this could account for genetically based phenotypic variation between cultures (Laland 1994). For example, if a preference for large noses arose within a population, other members and subsequent members of that population would observe the preferences and learn the trait was attractive, perpetuating a preference for large noses through a population and maintaining the preference over generations. These effects may help explain the diversity of preferences for seemingly arbitrary traits, such as tattooing or scarification.

Summary and Conclusions

Attraction is an important part of human social life; being more or less attractive has important social consequences and people generally agree on who is and who is not attractive. Beauty is unlikely to be entirely socially constructed. Many nonhuman animals are equally biased in mate selection. Like other animals, humans have come under the influence of sexual selection, driving our preferences.

There are many traits linked to attractiveness in humans and each may impart direct or indirect benefits to individuals who act on their preferences. If a trait reliably advertises some benefit to the perceiver, then we expect individuals in a population to find that trait attractive. This evolutionary view may postulate that some traits will be universally attractive; however, this does not preclude interesting variation. Indeed, it would be surprising if there was a template of the perfect mate that was not affected by environment, context, or the specific needs of an individual. Variation in preferences for some traits will prove adaptive and so be consistent with evolutionary theory. In this way, evolutionary theory can be married to the complexity and variation of human social behavior to present a fuller understanding of what we find attractive, why we find it attractive, and why, despite broad agreement, we see a wide variety of personal preferences.

References

Anderson, J. L., Crawford, C. B., Nadeau, J., & Lindberg, T. (1992). Was the Duchess of windsor right—a cross-cultural review of the socioecology of ideals of female body shape. *Ethology and Sociobiology, 13,* 197–227.

Andersson, M. (1994). *Sexual selection.* Princeton: Princeton University Press.

Apicella, C. L., Little, A. C., & Marlowe, F. W. (2007). Facial averageness and attractiveness in an isolated population of hunter-gatherers. *Perception, 36,* 1813–1820.

Bakker, T. C. M., Künzler, R., & Mazzi, D. (1999). Condition-related mate-choice in sticklebacks. *Nature, 401,* 234.

Bateson, P. (1983). Optimal outbreeding. In P. Bateson (Ed.), *Mate choice.* (pp. 257–277). Cambridge: Cambridge University Press.

Belsky, J., Steinberg, L., & Draper, P. (1991). Childhood experience, interpersonal development, and reproductive strategy—an evolutionary-theory of socialization. *Child Development, 62,* 647–670.

Berry, D. S., & McArthur, L. Z. (1985). Some components and consequences of a babyface. *Journal of Personality and Social Psychology, 48,* 312–323.

Berscheid, E., Dion, K., Walster, E., & Walster, G. W. (1971). Physical attractiveness and dating choice: A test of the matching hypothesis. *Journal of Experimental and Social Psychology, 7,* 173–189.

Botwin, M. D., Buss, D. M., & Shackelford, T. K. (1997). Personality and mate preferences: Five factors in mate selection and marital satisfaction. *Journal of Personality, 65,* 107–136.

Buss, D. M. (1989). Sex differences in human mate preferences: Evolutionary hypotheses tested in 37 cultures. *Behavioural and Brain Sciences, 12,* 1–49.

Buss, D. M., & Barnes, M. (1986). Preferences in human mate selection. *Journal of Personality and Social Psychology, 50,* 559–570.

Buunk, B. P., Dijkstra, P., Fetchenhauer, D., & Kenrick, D. T. (2002). Age and gender differences in mate selection criteria for various involvement levels. *Personal Relationships, 9,* 271–278.

Cash, T. F., & Kilcullen, R. N. (1985). The aye of the beholder—susceptibility to sexism and beautyism in the evaluation of managerial applicants. *Journal of Applied Social Psychology, 15,* 591–605.

Chiu, R. K., & Babcock, R. D. (2002). The relative importance of facial attractiveness and gender in Hong Kong selection decisions. *International Journal of Human Resource Management, 13,* 141–155.

Christensen, T. L., Djurhuus, C. B., Clayton, P., & Christiansen, J. S. (2007). An evaluation of the relationship between adult height and health-related quality of life in the general UK population. *Clinical Endocrinology, 67,* 407–412.

Cunningham, M. R. (1986). Measuring the physical in physical attractiveness: Quasi-experiments on the sociobiology of female facial beauty. *Journal of Personality and Social Psychology, 50,* 925–935.

Cunningham, M. R., Barbee, A. P., & Pike, C. L. (1990). What do women want? Facialmetric assessment of multiple motives in the perception of male facial physical attractiveness. *Journal of Personality and Social Psychology, 59,* 61–72.

Cunningham, M. R., Roberts, A. R., Barbee, A. P., & Druen, P. B. (1995). "Their ideas of beauty are, on the whole, the same as ours": Consistency and variability in the cross-cultural perception of female attractiveness. *Journal of Personality and Social Psychology, 68,* 261–279.

Darwin, C. (1871). *The descent of man, and selection in relation to sex* (1st ed.). London: John Murray.

DeBruine, L. M., Jones, B. C., Little, A. C., Boothroyd, L. G., Perrett, D. I., Penton-Voak, I. S., Cooper, P. A., Penke, L., Feinberg, D. R., & Tiddeman, B. P. (2006). Correlated preferences for facial masculinity and ideal or actual partner's masculinity. *Proceedings of the Royal Society B-Biological Sciences, 273,* 1355–1360.

DeBruine, L. M., Jones, B. C., Crawford, J. R., Welling, L. L. M., & Little, A. C. (2010). The health of a nation predicts their mate preferences: Cross-cultural variation in women's preferences for masculinized male faces. *Proceedings of the Royal Society B-Biological Sciences, 277,* 2405–2410.

Dion, K., Berscheid, E., & Walster, E. (1972). What is beautiful is good. *Journal of Personality and Social Psychology, 24,* 285–290.

Dixson, A. F., Halliwell, G., East, R., Wignarajah, P., & Anderson, M. J. (2003). Masculine somatotype and hirsuteness as determinants of sexual attractiveness to women. *Archives of Sexual Behavior, 32,* 29–39.

Downs, A. C., & Lyons, P. M. (1991). Natural observations of the links between attractiveness and initial legal judgments. *Personality and Social Psychology Bulletin, 17,* 541–547.

Eagly, A. H., Ashmore, R. D., Makhijani, M. G., & Longo, L. C. (1991). What is beautiful is good, but…: A meta-analytic review of research on the physical attractiveness stereotype. *Psychological Bulletin, 110,* 109–128.

Elder, G. H. J. (1969). Appearance and education in marriage mobility. *American Sociological Review, 34,* 519–533.

Enlow, D. M. (1982). *Handbook of facial growth* (2nd ed.). Philadelphia: Saunders.

Feinberg, D. R., Jones, B. C., Law-Smith, M. J., Moore, F. R., DeBruine, L. M., Cornwell, R. E., Hillier, S. G., & Perrett, D. I. (2006). Menstrual cycle, trait estrogen level, and masculinity preferences in the human voice. *Hormones and Behavior, 49,* 215–222.

Feingold, A. (1982). Do taller men have prettier girlfriends. *Psychological Reports, 50,* 810–810.

Feingold, A. (1992). Good-looking people are not what we think. *Psychological Bulletin, 111,* 304–341.

Fink, B., Grammer, K., & Matts, P. J. (2006). Visible skin color distribution plays a role in the perception of age, attractiveness, and health in female faces. *Evolution and Human Behavior, 27,* 433–442.

Fisher, R. A. (1915). The evolution of sexual preference. *Eugenics Review, 7,* 184–192.

Fisher, R. A. (1930). *The genetical theory of natural selection.* Oxford: Clarendon Press.

Ford, C. S., & Beach, F. A. (1951). *Patterns of sexual behaviour.* New York: Harper & Row.

Gangestad, S. W., & Simpson, J. A. (2000). The evolution of human mating: Trade-offs and strategic pluralism. *Behavioural and Brain Sciences, 23,* 573–644.

Geary, D. C., Vigil, J., & Byrd-Craven, J. (2004). Evolution of human mate choice. *Journal of Sex Research, 41,* 27–42.

Gibson, R. M. (1990). Relationships between blood parasites, mating success and phenotypic cues in male sage grouse. *American Zoologist, 30,* 271–278.

Grammer, K., & Thornhill, R. (1994). Human (*Homo sapiens*) facial attractiveness and sexual selection: The role of symmetry and averageness. *Journal of Comparative Psychology, 108,* 233–242.

Hensley, W. E. (1994). Height as a Basis for Interpersonal-Attraction. *Adolescence, 29,* 469–474.

Hill, C. T., Rubin, Z., & Peplau, L. A. (1976). Breakups before marriage: The end of 103 affairs. *Journal of Social Issues, 32,* 147–168.

Hinsz, V. B. (1989). Facial resemblance in engaged and married couples. *Journal of Social and Personal Relationships, 6,* 223–229.

Holmes, S. J., & Hatch, C. E. (1938). Personal appearance as related to scholastic records and marriage selection in college women. *Human Biology, 10,* 65–76.

Johnston, V. S., Hagel, R., Franklin, M., Fink, B., & Grammer, K. (2001). Male facial attractiveness: Evidence for a hormone-mediated adaptive design. *Evolution and Human Behavior, 22,* 251–267.

Jones, D., & Hill, K. (1993). Criteria of facial attractiveness in five populations. *Human Nature, 4,* 271–296.

Jones, B. C., Little, A. C., Penton-Voak, I. S., Tiddeman, B. P., Burt, D. M., & Perrett, D. I. (2001). Facial symmetry and judgements of apparent health—Support for a "good genes" explanation of the attractiveness-symmetry relationship. *Evolution and Human Behavior, 22,* 417–429.

Jones, B. C., Little, A. C., Burt, D. M., & Perrett, D. I. (2004). When facial attractiveness is only skin deep. *Perception, 33,* 569–576.

Jones, B. C., Little, A. C., Boothroyd, L., DeBruine, L. M., Feinberg, D. R., Law Smith, M. J., Cornwell, R. E., Moore, F. R., & Perrett, D. I. (2005a). Commitment to relationships and preferences for femininity and apparent health in faces are strongest on days of the menstrual cycle when progesterone level is high. *Hormones and Behavior, 48,* 283–290.

Jones, B. C., Perrett, D. I., Little, A. C., Boothroyd, L., Cornwell, R. E., Feinberg, D. R., Tiddeman, B. P., Whiten, S., Pitman, R. M., Hillier, S. G., Burt, D. M., Stirrat, M. R., Smith, M. J. L., & Moore, F. R. (2005b). Menstrual cycle, pregnancy and oral contraceptive use alter attraction to apparent health in faces. *Proceedings of the Royal Society B-Biological Sciences, 272,* 347–354.

Jones, B. C., DeBruine, L. M., Perrett, D. I., Little, A. C., Feinberg, D. R., & Smith, M. J. L. (2008). Effects of menstrual cycle phase on face preferences. *Archives of Sexual Behavior, 37,* 78–84.

Judge, T. A., & Cable, D. M. (2004). The effect of physical height on workplace success and income: Preliminary test of a theoretical model. *Journal of Applied Psychology, 89,* 428–441.

Kenrick, D. T., & Keefe, R. C. (1992). Age preferences in mates reflect sex differences in human reproductive strategies. *Behavioral and Brain Sciences, 15,* 75–133.

Korthase, K. M., & Trenholme, I. (1982). Perceived age and perceived physical attractiveness. *Perceptual and Motor Skills, 54,* 1251–1258.

Langlois, J. H., & Roggman, L. A. (1990). Attractive faces are only average. *Psychological Science, 1,* 115–121.

Langlois, J. H., Roggman, L. A., Casey, R. J., Ritter, J. M., Riser-Danner, L. A., & Jenkins, V. Y. (1987). Infant preferences for attractive faces: Rudiments of a stereotype? *Developmental Psychology, 23,* 363–369.

Langlois, J. H., Roggman, L. A., & Musselman, L. (1994). What is average and what is not average about attractive faces. *Psychological Science, 5,* 214–220.

Langlois, J. H., Ritter, J., Casey, J., & Solwin, D. (1995). Infant attractiveness predicts maternal behaviours and attitudes. *Developmental Psychology, 31,* 464–472.

Langlois, J. H., Kalakanis, L., Rubenstein, A. J., Larson, A., Hallamm, M., & Smoot, M. (2000). Maxims or myths of beauty? A meta-analytic and theoretical review. *Psychological Bulletin, 126,* 390–423.

Law-Smith, M. J., Perrett, D. I., Jones, B. C., Cornwell, R. E., Moore, F. R., Feinberg, D. R., Boothroyd, L. G., Durrani, S. J., Stirrat, M. R., Whiten, S., Pitman, R. M., & Hillier, S. G. (2006). Facial appearance is a cue to oestrogen levels in women. *Proceedings of the Royal Society B-Biological Sciences, 273,* 135–140.

Little, A. C., & Hancock, P. J. B. (2002). The role of masculinity and distinctiveness in judgments of human male facial attractiveness. *British Journal of Psychology, 93,* 451–464.

Little, A. C., & Jones, B. C. (2012). Variation in facial masculinity and symmetry preferences across the menstrual cycle is moderated by relationship context. *Psychoneuroendocrinology, 37,* 999–1008.

Little, A. C., & Mannion, H. (2006). Viewing attractive or unattractive same-sex individuals changes self-rated attractiveness and face preferences in women. *Animal Behaviour, 72,* 981–987.

Little, A. C., Burt, D. M., Penton-Voak, I. S., & Perrett, D. I. (2001). Self-perceived attractiveness influences human female preferences for sexual dimorphism and symmetry in male faces. *Proceedings of the Royal Society B-Biological Sciences, 268,* 39–44.

Little, A. C., Jones, B. C., Penton-Voak, I. S., Burt, D. M., & Perrett, D. I. (2002). Partnership status and the temporal context of relationships influence human female preferences for sexual dimorphism in male face shape. *Proceedings of the Royal Society B-Biological Sciences, 269,* 1095–1100.

Little, A. C., Burt, D. M., & Perrett, D. I. (2006a). Assortative mating for perceived facial personality traits. *Personality and Individual Differences, 40,* 973–984.

Little, A. C., Burt, D. M., & Perrett, D. I. (2006b). What is good is beautiful: Face preference reflects desired personality. *Personality and Individual Differences, 41,* 1107–1118.

Little, A. C., Apicella, C. L., & Marlowe, F. W. (2007a). Preferences for symmetry in human faces in two cultures: Data from the UK and the Hadza, an isolated group of hunter-gatherers. *Proceedings of the Royal Society B-Biological Sciences, 274,* 3113–3117.

Little, A. C., Jones, B. C., & Burriss, R. P. (2007b). Preferences for masculinity in male bodies change across the menstrual cycle. *Hormones and Behavior, 51,* 633–639.

Little, A. C., Jones, B. C., Burt, D. M., & Perrett, D. I. (2007c). Preferences for symmetry in faces change across the menstrual cycle. *Biological Psychology, 76,* 209–216.

Little, A. C., Jones, B. C., & DeBruine, L. M. (2011a). Facial attractiveness: Evolutionary based research. *Philosophical Transactions of the Royal Society B-Biological Sciences, 366,* 1638–1659.

Little, A. C., Jones, B. C., DeBruine, L. M., & Caldwell, C. A. (2011b). Social learning and human mate preferences: A potential mechanism for generating and maintaining between-population diversity in attraction. *Philosophical Transactions of the Royal Society B-Biological Sciences, 366,* 366–375.

Marlowe, C. M., Schneider, S. L., & Nelson, C. E. (1996). Gender and attractiveness biases in hiring decisions: Are more experienced managers less biased? *Journal of Applied Psychology, 81,* 11–21.

Mealey, L., Bridgestock, R., & Townsend, G. (1999). Symmetry and perceived facial attractiveness. *Journal of Personality and Social Psychology, 76,* 151–158.

Mitton, J. B., & Grant, M. C. (1984). Associations among proteins heterozygosity, growth rate, and developmental homeostasis. *Annual Review of Ecology and Systematics, 15,* 479–499.

Møller, A. P. (1990). Parasites and sexual selection: Current states of the Hamilton and Zuk hypothesis. *Journal of Evolutionary Biology, 3,* 419–428.

Møller, A. P., & Swaddle, J. P. (1997). *Asymmetry, developmental stability, and evolution.* Oxford: Oxford University Press.

Newcomb, T. M. (1961). *The acquaintance process.* New York: Holt, Rinehart & Winston.

Penton-Voak, I. S., & Chen, J. Y. (2004). High salivary testosterone is linked to masculine male facial appearance in humans. *Evolution and Human Behavior, 25,* 229–241.

Penton-Voak, I. S., Perrett, D. I., Castles, D. L., Kobayashi, T., Burt, D. M., Murray, L. K., & Minamisawa, R. (1999). Menstrual cycle alters face preference. *Nature, 399,* 741–742.

Penton-Voak, I. S., Little, A. C., Jones, B. C., Burt, D. M., Tiddeman, B. P., & Perrett, D. I. (2003). Measures of female condition influence preferences for sexual dimorphism in faces of male *Homo sapiens*. *Journal of Comparative Psychology, 117,* 264–271.

Penton-Voak, I. S., Jacobson, A., & Trivers, R. (2004). Populational differences in attractiveness judgements of male and female faces: Comparing British and Jamaican samples. *Evolution and Human Behavior, 25,* 355–370.

Perrett, D. I., Lee, K. J., Penton-Voak, I. S., Rowland, D. R., Yoshikawa, S., Burt, D. M., Henzi, S. P., Castles, D. L., & Akamatsu, S. (1998). Effects of sexual dimorphism on facial attractiveness. *Nature, 394,* 884–887.

Perrett, D. I., Burt, D. M., Penton-Voak, I. S., Lee, K. J., Rowland, D. A., & Edwards, R. (1999). Symmetry and human facial attractiveness. *Evolution and Human Behavior, 20,* 295–307.

Pierce, C. A. (1996). Body height and romantic attraction: A meta-analytic test of the male-taller norm. *Social Behavior and Personality, 24,* 143–149.

Puts, D. A. (2005). Mating context and menstrual phase affect women's preferences for male voice pitch. *Evolution and Human Behavior, 26,* 388–397.

Rhodes, G., Proffitt, F., Grady, J., & Sumich, A. (1998). Facial symmetry and the perception of beauty. *Psychonomic Bulletin Review, 5,* 659–669.

Rhodes, G., Hickford, C., & Jeffery, L. (2000). Sex-typicality and attractiveness: Are supermale and superfemale faces super-attractive. *British Journal of Psychology, 91,* 125–140.

Rhodes, G., Yoshikawa, S., Clark, A., Lee, K., McKay, R., & Akamatsu, S. (2001a). Attractiveness of facial averageness and symmetry in non-Western populations: In search of biologically based standards of beauty. *Perception, 30,* 611–625.

Rhodes, G., Zebrowitz, L. A., Clark, A., Kalick, S. M., Hightower, A., & McKay, R. (2001b). Do facial averageness and symmetry signal health? *Evolution and Human Behavior, 22,* 31–46.

Rhodes, G., Chan, J., Zebrowitz, L. A., & Simmons, L. W. (2003). Does sexual dimorphism in human faces signal health? *Proceedings of the Royal Society B-Biological Sciences, 270,* S93–S95.

Richerson, P. J., & Boyd, R. (2005). *Not by genes alone: How culture transformed human evolution.* Chicago: University of Chicago Press.

Riggio, R., & Woll, S. (1984). The role of non-verbal and physical attractiveness in the selection of dating partners. *Journal of Social and Personal Relations, 1,* 347–357.

Rikowski, A., & Grammer, K. (1999). Human body odour, symmetry and attractiveness. *Proceedings of the Royal Society B-Biological Sciences, 266,* 869–874.

Roberts, S. C., Little, A. C., Gosling, L. M., Perrett, D. I., Carter, V., Jones, B. C., Penton-Voak, I., & Petrie, M. (2005). MHC-heterozygosity and human facial attractiveness. *Evolution and Human Behavior, 26,* 213–226.

Samuels, C. A., Butterworth, G., Roberts, T., Graupner, L., & Hoyle, G. (1994). Facial aesthetics: Babies prefer attractiveness to symmetry. *Perception, 23,* 823–831.

Scheib, J. E. (2001). Context-specific mate choice criteria: Women's trade-offs in the contexts of long-term and extra-pair mateships. *Personal Relationships, 8,* 371–389.

Scheib, J. E., Gangestad, S. W., & Thornhill, R. (1999). Facial attractiveness, symmetry, and cues to good genes. *Proceedings of the Royal Society B-Biological Sciences, 266,* 1913–1917.

Seifert, T. (2005). Anthropomorphic characteristics of centerfold models: Trends towards slender, figures over time. *International Journal of Eating Disorders, 37,* 271–274.

Shepperd, J. A., & Strathman, A. J. (1989). Attractiveness and height—the role of stature in dating preference, frequency of dating, and perceptions of attractiveness. *Personality and Social Psychology Bulletin, 15,* 617–627.

Sigall, H., & Ostrove, N. (1975). Beautiful but dangerous: Effects of offender attractiveness and nature of the crime on juridical judgement. *Journal of Personality and Social Psychology, 31,* 410–414.

Singh, D. (1993). Adaptive significance of female physical attractiveness: Role of waist-to-hip ratio. *Journal of Personality and Social Psychology, 65,* 293–307.

Singh, D. (1995). Female judgment of male attractiveness and desirability for relationships—role of waist-to-hip ratio and financial status. *Journal of Personality and Social Psychology, 69,* 1089–1101.

Smith, F. G., Jones, B. C., Welling, L. L. W., Little, A. C., Vukovic, J., Main, J. C., & DeBruine, L. M. (2009). Waist-hip ratio predicts women's preferences for masculine male faces, but not perceptions of men's trustworthiness. *Personality and Individual Differences, 47,* 476–480.

Snyder, M., Tanke, E. D., & Berscheid, E. (1977). Social perception and interpersonal behaviour: On the self-fulfilling nature of social stereotypes. *Journal of Personality and Social Psychology, 35,* 656–666.

Swaddle, J. P., & Reierson, G. W. (2003). Testosterone increases perceived dominance but not attractiveness in human males. *Proceedings of the Royal Society B-Biological Sciences, 269,* 2285–2289.

Swami, V., & Tovee, M. J. (2006). Does hunger influence judgments of female physical attractiveness? *British Journal of Psychology, 97,* 353–363.

Symons, D. (1987). An Evolutionary approach: Can Darwin's view of life shed light on human sexuality? In J. H. Geer, & W.T. O'Donohue (eds.). *Theories of human sexuality* (pp. 91–126). New York: Plomin Press.

Thiessen, D., & Gregg, B. (1980). Human assortative mating and genetic equilibrium: An evolutionary perspective. *Ethology and Sociobiology, 1,* 111–140.

Thornhill, R., & Gangestad, S. W. (1993). Human facial beauty: Averageness, symmetry, and parasite resistance. *Human Nature, 4,* 237–269.

Thornhill, R., & Gangestad, S. W. (2006). Facial sexual dimorphism, developmental stability, and susceptibility to disease in men and women. *Evolution and Human Behavior, 27,* 131–144.

Tovee, M. J., Reinhardt, S., Emery, J. L., & Cornelissen, P. L. (1998). Optimum body-mass index and maximum sexual attractiveness. *Lancet, 352,* 548.

Townsend, J. M., & Levy, G.D. (1990). Effects of potential partners' physical attractiveness and socioeconomic status on sexuality and partner selection. *Archives of Sexual Behavior, 9,* 149–164.

Vukovic, J., Jones, B. C., DeBruine, L., Feinberg, D. R., Smith, F. G., Little, A. C., Welling, L. L. M., & Main, J. (2010). Women's own voice pitch predicts their preferences for masculinity in men's voices. *Behavioral Ecology, 21,* 767–772.

Walster, E., Aronson, V., Abrahams, D., & Rottman, L. (1966). Importance of physical attractiveness in dating behaviour. *Journal of Personality and Social Psychology, 4,* 508–516.

Evolutionary Developmental Perspectives on Male Androphilia in Humans

26

Paul L. Vasey and Doug P. VanderLaan

Male Androphilia is an Evolutionary Paradox

Androphilia refers to sexual attraction to adult males, whereas *gynephilia* refers to sexual attraction to adult females. Research indicates that male androphilia is influenced by genetic factors (e.g., Alanko et al. 2010; Hamer et al. 1993; Långström et al. 2010). Nevertheless, androphilic males reproduce at significantly lower rates than gynephilic males, and often they do not reproduce at all (e.g., King et al. 2005; Schwartz et al. 2010; Vasey et al. 2014).

Since male androphilia appears to have a genetic component, but male androphiles reproduce little, if at all, one would have expected genes for male androphilia to have become extinct given the relative reproductive costs associated with this trait and the reproductive benefits associated with male gynephilia. Any species-typical trait that has a genetic component, but that lowers direct reproduction and persists over evolutionary time requires explanation when viewed within the context of natural selection, a process that favors the evolution of reproductively viable traits. For this reason, the existence of male androphilia represents one of the outstanding paradoxes of evolutionary biology.

If it could be definitively demonstrated that male androphilia was a historically recent phenomenon that did not extend back into the evolutionary past, then one might reasonably dismiss the characterization of male androphilia as an *evolutionary paradox*. However, archaeological and cross-cultural evidence suggest that this conclusion lacks credibility. *Sexual orientations* such as gynephilia or androphilia are not part of the archaeological record, nor could they ever be, because sexual orientations cannot be preserved in the form of archaeological artifacts. However, depictions of *sexual behaviors* involving same-sex individuals do exist as part of the archaeological record, albeit rarely (e.g., Gebhard 1970; Nash 2001) and, on the basis of these depictions, it seems reasonable to suggest, at a very minimum, that some prehistoric peoples understood that such activity was within the realm of possibility. A somewhat stronger supposition would be that such depictions are, in fact, evidence that same-sex sexual behavior existed in prehistoric times.

Certain constellations of funerary remains may also be indicative of male androphilia in the ancestral past. For example, graves containing male skeletal remains and female-typical artifacts are indicative of transgender males in the

P. L. Vasey (✉)
Department of Psychology, University of Lethbridge, 4401 University Drive, Lethbridge, AB T1K 3M4, Canada
e-mail: paul.vasey@uleth.ca

D. P. VanderLaan
Gender Identity Service, Child, Youth and Family Services, Centre for Addiction and Mental Health, Beamish Family Wing, Intergenerational Wellness Centre, 80 Workman Way, 5th Floor, Toronto, ON M6J 1H4, Canada
e-mail: doug.vanderlaan@camh.ca

V. Zeigler-Hill et al. (eds.), *Evolutionary Perspectives on Social Psychology,* Evolutionary Psychology,
DOI 10.1007/978-3-319-12697-5_26, © Springer International Publishing Switzerland 2015

distant past (e.g., Hollimon 1997). Given what we know about the exclusive androphilic orientation of most transgender males from comparable populations (e.g., Harrington 1942), archaeological indicators of such individuals are once again suggestive of the presence of male androphilia in human antiquity.

All told, the archaeological evidence for male androphilia in the prehistoric past is suggestive, but limited. Perhaps more compelling is the research that suggests that male androphilia occurs in the majority of cultures for which data are available (e.g., Murray 2000) and its population prevalence rate appears to be similar (~ 1.5–5 %) across a variety of different cultures (e.g., Smith et al. 2003; VanderLaan et al. 2013a; Whitam 1983). Although male–male sexuality may truly be absent in a minority of cultures (e.g., Hewlett and Hewlett 2010), these exceptions do not invalidate the conclusion that male androphilia appears to be a predictably and reliably reoccurring phenomenon in the vast majority of human cultures. The cross-culturally widespread and consistent nature with which male androphilia is expressed suggests that it is not an evolutionarily recent aspect of the human sexual condition.

The Expression of Male Androphilia Varies Cross-Culturally

The manner in which male androphilia is publicly expressed varies across cultures (Murray 2000). This expression typically takes one of two forms, that are related to gender role enactment. These two forms are *sex-gender congruent* and *transgender* male androphilia.

Sex-gender congruent male androphiles occupy the gender role typical of their sex, behave in a relatively masculine manner, and identify as "men." In contrast, transgender androphilic males typically behave in an effeminate manner and often identify as neither "men" nor "women," but rather, as a member of some "third" gender category. In some cultures, transgender male androphilia is linked to particular institutionalized labor practices, which often involve specialized religious activities. Such transgender male androphilia has been referred to as "institutionalized role structured homosexuality" (Herdt 1997). For example, on the Indian subcontinent, transgender male androphiles known as *hijra* bestow blessings from Hindu gods and goddesses for luck and fertility at weddings and at the birth of baby boys (Nanda 1998). Similarly, in some cultures such as the Mohave and the Yorok, all *berdache* (transgender male androphiles) were recognized as shamans (e.g., Devereux 1937; Kroeber 1925). In Sulawesi, Indonesia, transgender androphilic males known as *bissu* are shamans who bless people for good health and successful journeys and who play important ritual roles in weddings. Historically, *bissu* were also guardians of sacred royal regalia and the protectors of nobility (Peletz 2009)[1].

Both sex-gender congruent and transgender male androphilia may occur within a given culture, but typically one or the other tends to predominate (Whitam 1983). For example, the sex-gender congruent form is more common in many Western cultures. In contrast, in many non-Western cultures, the transgender form appears to be more common (Murray 2000).

Cross-Culturally Invariant Correlates of Male Androphilia

Quantitative research indicates that the sex-gender congruent and transgender forms of male androphilia share numerous developmental and biodemographic correlates that are cross-culturally invariant. In terms of biodemographic correlates that exist across cultures, sex-gender congruent and transgender male androphiles tend to both be later born among their siblings (e.g., Blanchard 2004; VanderLaan and Vasey 2011; Vasey and VanderLaan 2007), have greater numbers of older biological brothers ("fraternal birth order effect[2]," e.g., Bogaert and Skorska

[1] These institutionalized religious roles sometimes carry with them the expectation of asceticism, but often this ideal is not realized (e.g., Nanda 1998; Peletz 2009).

[2] The *fraternal birth order effect* refers to the well-established finding that the number of older biological broth-

2011; VanderLaan and Vasey 2011; Vasey and VanderLaan 2007), exhibit larger family sizes (Blanchard and Lippa 2007; Camperio-Ciani et al. 2004; Iemmola and Camperio Ciani 2009; King et al. 2005; Rahman et al. 2008; Schwartz et al. 2010; VanderLaan et al. 2012; VanderLaan and Vasey 2011; Vasey and VanderLaan 2007), cluster within families (e.g., Schwartz et al. 2010; VanderLaan et al. 2013a, b), occur at similar prevalence rates across different populations (e.g., Smith et al. 2003; VanderLaan et al. 2013a; Whitam 1983) and produce few—if any—offspring (e.g., King et al. 2005; Schwartz et al. 2010; Vasey et al. 2013). In addition, the odds ratios associated with the fraternal brother effect in various populations of sex-gender congruent and transgender male androphiles are remarkably consistent, suggesting that the manner in which older brothers influence the development of male androphilia is constant across diverse populations (e.g., Cantor et al. 2002; VanderLaan and Vasey 2011).

Prospective and retrospective cross-cultural research on early psychosocial development among transgender and sex-gender congruent male androphiles has shown that the childhood behavior of such males is characterized by greater levels of female-typical behavior (e.g., nurturing play with dolls) and lower levels of male-typical behavior (e.g., rough-and-tumble play) compared to gynephilic males (Bailey and Zucker 1995; Bartlett and Vasey 2006; Cardoso 2005, 2009; Whitam 1983). In addition, both types of male androphiles express elevated cross-gender wishes in childhood (e.g., "I wish I was a girl"; Bailey and Zucker 1995; Vasey and Bartlett 2007; Whitam 1983). Furthermore, both sex-gender congruent and transgender male androphiles also experience elevated traits of childhood separation anxiety (i.e., anxiety related to separation from major attachment figures such as parents; VanderLaan et al. 2011a; Vasey et al. 2011; Zucker et al. 1996), which tend to be more common among girls compared to boys (e.g., Shear et al. 2006; VanderLaan et al. 2011a). In adulthood, male androphiles from a range of cultures exhibit preferences for a variety of female-typical occupations (e.g., florist) and hobbies (e.g., interior design; Lippa 2005; Whitam 1983).

Even though sex-gender congruent androphilic males are relatively feminine as boys compared to their gynephilic counterparts (Bailey and Zucker 1995), they behaviorally defeminize to varying degrees as they develop. It has been suggested that this behavioral defeminization probably occurs in response to culturally specific gender role expectations, which hold that male-bodied individuals should behave in a masculine manner (Bailey 2003; Berling 2001; Rieger and Savin-Williams 2012). In contrast, in cultures where transgender male androphilia is the norm, feminine boys develop into feminine adult males. Consequently, adult sex-gender congruent male androphiles are relatively masculine when compared to adult transgender male androphiles (Murray 2000). Conversely, they are, on average, relatively feminine when compared to adult male gynephiles (Bailey 2003; Lippa 2005). Thus, regardless of how it is manifested, male androphilia is associated with gender atypicality in childhood and adulthood. However, the strength of this association varies depending on the manner in which male androphilia is publicly expressed. Taken together, these numerous, cross-culturally invariant biodemographic and developmental correlates of male androphilia indicate that sex-gender congruent and transgender male androphilia share a common etiological basis despite being different in appearance.

Male Androphilia in the Ancestral Environment

Given that the manner in which male androphilia is publicly expressed varies cross-culturally, the question arises as to which form, sex-gender congruent or transgender was the ancestral form. Identifying the ancestral form of male androphilia is critical if we seek to test hypotheses pertaining to the evolution of this trait in an accurate manner. More derived forms of this trait might reflect historically recent cultural influences.

ers increases the odds of androphilia in later-born males (Blanchard 2004; Bogaert and Skorska 2011).

With this concern in mind, VanderLaan et al. (2013c) attempted to identify the ancestral form of male androphilia. They did so by examining whether societies in which transgender male androphilia predominates exhibit more of the socio-cultural features that are believed to have characterized the human ancestral past relative to a comparison group of societies in which transgender male androphilia did not predominate. Numerous researchers have presented evidence indicating that the ancestral human sociocultural environment was likely characterized by hunter-gatherers living in small groups with relatively egalitarian sociopolitical structures and animistic religious belief systems (e.g., Binford 2001; Hill et al. 2011; Marlowe 2005; McBrearty and Brooks 2000; Sanderson and Roberts 2008; Smith 1999; Winkelman 2010; Woodburn 1982). If these conditions are more often associated with societies in which transgender male androphilia predominates, then this would bolster the argument that male androphilia was predominantly expressed in the transgender form under ancestral conditions.

Using information derived from the Standard Cross-Cultural Sample (SCCS)[3], VanderLaan et al. (2013c) compared 46 societies in which transgender male androphiles were coded as predominating with 146 societies in which they were not. Their goal was to ascertain whether the former were more likely to be characterized by human ancestral sociocultural conditions (i.e., smaller group size, hunting and gathering, egalitarian political structure, and animistic religious beliefs) compared to the latter. Compared to non-transgender societies, transgender societies were characterized by a significantly greater presence of ancestral sociocultural conditions. Given the association between transgender male androphilia and ancestral human sociocultural conditions, it seems parsimonious to conclude that the ancestral form of male androphilia was the transgender form. Consistent with this conclusion is the fact that sex-gender congruent male androphilia appears to be a historically recent phenomenon with little precedent outside of a Western cultural context until very recently (Murray 2000). Accordingly, caution needs to be exercised in utilizing sex-gender congruent male androphiles, such as "gay" men, as models to test hypotheses pertaining to the evolution of male androphilia. This is particularly true if the hypotheses under consideration propound a role for the social behavior of male androphiles in the evolutionary maintenance of genes associated with same-sex sexual orientation.

The existence of two forms of transgender male androphilia (i.e., *institutionalized role structured* and *non-role structured*) raises the question as to which one preceded the other in evolutionary time. Given that less specialized forms of traits tend to precede more specialized ones in evolutionary time (Dean et al. 2014), it seems parsimonious to propose that institutionalized role structure transgender male androphilia is derived from a more ancestral form of transgender male androphilia that did not involve role specialization and was not institutionalized. Once transgender male androphilia originated in humans, it could then be culturally elaborated to serve any number of distinct social roles, which, in turn, could become institutionalized.

The Fa'afafine of Samoa

Translated literally, *fa'afafine* means "in the manner of a woman." Although they are biological males, within Samoan society, *fa'afafine* are not recognized as "men" nor are they recognized as "women" and, as such, they have been described as a type of "third" gender. From a Western cultural perspective, the vast majority of *fa'afafine* would be considered transgender individuals or, at the very least, highly effeminate males. Most *fa'afafine* do not experience dysphoria with respect to their genitals and, as such, could not be accurately characterized as transsexual (Vasey and Bartlett 2007).

Inclusion in the category *fa'afafine* is contingent on feminine gender role presentation,

[3] The SCCS provides data related to a subset of the world's nonindustrial societies and circumvents Galton's problem (i.e., common cultural derivation and cultural diffusion) when conducting cross-cultural comparisons.

not on same-sex sexual activity. Consequently, long before they engage in any sexual activity, prepubescent boys are identified as *fa'afafine* based on their tendencies to engage in female-typical activities (e.g., playing with girls) and their aversion toward male-typical activities (e.g., rough-and-tumble play). This process of recognition does not mean that Samoans make male children into *fa'afafine*. Rather, in Samoan culture, boyhood femininity is interpreted to mean that such individuals simply are *fa'afafine* and it is understood that they will not grow up to be "men." Some families react negatively to the presence of a *fa'afafine* child with corporal punishment, but the majority have a *laissez-faire* attitude; some even facilitate the child's feminine behavior by sewing dresses for the child, for example (Bartlett and Vasey 2006; Vasey and Bartlett 2007).

In adulthood, the vast majority of *fa'afafine* are exclusively androphilic and, consequently, they do not have children of their own (Vasey et al. 2014). All *fa'afafine* recognize the term "gay" although the precise meaning of this term varies depending on the individual asked. That being said, none of the *fa'afafine* use the term "gay" to describe themselves. "Gays" as one *fa'afafine* told the first author "sleep with each other, but *fa'afafine* don't do that." Indeed, *fa'afafine* express disgust at the thought of engaging in sexual activity with another *fa'afafine* and stress that they do not do so. Instead, they point out, in contrast to "gays," they have sex with "straight men."

In a Samoan cultural context, regardless of sexual orientation, "straight man" means a male who is masculine and who self-identifies as a "man." Some "straight men" in Samoa are gynephilic and only have sex with women. However, other men who are bisexual will have sex with *fa'afafine* when they are unable to access their preferred sexual partners (i.e., adult females). The majority of men who sleep with *fa'afafine* likely fall into this group (Petterson et al. 2015). The remaining minority of men who have sex with *fa'afafine* appear to be a combination of individuals who are androphilic or *gynandromorphophilic* (i.e., peak sexual attraction to individuals with penises and breasts). In short, the Samoan category of "straight man" is a very heterogeneous one with respect to sexual orientation.

In Samoa, *fa'afafine* enjoy a high level of social acceptance that, while by no means absolute, stands in stark contrast to the situation experienced by Western transgender male androphiles (e.g., Meyer 2003; Namaste 2000; Seil 1996). Indeed, the prime minister of Samoa, the Honorable Tuilaepa Sailele Malielegaoi, is patron of the National *Fa'afafine* Association and has spoken publically on several occasions about the value of *fa'afafine* for Samoan society. *Fa'afafine* are highly visible and active members of Samoan society. Although it is not unusual for *fa'afafine* to occupy certain occupations (e.g., florist) more than others (e.g., mechanic), they are not associated with any institutionalized social role. *Fa'afafine* occupy all manner of positions from stay-at-home caregivers to assistant chief executive officers in the government.

Kin Selection and the Evolution of Male Androphilia

To date, tests of evolutionary hypotheses pertaining to male androphilia that utilize transgender androphilic males as models have been conducted on a single population—the *fa'afafine* of Samoa. Our own group has conducted this research. The most prominent hypothesis that posits a role for the social behavior of male androphiles in the evolutionary maintenance of genes associated with same-sex sexual orientation is the kin selection hypothesis. This hypothesis holds that genes for male androphilia could be maintained in a population if enhancing one's indirect fitness offset the cost of not reproducing directly (Wilson 1975). Indirect fitness is a measure of an individual's impact on the fitness of kin (who share some identical genes by virtue of descent), weighted by the degree of relatedness (Hamilton 1963). Theoretically speaking, androphilic males could increase their indirect fitness by directing altruistic behavior toward kin, which, in principle, would allow such kin to increase their reproductive success. In particular, androphilic males should allocate altruistic behavior toward close kin because they share more genes in common with such individuals.

Research conducted on transgender male androphiles in Samoa has repeatedly furnished support for the kin selection hypothesis. Research demonstrates that the avuncular (uncle-like) tendencies of *fa'afafine* are elevated compared to those of Samoan gynephilic males (VanderLaan and Vasey 2012; Vasey et al. 2007; Vasey and VanderLaan 2010a). *Fa'afafine* also demonstrate elevated avuncular tendencies compared to the materteral (aunt-like) tendencies of Samoan women (Vasey and VanderLaan 2009). Elevated avuncular tendencies among *fa'afafine* were also documented when comparing them to control groups of childless women and gynephilic men (Vasey and VanderLaan 2009, 2010a). These latter comparisons indicated that the *fa'afafine's* elevated avuncular tendencies cannot be characterized as a simple by-product that is due to a lack of parental care responsibilities and, thus, greater availability of resources for avuncular investment. If this were true, then the avuncular tendencies of *fa'afafine* should have been similar to those of childless men and women, but this was not the case. Moreover, these same findings indicate that the elevated avuncular tendencies of *fa'afafine* could not be characterized as a simple by-product that is due to the male members of this "third" gender group adopting feminine gender roles, which included expectations for elevated childcare. If this were true, then the materteral tendencies of Samoan mothers and childless women should have been similar to the avuncular tendencies of *fa'afafine,* but again this was not the case.

We have also demonstrated that *fa'afafine's* avuncular tendencies are much higher than their altruistic interest in non-kin children (Vasey and VanderLaan 2010b). As such, *fa'afafine's* elevated avuncular tendencies are not a by-product of general altruistic interest in all children. If this were true, the *fa'afafine's* avuncular tendencies toward nieces and nephews and their altruistic tendencies toward non-kin children would have been similar, but this was not the case.

Additional research indicates that *fa'afafine* exhibit similar levels of sexual/romantic relationship involvement compared to Samoan women and gynephilic men (VanderLaan and Vasey 2012). As such, *fa'afafine's* relatively elevated avuncular tendencies cannot be characterized as a simple by-product of their failure to form, and invest in intimate sexual/romantic relationships, which, in turn, leaves them with more time and resources. If that were true, *fa'afafine* should have exhibited reduced levels of sexual/romantic relationship involvement compared to men and women, but once again, this was not the case.

Finally, there is no evidence that Samoans hold unique (trans)gender role expectations that *fa'afafine* will engage in elevated levels of avuncular activity compared to women and gynephilic men (VanderLaan et al. 2014a). Equally, there is no evidence that *fa'afafine* hold such expectations for themselves (VanderLaan et al. 2014a). Because Samoans in general, and *fa'afafine* themselves, did not believe that *fa'afafine* are primarily responsible for the care of nieces and nephews, elevated avuncular tendencies among *fa'afafine* cannot be explained in terms of such (trans)gender role expectations.

It should be clear from the research described above that much of our work has focused on falsifying the kin selection hypothesis for male androphilia by examining alternative explanations that might account for the *fa'afafine's* elevated avuncularity. It should be equally clear that none of the alternative explanations we have tested, to date, have been supported. Taken together, this body of work is not inconsistent with the conclusion that elevated avuncularity by androphilic males is an adaptation that evolved via kin selection. That being said, establishing that a given trait is an adaptation involves not only ruling out alternative explanations but also repeatedly satisfying adaptive design criteria empirically (Buss et al. 1998). Adaptive design implies complexity, economy, efficiency, reliability, precision, and functionality (Williams 1966).

We have conducted several studies that indicate that compared to Samoan women and gynephilic men, the avuncular cognition of *fa'afafine* appears to be more adaptively designed. First, the avuncular tendencies of *fa'afafine* are more dissociated from (i.e., covary less with) their altruistic interest in non-kin children, compared to Samoan women and gynephilic men (Vasey and VanderLaan 2010b). Such a dissociation would allow *fa'afafine* to channel resources toward nieces and nephews in a more optimal manner while minimizing resources directed toward non-kin children. Second, whereas Samoan men and women show a tendency to decrease their willingness to invest in nieces and nephews when they have sexual/romantic relationship partners, the cognition of *fa'afafine* appears to protect against this tendency by maintaining a high level of willingness to invest in nieces and nephews regardless of relationship status (VanderLaan and Vasey 2012). Third, due to the mechanics of human reproduction, individuals can always be certain that their sisters' offspring are their genetic relatives. Yet, due to the possibility of cuckoldry, individuals are necessarily less certain in the case of brothers' offspring. The elevated avuncular tendencies of *fa'afafine* are contingent on the presence of sisters, not brothers, which suggests the avuncular cognition of *fa'afafine* is sensitive to the relative fitness benefits of investing in sisters' versus brothers' offspring (VanderLaan and Vasey 2013). Fourth, compared to women and gynephilic men, *fa'afafine* are generally better at allocating investment toward indirect fitness-maximizing categories of kin (i.e., sisters' younger daughters) and they do so in a manner that reflects greater sensitivity to nonfrivolous versus frivolous investment contexts (VanderLaan and Vasey 2014).

Elevated avuncular tendencies must translate into real-world avuncular behavior if they are to have any impact on the fitness of nieces and nephews and the uncles themselves. Vasey and VanderLaan (2010c) used money given to, and received from, oldest and youngest siblings' sons and daughters as a behavioral assay of expressed kin-directed altruism. In line with the predictions of the kin selection hypothesis, compared to women and gynephilic men, *fa'afafine* gave significantly more money to their youngest siblings' daughters. No other group differences were observed for money given to, or received from, nieces and/or nephews. Moreover, among women and gynephilic men, there were no correlations between the number of children parented and monetary exchanges with the niece and nephew categories examined, suggesting, once again, that childlessness cannot account for why *fa'afafine* give more money to their youngest siblings' daughters.

Analyses by VanderLaan et al. (2013c) revealed that key aspects of the adaptively relevant environment (ARE) of transgender androphilic males likely facilitated the expression of elevated kin-directed altruism. AREs consist of those features of the environment that must be present in order for an adaptation to be functionally expressed (Irons 1998). VanderLaan et al. (2013c) found that societies in which transgender male androphilia predominates were more likely to show social characteristics that facilitate investment in kin, compared to non-transgender societies. For example, relative to non-transgender societies, transgender societies were more likely to exhibit bilateral[4] and double descent[5] systems than patrilineal, matrilineal, and ambilineal[6] descent systems. In addition, correlational analysis showed that as the presence of ancestral sociocultural conditions increased, so too did the presence of bilateral (and double) descent systems. Ethnologists have argued that bilateral decent systems and bilocal patterns of residence following marriage are maximally inclusive of kin because they do not bias individuals to interact with only one subset of relatives (Alvard 2002; Ember 1975; Kramer and Greaves 2011). Consequently, it is reasonable to deduce that these patterns of descent would have allowed for more altruistic interactions with a full range of genetically related kin. Taken together, these analyses

---

[4] In bilateral descent systems, ego's mother's and father's lineages are equally important for emotional, social, spiritual, and political support, as well as for transfer of property or wealth.

[5] In double descent systems, individuals receive some rights and obligations from the father's side of the family and others from the mother's side.

[6] Ambilineal descent systems are defined as existing when individuals have the option of choosing one of their lineages for membership.

are consistent with the conclusion that bilateral descent characterized the ancestral societies in which male androphilia was expressed in the transgender form.

VanderLaan et al. (2013c) also examined the acceptance of same-sex sexuality in 27 transgender societies for which information could be obtained. The vast majority of these societies expressed no negative reactions to same-sex sexual behavior. Overall then, the same-sex sexual orientation of transgender males appears to be socially tolerated in societies where this form of male androphilia predominates. Such tolerance, particularly on the part of the kin of transgender androphilic males, might be considered essential for kin selection to be deemed as a plausible contributing factor toward the persistence of male androphilia over evolutionary time. Unless transgender androphilic males are accepted by their families, their opportunity to invest in kin is likely mitigated.

In sum, transgender male androphilia is likely the ancestral form of male androphilia, key aspects of the transgender androphilic male ARE (i.e., bilateral and double descent systems, social tolerance of same-sex sexuality) would have facilitated elevated kin-directed altruism, and data from contemporary transgender male androphiles (*fa'afafine*) indicates that they exhibit elevated avuncularity. Given all of this, it seems reasonable to suggest that kin selection played some role in the evolution of male androphilia. As such, the elevated kin-directed altruism documented in Samoan *fa'afafine* is more likely to have characterized ancestral androphilic males compared to the lack thereof documented in sex-gender congruent androphilic men from industrialized cultures (Abild et al. 2014; Bobrow and Bailey 2001; Forrester et al. 2011; Rahman and Hull 2005; Vasey and VanderLaan 2012).

Our research has identified a number of features of the ARE that would have facilitated the expression of kin-directed altruism by androphilic males. What needs more careful consideration is the process by which this putative evolved trait develops over the life span. Research on childhood separation anxiety among gender nonconforming boys who grow up to be androphilic may provide insight in this regard.

Childhood Separation Anxiety: A Developmental Precursor of Elevated Kin-Directed Altruism?

Childhood separation anxiety occurs in response to separation from major attachment figures such as parents and it tends to be more commonly manifest by girls compared to boys (e.g., Shear et al. 2006; VanderLaan et al. 2011a). As such, it can be described as a female-typical characteristic. Interestingly, in clinical samples drawn from Western populations, it is not uncommon for extremely feminine boys who are diagnosed with gender dysphoria in children (GDC)[7] to exhibit elevated traits of childhood separation anxiety (Coates and Person 1985; Zucker et al. 1996). The majority of boys diagnosed with GDC grow up to be androphilic in adulthood (Green 1987; Wallien and Cohen-Kettenis 2008; Singh 2012; Steensma 2013).

Recall that androphilic males are relatively feminine compared to gynephilic males, although often not necessarily to the extreme that characterizes GDC boys (Bailey and Zucker 1995; Bartlett and Vasey 2006; Cardoso 2005, 2009; Lippa 2005; Vasey and Bartlett 2007; Whitam 1983). Consequently, it is perhaps not surprising that *nonclinical* samples of adult androphilic males recall more traits of childhood separation anxiety compared to their gynephilic counterparts. This pattern of recall holds for both nonclinical samples of sex-gender congruent androphilic males in Canada (VanderLaan et al. 2011a) and nonclinical samples of transgender androphilic males in Samoa (Vasey et al. 2011).

[7] According to the American Psychiatric Association's *Diagnostic and Statistical Manual of Mental Disorders* (DSM-V; American Psychiatric Association 2013), gender dysphoria in children (GDC) is a mental disorder that characterizes individuals who experience dysphoria with respect to their sexed bodies or assigned genders or both. In Western parlance, such individuals are commonly referred to as transsexual or transgender. The full diagnostic criteria for GDC can be found in the DSM-V (American Psychiatric Association 2013). For an entree into the substantial controversy surrounding this diagnosis, see, for example, Bartlett et al. (2000) and Vasey and Bartlett (2007).

When considering these clinical and nonclinical studies from an evolutionarily perspective, the question arises as to what the functional (i.e., adaptive) basis of elevated childhood separation anxiety might be in feminine, (pre)androphilic boys in general, as opposed to GDC boys more specifically. For some readers it may seem incongruous to entertain the idea that a "negative" emotion like separation anxiety might be adaptive. However, if one considers that emotions evolved to guide behavior toward adaptive courses of action, then there is no necessary reason why emotional states should be associated with positive affect in order to be considered adaptive (Keller and Miller 2006; Nesse 2005). Because separation anxiety occurs in response to separation from major attachment figures (Coates and Person 1985; Zucker et al. 1996), it seems reasonable to suggest that elevated traits of childhood separation anxiety in relatively feminine, (pre)androphilic boys are indicative of marked attachment to parents and other close family members.

In light of this literature, VanderLaan et al. (2011b) suggest that traits of elevated childhood separation anxiety in (pre)androphilic boys may be a developmental precursor of an evolved predisposition in adulthood for prosocial tendencies, particularly kin-directed altruism such as elevated avuncularity. According to this model, in childhood, concern for one's kin manifests as elevated separation anxiety in (pre)androphilic boys and is part of an overall pattern of feminine behavior. Later, in adulthood, concern for one's kin is expressed as elevated kin-directed altruism by adult male androphiles. The model stipulates that this adult pattern of elevated kin-directed altruism is contingent on the continued expression of femininity in adulthood. As such, elevated traits of childhood separation anxiety are predicted to occur in all (pre)androphlic boys, regardless of their cultural milieu. In contrast, elevated kin-directed altruism in adulthood is predicted to occur in transgender male androphiles such as *fa'afafine* who are feminine, but not in sex-gender congruent male androphiles such as gay men, who present publicly in a relatively masculine manner.

In support of this evolutionary developmental model, retrospective research has shown that Samoan *fa'afafine* recall more gender-atypical behavior and more traits of separation anxiety in childhood than gynephilic men (Bartlett and Vasey 2006; Vasey and Bartlett 2007; Vasey et al. 2011). *Fa'afafine* scored highest for items used to measure childhood separation anxiety involving worrying about parents (e.g., "I worried that something terrible might happen to my parents"). These findings are reinforced by qualitative data collected during interviews with adult *fa'afafine*. The anxiety that some *fa'afafine* recalled experiencing with respect to something terrible happening to their parents seemed to generalize into a pattern of extreme worry about all aspects of the parents' (especially the mothers') lives. For example, one *fa'afafine* participant recounted the following story:

> When my mom brought my lunch to school and she was wearing a *puletasi* [a traditional Samoan two-piece dress], I knew she wasn't too rushed and had time to make herself look pretty. But when she came wearing a *lavalava* [a colourful Samoan garment similar to a sarong] and a t-shirt, I knew she was too busy to make herself beautiful. I would ask her if I could go home with her to help but she would tell me to stay at school. I would be worried all afternoon and wouldn't be able to focus on my work. I just waited for that final bell to ring. I would have rather helped my mom at home but I had to stay behind.

Research conducted in Canada also furnishes support for VanderLaan et al.'s (2011b) evolutionary development model. For example, retrospective research in Canada indicates that sex-gender congruent androphilic men are also more gender-atypical in childhood compared to gynephilic men (Bailey and Zucker 1995; VanderLaan et al. 2011a). Moreover, they recalled significantly more traits of childhood separation anxiety compared to gynephilic men, but did not differ in this regard from women (VanderLaan et al. 2011a). Those who recalled higher levels of boyhood gender atypicality were more likely to also recall higher levels of childhood separation anxiety (VanderLaan et al. 2011a). Like *fa'afafine,* Canadian sex-gender congruent androphilic males also scored highest for items used to measure childhood separation anxiety involving worrying about parents, as opposed to items used to measure concern for one's own well-being (VanderLaan et al. 2011a).

In another Canadian study, VanderLaan et al. (2014b) demonstrated that elevated concern for parental well-being was a source of childhood separation anxiety that characterized androphilic males and females significantly more than gynephilic males. The heterosexual sex and male sexual orientation differences in concern about parental well-being were accounted for by childhood feminine behavior. These findings suggest that female-typical behavior in childhood is an important proximate factor in the expression of elevated concern for the well-being of kin among (pre)homosexual boys.

Also consistent with VanderLaan et al.'s (2011b) evolutionary developmental model is the finding that, unlike *fa'afafine* who are feminine in adulthood, sex-gender congruent androphilic men in Canada and other industrialized nations (i.e., USA, UK, Japan) do not exhibit elevated avuncular tendencies in adulthood (Abild et al. 2014; Bobrow and Bailey 2001; Forrester et al. 2011; Rahman and Hull 2005; Vasey and VanderLaan 2012). In these cultures, gender role expectations hold that male-bodied individuals should behave in a masculine manner and, as such, boys are socialized to behave accordingly (Bailey 2003; Berling 2001; McLelland 2000; Rieger and Savin-Williams 2012). VanderLaan et al. (2011b) have speculated that the behavioral masculinization and defeminization that characterizes the development of sex-gender congruent males in such cultures may lower the expression of elevated kin-directed altruism in adulthood.

Concluding Remarks

In recent years, progress has finally been made toward gaining an empirically based understanding of how male androphilia persists over evolutionary time. Although male androphilia varies dramatically with respect to the manner in which it is publicly expressed, there are multiple lines of developmental and biodemographic evidence indicating that different cultural forms of male androphilia (i.e., transgender sex-gender congruent) share the same etiological basis. Quantitative research indicates that the transgender form of male androphilia was likely ancestral to the sex-gender congruent form.

The most prominent hypothesis that posits a role for the social behavior of male androphiles in the evolutionary maintenance of genes associated with same-sex sexual orientation is the kin selection hypothesis. Research in Samoa has repeatedly furnished support for the kin selection hypothesis where transgender male androphiles known locally as *fa'afafine* exhibit elevated avuncular tendencies and behavior compared to women and gynephilic men. Research on Samoan *fa'afafine* has also furnished evidence that their avuncular cognition exhibits hallmarks of adaptive design.

VanderLaan et al. (2011b) proposed that elevated traits of childhood separation anxiety are part of a general constellation of feminine characteristics exhibited by androphilic males. Moreover, they argued that elevated traits of childhood separation anxiety in androphilic males primarily reflect concern for close kin. The research that exists is consistent with these predictions. On the basis of these ideas, VanderLaan et al. (2011b) argued, further, that childhood concern for kin, as manifested in terms of elevated traits of childhood separation anxiety, is a developmental precursor of elevated kin-directed altruism in adulthood. The expression of elevated adult kin-directed altruism by androphilic males is, however, contingent on the continued expression of femininity in adulthood. As such, elevated kin-directed altruism is expected to occur in transgender male androphiles, but not sex-gender congruent male androphiles. Again, existing research, while limited, is consistent with these predictions.

To provide more detailed tests of VanderLaan et al.'s (2011b) evolutionary developmental model, additional research is needed on other populations of sex-gender congruent and transgender male androphiles to ascertain whether the expression of elevated traits of childhood separation anxiety is indeed a cross-culturally invariant pattern of psychosexual development in such individuals. Future research is also needed to provide further tests of the hypothesis that childhood separation anxiety in androphilic males is primarily related to concern for kin, as opposed to concern for oneself. Similarly, more research is needed to explore the purported link between separation anxiety in childhood and kin-directed altruism in adulthood in androphilic males. Lastly, it will be important to test the kin selection hypothesis in additional populations of transgender male androphiles to ascertain whether other such populations exhibit elevated avuncular tendencies.

Acknowledgments We thank Liulauulu Faaleolea Ah Fook, Resitara Apa, Nancy Bartlett, Vester Fido Collins, Alice Dreger, Gardenia Elisaia, Vaosa Epa, Vaasatia Poloma Komiti, Anita Latai, Jean-Baptiste Leca, Tyrone Laurenson, Gaualofa Matalavea, Avau Memea, Sarah Faletoese Su'a, Nella Tavita-Levy, Palanitina Toelupe, Trisha Tuiloma, Avalogo Togi A. Tunupopo, Erin Zelinski, the Kuka family of Savai'i, the Samoan AIDS Foundation, the National University of Samoa, the Samoan Ministry of Health, and the Government of Samoa. We are grateful to all of the individuals who agreed to participate in our studies. We extend special thanks to Alatina Ioelu without whom this research could not have been conducted. Our research on the evolution of male androphilia has taken place over the past decade and has been supported by the University of Lethbridge and a variety of funding agencies. PLV received funding from an Alberta Provincial Government S.T.E.P. Award, an Alberta Innovates Health Solutions (AIHS) Sustainability Fund Grant, a Canadian Institutes of Health Research (CIHR) Catalyst Grant in Methods and Measures for Gender, Sex and Health, three Natural Sciences and Engineering Research Council (NSERC) of Canada Grants, and a Social Sciences and Humanities Research Council of Canada (SSHRC) Grant. DPV received funding from a NSERC of Canada Graduate Scholarship-D3, the Sigma Xi Scientific Research Society Grant-in-Aid-of-Research, a Ralph Steinhauer Award of Distinction, an American Psychological Foundation Henry David Travel Grant, and a Sexual Medicine Society of North America Post-Doctoral Fellowship Stipend.

References

Abild, M., VanderLaan, D. P., & Vasey, P. L. (2014). Does proximity influence the expression of avuncular tendencies in Canadian androphilic males? *Journal of Cognition and Culture, 14,* 40–62.

Alanko, K., Santtila, P., Harlaar, N., Witting, K., Varjonen, M., Jern, P., Johansson, A., von der Pahlen, B., & Sandnabba, N. K. (2010). Common genetic effects of gender atypical behavior in childhood and sexual orientation in adulthood: A study of Finnish twins. *Archives of Sexual Behavior, 39,* 81–92.

Alvard, M. S. (2002). Carcass ownership and meat distributions by big game hunters. *Research in Economic Anthropology, 21,* 99–131.

American Psychiatric Association. (2013). *Diagnostic and statistical manual of mental disorders* (5th ed.). Washington, DC: Author.

Bailey, J. M. (2003). *The man who would be queen: The science of gender-bending and transsexualism.* Washington, DC: Joseph Henry Press.

Bailey, J. M., & Zucker, K. J. (1995). Childhood sex-typed behavior and sexual orientation: A conceptual analysis and quantitative review. *Developmental Psychology, 31,* 43–55.

Bartlett, N. H., & Vasey, P. L. (2006). A retrospective study of childhood gender-atypical behavior in Samoan *fa'afafine. Archives of Sexual Behavior, 35,* 559–566.

Bartlett, N. H., Vasey, P. L., & Bukowski, W. M. (2000). Is gender identity disorder in children a mental disorder? *Sex Roles, 43,* 753–785.

Berling, T. (2001). *Sissyphobia: Gay men and effeminate behavior.* Philadelphia: Harrington Park Press.

Binford, L. R. (2001). *Constructing frames of references: An analytical method for archaeological theory building using hunter-gatherer and environmental data sets.* Berkley: University of California.

Blanchard, R. (2004). Quantitative and theoretical analyses of the relation between older brothers and homosexuality in men. *Journal of Theoretical Biology, 230,* 173–187.

Blanchard, R., & Lippa, R. A. (2007). Birth order, sibling sex ratio, handedness, and sexual orientation of male and female participants in a BBC Internet research project. *Archives of Sexual Behavior, 36,* 163–176.

Bobrow, D., & Bailey, J. M. (2001). Is male homosexuality maintained via kin selection? *Evolution and Human Behavior, 22,* 361–368.

Bogaert, A. F., & Skorska, M. (2011). Sexual orientation, fraternal birth order, and the maternal immune hypothesis: A review. *Frontiers in Neuroendocrinology, 32,* 247–254.

Buss, D. M., Haselton, M. G., Shackelford, T. K., Bleske, A. L., & Wakefield, J. C. (1998). Adaptations, exaptations, and spandrels. *American Psychologist, 53,* 533–548.

Camperio-Ciani, A., Corna, F., & Capiluppi, C. (2004). Evidence for maternally inherited factors favoring male homosexuality and promoting female fecundity. *Proceedings of the Royal Society of London B, 271,* 2217–2221.

Cantor, J. M., Blanchard, R., Paterson, A. D., & Bogaert, A. F. (2002). How many gay men owe their sexual orientation to fraternal birth order? *Archives of Sexual Behavior, 31,* 63–71.

Cardoso, F. L. (2005). Cultural universals and differences in male homosexuality: The case of a Brazilian fishing village. *Archives of Sexual Behavior, 34,* 103–109.

Cardoso, F. L. (2009). Recalled sex-typed behavior in childhood and sports preferences in adulthood of heterosexual, bisexual, and homosexual men from Brazil, Turkey, and Thailand. *Archives of Sexual Behavior, 38,* 726–736.

Coates, S., & Person, E. S. (1985). Extreme boyhood femininity: Isolated behavior or pervasive disorder? *Journal of the American Academy of Child Psychiatry, 24,* 702–709.

Dean, L. G., Vale, G. L., Laland, K. N., Flynn, E., & Kendal, R. L. (2014). Human cumulative culture: A comparative perspective. *Biology Review, 89,* 284–301.

Devereux, G. (1937). Institutionalized homosexuality of the Mohave Indians. *Human Biology, 9,* 498–527.

Ember, C. R. (1975). Residential variation in hunter-gatherers. *Cross-Cultural Research, 10,* 199–227.

Forrester, D. L., VanderLaan, D. P., Parker, J., & Vasey, P. L. (2011). Male sexual orientation and avuncularity in Canada: Implications for the kin selection hypothesis. *Journal of Culture and Cognition, 11,* 339–352.

Gebhard, P. H. (1970). Sexual motifs in prehistoric Peruvian ceramics. In T. Bowie & C. V. Christenson (Eds.), *Studies in erotic art* (pp. 109–144). New York: Basic Books.

Green, R. (1987). *The "sissy boy syndrome" and the development of homosexuality*. New Haven: Yale University Press.

Hamer, D. H., Hu, S., Magnunson, V. L., Hu, N., & Pattatucci, A. M. (1993). A linkage between DNA markers on the X-chromosome and male sexual orientation. *Science, 261,* 321–327.

Hamilton, W. D. (1963). The evolution of altruistic behavior. *American Naturalist, 97,* 354–356.

Harrington, J. P. (1942). Culture element distributions 19: Central California coast. *Anthropological Records, 7*(1), 1–46.

Herdt, G. (1997). *Same sex, different cultures*. Colorado: Westview Press.

Hewlett, B., & Hewlett, B. L. (2010). Sex and searching for children among Aka foragers and Ngandu farmers of Central Africa. *African Studies Monographs, 31,* 107–125.

Hill, K. R., Walker, R. S., Bozicevic, M., Eder, J., Headland, T., Hewlett, B., Hurtado, A. M., Marlow, F., Wiessner, P., & Wood, B. (2011). Co-residence patterns in hunter-gatherer societies show unique human social structure. *Science, 331,* 1286–1289.

Hollimon, S. E. (1997). The third gender in California: Two-spirit undertakers among the Chumash, their neighbours. In C. Claassen & R. A. Joyce (Eds.), *Women in prehistory: North America and Mesoamerica* (pp. 173–188). Philadelphia: University of Pennsylvania Press.

Iemmola, F., & Camperio Ciani, A. (2009). New evidence of genetic factors influencing sexual orientation in men: Female fecundity increase in the maternal line. *Archives of Sexual Behavior, 38,* 393–399.

Irons, W. (1998). Adaptively relevant environments versus the environment of evolutionary adaptiveness. *Evolutionary Anthropology, 6,* 194–204.

Keller, M. C., & Miller, G. (2006). Resolving the paradox of common, harmful, heritable mental disorders: Which evolutionary genetic models work best? *Behavioral and Brain Sciences, 29,* 385–452.

King, M. D., Green, J., Osborn, D. P. J., Arkell, J., Hetherton, J., & Pereira, E. (2005). Family size in white gay and heterosexual men. *Archives of Sexual Behavior, 34,* 117–122.

Kramer, K. L., & Greaves, R. D. (2011). Postmarital residence and bilateral kin associations among hunter-gatherers: Pumé foragers living in the best of both worlds. *Human Nature, 22,* 41–63.

Kroeber, A. L. (1925). Handbook of the Indians of California. *Bureau Ame Ethnol Bull, 78,* 1–995.

Långström, N., Rahman, Q., Carlström, E., & Lichtenstein, P. (2010). Genetic and environmental effects on same-sex sexual behavior: A population study of twins in Sweden. *Archives of Sexual Behavior, 39,* 75–80.

Lippa, R. A. (2005). *Gender, nature, nurture* (2nd ed.). Mahwah: Erlbaum.

Marlowe, F. W. (2005). Hunter-gatherers and human evolution. *Evolutionary Anthropology, 14,* 54–67.

McBrearty, S., & Brooks, A. S. (2000). The revolution that wasn't: A new interpretation of the origins of modern human behavior. *Journal of Human Evolution, 39,* 453–563.

McLelland, M. J. (2000). *Male homosexuality in modern Japan: Cultural myths and social realities*. London: RoutledgeCurzon.

Meyer, I. (2003). Prejudice, social stress and mental health in lesbian, gay, and bisexual populations: Conceptual issues and research evidence. *Psychological Bulletin, 129,* 674–697.

Murray, S. O. (2000). *Homosexualities*. Chicago: University of Chicago Press.

Namaste, V. (2000). *Invisible lives: The erasure of transsexual and transgender people*. Chicago: University of Chicago Press.

Nanda, S. (1998). *Neither man nor woman: The hijras of India*. Belmont: Wadsworth.

Nash, G. (2001). The subversive male: Homosexual and bestial images on European Mesolithic rock art. In L. Bevan (Ed.), *Indecent exposure: Sexuality, society and the archaeological record* (pp. 43–55). Glasgow: Cruithne Press.

Neese, R. M. (2005). Evolutionary psychology and mental health. In D. M. Buss (Ed.), *The handbook of evolutionary psychology* (pp. 903–927). Hoboken: Wiley.

Peletz, M. G. (2009). *Gender pluralism: Southeast Asia since early modern times*. New York: Routledge.

Petterson, L. J, Dixson, B. J., Little, A. C., & Vasey, P. L. (2015). Viewing time measures of sexual orientation in Samoan cisgender men who engage in sexual interactions with *fa'afine*. *PLoS ONE, 10*(2), e0116529.

Rahman, Q., & Hull, M. S. (2005). An empirical test of the kin selection hypothesis for male homosexuality. *Archives of Sexual Behavior, 34,* 461–467.

Rahman, Q., Collins, A., Morrison, M., Orrells, J. C., Cadinouche, K., Greenfield, S., et al. (2008). Maternal inheritance and familial fecundity factors in male homosexuality. *Archives of Sexual Behavior, 37,* 962–969.

Rieger, G., & Savin-Williams, R. C. (2012). Gender nonconformity, sexual orientation, and psychological well-being. *Archives of Sexual Behavior, 41,* 611–621.

Sanderson, S. K., & Roberts, W. W. (2008). The evolutionary forms of the religious life: A cross-cultural, quantitative analysis. *American Anthropologist, 110,* 454–466.

Schwartz, G., Kim, R. M., Kolundziji, A. B., Rieger, G., & Sanders, A. R. (2010). Biodemographic and physical correlates of sexual orientation in men. *Archives of Sexual Behavior, 39,* 93–109.

Seil, D. (1996). Transsexuals: The boundaries of sexual identity and gender. In R. P. Cabaj & B. Brenner (Eds.), *Textbook of homosexuality and mental health* (pp. 743–762). Washington, DC: American Psychiatric Press.

Shear, K., Jin, R., Ruscio, A. M., Walters, E. E., & Kessler, R. C. (2006). Prevalence and correlates of estimated DSM-IV child and adult separation anxiety disorder in the national comorbidity survey replication. *American Journal of Psychiatry, 163,* 1074–1083.

Singh, D. (2012). *A follow-up study of boys with gender identity disorder.* Unpublished doctoral dissertation. University of Toronto.

Smith, A. B. (1999). Archaeology and the evolution of hunter-gatherers. In R. B. Lee & R. Daly (Eds.), *The Cambridge encyclopedia of hunters and gatherers* (pp. 384–390). Cambridge: Cambridge University Press.

Smith, A. M., Rissel, C. E., Richters, J., Grulich, A. E., & de Visser, R. O. (2003). Sex in Australia: Sexual identity, sexual attraction, and sexual experience among a representative sample of adults. *Australian and New Zealand Journal of Public Health, 27,* 138–145.

Steensma, T. D. (2013). *From gender variance to gender dysphoria: Psychosexual development of gender atypical children and adolescents.* Unpublished doctoral dissertation. Vrije Universiteit, Amsterdam, the Netherlands.

VanderLaan, D. P., & Vasey, P. L. (2011). Male sexual orientation in Independent Samoa: Evidence for fraternal birth order and maternal fecundity effects. *Archives of Sexual Behavior, 40,* 495–503.

VanderLaan, D. P., & Vasey, P. L. (2012). Relationship status and elevated avuncularity in Samoan *fa'afafine. Personal Relationships, 19,* 326–339.

VanderLaan, D. P., & Vasey, P. L. (2013). Birth order and avuncular tendencies in Samoan men and *fa'afafine. Archives of Sexual Behavior, 42,* 371–379.

VanderLaan, D. P., & Vasey, P. L. (2014). Evidence of cognitive biases for maximizing indirect fitness in Samoan *fa'afafine. Archives of Sexual Behavior, 43,* 1009–1022.

VanderLaan, D. P., Gothreau, L., Bartlett, N. H., & Vasey, P. L. (2011a). Recalled separation anxiety and gender atypicality in childhood: A study of Canadian heterosexual and homosexual men and women. *Archives of Sexual Behavior, 40,* 1233–1240.

VanderLaan, D. P., Gothreau, L., Bartlett, N. H., & Vasey, P. L. (2011b). Separation anxiety in feminine boys: Pathological or prosocial? *Journal of Gay and Lesbian Mental Health, 15,* 1–16.

VanderLaan, D. P., Forrester, D. L., Petterson, L. J., & Vasey, P. L. (2012). Offspring production among the extended relatives of Samoan men and *fa'afafine. PLoS ONE,* 7(4), e36088.

VanderLaan, D. P., Forrester, D. L., Petterson, L. J., & Vasey, P. L. (2013a). The prevalence of *fa'afafine* relatives among Samoan men and *fa'afafine. Archives of Sexual Behavior, 42,* 353–359.

VanderLaan, D. P., Vokey, J. R., & Vasey, P. L. (2013b). Is male androphilia familial in non-Western cultures? The case of a Samoan village. *Archives of Sexual Behavior, 42,* 361–370.

VanderLaan, D. P., Ren, Z., & Vasey, P. L. (2013c). Male androphilia in the ancestral environment: An ethnological analysis. *Human Nature, 24,* 375–401.

VanderLaan, D. P., Petterson, L. J., Mallard, R. W., & Vasey, P. L. (2014a). (Trans)gender role expectations regarding childcare in Samoa. *Journal of Sex Research.* doi:10.1080/00224499.2014.884210.

VanderLaan, D. P., Petterson, L. J., & Vasey, P. L. (2014b). Elevated childhood separation anxiety: An early developmental expression of heightened concern for kin in homosexual men? *Personality and Individual Differences.* doi:10.1080/00224499.2014.884210.

Vasey, P. L., & Bartlett, N. H. (2007). What can the Samoan *fa'afafine* teach us about the Western concept of "Gender Identity Disorder in Childhood"? *Perspectives in Biology and Medicine, 50,* 481–490.

Vasey, P. L., & VanderLaan, D. P. (2007). Birth order and male androphilia in Samoan *fa'afafine. Proceedings of the Royal Society of London B, 274,* 1437–1442.

Vasey, P. L., & VanderLaan, D. P. (2009). Materteral and avuncular tendencies in Samoa: A comparative study of women, men and *fa'afafine. Human Nature, 20,* 269–281.

Vasey, P. L., & VanderLaan, D. P. (2010a). Avuncular tendencies in Samoan *fa'afafine* and the evolution of male androphilia. *Archives of Sexual Behavior, 39,* 821–830.

Vasey, P. L., & VanderLaan, D. P. (2010b). An adaptive cognitive dissociation between willingness to help kin and non-kin in Samoan *fa'afafine. Psychological Science, 21,* 292–297.

Vasey, P. L., & VanderLaan, D. P. (2010c). Monetary exchanges with nieces and nephews: A comparison of Samoan men, women, and *fa'afafine. Evolution and Human Behavior, 31,* 373–380.

Vasey, P. L., & VanderLaan, D. P. (2012). Male sexual orientation and avuncularity in Japan: Implications for the Kin Selection Hypothesis. *Archives of Sexual Behavior, 41,* 209–215.

Vasey, P. L., Pocock, D. S., & VanderLaan, D. P. (2007). Kin selection and male androphilia in Samoan *fa'afafine. Evolution and Human Behavior, 28,* 159–167.

Vasey, P. L., VanderLaan, D. P., Gothreau, L., & Bartlett, N. H. (2011). Traits of separation anxiety in childhood: A comparison of Samoan men, women and *fa'afafine*. *Archives of Sexual Behavior, 40,* 511–517.

Vasey, P. L., Parker, J. L., & VanderLaan, D. P. (2014). Comparative reproductive output of androphilic and gynephilic males in Samoa. *Archives of Sexual Behavior, 43*, 363–367.

Wallien, M. S., & Cohen-Kettenis, P. T. (2008). Psychosexual outcome of gender-dysphoric children. *Journal of the American Academy of Child and Adolescent Psychiatry, 47,* 1413–1423.

Whitam, F. L. (1983). Culturally invariant properties of male homosexuality: Tentative conclusions from cross-cultural research. *Archives of Sexual Behavior, 12,* 207–226.

Williams, G. C. (1966). *Adaptation and natural selection*. Princeton: Princeton University Press.

Wilson, E. O. (1975). *Sociobiology: The new synthesis*. Cambridge: Belknap Press.

Winkelman, M. (2010). *Shamanism: A biopsychosocial paradigm of consciousness and healing*. Santa Barbara: Praeger.

Woodburn, J. (1982). Egalitarian societies. *Man, 17,* 431–451.

Zucker, K. J., Bradley, S. J., & Sullivan, C. B. L. (1996). Traits of separation anxiety in boys with gender identity disorder. *Journal of the American Academy of Child and Adolescent Psychiatry, 35,* 791–798.

Familial Relationships

27

Catherine Salmon

Our most basic instinct is not for survival but for family. Most of us would give our own life for the survival of a family member, yet we lead our daily life too often as if we take our family for granted.

Paul Pearshall

The great advantage of living in a large family is that early lesson of life's essential unfairness.

Nancy Mitford

A fundamental focus of adaptationist research into social relationships has been that of kinship and the family. Anthropologists have long recognized the centrality of kinship to human relations and the overwhelming interest humans around the world devote to matters of sex and family (Leach 1966). Evolutionary biology and psychology have been profoundly influenced by the work of William Hamilton. Hamilton's (1964) seminal paper on the evolution of social behavior extended the concept of Darwinian fitness (one's personal reproductive success as measured by descent kin) to include fitness achieved through an actor's effects on the expected reproductive success of collateral as well as descendent kin, referred to as inclusive fitness. Rather than thinking of humans, or other organisms, as just reproductive strategists, they are seen as nepotistic strategists. An organism's genes are just as likely to be found in a brother as in a son and, as a result, fraternal investment would be expected to evolve much like paternal investment. This view of kinship has profound implications for our understanding of social relationships.

Because of the clear importance of family relationships to our social lives, one would have expected the study of the family to hold a central role in social psychology, not just evolutionary psychology, biology, and anthropology. Surprisingly, it does not. Despite human social life being dominated by interactions with family and friends, social psychology has been far more concerned with the interactions of strangers. A perusal of current textbooks of social psychology reveals social life broken down into social perception, influence, and relations. One might expect social relations to have a substantial focus on the family, but instead it is mainly concerned with attraction and close relationships, helping behavior, and aggression. An examination of the subject index of one popular text includes one mention of family (family violence), one mention of parental instinct, and one of kin selection. Though it has been open recently to evolutionarily informed studies, particularly in the area of mating, an examination of the *Journal of Personality and Social Psychology*'s articles reveals 120 articles published in

C. Salmon (✉)
Department of Psychology, University of Redlands, 1200 East Colton Avenue, 92223 Redlands, CA, USA
e-mail: catherine_salmon@redlands.edu

V. Zeigler-Hill et al. (eds.), *Evolutionary Perspectives on Social Psychology*, Evolutionary Psychology,
DOI 10.1007/978-3-319-12697-5_27,

2013, only three of which touch on some aspect of family, mostly the impact of parenting on adult attachment. While many areas of psychology are inclined to study college students (a convenient, easily accessible sample), one problem is that many of them are strangers, far from family. As a result, stranger interactions, dating, and hook-up relations are more easily studied. In addition, long-term social relationships like family can be messy sorts of data with lots of factors to control for that are not very open to experimentation. The past 20–30 years have seen a shift by some social psychologists to studying "close relationships" and one might assume that family would be a big part of this. But with a few exceptions (for an example, see Burnstein et al. 1994), the majority of this work has focused on sexual and/or romantic relationships as well as friendships.

Daly et al. (1997) raised a number of issues about the lack of a family focus in the study of social behavior by psychologists. This chapter highlights some of the work done since then that uses an adaptationist perspective to better understand social behavior in the family context. Different types of close relationships, whether they be sexual, parent–offspring, or friendship, are qualitatively distinct types of relationships that differ along dimensions other than intimacy. The features that make up an ideal mate are different from those of an ideal mother or brother, for example, and humans clearly process information about different types of intimates in different ways (Kenrick et al. 1998; Symons 1995). The mechanisms entailed by such a psychology would be specialized motivational and information processing systems designed to deal with the specific adaptive problems faced by being a mother, father, sibling, or grandparent. Evolutionarily informed research exploring these mechanisms and the problems they solve are highlighted.

Nepotistic Strategists and Fitness: What Is the Basis of an Evolutionary Psychology of the Family?

According to Hamilton (1964), if a heritable trait increases the inclusive fitness of individuals possessing it, the trait will spread due to its impact on the survival and reproduction of the focal individual (its direct fitness effects) as well as the effects it has on the survival and reproduction of the focal individual's kin weighted by the closeness of the relationship (indirect fitness effects). One's own reproduction can be seen, from this perspective, as a special case of kin-directed altruism (toward one's own offspring), one way that an individual can contribute to the proliferation of his or her relatives and genes within a population.

This can shed light on how parents and offspring behave with regard to parental investment. When Hamilton developed his concept of inclusive fitness, he noted that when we assess the fitness of a trait or behavior, we need to consider its contribution to the reproduction of that individual and whether it influences the reproductive prospects of its kin. The conditions under which such behavior would be expected to spread is $c<rb$, where c equals the fitness cost of the action (providing food) to the actor, b is the fitness benefit (getting to eat) to the recipient, and r is the degree of relatedness between the actor and recipient (0.5 for parent–offspring, 0.5 for full siblings, 0.25 for half-siblings, and so on). Clearly, acts of parental investment provide a benefit to the offspring, which increases the parent's inclusive fitness. As long as the cost of parental investment does not outweigh the benefit to the offspring times the degree of relatedness, it should continue.

Consider the case of siblings, A and B. From an inclusive fitness perspective, A should continue to take resources until its marginal gains drop to half those of B, who gets the remainder (Parker et al. 1989). For half-siblings, marginal gains drop to one fourth as they share only one parent. The key to this is the degree of relatedness. A child shares a given gene with itself with a probability of 1.0, but it shares the same gene with a probability of only 0.5 with a sibling. For this reason, a child is expected to try and monopolize a unit of resource unless the benefit of consuming an extra unit of resource is less than the benefit, weighted by relatedness, of giving the resource to its sibling. Parents, in contrast, share a given gene with each of their offspring with a probability of 0.5. Thus, they prefer to divide a unit of resource equally unless the benefit of the resource is greater for one child compared to the other. Though offspring are the vehicles by which parental genes are transported into future generations, offspring are not identical fitness vehicles. Some will be better able to survive or more likely to reproduce successfully. Such offspring are better bets for successfully moving parental genes into future generations. Additionally, some offspring benefit more from parental care than others (Beaulieu and Bugental 2008). As a result, selection has favored mechanisms of parental care that have the effect of increasing the fitness of the parent via the favoring of offspring who are likely to provide a higher reproductive return on their parents' investment (Daly and Wilson 1995), or at least, the allocation of resources to where they will have the greatest impact (Beaulieu and Bugental 2008).

At the heart of Hamilton's (1964) inclusive fitness theory is the idea that kin are valuable; that they share a commonality of interest. From this perspective, natural selection favored not only traits that promote individual survival and reproduction but also traits that increase the reproductive success of one's kin. While this is very clear in the case of parental–offspring relationships, it is also true for other family relationships, such as siblings, and grandparents.

An inherent feature of social behavior is that the interests of interacting individuals invariably come into conflict to some extent. Each individual behaves so as to increase its own inclusive fitness, even when such behavior may reduce the inclusive fitness of others. Social interactions typically entail cooperation, but they also involve competition, sometimes even during cooperative interactions. The interaction between parents and offspring, for example, involves a high level of cooperation, but is not conflict-free. In a similar vein, siblings may often disagree over how important each other is and the optimal allocation of parental resources between them.

Relationship-Specific Psychological Adaptations

An adaptation is an anatomical structure, a physiological process, or a behavior that contributed to ancestral individuals' ability to survive and reproduce in competition with members of their own species (Williams 1966; Wilson 1975). The beaks of Darwin's finches are the classic example of anatomical adaptations. The food options available dictated the survival of birds with different shapes and sizes of beaks, so that today we see birds with beaks that are designed by natural selection to crack large nuts in some environments, while other environmental niches are filled by birds with beaks well suited to small seeds or obtaining insects (Grant and Grant 2011; Sulloway 1982). Another way of looking at adaptations is in terms of processes that carry out the cost–benefit analyses required by ancestral organisms to survive environmental challenges. Consider the following behavioral example, the mating strategy of the male scorpion fly. The male has three mating tactics or options within its strategy: (1) Obtain a dead insect, offer it to a female and then copulate with her while she eats it; (2) generate a proteinaceous salivary mass, present it to the female and then copulate with her while she eats it; or (3) If he cannot obtain an insect or generate a salivary mass, he may attempt to force copulation (Thornhill 1980). In a variety of studies (Thornhill 1980; Thornhill and Alcock 1983; Thornhill and Sauer 1992), Thornhill et al. have shown that all three tactics are available to all scorpion fly males and that it is their success in the male–male competitive environment that determines which tactic is used by an individual male. Male success in such competition is influenced by internal and external factors (Crawford 1989). Similarly, the psychological adaptations for dealing with kin relations that will be discussed are also influenced by internal factors (of both participants in the relationship) as well as external environmental factors that influence investment in kin, such as resource availability.

When talking about adaptations for dealing with kin relations, we are focusing on psychological adaptations as decision makers, innate specialized information-processing mechanisms instantiated in our neural hardware. When activated by appropriate problem content from the environment, they focus attention, organize perception and memory, and call up specialized procedural knowledge that leads to domain appropriate inferences, judgments, and choices (Buss 1999). When we consider familial relationships as a group, the categorical distinctions between relationships are important. They signal that somewhat different domains are involved. Genealogical kinship is not just one discrete category of relationship, but rather is a collection of many different types of relationships. The adaptive problems that have faced human mothers, for example, are different from those confronting fathers or offspring or siblings or more distant relatives. As a result, we possess distinct sets of evolved psychological adaptations for dealing with the specific challenges of motherhood and offspringhood, as well as psychological adaptations specific to the demands of being fathers, siblings, and perhaps grandparents and other more distant kin.

Motherhood

The most essential of all mammalian relationships is that between mother and offspring. Thus, it is not surprising that this appears to be one of the relationships with the most specialized anatomical, physiological, and psychological mechanisms. Motherhood is the most demanding role that female mammals can have and these demands go beyond the required gestation and nursing. Not all offspring are equally capable of transforming parental care and investment into future generations and the long-term survival of parental genes. The result is strong selection for the strategic allocation of maternal effort. The adaptive motivational mechanisms that enable discriminative parental solicitude are sensitive to cues of likely offspring success, the physical and social environment, and the condition of the mother (Daly and Wilson 1988, 1995; Hrdy 1992, 1999). Evolution does not favor indiscriminate love or parental investment. Limited resources must be allocated wisely and parents channel their investment toward those offspring best equipped to provide a fitness return on that investment. An extreme example of discriminative parental solicitude is maternal infanticide, seen most frequently in harsh ecologies (Hrdy 1999). Daly and Wilson's (1985, 1988, 1998) studies of infanticide and child abuse statistics indicate greater risk when the mother is young and lacks social support (and will likely have better chances to raise a child in the future). Adaptationist-minded researchers have examined a number of characteristics influencing levels of maternal investment, including the sex, age (and related birth order), and health of the child, as well as the age and circumstances of the mother.

Factors Influencing Maternal Investment

Sex of Offspring Preferences for sons or daughters are also quite common in families and parents can benefit from investing preferentially in children of one sex depending on ecological variables. Trivers and Willard (1973) argued that when one sex has a greater variance in lifetime reproductive success than the other and parents (specifically mothers) vary in their physical condition or resource base, differences in offspring sex preferences are likely to evolve. If male reproductive success depends on the individual's condition, mothers in good condition who are able to invest heavily will be able to influence the reproductive success of their sons more successfully than mothers in poor condition (or with few resources). They should therefore prefer to have sons, or to invest more in their sons (Bercovitch et al. 2000; Trivers and Willard 1973). In contrast, mothers in poor condition should prefer daughters because daughters are reproductively less risky (lower variance). This is known as the Trivers–Willard effect.

The effect of maternal condition (e.g., nutritional) on the sex ratio at birth has received some attention in demographic studies of modern societies (Almond and Edlund 2007; Chacon et al. 1996; Gibson and Mace 2003). Some studies also demonstrate maternal condition predicting sex biases in infant mortality (Almond and Edlund 2007; Chacon et al. 1996; Voland et al. 1997); however, effect sizes tend to be small and a number of studies have failed to find Trivers–Willard effects (e.g., Beaulieu and Bugental 2008; Guggenheim et al. 2007; Sieff 1990). Cronk (2007) has highlighted the difficulties, both theoretical and methodological, of testing the Trivers–Willard hypothesis in large industrialized societies. The strongest evidence for Trivers–Willard effects comes from studies of small-scale societies.

Dickemann's (1979) review of historical data on infanticide and the Indian caste system reveals that infanticide was extremely common among the highest castes prior to the twentieth century, with female infants being the victims. These daughters had very few marriage options (had to marry within own subcaste). Among high caste Indian families, investment in males (who could marry females from lower subcastes) paid larger dividends in terms of grandchildren and parents heavily biased their investment toward males (Gupta 1987). For lower castes, the tendency toward males marrying down meant daughters outreproduced sons and parents biased their investment toward daughters (lower rate of female infanticide). Studies in the USA (Gaulin and Robbins 1991) and Kenya (Cronk 1989) have suggested that female infants from low-income families are nursed more than infant boys. Hungarian Gypsy populations also show a female-biased sex ratio (Bereczkei and Dunbar 1997, 2002). Like lower caste Indians, Gypsies are at the bottom of the social scale in Hungary and Gypsy women are more likely to marry up the social scale than men and, in doing so, provide their parents with more surviving grandchildren. Gypsy women who marry up have babies with higher birth weights, lower mortality rates, and lower rates of birth defects than Gypsy women who marry within their social group. Bereczkei and Dunbar (1997) found that compared to native Hungarians, Gypsy women were more likely to suckle their firstborn daughters for longer than sons, abort a subsequent pregnancy after a daughter than after a son, and allow their daughters to stay in school longer.

There are also examples where investment favors sons. In societies where the possession of resources has a significant impact on male reproductive success, a preference for sons will be seen among the affluent. This has been the case in the eighteenth-century northern German villages (Voland 1998) and has been noted in the records of probated wills among Canadians living in British Columbia (Smith et al. 1987). In terms of the parental payoff, Cameron and Dalerum's (2009) study of Trivers–Willard effects in Forbes list of billionaires indicated that people in the top economic bracket have more grandchildren via their sons than daughters and that mothers at this highest socioeconomic status have more sons.

Maternal Age Parental age is another factor influencing maternal investment. In species in which the probability of death increases systematically with age, a parent is selected to give an increasing proportion of parental investment to older offspring. Relative to older parents, younger parents should be harboring resources to maximize lifetime reproductive success. Some data show that older parents invest more than younger parents (Salmon and Daly 1998; Voland and Gabler 1994), and this is often particularly true of older mothers who face more of a reproductive constraint due to menopause. In humans, the age of the mother is a significant factor in the likelihood of perpetrating maternal infanticide (Daly and Wilson 1988). Young women, those likely to have many future opportunities to reproduce, might be expected to be more willing to sacrifice a current child when conditions for successfully raising the child are poor. Older women, close to the end of their reproductive years, who pass up the opportunity to invest may never have that chance again. As the likelihood of future reproduction decreases, delaying childbirth becomes more costly. Selection should favor older women who invest immediately and to a significant extent in children rather than delaying investment. The dramatic cross-culturally observed decrease in the rate of maternally perpetrated infanticide with increasing maternal age reflects the change over time of the weight the maternal psyche places on a current offspring versus possible future offspring (Daly and Wilson 1995; Lee and George 1999; Overpeck et al. 1998).

Age of Offspring There is often a greater fitness payoff from investing in older children. Any specific offspring's expected contribution to parental fitness is found mainly in their reproductive value (expected future reproduction). This value increases with age until puberty, making an older, immature offspring more valuable from the parental perspective than a younger one (Montgomerie and Weatherhead 1988). In humans, this increase is mainly due to the degree of childhood mortality experienced in developing societies and over most of our evolutionary history. The average teenager has a higher reproductive value than the average infant because some infants do not survive to become teenagers. However, on average, the older a particular offspring gets, the less valuable parental investment, especially certain kinds of investment (like breast milk), will be compared to its value to younger offspring. Parents must weigh these costs and benefits when there is more than one offspring to care for.

Studies of familial homicides support the idea that older children may be more highly valued. Daly and Wilson's (1988) examination of the risk of homicide of a child by a genetic parent in relation to offspring age revealed that infants were at a much higher risk of being killed than any other group of children. The rates drop dramatically, after 1 year of age, until they approach zero at 17 years of age. One might suggest that this is because it is easier to kill a baby than a teenager. However, the risk of a child being killed by a nonrelative shows a rather different pattern: 1 year olds are more likely to be killed than infants and teenagers are the most likely to be killed.

Birth Order The relevance of birth order to parental investment is related to several factors, including age of the offspring and age of the mother. An offspring's expected contribution to parental fitness rests mainly in their reproductive value. This value increases with age until puberty, making older immature offspring more valuable from a parental fitness perspective than younger ones. It is this assurance of parental favoritism, as well as an early absence of sibling contenders for a share of parental attention, that makes firstborn children defenders of parental values and the status quo, while laterborns are more likely to be rebellious.

However, offspring age is not the whole story. As parents themselves grow older, the fitness value of any one offspring increases relative to the parent's residual reproductive value. As parents grow older, their own chance of reproducing again drops, thus older parents have been observed to invest more in offspring, all else being equal, than younger parents. As a result, while firstborns may have an inherent advantage in terms of parental investment, there is a growing willingness of older parents to invest highly in their lastborn, their last chance to invest, so to speak. In fact, lastborns are the only birth order to receive their parental investment without the competing demands of a younger sibling. This would seem to imply that middleborns may lose out in terms of parental investment and attention and there are a number of studies that support this (Rohde et al. 2003; Salmon 2003; Salmon and Daly 1998; Sulloway 1996).

Offspring Need While offspring prospects, or the ability to turn maternal investment into future reproductive success, have always been assumed to be a strong predictor of maternal care, it has also been suggested that mother's investment in offspring could be contingent in that high-risk offspring will either receive more or less investment than low-risk offspring based on maternal resources (Beaulieu and Bugental 2008). Beaulieu et al. have tested this in several studies (Beaulieu and Bugental 2008; Bugental et al. 2010). Their results in samples including preterm babies/children and women with high or low resource availability suggest that mothers with low resources invest more in low-risk children whereas those mothers with higher resource levels invest more in high-risk children (as they have sufficient resources to care for other children as well).

Parent–Offspring Conflict

It is important to remember that mothers are not the only players in this relationship. Offspring also have a role to play in shaping parental resource allocation. Parent–offspring conflict (Trivers 1974) is a reliable characteristic of sexually reproducing species because of the inherent genetic asymmetries between individuals in the family. For example, a mother is equally related to any two of her children, but each child is more closely related to itself than to their sibling (unless they are part of a pair of identical twins). The result is that mother and any specific child do not see the fitness value of a sibling equally and therefore also disagree on the optimal allocation of resources between siblings. Such maternal–offspring conflict provides a clear explanation for evidence (such as weaning conflict and maternal–fetal conflict) that the relationship between mother and child is not as harmonious as often depicted.

Maternal–Fetal Conflict Although most people think of parental investment as something that occurs post-birth, mothers begin to invest in their offspring long before they are born. For 9 months, the mother's body provides all the nutrients for their baby's development as well as a safe haven in which to grow. At this stage, it would appear that the fetus and mother have identical interests, the continuing safety and development of the fetus. But their genetic interests are not identical. The fetus is more closely related to itself than to either its mother or any future siblings and, as a result, pregnancy becomes a balancing act between the fetus' attempts to secure a larger share of the mother's resources than she is willing to give and the mother's attempts to retain resources for herself and future offspring. Thus, selection will favor fetal genes that serve to increase the transfer of nutrients to the fetus and maternal genes that limit any transfers in excess of the ideal from the maternal perspective. The results of this balancing act can include a variety of unpleasant maternal symptoms and can occasionally create serious pregnancy complications.

Gestational diabetes affects up to 10% of women in the USA. When women are not pregnant, blood glucose levels rise after a meal, but rapidly return to fasting levels in response to the release of insulin. During the later stages of pregnancy, maternal blood glucose and insulin both reach higher levels and remain elevated for a longer duration. This occurs because the placental hormone human placental lactogen (hPL) acts on maternal prolactin receptors to increase maternal resistance to insulin. If there is no opposition, hPL will maintain higher blood glucose levels for longer periods after eating. However, this usually is opposed by increased maternal production of insulin. As a result, in the third trimester, the same meal will produce an exaggerated insulin response which is less effective at reducing blood glucose levels (Buchanan et al. 1990; Catalano et al. 1991).

This occurs because the mother is attempting to restrict fetal access to blood glucose. Why do mothers enact this restriction, and why do mothers increase insulin production while also becoming resistant to it? One approach to answering these questions is that if fetal demands for glucose are unopposed, the fetus may remove more glucose from maternal blood than is in the mother's interests to give. For much of human history, food was not an unlimited resource and so from both a maternal and fetal perspective, nutritional resources are in high demand. Each maternal meal entails conflict over the share of blood glucose mother and fetus will receive and the longer the mother takes to reduce blood sugar levels, the greater the share obtained by the fetus. The insulin resistance of late pregnancy is caused by placental hormones producing increased blood glucose levels and a corresponding increased production of insulin by the mother (Haig 1993). For pregnant women without preexisting diabetes, maternal glucose levels 2 h after a meal have been positively correlated with infant birth weight (Tallarigo et al. 1986). However, this benefit of increased maternal glucose levels for the fetus can come at a cost to the mother's health. If blood glucose levels remain elevated, gestational diabetes can develop when the mother becomes unable to increase her insulin production sufficiently to match the insulin resistance that developed during the pregnancy.

Fatherhood

While there are many similarities between paternal and maternal solicitude, there are also many differences. Both mothers and fathers have been selected to assess offspring quality and need.

Both possess evolved mechanisms designed to motivate solicitude in response to cues of the expected impact of such parental investment on offspring future success. Both mother and father have been selected to discriminate based on cues that any particular offspring is their genetic child. For mothers, the evidence has always been clear. Modern reproductive technology aside, if you gave birth to a baby, it is your biological child. Internal fertilization and relatively concealed ovulation make this situation less certain for men. Paternity would rarely have been 100% certain (at least in the ancestral environment with its lack of paternity tests). One study of men in New Mexico (Anderson et al. 2006), suggests than men are more likely to have low paternity confidence if the pregnancy was unplanned and they were not in a married or committed relationship. Their estimate of nonpaternity for these men was about 3.7% (as cited in Gray and Anderson 2010). Gray and Anderson's (2010) book *Fatherhood* is an excellent overview of the evolutionary psychology of fatherhood that also covers the cross-cultural variation in paternal care and the consequences of a lack of paternal presence.

Paternity Uncertainty Putative fathers must possess mechanisms that cue into sources of information about the mother's likely fidelity. One way to assess this is through the child's resemblance to his relatives or to himself. Given the relatively high levels of heritability in many physical traits, the more a child resembles the putative father, the greater the paternity confidence is likely to be. As a result, one might expect that paternal affection and investment will be influenced by paternal perceptions of resemblance. Several empirical studies have tested this, demonstrating that perceived father–child similarity is associated with higher degrees of paternal emotional closeness and investment, typically measured as time spent with the child, or involvement in education (Alvergne et al. 2010; Apicella and Marlowe 2004, 2007; Li and Chang 2007). Fox and Bruce (2001) also reported that a telephone sample of Tennessee men were more involved with children when they had greater certainty of paternity.

Data also suggest that people pay more attention to a child's paternal resemblance compared to maternal resemblance, despite the fact that the degree of actual resemblance between parents and infants is, in fact, quite low and, if anything, is slightly biased toward mother–child resemblance (Alvergne et al. 2007; Bressan and Grassi 2004). Greater resemblance to the mother makes sense if paternity confusion is beneficial for offspring (because they might be living with a social rather than biological father). Some evidence even suggests that men not only pay more attention to resemblance than women but that they are better at detecting it (Volk and Quinsey 2002). Despite the lack of actual resemblance, evidence suggests that mothers and maternal relatives are highly inclined to emphasize paternal resemblance in newborns. This is most often interpreted as an attempt to manipulate fathers' perceptions of paternal resemblance, increasing their paternal attachment and investment (Bressan 2002; Daly and Wilson 1982; McLain et al. 2000; Regalski and Gaulin 1993).

Sibship

An evolutionary perspective also adds a great deal of insight into our understanding of sibling relationships (Mock and Parker 1997; Pollet and Hoben 2011). Hamilton's (1964) analysis of the evolution of sociality and altruism in haplodiploid insects had at its core the shared genetic interests of sisters in such species. Although siblings, our close genetic kin, can be major allies, they can also be our fiercest competitors, especially for parental resources. The result is sibling relationships that are often somewhat ambivalent across the life span (Cicirelli 1995).

Sibling Conflict From an evolutionary perspective, this stems from rivalry over limited resources, specifically over limited parental resources. As such, more conflict would be expected in families that have more limited parental resources and more siblings. In relation to family size, evidence does indicate that although fewer siblings are associated with more severe acts of violence, more siblings are associated with more overall incidents of violence (Straus et al. 2006). Investigations of proximate explanations have found the most common sources of sibling conflict include issues of relative power, self-interest (e.g., sharing of personal items), violation of rules (e.g., perceived immaturity and inappropriate behavior), and interests outside the family (McGuire et al. 2000; Salmon and Hehman 2013). Interestingly, the most commonly cited source of conflict by both older and younger siblings has been the sharing of personal possessions, and the least commonly cited source has been competition over parental attention. This has been a consistent finding in studies conducted with toddlers and preschool-aged siblings (Dunn and Munn 1987), school-aged siblings (McGuire et al. 2000), and adolescent siblings who noted conflict over personal space and possessions as the most frequent and intense source of conflict (Campione-Barr and Smetana 2010).

The prevalence and the intensity of sibling conflict are influenced by many factors, including differential parental treatment, relatedness, gender, birth order, and birth spacing. Given that sibling conflict can be construed as rivalry over limited parental resources, one would predict that siblings would be very aware of differential treatment, and such disparities between siblings would lead to an increase in sibling conflict. By age 3, children are sensitive to differences in parental treatment between themselves and their siblings and actively monitor their siblings' relationships with their parents relative to their own (Dunn and Munn 1985). This differential treatment has been associated with higher levels of negativity within sibling relationships (Brody et al. 1992a, b).

Birth order and birth spacing appear to influence sibling relationships. Firstborns are more likely to maintain close contact with siblings and invest more in siblings relative to laterborns (Pollet and Nettle 2009), though some middleborns report feeling closer to their siblings than their parents (Salmon and Daly 1998). In addition, during childhood, greater birth spacing leads to a reduction in conflict. In adulthood, however, greater birth spacing is associated with less contact and less close relationships between siblings (Pollet 2007).

Sulloway (2001) has suggested that children adopt different roles or niches within the family and that such specialization of roles within the family, like specialization of species in the wild (e.g., Darwin's finches) reduces levels of sibling competition. Eldest siblings often occupy the role of surrogate parent with its responsibilities and adherence to rules. For laterborn children, there is no advantage to trying to duplicate the same role; they need to find their own niche, which is facilitated by their openness to experience with less adherence to rules and authority (Sulloway 1999, 2001). Healey and Ellis' (2007) study of the sibling niche theory provides supportive evidence for the role of niches in shaping personality with regard to firstborns and secondborns. This tendency for siblings to diversify makes adjacent siblings more different from each other in personality than those farther spaced. It has also been suggested that although parental influence may tend to create linear birth order effects, sibling competition and diversification in search of a family niche will tend to create quadratic effects. Pollet and Nettle's (2007) study of face-to-face contact with siblings reports that firstborns are more likely to take on the role of family contact, taking on the responsibility of keeping track of and informing siblings of family news (see also Salmon and Daly 1998).

Hamilton's kin selection theory (1964), discussed previously, predicts that greater genetic similarity should lead to increased levels of cooperation and altruism, whereas less genetic similarity would lead to increased competition. Indeed, monozygotic twins have higher levels of cooperation and closer relationships throughout childhood and into adulthood relative to dizygotic twins (for a review, see Segal 2005). While relatively few studies have investigated the effect of relatedness on sibling relationships, studies that have been conducted are also consistent with kin selection theory in that there is less conflict in full-sibling relationships relative to half-sibling and step-sibling relationships (Hetherington 1988; Pollet 2007).

When we examine the role of gender, boys seem to have more conflict with siblings than do girls (Brody et al. 1985) and opposite sex siblings have more conflict than same-sex siblings (Campione-Barr and Smetana 2010; Dunn and Kendrick 1982). Gender differences in closeness of sibling pairs continue into adulthood, with sister–sister pairs having closer and stronger relationships relative to brother–brother and brother–sister pairs (Campione-Barr and Smetana 2010; Pollet 2007).

Sibling cooperation: It is important to remember that siblings are resources as well as rivals. Siblings, especially older siblings, can be sources of emotional, social, and financial help. One way in which older siblings can provide support is through the caretaking of young siblings, similar to the helper at the nest phenomenon in a number of bird species, such as the scrub jay (Woolfenden and Fitzpatrick 1984). Hrdy (2005) has argued that cooperative breeding was a key component of our human reproductive past, but there has been debate over whether a significant role was played by female siblings. There is some cross-cultural evidence that suggests that older female siblings are frequent caretakers of their younger siblings (Cicirelli 1994), including Paul Turke's (1988) work with the Ifaluk of Micronesia where the presence of a firstborn daughter was found to be positively related to her parents' reproductive success. In a similar vein, Bereczkei and Dunbar's (2002) previously mentioned study of Hungarian Gypsies documented that having a firstborn daughter in the home shortened the mother's interbirth intervals, which could result in greater parental reproductive success. However, other studies have not found support for a significant impact on parental reproductive success from sibling childcare (Crognier 2001, 2002; Hames and Draper 2004). Siblings may also gain an additional benefit from sibling caretaking: improved social skills. Elder siblings engage in prosocial behavior, leadership activities, teach their younger siblings physical skills, and help with language acquisition (Azmitia and Hesser 1993; Cicirelli 1995). Younger siblings benefit from sibling nurturing and comfort (Samuels 1980; Stewart and Marvin 1984) and do better in school when taught by siblings rather than peers (Azmitia and Hesser 1993).

In general, sibling rivalry tends to decrease postadolescence and, as a result, adult siblings are more often seen as a source of support (White 2001). Perhaps an extreme example, Neyer and Lang (2003) suggest that after parents and children, siblings are typically the only kin for which we are willing to make extreme sacrifices (the kind that entail risks to our own health, such as organ donation).

Grandparenthood

Do we have adaptations designed specifically to deal with the problems faced by grandparental relationships? Or do these relationships merely co-opt adaptations for parenting? Postmenopausal women make significant contributions to the welfare of their grandchildren in many cultures (Lancaster and King 1985; Sears et al. 2000). Thus, it is reasonable to suspect that mental processes specific to the allocation of grandparental investment may have been the targets of natural selection (Hawkes et al. 1998; Smith 1988).

In fact, many researchers have suggested a specific role for grandmothers and that it may be responsible for the evolution of menopause in humans (see Euler 2011, for a more general review of the literature on grandparenting). In most other species, there is no substantial post-reproductive life span (see Cohen 2004, for examples in other mammals). The fact that human females experience many healthy productive post-reproductive years has seemed somewhat of a puzzle. Hamilton (1966) suggested that older women had special value and others have elaborated on this idea with various versions of the grandmother hypothesis that focus on the timing of menopause, the life span postmenopause (Hrdy 1999), or the importance of investment in grandchildren (Hrdy 1999; Peccei 2001). Despite the interest in menopause as an adaptation, there is a continuing debate over whether it is an adaptation, by-product, or artifact of the modern world and longer life spans (Voland et al. 2005). There is, however, evidence that grandmothers do contribute substantially to the survival of grandchildren, and thus to the fitness of mothers and the grandmothers themselves (Hawkes et al. 1989, 2000; Lahdenperä et al. 2004; Sear and Mace 2008).

Euler and Weitzel (1996) noted that paternity certainty could influence grandparental investment (in addition to its impact on paternal investment). To test their hypotheses, they asked adults to rate the degree of grandparental solicitude they experienced from each of their four grandparents. The results were striking, indicating a strong link between relatedness/paternity certainty and solicitude. Maternal grandmothers were rated the highest on solicitude, followed by maternal grandfathers, paternal grandmothers, and finally paternal grandfathers. From a theoretical perspective, a maternal grandmother has the greatest certainty of her grandchild's relatedness to her. A paternal grandfather faces a different dynamic. He endures two relationship links that can be broken by nonpaternity: the grandchild might not be his son's child and his son might not be his own biological child (see also Michalski and Shackelford 2005). Studies that examine contact frequency between grandparents and grandchildren reveal similar patterns: greater contact seen with maternal grandmothers and the least with paternal grandfathers (Pollet et al. 2007, 2008; Salmon 1999; Uhlenberg and Hamill 1998). This pattern of greatest investment from maternal grandmother and least from paternal grandfather has been demonstrated across a wide range of measures and methodologies (Bishop et al. 2009; DeKay 1995; Euler and Weitzel 1996; Laham et al. 2005; Mills et al. 2001; Monserud 2008; Pashos 2000; Pollet et al. 2006, 2007, 2008; Salmon 1999; Uhlenberg and Hamill 1998).

Conclusions

While this chapter could not possibly cover all of the interesting research that has been done in the past 20–30 years on the evolutionary psychology of the family, it has hopefully illustrated the insight that can be gained into family dynamics by taking an adaptationist perspective. Some people's greatest joys are found in their relationships with kin; for others, family can be a source of pain as well as joy. But our family relationships, particularly those between parent and child, are an emotionally intense essential part of our psychology. Sibling relationships can be some of the longest relationships we ever experience. An evolutionary perspective also helps us to explain why we can be willing to sacrifice ourselves for our kin and yet sacrifice them under certain conditions. Biological relatedness creates a bond. An understanding of the design of our evolved mechanisms for kin-directed solicitude allows us to predict where that bond will be intense, weak, and where conflict will arise.

References

Almond, D., & Edlund, L. (2007). Trivers–Willard at birth and one year: Evidence from US natality data 1983–2001. *Proceedings of the Royal Society of London B, 274,* 2491–2496.

Alvergne, A., Faurie, C., & Raymond, M. (2007). Differential facial resemblance of young children to their parents: Who do children look like more? *Evolution and Human Behavior, 28,* 135–144.

Alvergne, A., Faurie, C., & Raymond, M. (2010). Are parents' perceptions of offspring facial resemblance consistent with actual resemblance? Effects on parental investment. *Evolution and Human Behavior, 31,* 7–15.

Anderson, K. G., Kaplan, K., & Lancaster, J. B. (2006). Demographic correlates of paternity confidence and pregnancy outcomes among Albuquerque men. *American Journal of Physical Anthropology, 131,* 560–571.

Apicella, C. L., & Marlowe, F. W. (2004). Perceived mate fidelity and paternal resemblance predict men's investment in children. *Evolution and Human Behavior, 25,* 371–378.

Apicella, C. L., & Marlowe, F. W. (2007). Men's reproductive investment decisions. Mating, parenting and self-perceived mate value. *Human Nature, 18,* 22–34.

Azmitia, M., & Hesser, J. (1993). Why siblings are important agents of cognitive development: A comparison of siblings and peers. *Child Development, 64,* 430–444.

Beaulieu, D. A., & Bugental, D. (2008). Contingent parental investment: An evolutionary framework for understanding early interaction between mothers and children. *Evolution and Human Behavior, 29,* 249–255.

Bercovitch, F. B., Widdig, A. & Nurnberg, P. (2000). Maternal investment in rhesus Macaques (*Macaca mulatto*): Reproductive costs and consequences on raising sons. *Behavioral Ecology and Sociobiology, 48,* 1–11.

Bereczkei, T., & Dunbar, R. I. M. (1997). Female-biased reproductive strategies in a Hungarian Gypsy population. *Proceedings of the Royal Society, London, B, 264,* 17–22.

Bereczkei, T., & Dunbar, R. I. M. (2002). Helping-at-the-nest and sex-biased parental investment in a Hungarian Gypsy population. *Current Anthropology,* 43, 804–809.

Bishop, D. I., Meyer, B. C., Schmidt, T. M., & Gray, B. R. (2009). Differential investment behavior between grandparents and grandchildren. The role of paternity uncertainty. *Evolutionary Psychology, 7,* 66–77.

Bressan, P. (2002). Why babies look like their daddies: Paternity uncertainty and the evolution of self-deception in evaluating family resemblance. *Acta Ethologica, 4,* 113–118.

Bressan, P., & Grassi, M. (2004). Parental resemblance in 1-year-olds and the Gaussian curve. *Evolution and Human Behavior, 25,* 133–141.

Brody, G. H., Stoneman, Z., MacKinnon, C. E., & MacKinnon, R. (1985). Role relationships and behaviors between preschool-aged and school-aged sibling pairs. *Developmental Psychology, 21,* 124–129.

Brody, G. H., Stoneman, Z., & McCoy, J. K. (1992a). Associations of maternal and paternal direct and differential behavior with sibling relationships: Contemporaneous and longitudinal analyses. *Child Development, 63,* 82–92.

Brody, G. H., Stoneman, Z., & McCoy, J. K. (1992b). Parental differential treatment of siblings and sibling differences in negative emotionality. *Journal of Marriage and the Family, 54,* 643–651.

Buchanan, T. A., Metzger, B. E., Freinkel, N., & Bergman, R. N. (1990). Insulin sensitivity and B-cell responsiveness to glucose during late pregnancy in lean and moderately obese women with normal glucose tolerance or mild gestational diabetes. *American Journal of Obstetrics and Gynecology, 162,* 1008–1014.

Bugental, D. B., Beaulieu, D. A., & Silbert-Geiger, A. (2010). Increases in parental investment and child health as a result of an early intervention. *Journal of Experimental Child Psychology, 106,* 30–40.

Burnstein, E., Crandall, C., & Kitayama, S. (1994). Some neo-Darwinian decision rules for altruism: Weighing cues for inclusive fitness as a function of the biological importance of the decision. *Journal of Personality and Social Psychology, 67,* 773–789.

Buss, D. M. (1999). *Evolutionary Psychology: The new science of the mind* (1st ed.). New York: Allyn & Bacon.

Cameron, E. Z., & Dalerum, F. (2009). A Trivers-Willard effect in contemporary humans: Male-biased sex ratios among billionaires. *PLoS ONE, 4,* e4195.

Campione-Barr, N., & Smetana, J. G. (2010). "Who said you could wear my sweater?" Adolescent siblings' conflicts and association with relationship quality. *Child Development, 81,* 464–471.

Catalano, P. M., Tyzbir, E. D., Roman, N. M., Amini, S. B., & Sims, A. H. (1991). Longitudinal changes in insulin release and insulin resistance in nonobese pregnant women. *American Journal of Obstetrics and Gynecology, 165,* 1667–1672.

Chacon Puignau, G. C., & Jaffe, K. (1996). Sex ratio at birth deviations in modern Venezuela: The Trivers-Willard effect. *Social Biology, 43,* 257–270.

Cicirelli, V. G. (1994). Sibling relationships in cross-cultural perspective. *Journal of Marriage and the Family, 56,* 7–20.

Cicirelli, V. G. (1995). *Sibling relationships across the life span.* New York: Plenum Press.

Cohen, A. (2004). Female post-reproductive lifespan: A general mammalian trait. *Biological Reviews, 79,* 733–750.

Crawford, C. B. (1989). The theory of evolution: Of what value to psychology? *Journal of Comparative Psychology,* 103, 4–22.

Crognier, E., Baali, A. & Hilali, H. K. (2001). Do "helpers at the nest" increase their parents' reproductive success? *American Journal of Human Biology, 13,* 365–373.

Crognier, E., Villena, M. & Vargas, E. (2002). Helping patterns and reproductive success in Aymara communities. *American Journal of Human Biology, 14,* 372–379.

Cronk, L. (1989). Low socioeconomic status and female-based parental investment: The Mokogodo example. *American Anthropologist, 91,* 414–429.

Cronk, L. (2007). Boy or girl: Gender preferences from a Darwinian point of view. *Reproductive Biomedicine Online, 15,* 23–32.

Daly, M., & Wilson, M. (1982). Whom are newborn babies said to resemble? *Ethology and Sociobiology, 3,* 69–78.

Daly, M., & Wilson, M. (1985). Child abuse and other risks of not living with both parents. *Ethology and Sociobiology, 6,* 197–201.

Daly, M., & Wilson, M. (1988). *Homicide.* Hawthorne: Aldine de Gruyter.

Daly, M., & Wilson, M. (1995). Discriminative parental solicitude and the relevance of evolutionary models to the analysis of motivational systems. In M. Gazzaniga (Ed.), *The cognitive neurosciences* (pp. 1269–1286). Cambridge: MIT Press.

Daly, M., & Wilson, M. (1998). *The truth about Cinderella: A Darwinian view of parental love.* New Haven: Yale University Press.

Daly, M., Salmon, C. A., & Wilson, M. (1997). Kinship: The conceptual hole in psychological studies of social cognition and close relationships. In J. A. Simpson & D. T. Kenrick (Eds.), *Evolutionary social psychology* (pp. 265–296). Mahweh: Erlbaum.

DeKay, W. T. (1995, July). *Grandparent investment and the uncertainty of kinship.* Paper presented at the Seventh Annual Meeting of the Human Behavior and Evolution Society, Santa Barbara, CA.

Dickemann, M. (1979). Female infanticide, reproductive strategies, and social stratification: A preliminary model. In N. A. Chagnon & W. Irons (Eds.), *Evolutionary Biology and human social behavior* (pp. 321–367). North Scituate: Duxbury Press.

Dunn, J., & Kendrick, C. (1982). *Siblings: Love, envy, and understanding*. Cambridge: Cambridge University Press.

Dunn, J., & Munn, P. (1987). The development of justifications in disputes. *Developmental Psychology, 23,* 791–798.

Euler, H. (2011). Grandparents and extended kin. In C. Salmon & T. K. Shackelford (Eds.), *The Oxford handbook of evolutionary family psychology*. New York: Oxford University Press.

Euler, H., & Weitzel, B. (1996). Discriminative grandparental solicitude as reproductive strategy. *Human Nature, 7,* 39–59.

Fox, G. L., & Bruce, C. (2001). Conditional fatherhood: Identity theory and parental investment theory as alternative sources of explanation of fathering. *Journal of Marriage and the Family, 63,* 394–403.

Gaulin, S. J. C., & Robbins, C. J. (1991). Trivers-Willard effect in contemporary North American society. *American Journal of Physical Anthropology, 85,* 61–69.

Gibson, M. A., & Mace, R. (2003). Strong mothers bear more sons in rural Ethiopia. *Proceedings of the Royal Society of London B, 270,* S108–S109.

Grant, P. R., & Grant, R. (2011). *How and why species multiply: The radiation of Darwin's finches*. Princeton: Princeton University Press.

Gray, P. B., & Anderson, K. G. (2010). *Fatherhood: Evolution and human paternal behavior*. Cambridge: Harvard University Press.

Guggenheim, C. B., Davis, M. F., & Figueredo, A. J. (2004). Sons or daughters: A cross-cultural study of sex ratio biasing and differential parental investment. *Journal of the Arizona-Nevada Academy of Science, 39,* 73–90.

Gupta, D. (1987). Selective discrimination against female children in rural Punjab. *Population and Development Review,* 13, 77–100.

Haig, D. (1993). Genetic conflicts in human pregnancy. *The Quarterly Review of Biology,* 68, 495–532.

Hames, R. D., & Draper, P. (2004). Women's work, childcare and helpers at the nest in a traditional hunter–gatherer society. *Human Nature, 15,* 319–341.

Hamilton, W. D. (1964). The genetical evolution of social behavior. I and II. *Journal of Theoretical Biology,* 7, 1–52.

Hamilton, W. D. (1966). The moulding of senescence by natural selection. *Journal of Theoretical Biology, 12,* 12–45.

Hawkes, K., O'Connell, J. F., & Blurton Jones, N. G. (1989). Hardworking Hadza grandmothers. In V. Standen & R. A. Foley (Eds.), *Comparative socioecology: The behavioural ecology of humans and other mammals* (pp. 341–366). London: Basil Blackwell.

Hawkes, K., O'Connell, J. F., Blurton Jones, N. G., Alvarez, H., & Charnov, E. L. (1998). Grandmothering, menopause, and the evolution of human life histories. *Proceedings of the National Academy of Sciences of the United States, 95,* 1336–1339.

Hawkes, K., O'Connell, K. J. F., Blurton-Jones, N. G., Alvarez, H., & Charnov, E. (2000). The grandmother hypothesis and human evolution. In L. Cronk, N. Chagnon, & W. Irons (Eds.), *Adaptation and human behavior: An anthropological perspective* (pp. 237–258). Hawthorne: Aldine de Gruyter.

Healey, M. D., & Ellis, B. J. (2007). Birth order, conscientiousness, and openness to experience: Tests of the family-niche model of personality using a within-family methodology. *Evolution and Human Behavior, 28,* 55–59.

Hetherington, E. M. (1988). Parents, children, and siblings: Six years after divorce. In R. A. Hinde & J. Stevenson-Hinde (Eds.), *Relationships within families: Mutual influences* (pp. 311–331). Oxford: Oxford University Press.

Hrdy, S. B. (1992). Fitness tradeoffs in the history and evolution of delegated mothering with special reference to wet-nursing, abandonment, and infanticide. *Ethology and Sociobiology, 13,* 409–442.

Hrdy, S. B. (1999). *Mother Nature: A history of mothers, infants, and natural selection*. New York: Pantheon Books.

Hrdy, S. B. (2005). Evolutionary context of human development: The cooperative breeding model. In S. C. Carter, L. Ahnert, K. Grossman, S. B. Hrdy, M. E. Lamb, S. W. Porges, & N. Sachser (Eds.), *Attachment and bonding: A new synthesis* (pp. 9–32). Cambridge: MIT Press.

Kenrick, D. T., Sadalla, E. K., & Keefe, R. C. (1998). Evolutionary cognitive psychology: The missing heart of modern cognitive science. In C. Crawford & D. Krebs (Eds.), *Evolution and Human Behavior: Ideas, issues, and applications* (pp. 485–514). Hillsdale: Erlbaum.

Laham, S. M., Gonsalkorale, K., & von Hippel, W. (2005). Darwinian grandparenting: Preferential investment in more certain kin. *Personality and Social Psychology Bulletin, 31,* 63–72.

Lahdenperä, M., Lummaa, V., Helle, S., Tremblay, M., & Russell, A. F. (2004). Fitness benefits of prolonged post-reproductive lifespan in women. *Nature, 428,* 178–181.

Lancaster, J. B., & King, B. J. (1985). An evolutionary perspective on menopause. In J. K. Brown & V. Kern (Eds.), *In her prime: A new view of middle aged women* (pp. 13–20). Boston: Bergin and Garvey.

Leach, E. (1966). Virgin birth. *Proceedings of the Royal Anthropological Institute of Great Britain and Ireland, 1966,* 39–49.

Lee, B. J., & George, R. M. (1999). Poverty, early childbearing and child maltreatment: A multinomial analysis. *Children and Youth Services Review, 21,* 755–780.

Li, H., & Chang, L. (2007). Paternal harsh parenting in relation to paternal versus child characteristics: the moderating effect of paternal resemblance belief. *Acta Psychologica Sinica, 39,* 495–501.

McGuire, S., Manke, B., Eftekhari, A., & Dunn, J. (2000). Children's perceptions of sibling conflict during middle childhood: Issues and sibling (dis)similarity. *Social Development, 9,* 173–190.

McLain, D. K., Setters, D., Moulton, M. P., & Pratt, A. E. (2000). Ascription of resemblance of newborns by parents and nonrelatives. *Evolution and Human Behavior, 21,* 11–23.

Michalski, R. L., & Shackelford, T. K. (2005). Grandparental investment as a function of relational uncertainty and emotional closeness with parents. *Human Nature, 16,* 292–304.

Mills, T. L., Wakeman, M. A. & Fea, C. B. (2001). Adult grandchildren's perceptions of emotional closeness and consensus with their maternal and paternal grandparents. *Journal of Family Issues, 22,* 427–55.

Mock, D. W., & Parker, G. A. (1997). *The evolution of sibling rivalry.* New York: Oxford University Press.

Monserud, M. A. (2008). Intergenerational relationships and affectual solidarity between grandparents and young adults. *Journal of Marriage and Family, 70,* 182–95.

Montgomerie, R. D., & Weatherhead, P. J. (1988). Risks and rewards of nest defense by parent birds. *Quarterly Review of Biology,* 63, 167–187.

Neyer, F. J., & Lang, F. R. (2003). Blood is thicker than water. Kinship orientation across adulthood. *Journal of Personality and Social Psychology, 84,* 310–321.

Overpeck, M. D., Brenner, R. A., Trumble, A. C., Trifiletti, L. B., & Berendes, H. W. (1998). Risk factors for infant homicide in the United States. *New England Journal of Medicine,* 339, 1211–1216.

Parker, G. A., Mock, D. W., & Lamey, T. C. (1989). How selfish should stronger sibs be? *American Naturalist,* 133, 846–868.

Pashos, A. (2000). Does paternal uncertainty explain discriminative grandparental solicitude? A cross-cultural study in Greece and Germany. *Evolution and Human Behavior, 21,* 97–109.

Peccei, J. S. (2001). A critique of the grandmother hypotheses: Old and new. *American Journal of Human Biology, 13,* 434–452.

Pollet, T. V. (2007). Genetic relatedness and sibling relationship characteristics in a modern society. *Evolution and Human Behavior, 28,* 176–185.

Pollet, T. V., & Hoben, A. D. (2011). An evolutionary perspective on siblings: Rivals and resources. In C. Salmon & T. K. Shackelford (Eds.), *The Oxford handbook of evolutionary family psychology* (pp. 128–148). New York: Oxford University Press.

Pollet, T. V., & Nettle, D. (2007). Birth order and face-to-face contact with a sibling: firstborns have more contact than laterborns. *Personality and Individual Differences, 43,* 1796–1806.

Pollet, T. V., & Nettle, D. (2009). Birth order and family relationships in adult life: Firstborns report better sibling relationships than laterborns. *Journal of Social and Personal Relationships, 26,* 1029–1046.

Pollet, T. V., Nettle, D., & Nelissen, M. (2006). Contact frequencies between grandparents and grandchildren in a modern society: Estimates of the impact of paternity uncertainty. *Journal of Cultural and Evolutionary Psychology, 4,* 203–214.

Pollet, T. V., Nettle, D., & Nelissen, M. (2007). Maternal grandmothers do go the extra mile: Factoring distance and lineage into differential contact with grandchildren. *Evolutionary Psychology, 5,* 832–843.

Pollet, T. V., Nelissen, M., & Nettle, D. (2008). Lineage based differences in grandparental investment: Evidence from a large British cohort study. *Journal of Biosocial Science, 41,* 355–379.

Regalski, J. M., & Gaulin, S. J. C. (1993). Whom are Mexican infant said to resemble? Monitoring and fostering paternal confidence in the Yucatan. *Ethology and Sociobiology, 14,* 97–113.

Rohde, P. A., Atzwanger, K., Butovskaya, M., Lampert, A., Mysterud, I., Sanchez-Andres, A., & Sulloway, F. (2003). Perceived parental favoritism, closeness to kin, and the rebel of the family: The effects of sex and birth order. *Evolution and Human Behavior, 24,* 261–276.

Salmon, C. A. (1999). On the impact of sex and birth order on contact with kin. *Human Nature, 10,* 183–197.

Salmon, C. A. (2003). Birth order and relationships: Family, friends and sexual partners. *Human Nature, 14,* 73–88.

Salmon, C. A., & Daly, M. (1998). Birth order and familial sentiment: Middleborns are different. *Evolution and Human Behavior, 19,* 299–312.

Salmon, C. A., & Hehman, J. (2013). The evolutionary psychology of sibling conflict and siblicide. In T. K. Shackelford & R. D. Hansen (Eds.), *The evolution of violence* (pp. 137–158). New York: Springer.

Samuels, H. R. (1980). The effect of an older sibling on infant locomotor exploration of a new environment. *Child Development, 51,* 607–609.

Sear, R., & Mace, R. (2008). Who keeps children alive? A review of the effects of kin on child survival. *Evolution and Human Behavior, 29,* 1–18.

Sear, R., Mace, R., & McGregor, I. A. (2000). Maternal grandmothers improve nutritional status and survival of children in rural Gambia. *Proceedings of the Royal Society of London. Series B. Biological Sciences, 267,* 1641–1647.

Segal, N. L. (2005). Evolutionary studies of cooperation, competition, and altruism: A twin-based approach. In R. L. Burgess & K. B. MacDonald (Eds.), *Evolutionary perspectives on human development* (2nd ed., pp. 265–304). Thousand Oaks: Sage.

Sieff, D. F. (1990). Explaining biased gender ratios in human populations. *Current Anthropology, 31,* 25–48.

Smith, M. S. (1988). Research in developmental sociobiology: Parenting and family behavior. In K. MacDonald (Ed.), *Sociobiological perspectives on human development* (pp. 271–292). New York: Springer.

Smith, M. S., Kish, B. J., & Crawford, C. B. (1987). Inheritance of wealth and human kin investment. *Ethology and Sociobiology, 8,* 171–182.

Stewart, R. B., & Marvin, R. S. (1984). Sibling relations: The role of conceptual perspective taking in the ontogeny of sibling caregiving. *Child Development, 55,* 1322–1332.

Straus, M., Gelles, R. J., & Steinmetz, S. K. (2006). *Behind closed doors: Violence in the American family.* Piscataway: Transaction Publishers.

Sulloway, F. J. (1982). Darwin and his finches: The evolution of a legend. *Journal of the History of Biology, 15,* 1–53.

Sulloway, F. J. (1996). *Born to rebel: Birth order, family dynamics and creative lives.* New York: Pantheon.

Sulloway, F. J. (1999). Birth order. In M. A. Runco & S. Pritzker (Eds.), *Encyclopedia of creativity volume 1* (pp. 189–202). San Diego: Academic.

Sulloway, F. J. (2001). Birth order, sibling competition, and human behavior. In H. R. Holcomb III (Ed.), *Conceptual challenges in evolutionary psychology: Innovative research strategies* (pp. 39–83). Boston: Kluwer Academic Press.

Symons, D. (1995). Beauty is in the adaptations of the beholder: The evolutionary psychology of female sexual attractiveness. In P. R. Abramson & S. D. Pinkerton (Eds.), *Sexual nature sexual culture* (pp. 80–118). Chicago: University of Chicago Press.

Tallarigo, L., Giampietro, O., Penno, G., Miccoli, R., Gregori, G., & Navalesi, R. (1986). Relation of glucose tolerance to complications of pregnancy in nondiabetic women. *New England Journal of Medicine, 316,* 1343–1346.

Thornhill, R. (1980). Rape in *Panorpa* scorpionflies and a general rape hypothesis. *Animal Behavior, 28,* 52–59.

Thornhill, R., & Alcock, J. (1983). *The evolution of insect mating systems.* Cambridge: Harvard University Press.

Thornhill, R., & Sauer, P. (1992). Genetic sire effects on the fighting ability of sons and daughters and mating success of sons in a scorpionfly. *Animal Behavior, 43,* 255–264.

Trivers, R. L. (1974). Parent-offspring conflict. *American Zoologist, 14,* 249–264.

Trivers, R. L., & Willard, D. (1973). Natural selection of parental ability to vary the sex-ratio of offspring. *Science, 179,* 90–92.

Turke, P. W. (1988). Helpers at the nest: childcare networks on Ifaluk. In L. L. Betzig, M. Borgerhoff Mulder, & P. W. Turke (Eds.) *Human reproductive behaviour* (pp. 178–188). Cambridge: Cambridge University Press.

Uhlenberg, P., & Hammill, B. G. (1998). Frequency of grandparental contact with grandchild sets: Six factors that make a difference. *The Gerontologist, 38,* 276–285.

Voland, E. (1998). Evolutionary ecology of human reproduction. *Annual Review of Anthropology, 27,* 347–374.

Voland, E., & Gabler, S. (1994). Differential twin mortality indicates a correlation between age and parental effort in humans. *Naturwissenschaften, 81,* 224–225.

Voland, E., Dunbar, R. I. M., Engel, C., & Stephan, P. (1997). Population increase and sex-biased parental investment in humans: Evidence from 18th and 19th century Germany. *Current Anthropology, 38,* 129–135.

Voland, E., Chasiotis, A., & Schiefenhövel, W. (Eds.). (2005). *Grandmotherhood. The evolutionary significance of the second half of female life.* New Brunswick: Rutgers University Press.

Volk, A., & Quinsey, V. L. (2002). The influence of infant facial cues on adoption preferences. *Human Nature, 13,* 437–455.

White, L. (2001). Sibling relationships over the life course: A panel analysis. *Journal of Marriage and the Family, 63,* 555–568.

Williams, G. C. (1966). *Adaptation and natural selection.* Princeton: Princeton University Press.

Wilson, E. O. (1975). *Sociobiology: The new synthesis.* Cambridge: Harvard University Press.

Woolfenden, G. E., & Fitzpatrick, J. W. (1984). *The Florida scrub jay: Demography of a cooperative-breeding bird.* Princeton: Princeton University Press.

A Life History Approach to the Dynamics of Social Selection

28

Aurelio José Figueredo, Emily Anne Patch and Carlos Ernesto Gómez Ceballos

The conditions for the evolution and development of fast and slow life history strategies have been extensively studied (see Ellis et al. 2009), and it is the main premise of this chapter that many of the relevant ecological conditions have implications, both directly and indirectly, for the dynamics of social cooperation and conflict. Life history (LH) theory is an evolutionary-economic model of resource allocation governing the allocation of the bioenergetic and material resources available to organisms among the different components of fitness. For example, total reproductive output over the life span is a multiplicative product of survivorship and fecundity, integrated over time, meaning that some finite proportion of the organismic resources need to be allocated to each of these two components to obtain a fitness product that is greater than zero. However, there are many combinations of these two coefficients that will yield the same product, and the quantitative parameters of the trade-off involved in allocating resources between them are determined by the selective pressures of the ecological niche of the organism and thus shape LH evolution. The bioenergetic and material resources devoted to continued survival of the organism are collectively referred to as comprising *somatic effort,* the resources devoted to the production of new organisms (as vehicles for survival of the individual's genes) are collectively referred to as comprising *reproductive effort.* In sexually reproducing species, reproductive effort is also comprised of two components, where the resources devoted to obtaining and retaining sexual partners comprise *mating effort,* and those devoted to enhancing survival of any offspring produced by self or kin comprise *parental* or *nepotistic effort,* respectively.

The principal dimension along which LH strategies can be organized is *speed. Fast* (formerly "*r-selected*") LH strategies are those that allocate resources preferentially to: (1) reproductive effort over somatic effort, and (2) mating effort over parental/nepotistic effort. Thus, fast LH strategies emphasize the production of new propagules over the survival of existing ones. Among mammals, for example, rabbits are faster LH strategists characterized by: (1) rapid sexual development, (2) high fertility, (3) little parental care per offspring, (4) high infant mortality, and (5) low adult longevity. As one illustration of this pattern, a female rabbit might invest as little as two minutes a day in all her offspring *combined,* and this only for the first 25 days of life.

In contrast, *slow* (formerly "*K-selected*") LH strategies allocate resources preferentially to: (1) somatic effort over reproductive effort, and (2) parental/nepotistic effort over mating effort. Slow LH strategies emphasize the survival

A. J. Figueredo (✉) · E. A. Patch · C. E. Gómez Ceballos
Graduate Program in Ethology and Evolutionary Psychology, Department of Psychology, 1503 E. University Blvd., University of Arizona, Tucson, AZ 85721-0068, USA
e-mail: ajf@u.arizona.edu

E. A. Patch
e-mail: epatch@email.arizona.edu

V. Zeigler-Hill et al. (eds.), *Evolutionary Perspectives on Social Psychology,* Evolutionary Psychology, DOI 10.1007/978-3-319-12697-5_28, © Springer International Publishing Switzerland 2015

of propagules over the production of new ones. For another mammalian example, elephants are slower LH strategists characterized by: (1) very slow and delayed sexual development (as much as 14 years), (2) few new babies at a time (typically only one), (3) high and extended quantities of parental care per offspring (at least until puberty), (4) very low infant mortality (due to alloparental protection from predators by as many as 8–10 related females), and (5) very high life expectancy (as high as 70 years).

The ultimate causes of such divergent profiles of resource allocation can be found in the ecological niche in which both evolution and development occur. Fast LH strategies are naturally selected in unstable, unpredictable environments, where sources of morbidity and mortality are predominantly *extrinsic,* meaning uncontrollable by genetically influenced developmental processes. These conditions lead to highly variable population densities, in turn reinforcing this selective effect (Pianka 1970). Slow LH strategies are naturally selected in stable, predictable environments, where sources of morbidity and mortality are predominantly *intrinsic,* meaning controllable by genetically influenced (and hence evolvable) developmental processes. These conditions lead to highly stable population densities, in turn reinforcing this selective effect (Pianka 1970).

The conventional categories of resource allocation described above are informed by the theories of *natural selection* (e.g., somatic effort) and *sexual selection* (e.g., mating effort), with the theory of *kin selection* (e.g., nepotistic effort) often appended as a seeming afterthought (Darwin 1859, 1871; Hamilton 1964a, 1964b). We propose that an entire category is missing from this framework, one that we call *social effort,* meaning the resources devoted to social interactions (whether cooperative or competitive or a combination of both) with conspecifics. This category is based on the theory of *social selection,* which was implicit in Darwin's (1871) *Descent of Man,* and was further elaborated by West-Eberhard (1979) and most recently by Nesse (2007).

Under this set of presumptions, it is reasonable to ask what social selective pressures govern the allocation of social effort and regulate the quantitative trade-offs in investment entailed with the other components of fitness. We propose that a comprehensive model of multilevel selection must include the causal transactions among the different levels in the hierarchy, much like in Bronfenbrenner's (1979) *ecological systems theory*. We also propose the existence of the following hierarchical cascade of consequences, wherein *natural* selective pressures generate both *individual* and *social* sequelae, in turn producing *social* selective pressures that generate *sexual* sequelae, in turn producing *sexual* selective pressures that generate further *sexual* sequelae. Thus, the generative natural selective pressures *constrain* (but do not *determine*) the social selective pressures, which then constrain the sexual selective pressures that drive both LH evolution and development. As in the Bronfenbrenner model, the directionality of these causal transactions may occasionally operate in the opposite direction, from the lower to the higher levels of the hierarchy. All of the theoretically expected relations that follow should therefore be viewed a *probabilistic* in nature.

The Social and Sexual Sequelae of Faster LH Strategies

The evolution and development of LH strategies should be governed by the following selectionist principles. The limited time horizon available for social, nepotistic, and parental relations due to the adverse natural selective pressures specified for the evolution and development of faster LH strategies should lead to unstable, unpredictable, and uncontrollable social relationships. Under such regimes of social selection, individuals (both self and others) tend to evolve and develop the following characteristics: (1) higher levels of insecure (anxious or avoidant) attachment to kith and kin, (2) higher levels of opportunistic and exploitative interpersonal styles, (3) lower levels of kin-selected altruism, (4) lower levels of parental and nepotistic effort, (5) higher levels of social defection, (6) higher levels of social antagonism, (7) higher levels of social aggression, and (8) higher levels of more selfish general orientations towards social partners (Figueredo et al. 2006, 2013; Figueredo and Jacobs 2010). These socially selected sequelae will tend to be self-reinforcing (as in the theory of *r*- and *K*-selection proposed by Pianka 1970) due to the adverse social selective pressures generated in environments where the majority of conspecifics are also pursuing faster life histories and hence shorter-term social strategies.

These socially selected sequelae lead to the equivalent sexually selected sequelae. In social ecologies characterized by unstable, unpredictable, and uncontrollable sexual relationships, individuals (both self and others) tend to evolve and develop the following characteristics: (1) higher levels of insecure attachment to sexual partners, (2) higher levels of mating effort in the service of multiple short-term pairings, whether simultaneous or serial or both, (3) higher levels of opportunistic and exploitative sexual relations, including deceptive and coercive sexuality, (4) higher levels of cross-sexual defection, (5) higher levels of cross-sexual antagonism, including low cross-sexual cooperation and coparenting, (6) higher levels of cross-sexual aggression, including "intimate partner violence," and (7) higher levels of more selfish general orientations towards sexual partners (Figueredo et al. 2006, 2013; Figueredo and Jacobs 2010). As with the socially selected sequelae of fast LH, these sexually selected sequelae are self-reinforcing (again as in Pianka 1970) due jointly to the limited time horizon available for sexual relationships and the adverse social and sexual selective pressures generated in environments where the majority of conspecifics are also pursuing faster LH and hence shorter-term social and sexual strategies.

The traditional social and psychological sciences seek to understand the underlying reasons for which some families, children, and adolescences are at disproportionately higher risk for violence, conflict, and abuse than others. An evolutionary perspective using the LH theory can help inform social science research into these important questions. For illustrations, we briefly review and reappraise the relevant literatures on adolescent delinquency in males, teenage pregnancy in females, and child abuse in both sexes.

Delinquency in Adolescent Males

Felson and Haynie (2002) begin their discussion of adolescent male delinquent behavior by noting that boys who achieve sexual maturity earlier are more likely to engage in socially deviant behavior. Nevertheless, they go on to state that the literature is "unclear" as to why early pubertal development should be associated with delinquent behavior. The judicious application of LH theory would suggest that this relation might be spurious rather than directly causal because earlier sexual maturity is an indicator of a faster LH strategy: Faster LH individuals, who are more likely to reach puberty earlier and consequently engage in sexual behavior at a younger age, are also more likely to engage in higher levels of antisocial and delinquent behavior (Brumbach et al. 2007, 2009; Rowe 1997).

Alternative explanations have included the claim that adolescent males are put in positions where they are required to face challenges and perform tasks for which they are developmentally unprepared. However, this begs the question as to *why* these early-developing young males are so unprepared? Similarly, young boys who exhibit aggressive behaviors are said to become deviant and delinquent later in life. Nagin and Tremblay (1999) described a longitudinal study demonstrating that childhood disruptive behavior is one of the best predictors of adolescent and adult criminality. Once again, however, we are left wondering *why* these particular children become aggressive to begin with?

According to LH theory, all these social sequelae are attributable to the circumstance that an unstable, unpredictable, and uncontrollable environment does not provide an adequate context for the development of a *mutualistic* cognitive social schema that involves relying on cooperative and reciprocally supportive relations with other people based on perceived commonality of interests (Figueredo and Jacobs 2010). Faster LH strategists instead tend to develop *antagonistic* cognitive social schemata that conceptualize any given individual as being in a perpetual state of conflict of interests with all others.

Early ("teenage") Pregnancy in Adolescent Females

Early reproduction itself is one of the hallmarks of a faster LH strategy. If the environment is unstable, and the hazards of extrinsic morbidity and mortality are high, a strategy that includes early initiation of reproductive activity will be subject to positive selective pressure. Faster LH strategists adapt to their unstable and unpredictable environments by endeavoring to pass on their genes before some external and uncontrollable hazard occasions their incapacitating illness or untimely death.

Moreover, many of the predictors of early teenage pregnancy reported in the social science literature are equally related to faster LH strategies. For example, Woodward et al. (2001) reported that pubertal timing is a characteristic associated with teenage pregnancy: Girls who start menstruating earlier are at a higher risk for teenage pregnancy. As with the delinquent adolescent males, earlier sexual maturity is also a classic indicator of a faster LH strategy, because any physiological mechanism that biases development towards earlier puberty will be subject to positive selective pressure in unstable environments if it leads to an earlier onset of sexual and reproductive behaviors. Furthermore, Woodward et al. (2001) noted that females who were raised by a teenage mother had an earlier time of pregnancy themselves. This is also not surprising because human LH strategy is highly heritable ($h^2 \sim 65$; Figueredo et al. 2004; Figueredo and Rushton 2009).

Woodward et al. (2001) also found that both drug use and deviant behavior are contributing factors to the aggregate risk of teenage pregnancy. In addition, Vernon et al. (1983) reported that low religiosity appears to facilitate teenage pregnancy. Again, these relations might all be spurious rather than directly causal because faster LH strategists of both sexes are more likely to exhibit antisocial and socially deviant behaviors, including substance abuse and other risk-taking behaviors, and be lower in conventional religiosity, nontraditional spirituality, and moral intuitions such as moral dumbfounding, disgust sensitivity, and the ethics of autonomy, community, and divinity (see Figueredo et al. 2006; Gladden et al. 2009; Wenner et al., 2013).

Child Abuse

Child abuse has been related to a number of factors, such as poverty, lack of education, and substance abuse. As with the alternative hypotheses considered above, however, these *proximate*-level explanations beg for *ultimate*-level explanation. For example, *why* would poverty and lack of education lead to child abuse? Are those relations directly causal or spurious?

LH theory offers a more comprehensive and contextualized view of these risk factors. If an organism evolves and develops in an unstable and unpredictable environment, where morbidity and mortality are high and uncontrollable, LH theory reminds us that it is not productive to engage in long-term planning under such adverse circumstances. A cascade of consequences follows from that simple fact: (1) Completing an education in an industrial or postindustrial society typically requires long-term foresight, planning, and delay of gratification, (2) a lack of sufficient education diminishes opportunities for employment and advancement; and (3) insufficient education might lead to unemployment or underemployment and may therefore lead to poverty. Thus, if child abuse is more prevalent in environments favoring faster LH strategies, the role of these additional dimensions needs to be considered (see Frías-Armenta et al. 1996; Gaxiola-Romero et al. 2011).

Within these more general social circumstances, men are the likely perpetrators of child abuse, and male infants (under 1 year of age) are more likely to be the victims. Children living in father-only households are at high risk for abuse and neglect (Weghorst 1980), and children living with an unrelated male are 50 times more likely to suffer a fatal injury than children living with their two genetic parents (Schnitzer and Ewigman 2005). Some researchers even suggest that this is due to the fact that fathers are not *meant* to be the figureheads providing parental care to an infant (Weghorst 1980). Again, *why* might males be more likely to abuse children under these conditions?

Evolutionary theory reminds us that a male can never be certain he is the genetic father of any particular child (at least without recourse to modern molecular-genetic methods of paternity testing). Investing in a child that is not genetically one's own is costly to the Darwinian fitness of any organism, and a male typically incurs the additional risk that he would be providing a portion of his limited resources to a genetically unrelated child.

The fact that males are the most likely perpetrators of fatal child abuse (and not just abuse in general) is not surprising. Infanticide is common among nonhuman primates (Palmobit 1999; Van Schaik and Kappeler 1997). Male nonhuman primates often kill infants to bring females into estrus because most females will not ovulate while nursing and can therefore not be impregnated. In addition, killing male infants decreases future competition for mates. Although these are not likely to be the same specific causes for child abuse in humans, similar LH dynamics might be involved. For example, the presence of maternal half-siblings in the home is associated with greater parent–offspring conflict between mothers and their genetic offspring than the presence of full siblings. This relation is obtained when the stepfathers (presumably the genetic fathers of the added half-siblings) are not present in the home (presumably to defend their interests), but is not influenced by family size, socioeconomic status, or maternal depression (Schlomer et al. 2010). It is therefore likely that conflict over allocation of parental resources among offspring of mixed paternity is conducive to higher levels of child abuse.

The Social and Sexual Sequelae of Slower LH Strategies

The more distant and foreseeable time horizon available for social, nepotistic, and parental relations due to the relatively safe and favorable natural selective pressures specified for the evolution and development of slower LH strategies should lead to more stable, predictable, and controllable social relationships. Under such regimes of social selection, individuals (both self and others) tend to evolve and develop the following characteristics: (1) higher levels of secure attachment to kith and kin, (2) higher levels of mutually and reciprocally rewarding interpersonal styles, (3) higher levels of kin-selected altruism, (4) higher levels of parental and nepotistic effort, (5) higher levels of social reciprocity, (6) higher levels of social mutualism, and (7) higher levels of more altruistic general orientations towards social partners (Figueredo et al. 2006, 2013; Figueredo and Jacobs 2010). These socially selected sequelae tend to be self-reinforcing (as in the theory of *r*- and *K*-selection proposed by Pianka 1970) due to the relatively safer and more favorable social selective pressures of environments where the majority of conspecifics are also pursuing slower life histories and longer-term social strategies.

Consequently, the relatively safe and favorable natural selective pressures specified for the evolution and development of slower LH strategies should lead to more stable, predictable, and controllable sexual relationships. Under such regimes of social selection, individuals (both self and others) tend to evolve and develop the following characteristics: (1) higher levels of secure attachment to romantic, not just sexual, partners, (2) lower levels of mating effort in the service of a reduced number of long-term pairings, although perhaps not perfectly monogamous ones, (3) higher levels of mutually and reciprocally rewarding sexual relations, (4) higher levels of strong and committed cross-sexual bonds, (5) higher levels of cross-sexual reciprocity, (6) higher levels of cross-sexual mutualism, including cross-sexual cooperation and coparenting, (7) lower levels of cross-sexual antagonism, and (8) higher levels of more altruistic general orientations towards sexual partners (Figueredo et al. 2006, 2013; Figueredo and Jacobs 2010). As with the socially selected sequelae of slow LH, these sexually selected sequelae are self-reinforcing (again as in Pianka 1970) due jointly to the more distant and foreseeable time horizon available for sexual relationships and the safer and more favorable social and sexual selective pressures in environments where the majority of conspecifics are also pursuing slow LH and short-term social and sexual strategies.

Just as we routinely investigate the causes of many socially problematic behaviors, the social and psychological sciences should seek to understand the underlying reasons for which some romantic couples, parents, and children are at *lower* risk for many perceived social problems. Why are *these* particular individuals somehow resistant and often virtually immune to these afflictions? An evolutionary perspective using the LH theory perspective can help inform social science research into these questions: We might get a better handle on the *problem* if we examine some of the *solutions* that seem to have been independently discovered by the evolutionary process. For illustrations, we briefly review and reappraise the relevant literatures on parent–child and romantic partner attachment, relationship satisfaction and relationship stability in pair-bonded romantic couples, and the dynamics and developmental consequences of cooperative parenting among both slow LH mothers and fathers.

Attachment Styles

Attachment theorists have identified three attachment styles in infants: (1) secure attachment style, characterized by trust, a lack of concern with being abandoned, and a belief that one is worthy and well-liked; (2) avoidant attachment style, characterized by a suppression of attachment needs, presumably because attempts at being intimate have been rebuffed, as well as the consequent difficulties in developing intimate relationships; and (3) anxious/ambivalent attachment style, characterized by higher levels of anxiety, presumably caused by the fear that their desire for intimacy will not be reciprocated (Aronson et al. 2007). Attachment theory presumes that the bonds that people create with peers as adults are influenced by the bonds created with their primary caregivers early in life, and most of the relevant empirical research shows that attachment styles remain relatively consistent through life (Aronson et al. 2007).

An interpretation of these findings informed by LH theory might instead view some of these relations as spurious rather than causal. Due to the high heritability of human LH strategies, it should come as no surprise that secure-attachment-style mothers typically produce secure-attachment-style infants. Although such an effect could be produced by either "nature" or "nurture," it is unwarranted to presume that the mother–infant attachment behaviors are transmitted in a purely environmental fashion through differential rearing practices. The "nurturing" high parental investment behaviors of the slower LH mothers might instead be genetically correlated with the secure attachment behaviors of their slower LH infants. The later attachment behaviors of these slower LH offspring as adults, as with attachment to their future romantic partners, might also be genetically correlated with their original attachment behaviors towards parents during infancy and, in turn, with their own "nurturing" high parental investment behaviors when they eventually produce slower LH offspring of their own. Factor analyses of the genetic variance-covariance matrices of these behaviors performed on nationally representative samples of monozygotic and dizygotic twins provide substantial empirical support for this alternative hypothesis (e.g., Figueredo et al. 2004).

Because even a high heritability coefficient does not imply "genetic determinism," however, it is reasonable to then ask whether the environmental influences on attachment behaviors are consistent with the interpretations derived from LH theory. Such studies (e.g., Vaughn et al. 1979) find that an increase in the frequency of stressful events is related to change from secure attachment-related behaviors to insecure attachment-related behaviors in infants aged 12–18 months. On the other hand, a decrease in stressful events, although presumably conducive to secure attachment, was not enough for "improved" patterns of social interaction. Related research (e.g., Mikulincer and Shaver 2005) has nonetheless suggested that environmental factors may affect attachment behaviors even in adults, at least temporarily: contextual activation of attachment security, as by subliminal exposure to words related to secure attachment (e.g., *love, hug*) or by asking individuals to imagine themselves in safe environments, increases *compassion* towards people in distress as well as the endorsement of prosocial values, such as *benevolence* (defined as concern for those close to us) and *universalism* (defined as concern for all humanity). This is consistent with findings that slower LH strategists are lower than faster LH strategists in both negative ethnocentrism (Figueredo et al. 2011) and negative androcentrism (Gladden et al. 2013). Cabeza de Baca et al. (2012) recently reviewed the wider nomological network of human LH strategy as a latent hypothetical construct. These environmental effects in both infants and adults are what one might expect if selection had shaped developmental mechanisms to be responsive to environmental cues signaling increases in extrinsic morbidity and mortality ("stressful events") by shifting the speed of LH strategy accordingly, as indicated by attachment-related behaviors.

Romantic Relationship Satisfaction and Stability

So what happens when one possesses more secure interpersonal attachment as a consequence of a slower LH strategy? A mediational model (Figueredo et al. 2010) examined the hypothesized causal pathways from slower LH strategy to higher executive functioning, through higher emotional intelligence, to short-term and long-term sociosexual orientations. Slower LH strategy suppressed dispositions towards short-term mating through enhanced executive functioning (as in impulse control and delay of gratification), whereas it facilitated dispositions towards long-term mating through enhanced emotional intelligence. Direct effects were also found from slower LH strategy to both short-term and long-term mating dispositions, presumably reflecting the *conative* preference for long-term mating as well as the *cognitive* abilities required to preserve the long-term pair bonds. There was also a direct contribution from enhanced executive functioning to increased emotional intelligence, as expected by theory, but there were no direct effects of either enhanced executive functioning on long-term mating or increased emotional intelligence on short-term mating. Only an indirect effect was found between executive functioning and long-term mating because short-term mating (which executive functioning served to suppress) strategically interfered with long-term mating.

A cross-sectional study (Olderbak and Figueredo 2009) found that, once a long-term pair bond was established, a slow LH shared by both romantic partners enhanced relationship satisfaction, and that this effect was partially mediated by secure romantic partner attachment and supportive communication among partners. Again, a presumably conative direct effect of slow LH on relationship satisfaction was also found. A subsequent longitudinal study (Olderbak and Figueredo 2010) linked slower LH strategies to enhanced levels of romantic relationship satisfaction over time. The strongest effect was on the average level of romantic relationship satisfaction, which in turn exerted the largest direct influence upon both: (1) the slope of relationship satisfaction, with slower LH strategists having flat slopes, indicating little change over time, and (2) the residual variability in relationship satisfaction, with slower LH strategists having less variability, indicating little relationship instability over time. This means that romantic couples who share slower LH strategies tend to be high in relationship satisfaction, stay that way over time, and show fewer ups-and-downs in the quality of their relationships. It was also found that shared slow LH decreased the probability of relationship dissolution during the study period of two years, presumably because the romantic partners were still happy together. The opposite was true for faster LH couples, for whom relationship satisfaction was lower on average for the entire duration of the relationship, the slope was more negative (indicating a systematically decreasing level of relationship satisfaction over time), and a high degree of residual variability in relationship quality over time (indicating more "rocky" and unstable relationships among faster LH strategists). All this led to a higher rate of relationship dissolution for faster LH strategists over the study period. These outcomes are consistent with faster LH strategies in that they facilitate re-pairings with alternative sexual partners and the consequent achievement of the greater genetic diversity among one's offspring that is theoretically optimal in unpredictable environments (see Wolf and Figueredo 2011).

But what happens if the romantic partners do *not* share the same LH speed? Both model-based theoretical predictions (Wolf and Figueredo 2011) and cross-cultural empirical tests replicated in Mexico, Costa Rica, and the USA (Figueredo and Wolf 2009) indicate that slower LH strategists appear to possess behavioral adaptations to prevent mismatch in reproductive strategy with their romantic partners. In these studies, slower LH strategies were associated cross-culturally with higher levels of positive assortative mating among romantic partners and positive assortative pairing among social partners on both speed of LH strategy and overall mate value (Wolf and Figueredo 2009). These results were found to be consistent with a mathematical model developed for the fitness benefits of mating with genetically similar individuals under ecological conditions favoring the evolution of slower LH strategies and thus with slow LH strategy traits (Wolf and Figueredo, 2011). This mating pattern also increases the coefficient of relatedness among mothers and their infants to exceed the $r_g = 0.50$ typically expected under the combination of diploidy and panmixia, further buttressing the mother–infant phenotypic similarity in LH speed alluded to in relation to attachment styles.

Shared Parenting: "Baby Makes Three"

A subsequent cross-cultural study (Sotomayor-Peterson et al. 2011) carried out in Mexico, Costa Rica, and the USA, revealed what happens when romantic partners with shared slow LH strategies reproduce. The quantitative results of this study replicated well, with the exception that the Costa Rican sample had lower average reported levels of total parental effort than the Mexican sample, whereas the USA sample did not. A path model produced the following results: (1) higher levels of total parental effort (meaning the amount jointly contributed by both the father and the mother) predicted higher levels of shared parenting (meaning more equally distributed between the father and the mother); (2) higher levels of shared parenting and of total parental effort predicted higher, more positive levels of family emotional climate; and (3) higher and more positive levels of family emotional climate, shared parenting, and total parental effort predicted slower LH strategies in the offspring later on as young adults.

This last finding is confounded by the possible effects of the genetic transmission of slow LH characteristics rather than the presumed environmental effects of parental rearing practices. Again, the observed positive assortative mating for genetic similarity among slower LH strategists elevates both the father–mother and (in consequence) the parent–offspring coefficients of relatedness above the otherwise expected levels and thus favors both higher degrees of cooperation among parents and higher degrees of kin-selected altruism towards offspring. Nevertheless, the overall pattern of intergenerational transmission of slower LH strategy is quite clear, even if the alternative (and perhaps partially complementary) mediating mechanisms remain difficult to disentangle.

Summary and Conclusions

We hope to have illustrated with several empirical examples how an approach based on the judicious application of LH theory can help elucidate several thorny problems in the traditional social and psychological sciences. As in the conventional biological sciences, LH theory can serve as an integrative framework with which to organize and better understand our data. These contributions should therefore be viewed as complementing rather than competing with traditional approaches, providing a supportive scaffolding on which to build and elaborate on our theoretical superstructures. By arranging our social science findings in a biologically meaningful way, we can often detect patterns in the data that were not previously self-evident, and better understand the ultimate level causal forces underlying the observed and often puzzling associations we encounter. LH theory thus provides a "big picture" backdrop with which to view our existing knowledge as well as offering a more coherent view of social and psychological phenomena that can serve as a heuristic for the generation of novel testable hypotheses regarding the latent structural relations among them that might not have been apparent otherwise.

We have argued that the natural selective pressures driving both LH evolution and development constrain the social selective pressures, which then constrain the sexual selective pressures. We use the word *constrain* advisedly, in that we do not suggest determination of one level by the other. If that were the case, one would hardly need a multilevel model, because a single and all-powerful level of explanation would suffice. As seen in the hierarchically nested level of biological organization (from cells to tissues to organs to ecosystems; see Mayr 1982), novel *emergent properties* arise with each new level of behavioral and social complexity. Due to the reciprocal causal transactions between levels, the emergent properties arising at a higher level can also constrain those of the lower (also as in Bronfenbrenner 1979). In neuropsychology, for example, we see that the later evolving and developing prefrontal cortex regulates the more ancestrally and developmentally primitive areas of the brain, primarily through the mechanisms of differential inhibition that we collectively label executive functioning. These higher-level processes do not shut down, render irrelevant, or somehow supersede the functions of the lower-level systems of the brain, such as the cerebellum.

Thus, these superimposed layers of selective pressure do not always "push" or "pull" in the same direction. As in the classic case of the length of the peacock's tail, the final product of selection might represent a compromise between opposing evolutionary forces. As described by Darwin (1871), *sexual* selection favors longer peacock tails due to female mating preferences for extravagant displays, whereas *natural* selection favors shorter peacock tails due to predation pressures by carnivores such as tigers. Similarly, many conflicting individualist and collectivist human impulses might be seen as generated by the opposing forces of *individual* and *group* selection, as also originally described by Darwin (1871), albeit in more antiquated terminology. The social and behavioral phenomena that we finally observe might thus represent the resultant vector sum, as in classical Newtonian physics, of the sometimes opposing and discrepant evolutionary forces jointly shaping them.

References

Aronson, E., Wilson, T. D., & Akert, R. M. (2007). *Social psychology* (6th ed.). Upper Saddle River: Pearson.

Bronfenbrenner, U. (1979). *The ecology of human development: Experiments by nature and design*. Cambridge: Harvard University Press.

Brumbach, B. H., Walsh, M., & Figueredo, A. J. (2007). Sexual restrictedness in adolescence: A life history perspective. *Acta Psychologica Sinica, 39,* 481–488.

Brumbach, B. H., Figueredo, A. J., & Ellis, B. J. (2009). Effects of harsh and unpredictable environments in adolescence on development of life history strategies: A longitudinal test of an evolutionary model. *Human Nature, 20,* 25–51.

Cabeza de Baca, T., Figueredo, A. J., & Ellis, B. J. (2012). An evolutionary analysis of variation in parental effort: Determinants and assessment. *Parenting: Science and Practice, Special Issue: The Arc of Parenting from Epigenomes to Ethics, 12,* 94–104.

Darwin, C. (1871). *The descent of man, and selection in relation to sex*. London: Appleton.

Darwin, C. (1959). *On the origin of species by means of natural selection*. London: Murray.

Ellis, B. J., Figueredo, A. J., Brumbach, B. H., & Schlomer, G. L. (2009). Fundamental dimensions of environmental risk: The impact of harsh versus unpredictable environments on the evolution and development of life history strategies. *Human Nature, 20,* 204–268.

Felson, R. B., & Haynie, D. L. (2002). Pubertal development, social factors, and delinquency among adolescent boys. *Criminology, 40,* 967–988.

Figueredo, A. J., & Jacobs, W. J. (2010). Aggression, risk-taking, and alternative life history strategies: The behavioral ecology of social deviance. In M. Frias-Armenta & V. Corral-Verdugo (Eds.), *Bio-psycho-social perspectives on interpersonal violence* (pp. 3–28). Hauppauge: Nova Science Publishers.

Figueredo, A. J., & Rushton, J. P. (2009). Evidence for shared genetic dominance between the general factor of personality, mental and physical health, and life history traits. *Twin Research and Human Genetics, 12,* 555–563.

Figueredo, A. J., & Wolf, P. S. A. (2009). Assortative pairing and life history strategy: A cross-cultural study. *Human Nature, 20,* 317–330.

Figueredo, A. J., Vásquez, G., Brumbach, B. H., & Schneider, S. M. R. (2004). The heritability of life history strategy: The K-factor, covitality, and personality. *Social Biology, 51,* 121–143.

Figueredo, A. J., Vásquez, G., Brumbach, B. H., Schneider, S. M. R., Sefcek, J. A., Tal, I. R., Hill, D., Wenner, C. J., & Jacobs, W. J. (2006). Consilience and life history theory: From genes to brain to reproductive strategy. *Developmental Review, 26,* 243–275.

Figueredo, A. J., Andrzejczak, D. J., Jones, D. J., Smith-Castro, V., & Montero-Rojas, E. (2011). Reproductive strategy and ethnic conflict: Slow life history as a protective factor against negative ethnocentrism in two contemporary societies. *Journal of Social, Evolutionary, and Cultural Psychology, 5,* 14–31.

Figueredo, A. J., Cabeza de Baca, T., & Woodley, M. A. (2013). The measurement of human life history strategy. *Personality and Individual Differences, 55,* 251–255.

Frías-Armenta, M., Corral-Verdugo, V., & Figueredo, A. J. (1996). Comparación de modelos explicativos de la relación entre maltrato infantil y el desarollo de caracteristicas "especiales" en niños (Comparing explanatory models of the relation between child abuse and the development of "special" characteristics in children). *Psicología y Salud, 8,* 33–44.

Gaxiola-Romero, J., Frías-Armenta, M., & Figueredo, A. J. (2011). Factores protectores y los estilos de crianza: Un modelo bioecológico (Protective factors and parenting styles: A bio-ecological model). *Revista Mexicana de Investigación en Psicología Social y de la Salud, 1,* 28–40.

Gladden, P. R., Welch, J., Figueredo, A. J., & Jacobs, W. J. (2009). Moral intuitions and religiosity as spuriously correlated life history traits. *Journal of Evolutionary Psychology, 7,* 167–184.

Gladden, P. R., Figueredo, A. J., Andrejzak, D. J., Jones, D. N., & Smith-Castro, V. (2013). Reproductive strategy and sexual conflict: Slow life history strategy inhibits negative androcentrism. *Journal of Methods and Measurement in the Social Sciences, 4,* 48–71.

Hamilton, W. (1964a). The genetical evolution of social behaviour: I. *Journal of Theoretical Biology, 7,* 1–16.

Hamilton, W. (1964b). The genetical evolution of social behaviour: II. *Journal of Theoretical Biology, 7,* 17–52.

Mayr, E. (1982). *The growth of biological thought: Diversity, evolution, and inheritance*. Cambridge: Belknap.

Mikulincer, M., & Shaver, P. R. (2005). Attachment security, compassion, and altruism. *Current Directions in Psychological Science, 14,* 33–38.

Nagin, D., & Tremblay, R. E. (1999). Trajectories of boys' physical aggression, opposition, and hyperactivity on the path to physically violent and nonviolent juvenile delinquency. *Child Development, 70,* 1181–1196.

Nesse, R. M. (2007). Runaway social selection for displays of partner value and altruism. *Biological Theory, 2,* 143–155.

Olderbak, S. G., & Figueredo, A. J. (2009). Predicting romantic relationship satisfaction from life history strategy. *Personality and Individual Differences, 46,* 604–610.

Olderbak, S. G., & Figueredo, A. J. (2010). Life history strategy as a longitudinal predictor of relationship satisfaction and dissolution. *Personality and Individual Differences, 49,* 234–239.

Palombit, R. A. (1999). Infanticide and the evolution of pair bonds in nonhuman primates. *Evolutionary Anthropology, 7,* 117–129.

Pianka, E. R. (1970). On r and K selection. *American Naturalist, 104,* 592–597.

Rowe, D. C., Vazsonyi, A. T., & Figueredo, A. J. (1997). Mating effort in adolescence: Conditional or alternative strategy? *Personality and Individual Differences, 23,* 105–115.

Schlomer, G. L., Ellis, B. J., & Garber, J. (2010). Mother-child conflict and sibling relatedness: A test of hypotheses from parent-offspring conflict theory. *Journal of Research on Adolescence, 20,* 287–306.

Schnitzer, P. G., & Ewigman, B. G. (2005). Child deaths resulting from inflicted injuries: Household risk factors and perpetrator characteristics. *Pediatrics, 116,* e687–e693.

Sotomayor-Peterson, M., Cabeza de Baca, T., Figueredo, A. J., & Smith-Castro, V. (2012). Shared parenting, parental effort, and life history strategy: A cross-cultural comparison. *Journal of Cross-Cultural Psychology, 44,* 620–639.

Van Schaik, C., & Kappeler, P. M. (1997). Infanticide risk and the evolution of male-female association in primates. *Proceedings of the Royal Society B, 264,* 1687–1694.

Vaughn, B., Egeland, B. L., Sroufe, A., & Waters, E. (1979). Stability and change in families under stress. *Child Development, 50,* 971–975.

Vernon, M. E., Green, J. A., & Frothingham, T. E. (1983). Teenage pregnancy: A prospective study of self-esteem and other sociodemographic factors. *Pediatrics, 72,* 632–635.

Weghorst, S. J. (1980). Household composition and the risk of child abuse and neglect. *Journal of Biosocial Science, 12,* 333–340.

Wenner, C. J., Bianchi, J., Figueredo, A. J., Rushton, J. P., & Jacobs, W. J. (2013). Life history theory and social deviance: The mediating role of Executive Function. *Intelligence, 41,* 102–113.

West-Eberhard, M. J. (1979). Sexual selection, social competition, and evolution. *Proceedings of the American Philosophical Society, 123,* 222–234.

Wolf, P. S. A., & Figueredo, A. J. (2011). Fecundity, offspring longevity, and assortative mating: Parametric tradeoffs in sexual and life history strategy. *Biodemography and Social Biology, 52,* 171–183.

Woodward, L., Fergusson, D. M., & Horwood, L. J. (2001). Risk factors and life processes associated with teenage pregnancy: Results of a prospective study from birth to 20 years. *Journal of Marriage and Family, 63,* 1170–1184.

Part VII

Violence and Aggression

War and Aggression

29

John M. Friend and Bradley Thayer

War and aggression are defining features of international relations, be it the numerous terrorist attacks worldwide, the high number of ethnic conflicts, or the resurgence of violent nationalist sentiment. Von Clausewitz (1989) once famously argued that "war is merely the continuation of policy by other means" (p. 87). When diplomacy breaks down, when all else fails, war is just another rational policy option. International relations scholars such as Waltz (1979) and Mearsheimer (2001) share von Clausewitz's conclusion, arguing that war and aggression in great power politics are simply a fact of life in an anarchic system, a way to maximize power and protect national interests.

However, the high cost in blood and treasure of war calls into question the rationality of war. Fearon (1995) correctly points out that this rational approach to war is incapable of adequately addressing the "central puzzle," that is to say, "war is costly and risky, so rational states should have incentives to locate negotiated settlements that all would prefer to the gamble of war" (p. 380). Simply, it would be more rational and cost-effective to avoid war and make mutually beneficial settlements than to wage war and risk economic collapse and possible annihilation, an even greater concern today. Thus, the prevalence of conflict in international politics suggests that war is not merely a continuation of policy, but rather a central component of the human condition.

J. M. Friend (✉)
Department of Political Science, University of Hawai'i at Mānoa, 2424 Maile Way, Saunders 640, Honolulu, HI 96822, USA
e-mail: jfriend@hawaii.edu

B. Thayer
Department of Political Science, Utah State University, 0700 Old Main Hill, Logan, UT 84322–0700, USA
e-mail: bradley.thayer@usu.edu

Since war is one of the oldest and most ubiquitous themes in human civilization (Keeley 1997), this puzzle identified by Fearon (1995) has been a long time interest of many in the fields of political science and international relations. Indeed, since the behavioral revolution of the 1960s, those interested in the causes of international conflict have drawn heavily from the life sciences, particularly from the fields of social psychology and evolutionary theory (Masters 1991; Peterson and Somit 1978; Schubert 1983; Somit 1968, 1976). This emphasis on studying human nature and individual differences to understand why leaders make "irrational decisions" that lead countries to war would later become the hallmark of political psychology during the 1970s and 1980s. No longer satisfied with rational choice models of decision making, international relations scholars turned to the individual level of analysis of political psychology to explain "credible" deterrence failures, alliance formations, and why political leaders eagerly chase *fait accompli* strategies (Gross-Stein and Tanter 1980; Jervis 1976; Jervis et al. 1989).

The work of these scholars highlighted the various cognitive mechanisms involved in the decision making process, such as motivated and

V. Zeigler-Hill et al. (eds.), *Evolutionary Perspectives on Social Psychology,* Evolutionary Psychology,
DOI 10.1007/978-3-319-12697-5_29, © Springer International Publishing Switzerland 2015

unmotivated biases, that can produce differences in rationality and, in turn, lead to deterrence failures and conflict. While many in the field of political psychology acknowledged the advantages of the rigor and parsimony provided by the traditional deterrence paradigm, they also considered a cognitive analysis (with its emphasis on human psychological attributes) to be a much-needed supplement to the study of war and aggression.

Recent breakthroughs in the fields of neuroscience and behavioral genetics have shown us that human behavior is, according to McDermott (2004), the product of "emotional rationality," that is to say, a result of adaptive "reflexive and instinctual behavior" (p. 697), not deliberate cost–benefit calculations. With this new understanding of human nature and groundbreaking work that revisits the brain–body relationship (Damasio 2005; Gazzaniga 2006; Kurzban 2012; LeDoux 2003), we are currently experiencing a new behavioral revolution in the social sciences, with particular resurgence in the fields of international relations and American politics (Friend and Thayer 2012; Hatemi and McDermott 2011; Johnson and Tierney 2006; 2004). Indeed, as Stavridis (2014) points out, we are currently experiencing the dawning of the age of biology.

In *The Politics,* Aristotle was the first to suggest that man is, by nature, a political animal and recognize the biological underpinning of human political behavior and social development. Today, evolutionary psychology and the new brain sciences provide scientific theory and evidence to Aristotelian philosophy. According to Fowler and Schreiber (2008), neuroscience's investigation of genetic and neural mechanisms is both inherently political and biological. It is political due to the neurobiological interest in human decision making and organization to achieve ingroup goals and stability, and biological because questions remain unanswered about the evolution of cooperative behavior, coalition formation, and intergroup conflict. Evolutionary perspectives offer much insight into the causes of war and aggression. In fact, a recent review of the literature on violence, homicide, and war in humans and nonhumans by Liddle et al. (2012) found that evolutionary theory can "substantially enhance our understanding of these behaviors" (p. 24). Therefore, by approaching war and aggression as the product of evolved adaptations (Bowles 2009; Otterbein 1997), we can begin to see not only that human aggression has evolutionary roots but also that war and international conflicts are, in part, a product of these roots. Thus, despite von Clausewitz's (1989) claim, judgments about whether to go to war do not necessarily follow instrumental rationality; rather, evolutionary psychology tells us that humans are "relatively insensitive to material consequences or to instrumental preferences regarding risk when making choices about the use of intergroup violence" (Ginges and Atran 2011, p. 2937).

By acknowledging that war and aggression are produced by evolved mechanisms, we are not suggesting that violence, such as ethnic conflict, is justified or acceptable, nor are we positing, as many dystopian films and novels hint, that humans are doomed to a constant state of war that is nasty, brutish, and short. Rather, we are arguing that the theories and methods of evolutionary psychology allow us to study the causes of aggression and violence with the goal of better understanding conditions for cooperation and peace. To promote the better angels of our nature, as Pinker (2011) puts it, we need to analyze the biological and cultural evolution of warfare.

Through the perspectives of evolutionary psychology and findings from the field of social neuroscience, we can begin to see that "anger is part of the basic biology of the human species" (Sell et al. 2009, p. 15073). Recent studies using contemporary brain imaging techniques, such as functional magnetic resonance imaging (fMRI), have shown this to be true by revealing an underlying neurobiology of aggression in human social behavior (Siever 2008). For example, specific areas of the brain have been linked to different types of aggressive and violent behaviors. Most notably, in an online article published by *Reuters,* Mozes (2001) has noted that the prefrontal cortex (PFC) "has been recognized as an important regulator of social and aggressive behavior," and evidence from brain imaging studies suggests that this region of the brain "functions as a critical filter between the violent images themselves and the decisions people make in choosing how to respond to them." The role of the prefrontal region of the brain in aggressive and violent behavior can be clearly seen in studies of patients with lesions to the PFC that display antisocial behavior similar to psychopathy (Anderson et al. 1999).

While Phineas Gage is the most famous subject who displayed such symptoms after experiencing trauma to the ventromedial prefrontal cortex (VMPFC), more recently fMRI studies have revealed that drug abuse can also impair the orbitofrontal cortex and cause psychopathic-like behavior and impulsive decision making (Anderson et al., 1999). These studies demonstrate that violent acts have genetic components, such as in the case of impulsive aggression. However, it is important to note that the causes of human aggression are multifactorial, and include a wide array of cultural, socioeconomic, political, medical, psychological, and historical factors. Nonetheless, through the intersection of evolutionary psychology and social neuroscience, we can begin to better understand the biological and cultural evolution of aggression and warfare, which in turn provides insight into the intergroup competition and ethnic and cultural conflicts that appear regularly in international politics.

The debate around the causes of war has shaped the field of international relations for decades. While overlooked until more recently, evolutionary psychology and the new brain sciences have much to offer to this debate, providing empirical evidence to an age-old philosophical question. As Cosmides and Tooby (2013) point out, evolutionary psychology views "the brain as composed of evolved computational systems engineered by natural selection to use information to adaptively regulate physiology and behavior" (p. 201). These computational systems that shape our behavior today were selected in response to specific and reoccurring adaptive problems faced by our ancestors related to survival and reproduction (Buss 2013). From this perspective, according to Buss and Shackelford (1997), we can understand that human aggression and war are "context-sensitive solutions to particular adaptive problems of social living" (p. 605), such as competing for resources, defending against attack, deterring rivals from future aggression, and negotiating status and power hierarchies.

Evolutionary Perspectives on Intergroup Competition

For decades, primate models have been used to better understand the causes of human aggression (Kalin 1999). In particular, Kalin (1999) notes that these models have shown that "aggressive behavior is related to other emotional states and affective disorders" (p. 29) and can be classified into three categories that involve different neural mechanisms: defensive and fear motivated behavior, offensive and impulsive behavior, and self-injurious behavior. More recently, Wrangham and Glowacki (2012) argue that the chimpanzee model is an appropriate starting point for investigating the evolutionary roots of war and aggression. Simply, this model suggests that intergroup killing serves a strategic function, that is, "success in killing shifts the long-term balance of power toward the aggressor by increasing their numerical superiority, and hence their ability to win future contests over resources" (Wrangham and Glowacki 2012, p. 6). With this shift in power and status, individuals in the stronger coalition experience a rise in survival and reproductive success. Because of this, "selection has accordingly favored male tendencies to search for and take advantage of safe circumstances to cooperate in killing members of neighboring rival groups" (Wrangham and Glowacki 2012, p. 6).

Along these lines, Tooby and Cosmides (1988) suggest that in-group cooperation was most likely promoted through intergroup warfare, since conflict enabled a coalition to "coalesce, function, and sustain itself as a group of cooperating individuals" when attempting to gain access to competitive "reproductive enhancing resources" (p. 2). Moreover, Bowles (2006) proposes that lethal intergroup competition and the resulting consequence of selective group extinction can account for the evolution of altruism, since groups with more altruists survive when groups engage in conflict. That is to say, intergroup aggression is interlinked with altruism in that "an individual adopting these behaviors incurs mortal risks or foregoes beneficial opportunities for coalitions, coinsurance, and exchange, thereby incurring a fitness loss by comparison to those who eschew hostility towards other groups" (Choi and Bowles 2007, p. 636).

In other words, cooperation is, in part, a by-product of intergroup conflict. However, the chimpanzee model does not suggest that aggression is uncontrollably released periodically or that we suffer from a death instinct as Lorenz (1974) and Freud (1922) once posited. Rather, human behavior such as violence is sensitive to context and, thus, directed towards out-group members only when it is perceived to be safe and beneficial, since miscalculation of these factors could have a tragic outcome. Unfortunately, within the complex warfare that defines the modern era (Otterbein 2004), miscalculation occurs often. What we continuously see among political leaders is a misreading of the enemies' intentions and, consequently, a miscalculation of the likelihood of success following an attack. For this alone, deterrence can be difficult to maintain and surprise attacks hard to predict, with two obvious cases being Japan's attack on Pearl Harbor in 1941 and Israel's failure to anticipate the preemptive attack by its neighbors during the Yom Kippur War in 1973. The persistence of warfare in the international system suggests that deterrence and political decision making are much more complicated than the view of human nature provided by rational choice models that assume decisions on the use of violence are the product of deliberate cost–benefit calculations.

Evolutionary perspectives tell us that determining a safe and beneficial time to attack is often plagued with cognitive errors. For Johnson and his colleagues (2006), since incidences of war occur outside of the explanatory power of a rational approach, "states appear to overestimate their relative power…a recurrent theme among studies of the causes of war is that overconfidence is frequently associated with the outbreak of violence" (p. 2513). For some rationalists, these outbreaks cannot be explained or are considered to be a product of miscalculations caused by limited or distorted information. For others, they are simply a result of irrationality on behalf of the decision maker. However, evolutionary theory tells us that overestimation is not always an act of irrationality out of desperation, or a *fait accompli* strategy, but can be a product of evolved mechanisms. For example, evolutionary psychology posits that human social and political behavior is best understood "as the product of evolved psychological mechanisms that depend on internal and environmental input for their development, activation, and expression in manifest behavior" (Confer et al. 2010, p. 110). Like our most basic intuitive feelings, advances in the neurological and biological sciences have revealed that complex political behaviors, such as coalition building and intergroup warfare, may be interconnected with evolved mechanisms shaped by natural selection (Alford and Hibbing 2004).

In this sense, the overconfidence that leads a political leader to wage an unwinnable war can be seen as a product of a "positive illusion," that is, a motivational bias associated with perceived invulnerability to risk and an exaggeration of one's capabilities that can cause an illusion of control over events (Johnson and Fowler 2011). Positive illusions among individuals, groups, and nations offer, in part, a solution to the puzzle proposed by Fearon (1995) that falls outside of the explanatory power of traditional approaches to the causes of war. In other words, "the theory of positive illusions predicts that decision-makers will not rationally calculate the correct outcomes; rather, they will tend to overestimate the probability and/or the ease of their own victory and thus prefer war to any negotiated settlement that their adversary would accept" (Johnson 2004, p. 27).

Although rational choice theorists will most likely note that overconfidence violates conventional formulations of rationality, Johnson et al. (2011, p. 5) point out that "the appropriate metric of success in competitive situations is 'ecological rationality,'" that is to say, "the strategy that best exploits the prevailing environment." From an evolutionary perspective, we can see how overconfidence may have been favored by natural selection since exaggerating personal capabilities can have fitness enhancing qualities by improving the overall competitiveness and success of an individual among rivals.

However, there is a dark side to positive illusions. Overconfidence can also have a strategic disadvantage by putting greater emphasis on the use of aggression and conflict to achieve one's goals. This can lead to costly misperceptions and misjudgments about an enemy's capabilities and chances of winning. Overconfidence may cause policymakers to perceive the international security environment as offense dominant when in actuality it is defense dominant—the "cult of the offensive," or the strategy of the Allies during the First World War, is a clear example (Van Evera 1984).

In addition, Johnson and Tierney (2011) argue that overconfidence can trigger a switch from a "deliberative" to an "implemental" mindset, which causes decision makers to believe they have crossed a "psychological Rubicon," or a point of no return, and perceive war to be imminent. Once in this mindset, according to the authors, the chances of war increase significantly because the perceived high probability of military victory encourages the implementation of hawkish policies and aggressive stances. The research on positive illusion and the Rubicon theory of war provides us with a deeper understanding of why deterrence fails and nations go to war.

Supporting many of the hypotheses of evolutionary perspectives, recent studies from the field of social neuroscience have offered a great deal of insight into the neural content associated with human aggression. For example, dysfunction in testosterone levels has long been implicated in aggressive and violent behavior (Archer 2006). Testosterone is an androgenic steroid found in both men and women, but with much higher concentrations in the former. Among men, however, young men tend to show higher rates of aggression and physical violence, such as fighting and homicide, compared to older men (Archer 2004; Daly and Wilson 1988), especially those that are married with children (Gray et al. 2002). Differences in the testosterone levels between individuals can be attributed to both social and hereditary factors, but while both animal and human studies suggest that testosterone levels are linked to aggressive acts, such as fighting, assault, and dominance behavior, the role testosterone plays in aggression remains a polarized debate in the social science literature (Archer 1991). However, despite the controversy over the existence of a direct link between violence and testosterone, high levels of testosterone have been reported in populations of aggressive individuals, such as criminals with personality disorders, alcoholics, and spouse abusers (Siever 2008).

Furthermore, testosterone appears to play a decisive role in intergroup competition. A study of competing males found that "aggressive behavior and change in testosterone concentrations predicted willingness to reengage in another competitive task" (Carré 2008, p. 408). Moreover, Salvador and colleagues (2003) posit that accompanying this desire for competition associated with increased testosterone levels are psychological variables that increase performance success, such as high self-confidence and motivation to win, which in turn suggests "an adaptive psychobiological response to competition" (p. 373). Likewise, within the context of a simulated crisis game, a study by McDermott and colleagues (2007) found that "high-testosterone subjects are much more likely to engage in provoked attacks against their opponents than their lower-testosterone counterparts" (p. 30). Furthermore, the authors found that while the female participants were just as likely as the men to fight back once they were provoked, men were much more likely to initiate a conflict. More recently, a study by Flinn and his colleagues (2012) found that testosterone levels during competition were linked to whether the opponent was a friend or foe, which suggests that nuanced neuroendocrine mechanisms are sensitive to social context and linked to specific coalitionary behaviors of humans. Thus, "testosterone may enable physiological and psychological responses for fighting or mating, but also for the comradeship among a 'band of brothers'" (Flinn et al. 2012, p. 80).

Supporting these findings, Mehta and Beer (2010) have shown that testosterone increases aggressive behavior by reducing the ability of the medial orbito-frontal cortex (OFC) to govern self-regulation and impulse control following social provocation. In addition to affecting the OFC, a study by Derntl and colleagues (2009) found a correlation between testosterone levels and amygdala activation. Similar to its influence on the OFC, increased levels of testosterone improved the amygdala's ability to process threat-related stimuli, especially during episodes of anger and fear. Essentially, the higher the testosterone level, the faster, with more accuracy, the response, which suggests that "when confronted with human facial expressions, testosterone prepares females and males for further behavioral action by enforcing more automatic and autonomic processes leading to attentional shifts and decrease of subconscious fear thereby facilitating approach behavior" (Derntl et al. 2009, p. 691).

The Causes of Ethnic Conflict

One specific form of intergroup competition that has received a great deal of attention is ethnic conflict. This growing interest is no surprise given that since the end of the Cold War, we have witnessed an increase in ethnic conflicts around the world (Brown 2010). Indeed, as Figueredo and colleagues (2011) suggest, "negative ethnocentrism remains a major source of social conflict in the twenty-first century. Age-old ethnic rivalries continue to plague the modern world, including persistent and seemingly intractable conflicts in the Indian Subcontinent, Rwanda, the former Soviet Union, the former Yugoslavia, Palestine, and most recently in the Sudan and in Iraq" (p. 15). While there are many theoretical perspectives available for studying ethnic conflict, some more insightful than others, evolutionary perspectives combined with recent neuroscientific findings are particularly valuable for understanding the causes and implications of ethnic conflicts.

Evolutionary theory suggests that xenophobia (fear of foreigners) may have helped our ancestors compete against out-group members for resources and territory and avoid threats to survival posed by strangers (Pitman 2011; Thayer 2004). As a result, our brains are hardwired for prejudicial behavior when faced with uncertain or unclear situations involving out-group members, most commonly seen in unintended racial or discriminatory practices. Thus, we can see that bias in intergroup relations is an automatic response across populations because, as Tooby and Cosmides (1988) point out, coalitional aggression and prejudice (against different racial and ethnic groups) are produced by evolved mechanisms that improved overall fitness by enabling members of a coalition to gain access to reproduction-enhancing resources and detect coalitions and alliances (Kurzban et al. 2001).

Advances in neuroscience theory and method, such as the use of brain imaging techniques, provide us with a better understanding of the neuronal activity influencing xenophobic behavior, such as discrimination and prejudice, which in the right socio-political conditions can result in hyper-nationalism and intense ethnic conflict. Through these new approaches, we can begin to "explore the role of specific neural regions and systems in complex social psychological phenomena such as a person's perceptions and racial prejudice" (Derks et al. 2008, p. 164). Through an examination of the cognitive, affective, and behavioral structures associated with stereotyping and xenophobic responses, we can build a more accurate theory of how these structures influence people's beliefs and expectations about out-groups (Ochsner and Lieberman 2001). In fact, many neuroscience and social psychology studies have found that intergroup bias occurs automatically under minimal conditions among relatively unprejudiced people (Ashburn-Nardo et al. 2001; Fiske 2002; Ronquillo et al. 2007).

For example, the work of Harris and Fiske (2006) tells us that we first need to uncover the neural and biological mechanisms that trigger automatic biases to better understand the causes of ethnic conflicts. Evidence from brain imaging studies of extreme out-group bias concluded that severe prejudice can dehumanize targets and possibly lead to genocidal actions. Using the stereotype content model, Harris and Fiske (2006) found that in-group/out-group interactions trigger four distinct emotional responses within the contexts of friend–foe judgment (level of warmth) and capability judgment (level of competence): pride, envy, pity, and disgust.

Harris and Fiske (2006) found that some groups stereotyped as highly competent and warm, "elicit the in-group emotions of pride and admiration" (p. 852), while, on the other end of the spectrum, those stereotyped as significantly incompetent with little compassion, or warmth, evoke absolute disgust to the extent that the group members were viewed as less human, or were completely dehumanized. Interestingly, it is with this latter discriminatory categorization and the emotional responses it evokes that the conditions for severe violence and brutality against a specific population or small group of people are made possible, that is to say "the all-too human ability to commit atrocities such as hate crimes, prisoner abuse, and genocide against people who are dehumanized" (Harris and Fiske 2006, p. 847).

At the neuronal level, fMRI scanning shows that extreme discrimination and disgust not only evoke significant response in the amygdala (signifying fear and threat), but also decrease activation of the medial prefrontal cortex (mPFC). Since mPFC activation has been observed in "social cognition tasks in which participants form an impression of a person, rather than an object" (Mitchell et al. 2005, p. 255), little to no activity in the mPFC during interactions with a specific group possibly suggests that the individuals of the target group are valued more as objects than humans.

Along similar lines, a growing number of studies have begun to unravel the neural correlates of processing race. A review by Ito and Bartholow (2009) found that brain imaging and electrophysiological methods have become important tools for studying racial stereotypes and prejudice. For example, in a study by Hart and his colleagues (2000) addressing how perceptions of out-group members differ from in-group members, White and Black participants viewed photographs of unfamiliar White and Black faces while undergoing fMRI. For all participants, "the rate of response habituation within the amygdala to face stimuli [was] dependent upon an interaction between the race of the subjects and the perceived race of the face stimuli" (p. 2353). These results suggest that the amygdala exhibits greater response to unfamiliar, and possibly threatening, faces than to familiar faces. Given the amygdala's role of "relevance detector" (Sander et al. 2003), which includes, but is not limited to, fear-related stimuli, the prejudice and anxiety that occurs between in-group and out-group members during initial interactions can lessen over time through prolonged exposure or, as a study by Kurzban and colleagues (2001) found, by manipulating coalition formation and reestablishing coalition membership across racial cleavages.

It is important to note, however, that even though evidence suggests that attention to race is a byproduct of mechanisms that allowed our ancestors to distinguish alliances and detect threats, discrimination can occur between members of the in-group as well. For example, an fMRI study of the amygdala's sensitivity to race revealed that both African-American and Caucasian-American participants showed greater amygdala response to Black faces than to White faces (Lieberman et al. 2005). Since amygdala activity in African-American participants exhibited greater response to the Black target faces, the authors speculate: "the amygdala activity typically associated with race-related processing may be a reflection of culturally learned negative associations regarding African-American individuals" (Lieberman et al. 2005, p. 722). Supporting this finding, a recent fMRI study by Schreiber and Iacoboni (2012) suggests that the amygdala activity associated with negative racial attitudes appears to be driven more by norm violations than race, such as political and sociocultural differences. In other words, intergroup prejudice and discrimination is a biological and cultural phenomenon.

This can be further seen in a study on social cognition in people from different cultural backgrounds that found increased activation in the precuneus (PC) among Israeli and Arab participants as they read pro-out-group versus pro-in-group statements (Bruneau and Saxe 2010). Activation in the PC is believed to signify emotional reasoning during difficult moral judgments of harmful behavior (Greene et al. 2001), which suggests, according to the authors, "strong ingroup bias in evaluating the reasonableness of partisan statements [about the Middle East]" (Bruneau and Saxe 2010, p. 1709). Although these findings support previous research on neuronal and evolutionary reasons for prejudice and stereotypes in intergroup relations, the particularly high level of in-group bias among Israelis and Arabs is undoubtedly exacerbated by the politically hostile context that those participants interact within on a daily basis, which in turn can make extremely aggressive conflict between such groups significantly more likely and harder to mitigate.

The Neurobiology of Cultural Conflict

With these findings that the xenophobia and prejudice underlying ethnic conflict is, in part, caused by perceptions of norm violations, it is necessary to now turn our attention to the neurobiology of cultural conflict. Although "biology" and "culture" have traditionally been approached separately, giving way to the famous nature versus nurture debate, Berns and Atran (2012) posit that advances in the life sciences suggest that these two forms of the human condition are intertwined and cannot be easily separated. Rather, according Berns and Atran (2012), it is important to recognize that cultural conflicts occur when the beliefs and traditions of an in-group are challenged by individuals of an out-group, which has been shown to elicit brain activity involved in "cognitive decision-making, emotional activation and physiological arousal associated with the outbreak, conduct and resolution of conflict" (p. 633). In fact, cultural and physical anthropologists are collaborating to produce evolutionary perspectives on cross-cultural anthropology, in turn providing explanations for "the ultimate causes" of human behaviors and cultural traits (Jordan and Huber 2013). However, this approach to cultural conflict is not synonymous with Huntington's (1993) class of civilization thesis, or other generalized understandings of cultural difference, but rather suggests that cultural processes and capabilities, such as social learning, can, in part, be explained by Darwinian-like processes (Whiten et al. 2011).

For example, Gelfand and colleagues (2012) propose a cultural transmission model of intergroup conflict in which "conflict contagion" is argued to be a consequence of universal human traits, such as in-group preference, out-group hostility, and parochial altruism. For example, the authors found that an individual's honor is more intertwined in collectivist than individualist cultures, in which "harming a person creates a contagion effect that involves a large web of people in collectivistic groups…honour is interchangeable, especially among one's family and extended networks; and it is contagious, one person's honour harm is capable of harming others throughout the broader society" (Gelfand et al. 2012, p. 698). In fact, studies of young children have found evidence of parochialism and preference for one's own social group (Fehr et al. 2008), as well as that even young children expect category membership to more strongly constrain prosocial (group obligations) and antisocial behaviors and link identity and behavior to category membership (Rhodes and Brickman 2011).

According to Bowles and Gintis (2011), protecting sociocultural norms, and punishing those that break them, has an evolutionary explanation. In the context of shared social tasks, to cooperate with others and punish those who violate cooperative norms, even at a personal cost, allowed for the adaption of a universal structure of human morality. Bowles and Gintis refer to this adaptive behavior of protecting norms and punishing violators as strong reciprocity, and argue that through this structure of morality, cooperation both within and between groups increases, which is especially beneficial in an ancestral environment defined by intergroup competition for resources and survival (Gintis et al. 2008).

Within the context of cultural conflict, in-group members seek to delegitimize the competing values and beliefs of out-groups in order to protect the social norms that unite the group, which often results in lack of compassion for out-group members. Cikara and Fiske's (2012) work demonstrates how the failure to empathize with out-groups during competition and conflict produces *Schadenfreude* (pleasure in response to another's misfortunes) toward out-group individuals, specifically against high-status, competitive groups. Cikara et al. (2011) note that these findings suggest that our brains consist of "evolutionary old neural systems, which may have developed to respond to physically rewarding and painful stimuli in the service of reinforcing adaptive behavior" (p. 311), and have evolved to "encode group-level rewards and punishments" (p. 311). A similar fMRI study by Takahashi and colleagues (2009) found that envy of a competitor's superior and self-relevant characteristics was linked to stronger anterior cingulate cortex (ACC) activation and, in the case of stronger feelings of *Schadenfreude,* increased striatum activation occurred when misfortune happened to envied persons.

With the changing political and socio-cultural landscapes brought on by globalization, we can expect that the increasing number of migrants traveling to host countries for employment and access to better resources will exacerbate historical and contemporary cultural tensions and, more than likely, cause political instability. Numerous studies have shown that decision making within a condition of uncertainty causes actors to make emotionally biased decisions that are often absent of rational calculations. Cryder and Lerner (2009) point out that emotions like fear and surprise increase during conditions of uncertainty and have been linked with "increased depth of information processing and increased perceptions of risk" (p. 395), which can influence how individuals predict and understand a situation. At the neuronal level, during periods of increased stress, fear, and anxiety, catecholamines, a family of neurotransmitters that include epinephrine, norepinephrine, and dopamine, are released into the peripheral and central nervous systems, and this increase causes the body to prepare for a fight-or-flight situation. During this time, the amygdala is activated and the prefrontal cortex (or the higher cognitive center) is shutdown, enabling posterior cortical and subcortical mechanisms to significantly influence behavior in an emotionally biased way with limited, if any, "rational" oversight (Arnsten 1998).

Such research on the neuropsychological underpinnings of extreme prejudice, *Schadenfreude,* and uncertainty speaks to why the Israeli–Palestine and Uighur–Han Chinese conflicts (among many others) persist and why political leaders on both sides continue to take aggressive stances towards the other in the attempt to protect and assert in-group norms, beliefs, and values.

Conclusion

This chapter provided an overview of evolutionary perspectives on conflict. We conclude by offering two observations about the significance of this chapter and its influence on the study of war and aggression. First, evolution provides important and largely neglected insights for this field of study. It is important to understand both the ultimate and proximate causes of conflict as illuminated by evolutionary theory so that scholars and policymakers can better predict the circumstances in which it may occur. Such a comprehension of the ultimate and proximate causes of warfare will help policymakers prevent war in some instances, or else to advance policies designed to minimize suffering. Given the crucial importance of conflict in international politics, scholars should explore every major explanation that contributes to understanding its origins. In essence, to prevent the deleterious consequences that stem from war, including violence against noncombatants and human rights abuses, we need to understand the origins of these behaviors.

Social science theories that depend heavily on psychology—such as theories of decision making and of cognitive misperception—will benefit by incorporating both evolutionary theory and the advances in other fields we have identified in this chapter. As the life sciences advance, we will understand more of human behavior as evolutionary theorists, biologists, and geneticists discover and map evolution's full impact on the human mind. Great advances will be made in both evolutionary psychology and psychiatry as the mind is mapped, and we will better comprehend both its physiology and the ways it evolved to solve problems our ancestors encountered in past environments. As one consequence of this research, theories of decision making will be greatly improved as scientists discover how the mind makes decisions, weighs preferences, and prioritizes data or information. These advances hold great promise for the study of war and aggression, perhaps most importantly for scholarship on leaders' decision making: How do they form psychological images of threats? Why do they form these images? What are the cognitive origins of conflict and misperception?

Second, and more broadly, the more we learn about human evolution the more we recognize what makes us human. Recognizing this, we can better understand life in the natural world: what makes us unique as humans and what makes us akin to other animals, from our "cousin" the chimpanzee, to our more distant relatives. As Wilson (1984) explains in his wonderfully titled *Biophilia:* "Humanity is exalted not because we are so far above other living creatures, but because knowing them well elevates the very concept of life" (p. 22). Humans are not separate from evolution and the ecology of the natural world; it influences us in countless ways, from natural selection to the blowback effect of environmental destruction. Understanding the evolutionary origin of warfare, ethnic conflict, and other forms of aggression is a first and necessary step to reducing their likelihood and deleterious effects.

References

Alford, J. R., & Hibbing, J. R. (2004). The origin of politics: An evolutionary theory of political behavior. *Perspectives on Politics, 2,* 707–723.

Arnsten, A. F. T. (1998). The biology of being frazzled. *Science, 280,* 1711–1712.

Anderson, S. W., Bechara, A., Damasio, H., Tranel, D., & Damasio, D. (1999). Impairment of social and moral behavior related to early damage in human prefrontal cortex. *Nature Neuroscience, 2,* 1032–1037.

Archer, J. (1991). The influence of testosterone on human aggression. *British Journal of Psychology, 82,* 1–28.

Archer, J. (2004). Sex differences in aggression in real-world settings: A meta-analysis. *Review of General Psychology, 8,* 291–322.

Archer, J. (2006). Testosterone and human aggression: An evaluation of the challenge hypothesis. *Neuroscience and Biobehavioral Reviews, 30,* 319–345.

Ashburn-Nardo, L., Voils, C. I., & Monteith, M. J. (2001). Implicit associations as the seeds of intergroup bias: How easily do they take root? *Journal of Personality and Social Psychology, 81,* 789–799.

Berns, G. S., & Atran, S. (2012). The biology of conflict. *Philosophical Transactions of the Royal Society B, 367,* 633–639.

Bowles, S. (2006). Group competition, reproductive leveling, and the evolution of human altruism. *Science, 314,* 1569–1572.

Bowles, S. (2009). Did warfare among ancestral hunter-gatherers affect the evolution of human social behavior. *Science, 324,* 1293–1298.

Bowles, S., & Gintis, H. (2011). *A cooperative species: Human reciprocity and its evolution.* Princeton: Princeton University Press.

Brown, M. E. (2010). Causes and implications of ethnic conflict. In M. Guibernau & J. Rex (Eds.), *The ethnicity reader: Nationalism, multiculturalism, & migration* (2nd ed., pp. 92–109). United Kingdom: Polity Press.

Bruneau, E. G., & Saxe, R. (2010). Attitudes towards the outgroup are predicted by activity in the precuneus in Arabs and Israelis. *NeuroImage, 52,* 1704–1711.

Buss, D. M. (2013). *Evolutionary psychology: The new science of the mind* (4th ed.). Boston: Pearson.

Buss, D., & Shackelford, T. K. (1997). Human aggression in evolutionary psychological perspective. *Clinical Psychology Review, 17,* 605–619.

Carré, J. M., & McCormick, C. M. (2008). Aggressive behavior and change in salivary testosterone concentrations predict willingness to engage in a competitive task. *Hormones and Behavior, 54,* 403–409.

Choi, J. K., & Bowles, S. (2007). The coevolution of parochial altruism and war. *Science, 318,* 636–640.

Cikara, M., & Fiske, S. T. (2012). Stereotypes and schadenfreude: Affective and physiological markers of pleasure at outgroup misfortunes. *Social Psychological and Personality Science, 3,* 63–71.

Cikara, M., Botvinick, M. M., & Fiske, S. T. (2011). Us versus them: Social identity shapes neural responses to intergroup competition and harm. *Psychological Science, 22,* 306–313.

Confer, J. C., Easton, J. A., Fleischman, D. S., Goetz, C. D., Lewis, D. M. G., Perilloux, C., & Buss, D. (2010). Evolutionary psychology: Controversies, questions, prospects, and limitations. *American Psychologist, 65,* 110–126.

Cosmides, L., & Tooby, J. (2013). Evolutionary psychology: New perspectives on cognition and motivation. *Annual Review of Psychology, 64,* 201–229.

Cryder, C., & Lerner, J. (2009). Uncertainty. In K. Scherer & D. Sander (Eds.), *Oxford companion to emotion and the affective sciences* (p. 395). New York: Oxford University Press.

Daly, M., & Wilson, M. (1988). *Homicide.* New York: Aldine de Gruyter.

Damasio, A. (2005). *Descartes' error: Emotion, reason, and the human brain.* New York: Penguin Books.

Derks, B., Inzlicht, M., & Kang, S. (2008). The neuroscience of stigma and stereotype threat. *Group Processes and Intergroup Relations, 11,* 161–181.

Derntl, B., Windischerger, C., Robinson, S., Kryspin-Exner, I., Gur, R. C., Moser, E., & Habel, U. (2009). Amygdala activity to fear and anger in healthy young males is associated with testosterone. *Psychoneuroendocrinology, 34,* 687–693.

Fearon, J. D. (1995). Rationalist explanations for war. *International Organizations, 49,* 379–414.

Fehr, E., Bernhard, H., & Rockenbach, B. (2008). Egalitarianism in young children. *Nature, 454,* 1079–1083.

Figueredo, A. J., Andrzejczak, D. J., Jones, D. N., Smith-Castro, V., & Montero, E. (2011). Reproductive strategy and ethnic conflict: Slow life history as a protective factor against negative ethnocentrism in two contemporary societies. *Journal of Social, Evolutionary, and Cultural Psychology, 5,* 14–31.

Fiske, S. T. (2002). What we know about bias and intergroup conflict, the problem of the century. *Current Directions in Psychological Science, 11,* 123–128.

Flinn, M. V., Ponzi, D., & Muehlenbein, M. P. (2012). Hormonal mechanisms for regulation of aggression in human coalitions. *Human Nature, 23,* 68–88.

Fowler, J., & Schreiber, D. (2008). Biology, politics and the emerging science of human nature. *Science, 322,* 912–914.

Freud, S. (1922). *Beyond the pleasure principle* (trans. C. J. M. Hubback). London: International Psycho-Analytical Press.

Friend, J. M., & Thayer, B. A. (2012). Evolution and foreign policy: Insights for decision-making models. In A. Somit & S. A. Peterson (Eds.), *Biopolicy: The life sciences and public policy* (pp. 97–118). United Kingdom: Emerald.

Gazzaniga, M. S. (2006). *The ethical brain: The science of our moral dilemmas*. New York: Harper Perennial.

Gefland, M., Shteynberg, G., Lee, T., Lun, J., Lyons, S., Bell, C., & Chiao, J. Y., et al. (2012). The cultural contagion of conflict. *Philosophical Transactions of Royal Society B, 367,* 692–703.

Ginges, J., & Atran, S. (2011). War as a moral imperative (not just practical politics by other means). *Proceedings of the Royal Society B, 278,* 2930–2938.

Gintis, H., Henrich, J., Bowles, S., Boyd, R., & Fehr, E. (2008). Strong reciprocity and the roots of human morality. *Social Justice Research, 21,* 241–253.

Gray, P. B., Kahlenberg, S. M., Barrett, E. S., Lipson, S. L., & Ellison, P. T. (2002). Marriage and fatherhood are associated with lower testosterone in males. *Evolution and Human Behavior, 23,* 193–201.

Greene, J. D., Sommerville, B. R., Nystrom, L. E., Darley, J. M., & Cohen, J. D. (2001). An fMRI investigation of emotional engagement in moral judgment. *Science, 293,* 2105–2108.

Gross-Stein, J., & Tanter, R. (1980). *Rational decision-making: Israel's security choices, 1967*. Columbus: The Ohio State University Press.

Hatemi, P. K., & McDermott, R. (2011). Man is by nature a political animal: Evolution, biology, and politics. Chicago: The University of Chicago Press.

Harris, L. T., & Fiske, S. T. (2006). Dehumanizing the lowest of the low: Neuroimaging responses to extreme out-groups. *Psychological Science, 17,* 847–853.

Hart, A. J., Whalen, P. J., Shin, L. M., McInerney, S. C., Fischer, H., & Rauch, S. L. (2000). Differential response in the human amygdala to racial outgroup vs ingroup face stimuli. *NeuroReport, 11,* 2351–2354.

Huntington, S. P. (1993). The class of civilizations? *Foreign Affairs, 72,* 22–49.

Ito, T. A., & Bartholow, B. D. (2009). The neural correlates of race. *Trends in Cognitive Science, 13,* 524–531.

Jervis, R. (1976). *Perceptions and misperception in international politics*. Princeton: Princeton University Press.

Jervis, R., Lebow, R. N., & Gross-Stein, J. (1989). *Psychology and deterrence*. Baltimore: Johns Hopkins University Press.

Johnson, D. D. P. (2004). *Overconfidence and war: The havoc and glory of positive illusions*. Cambridge: Harvard University Press.

Johnson, D. D. P., & Fowler, J. (2011). The evolution of overconfidence. *Nature, 477,* 317–320.

Johnson, D. D. P., & Tierney, D. (2011). The rubicon theory of war: How the path to conflict reaches the point of no return. *International Security, 36,* 7–40.

Johnson, D. D. P., & Tierney, T. (2006). *Failing to win: Perceptions of victory and defeat in international politics*. Cambridge: Harvard University Press.

Johnson, D. D. P., McDermott, R., Barrett, E. S., Cowden, J., Wragham, R., McIntyre, M. H., & Rosen, S. P. (2006). Overconfidence in wargames: Experimental evidence on expectations, aggression, gender, and testosterone. *Proceedings of the Royal Society B, 272,* 2513–2520.

Johnson, D. D. P., Weidmann, N. B., & Cederman, L. E. (2011). Fortune favours the bold: An agent-based model reveals adaptive advantages of overconfidence in war. *PLoS ONE, 6,* e20851.

Jordan, F. M., & Huber, B. R. (2013). Evolutionary approaches to cross-cultural anthropology. *Cross-Cultural Research, 47,* 91–101.

Kalin, N. H. (1999). Primate models to understand human aggression. *Journal of Clinical Psychiatry, 60,* 29–32.

Keeley, L. H. (1997). *War before civilization: The myth of the peaceful savage*. United Kingdom: Oxford University Press.

Kurzban, R. (2012). *Why everyone (else) is a hypocrite: Evolution and the modular mind*. Princeton: Princeton University Press.

Kurzban, R., Tooby, J., & Cosmides, L. (2001). Can race be erased? Coalitional computation and social categorization. *Proceedings of the National Academy of Science, 98,* 15387–15392.

LeDoux, J. (2003). *Synaptic self: How our brains become who we are*. New York: Penguin.

Liddle, J. R., Shackelford, T. K., & Weekes-Shackelford, V. A. (2012). Why can't we all just get along? Evolutionary perspectives on violence, homicide, and war. *Review of General Psychology, 16,* 24–35.

Lieberman, M. D., Hariri, A., Jarcho, J. M., Eisenberger, N. I., & Bookheimer, S. Y. (2005). An fMRI investigation of race-related amygdala activity in African-American and Caucasian-American individuals. *Nature Neuroscience, 8,* 720–722.

Lorenz, K. (1974). *On aggression* (trans. M. K. Wilson). New York: Mariner Books.

Masters, R. D. (1991). *The nature of politics*. New Haven: Yale University Press.

McDermott, R. (2004). The feeling of rationality: The meaning of neuroscientific advances for political science. *Perspectives on Politics, 2,* 691–706.

McDermott, R., Johnson, D., Cowden, J., & Rosen, S. (2007). Testosterone and aggression in a simulated crisis game. *The Annals of the American Academy of Political and Social Science, 614,* 15–33.

Mearsheimer, J. (2001). *Tragedy of great power politics*. New York: W.W. Norton & Company.

Mehta, P. H., & Beer, J. (2010). Neural mechanisms of the testosterone-aggression relation: The role of orbitofrontal cortex. *Journal of Cognitive Neuroscience, 22,* 2357–2368.

Mitchell, J. P., Banaji, M. R., & Macrae, C. N. (2005). The link between social cognition and self-referential thought in the medial prefrontal cortex. *Journal of Cognitive Neuroscience, 17,* 1306–1315.

Mozes, A. (2001). Violent images activate brain region: Study. *Reuters*, 18 November 2001.

Ochsner, K. N., & Lieberman, M. D. (2001). The emergence of social cognitive neuroscience. *American Psychologist, 56,* 717–734.

Otterbein, K. F. (1997). The origins of war. *Critical Review: A Journal of Politics and Society, 11,* 251–277.

Otterbein, K. F. (2004). *How war began*. College Station: Texas A & M University press.

Peterson, S. A., & Somit, A. (1978). Methodological problems associated with a biologically-oriented social science. *Journal of Social and Biological Structures, 1,* 11–25

Pinker, S. (2011). *The better angels of our nature: Why violence has declined*. New York: Viking.

Pitman, G. R. (2011). The evolution of human warfare. *Philosophy of the Social Sciences, 41,* 352–379.

Rhodes, M., & Brickman, D. (2011). The influence of competition on children's social categories. *Journal of Cognition and Development, 12,* 194–221.

Ronquillo, J., Denson, T. F., Lickel, B., Lu, Z. L., Nandy, A., & Maddox, K. B. (2007). The effects of skin tone on race-related amygdala activity: An fMRI investigation. *SCAN, 2,* 39–44.

Salvador, A., Suay, F., Gonzalez-Bono, E., & Serrano, M. A. (2003). Anticipatory cortisol, testosterone and psychological response to judo competition in young men. *Psychoneuroendocrinology, 28,* 364–375.

Sander, D., Grafman, J., & Zalla, T. (2003). The human amygdala: An evolved system for relevance detection. *Reviews in the Neurosciences, 14,* 303–316.

Schreiber, D., & Iacoboni, M. (2012). Huxtables on the brain: An fMRI study of race and norm violation. *Political Psychology, 33,* 313–330.

Schubert, G. (1983). Evolutionary politics. *Political Research Quarterly, 36,* 175–193.

Sell, A., Tooby, J., & Cosmides, L. (2009). Formidability and the logic of human anger. *Proceedings of the National Academy of Science, 106,* 15073–15078.

Siever, L. J. (2008). Neurobiology of aggression and violence. *American Journal of Psychiatry, 165,* 429–442.

Somit, A. (1968). Toward a more biologically-oriented political science: Ethology and psychopharmacology. *Midwest Journal of Political Science, 12,* 550–567.

Somit, A. (1976). *Biology and politics: Recent explorations*. The Hague: Mouton.

Stavridis, J. (2014). The dawning of the age of biology. Financial Times, 19 January 2014.

Takahashi, H., Kato, M., Matsuura, M., Mobbs, D., Suhara, T., & Okubu, Y. (2009). When your pain is my pain and your pain is my gain: Neural correlates of envy and schadenfreude. *Science, 323,* 937–939.

Thayer, B. A. (2004). *Darwin and international relations: On the evolutionary origins of war and ethnic conflict*. Lexington: The University Press of Kentucky.

Tooby, J., & Cosmides, L. (1988). The evolution of war and its cognitive foundations. Institute for Evolutionary Studies Technical Reports 88–1.

Van Evera, S. (1984). The cult of the offensive and the origins of the First World War. *International Security, 9,* 58–107.

von Clausewitz, C. (1989). *On war* (trans. M. E. Howard & P. Paret). Princeton: Princeton University Press.

Waltz, K. (1979). *Theory of international politics*. New York: McGraw-Hill.

Whiten, A., Hinde, R. A., Laland, K., & Stringer, C. B. (2011). Culture evolves. *Philosophical Transactions of Royal Society B, 366,* 938–948.

Wilson, E. O. (1984). *Biophilia*. Cambridge: Harvard University Press.

Wrangham, R., & Glowacki, L. (2012). Intergroup aggression in chimpanzees and war in nomadic hunter-gatherers. *Human Nature, 23,* 5–29.

Social Competition and Bullying: An Adaptive Socioecological Perspective

30

Anthony A. Volk, Victoria Della Cioppa, Megan Earle and Ann H. Farrell

The human brain evolved, in part, to deal with other human brains. While humans are perhaps the most cooperative species (Hrdy 2009), they are also quite competitive (Pinker 2011). One expression of this competition is deliberate, harmful aggression in the context of power imbalance, also known as bullying. At its minimum, bullying is a dyadic process. At its maximum, it can involve entire communities. Thus, bullying is an inherently social process, making a social psychological perspective exceptionally helpful for understanding human bullying.

In this chapter, we examine bullying from multiple social perspectives, drawing from an evolutionary socioecological framework that emphasizes the adaptive fit of an organism to multiple layers of social context (Bronfenbrenner 2009; Volk et al. 2012a, 2012b). We examine factors at the microsystem (Bronfenbrenner 2009) where individual personality factors influence bullying. We then turn to the influence of competition in the immediate social environment, or mesosystem, among peers at school and in sports. We follow this by examining an even broader social context in the exosystem, or community level, by studying the impact of wealth and income inequality on bullying. Finally, we examine the macrosystem, where cultural factors wield influence. Together, these multiple socioecological contexts yield a rich picture of the influence of various social factors on bullying built upon an adaptive understanding of bullying. First, however, we review the general evidence for bullying as adaptive behavior.

Bullying in Animals

Before turning to bullying in humans, we begin by examining the social context of bullying in nonhuman animals as a means of illustrating the potential evolutionary benefits of bullying. While examples of bullying abound across many forms of life, bullying is particularly common in social mammals (Volk et al. 2012a). Most mammals operate under a polygynous mating system whereby a dominant male can monopolize access to reproductive females at the expense of other males (Alcock 1989). The intimidation and physical dominance by more powerful males against weaker males is an intentional behavior that harms the nondominant animals' reproduc-

A. A. Volk (✉)
Department of Child and Youth Studies, Brock University, 344 Cairns, St. Catharines, ON L2S 3A1, Canada
e-mail: tony.volk@brocku.ca

V. Della Cioppa
Department of Psychology, Queen's University, K7L 3N6 Kingston, ON, Canada
e-mail: 13vdc@queensu.ca

A. H. Farrell · M. Earle
Department of Psychology, Brock University, 344 Cairns, L2S 3A1 St. Catharines, ON, Canada
e-mail: af08tl@badger.ac.brocku.ca

M. Earle
me11tt@badger.ac.brocku.ca

V. Zeigler-Hill et al. (eds.), *Evolutionary Perspectives on Social Psychology,* Evolutionary Psychology, DOI 10.1007/978-3-319-12697-5_30, © Springer International Publishing Switzerland 2015

tive success, making it a clear form of bullying. The importance of bullying as an adaptive male behavior is reflected in the disparity between the size and strength of the sexes in most mammals, with males' larger body size reflecting their more frequent sexual conflict (Alcock 1989). Larger body size is advantageous in a physical competition of near-equals, but its most significant function may be deterring competition from those who are significantly weaker.

Bullying over reproductive opportunities is not the exclusive domain of males. In a number of social mammalian carnivores (e.g., wolves: Mech 1970; African wild dogs: Scott 1991, Creel and Creel 2002; banded mongoose: Bell et al. 2012) the dominant female will harass and attack subordinates who try to breed, as well as kill infants who are not their own. Again, this is a clear case of bullying whereby a more powerful animal causes harm to a weaker individual. Dominant females may be joined by other females, turning the bullying from a dyadic event to a group event. In a primate example, a mother and daughter chimpanzee (Passion and Pom) were observed teaming up to attack other females and kill their offspring (Goodall 1986). Initially believed to be a pathological behavior, dominant or team female infanticide has since been seen in other chimpanzees (Townsend et al. 2007), suggesting it is an evolved form of bullying that harms the reproductive success of rivals, rather than a pathological behavior.

Bullying also occurs over nonreproductive resources. Male lions use their larger size to harass and intimidate female lions from feeding (Scheel and Packer 1991). Female hyenas also use their larger size and dominance to monopolize food resources from males and other females (Stewart 1987). Among primates, male chimpanzees not only bully other males over resources but they also attempt to monopolize valued and scarce resources, such as monkey flesh (Goodall 1986). Similar food-related bullying behaviors are seen in many primate species (e.g., yellow baboons: Post et al. 1980).

Finally, although rare, animals sometimes bully for status in the absence of immediate or imminent mating or feeding opportunities. Dominance hierarchies are often used as an example of the link between bullying and social status (Kolbert and Crothers 2003), but most mammalian dominance hierarchies exist within the content of immediate or imminent access to food or mates. There are some examples of bullying in the absence of immediate or imminent rewards, and most are found amongst primates. Female hanuman langurs harass male newcomers in support of an existing dominant male (Hrdy 1999), presumably to hinder the new male's ability to rise in the dominance hierarchy. Another example of bullying in the absence of immediate rewards is the example of Frodo, a chimpanzee observed by Goodall (1986) at Gombe. Unlike other males who used a combination of physical strength, social displays, and social coalitions to obtain and maintain dominance, Frodo appeared to rely solely on physical bullying to maintain his status as alpha male. He regularly attacked and harassed weaker individuals within his group in the absence of imminent mating or feeding opportunities. There is therefore considerable evidence for bullying serving an adaptive function in securing mating, feeding, and dominance opportunities in animals. But is there evidence for bullying being similarly adaptive for humans?

Bullying in Humans: Evidence for an Adaptation

There is indeed evidence suggesting that bullying in humans may be, at least in part, an evolutionary adaptation (Volk et al. 2012b). Similar to other animals, humans bully for resources, mates, and dominance status. Adolescent bullies are able to get physical resources, such as food, money, consumer goods, and preferred playing or eating areas (Volk et al. 2012b). Adolescent bullies also get more dates, more dating partners, and are more likely to have lost their virginity (Connolly et al. 2000; Volk et al. submitted). Finally, adolescent bullies not only start with high levels of popularity and dominance (Salmivalli 2010) but they also increase their popularity and dominance over time due to their bullying behavior (Reijntjes et al. 2013). Thus, bullying offers advantages relevant to evolutionary selection. Bullying also is relatively low in terms of its costs, as several studies note that pure bullies (i.e., individuals who bully others, but who are not bullied in return) report equal or better mental health than uninvolved adolescents and victims (Berger 2007; Ireland 2005; Juvonen et al. 2003; Volk et al. 2006; Wolke et al. 2001). Bullying is also positively linked with other social/mental traits, such as theory of mind ability, cognitive empathy, leadership, social competence, and self-efficacy (Caravita et al. 2009, 2010; Vaillancourt et al. 2003).

Bullying is ubiquitous, having been found in every modern society in which its measurements have been undertaken (e.g., Elgar et al. 2009). When combined with the ubiquity of bullying across historical time and cultures (Volk et al. 2012a), this lends credence to bullying being an evolved adaptation. Bullying is also remarkably resistant to interventions (Merrell et al. 2008; Ttofi and Farrington 2011), with some data suggesting that bullying is more similar to an evolved predisposition than to a socially learned behavior (Garandeau et al. 2013). Lastly, bullying is strongly heritable (Ball et al. 2008), which suggests that there is sufficient genetic linkage with the behavior for selection to act upon.

Taken together, the evidence is compelling that bullying in humans is, at least in part, an adaptation. We seek to expand this evidence by examining bullying from a socioecological perspective that emphasizes the importance of personality as well as environmental factors. Inspired by Bronfenbrenner's (2009) socioecological model that views the individual in the center of expanding concentric circles of social influence, we examine how bullying is adaptive across a variety of socioecological contexts. We begin by examining the innermost circle, the microsystem, to determine how individual differences in personality relate to differences in bullying behavior from an adaptive perspective.

Bullying and Personality

There have been few studies of bullying and personality. Personality is an important predictor of individual behavior that has a strong degree of heritability (Veselka et al. 2010). Early studies of bullying using the Eysenck measure of personality (Eysenck and Eysenck 1975) reported heightened levels of psychoticism and modest increases in extraversion and neuroticism amongst bullies compared to controls (Connolly and O'Moore 2003; Mynard and Joseph 1997; Slee and Rigby 1993). There have also been a few studies of bullying and the Big Five personality traits that demonstrated a strong link between bullying and low levels of agreeableness, as well as weaker links (in some studies) with higher neuroticism and lower conscientiousness (Bollmer et al. 2006; Menesini et al. 2010; Tani et al. 2003). However, the strong personality link with Agreeableness is, in a sense, circular because bullying is by its nature disagreeable behavior, making the Big Five a potentially poor choice for examining bullying.

In contrast, the Honesty-Humility, Emotionality, Extraversion, Agreeableness, Conscientiousness, Openness to Experience (HEXACO) scale of personality differs from the Big Five in that it is a six-factor model of personality that has greater cross-cultural validity (Ashton and Lee 2001) and an evolutionary theoretical foundation (Ashton and Lee, 2007). Specifically, the HEXACO posits that personality traits exist upon a continuum, with different adaptive advantages for individuals across the continuum (Ashton and Lee 2007). There is a primary domain related to kin selection (Emotionality) and reciprocal altruism (Honesty-Humility and Agreeableness). This helps differentiate a willingness to exploit (Honesty-Humility, predatory behavior) from a willingness to be exploited (Agreeableness, retaliatory behavior). When the HEXACO was applied in a study of bullying (Book et al. 2012), it was found that bullying was predicted by Honesty-Humility (i.e., a willingness to exploit), but not by Agreeableness (i.e., a willingness to be exploited). This fits with a description of successful general aggression as being bistrategic, whereby individuals employ aggressive strategies while remaining open to cooperation (Hawley 1999). Indeed, bullying is predicted by proactive (predatory), but not reactive (retaliatory) aggression (Book et al. 2012).

While general bullying (along with verbal, social, and sexual bullying) is best predicted by low levels of Honesty-Humility, some subtypes of bullying are best predicted by different aspects of the HEXACO (Farrell et al. in press). Physical bullying is predicted by low levels of Conscientiousness, presumably because it is a riskier form of aggression engaged in by individuals who lacked a strong concern about rules or self-regulation. Racial bullying is predicted by low levels of Emotionality, presumably because it represents a low level of empathy and concern for other individuals combined with a low worry about escalating conflict between groups. Thus, bullying is related to individual differences in personality. This helps explain why not all individuals engage in bullying, as it appears that different levels of personality traits may vary in how adaptive they are in different contexts (Farrell et al. in press). For example, a low level of Honesty-Humility allows individuals to bully and exploit other individuals, but it may hinder cooperative efforts as the low Honesty-Humility individual develops a reputation for being selfish and untrustworthy. A low level of Conscientiousness may allow for less effort in maintaining self-control, but it increases the risks an individual faces, such as adult punishment. A low level of Emotionality may facilitate aggression towards out-group members, but it may inhibit concern and care for members of one's in-group.

In summary, bullying is predicted by different levels of personality traits. From an adaptive perspective, the HEXACO appears to be the best model for studying bullying and personality, particularly given that the strongest personality predictor of bullying is a willingness to exploit others (Honesty-Humility) rather than reactive anger (Agreeableness). Different forms of bullying may be predicted by different personality factors, emphasizing how individual factors can influence not only the presence of bullying behavior but also the form of that behavior. An important avenue of future study may be to examine whether certain forms of bullying are more adaptive (i.e., offer greater benefits and fewer costs) to individuals with different types of personality. For example, is physical bullying more adaptive when an individual has low Conscientiousness than when they have high Conscientiousness? While these are important questions to be answered, we now turn to looking at how the immediate environment beyond the individual influences bullying.

Bullying and the Immediate Social Environment

From an evolutionary perspective, successful competition in one's immediate environment can serve to achieve status and resources (Warren et al. 2005). Specifically, competition allows individuals to establish a hierarchy, with those at the top being favored, respected, and having the greatest access to resources (Alcock 1989; Hawley 1999). Furthermore, this dominance hierarchy reflects who has the greatest competitive ability and, in turn, who may have the greatest reproductive success (Ellis 1995; Hawley 1999; Hrdy 2009). As individuals interact with peers in their immediate environment, they recognize their own abilities and ranking within this dominance hierarchy. However, some environments may emphasize competition more than others, resulting in the use of greater aggressive behaviors, such as bullying, to respond to the heightened competition. This relationship between competition, aggression, and bullying will be discussed within the ecological context of students in a school setting.

School is a noteworthy environment in which children and adolescents spend the majority of their time and establish social hierarchies with their peers. From an ecological framework, school climate is a component of the mesosystem, or the immediate setting in which children and adolescents have interactions (Hong and Espelage 2012). An important aspect of the school environment is the degree to which it is perceived as having a climate of competition versus cooperation (Koth et al. 2008). The former may favor bullying (and low Honesty-Humility), while the latter may facilitate positive peer interactions (and high Honesty-Humility). Competitive school environments can include comparing students to one another on academic and social outcomes, or providing rewards and acknowledgment only to students who have more achievements than other students (Butler and Kedar 1990). These competitive school environments promote an emphasis on performance versus positive social relationships, as students are encouraged to compare their own accomplishments with the accomplishments of their peers rather than adopting a less zero-sum approach (Roseth et al. 2008).

In schools, adolescents may compete for both social and academic accomplishments. For example, adolescents may compete sexually for dates and intersexual partners (Leenaars et al. 2008) or social dominance (Pellegrini et al. 2007), as well for postsecondary academic success (Sutton and Keogh 2000). Competitive behavior often takes the form of bullying. We know that this competition frequently occurs intrasexually, as individuals compete with and are aggressive towards peers whom they believe are important targets that they can beat in a conflict (Archer 2004; Veenstra et al. 2010). For example, a study by Leenaars and colleagues (2008) found that adolescent females in high school were more likely to perceive attractive adolescent females as rivals when competing for male partners, and were more likely to be indirectly aggressive (e.g., gossiping, spreading rumors) towards them. Furthermore, female adolescents who rated themselves as attractive reported that they were victimized by other female peers. Similarly, a study by Shute et al. (2008) found evidence for 14- and 15-year-old girls as recipients of indirect sexual bullying (e.g., rumors about promiscuity). Researchers suggest that sexual bullying is a way to make competitors appear unattractive to potential partners and increase one's own likelihood of finding a partner (Volk et al. 2012b). Indeed, Veenstra and colleagues (2010) noted that intra-sexual bullying was viewed more positively by members of the opposite sex than intersexual bullying. Thus, these studies demonstrate that during adolescence, a time of increased dating and sexual activity, adolescents may use bullying to compete for partners in the school setting.

In addition to dominance for the purposes of finding a partner, researchers have found evidence for the use of bullying for global social dominance within highly competitive schools. For example, Sutton and Keogh (2000) found that students who had competitive attitudes also had pro-bullying attitudes. In comparison to non-bullies, bullies rated higher in a desire for social success and Machiavellianism, a trait associated with low Honesty-Humility and one that emphasizes how individual differences can relate to an adaptive fit with one's environments (Lee and Ashton 2005). Similarly, Merten (1997) found that when adolescent girls compete with each other they used indirect bullying to gain social status in their school. Specifically, girls preferred to have a reputation as being "mean" if it meant that they gained popularity. This popularity can relate not only to dominance over peers but also to positive recognition from teachers who promote competition and favor only successful students (Butler and Kedar 1990; Kolbert and Crothers 2003). Researchers explained that when students perceive only the best accomplishments to be rewarded with resources, success, and respect, with all other accomplishments associated with shame and failure, students will increase their competitive behavior to ensure a better chance of achieving the goals that are reinforced by the environment (Brady et al 1983; Warren et al. 2005).

Competition can also occur in a variety of peer networks outside of school (that border between the meso- and exosystems of social influence; Hong and Espelage 2012). In this context, one of the most salient groups in which to observe competition is a sports team. Within sports, hazing is a common occurrence that has been labeled a form of bullying both in historical (Volk et al. 2012a) and modern societies (Malszecki 2004; Rees 2010). Recent studies have reported that the number of hazing incidents in sports environments have persisted (Allan and Madden 2008) despite new legislation and strict penalties for this behavior. In the USA, 44 states have enforced anti-hazing laws (Van Raalte et al. 2007), while in Canada athletes are penalized under the Criminal Code for acts of hazing (Johnson 2011). Additionally, both Vermont State University and McGill University have canceled their men's hockey and football seasons, respectively, for incidents of hazing (Johnson 2011), while other teams have distributed fines and even expulsion for this violation (Crow and Rosner 2002). Additionally, a recent case of racial hazing in the National Football League (NFL, Miami Dolphins) received national media coverage (Jonsson 2013). All of this takes places under the light of recent evidence that suggests that hazing does not increase team cohesion, which many had thought was its purpose (Van Raalte el al. 2007). Instead, hazing appears to diminish team cohesion (Van Raalte et al. 2007). This raises an interesting question: if hazing fails to build team cohesion, why do sports teams persist in hazing new individuals?

From an evolutionary perspective, there are several different reasons why hazing might remain common. As social animals, the need to belong and the ability to maintain in-group distinctions between different coalitions may be important outcomes of hazing (Keating et al. 2005). The underlying motivation to bond with those undergoing a similar experience is a powerful feature that veterans utilize when recycling hazing practices, making them a ritualized force of sociability (Johnson 2011; Keating et al. 2005). The ritualized initiations, often likened to rites of passage, are used to educate newcomers or "rookies" as to their place in the hierarchy and reaffirm the veterans' dominant position (Cimino 2011; Johnson 2011). This practice is a system of control where newcomers must acknowledge that veterans hold the power, as status is achieved through experience with the team (Holman 2004). Those with more years of experience have greater power and privilege and this dynamic is enforced immediately upon the rookie's arrival at the beginning of each year. This relationship operates as a social control aimed at educating newcomers of their submissive roles (Holman 2004). Newcomers are often subjected to tests of fortitude that include pain, violence, heavy drinking, and humiliation that reinforce their submissive position relative to the dominant positions of the veterans, allowing for a pyramid-type scheme where those at the top benefit at the expense of the newcomers (Crow and Macintosh 2009; Johnson 2011). The newcomers are driven by a motivation to obtain a limited resource, that is, membership on a desired sports team (Johnson 2011).

These tests of fortitude can also serve to highlight the newcomers' commitment to the coalition (Cimino 2011). Belonging to an in-group generally carries certain benefits and members seek to ensure that newcomers are not "free riding" (i.e., receiving the benefits associated with becoming a member of the team without incurring any of the costs; Cimino 2011). By imposing hazing rituals, teams may be enhancing a better pool of applicants because those who are not willing to incur the costs of belonging to a sports team may not be worth cooperative efforts (Kiyonari and Barkclay 2008). Cooperation can be maintained in most groups by carefully imposing punishment that often includes physical pain. Researchers propose that punishment may be an evolved human psychology intended to preserve cooperation in groups (Kiyonari and Barkclay 2008). By guaranteeing that the coalition consists of the most dedicated members, hazing helps secure a better flow of resources to existing group members who, by virtue of those resources, make the group more competitive (e.g., ancient Spartan warriors, Golden 1990).

At the group level, even though hazing does not increase team cohesion, it might play a critical role in augmenting groupthink. Within groups, camaraderie boosts productivity and team spirit helps with morale, however coalitions with high levels of groupthink may not want to jeopardize the esprit de corps of the group (Janis 1972, 1982). Therefore, members become afraid to voice contrary views for fear of being criticized. This creates an illusion of invulnerability that may be useful in conflicts with other groups (Myers et al. 2009) and extends beyond sports to hazing in the military, where once initiated in a combat unit, individual goals are set aside to accomplish a common one as an example of groupthink (Malszecki 2004). Furthermore, the imposed obedience of groupthink is also highly visible in the classic obedience studies by Milgram (reviewed in Milgram 2004). Here, authority figures are perceived as creditable, legitimate, and knowledgeable. Thus, individuals are willing to administer excessive amounts of pain simply because the authority figure urges the person to continue. This, coupled with depersonalization may explain why hazing persists amongst individuals despite a reduction in team cohesion. Dominant individuals (e.g., team captains) lead the way by making hazing seem appropriate and thereby reinforce the behavior through a combination of obedience and normative thinking (Asch 1956). This social influence of the collective may make it difficult for individuals to speak out against hazing along the lines of bystander theory (Darley and Latané 1968). While this may play a role in explaining bullying bystanders in general (Salmivalli 2010), it may be of particular importance among institutions where hazing is a ritualized part of the environment.

Hazing in sports may persist because the competitive nature of sports often creates situations that foster increased bullying (Shannon 2013; Volk and Lagzdins 2009), especially if the competitive sports program involves physical contact (Waldron and Kowalski 2010). However, even competitive extracurricular programs that were noncontact promoted bullying (Shannon 2013). High school and collegiate level athletes were clear in their opinions that more hazing would occur in competitive team and contact sports (Waldron and Kowalski 2010), but even recreational sports programs fostered increased bullying in a competitive setting. It appears that, as in schools, a competitive environment in sports or extracurricular activities serves as a trigger for bullying and hazing behaviors, although specific reasons for this outcome are unknown. Overall then, competitive environmental factors are an important component of the mesosystem.

A non-peer component of the competitive sports mesosystem can be coaches. Even though numerous anti-hazing laws have been put in place, it is usually the responsibility of each individual coach to detect hazing and enforce the penalties associated with violations (Crow and Macintosh 2009). Therefore, athletes' misconduct is often at the discretion of the coach. Some athletes feel that coaches turn a blind eye to hazing, thereby tolerating and allowing hazing rituals, making it easier for veteran athletes to carry out these harmful acts (Kowalski and Waldron 2010). Certainly, coaches play an instrumental role in building team cohesion and dissuading harmful hazing behavior (Fields et al. 2010; Keegan et al. 2009; Kowalski and Waldron 2010). Similarly, in school, teachers who set boundaries for inappropriate conduct direct children towards moral reasoning through their ability to anticipate interpersonal problems by knowing their students' social status and peer groups (Rodkin and Hodges 2003). Thus, the social interactions (including obedience and normative influence) between significant adult figures and athletes/youth in the mesosystem can also influence the amount and degree to which hazing or bullying occurs.

Bullying and the Broader Social and Cultural Contexts

Research suggests that adolescents do indeed learn their positions in the social hierarchy from their parents and other adults in their social environments (Due et al. 2009; Elgar et al. 2013). For example, adolescents from wealthy families can learn that they have a competitive advantage over those from lower income families, and subsequently use that economic advantage as a means to express and maintain dominance over their economically disadvantaged peers. Empirical research suggests that, when comparing adolescents from different socioeconomic backgrounds, adolescents from high-income families are most likely to be bullies, whereas adolescents from low income families are more likely to be victims of bullying (Barboza et al. 2009; Due et al. 2009; Elgar et al. 2009, 2013). This association has been found cross-culturally (Due et al. 2009; Elgar et al. 2009, 2013), suggesting a persistent pattern of bullying behavior in which high-status adolescents use acts of intimidation and harassment to exert dominance over their peers of lower status. Furthermore, adolescents from low socioeconomic status families may make ideal victims as they lack the ability to fight back from an economic perspective. For high-income bullies, this minimizes some of the risks associated with bullying, making it a more adaptive strategy. In contrast, middle-income adolescents are typically neither bullies nor victims (Due et al. 2009), presumably because these individuals are neither in a position to express dominance over others, nor are they the ideal victims, as they are more likely to retaliate compared to peers of low economic status.

Thus, it appears that the most important aspect of socioeconomic status, in terms of predicting adolescent bullying patterns, is not overall wealth, as some would suggest. Typically, studies focused on comparing bullying rates between low-income communities and high-income communities find weak or insignificant results (Jankauskiene et al. 2008; Menzer and Torney-Purta 2012; Shetgiri et al. 2012). Instead of comparing between communities, the most important factor appears to be an individual's income status relative to those within the social environment. In terms of Bronfenbrenner's (2009) terminology, the exosystem therefore appears to be more predictive than the macrosystem when it comes to the importance of wealth. For example, in cross-cultural studies, strong associations persist between Gini coefficients and the prevalence of bullying despite differences in culture, such that as income inequality increases, so does the rate of bullying (Due et al. 2009; Elgar et al. 2009, 2013). A similar pattern appears to exist in schools, such that more bullying is reported in economically diverse schools relative to schools in which students' family income levels are more homogeneous (Menzer and Torney-Purta 2012). There are two possible reasons for this. First, greater levels of income inequality lead to greater levels of power imbalances in favor of wealthier students. A second possibility is that greater income inequality fosters greater competition for resources (Daly and Wilson 2010). Thus, it becomes more reward for bullies to gain status, as it can be associated with greater material/social gains than in a more egalitarian context (Wilkinson 2004).

This pattern also highlights humans' ability to respond adaptively to their environment. As greater inequality fosters dominance hierarchies and greater competition for scarce resources, it may be adaptive for relatively wealthy adolescents to exert dominance over their peers of lower status, both to maintain their status and to secure access to scarce resources (Ellis et al. 2012). Furthermore, in places of high income inequality, adolescent dominance hierarchies are often enforced by their parents and other adults around them (Due et al. 2009; Elgar et al. 2013). For example, adolescents may learn that punishment for bullying is less likely in places of greater income inequality, as wealthy adults also express dominance over low-income adults. This creates a competitive climate that tolerates bullying based on economic status, reducing the risks of punishment for high socioeconomic status adolescents who bully those of lower status (Due et al. 2009).

In contrast, in locations where income inequality is lower, the benefits for competing over resources are also lower. In these situations, using bullying as a means to exert dominance and status over others may not be the most adaptive choice for adolescents, as victims are more likely to be capable of successfully retaliating, given the smaller power imbalance between bully and victim. Furthermore, the risk of punishment for bullying may be greater, as adults may be more likely to deem dominance hierarchies and the expression of dominance as unacceptable in a society where most people are considered nearly equal in status (e.g., Scandinavian countries: Ttofi and Farrington 2011). Therefore, it may be adaptive for adolescents to act more altruistically towards their peers under broad social conditions of equality so that acts of reciprocity and sharing of resources become more likely (Barber 2008; Wilkinson 2004). When dominance hierarchies are not emphasized in the wider society, then forming bonds with peers allows adolescents to enjoy greater cooperative benefits such as non-zero-sum access to resources through reciprocity and avoiding the risks that come with bullying, such as punishment or retaliation.

Perhaps at the broadest level of social influence (macrosystem), one's culture can have a significant impact on bullying behavior. Warlike hunter–agricultural cultures, such as the Grand Valley Dani or Yanamamo, appear to encourage higher levels of bullying (Napoleon Chagnon, personal communication, July 2013) than do more peaceful hunter–gatherer cultures, such as the !Kung or Labrador Inuit (although the latter still have bullying, despite a cultural ban on "anger"; Volk et al. 2012a). Scandinavian countries appear to have lower levels of bullying due to a greater national/cultural emphasis on anti-bullying efforts than other Western countries (Berger 2007; Ttofi and Farrington 2011). Thus, cultural differences appear to play a role in the expression of bullying.

From an evolutionary perspective, there are reasons to suspect that modern culture has exerted forces that both increase and decrease bullying. The lack of genetic relatedness among most child/adolescent groups removes an important brake on violence: kin selection (Daly and Wilson 1988). Youth today also are less likely to need to rely upon the youth that they grow up with for their survival, reducing the need for cooperative reciprocal altruism in place of aggression. When combined with an increased pool of potential victims, this allows for more opportunities to bully someone without suffering a personal cost in the future. Finally, youth today tend to compete for more zero-sum rewards, such as scholarships, coveted awards, and entrance to universities (Flanagan 2007).

On the other hand, general levels of violence have declined markedly over the last few centuries (Pinker 2011). Hazing rituals used to be a common fact of life for all students, and for many adults as well (Cunningham 2005; Pinker 2011). Yet, outside of sports, many organizations, from schools to the military, have reduced the intensity of or eliminated hazing rituals. For example, "Slave Day" (a day when senior students could donate money to a charity to buy the services of a freshman for a day) has been eliminated from Ontario schools since 1990 while hazing practices have been officially forbidden in the Canadian military since the early 1990s. Adults used to view bullying as a "fact of life," or a test to be overcome, but increasingly adults are no longer sanctioning this kind of behavior as either necessary or harmless (Bazelon 2013; Pinker 2011). That said, there is no evidence that bullying rates have decreased within the last 20 years, suggesting that the recent focus on bullying has done little to reduce actual levels of bullying (Berger 2007). We suggest that this may be due to the fact that bullying is, in part, an evolutionary adaptation that occurs "naturally" amongst most adolescents.

Indeed, a recent natural experiment was conducted in Norway. An anti-bullying program was initiated in 2002 that reduced the levels of bullying by 20 % within 4 years (victimization dropped by 60 %; Roland 2011). Yet, the success of this intervention was its own worst enemy as the government decided to cut back funding for anti-bullying interventions in 2006 (Roland 2011). After having several years of low levels of bullying, this was a good test of whether bullying was a socially learned phenomenon, as suggested by Bandura (1978), in which case bullying rates would stay low given the lack of visible social exemplars. On the other hand, if bullying was largely driven by some other cause, such as an internal predisposition that was flexibly expressed in the right environmental context, then bullying rates would increase once environmental conditions became favorable again (Volk et al. 2012b). The latter proved accurate, as bullying rates returned to normal as soon as the more lax environmental conditions of the second intervention replaced the highly monitored and punitive environmental conditions of the first intervention (Roland 2011). Once again, this emphasizes bullying's flexible and adaptive fit to local and broad socioecological conditions, and the importance of social factors in understanding bullying.

Concluding Thoughts

Bullying is an important issue not only for today's adolescents but also for society in general. Bullying is not simply a childhood issue; it also occurs in the work place (Einarsen et al. 2010). Social psychology offers valuable tools for understanding how and why individuals engage in bullying. A socioecological approach (Bronfenbrenner 2009) reveals multiple levels of social and cultural influences on the expression and adaptiveness of bullying. Classic social psychology studies on normative influence (Asch 1956) and obedience

(Milgram 2004) offer some insights as to why some children engage in bullying, particularly in the context of increased social competition, while other social theories (e.g., Bandura 1978) appear to be less salient in some social contexts (e.g., peers) versus others (e.g., adults). Personality theories further help to explain why some children choose to engage in bullying (i.e., because it suits their individual personalities to do so), as well as what form of bullying.

In summary, social psychology is valuable for understanding the social phenomenon that is bullying. When combined with an adaptive ecological perspective, it offers potentially the best window for understanding and preventing bullying. This approach is currently being adopted by a growing number of researchers who believe that bullying, along with other adolescent risk-taking, is not simply the result of maladaptive behavior. Instead, it is the adaptive interaction between individuals and their environments (Ellis et al. 2012). Recent interventions suggest that adaptive differences between individuals can affect the efficacy of intervention programs. For example, Garandeau et al. (2013) found that bullying interventions were more successful with unpopular bullies than popular bullies (who were benefiting more from bullying). This highlights how a better understanding of the nature of bullying should be a priority for researchers and practitioners. From an evolutionary psychological perspective, the study of bullying offers strong support for the utility of applying an adaptive lens to social psychological problems.

References

Alcock, J. A. (1989). *Animal behavior* (4th Ed.). Sunderland: Sinauer Associates.

Allan, E., & Madden, M. (2008). Hazing in view: College students at risk, initial findings from the national study on student hazing. http://www.hazingstudy.org. Accessed 6 Dec 2013.

Archer, J. (2004). Sex differences in aggression in real-world settings: A meta-analytic review. *Review of General Psychology, 8,* 291–322. doi: 10.1037/1089-2680.8.4.291.

Asch, S. E. (1956). Studies of independence and conformity: I. A minority of one against a unanimous majority. *Psychological Monographs: General and Applied, 70,* 1–70. doi: 10.1037/h0093718.

Ashton, M., & Lee, K. (2001). A theoretical basis for the dimensions of personality. *European Journal of Personality, 15,* 327–353.

Ashton, M. C., & Lee, K. (2007). Empirical, theoretical, and practical advantages of the HEXACO model of personality structure. *Personality and Social Psychology Review, 11,* 150–166.

Ball, H. A., Arseneault, L., Taylor, A., Maughan, B., Caspi, A., & Moffitt, T. E. (2008). Genetic and environmental influences on victims, bullies and bully-victims in childhood. *Journal of Child Psychology and Psychiatry, 49,* 104–112. doi:10.1111/j.1469-7610.2007.01821.x.

Bandura, A. (1978). Social learning theory of aggression. *Journal of Communication, 28,* 12–29. doi:10.1111/j.1460-2466.1978.tb01621.x.

Barber, N. (2008). Evolutionary social science: A new approach to violent crime. *Aggression and Violent Behavior, 13,* 237–250. doi:10.1016/j.avb.2008.04.002.

Barboza, G., Schiamberg, L. B., Oehmke, J., Korzeniewski, S. J., Post, L. A., & Heraux, C. G. (2009). Individual characteristics and the multiple contexts of adolescent bullying: An ecological perspective. *Journal of Youth and Adolescence, 38,* 101–121. doi:10.1007/s10964-008-9271-1.

Bazelon, E. (2013). *Sticks and stones*. New York: Random House.

Bell, M. B., Nichols, H. J., Gilchrist, J. S., Cant, M. A., & Hodges, S. J. (2012). The cost of dominance: Suppressing subordinate reproduction affects the reproductive success of dominant female banded mongooses. *Proceedings of the Royal Society (B), 270,* 619–624. doi:10.1098/rspb.2011.1093.

Berger, K. S. (2007). Update on bullying at school: Science forgotten? *Developmental Review, 27,* 90–126. doi:10.1016/j.dr.2006.08.002.

Bollmer, J. M., Harris, M. J., & Milich, R. (2006). Reactions to bullying and peer victimization: Narratives, physiological arousal, and personality. *Journal of Research in Personality, 40,* 803–828. doi:10.1016/j.jrp.2005.09.003.

Book, A., Volk, A. A., & Hosker, A. (2012). Adolescent bullying and personality: An adaptive approach. *Personality and Individual Differences, 52,* 218–223. doi:10.1016/j.paid. 2011.10.028.

Brady, J. E., Newcomb, A. F., & Hartup, W. W. (1983). Context and companion's behavior as determinants of cooperation and competition in school-age children. *Journal of Experimental Child Psychology, 36,* 396–412. doi:10.1016/0022-0965(83)90042-5.

Bronfenbrenner, U. (2009). *The ecology of human development: Experiments by nature and design*. Cambridge: Harvard University Press.

Butler, R., & Kedar, A. (1990). Effects of intergroup competition and school philosophy on student perceptions, group processes, and performance. *Contemporary Educational Psychology, 15,* 301–318.

Caravita, S. C. S., Di Blasio, P., & Salmivalli, C. (2009). Unique and interactive effects of empathy and social status on involvement in bullying. *Social Development, 18,* 140–163.

Caravita, S. C. S., Di Blasio, P., & Salmivalli, C. (2010). Early adolescents' participation in bullying: Is ToM involved? *Journal of Early Adolescence, 30,* 138–170.

Cimino, A. (2011). The evolution of hazing: Motivational mechanisms and the abuse of newcomers. *Journal of Cognition and Culture, 11,* 241–267. doi:10.1163/156853711X591242.

Connolly, I., & O'Moore, M. (2003). Personality and family relations of children who bully. *Personality and Individual Differences, 35,* 559–567.

Connolly, J., Pepler, D., Craig, W., & Taradesh, A. (2000). Dating experiences of bullies in early adolescence. *Child Maltreatment, 5,* 299–310.

Creel, S., & Creel, N. M. (2002). *The African wild dog.* Princeton: Princeton University Press.

Crow, B. R., & Macintosh, E. W. (2009). Conceptualizing a meaningful definition of hazing in sport. *European Sports Management Quarterly, 9,* 433–451. doi:10.1080/16184740903331937.

Crow, R. B., & Rosner, S. R. (2002). Institutional and organizational liability for hazing in intercollegiate and professional team sports. *St. John's Law Review, 76,* 87–114.

Cunningham, H. (2005). *Children and childhood in western society since 1500* (2nd ed.). Toronto: Pearson-Longman Press.

Daly, M., & Wilson, M. (1988). *Homicide.* New Brunswick: Transaction Publishers.

Daly, M., & Wilson, M. (2010). Cultural inertia, economic incentives, and the persistence of 'southern violence'. In M. Schaller, A. Norenzayan, S. J. Heine, T. Yamagishi, T. Kameda (Eds.), *Evolution, culture and the human mind* (pp. 229–241). New York: Psychology Press.

Darley, J. M., & Latané, B. (1968). Bystander intervention in emergencies: Diffusion of responsibility. *Journal of Personality and Social Psychology, 8,* 377–383.

Due, P., Merlo, J., Harel-Fisch, Y., Damsgaard, M., Holstein, B. E., Hetland, J., Currie, C., Gabhainn, S. N., Des Matos, M. G., & Lynch, J. (2009). Socioeconomic inequality in exposure to bullying during adolescence: A comparative, cross-sectional, multilevel study in 35 countries. *American Journal of Public Health, 99,* 907–912.

Einarsen, S., Hoel, H., Zapf, D., & Cooper, C. (Eds.), (2010). *Bullying and harassment in the workplace: Developments in theory, research, and practice.* Boca Raton: Taylor-Francis.

Elgar, F., Craig, W., Boyce, W., Morgan, A., & Vella-Zarb, R. (2009). Income inequality and school bullying: Multilevel study of adolescents in 37 countries. *Journal of Adolescent Health, 45,* 351–359. doi:10.1016/j.jadohealth.2009.05.004.

Elgar, F. J., Pickett, K. E., Pickett, W., Craig, W., Molcho, M., Hurrelmann, K., & Leniz, M. (2013). School bullying, homicide and income inequality: A cross-national pooled time series analysis. *International Journal of Public Health, 58,* 237–245. doi:10.1007/s00038-012-0380-y.

Ellis, L. (1995). Dominance and reproductive success among nonhuman animals: A cross-species comparison. *Ethology and Sociobiology, 16,* 257–333.

Ellis, B. J., Del Giudice, M., Dishion, T. J., Figueredo, A. J., Gray, P., Griskevicious, V., Hawley, P. H., Jacobs, J., James, J., Volk, A. A., & Wilson, D. S. (2012). The evolutionary basis of risky adolescent behavior: Implications for science, policy, and practice. *Developmental Psychology, 48,* 598–623.

Eysenck, H. J., & Eysenck, S. B. G. (1975). *Manual of the eysenck personality questionnaire.* London: Hodder and Stoughton.

Farrell, A. H., Della Cioppa, V., Volk, A. A., & Book, A. S. (in press). Predicting bullying heterogeneity with the HEXACO model of personality. *International Journal of Advances in Psychology.*

Fields, S. K., Collins, C. L., & Comstock, R. D. (2010). Violence in youth sports: Hazing, brawling and foul play. *British Journal of Sports Medicine, 44,* 32–37. doi:10.1136/bjsm.2009.068320.

Flanagan, R. (2007). Lucifer goes to law school: Towards explaining and minimizing law student peer-to-peer harassment and intimidation. *Washburn Law Journal, 47,* 453–469.

Garandeau, C. F., Lee, I. A., & Salmivalli, C. (2013). Differential effects of the KiVa anti-bullying program on popular and unpopular bullies. *Journal of Applied Developmental Psychology.* doi:10.1016/j.appdev.2013.10.004.

Golden, M. (1990). *Children and childhood in classical Athens.* Baltimore: The John Hopkins University Press.

Goodall, J. (1986). *The chimpanzees of Gombe.* Cambridge: Harvard University Press.

Hawley, P. H. (1999). The ontogenesis of social dominance: A strategy-based evolutionary perspective. *Developmental Review, 19,* 97–132. doi:10.1006/drev.1998.0470.

Holman, M. (2004). A search for a theoretical understanding of hazing practices in athletics. In J. Johnson & M. Holman (Eds.), *Making the team: Inside the world of sports initiations and hazing* (pp. 50–60). Toronto: Canadian Scholars' Press Inc.

Hong, J. S., & Espelage, D. L. (2012). A review of research on bullying and peer victimization in school: An ecological system analysis. *Aggression and Violent Behaviour, 17,* 311–322. doi:10.1016/j.avb.2012.03.003.

Hrdy, S. B. (1999). *Mother nature: A history of mothers, infants, and natural selection.* Toronto: Pantheon.

Hrdy, S. B. (2009). *Mothers and others: The evolutionary origins of mutual understanding.* Cambridge: Harvard University Press.

Ireland, J. L. (2005). Psychological health and bullying behavior among adolescent prisoners: A study of young and juvenile offenders. *Journal of Adolescent, 36,* 236–243.

Janis, I. L. (1972). *Victims of groupthink.* Boston: Houghton Mifflin.

Janis, I. L. (1982). *Groupthink* (2nd ed.). Boston: Houghton Mifflin.

Jankauskiene, R., Kardelis, K., Sukys, S., & Kardeliene, L. (2008) Associations between school bullying and psychosocial factors. *Social Behaviour & Personality: An International Journal, 36,* 145–161. doi:10.2224/sbp.2008.36.2.145.

Johnson, J. (2011). Through the liminal: A comparative analysis of communitas and rites of passage in sports hazing and initiations. *Canadian Journal of Sociology, 36,* 199–226.

Jonsson, P. (2013, November 8). Muscle and meanness: Incognito hazing comes down to 'What's a real man?' *The Christian Science Monitor*. http://www.csmonitor.com/USA/Sports/2013/1108/Muscle-and-meanness-Incognito-hazing-comes-down-to-What-s-a-real-man.

Juvonen, J., Graham, S., & Schuster, M. A. (2003). Bullying among young adolescents: The strong, the weak, and the troubled. *Pediatrics, 112,* 1231–1237.

Keating, C. F., Pomerantz, J., Pommer, D., Ritt, S. J. H., Miller, L. M., & McCormick, J. (2005). Going to college and unpacking hazing: A functional approach to decrypting initiation practices among undergraduates. *Group Dynamics: Theory, Research and Practice, 9,* 104–126. doi:10.1037/1089-2699.9.2.104.

Keegan, R., Spray, C., Harwood, C., & Lavallee, D. (2009). The motivational atmosphere in youth sport: Coach, parent and peer influences on motivation in specializing sport participants. *Journal of Applied Sport Psychology, 22,* 87–105. doi:10.1080/10413200903421267.

Kiyonari, T., & Barkclay, P. (2008). Cooperation in social dilemmas: Free riding may be thwarted by second-order reward rather than by punishment. *Journal of Personality and Social Psychology, 95,* 826–842. doi:10.1037/a0011381.

Kolbert, J. B., & Crothers, L. M. (2003). Bullying and evolutionary psychology. *Journal of School Violence, 2,* 73–91. doi:10.1300/J202v02n03_05.

Koth, C. W., Bradshaw, C. P., & Leaf, P. J. (2008). A multilevel study of predictors of student perceptions of school climare: The effect of classroom-level factors. *Journal of Educational Psychology, 100,* 96–104. doi:10.1037/0022-0663.100.1.96.

Lee, K., & Ashton, M. C. (2005). Psychopathy, Machiavellianism, and Narcissism in the Five Factor Model and the HEXACO model of personality structure. *Personality and Individual Differences, 38,* 1571–1582. doi:10.1016/paid.2004.09.016.

Leenaars, L. S., Dane, A. V., & Marini, Z. A. (2008). Evolutionary perspective on indirect victimization in adolescence: The role of attractiveness, dating and sexual behaviour. *Aggressive Behavior, 34,* 404–415. doi:10.1002/ab.20252.

Malszecki, G. (2004). "No mercy shown nor asked"-toughness test or torture? Hazing in military combat units and its "collateral damage". In J. Johnson & M. Holman (Eds.), *Making the team: Inside the world of sports initiations and hazing* (pp. 32–49). Toronto: Canadian Scholars' Press Inc.

Mech, D. L. (1970). *The wolf: The ecology and behavior of an endangered species*. Garden City: Natural History Press.

Menesini, E., Camodeca, M., & Nocentini, A. (2010). Bullying among siblings: The role of personality and relational variables. *British Journal of Developmental Psychology, 28,* 921–939. doi:10.1348/026151009X479402.

Menzer, M., & Torney-Purta, J. (2012). Individualism and socioeconomic diversity at school as related to perceptions of the frequency of peer aggression in fifteen countries. *Journal of Adolescence, 35,* 1285–1294. doi:10.1016/j.adolescence.2012.04.013.

Merrell, K. W., Gueldner, B. A., Ross, S. W., & Isava, D. M. (2008). How effective are school bullying intervention programs? A meta-analysis of intervention research. *School Psychology, 23,* 26–42. doi:10.1037/1045-3830.23.1.26.

Merten, D. E. (1997). The meaning of meanness: Popularity, competition and conflict among junior high school girls. *Sociology of Education, 70,* 175–191. doi:10.2307/2673207.

Milgram, S. (2004). *Obedience to authority: An experimental view*. New York: Harper Collins.

Myers, D. G., Spencer, S. J., & Jordan, C. (2009). *Social psychology* (4th ed.). Toronto: McGraw-Hill Ryerson.

Mynard, H., & Joseph, S. (1997). Bully/victim problems and their associations with Eysenck's personality dimensions in 8 to 13 year-olds. *British Journal of Educational Psychology, 67,* 51–54. doi:10.1111/j.2044-8279.1997.tb01226.x.

Pellegrini, A. D., Roseth, C. J., Milner, S., Bohn, C. M., Van Ryzin, M., Vance, N., Cheatham, C. L., & Tarullo, A. (2007). Social dominance in preschool classrooms. *Journal of Comparative Psychology, 121,* 54–64. doi:10.1037/0735-7036.121.1.54.

Pinker, S. (2011). *The better angels of our nature: Why violence has declined*. Toronto: Penguin.

Post, D. G., Hausfater, G., & McCuskey, S. A. (1980). Feeding behavior of yellow baboons (Papio cynocephalus): Relationship to age, gender and dominance rank. *Folia Primatologica, 34,* 170–195.

Rees, R. C. (2010). Bullying and hazing/initiation in schools: How sports and physical education can be part of the problem and part of the solution. *Journal of Physical Education, 43,* 24–27.

Reijntjes, A., Vermande, M., Olthof, T., Goosens, F. A., van de Schoot, R., Aleva, L., & van der Meulen, M. (2013). Costs and benefits of bullying in the context of peer group: A three wave longitudinal analysis. *Journal of Abnormal Child Psychology, 41,* 1217–1229. doi:10.1007/s10802-013-9759-3.

Rodkin, P. C., & Hodges, E. V. E. (2003). Bullies and victims in the peer ecology: Four questions for psychologist and school professionals. *School Psychology Review, 32,* 384–400.

Roland, E. (2011). The broken curve: Effects of the Norwegian manifesto against bullying. *International Journal of Behavioral Development, 35,* 383–388.

Roseth, C. J., Johnson, D. W., & Johnson, R. T. (2008). Promoting early adolescents' achievement and peer relationships: The effects of cooperative, competitive,

and individualistic goal structures. *Psychology Bulletin, 134,* 223–246. doi:10.1037/0033 2909.134.2.223.
Salmivalli, C. (2010). Bullying and the peer group: A review. *Aggression and Violent Behavior, 15,* 112–120. doi:10.1016/j.avb.2009.08.007.
Scheel, D., & Packer, C. (1991). Group hunting behaviour of lions: A search for cooperation. *Animal Behaviour, 41,* 697–709.
Scott, J. (1991). *Painted wolves.* Toronto: Penguin Books.
Shannon, C. S. (2013). Bullying in recreation and sport setting: Exploring risk factors, prevention efforts, and intervention strategies. *Journal of Parks and Recreation Administration, 31,* 15–33.
Shetgiri, R., Lin, H., Avila, R. M., & Flores, G. (2012). Parental characteristics associated with bullying perpetration in US children aged 10 to 17 years. *American Journal of Public Health, 102,* 2280–2286. doi:10.2105/AJPH.2012.300725.
Shute, R., Owens, L., & Slee, P. (2008). Everyday victimization of adolescent girls by boys: Sexual harassment, bullying, or aggression? *Sex Roles, 58,* 447–489. doi:10.1007/s11199-007-9363-5.
Slee, P. T., & Rigby, K. (1993). The relationship of Eysenck's personality factors and self- esteem to bully/victim behaviour in Australian school boys. *Personality and Individual Differences, 14,* 371–373.
Stewart, K. J. (1987). Spotted hyenas: The importance of being dominant. *Trends in Ecology and Evolution, 2,* 88–89.
Sutton, J., & Keogh, E. (2000). Social competition in school: Relationships with bullying, Machiavellianism, and personality. *British Journal of Educational Psychology, 70,* 443–456. doi:10.1348/000709900158227.
Tani, F., Greenman, P. S., Schneider, B. H., & Fregoso, M. (2003). Bullying and the Big Five: A study of childhood personality and participant roles in bullying incidents. *School Psychology International, 24,* 131–146.
Townsend, S. W., Slocombe, K. E., Emery Thompson, M., & Zuberbühler, K. (2007). Female-led infanticide in wild chimpanzees. *Current Biology, 17,* R355–R356. doi:0.1016/j.cub.2007.03.020.
Ttofi, M. M., & Farrington, D. P. (2011). Effectiveness of school-based programs to reduce bullying: A systematic and meta-analytic approach. *Journal of Experimental Criminology, 7,* 27–56.
Vaillancourt, T., Hymel, S, & McDougall, P. (2003). Bullying Is power: Implications for school-based intervention strategies. *Journal of Applied School Psychology, 19,* 157–176. doi:10.1300/J008v19n02_10.
Van Raalte, J. L., Cornelius, A. E., Linder, D. E., & Brewer, B. W. (2007). The relationship between hazing and team cohesion. *Journal of Sports Behavior, 30,* 491–504.
Veenstra, R., Lindenberg, S., Munniksma, A., & Dijkstra, J. K. (2010). The complex relation between bullying, victimization, acceptance, and rejection: Giving special attention to status, affection, and sex differences. *Child Development, 81,* 480–486.
Veselka, L., Schermer, J. A., Martin, R. A., Cherkas, L. F., Spector, T. D., & Vernon, P. A. (2010). A behavioral genetic study of relationships between humor styles and the six HEXACO personality factors. *Europe's Journal of Psychology, 6,* 9–33.
Volk, A. A., & Lagzdins, L. (2009). Bullying and victimization among adolescent girl athletes. *Athletic Insight, 11,* 15–33.
Volk, A. A., Craig, W., Boyce, W., & King, M. (2006). Adolescent risk correlates of bullying and different types of victimization. *International Journal of Adolescent Medicine and Health, 21,* 575–588. doi:10.1515/IJAMH.2006.18.4.575.
Volk, A., Camilleri, J., Dane, A., & Marini, Z. (2012a). If, when, and why bullying is adaptive. In T. Shackelford & V. Shackelford (Eds.), *Oxford handbook of evolutionary perspectives on violence, homicide, and war* (pp. 270–288). Toronto: Oxford University Press.
Volk, A. A., Camilleri, J. A., Dane, A. V., & Marini, Z. A. (2012b). Is adolescent bullying an evolutionary adaptation? *Aggressive Behaviour, 38,* 222–238. doi:10.1002/ab.21418.
Volk, A. A., Dane, A. V., Marini, Z. A., & Vaillancourt, T. (Submitted). Adolescent bullying, dating, and mating: An evolutionary hypothesis. *Evolution and Human Behavior.*
Waldron, J., & Kowalski, C. (2010). Looking the other way: Athletes' perceptions of coaches' responses to hazing. *International Journal of Sports Science & Coaching, 5,* 87–100.
Warren, K., Schoppelrey, S., Moberg, D. P., & McDonald, M. (2005). A model of contagion through competition in the aggressive behavior of elementary school students. *Journal of Abnormal Child Psychology, 33,* 283–292. doi:10.1007/s10802-005-3565-5.
Wilkinson, R. (2004). Why is violence more common where inequality is greater? *Annals of the New York Academy of Sciences, 1036,* 1–12. doi:10.1196/annals.1330.001.
Wolke, D., Woods, S., Bloomfield, L., & Karstadt, L. (2001). Bullying involvement in primary school and common health problems. *Archives of Disease in Childhood, 85,* 197–201.

Dangerous Terrorists as Devoted Actors

31

Scott Atran and Hammad Sheikh

This chapter harnesses our recent cross-cultural experiments and fieldwork to better understand some of today's most dangerous terrorists as "devoted actors" (Atran et al. 2007; Sheikh et al. 2013) motivated by "sacred values" (Ginges et al. 2007; Atran and Ginges 2012). Sacred values (SVs) are nonnegotiable preferences whose defense compels actions beyond evident reason, that is, regardless of risks or costs.

People committed to SVs show: (1) commitment to a rule-bound logic of moral appropriateness to do what is morally right no matter the likely risks or rewards, rather than following a utilitarian calculus of costs and consequences (Atran 2003; Bennis et al. 2010; Ginges and Atran 2011; Hoffman and McCormick 2004); (2) immunity to material trade-offs, coupled with a "backfire effect," where offers of incentives or disincentives to give up SVs heighten refusal to compromise or negotiate (Dehghani et al. 2010; Ginges et al. 2007); (3) resistance to social influence and exit strategies (Atran and Henrich 2010; Sheikh et al. 2013), which leads to unyielding social solidarity, and binds genetic strangers to voluntarily sacrifice for one another; (4) insensitivity to spatial and temporal discounting, where considerations of distant places and people, and even far past and future events, associated with SVs significantly outweigh concerns with here and now (Atran 2010a; Sheikh et al. 2013); and (5) brain-imaging patterns consistent with processing SVs as rules rather than as calculations of costs and benefits, and with processing perceived violations of SVs as emotionally agitating and resistant to social influence (Berns et al. 2012, 2013).

Our research indicates that when SVs become embedded in fused groups of imagined kin who consider themselves in existential competition with other groups, then individuals in such groups (e.g., bands of brothers) become empowered to make great sacrifices and exertions, for ill or good (Atran 2010a; Atran et al. 2014a, b). Devoted actors are most likely to commit themselves to extreme actions—and thus to be most dangerous—if they perceive themselves to be under existential threat from outside groups (Sheikh et al. 2012), and if their primary reference group forms around a prior action-oriented association, such as shared combat experience or even membership in a sports team (Atran 2010a).

There is an evolutionary rationale behind the willingness to make costly sacrifices for the group, even unto death and against all odds. When a perceived outside threat to one's primary reference group is very high, and

S. Atran (✉)
Centre National de la Recherche Scientifique, Institut Jean Nicod-Ecole Normale Supérieure, 29 rue d'Ulm, 75005 Paris, France
e-mail: satran@umich.edu

H. Sheikh
ARTIS Research, 38400 North School House Road, Unit 7278, Cave Creek, AZ 8532
e-mail: sheikh60@newschool.edu

V. Zeigler-Hill et al. (eds.), *Evolutionary Perspectives on Social Psychology*, Evolutionary Psychology, DOI 10.1007/978-3-319-12697-5_31, © Springer International Publishing Switzerland 2015

survival prospects are very low, then only when a sufficient number of group members are endowed with such a willingness to extreme sacrifice can the group hope to parry stronger but less devoted enemies who are less inclined to disregard the costs of action. SVs mobilized for collective action by devoted actors enable outsize commitment in low-power groups to resist and often prevail against materially more powerful foes who depend on standard material incentives, such as armies and police that rely on pay and promotion (Atran and Ginges 2012).

Thus, for Darwin (1871), moral virtue was not most clearly associated with intuitions, beliefs, and behaviors about fairness and reciprocity, emotionally supported by empathy and consolation, all of which most of the recent work in the philosophy, psychology, and the neuroscience of morality focus on (Gazzaniga 2009; Baumard et al. 2013; Van Slyke 2014). Rather, Darwin (1871) associated the virtue of "morality…patriotism, fidelity, obedience, courage, and sympathy" (pp. 163–165) with a propensity to what we now call "parochial altruism" (Choi and Bowles 2007; Ginges and Atran 2009). Parochial altruism is especially evident in extreme self-sacrifice in war and other intense forms of human conflict, where likely prospects for individual and even group survival may have very low initial probability. Heroism, martyrdom, and other forms of self-sacrifice for glory and group appear to go beyond the mutualistic, *golden rule* principles of cooperation and distributive justice of overriding concern for universalist religions and ideologies, including modern liberal democracy (Rawls 1971).

People often make their greatest exertions and sacrifices, including killing or dying for ill or good, not just in order to preserve their own lives or kin and kith, but for the sake of an idea—the abstract conception they have formed of themselves, of "who we are." This is "the privilege of absurdity; to which no living creature is subject, but man only" (p. 29) of which Thomas Hobbes (1651/1901) wrote in *Leviathan*. For most of human history, and for most cultures, religion has been the locus of this privilege and power of absurdity. For Hobbes, as for countless other religious and nonreligious thinkers, from Augustine to Kierkegaard and Aristotle to Ayer, the "incomprehensible" nature of core religious beliefs, such as belief in a sentient but bodiless deity, renders such beliefs immune to empirical or logical verification or falsification. Religious consensus does not primarily involve fact-checking or reasoned argument, but ensues from ritual communion and emotional bonding (Atran and Norenzayan 2004).

Costly ritual commitment to apparently absurd beliefs can deepen trust by reliably identifying cooperators with sacred symbols, while galvanizing group solidarity for common defense (Atran and Henrich 2010; Norenzayan and Shariff 2008). The more belligerent a group's environment, however, the more proprietary the group's SVs and rituals, increasing in-group reliance, but also disbelief, distrust, and potential conflict towards other groups (Sosis et al. 2007; Wilson 2002). By contrast, fully reasoned social contracts that regulate individual interests to share costs and benefits of cooperation can be less distancing between groups but also more liable to collapse: Awareness that more advantageous distributions of risks and rewards may be available in the future makes defection more likely (Atran and Axelrod 2008). This is why even ostensibly secular nations and transnational movements usually contain important quasi-religious rituals and beliefs (Anderson 1983). Therefore, while the term "sacred values" intuitively denotes religious belief, in line with recent work we use the term to refer to any preferences regarding objects, beliefs, or practices that people treat as either incompatible or nonfungible with profane issues or economic goods, as when land becomes "sacred land."

Whether for cooperation or conflict, SVs—like devotion to God or a collective cause—signal group identity and operate as moral imperatives that inspire nonrational exertions independent of likely outcomes. In research involving Palestinians, Israelis, Indonesians, Indians, Afghans, and Iranians, our studies find that offering people material incentives (large amounts of money, guarantees for a life free of political violence) to compromise SVs can backfire, increasing stated willingness to use violence towards compromise (Atran 2010b;

Atran and Axelrod 2008; Ginges et al. 2007). Backfire effects occur both for SVs with clear religious investment (Jerusalem, Sharia law) and those with initially none (Iran's right to nuclear capability, Palestinian refugees' right of return). For example, Dehghani et al. (2010) found that for most Iranians having a nuclear program has nothing sacred about it, but it had become a sacred subject through religious rhetoric for about 13 % of the population. This group, which tends to be close to the regime, now believes a nuclear program is bound up with the national identity and with Islam itself, so that offering material rewards or punishments to abandon the program only increases anger and support for it.

Our fieldwork with suicide terrorists and political and militant leaders and supporters in violent conflict situations suggests that some behaviors that punctuate the history of human intergroup conflict do indeed go beyond instrumental concerns. Historical examples include the self-sacrifice of Spartans at Thermopylae, the Jewish Zealots in revolt against Rome, defenders of the Alamo, the Waffen SS "volunteer death squads" during the Soviet siege of Budapest, some cohorts of Japanese Kamikaze, and the Jihadi pilot bombers of 9/11 (Atran 2010a; Ginges et al. 2011). Such events exemplify that humans fight and kill in the name of abstract, often ineffable values—like God, national destiny, or salvation (Atran and Ginges 2012).

Most theories and models related to violent intergroup conflict assume that civilians and leaders make a rational calculation (Caplan, 2006; Fearon 1995; von Clausewitz 1832/1956). If the total cost of the war is less than the cost of the alternatives, they will support war. But in another set of studies (Ginges and Atran 2011), we found that when people are confronted with violent situations, they consistently ignore quantifiable costs and benefits, relying instead on SVs. We asked a representative sample of 650 Israeli settlers in the West Bank about the dismantlement of their settlements as part of a peace agreement with Palestinians. Some subjects were asked about their willingness to engage in nonviolent protests, whereas others were asked about violence. Besides willingness to violently resist eviction, subjects rated how effective they thought the action would be and how morally right the decision was. When it came to nonviolent options such as picketing and blocking streets, rational behavior models predicted settlers' decisions. In deciding whether to engage in violence, the settlers reacted differently. Rather than how effective they thought violence would be in saving their homes, the settlers' willingness to engage in violent protest depended only on how morally correct they considered that option to be. We found similar patterns of "principled" resistance to peace settlements and support for violence, including suicide bombings, among Palestinian refugees who felt SVs were at stake (e.g., recognizing their moral right of return to homes in Israel even if they expressed no material or practical interest in resettling).

In a series of follow-up surveys among the US and Nigerian participants, we confronted subjects with hypothetical hostage situations and asked them if they would approve of a solution—which was either diplomatic or violent—for freeing the prisoners. The chance of success varied in terms of the number of hostages who might die. For example, in one version of the survey, when told that their action would result in all hostages being saved, people endorsed the plan presented to them, whether it used diplomacy or military action. When told that one hostage would die, however, most people were reluctant to endorse the diplomatic response, whereas people pondering military action had no such qualms. In fact, the most common response supported military action even if 99 of 100 hostages died as a consequence.

These and other studies suggest that social groups have "sacred rules" for which their people would fight and risk serious loss/death rather than compromise. In another study with a representative sample of over 700 adults in the West Bank and Gaza, we asked:

> What if a person wanted to carry out a bombing (which some…call suicide attacks) against the enemies of Palestine but his father becomes ill, and his family begs the chosen martyr to take care of his father, would it be acceptable to delay the attack indefinitely?

> What if a person wanted to carry out a bombing (which some…call suicide attacks) against the enemies of Palestine but his family begs him to delay martyrdom indefinitely because there was a significantly high chance the chosen martyr's family would be killed in retaliation, would it be acceptable to delay the attack indefinitely?

Palestinians tended to reason about political violence in a noninstrumental manner by showing more disapproval over a delay of a martyrdom attack to rescue an entire family than over a delay of a martyrdom attack to take care of an ill father. These results indicate that when people are reasoning between duty to war or to family, they are not making instrumental decisions, but decisions based on perceptions of moral obligations that can change as a result of instrumentally irrelevant alterations in context (Ginges and Atran 2009).

If people perceive a sacred rule was violated, they may feel morally obliged to retaliate against the wrongdoers—even if the retaliation does more harm than good. Such moral commitment to SVs ultimately can be the key to the success or failure of insurgent or revolutionary movements with far fewer material means than the armies or police arrayed against them (which tend to operate more on the basis of typical "rational" reward structures, such as calculated prospects of increased pay or promotion). After WWII, revolutionary movements have, on average, emerged victorious with as little as ten times less firepower and manpower than the state forces arrayed against them (Arreguín-Toft 2001). Ever since the nineteenth-century anarchists, science education in engineering and medical studies has been a frequent criterion of leadership for these movements because such studies demonstrate hands-on capability and potential for personal and costly sacrifice through long-term commitment to a course of study that requires delayed gratification. Al-Qaeda, like other revolutionary groups, was initially formed and led by fairly well-off and well-educated individuals, the plurality of whom studied engineering and medicine (Bergen and Lind 2007; Gambetta and Hertog 2007).

The Importance of Group Dynamics and Identity Fusion

Understanding the way SVs influence decision making, leading to deontic judgments and choices in disregard for material interests, is necessary but not sufficient to explain how they may influence extreme and costly behaviors. We suggest that SVs may influence extreme behavior particularly to the extent that they become embedded or fused with identity and internalized. When internalized, SVs lessen societal costs of policing morality through self-monitoring, and further blind members to exit strategies (Atran and Henrich 2010).

There is more to group dynamics than just the weight and mass of people, their behavior, and ideas. There are also the structural relationships between group members that make the group more than the sum of its individual members (Magouirk et al. 2008). It is also the networking among members that distributes thoughts and tasks that no one part may completely control or even understand. Case studies of suicide terrorism and related forms of violent extremism suggest that "people almost never kill and die [just] for the cause, but for each other: for their group, whose cause makes their imagined family of genetic strangers—their brotherhood, fatherland, motherland, homeland" (Atran 2010a, p. 33).

In line with these observations, a promising new theory holds that when people's collective identities become fused with their personal self-concept, they subsequently display increased willingness to engage in extreme pro-group behavior when the group is threatened (Swann et al. 2012). Swann and colleagues have dubbed this powerful form of personal investment in the group "identity fusion." Fusion theory is markedly different from various social identity theories in its privileging of group cohesion through social networking and emotional bonding of people and values rather than through processes of categorization and association, thus empowering individuals and their groups with sentiments of exceptional destiny and invulnerability.

To test the relationship between identity fusion and parochial altruism in a threatening environment (i.e., spillover from the Syrian civil war), we interviewed 62 Lebanese youth in Beirut and Byblos (Sheikh et al., 2014). Participants were asked to pick the pictorial representation that best represents how essential the relationship is between them and the given group (Fig. 31.1).

Support for costly sacrifices was assessed with questions about whether their community would approve of a list of extreme actions in the context of conflict (e.g., "a person who risks the safety of their family or children to defend the group"). People who fused with their religious group expressed greater willingness to make costly sacrifices than people not fused (Fig. 31.2).

To examine this effect in more detail, we assessed *parochial morality,* by contrasting respondents' moralizing a tight set of "parochial" values (i.e., patriotism, purity, divinity, sacrifice for your group, fighting for your group, modesty, selling land to outgroup, worship, and loyalty) with their moralizing an equally tight set of "universal" values (i.e., emotional harm, discrimination, caring for others, individual rights, tolerance, democracy, free speech, theft, respecting parents, murder). Although we did not test if subjects held important parochial values to be immune to trade-offs and social influence, hence sacred, independent research indicates that group-defining SVs are also morally most important (Graham and Haidt 2013). We also assessed threat and superiority by asking participants to pick a group they most identified with, and respond to questions about it, such as: "I believe the group is superior to other groups or communities in this country in many ways." Finally, we measured religiosity using questions tapping into

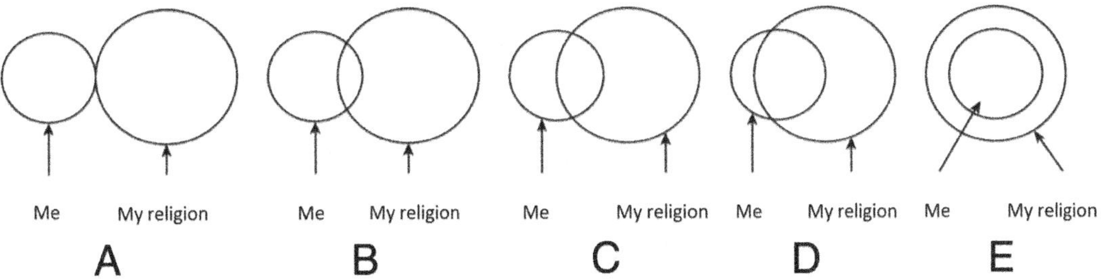

Fig. 31.1 Pictorial measure of fusion with group. Responses show a dichotomous distribution: nonfused (*A, B, C, D*) versus fully fused (*E*). This is replicated even with a continuous measure (e.g., sliding a smaller circle into a larger circle on a smart phone)

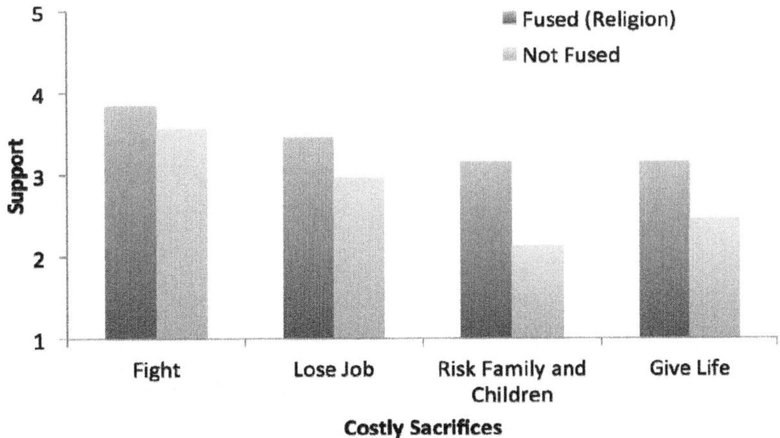

Fig. 31.2 Fusion with religious group and support for costly sacrifice in Lebanon

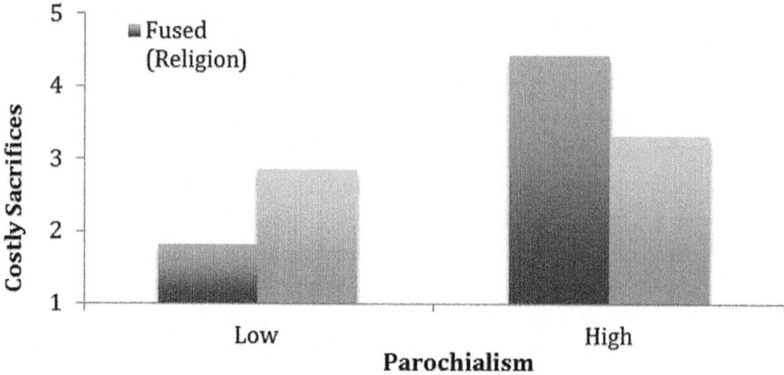

Fig. 31.3 Fusion, parochialism, and costly sacrifices

religious beliefs and participation in religious rituals. Parochial morality, belief in group superiority, and religiosity showed a similar interaction pattern with fusion. Accordingly, we created a parochialism score by combining these three measures. There was a reliable interaction effect: the more parochially fused people were, the more they supported costly sacrifices, but if fused people were not parochial, they showed decreased support of costly sacrifices (Fig. 31.3).

These findings paint a picture of value-driven actors willing to make costly sacrifices to defend their group, who are motivated by a belief in their community's superiority and who moralize parochial values. When they are fused with their community, they are especially likely to support costly sacrifices. Fusion theory argues that fused actors are most prone to extreme actions, whereas our findings suggest that fused actors may be least prone to extreme actions under certain conditions. For example, in the case of groups that do not feel superior to others, do not bind their identity to particular religious beliefs and rituals, and which favor universal values over parochial values, such as some religious liberal and civil and human rights groups. It is possible that people may fuse not only with groups of people but also with particular issues and values (Fig. 31.4).

In an ongoing collaboration with fusion theorists Ángel Gomez and Juan Jiménez (reported in Atran & Ginges , 2015), we find highly convergent measures of SVs: resistance to monetary payoffs, alternative benefits to society, and social pressure are strongly related to one another. Fusion with values (internalization) is a complementary but somewhat independent phenomenon. Table 31.1 gives the conditional probabilities calculated from these measures in a recent study of 1600 *pro-choice* and *pro-life* supporters in Spain in early 2014, at a time where rival demonstrations were an almost daily occurrence. These interrelations tend to be maximized among individuals who are fully fused with their group.

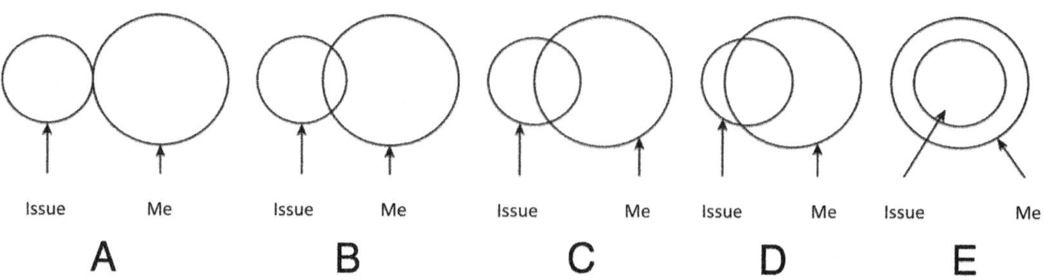

Fig. 31.4 Measuring fusion with issue/value. Responses show a dichotomous distribution: nonfused (*A, B, C, D*) versus fully fused (*E*)

Table 31.1 Conditional probabilities of commitments to issues/values. Predictors are in rows and outcomes in columns. For example, the second row of the fourth column shows that when people were immune to social influence, there was an 84 % chance they would refuse monetary rewards, as compared to just an 8 % chance when they were not immune to social influence

	Fusion with value	Resistance to social influence	Resistance to societal benefit	Resistance to money trade-off
Fusion with value	0 % → 100 %	60 % → 95 %	28 % → 74 %	36 % → 80 %
Resistance to social influence	26 % →75 %	0 % → 100 %	6 % → 78 %	8 % → 84 %
Resistance to societal benefit	37 % → 82 %	59 % → 99 %	0 % → 100 %	11 % → 96 %
Resistance to money trade-off	39 % →78 %	48 % → 98 %	12 % → 88 %	0 % → 100 %

In a recent set of cross-cultural experiments, Swann et al. (2014) found that when fused people perceive that group members share core attributes and values, they are more likely to project familial ties common in smaller groups onto the extended group, and this enhances expressed willingness to fight and die for the larger group, echoing field research with militant and terrorist groups (Atran 2010a). We found that for the relevant group-defining values (pro-life or pro-choice), the greater the fusion with those values, the greater the willingness to take extreme action and engage in sacrifice (except for risking physical harm to one's own children). In addition, we found that fusion with values mediates the relationship between fusion with family-like groups of "imagined kin" and costly sacrifices. We also found that SVs mediate the relationship between fusion with values and costly sacrifices. These findings suggest the devoted actor's pathway to costly sacrifices and extreme actions (Fig. 31.5). More recent findings in Morocco among prospective volunteers for the Islamic State support the idea that SVs (Sharia and the Caliphate) interact with fusion in family-like groups to drive costly sacrifices (Atran et al. 2014a, b).

Of course, the move from reports of willingness to engage in costly sacrifices and extreme behavior to actual actions under appropriate conditions is by no means guaranteed; however, compatibility of our findings with field studies of violent extremists makes the exercise relevant to understanding actual trends and cases in contemporary terrorism.

Terrorism Trends and Cases: Search for Glory and the Limits of Economic and Genetic Rationality

A main problem in studies of violent religious and political extremism is that most "experts" have little field experience and otherwise lack the required level of details that statistical and trend analyses could properly mine. Under sponsorship by the National Science Foundation and the US Department of Defense, our multidisciplinary, multinational research team has been conduct-

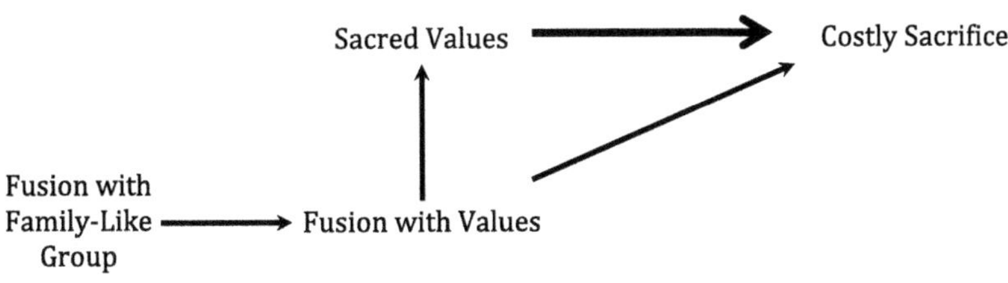

Fig. 31.5 Theoretical model of devoted action (based on empirical findings discussed)

ing field studies and analyses of the mental and social processes involved in pathways to violent extremism. Our findings indicate that terrorist plotters against Western civilian populations tend not to be part of sophisticated, foreign-based command-and-control organizations. Rather, they belong to loose, homegrown networks of family and friends who die not just for a cause, but for each other.

Most academic attempts to explain the behavior of violent extremists, including suicide bombing, tend to rely on some simple utilitarian calculation or another, whether in terms of economic self-interest (Frey 2004; Ganor 2009; Wintrobe 2006) or evolutionary strategies to enhance genetic fitness (Brin 2012; Kanazawa 2007; Rushton 2005). On many of these accounts, it does not matter even if the material preferences and goals are more imaginary than real; it suffices that a would-be terrorist *believes* they are real. We have no objection to the idea that imaginary preferences can function psychologically as real instrumental preferences. The problem is that little beyond sheer speculation indicates that terrorists are chiefly motivated by such simple preferences.

For example, the desire of young men to seek virgins in Paradise as a goal of suicide bombers is often proffered by analysts who have never met anyone involved with suicide bombing, and who provide no empirical evidence beyond an occasional anecdote for this or related notions (e.g., tensions built up from intra-sexual competition) as significant motivators. In fact, in our interviews across Eurasia and North Africa with numerous would-be suicide bombers, captured suicide bombers, and leaders of suicide-bombing organizations, no one ever invoked maidens in heaven as a principal motivating reason for martyrdom actions. On the contrary, apart from a few exceptional cases—an operative from Palestinian Fateh's Aqsa' Martyrs Brigades who said he would take "anyone he could get for whatever reason," a young Taliban commander who said the same, and veterans of the Zarqawi-led al-Qaeda affiliate in Iraq who preferred young volunteers without real fighting experience for suicide attack—sponsors of suicide attacks systematically informed us that they would reject anyone who sought martyrdom for such a reason (with no evidence to suspect deception on this score).

Other widespread—but empirically unsupported—utilitarian explanations concern kin selection. The idea is that young, unmarried men sacrifice themselves so that genetic relatives may have better access to scarce resources and thereby increase the prospects for survival of the martyr's genes via his close relatives. This occurs by way of reducing the competition among siblings for scarce resources, or by enhancing surviving family's social status, thereby increasing the family's access to scarce resources. To explore this in one study with a representative sample of nearly 1300 Palestinian Muslim adults, we measured whether it was permissible or taboo in Palestinian society to think about material gains of involvement in acts of violence against the Israeli occupation (Ginges and Atran 2009). We asked:

> In your view would it be acceptable for the family of a martyr to request compensation in the amount of JD (Jordanian Dinars) _________ after their son carried out a martyrdom operation? Would it be certainly acceptable, acceptable, unacceptable, or certainly unacceptable?

We randomly varied between participants the amount of money requested in this scenario in order of magnitude increments of Jordanian dinars: JD 10,000, JD 100,000, or JD 1,000,000. Across experimental conditions, more than 90 % of the sample regarded a request for compensation, regardless of the amount, to be unacceptable. This indicates that it is not normative to think about martyrdom in material terms. Analysis of variance indicated a significant linear trend (JD 10,000 < JD 100,000 < JD 1,000,000) such that as the amount of financial compensation increased, so too did the perception that the request was unacceptable. In brief, Palestinians regard material-selective incentives for participating in acts of martyrdom as taboo.

Rather than support strictly instrumentalist explanations of terrorism, the increasing involvement of marginal youth (Atran 2010a)—especially from the petty criminal world—actually undermines such explanations. Thus, international success at stopping large transfers of money to terrorist organizations (Zarate 2013) have compelled the new wave of terrorists to seek financing where they can (while the cost of 9/11 exceeded US$ 400,000 and the cost of the 2002 Bali and 2004 Madrid bombings were at about US$ 50,000 each, more recent attacks were considerably less costly). As a result, many operations nowadays ride piggyback on available petty criminal networks. Most significantly, marginalized Muslim youth who first become petty criminals because of "opportunity costs" (Becker 1962), and then get involved in aiding jihadis, often volunteer for violent jihad, including suicide bombings, because of the promise of achieving a greater sense of personal significance in a glorious cause. Indeed, it is these young petty criminals, even more than the "ideological" students and others, who often prove themselves most ready to kill and die (Atran 2010a; see Box 31.1 on the 2004 Madrid plot and its aftermath). This trend towards involvement of marginalized youth contrasts starkly with the fairly well-educated and well-off founders and members of al-Qaeda before 9/11.

Jihadis span the population's normal distribution: There are very few psychopaths and sociopaths, and few brilliant thinkers and strategists. Unlike the founding members of al-Qaeda, today's jihadi wannabes are mostly emerging adults in transitional stages of their lives—students or immigrants who are in search of jobs or companions—who are especially prone to movements that promise a meaningful cause, camaraderie, adventure, and glory. Most have a secular education, becoming "born again" into the jihadi cause in their late teens or 20s. The path to radicalization can take years, months, or just days, depending on personal vulnerabilities and the influence of others. Occasionally, there is a hook-up with a relative, or an acquaintance, who has some overseas connection to someone who can get them a bit of training and motivation to pack a bag of explosives or pull a trigger, but the Internet and social media can be sufficient for radicalization and even operational preparation (Atran 2011).

Soccer, paintball, camping, hiking, rafting, body building, martial arts training, and other forms of physically stimulating and intimate group action create a bunch of buddies (usually not less than 4 and not more than 12, with a median of 8), who become a "band of brothers" in a glorious cause (Atran 2010a). It usually suffices that a few (usually at least two) of these action buddies come to believe in the cause, truly and uncompromisingly, for the rest to follow even unto death. This is because humans, like all primates, need to socially organize, lead and be led. This is in contrast to exaggerated notions of "charismatic leaders" going out or sending recruiters to "brainwash" unwitting minds into joining well-structured organizations with command and control. Standard counterterrorism notions of "cells" and "recruitment"—and to some degree even "leadership"—often reflect more the psychology and organization of people analyzing terrorist groups than terrorist groups themselves (see Box 31.2 on the decentralized attack networks of Jemaah Islamiyah). Of course, some inspirational leaders like the late Osama Bin Laden or, more recently, Abu Bakr al-Baghdadi, head of the Islamic State in Syria and the Levant (ISIL), demand formal oaths of loyalty and agreement with their strategic vision and have ultimate control over operational decisions; however, enlistment into the group is usually elective and even reversible, and tactical decision making is generally decentralized.

More recently, "lone wolves" have begun carrying out actions on their own, inspired by jihadi icons, such as the late American born Islamist preacher Anwar al-Awlaki, but without being directed by them (e.g., Maj. Nadal Hassan, who killed fellow soldiers at Fort Hood in the name of Jihad, sent over a score of emails to Awalki who responded only twice with no specific recommendations or direction). Indeed, Awlaki is perhaps more of an attractor on the Internet since his death than when he was alive. More than 80% of plots in both Europe and the USA were concocted from the bottom up by mostly young people just hooking up with one another, and increasingly over the Internet, in search of personal significance and eternal glory through devoted action (Atran 2013; Sageman 2009).

For the first time in history, a massive, media-driven political awakening has been occurring—spurred by the advent of the Internet, social media, and cable television—that can, on the one hand, motivate universal respect for human rights while, on the other hand, enable, say, Muslims from Sulawesi to sacrifice themselves for Palestine, Afghanistan, or Chechnya (despite almost no contact or shared history for the last 50,000 years or so). When perceived global injustice resonates with frustrated personal aspirations, moral outrage gives universal meaning and provides the push to radicalization and violent action. But the popular notion of a "clash of civilizations" between Islam and the West is woefully misleading. Violent extremism represents not the resurgence of traditional cultures, but their collapse, as young people unmoored from millennial traditions flail about in search of a social identity that gives personal significance and glory. This is the dark side of globalization.

Especially for young men, mortal combat with a "band of brothers" in the service of a great cause is both the ultimate adventure and a road to esteem in the hearts of their peers. For many disaffected souls today, jihad is a heroic cause—a promise that anyone from anywhere can make a mark against history's most powerful country and its perceived allies. But because would-be jihadists best thrive in small groups and among family, friends, and fellow travelers—not in large movements or armies—their threat can only match their ambitions if fueled beyond actual strength. Publicity hyped by political and media frenzy is the oxygen that fires modern terrorism.

Unfortunately, standard US military and counterterrorism strategies (e.g., the Quadrennial Defense Review, 2014) continue to focus on minimizing US costs in lives and treasure, while "impos[ing] unacceptable costs" on the enemy (p. 22). This classic instrumentalist approach is often wrong-headed when applied to devoted actors. To a significant degree, jihadis do not respond to utilitarian cost–benefit strategies (e.g., airport plotters may knowingly choose the targets that are most watched, plotters who know they are being watched sometimes openly flaunt this knowledge, European volunteers for Syria are up front about their readiness to die). They respond to moral values, are more than willing to die for the cause, and each death is publicized to inspire more young Muslims to join the cause. Indeed, utilitarian perspectives (offers of jobs, housing, money) often play into the hands of terrorists, who say that the USA and allies try to reduce people to material matters rather than moral beings.

Conclusion

Recent cross-cultural experiments and fieldwork related to costly group sacrifices and violent extremism favor consideration of today's most dangerous terrorists as devoted actors motivated by SVs, nonnegotiable preferences whose defense compels actions regardless of risks or costs. When SVs become embedded in fused groups of imagined kin who consider themselves in existential competition with other groups, then individuals in such groups (e.g., bands of brothers) become empowered to make great sacrifices and exertions, especially if they perceive themselves to be under existential threat from outside groups and if their primary reference group forms around a prior action-oriented association.

There is an evolutionary rationale to the willingness to make costly sacrifices for the group, unto death and against all odds. As Darwin (1871) suggested in *The Descent of Man,* only if sufficiently many members of a group are endowed with such a willingness to extreme sacrifice can the group hope to parry stronger but less devoted enemies who are less committed to disregarding the costs of action. SVs mobilized for collective action by devoted actors enables outsize commitment in low-power groups to resist and often prevail against materially more powerful foes who depend on standard material incentives, such as armies and police that rely on pay and promotion. Recent changes in the composition of some terrorist groups from fairly well-educated and well-off founders to increasingly marginalized youth in transitional stages of life continue to follow this evolutionary rationale.This goes for many foreign fighter volunteers from Europe and North Africa who join the Islamic State or Al Qaeda , or who act out their ideals, such as recent targeting of Jews and expressions of free speech that ostensibly hurt Muslim sensibilities.

Box 31.1: The 11 March 2004 Madrid Train Bombing Plot and the Link to Iraq

Through a series of unplanned events, two young North African immigrants bonded to plot an attack in Spain. They lived in separate worlds—religious extremism (Serhane Fakhet, "The Tunisian") and the criminal underworld (Jamal Ahmidan, a Moroccan fugitive known as "The Chinaman" for his sloping eyes and buck teeth)—until their paths crossed 6 months before the bombing. A detailed plot only began to coalesce in late December 2003, shortly after the Internet tract "Iraqi Jihad, Hopes and Risks" circulated on a Zarqawi-affiliated website. The tract called for "two or three attacks…to exploit the coming general elections in Spain in March 2004." The plot, which brought together a bunch of radical students and hangers on, drug traffickers, small-time dealers in stolen goods and other sorts of petty criminals, improbably succeeded precisely because it was so improbable. Indeed, Spanish police were following the three main groups of actors (Chinaman's friends, Tunisian's friends, Spaniards) but never realized they were connected. For example, the substitute Imam (codename "Cartagena") at the mosque where the Tunisian's friends met, periodically reported on informal meetings of their self-styled "Salafi Movement" for martyrdom action. In fact, the police helped to set up the plot: They arranged for a drugs-for-explosives exchange involving Spanish ex-cons who stole dynamite from a mine where they worked and a former cellmate (Rafa Zuheir) with ties to the Chinaman's Moroccan underworld of hashish and ecstasy traffickers. There was no real cell structure, hierarchy, recruitment, brainwashing, coherent organization, or al-Qaeda involvement. Yet, this half-baked conspiracy, concocted in a few months, with a target likely suggested over the Internet, was the immediate cause of regime change in a major democratic society.

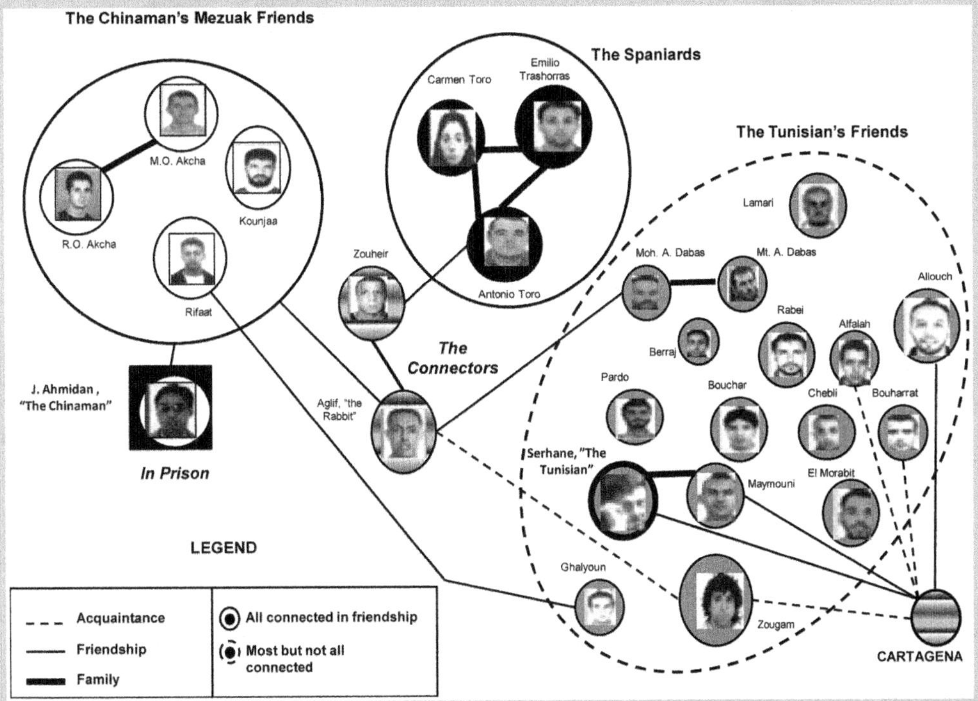

Three Main Circles of Friends Linked to the 11 March 2004 Madrid Train Bombing (Network relations in mid-2003, just before the Chinaman's jail release)

Five of the seven plotters who blew themselves up when cornered by police grew up within a few blocks of one another in the Chinaman's tumble-down neighborhood of Jemaa Mezuak in Tetuan, Morocco. Beginning in the summer of 2006, we found that at least a dozen other young men had volunteered to become martyrs in Iraq. We confirmed the names and itineraries of five who attended the same elementary school that Madrid's Moroccan bombers attended. All were soccer buddies. The cousin of one of the Iraq-bound group (Hamza) was married to one of the Madrid plotters (Kounjaa). Friends say the young men bound for Iraq all respected the courage of the Madrid plotters, but disagreed about civilian targets and believed that action in Iraq would be more just and "soldierly" than in Europe. Like the Madrid plotters (and the Hamburg and London plotters), they were buddies, hung out together at local cafés and restaurants, and mingled in the same barbershops (where young men gather and talk).

The Jamaa Mezuak Connection: After the Madrid plotters from Mezuak blew themselves up (April 3, 2004), friends in the neighborhood began contemplating their own "martyrdom actions" in Iraq (beginning in summer 2006)

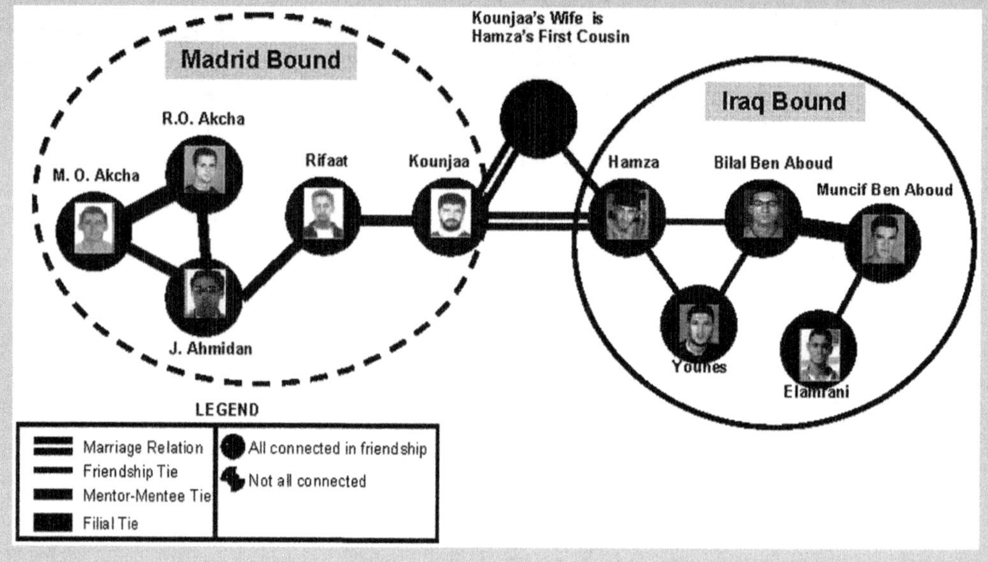

Box 31.2: The Attack Networks of Jemaah Islamiyah and Its Splinters

Jemaah Islamiyah (JI) is Al-Qaeda's most important Southeast Asian ally. We analyzed every attack by Southeast Asia's JI between 1999 and the second Bali bombing of 2005 and entered demographic details on all known operatives. Of about 180 people implicated in JI attacks, 78 % worked in unskilled jobs and 23 % had education beyond high school.

We found that operational associations in JI are determined by four variables: (1) being a member of the self-styled "Afghan Alumni," that is, someone who went through training with the Indonesia volunteers in the Abu Sayyaf's Sadah training camp during the Soviet–Afghan War and its immediate aftermath; (2) continuing to work together (e.g., on the Malaysian chicken farm of JI cofounder Abdullah Sungkar, who died in 1999) or play soccer together after demobilization from Afghanistan (and before JI was officially established); (3) having studied or taught in at least one of the two religious schools established by JI's cofounders, Sungkar and Abu Bakr Ba'asyir (al-Mukmin in Java and Lukman al-Hakiem in Malaysia); and (4) being related by kinship or marriage to someone else in the network (e.g., there are more than 30 marriages woven through 10 attacks). In contrast with these factors, we find that the knowledge of JI's "official" organizational structure is largely uninformative in helping us to understand the networks involved in JI attacks.

JI Family Ties—Attack View: The graph below shows the main clusters of family ties among important JI members and associates, as well as the positioning and connection among family clusters across three attacks: the 2000 bombing of the Philippines Ambassador's Residence (PAR), the 2002 Bali bombing, and the 2004 Australian Embassy bombing:

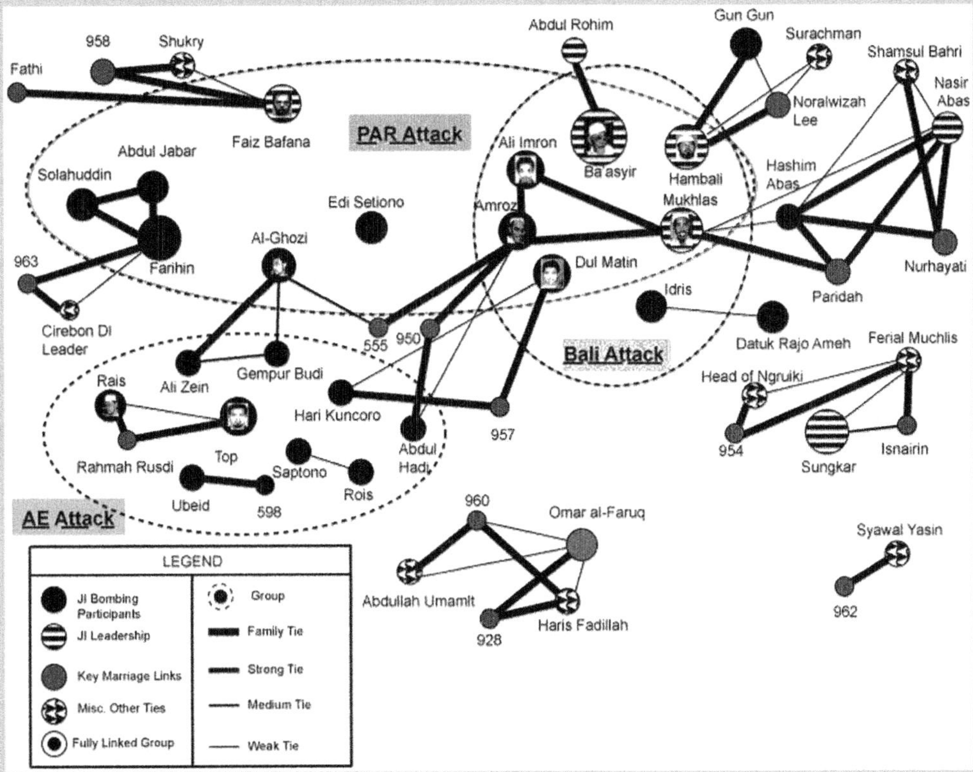

Following the arrest of JI emir (leader) Ba'aysir and the Bali bombing coordinator and al-Qaeda liaison, Hambali, splinters of the JI attack network reconstituted themselves around Noordin Top. The opening scene of the book and movie *The Godfather* sets the stage for the intrigue and action that will follow, just as do mafia marriages and marriage ceremonies in real life. And the same goes for terrorist groups: Marriages are convivial events for establishing rapport and trust among "friends of the family," and for reconstituting networks that have been torn up by police. This is how Noordin began to rebuild the attack network after the arrests that followed the first Bali and Marriot bombings. Four of the principal actors in the 2009 Jakarta Marriot and Ritz Carlton hotel bombings (also meant to kill Indonesian President Yudhoyono) were part of one village family: Syaifudin Jaelani, a herbal healer and Yemeni-trained imam of a local mosque, chose the suicide bombers. Amir Ibrahim, married to Jaelani's sister, booked room 1808 in the Marriott hotel where the suicide bombers stayed. Ibrohim, married to another of Jaelani's sisters, was the hotel florist who smuggled in the bombs. Jaelani's older brother, Mohamad Sjahir, was a technician who had infiltrated Garuda, Indonesia's national airline.

According to General Tito Karnavian, head of Indonesian police strike team that tracked down and eventually killed Noordin: "*Knowledge of the interconnected networks of Afghan Alumni, friendship, kinship and marriage groups was very crucial to uncovering the inner circle of Noordin*" (personal communication, December 10, 2009). Increasing success has depended on closer scrutiny and exploitation of social connections, not in directly attacking or challenging ideas and values. Those ideas and values continue to circulate and diffuse freely, and their potential for bringing in new blood remains. The problem for the future is how to prevent these values from embedding in tight-knit, action-oriented networks of youth.

2009 Jakarta Marriott and Ritz Carlton Hotel Bombings

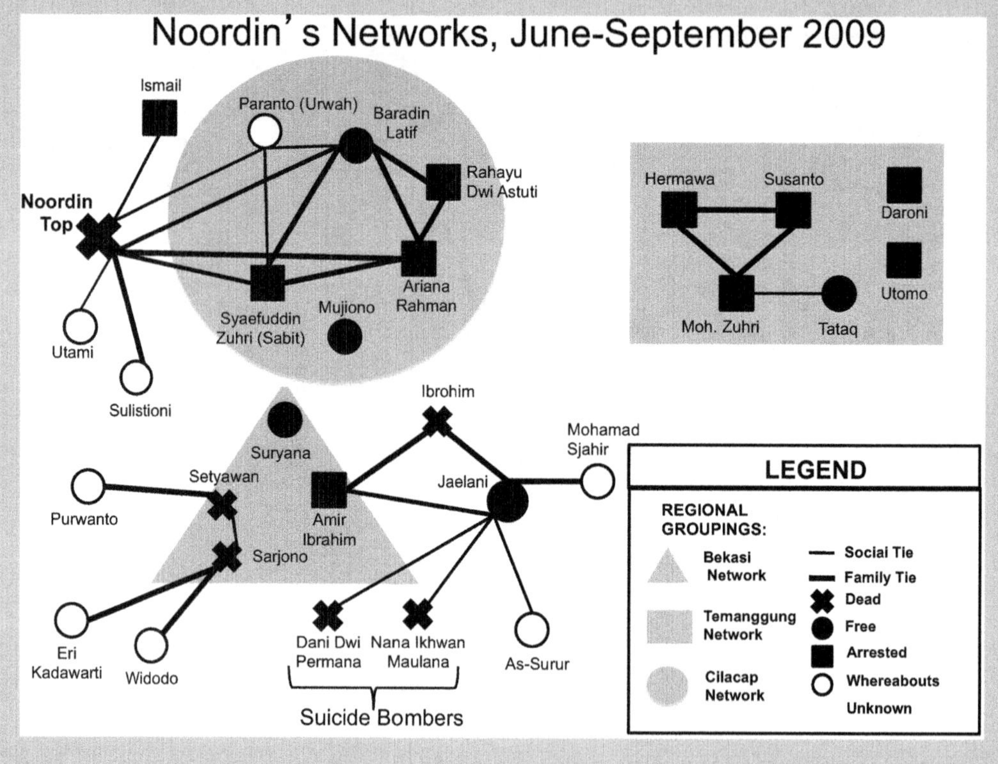

Acknowledgment Research was supported by grants from the National Science Foundation (BCS-827313, SES-0962080), the MINERVA programs of the Office of Naval Research (N000141310054), and the Air Force Office of Scientific Research (FA9550-14-1-0030 DEF).

References

Anderson, B. (1983). *Imagined communities*. New York: Verso.

Arreguín-Toft, I. (2001). How the weak win wars. *International Security, 26*, 93–128.

Atran, S. (2003). Genesis of suicide terrorism. *Science, 299*, 1534–1539.

Atran, S. (2010a). *Talking to the enemy: Violent extremism, sacred values, and what it means to be human*. London: Penguin.

Atran, S. (2010b). A question of honor: Why the Taliban fight and what to do about It. *Asian Journal of Social Science, 38*, 341–361.

Atran, S. (2011). *US Government Efforts to Counter Violent Extremism*, US Senate Armed Services Committee, 2010–2011 (Testimony, Response to Questions); http://www.jjay.cuny.edu/US_Senate_Hearing_on_Violent_Extremism.pdf.

Atran, S. (2013). Black and white and red all over: How the hyperkinetic media is breeding a new generation of terrorists. *Foreign Policy*. http://www.foreignpolicy.com/articles/2013/04/22/black_and_white_and_red_all_over_boston_bombing_terrorists_media.

Atran, S., & Axelrod, R. (2008). Reframing sacred values. *Negotiation Journal, 24,* 221–246.

Atran, S., & Ginges, J. (2012). Religious and sacred imperatives in human conflict. *Science, 336,* 855–857.

Atran, S., & Henrich, J. (2010). The evolution of religion. *Biological Theory, 5,* 18–30.

Atran, S., & Norenzayan, A. (2004). Religions evolutionary landscape. *Behavioral and Brain Sciences, 27,* 713–770.

Atran, S., Axelrod, R., & Davis, R. (2007). Sacred barriers to conflict resolution. *Science, 317,* 1039–1040.

Atran, S., & Ginges, J. (2015). Devoted actors and the moral foundations of intractable inter-group conflict. In J. Decety & T. Wheatley (Eds.), *The moral brain* (pp. 69-85). Cambridge: MIT Press.

Atran, S., Sheikh, H., & Gómez, Á. (2014a). Devoted actors fight for close comrades and sacred cause. Proceedings of the *National Academy of Sciences, USA, 111,* 17702–17703.

Atran, S., Sheikh, H., & Gómez, Á. (2014b). For cause and comrade: Devoted actors and willingness to fight. *Cliodynamics, 5,* 23–40.

Baumard, N., André, J., & Sperber, D. (2013). A mutualistic theory of morality. *Behavioral and Brain Sciences, 36,* 59–122.

Becker, G. (1962). Irrational behavior and economic theory. *The Journal of Political Economy, 70,* 1–13.

Bergen, P., & Lind, M. (2007). A matter of pride: Why we can't buy off Osama Bin Laden. *Democracy Journal*. www.democracyjournal.org/article.php?ID†=6496.

Bennis, W., Medin, D., & Bartels, D. (2010). The costs and benefits of calculations and moral rules. *Perspectives on Psychological Science, 5,* 187–202.

Berns, G. S., Bell, E., Capra, C. M., Perietula, M. J., Moore, S., Anderson, B., Ginges, J, & Atran, S. (2012). The price of your soul: Neural evidence for the nonutilitarian representation of sacred values. *Philosophical Transactions of the Royal Society–B, 367,* 754–762.

Berns, G., Bell, E., & Capra, M. (2013). *Moral outrage and the neurobiological antecedents to political conflict*. Presented to AFOSR Annual Trust and Influence Review, Dayton, OH, January 16.

Brin, D. (2012). A contrarian perspective on altruism. In B. Oakley, A. Knafo, G. Muadhavan, & D. S. Wilson (Eds.), *Pathological altruism* (pp. 77–84). New York: Oxford University Press.

Caplan, B. (2006). Terrorism: The relevance of the rational choice model. *Public Choice, 128,* 91–107.

Choi, J.-K., & Bowles, S. (2007). The coevolution of parochial altruism and war. *Science, 318,* 636–640.

Darwin, C. (1871). *The descent of man, and selection in relation to sex*. London: John Murray.

Dehghani, M., Atran, S. Iliev, Sachdeva, R., Ginges J., & Medin, D. (2010). Sacred values and conflict over Iran's nuclear program. *Judgment and Decision Making, 5,* 540–546.

Fearon, J. (1995). Rationalist explanations for war. *International Organization, 49,* 379–414.

Frey, B. (2004). *Dealing with terrorism: Stick or Carrot?* Northhampton: Edward Elgar Publishing.

Gambetta, D., & Hertog, S. (2007). *Engineers of Jihad*. Sociology Working Papers, no. 2007–10; http://www.nuff.ox.ac.uk/users/gambetta/Engineers%20of%20Jihad.pdf.

Ganor, B. (2009). Terrorism in the twenty-first century. In S. Shapira, J. Hammond, & L. Cole (Eds.), *Essentials of terror medicine* (pp. 13–26). New York: Springer.

Gazzaniga, M. S. (Ed.). (2009). *The cognitive neurosciences*. Cambridge: MIT Press.

Ginges, J., & Atran, S. (2009). Why do people participate in violent collective action? *Annals of the New York Academy of Sciences, 1167,* 115–123.

Ginges, J., & Atran, S. (2011). War as a moral imperative. *Proceedings of the Royal Society–B, 278,* 2930–2938.

Ginges, J., Atran, S., Medin, D., & Shikaki, K. (2007). Sacred bounds on rational resolution of violent political conflict. *Proceedings of the National Academy of Sciences, USA, 104,* 7357–7360.

Ginges, J., Atran, S., Sachdeva, S., & Medin, D. (2011). Psychology out of the laboratory: The challenge of violent extremism. *American Psychologist, 66,* 507–519.

Graham, J., & Haidt, J. (2013). Sacred values and evil adversaries. In P. Shaver & M. Mikulincer (Eds.), *The social psychology of morality* (pp. 11–31). New York: APA Books.

Hobbes, T. (1651/1901). *Leviathan*. New York: E.P. Dutton.

Hoffman, B., & McCormick, G. (2004). Terrorism, signaling, and suicide attack. *Studies in Conflict & Terrorism, 27,* 243–281.

Kanazawa, S. (2007). The evolutionary psychological imagination. *Journal of Social, Evolutionary, and Cultural Psychology, 1,* 7–17.

Magouirk, J., Atran, S., & Sageman, M. (2008). Connecting terrorist networks. *Studies in Conflict and Terrorism, 31,* 1–16.

Norenzayan, A., & Shariff, A. (2008). The origin and evolution of religious prosociality. *Science, 322,* 58–62.

Rawls, J. (1971). *A theory of justice*. Cambridge: Harvard University Press.

Rushton, J. P. (2005). Ethnic nationalism, evolutionary psychology and genetic similarity theory. *Nations and Nationalism, 11,* 489–507.

Sageman, M. (2004). *Understanding terror networks*. Philadelphia: University of Pennsylvania Press.

Sageman, M. (2009). Confronting al-Qaeda. Testimony to the Senate Foreign Relations Committee, October 7; http://www.ebookdb.org/reading/31347CGA1773512938272C69/Confronting-Al-Qaeda-Understanding-The-Threat-In-Afghanistan-And-Beyond–Congres.

Sheikh, H., Atran, S., Ginges, J., Wilson, L., Obeid, N., & Davis. R. (2014). The devoted actor as parochial altruist: Sectarian morality, identity fusion, and support for costly sacrifices. *Cliodynamics, 5,* 23–40.

Sheikh, H., Ginges, J., & Atran, S. (2013). Sacred values in intergroup conflict. *Annals of the New York Academy of Sciences, 1299,* 11–24.

Sheikh, H., Ginges, J., Coman, A., & Atran, S. (2012). Religion, group threat and sacred values. *Judgment and Decision Making, 7,* 110–18.

Sosis, R., Kress, H., & Boster, J. (2007). Scars for war: Evaluating alternative signaling explanations for cross-cultural variance in ritual costs. *Evolution and Human Behavior, 28,* 234–247.

Swann, W., Jetten, J., Gómez, Á., Whitehouse, H., & Bastian, B. (2012). When group membership gets personal: A theory of identity fusion. *Psychological Review, 119,* 441–456.

Swann, W., Buhrmester, M., Gómez, Á., Jetten, J., Bastian, B., Vázquez, A., & Zhang, A. (2014). What makes a group worth dying for? *Journal of Personality and Social Psychology, 106,* 912–926.

Van Slyke, J. (2014). Moral psychology, neuroscience, and virtue. In K. Timpe & C. Boyd (Eds.), *Virtues and their vices* (pp. 459–480). New York: Oxford University Press.

von Clausewitz, C. (1832/1956). *On war*. New York: Barnes & Noble.

Wilson, D. S. (2002). *Darwin's cathedral*. Chicago: University of Chicago Press.

Wintrobe, R. (2006). *Rational extremism*. New York: Cambridge University Press.

Zarate, J. (2013). *Treasury's war*. New York: PublicAffairs.

Part VIII

Health and Psychological Adjustment

The Parasite-Stress Theory of Sociality and the Behavioral Immune System

32

Randy Thornhill and Corey L. Fincher

People are parasitically modified animals as a result of their interactions with parasites (i.e., infectious diseases of all types) during evolutionary historical generations and during their individual lifetimes. The evolutionary ancestral interactions with parasites gave rise to the Darwinian selection that crafted the classical immune system and the behavioral immune system of humans, as well as the functional integration and synergy of these two systems in defending against parasites. During the lifetime of individual humans, their interactions with cues correlated with risk of infectious disease proximately cause the values or preferences and associated emotions and cognitions that function to yield the personal social psychology and behavior to match the infectious-disease level locally. This perspective on humans as parasitically modified animals is strongly supported by a rapidly growing literature.

We have called the relatively new set of concepts and associated evidence supporting this perspective "the parasite-stress theory of sociality." This theory appears to be a general theory of human culture and sociality. In novel ways, it informs and synthesizes knowledge of some major categories of social life and societal-level affairs of people, ranging from prejudice and egalitarianism to personality, economic patterns, core values, interpersonal and intergroup violence, governmental systems, gender relations, family structure, and the genesis and maintenance of cultural diversity across the world. The theory's generality also illuminates important features of nonhuman animals, particularly family organization, kinship behavior, patterns of movement, and the origin of new species. The empirical evidence for this broad application of the parasite-stress theory of sociality is reviewed fully by Thornhill and Fincher (2014; partial reviews in Fincher and Thornhill 2012a, b).

In this chapter, the parasite-stress theory and some related empirical patterns discovered by the theory are discussed, with focus on human sociality. Also, we expand and clarify the theory by identifying how human behavioral immunity affects the evolution of genetic immunity to infectious diseases, the virulence and host-to-host transmission rate of these diseases, and the linkage of host traits of genetic immunity and behavioral immunity; these added features, we argue, result in effective mechanisms of in-group defense against parasites and promote intergroup divergence and the resultant emergence of new cultures.

In addition, we expand the typical conception of human behavioral immunity discussed in the recent literature to incorporate more of the phenotypic traits that function to defend against

R. Thornhill (✉)
Department of Biology, University of New Mexico, Castetter Hall, Albuquerque, NM 87131-1091, USA
e-mail: rthorn@unm.edu

C. L. Fincher
Department of Psychology, University of Warwick, Coventry CV4 7AL, UK
e-mail: c.fincher@warwick.ac.uk

V. Zeigler-Hill et al. (eds.), *Evolutionary Perspectives on Social Psychology,* Evolutionary Psychology, DOI 10.1007/978-3-319-12697-5_32, © Springer International Publishing Switzerland 2015

infectious disease. Schaller (2006) coined the term "behavioral immune system" and proposed that it consists of a group of psychological adaptations that function to regulate infectious-disease-avoidance behaviors. We show that the human behavioral immune system is much more diverse in its psychological and behavioral repertoires than Schaller emphasized. In addition to infectious-disease-avoidance adaptations, the behavioral immune system includes adaptations for managing infectious diseases that invade a group. Also, the disease-avoidance component of the behavioral immune system includes adaptations that regulate dispersal from the natal region dependent upon local infectious-disease adversity. We discuss, too, some other features of behavioral immunity that may be overlooked when the focus is only on avoidance of contact with contagion.

Finally, we consider and reject an alternative hypothesis—the parasite-manipulation hypothesis—for traits that we interpret as human adaptations of behavioral immunity. We conclude that people are psychologically and behaviorally modified by parasites in ways that defend against infectious disease rather than parasitically manipulated to promote the reproductive interest of parasites by increasing their transmission to new hosts.

The Parasite-Stress Theory of Sociality

Immunity

Established knowledge of the ecology and evolution of parasitic diseases provides part of the foundation for the parasite-stress theory of sociality (also referred to as the parasite-stress theory of values; Thornhill et al. 2009). Infectious diseases are significant causes of Darwinian selection acting on all life. For modern humans, parasites appear to be the predominant cause of evolutionary change. Geneticists who study evolutionary changes in genes of the human genome report that parasites account for more evolutionary action across the genome than other environmental factors that are also sources of selection. Recently, Fumagalli et al. (2011) reviewed much of the published evidence of recent evolution in the human genome in response to infectious diseases. They report, too, their extensive study across 55 contemporary human populations showing that compared to genes involved in dealing with 13 other environmental challenges (climatic and geographic factors, diet, metabolic traits, subsistence strategies), genes related to immunity exhibit significantly more allelic variation and hence evolutionary change across geographic regions. Immunity genes are evolutionary hotspots, and forces of Darwinian selection that are region-specific act more strongly on those genes than other genes so far studied. Indeed, a large portion of the current morbidity and mortality across the world and even across regions of the USA may be attributable to parasitic diseases (Thornhill and Fincher 2011).

In addition, infectious diseases also were a major source of morbidity and mortality, and hence of natural selection, in human evolutionary history (Anderson and May 1991; Dobson and Carper 1996; Ewald 1994; McNeill 1998; Volk and Atkinson 2013; Wolfe et al. 2007). Volk and Atkinson (2013) recently published an important review of rates and causes of human juvenile mortality in three ethnographic samples representative of ecological conditions in human evolutionary history: hunter–gatherer societies without contact with modern technology that can affect mortality (e.g., medicine, sanitation, education, birth control); agriculturalist societies with very limited access to modern technology; and ancient historical populations, extending in some cases as far back as several 100 years BC The data on rates of infant and child mortality reflected the probability of mortality by age 1 year and by approximate sexual maturity at age 15 years, respectively. Across the three samples combined, infant mortality was about 25% and child mortality about 50%, and similar mortality patterns were seen across the three samples. Volk and Atkinson limited their study to samples with relatively large sample sizes from reliable sources, and emphasized that their estimates are likely considerably below the actual mortality rates. The two largest mortality factors were infectious disease (especially gastrointestinal and respiratory illnesses) and infanticide, with the former greatly predominating. In sum, infectious disease was the chief cause of juvenile mortality in the evolutionary historical settings comprising the juvenile mortality data reviewed by Volk and Atkinson. Finally, the existence of complex, evolved human adaptations that are organized functionally to defend against parasites documents that natural selection acting in the deep-time past of human evolutionary history directly favored individuals with defenses against infectious diseases.

Humans have two immune systems. One is the *classical immune system:* the biochemical, physiological, cellular, and tissue-based mechanisms of defense against parasites discussed in traditional textbooks for immunology courses taught at universities. The second is the *behavioral immune system*. It is comprised of the psychological features and behaviors for infectious-disease avoidance (Schaller 2006; Schaller and Duncan 2007) as well as for managing the effects of infectious diseases (Fincher and Thornhill 2008a). The human behavioral immune system has only recently been researched in detail, and the resulting cornucopia of findings will require major expansion of immunology textbooks. Furthermore, behavioral immunity research is connecting knowledge on behavioral immunity, classical immunity, and sociality by anchoring the three topics in shared proximate and ultimate causation of infectious-disease adversity.

Host–Parasite Coevolution

Hosts and their parasites coevolve in antagonistic and perpetual races with adaptation, counter-adaptation, counter-counter-adaptation, and so on; there is no lasting adaptive solution that can be mounted by either side against the other (Ewald 1994; Ridley 1993; Thompson 2005; Van Valen 1973). In the human case, this dynamic, antagonistic interaction is illustrated by the fact that, despite the huge somatic allocation made to the classical immune system, people still get sick and even small reductions in immunocompetence increase vulnerability to infectious disease.

Furthermore, host–parasite arms races typically are localized geographically across the range of a host species and its parasite, creating a coevolutionary mosaic involving genetic and phenotypic differences in host immune adaptation and corresponding parasite counter-adaptation (Thompson 2005). An important outcome of the geographical localization of parasite–host coevolutionary races is that host defense works most effectively, or only, against the local parasite species, strains, or genotypes, and not against those evolving in nearby host groups. Hence, out-groups may often harbor novel parasites that cannot be defended against very well or at all by an individual or his or her immunologically similar in-group members (Fincher et al. 2008; Fincher and Thornhill 2008a, b). Out-group individuals pose the additional infectious-disease threat of lacking knowledge of local customs, manners, and norms in general, many of which, like methods of hygiene or food preparation, may prevent infection from local parasites; also, individuals with out-group norms may carry out-group parasites (Fincher et al. 2008; Schaller and Neuberg 2008). Norms of many types—culinary, linguistic, moral, sexual, nepotistic, religious, dress, and so on—are used by people both to display in-group affiliation and associated values and to distinguish in-group from out-group members. Norm differences between groups are often the basis of intergroup prejudice and hostility (i.e., xenophobia). Likewise, norm similarity is the basis of positive valuation of and altruism toward people (Murray et al. 2011; Norenzayan and Shariff 2008; Park and Schaller 2005).

The emotion of disgust is not only evoked in the context of perception of disease-laden cues, such as contaminated foods, sick people, parasites (e.g., worms), or parasite reservoirs (e.g., cockroaches), but also is commonly generalized to include: (a) groups of people who are perceived as harboring infectious disease and (b) cultural behaviors that are different or unfamiliar (Curtis 2007; Curtis et al. 2004). Thus, disgust directed toward out-group people appears to be a component of behavioral immunity that provides a boundary between in-group and out-group and promotes out-group avoidance. This includes so-called moral disgust toward others in which others' beliefs, norms, values, manners, or behavior are deemed morally undesirable or repugnant (Curtis et al. 2011; Inbar et al. 2012; Oaten et al. 2009; Schnall et al. 2008).

Evidence for geographically localized host–parasite coevolutionary races is abundant. On the parasite side of the race, a parasite geographical mosaic was found, for example, in research on the human protozoan parasite *Leishmania braziliensis*. Rougeron et al. (2009) described the high genetic diversity and subdivided population structure of this parasite across both Peru and Bolivia. They found high levels of microgeographic variation identifiable by at least 124 highly localized, physiologically and genetically distinct strains.

The extremely fine-grained geographic mosaic in *L. braziliensis* implies a similar microgeographic immunological genetic mosaic in human hosts. This type of spatial variation in host adaptation against local parasites, or, said differently, in host immune maladaptation against out-group-typical parasites, is a common pattern in the animal and plant infectious disease literature (e.g., Corby-Harris and Promislow 2008; Dionne et al. 2007; Kaltz et al. 1999; Thompson 2005; Tinsley et al. 2006). Specific human cases showing this include the caste-specific infectious diseases and associated caste-specific immunity among Indian castes in the same geographic locale (Pitchappan 2002). Another case is found in the village-specific immune defenses against *Leishmania* parasites in adjacent Sudanese villages (Miller et al. 2007). In particular regions, the localization of host immunity to local parasites is so fine-grained that people inbreed, risking the potential costs of inbreeding depression, to maintain coadapted gene complexes important for coping with parasite infection in their offspring, as Denic and et al. have shown for malaria across regions (Denic and Nicholls 2007; Denic et al. 2008a, b), and we—along with our colleagues—have proposed and found empirical support for parasite stress in general across countries (Hoben et al. 2010; also Hoben 2011). On a broad scale, the localization of host–parasite coevolutionary races in humans is seen dramatically in the findings of the human genetic research noted above: There is more regional variation in genes affecting classical immunity than in many other human genes affecting fitness.

There are other bodies of evidence of localized host immunity. One familiar type of evidence involves events where individuals from isolated groups interact with novel groups by conquest or trade and infectious disease transmission ensues, sometimes with drastic effects. This has occurred after the intra- and intercontinental movement of individuals brought about intergroup contact (Diamond 1998; Good 1972; McNeill 1998). Some other human examples of localized immunity are discussed by Fincher and Thornhill (2012a).

Assortative Sociality: An Aspect of the Behavioral Immune System

In an ecological setting of high disease stress, reduced dispersal, xenophobia, and ethnocentrism reflect evolved preferences/values and motivate behaviors for avoidance of novel parasites contained in out-groups and for the management of local infectious disease (Fincher and Thornhill 2008a, b, 2012a). Philopatry is psychological preference for the natal locale. It is manifested in behaviors that reduce movements away from the natal location. In areas of high parasite adversity, compared to areas of low parasite adversity, philopatry will be the optimal habitat preference because of the correspondent increase in social association with immunologically similar individuals and decreased contact with more distant, and differently parasitized, individuals and their habitats. Likewise, xenophobia—the avoidance and dislike of out-group members—discourages contact with out-groups and their likely different parasites. Neophobia—the dislike of new ideas and ways of doing—is a component of xenophobia; according to the parasite-stress theory of sociality, neophobia functions like xenophobia. Ethnocentrism is in-group favoritism entailing nepotism toward both nuclear and extended family and altruism toward other immunologically similar in-group members. This support and loyalty toward in-group members defends against the morbidity and mortality effects of parasites (Navarrete and Fessler 2006; Sugiyama 2004; Sugiyama and Sugiyama 2003). Sugiyama (2004) reported that in the Shiwiar, an indigenous society without ready access to modern medicine, health care in the forms of food and other assistance from in-group members to persons suffering from infectious disease is a major factor lowering mortality. This parasite-management benefit of embeddedness in the local in-group seems to characterize numerous traditional societies in the ethnographic record (Gurven et al.2000; Sugiyama 2004; Sugiyama and Sugiyama 2003). To paraphrase Navarrete and Fessler (2006), in human evolutionary history, under high parasite stress, in-group members were the only health insurance one had, and it was adaptive to have always paid your premiums—in terms of social investment and loyalty toward in-group allies that buffer one and one's family against the morbidity and mortality of infectious disease.

Hence, philopatry, xenophobia (including neophobia), and ethnocentrism—the basic features of assortative sociality and important features of the behavioral immune system—are expected to be values and normative behaviors predominantly in areas of high parasite stress (Fincher et al. 2008; Fincher and Thornhill 2008a; Thornhill et al. 2009). Yet, humans have experienced parasite gradients throughout history and continue to do so today (Dobson and Carper 1996; Guernier et al. 2004; Lopez et al. 2006; Low 1990; McNeill 1998; Smith et al. 2007; Wolfe et al. 2007). Thus, we expect that the benefits and costs of assortative sociality will shift along the parasite-stress gradient such that in ecological settings of high parasite stress, high levels of assortative sociality will be more beneficial than in circumstances of low parasite stress. As parasite stress declines, the infectious-disease risks to individuals of dispersal and interaction with out-groups decrease. Consequently, for individuals in ecological settings that are relatively low in parasite stress, out-group contacts and alliances can provide greater benefits than costs. The benefits of out-group interactions include gains through access to goods, services, and ideas of other groups, as well as through diversified and sometimes larger social networks for marriage and other social alliances (Fincher et al. 2008; Thornhill et al. 2009). Research discussed later in this chapter has shown that the components of assortative sociality or behavioral immunity respond quantitatively to regional variation in parasite adversity, as predicted by this reasoning.

Conditional Behavioral Immunity

The parasite-stress theory of sociality posits an ancestrally adaptive, condition-dependent adoption of in-group and out-group values and related social tactics by individuals, dependent on variable local parasite stress. This condition-dependent adaptation, like other condition-dependent adaptations, requires for its evolution, local variation on a short time scale in the selection pressures responsible for it. Hence, evolutionary historical selection due to morbidity and mortality from parasites varied locally in individual lifetimes and thereby favored contingent behavioral and psychological adaptations for assortative sociality.

The evolution of conditionality as an important feature of assortative sociality's functional design, rather than a region-specific genetically distinct adaptation, is consistent with knowledge about infectious diseases. The dynamics of an infectious disease can generate considerable variation in prevalence, transmissibility, and pathogenicity of the disease agent across the range of its host species, as well as on a fine-grained, local scale within an individual's lifetime. Important factors affecting this variability at a single locale and in a single generation are temporal changes in host group size, weather, disease-vector abundance and behavior, and the number, virulence and dynamics of the different diseases infecting hosts (Anderson and May 1991; Corby-Harris and Promislow 2008; Ewald 1994; Guernier et al. 2004; Loker 2012; Prugnolle et al. 2005). Thus, in-group assortative sociality is an example of evolved phenotypic plasticity within individuals. That is, the individual possesses a conditional strategy with multiple contingent tactics (Fincher et al. 2008; Schaller and Murray 2008; Thornhill et al. 2009). Such plasticity in traits is favored by

Darwinian selection when phenotypic change allows the individual to modify its phenotypic expression in directions that give greater net inclusive fitness benefit than that achieved by a single static phenotype.

A considerable body of research supports the hypothesis of an evolved contingent assortative sociality in people that functions against contagion. In some of the earliest studies of behavioral immunity, Faulkner et al. (2004) and Navarrete and Fessler (2006) provided evidence, based on numerous and diverse Western samples, that scores among individuals on scales that measure the degree of xenophobia and ethnocentrism correspond to chronic individual differences in worry about contracting or catching infectious disease (measured by the perceived-vulnerability-to-disease scale, see Duncan et al. 2009); those who perceive high infectious-disease risk are more xenophobic and ethnocentric than those who perceive low disease risk. Importantly, this research also showed that xenophobia and ethnocentrism within individuals increase under experimental primes of greater parasite salience in the current environment.

Other research has documented within-individual shifts in personality—toward greater introversion and avoidance of novelty—and in heightened classical immune responses as well as behavioral avoidance of strangers immediately after research participants view cues of infectious-disease salience. Mortensen et al. (2010) reported that subjects viewing slides with disease-salient cues immediately exhibited greater feelings promoting between-person avoidance (i.e., extraversion, openness to experience, and agreeableness were reduced) in comparison to these subjects' feelings upon viewing control slides. These researchers also found that subjects with high scores on the scale of perceived vulnerability to disease showed greater feelings of interpersonal avoidance than did subjects with low scores on the same scale. Finally, these researchers reported that viewing disease-salient slides resulted in increased avoidant arm movements when subjects viewed facial photos of strangers, especially for subjects high in perceived vulnerability to disease. Schaller et al. (2010) reported that participants who observed slides of people with infectious disease symptoms (e.g., pox, skin lesions, sneezing) immediately mounted a classical immune response. Their white blood cells produced elevated amounts of inflammatory cytokine-interleukin-6 when exposed to bacterial antigens. This immune response was not seen in participants who viewed control slides, including those who viewed slides depicting a person pointing a gun directly at them. Hence, the immune response was not a general reaction to danger or threat, but was specific to cues of other people with symptoms of parasitic infection. Research by Stevenson et al. (2011) compared salivary immune markers between research participants in whom disgust was induced by disease-relevant pictorial cues documented to be disgust-elicitors (e.g., a dirty toilet, an eye infection) and other participants who were exposed to either negative, but disease-irrelevant, pictures or neutral pictures. The disgust-primed group showed an oral classical immune response, but the other groups did not.

When considered together, these studies by Mortensen et al. (2010), Schaller et al. (2010), and Stevenson et al. (2011) reveal that visually perceiving cues pertinent to risk of parasitic infection generate immediate cellular and biochemical classical immune responses, change in perceptions of one's own personality, change in disgust sensitivity, and behavioral actions that defend against contagion and motivate avoidance of infectious people. Hence, such cues activate markedly the classical immune system as well as the behavioral immune system, and the dual activation is functionally coordinated to defend against infectious-disease threat.

In sum, there is considerable evidence of both interindividual stable differences and within-individual conditionality in xenophobic and ethnocentric values and related personality features and behaviors, and evidence that both the interindividual consistency and within-individual contingency are caused by infectious-disease problems in the local environment. The proximate means by which individuals assess local parasite stress—and thereby ontogenetically and contingently express the locally adaptive degree of assortative sociality—may include immune system activation (such as, the frequency of infection; Stevenson et al. 2009) and social learning of local disease risks (Fincher et al. 2008). Both these causes may act typically during an individual's development and account for the interindividual and within-individual variation in values affecting in- and out-group behavioral preferences and degree of philopatry. In regard to immune system activation, Stevenson et al. (2009) found that people with high contamination sensitivity (an individual-difference variable related to perceived vulnerability to disease), reported a history of high infectious diseases (but not recency of infections), implying that an ontogeny of repeated activation of the classical immune system may underlie the adoption of assortative-sociality values and associated behavior. These researchers also reported that people with high contamination sensitivity and disgust sensitivity had fewer recent infectious diseases than people with low sensitivities, providing evidence of a protective function of these emotions against these diseases.

Our emphasis on adaptive contingency in the adoption and use of assortative-sociality tactics does not imply that we expect no variation across human groups in genetic adaptation for assortative sociality. As outlined by Durham (1991) and Blute (2010), culture–gene coevolution involves allelic frequency changes (i.e., evolution) that correspond to changes in cultural traits. Culture–gene coevolution may produce genetically differentiated cross-cultural variation in the values and behaviors of assortative sociality. For example, in areas of consistently high parasite prevalence, cultural practices of xenophobia, philopatry, and ethnocentrism may select for alleles affecting psychological features that promote the learning and effective use of these values (Fincher et al. 2008). Our argument is that infectious-disease problems are locally variable on a short time scale as a result of temporal changes mentioned above, and hence significant conditionality will be favored and maintained by selection even in the presence of localized genetic adaptation functioning in adoption and use of local values and behaviors. There is some evidence that culture–gene coevolution may play a role in cross-national variation in assortative sociality, specifically in the value dimension collectivism–individualism (Chiao and Blizinsky 2010; Way and Lieberman 2010). That genetically distinct adaptations for coping with an ecological problem and condition-dependent adaptation for the same problem domain can co-occur within individuals is well established in the literature of alternative reproductive tactics (recent review in Oliveira et al. 2008).

Behavioral Immunity Adaptively Manages False Positives

Only fairly recently has it been demonstrated scientifically that parasites, most of which are microscopic, cause disease. Natural selection in all animal species favors individuals with indirect knowledge of infectious-disease risk and the avoidance of such risks. Hence, there are directly selected human psychological features that attend to, and process information about, environmental cues that, across generations of human evolutionary history, corresponded with risk of contagion. Moreover, given that an error in judging a contagion risk can be grave, selection has built behavioral immunity to adaptively accept many false positives—i.e., deduce contagion risk when it is absent (Curtis 2007; Duncan and Schaller 2009; Oaten et al. 2009). As a result, people's behavioral immune system sometimes overreacts to even the hint of contagion danger in our environment, including our social environment. This is why a person's encounter with a stranger who speaks a different dialect or possesses a different value system may evoke strong xenophobia toward the stranger. This, too, is a cause of disgust and associated prejudice of many people toward sexual minorities (homosexuals and bisexuals), obese or very thin people, the elderly, people with noncontagious diseases, or physically or mentally challenged people who show behavior that deviates from the norm (for reviews, see Duncan and Schaller 2009; Kouznetsova et al. 2012; Ryan et al. 2012; Terrizzi et al. 2010, 2012).

New Additions to the Parasite-Stress Theory

We expand in this section on the basic parasite-stress theory of sociality by making explicit some important features that were not included in earlier published discussions of the theory. As discussed above, in a region of high parasite adversity, the localized coevolutionary parasite–host races result in Darwinian selection favoring individuals with alleles that contribute to classical immunity against local parasites. Also, behavioral immunity in the form of cultural values and behaviors that promote parasite avoidance and management are originated, adopted widely, and increase in frequency in descendant generations because of their adaptive value. These values and behaviors function in: (a) avoidance of out-group members that are infected or potentially infected with novel parasites to which local classical immunity is reduced (i.e., xenophobia); (b) developing strong and interdependent social ties with local people (and hence immunologically locally adapted individuals), which provide social investment and protection against the effects of parasitic infection (i.e., ethnocentrism or parochialism); and (c) restricting movements to the local habitat (i.e., philopatry).

Note that there are two types of preferences or values at work. One is social preference for individuals who manifest the locally adaptive antiparasite values and behaviors. Social interactions are biased toward these individuals because they have classical and behavioral immunity to local parasites and hence present less contagion risk than occurs in interactions with behaviorally dissimilar individuals. This in-group social preference refers to the preferential alliance and transaction with similar and local others, including mating and other social contact (e.g., nepotism, reciprocity, cooperative hunting, cooperative breeding). In humans, this includes behaviors of discriminative affiliation based on the presence of similar normative behavior (norms), styles of adornment, religious and other values, dialects and other language use, or other cultural traits that distinguish local from nonlocal people. The second type of preference involved is for the acquisition by individuals of cultural values and behaviors that are locally defensive against infectious disease. In humans, this discriminative enculturation is regulated by psychological adaptations functionally designed for the strategic adoption of values and other cultural items through learning that promote survival and reproductive success in the local culture.

Note, too, that in ecological settings of parasite adversity the values and behaviors of in-group embeddedness, xenophobia, and philopatry generate localized population structuring. Xenophobia generates in-group boundary. In-group social preference and philopatry localize social interactions and reproduction to the natal region. Local reproduction increases genetic relatedness among in-group members. In turn, the increased genetic similarity promotes natural selection for kin altruism (nepotism) as well as the adaptiveness of engaging in kin altruism, because increased relatedness of interacting individuals raises the reproductive gains (inclusive reproductive success) from altruism (Hamilton 1964). The localized population structuring arising from assortative sociality, through the increased genetic relatedness within a group it creates, fosters nepotistically embedded extended families.

Note also that increased relatedness among locals arising from assortative sociality and local reproduction not only magnifies the adaptive value of nepotism but also promotes the rapid spread of new mutant alleles that confer resistance to local parasites, as first suggested by Best et al. (2011). Given the increased relatedness of individuals in a group, when such a mutant arises, its bearers likely will be in close proximity to other individuals who also have the mutant allele. Then, local reproduction and in-group assortative social favoritism and altruism will magnify the natural selection for the mutant, providing rapid and widespread immunity in the in-group against local parasites. As alleles for resistance to local parasites increase in frequency in the local group as a result of this natural selection, the parasite severity (number of cases of the disease) declines. In turn, as Best et al. (2011) discussed, declining parasite severity corresponds to lower host-to-host transmission rate of the parasite.

Reduced transmission rate of a parasite is an ecological context in which natural selection favors lower virulence in the parasite (Ewald 1994). Hence, the combination of localized population structure and increased genetic relatedness of in-group members, in-group assortative sociality, and selection for both local parasite resistance in hosts and low virulence in parasites produces an encompassing defense against local contagion. Hence, the benefits of in-group assortativeness in coping with contagion extend beyond the behavioral immunity features of xenophobia, ethnocentrism, and philopatry. Its long-term beneficial consequences are the reduction of the prevalence and virulence of parasitic diseases that are present in the local group.

Moreover, at the same time, the traits of: (a) local genetic immunity, (b) preference for the local habitat (philopatry), (c) social preference for in-group members with local behaviors, and (d) avoidance of out-group members will become coupled within individuals. Each of the four traits corresponds to high inclusive fitness of individuals and hence becomes increasingly represented in descendant generations. Also, mating is nonrandom; specifically, mating and reproduction are local and hence produce inbreeding. Inbreeding may have the selective advantage of coupling coadapted alleles that defend against local infectious diseases (Fincher and Thornhill 2008a). Supporting this reasoning is the evidence that the frequency of consanguineous marriages is related positively to parasite stress both across contemporary countries of the world and indigenous societies (Hoben 2011; Hoben et al. 2010).

The coupling of traits of genetic and behavioral immunity, we propose, plays an important role in creating effective local defense against parasites. Consider a human society living in a setting of high parasite adversity and associated localized parasite–host antagonistic coevolution. Suppose discriminating in-group members from other people can be achieved by a local cultural innovation, such as a new religious belief or dialect. Both acquiring the new cultural item and preferring those who show it in their behavior are defensive against novel parasites in out-groups because the cultural item is not available to and used by the out-group people who may possess novel parasites; therefore, the cultural item distinguishes the in- versus out-group. In this scenario, individuals who adopt the new cultural item and prefer its presence in others with whom social interactions occur have more descendants than individuals who do not, and the predominant descendants socially learn the adaptive cultural item and the bias favoring in-group social interactions. With time, both the cultural item and the preference for others with it become common in the locale. Within individuals, the cultural item will be linked with the preference for others with it, as well as with any present genetic resistance against local parasites. Simultaneously, cultural ideas that limit dispersal, as well as cultural values that focus social investment on in-group members and motivate avoidance of out-group individuals, arise and become common because they are adaptive against local infectious disease. Genetic immunity and all the cultural traits of assortative sociality are linked within individuals and hence mutually reinforce each other (i.e., when any one increases in descendant generations, all others are simultaneously favored). In addition, when an individual expresses a social preference (in altruism or mating) for another person with a cultural trait of local behavioral immunity, the preference reinforces itself, because the preferred individual has the same preference, and the benefactor's reproductive success is increased by the assistance received.

We suggest here some new labels for the processes just described by linkage and self-reinforcement of traits. We call the process of the linkage of cultural traits of behavioral immunity within individuals "cultural linkage disequilibrium." We define it as the nonrandom association of cultural preferences or values within the minds of individual people. It is analogous to classical (genetic) linkage disequilibrium (the nonrandom association in an individual's gametes of alleles of unlinked loci, i.e., loci on different chromosomes). We label the self-reinforcing elements of cultural assortative sociality "cultural self-reinforcement."

Boyd and Richerson (1985) recognized that a cultural trait and the socially learned preference for others with the same trait can become coupled within individuals. They explored in mathematical models this coupling's positive effect on the rapid spread within a culture, and divergence between cultures, of cultural traits. McElreath et al. (2003) also recognized this coupling's role in the divergence of ethnic cultural markers. We extend this earlier research by connecting their ideas to those comprising the parasite-stress theory of sociality.

Empirical evaluation of cultural linkage disequilibrium is straightforward. Consider a human society with a cultural repertoire consisting of the following: prefer local people as mates and as beneficiaries of aid, prefer natal locale, dislike and avoid strangers (out-group people). Each of these values may be possessed exclusively by different groups of the society in one extreme. In another extreme, all the values may be within the minds of all societal members. The degree to which the items correspond to the cognitive preferences within individuals versus between individuals or groups is the magnitude of cultural linkage disequilibrium. The prediction is that as parasite adversity increases across human cultures there will be an elevated cultural linkage disequilibrium among traits of assortative sociality and an elevated covariation within individuals of alleles for local parasite resistance and local cultural behaviors of behavioral immunity.

Thus, the parasite-stress theory includes various subtle mechanisms of defense against local parasites that enhance the basic defense provided by cultural immunity behaviors (philopatry, xenophobia, and social preferences for local conspecifics). These enhancements involve the coupling of these immunity-providing behaviors with each other and with genetic immunity, mutual reinforcement of all traits involved, and self-reinforcement of preferences for others with behavioral immunity. The theory also implies: (a) mechanisms that promote the evolution and adaptive significance of nepotism (through local reproduction and associated increased relatedness of local people), which promotes parochial embeddedness and reliability of the local social network, (b) increased frequency of new mutants for resistance, and (c) reduced parasite transmission and virulence.

Additional Evidence Supporting the Parasite-Stress Theory of Sociality

Above we mentioned several published empirical findings that support the parasite-stress theory of sociality. In this section, we discuss some additional supportive empirical results from the literature. The cultural variable collectivism–individualism is a major variable in psychology and sociology for describing cross-cultural differences in values. This unidimension corresponds closely with what political scientists call the rightist–leftist or conservatism–liberalism, dimension with high collectivism mapping on to high conservatism (low liberalism) and low collectivism mapping on to high liberalism/individualism (Fincher and Thornhill 2012b). Fincher et al. (2008) hypothesized that regional differences in parasite adversity proximately cause variation in this dimension of values, with the following reasoning. The values and behaviors that define collectivism, such as ethnocentrism, xenophobia, and interdependent thinking dictated by the cognitive preferences of the in-group and related conformity with traditional ideas and ways, provide antiparasite defenses, and thus are optimal under conditions of high parasite adversity. Collectivist values and behavior, we reasoned, function in behavioral immunity. In contrast, individualism confers benefits upon individuals such as personal autonomy and independent thinking, openness to new and nontraditional ideas and ways, and willingness to interact with a diversity of people. These individualistic/liberal traits, however, have the cost of an enhanced likelihood of contracting infectious disease. Thus, the lower the parasite stress, the greater the benefits of individualism relative to its costs. Specifically, Fincher et al. (2008) predicted a positive correlation between parasite stress and collectivism (negative with individualism) across cultures.

Across multiple measures of collectivism–individualism, Fincher et al. (2008) found, as hypothesized, that worldwide variation in parasite stress robustly predicted cross-national values of collectivism–individualism. Within regions with high severity of infectious diseases, human cultures are characterized by high collectivism, whereas regions of low parasite stress cultures are highly individualistic. This pattern remained statistically significant when controlling for potential confounding variables, including societal wealth, population size, and latitude.

Subsequently, Thornhill et al. (2010) computed separate indices assessing the number of human parasitic diseases in each of the two distinct categories, nonzoonotic and zoonotic, and examined the extent to which each index uniquely predicted cross-national differences in collectivism–individualism. The parasite-stress theory of values proposes that infectious diseases transmissible among humans (nonzoonotics) will be more important in predicting collectivism–individualism than those that humans can contract only from nonhuman animals and not subsequently pass to other humans (zoonotics). As hypothesized, nonzoonotics predicted uniquely cross-national differences in collectivist–individualist values. Zoonotic parasite richness contributed little to cross-national relationships between parasite adversity and these values. Thus, worldwide variation in these values predicted by parasite adversity appears to be attributable almost entirely to the prevalence of nonzoonotic diseases. These cross-national results for numbers of diseases in the transmission categories in relation to collectivism–individualism were repeated with parasite-severity measures (measures of number of infectious-disease cases, not number of diseases). Nonzoonotic severity related much more strongly to collectivism–individualism than did zoonotic severity. Also, the measures of parasitic disease numbers were strongly and positively correlated with measures of parasite severity (Thornhill and Fincher 2014).

Moreover, across the 50 states of the USA and 186 indigenous societies in the standard cross-cultural sample, collectivism correlated positively with parasite stress (individualism negatively; Cashdan and Steele 2013; Fincher and Thornhill 2012a). Furthermore, as with the cross-national results, collectivism across the US states correlated more strongly with nonzoonotic than with zoonotic human diseases (Fincher and Thornhill 2012a).

The "strength of family ties," a measure of collectivism developed by Fincher and Thornhill (2012a) and focused on extended-family loyalty and support, also showed robust positive correlation with parasite stress, across nations and across states of the USA. And, as predicted, in both the cross-national analysis and analysis across the US states, the strength of family ties was correlated more strongly with nonzoonotic infectious diseases than with zoonotic infectious diseases (Thornhill and Fincher 2014).

The potential confounds examined in our analyses did not change any of the conclusions we have mentioned. Also, the basic relationships of values and parasite stress are robust at regional levels both cross-nationally (e.g., Murdock's six world regions) and across the USA (nine US census regions; Fincher et al. 2008; Fincher and Thornhill 2012a; Thornhill et al. 2010).

Guided by the parasite-stress theory of sociality, we have also investigated religiosity (religious commitment and participation) across nations and states of the USA. We hypothesized that religiosity is a collectivist/conservative value that functions to enhance in-group embeddedness and in-group boundary formation and maintenance and, hence, in defense against parasites. As hypothesized, the degree of religiosity at each of the two regional levels is strongly positively related to collectivism (negatively with individualism) and parasite adversity (Fincher and Thornhill 2012a, b). Thus, religiosity reflects and promotes behavioral immunity (also see Terrizzi et al. 2012).

As mentioned, we have hypothesized that absence of dispersal (philopatry) is a behavioral immunity defense against contact with novel parasites harbored in out-groups and the habitats they frequent, and that philopatry is the optimal habitat preference under high parasite stress. Evidence in support of this hypothesis is seen in movement patterns of people from both cross-national analysis (see Fincher and Thornhill 2012a) and analyses across indigenous societies (Cashdan and Steele 2013; Fincher and Thornhill 2008a).

With colleagues, we extended the parasite-stress theory of sociality to explain cross-national variation in degree of democratization, gender equality, sexual permissiveness, and property rights, and in personality (Fincher and Thornhill 2012a; Thornhill et al. 2009, 2010; also see Gangestad et al. 2006; Schaller and Murray 2008). Parasite stress and collectivism positively correlate with undemocratic (autocratic or authoritarian) governance, sexual restrictiveness (especially in women), property rights' restriction to elites, and the personality traits of introversion and closed-mindedness to new experiences. Hence, the behavioral immunity values characterizing collectivism give rise at the societal level to autocratic governance, illiberal sexuality of women, restricted property rights, and certain personality traits.

In separate studies with a colleague, we showed that parasite stress positively predicts frequencies of civil and other intrastate warfare, revolutions, coups, and the absence of peace across countries of the world (Letendre et al. 2010, 2012). This work supported our hypothesis that the collectivism generated by parasite adversity, in particular the xenophobic component of collectivism, is a proximate cause of intergroup coalitional violence. Hence, this research indicates that certain features of behavioral immunity are causes of warfare and other intergroup coalitional violence.

Recent research on conformity in relation to infectious-disease risk is another example of the generality of the parasite-stress theory of sociality and associated behavioral immunity. Conforming to the beliefs and values of the majority has benefits and costs. Benefits of socially navigating in a conformist group include the predictability of the way people think and behave. Moreover, when conformity is coupled with aversion and prejudice toward those who do not conform to the majority behavior, as it typically is, conformity will be protective against novel parasites in out-groups to which the conforming in-group is not immune (Fincher et al. 2008; Murray et al. 2011; Murray and Schaller 2012; Wu and Chang 2012). Costs of conformity include the low rate of generating and adopting ideas, especially ideas that are unfamiliar locally. However, preferring traditional ways of thinking and avoiding foreign ideas can be defenses against novel parasites in out-groups by way of reduced contact with out-groups. In line with this reasoning that conformity is an aspect of behavioral immunity, and supporting the parasite-stress theory of sociality, Murray et al. (2011) showed that cross-national variation in conformity correlates positively with parasite adversity. Also, using a Canadian and a Chinese sample, respectively, Murray and Schaller (2012) and Wu and Chang (2012) examined individual differences in conformity values and found that scores on the scale that measures perceived vulnerability to disease correlate positively with conformity. Each of these two studies also included experiments that made infectious-disease risk salient to research participants. The participants immediately became more conformist, but this change in values was not observed in control groups of participants, including controls presented with disease-irrelevant threat cues. In the Murray and Schaller study, the participants exposed to parasite-salient cues showed increased positivism toward conforming others. Murray and Schaller's and Wu and Chang's findings indicate that an individual's perception of threat of infectious disease, arising either from individual differences in perceived vulnerability to disease or due to immediate stimuli of parasite presence, causes the individual to adopt conformist values. The Murray and Schaller study also showed that individuals presented with cues of parasite presence in their immediate environment become prejudiced in favor of others with conformist values.

Other recent research also reveals the heuristic nature of the parasite-stress theory of sociality and associated behavioral immunity. Terrizzi et al. (2010, 2012) investigated individual differences in the relationship of disgust sensitivity with the conservative values of religiosity and prejudice against sexual minorities (homosexuals and bisexuals). They reported that disgust sensitivity positively predicts these values and argued that disgust, religiosity, and prejudice against sexual out-groups are components of the human behavioral immune system. In a complementary work, Clay et al. (2012) showed that individual differences in disgust sensitivity and perceived vulnerability to disease positively correlate with collectivism and several other variables that reflect conservativism (e.g., traditionalism, conformity, and importance of societal stability and security). Moreover, Terrizzi et al. (2013) conducted a meta-analysis of 22 studies of individual differences in components of collectivism or of conservatism in relation to perceived vulnerability to disease or disgust sensitivity. They reported robust positive relationships among the variables. Consistent with our arguments and with the evidence presented above, Terrizzi et al. (2013) concluded that conservative values are defenses that reduce contact with infectious diseases.

Inspired by the parasite-stress theory of sociality, Reid et al. (2012) made a significant discovery for the scholarly discipline of linguistics. Reid et al. researched disgust sensitivity in relation to sound perception of dissimilarity to self's accent of foreign-accented English. Americans of high disgust sensitivity rated foreign-accented English as more dissimilar to their own accent than did Americans of low disgust sensitivity, even though the study participants were listening to the same speakers. The study also showed that research participants who viewed parasite-salient stimuli perceived a greater difference in foreign-accented English compared to their own accent, but participants viewing other threat stimuli (unrelated to parasite threat) did not. Given the positive relationship between conservatism and disgust (e.g., Terrizzi et al. 2013), these results imply that conservatives perceive greater differences between in-group and out-group spoken language than do liberals. We hypothesize from the parasite-stress theory of sociality that the greater sensitivity of high-disgust people to differences between us and them, which was documented by Reid et al. for accents, may extend to many differences outside of language, such as the perception of value differences, skin color, and behavior. Such perception biases may underlie the xenophobia-sensitivity of conservatives.

Prokop et al. (2010a, b) showed that the human behavioral immune system includes avoidance and regulation of contact with pets that pose human infectious-disease threats. Research subjects in Turkey reported lower rates of pets-in-home (which included dogs) than did Slovakians; parasite stress is higher in Turkey than in Slovakia. Furthermore, in the same study, in each of the two countries, having pets in the home was related negatively with individual differences in perceived vulnerability to disease.

Billing and Sherman (1998) and Sherman and Billing (1999) hypothesized that the value people place on the use of spices in cooking is a defense against food-borne human parasites. To test this, they investigated the types and numbers of spices used in recipes across many regions of the world. They found that temperature positively correlates with anti-pathogen spice use across regions. Regional temperature is a useful surrogate for parasite stress, with warmer equating with more parasite adversity (Billing and Sherman 1998; Guernier et al. 2004). Later research by Murray and Schaller (2010) reported a robust positive relationship across countries between spice use and parasite stress per se. Additional evidence that spicing foods is a form of behavioral immunity has been found by Prokop and Fačovičová (2011). They showed that individual differences in preference for and use of spiced food corresponded with concern about infectious diseases. Individuals who are high in worry about contagion (high scorers on the perceived-vulnerability-to-disease scale) had stronger preference for and greater consumption of spicy foods than individuals who are low on concern about contagion.

The parasite theory of sexual selection was proposed by Hamilton and Zuk (1982). It treats the component of sociality involved in competition for mates and mate choice and hence is a subtheory of the parasite-stress theory of sociality. The parasite theory of sexual selection argues that variation among individuals in genetic immunity to parasites and related phenotypic quality gives rise to sexual selection, which favors resistant individuals. Relative resistance of individuals is honestly depicted in traits such as the rooster's comb and the peacock's tail, and in humans in the traits affecting sexual attractiveness, especially developmental stability (bilateral symmetry) and the sexually dimorphic hormone markers on the face and body (estrogen markers in women and testosterone markers in men; see Thornhill and Gangestad 2008).

Gangestad and Buss (1993) and Gangestad et al. (2006) conducted cross-national research inspired by the parasite theory of sexual selection that empirically linked human mate choice, parasite stress, and behavioral immunity. They reported a positive correlation across countries between human parasite stress and the importance people place on physical attractiveness (good looks) in mate choice. This finding was hypothesized from their reasoning that physical attractiveness is a certification of genetic resistance to parasites—good genes for parasite resistance—and hence is expected to be valued more in high than low parasite-stress regions (see Thornhill and Gangestad 2008 for a review of literature on the positive relationship between attractiveness and genetic quality in humans.)

Consistent with this finding, DeBruine et al. (2012) showed that high parasite stress evokes in women an enhanced mate preference for facially masculine men and hence for men's facial markers of phenotypic and genetic quality. Women's preference for testosteronization/masculinity of the male faces correlates significantly and positively with parasite stress across countries and across the US states. In related research, Jones et al. (2013a) linked masculinity preferences of women to pathogen disgust sensitivity. They reported that, in women, pathogen disgust positively correlates with their attractiveness ratings of masculinity in men's faces, bodies, and voices. In other research, Jones et al. (2013b) showed men's preferences for femininity in women's faces, also apparent markers of phenotypic and genetic quality, were positively correlated with men's pathogen disgust sensitivity.

Research findings reported by de Barra et al. (2013) reveal more about the mechanisms of the behavioral immune system that act during individuals' ontogeny and account for the regional differences in priority of good looks in mate selection. Compared to adults with a low infectious-disease ontogenetic history, adults with a childhood background of high infectious disease incidence showed stronger attractiveness preference for mates with enhanced sex-typical facial hormone markers, and hence with relatively high phenotypic and genetic quality, including parasite resistance.

Little et al. (2010) experimentally presented to research participants pictures of high and absent parasite salience, after which they recorded the participants' attractiveness ratings of human faces that varied in symmetry and hormone markers. Symmetry, like sex-specific hormone markers in the face, is a likely marker of phenotypic and genetic quality. Little et al. found that people who were exposed to cues of high contagion risk, compared to those seeing no contagion risk, immediately showed increased attractiveness preferences for opposite-sex individuals with greater sex-specific hormone markers and symmetry. Young et al. (2011) replicated the Little et al. finding for symmetry.

Lee and Zeitsch's (2011) research indicates that women primed to perceive contagion in their current environment immediately adjusted their mate preferences for men with resources versus men with high genetic quality. Showing women contagion cues activated the aspect of their behavioral immune system that increases their psychological preference for a mate of high genetic quality and reduces their preference for a mate with resources to provide.

Welling et al.'s (2007) research, like that of Gangestad et al., DeBruine et al., Jones et al., de Barra et al., Little et al., and Lee and Zeitsch, indicates that physical attractiveness judgments are a part of the behavioral immune system. Welling et al. reported that men and women who perceived themselves to be more vulnerable to infectious disease had stronger attractiveness preferences for healthy faces than did individuals who perceived themselves to be less vulnerable to disease.

As a theory of cultural diversity, the parasite-stress theory of sociality informs the processes causing new cultures to originate. We propose that, given the ecological localization of host defenses against parasites, the components of assortative sociality—limited dispersal, ethnocentrism, and xenophobia—by functioning in parasite avoidance and management, fractionate or segment and also factionalize an original culture's range and thereby contribute to the independence of the resulting segments (Fincher and Thornhill 2008a, b). Thus, the parasite-stress theory of sociality includes a hypothesis about the genesis of cultural or ethnic diversity.

Accordingly, infectious diseases can transform an ancestral culture into new cultures that arise side by side and without segmentation of the ancestral culture by a geographic barrier. We have called the process involved "the parasite-driven wedge" (Fincher and Thornhill 2008a, b; Thornhill and Fincher 2013a). The geographically localized host–parasite races and corresponding localized behavioral immunity traits are the basic features of the wedge. The new additions to the parasite-stress theory of sociality presented earlier in this chapter are important too in the genesis of new cultures by the wedge mechanism. Thus, the parasite-driven wedge consists of behaviors (philopatry, xenophobia, and preference for in-group transaction and embeddedness), the coupling within individuals of these immunity-providing behaviors with each other and with genetic immunity, mutual reinforcement of the traits involved, and self-reinforcement of assortative sociality. The wedge subdivides an ancestral species or culture and thereby pushes segments apart, creating new cultures in the absence of segmentation created by mountains or other geographic barriers.

Several predictions of the parasite-driven wedge hypothesis have been supported empirically. We have shown that the numbers of endemic religions (both major religions and ethnoreligions), as well as the numbers of endemic languages, across contemporary countries worldwide, are related strongly and positively to parasite stress (Fincher and Thornhill 2008a, b). Also consistent with this aspect of the parasite-stress theory of sociality was the earlier finding by Cashdan (2001) that high parasite-stress regions have more indigenous ethnic groups than low parasite-stress regions. Our own and Cashdan's research on the diversity of human cultures across the world indicates that the behavioral immune system is a cause of the genesis of new cultures.

An Alternative Hypothesis: Host Manipulation by Parasites

For completeness, we consider a causally distinct alternative hypothesis for aspects of human sociality that we propose are adaptations of behavioral immunity. In numerous parasite–host associations, the parasite manipulates the host's psychology, behavior, or external morphology as an adaptation to increase transmission to new hosts (Moore 2002). This is in the reproductive interests of the parasite, but often maladaptive for the host. Effective host manipulation is seen in a wide range of parasite types, from viruses and bacteria to fungi and helminths ("worms"), and in a wide range of host taxa. The nature of parasitic host-manipulation adaptations depends on whether the parasite has a direct or an indirect life cycle. In the case of a parasite with an indirect life cycle, the parasite's host-manipulation adaptations function to increase the intermediate host's probability of being eaten by a species of predator that is the definitive host of the parasite—that is, the host in which sexual reproduction of the parasite occurs. In the case of direct life cycle parasites (those without an intermediate host), the host-manipulation adaptations function to transmit the parasite to susceptible members of the host species. Humans are not known to be the host of any parasite that is transmitted by predation of humans to a definitive host. Nonetheless, the host-manipulation strategy of parasites to increase direct transmission among members of a host species is a possibility for human parasites. A recent study by Rode et al. (2013) reported that brine shrimp increase temporary grouping behavior (referred to as swarming) when parasitized and that this promotes transmission of the parasite involved among group members. This raises the question: Is in-group assortative sociality (ethnocentrism, xenophobia, and philopatry) produced by a parasite-manipulation adaptation that functions to promote transmission to new local hosts?

There are good reasons to reject the parasite-manipulation hypothesis applied to human assortative sociality. The hypothesis requires that in-group sociality will be maladaptive for hosts and adaptive for the parasite by promoting parasite transmission (Poulin 2010). This is negated in the human case by the diverse and copious evidence indicating that the values comprising in-group sociality are effective means of avoiding and managing infectious diseases and are thereby functional for human hosts in high parasite-adversity regions. Furthermore, as we explained, the in-group values and associated local reproduction promote the evolution of genetic immunity to the parasite, which reduces host-to-host transmission of a parasite in an in-group; the reduced transmission, in turn, selects for reduced parasite virulence.

Concluding Comments

The parasite-stress theory of sociality is a relatively new perspective on human social psychology and behavior. As an ecological and evolutionary theory of values or core preferences it applies widely across domains of human sociality and human affairs. It has produced a cornucopia of newly discovered patterns and informed previously described patterns in the behavior of individuals and in features at the level of cultures and regions. It is a general theory of sociality. We have addressed its application to nonhuman animal sociality in Fincher and Thornhill (2008a) and Thornhill and Fincher (2013a), and have addressed the recent criticisms of the theory applied to human sociality in Fincher and Thornhill (2012b) and Thornhill and Fincher (2013b).

Fundamental to the theory is the behavioral immune system. In this chapter, we have explained that the human behavioral immune system is not restricted to psychological features and behaviors for avoiding contact with infectious disease. It includes behaviors of in-group social preference, altruism, alliance, and conformity that manage the negative effects of infectious diseases; mate choice to increase offspring defense against parasites; the regulation of interaction with pets; culinary behavior; and components of personality. The contagion-avoidance aspect of behavioral immunity is richer than usually conceived as well, as it includes the preference for local region (philopatry) and hence avoidance of foreignness in people and places where novel parasites may occur. Furthermore, it is unlikely that any features of human behavioral immunity are adaptations of parasites for increasing transmission to new hosts because the behavioral immune system promotes genetic immunity to parasites and results in reduced transmission of parasites within the in-group.

References

Anderson, R. M., & May, R. M. (1991). *Infectious disease of humans: Dynamics and control*. Oxford: Oxford University Press.

Best, A., Webb, S., White, A., & Boots, M. (2011). Host resistance and coevolution in spatially structured populations. *Proceedings of the Royal Society B, 278,* 2216–2222.

Billing, J., & Sherman, P. W. (1998). Antimicrobial functions of spices: Why some like it hot. *Quarterly Review of Biology, 73,* 3–49.

Blute, M. (2010). *Darwinian sociocultural evolution: Solutions to dilemmas in cultural and social theory*. Cambridge: Cambridge University Press.

Boyd, R., & Richerson, P. J. (1985). *Culture and the evolutionary process*. Chicago: Chicago University Press.

Cashdan, E. (2001). Ethnic diversity and its environmental determinants: Effects on climate, pathogens, and habitat diversity. *American Anthropology, 103,* 968–991.

Cashdan, E., & Steele, M. (2013). Pathogen prevalence, group bias, and collectivism in the standard cross-cultural sample. *Human Nature, 24,* 59–75.

Chiao, J. Y., & Blizinsky, K. D. (2010). Culture–gene coevolution of individualism–collectivism and the serotonin transporter gene. *Proceedings of the Royal Society B, 277,* 529–537.

Clay, R., Terrizzi, J. A., Jr., & Shook, N. J. (2012). Individual differences in the behavioral immune system and the emergence of cultural systems. *Journal of Social Psychology, 43,* 174–184.

Corby-Harris, V., & Promislow, D. E. L. (2008). Host ecology shapes geographical variation for resistance to bacterial infection in *Drosophila melanogaster*. *Journal of Animal Ecology, 77,* 768–776.

Curtis, V. A. (2007). Dirt, disgust and disease: A natural history of hygiene. *Journal of Epidemiology and Community Health, 61,* 660–664.

Curtis, V., Aunger, R., & Rabie, T. (2004). Evidence that disgust evolved to protect from risk of disease. *Proceedings of the Royal Society B, 271*(Supplement), 17–31.

Curtis, V. A., de Barra, M., & Aunger, H. (2011). Disgust as an adaptive system for disease avoidance behaviour. *Philosophical Transactions of the Royal Society B, 366,* 389–401.

de Barra, M., DeBruine, L., Jones, B., & Curtis, V. A. (2013). Illness in childhood predicts face preferences in adulthood. *Evolution and Human Behavior, 34,* 384–389.

DeBruine, L. M., Little, A. C., & Jones, B. C. (2012). Extending parasite-stress theory to variation in human mate preferences. *Behavioral and Brain Sciences, 35,* 86–87.

Denic, S., & Nicholls, M. G. (2007). Genetic benefits of consanguinity through selection of genotypes protective against malaria. *Human Biology, 79,* 145–158.

Denic, S., Nagelkerke, N., & Agarwal, M. M. (2008a). Consanguineous marriages and endemic malaria: Can inbreeding increase population fitness? *Malaria Journal, 7,* 150.

Denic, S., Nagelkerke, N., & Agarwal, M. M. (2008b). Consanguineous marriages: Do genetic benefits outweigh its costs in populations with alpha(+)-thalassemia, hemoglobin s, and malaria? *Evolution and Human Behavior, 29,* 364–369.

Diamond, J. (1998). *Guns, germs and steel: The fates of human societies*. New York: W.W. Norton.

Dionne, M., Miller, K. M., Dodson, J. J., Caron, F., & Bernatchez, L. (2007). Clinical variation in MHC diversity with temperature: Evidence for the role of host–pathogen interaction on local adaptation in Atlantic salmon. *Evolution, 61,* 2154–2164.

Dobson, A. P., & Carper, E. R. (1996). Infectious diseases and human population history. *BioScience, 46,* 115–126.

Duncan, L. A., & Schaller, M. (2009). Prejudicial attitudes toward older adults may be exaggerated when people feel vulnerable to infectious disease: Evidence and implications. *Analysis of Social Issues and Public Policy, 9,* 97–115.

Duncan, L. A., Schaller, M., & Park, J. H. (2009). Perceived vulnerability to disease: Development and validation of a 15-item self-report instrument. *Personality and Individual Differences, 47,* 541–546.

Durham, W. H. (1991). *Coevolution: Genes, culture and human diversity*. Stanford: Stanford University Press.

Ewald, P. W. (1994). *Evolution of infectious disease*. New York: Oxford University Press.

Faulkner, J., Schaller, M., Park, J. H., & Duncan, L. A. (2004). Evolved disease-avoidance mechanisms and contemporary xenophobic attitudes. *Group Processes and Intergroup Relations, 7,* 333–353.

Fincher, C. L., & Thornhill, R. (2008a). A parasite-driven wedge: Infectious diseases may explain language and other biodiversity. *Oikos, 117,* 1289–1297.

Fincher, C. L., & Thornhill, R. (2008b). Assortative sociality, limited dispersal, infectious disease and the genesis of the global pattern of religion diversity. *Proceedings of the Royal Society of London, Biological Sciences, 275,* 2587–2594.

Fincher, C. L., & Thornhill, R. (2012a). Parasite-stress promotes in-group assortative sociality: The cases of strong family ties and heightened religiosity. *Behavioral and Brain Sciences, 35,* 61–79.

Fincher, C. L., & Thornhill, R. (2012b). The parasite-stress theory may be a general theory of culture and sociality Response. *Behavioral and Brain Sciences, 35,* 99–119.

Fincher, C. L., Thornhill, R., Murray, D. R., & Schaller, M. (2008). Pathogen prevalence predicts human cross-cultural variability in individualism/collectivism. *Proceedings of the Royal Society of London Biological Sciences, 275,* 1279–1285.

Fumagalli, M., Sironi, M., Pozzoli, U., Ferrer-Admettla, A., Pattini, L., & Nielsen, R. (2011). Signatures of environmental genetic adaptation pinpoint pathogens as the main selective pressure through human evolution. *PLoS Genetics, 7,* e1002355.

Gangestad, S. W., & Buss, D. M. (1993). Pathogen prevalence and human mate preference. *Ethology and Sociobiology, 14,* 89–96.

Gangestad, S. W., Haselton, M. G., & Buss, D. M. (2006). Evolutionary foundations of cultural variation: Evoked culture and mate preferences. *Psychological Inquiry, 17,* 75–95.

Good, C. M. (1972). Salt, trade, and disease: Aspects of development in Africa's northern Great Lakes region. *International Journal of African Historical Studies, 5,* 543–586.

Guernier, V., Hochberg, M. E., & Guegan, J. (2004). Ecology drives the worldwide distribution of human diseases. *PLoS Biology, 2,* e141.

Gurven, M., Allen-Arave, W., Hill, K., & Hurtado, M. (2000). "It's a Wonderful Life": Signaling generosity among the Ache of Paraguay. *Evolution and Human Behavior, 21,* 263–282.

Hamilton, W. D. (1964). The genetical evolution of social behaviour, I & II. *Journal of Theoretical Biology, 7,* 1–52.

Hamilton, W. D., & Zuk, M. (1982). Heritable true fitness and bright birds: A role for parasites? *Science, 218,* 284–387.

Hoben, A. D. (2011). An evolutionary investigation of consanguineous marriages. Doctoral dissertation, University of Groningen.

Hoben, A. D., Buunk, A. P., Fincher, C. L., & Thornhill, R. (2010). On the adaptive origins and maladaptive consequences of human inbreeding: Parasite prevalence, immune functioning, and consanguineous marriage. *Evolutionary Psychology, 8,* 658–676.

Inbar, Y., Pizarro, D. A., Iyer, R., & Raidt, J. (2012). Disgust sensitivity, political conservatism, and voting. *Social Psychological and Personality Science, 5,* 537–544.

Jones, B. C., Feinberg, D. R., Watkins, C. D., Fincher, C. L., Little, A. C., & DeBruine, L. M. (2013a). Pathogen disgust predicts women's preferences for masculinity in men's voices, faces, and bodies. *Behavioral Ecology, 24,* 373–379.

Jones, B. C., Fincher, C. L., Welling, L. L. M., Little, A. C., Feinberg, D. R., Watkins, C. D., Al-Dujaili, E. A. S., & DeBruine, L. M. (2013b). Salivary cortisol and pathogen disgust predict men's preferences for feminine shape cues in women's faces. *Biological Psychology, 92,* 233–240.

Kaltz, O., Gandon, S., Michalakis, Y., & Shykoff, J. A. (1999). Local maladaptation in the anther-smut fungus *Microbotryum violaceum* to its host plant *Silene latifolia*: Evidence from a cross-inoculation experiment. *Evolution, 53,* 395–407.

Kouznetsova, D., Stevenson, R. J., Oaten, M. J., & Case, T. I. (2012). Disease-avoidant behaviour and its consequences. *Psychology and Health, 27,* 491–506.

Lee, A. J., & Zietsch, B. P. (2011). Experimental evidence that women's mate preferences are directly influenced by cues of pathogen prevalence and resource scarcity. *Biology Letters, 7,* 892–895.

Letendre K., Fincher, C. L., & Thornhill, R. (2010). Does infectious disease cause global variation in the frequency of intrastate armed conflict and civil war? *Biological Reviews, 85,* 669–683.

Letendre, K., Fincher, C. L., & Thornhill, R. (2012). Infectious disease, collectivism, and warfare. In T.

Shackelford & V. Weekes-Shackelford (Eds.), *The Oxford handbook on evolutionary perspectives on violence, homicide, and warfare* (pp. 351–371). New York: Oxford University Press.

Little, A. C., DeBruine, L. M., & Jones, B. C. (2010). Exposure to visual cues of pathogen contagion changes preferences for masculinity and symmetry in opposite-sex faces. *Proceedings of the Royal Society of London B, 278,* 2032–2039.

Loker, E. S. (2012). Macroevolutionary immunology: A role for immunity in the diversification of animal life. *Frontiers in Immunology, 3,* 25.

Lopez, A. D., Mathers, C. D., Ezzati, M., Jamieson, D. T., & Murray, C. J. (2006). Global and regional burden of disease and risk factors, 2001: Systematic analysis of population health data. *Lancet, 367,* 1747–1757.

Low, B. S. (1990). Marriage systems and pathogen stress in human societies. *American Zoologist, 30,* 325–339.

McElreath, R., Boyd, R., & Richerson, P. J. (2003). Shared norms and the evolution of ethnic markers. *Current Anthropology, 44,* 122–129.

McNeill, W. H. (1998). *Plagues and peoples.* Harpswell: Anchor.

Miller, E. N., Fadl, M., Mohamed, H. S., Elzein, A., Jamieson, S. E., Cordell, H. J., et al. (2007). Y chromosome lineage- and village-specific genes on chromosomes 1p22 and 6q27 control visceral leishmaniasis in Sudan. *PLoS Genetics, 3,* 679–688.

Moore, J. (2002). *Parasites and the behavior of animals.* New York: Oxford University Press.

Mortensen, C. R., Becker, D. V., Ackerman, J. M., Neuberg, S. L., & Kenrick, D. T. (2010). Infection breeds reticence: The effects of disease salience on self-perceptions of personality and behavioral avoidance tendencies. *Psychological Science, 21,* 440–447.

Murray, D. R., & Schaller, M. (2010). Historical prevalence of infectious diseases within 230 geopolitical regions: A tool for investigating origins of culture. *Journal of Cross-Cultural Psychology, 41,* 99–108.

Murray, D. R., & Schaller, M. (2012). Threat(s) and conformity deconstructed: Perceived threat of infectious disease and its implications for conformist attitudes and behavior. *European Journal of Social Psychology, 42,* 180–188.

Murray, D. R., Trudeau, R., & Schaller M. (2011). On the origins of cultural differences in conformity: Four tests of the pathogen prevalence hypothesis. *Personality and Social Psychology Bulletin, 37,* 318–329.

Navarrete, C. D., & Fessler, D. M. T. (2006). Disease avoidance and ethnocentrism: The effects of disease vulnerability and disgust sensitivity on intergroup attitudes. *Evolution and Human Behavior, 27,* 270–282.

Norenzayan, A., & Shariff, A. F. (2008). The origin and evolution of religious prosociality. *Science, 322,* 58–62.

Oaten, M., Stevenson, R. J., & Case, T. I. (2009). Disgust as a disease-avoidance mechanism. *Psychological Bulletin, 135,* 303–321.

Oliveira, R. F., Taborski, M., & Brockman, H. J. (2008). *Alternative reproductive tactics: An integrated approach.* Cambridge: Cambridge University Press.

Park, J. H., & Schaller, M. (2005). Does attitude similarity serve as a heuristic cue for kinship? Evidence of an implicit cognitive association. *Evolution and Human Behavior, 26,* 158–170.

Pitchappan, R. M. (2002). Castes, migration, immunogenetics and infectious diseases in south India. *Community Genetics, 5,* 157–161.

Poulin, R. (2010). Parasite manipulation of host behavior: An update and frequently asked questions. *Advances in the Study of Behavior, 41,* 151–186.

Prokop, P., & Fančovičová, J. (2011). Prererences for spicy foods and disgust of ectoparasites are associated with reported health in humans. *Psihologija, 44,* 281–293.

Prokop, P., Usak, M., & Fančovičová, J. (2010a). Health and the avoidance of macroparasites: A preliminary cross-cultural study. *Journal of Ethology, 28,* 345–351.

Prokop, P., Usak, M., & Fančovičová, J. (2010b). Risk of parasite transmission influences perceived vulnerability to disease and perceived danger of disease-relevant animals. *Behavioural Processes, 85,* 52–57.

Prugnolle, F., Manica, A., Charpentier, M., Guegan, J. F., Guernier, V., & Balloux, F. (2005). Pathogen-driven selection and worldwide HLA Class I diversity. *Current Biology, 15,* 1022–1027.

Reid, S. A., Zhang, J., Anderson, G. L., Gasiorek, J., Bonilla, D., & Peinado, S. (2012). Parasite primes make foreign-accented English sound more distant to people who are disgusted by pathogens (but not by sex or morality). *Evolution and Human Behavior, 33,* 471–478.

Ridley, M. (1993). *The red queen: Sex and the evolution of human nature.* New York: Macmillan Publishing Company.

Rode, N. O., Lievens, E. J. P., Flaven, E., Segard, A., Jabbour-Zahab, R., Sanchez, M. I., et al. (2013). Why join groups? Lessons from parasite-manipulated Artemia. *Ecology Letters, 16,* 493–501.

Rougeron, V., De Meeus, T., Hide, M., Waleckx, E., Bermudez, H., Arevalo, J., et al. (2009). Extreme inbreeding in *Leishmania braziliensis. Proceedings of the National Academy of Sciences USA, 106,* 10224–10229.

Ryan, S., Oaten, M., Stevenson, R. J., & Case, T. I. (2012). Facial disfigurement is treated like an infectious disease. *Evolution and Human Behavior, 33,* 639–646.

Schaller, M. (2006). Parasites, behavioral defenses, and the social psychological mechanisms through which cultures are evoked. *Psychological Inquiry, 17,* 96–101.

Schaller, M., & Duncan, L. (2007). The behavioral immune system: Its evolution and social psychological implications. In J. P. Forges, M. G. Haselton, & W. Von Hippel (Eds.), *Evolution and the social mind: Evolutionary psychology and social cognition* (pp. 293–307). New York: Psychology Press.

Schaller, M., & Murray, D. (2008). Pathogens, personality, and culture: Disease prevalence predicts worldwide variability in sociosexuality, extraversion, and openness to experience. *Journal of Personality and Social Psychology, 95,* 212–221.

Schaller, M., & Neuberg, S. L. (2008). Intergroup prejudices and intergroup conflicts. In C. Crawford & D. L.

Krebs (Eds.), *Foundations of evolutionary psychology* (pp. 399–412). New York: Erlbaum.

Schaller, M., Miller, G. E., Gervais, W. M., Yager, S., & Chen, E. (2010). Mere visual perception of other people's disease symptoms facilitates a more aggressive immune response. *Psychological Science, 21,* 649–652.

Schnall, S., Haidt, J., Clore, G. L., & Jordan, A. H. (2008). Disgust as embodied moral judgment. *Personality and Social Psychology Bulletin, 34,* 1096–1109.

Sherman, P. W., & Billing, J. (1999). Darwinian gastronomy: Why we use spices. *BioScience, 49,* 453–463.

Smith, K. F., Sax, D. F., Gaines, S. D., Guernier, V., & Guégan, J. F. (2007). Globalization of human infectious disease. *Ecology, 88,* 1903–1910.

Stevenson, R. J., Case, T. I., & Oaten, M. J. (2009). Frequency and recency of infection and their relationship with disgust and contamination sensitivity. *Evolution and Human Behavior, 30,* 363–368.

Stevenson, R. J., Hodgson, D., Oaten, M. J., Barouei, J., & Case, T. I. (2011). The effect of disgust on oral immune function. *Psychophysiology, 48,* 900–907.

Sugiyama, L. S. (2004). Illness, injury, and disability among Shiwiar forager–horticulturalists: Implications of human life history. *American Journal of Physical Anthropology, 123,* 371–389.

Sugiyama, L. S., & Sugiyama, M. S. (2003). Social roles, prestige, and health risk: Social niche specialization as a risk-buffering strategy. *Human Nature, 14,* 165–190.

Terrizzi, J. A., Jr., Shook, N. J., & Ventis, W. L. (2010). Disgust: A predictor of social conservatism and prejudicial attitudes toward homosexuals. *Personality and Individual Differences, 49,* 587–592.

Terrizzi, J. A., Jr., Shook, N. J., & Ventis, W. L. (2012). Religious conservatism: an evolutionarily evoked disease-avoidance strategy. *Religion, Brain and Behavior, 2,* 105–120.

Terrizzi, J. A., Jr., Shook, N. J., & McDaniel, M. A. (2013). The behavioral immune system and social conservatism: A meta-analysis. *Evolution and Human Behavior, 34,* 99–108.

Thompson, J. N. (2005). *The geographic mosaic of coevolution.* Chicago: University of Chicago Press.

Thornhill, R., & Fincher, C. L. (2011). Parasite stress promotes homicide and child maltreatment. *Philosophical Transactions of the Royal Society: Biological Sciences, 366,* 3466–3477.

Thornhill, R., & Fincher, C. L. (2013a). The parasite-driven-wedge model of parapatric speciation. *Journal of Zoology, 291,* 23–33.

Thornhill, R., & Fincher, C. L. (2013b). Commentary on Hackman, J., & Hruschka, D. (2013) Fast life histories, not pathogens, account for state-level variation in homicide, child maltreatment, and family ties in the U.S. *Evolution and Human Behavior, 34,* 314–315.

Thornhill, R., & Fincher, C. L. (2014). *The parasite-stress theory of values and sociality: Infectious disease, history and human values worldwide.* New York: Springer.

Thornhill, R., & Gangestad, S. W. (2008). *The evolutionary biology of human female sexuality.* New York: Oxford University Press.

Thornhill, R., Fincher, C. L., & Aran, D. (2009). Parasites, democratization, and the liberalization of values across contemporary countries. *Biological Reviews, 84,* 113–131.

Thornhill, R., Fincher, C. L., Murray, D. R., & Schaller, M. (2010). Zoonotic and non-zoonotic diseases in relation to human personality and societal values: Support for the parasite-stress model. *Evolutionary Psychology, 8,* 151–169.

Tinsley, M. C., Blanford, S., & Jiggins, F. M. (2006). Genetic variation in *Drosophila melanogaster* pathogen susceptibility. *Parasitology, 132,* 767–773.

Van Valen, L. (1973). A new evolutionary law. *Evolutionary Theory, 1,* 1–30.

Volk, A. A., & Atkinson, J. A. (2013). Infant and child death in the human environment of evolutionary adaptation. *Evolution and Human Behavior, 34,* 182–192.

Way, B. M., & Lieberman, M. D. (2010). Is there a genetic contribution to cultural differences? Collectivism, individualism and genetic markers of social sensitivity. *Social Cognitive and Affective Neuroscience, 5,* 203–211.

Welling, L. L. M., Conway, C. A., DeBruine, L. M., & Jones, B. C. (2007). Perceived vulnerability to disease is positively related to the strength of preferences for apparent health in faces. *Journal of Evolutionary Psychology, 5,* 131–139.

Wolfe, N. D., Dunavan, C. P., & Diamond, J. (2007). Origins of major human infectious diseases. *Nature, 447,* 279–283.

Wu, B., & Chang, L. (2012). The social impact of pathogen threat: How disease salience influences conformity. *Personality and Individual Differences, 53,* 50–54.

Young, S. G., Savvo, D. F., & Hugenberg, K. (2011). Vulnerability to disease is associated with a domain-specific preference for symmetrical faces relative to symmetrical non-face stimuli. *European Journal of Social Psychology, 41,* 558–563.

Happiness

33

Bjørn Grinde

Happiness is presumably the key ingredient in quality of life. It has been a focal topic in philosophy for thousands of years, but only recently have several lines of scientific inquiry approached the issue. In the social sciences, the subject is typically referred to as positive psychology, and measured by questionnaires probing subjective well-being (Diener et al. 2003; Seligman et al. 2005). Based on an evolutionary perspective, the term Darwinian happiness has been used in an attempt to understand why evolution endowed the human species with the capacity to have pleasant and unpleasant experiences (Grinde 2002, 2012). Neuroscientists have been able to locate and describe some of the neural networks involved (Leknes and Tracey 2008). The present chapter draws on these lines of investigation in an attempt to generate a model of what happiness is about.

In certain traditions within philosophy and psychology, happiness is viewed as either hedonic, which reflects sensual pleasures, or eudemonic, which is a question of flourishing and experiencing inner contentment (Deci and Ryan 2008). The dichotomy typically differentiates between pleasure derived from the senses and forms of "deeper" satisfaction. The latter is associated with having a meaningful life and appears to be partly equivalent to the mental condition referred to as "flow" (Csikszentmihalyi 1990). I argue that key neural structures are engaged regardless of the causes of pleasure or pain, and regardless of whether the positive emotions would be conceived as hedonic or eudemonic. Apparently, these structures first evolved in the early amniotes (i.e., ancestors of present reptiles, birds, and mammals) and their purpose was to create a more advanced platform for orchestrating behavior.

B. Grinde (✉)
Division of Mental Health, Norwegian Institute of Public Health, PO Box 4404, Nydalen, 0403 Oslo, NORWAY
e-mail: bjgr@fhi.no

The Concept of Brain Modules

Modules as Units of Evolutionary Function

The brain has been shaped by evolution to provide various functions. Thus, a possible approach aimed at understanding the brain is to consider it as divided into numerous modules (Nesse 2008; Philipson 2002). Each module deals with a particular need that arose during our evolutionary history and can be engaged when required, somewhat like a Swiss army knife. Unlike the knife, a particular brain module may involve dispersed neural circuitry, and the same nerve cells may be active in several modules. The concept of modules simply provides an alternative, evolution-based framework for organizing present knowledge in neurobiology and psychology. Neuronal networks are the physical substrate for brain modules, but the actual anatomical location and neurochemistry

V. Zeigler-Hill et al. (eds.), *Evolutionary Perspectives on Social Psychology*, Evolutionary Psychology,
DOI 10.1007/978-3-319-12697-5_33, © Springer International Publishing Switzerland 2015

of the neurons involved in any given function is, at best, vaguely understood. Moreover, how to categorize modules is to a large extent a question of whether to lump related functions together or divide them into sub-modules.

Some 300 million years ago, evolution built a new type of module that gave the organism the capacity to experience feelings and, as a by-product, early forms of consciousness (Grinde 2013). Prior to that time, behavior was likely produced more in terms of reflexes, fixed action patterns, and nonemotional instincts.

Nervous systems most likely first appeared more than 600 million years ago to control locomotion in early multicellular animals (Jékely 2011). Primitive, bilaterian nervous systems were presumably akin to those still found in, for example, nematodes. Their primary purpose was either to direct the organism toward something or to cause aversion, as exemplified by obtaining food and escaping danger, respectively. These two alternatives—attraction and aversion—are still a key ingredient in even the most advanced brains; that is, as a reasonable approximation, the brain directs attention and actions either toward or away from particular situations and opportunities. Evolution gradually designed more advanced control mechanisms to motivate behavior. Feelings, in the form of brain rewards and punishments, arose for that purpose (Watson and Platt 2008). In effect, they work as a "common currency" that allows the organism to weigh advantages against risks; for example, in relation to whether one ought to hunt down a large prey (Cabanac 1979). In short, whatever is detrimental for the organism (or the genes) is given a negative value—it feels bad, whereas whatever helps survival and reproduction feels good. The brain is set up to weigh the expected outcomes of actions based on the principle of maximizing positive feelings. The brain modules involved in generating positive or negative affect are hereafter referred to as *mood modules*.

Mood Modules

Rewards elicit approach and consummatory behavior, whereas punishment elicits avoidance; pleasure and pain represent the accompanying, subjective hedonic value. In some situations, the instigations have an immediate effect on behavior, but they also help classify information relevant for dealing with future choices—the pleasure of success helps the organism remember that the strategy worked, whereas the pain of failure suggests a change in strategy. Based partly on innate dispositions and partly on past experience, the organism learns what is likely to yield either pleasure or pain.

It seems pertinent to define happiness as the net output of the mood modules, but the definition requires clarification. Mood is here considered to be an aspect of the mind that moves up or down a scale that ranges from pleasant to unpleasant. Positive and negative affect may be used somewhat synonymously with rewards and punishment, or with mood value. Affect, however, like emotion, typically focuses on the particular functional role (for example, love, grief, or anger), whereas mood points to the actual positive or negative quality of affects, emotions, and sensations. As will be discussed below, there are independent neuronal networks regulating the particulars of each type of emotion or sensation, but they converge on partly shared structures responsible for their mood value.

Positive mood is best understood as depending on two distinct modules, referred to as *seeking* (or wanting) and *liking* (the feelings associated with the actual consumption; Berridge 2003; Panksepp 1998). Even in primitive organisms, seeking and liking presumably reflect two independent functions: The animals are instigated first to search for relevant items in the environment, such as food, and subsequently to devour. As the two functions were separated at an early stage in the evolution of nervous systems, they are expected to have distinct neurobiology, which appears to be the case (Kringelbach and Berridge 2009).

The various mood modules need to cooperate to orchestrate behavior. A minor pain should, for example, not ruin the chance for a major reward; thus, the pain should be subdued to direct the mind toward the benefit. Similarly, a small reward is not worth a life-threatening situation, and should consequently be ignored to secure escape. As reviewed by Leknes and Tracey (2008), various lines of research have demonstrated these principles. Pleasure-related analgesia implies suppression of pain, whereas various forms of pain reduce or obliterate the capacity to experience gratification, a condition referred to as *anhedonia*.

The Neurobiology of Mood Modules

The neurobiology of brain rewards and punishments has been covered in recent reviews (Kringelbach and Berridge 2009; Leknes and Tracey 2008; Russo and Nestler 2013). Below is a brief outline.

The main neurotransmitters involved in the mood modules—dopamine, serotonin, and opioids—apparently serve the homologous functions of attraction and avoidance even in the most primitive, nonemotional neural system, such as that of nematodes (Chase and Koelle 2007; Nieto-Fernandez et al. 2009). This observation strengthens the notion that the human mood modules represent an evolutionary expansion of processes involved in directing animals either toward opportunities or away from dangers.

For the mammalian brain, there are extensive data pertaining to the neuroanatomical correlates of mood modules. The information is based on a range of techniques, including various types of brain scans, neurochemical modulators, and electrical stimulation—exploring both humans and animals. The more ancient neural circuitries involved are located in subcortical parts of the brain, such as the thalamus, hypothalamus, amygdala, nucleus accumbens, and the ventral tegmental area. The cortical extensions include the orbitofrontal, lateral prefrontal, and anterior cingulate structures. The subcortical parts are presumably essential for generating positive and negative feelings, and the cortex enables conscious awareness as well as a capacity to modulate. The various sub-modules involved in mood have apparently retained a partly shared neurobiology with regard to anatomical features and neurochemistry. This observation testifies to their common evolutionary origin, as well as to the need for a close collaboration between rewards and punishment to derive optimal behavioral instigations. Although the various mood modules have shared features, it is possible to describe distinct neurobiology for the two pleasure modules (seeking and liking) and the pain module. For example, the opioid system serves a key role in liking, whereas dopaminergic nerve cells are important in the seeking module (Leknes and Tracey 2008).

There is cumulating evidence supporting the notion that the various forms of pleasures and pains converge on key neurobiological features. For example, experiencing envy of another person's success activates pain-related circuitry, whereas experiencing delight at someone else's misfortune (*schadenfreude*) activates reward-related circuits (Takahashi et al. 2009). Similarly, being excluded or treated unfairly activates pain-related neural regions (Eisenberger et al. 2003; O'Connor et al. 2008). On the other hand, positive social feelings—such as obtaining a good reputation, being treated fairly, or cooperating with others—offer rewards similar to those obtained from desirable food (Izuma et al. 2010; Tabibnia et al. 2008).

Several parts of the brain are engaged in generating reward-related experiences, but only a few "hotspots" are known to cause enhanced pleasure upon direct stimulation (Smith and Berridge 2007). These hotspots are found in structures such as the nucleus accumbens and the ventral pallidum. The same regions appear to be involved in both liking and seeking, but whereas opioids and cannabinoids stimulate liking, dopamine amplifies seeking. Their subcortical location supports the notion that the mood "motor" is subcortical, whereas the cortical regions act more like a "dashboard" (Grinde 2012).

Understanding Happiness

An Evolutionary Perspective

The evolutionary advantage of feelings rests with the power of a more flexible response to environmental challenges, which may have helped ancestral animals survive under varying and unexpected conditions. In other words, installing rewards and punishment was a strategy that promoted adaptive behavior by improving the plasticity of response. The individual animal would, in effect, select an option based on the expected hedonic value of various alternatives, the expectations being based on innate guidance and on previous experiences. Over time, the individual would learn to adjust behavior according to the potential harvest of pleasure, which—in a natural environment—should reflect what is best for the genes. The prospect of happiness, and very likely the capacity for consciousness (Grinde 2013), appears to be no more than peculiar side effects of this evolutionary strategy.

Various lines of evidence suggest that feelings first appeared in the amniotes some 300 million years ago (Cabanac et al. 2009). Presumably, evolution gradually expanded the role of the mood modules moving toward present mammals. Not only did the mood increase in strength, but the modules also became engaged in an increasing variety of situations. This expansion probably correlated with an increase in the size and significance of the cortex, while subcortical elements of the modules were retained. The subcortical elements may deliver a tonus of positive and negative feelings, while the cortex adds the "flavor" associated with the various experiences. A good meal, for example, produces a rather different impression compared to the joy of an aesthetic object, yet the pleasure itself may in both cases be generated by the same reward circuitry. In other words, brain mechanisms involved in the instigation of fundamental behavior, such as eating or sex, also cater to behavior considered specific to humans, such as enjoying music or gossiping. Evolution has apparently erected all pleasures and pains on the same neurobiological framework.

It may be hypothesized that with the advent of more advanced cognitive functions, such as those reflected in self-awareness and free will, a further enhancement of the mood value was called for, as the individual might otherwise use the elevated level of free will to choose options that diverge from the interest of the genes. That is, the higher cognitive functions imply a gain in flexibility, but at the risk of ending up with behavior that is less conducive to reproduction—particularly if the environment changes. The conjecture implies that humans may have the capacity to be the most happy—and most unhappy—of any animal. The assumption is in line with the observation that endorphins, key neurotransmitters in relation to reward and pain, are expressed at higher levels in human brains as compared to other apes (Cruz-Gordillo et al. 2010). Perhaps, the capacity for happiness has been boosted in the human lineage by sexual selection; that is, people may have preferred partners displaying good mood.

Cognitive Control

The function of the mood modules can be described as telling the individual whether it is on the right or wrong track toward survival and reproduction. In humans, however, there is a considerable element of cognitive assessment that influences what is construed as beneficial or detrimental. Collecting stamps may not improve the chance of survival, but it is possible to prime the brain to accept that finding a rare stamp is the most important thing to do and, consequently, harvest a solid reward for doing so. The human mind is susceptible to this sort of learning and molding. In an environment that differs from what evolution has prepared us for, such as an industrialized society, the system easily causes behavior at odds with the interest of the genes; fortunately, however, not necessarily at odds with maximizing happiness.

The mood modules may be activated directly from a sensory experience, such as tasting sweet food or burning a finger, or cognitive modulation may intervene to the effect of either subduing or enhancing the rewarding or punishing feelings. Minor alterations in a situation or a line of thought—whether due to conscious input, subconscious brain activity, or external factors—can change the net effect abruptly from a positive to a negative experience. Fear, for example, is normally an unpleasant feeling because it is meant to keep you away from dangerous situations. If you see something resembling a snake on the ground in front of you, it creates an unpleasant startle. When, upon closer examination, you realize it is only a twig, the relief is pleasant. In certain situations, the fear itself may be pleasurable—a mountaineer appreciates the adrenalin kick of the challenge of a dangerous mountain. The link between danger and the reward module is explained in evolutionary terms by the advantage of occasionally facing treacherous situations, for example, in connection with hunting. If the climber loses control over the situation, the feeling abruptly turns disagreeable.

Grief provides another interesting example. Normally, this is a negative experience, as it is evoked by events that are unfortunate for the genes, such as the loss of a child or support system. The brain reacts by marking the occurrence as something you should learn to avoid. But grief also serves a purpose in that it may help the individual overcome the situation; furthermore, as the emotion is visible in the face, it can be used to elicit support. The idea that grief may improve fitness implies that, in the appropriate context, the individual is served by engaging in the emotion and a reward is necessary to instigate this state of mind. In other words, grief may feel either good or bad. When your own situation is not jeopardized, the rewarding facet of grief may overwhelm the negative aspects, which helps explain why people willingly attend sad movies. O'Connor et al. (2008) have shown that although grief normally activates pain-related areas of the brain, in some people it activates reward centers.

The above examples illustrate that it is not obvious whether a particular situation will add or subtract to the level of happiness; that is, whether the situation will activate positive or negative mood modules. Various factors, including the context and the cognitive assessment, can move the experience toward being either pleasant or unpleasant.

Setpoint of Happiness

Much of daily conscious activity has only limited relevance for the level of happiness. Simply put, people do not experience life as a stream of either good or bad events, but rather as a relatively steady state. Mood may move slightly up or down, as when respectively working on an interesting task or feeling bored. Occasional incidents may cause a particular surge of pleasure or pain. In short, for most of the day the mood modules do not dominate the mind; however, that does not mean they are inactive. It seems more pertinent to envision a permeating tonus of mood caused by the net, (more or less) steady-state activity of the reward and punishment modules. This steady-state tonus presumably reflects what some scientists refer to as a *setpoint of happiness* (Lykken 2000). Although it is easy to find a stimulus that sends happiness temporarily beyond the setpoint, it is more difficult to enhance the setpoint itself.

The human mind receives a vast variety of input. Some information is received by the sense organs and reaches consciousness via the corresponding processing centers; other input is internally initiated, for example, hunger and thirst as part of a homeostatic system. Most inputs—as well as the experiences, thoughts, and sensations they generate—may connect with the mood modules, but only some have sufficient impact to be consciously regarded as pleasure or pain. Occasionally, the effect on mood can be considerable, but it is still not recognized; one example is when a situation causes a person to worry without any conscious awareness of the apprehension. The activity of the positive and negative mood modules can change without even alerting the conscious brain; that is, both external and internal signals can have an impact on emotions in the absence of attention (Tamietto and de Gelder 2010).

Default Contentment

According to the present model, both hedonic and eudemonic forms of happiness operate via the same mood modules of the brain. The idea is supported by the presumed prudence of the evolutionary process, meaning that it seems unlikely that evolution devised several independent systems aimed at putting the mind in a positive (or negative) state. Moreover, as pointed out above, a shared "reward circuitry" appears to be involved in all types of pleasure, including those often considered as eudemonic, such as friendship and compassion. The observation that people suffering from anhedonia have reduced ability to experience any form of happiness further supports the contention (Gorwood 2008; Kringelbach and Berridge 2009).

On the other hand, the above reasoning does not imply that the hedonia–eudemonia dichotomy is unwarranted, as the sources and nature of eudemonia may differ appreciably from typical hedonic pleasures. Whereas the early nervous systems responded primarily to the basal requirements of life (e.g., danger, food, and mating), in the human lineage the complexity and repertoire of behavioral instigations have expanded considerably. For example, having a "meaningful life" typically produces a pleasant feeling, presumably because evolution has attached positive feelings to utility: We are rewarded for doing something the brain considers constructive. Finding a meaning of life is considered a eudemonic type of contentment. In short, the types of positive affects considered to be eudemonic may simply reflect a subset of the vast array of stimuli that connect to a common reward motor.

Hedonism, in the form of sensual pleasures, tends to be frowned upon in Western society. This sentiment makes sense in that the pleasures associated with eudemonia have some preferred characteristics: They tend to be either more lasting, less likely to cause harm by misuse, or considered virtuous by being beneficial to society. Thus, the penchant for eudemonic values may reflect an attempt to coach people toward choosing particular types of rewards. The list would include those more likely to ensure optimal long-term happiness, and those favored due to social or political priorities.

There is one more feature as to the design of the brain that helps explain why people tend to consider eudemonia as different from hedonia. In the absence of adverse factors, humans (and other mammals) are apparently designed to be in a good mood—what has been referred to as a *default state of contentment* (Grinde 2004). It is most probably in the interest of the genes to reside in a body/mind with a positive attitude to life, as this condition is more likely to instigate pursuits required for survival and procreation. The individual is more willing to take the trouble of looking for food or a mate if in a good mood. In support of the notion of default contentment, there is considerable data suggesting that people tend to be happy and optimistic (Diener and Diener 1996; Lykken 2000). The point is reflected in their tendency to gamble, as well as in their personal assessment of happiness; when asked about subjective well-being, people claim (on the average) to be on the happy side of neutral.

The default contentment is likely to be associated with eudemonia rather than hedonia, as it does not require any pleasurable stimuli, and is not detrimental for the individual or the community. Furthermore, retaining this state of mind is probably more important for the level of happiness than pursuing typical hedonic pleasures. Hedonic stimuli are generally fleeting and often at odds with long-term happiness, while a positive default state implies a continuous and wholesome source of satisfaction. It seems likely that the default contentment simply reflects that the mood modules are designed to operate with a net positive value as long as the negative modules are not activated. That is, in a person with proper mental health, whose basal needs are cared for, the setpoint of happiness is positive. The construct referred to as "eudemonic happiness" apparently combines this default state of contentment with positive stimuli regarded as wholesome, such as friendship, empathy, and a meaning of life.

Implementing Happiness

Consciousness implies a capacity to influence affective neural activity and, thus, to some extent control how we feel. In theory, we have the opportunity to manipulate the mind, and consequently our level of happiness. In practice, however, most people are swayed by environmental stimuli, as well as by processes initiated in the subconscious parts of the brain. In short, it is within the design of the brain to allow us to influence the modules involved with positive and negative feelings, but having the desired impact requires special knowledge and skills.

The more common causes of reduced mental quality of life are related to excessive activity of the punishment modules, particularly in the form of anxiety, depression, and chronic pain (Wittchen et al. 2011). This observation presumably reflects that these sub-modules easily become distorted in industrialized societies. Even a subclinical level of unwarranted activity is likely to diminish happiness. Thus, the diagnosable conditions may be the tip of the iceberg as to reduced quality of life. As expected, psychological indicators suggest that a tendency toward anxiety or depression correlates negatively with subjective well-being (Nes et al. 2008; Watson and Naragon-Gainey 2010).

The size and strength of muscles improve upon exercise, and a similar effect is also seen in neuronal tissue (Pascual-Leone et al. 2005). The expansion of relevant brain areas upon use is easily demonstrated in animals where it is possible to apply experimentally controlled stimuli and subsequently remove the brain for anatomical analyses (Hensch 1999), but the general principle has been confirmed in humans. For example, hippocampal gray matter is increased as a consequence of exercising navigational skills (Maguire et al. 2000). It seems reasonable to assume that by exercising a brain module—that is, activating it regularly—the module will tend to be strengthened and have a concomitant greater impact on consciousness. For instance, by regularly stimulating the fear module, one is more likely to end up suffering from excessive activity of this module meaning that one is more likely to become anxious. This point has been documented in connection with research on early life stress (Bremne and Vermetten 2001).

Anxiety may be regarded as perverted activity of the fear module, whereas depression is presumably a question of similar hyperactivity in a "low mood" module. Although fear has an obvious biological function, it is less clear why humans need a module for low mood. A likely purpose is to help direct the individual toward reasonable strategies of living, particularly in relation to social life and task achievement. For the Paleolithic hunter-gatherer, a lack of a strong social network would be a serious threat to survival. The low mood induces a negative feeling (loneliness) to teach the individual to seek companionship with others. The low-mood module is probably also activated when unsuccessful in a task. Physical pain is a permeating feature of amniotes and important for survival. Interestingly, the prevalence of chronic pain is reported as even higher than that of anxiety and depression (Breivik et al. 2006; Wittchen et al. 2011).

Unwarranted activity in these three sub-modules tends to diminish rewarding sensations and demolish the default state of contentment. Preventing or treating these conditions is arguably the most compelling way to improve happiness in society. Indeed, the prevalence of diagnosable cases is considerable, but excessive, nonfunctional activity probably bothers a much larger percentage of the population. It may manifest itself as undue rumination on worries, a vague gloom, or occasional aching.

As pointed out above, neural circuits are "exercised" by frequent activation. This is useful in the case of improving navigational skills, but unfortunate when the result is to enhance the activity of negative emotions. As the default mood is positive, well-being depends primarily on avoiding excessive activity in the punishment modules. The first years of life are by far the most relevant when it comes to molding the brain. Early environment is consequently of primary importance for laying the foundations for later emotional life—and well-being. The plasticity of the human brain allows adults to compensate for a less than optimal childhood, but for the average person childhood experiences will have a considerable impact (Shonkoff and Phillips 2000).

The problem with the punishment modules is that their function implies they are easily triggered: For the sake of the genes, it is more important to avoid a threatening situation than to exploit a potential benefit. In other words, you react faster and more intensely to the sight of a snake than the sight of a fruit. Negative feelings are therefore easily exercised. The high prevalence of anxiety and depression may reflect that the present way of handling infants in industrialized society is not optimal for the development of these modules (Grinde 2005).

Presumably, there are particular neural circuits whose function is to either switch on or switch off the various modules. In nature, a frightening situation will generally resolve itself within a short time. To avoid that the accompanying fear obstructs other activities, the fear module will subsequently be turned off. Inappropriate development of the fear function (i.e., anxiety) presumably results when the "on-button" is exercised, but not the "off-button." A reasonable therapeutic strategy would therefore be to exercise the capacity to turn off the punishment modules.

It is also possible to exercise the reward modules in order to improve the mood tonus or set-point of happiness. Meditation appears to be a relevant exercise in this respect. Certain forms of meditation, such as that based on the Tibetan Buddhist tradition, have been claimed to install in the brain a sufficiently strong reward module to allow for a positive sentiment regardless of the external situation (Ricard 2007). The positive effect of meditation is partly substantiated by measuring activity in brain centers associated with rewards in Buddhist monks (Lutz et al. 2004).

Final Comments

Once evolution established emotions as an upgraded version of behavioral control, the mood modules became an integral part of the brain. Happiness can be construed as the net output of these modules integrated over a lifetime. The more salient feature of this model is that it points toward a strategy for improving the quality of life. A key element in this respect is the idea that appropriate "brain exercise" can lead to an enhancement of relevant nerve circuitry.

Other mammals apparently have more or less the same repertoire of feeling that we find in humans, including the capacity for a wide range of pleasure and pain (Panksepp 1998). The positive and negative mood values may be stronger in humans, but the more important difference is that humans have the competence to understand, and to use that insight to make the most of the situation. According to an evolutionary theory of happiness, strategies for improvement should focus primarily on how to reduce the activity of the punishing sub-modules (particularly anxiety, depression, and pain), and secondarily on how to stimulate reward modules. The reason why the former should be the main target is that in the absence of punishing activity, happiness will prevail in the form of the default state of contentment.

References

Berridge, K. C. (2003). Pleasures of the brain. *Brain Cognition, 52,* 106–128.

Breivik, H., Collett, B., Ventafridda, V., Cohen, R., & Gallacher, D. (2006). Survey of chronic pain in Europe: Prevalence, impact on daily life, and treatment. *European Journal of Pain, 10,* 287–333.

Bremne, J. D., & Vermetten, E. (2001). Stress and development: Behavioral and biological consequences. *Developmental Psychopathology, 13,* 473–489.

Cabanac, M. (1979). Sensory pleasure. *The Quarterly Review of Biology, 54,* 1–29.

Cabanac, M., Cabanac, A. J., & Parent, A. (2009). The emergence of consciousness in phylogeny. *Behavioral Brain Research, 198,* 267–272.

Chase, D. L., & Koelle, M. R. (2007). Biogenic amine neurotransmitters in *C. elegans*. *WormBook, 20,* 1–15.

Cruz-Gordillo, P., Fedrigo, O., Wray, G. A., & Babbitt, C. C. (2010). Extensive changes in the expression of the opioid genes between humans and chimpanzees. *Brain Behavior and Evolution, 76,* 154–162.

Csikszentmihalyi, M. (1990). *Flow: The psychology of optimal experience*. New York: Harper and Row.

Deci, E. L., & Ryan, F. M. (2008). Hedonia, eudaimonia, and well-being: An introduction. *Journal of Happiness Studies, 9,* 1–11.

Diener, E., & Diener, C. (1996). Most people are happy. *Psychological Science, 7,* 181–185.

Diener, E., Oishi, S., & Lucas, R. E. (2003). Personality, culture, and subjective well-being: Emotional and cognitive evaluations of life. *Annual Review of Psychology, 54,* 403–425.

Eisenberger, N. I., Lieberman, M. D., & Williams, K. D. (2003). Does rejection hurt? An fMRI study of social exclusion. *Science, 302,* 290–292.

Gorwood, P. (2008). Neurobiological mechanisms of anhedonia. *Dialogues in Clinical Neuroscience, 10,* 291–299.

Grinde, B. (2002). Happiness in the perspective of evolutionary psychology. *Journal of Happiness Studies, 3,* 331–354.

Grinde B. (2004). Darwinian happiness: Can the evolutionary perspective on well-being help us improve society? *World Futures—Journal of General Evolution, 60,* 317–329.

Grinde, B. (2005). An approach to the prevention of anxiety-related disorders based on evolutionary medicine. *Preventive Medicine, 40,* 904–909.

Grinde B. (2012). *The biology of happiness*. Dordrecht: Springer.

Grinde, B. (2013). The evolutionary rationale for consciousness. *Biological Theory, 7,* 227–236.

Hensch, T. K. (1999). Whisking away space in the brain. *Neuron, 24,* 623–637.

Izuma, K., Saito, D. N., & Sadato, N. (2010). Processing of the incentive for social approval in the ventral striatum during charitable donation. *Journal of Cognitive Neuroscience, 22,* 621–631.

Jékely, G. (2011). Origin and early evolution of neural circuits for the control of ciliary locomotion. *Proceedings of the Royal Society B, 278,* 914–922.

Kringelbach, M. L., & Berridge, K. C. (2009). Towards a functional neuroanatomy of pleasure and happiness. *Trends in Cognitive Science, 13,* 479–487.

Leknes, S., & Tracey, I. (2008). A common neurobiology for pain and pleasure. *Nature Reviews Neuroscience, 9,* 314–320.

Lutz, A., Greischar, L. L., Rawlings, N. B., Ricard, M., & Davidson, R. J. (2004). Long-term meditators self-induce high-amplitude gamma synchrony during mental practice. *Proceedings of the National Academy of Science USA, 101,* 16369–16373.

Lykken, D. (2000). *Happiness: The nature and nurture of joy and contentment*. New York: St. Martin's Griffin.

Maguire, E. A., Gadian, D. G., Johnsrude, I. S., Good, C. D., Ashburner, J., Frackowiak, R. S., & Frith, C. D. (2000). Navigation-related structural change in the hippocampi of taxi drivers. *Proceedings of the National Academy of Science USA, 97,* 4398–4403.

Nes, R. B., Roysamb, E., Tambs, K., Harris, J. R., & Reichborn-Kjennerud, T. (2008). Well-being and ill-being: Shared environments, shared genes? *Journal of Positive Psychology, 3,* 253–265.

Nesse, R. M. (2008). Natural selection, mental modules and intelligence. In G. R. Bock, J. A. Goode, & K. Webb (Eds.), *The nature of intelligence: Novartis foundation symposium 233* (pp. 96–115). Chichester: Wiley.

Nieto-Fernandez, F., Andrieux, S., Idrees, S., Bagnall, C., Pryor, S. C., & Sood, R. (2009). The effect of opioids and their antagonists on the nocifensive response of *Caenorhabditis elegans* to noxious thermal stimuli. *Invertebrate Neuroscience, 9,* 195–200.

O'Connor, M. F., Wellisch, D. K., Stanton, A. L., Eisenberger, N. I., Irwin, M. R., & Lieberman, M. D. (2008). Craving love? Enduring grief activates brain's reward center. *Neuroimage, 42,* 969–972.

Panksepp, J. (1998). *Affective neuroscience*. Oxford: Oxford University Press.

Pascual-Leone, A., Amedi, A., Fregni, F., & Merabet, L. B. (2005) The plastic human brain cortex. *Annual Review of Neuroscience, 28,* 377–401.

Philipson, L. (2002). Functional modules of the brain. *Journal of Theoretical Biology, 215,* 109–119.

Ricard, M. (2007). *Happiness—A guide to developing life's most important skill*. Boston: Atlantic Books.

Russo, S. J., & Nestler, E. J. (2013). The brain reward circuitry in mood disorders. *Nature Reviews Neuroscience, 14,* 609–625.

Seligman, M. E., Steen, T. A., Park, N., & Peterson, C. (2005). Positive psychology progress: Empirical validation of interventions. *American Psychologist, 60,* 410–421.

Shonkoff, J. P., & Phillips, D. A. (2000). *From neurons to neighborhoods. The science of early childhood development*. Washington, DC: National Academy Press.

Smith, K. S., & Berridge, K. C. (2007). Opioid limbic circuit for reward: Interaction between hedonic hotspots of nucleus accumbens and ventral pallidum. *Journal of Neuroscience, 27,* 1594–1605.

Tabibnia, G., Satpute, A. B., & Lieberman, M. D. (2008). The sunny side of fairness—preference for fairness activates reward circuitry (and disregarding unfairness activates self-control circuitry). *Psychological Science, 19,* 339–347.

Takahashi, H., Kato, M., Matsuura, M., Mobbs, D., Suhara, T., & Okubo, Y. (2009). When your gain is my pain and your pain is my gain: Neural correlates of envy and schadenfreude. *Science, 323,* 937–939.

Tamietto, M., & de Gelder, B. (2010). Neural bases of the non-conscious perception of emotional signals. *Nature Reviews Neuroscience, 11,* 697–709.

Watson, D., & Naragon-Gainey, K. (2010). On the specificity of positive emotional dysfunction in psychopathology: Evidence from the mood and anxiety disorders and schizophrenia/schizotypy. *Clinical Psychology Review, 30,* 839–848.

Watson, K. K., & Platt, M. L. (2008). Neuroethology of reward and decision making. *Philosophical Transactions of the Royal Society of London B, 363,* 3825–3835.

Wittchen, H. U., Jacobi, F., Rehm, J., Gustavsson, A., Svensson, M., Jönsson B., Olesen, J., Allgulander, C., Alonso, J., Faravelli, C., Fratiglioni, L., Jennum, P., Lieb, R., Maercker, A., van Os, J., Preisig, M., Salvador-Carulla, L., Simon, R., Steinhausen, H. C. (2011). The size and burden of mental disorders and other disorders of the brain in Europe 2010. *European Neuropsychopharmacology, 21,* 655–679.

Part IX
Individual Differences

Evolutionary Game Theory and Personality

34

Pieter van den Berg and Franz J. Weissing

Personality psychology and evolutionary game theory may not seem to be closely connected. Evolutionary game theory is a set of tools for helping us understand the evolution of social behavior; personality psychologists are mostly interested in comprehensively describing consistent individual differences between people (and in predicting the ramifications of these differences for various life outcomes). Traditionally, evolutionary game theory has been used by biologists in their pursuit of understanding the evolutionary origins of animal behavior, but has received much less attention from psychologists trying to understand human behavior. Conversely, the study of personality and individual differences has been a prime interest of psychologists, but has largely been neglected by biologists.

In recent years, however, this has changed and the study of individual differences has become a hot topic in various subdisciplines within biology. In particular, behavioral studies across the animal kingdom have revealed that the individuals in virtually all species differ systematically and consistently in their behavior (Gosling 2001; Sih et al. 2004a, b; Réale et al. 2007). This has produced a literature in which these differences are not only described but also interpreted from an evolutionary perspective. A number of hypotheses about the evolutionary emergence of individual variation have been advanced. Recent years have also seen increased attention to evolutionary explanations of personality differences in psychology, but these literatures have remained segregated (although some cross-references have certainly been made (e.g., Nettle and Penke 2010)). In comparison to psychologists, biologists base their arguments more strongly on formal theory, and in particular on evolutionary game theory, when suggesting explanations for individual differences.

In this chapter, we show that evolutionary game theory is a suitable tool to study the adaptive significance of individual differences. To do this, we first give a brief overview of evolutionary game theory and the study of individual differences in both humans and animals. Next, we discuss a number of evolutionary arguments that provide an adaptive explanation for the existence of individual differences and the structure of personalities. Most of these explanations are based on models from evolutionary game theory. Then, we discuss the evolutionary implications of personality differences for the course and outcome of evolution. By means of examples, we demonstrate that evolutionary predictions (including those of evolutionary game theory) can be far off target when individual differences are neglected.

P. van den Berg (✉) · F. J. Weissing
Theoretical Biology Group, Groningen Institute for Evolutionary Life Sciences, University of Groningen, Nijenborgh 7, 9747 AG Groningen, The Netherlands
e-mail: pieter.van.den.berg@rug.nl

F. J. Weissing
e-mail: f.j.weissing@rug.nl

V. Zeigler-Hill et al. (eds.), *Evolutionary Perspectives on Social Psychology,* Evolutionary Psychology, DOI 10.1007/978-3-319-12697-5_34, © Springer International Publishing Switzerland 2015

Evolutionary Game Theory

For many decades, economists have used game theory as their main tool for modeling and analyzing strategic interactions. Economic game theory (Rasmusen 2007) is generally normative; it is aimed at identifying optimal decisions, assuming that all involved parties act according to their own interests and in line with *Homo economicus* (i.e., fully rational and with unlimited computational ability). The central concept is that of Nash equilibrium: a combination of strategies where none of the players can obtain a better payoff by changing their behavior (Nash 1951).

Maynard Smith and Price (1973) realized that the insights from game theory could be applied to studying interactions between animals in evolutionary biology. For this, the concept of Nash equilibrium had to be adjusted. To apply it to animals, the definition of equilibrium could no longer be based on assumptions of rationality, but rather on fitness considerations. To achieve this, they introduced the concept of evolutionarily stable strategy (ESS). If all individuals in a population adopt an ESS, natural selection does not favor the invasion of any mutant strategy that is initially rare.

Evolutionary game theory is based on the insight that selection in a social context is "frequency dependent" (Heino et al. 1998): The Darwinian fitness of a strategy does depend not only on an individual's own behavior but also on the behavior of others in the population. This has important implications. For example, Maynard Smith and Price presented an evolutionary game theoretical model of animal conflict nowadays called the Hawk–Dove game (Maynard Smith 1982; Maynard Smith and Price 1973, see Fig. 34.1 for the payoff structure of this game). Pairs of individuals compete for a resource, and each individual has to decide whether to do this in a relatively peaceful ritualized manner ("Dove") or to employ dangerous weapons ("Hawk")[1]. When a Dove meets a Hawk, it is overpowered by the Hawk and gives away the resource without fight. The mean fitness of a population is maximized in the absence of Hawks, since Hawk–Hawk interactions may lead to injury and, hence, a reduction in fitness. Yet, a population of Doves is not evolutionarily stable, since in a population of Doves a single Hawk has a higher fitness than the Dove individuals. As long as Hawks are rare, they will typically meet Doves and therefore easily get access to the resource. Hence, the Hawk strategy will have a selective advantage and will spread when rare. When the Hawk strategy becomes more frequent, however, the risk of injury by getting involved in a Hawk–Hawk interaction increases. If the fitness costs of such injuries are high, the Dove strategy will have a selective advantage in a population of Hawks and, hence, will also spread when rare. Consequently, neither a pure Dove population nor a pure Hawk population is evolutionarily stable. The only evolutionarily stable population is a mixture of Hawks and Doves, or a population in which each individual plays Hawk and Dove with some intermediate probability. This simple example illustrates two points. First, when fitness is frequency dependent, evolution will typically not lead to a state where the mean fitness of the population is maximized; in the majority of all social interactions, such fitness maxima are not evolutionarily stable. Second, frequency-dependent selection will often lead to a polymorphic population where different individuals employ different strategies. Since the 1980s, the Hawk–Dove game has been studied widely—sometimes "disguised" as other games that have the same basic payoff structure, such as the Snowdrift game (which is framed as a context of cooperation rather than conflict; see Fig. 34.1).

Evolutionary game theory has been used to study many types of interactions (Broom and Rychtár 2013; Maynard Smith 1982), but the game that has received by far the most scientific attention is the Prisoner's Dilemma (Axelrod and Hamilton 1981). This game exemplifies why cooperation may be difficult to achieve, even if mutual cooperation is more beneficial for all parties than mutual restraint from cooperation. In the Prisoner's Dilemma, two players simultaneously decide on whether to "cooperate" or to "defect." If a player cooperates, the other player receives a

[1] Notice that Hawk and Dove indicate strategies and not different species of animals; evolutionary game theory is typically concerned with interactions within one species.

benefit *b*, while the cooperator has to pay a cost *c* (where $b > c$). A defector does not create benefits and does not have to pay a cost (see Fig. 34.1). Since $b > c$, the payoff in case of mutual cooperation $(b-c)$ is larger for both players than the payoff in case of mutual defection (zero). Yet, defection is a dominant strategy: Whatever the other player is doing, defection yields a higher payoff than cooperation (see Fig. 34.1). This outcome reflects the "Tragedy of the Commons" (Hardin 1968): At evolutionary equilibrium, everybody will defect, while mutual cooperation would be a more favorable outcome.

Matters change if the same two players interact with each other repeatedly (the Iterated Prisoner's Dilemma (IPD) game). Now more sophisticated strategies can emerge that make the behavior of an individual dependent on the history of the game and, in particular, on the cooperativeness of the other player. Human players often employ a simple strategy called tit-for-tat (TFT; Axelrod and Hamilton 1981). TFT always cooperates unless the other player has defected in the previous round; in that case, a TFT player defects in the next round. Hence, a population of TFT players will always cooperate, but since this cooperation is conditional on the behavior of the other player, a TFT player can less easily be exploited by a free-riding defector. Notice that superior features of a conditional strategy like TFT may not be immediately apparent to an outside observer, since a population of TFT players behaves in exactly the same way as a population of indiscriminate cooperators. This is another general insight from game theory: crucial aspects of a successful strategy may be hidden below the surface.

While TFT plays a prominent role in treatments of the IPD, this strategy is vulnerable, since the slightest mistake made by one of two

a Hawk-Dove game

	Dove	Hawk
Dove	$\frac{b}{2}$	0
Hawk	b	$\frac{b-c}{2}$

b Snowdrift game

	Cooperate	Defect
Cooperate	$b-\frac{c}{2}$	$b-c$
Defect	b	0

c Prisoner's Dilemma game

	Cooperate	Defect
Cooperate	$b-c$	$-c$
Defect	b	0

Fig. 34.1 Payoff structures of three prominent two-player games. Payoffs to the row player are shown; arrows indicate the best choice for the row player for both possible actions of the column player. **a** The Hawk-Dove game: two individuals are competing for a resource of value *b*. Hawks pursue the resource aggressively, while Doves try to resolve the conflict peacefully, and retreat from the conflict when competing with a Hawk. *c* denotes the cost of getting injured in a Hawk-Hawk fight. In this game, it is usually assumed that $c > b$, in which case it is most favorable to play Dove when the opponent plays Hawk, and vice versa. Hence, neither a population of Hawks nor a population of Doves is evolutionarily stable. The evolutionarily stable strategy (ESS) for this game corresponds to a mixed strategy where individuals play Hawk with a probability $p_H = b/c$. **b** The Snowdrift game: two individuals decide whether to perform a cooperative act that benefits both players (with benefit *b*, regardless of whether one or both individuals perform it), but comes at a cost of *c*. If both players cooperate, they share the cost. In this game, it is usually assumed that $b > c$. The ESS corresponds to a mixed strategy where individuals cooperate with probability $p_C = (2b-2c)/(2b-c)$. **c** The Prisoner's Dilemma game: two individuals decide whether to perform a cooperative act that provides a benefit *b* to the other player, and comes at a cost *c* to the cooperator. As in the Snowdrift game, it is usually assumed that $b > c$. Defect is always the best option, regardless of the behaviour of the other player. Therefore, the ESS is to cooperate with probability $p_C = 0$.

interacting TFT players results in a sequence of alternations between cooperation and defection. Other strategies, notably "generous tit-for-tat," which only retaliate against defection with a certain probability, and "Pavlov," which starts with cooperation and switches behavior when the other player defected in the previous round (the name "Pavlov" refers to the fact that the strategy continues behavior that is "rewarded" with good payoffs, but switches behavior after bad payoffs) have been found to be relatively robust outcomes of evolutionary simulations (Nowak and Sigmund 1992, 1993). However, even in this simple kind of interaction, the evolutionary dynamics can be complex. This reflects the fact that the IPD and virtually all games with a rich strategic structure have a multitude of Nash equilibrium strategies. In fact, for *any* outcome between 0 (mutual defection) and $b-c$ (mutual cooperation) a Nash equilibrium can be found that realizes it. This "folk theorem" of game theory (Gintis 2009) is still underappreciated in the behavioral sciences, although it has important implications. First, it is not self-evident that the iteration of a cooperation game leads to mutual cooperation; there are many alternative equilibrium outcomes. Second, the fact that many game models have a huge number of potential Nash equilibria makes the choice of equilibrium (i.e., equilibrium selection; Samuelson 1997) a much harder task than the identification of Nash equilibrium strategies. Even rational players who are able to compute all possible equilibrium strategies have to find ways to coordinate their behavior and to settle on one of these strategies. Personality may be important for resolving the coordination problems that are associated with the complexities of social interactions (discussed below).

There are numerous examples of evolutionary game theoretical analyses that have led to insights that can be overlooked when developing arguments without a basis in formal techniques (McNamara and Weissing 2010). A striking example is biparental care, in which a male and a female have to decide whether they should care for their common offspring, or invest their reproductive effort elsewhere. An evolutionary game theoretical model by McNamara and Houston (2002) found that the outcome of the interaction depends on the order of decision making of the players. Figure 34.2 shows the payoffs to the male and the female for a generalized version of this model, contingent on the decisions of each parent to either care for the young or desert the nest. If both parents make their choice simultaneously, the female should always care, because this is the best response, both if the male cares and if he deserts. Consequently, given the fact that the female cares, the male will desert. However, if the female decides first, the situation changes, because the male now knows the decision of the female. The male does best to respond to the female's desertion by caring, and to her caring by desertion. Because of this, the female chooses between a situation in which she cares and the male deserts, and a situation in which the male cares and she deserts. Because the latter situation is the best outcome for her, the female will desert, and the male will respond by caring. Although the male has more information than the female in the latter situation, this works to his disadvantage. This

a

	Male cares	Male deserts
Female cares	B − c (5)	b − c (3)
Female deserts	b (4)	0

b

	Female cares	Female deserts
Male cares	B − c (5)	b − c (3)
Male deserts	b + a (6)	a (2)

Fig. 34.2 Payoffs to the female **a** and the male **b** in a parental care game (inspired by a game considered by McNamara and Houston 2002). In this model, B represents the benefit of biparental care, b represents the benefit of uniparental care, c represents the cost of providing care, and a represents the fitness accrued through additional mating (we assume that such extra-pair mating opportunities are only available to males). In the model, $B>b>c$ and $B<2b$ (uniparental care provides more benefit per invested effort than biparental care). In the example (digits shown in red), we assume that $B=6$, $b=4$, $c=1$, and $a=2$

shows that having more information can have negative consequences.

Although evolutionary game theory has generated valuable insights over the years, there are also limitations of the approach. Game theoretical analyses focus on fitness considerations, without regard for the mechanisms that underlie traits. This has been referred to as the "phenotypic gambit": sacrificing realism of mechanisms for tractability of the evolutionary process. It fits in the tradition in biology to separate questions of proximate causation (How is a trait caused by immediate factors? What are the underlying mechanisms?) from ultimate causation (Why did a trait emerge in evolution? Why does it provide a fitness advantage?; Mayr 1961; Tinbergen 1963). However, the relative neglect of mechanisms in evolutionary studies is receiving increasing criticism (Bateson and Laland 2013; Fawcett et al. 2012; Laland et al. 2011; McNamara 2013). Mechanisms are of particular importance when considering the evolution of social traits, because they influence the probabilities with which strategies arise through mutation (van den Berg and Weissing, submitted). This is important, because in social contexts the success of a mutant strategy often strongly depends on the probability that it encounters itself in a resident population.

Another aspect of evolutionary game theory that has come under recent criticism is its focus on finding stable strategies for isolated contexts. Animals are faced with a complex and dynamic world, and it is unlikely that natural selection has equipped them with a perfect behavioral answer to every possible situation that they encounter (Fawcett et al. 2012, 2014). Indeed, animals often value immediate gains over long-term gains in a suboptimal way (Henly et al. 2008), make different decisions when there are "decoy" options available (Bateson and Healy 2005), and value food options differently depending on whether they were hungry when they previously encountered them (Marsh et al. 2004). Human behavior is also known to be subject to numerous psychological biases, causing them to deviate from rational behavior (Kahneman 2011; Tversky and Kahneman 1974). It seems likely that natural selection has equipped organisms with simple heuristics that perform relatively well when faced with a range of contexts (Gigerenzer et al. 1999).

Individual differences are often overlooked in evolutionary game theoretical analyses. Evolutionary game theoretical models consider the fate of mutants in monomorphic resident populations. However, behavioral variation can have a profound effect on the outcome of evolution, for instance in the case of cooperative behavior (McNamara and Leimar 2010). If variation in a social trait is present in a population, it can be advantageous to be choosy about with whom to interact. If this social sensitivity indeed evolves, it may in turn affect the evolution of the social trait (Wolf et al. 2011). For this reason and others mentioned below, it is important to consider individual variation when constructing evolutionary game theoretical models (McNamara 2013; McNamara and Weissing 2010).

Human and Animal Personality

The study of individual differences has been one of the main areas of study in psychology for decades. The field of personality psychology has a long and diverse history, its prominence reflected by the large number of scientific journals, books, and conferences dedicated to it today. The study of personality addresses individual differences in characteristics that are relatively stable over time, but how those characteristics should be defined and measured has remained a matter of controversy (Engler 2009). Personality research is characterized by a large variation in objectives. Much research is focused on comprehensively describing the individual variation in a population, but much research is also dedicated to correlating outcomes (in education, work, or personal life) with personality factors. Over time, a number of influential systems for describing personality variation have been devised, of which the five-factor model (Digman 1990; McCrae and John 1992; Tupes and Christal 1961) is the most used and confirmed. Personality is most often measured using self-report data, although ratings by others and behavioral observations are also used.

In biology, research concerning individual differences is a more recent phenomenon. Individual differences between animals of the same species have long been ignored or treated as irrelevant behavioral noise. The idea that evolution does not lead to variation, but rather depletes variation and leads to a single optimal type, is likely to have contributed to this attitude. However, in the last few decades, evidence has accumulated that patterned variation in animal behavior (dubbed "coping style," "behavioral syndrome," or "animal personality") occurs across a wide range of taxa (Gosling 2001; Groothuis and Carere 2005; Koolhaas et al. 1999; Réale et al. 2007; Sih et al. 2004a; Wolf and Weissing 2012). Animal personality has been defined as behavioral variation that is consistent through time as well as across different contexts. It is defined in terms of measurable behavioral tendencies; the fact that self-report data are impossible with animals has helped avoid some of the controversy about the concepts of personality in psychology. Perhaps more importantly, animal personality research distinguishes itself from personality psychology by acceptance of the overarching framework of evolutionary theory. Questions are often inspired from an evolutionary perspective, and the relevance of different characteristics is determined accordingly.

In recent years, there has been some cross-pollination between the fields of personality psychology and animal personality research, particularly in the development of theory to explain the evolution of individual variation (Buss 2009; Figueredo et al. 2005; Gosling 2001; Michalski and Shackelford 2010; Nettle 2006; Penke et al. 2007). Recently, Nettle and Penke (2010) have argued that personality psychologists can benefit much from behavioral ecology, especially in adopting an evolutionary perspective. They also argue that adopting the concept of the reaction norm from biology (a rule that defines the response of an organism to environmental conditions) can help solve the long-standing debate in psychology about whether personality or situational parameters are more important in shaping human behavior. Conversely, biologists can learn from the 100 years of experience that psychologists have with devising comprehensive descriptions of behavioral variation. Some have argued that personality differences are especially prevalent in highly social species (Figueredo et al. 1995, 2005; Penke et al. 2007). Since the evolution of social behavior is governed by frequency-dependent selection, evolutionary game theory is a preeminent tool to formally study the evolutionary emergence of personality differences. Moreover, the use of formal techniques such as evolutionary game theory is important for further developing verbal arguments, so that they mature into theories that generate testable predictions.

Evolutionary Causes of Personality Differences

Consistent individual differences are challenging to explain from an evolutionary point of view. First, there is the question of variation: Why are there individual differences between members of the same species, where one would expect evolution to deplete variation, leading to a single optimal type? Second, there is the question of consistency: Why do individuals behave in the same way across different contexts and over their lifetime, instead of being flexible and optimally adapting their behavior to each specific circumstance? Adaptive explanations for individual differences have started to emerge in both evolutionary psychology and evolutionary biology over the last two decades. In recent years, both fields have started recognizing the same evolutionary mechanisms that can lead to consistent variation. In biology more than in psychology, evolutionary explanations have often been backed by formal theory—often evolutionary game theoretical models.

Buss (1984) remarked that evolutionary biology and personality psychology are connected in an interesting way: personality psychology studies variation, which is the substrate that evolution acts on. Tooby and Cosmides (1990) argued that personality differences are unlikely to have resulted from natural selection, and consider personality variation to be random noise. However, since then, adaptive explanations for personality differences have started emerging in the literature. Notable examples from psychology include the theories of sociosexuality (Gangestad and Simpson 1990) and sociopathy (Mealey 1995). The biological literature of the 1990s also saw an increased interest in adaptive explanations for variation in reproductive strategies (see Gross 1997, for a review), often accompanied by evolutionary game theoretical models, and other studies invoking adaptive arguments for individual differences (e.g., Morris 1998). More recently, Nettle (2006) took the first steps towards more explicitly connecting the fields of evolutionary biology and personality psychology by offering a number of potentially adaptive explanations for the variation in human personality using the five-factor model.

Recent reviews from evolutionary psychology (Buss 2009) and evolutionary biology (Wolf and Weissing 2010) reveal that a similar range of adaptive explanations for individual variation is currently being considered in both fields. Three types of adaptive explanations prominently figure in both reviews: (1) state-dependent behavior that is contingent on nonevolved differences, (2) environmental heterogeneity in fitness optima through space and/or time, and (3) negative frequency-dependent selection. These are not all the explanations that are considered in either paper. Buss also includes costly signaling, but this can be considered as a subset of state-dependent behavior, and some nonadaptive explanations such as mutation load. Wolf and Weissing, in turn, also discuss the emergence of individual variation as a result of nonequilibrium dynamics. Below, we elaborate on these three explanations, and give examples of evolutionary game theoretical models that support each of them.

State-Dependent Behavior

The idea that individual variation may arise from underlying differences in state is not new. In fact, it is central to the handicap theory of sexual selection (Zahavi 1975). In handicap models, it is assumed that there is some kind of variation in quality between males; either heritable ("good genes") or nonheritable (e.g., the amount of resources a male has available to invest in offspring). In these models, evolution leads to the development of a costly indicator trait that signals quality in males, and a costly preference for the degree of exaggeration of that indicator trait in females. Thus, the measurable individual variation in the indicator trait is contingent on the underlying variation in male quality.

A more recent example is the idea that individual differences in social dominance may result from minute differences in fighting ability, or even from chance asymmetries regarding who happens to win most fights early in life. Van Doorn et al. (2003) considered the iterated version of the Hawk–Dove game (see Fig. 34.1): The same two individuals repeatedly had to fight over resources and in each round could choose between playing Hawk or Dove. In the majority of their simulations, a strategy emerged that resembles the so-called winner–loser (WL) effect that has been described in many animal populations (Chase et al. 1994). According to this WL strategy, individuals play Hawk with a certain probability in their first rounds, until they are involved in a Hawk–Hawk interaction. From this round onwards, the winner of this interaction plays Hawk in all remaining rounds, while the loser sticks to playing Dove. If both players of an iterated Hawk–Dove interaction adopt the strategy WL, the outcome is a stable dominance convention: the individual that happens to win the first fight keeps obtaining the resource in subsequent interactions, while the other individual keeps losing the contest. This happens despite of the fact that there are no initial differences in strength or fighting ability. The evolved strategy WL is a strategic convention that leads to consistent individual differences in social dominance on the basis of a single event, the random assignment of a winner, or loser position in one escalated fight.

Environmental Heterogeneity

If there is variation in fitness optima through space and/or time, this may lead to variation in behavior. However, exactly how phenotypic variation is expected to emerge depends on the details of the situation (Wolf and Weissing 2010). If individuals have reliable knowledge of their environment and the costs of adapting behavior to environmental conditions are low, phenotypic plasticity is likely to evolve. In this case, the resulting individual variation is a consequence of a form of state-dependent behavior, where "states" correspond to environmental conditions. If information on the environment is noisy or the costs of plasticity are high, polymorphism will typically arise, where different types of individuals coexist that are adapted to some but not all environmental conditions. This polymorphism may reflect either genetic diversity (different genotypes specifying phenotypes adapted to different conditions) or a bet-hedging strategy (where a single genotype produces phenotypically variable offspring).

Olofsson et al. (2009) present an evolutionary model to explain the evolution of bet-hedging strategies. In their model, a population of individuals is living in a temporally variable environment. The variation between years is implemented as a variable minimal weight for the viability of offspring; any offspring below that threshold does not survive. In addition, only a limited number of offspring can survive in each year. In the model, each individual can produce the same total weight of offspring, but has three genes to determine how many offspring to produce. One gene determines the average weight of one offspring, one determines the variability in weight among offspring in a given year, and one determines the variability in weight between years. The outcome of evolution in the model is that individuals produce variable offspring both within and across the generations. The result is a population in which there are individual differences in size, that are not conditional responses to the current environment, but that are also not based on a genetic polymorphism.

Frequency-Dependent Selection

Frequency-dependent selection is arguably the only ultimate explanation of the sustained persistence of heritable variation. Competing strategies will easily coexist (resulting in individual variation) if each strategy has a fitness advantage when occurring in a low frequency. Such a rareness advantage arises, for example, in case of frequency-dependent selection where the fitness of each strategy decreases with the frequency of this strategy in the population ("negative" frequency-dependent selection). Both Gangestad and Simpson's (1990) theory of sociosexuality and Mealey's (1995) theory of sociopathy are based on arguments of negative frequency dependence. Evolutionary game theory is a particularly useful tool for studying the implications of negative frequency-dependent selection.

An example of a game theoretical model that explains the evolution of individual differences by negative frequency-dependent selection is the model of Johnstone and Manica (2011) for the emergence of leaders and followers (but see Weissing 2011). With their model, they consider a population in which individuals are grouped at random and have to play an n-person version of the game "battle of the sexes." The original context of this game is a situation where a couple has to decide how to spend their evening. The man would like to go to the prizefight, the woman would prefer to go to the ballet, but above all they want to spend their evening together. In the model, there is a group of individuals that each have their own preference, but also obtain benefits when they coordinate on the same option with many fellow group members. Each individual has a genetically determined value of leadership: if it is high, the individual tends to choose their own preferred option; if it is low, the individual copies the most recent choice of a randomly selected group member. In this case, leadership is subject to negative frequency-dependent selection; the fewer leaders there are, the more it pays to be a leader. The outcome of their model is individual variation because of a genetic polymorphism in leadership; some individuals are leaders, some are followers. Indeed, for some parameter combinations, as many as five different types can arise.

Overall, constraints play an important role in the evolution of consistent individual differences. If the optimal strategy cannot be attained, because of imperfect information, cognitive limitations, costs of plasticity, or for whatever other reason, frequency-dependent selection will often lead to the emergence of consistent individual variation. For a simple way of illustrating this, again consider the Hawk–Dove game. If individuals can have mixed strategies (their strategy can be to play Hawk with a certain probability), evolution leads to the emergence of a single type (Wolf et al. 2011). However, the strategy space is constrained so that only pure strategies are allowed (individuals can only always play Hawk or always play Dove), evolution leads to a population that consists of some individuals that always play Hawk, and some that always play Dove. Because of a constraint on the flexibility of behavior, both variation and consistency in behavior emerge.

Most animals are faced with numerous different contexts throughout their lives, and they usually lack detailed information about the specific context that they are in. It is not difficult to see that informational and cognitive constraints render it close to impossible for animals to have a perfect behavioral response for each possible context that they may face. Instead, they often resort to imperfect behavioral responses: general-purpose mechanisms or "rules of thumb." These imperfect mechanisms leave room to be exploited by other imperfect mechanisms, and individual variation can emerge as a result (Botero et al. 2010). A recent empirical example of variation in general-purpose mechanisms in human behavior is individual variation in social learning strategies (Molleman et al. 2014; Van den Berg et al. 2015). These authors show experimentally that humans are different in the extent to which they are interested in social information. Moreover, there is variation in the type of information individuals are interested in; some try to identify the type of behavior that is associated with the highest payoffs, whereas others are only interested in finding out what the majority is doing. Interestingly, these differences were consistent across a number of different contexts that the subjects were confronted with. This indicates that there may be limitations to flexibly adapting social learning strategies to each different context, potentially explaining the observed variation.

Evolutionary Consequences of Personality Differences

Even though there has recently been interest in evolutionary explanations for personality differences, questions concerning the evolutionary consequences of individual variation have received less attention. However, as summarized in two recent reviews (Sih et al. 2012; Wolf and Weissing 2012), there are many potential ecological and evolutionary consequences of the presence of behavioral variation in a population. Consequences of individual differences can impact three qualitatively different domains. First, it can affect ecological parameters, such as population density, the spatial distribution of different behavioral types over different habitats, and disease transmission dynamics. Second, it can affect qualitative aspects of the evolutionary process, such as evolvability, constraints on evolution, and the likelihood of evolution to lead to speciation. Third, the presence of consistent individual variation can alter selective forces acting within populations. This latter consequence of consistent individual variation is especially suited for analysis with formal techniques from evolutionary game theory. Below, we elaborate on the consequences of both consistency and individual variation for the outcome of evolution, giving examples of evolutionary game theoretical models in both cases.

Implications of Individual Variation

To illustrate the evolutionary consequences of individual differences, we can again refer back to handicap models of sexual selection (Zahavi 1975). In those models, males signal their mate value (whether heritable or not) with a costly indicator trait. In response, a costly female preference for the extent of expression of this trait can emerge. Under the right circumstances, the benefits of such a preference (leading to mating with higher-quality males) will outweigh the cost of being choosy. However, a costly female preference can only be maintained if there is something to choose—there must be variation between males for the preference to have a selective advantage. Without individual variation in male quality, female preference for the indicator trait will be lost from the population. As a result, male investment in the indicator trait also loses its selective advantage, and will also be lost. In summary, without individual differences in male quality, there can be no evolution of exaggerated indicator traits and female preferences for those traits. Noe and Hammerstein (1994, 1995) recognized the importance of the evolution of choosiness in "biological markets," where one class of individual has something to offer for another class of individuals. They consider the case of mating, but also of cooperation and mutualism between different species. However, although variation is a prerequisite for any market to function, they do not explicitly consider the importance of variation in their models.

Recently, McNamara et al. (2008) developed an evolutionary game model that explicitly considers the importance of individual variation for the evolution of choosiness in the context of cooperation. In the model, they consider a population in which pairs of individuals engage in a variant of the IPD. Each individual carries two genetically determined traits: degree of cooperativeness and degree of choosiness. At the beginning of each interaction, both individuals simultaneously invest an amount of effort, which is determined by their degree of cooperativeness. Both individuals incur a cost for the amount of effort that they invest, but gain a benefit from the amount of effort invested by the other player. The degree of choosiness next determines the minimal cooperative effort that is accepted from the other player. If the choosiness of both players is satisfied, the two players interact again—unless one of them does not survive to the next round, which happens with a small fixed probability. If the choosiness of at least one of the players is not satisfied, both players find a new interaction partner, at a small cost. The outcome of the model is that the evolution of choosiness and cooperation strongly depend on the mutation rate, which determines the amount of individual variation in the population. If the mutation rate is high enough, there are sufficient individual differences in cooperativeness, which provides a selective advantage for being choosy. Consequently, as a result of the evolution of increased choosiness, it pays to cooperate more, and high levels of cooperativeness evolve. In contrast, if the mutation rate is too low, choosiness does not pay, and levels of cooperation remain low as a consequence. In summary, this model shows that the amount of individual variation that is present in a population can profoundly affect the evolution of cooperation and choosiness.

Implications of Behavioral Consistency

As noted, many types of interactions have a huge number of Nash equilibria. Even if there are several Nash equilibria that are favorable for all individuals involved, the participants of an interaction first have to zoom in on one particular equilibrium. In the absence of efficient and reliable communication, this may be a difficult task, corresponding to a "coordination game." (A classic example of a coordination game with different equilibria is whether to drive on the left side or the right side of the road; see McNamara and Weissing 2010.) Behavioral consistency can be helpful in solving problems of coordination. By being consistent, individuals can inform others about how they are likely to behave in the future. Others can use this information to choose their own behavior in such a way that successful coordination is the result.

By means of an evolutionary game model, Wolf et al. (2010) show how consistency and responsiveness to consistency may arise in evolution, and how a small amount of consistency may lead to the emergence of even more consistent strategies. They model a population in which individuals are engaged in pairwise Hawk–Dove game interactions. Each individual has a genetically determined trait that dictates with what probability they play Hawk. As described before, the evolutionary outcome in the simplest version of this model is a population in which each individual plays Hawk with some intermediate probability (the exact value depends on the specifics of the payoff parameters; see Fig. 34.1). In an expanded version of the model, each individual also carries a gene that allows for social responsiveness. Responsive individuals watch their future interaction partners in one interaction with a third individual and subsequently make their behavior contingent on the choice of strategy in this interaction: if the future interaction partner played Hawk, the responsive individual plays Dove, and vice versa. Surprisingly low levels of individual variation in the probability to play Hawk already provide social responsiveness with a selective advantage. The ensuing presence of responsive individuals in the population selects for consistency, since the best reply to the strategy employed by responsive individuals is to stick to one's previous behavior. In turn, responsive individuals profit from the consistency of their interaction partners. Accordingly, there is a positive feedback loop: the more consistent individuals there are, the more it pays to be socially responsive, which can in turn lead to even greater consistency. In the end, a population may result that differs substantially from the original population (e.g., in the frequency of Hawk–Hawk interactions).

Conclusions and Future Directions

We have given a number of examples where evolutionary game theory has been used as a formal tool to support arguments for the adaptive significance of consistent individual differences. Both when studying the evolutionary causes and the consequences of consistent individual variation, evolutionary game models can be used to sharpen intuition, make arguments more precise, and help formulate predictions and new questions. Personality psychologists can benefit from the use of evolutionary game models in advancing our understanding of individual differences in human populations. Especially in humans, where the study of individual variation has a long and rich tradition, there is a huge amount of empirical substrate for formulating evolutionary hypotheses that could benefit from formal approaches.

We have argued that a better understanding of evolutionary constraints is crucial for getting a better grasp on the evolution of individual variation. Mechanistic constraints are often (perhaps even always) at the basis of the evolution of heritable individual differences. However, developing such a theory of constraints is a rather unfamiliar practice to evolutionary biologists. Traditionally, evolutionary biologists have separated proximate (how does it work?) and ultimate (why does it exist?) questions, and evolutionary models have reflected this separation in their neglect of mechanistic constraints. However, there is now a growing appreciation that asking evolutionary questions without regard for proximate mechanisms can be misleading. We contend that the study of the evolution of individual differences would be an ideal test case for the development of a more mature theory of the relation between ultimate explanations and proximate mechanisms.

References

Axelrod, R., & Hamilton, W. D. (1981). The evolution of cooperation. *Science, 211,* 1390–1396.

Bateson, M., & Healy, S. D. (2005). Comparative evaluation and its implications for mate choice. *Trends in Ecology and Evolution, 20,* 659–664.

Bateson, P., & Laland, K. N. (2013). Tinbergen's four question: An appreciation and an update. *Trends in Ecology and Evolution, 28,* 712–718.

Botero, C., Pen, I., Komdeur, J., & Weissing, F. J. (2010). The evolution of individual variation in communication strategies. *Evolution, 64,* 3123–3133.

Broom, M., & Rychtár, J. (2013). *Game-theoretical models in biology*. New York: Chapman & Hall.

Buss, D. M. (1984). Evolutionary biology and personality psychology: Towards a conception of human nature and individual differences. *American Psychologists, 39,* 1135–1147.

Buss, D. M. (2009). How can evolutionary psychology successfully explain personality and individual differences. *Perspectives on Psychological Science, 4,* 359–366.

Chase, I. D., Bartolomeo, C., & Dugatkin, L. A. (1994). Aggressive interactions and inter-contest interval—how long do winners keep winning. *Animal Behaviour, 48,* 393–400.

Digman, J. M. (1990). Personality structure: Emergence of the Five-Factor Model. *Annual Review of Psychology, 41,* 417–440.

Engler, B. (2009). *Personality theories* (8th ed.). Belmont: Wadsworth.

Fawcett, T. W., Hamblin, S., & Giraldeau, L. (2012). Exposing the behavioral gambit: The evolution of learning and decision rules. *Behavioral Ecology, 24,* 2–11.

Fawcett, T. W., Fallenstein, B., Higginson, A. D., Houston, A. I., Mallpress, D. E. W., Trimmer, P. C., & McNamara, J. M. (2014). The evolution of decision rules in complex environments. *Trends in Cognitive Sciences, 18,* 153–161.

Figueredo, A. J., Cox, R. L., & Rhine, R. J. (1995). A generalizability analysis of subjective personality assessments in the stumptail macaque and the zebra finch. *Multivariate Behavioral Research, 30,* 167–197.

Figueredo, A. J., Sefcek, J. A., Vasquez, G., Brumbach, B. H., King, J. E., & Jacobs, W. J. (2005). Evolutionary personality psychology. In D. M. Buss (Ed.), *Handbook of evolutionary psychology* (pp. 851–877). New York: Wiley.

Gangestad, S. W., & Simpson, J. A. (1990). Toward an evolutionary history of female sociosexual variation. *Journal of Personality, 58,* 69–96.

Gigerenzer, G., Todd, P. M., & ABC Research Group. (1999). *Simple heuristics that make us smart.* New York: Oxford University Press.

Gintis, H. (2009). *Game theory evolving.* Princeton: Princeton University Press.

Gosling, S. D. (2001). From mice to men: What can we learn about personality from animal research? *Psychological Bulletin, 127,* 45–86.

Groothuis, T. G. G., & Carere, C. (2005). Avian personalities: Characterization and epigenesis. *Neuroscience and Behavioural Reviews, 29,* 137–150.

Gross, M. R. (1997). Alternative reproductive strategies and tactics: Diversity within the sexes. *Trends in Ecology and Evolution, 11,* 92–98.

Hardin, G. (1968). The tragedy of the commons. *Science, 162,* 1243–1248.

Heino, M., Metz, J. A. J., & Kaitala, V. (1998). The enigma of frequency-dependent selection. *Trends in Ecology and Evolution, 13,* 367–370.

Henly, S. E., Ostdiek, A., Blackwell, E., Knutie, S., Dunlap, A. S., & Stephens, D. W. (2008). The discounting-by-interruptions hypothesis: Model and experiment. *Behavioural Ecology, 19,* 154–162.

Johnstone, R. A., & Manica, A. (2011). Evolution of personality differences in leadership. *Proceedings of the National Academy of Sciences of the United States of America, 108,* 8373–8378.

Kahneman, D. (2011). *Thinking, fast and slow.* New York: Farrar, Straus, and Giroux.

Koolhaas, J. M., Korte, S. M., De Boer, S. F., Van der Vegt, B. J., Van Reenen, C. G., Hopster, H., De Jong, I. C., & Blokhuis, H. J. (1999). Coping styles in animals: Current status in behavior and stress-physiology. *Neuroscience and Biobehavioral Reviews, 23,* 925–935.

Laland, K. N, Sterelny, K., Odling-Smee, J., Hoppitt, W., & Uller, T. (2011). Cause and effect in biology revisited: Is Mayr's proximate-ultimate dichotomy still useful? *Science, 224,* 1512–1516.

Marsh, B., Schuck-Paim, C., & Kacelnik, A. (2004). Energetic state during learning affects foraging choices in starlings. *Behavioural Ecology, 15,* 396–399.

Maynard Smith, J. M. (1982). *Evolution and the theory of games.* Cambridge: Cambridge University Press.

Maynard Smith, J. M., & Price, G. R. (1973). The logic of animal conflict. *Nature, 246,* 15–18.

Mayr, E. (1961). Cause and effect in biology. *Science, 134,* 1501–1506.

McCrae, R. R., & John, O. P. (1991). An introduction to the five-factor Model and its applications. *Journal of Personality, 60,* 175–215.

McNamara, J. M. (2013). Towards a richer evolutionary game theory. *Journal of the Royal Society Interface, 10,* 20130544.

McNamara, J. M., & Houston, A. I. (2002). Credible threats and promises. *Philosophical Transactions of the Royal Society: Biological Sciences, 357,* 1607–1616.

McNamara, J. M., & Leimar, O. (2010). Variation and the response to variation as a basis for successful cooperation. *Philosophical Transactions of the Royal Society: Biological Sciences, 365,* 2627–2633.

McNamara, J. M., & Weissing, F. J. (2010). Evolutionary game theory. In T. Székely, A. J. Moore, & J. Komdeur (Eds.), *Social behaviour: Genes, ecology and evolution* (pp. 109–133). Cambridge: Cambridge University Press.

McNamara, J. M., Barta, Z., Fromhage, L., & Houston, A. I. (2008). The coevolution of choosiness and cooperation. *Nature, 451,* 189–192.

Mealey, L. (1995). The sociobiology of sociopathy: An integrated evolutionary model. *Behavioral and Brain Sciences, 18,* 523–541.

Michalski, R. L, & Shackelford, T. K. (2010). Evolutionary personality psychology: Reconciling human nature and individual differences. *Personality and Individual Differences, 48,* 509–516.

Molleman, L., Van den Berg, P., & Weissing, F. J. (2014). Consistent individual differences in human social learning strategies. *Nature Communications, 5,* 3570.

Morris, D. W. (1998). State-dependent optimization of litter size. *Oikos, 83,* 518–528.

Nash, J. (1951). Non-cooperative games. *Annals of Mathematics, 54,* 286–295.

Nettle, D. (2006). The evolution of personality variation in humans and other animals. *American Psychologist, 61,* 622–631.

Nettle, D., & Penke, L. (2010). Personality: Bridging the literatures from human psychology and behavioural ecology. *Philosophical Transactions of the Royal Society B, 365,* 4043–4050.

Noe, R., & Hammerstein, P. (1994). Biological markets—Supply-and-demand determine the effect of partner choice in cooperation, mutualism and mating. *Behavioral Ecology and Sociobiology, 35,* 1–11.

Noe, R., & Hammerstein, P. (1995). Biological markets. *Trends in Ecology and Evolution, 10,* 336–339.

Nowak, M. A., & Sigmund, K. (1992). Tit-for-tat in heterogeneous populations. *Nature, 355,* 250–253.

Nowak, M. A., & Sigmund, K. (1993). A strategy of win stay, lose shift outperforms tit-for-tat in the Prisoner's Dilemma game. *Nature, 364,* 56–58.

Olofsson, H., Ripa, J., & Jonzén, N. (2009). Bet-hedging as an evolutionary game: The trade-off between egg size and number. *Proceedings of the Royal Society B, 276,* 2963–2969.

Penke, L., Dennissen, J. J. A., & Miller, G. F. (2007). The evolutionary genetics of personality. *European Journal of Personality, 21,* 549–587.

Rasmusen, E. (2007). *Games and information—An introduction to game theory.* New York: Wiley-Blackwell.

Réale, D., Reader, S. M., Sol. D., McDougall, P. T., & Dingemanse, N. J. (2007). Integrating animal temperament within ecology and evolution. *Biological Reviews, 82,* 291–318.

Samuelson, L. (1997). *Evolutionary games and equilibrium selection.* Boston: MIT Press.

Sih, A., Bell, A. M., & Johnson, J. C. (2004a). Behavioral syndromes: An ecological and evolutionary overview. *Trends in Ecology and Evolution, 19,* 372–378.

Sih, A., Bell, A. M., Johnson, J. C., & Ziemba, R. E. (2004b). Behavioral syndromes: An integrative overview. *Quarterly Review of Biology, 79,* 241–277.

Sih, A., Cote, J., Evans, M., Fogarty, S., & Pruitt, J. (2012). Ecological implications of behavioural syndromes. *Ecology Letters, 15,* 278–289.

Tinbergen, N. (1963). On aims and methods of ethology. *Zeitschrift für Tierpsychologie, 20,* 410–433.

Tooby, J., & Cosmides, L. (1990). On the universality of human nature and the uniqueness of the individual: The role of genetics and adaptation. *Journal of Personality, 58,* 17–67.

Tupes, E. C., & Christal, R. E. (1961). Recurrent personality factors based on trait ratings. USAF ASD Technical Report (no 61–97).

Tversky, A., & Kahneman, D. (1974). Judgment under uncertainty: Heuristics and biases. *Science, 185,* 1124–1131.

Van den Berg, P., Molleman, L., & Weissing, F. J. (2015). Focus on the success of others leads to selfish behavior. *Proceedings of the National Academy of Sciences of the United States of America.* In press.

Van Doorn, G. S., Hengeveld, G. M., & Weissing, F. J. (2003). The evolution of social dominance—I: Two-player models. *Behaviour, 140,* 1333–1358.

Weissing, F. J. (2011). Born leaders. *Nature, 474,* 288–289.

Wolf, M., Van Doorn, G. S., & Weissing, F. J. (2011). On the coevolution of social responsiveness and behavioural consistency. *Proceedings of the Royal Society B: Biological Sciences, 278,* 440–448.

Wolf, M., & Weissing, F. J. (2010). An explanatory framework for adaptive personality differences. *Philosophical Transactions of the Royal Society: Biological Sciences, 365,* 3959–3968.

Wolf, M., & Weissing, F. J. (2012). Animal personalities: Consequences for ecology and evolution. *Trends in Ecology and Evolution, 27,* 452–461.

Zahavi, A. (1975). Mate selection—A selection for a handicap. *Journal of Theoretical Biology, 53,* 205–214.

Evolutionary Perspectives of Personality

35

Jon A. Sefcek, Candace J. Black and Pedro S. Wolf

Personality in Context

Personality, as a whole, refers to an individual's characteristic pattern of behavior that arises from the interplay among psychological mechanisms, thoughts, and emotions. It is an individual difference variable that is stable across time and context, varying across individuals at the level of specific behaviors, but similar across individuals at the level of overarching traits. At first glance, this may seem outside the scope of evolutionary psychology, which has largely focused on explaining human universals. However, a more contemporary view of evolutionary mechanisms has emerged focusing on the types of individual differences that are important to traditional personality researchers. This understanding has led to an increasing role of evolutionary theory in personality and social psychology (reviewed in Webster 2007).

J. A. Sefcek (✉)
Department of Psychology, Kent State University at Ashtabula, 3300 Lake Road West, Ashtabula, OH 44004, USA
e-mail: jsefcek@kent.edu

C. J. Black
Department of Psychology, University of Arizona, Ethology and Evolutionary Psychology, 1503 E. University Blvd., Tucson, AZ 85721, USA
e-mail: cjblack@email.arizona.edu

P. S. Wolf
Methodology Center at the Pennsylvania State University, 204 E Cader Way, Suite 400, State Colege, PA 16801, USA
e-mail: pedrosaw@gmail.com

Major players in personality research successfully developed and tested generative theories in the area long before evolutionary psychology branched out to become an independent approach to studying psychological phenomena. The social psychologist may ask why the evolutionary perspective should be considered at all when established theories perform reasonably well with regard to predicting behavior. The value added by evolutionary psychology to the measurement of personality is a key argument we hope to make in this chapter. We aim to illustrate that there is substantial explanatory power to be gained by applying evolutionary theory to the understanding of personality. In addition, evolutionary perspectives may serve the dual purpose of data reduction by way of consolidating lower-order factors in a theoretically coherent fashion and providing overarching theory that describes a broader swath of behavior than extant personality theories.

The Dispositional Approach

Personality is a concept that requires social interaction. As described by *Socioanalytic Theory,* personality requires both an actor and an observer, a signal producer and a signal receiver (Hogan 1983). The actor produces signals based on their identity (the set of characteristics that makes them who they think they are), while the observer interprets these signals, which creates one's reputation in the world (i.e., who others think they are). This reputation is therefore an

V. Zeigler-Hill et al. (eds.), *Evolutionary Perspectives on Social Psychology,* Evolutionary Psychology,
DOI 10.1007/978-3-319-12697-5_35, © Springer International Publishing Switzerland 2015

indication of one's observable, behavioral, individual differences. McAdams (1995) describes these personality characteristics at multiple levels, including: (1) traits (i.e., descriptive, dispositional characteristics that allow a quick read of an individual), (2) personal concerns (i.e., an individual's values, motives, goals, and concerns that give us a sense of how they behave in the world), and (3) identity as a life story (i.e., the changing narrative of an individual's life that is influenced by their cultural interactions and sense of purpose in the world). While each of these is important for a deep understanding of an individual, a person's disposition will affect their motives and goals, and their motives and goals will in turn affect their interactions in the world. We focus on the level of traits, as they are largely based on temperamental characteristics that serve as the foundation of personality.

A focus on trait-based approaches is rooted in the history of personality research. Since at least the early twentieth century, fundamental patterns of individual differences have been explored. Largely guided by Galton's (1884) *Lexical Hypothesis,* personality psychologists have conceptualized a variety of trait-based models exploring the structure of universal dispositional dimensions that had the capacity to distinguish the behavior between different individuals (e.g., Cattell 1946; Eysenck and Eysenck 1976; Goldberg 1993; McCrae and Costa 1987).[1] While the number of these traits has varied from model to model, they have been shown to have a biological basis. For example, Eysenck (1967) argues that the arousability of the reticular activating and limbic systems causes individuals to behave in ways to either lessen stimulation (introversion) or increase stimulation (extraversion) to obtain optimal levels of cortical arousal. So the reputation of an extravert is of an individual who seeks-out social gatherings or stimulating activities to increase arousal to an optimal level.

[1] The lexical hypothesis refers to the concept that individual differences that are important within a culture will become encoded in language, with the more important ones becoming encoded in a single word. In the English language, we refer to these words as adjective descriptors.

Other factor models have been used to study the genetic basis of personality. For instance, McCrae and Costa's (1987) *five-factor model* (FFM) has received a large amount of attention across both clinical and community samples. These five, broad dimensions (and their opposite poles) are Openness to Experience (closed-mindedness), Conscientiousness (disorganization), Extraversion (introversion), Agreeableness (disagreeableness), and Neuroticism (emotional stability). Rotated to be orthogonal to one another, it has been argued that an individual's level of a particular dimension need not be related to their level of other dimensions. Research has shown these factors are stable across time, context, and culture, as well as heritable (h^2 ranging from 0.41 to 0.61; Jang et al. 1996). Further, this taxonomy has shown good predictive validity for a variety of behavioral measures and life outcomes (e.g., see Poropat 2009, for a meta-analysis of academic performance). We make no argument that the FFM is all encompassing or the sole approach necessary for understanding personality because it is a descriptive model. However, due to the robust nature of this model, its biological basis, and predictive abilities, taxonomies of personality—especially those based on evolutionary mechanisms—should not fail to address it (Buss 1991). As such, we use it as a unifying theme of this chapter and offer it as a starting point for an exploration of how evolutionary principles might inform our understanding of individual differences such as personality.

Proximate Versus Ultimate Causes of Behavior

The question of relevant variables of inquiry is at the heart of the scientific process. Practitioners of scientific methods understand that one must begin by identifying potential causal variables for the phenomenon of interest in order to reach the broader goals of prediction and control. Much of the empirical work in psychology is successful in that it identifies *necessary* causes or, in other words, predictors that are necessary for an effect to occur. Collectively, however, we have a poorer grasp on *sufficient* causes, or those variables that, if present, guarantee a particular outcome.

Tinbergen (1963) distinguished between four types of questions that must be asked if one has any hope of gaining a comprehensive understanding of animal behavior. Most empiricists are familiar with the one termed "causality," but to avoid confusion we refer to it as *mechanism*. This suggests a more proximate association between antecedent and subsequent events that are proposed to be causally related. By examining mechanism, a researcher examines *how* a particular behavior might be produced. Within personality psychology, a mechanism might refer to physiological, cognitive, and social phenomena that influence behavioral patterns. For example, Phineas Gage, whose personality changed drastically after incurring damage to the left frontal lobe, illustrated to researchers such as Dr. John Harlow that personality is at least partially controlled by particular regions in the brain. The second question proposed by Tinbergen was that of the developmental trajectory, or ontogeny, of a behavior. This approach is akin to that taken by personality development theorists such as Erikson (1950), who proposed that personality is constructed of particular characteristics produced during eight different developmental windows. One may note that explaining behavior using either the mechanistic or the developmental approach does not preclude understanding the behavior from the other approach. Rather, these approaches are complementary and provide different information based on the level of analysis. Together, the mechanistic and developmental questions constitute *proximate* causes of behavior.

Many personality theorists proceed by examining the types of proximate causes described above. However, Tinbergen (1963) offers two additional levels of analysis necessary for a comprehensive understanding of a behavior. These *ultimate* causes are composed of the behaviors' phylogenetic causes and the survival value or adaptive function. These are the *why* questions examining which evolutionary forces have shaped the existence (or capacity) of the phenomena to exist at all. Such an approach may seek to understand the evolutionary history of a particular behavior, exploring how it is conserved or has diverged in closely related species; or it might seek to understand which selective pressures have shaped the formation of a particular behavior.

The teleological question mentioned above asks what *binds* events (i.e., what are the *sufficient* causes of behavior?) and we offer evolutionary theory as a plausible adhesive. In doing so, we move to a teleonomic approach that seeks to understand the past selective forces that have shaped the expression of the trait in the present environment. This nuance is often missing in the psychological literature. This evolutionary glue gives researchers, across disparate scientific fields, the same theoretical foundation upon which to formulate testable hypotheses. With this we turn to the evolutionary principles that help to shape individual differences in personality.

Evolutionary Principles

Species-Typical Products of Natural and Sexual Selection

Personality theories have tended toward explanations that encompass all humans (Buss 1984). For instance, Erikson's (1950) developmental stage theory was global in its intent to explain personality development and Maslow's (1943) theory of human motivation (or anyone in the aptly termed *humanist* school of thought) focused on those characteristics thought to be uniquely human. In ethological or evolutionary terms, this approach examines "species-typical" components of personality. It was perhaps not surprising then that evolutionary psychologists were able to propose ultimate causes of personality with relative ease. Buss (1984) and Tooby and Cosmides (1990) were among the earlier proponents of a marriage between personality research and evolutionary theory with the latter arguing that personality must be nested within a "universal human psychological architecture" (p. 40). While this quest to identify human nature was not new to the field, the implication that a personality system was produced out of natural and sexually selective forces was in its infancy.

Role of Selection and Fixation

Part of the perplexity in understanding personality from an evolutionary perspective lies in the vast observable differences seen in human behavior. On the one hand, as Tooby and Cosmides (1990) argue, the adaptive significance of a characteristic is a function of its prevalence in the population. Those characteristics that were quite adaptive in evolutionary history should approach fixation in the population. In other words, if it is so adaptive, everyone should have it. On the other hand, to what evolutionary process can we attribute different behavioral patterns and tendencies? One popular illustration is the Hawk versus Dove paradigm (Maynard Smith and Price 1973, who actually employed a hawk/mouse taxonomy in their original paper), wherein the proportion of individuals who will escalate conflicts ("hawks") relative to those who will yield from it ("doves" or "mice") may reach equilibrium under frequency-dependent selection. Further examination of selective forces with the capability of producing variable phenotypic (i.e., observable characteristics) outcomes is described below.

Socioecology and the Evolution of Individual Differences

An evolutionary approach to personality must take into account the ecological niche that a species occupies. An ecological niche refers to both living and nonliving aspects of an environment that affect the fitness of individuals within a particular species or population (Figueredo et al. 2007). These aspects include micro- and macropredators, prey and other food sources, cooperative allies, hostile conspecifics, and temporal and spatial dimensions, such as climate, latitude, and expected longevity. Within a population, individuals will compete for access to particular fitness-enhancing resources (e.g., seek out high-quality foods or mates, avoid dangerous predators). *Niche splitting,* or partitioning an ecological niche into smaller, less competitive niches, is adaptive when the competition costs within a particular niche are too high. In so doing, a multidimensional niche space is created, where individuals can differentiate and specialize in exploiting the resources of a smaller, less competitive niche. The evolutionary products of such niche-splitting specializations may be physical (e.g., body size or coloration) or behavioral (e.g., being cooperative and agreeable in social interactions versus being exploitative and manipulative), and may be either more constrained by genes (producing less variation given a particular genotype) or more developmentally plastic (permitting more behavioral flexibility). This may be further illustrated through consideration of the process of balancing selection.

Balancing Selection

A variety of evolutionary processes may lead to heritable individual differences in traits. Among these, balancing selection causes phenotypic variations to be maintained within a population due to no single alternative producing a fitness optimum. As such, a population will produce more than one variant with equal fitness payoffs. Different forms of balancing selection exist, producing specific outcomes in relation to the speed of evolution and population variations. As argued by Buss (2009) and others (e.g., Penke et al. 2007), the two types of balancing selection of primary importance in understanding personality variation are frequency-dependent selection and environmental heterogeneity of selective optima (i.e., variation in traits due to variation in ecological niche).

Environmental Heterogeneity of Selective Optima

Environmental heterogeneity of selective optima refers to phenotypic variations being maintained due to fluctuations in selective pressures (or available ecological niches) over time and space

(Buss 1991). These changing pressures create a temporal environment where no single adaptive solution is best, and therefore no single solution takes hold. The products, therefore, are a variety of phenotypes that allow some organisms an adaptive advantage depending on the particular environmental challenges. Buss (2009) provides an example using molecular genetics research that examines the 7R allele of the DRD4 gene. Associated with the dopaminergic system, this gene is related to extraversion and novelty-seeking behavior (Ebstein 2006, as reported by Buss). In a variety of studies, migratory human populations (e.g., nomadic tribes) show a far higher proportion of this genetic variant than populations that have been traditionally nonmigratory (even when compared to recently settled groups; e.g., Eisenberg et al. 2008). More recently, Matthews and Butler (2011) showed that the long-repeat allele is associated with the distance of ancestral human population migrations out of Africa, such that further distance from Africa is correlated with a higher proportion of this variant in the population. Their analysis further found that these polymorphisms were accounted for by natural selection rather than genetic drift or recent admixture.

The above example illustrates the relationship between the behavioral outputs of extraversion and novelty seeking (e.g., low neuronal reactivity to novel stimuli and increased exploratory behavior) in relation to overarching behavioral strategies. Those who had the long-repeat allele were more successful adopting a nomadic lifestyle, while those who had the short-repeat allele were more successful adopting a more sedentary one. Put simply, one's personality characteristics direct them toward particular behaviors, which, in turn, direct them toward different environmental niches. A more detailed account of this niche-splitting has been dealt with in detail elsewhere (see Figueredo et al. 2012).

Frequency-Dependent Selection

Frequency-dependent selection occurs when the relative fitness of a phenotype is dependent on the frequency of alternative phenotypes within a population. As a phenotype becomes more common, competition among individuals with shared phenotypes increases because they need to exploit the same resources. Rather than invest in costly traits that would make individuals more competitive within a single niche, a more cost-effective strategy is to seek-out a novel niche with different resource availabilities and requirements for obtaining those resources. In terms of the FFM, the universal personality dimension of extraversion/introversion may serve as an example. As the number of socially outgoing, dominant extraverts increase, competition among them for access to resources (e.g., food, mates) will also increase. As this population grows, the fitness costs associated with this phenotype increases, eventually reaching a point where the costs of being extraverted outweigh the benefits. This opens a niche for the less outgoing, lower dominance introverts who can exploit a less-competitive niche. The persistence of such a selective pressure over time can lead to the development of a gene–environment correlation, whereby an individual's genotype influences the niche that it both seeks and exploits (Figueredo et al. 2012). A population balance is therefore maintained where individual variation leading to alternative strategies develops to decrease the relative fitness costs of increasing competition.

Individual Differences as Products of Natural and Sexual Selection

We have evidence that at least some personality traits are under genetic influence (Bouchard and McGue 1990; Eysenck 1990; Loehlin et al. 1990; Plomin and Nesselroade 1990), lending additional support to selectionist models. Behavior geneticists employ heritability coefficients to estimate the proportion of variance in a trait within a population that can be attributed to genetic variance. For example, heritability estimates for the FFM factors range between 40 and 60% for Neuroticism, Extraversion, Openness, Agreeableness, and Conscientiousness (Jang et al. 1996). At least three of these factors (Emotional

Stability, Agreeableness, and Conscientiousness) play an important role in mate choice, which is a key component of fitness-related outcomes (Buss 1999). Other stable individual differences predicted to be important for survival or reproductive outcomes also show heritability, such as altruism, empathy, nurturance, aggressiveness, and assertiveness (Rushton et al. 1986).

Parental Investment Theory and Personality

The heritability estimates above indicate that there is genetic variation underlying these phenotypic individual differences. This variation gives the processes of natural and sexual selection something to act upon. The evolutionary perspective also provides predictions about the patterns these selective forces will produce. One particularly effective example stems from Trivers' (1972) *Parental Investment Theory,* which offers a biologically grounded framework from which to derive predictions about sex differences in the allocation of bioenergetic and material resources toward mating and parenting. Due to fundamental reproductive biology, there is differential parental investment between males and females, such that the minimum investment required for females is much greater than it is for males (in most species, at least, including humans). Consequently, reproductive opportunities are also sex-differentiated because males have the potential to sire many more offspring than a female could reasonably produce in her lifetime. As a result, unique behavioral patterns are predicted to reflect the differences in trade-offs faced by each sex.

In this view, males and females occupy different ecological niches with sex-specific distributions of resources and competition. Given this, it is reasonable to predict that there will be sex differences in desires, attitudes, and behavior relating to fitness outcomes. Penke and Asendorpf (2008) showed that males scored higher than females on the desires and attitudes dimensions of the sociosexual orientation inventory, which measures overall orientation toward uncommitted sex. Schmitt and Buss (2000) identified seven sexuality factors of personality. In four of these dimensions, significant sex differences were found, with females scoring higher on gender orientation, relationship exclusivity, and emotional investment and males scoring higher on erotophilic disposition (no sex differences were found for the constructs of sexual attractiveness, sexual restraint, and sexual orientation). Taken together, these findings support parental investment theory. Importantly, sexually based personality constructs were neglected virtually entirely by personality researchers until evolutionary theorists applied the theoretical frameworks of sexual selection and parental investment theory to make predictions about stable individual differences.

Personality Systems

How might we reconcile the diversity of individual differences attributed to personality with a universal human nature produced by evolution? MacDonald (1995, 1998, 2005, 2012) proposes the concept of universal personality systems that would have evolved like any other biological system (e.g., circulatory system or cardiovascular system) or psychological system for which we have evidence (e.g., motivational system or emotional system; Panksepp 1998). Viewed this way, personality systems are responsive to situational (Mischel 1968) and developmental contexts, resulting in a suite of potential responses. This conceptualization is compatible with both the universalist perspective and the variation of individual differences. Moreover, it also accommodates multiple models of personality that may compete with one another or operate hierarchically. This latter characteristic of personality systems is especially relevant when discussing a proper integration of evolutionary biology and extant personality models, which we will elaborate upon in subsequent sections.

While some researchers like those described above investigate personality factors beyond traditional formulations of personality, such as the FFM, others have approached the problem from a different angle. MacDonald (1995,

1998) proposed rotating the factor structure of the FFM based on evolutionary predictions about sex differences. He argues that this novel conception of personality structures is consistent with research on neural systems, such as the behavioral approach/inhibition systems and arousal/reactivity systems. Specifically, dominance/sensation-seeking and nurturance/love dimensions are sex-specific manifestations of the behavioral approach system (BAS), Conscientiousness reflects interactions between the BAS and the behavioral inhibition system (BIS), and Neuroticism is produced by arousal/reactivity systems.

One particular advantage of MacDonald's proposal is that this revised model of personality better reflects observed individual differences in the construct Extraversion than the standard FFM. Under this new model, Dominance and Nurturance/Love are biologically founded alternative conceptualizations of the Extraversion and Agreeableness constructs of the FFM. MacDonald (2005) points out that one of the reasons we observe only modest sex differences in Extraversion is because typical scales include items about dominance/risk-taking as well as items about warmth/affiliation, thus failing to address the fact that dominance and risk-taking behaviors are more prevalent among males whereas warmth and affiliation behaviors are more prevalent among females. Moreover, the BAS underlying dominance and sensation-seeking behaviors appears to be under the influence of the dopaminergic reward system while certain manifestations of the Nurturance/Love system, such as pair-bonding are influenced by specific neurochemical substrates like oxytocin. Additionally, while Extraversion appears to be stable over the lifespan, the rotated factor structure captures age-related changes in risk-taking among males that are predicted by evolutionary theory and reflect the period when males are most likely to be striving to attract mates and establish themselves in a dominance hierarchy. Thus, combining these characteristics into a single construct is incompatible with the evolved systems perspective proposed by MacDonald.

The Sociality Hypothesis

Evolutionary psychology asserts that social competition within species underlies the behavioral manifestations of individual differences. Extending this idea, Figueredo (1995) and Figueredo and King (2001) have proposed the *sociality hypothesis:* that as populations become more social, increasing both the duration and intensity of social interaction, noticeable individual differences will become more important, socially relevant, and pronounced (reviewed in Figueredo et al. 2005). Such pronounced variations would allow signal producers and signal receivers alike to quickly predict those who would best benefit them as coalitional partners (e.g., group leaders, friends), reproductive vessels (e.g., mates, genetic relatives), or who poses the highest fitness cost (e.g., same-sex rivals, unhealthy mates). Such variation would help an individual differentially allocate resources toward those who would give them the greatest fitness payoff.

The strengths of this frequency-dependent model are that, based on *parental investment theory,* it predicts sex differences in personality traits, as well as offers a framework for comparative research across species. As a group becomes more social, intersexual and intrasexual competition will increase variation within species, especially for the sex that competes more for access to mates. For example, species which tend more toward monogamy would show decreased variation in personality traits across members of the species (there is relatively less competition for access to mates); whereas in species with multimale social structures, we would see more variation in traits that aid social competition, especially in males (there is relatively more competition among males for access to mates).

Studies examining the nature of sex differences in personality traits have largely been inconclusive (Borkenau et al. 2013). Critiques of this body of research have ranged from ideological to methodological, with some studies supporting sex differences and others failing to find them. A recent study by Del Giudice et al. (2012) accounted for these concerns by pitting predictions made by the "gender similarities hypothesis" and the predictions made by evolutionary psychology's view of sex differences against each other. By using a large sample size ($N = 10{,}261$) and sophisticated multivariate modeling techniques, the researchers identified robust sex differences. These analyses illustrated an overlap of only between 10 and 24% in the distribution between males and females, suggesting much larger sex differences than previous studies using smaller samples and weaker statistical methods. Further evidence in favor of sex differences in personality includes a recent study that used informant reports rather than self-reports, and found that men showed significantly more variation for the FFM dimensions of Openness, Conscientiousness, Extraversion, and Agreeableness, but not Neuroticism, across four European samples (Borkenau et al. 2013). Additionally, Budaev (1999) found more variation in male aggression and a factor of personality combining Agreeableness and low Neuroticism. While not conclusive, these recent studies suggest that sex differences in personality traits may be more robust than earlier research has suggested. That the sex differences tended to illustrate more within-sex variation in men also lends support for the sociality hypothesis; however, more research directly examining this prediction needs to be conducted.

Research on nonhuman personality has offered phylogenetic evidence for an evolutionary function of stable individual differences. In a meta-analysis, Gosling (2001) showed that many of the FFM personality traits have been identified across species, ranging from octopi to chimpanzees. Across the 12 species studied, Extraversion and Agreeableness were identified in ten species, Neuroticism in nine, Openness in two, and Conscientiousness only in chimpanzees and humans. Additionally, Dominance was identified in ten species, but not humans. Consistent with the *sociality hypothesis,* the multi-male, social chimpanzee displays six traits (Dominance, Surgency, Agreeableness, Dependability, Emotionality, and Openness; King and Figueredo 1997), the mostly solitary orangutan displays five traits (Extraversion, Dominance, Neuroticism, Agreeableness, and Intellect; Weiss et al. 2006), and the extremely polygynous gorilla displays four traits (Extroversion, Dominance, Fearfulness, and Understanding; Gold and Maple 1994). Of notable importance, the orangutan seems to be missing a factor that specifically displays how dependable and trustworthy one is in repeated interactions, which fits into an evolutionary history of little social interaction and little male parental investment.

A Factor-Analytic Evolutionary Model of Personality

Although the FFM has become the most widely used personality taxonomy since the late 1980s, there is still some disagreement concerning the number of higher-order personality dimensions. There is factor analytic evidence supporting six (e.g., HEXACO; Lee and Ashton 2004), five (e.g., FFM; McRae and Costa 1987), three (e.g., PEN; Eysenck 1992), two (e.g., Alpha and Beta Model; Digman 1997), and even one-dimensional taxonomies (e.g., Musek's general factor of personality). Further, none of these approaches have attempted to incorporate an evolutionary basis as to why these identifiable common factors would have been shaped to aid survival or reproduction. Below we offer an integrative model.

The General Factor of Personality

Using exploratory factor-analytic techniques, Musek (2007) identified a hierarchical model of personality with a single global personality factor at the top, Digman's factors of Stability (Alpha) and Plasticity (Beta) in the middle, and the FFM at the bottom. As such, the FFM personality dimensions are absorbed by Stability (Conscientiousness, Agreeableness, and Neuroticism) and Plasticity (Extraversion and Openness), and a general factor of personality (GFP) absorbing each of these. In the end, this data-driven approach led Musek to question the interpretability of a single factor of personality. By considering the possibility of evolutionary forces shaping the GFP, he produced a plausible argument that selective forces facilitated the evolution of socially desirable personality characteristics, which fit with the pattern of human evolution.

Evolutionary Psychology and the General Factor of Personality

Although we believe that efforts by researchers like Musek are valuable as a first step, we argue that taking a theory-driven approach that integrates Tinbergen's four questions within a research program and is consistent with a meta-theory as powerful as evolutionary theory leads to more interpretable scientific results. As an example, we present a synthesis of the research on the GFP and *life history theory* (LHT; see Chap. 29 in this volume for full consideration of LHT).

LHT is a midlevel evolutionary theory of resource allocation wherein individuals have limited bioenergetic and material resources (e.g., time, energy, food) which constrain reproductive strategies. Under this framework, an individual may allocate their resources toward two major fitness categories: somatic effort and reproductive effort. Somatic effort entails all allocation of resources that are devoted to keeping the organism alive (e.g., food acquisition, predator avoidance, investment in one's immune system), whereas reproductive effort is devoted to producing and maintaining new genetic variants (i.e., mating, parenting, and aiding genetic relatives; Figueredo et al. 2004). As resources are limited, the relative cost of devoting effort to one category over the other is an important consideration. LHT therefore predicts that natural selection drives species to evolve overall adaptive strategies that are shaped by the evolutionary history of the species or a particular genetic lineage.

These reproductive strategies lie on a continuum of fast and slow. On the fast end of the continuum, individual organisms put a premium on mating effort and reproductive output, whereas on the slow end of the continuum a premium is placed on somatic and parental effort (Figueredo and Rushton 2009). Environments that shape fast life history (LH) strategies tend to have high infant mortality, high pathogen load, and high extrinsic mortality (i.e., threats to mortality that cannot be prevented by behavior or investment in additional somatic resources), whereas slow LH strategies are shaped by environments that are more stable and threats to mortality may be avoidable by allocating resources toward behavioral or physiological outputs that would lower risk (Brumbach et al. 2009). Further, LHT predicts that natural selection shaped the capacity to systematically respond to environmental cues during development and calibrate an individual's LH strategy to better fit the contingencies in the immediate environment. Evidence for this early calibration comes from Belsky et al. (1991) who showed that being raised in a stressful environment increased the probability of early pubertal development, precocious sexuality, unstable pair bonds, and limited investment in childrearing. Conversely, being raised in a non-stressful rearing environment tended to produce the opposite outcomes (Ellis 2004; Ellis et al. 2009).

From this perspective, events during early development serve as cues to how bioenergetics and material resources should be allocated to maximize fitness. Brunswikian evolutionary development (BED) theory provides an additional framework for predicting differences in the level of preparedness and plasticity of a phenotype based on two statistical parameters that describe the history of an adaptive problem over evolutionary time. The parameter that shapes the preparedness of an adaptation is related to the *mean* of the ecological conditions the species faced during its evolution. In other words, if on average, it is better to have a certain phenotype, that average phenotype should be more represented in the population. The parameter that shapes the plasticity of an adaptation is related to the *variance* of the ecological conditions the species faced during its evolutionary development. An adaptation shaped by ecological conditions with high variances should produce high developmental plasticity, and those with low variances should produce low developmental plasticity (Figueredo et al. 2006). An individual adaptation, shaped by an adaptive problem with a high *variance* environmental history, will be set by the *mean* ecological condition at birth, and be sensitive to relevant ecological cues, the species faced over evolutionary time, that allow it to develop a phenotype that solves the adaptive problem set in the current environment. Those adaptations shaped by adaptive problems with low *variance* environmental histories should not be sensitive to ecological cues and not change in response to them.

To date, most evolutionary psychologists concentrate on traits that evolved under ecological conditions with a high mean and *low variance* in the importance of an adaptive problem. From the perspective of BED theory, this type of evolutionary history would produce fixed adaptations and human universals. For example, regardless of geographic or temporal location, human males have faced the recurring problem of paternal uncertainty. As such, evolutionary psychologists have developed research programs studying possible psychological adaptations in response to paternity uncertainty, such as jealousy and associated behavioral outputs (e.g., mate guarding and retention tactics; Buss 1991). However, the additional view of exploring the behavioral products of evolution under ecological conditions with a high mean and *high variance* offers a different prediction.

Research on LH strategy has suggested that it is a phenotype shaped by an ecological history that has a high mean ecological validity and a high variance. In other words, an organism's genes do not know what environment they will be born into, and in response, humans have evolved a level of adaptive developmental plasticity that is able to respond to recurring, normal environmental variation. This developmental plasticity requires developmental inputs that, over evolutionary time, reliably signaled to the organism that a particular pattern of bioenergetics and material resource allocation would best fit the environment. These environmental inputs include father absence, stressful child-rearing environments (Belsky et al. 1991), exposure to violence, and frequency of changes in childhood environments (Brumbach et al. 2009). Presumably, each of these cues has, over evolutionary time, predicted an unstable environment where the child cannot count on long-term parental investment or long-term outcomes. This mechanism is another way that individual differences may be sustained in a population, by calibrating an individual's developmental trajectory with recurring environmental cues.

Life History Strategy and the General Factor of Personality

In humans, LH strategy is represented by a long-term, developmental pattern of behaviors and trait development that must be coordinated to maximize fitness. With this in mind, a thread of research has emerged linking LHT, a suite of mental and physical health-related variables that make up a factor they called *covitality* (comprised of overall good physical and mental health, prosocial relationships, more "favorable" behaviors), and the GFP. The underlying hypothesis is that there has been recent directional selection toward slow LH strategies in humans (Rushton et al. 2008). A slow LH strategist needs to score highly on the GFP (high Conscientiousness, Openness, Extraversion, and Agreeableness; low Neuroticism) because these traits are essential for making and retaining long-term, reciprocally altruistic friendships as well as retaining long term mating partners (Figueredo and Jacobs 2009). This mutualistic social strategy is not as conducive for fast LH strategists living in unstable environments with high mortality rates where the adaptive response is maximizing reproductive success through short-term mating strategies.

Figueredo and Rushton (2009) confirmed the hierarchical structure of these traits with a common higher order factor they called the Super-*K*. They argued that this higher order factor, comprising high parental investment, covitality, and the prosocial aspects of personality, illustrated an overarching LH strategy shaped by selective pressures favoring a slower, *K* selected, LH strategy. In this twin study, they also presented evidence that the three factors that make up the Super-*K* share nonadditive genetic variance, providing evidence for recent directional selection on this suite of traits. A recent study tested a hypothesis derived from the super-*K* theory and found a relationship between the GFP and increased parental support, an important component of a slow LH strategy (van der Linden et al. 2012). Other research has found that couples that share a slow LH strategy have higher levels of relationship satisfaction, and are less like to experience relationship dissolution (Olderbak and Figueredo 2010). Still other work has tested the relationships between LH strategy, personality, and its role in positive assortative mating in humans (Figueredo and Wolf 2009).

Given our theme that highlights Tinbergen's (1963) four questions, we want to highlight a test of theory that contradicts the evolutionary underpinnings of the GFP. If the GFP has an evolutionary basis, as we have seen in relation to the FFM, we should find evidence of the GFP in closely related species. Using informant reports, Weiss et al. (2011) tested whether there was evidence of a GFP in chimpanzees, orangutans, and rhesus macaques. Their results were not consistent with a GFP. Although these findings are not a deathblow to the theoretical link between LHT and the GFP, they do suggest that the relationship between LHT and GFP is not as straightforward as proposed. It is possible that in the 6–34 million years since humans shared a common ancestor with these species, humans have evolved a human-specific system of organized individual differences.

In an effort to further explore this theoretical link, we would like to offer a novel evolutionary prediction about the ontogenetic development of the GFP. We propose integrating theory outlining the existence of a Super-*K* factor and the adaptive calibration model related to LHT. In twin studies, it is estimated that about a third of variation in personality is due to non-shared environments (Bouchard 1994). As such, we propose that these differences may not be entirely random, but instead a result of adaptive calibration. More specifically, because the GFP is part of an overarching LH strategy, the same environmental indicators that shape a fast LH strategy over development should decrease an individual's scores on the GFP. If this hypothesis is valid, we should observe the following pattern: Individuals who are raised in a fast LH environment marked by stressful events and high levels of extrinsic mortality should not only have faster LH strategy, but their GFP should be lower than individuals not raised in a fast LH environment.

Summary and Conclusions

The objective of this chapter was to illustrate the utility of evolutionary perspectives in personality psychology. To this end, we reviewed some of the major theoretical approaches in mainstream personality psychology, including trait-based models such as the FFM, and showed how incorporating evolutionary theory can produce novel, testable predictions and provide additional, integral explanatory power to the understanding of personality and individual differences.

An additional objective of this chapter was to highlight how a research program can be evaluated using multiple levels of analysis that are informed by evolutionary biology. By asking Tinbergen's four questions, evolutionary psychologists are forced to tackle topics related to ontogeny and proximate mechanisms, levels of analysis more familiar to social psychologists. We hope that in turn social psychologists begin considering the roles that their typical proximate hypotheses have, in a broader picture of human behavior that incorporates ultimate (adaptive) explanations.

References

Belsky, J., Steinberg, L., & Draper, P. (1991). Childhood experience, interpersonal development, and reproductive strategy: An evolutionary theory of socialization. *Childhood Development, 62,* 647–670.

Borkenau, P., Hřebíčková, M., Kuppens, P., Realo, A., & Allik, J. (2013). Sex differences in variability in personality: A study in four samples. *Journal of Personality, 81,* 49–60.

Bouchard, T. J., Jr. (1994). Genes, environment, and personality. *Science, 264,* 1700–1701.

Bouchard, T. J., & McGue, M. (1990). Genetic and rearing environmental influences on adult personality: An analysis of adopted twins reared apart. *Journal of Personality, 58,* 263–292.

Brumbach, B.H., Figueredo, A.J., & Ellis, B.J. (2009). Effects of harsh and unpredictable environments in adolescence on development of life history strategies: A longitudinal test of an evolutionary model. *Human Nature, 20,* 25–51.

Budaev, S. V. (1999). Sex differences in the big five personality factors: Testing an evolutionary hypothesis. *Personality and individual differences, 26,* 801–813.

Buss, D. M. (1984). Evolutionary biology and personality psychology: Toward a conception of human nature and individual differences. *American Psychologist, 39,* 1135–1147.

Buss, D. M. (1991). Evolutionary personality psychology. *Annual Review of Psychology, 42,* 459–491.

Buss, D. M. (1999). Adaptive individual differences revisited. *Journal of Personality, 67,* 259–264.

Buss, D. M. (2009). How can evolutionary psychology successfully explain personality and individual differences? *Perspectives on Psychological Science, 4,* 359–366.

Cattell, R. B. (1946). *The description and measurement of personality*. New York: World Book.

Del Giudice, M., Booth, T., & Irwing, P. (2012). The distance between Mars and Venus: Measuring global sex differences in personality. *PLoS ONE, 7,* 1–8.

Digman, J. M. (1997). Higher-order factors of the Big Five. *Journal of Personality and Social Psychology, 73,* 1246–1256.

Eisenberg, D. T. A., Campbell, B., Gray, P. B., & Sorenson, M. D. (2008). Dopamine receptor genetic polymorphisms and body composition in undernourished pastoralists: An exploration of nutrition indices among nomadic and recently settled Ariaal men of northern Kenya. *BioMed Central Evolutionary Biology, 8*(1), 173.

Ellis, B.J. (2004). Timing of pubertal maturation in girls: An integrated life history approach. *Psychological Bulletin, 130*, 920–958.

Ellis, B.J., Figueredo, A.J., Brumbach, B.H., & Schlomer, G.L. (2009). Fundamental dimensions of environmental risk: The impact of harsh versus unpredictable environments on the evolution and development of life history strategies. *Human Nature, 20*, 204–268.

Erikson, E. H. (1950). *Childhood and society*. New York: Norton.

Eysenck, H. J. (1967). *The biological basis of personality*. Springfield: Thomas.

Eysenck, H. J. (1990). Genetic and environmental contributions to individual differences: The three major dimensions of personality. *Journal of Personality, 58,* 245–261.

Eysenck, H. J. (1992). A reply to Costa and McCrae: P or A and C—the role of theory. *Personality and Individual Differences, 13,* 867–868.

Eysenck, H. J., & Eysenck, S. B. G. (1976). *Psychoticism as a dimension of personality*. London: Hodder & Stoughton.

Figueredo, A. J. (1995). *The evolution of individual differences*. Paper presented at Jane Goodall Institute ChimpanZoo annual conference, Tucson, Arizona.

Figueredo, A.J., & Jacobs, W.J.(2009) Aggression, risk-taking, and alternative life history strategies: The behavioral ecology of social deviance. In Frias-Armenta M, Corral-Verdugo V, (Eds.), *Biopsychosocial perspectives on aggression*. Hauppauge, NY: Nova Science Publishers.

Figueredo, A. J., & King, J. E. (2001). The evolution of individual differences. In S. D. Gosling & A. Weiss (Chairs), *Evolution and individual differences*. Symposium conducted at the annual meeting of the Human Behavior and Evolution Society, London, England, United Kingdom.

Figueredo, A. J., & Rushton, J. P. (2009). Evidence for shared genetic dominance between the general factor of personality, mental and physical health, and life history traits. *Twin Research and Human Genetics, 12,* 555–563.

Figueredo, A. J., & Wolf, P. S. A. (2009). Assortative pairing and life history strategy. *Human Nature, 20,* 317–330.

Figueredo, A.J., Vásquez, G., Brumbach, B.H., & Schneider, S.M.R. (2004). The heritability of life history strategy: The K-factor, covitality, and personality. *Social Biology, 51*, 121–143.

Figueredo, A. J., Sefcek, J., Vasquez, G., Brumbach, B. H., King, J. E., & Jacobs, W. J. (2005). Evolutionary personality psychology. In D. M. Buss (Ed.), *Handbook of evolutionary psychology* (pp. 851–877). Hoboken: Wiley.

Figueredo, A. J., Vásquez, G., Brumbach, B. H., Schneider, S., Sefcek, J. A., Tal, I. R., Hill, D., Wenner, C. J., & Jacobs, W. J. (2006). Consilience and life history theory: From genes to brain to reproductive strategy. *Developmental Review, 26* (2), 243–275.

Figueredo, A.J., Brumbach, B.H., Jones, D.N., Sefcek, J.A., Vásquez, G., & Jacobs, W.J. (2007). Ecological constraints on mating tactics. In Geher, G., & Miller, G.F., (Eds.), *Mating Intelligence: Sex, Relationships and the Mind's Reproductive System* (pp. 335–361). Mahwah, NJ: Lawrence Erlbaum.

Figueredo, A. J., Sefcek, J. A., Black, C. J., Garcia, R. A., & Jacobs, W. J. (2012). Evolutionary personality psychology. In V. S. Ramachandran (Ed. In Chief), *The encyclopedia of human behavior* (2nd ed., pp. 111–117). San Diego: Academic.

Galton, F. (1884). Measurement of character. *Fortnightly Review, 36*, 179–185.

Gold, G. C., & Maple, T. L. (1994). Personality assessment in the gorilla and its utility as a management tool. *Zoo Biology, 13,* 509–522.

Goldberg, L. R. (1993). The structure of phenotypic personality traits. *American Psychologist, 48,* 26–34.

Gosling, S. D. (2001). From mice to men: What can we learn about personality from animal research? *Psychological Bulletin, 127,* 45–86.

Hogan, R. (1983). A socioanalytic theory of personality. In M. M. Page (Ed.), *1982 Nebraska symposium on motivation: Personality—current theory and research* (pp. 55–89). Lincoln: University of Nebraska Press.

Jang, K. L., Livesley, W. J., & Vernon, P. A. (1996). Heritability of the Big Five personality dimensions and their facets: A twin study. *Journal of Personality, 64,* 577–591.

King, J. E., & Figueredo A. J. (1997). The five-factor model plus dominance in chimpanzee personality. *Journal of Research in Personality, 31,* 257–271.

Lee, K., & Ashton, M. C. (2004). Psychometric properties of the HEXACO personality inventory. *Multivariate Behavioral Research, 39*(2), 329–358.

Loehlin, J. C., Horn, J. M., & Willerman, L. (1990). Heredity, environment, and personality change: Evidence from the Texas Adoption Project. *Journal of Personality, 58,* 221–243.

MacDonald, K. (1995). Evolution, the five factor model, and levels of personality. *Journal of Personality, 63,* 525–567.

MacDonald, K. (1998). Evolution, culture, and the Five-Factor Model. *Journal of Cross-Cultural Psychology, 29,* 119–149.

MacDonald, K. (2005). Personality, evolution, and development. In R. Burgess & K. MacDonald (Eds.), *Evolutionary perspectives on human development* (2nd ed., pp. 9–12). Thousand Oaks: Sage.

MacDonald, K. (2012). Temperament and evolution. In M. Zentner (Ed.), *Handbook of temperament* (pp. 273–296). New York: Guilford.

Maslow, A. H. (1943). A theory of human motivation. *Psychological Review, 50,* 370–396.

Matthews, L. J., & Butler, P. M. (2011). Novelty-seeking DRD4 polymorphisms are associated with human migration distance out-of-Africa after controlling for neutral population gene structure. *American Journal of Physical Anthropology, 145,* 382–389.

Maynard Smith, J., & Price, G. R. (1973). The logic of animal conflict. *Nature, 246,* 15–18.

McAdams, D. P. (1995). What do we know when we know a person. *Journal of Personality, 63,* 365–396.

McCrae, R. R., & Costa, P. T. (1987). Validation of the Five-factor model of personality across instruments and observers. *Journal of Personality and Social Psychology, 52,* 81–90.

Mischel, W. (1968). *Personality and assessment.* London: Wiley.

Musek, J. (2007). A general factor of personality: Evidence for the big one in the five-factor model. *Journal of Research in Personality, 41,* 1213–1233.

Olderbak, S. G., & Figueredo, A. J. (2010). Life history strategy as a longitudinal predictor of relationship satisfaction and dissolution. *Personality and Individual Differences, 49,* 234–239.

Panksepp, J. (1998). *Affective neuroscience: The foundations of human and animal emotions.* New York: Oxford University Press.

Penke, L., & Asendorpf, J. B. (2008). Beyond global sociosexual orientations: A more differentiated look at sociosexuality and its effects on courtship and romantic relationships. *Journal of Personality and Social Psychology, 95,* 1113–1135.

Penke, L., Denissen, J. J. A., & Miller, G. F. (2007). The evolutionary genetics of personality. *European Journal of Personality, 21,* 549–587.

Plomin, R., & Nesselroade, J. R. (1990). Behavioral genetics and personality change. *Journal of Personality, 58,* 192–220.

Poropat, A. E. (2009). A meta-analysis of the five-factor model of personality and academic performance. *Psychological Bulletin, 135,* 322–338.

Rushton, J., Bons, T.,& Hur, Y. (2008). The genetics and evolution of the general factor of personality. *Journal of Research in Personality 42*(5): 1173–1185.

Rushton, J. P., Fulker, D. W., Neale, M. C., Nias, D. K. B., & Eysenck, H. J. (1986). Altruism and aggression: The heritability of individual differences. *Journal of Personality and Social Psychology, 50,* 1192–1198.

Schmitt, D., & Buss, D. M. (2000). Sexual dimensions of person description: Beyond or subsumed by the Big Five? *Journal of Research in Personality, 34,* 141–177.

Tinbergen, N. (1963). On aims and methods of ethology. *Zeitschrift fur Tierpsychologie, 20,* 410–433.

Tooby, J., & Cosmides, L. (1990). On the universality of human nature and the uniqueness of the individual: The role of genetics and adaptation. *Journal of Personality, 58,* 17–67.

Trivers, R. L. (1972). Parental investment and sexual selection. In B. Campbell (Ed.), *Sexual selection and the descent of man,* 1871–1971 (pp. 136–207). Chicago: Aldine.

van der Linden, D., Figueredo, A. J., de Leeuw, R. N. H., Scholte, R. H. J., & Engels, R. C. M. E. (2012). The general factor of personality (GFP) and parental support: Testing a prediction from life history theory. *Evolution and Human Behavior, 33,* 537–546.

Webster, G. D. (2007). Evolutionary theory's increasing role in personality and social psychology. *Evolutionary Psychology, 5,* 84–91.

Weiss, A., King, J. E., & Perkins, L. (2006). Personality and subjective well-being in orang-utans (*Pongo pygmaeus and Pongo abelii*). *Journal of Personality and Social Psychology, 90,* 501–511.

Weiss, A., Adams, M. J., & Johnson, W. (2011). The big none: No evidence for a general factor of personality in chimpanzees, orangutans, or rhesus macaques. *Journal of Research in Personality, 45*(4), 393–397.

The Roots of Narcissus: Old and New Models of the Evolution of Narcissism

36

Nicholas S. Holtzman and M. Brent Donnellan

What are the evolutionary roots of narcissism? Finding answers to this question will require some serious digging. Current explanations for the origins of narcissism tend to emphasize environmental and experiential explanations (e.g., Kohut 1971) with little attention given to biological and evolutionary factors. Many papers suggest that narcissism is created by particular parenting styles (either indulgent or neglectful), cultural trends toward a heightened importance of individualism, increased usage of social media, and/or exposure to the antics of narcissistic celebrities. These kinds of explanations are incomplete because they do not address the role that biological factors might play in the development of narcissism. Although the modern environment matters in shaping narcissism, as all traits are inseparable from their environments (Roberts and Jackson 2008), biological factors also are relevant to its development. Indeed, narcissism, like most individual differences in personality, is heritable (Coolidge et al. 2001, 2004; Livesley et al. 1993; Vernon et al. 2008). Accordingly, the goal of the present chapter is to draw on recent advances in evolutionary personality psychology (Buss 1991, 2009; Buss and Hawley 2011; Keller and Miller 2006; Nettle 2006; Penke et al. 2007) to consider biologically informed accounts of the origins of narcissism. Our overarching point is that narcissism has a biological component that should be factored into any comprehensive account of the origins of this multifaceted construct.

The plan for this chapter is to define narcissism, outline the largely unsuccessful search for a specific gene for narcissism, and then provide an overview of the various ways that researchers have started thinking about how genetic and environmental factors work together to influence the development of narcissism. In particular, we cover three explanations for the origin of narcissism: (1) Narcissism is rooted in physical characteristics that, in turn, shape one's psychological development; (2) narcissism is shaped by complex gene × environment interactions; and (3) narcissism is related to numerous genes with small effects that have been subjected to selection pressures over the course of human evolutionary history. Building on this third explanation, we propose a model for the origins of narcissism. Namely, narcissism is a function of selection for short-term mating (Holtzman and Strube 2011) and dominance (Tracy et al. 2011), as these two attributes facilitate their reproduction and survival, respectively.

N. S. Holtzman (✉)
Department of Psychology, Georgia Southern University, P.O. Box 8041, Statesboro, GA 30460-8041, USA
e-mail: nick.holtzman@gmail.com

M. B. Donnellan
Department of Psychology, Texas A&M University, College Station, TX, USA
e-mail: mbdonnellan@tamu.edu

Defining Narcissism

Narcissism is a complex construct that involves attributes such as arrogance, assertiveness, a sense of authority, entitlement, exhibitionism, exploitativeness, forcefulness, self-absorption,

V. Zeigler-Hill et al. (eds.), *Evolutionary Perspectives on Social Psychology*, Evolutionary Psychology,
DOI 10.1007/978-3-319-12697-5_36,

social potency, and vanity (Emmons 1984; Raskin and Terry 1988). Given the burgeoning work on the evolutionary underpinnings of the Big Five domains, it is useful to consider how narcissism relates to this taxonomy of traits. In particular, narcissists tend to score high on extraversion and low on agreeableness (Paulhus 2001), a finding that generalizes from self-report studies to research that measures the Big Five traits behaviorally (Holtzman et al. 2010). Individuals high in narcissism also tend to score low on conscientiousness, with the exception of a relatively high score on the achievement-striving facet (Lynam and Widiger 2001). Thus, narcissism can be understood as a pattern of thoughts, feelings, and behaviors that empirically overlap with extraversion, disagreeableness, and, to some extent, low conscientiousness.

Narcissism can be distinguished from the neighboring constructs that constitute the other two components of the "Dark Triad"—Machiavellianism and psychopathy (Furnham et al. 2013; Paulhus and Williams 2002). Machiavellianism is characterized by scheming. Machiavellians operate "behind the scenes" and tend to be manipulative. Machiavellians are less extraverted than narcissists. Also noteworthy, Machiavellianism appears to be less heritable than narcissism (Vernon et al. 2008), although more research is needed to provide conclusive data on this point. The correlation between narcissism and Machiavellianism is approximately.25 (Paulhus and Williams 2002). Thus, there is little reason to suspect that narcissism and Machiavellianism are the same construct.

Psychopathy is characterized by callousness and a lifestyle that is often reckless, and—quite unlike narcissism—explicitly antisocial (Furnham et al. 2013). Psychopaths tend to be less conscientious than narcissists (Lynam and Widiger 2001, 2007; Paulhus and Williams 2002) and, in particular, they are lower in the achievement-striving facet of conscientiousness. Nevertheless, the constructs empirically overlap, with correlations as high as .50 (Paulhus and Williams 2002). In particular, the first factor ("primary psychopathy"), and to a lesser extent the second factor ("secondary psychopathy"), overlap with narcissism (see Table 2 in Jakobwitz and Egan 2006). For a review on the conceptual and empirical differences between psychopathy and narcissism, see Furnham and colleagues (2013). For evolutionary accounts of psychopathy, see Mealey (1995) or Lalumiere et al. (2008).

The Search for Genes That Code for Narcissism

Any reader who wants replicable evidence for the existence of a specific gene for narcissism will be disappointed. Large genome-wide association studies (GWAS) have not identified single gene linked to extraversion or (low) agreeableness (de Moor et al. 2012). Just as there is no single gene for personality traits and most psychiatric disorders (Kendler 2005), there probably is no single gene for narcissism. One reason is that narcissism is not a single entity or taxon, such that the narcissist can be distinguished from the nonnarcissist (Foster and Campbell 2007). When researchers talk about the proverbial narcissist, they are using shorthand to refer to people who report possessing a large number of narcissistic attributes. Multiple genes are likely to be responsible for creating variation in this complex phenotype.

Nonetheless, genetically informed studies are important because they highlight the importance of biological factors for understanding the origins of narcissism. Researchers are now proposing theoretical models that delineate how heritable factors work with environmental factors to explain the development of narcissistic tendencies. There are currently three primary explanations: (1) genetic factors might influence physical characteristics, which then contribute to the development of narcissistic characteristics (reactive heritability); (2) particular genetically influenced attributes interact with environmental factors to produce narcissistic characteristics (gene × environment interactions); or (3) numerous genes combine additively and interactively to produce narcissistic attributes (gene × gene interactions). This third explanation raises interesting questions about the selective pressures that produce variability in narcissistic attributes, a key question in evolutionary personality psychology. Before describing these explanations, however, we note that these explanations are neither exhaustive nor mutually exclusive. Indeed, we believe there is validity in each of these accounts.

Explanation #1: Reactive Heritability

One way to explain the origins of narcissism draws on the idea that organisms pursue different kinds of interpersonal strategies based on their physical features. Buss (2009) noted that an aggressive interpersonal strategy may prove more successful for larger and more physically formidable children as opposed to more diminutive children. Using force to obtain resources works better for larger individuals than smaller individuals. These insights are acquired early in the life span and are then elaborated into personality attributes over the course of development. This is the gist of the notion of reactive heritability (Tooby and Cosmides 1990) or the idea that the physical self provides constraints and opportunities that shape the development of personality attributes. The traits that reactive heritability impact are called facultatively calibrated traits (Lukaszewski 2011).

According to the reactive heritability explanation, narcissism might be a psychological profile that develops because of certain physical attributes (Holtzman 2011). The viability of this explanation begins with a physical profile associated with narcissism. Absent reliable physical correlates the idea that narcissistic attributes are facultatively calibrated traits that cannot gain traction. As it stands, narcissists tend to be strong (Gangestad et al. 2007), they move in a smooth way—perhaps indicative of athleticism (Back et al. 2010; Table 3), and they tend to have a particular facial appearance (Holtzman 2011). Anecdotally, narcissistic attributes are linked to sharper features in women, whereas narcissism appears to correlate with a larger head, thinner lips, a thicker jaw, and fuller brows in men (see Fig. 1 in Holtzman 2011). Male narcissists self-report that they are hairier and self-report having a larger penis (Moskowitz et al. 2009) than nonnarcissists. Although self-reports of a larger penis might be explained by the self-enhancing tendencies of narcissists, other findings are more difficult to explain as artifacts of reporting. Thus, some connection between physical characteristics and narcissistic attributes may exist. The reactive heritability account would further suggest that much of the overlap between physical traits and narcissistic traits should be attributable to shared genetic influences. This hypothesis could be tested using a multivariate model applied to twin data, and this strikes us as an important test for future studies.

There are at least two developmental processes that can link heritable physical features to individual differences in narcissism. First, physical features may afford certain opportunities and cues that cause a person to think about the self in a certain way (self-reflection). For example, a strong person may learn that he or she can act in a particular way with less interference from others. An athletic youth might succeed at sports and earn status among her or his peers. This status may translate to feelings of power and social dominance. Second, social evocation might be a factor that elicits narcissism, as certain physical attributes generate expectations in others that are more or less independent of how the target actually acts in the first place (Snyder et al. 1977; Zebrowitz et al. 2002; Zebrowitz et al. 1996). For example, others may expect a physically strong person to take a leadership role regardless of the individual's initial preferences for leadership. Once thrust into the leadership role, the individual will be subjected to particular rewards and punishments, which might shape psychological development. Being expected to act as a leader could eventually shape a person into a leader—and leadership is one facet frequently captured by measures of narcissism (Emmons 1984). In sum, physical characteristics (e.g., strength and attractiveness), which have been partially shaped by evolution (Liu et al. 2012; Silventoinen et al. 2008), may impact self-reflective processes and social processes, thereby influencing personality development in general and narcissism in particular.

Explanation #2: Gene × Environment Interactions

A second explanation for the origin of narcissism is that genetically influenced tendencies and environmental features may interact to produce variation in personality (Penke et al. 2007), including attributes linked with narcissism (for a similar argument about antisocial tendencies, see Caspi et al. 2002; Sadeh et al. 2010). According to this perspective, people vary in their genotypes, with different people having more or less potential to become narcissistic because of their genetic endowment. The expression of narcissistic tendencies, however, depends on environmental contingencies. The development of a narcissistic phenotype may depend upon genotypic factors acting with environmental factors in a developmental process.

One example of this process draws on work by Cramer (2011; see also Tracy and Robins 2003). There are now hints that young children (age 3–4 years) vary in temperamental proclivities toward narcissism. Temperament—for the purposes of positing an evolutionary account, and based on the average heritability of narcissism in children (33 %; Coolidge et al. 2001, 2004)—is assumed to be under at least some nontrivial genetic influence. These early childhood individual differences may interact with parenting strategies (authoritarianism, indulgence) to produce narcissistic attributes in adolescence and adulthood. Thus, although there is evidence of temperamental correlates of adult narcissism at an early age, the development of high levels of narcissism depends on the interaction between temperament and parenting (or other environmental factors). Under certain conditions, people who are genetically predisposed to become narcissistic, because of dispositional tendencies toward exuberance and confidence (or even a dispositional tendency toward emotional brittleness), will not develop high levels of narcissistic traits if they are raised in environments that feature developmentally appropriate levels of parental demandingness and responsiveness. According to this kind of model, parenting may be relevant to the development of narcissism for only those children with certain genotypes.

Readers familiar with the behavior genetics literature may find any suggestion of a role for parenting as inconsistent with the evidence of near-zero shared environmental effects for most aspects of adult personality (Harris 1995, 2000). This may not, however, be the correct way to interpret behavioral genetic research. As it stands, gene × environment effects are captured by the additive genetic component of the basic twin model used in behavioral genetic studies to partition observed variation into underlying additive genetic effects, shared environment effects, and unique environmental effects (plus measurement error; Johnson et al. 2011; Purcell 2002). In other words, gene × shared environmental factors like parenting styles end up being captured by the additive genetic factor in the common twin model. This means that "heritability" estimates may reflect, in part, environmental inputs that interact with genetic factors. Thus, researchers who espouse the importance of the gene × environment interactionist paradigm tend to argue that the environmental factors may have been underemphasized in the behavioral genetic literature (Penke et al. 2007; Roberts and Jackson 2008). This is also one reason why Jackson and colleagues argue that heritability does not unequivocally mean that there is a "genetic substrate" for a trait (Jackson et al. 2011). Nonetheless, our point is that genetic factors are likely to be relevant for understanding the origins of narcissism with the caveat that the critical issues often amount to how genetically influenced proclivities are translated into phenotypic personality attributes in concert with environmental factors.

Explanation #3: Evolutionary Selection

We propose that genetically influenced attributes are part of the explanation for the origins of narcissism. This perspective leads to questions about the evolutionary significance of heritable variation in the tendency to exhibit narcissistic attributes. A set of theories concerning the evolutionary origin and functions of narcissism relies on different models of evolutionary selection. In this section, we consider two key types of selection pressures: Direct selection (i.e., mutation–selection balance) and balancing selection. Direct selection operates by favoring particular variants in the population in general, while (typically) selecting against mutation; the constant influx of mutations across generations creates phenotypic variance within the population (Keller and Miller 2006; Lande 1975). That is, some people carry higher mutation loads. These models are gaining support (Verweij et al. 2012), as traits that are clearly socially undesirable tend to accrue in populations where inbreeding is common, suggesting that direct selection is operating.

Direct selection models, however, do not seem to apply particularly well to narcissism; instead, evolutionary models that invoke concepts related to balancing selection appear to hold more promise for explaining narcissism. Balancing selection occurs when two (or more) alternative strategies are seemingly viable. This is the case if the optima for traits differ between environments (Nettle 2006). For example, high levels of trait neuroticism might facilitate survival in especially dangerous environments in which risks of bodily injury are great (see Nettle 2006). Organisms who are highly sensitive to threat (i.e., highly vigilant) will be less likely to die in such a high-threat context when compared to less reactive conspecifics. On the other hand, high levels of neuroticism may not confer such advantages in relatively safe environments. In these cases, a highly reactive nervous system may impart more costs than benefits because of the inherent biological costs associated with heightened stress reactivity, as well as any opportunity costs due to missed opportunities to explore the environment. In short, the costs and benefits of a particular trait level seem to depend on the particular context. This kind of situation tends to preserve personality variation across generations, especially to the extent that humans have inhabited a wide range of environments over the course of their evolutionary history.

Balancing selection may even happen within a single environment. For instance, frequency-dependent selection is a type of balancing selection in which the number of organisms who exhibit a strategy determines whether that variant will be selected (Keller and Miller 2006); the evolutionary advantages of a particular strategy depend on the frequencies of all possible strategies in the local ecology. Howard (1984) discusses the case of bullfrogs with alternative mating strategies (see also Simpson and Gangestad 1992). If a large number of frogs adopt one type of mating strategy (such as croaking loudly to attract females), then there will be opportunities for alternative strategies to find success (such as circling the croaking male and intercepting the approaching females). If there are too many frogs that have evolved to fill one niche, then there is an opportunity for frogs with a different strategy to exploit a different niche. If these mating strategies also have a genetic basis, then they exemplify frequency-dependent selection and thus provide an example of balancing selection. Balancing selection for polygenic traits does indeed appear to be viable in certain circumstances (Turelli and Barton 2004).

In sum, narcissism is typically understood with reference to balancing selection (rather than direct selection) when considering the selective pressures that shape this construct. In other words, we suspect that variability in narcissism has been preserved across evolutionary history because the particular costs and benefits associated with narcissistic attributes depend on a wide range of environmental factors. Variation exists because narcissistic attributes can be beneficial for survival and reproduction in certain contexts. As it stands, there are a number of specific possibilities that might explain the origins of narcissistic traits rooted in balancing selection models. We described a few of these explanations in this section. However, we do not intend this to be an exhaustive summary of the possibilities.

Explanation #3A: Narcissism and Short-Term Mating

Holtzman and Strube (2011) argued that narcissistic strategies were maintained over generations due to the viability of short-term mating (e.g., promiscuity, one-night stands). The 2011 version of the theory is a frequency-dependent selection argument that is consistent with life history theory (Ellis et al. 2012; Jonason et al. 2012; McDonald et al. 2012; Simpson et al. 2011), and it was partially inspired by key developments in the psychopathy literature (e.g., Lalumiere et al. 2001; Mealey 1995). In particular, Holtzman and Strube (2011) argued that there may have been frequency-dependent selection for short-term mating among a population of people who largely engaged in long-term relationships (see also Eastwick 2009). This evolutionary context included a tension between selection for short-term mating (part of a fast life history strategy) versus selection for long-term mating (part of a slow life history strategy). There is some evidence consistent with Holtzman and Strube's (2011) evolutionary account, given that narcissism is associated with many traits that theoretically would have been selected in short-term mating contexts: coercion, attractiveness, and unique physical traits.

First and foremost, narcissism is positively associated with short-term mating behaviors (Buss and Shackelford 1997; Foster et al. 2006; Jonason et al. 2009; Reise and Wright 1996). Perhaps the most convincing evidence of this link comes from Dufner et al. (2013), who demonstrated that, compared to male nonnarcissists, male narcissists tend to be more likely to obtain contact information from random females on a city street. This behavioral evidence suggests that male narcissists are successful at achieving a crucial first step in short-term mating—gaining access to potential mates. Narcissism is also associated with sexually coercive tendencies (Bushman et al. 2003; Williams et al. 2009). Moreover, Holtzman and Strube (2010) argue that narcissism should be associated with attractiveness, given that people in short-term mating contexts tend to weigh attractiveness more heavily (Li et al. 2002; Li and Kenrick 2006). Narcissism is indeed associated with attractiveness (Dufner et al. 2013; Holtzman and Strube 2010; Rauthmann and Kolar 2013), an effect that has been replicated by various independent research groups.

It is important to point out a few findings that are inconsistent with Holtzman and Strube's (2011) evolutionary account. Perhaps the most important finding that contradicts the original account is that narcissism was not clearly related to unadorned physical attractiveness—operationalized as attractiveness when one dresses in a neutral gray outfit (Holtzman and Strube 2013). This suggests that the attractiveness of narcissists is explained by something other than their "inherent beauty" per se, such as the tendency of narcissists to adopt flattering styles. A second piece of evidence also runs counter to the original hypothesis: Although socially aversive traits are associated positively with symmetry (Holtzman et al. 2011), narcissism was not clearly positively associated with physical symmetry. All in all, little evidence at this juncture suggests that narcissism is tied to unadorned attractiveness.

Thus, these findings beg for an explanation: The correlation between narcissism and raw attractiveness hovers around zero. However, when allowed to control and modify their own appearances (i.e., adorned attractiveness), narcissists are rated as physically attractive by observers. Holtzman and Strube (2013) recommend that dynamic self-regulatory theories of narcissism (Morf and Rhodewalt 2001) or the conspicuous consumption literature (Sedikides et al. 2011; Sedikides et al. 2007; Sundie et al. 2011) may be useful for trying to explain the link between narcissism and adorned attractiveness. The link between attractiveness and narcissism may in part hinge on cultural inputs, such as manipulating one's appearance and signaling that the individual has resources (i.e., conspicuous consumption). In turn, manipulating one's image may itself hinge on evolutionarily grounded motives; see the conspicuous consumption literature for further reading (Sundie et al. 2011).

Explanation #3B: Narcissism and Dominance

An alternative to the short-term mating account for the evolutionary origins of narcissism is offered by Tracy et al. (2011). This perspective argues that narcissism is related to dominance and that this explains the origins of narcissism. Dominance was selected because it is one route to the attainment of status (Henrich and Gil-White 2001); simultaneously, there was selection for the emotion systems that enable humans to feel and exhibit hubristic pride—one of the core emotional correlates of narcissism (Tracy et al. 2009; Tracy and Robins 2003). According to this model, it was the expression of hubristic pride that helped narcissists appear dominant, which led to narcissists' social elevation. This rise in status hierarchies led to resource acquisition (food, desirable living locations, material goods) and these resources promoted survival.

There is indeed evidence that narcissism is tied to dominance (Bradlee and Emmons 1992). The two constructs are so similar that sometimes the labels are interchangeable, as in the California Psychological Inventory (Havlicek et al. 2005). However, one problem with the dominance model of narcissism is that it may treat dominance as an ultimate end in itself rather than as a means to achieving reproductive success. A devil's advocate would argue that dominant narcissists who never reproduced would never directly pass along genes to the next generation. Therefore, dominance by itself is unlikely to be an evolutionary endpoint; the dominant form of narcissism cannot evolve without conferring reproductive success. Essential to this argument is that dominance may constitute a crucial element of a larger strategy that involves both reproductive strategies and increased survival. This gives rise to an integrative third model that combines the dominance and the short-term mating explanations.

Explanation #3C: Selection for Short-Term Mating and Dominance-Shaped Narcissism

The novel idea here is that short-term mating strategies and dominance were dually selected. Short-term mating traits directly helped narcissists pass on their genes to the next generation, enabling reproductive success. Dominant traits helped narcissists strive for status, which had effects primarily on the likelihood of survival (and more secondarily or indirectly on their likelihood of reproductive success). Across evolutionary time, selection for each of these traits would have led to their covariation. This gives rise to an integrative theoretical model. Holtzman and Strube (2011) provide an explanation of the reproductive means by which narcissism is transmitted from one generation to the next, whereas Tracy and colleagues (e.g., Tracy and Robins 2003) primarily explain how narcissists survive and thrive. This integration directly answers the call for "a concern with the impact of personality variation on survival and reproductive success" (Nettle and Penke 2010, p. 4043).

This integration yields testable predictions. Namely, both short-term mating and dominance should significantly mediate the effects of narcissistic traits on behavior. Putting this theory to the test should reveal that in reproductively relevant domains, such as speed-dating paradigms, short-term mating should be a bigger mediator. In survival-relevant domains, such as physical aggression paradigms, dominance should be a bigger mediator. This theory makes the falsifiable prediction that one or the other proposed mediators will be significant for most narcissism–behavior relationships.

More broadly, this model of narcissism is representative of the emerging paradigm of social-cognitive evolutionary psychology. With respect to the narcissism literature, the model suggests that it is not short-term-mating motives that are always the most predictive of narcissistic behavior; nor are dominance motives always the most important way to explain narcissistic behavior. Instead, the inputs from the environment will determine which evolved program (a mating-relevant one or a survival-relevant one) is active at a given time.

Summary and Conclusions

Behavioral genetic evidence demonstrates that narcissism is heritable. This provides support for the idea that narcissism has a biological component, but, simultaneously, there is little reason to believe that narcissism will be explained by single genes. Instead, genetically informed research highlights the importance of biological factors and provides a set of tools that can be used to test some theoretical propositions. The key is that biological components should be included in theorizing about the origins of this complex phenotype. In short, evolutionary personality psychology can make important contributions to the current understanding of narcissism.

Accordingly, we outlined three primary explanations of the evolutionary roots of narcissism: (1) Narcissism may reflect a strategic reaction to one's heritable physical characteristics rather than being directly a function of one's genes; (2) narcissism may be the outcome of gene × environment interactions; and (3) narcissism may be rooted in selection for strategies that have different cost and benefit ratios depending on environmental conditions. Expanding this third explanation, we forwarded the novel idea that narcissism has been selected for two primary advantages—because it facilitates short-term mating and helps to elevate a person within a dominance hierarchy. This integrative perspective on the evolutionary roots of narcissism will hopefully generate more attention to the role that biological factors play in the origins of narcissism.

In sum, the goal of this chapter was to ground narcissism in contemporary evolutionary psychology to provide biologically informed insights into the origins of narcissistic attributes. This is a challenging task and we have outlined several possibilities for understanding how and why narcissistic traits may have evolved. Our overarching goal is to encourage psychologists to entertain the possibility that narcissism has some biological roots. Indeed, if the psychological construct "narcissism" is anything like the narcissus plant, it will have a number of deep roots and involve a complicated development from seed to flower.

Acknowledgments The authors thank Joy Losee and Bradley R. Sturz as well as the editors—Todd Shackelford, Lisa Welling, and Virgil Zeigler-Hill—for their insightful comments on previous drafts of this chapter.

References

Back, M. D., Schmukle, S. C., & Egloff, B. (2010). Why are narcissists so charming at first sight? Decoding the narcissism-popularity link at zero acquaintance. *Journal of Personality and Social Psychology, 98*, 132–145. doi:10.1037/a0016338.

Bradlee, P. M., & Emmons, R. A. (1992). Locating narcissism within the interpersonal circumplex and the 5-factor model. *Personality and Individual Differences, 13*, 821–830. doi:10.1016/0191-8869(92)90056-U.

Bushman, B. J., Bonacci, A. M., van Dijk, M., & Baumeister, R. F. (2003). Narcissism, sexual refusal, and aggression: Testing a narcissistic reactance model of sexual coercion. *Journal of Personality and Social Psychology, 84*, 1027–1040. doi:10.1037/0022-3514.84.5.1027.

Buss, D. M. (1991). Evolutionary personality psychology. *Annual Review of Psychology, 42*, 459–491. doi:10.1146/annurev.ps.42.020191.002331.

Buss, D. M. (2009). How can evolutionary psychology successfully explain personality and individual differences? *Perspectives on Psychological Science, 4*, 359–366.

Buss, D. M., & Hawley, P. H. (2011). *The evolution of personality and individual differences*. Oxford: University Press.

Buss, D. M., & Shackelford, T. K. (1997). Susceptibility to infidelity in the first year of marriage. *Journal of Research in Personality, 31*, 193–221. doi:10.1006/jrpe.1997.2175.

Caspi, A., McClay, J., Moffitt, T. E., Mill, J., Martin, J., Craig, I. W., Taylor, A., & Poulton, R. (2002). Role of genotype in the cycle of violence in maltreated children. *Science, 297*, 851–854. doi:10.1126/science.1072290.

Coolidge, F. L., Thede, L. L., & Jang, K. L. (2001). Heritability of personality disorders in childhood: A preliminary investigation. *Journal of Personality Disorders, 15*, 33–40. doi:10.1521/pedi.15.1.33.18645.

Coolidge, F. L., Thede, L. L., & Jang, K. L. (2004). Are personality disorders psychological manifestations of executive function deficits? Bivariate heritability evidence from a twin study. *Behavior Genetics, 34*, 75–84. doi:10.1023/b:bege.0000009486.97375.53.

Cramer, P. (2011). Young adult narcissism: A 20 year longitudinal study of the contribution of parenting styles, preschool precursors of narcissism, and denial. *Journal of Research in Personality, 45*, 19–28. doi:10.1016/j.jrp.2010.11.004.

de Moor, M. H. M., Costa, P. T., Terracciano, A., Krueger, R. F., de Geus, E. J. C., Toshiko, T., Penninx, B. W. J. H., Esko, T., Madden, P. A. F., Derringer, J., Amin, N., Willemsen, G., Hottenga, J. J., Distel, M. A., Uda, M., Sanna, S., Spinhoven, P., Hartman, C. A., Sullivan, P., Realo, A., Allik, J., Heath, A. C., Pergadia, M. L., Agrawal, A., Lin, P., Grucza, R., Nutile, T., Ciullo, M., Rujescu, D., Giegling, I., Konte, B., Widen, E., Cousminer, D. L., Eriksson, J. G., Palotie, A., Peltonen,

L., Luciano, M., Tenesa, A., Davies, G., Lopez, L. M., Hansell, N. K., Medland, S. E., Ferrucci, L., Schlessinger, D., Montgomery, G. W., Wright, M. J., Aulchenko, Y. S., Janssens, A. C. J. W., Oostra, B. A., Metspalu, A., Abecasis, G. R., Deary, I. J., Raikkonen, K., Bierut, L. J., Martin, N. G., van Duijn, C. M., & Boomsma, D. I. (2012). Meta-analysis of genome-wide association studies for personality. *Molecular Psychiatry, 17,* 337–349. doi:10.1038/mp.2010.128.

Dufner, M., Rauthmann, J. F., Czarna, A. Z., & Denissen, J. J. A. (2013). Are narcissists sexy? Zeroing in on the effect of narcissism on short-term mate appeal. *Personality & Social Psychology Bulletin, 39,* 870–882. doi:10.1177/0146167213483580.

Eastwick, P. W. (2009). Beyond the pleistocene: Using phylogeny and constraint to inform the evolutionary psychology of human mating. *Psychological Bulletin, 135,* 794–821. doi:10.1037/a0016845.

Ellis, B. J., Del Giudice, M., Dishion, T. J., Figueredo, A. J., Gray, P., Griskevicius, V., Hawley, P. H., Jacobs, W. J., James, J., Volk, A. A., & Wilson, D. S. (2012). The evolutionary basis of risky adolescent behavior: Implications for science, policy, and practice. *Developmental Psychology, 48,* 598–623. doi:10.1037/a0026220.

Emmons, R. A. (1984). Factor-analysis and construct-validity of the narcissistic personality inventory. *Journal of Personality Assessment, 48,* 291–300. doi:10.1207/s15327752jpa4803_11.

Foster, J. D., & Campbell, W. K. (2007). Are there such things as "Narcissists" in social psychology? A taxometric analysis of the narcissistic personality Inventory. *Personality and Individual Differences, 43,* 1321–1332. doi:10.1016/j.paid.2007.04.003.

Foster, J. D., Shrira, I., & Campbell, W. K. (2006). Theoretical models of narcissism, sexuality, and relationship commitment. *Journal of Social and Personal Relationships, 23,* 367–386. doi:10.1177/0265407506064204.

Furnham, A., Richards, S. C., & Paulhus, D. L. (2013). The dark triad of personality: A 10 year review. *Social and Personality Psychology Compass, 7,* 199–216. doi:10.1111/spc3.12018.

Gangestad, S. W., Garver-Apgar, C. E., Simpson, J. A., & Cousins, A. J. (2007). Changes in women's mate preferences across the ovulatory cycle. *Journal of Personality and Social Psychology, 92,* 151–163. doi:10.1037/0022-3514.92.1.151.

Harris, J. R. (1995). Where is the child's environment: A group socialization theory of development. *Psychological Review, 102,* 458–489. doi:10.1037/0033-295x.102.3.458.

Harris, J. R. (2000). The outcome of parenting: What do we really know? *Journal of Personality, 68,* 625–637. doi:10.1111/1467-6494.00110.

Havlicek, J., Roberts, S. C., & Flegr, J. (2005). Women's preference for dominant male odour: Effects of menstrual cycle and relationship status. *Biology Letters, 1,* 256–259. doi:10.1098/rsbl.2005.0332.

Henrich, J., & Gil-White, F. J. (2001). The evolution of prestige—Freely conferred deference as a mechanism for enhancing the benefits of cultural transmission. *Evolution and Human Behavior, 22,* 165–196. doi:10.1016/s1090-5138(00)00071-4.

Holtzman, N. S. (2011). Facing a psychopath: Detecting the dark triad from emotionally-neutral faces, using prototypes from the personality faceaurus. *Journal of Research in Personality, 45,* 648–654. doi:10.1016/j.jrp.2011.09.002.

Holtzman, N. S., & Strube, M. J. (2010). Narcissism and attractiveness. *Journal of Research in Personality, 44,* 133–136. doi:10.1016/j.jrp.2009.10.004.

Holtzman, N. S., & Strube, M. J. (2011). The intertwined evolution of narcissism and short-term mating: An emerging hypothesis. In W. K. Campbell & J. D. Miller (Eds.), *The handbook of narcissism and narcissistic personality disorder: Theoretical approaches, empirical findings, and treatments* (pp. 210–220). Hoboken: Wiley.

Holtzman, N. S., & Strube, M. J. (2013). Dark personalities tend to create a physically attractive veneer. *Social Psychological and Personality Science, 4,* 461–467. doi:10.1177/1948550612461284.

Holtzman, N. S., Vazire, S., & Mehl, M. R. (2010). Sounds like a narcissist: Behavioral manifestations of narcissism in everyday life. *Journal of Research in Personality, 44,* 478–484. doi:10.1016/j.jrp.2010.06.001.

Holtzman, N. S., Augustine, A. A., & Senne, A. L. (2011). Are pro-social or socially aversive people more physically symmetrical? Symmetry in relation to over 200 personality variables. *Journal of Research in Personality, 45,* 87–91. doi:10.1016/j.jrp.2011.08.003.

Howard, R. D. (1984). Alternative mating behaviors of young male bullfrogs. *American Zoologist, 24,* 397–406.

Jackson, J. J., Hill, P. L., & Roberts, B. W. (2011). Sociogenomic theory as an answer to the heritability problem. *European Journal of Personality, 25,* 274–276.

Jakobwitz, S., & Egan, V. (2006). The dark triad and normal personality traits. *Personality and Individual Differences, 40,* 331–339. doi:10.1016/j.paid.2005.07.006.

Johnson, W., Penke, L., & Spinath, F. M. (2011). Heritability in the era of molecular genetics: Some thoughts for understanding genetic influences on behavioural traits. *European Journal of Personality, 25,* 254–266. doi:10.1002/per.836.

Jonason, P. K., Li, N. P., Webster, G. D., & Schmitt, D. P. (2009). The dark triad: Facilitating a short-term mating strategy in men. *European Journal of Personality, 23,* 5–18. doi:10.1002/per.698.

Jonason, P. K., Webster, G. D., Schmitt, D. P., Li, N. P., & Crysel, L. (2012). The antihero in popular culture: Life history theory and the dark triad personality traits. *Review of General Psychology, 16,* 192–199. doi:10.1037/a0027914.

Keller, M. C., & Miller, G. (2006). Resolving the paradox of common, harmful, heritable mental disorders: Which evolutionary genetic models work best? *Behavioral and Brain Sciences, 29,* 385–452. doi:10.1017/s0140525x06009095.

Kendler, K. S. (2005). "A gene for…": The nature of gene action in psychiatric disorders. *American Journal of Psychiatry, 162,* 1243–1252. doi:10.1176/appi.ajp.162.7.1243.

Kohut, H. (1971). *The analysis of the self: A systematic approach to the psychoanalytic treatment of Narcissistic Personality Disorders*. New York: International Universities Press, Inc.

Lalumiere, M. L., Harris, G. T., & Rice, M. E. (2001). Psychopathy and developmental instability. *Evolution and Human Behavior, 22,* 75–92. doi:10.1016/s1090-5138(00)00064-7.

Lalumiere, M. L., Mishra, S., & Harris, G. T. (2008). In cold blood: The evolution of psychopathy. In J. Duntley & T. K. Shakelford (Eds.), *Evolutionary forensic psychology: Darwinian foundations of crime and law* (pp. 139–159). New York: Oxford University Press.

Lande, R. (1975). Maintenance of genetic-variability by mutation in a polygenic character with linked loci. *Genetical Research, 26,* 221–235.

Li, N. P., & Kenrick, D. T. (2006). Sex similarities and differences in preferences for short-term mates: What, whether, and why. *Journal of Personality and Social Psychology, 90,* 468–489. doi:10.1037/0022-3514.90.3.468.

Li, N. P., Bailey, J. M., Kenrick, D. T., & Linsenmeier, J. A. W. (2002). The necessities and luxuries of mate preferences: Testing the tradeoffs. *Journal of Personality and Social Psychology, 82,* 947–955. doi:10.1037//0022-3514.82.6.947.

Liu, F., van der Lijn, F., Schurmann, C., Zhu, G., Chakravarty, M. M., Hysi, P. G., Wollstein, A., Lao, O., de Bruijne, M., Ikram, M. A., van der Lugt, A., Rivadeneira, F., Uitterlinden, A. G., Hofman, A., Niessen, W. J., Homuth, G., de Zubicaray, G., McMahon, K. L., Thompson, P. M., Daboul, A., Puls, R., Hegenscheid, K., Bevan, L., Pausova, Z., Medland, S. E., Montgomery, G. W., Wright, M. J., Wicking, C., Boehringer, S., Spector, T. D., Paus, T., Martin, N. G., Biffar, R., Kayser, M., & Int Visible Trait Genetics, V. (2012). A genome-wide association study identifies five loci influencing facial morphology in Europeans. *Plos Genetics, 8*. doi:10.1371/journal.pgen.1002932.

Livesley, W. J., Jang, K. L., Jackson, D. N., & Vernon, P. A. (1993). Genetic and environmental contributions to dimensions of personality disorder. *American Journal of Psychiatry, 150,* 1826–1831.

Lukaszewski, A. W. (2011). The concept of 'reactive heritability': How heritable personality variation may arise from a universal human nature. *European Journal of Personality, 25,* 277–278.

Lynam, D. R., & Widiger, T. A. (2001). Using the five-factor model to represent the DSM-IV personality disorders: An expert consensus approach. [Article]. *Journal of Abnormal Psychology, 110,* 401–412. doi:10.1037//0021-843x.110.3.401.

Lynam, D. R., & Widiger, T. A. (2007). Using a general model of personality to identify the basic elements of psychopathy. *Journal of Personality Disorders, 21,* 160–178. doi:10.1521/pedi.2007.21.2.160.

McDonald, M. M., Donnellan, M. B., & Navarrete, C. D. (2012). A life history approach to understanding the dark triad. *Personality and Individual Differences, 52,* 601–605.

Mealey, L. (1995). The sociobiology of sociopathy: An integrated evolutionary model. *Behavioral and Brain Sciences, 18,* 523–541.

Morf, C. C., & Rhodewalt, F. (2001). Unraveling the paradoxes of narcissism: A dynamic self-regulatory processing model. *Psychological Inquiry, 12,* 177–196. doi:10.1207/s15327965pli1204_1.

Moskowitz, D. A., Rieger, G., & Seal, D. W. (2009). Narcissism, self-evaluations, and partner preferences among men who have sex with men. *Personality and Individual Differences, 46,* 725–728. doi:10.1016/j.paid.2009.01.033.

Nettle, D. (2006). The evolution of personality variation in humans and other animals. *American Psychologist, 61,* 622–631. doi:10.1037/0003-066x.61.6.622.

Nettle, D., & Penke, L. (2010). Personality: Bridging the literatures from human psychology and behavioural ecology. [Review]. *Philosophical Transactions of the Royal Society B-Biological Sciences, 365,* 4043–4050. doi:10.1098/rstb.2010.0061.

Paulhus, D. L. (2001). Normal narcissism: Two minimalist accounts. *Psychological Inquiry, 12,* 228–230.

Paulhus, D. L., & Williams, K. M. (2002). The dark triad of personality: Narcissism, Machiavellianism, and psychopathy. *Journal of Research in Personality, 36,* 556–563. doi:10.1016/S0092-6566(02)00505-6.

Penke, L., Denissen, J. J. A., & Miller, G. F. (2007). The evolutionary genetics of personality. *European Journal of Personality, 21,* 549–587. doi:10.1002/per.629.

Purcell, S. (2002). Variance components models for gene-environment interaction in twin analysis. [Article]. *Twin Research, 5,* 554–571. doi:10.1375/136905202762342035.

Raskin, R., & Terry, H. (1988). A principal-components analysis of the narcissistic personality-inventory and further evidence of its construct-validity. *Journal of Personality and Social Psychology, 54,* 890–902. doi:10.1037/0022-3514.54.5.890.

Rauthmann, J. F., & Kolar, G. P. (2013). The perceived attractiveness and traits of the Dark Triad: Narcissists are perceived as hot, Machiavellians and psychopaths not. [Article]. *Personality and Individual Differences, 54,* 582–586. doi:10.1016/j.paid.2012.11.005.

Reise, S. P., & Wright, T. M. (1996). Personality traits, cluster B personality disorders, and sociosexuality. [Article]. *Journal of Research in Personality, 30,* 128–136. doi:10.1006/jrpe.1996.0009.

Roberts, B. W., & Jackson, J. J. (2008). Sociogenomic personality psychology. *Journal of Personality, 76,* 1523–1544. doi:10.1111/j.1467-6494.2008.00530.x.

Sadeh, N., Javdani, S., Jackson, J. J., Reynolds, E. K., Potenza, M. N., Gelernter, J., Lejuez, C. W., & Verona, E. (2010). Serotonin transporter gene associations with psychopathic traits in youth vary as a function of socioeconomic resources. *Journal of Abnormal Psychology, 119,* 604–609. doi:10.1037/a0019709.

Sedikides, C., Gregg, A. P., Cisek, S., & Hart, C. M. (2007). The I that buys: Narcissists as consumers. *Journal of Consumer Psychology, 17,* 254–257. doi:10.1016/S1057-7408(07)70035-9.

Sedikides, C., Cisek, S., & Hart, C. M. (2011). Narcissism and brand name consumerism. In W. K. Campbell & J. D. Miller (Eds.), *The handbook of narcissism and narcissistic personality disorder: Theoretical approaches, empirical findings, and treatments* (pp. 382–392). Hoboken: Wiley.

Silventoinen, K., Magnusson, P. K. E., Tynelius, P., Kaprio, J., & Rasmussen, F. (2008). Heritability of body size and muscle strength in young adulthood: A study of one million Swedish men. *Genetic Epidemiology, 32,* 341–349. doi:10.1002/gepi.20308.

Simpson, J. A., & Gangestad, S. W. (1992). Sociosexuality and romantic partner choice. *Journal of Personality, 60,* 31–51. doi:10.1111/j.1467-6494.1992.tb00264.x.

Simpson, J. A., Griskevicius, V., & Kim, J. S. (2011). Evolution, life history, and personality. In L. Horowitz & S. Strack (Eds.), *Handbook of interpersonal psychology: Theory, research, assessment, and therapeutic interventions* (pp. 75–89). New York: Wiley.

Snyder, M., Tanke, E. D., & Berscheid, E. (1977). Social perception and interpersonal behavior: On self-fulfilling nature of social stereotypes. *Journal of Personality and Social Psychology, 35,* 656–666.

Sundie, J. M., Griskevicius, V., Vohs, K. D., Kenrick, D. T., Tybur, J. M., & Beal, D. J. (2011). Peacocks, porsches, and thorstein veblen: Conspicuous consumption as a sexual signaling system. *Journal of Personality and Social Psychology, 100,* 664–680. doi:10.1037/a0021669.

Tooby, J., & Cosmides, L. (1990). On the universality of human nature and the uniqueness of the individual: The role of genetics and adaptation. *Journal of Personality, 58,* 17–67.

Tracy, J. L., & Robins, R. W. (2003). "Death of a (narcissistic) salesman": An integrative model of fragile self-esteem. *Psychological Inquiry, 14,* 57–62.

Tracy, J. L., Cheng, J. T., Robins, R. W., & Trzesniewski, K. H. (2009). Authentic and hubristic pride: The affective core of self-esteem and narcissism. *Self and Identity, 8,* 196–213. doi:10.1080/15298860802505053.

Tracy, J. L., Cheng, J. T., Martens, J. P., & Robins, R. W. (2011). The emotional dynamics of narcissism: Inflated by pride, deflated by shame. In W. K. Campbell & J. D. Miller (Eds.), *The handbook of narcissism and narcissistic personality disorder: Theoretical approaches, empirical findings, and treatments.* Hoboken: Wiley.

Turelli, M., & Barton, N. H. (2004). Polygenic variation maintained by balancing selection: Pleiotropy, sex-dependent allelic effects and GxE interactions. *Genetics, 166,* 1053–1079. doi:10.1534/genetics.166.2.1053.

Vernon, P. A., Villani, V. C., Vickers, L. C., & Harris, J. A. (2008). A behavioral genetic investigation of the dark triad and the big 5. *Personality and Individual Differences, 44,* 445–452. doi:10.1016/j.paid.2007.09.007.

Verweij, K. J. H., Yang, J., Lahti, J., Veijola, J., Hintsanen, M., Pulkki-Raback, L., Heinonen, K., Pouta, A., Pesonen, A.-K., Widen, E., Taanila, A., Isohanni, M., Miettunen, J., Palotie, A., Penke, L., Service, S. K., Heath, A. C., Montgomery, G. W., Raitakari, O., Kahonen, M., Viikari, J., Raikkonen, K., Eriksson, J. G., Keltikangas-Jarvinen, L., Lehtimaki, T., Martin, N. G., Jarvelin, M.-R., Visscher, P. M., Keller, M. C., & Zietsch, B. P. (2012). Maintenance of genetic variation in human personality: Testing evolutionary models by estimating heritability due to common causal variants and investigating the effect of distant inbreeding. *Evolution, 66,* 3238–3251. doi:10.1111/j.1558-5646.2012.01679.x.

Williams, K. M., Cooper, B. S., Howell, T. M., Yuille, J. C., & Paulhus, D. L. (2009). Inferring sexually deviant behavior from corresponding fantasies: The role of personality and pornography use. *Criminal Justice and Behavior, 36,* 198–222. doi:10.1177/0093854808327277.

Zebrowitz, L. A., Voinescu, L., & Collins, M. A. (1996). "'Wide-eyed" and "crooked-faced": Determinants of perceived and real honesty across the life span. *Personality and Social Psychology Bulletin, 22,* 1258–1269. doi:10.1177/01461672962212006.

Zebrowitz, L. A., Hall, J. A., Murphy, N. A., & Rhodes, G. (2002). Looking smart and looking good: Facial cues to intelligence and their origins. *Personality and Social Psychology Bulletin, 28,* 238–249. doi:10.1177/0146167202282009.

Part X

Conclusion

37 Integrating Evolutionary Psychology and Social Psychology: Reflections and Future Directions

Lisa L. M. Welling, Virgil Zeigler-Hill and Todd K. Shackelford

Using a present-oriented perspective sometimes provides a poor guide when investigating modern social behavior because the psychological mechanisms that produce these behaviors have been shaped over a long ancestral past, rather than molded recently in accordance with modern conveniences. By adopting the design stance, standard social psychological principles can reach a broader audience (e.g., evolutionary biologists) and consider broader questions. Thus, an evolutionary perspective—which suggests that our minds were designed by past, rather than present, environmental demands (Tooby and Cosmides 1990)—sensibly accounts for the history of our species when positing explanations for social behavior and development. Indeed, it is not possible to properly consider the ultimate causation—questioning *how* a behavior came to be—for any aspect of social psychology without considering evolutionary explanations. Nonetheless, evolutionary psychology and social psychology have progressed somewhat independently.

L. L. M. Welling (✉) · V. Zeigler-Hill · T. K. Shackelford
Department of Psychology, Oakland University,
212 Pryale Hall, Rochester, MI 48309, USA
e-mail: welling@oakland.edu

V. Zeigler-Hill
e-mail: zeiglerh@oakland.edu

T. K. Shackelford
e-mail: shackelf@oakland.edu

Throughout this volume, various experts have outlined what an evolutionary perspective offers mainstream social psychologists. The current chapter provides a brief overview of the different sections of this volume, namely social cognition, the self, attitudes and attitude change, interpersonal processes, mating and relationships, violence and aggression, health and psychological adjustment, and individual differences. Within each section, we highlight advantages of an evolutionary perspective when considering social psychological questions. Additionally, we suggest avenues for future research that apply a Darwinian rationale to conventional social psychological matters.

Social Cognition

Social cognition is a multifaceted topic within social and cognitive psychology that contains many subtopics, including adult (Fiddick, Chap. 2) and child (Machluf and Bjorklund, Chap. 3) cognition, comparative cognition (Vonk et al., Chap. 7), modularity (Barrett, Chap. 4), emotion (Ketelaar, Chap. 5), and religiosity (Kirkpatrick, Chap. 6). Despite arguments that social psychology has nothing to contribute to the study of cognition (Kelley 1973), research into social cognition has made important strides by integrating social psychological concepts and evolutionary reasoning. For instance, the modularity of the mind view—the idea that the mind is composed of neural structures or modules with specialized

V. Zeigler-Hill et al. (eds.), *Evolutionary Perspectives on Social Psychology,* Evolutionary Psychology,
DOI 10.1007/978-3-319-12697-5_37, © Springer International Publishing Switzerland 2015

functions—has recently expanded from equating the mind to a series of fixed, independent systems to evolved interconnected biological modules that are interactive, flexible, and shaped by learning (e.g., Barrett 2005, 2006, 2012; Barrett, Chap. 4). This view of modularity allows for a complementary overlap of related evolutionary, biological, and social psychological concepts. Similarly, adaptationist accounts of emotion (i.e., the position that emotions are evolved defenses rather than defects; see Ketelaar, Chap. 5) enable an understanding of the social utility of emotions, such as guilt and anger, and why some moral sentiments are absent in some individuals (e.g., psychopaths; Mealey 1995). Thus, it is clear that research concerning social cognition has and will continue to benefit from an evolutionary perspective.

Human social behavior and cognition develops in infancy and early childhood (reviewed in Machluf and Bjorklund, Chap. 3), making the study of social cognitive development an important aspect of understanding the evolution of human social psychology. Human preferences for social interaction begin in infancy such that newborns selectively attend to faces and face-like stimuli relative to other stimuli (e.g., Mondloch et al. 1999), are more attentive to depictions of biological versus other motion (Bardi et al. 2011; Simion et al. 2008), and match facial expressions made by adults (Abravanel and Sigafoos 1984; Bjorklund 1997; Oppenheim 1981). The human ability to view others as intentional agents (e.g., Bandura 2006; Tomasello 2009; Tomasello and Carpenter 2007) serves as the foundation for theory of mind (i.e., the ability to attribute psychological states to others), which develops over the preschool years (Bjorklund et al. 2010). These skills are honed during our extended childhood and solve various adaptive problems (Bjorklund 2003) and may have been observed to varying extents in some nonhuman species (e.g., Nielsen 2012; cf. Povinelli and Vonk 2003).

Comparative work on varied species provides insight into the evolution of social cognition and has led to several hypotheses about how the mechanisms of social cognition evolved (reviewed in Vonk et al., Chap. 7). For example, the domestication hypothesis—that social behaviors and cognitive traits in nonhumans were shaped over a long domestication process that selected for strong social aptitudes (Hare and Tomasello 2004; Hare et al. 2010)—highlights the superiority of domestic dogs in reading human pointing gestures when compared to other animals, such as wolves, coyotes (Udell et al. 2012), and chimpanzees (Kirchhofer et al. 2012). Additional research should continue to investigate social cognitive ability and development in adult and juvenile nonhuman animals. However, most comparative research into social cognition has focused on highly social species, often using the social intelligence hypothesis (i.e., that social ability and predicting the behavior of others stems from associated increased benefits in a group setting; Humphrey 1976; Jolly 1966) to predict social cognitive ability, and have neglected solitary species (Vonk et al., Chap. 7). A measure of social cognitive ability that considers a full range of socially diverse species will provide more compelling evidence of the evolutionary bases of social behavior.

The Self

The psychology of the self is the study of the conative, cognitive, and affective aspects of identity or subjective experience. The concept of the self does not appear to be unique to humans (Neubauer, Chap. 8). Many animals—including other primates (e.g., Boesch and Boesch-Achermann 2000; Suddendorf and Butler 2013), land mammals (e.g., McComb et al. 2000; Plotnik et al. 2006) and marine mammals (e.g., Connor 2007; Reiss and Marino 2001), and certain birds (e.g., Fraser and Bugnyar 2010; Prior et al. 2008)—show evidence of self-awareness. Mechanisms underlying human and nonhuman psychology, including self-concept, evolved because they solved ancestral adaptive problems (e.g., Barrett and Kurzban 2006), making investigation into other animals of varying cognitive ability and social structures important. An evolutionary perspective can shed light on the self by providing a theoretically sound framework from which to scrutinize the formation of social identity (i.e., the portion of self-concept derived from membership to specific social groups; Park and van Leeuwen, Chap. 9), self-esteem (Kavanagh and Scrutton, Chap. 10), and self-deception (von Hippel, Chap. 12). Further investigation into whether critical periods of development (e.g., puberty) relate to a solidification of different social identities could increase our understanding of the formation of social roles. Moreover, research could address the integration of private versus public social identities in strategically influencing others and in self-deception. Self-deception may have evolved to facilitate deception of others, because it eliminates the taxing cognitive load associated with active deception (Trivers 2011; von Hippel, Chap. 12), but it may also function to amalgamate private expectations with public realities to facilitate the attainment of desirable social identities. Future research can investigate these possibilities, along with the role of self-deception in the development of negative personality traits (e.g., narcissism), mate selection, intrasexual competition, and self-esteem.

Research concerning self-esteem has a rich history in social psychology (see Zeigler-Hill 2013, for a review). Grounded in an evolutionary perspective, sociometer theory (Kavanagh and Scrutton, Chap. 10; Leary and Downs 1995; Stinson et al., Chap. 11) proposes that state self-esteem is a gauge (or sociometer) of interpersonal relationships (i.e., a reflection of a person's perception of how others view him/her) that functions to make individuals aware of their social inclusion and motivate corrective action in advance of social rejection. However, human interactions have changed substantially with the increasing popularity of online social networking (see Piazza and Ingram, Chap. 13) which has led to increased research concerning cyberpsychology. Technology offers novel outlets for social behavior (e.g., cyberbullying; Piazza and Bering 2009) and many online behavioral patterns mirror offline ones (e.g., sex ratios of stalking perpetrators versus victims; Dreßing et al. 2014). Consequently, cyberpsychological research is a fruitful direction for exploring social questions from an evolutionary perspective.

Attitudes and Attitude Change

A person's attitudes—their assessments of a person, place, object, or event—are relatively stable, but can change according to context in flexible and adaptively patterned ways (reviewed in Lord et al., Chap. 14). For example, despite prior beliefs, people tend to obey the requests of authority figures (e.g., Milgram 1963). Depending on the context, obedience to authority can be adaptively patterned (e.g., when a child obeys their parent), making an evolutionary perspective sensible and informative (see Coultas and van Leeuwen, Chap. 15). An evolutionary perspective can also inform research into cultural shifts in attitude, such as those pertaining to women's rights and other social movements (Nicolas and Welling, Chap. 16). Given that violence has been steadily declining (Pinker 2011) and that this decline overlaps with social movements that aim to minimize aggression towards others, it is likely that social revolutions have curbed our violent inclinations and are a reflection of human cultural evolution and social learning (see Morgan et al., Chap. 17). Evolutionary psychology offers sound theoretical bases for addressing questions aimed at understanding human attitudes and social change. An evolutionary perspective, which can potentially explain (but not excuse) social inequalities, may be particularly useful for scholars interested in revising public policy.

Interpersonal Processes

Statistical models of purely self-interested decision making among human groups fail consistently across human cultures (Henrich et al. 2005). As the quintessential social species, humans rely on others in our social groups. It is perhaps unsurprising, then, that people spend a great deal of their time behaving prosocially (Krebs, Chap. 18). An evolutionary perspective suggests that the prosocial behaviors studied by social psychologists are produced by evolved mechanisms. Prosocial behaviors facilitate group living (Kameda et al., Chap. 19), and living in groups enhances survival (Van Vugt and Kameda 2014).

Thus, it is likely that many aspects of human cognition are the result of having to navigate complex social interactions with kith, kin, and other group members and of the need to solve the associated recurrent problems (e.g., group coordination, status, cohesion, decision making; Kameda et al., Chap. 19) that ancestral humans encountered via group living (e.g., Dunbar 1993).

Friendship (Hruschka et al., Chap. 20) and cooperation (Prentice and Sheldon, Chap. 21) facilitate group living. Although people are more generous to kin than non-kin of the same level of social closeness (Curry et al. 2012; Rachlin and Jones 2008), individuals regularly build discerning and lasting relationships with others (who may or may not be kin) with whom they mutually express affectionate regard and help (Hruschka 2010). Several theories have addressed why friendships exist, including expectations of reciprocity (e.g., Tooby and Cosmides 1996) or reputation maintenance (Roberts 1998), and additional research is needed to dissociate the various possibilities. Nonetheless, prosociality, friendship, and cooperation offered ancestral advantages, such as the ability to form and maintain alliances (DeScioli and Kurzban 2009, 2012). Future research should investigate the influence of our modern environment—with its unprecedented crowding and decreased reliance on face-to-face social interactions (and increased preference for online social interactions)—on interpersonal processes.

Evolutionary reasoning also informs language and communication (Scott-Philips, Chap. 22). Human communication involves the expression and inference of intentions, and functions to assist social navigation (e.g., Scott-Phillips et al. 2012), but communication is not limited to language. Status hierarchies of human face-to-face groups bear striking similarities to those observed among other primates (reviewed in Mazur, Chap. 24) and are established through varied forms of communication (e.g., language, dominance displays, expression). Moreover, stereotypes are template-like cognitive representations that function to quickly communicate information about social group membership (Hutchison and Martin, Chap. 23). In the absence of person-specific information, stereotypes facilitate rapid and efficient categorization and judgment of others (Fiske and Neuberg 1990), including information about sex, ethnicity, and social status. Cultural evolutionary approaches permit and should continue to enlighten the practical examination of the origin and development of different types of communication in the laboratory.

Mating and Relationships

Mating and relationships have shaped human evolution through sexual selection and are key aspects of human social behavior. Far from being arbitrary, there is a great deal of cross-cultural agreement regarding what is attractive (Langlois et al. 2000). Attractive people are more likely to be hired for jobs (Cash and Kilcullen 1985; Chiu and Babcock 2002; Marlowe et al. 1996), are treated more favorably in criminal proceedings (Downs and Lyons 1991), and receive better care as infants (Langlois et al. 1995) than less attractive people. Physically attractive qualities, such as symmetry and sexually dimorphic traits (reviewed in Little, Chap. 25), are indicators of good physical condition, such that attractive people may have better genes for immunocompetence that could be passed on to offspring and enhance fitness (e.g., Thornhill and Gangestad 1993, 2006). However, although there is evidence of a genetic influence (e.g., Alanko et al. 2010; Långström et al. 2010), evolutionary psychology has had a more difficult time explaining same-sex attraction, as homosexual men and women reproduce less than heterosexual individuals (e.g., Schwartz et al. 2010). Recently, research on the *fa'afafine* of Samoa—a group of transgendered androphilic men recognized in Samoan culture as belonging to a third gender—provides evidence that same-sex sexual orientation may function to enhance indirect fitness by motivating care for closely related kin (Vasey and VanderLaan, Chap. 26). In other words, the benefits associated with providing additional care to kin (e.g., the offspring of siblings) may offset the costs of not reproducing directly. However, more research is needed, particularly across other cultures and among gynephilic women.

Familial relationships have received relatively little attention within social psychology (discussed in Salmon, Chap. 27). Given our slower life history strategy relative to other mammals and even other primates (reviewed in Figueredo et al., Chap. 28), humans experience extended childhoods and, thus, familial relationships can have a dramatic effect on survival. Adaptationist-minded researchers provide evidence-based explanations for family-related social issues, including preferences for offspring of one sex over the other (e.g., Gaulin and Robbins 1991; Smith et al. 1987; Trivers and Willard 1973), infanticide (Daly and Wilson 1998), and higher parental investment in first- and last-born children compared to middle-born children (Rohde et al. 2003; Salmon 2003). Scientists should continue to investigate diverse aspects of mating and relationships from an evolutionary perspective, particularly because such research surrounds questions that are important to personal and relational well-being.

Violence and Aggression

The human capacity for affiliative behaviors notwithstanding, one need only scan the headlines of any news source for examples of the human potential for violence and aggression. War and aggression are ubiquitous throughout history, and an evolutionary perspective offers telling insight into these phenomena (reviewed in Liddle et al. 2012; Friend and Thayer, Chap. 29). Terrorism provides one such example. When survival prospects are low and the "sacred values" held by violent extremists mobilizes collective action against a perceived outside threat to their primary reference group, extreme sacrifice by a sufficient number of individuals may afford the group hope to circumvent stronger but less devoted adversaries (Atran and Sheikh, Chap. 31). In other words, aggressive behaviors are often rooted in survival-related problems, such as competition for resources and mates, and, although destructive in nature, they are not necessarily maladaptive.

One form of aggression that has received considerable media attention in recent years is bullying (Volk et al., Chap. 30). Bullying is an inherently social process that involves deliberate, harmful aggression toward another to cause a power imbalance that favors the aggressor (Volk et al. 2012a). Like other social species, humans bully each other in diverse situations and at various ages (e.g., in the work place; Einarsen et al. 2010) for social status, mates, and resources (Volk et al. 2012b). As with war and other forms of aggression, understanding the evolutionary origins of bullying is a first step to reducing its incidence. More fundamentally, research can inform theories about decision making by using a combined social evolutionary perspective to investigate how and why people engage in aggression, including perceptions and misperceptions of threat.

Health and Psychological Adjustment

Mental health and affect play a major role in human social psychology. Positive psychologists endeavor to scientifically explain positive human development and happiness, and understanding why evolution bestowed humans and other sentient creatures with the capacity for both pleasant and unpleasant experiences is theoretically and empirically important (Grinde, Chap. 33). The default state of contentment displayed by humans and other animals in the absence of adverse factors (Diener and Diener 1996; Grinde 2004) may reflect the fact that a positive attitude is more conducive to the pursuits required for survival and reproduction. Conversely, negative affect may function to encourage the individual to seek a more advantageous environment or situation (e.g., feelings of loneliness encourage group living which enhances survival; Grinde, Chap. 33). Investigation into positive and negative affect using Darwinian reasoning may facilitate efforts to improve the well-being of individuals suffering from conditions such as anxiety and depression, which is especially important given the prevalence of these and related mental health issues in modern society (e.g., Grant et al. 2005).

Physical health also may affect the selection of social behavioral traits. Research suggests that psychological mechanisms evolved during ancestral interactions with parasites to allow individuals to detect the presence of disease-causing agents and to motivate behaviors that reduce the individual's risk of infection. This set of evolved health-related behaviors, known collectively as the behavioral immune system (Schaller 2006), broadly influences social exchanges, preferences, and prejudices (reviewed in Thornhill and Fincher, Chap. 32). Thornhill and Fincher (Chap. 32; see also Fincher and Thornhill 2012a, b; Thornhill and Fincher 2014) have expanded on this perspective, dubbing it *the parasite-stress theory of sociality,* by presenting evidence that human interactions with infectious disease risk factors across the lifespan directly cause and track changes in morals and preferences and their associated emotions, cognition, and social behavior. For instance, work by DeBruine et al. (2010, 2011, 2012) demonstrates a link between women's preferences for masculinity in a potential partner, a putative indicator of male genetic quality (e.g., Thornhill and Gangestad 2006), and high levels of environmental parasite stress. This suggests that negative health-related environmental cues may increase women's preferences for cues to immunocompetence that may be passed on to potential offspring (see also Penton-Voak et al. 2004). Although support for the parasite-stress theory of sociality is accumulating, further investigation into the impact of health-related environmental cues on individual differences in preferences, social behavior, and personality is warranted.

Individual Differences

Although evolutionary psychology has largely focused on explaining universal human psychological mechanisms, individual differences are of interest to social and evolutionary psychologists alike. A key topic within individual differences research is the development of differences in personality (Sefcek et al., Chap. 35; van den Berg and Weissing, Chap. 34). Personality traits are relatively stable over time and are heritable (e.g., Jang et al. 1996; Vernon et al. 2008), but show marked variation across individuals. Evolutionary game theory is a set of methods (traditionally used by biologists to understand the origins of social behavior in animals) that has recently been applied to human social behavior and differences in personality (van den Berg and Weissing, Chap. 34). Games such as the Prisoner's Dilemma (Axelrod and Hamilton 1981) explore within-species variation in traits and enable scientists to disentangle the complexities of social interactions while accounting for psychological and behavioral variation (i.e., differences in personality; van den Berg and Weissing, Chap. 34). An evolutionary perspective also provides an explanation for variance in negative, seemingly maladaptive social traits, such as psychopathy (e.g., Lalumiere et al. 2008) and narcissism (Holtzman and Donnellan, Chap. 36), and generates novel hypotheses. Narcissism, for example, may reflect a strategic response to an individual's heritable physical traits (e.g., a dominant stature), may result from a genetic predisposition interacting with environmental triggers, or may originate in selection for specific strategies that have different cost–benefit ratios depending on ecological conditions (e.g., short-term mating; reviewed in Holtzman and Donnellan, Chap. 36). Understanding the ultimate causation behind negative personality traits may inform clinical treatment of personality disorders. More broadly, an evolutionary perspective enables a more thorough comprehension of the sources and influences of individual differences.

Conclusion

We outlined several research themes found within social psychology and emphasized how an evolutionary perspective can generate novel interpretations and research questions within the respective areas. The chapters in this volume expertly outline many pertinent social psychological issues using compelling evolutionary logic. Future research should continue to promote the integration of social psychology and evolutionary psychology. These complementary approaches combine to deliver exciting new insights into long-standing social subjects. The amalgamation of evolutionary and social psychology can be of tremendous value to scholars, as it speaks to both the proximate and ultimate mechanisms underlying human social emotion, cognition, and behavior.

References

Abravanel, E., & Sigafoos, A. D. (1984). Exploring the presence of imitation during early infancy. *Child Development, 55,* 381–392.

Alanko, K., Santtila, P., Harlaar, N., Witting, K., Varjonen, M., Jern, P., Johansson, A., von der Pahlen, B., & Sandnabba, N. K. (2010). Common genetic effects of gender atypical behavior in childhood and sexual orientation in adulthood: A study of Finnish twins. *Archives of Sexual Behavior, 39,* 81–92.

Axelrod, R., & Hamilton, W. D. (1981). The evolution of cooperation. *Science, 211,* 1390–1396.

Bandura, A. (2006). Toward a psychology of human agency. *Perspectives on Psychological Science, 1,* 164–180.

Bardi, L., Regolin, L., & Simion, F. (2011). Biological motion preference in humans at birth: Role of dynamic and configural properties. *Developmental Science, 14,* 353–359.

Barrett, H. C. (2005). Enzymatic computation and cognitive modularity. *Mind & Language, 20,* 259–287.

Barrett, H. C. (2006). Modularity and design reincarnation. In P. Carruthers, S. Laurence, & S. Stich (Eds.), *The innate mind: Culture and cognition* (Vol. 2, pp. 199–217). New York: Oxford University Press.

Barrett, H. C. (2012). A hierarchical model of the evolution of human brain specializations. *Proceedings of the National Academy of Sciences, 109*(Suppl. 1), 10733–10740.

Barrett, H. C., & Kurzban, R. (2006). Modularity in cognition: Framing the debate. *Psychological Review, 113,* 628–647.

Bjorklund, D. F. (1997). The role of immaturity in human development. *Psychological Bulletin, 122,* 153–169.

Bjorklund, D. F. (2003). Evolutionary developmental psychology: A new tool for better understanding human ontogeny. *Human Development, 46,* 259–281.

Bjorklund, D. F., Causey, K., & Periss, V. (2010). The evolution and development of human social cognition. In P. Kappeler & J. Silk (Eds.), *Mind the gap: Tracing the origins of human universals* (pp. 351–371). Berlin: Springer.

Boesch, C., & Boesch-Achermann, H. (2000). *The chimpanzees of the Taï Forest: Behavioural ecology and evolution.* New York: Oxford University Press.

Cash, T. F., & Kilcullen, R. N. (1985). The aye of the beholder—Susceptibility to sexism and beautyism in the evaluation of managerial applicants. *Journal of Applied Social Psychology, 15,* 591–605.

Chiu, R. K., & Babcock, R. D. (2002). The relative importance of facial attractiveness and gender in Hong Kong selection decisions. *International Journal of Human Resource Management, 13,* 141–155.

Connor, R. C. (2007). Dolphin social intelligence: Complex alliance relationships in bottlenose dolphins and a consideration of selective environments for extreme brain size evolution in mammals. *Philosophical Transactions of the Royal Society B-Biological Sciences, 362,* 587–602.

Curry, O., Roberts, S. G., & Dunbar, R. I. (2012). Altruism in social networks: Evidence for a 'kinship premium'. *British Journal of Psychology, 104,* 283–295.

Daly, M., & Wilson, M. (1998). *The truth about Cinderella: A Darwinian view of parental love.* New Haven: Yale University Press.

DeBruine, L. M., Jones, B. C., Crawford, J. R., Welling, L. L. M., & Little, A. C. (2010). The health of a nation predicts their mate preferences: Cross-cultural variation in women's preferences for masculinized male faces. *Proceedings of the Royal Society of London B, 277,* 2405–2410.

DeBruine, L. M., Jones, B. C., Little, A. C., Crawford, J. R., & Welling, L. L. M. (2011). Further evidence for regional variation in women's masculinity preferences. *Proceedings of the Royal Society of London B, 278,* 813–814.

DeBruine, L. M., Little, A. C., & Jones, B. C. (2012). Extending parasite-stress theory to variation in human mate preferences. *Behavioral and Brain Sciences, 35,* 86–87.

DeScioli, P., & Kurzban, R. (2009). The alliance hypothesis for human friendship. *PLoS One, 4,* e5802.

Descioli, P., & Kurzban, R. (2012). The company you keep: Friendship decisions from a functional perspective. In J. Krueger (Ed.), *Social judgment and decision-making* (pp. 209–226). New York: Taylor and Francis Group.

Diener, E., & Diener, C. (1996). Most people are happy. *Psychological Science, 7,* 181–185.

Downs, A. C., & Lyons, P. M. (1991). Natural observations of the links between attractiveness and initial legal judgments. *Personality and Social Psychology Bulletin, 17,* 541–547.

Dreßing, H., Bailer, J., Anders, A., Wagner, H., & Gallas, C. (2014). Cyberstalking in a large sample of social network users: Prevalence, characteristics, and impact upon victims. *Cyberpsychology, Behavior & Social Networking, 17,* 61–67.

Dunbar, R. I. M. (1993). Coevolution of neocortical size, group size, and language in humans. *Behavioral and Brain Sciences, 16,* 681–735.

Einarsen, S., Hoel, H., Zapf, D., & Cooper, C. (2010). *Bullying and harassment in the workplace: Developments in theory, research, and practice.* Boca Raton: Taylor-Francis.

Fincher, C. L., & Thornhill, R. (2012a). Parasite-stress promotes in-group assortative sociality: The cases of strong family ties and heightened religiosity. *Behavioral and Brain Sciences, 35,* 61–79.

Fincher, C. L., & Thornhill, R. (2012b). The parasite-stress theory may be a general theory of culture and sociality Response. *Behavioral and Brain Sciences, 35,* 99–119.

Fiske, S. T., & Neuberg, S. L. (1990). A continuum of impression formation, from category-based to individuating processes: Influences of information and motivation on attention and interpretation. In M. P. Zanna (Ed.), *Advances in experimental social psychology* (Vol. 23, pp. 1–74). San Diego: Academic Press.

Fraser, O. N., & Bugnyar, T. (2010). Do ravens show consolation? Responses to distressed others. *PLoS One, 5,* e10605.

Gaulin, S. J. C., & Robbins, C. J. (1991). Trivers-Willard effect in contemporary North American society. *American Journal of Physical Anthropology, 85,* 61–69.

Grant, B. F., Hasin, D. S., Stinson, F. S., Dawson, D. A., Ruan, W. J., Goldstein, R. B., Smith, S. M., Saha, T. D., & Huang, B. (2005). Prevalence, correlates, co-morbidity, and comparative disability of DSM-IV generalized anxiety disorder in the USA: Results from the National Epidemiologic Survey on Alcohol and Related Conditions. *Psychological Medicine, 35,* 1747–1759.

Grinde B. (2004). Darwinian happiness: Can the evolutionary perspective on well-being help us improve society? *World Futures—Journal of General Evolution, 60,* 317–329.

Hare, B., & Tomasello, M. (2004). Chimpanzees are more skillful in competitive than cooperative cognitive tasks. *Animal Behaviour, 68,* 571–581.

Hare, B., Rosati, A., Kaminski, J., Bräuer, J., Call, J., & Tomasello, M. (2010). The domestication hypothesis for dogs skills with human communication: A response to Udell et al. (2008) and Wynne et al. (2008). *Animal Behaviour, 79,* e1–e6.

Henrich, J., Boyd, R., Bowles, S., Camerer, C., Fehr, E., Gintis, H., McElreath, R., Alvard, M., Barr, A., Ensminger, J., Henrich, N. S., Hill, K., Gil-White, F., Gurven, M., Marlowe, F. W., Patton, J. Q., & Tracer, D. (2005). Models of decision-making and the coevolution of social preferences. *Behavioral and Brain Sciences, 28,* 838–855.

Hruschka, D. J. (2010). *Friendship: Development, ecology, and evolution of a relationship* (Vol. 5). Berkeley: University of California Press.

Humphrey, N. (1976). The social function of intellect. In P. P. G. Bateson & R. A. Hinde (Eds.), *Growing points in ethology* (pp. 303–317). Cambridge: Cambridge University Press.

Jang, K. L., Livesley, W. J., & Vernon, P. A. (1996). Heritability of the big five personality dimensions and their facets: A twin study. *Journal of Personality, 64,* 577–591.

Jolly, A. (1966). Lemur social behavior and primate intelligence. *Science, 153,* 501–506.

Kelley, H. H. (1973). The process of attribution. *American Psychologist, 28,* 107–128.

Kirchhofer, K. C., Zimmermann, F., Kaminski, J., & Tomasello, M. (2012). Dogs (*Canis familiaris*), but not chimpanzees (*Pan troglodytes*), understand imperative pointing. *PloS One, 7,* e30913.

Lalumiere, M. L., Mishra, S., & Harris, G. T. (2008). In cold blood: The evolution of psychopathy. In J. Duntley & T. K. Shakelford (Eds.), *Evolutionary forensic psychology: Darwinian foundations of crime and law* (pp. 139–159). New York: Oxford University Press.

Langlois, J. H., Ritter, J., Casey, J., & Solwin, D. (1995). Infant attractiveness predicts maternal behaviours and attitudes. *Developmental Psychology, 31,* 464–472.

Langlois, J. H., Kalakanis, L., Rubenstein, A. J., Larson, A., Hallamm, M., & Smoot, M. (2000). Maxims or myths of beauty? A meta-analytic and theoretical review. *Psychological Bulletin, 126,* 390–423.

Långström, N., Rahman, Q., Carlström, E., Lichtenstein, P. (2010). Genetic and environmental effects on same-sex sexual behavior: A population study of twins in Sweden. *Archives of Sexual Behavior, 39,* 75–80.

Leary, M. R., & Downs, D. L. (1995). Interpersonal functions of the self-esteem motive: The self-esteem system as a sociometer. In M. H. Kernis (Ed.), *Efficacy, agency, and self-esteem* (pp. 123–144). New York: Plenum Press.

Liddle, J. R., Shackelford, T. K., & Weekes-Shackelford, V. A. (2012). Why can't we all just get along? Evolutionary perspectives on violence, homicide, and war. *Review of General Psychology, 16,* 24–35.

Marlowe, C. M., Schneider, S. L., & Nelson, C. E. (1996). Gender and attractiveness biases in hiring decisions: Are more experienced managers less biased? *Journal of Applied Psychology, 81,* 11–21.

McComb, K., Moss, C., Sayialel, S., & Baker, L. (2000). Unusually extensive networks of vocal recognition in African elephants. *Animal Behaviour, 59,* 1103–1109.

Mealey, L. (1995). The sociobiology of sociopathy: An integrated evolutionary model. *Behavioral and Brain Sciences, 18,* 523–599.

Milgram, S. (1963). Behavioral study of obedience. *Journal of Abnormal and Social Psychology, 67,* 371–378.

Mondloch, C. J., Lewis, T. L., Budreau, D. R., Maurer, D., Dannemiller, J. L., Stephens, B. R., & Kleiner-Gathercoal, K. A. (1999). Face perception during early infancy. *Psychological Science, 10,* 419–422.

Nielsen, M. (2012). Imitation, pretend play, and childhood: Essential elements in the evolution of human culture? *Journal of Comparative Psychology, 126,* 170–181.

Oppenheim, R. W. (1981). Ontogenetic adaptations and retrogressive processes in the development of the nervous system and behavior. In K. J. Connolly & H. F. R. Prechtl (Eds.), *Maturation and development: Biological and psychological perspectives* (pp. 73–108). Philadelphia: International Medical Publications.

Penton-Voak, I. S., Jacobson, A., & Trivers, R. (2004). Populational differences in attractiveness judgements of male and female faces: Comparing British and Jamaican samples. *Evolution and Human Behavior, 25,* 355–370.

Piazza, J., & Bering, J. M. (2009). Evolutionary cyber-psychology: Applying an evolutionary framework to

Internet behavior. *Computers in Human Behavior, 25,* 1258–1269.

Pinker, S. (2011). *The better angels of our nature: Why violence has declined.* New York: Penguin.

Plotnik, J. M., de Waal, F. B. M., & Reiss, D. (2006). Self-recognition in an Asian elephant. *Proceedings of the National Academy of Sciences of the United States of America, 103,* 17053–17057.

Povinelli, D. J., & Vonk, J. (2003). Chimpanzee minds: Suspiciously human? *Trends in Cognitive Science, 7,* 157–160.

Prior, H., Schwarz, A., & Gunturkun, O. (2008). Mirror-induced behavior in the magpie (Pica pica): Evidence of self-recognition. *PLoS Biology, 6,* 1642–1650.

Rachlin, H., & Jones, B. A. (2008). Altruism among relatives and non-relatives. *Behavioural Processes, 79,* 120–123.

Reiss, D., & Marino, L. (2001). Mirror self-recognition in the bottlenose dolphin: A case of cognitive convergence. *Proceedings of the National Academy of Sciences of the United States of America, 98,* 5937–5942.

Roberts, G. (1998). Competitive altruism: From reciprocity to the handicap principle. *Proceedings of the Royal Society of London, Series B: Biological Sciences, 265,* 427–431.

Rohde, P. A., Atzwanger, K., Butovskaya, M., Lampert, A., Mysterud, I., Sanchez-Andres, A., & Sulloway, F. (2003). Perceived parental favoritism, closeness to kin, and the rebel of the family: The effects of sex and birth order. *Evolution and Human Behavior, 24,* 261–276.

Salmon, C. A. (2003). Birth order and relationships: Family, friends and sexual partners. *Human Nature, 14,* 73–88.

Schaller, M. (2006). Parasites, behavioral defenses, and the social psychological mechanisms through which cultures are evoked. *Psychological Inquiry, 17,* 96–101.

Schwartz, G., Kim, R. M., Kolundziji, A. B., Rieger, G., & Sanders, A. R. (2010). Biodemographic and physical correlates of sexual orientation in men. *Archives of Sexual Behavior, 39,* 93–109.

Scott-Phillips, T. C., Blythe, R. A., Gardner, A., & West, S. A. (2012). How do communication systems emerge? *Proceedings of the Royal Society of London, Series B, 279,* 1943–1949.

Simion, F., Regolin, L., & Bulf, H. (2008). A predisposition for biological motion in the newborn baby. *Proceedings of the National Academy of Sciences, 105,* 809–813.

Smith, M. S., Kish, B. J., & Crawford, C. B. (1987). Inheritance of wealth and human kin investment. *Ethology and Sociobiology, 8,* 171–182.

Suddendorf, T., & Butler, D. L. (2013). The nature of visual self-recognition. *Trends in Cognitive Sciences, 17,* 121–127.

Thornhill, R., & Fincher, C. L. (2014). *The parasite-stress theory of values and sociality: Infectious disease, history and human values worldwide.* New York: Springer.

Thornhill, R., & Gangestad, S. W. (1993). Human facial beauty: Averageness, symmetry, and parasite resistance. *Human Nature, 4,* 237–269.

Thornhill, R., & Gangestad, S. W. (2006). Facial sexual dimorphism, developmental stability, and susceptibility to disease in men and women. *Evolution and Human Behavior, 27,* 131–144.

Tomasello, M. (2009). *Why we cooperate.* Cambridge: MIT Press.

Tomasello, M., & Carpenter, M. (2007). Shared intentionality. *Developmental Science, 10,* 121–125.

Tooby, J., & Cosmides, L. (1990). The past explains the present: Emotional adaptations and the structure of ancestral environments. *Ethology and Sociobiology, 11,* 375–424.

Tooby, J., & Cosmides, L. (1996). Friendship and the banker's paradox: Other pathways to the evolution of adaptations for altruism. *Proceedings of the British Academy, 88,* 119–143.

Trivers, R. (2011). *The folly of fools: The logic of deceit and deception in human life.* New York: Basic Books.

Trivers, R. L., & Willard, D. (1973). Natural selection of parental ability to vary the sex-ratio of offspring. *Science, 179,* 90–92.

Udell, M. A. R., Spencer, J. M., Dorey, N. R., & Wynne, C. D. L. (2012). Human-socialized wolves follow diverse human gestures… and they may not be alone. *International Journal of Comparative Psychology, 25,* 97–117.

Van Vugt, M., & Kameda, T. (2014). Evolution of the social brain: Psychological adaptations for group living. In M. Mikulincer & P. Shaver (Eds.), *Mechanism of social connection: From brain to group* (pp. 335–355). Washington, DC: American Psychological Association.

Vernon, P. A., Villani, V. C., Vickers, L. C., & Harris, J. A. (2008). A behavioral genetic investigation of the Dark Triad and the Big 5. *Personality and Individual Differences, 44,* 445–452.

Volk, A., Camilleri, J. A., Dane, A. V., & Marini, Z. A. (2012a). If, when, and why bullying is adaptive. In T. Shackelford & V. Shackelford (Eds.), *Oxford handbook of evolutionary perspectives on violence, homicide, and war* (pp. 270–288). Toronto: Oxford University Press.

Volk, A., Camilleri, J. A., Dane, A. V., & Marini, Z. A. (2012b). Is adolescent bullying an evolutionary adaptation? *Aggressive Behaviour, 38,* 222–238.

Zeigler-Hill, V. (2013). The importance of self-esteem. In V. Zeigler-Hill (Ed.), *Self-esteem* (pp. 1–20). London: Psychology Press.

Index

V. Zeigler-Hill et al. (eds.), *Evolutionary Perspectives on Social Psychology*, Evolutionary Psychology,
DOI 10.1007/978-3-319-12697-5, © Springer International Publishing Switzerland 2015

Printed by Printforce, the Netherlands